THE WINNING MANAGER

Gulf Publishing Company
Houston, Texas

WINNING MANAGER

LEADERSHIP SKILLS FOR GREATER INNOVATION, QUALITY, AND EMPLOYEE COMMITMENT

JULIUS E. EITINGTON

THE WINNING MANAGER

Leadership Skills for Greater Innovation, Quality, and Employee Commitment

Gulf Publishing Company
Book Division
P.O. Box 2608 □ Houston, Texas 77252-2608

10   9   8   7   6   5   4   3   2   1

Library of Congress Cataloging-in-Publication Data
Eitington, Julius E.
　　The winning manager : leadership skills for greater innovation,
　quality, and employee commitment / Julius Eitington.
　　　　p.　cm.
　　Includes index.
　　ISBN 0-88415-902-7
　　1. Management.　2. Leadership.　I. Title.
HD31.E477　1997
658.4′092—dc21
96-48028
CIP

Contents

ence. Self-Esteem. Commitment to Quality and Continuing Improvement. Employee Involvement Teams for Continuous Improvement. Using Career Planning Tools for Motivation. Environmental Focus. Payoffs for Effort. Complaint Conversion. What About Competition? What About Money? Your Reward System. How to Decrease or Eliminate an Undesired Behavior. Motivation and Morale.

5

The Woman Worker. Valuing Workforce Diversity. The Older Worker. The Baby Boomer. The Baby Buster. Peak Peformers. The Technical Professions. The Plateaued Worker. The Support Staff. People with Disabilities. The Rehabilitated Mentally Ill Person. Custodial Workers and Others in Boring Jobs. The "Temp" Worker. Survivors of Downsizing and Mergers. Managing Volunteers. A Few Thoughts on the Checksheets. Key Summary Concepts. Exercises.

6

Why Delegate? Some Logical Reasons for Non-Delegation. Barriers to Delegation. R_x for Effective Delegation: Requisite Attitudes. R_x for Effective Delegation: Requisite Techniques. Delegation and Control. Delegation Taboos. What Our Delegation Practices Communicate. Your Delegation Quotient. Key Points. Exercises.

7

Using Job Design for Empowerment and Work Improvement. Selecting Staffers Selectively. Orientation. Communicating Expectations. Building Trust. Modeling. Giving Support. Providing Accessibility. Observing Behavior/Performance. Reviewing Work and Giving Feedback. Confronting Undesirable Performance/Behavior. The Coach as Developer of People. The Coach as Trainer. Conducting the Annual Perfor-

mance Review. Confrontation. Guidelines for Effective Discipline. How to See Yourself as Your Staff Does. Key Points. Exercises.

8

Close Encounters of the "Impossible Kind": How to Work with Difficult People. Working with the Troubled Employee. Counseling Employees on Their Careers. Mentoring: Getting the "Big Picture" the "Hands-on" Way. Directive vs. Non-directive Counseling. Your Counseling Skill: A Self-Assessment. Exercises.

9

What Makes an Effective Team. Barriers to Teamwork: Are We Alert to Them? Team Building: Why Do It? The Management Team: Various Techniques to Upgrade Its Effectiveness. Types of Teams. Self-Directed Teams: How to Organize and Manage Them. How to Manage the Project Team. Concurrent Engineering: Using Team Collaboration for Product Development. Team Selling: How to Make It Work. Gearing Up the Team for Quality. Resolving Inter-Group Conflict. Overcoming the "Group Think" Trap. Exercises.

10

The World of the Problem Solver. The Mind of the Problem Solver. A Problem-Solving Model. Step 1: Identifying and Defining/Formulating Our Problem. Are We Solving the Right Problem? Step 2: Gathering Information About the Problem. Step 3: Developing/Generating Alternate Solutions. Step 4: Assessing Alternate Solutions. Step 5: Choosing (Deciding) Among Alternatives. Step 6: Implementation—Converting Hope Into Reality. Step 7: Evaluation: Did Whatever You Did, Work?

Preface

Rare is the manager in today's rapidly changing world who is not constantly reminded by his pressure-ridden superiors that the organization is operating on a "lean and mean" basis and that he* is expected to be "doing more with less." This book, then, is dedicated to the serious, conscientious manager (or would-be manager) who wishes to do well in an era of global competition, global markets, shrinking product life cycles, instant communication, technological change, organizational turbulence (restructuring, reorganizing, delayering, downsizing, outsourcing, implementing divestitures, mergers and acquisitions), and a changing workforce marked by higher education and resultant higher expectations, as well as increasing diversity.

NEW AND CHALLENGING VALUES, ROLES AND WORK FORMS

To be effective, then, today's manager must adapt to:

New values. Sharing information fully rather than doling it out selectively is a must: "Secrets" and less-than truth telling are counter-productive for staffers who need a robust supply of accurate information to be effective. Involving staff in problem solving and decision making—participative management—is essential to meeting employee expectations and to ensuring high-quality decisions as well. Building continuous quality improvement into all products and services is another imperative.

Also to be stressed, value-wise, is an expanded concept of work—that people, to be effective and creative, need to be listened to, supported, permitted to function in an atmosphere of fun and freedom, encouraged to experiment and take risks, and helped to grow both as persons and performers. Diversity of viewpoints and staff member make-up is to be fostered rather than frowned upon. And as a final value, change and unpredictability are to be regarded as positive proof of vitality and as an inevitable, natural process of growth.

New, multiple roles. The manager is no longer someone who is totally "in charge" and thus can automatically command productivity and quality. Rather, he can be effective only to the extent that he *consciously* looks at himself as being and functioning in a multiplicity of demanding roles: The Manager of One's Boss, The Manager as a Collaborator with Peers/Colleagues, The Manager as a Communicator, The Manager as a Motivator, The Manager as a Coach and Trainer, The Manager as a Counselor, The Manager as a Delegator, The Manager as a Team Leader, The Manager as a Problem Solver and Decision Maker, The Manager as a Change Agent, and the Manager as a Force for Innovation and Creativity.

All of which is a far cry from the manager of old who could decree "My Way or the Highway" and have his authoritarian directives go unchallenged. In essence, managing by *influence* rather than by command and control is the new learning requirement.

New work forms. To maximize performance, the manager must operate his unit in a collegial, team-oriented way. New requirements also may include extensive use of and participation in project teams, task forces, and cross-functional teams, and possibly the creation of self-directed teams, too.

*To avoid awkward references (i.e., "he/she," "him/her," etc.), "he" will be used as an inclusive pronoun in most instances throughout this book.

WHAT THE BOOK IS LIKE AND ASPIRES TO

The author would like to think of this book as both a "how to" and a "why to." That is to say, although each chapter offers many practical skill pointers on how to manage a particular leadership skill area better, there are also conceptual underpinnings to provide the rationale for the use of the suggested techniques. As has been said, to know practice without knowing theory is not to know practice.

Another attribute of this work is a heavy emphasis on the use of self-assessment devices, or self-quizzes if you will. They are designed to maximize the reader's "take" from the book by providing him with an opportunity to "check out" (take a fresh look at) his own attitudes, values, behaviors, and/or current leadership skills in relation to the skills and concepts advanced in the text. This *introspection* (an inward look), if followed by *reflection* (seeking meaning) on the results of the quizzes, can provide a significant potential for the upgrading of one's current skill in the various areas of leadership presented in the book. A useful metaphor for this learning process is the holding up of a mirror to see one's conduct and, possibly too, how others see it.

The volume's underlying convictions are that many managers are:

- ☐ Seriously concerned about their effectiveness and probably feel that they can manage better than they do now. They thus:
- ☐ Wish to learn about and try out new, different or added ways of managing and are:
- ☐ Willing to step back and assess their past and current managerial experience and examine it in light of a number of (possibly newer) concepts and skills presented in this book, and:
- ☐ Have the courage to confront themselves where there are voids and minuses in their experience and plug those gaps with new or different approaches and, most importantly:
- ☐ Recognize the need to put themselves into a more active state of management learning. This is vital to avoiding or overcoming any static tendencies that serve to support the status quo and deprive one of continuing growth and self-development.

WHAT THE BOOK COVERS

This book stresses that to be fully effective the manager cannot only think in terms of managing his staff.

Rather, he must think in much broader terms and also be concerned with:

- ☐ **The Boss** (Chapter 1): Who can afford to take the boss for granted, whether he is or is not perfect?
- ☐ **Peers/Colleagues** (Chapter 2): With whom (and how) must you interface to get your job done well.

Additionally, the future—change (Chapter 12) and innovation/creativity (Chapter 13)—must also be consciously managed. Either we prepare sophisticatedly for what's up ahead, or we get left behind by our competition and our customers/clients who demand better quality and service each day.

Also, the manager must not neglect to manage assiduously himself, which entails concern with:

- ☐ **Ethics** (Chapter 11): Is this a significant leadership value and, if it is, how do you manage yourself and your team for it?

And finally, underlying everything you do or try to do, is a need to be sensitive to:

- ☐ The nuances of **communication** (Chapter 3): How do you ensure true and full understanding of the messages that you send? How do you tune in successfully to other people's wavelengths?
- ☐ The **motivation** of people (Chapter 4): How do you kindle and maintain that all-important "will to do"?
- ☐ A changing, culturally **diverse workforce** (Chapter 5): How do you use that potentially potent person-power fully to strengthen your overall operation?
- ☐ The need for true **team** leadership (Chapter 9): Can the traditional one-on-one leadership style serve adequately given the complexities and challenges you now face?

WHO CAN PROFIT FROM THIS BOOK?

As the author sees it, the audience for this volume is adequately varied. It is directed at and should be of interest and value to:

- ☐ **Experienced or long-tenured managers:** Those who have been managing for a good while, but feel that a new look, an updating, may have real value, particularly in these changing and demanding times. Some of these managers may not have been exposed previously to management ideas in any formal way, that is, via training courses, systematic reading of the management literature, viewing films or videos, and so on. For this latter group, it may be a worthwhile first opportunity to explore what all the management writers drawn upon in the book have to say.

- ☐ **New or beginning managers:** Those who want to get off on "the right foot" and avoid the mistakes that they, as non-managers, have experienced, observed, heard or read about. They may also see the need for guides to help develop a strong set of convictions or philosophy about modern, progressive, effective management.

- ☐ **Aspiring managers:** Those who expect to enter management in the near or not-too-distant future and want to be prepared when that big event arrives.

- ☐ **Management trainers** who are the lookout for practical, experiential training material—self-assessment devices, exercises, checklists, how-to-do-it guides, problems, and discussion questions—plus current behavioral science-oriented textual material for use in corporate, government, or non-profit organization programs in management or supervision.

- ☐ **College/university professors and instructors in management** who can enrich their course offerings via the large number of practical, application-type activities featured in the book.

If this volume serves the purpose of exciting and educating the reader (whether a busy manager, a future manager or a college/university student) and expanding and updating his leadership outlook and style, it will have served a worthwhile purpose.

This preface provides an opportunity to acknowledge the savvy inputs of the many managers with whom I have been associated and privileged to work with and train. Unknowingly, they have enriched this work via their insightful comments and observations, pointed questions, presentation of painful dilemmas, candid expression of concerns, and spirited disagreements with the author's viewpoints, all of which became grist for my learning from them.

Their contacts over the years with me occurred in my varied roles of management trainer, training director in the corporate and government sectors, management consultant, college and university instructor, periodical editor *(Personnel Administration* and *The Bulletin of Training)* and author of numerous articles for business/professional management, personnel, and training journals.

ACKNOWLEDGMENT

Dr. Norma Jo Eitington, my wife and Director of Learning Services, Georgetown University, gave generously of her precious time to critique and advise on each of the book's chapters. Her patience, interest, and understanding helped significantly to make this work a more insightful and useful one.

How to Manage the Boss

No doubt, some subordinates will resent that on top of all their other duties, they also need to take time and energy to manage their relationships with their bosses. Such managers fail to realize the importance of this activity and how it can simplify their jobs by eliminating potentially severe problems. Effective managers recognize that this part of their work is legitimate. Seeing themselves as ultimately responsible for what they achieve in an organization, they know they need to establish and manage relationships with everyone on whom they depend—and that includes the boss.

> —John J. Gabarro and John P. Kotter,
> "Managing Your Boss," *Harvard Business Review,* May–June 1993

When you take the king's shilling, you do the king's bidding.

> —Old English maxim

MANAGERS accept as a given that they must direct or manage their *subordinates* (downward management). Many also recognize that they must concern themselves, to varying degrees, with the management of *peer or collegial relations* (horizontal management). However, relatively few consciously recognize that they must also *manage the boss* (upward management).

WHY MANAGE THE BOSS?

Here are some vital reasons:

To help meet his* needs as a person. Bosses, like ourselves, are human and thus need support, encouragement, recognition, attention, contact. (Many bosses are lonely people.)

---

*To avoid awkward references (i.e., "he/she," "him/her," etc.), "he" will be used as an inclusive pronoun in most instances throughout this book.

To bridge the gap in the boss' experience. Some observers refer to this process as "managing upward." Your boss may be very able and intelligent, but he can't know it all. If he did, you wouldn't have to be on the payroll. So your job is to ensure that he profits to the fullest from your talents and experience.

To keep him out of trouble. Bosses appreciate the prevention of crises before they arise. Again, your perception and know-how can help minimize the unexpected and the unwanted.

To form an interdependent team. Both parties have special resources that can be used to help one another. Cooperation based on mutual trust and mutual respect will have a synergistic effect.

To make the boss successful and thus "look good." The boss who is anxious about his status in the organization is not likely to be an easy person with whom to work.

To increase the degree of confidence and trust your superior has in you. This, in turn, will help your relationship with the boss.

To increase your upward influence. This is essential to ensure that you have the power and resources you need to get things done in your job. Since bosses can help, hinder, or be indifferent to your operation, it's good business to cultivate your relationship with the boss and have him in your corner. So whether it's getting your program ideas accepted or a greater share of the budget, exceptions to rules and regulations, new equipment, more space, promotions or transfers for your subordinates, or whatever, the likelihood of any of this happening is directly related to how influential you are with your boss. In fact, the available research tells us that the more successful supervisors are those who have influence up the line.

To increase your likelihood of advancement. Rare is the promotion of someone who is perceived as not being on the same team. Being sensitive to the boss' needs grants you solid team membership automatically.

It should be clear, then, that when we talk about managing the boss we are not talking at all about manipulating, out-foxing, or doing end-runs around him, or buttering up or bossing the boss. Essentially, we are suggesting that you, as a manager, should ask yourself

whether you are doing enough to ensure that your upward relations are strong, supportive, and facilitating, and are so perceived by your superior.

To augment your assurance that you are operating in a helpful manner:

1. Reflect upon the three things your boss has—a job, leadership and operating style, and a needs system*—and then
2. Look at your own style of operating and your needs system to see where matching possibilities exist.

The following paragraphs and worksheet will help you make such an analysis.

YOUR BOSS' JOB

Have you ever thought very much about your boss' job? What is it really like? What demands does it include? What is his work schedule like? How much traveling must he do? How extensive are his meeting requirements? To what degree is your superior really his own boss? In what areas does he need the most help?

Your boss may not meet your standards of the ideal supervisor. But have you attempted to enter his world to understand his job requirements, anxieties, pressures, or problems? If not, you probably are not able to help your boss meet his job needs nor his needs as a person.

Take a few minutes to zero in on the character of your boss' job with Worksheet 1-1, "My Boss' Job."

After conscientiously responding to the questions in Worksheet 1-1 (page 32), you should see that your boss has concerns that may require your help and understanding to a greater degree than you previously appreciated.

A needs system relates to motivations, drives, hopes, etc., one has. These internal forces trigger behavior. Obviously, some needs may be stronger than others, some may be recognized and verbalized upon, and some may exist subconsciously. Healthy needs relate to achievement, recognition, and self-esteem; and contact, cooperation, and sharing with, and concern for others. Less healthy needs include punishing others, pursuing power for the sake of power, being self-centered, besting others, and functioning in isolation or privacy in an extreme way. Needs for security, order, predictability, and self-worth are present in all of us; however, an overemphasis on any of these latter needs will produce behaviors that may range from the unattractive to the destructive.

YOUR BOSS' LEADERSHIP STYLE AND NEEDS SYSTEM

Now focus on your boss' leadership and operating style, and the needs he has as a person and as a boss. What is your boss' style of operating? Is there a preference for reading and writing memos, or are face-to-face contacts preferred? Does he favor exhaustive memoranda or are one-pagers desired? Is he a morning or afternoon person? Does he prefer personal interactions to be formal or informal, short or long?

What are his likes, dislikes, pet peeves? What are his objectives, interests, hopes, fears, aspirations, anxieties, drives, motivations? What is his tolerance for surprises? What procedures or protocols does he favor? Is he a detail person or a "loose," relaxed operator? Does he work rapidly or slowly? Is he the prime initiator of activities, or does he expect you to initiate things? How important are deadlines? How does he respond to "bad" news? Is he a workaholic, a golf course devotee, or simply a 9-to-5 functionary? Is he a planner, a risk-taker, an initiator, or a responder to crises? How receptive is he to change, suggestions, criticisms?

If you understand your boss' style and needs system well, you are in a good position to cope with and adjust to him. For example, assume your boss is a very busy person. He thus is difficult to see for a period long enough to resolve matters that are important to you. What can you do? You've tried setting up appointments to see him, but he is generally harassed by phone calls and visitors and can't give you his undivided attention. You know that he is a late-afternoon person and enjoys working after 5 p.m., even though the office is empty at that time. You don't particularly want to get involved in lengthy discussions at that late hour. Nevertheless, this may be the best time to transact more complex business matters or possibly to persuade him to adopt your sparkling new idea.

Worksheet 1-2, "My Boss' Leadership Style and Needs System" (page 33), should help you think through your boss' style, how he operates, and what seems to make him "tick."

YOUR OWN STYLE AND NEEDS SYSTEM

Along with an appreciation of your boss' job and an understanding of his leadership style and needs system, you should be sensitive to your own operating style and needs system. Insight should enable you to recognize where you can and cannot mesh your style and needs with those of your boss. For example, if you enjoy receiving praise for significant accomplishment of work but your boss is stingy in doling out psychic rewards, you can anticipate your need for praise will not be satisfied very often. This may well be a constant source of irritation and frustration for you. You thus may have to figure out other ways to get your strokes, e.g., via participation in community affairs, writing articles, teaching, or serving on or chairing committees in professional, trade, civic, church, or other groups, etc.

It might also be productive to engage in some realistic soul-searching concerning your own attitudes and behaviors vis-à-vis yourself and the boss. Certainly all of us may feel, at times, that we haven't applied enough empathy in our understanding of the boss' needs and how our behaviors work in contradiction to those needs. For examples, see Figure 1-1 (page 4).

Now go ahead and complete Worksheet 1-3, "My Boss and My Need System" (page 34). It should prove useful to you in developing data-based strategies to deal more effectively with your boss.

HELPFUL ATTITUDES AND BEHAVIORS

. . . don't ever underrate the boss, and don't ever just conform. That is the quickest way to lose the boss' respect and support.

—Peter Drucker, management consultant, educator, and prolific author, *The Bulletin on Training.* March/April 1977.

If you really want to impress your boss with your attitude and behavior—that you care about him as a person, his problems and priorities, his job successes, his "looking good"—score the items carefully in Figure 1-2 (page 35), "My BMQ (Boss Management Quotient)—A Self Quiz." Your scores on the quiz will serve as a useful point of departure for making such changes in attitude/behavior as may be indicated.

It should be apparent from the BMQ quiz that we are talking about a high form of "constructive subordinancy" or, as human relations consultant William J. Crockett terms it (*Industry Week,* November 15, 1976), "pro-active followership." Crockett, in fact, sees the role of management training as a means of developing people who can:

My Feelings and Behavior	Possible Overlooked Needs
"I wonder if the boss knows what's really going on?"	"Have I done enough to make certain he is informed?"
"I don't think the boss wants the bad news. So I'll soft-pedal it."	"Have I been too protective in acquainting him with the bad news as well as the good?"
"I'll spare the boss all the details."	"Have I been overlooking the need to send data upward that bears on possible problems, potential crises, new trends, PR headaches, etc.?"
"I'll just dash off a quickie memo on this. He can always come back to me for more info if needed."	"Have I overlooked the need to provide completed staff work, providing a formal report with explanatory headings?"
"The boss believes he delegates, but the reins are held tightly on whatever I do."	"Have I really tried to solve tough problems on my own, or have I dropped a good share of them in my boss' lap?"
"I dont't think the boss wants any argument out of me on this."	"Have I become a 'yes' man?"
"I don't think he wants any new ideas so I'll bury them."	"Have I fallen into the trap of assuming I'm powerless and that I have zero influence with the boss?"
"My boss turns down my ideas because he lacks the imagination to appreciate them."	"Have I taxed my boss' imagination by presenting partially developed ideas?"
"I can't predict the reaction to my proposals."	"Have I really analyzed the boss' philosophy, values, and attitudes, so that I can upgrade my prediction quotient and meet his needs better?"
"I don't know what the boss expects of me."	"Have I made a conscientious effort to establish or clarify goals, to report back on my goal accomplishment, and to get feedback on results?"
"The boss says one thing but means something else."	"Am I overstating my prowess as a mind reader? If a request or an assignment requires clarification, have I truly sought it out?"

Figure 1-1

☐ Produce a genuine climate of win/win with the boss so that there are not feelings of competition.

☐ Be valued as a devil's advocate by challenging the boss' decisions and approaches.

☐ Confront the boss' values, facts, behavior and be rewarded for the courage and openness exhibited.

☐ Obey the boss' orders and still not become subservient.

☐ Account to the boss for his stewardship candidly and factually, while retaining a sense of freedom and dignity.

☐ Fulfill a responsibility without claiming ownership to the "territory" created so skillfully.

☐ Retain self-esteem despite the ever-present, subtle appeals of power, ambition, and success.

☐ Depart when the boss' values, behavior, and decisions are no longer supportable by the subordinate's own value system.

Note that one researcher (Robert E. Kelley, "In Praise of Followers," *Harvard Business Review,* November-December 1988) found, surprisingly, that the traits of a good follower are almost identical to those of a good leader. Effective followers, per Kelley's research, had these characteristics: They manage themselves effectively; they have commitment to the firm and to a person, principle, or purpose other than themselves; they build their competence and concentrate/target their efforts for maximum results; and they are courageous, believable, and engage in truth telling.

HOW TO BUILD A RELATIONSHIP WITH YOUR BOSS

Your effectiveness as a manager is no better or stronger than the relationship you have developed with your boss. A solid relationship, obviously, can help you succeed in your assignments and responsibilities and help to advance your career. It thus is essential that you actively cultivate and maintain the best possible relations with your boss.

Note the terms "actively," "developed," and "cultivate." Our thought is that a healthy relationship doesn't occur by chance. It has to be worked on initially and maintained vigorously thereafter. A good analogy is a successful marriage. (In this connection you may recall the anecdote concerning the marriage counselor who advised the constantly battling couple to look for things they have in common instead of dwelling on "irreconcilable differences." Whereupon one of the quarrelsome partners said, "Hey, doc, if it weren't for our irreconcilable differences we wouldn't have a thing in common!")

The best way to get along with your boss is this: Size up his strengths. Sure, your boss may micromanage, or act in a laissez-faire way at times, or in certain areas, resist some of your new ideas, not be available as much as you would like, and so on. But everyone—yes, even bosses—has certain strengths. So why not identify those strengths and appreciate them to the fullest, for they may well more than compensate for weak or less-attractive skills or traits. For example, a colleague of mine has an overextended boss who wears several hats and thus practically abdicates his responsibilities insofar as my colleague's particular work is concerned. But what more than compensates for this perceived shortcoming is that his boss supports him in his decisions. And for my colleague that characteristic is extremely valuable, for his work requires a great deal of decision making, much of it impinging on the functions of other offices.

Several things you might do to make your relationship with your boss bloom are discussed below.

Relationship Building—Can You Think Like Your Boss?

No, we don't mean marching in lockstep to his fife and drum with a resultant surrender of your own uniqueness and creativity. What we do have in mind is can you put yourself in his boots—empathy, if you will—so that:

☐ You can understand readily where the boss is coming from—his values, beliefs, goals, priorities, style—the WHY or basis of his needs and expectations.
☐ You can anticipate his approach to problem solving and decision making. ("Given circumstances A, B and C, I bet the boss would favor approach X rather than Y.")

☐ Your managerial radar can pick up those early warning signs concerning his problems, concerns, pressures, frustrations, anxieties, preferences, dissatisfactions, ambitions—the WHAT of his needs and demands.

So if you find yourself saying, "I just can't understand that person . . ." it may be that you are not elevating your antenna high enough so that you can "read" your boss more often than not. If nothing else, some would say that the truly "unpredictable" boss *is* predictable in his unpredictabilities. Although the odds, more realistically speaking, are that there are patterns, values, and approaches you may not have worked through hard enough to discern.

A good question to pose to yourself daily is this: What can I do to help my superior meet better today's needs, problems, demands? Obviously, you can't anticipate all of those needs. But most likely you can ease some of today's burden on him by attending to or providing items such as the following:

☐ Background information for a scheduled conference, staff meeting or interview.
☐ Inputs concerning an inspection, field trip, or plant visit.
☐ Information regarding the status of projects in which he is particularly interested.
☐ Data concerning a competitor, a new market trend, or how a sister unit is faring.

If you are not sure of what support the boss may need on a particular day, consider asking about it the prior afternoon or the first thing in the morning. (If the boss is an early arriver, you may have to arrive early to learn of his needs for the day.) Or check with the boss' secretary regarding his schedule to provide clues.

One way to impress the boss that you understand his needs, pressures, and concerns is to offer to carry out chores he shies away from. For example, if the boss dislikes attending routine, time-consuming committee meetings, offer to take on that task. Or if he is readying himself for a field trip, offer to assist with any details to facilitate the departure. Or if the boss gets bogged down with recurring reports, offer to lighten his load by preparing the more routine portions. Other possibilities include: offering to pinch-hit on low-priority speaking engagements; developing agendas for conferences; conducting surveys on internal personnel and office management matters; researching topics requiring special data; visiting other offices, plants, or laboratories inside or outside the organization to learn of particular practices, procedures, policies, etc.

The bottom line, then, is that if you can think like the boss you can do a better job of giving him solid staff assistance. This should result in the boss' placing greater trust and reliance on your relationship with him and future success rather than stress in your job life.

Keeping Up on Your Boss' Interests

Bosses, like everyone else, have particular interests, not all of which are directly job related. So it behooves you to learn of them, for you don't want to be caught with a blank look on your face when the boss asks, "Did you see that report in this morning's paper on the Briggs/Allen merger? I never thought that . . ."

Obviously, you can't anticipate every external event that may intrigue your boss. But you should have a fairly good idea on a number of his interests. So ask yourself these questions: What are the boss' interests of a general sort? Business happenings, economic news, national or international affairs, sports, hobbies, or what? How can I best keep informed in these areas? Besides the daily newspaper, should I read *The Wall Street Journal,* a particular weekly news magazine, trade periodicals, and so on?

If your boss finds that he can converse with you on a broad range of issues, he will feel that you are on his wavelength and likely will rely on you to a greater degree than if you don't seem to be up on the things he is.

Respecting the Boss' Time

Whether it's a memo, a one-on-one briefing, a report, or anything else that consumes time, recognize that your boss has no more hours in the day than you do. In fact, he may have less discretionary time than you because of a greater number of meetings, appointments, interviews, field visits, assorted demands from his manager, and so on.

So plan accordingly. Prior to meeting with your boss, develop an outline to keep things on track. Try to time your meetings so that they fit into the best time frame for your boss. If you have a fair amount to discuss, there's no point meeting with the boss just before he has to take off for his boss' staff meeting.

Learn his preference as to written progress reports, which he can peruse when time allows, versus informal, verbal briefings.

And observe his body language—paper shuffling, clock glancing, and general fidgeting are signals that the meeting is ready to be wrapped up. If you have more to cover, suggest an additional meeting later on and commence your exit.

Conveying Compliments

If you accept the concept that bosses, like the rest of us, are human, you will recognize that they, too, crave praise. The odds are that your boss' manager is very busy and of "the old school" and thus has neither the time nor the inclination to pass along any positive strokes. (Negative strokes, yes, but hardly positive ones.)

So if it's to be, it's up to thee. You work closely with the boss. You know of his accomplishments, so why not provide some applause when it's merited? This may be awkward at first, but after a couple of renderings, you'll be able to do it with minimal embarrassment. You don't have to pile it on, of course. Keep it short, simple, specific, and sweet: "I thought your talk to the suppliers went over well. I particularly liked your statement on . . ."

Of course, the praise should be *earned* and doled out intermittently, not as a routine matter. You don't want your pats on his back to be regarded as insincere flattery. A good opportunity to provide praise is when he was particularly helpful in contributing to the success of a project of yours.

You also can use positive reinforcement (praise) to alter a particular behavior of your boss. For example, assume your boss typically comes down hard on a staffer who is slow in stating her problems or concerns at staff meetings. But in this instance the boss was very patient and encouraging of Mary. So after the meeting you let your boss know that the new behavior was effective and appreciated by everyone: "Boss, I couldn't help but notice how Mary beamed when you told her to take all the time she needed to tell her story. And the rest of us felt good about the fact that you were very patient with her and helped to draw her out."

Note: You may anticipate a by-product from your providing praise. Your boss may loosen up and start to pass some of it along to you and your fellow staffers! And he may be delightfully surprised to get compliments rather than complaints.

Deferring to Your Boss' Style

It may cramp your own style a bit, but it's good business to massage your boss' ego by showing him that you appreciate his style to the point that you are adopting certain aspects of his style/behavior/manner. **Examples:** If he operates in the office in "full dress" as opposed to coatless or possibly only wears a vest, do the same. Also try to approximate his arrival and departure times.

Other practices that may merit imitating: Your boss prefers to send notes rather than to communicate face to face; the boss keeps a super-clean desk; your superior holds socials at his house on occasion; your boss is a visual person so he uses phrases and words like "the big picture," "it looks to me," "point of view," etc.

How to "Look Good" and Be Effective at a Meeting with Your Boss in Attendance

When you attend meetings with your boss present, he probably is "grading" your performance. If you want a big fat "A," here is some perceptive advice from Marilyn Moats Kennedy, in her newsletter *Kennedy's Career Strategist* (reported in "How Would Your Boss Grade Your Meeting Attendance?", *Supervisory Management*, January 1995):

☐ Sit opposite the boss, providing eye contact and a message of your involvement and enthusiasm.

☐ When you talk to your boss, include the others who are present by varying your eye contact between him and the other attendees.

☐ Be prepared. Take pertinent notes along.

☐ Watch your disagreements. Do it, but do it gracefully: Not "I disagree," but "I can see that point, but had you considered . . . "

☐ Also help co-workers in attendance "get off the hook" with a graceful comment such as, "Your viewpoint is commendable, but did you know that . . . ?" This will show your boss that you respect your teammates and their positions and that you are not engaging in any onerous one-upmanship.

☐ If you are bored, don't show it. Take notes instead. But no doodling, for that communicates to everyone that you'd rather be out on the golf course or at the ball game.

How to Manage Your Boss in Times of Adversity

Rare is the organization in which managers only experience successes and triumphs as opposed to intermittent defeats and occasional setbacks. You thus should anticipate your boss may also be subject to assorted organizational ups and downs—reorganizations that shrink his authority, cutbacks that severely affect budget and staff, priorities and new policies from on high that suddenly alter on-going activities and curtail plans for new or anticipated programs.

The net result of any of these changes and pressures is that your boss may be subject to stress, anxiety, and insecurity. His reactions to stress may produce coping behaviors that may make him difficult to live with: irritability, moodiness, unpredictability, withdrawal of delegated authority, decreased willingness to share information, more unilateral decision making, and the like. Your boss, in short, may be "running scared."

While you may feel that it is "unfair" for your boss to "dump" his anxieties on a subordinate, nevertheless, this is a time when your boss needs you the most. These needs, of course, relate to a greater-than-ever degree of understanding, support, patience, and tolerance of less-attractive behaviors. Tell yourself that your boss currently is in a predicament brought on by events over which he has little or no control; that you thus fully understand his moods and behaviors; and that you not only intend to live with these difficult circumstances, but that you intend to do everything you can to help the boss weather the storm.

If your boss survives the setback, the odds are that he will always remember your support. If he should be forced to bow out, you will have the satisfaction of knowing that you functioned as a mature and understanding subordinate as opposed to contributing to his anxieties in a stressful period.

How to Get Back into Your Boss' Loop

Due to restructuring and reorganizing, your sphere of operation may have changed. Your accessibility to your boss may have changed, too. You feel, however, that you still can contribute significantly to the firm's objectives, particularly if you were more "in" on things. What might you do about this?

In an article "Getting Back Into the Boss's Loop" (*Supervisory Management*, October 1994), two strategies are suggested:

1. Whenever you run into your boss in the hall or cafeteria, suggest casually that although now on the "sidelines," you are rooting for him and the issues with which he is currently confronted. You thus would like to help him on one or two of them. Don't offer specifics; just let the boss wonder about what you might accomplish unofficially. He respected your abilities in the past so your offer may intrigue him a bit. Smart bosses are eager to get all the help they can.

2. Take a bolder tack, meet with your former boss and remind him of your capabilities and past accomplishments. Indicate you feel somewhat slighted and would like a fair shake to reprove your worth.

How to Work Under a Younger Boss

Psychologically speaking, it is understandable that an older manager may have some resentments working for "a brash upstart whose career is racing ahead faster than their own," says business writer Joann S. Lublin in her article "You Can Flourish Under Younger Boss By Avoiding Pitfalls" (*The Wall Street Journal,* September 1, 1993). Her advice to senior managers who find themselves hooked up with a younger boss is to do the following:

☐ Don't belittle the younger boss. Don't toss in frequent references to your many years of experience, implying that the young upstart has an awful lot to learn.

☐ Don't leave the impression that you will be tough to manage because "you are rigidly set in your ways." Instead, show your flexibility wherever you can.

☐ Consider updating your wardrobe, your familiarity with current management gurus (invest in and read the latest management books), and make a point of writing snappier rather than long-winded memos.

☐ Speak up enthusiastically in staff meetings rather than sitting there glumly with arms crossed.

☐ Try not to resist your boss' ideas. They may appear radical, even less than workable. But if the outfit wants the benefit of the younger person's ideas, you have to salute them and do your best to make them succeed.

☐ Shed any appearance of having a know-it-all attitude based on your long experience.

☐ Avoid references to "the good old days."

☐ Pick up newer ways of doing things, e.g., working readily with computers.

Human resource consultants offer some added advice (Rhoda Amon, "Older Concerns Over the Young and Restless," *The Washington Post,* February 16, 1992):

☐ Don't "mother" or "father" the boss. Trying to make points with the younger boss in this manner will merely aggravate matters. It will just revive memories of unresolved conflicts—the young boss pins the faults of his parents on the older person and the older employee expects the (young) boss to have the same faults as his kids.

☐ Be glad you're out of the pressure cooker your young boss is now in. The best tack is to sit down with your young boss, talk things out and assure him that you're eager to help him succeed.

☐ If you're an older woman returning to the work force, you may resent working for a younger female boss more so than working for a younger man. But your best attitude should be to recognize that women need to support other women just as men need to support other men.

☐ Try to forget financial rewards (salary increases, promotions). Instead opt for job satisfaction, which comes from making a real contribution to the firm.

How to Get Your Boss to OK Your Budget Without Trauma

Money is the lubricant to get and keep your unit's wheels going. So you want to use the best strategies possible to secure what your unit needs. Management writer Joseph D. O'Brian offers these suggestions ("Getting Your Budget Accepted," *Supervisory Management,* November 1992):

☐ Your first step is to ask what is needed to render the best service possible.

☐ Learn of your boss' priorities. If it's to ensure repeat business, address that issue in specific terms, e.g., new equipment, better ordering procedures, etc.

☐ Base your presentation on research, including statistics about work volume, customers' waiting time, and the like to justify possible added staffing.

☐ Use other departments' budgets to support budgetary increases.

☐ Tie your requests to overall company priorities and objectives spelled out in the annual report.

☐ Echo the tactics of other supervisors who have been successful in getting budgetary increases.

☐ Watch allocation of overhead to your budget. Is your unit actually responsible for the amount charged to it? If not, seek a change in the allocation to reflect actual costs, thereby achieving a better bottom line.

☐ Learn informally if more money is likely to be forthcoming for one of your projects. If things look good, draft a formal proposal.

☐ Don't hesitate to propose new costly expenditures if they are essential investments to produce greater customer satisfaction or increased sales, such as a toll-free telephone line.

☐ Cut things before people in an effort to keep trained people and preserve morale.

☐ Set your sights high, but don't be upset if you don't get everything you asked for.

How to Negotiate a Pay Raise

If there is one single universally espoused management principle, it is that bosses should take the initiative to recognize above-average performance and offer subordinates appropriate pay increases. Unfortunately, this ideal behavior may not always occur for reasons ranging from budget constraints or the lack of a formal organizational policy on salary increases, to sheer insensitivity. If you feel that you have been bypassed for a raise unfairly and want to broach the subject with your boss, here are some procedures that may prove helpful:

1. Work at your interest in a salary increase *all year long*. That is to say, feed your boss regularly information regarding your accomplishments in the form of memos and reports. Emphasize cost savings and your contributions to the bottom line. Pass along copies of any letters of commendation or appreciation you have received. Better still, ask the letter writer to address the letter of appreciation directly to your boss. In general, your request for a raise should flow logically because of your superior performance all year long.

2. Consider your timing. A good time is when the firm is doing well. A banner year eliminates the possible rebuttal of "We're barely in the black."

3. A week or so prior to the time a raise is in order, present your boss with a written statement detailing your past performance. Try to stress the growth in your job and its importance to the organization. Cite any significant innovations you have introduced. Your memo will set the stage for a "negotiation" meeting.

4. Your accomplishments should be expressed in terms of "hard data"—increases in production, sales quality, customer satisfaction, and profit and/or decreases in cost, waste, rejects, returns, complaints, turnover, absenteeism. *Results* are hard to ignore, even by the most obstinate of bosses.

5. Avoid any requests for an increase based on essentially extraneous personal factors such as seniority, loyalty, lapse of time since the last raise, a pending marriage or other financial needs ("I have three kids in college," or "I need to make a down payment on a house"). Another *non sequitor* is proper completion of assigned projects. This is expected of everyone all the time.

6. Request an appointment to discuss your interest. Try to schedule the meeting at a time when your boss is not rushed. Your boss' secretary should be able to help out on this. (We are assuming that you have been "cultivating" your boss' secretary all along for this and other reasons.)

7. Present an attitude of confidence in your meeting. The perception of power is often its own reality. So if you appear to have doubts about yourself or your data, you enter the negotiation session without power. **Note:** Your boss, obviously, is in the more powerful position because he (a) controls the purse strings and (b) has an "experience edge," i.e., operating from the vantage point of having dealt with the other staffers on the same problem. Nevertheless, you have the advantage of knowing your job and your accomplishments better than anyone else.

8. Let your boss know that you like the outfit, your job, and the direction and support you have been receiving. (But if you can't say it honestly, skip this assertion.)

9. You may wish to cite comparative pay data—the going rate for your type of work in the industry and/or pay rates for peers elsewhere in the organization. Anticipate, however, that not all bosses will be overwhelmed with appeals based on equity or justice. Pay comparisons with your immedi-

ate colleagues are to be avoided. You may be treading on sensitive ground.

10. If your position has changed considerably, take your updated job description along to help point out growth in your area of responsibility.

11. Try to anticipate reluctance to your request such as "the budget won't stand it," "we only had a mediocre year," "we're not doing much about raises this year," etc. Show that you understand his problems or concerns. But steer the conversation back to the highlights and tangible aspects of your banner year. Try to secure agreement that you *did* perform in a superior way. A skill point: Role play the area of objections/resistance with a colleague or your spouse in advance of your formal session.

12. Put yourself in your boss' moccasins and consider some of the questions which he might ask himself: "What risks do I run if I deny the request?" "Will it impact morale or motivation?" "Will the turn-down stimulate a search for another job? If so, how long will it take me to locate and train a suitable replacement?" Obviously, to the extent that you are a "valuable property" you have power. I recall the case of a colleague who had an inflated opinion of her worth to the organization. She attempted to use a job offer with another firm to bludgeon the boss into granting her a handsome raise. The boss simply smiled and, calling her bluff, asked politely: "When are you planning to leave us?" The poor woman practically fell out of her teeth. In this connection, *The Washington Post* columnist Richard Cohen ("Want a Raise? Vote for It," January 27, 1989) has observed, "The ultimate horror is not to be turned down; it is to be told that we are not even worth the money we are already getting."

13. Don't push for an immediate response. Your boss may need a little time to internalize the idea or to get various clearances on your request.

14. If your raise request is denied, don't regard it as the end of the world. Managers, like salespersons, have to be able to accept a certain amount of rejection. On the positive side, you may have dropped a seed that will bear fruit later on. Dawn Pendfold, a personnel placement specialist, offers this added advice ("Negotiating for Dollars," *Meeting News,* April 10, 1995): (1) Ask how you can increase your value to the outfit, or (2) bar-

gain for other benefits you favor such as extra vacation time, flextime, training opportunities in outside institutions, subscriptions to pertinent publications, and/or membership in professional associations.

15. Try harder to manage the boss well, continue to be a cheerful, supportive subordinate, and communicate your accomplishments more systematically throughout the next year.

Note: The above paragraphs provide skill approaches in convincing your boss that you're worth more than you're being paid. But a pay increase in today's organizational climate might actually be hazardous to your job health. Julie A. Lopez, in an article entitled "Raising Your Salary Could Help Sink Your Career" (*The Wall Street Journal,* March 9, 1994), cites instances of managers who were dropped shortly after receiving generous pay increases. The reason? They had become too expensive for their firms to keep!

So take stock of your company's economic climate and your salary before your try for another pay increase. If the company is substituting temps for permanent workers, or giving more work to outside contractors, or the grapevine is providing rumors about pending layoffs, that certainly would indicate a bad time to opt for that raise.

If you decide that a pay raise may make you vulnerable to a job loss, e.g., a newcomer may be brought in for less money, you do have several alternate routes to greater compensation:

1. You could seek a promotion that entails greater responsibility.

2. You could suggest taking more of your pay in bonus form. In this manner you increase your income without boosting your official salary.

3. You could opt for a company-funded educational program, e.g., to secure a higher degree or to attend an advanced management training program at a leading university.

And a final point: If you're doing high quality work and it goes unappreciated over a several year period, sharpen up your resume, tap your network, and consider relocating to a greener and friendlier pasture.

How to Communicate Effectively with Your Boss

I don't want any "yes" men around me. I want people to tell me the truth even if it costs them their jobs.

—Attributed to movie mogul Samuel Goldwyn

A number of the topics previously discussed relate to communicating with the boss. The following general principles or guidelines will serve to round out this vital skill area. Management consultant Terry Van Tell ("Communicating with Your Employees and Boss," *Supervisory Management,* October 1989), offers these skill pointers:

Respect your boss' communication style and avoid superimposing your own. Examples: Is he interested primarily in general information (a bottom-liner) or a lot of specifics (detail oriented)? Does he think short or long range?

Respect your boss but don't be afraid of him. In any case, don't exhibit your fear.

Risk candor. Most managers respect people who present rather than conceal their true convictions. **Note:** Temper this advisory with your prior history with the boss and also the nature of the current problem.

Connect yourself actively with your accomplishment. Don't say passively, "The Alpha project was done in record time and was under budget, too." **Better:** "I'm really proud that we completed the Alpha project ahead of time and below budget as well."

When complaining, use these guides: Keep your anger under control; prepare an outline of what you intend to say; start out by stating/acknowledging the boss' view of the difficulty; express your feelings via the use of "I messages"; don't get defensive; indicate what would be a proper outcome/end result; suggest more than one solution, as appropriate; ask for a follow-up meeting to gauge progress on resolution of the problem.

Another aspect of communicating with the boss is communicating failure. Management writers/consultants Jay T. Knippen, Thad B. Green, and Kurt Sutton ("How to Communicate Failures to Your Boss," *Supervisory Management,* September 1991) suggest the following:

☐ Present your non-success as quickly as possible. You're much better off if the bad news comes from you than someone else. There are two advantages to this approach: 1) It demonstrates your candor and cooperation, and 2) it makes certain that the relevant facts in the case come from you because you know the most about the circumstances surrounding the event.

☐ When meeting with the boss, be direct. Tell what you want to discuss and why.

☐ Provide sufficient background on the happening—when and how things began, and what led to the unfortunate situation.

☐ Secure the boss' reaction. It may be that the mistake isn't as grave as you think.

☐ Discuss ways to remedy the situation. Advise what you've already done to mend things and what else needs repair.

☐ Take full responsibility for the problem. You can't blame another staffer for the error.

☐ Tell your boss what you've learned from the experience.

☐ Advise of any possible positive results, if any, that accrued.

☐ Summarize the steps you plan to take to secure remedial action.

☐ Thank your boss for any support, understanding and encouragement he may have shown, including any help offered to find a solution.

How to Resolve Problems with Your Boss

Bosses may or may not mean well; but problems may still arise. A number of common problems are discussed below with suggestions on how to deal with them.

Your Boss Ignores Your Accomplishment

This is a vexing situation, indeed, for you are more than on top of your job. In fact, you are an outstanding performer. But rather than psychoanalyze the boss in an attempt to ferret out his reason(s) for not recognizing your A-1 performance and singing your praises, you will do better to take steps such as the following ("When Your Boss Won't Recognize Your Success," *Supervisory Management,* January 1994):

☐ **Self-promote yourself.** You may feel awkward about tooting your own horn, but if your boss won't, you have no other alternative. So let the in-house newsletter editor know how well one of your projects is proceeding. In fact, give the editor a write-up on one of your successes. (Editors are always looking for worthy success stories.) Once you break out into print, you may trigger praise from your reluctant boss.

☐ **Let colleagues do your P.R. work.** Another tack is to get your co-workers to go to bat for you. This, again, may encourage your boss to loosen up on his puny praise practices.

☐ **Talk candidly to your boss.** If your boss basically is approachable, talk to him on an open, face-to-face basis. State that you are disappointed that no recognition has been forthcoming. Assure him that you will continue trying to excel, but that it does hurt to be overlooked. In your discussion, be certain to ascertain whether the value you place on your accomplishment is in sync with the way he sees it. Learn, too, whether your time, talent and energies are being properly placed.

The author would add this tactic: Provide periodic (possibly monthly) reports about your accomplishments so there's no question that he knows that you want him to be cued into your stellar performance. Also, offer to meet with your boss to further clarify any fuzzy items in your report. Indicate, too, your plans for the next month or quarter and ask him if they are in line with his own views. In general, you want to stimulate his thinking about what you've achieved and hope to accomplish.

You Have an Incompetent Boss

Less-than-able bosses come in all shapes, sizes, attitudes, and behaviors. We'll enumerate some of the more common ones with suggestions for managing them.

☐ **The unorganized boss.** Your boss is a messy, poorly organized operator. He loses your memos, forgets to keep appointments you have made with him, ignores agreed-upon priorities, gives "heavy" assignments on short or no notice, suddenly cancels staff meetings, and more. **Your best strategies:** Enlist his secretary to better organize his life. Also, try to engineer an off-site team-building session where you and your fellow staffers can appropriately let your hair down about his peccadilloes and try to get some relief. What you can't do is send him to a time management course or psycho-

analyze him to learn whether his early toilet training had proceeded properly.

☐ **The overly zealous delegator.** As managers we want our bosses to delegate to us in depth—full freedom, no strings attached. But if we are given full responsibility without any guidelines/expectations from the boss, we may be faced with a murky, impossible task. **Your best strategy:** Politely confront your boss with the fact that you cannot do the A-1 job he expects, and you would like to deliver, without some real guidance. Stay with him until you understand what his expectations are.

☐ **The "wishy-washy" boss.** You have a boss who is very much on the ineffectual side, and tends to go off on minor tangents. **Your best strategy:** Give him the most important question/issue to resolve first. In this manner, he won't get sidetracked by minor areas of concern.

☐ **The perfectionist.** "Nothing can move since nothing is perfect" is the boss' unstated but real mantra. However, if we can't live with an endless stall, we have to help the boss act or decide. **Your best strategy:** Assure the boss that "it's OK to let go," that the completed job looks great, that there's little risk in moving ahead, and that the greater risk is in inaction.

☐ **The fire-fighting boss.** If you have a boss who seems to thrive on rapid movement, chaos, and pandemonium—everything is urgent and should have been accomplished yesterday—your challenge is to sit the boss down and get some planning into the operation. **Your best strategy:** Use the team approach, letting the boss know that (a) everyone is experiencing total job misery and (b) that with a modicum of planning things will actually get done better. But you must offer concrete examples of how planning is superior to turmoil.

☐ **The procrastinator.** Delays, on matters you need to get done or get moving on, may well impact negatively on your area of responsibility. **Your best strategy:** Shake your boss up a bit by communicating that if we don't get going on this activity, the big boss will land all over us and we'll all look like a bunch of dodoes.

Another way to jar your stalling boss into action is to give him a memo with a "time bomb" attached to it: "I'll go ahead on this unless you tell me otherwise by the 15th."

You Have a Timid Boss

You have a boss who lacks confidence in himself and is reluctant to act, to push things up the line, and so on. **Your best strategy:** Build his ego whenever you can. Compliment him whenever he does something you like; e.g., he successfully sells an idea of yours up the line. Of course, it wasn't his idea, but he did move it upward successfully. Your (earned) compliment to him should help improve relations with the boss as well as build his courage a bit for future transactions.

Your Boss Makes Hasty Decisions

While you may have the all-too-common misfortune to have a boss who is painfully slow to decide things, it is also possible to be subjected to a superior who is too impulsive. Too fast decisions, of course, can give you problems you hardly need. So what to do? Management writers Jay T. Knippen and Thad B. Green ("What to Do About a Boss Who Makes Decisions Too Fast," *Supervisory Management,* April 1994) assert that you have to level with your boss and convince him that more time is required to research and analyze the problem under consideration. These procedures should prove helpful:

1. State the nature of the problem and point out fully why it needs more consideration before things are finalized.

2. Cite the potential impact of the decision on costs and profits plus other key points such as risk, far-reaching consequences, long-term influences, and how a bad decision will impact your unit.

3. Point out the specific areas where vital information is in short supply and that it is essential for a sound decision. Advise where, how, and when that information can be garnered. Suggest who can get the information or offer to do it yourself.

4. Suggest a time frame to secure the needed information. Don't let the boss impulsively set a premature date that will handicap the quest for the needed information. Provide reasons to justify your more cautious date. You'll also want to avoid setting a date later than is necessary.

Key point: Your emphasis is to prevent the boss from committing a hasty blunder that in all likelihood will bomb, really make him look bad. Conversely, by slowing things down, you keep him out of trouble and ensure that he will look good as a result of the added research and time invested in it.

Your Boss Gives You an "Impossible" Assignment

Your boss may or may not be aware that he has given you a complex assignment that you regard as "impossible." This is primarily because of the short time frame he has indicated. If so, these procedures may help you to get some "relief":

☐ Ask enough questions so that you are fully certain what is actually involved in taking on this responsibility.

☐ Give your boss the benefit of the doubt that he doesn't realize that the demand is unreasonable. Why would your boss want to work you to death, anyhow?

☐ Meet with your boss and calmly tell him that you are intrigued with the nature of the assignment—possibly its novelty for you, its ramifications, its overall challenging aspects.

☐ Indicate that you wish to start on this project now, but that its nature is such that a quality job will not be assured if you are required to operate within the unrealistic deadline provided.

☐ Also, tell your boss up front that you will need added resources (possibly staff, budget, special equipment, an added room) to do all that's entailed.

By realistically presenting him with your circumstances as to time and needed resources, you are putting the monkey on his back where it properly belongs—he now has to decide priorities and how much resources he is willing to commit to allow the new project to fly successfully. Keep in mind the following:

1. If you let your boss pressure or seduce you into taking on an impossible job, you run the risk of producing failure. And who needs that? Sure, there may be a risk in challenging your boss on the nonworkability of the assignment. But the greater risk is to assume responsibility and end up with a fiasco that certainly won't help your reputation any.

2. Present "the facts of life," in writing as well as orally. This will demonstrate that you have given the matter serious thought. Additionally, a written document is likely to be more impressive than a verbal plea.

3. In responding to the boss on the impossible assignment, the natural reaction is to say "No." Management consultant Tim Gosselin ("Negotiating with Your Boss," *Training and Development,* May 1993) advises to learn to say "Yes, and here's what the costs or results will be . . ." In effect, you are testing the deadline, budget, or other constraints. You are trying to find out how much "give" there is in the limits the boss (unthinkingly) has set. In addition to negotiating for more time and resources, you may wish to suggest that certain aspects of your current work might be assigned to someone else or possibly be subcontracted out to help free you up to take on the new "hot" project.

You Have Conflict with Your Boss

Disagreements with one's boss do arise. How best to cope with them? Business writer Joseph T. Straub ("Coping with Conflict with Your Boss," *Supervisory Management* in Quick Tips, August 1993) suggests these approaches:

1. After your meetings, make detailed notes for analysis of who said what and in what context. Use them for future reference to predict how your boss will respond to like situations later on.

2. Contact co-workers to learn if they have experienced similar conflicts, how they handled them, and what they would advise to help you to cope better.

3. Make certain your assignments are clear as to desired end results. Use the technique of restatement to ensure that you are on the same wavelength as your boss: "As I understand the thrust of this assignment, you expect me to . . ."

The author would add that it often is essential to carefully think through how to present your point of view. The phraseology you choose or the questions posed can inflame, garner apathy, or elicit agreement. Consider the following anecdote:

It seems that a monk in a monastery asked the abbot if it is OK to smoke while praying. The superior replied authoritatively, "Definitely not." The following day the monk asked the abbot if it is permissible to pray while smoking. Replied the superior, "It is not only permissible, but highly admirable."

You Have to Cope with Criticism from the Boss

When we feel intimidated by negative feedback, we may respond in less-than-helpful ways—we may tend to defend ourselves, attack in retaliation, or escape the confrontation as best we can. But there are better ways of managing criticism. Consider these situations ("How to Take Criticism," *Supervisory Management,* October 1994):

☐ **You are totally wrong.** Your only action here is to grin and bear it, admit your error, and indicate what you will do next time so that you don't blunder again. **Advantage:** It shows that you can accept criticism and that you have enough confidence in your ability to learn from error and to improve. **Note:** There's little to be gained by providing the reasons for your boo-boo unless your boss wants that detail.

☐ **Your boss unloads with vague criticism.** Your best response is to insist on feedback that is specific. So tell your boss, "It would help me to learn from my mistake and thus to improve if you could provide me with specific examples (or data) about my ineffective behaviors." **Advantage:** You are communicating to your boss that (a) you want to improve and (b) if he wants change/improvement, he can't engage in unhelpful, vague generalities about your performance.

☐ **You goofed, but don't know how to remedy it.** Your goal here is to show the boss that you're not a complete washout. One error does not a failure make. So you want to show that you do have "smarts," which you can demonstrate by describing what you learned from the error(s). Also, suggest the added skills you need to prevent future goofs and possibly how you can acquire those skills. **Advantage:** You create your own opportunities for upgrading your capabilities.

☐ **You are blamed unfairly for something that you didn't do.** One's natural reaction is to say defensively, "I didn't do that, boss." To avoid a defensive response, drop the "I" and start with "You," putting responsibility for the erroneous assumption back on your critic: "You are in error about who did it." Follow up your polite denial with an offer to help solve the problem: "I wasn't involved, but I would be glad to help clean it up. How might I help?" **Advantage:** You avoid defensiveness and end up, instead, on a positive note, offering to help your boss out of the difficulty.

☐ **You solved a problem, but in an unorthodox, unauthorized way.** Instead of getting defensive when the criticism comes your way for not following standard procedure ("I did solve the problem, didn't I?"), simply admit that you departed from the usual approach. Then indicate the advantage that ensued by plowing new ground and ask if you can continue to operate in the new mode. **Advantage:** You can accept the criticism as legitimate, but offer a counter procedure and explain why it is superior. If your system works, it will be hard for the boss to insist that things be done in the old, less-effective way.

Of course, the "healthy" way of looking at criticism is to regard it as a fundamental means of achieving growth. Communication authority Dr. Walter O. St. John ("Profit from Criticism," *Personnel Journal,* July 1990), suggests that we use these principles and techniques to help us remain open to feedback:

☐ **Gain control of your emotions.** Remain calm, cool, and collected. Look at the data coming your way as help, not pain.

☐ **Show that you're sincere.** Evidence by work and deed that you want suggestions and criticism. Make a positive statement like: "I'm sure I can do better. I look forward to your ideas that will be of help." Listen, smile, look interested, and nod frequently.

☐ **Assess the source.** Is your critic sincere and qualified to offer criticism? If the feedback is similar to what others have said, you can be quite certain that it is valid.

☐ **Listen carefully to the words and voice tone.** Watch body language, too. Don't jump to conclusions, interrupt, or refute what is being said.

☐ **Assess the criticism.** Is it constructive or destructive? Is it general or specific? Are there suggestions for improvement as well as criticisms?

☐ **Ask for examples.** You can't be helped if you only receive vague generalities. Use statements like: "Could you explain in more detail . . ." or "Could you elaborate on your point about . . . ."

☐ **Check your understanding of what was said.** It's all too easy to miss something or misunderstand what is presented. Restate what was said to be certain you fully received what was presented. Ask for clarification if necessary.

☐ **Request help.** Ask: "What should I do now?" or "Where do we go from here?"

☐ **Summarize what was said.** This will ensure both you and the critic that you didn't miss an important point.

☐ **Ask for time to absorb what was said.** Arrange for another meeting in a day or two. Do this before you react to the criticism.

☐ **Present thanks for the data.** Show your appreciation. This will keep the valuable pipeline open.

☐ **Assess the criticism.** If it's factual and helpful, try to implement it. If it's unfair, let the feedback giver know why you find it difficult to accept it, either in whole or in part.

Your Boss is an Unfair Complainer

Your boss is not really up on what you do or what you go through to get things done. One day he unloads on you and testily says, "You could have finished those two projects a week ago if you'd worked harder on them." **Your best strategy:** Don't become defensive. That kind of behavior will blow it for you. Instead, (agree with) join him in his assertion, but then say, "I agree that I could have worked harder. But are you aware that besides my overtime most evenings, I had to work two of the last three weekends to accomplish as much as I did?" In effect, you are being assertive, standing up for your rights as opposed to letting your unknowing, insensitive boss walk all over you.

Your Boss Unfairly Passes Blame on to You

If your boss blunders and tries to dodge responsibility by pinning the blame on you, you have a real problem, one that's near insoluble. Business writer Joann S. Lublin ("Bosses Who Deflect Blame Put Employees in a Tough Spot," *The Wall Street Journal,* August 11, 1993) offers these suggestions:

☐ If blaming you for his mistakes is a recurring behavior, you may want to decide if your boss is the kind of employer you want to live with. But short of a departure, you do have other options.

☐ You can always suffer in silence, just frown and bear it. It's always possible that your boss may feel guilty enough about his less-than-gallant behavior and try to make amends in some way. In effect, the boss "owes you one." By taking the heat you show your loyalty, that you're a super team player and, as your reward, you may receive widened duties and responsibilities. Of course, there is a risk that your silence may backfire. Someone up the line may want to know why you didn't let others know what happened.

☐ You can accept the blame, but let colleagues or those who can help your advancement know of your innocence. But in this plan you try not to implicate your boss. You don't want any apparent act of disloyalty on your part to get back to your boss.

☐ It may be of value to meet privately with your boss, to clear the air in a diplomatic way. But weigh the risks carefully before you try this tack.

☐ You can protect yourself by keeping a "CYA" file. The "cover your anatomy" documentation about the incident may ward off later trouble, particularly at performance review time.

☐ A procedure that may help, in some cases, is to inform your boss that you feel you need to meet with senior management about the mistake. Of course, this is a high-risk tactic and should be weighed carefully in light of a myriad of factors—your reputation in the firm, your boss' standing, how well you know your boss' manager, how your boss might feel about being circumvented, the seriousness of being scapegoated for the boss' blunder, etc.

Your Boss Doesn't Like to Hear the "Bad News"

Some bosses don't want anyone to tell it as it is. For example, if certain items in the product line are real duds, it's almost suicidal to hint at them. Or if certain staffers are not pulling their weight or are totally obnoxious, again the boss would rather not hear about it. So what might be done? Consider these suggestions:

First, soul search and assure yourself the issue is important enough to alert the boss to some of the real facts of life.

Second, meet with the boss when he is in his most relaxed state.

Third, broach the subject gently: "Bob, I hate to be the messenger bearing bad news, but I've thought it over and I think you should know about a bad situation." (Assuming you get a go-ahead sign, continue to the next step.)

Fourth, confront the boss with the matter and point out the consequences that are likely to ensue if corrective action isn't taken, and possibly that he will end up with egg on his face.

Fifth, present a solution or possibly a set of options to the problem. Presenting a possible solution is more effective than merely dumping the problem in the boss' lap and then exiting.

Your Boss Defines Certain Topics as "Undiscussables"

As every sensitive subordinate knows, some topics simply are off limits. One's superior need not issue memoranda to that effect, but the message is communicated to staff one way or another, loud and clear.

But if the taboo topic(s) needs airing for unit effectiveness, what can a conscientious subordinate do about it? Some might say "not much"—"undiscussables" mean exactly that. On the other hand, given the right timing, it may be possible to bring to the surface that which isn't normally spoken about. How might this be done?

One possibility is to use the team as a vehicle for overcoming the usual inhibitions on truth-telling. Thus, at a staff meeting, or better still at a team-building session with an outside facilitator present, some of the "risk" of leveling with the boss may be reduced. The advantage of the team approach is that feedback to the boss from a number of staffers is less likely to produce defensiveness, anger, and recrimination than if a lone staffer dares to pierce the iron communication curtain. Also, because the purpose of team-building sessions is problem identification and problem solving, all topics presumably are now on the table. The undiscussables become fair game.

If things are going badly and consultants are brought in to collect data about what seems to be bugging the outfit, this, too, would be a good opportunity to ventilate about taboo topics.

Note: Skipping channels and going directly to the boss' boss on an issue is a high-risk approach and ordinarily isn't recommended. Similarly, sending unsigned memos to the boss' superior is a doubtful procedure because it may create new problems.

You Have Trouble Getting Projects Approved by Your Boss

One possibility for this is the nature of the projects, of course. But more likely, it may be the way you've treated the plan meeting. Management consultant Paul D. Lovett (in "Meetings That Work: Plans Bosses Can Approve," *Harvard Business Review,* November-

December 1988) says that the manager you report to wants four questions answered before an approval will be forthcoming:

1. What is the plan?
2. Why is it recommended?
3. What are its goals?
4. What will it cost to implement it?

Focus on these four elements to avoid overloading your presentation with unimportant facts or tons of paper. Provide specifics—no waffling and expecting your boss to supply the answer.

Recognize that the real planning occurs *before* the meeting. You and your staff must think through your grand plan carefully and boil it down to a sharp, concise and convincing presentation. Use a lot of empathy. Ask yourself: What does the boss really need to know, no more and no less, before he can sign off on the plan?

If you answer these four questions clearly, it will lead to a logical conclusion and an agreed-upon course of action to achieve the desired results.

Your Boss is Reluctant to Provide Feedback About Your Work

As a subordinate, you are entitled to know (a) how your boss perceives your work and (b) what you might do to perform more effectively. Of course, we know that not all bosses are willing to provide such feedback. This may be due to being busy with other matters, not really being up on the subordinate's work results, and/or simply being insensitive to the fact that people want and need feedback.

In any case, if feedback isn't readily forthcoming, you might try these approaches:

☐ Meet with your boss and tell him that you could be more effective with regular feedback from him.
☐ Specify the particular areas where feedback would be valuable and would make a real difference in your performance.
☐ Try to set up a periodic meeting time for such discussions. Indicate that you're even willing to do this after 5 p.m. because you regard the need so highly.

Your Boss Takes Credit for Your Ideas

This is a touchy situation, for confronting the boss on what is essentially a character flaw may well backfire.

One possibility, but a risky one, is to talk to your boss' manager about the series of thefts. Seeking employment elsewhere may be a more appropriate course of action. Or you may stay on and comfort yourself with the thought that "it is far more serious to have to steal than to be stolen from." (At least this was the advice the old music professor in the movie *The Red Shoes* (1948) gave to a student of his who complained to him that a choreographer had stolen his music for the ballet.)

While we would not recommend seeking revenge for the theft as a realistic option, there is a pertinent old anecdote about a disgruntled speech writer who did so.

It seems that a self-centered politician took credit for speeches he had not written or even reviewed before delivery. On one occasion, his speech writer wrote a speech for an unusually big audience of the politician's constituents. The politician read the speech which began as follows: "I'm going to tell you how to have prosperity and absolutely no inflation, at the same time. I'm going to tell you how to restore traditional morality and yet let everyone do his or her own thing." And then he flipped over to the next page, which was entirely blank except for the line: "Guess what—you're on your own."

Your Boss Appears Unhappy with Your Performance and Seems Ready to Fire You

Robert Half of Robert Half International Inc., which recruits accounting, financial, and data processing personnel, suggests you look for danger signals (e.g., you're not invited to important meetings) and listen to the grapevine regarding your status. To head off dismissal, says Half, you might pursue these steps (reported in "Odd Jobs," *The Washington Post,* June 7, 1992):

☐ Preempt the firing by leveling with your boss: "John, I get the feeling you're not happy with what I'm doing. What can I do to make you happy with me?"
☐ Summarize your work accomplishments and present them to your boss. State: "I've done these things, I can do more. Give me the XYZ project. I'll do it even if I have to work Saturday and Sunday."
☐ Ask for more responsibilities at your current pay or volunteer to work in other functions.
☐ Soul search: "Is it my attitude that has the boss upset?"
☐ If the ax is really about to fall, ask for a transfer to another part of the company.

☐ If others in your unit have been complaining about your boss and you're sure you are to be dropped, you might talk to your boss' manager. At this late stage you have nothing to lose.

Your Boss Demands Prompt Answers on Details of Your Operation

A boss who constantly keeps asking for details on this, updates on that, what the vendor said on that last shipment, what you told A, B, and C, etc., can certainly induce an Excedrin-sized headache. Nevertheless, if the boss has an endless need to know of the minutiae of operations, you have to be fully organized to feed him the data that he believes are necessary. So keep clear records within easy reach, following these guidelines ("Just-In-Time in the Information Age," *Training,* January 1992):

1. **Establish a personal filing system that allows you to collect and locate information easily.** These files will serve as an index, a rapid locator to tell you where to find what. Our assumption here is that the information is available, but scattered in several locations—in a locked cabinet, in your desk, with a particular subordinate, in personnel files, etc. For example, the contracts file you set up might contain the locations of many individual contracts.

2. **Be sure your staff is cued into your personal filing system.** Have them know its purpose and characteristics, and their responsibilities to help keep it current. If they have to move or redirect a file, they should insert a note in its place.

3. **Get in the habit of recording information.** Don't rely on memory. Use your telephone log to record what you said, when, and to whom. Record longer phone conversations on a steno pad.

The bottom line: If you're properly organized file-wise, you can keep your boss happy, avoid crises, and save time for your staff and yourself.

Your Boss Engages in Angry Screaming

Being abused verbally by one's boss is hardly a picnic. But there are ways to cope with a boss' tirades and tantrums, says human resources writer Carol Kleiman in "What to Do When the Big Bad Boss Gets All Steamed Up" (*The Washington Post,* September 19, 1993). She draws on the suggestions of Andra Medea, a conflict management consultant, whose ideas can help you to survive in a hostile workplace.

☐ Respond with a "flat surface," i.e., show little reaction to the temper tantrum. Why? Because screamers feed off your reaction. They require it because it stops them from examining their own behavior. If you show anger, fear, being upset, fidgeting, or other stress signs, it will only worsen matters. In the absence of a reaction by you, they have to listen to themselves.

☐ Do something surprising. One client of Medea's really shook up her screaming boss by reaching for his wrist and then taking his pulse. He was so shocked, he couldn't recall the reason for his anger.

☐ Talk to a neutral voice at a higher level of management about the problem. But this may be risky, so proceed with caution.

☐ Document each incident. It may come in handy at a later date, e.g., in a wrongful termination case or a worker's compensation case.

☐ Try to defuse the situation with humor, if you have that gift. But a boss in rage may have no humor.

Psychologist Leonard Felder (quoted in "Odd Jobs," *The Washington Post,* August 8, 1993) suggests that you employ either of these rejoinders when your boss is foaming at the mouth:

☐ "Time out! I want to hear what you have to say but I need you to slow down a bit."

☐ "I'm very interested in what you're saying but I'll wait until you're done (to respond)."

Either approach, says Felder, "Makes you the facilitator and the manager. You've broken out of being treated like a scolded child."

Taboos—Tread Tenderly and Thoughtfully

Part of the art of boss management is to avoid behaviors that clearly raise red flags for the boss. Included in this batch of "no-nos" are:

Going Around End

If you work for a "problem boss" and can't get your needs met, there may be a temptation to short-circuit your supervisor and contact the boss' manager about the difficulty. Skipping the established chain of command is a high-risk procedure, unless (a) the situation is so urgent that you have to get an answer immediately or possibly a radically superior one, (b) you do have a special "in" with your boss' boss, or (c) it seems to be standard operating procedure.

Of course, in all of these circumstances you are going around him. And if you are interested in furthering your career, your boss is unlikely to regard this action with merit. In fact, you may have to think in terms of a possible departure to another firm without the prospect of obtaining a good reference from the boss.

But if you do decide to see your boss' manager directly on a rare occasion, you should:

☐ Carefully think through why you are doing it and what you will say.

☐ Assure your boss that you dislike going over his head.

☐ Provide detailed documentation as to how bad the situation has become or how urgent the matter is.

☐ Indicate how the manager's boss can help matters now clearly in disarray.

Note: A rare boss, with an unusually strong ego, may have no objections to his staffers seeing his boss directly on matters where the boss' manager is in a better position to provide advice or make a decision. Under these circumstances, the boss may only request that (a) you let him know that you are seeing his boss and (b) you inform him of the results of your special meeting.

Becoming the "Teacher's Pet"

While you may think that being chummy with the boss is the acme of on-the-job bliss, the realities are that it is more likely to be a no-win relationship. As the title of Julie A. Lopez's article in *The Wall Street Journal* (June 8, 1994) puts it, "Being Your Boss' Pal May Be Hazardous to Your Career." Why? Consider these realities.

A good relationship with the boss is crucial. But when it's flaunted or exploited, you are very likely to alienate your colleagues. Some may feel that you are getting inside information. They may stop trusting you and withhold important business information for fear that you will communicate it prematurely to the boss. Or, out of envy, they may not invite you to important meetings. In today's all-important team operation, your effectiveness will drop without trust and respect from your co-workers.

Becoming the boss' pal—spending extra time with him, joking around, etc.—may result in the boss' regarding you only as a friend, not as a true professional. A possible result: promotions may stop coming. What happens if your boss gets dropped or leaves for another job? You're totally alone, left without anyone—boss or peers—to support you.

If being the boss' crony should backfire, it may be hard to restore your reputation and your prior healthy relationships with your peers. Lopez recommends as "damage control" a friendly confrontation with your fellow staffers. Admit that you erred, that you alienated them and ask how you can make amends so that you can get back "into the loop."

Socializing Indiscreetly

An easy "boo-boo" to commit is to lunch or otherwise socialize with people from another office who your boss detests or is in conflict with for one reason or another. Career strategist Marilyn Moats Kennedy warns, "Illogical as it is, if you are good pals with a peer in a rival department, your boss will question your loyalty" (quoted in "The Enemy of My People . . .", *Supervisory Management,* March 1985).

Sure, no one should tell you who to shun for luncheon dates. But if you want to avoid rubbing your boss the wrong way, do it on the QT. Adds Kennedy, "Office politics thrives on both fear and reality. Pursue an open friendship at your peril."

Communicating Your Complaints Candidly

Inevitably, many of us will develop certain negative feelings about the company, the operation we're in, or even the boss. Generally, we're pretty cautious about how and to whom we vent our complaints. But a trap to approach warily is when the boss smilingly asks, "What do you really think?" Business writer Joan E. Rigdon offers some perceptive advice about candor in her article titled "Even When They Ask, Bosses Don't Want Your Complaints," (*The Wall Street Journal,* August 10, 1994).

Obviously, you don't want to give your boss any negative feedback in a public situation, e.g., in a group meeting. You're better off presenting complaints or criticism in private, one-on-one. But this, too, may be high risk, even if the criticism is requested and delivered with great tact. The reason? Most people, including bosses, don't relish direct criticism of themselves. Egos are very easily bruised by negative feedback.

If you do decide to level with the boss, very carefully think through (a) your motives—e.g., are they punitive?—and (b) what are the possible benefits and risks?

If there is an anonymous electronic suggestion box, you may wish to use it. Or a management retreat or team-building session, with the aid of a trained facilitator, may provide an opportunity for candor. But if you do provide the boss with feedback, try to couch it in terms he will regard as helpful. For example, you may feel that your boss should delegate more responsibility on certain recurring projects. So you diplomatically state, "We could get these projects done more quickly and make more money if I had full authority to . . ."

Note: Part of managing well is to overcome the impulse to criticize without ascertaining the realities of the situation. Although a decision by your boss may be off-base, it is also possible the decision was based on factors to which you were not privy—broader considerations, pressures from within or outside the organization, future needs, etc. Perhaps British Prime Minister Benjamin Disraeli said it best: "It's much easier to be critical than to be correct."

Talking "Out Of School"

Be exceedingly careful to whom and what you say—even socially—about your work, the office's work, and your boss. While you may not intend to communicate dissatisfaction, disenchantment, doubt, or disloyalty, the listener may interpret your statements in such a way. He may then acquaint your boss with your feelings. The data regarding your "disgruntlement," transmitted to your boss, may be intended, unintended or merely hinted at in a matter-of-fact, very innocent, casual way. But the impact on the boss may well be the same: "What's eating Pat anyhow?"

Personal note: This incident happened to the author. I raised a very minor question about a new service the firm had launched. The next day my boss said to me, "George says that you think our new service is a mistake, that we should never have gotten into it." I had a hard time explaining what I had really meant.

Showing Up The Boss

If your boss blunders in some way, you can let him stew in his juices, or you can bail him out. Here are several strategies to consider, depending on your preferred outcome (presented in "Showing Up the Boss," *Supervisory Management,* February 1994, based on material for *Executive Strategies*):

1. Correct the error, telling the boss about it in private. **Advantage:** Your boss will feel that you can be trusted.
2. Again, correct the mistake, and keep quiet about it. **Advantage:** This is a wise and safe procedure if your boss doesn't accept criticism well or if your relations with your superior are on the weak side.
3. Correct the boss' boo-boo and tell his boss about it. But only do this if you believe that your boss is holding you back.
4. Skip making the correction, but promptly tell the boss about his error. **Advantage:** You save the boss from embarrassment by highlighting the error while it is still correctable.

Inflaming an Insecure Boss

Some bosses may have serious insecurities or self-doubts. So how do you cope? For starters, don't play psychologist and try to ascertain the causes for the feelings of inadequacy. Your better tack is to avoid incidents that trigger those feelings.

Management professor Jay T. Knippen (in "Dealing with an Insecure Boss," *Supervisory Management,* March 1995) suggests this sensitive approach:

First, identify (recall) those situations wherein your boss' statements or behaviors that illuminated his insecurity, e.g., uneasiness about making certain decisions, not taking a stand on a controversial issue, not seeking advice from staff when he clearly should have, etc.

Second, skip complaining about the behavior. Instead, behave in ways that don't ignite his insecurities, behaviors that might negatively impact your group. Before acting, then, ask yourself: Will my action be threatening to the boss? In effect, have a workable, responsible plan before you unload it on your superior.

Third, when you implement your plan, do it carefully. Watch each step for beginning signs of insecurity. If the boss seems to be uneasy at any point, back off and modify your tack.

Fourth, evaluate what took place—which behaviors on your part worked and which did not. Keep these data in reserve for future use. Your next session with the boss will profit from your efforts at eruption prevention.

Note: Besides guarding against situations that trigger insecurities, it's also good business to behave in a way to bolster the boss' feelings of self-worth and self-confidence. Don't hesitate to provide a compliment when merited.

Whining about the Boss

Don't complain to others about your boss. A good percentage of your listeners may well feel that you should know how to cope effectively with your boss. Others may believe your boss is totally blame-free and that you are wailing unnecessarily. The few who would support your perception in all its sincerity probably would accept your view, too, that your boss puts ground glass in his coffee as to come across more abrasively! In other words, you have little to gain by carping about your supervisor to others. If you need sympathy, seek it at home or among friends off the job.

Signaling a Departure

In these days of various cutbacks in organizations, opportunities to move ahead may be slowed down. Understandably, then, we may look for greener pastures elsewhere. However, many managers view the prospect of a subordinate manager leaving as a supreme act of disloyalty.

The best tack, then, is to fully hide your job search or offer for as long as possible. Make certain your prospective employer doesn't spill the beans prematurely. Once your boss gets wind of your "treasonous" desire to jump ship, he may write you off—no more training, travel money, pay increases—even if the new job possibility doesn't pan out.

COPING WITH INTOLERABLE BOSSES

To keep our topic of managing the boss in proper perspective, it should be recognized that not all bosses can be readily helped or even merit help. Michael M. Lombardo and Morgan W. McCall, Jr., *Coping with an Intolerable Boss* (Greensboro, N.C.: The Center for Creative Leadership, 1984) conducted a study of 54 executives who had an unbearable boss at a given stage in their careers. The respondents' descriptions of atrocious bosses were grouped into categories such as these:

Snakes in the grass. This largest category describes managers who lack integrity and simply can't be trusted.

Some characteristics: lying, failing to keep their word, and using their power to extort confidential information.

Attilas. Also known as dictators, little Napoleons, martinets, and ex-Marine types, they tend to ignore their own mistakes and become highly irritated if a subordinate made a decision or reaped any glory.

Heel grinders. These managers relish in treating people like dirt. They love to rake others over the coals and specialize in belittling, humiliating, and demeaning their subordinates.

Dodgers. Their bag is to evade responsibility and refuse to make decisions.

Detail drones. Strictly by-the-book types, they revel in petty detail.

Incompetents. Can you visualize superiors who don't know their jobs and won't admit it? If you can, you'll understand the "Peter Principle." (According to management writer/satirist Dr. Lawrence J. Peter: "In a hierarchy, each employee tends to rise to his level of incompetence. Every post tends to be occupied by an employee incompetent to execute its duties.")

Slobs. Their pecadilloes entail slovenly personal habits and boorish behaviors.

Other categories described by Lombard and McCall were "The Not Respected" and "Personality Clash."

The bad boss problem does not seem to go away—at least, the management literature treats this topic repeatedly. Stanley Foster Reed in *The Toxic Executive* (New York: HarperCollins, 1993) describes management types such as "The Narcissistic T.E.," "The Super-Jealous T.E.," "The Nitpicker T.E.," "The Toady T.E.," etc. Dr. Robert Bramson, author of *Coping with Difficult Bosses* (New York: Simon and Schuster, 1993) adds some more: "The Fire Eaters," "The Wafflers," "The Power Clutchers," "The Super Delegators."

A later study (reported in "Odd Jobs," *The Washington Post,* April 9, 1995) asked people to describe their worst and best bosses. The human resources consulting firm, Hammes and Associates, Deerfield, Illinois, found that the "worst" traits were:

Control obsession. This personality entails domination, micromanagement, and very low trust of subordinates.

Inaccessibility. This behavior consists of spending little time with staff, avoiding subordinates, and failing to share information.

Authority obsession. There is a heavy emphasis on criticizing subordinates and strongly asserting authority.

How do you cope with a bad boss? Typically, we might pursue one of these three less-than-productive approaches:

1. Simply complain about it. We can button-hole anyone who will listen—colleagues, subordinates, friends, family members, the friendly bartender—and constantly unload on them. Although this approach may have some cathartic effect, it will hardly make a dent in the problem. It may also "turn off" those who don't particularly wish to listen to "bad-mouthing whiners."

2. Retaliate by withdrawing our cooperation. We can delay things, withhold useful information, subtly lower quality, take advantage of the sick leave system, etc. These activities would be covert and intermittent so as to proceed unnoticed, but they would be frequent enough to ensure that the boss stews in his own juices. Again, although we might feel better by executing this vengeful act of polite sabotage, the situation would probably be aggravated rather than alleviated.

3. Accept one's fate and stoically suffer in silence. We can always tell ourselves that there probably aren't too many "good" bosses anyway. Also, maybe the boss will leave via transfer, promotion, retirement, or illness. Or maybe we can sweat it out until our own retirement.

A more practical approach is to use the insufferable situation as a learning experience. In fact, Lombardo and McCall say their interviewees learned two kinds of lessons from dealing with their intolerable bosses: (1) how to cope with adversity and (2) how to do things better by watching their bosses' negative behaviors. Following are some of the coping strategies they learned:

☐ Time suggestions/actions with the upswing period of "roller coaster"-type bosses.
☐ Keep interactions on a professional rather than a personal basis.
☐ Be confrontational on major issues only and yield on less vital ones.

☐ Give yourself regular morale-building reminders that "I work for the organization, not the boss."
☐ Exercise a great deal of patience, adopt a low profile, and leave as a last resort.

MANAGING UPWARD

Coping strategies, such as those cited above, obviously are essential if you have a true bear of a boss. But any manager is advised to hone his skills of "upward management" to deal with the boss in a professional, positive and productive way. Consider these two examples concerning bosses who were not "total horrors" at all, but had less-than-attractive traits requiring a need for careful upward management.

☐ I worked for a boss who was pleasant enough on a face-to-face basis. But when he was alone in his office and encountered something that bothered him, he typically would pen extremely nasty memos to his subordinate managers, including me. As might be imagined, this one-way, hit-and-run communication procedure was as difficult to cope with as it was irritating. I found, for example, that when I replied with a memo of my own that he really didn't read it or, if he did, he invariably would misinterpret what I had written or soon forgot its contents.

I ultimately learned to cope with his menacing memoranda by simply walking into his office to explain my position. Typically, he would back down and politely say: "Oh, I see what the problem (or situation) really is. Thanks for telling me." And later I developed a still more effective technique which entailed going on the offensive to even a greater degree. Specifically, I would make a point of visiting him in his office each day, chat a bit and ask if there was anything I could help him with, anything I should know about, were there any pending problems involving my unit, etc. In effect, by maintaining daily contact and confronting him on current or potential problems, real or imaginary, I defused his tendency to "discipline" me with "poison pen" letters. By virtue of these daily visits, my boss' behavior was modified—he had learned to hold his problems involving my unit until I came to see him. The problem could then be discussed rationally and disposed of on its merits.

☐ Fred, a colleague of mine, had a boss who was reluctant to offer praise. Fred used a "behavior modification" approach to secure an occasional stroke. Whenever Fred's boss, Gordon, expressed any degree of satisfaction with a completed task, he made a point of expressing warmly to Gordon his appreciation for the praise, even though the comment was terse and given begrudgingly. His tack: "Gordon, I really appreciated your reference at this morning's staff meeting to my early completion of the A-4 project. I'm the kind of guy who thrives on recognition and your statement about my work before the group was very rewarding to me." And not only did Gordon give Fred an occasional stroke or two, but he doled out some to other staff members, too. Gordon never seemed too comfortable rewarding anyone publicly, but he did do it on occasion.

The significance of these two examples is not that they represent the use of unusual degrees of skill to cope with self-centered, somewhat withdrawn bosses. Rather, they point out that more often than we may think possible, strategies can be devised to cope with the less-attractive and less-effective behavior of our bosses.

Part of your effectiveness in coping, obviously, is to know when to be assertive and confront the boss on an undesirable behavior and when to simply live with it. The quiz, "Confronting the Boss—A Problem Solving Exercise," will provide you with skill practice and serve to stimulate your thinking about this boss-subordinate relationship. Take a few minutes to tackle the quiz on page 24.

Another coping strategy suggested by a witty colleague of mine: Get rid of an undesirable boss by making that person look so good that he will get promoted—up and out and gone!

WEIGHING A DEPARTURE

There is very little future in being right when your boss is wrong.

—Anonymous

If coping strategies are not possible in dealing with the truly bad boss, the obvious last resort is to leave. However, before you adopt such a drastic course of action, you may wish to make a final attempt to see whether the situation is at all salvageable. Here are several suggested procedures to implement the final effort.

Take Worksheet 1-2 (page 33), "My Boss' Leadership Style and Needs System," which you have already completed. Study Item 1, "His/Her Leadership Style." Compare elements (a) and (b). Which element has more items in it? What is the significance of this? Now look at the items in the element (b) space. Check those items as follows: "L" for those you can live with and "C" for those for which a coping plan can be devised if you make a serious effort to do so.

Now look at those items you did not check. How significant are they? Are they "bearable" at all? If you believe them to be highly harassing or unbearable, keep in mind the options below.

1. Talk to your boss about one or more of his leadership behaviors in a constructive way. In such a meeting you must avoid the temptation of merely applying negative labels. You certainly don't want to put your boss on the defensive. Instead, focus on your needs for greater effectiveness on the job that are not being met. Also, in giving the boss feedback, present your complaint(s) in the "I message" format: "When you . . . I feel . . . because . . ." Describe his behavior, tell your feeling about it and how it affects you: "When you run your staff meeting an hour past quitting time, I get upset because it means I will have to miss my evening class at the college." As a basis for your discussion, use Worksheet 1-3, "My Boss and My Needs System" (page 34).

2. Look for opportunities to bring up some of these harassments at staff meetings or team-building sessions, where you are likely to get some support from one or more colleagues.

3. Consider pulling the plug. But leaving is not an easy decision to make, particularly if you have a rather heavy investment of time in the job or, possibly, you feel strongly about the worth of your organization's mission. You thus may ask yourself: "Is my department better off with me or without me?"

Personnel consultant Ellen Lemer (in "The Bad Boss," *Meetings and Conventions,* June 1992) suggests that when you are considering departure, be certain to do some serious soul searching, separating fact from fiction. Then ask yourself these questions: Absent the bad boss, would I still want to work there? If he were gone, would the job be perfect? Am I dumping on him, using the boss as a scapegoat? And do I really like what I do?

If I became a big lottery winner tomorrow, would I exit promptly or stay on as previously?

The author would add this question: What advice would I give to a friend/colleague who was in my situation?

In any case, if your boss has a style that you simply cannot tolerate, or you cannot respect his values, or the boss is a corrupting influence, it would seem appropriate to extricate yourself from this frustrating situation and quit punishing yourself.

In this connection, the Research Institute of America, a New York consulting firm, offered the following advice (reported by Linda Grant and Lois Timnick, "A Nightmare Working for a 'Crazy' Boss," *The Washington Post,* September 17, 1980): "If getting away from a raging boss is the only way for you to keep your sanity, it's better to go sooner rather than later. Putting up with irrational behavior over a long period of time will utterly destroy your self-respect. What's more, you are almost certain to become emotionally involved if you live with constant turmoil for years. Then you are quitting not because of the boss' emotionality, but because of your own."

Note: Your departure may be via internal transfer, if possible, or by total separation from the organization.

If you do decide to leave, be sure to (a) have your new job offer in writing and (b) provide the usual notice of departure of two to four weeks. Or better still, ask your boss what he feels is appropriate in light of his and general office needs. Offer to train a replacement, if the situation requires it. **Rationale:** You don't want to leave on harsh terms if you can avoid it. Also, "clean up" outstanding projects before you depart.

Confronting the Boss—A Problem-solving Exercise

Listed below are a dozen irksome situations involving a boss-subordinate relationship. Your procedure: Insert an "L" before a statement if you could "live" with the situation. Insert an "AC" if you would be assertive and confront your boss on it. Provide a rationale for each course of action. Then compare your approaches with those appearing after the problems. If you are in a group training program, the trainer may ask you to compare your responses with your colleagues in a small group prior to checking the author's solutions.

Problem Situations

1. [   ] Your boss edits your letters (or other written work) almost to the point of re-writing them. You don't feel at all that your writing is that atrocious.
Comment: _____
_____
_____
_____

2. [   ] Your boss ribs you quite regularly at staff meetings. This makes you feel quite uncomfortable, for you regard his comments as "put downs." The group generally laughs at his remarks, which hardly helps matters.
Comment: _____
_____
_____
_____

3. [   ] You are a non-smoker, as are four others at your boss' staff meetings. The boss and three others are smokers. The ventilation is not the greatest, and typically the smoke buildup becomes pretty heavy. You don't care very much for this secondary smoke imposed upon you.
Comment: _____
_____
_____
_____

4. [   ] You work hard to turn in various assigned projects. You want feedback, but invariably the boss is slow (10–15 workdays) in reviewing and returning them to you.
Comment: _____
_____
_____
_____

5. [   ] Your boss is generally slow in responding to your requests for leave, either for a single day or for a week or two of vacation time.
Comment: _____
_____
_____
_____

6. [   ] Your boss ignores company policy concerning a full discussion of performance at year's end.

Typically, the various adjectives on the performance rating form are merely checked off and the form is returned to you. Although the adjectives your boss provides are generally acceptable to you, you wish that there were a real discussion concerning past accomplishments and growth on the job, possible training opportunities, plans for the next year, etc.

Comment: _____

_____

_____

_____

7. [   ] Your boss is not particularly training minded and rarely approves attendance at training courses, either in-house or those offered by outside organizations. You are a high achiever and are strongly motivated toward self-development.

Comment: _____

_____

_____

_____

8. [   ] Your boss eats lunch at her desk, unless she is away from the building or out of town. You wish the boss would ask you to have lunch on occasion.

Comment: _____

_____

_____

_____

9. [   ] Your desk is in a large room. Your boss frequently closes the door to his office to take certain phone calls, to talk to a visitor, to work on the report for the period, etc. The overall effect, as you and others see it, is that he seems to want to keep things overly private and confidential.

Comment: _____

_____

_____

_____

10. [   ] The boss' staff meetings are a big bore. Most of the talking comes from the boss: the last field trip, her boss' staff meetings, plus a lot of trivia on minor matters. You feel that at least some, if

not most, of the time should be devoted to real problem solving.

Comment: _____

_____

_____

_____

11. [   ] The boss typically adopts your ideas and credits himself with their origin.

Comment: _____

_____

_____

_____

12. [   ] You try to be honest with your boss on a bad situation that has developed. It seems that customers are complaining about the boss' new "pet" product. Unfortunately, your good intentions backfire—he jumps all over you for bringing him "the bad news."

Comment: _____

_____

_____

_____

Author's Solutions

One way to approach these irritating situations is to consider how ingrained the boss' behaviors are, and to what degree they are basic to the boss' style and personality. If they are basic elements of the boss' operating style and needs system, he probably won't change them very much merely because a subordinate challenges or confronts him. On the other hand, if these behaviors reflect primarily a lack of sensitivity or empathy on his part, it may be that the boss can be reached on them. In the latter circumstance, a change might be possible if a particularly egregious behavior is a somewhat isolated trait and the boss is a "healthy" person (considerate, understanding) in practically all other respects.

Note: Anticipate that you won't agree with all of my responses. Not only are our operating styles, personalities, and job experiences different, but your thinking will be influenced by your knowledge of your boss and his turf.

1. My hunch is that the boss who loves to edit in depth is doing it to meet various personal needs and abnormal ones at that—perfectionism that

reflects a fear of "letting go," the need to exercise power over others, the need to demonstrate superior competency, and the like. Obviously, "comma chasing" is hardly the best use of a manager's time. Nor is it conducive to any learning by subordinates. I would live with the behavior despite its annoying aspects and philosophically tell myself: "Any time I can get an upper-level manager to do my low-level editorial work, I guess I'm ahead of the game."

2. Any time anyone makes you feel uncomfortable, you have a right, as a person, to express your feelings about it. I thus might take this tack: "Pat, may I talk to you about one aspect of our staff meetings? (Pat nods agreement.) Well, I become very uncomfortable when you tease me at our meetings. The group generally laughs at your comments, which only helps to make me feel even worse. I become so upset that I usually withdraw and don't contribute anything thereafter." The odds are that if the boss is anything of a human being, he will get off the subordinate's back as a result of the feedback. **Note:** It is not unusual at all for any one of us to engage in behavior without an awareness of its impact upon others.

3. I would certainly mention the smoking issue at a staff meeting. If your boss wants to be a considerate person, he would indeed enact a ban at the meetings. You may lose on this one, but it's worth a try since it is essentially an "environmental" issue rather than a substantive (work-related) one.

4. The boss may not be aware of his behavior, but he is communicating, nevertheless, that your work is not very important. He is insensitive to your very healthy need to know how he, as your boss, feels about your accomplishment. One possible solution is to bring it up gently at a staff meeting because the odds are that it is a problem that affects the total management team. As an alternative, you could confront the boss on a one-on-one basis and present your case along these lines: "Boss, I would like to get your help on a problem that's really bugging me. It's these projects that I complete and turn in. I work very hard on them, including work at home, to meet the deadlines. I think it's only fair that I get your reaction to them in two or three days, rather than having to wait two or three weeks for any feedback. I know

you're real busy, but do you really think it's fair to keep me in suspense all that time?" The twin appeal to fairness and the "need to know" may be adequately effective. Another possibility might be to set more realistic turn-in dates to reduce the boss' response time.

5. This is another example of a boss' insensitivity to the need of a subordinate to know. Nevertheless, it is not a work matter, and is not really worth making an issue over. One possibility is to ask his secretary or assistant to help get the approval of the leave request in memo form as a routine matter: "I expect to be away on leave the day after Thanksgiving since Jean and I are driving to her parents' house in Bellville. The leave slip is attached. Thank you for your approval of this request."

6. This is a tough one to deal with. All the available research indicates that many managers shy away from full, candid and timely performance review sessions. One tack might be to meet with him and point out that you could be more effective in your job if you were to receive feedback about your performance. And if you are interested in developmental feedback, state at the outset of the interview, "I see this as an opportunity to learn of my strengths and weaknesses. May I assume you will cover both aspects of my performance?" The problem of perfunctory performance reviews might also be broached at a staff meeting because it is probably a group-wide problem. However, it may be pointless to push too hard on this practice since it would seem to be a basic element of the boss' operating style. The odds are that the manager doesn't receive a true performance review from his own boss, so why should he give one to anyone else? In any case, give it a try.

7. The boss who is not training-minded may be reached, but only with some well-thought strategies. One possibility is to offer to share the cost. Another is to pay for it all, but to attend on organization time. A third is to detail the importance of the training program (expected end results) and how your attendance will benefit the operation. Add that you feel so strongly about the value of the training that you will pay for it yourself. The later approach may "shame" the boss into an approval, either in whole or in part.

8. Let sleeping dogs lie! The "loner" boss has a strong need to function privately, to minimize contacts with others. Her insecurity and concern for her status probably won't permit any contact that smacks of "fraternization" with the low-status, hired help. (The odds are that she would not be adverse to lunch with her boss, for this would be a more prestigious outing.)

9. The physical setup may not be the best for reasonable amounts of privacy, quiet, and freedom from distraction. This may be the motivation behind the closed-door practice. In any case, even if there is an excessive need for privacy, it still is a matter of operating style, and you can certainly learn to live with it.

10. Try to encourage the boss to have the group assess the effectiveness of the meetings. If agreement to do so is forthcoming, you might bring up the need for a different emphasis—possibly 50% sharing of routine information and 50% problem solving. If this procedure is not possible, simply recognize that this is a matter of style and live with it. There are worse calamities than deadly staff meetings!

11. Stealing, whether it's someone's property or ideas, represents a character deficiency. However, it is not a matter on which you can confront the boss, for you would be calling him a thief. You may have to live with the situation and accept the dictum, "It is far more serious to have to steal than to be stolen from." On the other hand, if this behavior is one that you cannot tolerate, coming from a person you can't respect, and if there are other serious irritants projected by the boss, perhaps you would be better off leaving the outfit.

12. Depending on how "rigid" your boss is, you may wish to confront him later when he has cooled off. You might say something like: "Boss, I think it's good business and it helps our relationship if we both level with one another. I have leveled and have incurred your wrath. Would you rather I not be truthful with you?"

Key Skill Pointers

The manager who understands fully the importance of managing his boss will engage in the following behaviors:

1. Analyze his boss' job, leadership/operating style, and needs system to gain a better feel for where the boss is coming from.

2. As a consequence of this analysis, you should understand the boss' aspirations, goals and plans, concerns, problems, and priorities, and so perform to increase the likelihood of his boss' success.

3. Recognize that the boss is a human being and thus has need for support, encouragement, attention, and sincere praise, as well as for the expected technical assistance. Also, you will avoid backing him into a corner with possible loss of face.

4. Keep the boss fully informed as to progress on and problems with assignments and, above all, avoid embarrassing the boss with surprises.

5. Present solutions to problems as opposed to merely highlighting them.

6. Function in a positive and facilitating manner, but do not hesitate to challenge the boss and offer constructive criticism when needed.

7. Ensure that the boss gets the credit for success and thus is made to feel and look good.

8. Should you get a new boss, show him how indispensible you are and intend to remain so.

9. In all transactions involving the boss, ask yourself: "Will my action strengthen or weaken my boss' perception that I am an understanding and supportive subordinate?"

10. To the extent practicable, develop strategies to cope with the less attractive aspects of the boss' behavior.

11. Use "I messages" when it is essential to confront your boss regarding behaviors you find inconsiderate or possibly punishing.

12. Use positive "self-talk" to bolster your feelings about your supervisor, avoiding self-sabotaging messages ("can't," "don't know how," "it's too hard"). A good verbal guide: "What you say is what you get!"

13. Change yourself because your ability to change your boss, who has the power, is necessarily limited. **Example:** Assume your boss is a slow decision maker. Shift your self-talk from "That guy dreads making a decision," to "Hey, this gives me a lot of freedom to fill that void."

Problems, Exercises, and Questions for Discussion at In-house Management Workshops and College/University Classes in Management

1. Start the session by asking participants to state their understanding and significance of the concept of managing the boss.

2. Assign your participants to trios. Have them respond in writing to this question: What is the most difficult task you face in managing your boss? Then have each member of the trio pass his written statement to the person on his right for possible resolution of the stated difficulty. To wrap up the activity, have the trios share their learnings with the entire group.

3. What are some of the things we might do that would rub our boss the "wrong" way?

4. Ask the group to list (on flipcharts) their bosses' "pet peeves."

5. Assume that there has been a major reorganization and a slew of reassignments at the top. Your boss, unfortunately, was one of the losers in this reshuffling. Your boss is no longer "in the loop" and seems somewhat depressed. He no longer provides the guidance you need, nor does he act promptly on decisions affecting your unit. What are the options available to you in this situation? Which option would you choose?

6. Assume that you have a performance review with your boss in two weeks. What preparations might you make to ensure that things go well?

7. Assume your boss quite often pops into your office with a cheery smile around 4 p.m. to give you assignments he expects the same day. How might you deal with this harassing situation?

8. Your boss asks for your opinion on a matter, but you are quite certain that your answer won't jibe with what he wants to hear. What do you do?

9. What are the pros and cons of engaging in various sports activities (golf, tennis, jogging, power walking) with the boss?

10. How important is it for you to get your boss back on track after his field trip? And if it is important, what might you do?

11. Assume your boss "sits" on proposals requiring approval by his superior. You feel action is badly required. What are your options for action? Which would you choose?

12. Have participants complete the "My BMQ (Boss Management Quotient)—A Self-Quiz." Then have them discuss their scores in small groups.

13. Assign one or more problem situations for small group discussion and resolution given in "Confronting the Boss—A Problem Solving Exercise" (page 24). Secure feedback from the teams for their "solutions."

14. A colleague from another office passes this "scuttlebutt" along to you: He has been told that your boss feels you are trying to get his job. What are your options for response/action? Which would you choose?

15. Time and Your Boss.

As a result of your attendance at a time management program, you have been concerned with various procedures to conserve your time. As a good subordinate, however, you also wish to conserve the time of *your supervisor.*

Step 1

List below several ways in which you can save your supervisor's time. You have 15 minutes for this task.

1. _____
   _____
   _____
2. _____
   _____
   _____
3. _____
   _____
   _____
4. _____
   _____
   _____
5. _____
   _____
   _____

Step 2

Meet in small groups to compare and discuss your time-saving ideas (20–25 minutes). Record the group's ideas on flipcharts and post them on the wall for discussion.

Step 3

If the participant group wishes, the trainer will consolidate the several lists and distribute the complete list as a group-prepared handout.

16. The Case of the Over-supervised Manager.

Assume that you have just been appointed the head of Human Resource Management in a fast-growing R&D concern. You report directly to the company president. In fact, one of the reasons you left your prior firm is that you could report to the C.E.O. However, his two assistants are quite active in giving you assorted instructions and advice, even though they are not specialists in your field. You don't like this meddling situation at all. You decide to:

1. Not take any action since you are new, and besides this may be the way the big boss expects his key assistants to operate in relation to you.
2. Confront your boss with your concerns about "multiple supervision." Ask him directly what your relationship should be with the two assistants.
3. Confront the two assistants on the matter and advise them politely that your understanding of the lines of authority are that all instructions to you are to come directly from the big boss.
4. Conduct a "campaign" to become "buddies" with the two assistants. Shower them with attention, ask them for advice, "butter them up," and the like. Conceivably, after you've won them over, they won't have a need to flaunt their "authority."
5. ?? (Your option.)

17. The Case of the Reluctant Retiree.

You are 55 years of age and have been in the company 22 years. Your boss keeps dropping hints that people over 50 should seek "the good life" on the outside while they are young enough to enjoy it. You really have no desire at all to take an early "voluntary" retirement. You decide to pursue this course of action:

1. Ignore the boss' fatherly advice. Since your work is top notch, regard it as *his* problem, not yours.
2. Fight fire with fire. Respond with facetious comments about retirement such as, "I'd retire early but my wife wouldn't want me around the house all day," or "I agree, but I'm allergic to the smell of golf balls."
3. At the next performance review, subtly advise your boss that you like the work very much, that you hope to be with the firm for quite a few years to come, and that you are enjoying great health. In connection with the health angle, also make a reference to some very active physical things you are doing—tennis, jogging, long distance swimming, etc.
4. ?? (Your option.)

18. The Case of the Demoted Boss.

You are working in a company that has just gone through a merger and two major reorganizations. In the latest organizational shuffle your boss got the ax and is now a peer. What should your communication with your ex-boss about his "downfall" be like?

1. Show sympathy. Tell him you know he got a "bum" deal.
2. Indicate that all this is temporary and that he'll probably be back on top once management gets its act together.
3. Grieve with the boss. Your expression of sorrow will probably bolster his spirits.
4. Use this event as an opportunity to remind your former boss of his unfair treatment of you and others. Justice does have a way of being served over time.
5. Merely show empathy, candidly stating that undoubtedly the next few months will be a rough period to go through.
6. ?? (Your option.)

19. The Case of the Eager Subordinate.

A colleague of yours, Kim, comes to you for advice relative to the following problem:

Kim is an artist-illustrator in a direct-mail marketing organization. Kim has been with the company for eight years, having developed the basic approaches, procedures, and illustrative formats for the direct mailings.

Kim's boss, promotion manager Fran Best, has unilaterally hired a part-time illustrator to assist Kim since the operation has grown and Kim seems to have a bit of an overload. At times, the mailing of some promotional materials has been delayed because of the overload. The new assistant, Pat West, reports to Kim's boss, Fran—a source of minor irritation to Kim—since Fran likes to keep fully on top of all staff activities. After nine months on the job, Pat has complained to Fran about under-utilization, both qualitatively and volume-wise.

Kim has been concerned about Pat's style of operation: At times Pat has made commitments to others which were inappropriate, and on several occasions has tried to engage in activities clearly beyond Pat's experience level, expected duties, and responsibilities. Kim, who just turned 60, feels that Pat may be trying to take over the head illustrator job. Kim wonders if that is why Fran brought Pat in. Pat is 35 years old, sharp and, with training, would in time head up the art shop.

Fran has told Kim that there will be a meeting next week involving the three of them to discuss Pat's complaint about under-utilization.

Your advice to Kim is:

1. Do nothing at this point. Wait until the meeting to see what actually develops.
2. Talk to Pat before the meeting to find out what added duties Pat would like to perform, if any, taking into account Pat's interests and experience level.
3. Try to meet with the boss before the meeting to learn how Fran views the situation and what expectations Fran has from the forthcoming meeting.
4. Meet with Fran in advance of the meeting and lay your cards on the table. After all, you started the operation, it is going well, and your relations with Fran have been very good. Advise Fran that Pat is not an easy person to work with, getting into deep water unnecessarily. Pat's style may well embarrass the whole promotion function. **Rationale:** Head off improper assignments to Pat before they are made.
5. Meet with Fran and frankly express your anxiety that Pat, a very ambitious person, seems to be trying to take over and you wonder if that is Fran's intent, too.

20. The Case of the Aloof Superior.

You are Terry Williams, administrative aide to the chief of purchasing. You have performed well in the five years you have been on the job. You have enjoyed good relations with your boss. A subordinate of yours, Ian Bright, uses every opportunity he can to speak directly to your boss about day-to-day matters. You don't know what Ian is up to. You don't like Ian's behavior one bit and as a consequence you don't feel you can trust him. On one recent occasion when this occurred, you reminded Ian that you are his boss and that you would appreciate it if he took up all matters directly with you; and if the chief of purchasing is to

be involved, that you would still want to be the point of that contact.

Since that incident occurred, you have felt something of a chill between you and your boss. He has been sharp with you at times, seems less friendly, generally, and contacts you, it seems, less frequently than previously on matters where you could provide some helpful input.

You have discussed your problem with a colleague and collectively you see several possible courses of action. Which of these would you choose? Why?

1. Say and do nothing. Time itself may straighten things out. Maybe your boss is just upset about other things and not necessarily with you.
2. Try very hard to improve relations with your boss. Maybe this will turn things around.
3. Try very hard to improve relations with your subordinate. If you can "soften him up," maybe he'll be a good ambassador for you vis á vis your boss and yourself.
4. Confront your boss directly. Tell him you feel that he is cool toward you and you wonder what you did to create this new, colder relationship. Assure him that you are on his team 100% and want to perform totally as he wishes.
5. ?? (Your option.)

21. The Case of the Explosive Boss.

A friend tells you that her boss has a hard time dealing with pressure. When her boss is under stress he is likely to unload on a subordinate, any subordinate. Your friend says she has a hard time coping with these unnecessary, irritating and totally unprofessional outbursts. Which of these courses of action would you recommend?

1. Say and do nothing. Since you understand that the boss is essentially venting his emotions and is not mad at anyone, why not just accept the boss as he is, that his tantrums go with the territory?
2. Secure an appointment with your boss' superior and advise him of the childish, irritating scenes his subordinate makes. Hopefully, the big boss will counsel his subordinate regarding the need to try to keep his cool. **Rationale:** Managers at upper levels

frequently are unaware of less-than-desirable behaviors of their subordinate supervisors.

3. If attacked, strike back, but in a polite way: "Mr. Brown, you are making me feel uncomfortable. I understand you are upset but I don't believe you should talk to me or anyone else in that way." **Rationale:** The boss could use some stern, candid feedback about his irksome behavior.

4. Assuming you have a good relationship with your boss, speak to your boss about the problem when he is calm. Point out that while you can take the abuse, you think that his berating behavior lowers his image in the eyes of everyone in the shop.

5. ?? (Your option.)

Worksheet 1-1
My Boss' Job

Describe and analyze your boss' job to give you a better appreciation of his role, responsibilities, and concerns.

Major Responsibilities (List 5–7):

_____

_____

_____

_____

Priorities (List 3–4):

_____

_____

_____

_____

Major Problems (List 2–5):

_____

_____

_____

_____

Pressures and/or Headaches

a) Internal (List 2–3):

_____

_____

_____

_____

b) External (List 2–3):

_____

_____

_____

_____

Worksheet 1-2
My Boss' Leadership Style and Needs System

1. His Leadership Style

In the space below list as objectively as you can the major characteristics of your boss' leadership style.

a) **Elements of strength** (**Note:** Try to be fair. Give full credit for traits/characteristics that make him successful—e.g., goal oriented, decisive, etc.)

_____
_____
_____
_____
_____
_____
_____

b) **Elements which are of concern to me** (e.g., reluctance to delegate, inconsistent communication patterns, etc.)

_____
_____
_____
_____
_____
_____
_____

2. His Needs System

In the space below list the needs your boss has.

a) **Needs that facilitate operations** (e.g., to accomplish, to complete things, to embark on new ventures, projects, etc.)

_____
_____
_____
_____
_____
_____

b) **Needs that hinder operations** (e.g., to look good, to punish, to feel superior, etc.)

_____
_____
_____
_____
_____
_____

Worksheet 1-3
My Boss and My Needs System

Describe your relations with your boss in respect to your needs system. Try to be specific, objective, and realistic. Try to give credit where credit is due.

1. What I need from my boss that I am now getting:

_____

_____

_____

_____

_____

_____

_____

_____

2. What I need from my boss that I am now *not* getting:

_____

_____

_____

_____

_____

_____

_____

_____

3. What I need *less* of from my boss:

_____

_____

_____

_____

_____

_____

_____

_____

Figure 1-2
My BMQ (Boss Management Quotient)—A Self Quiz

Listed below are 32 statements that describe boss-subordinate relationships from the standpoint of managing the boss. Read each statement carefully and provide a letter grade for the statements according to the scoring guide. Be as candid as you possibly can in making your responses, thinking in terms of *how your boss would see a particular attitude or behavior of yours.*

Scoring guide:
 F = Your attitude or behavior is facilitating or healthy.
 I = Your attitude or behavior could be improved upon.
 N = Your attitude or behavior is negative (non-facilitating) in character.
 U = You are uncertain how to label a particular attitude or behavior.

1. [   ] I know precisely what my boss expects of me. If at any time I'm unclear, I present a goals or procedures statement for him to review, discuss, and clarify.
2. [   ] I understand my boss' job, pressures, schedule, deadlines, priorities.
3. [   ] I recognize that my boss may have a broader view of a problem than I do.
4. [   ] I operate on the assumption that my boss doesn't like surprises.
5. [   ] I try to keep my boss out of trouble.
6. [   ] A key role for myself is to make my boss succeed.
7. [   ] I operate so that my boss gets credit for my accomplishments.
8. [   ] My boss sees me as a reliable person. He knows that I will carry through on all assignments.
9. [   ] I make no promises that I cannot fulfill.
10. [   ] I always provide my boss with completed staff work.
11. [   ] I have developed a habit of saying: "I don't know, but I will try to find out."
12. [   ] I avoid using jargon my boss doesn't understand or words that may raise a "red flag."
13. [   ] I operate so that my boss sees me as a key resource and thus taps my expertise regularly.
14. [   ] I use my boss fully as a resource.
15. [   ] I try to show my boss how he will personally benefit from any proposals that I may make.
16. [   ] I accept my boss as he is—weaknesses and strengths, good and bad moods. (After all, everyone has a few rough edges.)
17. [   ] I maintain regular contact with my boss so that he knows that I'm available, interested, eager to assist, and generally a "good subordinate."
18. [   ] If my boss is wrong, I don't hesitate to tell him so. I do this by presenting facts and showing respect for his opinion, approach, perspective.
19. [   ] I seek out by boss' viewpoint when I know that he would like to have input on a particular problem or project.
20. [   ] I seek and offer help so my boss sees me as an ally.
21. [   ] When I recognize that my boss is determined to proceed in a particular direction, I avoid prolonged debate to advance my viewpoint.
22. [   ] I support and carry out my boss' decisions even if I may have reservations about them.
23. [   ] If my boss is not ready to decide something, I readily go along with his deferral.
24. [   ] I operate so that I conserve my boss' time.
25. [   ] When I "goof," I candidly let my boss know of it. "Cover-ups" are not part of my style.
26. [   ] I expect my boss to criticize my work. I see that as a way to grow.
27. [   ] I don't take my relationship with my boss for granted. I constantly try to improve on it by giving information, support, respect, appreciation, and praise.
28. [   ] I am not in competition with my boss in any way.
29. [   ] I show my boss a high degree of respect—for his ideas and also as a person.
30. [   ] I never communicate to my boss that he is not a bright person.
31. [   ] I make it a point to never bad-mouth the boss.
32. [   ] I always try to accept any social engagements which my boss may offer me.

Now that you have completed grading all the items concerning your attitudes and behaviors, tally the scores for each letter grade and enter your scores below:

F for facilitating [   ]   I for improvement warranted [   ]
N for negative [   ]   U for uncertain [   ]

You now should know where and to what degree you should make changes in your attitudes and behaviors to be effective in managing your boss.

2 How to Work with Peers/Colleagues and Manage Conflict Constructively

A good name, like good will, is got by many actions and lost by one.

—Lord Francis Jeffrey (1773–1850), Scottish critic,
editor, and jurist

I learned on our old basketball court how to resolve disputes. It was pretty obvious that when we'd start fighting, or somebody decided to take their ball and go home, everybody lost. But if you could show a little patience, back off an emotional situation, think it through and maybe even change the rules so that everybody could be left standing with a sense of dignity, the game could continue. And after all, wasn't that the objective? For everybody to play fair?

—Carl Stewart, Judge of the 5th Circuit Court of Appeals in New Orleans (quoted in *The Washington Post*, May 22, 1994)

This chapter is designed to:

☐ Provide key concepts relative to maintaining effective relations with colleagues and resolving conflicts should differences arise.
☐ Provide an opportunity to assess your current style and practices in resolving conflict situations, thereby augmenting your skill in this important area of interpersonal relations.

Your reading of the text and completion of the worksheets and self-assessment inventory should help you reach these objectives.

The topics covered in this chapter are:

☐ How to Build Relations with Colleagues.
☐ Causes for Conflict.
☐ My Conflict Resolution Style.
☐ How Managers Regard Conflict.
☐ Conflict Management via Ad Hoc Learning.
☐ Approaches to Conflict Resolution.
☐ Added Concepts for Clash Control.
☐ Managing Inter-Group Conflict.
☐ Several Problem-Solving Models.
☐ Taboo Approaches.
☐ Application (Skill-Building) Activities.

HOW TO BUILD RELATIONS WITH COLLEAGUES

As organizations become more complex, fast-paced, and demanding, managers find that they have to not only manage their subordinates but also work effectively with their fellow managers. Thus, one middle manager described his pressure-laden job in these terms:

I have a terrible time trying to explain what I do at work when I get home. My wife thinks of a manager in terms of someone who has authority over those people who work for him and who in turn gets his job done for him. You know, she thinks of those nice, neat organization charts, too. She also expects that when I get promoted, I'll have more people working for me.

Now, all of this is unrealistic. Actually, I only have eighteen people directly reporting to me. These are the only ones I can give orders to. But I have to rely directly on the services of seventy-five or eighty other people in this company, if my project is going to get done. They in turn are affected by perhaps several hundred others, and I must sometimes see some of them, too, when my work is being held up.

So I am always seeing these people, trying to get their cooperation, trying to deal with delays, work out compromises on specifications, etc. Again, when I try to explain this to my wife, she thinks that all I do all day is argue and fight with people.

—Leonard R. Sayles, *Managerial Behavior— Administration in Complex Organizations* (McGraw-Hill, New York, 1964), p. 43.

Contacts with peers across organizational lines may make considerable demands on the manager's time. In fact, management authority Peter Drucker states that this is how a manager spends most of his time. All of which means that the manager has to acquire considerable skill to carry out such tasks as conferring, informing, explaining, relationship-building, bargaining, pleading, trading, negotiating, influencing, monitoring, representing (his work unit), expediting, coordinating, buffering, soothing, smoothing, and the like.

Seasoned and sophisticated managers know that effective relations with peers and colleagues are basic to getting things done. They are essential to avoid mix-ups, delays, misunderstandings, and missed opportunities. Relationship-building, obviously, is a form of conflict prevention. Here, then, are some procedures that, if followed, should make for smoother, more satisfying horizontal interactions:

☐ Define/clarify job roles, responsibilities, authority, and accountability between/among those with whom you are in lateral contact.
☐ Keep in close touch with those whom you must have cooperative relationships. To the extent that they know who you are—your attitudes, values, collaborative approaches, program goals, and responsibilities—and thus appreciate better where you are coming from, they are less likely to be surprised or disturbed should differences arise. In effect, we are talking about building and increasing *trust*.
☐ Reduce barriers to understanding and appreciating other functional units via such on-going activities for your subordinates as personnel exchange, job rotation, temporary assignment, joint task force or study teams, and planned discussion sessions with colleagues about allied responsibilities, programs, projects, problems, etc.
☐ Use your lunch periods as opportunities to exchange information and to build relations. But don't fall into the comfortable trap of lunching

with the same colleagues routinely. Instead, diversify and broaden your contacts.

☐ Make certain that you and your staff think constantly in these terms:

1) Who (laterally) should we keep posted on this development or decision ("I wonder how Frank in Operations will feel about this?").

2) Who (laterally) should we contact for additional information or even joint decision making? **Note:** Most managers think almost automatically about touching base with the boss on matters of importance. **Question:** Is the same kind of reflexive thinking being applied to peer/colleague relationships?

☐ Adhere religiously to any and all commitments you make with your colleagues. There is no faster way to reduce trust than to renege on your promises. If circumstances arise that prevent you from keeping an agreement, contact the other party and explain the nature of and cause for the change on your part. Remember, trust is hard to develop, but quite easy to lose. Also, some of your less-cooperative colleagues may be looking for reasons to institute "warfare." ("You can't count on Unit X for anything.") Don't feed that need by tendering a broken promise.

It is quite apparent, then, that unless you, as manager, assume full responsibility for your lateral relations, no one else is likely to. Peter Drucker suggests that it is the manager's job to ponder carefully and reduce to writing 1) what your fellow managers need from you in the way of information and support, and 2) what you require from them. It is then essential to meet jointly to secure agreement on these mutual requirements. Such a proactive (as opposed to a reactive) stance is required because no one is a mind reader. Anticipating possible friction points is certainly more efficient and less painful than working through delicate conflict situations via assorted soothing and smoothing procedures.

Commitments to receive help and to assist others may range from meeting deadlines for information (e.g., for reports) and arranging for interacting schedules, to emergency planning entailing sharing of personnel, and equipment and/or facilities. Agreements to provide specialized advice, counsel, information, technical assistance, and cooperation of various sorts may also be appropriate. In general, the operative concept is "synergy," which means

that the whole is greater than the sum of its parts when cooperative (interdependent) rather than unilateral (independent) action is planned and implemented.

The above paragraphs emphasize the importance of inter-collegial communication, planning, and action to ensure smooth interactions with your fellow managers. However, the facts of organizational life are that even with the best of intentions and concern with planning, conflict with lateral associates is quite likely to arise from time to time. In fact, Roy Pneuman and Margaret Bruehl, authors of *Managing Conflict* (Englewood Cliffs, NJ: Prentice-Hall, 1982) assert: "There is no conceivable human relationship in which the goals, values, needs, behaviors, and attitudes of two parties could be constantly and continuingly identical. Therefore, conflict is inherent in all interdependent relationships, whether work or personally oriented."

CAUSES FOR CONFLICT

Conflict in organizations is to be expected, then, for these reasons:

☐ **Informational factors.** The parties to a controversy often have different or partial data, or possibly none at all. They thus may make different assumptions about the issue(s) involved. We typically call conflicts of this sort "misunderstandings."

☐ **Perceptual factors.** Even if the same information/facts/events are available to or experienced by all concerned, the data may still be seen differently. Why? Because each of us interprets the data through our personal set of filters. Different perceptions or interpretations may arise from a variety of factors, as explained below.

☐ **Role-related factors.** How you or I see an issue often depends on "where we sit" in the organization. Thus, conflicts often arise between line and staff units, sales and production, R&D and financial/budgetary control, headquarters and field, and so on. And to complicate matters, roles in organizations may be poorly defined, which leads to clashes of various sorts.

☐ **Values.** To the extent that we embrace different values, e.g., cost vs. quality, social responsibility/ethics vs. the bottom line, concern with human factors vs. production/results, we are quite likely to develop strong feelings about an issue and thus choose different solutions to it.

☐ **Goals.** Differences in unit goals may produce conflicts over our "turf." ("Are *you* telling us what *we* should be doing in marketing?") Additionally, personal or career goals typically influence our outlooks on a given subject/situation/event. Thus, if one's career goal is to advance rapidly in the organization, one may engage in behaviors at odds with the goals of others.

Organizational goals may be ambiguous and thus become a fertile source of conflict. For example, an overall organization goal may be improved community relations. Yet organization leaders may be lukewarm to participation in community affairs and thus reluctant to provide the necessary time off and funding basic to the actual furtherance of such a goal.

☐ **Personality differences.** While ideally every manager should be able to work well with every other manager, in the real world not everyone can relate well to everyone else. Personality attributes, both tangible and intangible, can generate serious friction points. Hence, we hear expressions such as "I hate his guts," "She really turns me off," "He's a pompous ass," "She takes everything so seriously," "If only he weren't so abrasive," "I don't see how anyone can work with that man."

That these differences are not totally rational, as illustrated by the well-known doggerel about Dr. Fell:

I do not love thee, Dr. Fell
The reason why I cannot tell
But this alone I know full well
I do not love thee, Dr. Fell.

☐ **Communication bottlenecks/barriers.** The formal organization with its emphasis on chain of command may impede swift and easy communication between horizontal units and breed misunderstandings and conflict. Differences in physical location, producing a lack of face-to-face contact, may also encourage friction.

☐ **Methods and procedures.** Even though there may be agreement on goals, conflicts may arise from strong feelings over how to get things done. For example, do we expand the sales force or do we rely more on direct mail marketing? Do we increase, decrease, or retain our product line as it is? Do we conduct attitude surveys to learn of employee morale or do we use the data already available to us? If we do conduct attitude surveys, do we use an outside firm for this or do we do it internally? Do we centralize, decentralize, or recentralize?

☐ **Responsibility and authority issues.** It is not unusual for organizations to fail to clarify which unit has responsibility for a given activity. Or if responsibility is clear, the authority for its execution may be ambiguous or overlapping. Or competition may arise to take over a new activity. ("We know more about supervising field units than they'll ever know.") The result, unfortunately, is likely to be an unhealthy competition to assert aegis over the function or project.

☐ **Limited resources.** Conflict can readily arise over scarce or limited resources: budgets, space, equipment, personnel, etc. Managers are in competition with one another for such resources all the time. And if one colleague is actually dependent on the other for the allotment of a given resource, an opportunity for conflict is almost built into the process.

☐ **Power and/or prestige.** Conflict may arise because individuals and units are in competition for influence, authority, power, status, visibility, or access to top management. For example, staff units may compete over the "right" to report directly to the C.E.O.

☐ **History.** Longstanding disagreements may exist between individuals or groups. These unresolved clashes of years back may take on a life of their own. The cause(s) for the difference(s) may have long since been forgotten, but a proposal by A is certain to be "shot down" by B and vice versa. The warring parties may even seek allies for their sides and thereby infect others in a hostile, non-productive way.

☐ **The economy.** A downturn in the economy may impact negatively on people, causing many forms of stress and anxiety. Thus, people may over-react to their needs for job security and become overly protective of their function. ("Why cut data processing when those people in R&D have all the high salaries and never come up with anything anyway?")

☐ **Climate.** The overall organizational climate, particularly the reward system, may be such that it fosters severe competition (over turf, resources) or rivalry between units. The situation may be aggravated by one unit or function being favored over another. ("Those people in Branch X can get anything they want.") The favoritism may be a result of a top manager who came up the line through a particular function and thus is protective of it.

☐ **Need for contact.** Due to a need for an interdependent relationship, two parties may be forced into frequent association and interaction. But because of personality differences or the lack of skill to resolve disagreements, conflict may become the norm. On the other hand, a relationship that permits only occasional contact but requires much more intimacy to provide experience in developing collaborative procedures, may flounder because of the intermittent contact.

☐ **Career advancement.** At times rivalries may develop over who gets special training, promotions, desired field or foreign assignments, committee and task force appointments (which may provide high visibility, special experience, and the opportunity to make worthwhile contacts).

☐ **Ambiguity.** Reference has been made to ambiguity in role, goals, responsibility, and authority, which lead to conflict. Ambiguous organizational structure also may lead to conflict. For example, in a "matrix" organization, i.e., one consisting of numerous special project teams, special study groups, task forces, committees, etc., the usual chain of command or lines of authority are disregarded to provide flexibility in communication and certain decision making. Under these conditions, conflict is practically built into the established organizational pattern.

MY CONFLICT RESOLUTION STYLE

Before we explore conflict in more detail—that is, how managers typically regard it and the various modes of conflict resolution—it will be helpful to you to assess your own style of conflict resolution by completing "How I Manage (Deal With) Conflict—A Self-Quiz."

After you have taken the self-test, you may have a number of questions regarding conflict in general and conflict resolution styles in particular. If you will continue reading the text, a clear picture about conflict management should emerge.

How I Manage (Deal with) Conflict—A Self-quiz

Listed below are a number of statements that relate to feelings, attitudes, and actual or possible behaviors in situations involving conflict or disagreement with another person. Check those you agree with quite strongly. Leave blank those which you favor or agree with only in a mild way. Try to be as candid as you can. **Note:** You may not have encountered all of the situations described in the quiz. If so, respond *as you would be likely* to behave or feel in such situations.

[ ] 1. If I have a difference/disagreement with someone, I tend to use whatever skill or power it takes to win out.

[ ] 2. In conflict situations I prefer yielding to the other person to obtain his good will.

[ ] 3. In a difference with another party, I see no reason why we can't engage in enough give and take so that both of us get something out of the negotiation.

[ ] 4. I am proud of my persuasion skills. I believe they can help me to be "top dog" in a conflict situation.

[ ] 5. A good way to deal with a conflict situation is to try to avoid or defer it. Time often takes care of these things.

[ ] 6. Most confrontations over a difference or disagreement pose greater risks than potential rewards.

[ ] 7. My approach to conflict resolution is to define and explore differences candidly, and to work jointly toward a mutually acceptable solution of those differences.

[ ] 8. A difference with someone can be resolved reasonably and amicably by looking for midpoints to agree upon, as opposed to opting for extreme positions that make any agreement unlikely.

[ ] 9. It is more important for me to preserve harmony and avoid disruption than it is to win out in a conflict. I would thus readily accede to the needs of the other party.

[ ] 10. Although some people tend to wade right in to a conflict situation, my own preferences are to sidestep it or at least defer it, if at all possible.

[　] 11. To avoid a confrontation over a dispute is a sign of weakness. It will hardly get you what you need to be a winner.

[　] 12. The purpose of conflict resolution is not only to attack a problem mutually to achieve a superior, creative solution, but also to build trust and strengthen relations for the future.

[　] 13. Conflicts cannot be settled by running away from them, yielding totally, or beating the other party down. Rather, it takes a certain amount of sophisticated "horse trading" so that both parties emerge as victorious in some—but not all—ways.

[　] 14. It is important to be perceived as a reasonable person. Thus, if a difference arises with another person, I am likely to give priority to his needs.

[　] 15. My approach to conflict is "to let sleeping dogs lie" rather than to "beard the lion in his den."

[　] 16. When I have a difference with someone, I like to put our heads together to work out a solution superior to that which either one of us could come up with alone.

[　] 17. By letting the other party have his way in a matter of disagreement, future cooperation and good relations are likely to be obtained.

[　] 18. In a disagreement or conflict with another person, it is important to come out on top. Winning is the American way.

[　] 19. If I were to engage in direct confrontation with someone over a disagreement, it would only add fuel to the fire.

[　] 20. A good way to resolve a difference or disagreement, without spending a lot of time on it, is to settle for "half a loaf," which is certainly better than none at all.

[　] 21. Both parties to a dispute or conflict can produce a creative solution to their difference if there is a great deal of mutuality, sharing, caring, openness, and trust.

[　] 22. If I have a disagreement with another person, it is more important for me to come out ahead than to worry about how the losing party might feel.

[　] 23. I am not the kind of person who has to "protect my turf," debate over differences endlessly and have my way over things. I thus can yield to the needs of the other party without feeling that "I have given away the store."

[　] 24. When I have a conflict with another person, I'm more than willing to settle it via some kind of compromise.

[　] 25. If I have a dispute with another person, I believe in calling a spade a spade, even if it may hurt a bit. No one ever resolved a conflict by being a shrinking violet.

[　] 26. Disagreement can lead to hard feelings or to creativity. The latter is more likely if we opt for a solution that is best for the organization as well as ourselves. So I say: "Let the sparks fly" to release the energy needed for creative ideation.

[　] 27. The best way to resolve a difference with another person is to meet him half way, "to split the difference."

[　] 28. Because I don't have the skills to work through a conflict successfully with another person, my tendency is to withdraw from it if at all possible.

[　] 29. In a conflict with someone, the best approach is to generate a lot of alternatives to the issue and select one that we both agree to be a high-quality solution.

[　] 30. In a conflict with another person it is very important for me to have my way. I thus will use any legitimate means to be the winning party.

[　] 31. I am not the kind of person who needs to win all battles. I thus would prefer to smooth things over, to let the other person have his way, rather than to engage in a confrontation over the disagreement.

[　] 32. I see myself as a person who is flexible enough to stand up for the things I believe in, but not to the point where it produces an impasse. So as a rule, I am willing to "give in" if the other party does the same.

[　] 33. In a conflict situation I try to avoid the mindset of a "fixed pie" to be divided or fought over. Instead, I work with the other party to think in terms of an "expandable" pie. This permits two winners, not half-winners and one loser.

[　] 34. In a difference with another person I may work out a compromise on occasion. But my real preference is to go all out and have the winner—me—take all.

[ ] 35. It is difficult for me to talk with people who are angry with me about something.

[ ] 36. I am more than willing to recognize the needs of the other person in a conflict situation. I thus am quite willing to let that person have his way.

[ ] 37. In a dispute with another person, I will try to settle for a middle-ground position to avoid straining relationships.

[ ] 38. In a difference with another person, I favor joining with him to combine our perspectives for a creative solution.

[ ] 39. I am not bothered at all that a conflict with another person may lead to "hard feelings" because I was the winner.

[ ] 40. Because it is more important to get along with others than it is to challenge them over a difference, I often tend to recognize their needs rather than my own.

[ ] 41. To resolve a difference with another party, I rely on bargaining or trading on the issues involved. This gives both parties some gains and no one leaves feeling "mad."

[ ] 42. The best way to resolve a conflict is to work toward a solution that addresses the needs and concerns of both parties.

[ ] 43. My concern about confronting conflict is that it may lead to a lot of bad feelings rather than resolve anything.

[ ] 44. If I have a serious dispute with another unit I prefer to avoid any direct confrontation. At the most, I may use a staff member or possibly my boss to try to resolve it.

[ ] 45. I see nothing wrong with acceding fully to another person's views or needs should a conflict arise. This saves a lot of time haggling over differences and avoids the hard feelings certain to arise should a confrontation take place.

[ ] 46. Settling a conflict with a person is like resolving a labor dispute: You may start with an extreme position, give a little, maybe a little more, and in time you reach a midpoint that satisfies both parties.

[ ] 47. The purpose of a conflict resolution meeting is not to opt for half a loaf or to become top dog. Rather, its goal is to produce a top-quality solution to which both parties have contributed and thus will now support fully.

[ ] 48. When I have a problem with another person, my preferences/tendencies are to avoid a direct confrontation rather than to challenge him on the disagreement.

[ ] 49. I don't care to engage in conflict with a more powerful person. I thus observe the motto "discretion is the better part of valor" and let the other party have his way.

[ ] 50. A conflict can only be resolved by someone winning and someone losing. I don't care at all to be the loser.

Scoring

Please transfer each of the numbered items you have checked to the columns below. Use check marks again for this. Then add the check marks for all five columns. Each column should have 10 or fewer check marks.

A/W	AC	CO	COMP	COLL/PS
5. ( )	2. ( )	3. ( )	1. ( )	7. ( )
6. ( )	9. ( )	8. ( )	4. ( )	12. ( )
10. ( )	14. ( )	13. ( )	11. ( )	16. ( )
15. ( )	17. ( )	20. ( )	18. ( )	21. ( )
19. ( )	23. ( )	24. ( )	22. ( )	26. ( )
28. ( )	31. ( )	27. ( )	25. ( )	29. ( )
35. ( )	36. ( )	32. ( )	30. ( )	33. ( )
43. ( )	40. ( )	37. ( )	34. ( )	38. ( )
44. ( )	45. ( )	41. ( )	39. ( )	42. ( )
48. ( )	49. ( )	46. ( )	50. ( )	47. ( )
Totals [ ]	[ ]	[ ]	[ ]	[ ]

Score interpretation. If your responses fall into one column primarily, that is your primary style of conflict resolution. If you are "heavy" in one column and somewhat less heavy in another column, the former is your primary style and the latter your backup style. If your scores are somewhat equally divided among two or more columns, it would indicate that you do not have a clear-cut approach to or philosophy in conflict management.

Heavy scores in the first two columns indicate a generally passive approach to conflict resolution. Conversely, high scores in the last three columns indicate a willingness to confront a conflict. The five styles are as follows:

A/W = Avoidance/Withdrawal

AC = Accommodation

CO = Compromise

COMP = Competition

COLL/PS = Collaboration/Problem Solving

How Managers Regard Conflict

Conflict is typically regarded by managers (and others) in a pejorative or negative way. The term conjures up dreadful images normally associated with combat, collision, hostility, destruction, and severe pain. Because conflict is deemed to be unnecessary and harmful, it thus becomes an interpersonal (or inter-group) interaction to be avoided at all costs. The result: a lot of energy may be expended to conceal it or deny its existence. ("Conflicts? We don't have any conflicts. We're really one big happy family. Everybody always cooperates with everyone else.")

A discomforting result of a "sweep it under the rug" posture may well be that we are forced into facing up to the conflict at a time when we are ill-prepared to cope with it or, worse still, the situation may have greatly deteriorated.

Certainly conflict has the potential to be destructive—it can create hard feelings and destroy important relationships irreparably. However, behavioral scientists and a growing number of managers see conflict more positively. This is not to say that they purposefully provoke disagreement or seek it out. Rather, they see conflict as a natural consequence of an organization that is 1) dynamic, alert, motivated, growing, and "on the march," and 2) staffed by individuals who inevitably have different ideas, values, ways of approaching problems and challenges, and have strong convictions about their worth. In short, they see conflict as having potential for "constructive controversy." As someone once put it: "When everyone in the room thinks the same thing, no one is thinking very much."

In more specific terms, Dr. Dean Tjosvald ("Making Conflict Productive," *Personnel Administrator,* June 1984) sees these potential benefits from conflict:

- [ ] It increases the awareness of problems, who is involved, and ways of resolving these disagreements.

- [ ] It serves as a motivating/energizing force to treat identified problems.

- [ ] It enhances morale and cohesion by clearing up confusion, frustration, and resentments. People learn that their relationships are strong enough to manage their differences and difficulties. They also learn of their colleagues' needs, goals, and values.

- [ ] It makes possible high-quality decisions because people can "open up" and get their ideas into the hopper.
- [ ] It stimulates interest, creativity, curiosity, spontaneity. People see a problem from new perspectives and combine the best views for a truly creative solution.
- [ ] It is a source of fun and excitement, for the approach is one of positive confrontation and sharing.

I recently asked a managerial group attending a leadership workshop to brainstorm the case for conflict. Here are the more than 20 ideas they generated:

- [ ] A means for different personalities to express themselves.
- [ ] Forces change, thought, and a "facing up" to issues.
- [ ] A positive way of reacting to change.
- [ ] Broadens understanding of the problem/issue.
- [ ] Encourages a realistic definition of the problem.
- [ ] Serves as a creative force.
- [ ] Ensures involvement in the problem-solving process.
- [ ] It is energizing (gets the feelings out and the adrenaline flowing).
- [ ] Works as a catalyst to improve relations and cooperation.
- [ ] Clarifies issues and differences.
- [ ] Builds authentic relationships by its insistence on candor.
- [ ] Brings out the best in us via challenge and stretch.
- [ ] Keeps us from denying problems.
- [ ] Good for our mental health—gets the anger and other "garbage" out.
- [ ] Develops character and integrity.
- [ ] A way to grow—overcoming fear of conflict strengthens us as persons.
- [ ] Permits discovery of new options as opposed to doing it "my way" or "your way."
- [ ] Ultimately creates trust, the basis for any intimate and lasting relationship.
- [ ] Prevents loss of self-esteem, for if we can resolve our difficulties we feel a sense of power.

In sum, without conflict a tremendously powerful source of energy and creativity would vanish. The clash of differences is essential to avoid stagnation, apathy and luke-warm support for decisions. Out of conflict sparkling new ideas can arise. As has been said, the only place conflict does not exist is in a cemetery. So rather than smothering or denying conflict, we should learn to expect it, to manage it wisely and thus profit from it.

The nub of it all: disagreement can lead to hard feelings or to creativity. It is our job as managers to operate in a way that produces the latter rather than the former result. The pages which follow can help you to develop the mindset and provide a basis for the acquisition of the skills needed to manage conflict effectively.

CONFLICT MANAGEMENT VIA AD HOC LEARNING

The significant problems we face cannot be solved at the same level of thinking we were at when we created them.

—Albert Einstein

All of us, as managers, acquire attitudes about conflict sooner or later. We also develop typical ways of behaving or responding in a conflict situation. But the odds are that 1) we never received any formal training or even coaching by the boss on conflict resolution, and 2) we have not given much time or thought to the articulation of a philosophy about it.

Because differences with others do arise, we obviously must deal with them in some fashion. This question, then, logically arises: How did we learn what our attitude and approach (behavior) should be when we are face-to-face with a conflict situation? In all probability, our learning came directly or indirectly from such influential role models as parents, siblings, clergymen, teachers, and bosses. Heroes/stars in the movies, and players and coaches on big-time athletic teams also may have guided us. At work, too, the culture at large generously provided us with pat formulas and clichés such as: "Nice people don't fight," "Turn the other cheek," "You can catch more flies with honey than vinegar," "Never walk away from a fight," "Don't start a fight, but if you do make sure you win it," "Make sure you get him before he gets you," "Always fight your own battles," "It's a dog eat dog world," and so on.

Of course, the problem with these adages is that each unhesitatingly espouses the "right" course of action or inaction and in the aggregate they add up to a bundle of mixed or contradictory messages. Fortunately, we can improve on these well-intentioned bits of advice by drawing on the newer, behavioral-science based ideas and techniques about conflict resolution. Hopefully, the reader will find these approaches more realistic and productive than the management of conflict by maxim.

APPROACHES TO CONFLICT RESOLUTION

Men are never so likely to settle a question rightly as when they discuss it freely.

—Lord Thomas Babington Macauley (1800–1859), English essayist, historian, poet, and statesman

When we have a conflict with a subordinate we can, if we wish, resort to various forms of selling and telling to get our way. But when dealing with with a peer, our formal power as a supervisor has little utility or relevance. Hence the need to apply methods that do not rely on dominance.

It is to be noted that most of us have a typical style in our approach to conflict resolution. The self-quiz you took earlier gave you an indication of your own style. But depending on the problem, the personality of the other party and the available time, we also may resort at times to our secondary or back-up style.

In any case, here are the various ways managers deal with peer conflict, each of which is discussed in this section:

☐ Avoidance	☐ Collaboration (consensus seeking)
☐ Accommodation	☐ Resolution with the aid of a third party
☐ Compromise	☐ Resolution by or with the aid of a higher authority
☐ Competition	☐ Taboo approaches

Avoidance ("I'm not up to being a fighter.")

Avoidance or withdrawal is certainly a "natural" response to an actual or potential conflict situation. That is to say, "flight" may be an easier and more satisfying course of action than "fight" (or confrontation). As has been stated: "If your head and your gut augur disaster, then run."

However, the more basic motivations for avoidance, psychologically speaking, are a low self-image ("I'm not OK, you're OK" or "I'm not up to being a fighter"); feelings of powerlessness ("I don't stand a chance with someone so self-assured as Pat"); or possibly a personal history of defeats in prior conflict situations ("I'm not likely to win this one either").

Rationalization and denial thus become the mechanisms to avoid facing up to things. We may tell ourselves (negative self-talk) that "the problem really isn't that serious," "things are hardly so bad to merit a fight over them," "the problem will go away in time," "let's wait and see," "there's no point in adding fuel to the fire," and so on. But the "if it isn't broken, don't fix it" philosophy may really mean that we have been doing it this way (or living with it) for 20 years. So the issue isn't whether something is or isn't broken, but whether it should and can be improved upon.

Of course, at times any of the above arguments for inaction may be quite valid. For example, some problems are resolved through time, waiting things out, e.g., the person with whom we are in conflict may transfer out or if there is a conflict over budget we may get the boost next year. Certainly managers don't have the time and energy to confront all conflicts. What is needed, then, is a realistic and courageous sorting out of which areas of disagreement merit active resolution.

Management consultant Dr. Martin B. Ross ("Coping With Conflict," *The 1982 Annual for Facilitators, Trainers, and Consultants,* San Diego, University Associates, 1982) believes *selective* avoidance of conflict may be a good tactic to use. He states: "Those who confront every conflict head on can hurt others' feelings and stir up their hostilities. Selective avoidance is also the best way to keep from becoming overwhelmed by conflict, a distinct possibility in our society."

The avoidance stance may be appropriate for totally healthy and realistic motivations, e.g., one may lack the requisite confrontation skills or the adversary may be too powerful or unreasonable to cope with. Also, the time may not be right for confrontation due to lack of vital information, the need for greater preparation, the press of other business, or simply to allow emotions to cool a bit. In these situations, of course, we are talking about postponement rather than total avoidance. **Deferral** is certainly a useful phase of any sophisticated strategy for conflict resolution.

But avoidance, as one's dominant style in dealing with conflict, is hardly likely to be a satisfying one. For one thing, it is a confession that one has little courage, harbors weak convictions and possesses little or no skill "to set matters right." Self-doubt and self-blame may readily set in: "I should have had the guts to face up to it and work it through."

Avoidance also represents an anti-growth stance. One can hardly grow as a person by engaging in flight or withdrawal. Rather, growth is more likely to ensue from facing up to reality, active coping (working things through to a decisive end), persevering, risk-taking, and interacting vigorously with others on a thorny problem or difference.

Finally, if avoidance becomes *the* style of conflict management, your image as a manager, as seen by subordinates, peers and even the boss, may be perceived to be that of a Caspar Milquetoast, the traditional well-worn door mat.

In essence, avoidance is a "lose-lose" style in that nothing is ventured and nothing is gained. Sure, one party may have achieved his way and thus a certain gain because he was not challenged or confronted. But in the absence of a greater potential gain, which might have ensued by "letting the sparks fly" and working things through mutually to a more creative solution, the gain by default is likely to be a minimal, one-sided one.

Accommodation ("Go along to get along.")

In this mode we avoid a direct confrontation and decide instead to de-emphasize differences, smooth things over, downplay the importance of our own needs, and yield to and accommodate the other party. We may do this because we sincerely believe the needs of the other person are superior to our own or out of a desire to maintain a good working relationship. We may even rationalize our concession by telling ourselves: "Well, he owes us one now. Next time we'll be top dog."

But regardless of our motivation, the basic cause for the conflict is not addressed or confronted, and a search for a high-quality, mutually beneficial solution ("win-win") is not strived for at all.

Satisfaction with our decision to accommodate may be fairly high if we yielded to meet the other person's greater needs. It will be lower if our behavior is motivated by less-altruistic motivations, such as our desire to "go along to get along" with the other party or to get on to "more important" things.

Accommodation does little to augment personal growth because it provides no practical experience in working through a difference with someone. And like avoidance, it is likely to produce a lose-lose situation.

Conflict Resolution Via Confrontation

As is apparent from the previous paragraphs, conflicts can be "resolved" via such passive strategies as ducking the issue (avoidance) and capitulating (accommodation). These approaches represent the "peace at any price" school of thought. More realistic and productive devices require a more active stance entailing some form of *confrontation*. Confrontation may conjure up combative images of "telling the other party off," "shouting the other party down," "not letting anyone walk over us without a fight," "straightening the other guy out," and so on.

In reality, however, confrontation is not a means of raising the adrenaline levels of the "combatants." Rather, it is a systematic effort/process by which the parties to a conflict situation try to resolve their differences by facing up to them.

Confrontation may entail compromise, competition, or collaboration. Each of these techniques is discussed below.

Compromise ("Let's split the difference.")

In this mode we discuss, argue, bargain, negotiate, and then mutually decide to "split the difference," to exchange concessions. Both parties achieve some degree of satisfaction, for some needs are met and no one is totally beaten. So we may tell ourselves that "half a loaf is better than none." But a top-quality, creative solution is not achieved if we are striving for a relatively easy way out—a compromise.

Of course, a middle-ground position, while hardly perfect, may be essential if continuation of the conflict may be injurious to relationships or merely produce a deadlock. It may also be appropriate as an interim or temporary solution due to lack of time to work toward a qualitatively superior resolution of the difference.

Finally, when strong differences exist and fixed positions have been taken, it may be the best way to avoid creating a winner and a loser, and thereby allow for necessary face-saving. Compromise is the way parliamentary and legislative bodies such as the U.S. Congress reach most of their decisions. "Under the circumstances this was the best bill we could get" is a statement legislators often present to their constituents.

Political columnist Mary McGrory, writing on the convening of the 100th Congress ("The Cuisinart of Public Issues," *The Washington Post,* January 6, 1987) described the staid U.S. Senate in these terms: "But it was the old Senate to the life, tightly corseted in its rules, consumed with its own concerns, certain, as it has been for 100 years, that it is the 'world's greatest deliberative body' and its best club. Actually, it is the great Cuisinart of public issues. They are chopped, pureed, sliced, and minced to the point where those outside the chamber can hardly recognize them."

An interesting example of a compromise approach to a heated situation took place in a small factory in Southern Texas, which had a workforce of African and Mexican Americans, equal in numbers. Problems developed in the production area: production was down, spoilage was up, and fighting between the two groups broke out at various times during the day. The problem was over which radio station the workers could tune their portable radios. Tensions had risen over conflicting musical preferences—Hispanic vs. black music. Management met with the workers on both a group and individual basis to learn of their disagreements. A solution was arrived at that satisfied everyone and restored production to normal levels—black music could be listened to on Monday morning and Hispanic music in the afternoon, and the next day the order was reversed.

We say the solution was a compromise because both sides had to surrender something. A possible win-win solution would have been to have all those who want the music to listen with headphones. (Of course, problems of cost would be involved.) A lose-lose approach would have been for management to have banned all music playing "since there's too much squabbling here over the music so we won't have it at all."

A disadvantage of compromise, in addition to settling for a lower quality solution, is that hard feelings may arise due to the tough bargaining entailed. This may affect future relations. Or if relations were strained at the outset, they are likely to continue in that vein. Why do bad feelings arise or persist? Since the negotiating effort failed to provide a joint learning experience based on mutuality, sharing, caring, and intimacy, the conflict engenders an "every man for himself" feeling. The prime concern, unfortunately, is to get *some kind of agreement.* Period.

In general, compromise should be looked at as a "lose-lose" approach because a true, high-quality solution is not achieved, both parties surrender some or much of what they have, and the result may be a settling for little of what was originally desired. And to aggravate things, both parties are likely to resolve to prepare themselves more thoroughly to get a better deal next time around. All of which will lead to reduced communication and lower trust. Thus, the lose-lose cycle continues unimpeded.

Competition ("Winning isn't everything, it's the only thing.")

In this stance we attempt to meet our own needs totally, and we strive for this end at the expense of the other party. We typically try to exert *power* based on seniority, age, connections with influential figures, subject matter expertise, use of carefully selected facts, debating skills, persuasion, and the like. Reason is likely to suffer in this "we against them" interchange. This, of course, is the classic "win-lose" mode. Accommodation or compromise is not resorted to at all. The philosophy at work is that of late football coach Vince Lombardi: "Winning isn't everything, it's the only thing."

The "winner take all" approach may be appropriate if quick, decisive action is essential. However, it may have only short-term advantages as relations with the other party may be damaged from this point on. Losers do tend to store up resentments for a long time; they may unleash them when the first opportunity arises.

In a competitive climate, individuals vie to "get it all." My ideas are presumed to be better than your ideas. "Having my way" is more important than joint exploration of ideas. Winners and losers are to be expected. This *is* the "American way," isn't it?

Since winning is more important than rational, mutual problem solving, we may expect these behaviors in the negotiating session: delving into the past; launching of personal attacks via blaming, shaming, ridiculing, and put-downs; belittling of ideas; nit-picking; non-listening; interrupting; lecturing and endless debating; playing games; scoring points; stubbornness; fault-finding; withdrawing and pouting; becoming defensive. Needless to say, these behaviors are hardly useful to build trust and improve the future relationships of the parties involved.

Collaboration ("What if we were to try this...?")

In this mode, we adopt a mutual problem-solving approach. The goal of both parties is to strive conscientiously for a solution that is neither a surrender, a quick fix, nor a besting of the other person. Rather, it is one that recognizes the creative capabilities (strengths) of both parties to the conflict. Differences in needs and personality are accepted and exploited to opt for a top-quality solution, i.e., one which meets the needs, goals and aspirations of both the individuals *and* the organization. In short, both parties opt for mutual goals and mutual gains.

Underlying this approach is the assumption that the issue is too important to be compromised and that commonalties must and can be located. The end result is win-win, both parties benefitting (satisfying needs) from a creative, high-quality solution. Strategies are then developed jointly to reach agreed-upon goals.

Procedurally, collaboration is a joint consensus-seeking quest for high-quality options. The guide for action is this challenging question: "Now that we have identified the issues, what can we do collectively to resolve them in a way that will allow both us and the organization to come out ahead?" As people in the farm community might put it: "We all have to work together to get the ox out of the ditch." In essence, we bury our differences to achieve a *superordinate* goal—that is, one marked by interests that transcend those of one party.

Consensus-seeking is facilitated by posing this catalytic question: "What if we were to try . . .?" The strength of this question lies in the fact that it encourages exploration and exchange as opposed to operating from a fixed position.

A key to win-win, collaborative problem solving is to overcome the mental set of the "fixed pie," to divide or fight over. Instead, both parties can profit by thinking of a potentially expanded pie. As has been stated by win-win negotiators: "Why divide (or fight over) the apples on the ground, when we can collectively shake the tree and harvest more of them?"

Organizational behavior professor Dr. Max H. Bazerman thus suggests we think in terms of *integrative* rather than *distributive compromise* type solutions. He offers these examples ("Why Negotiations Go Wrong," *Psychology Today,* June 1986):

> **Sharing the orange.** Two sisters had one orange to share, but each had a different use for it. One wanted orange juice, the other the peel for a cake. They discussed the matter at length and could only come up with a distributive compromise. This entailed dividing the orange in half, one sister ending up with a small glass of juice, and the other enough peel for a small cake.

But an integrative solution would have been to allow one sister to have all of the juice and the other all of the peel. This procedure would have permitted each sister to receive twice what she actually got.

The sisters' narrow reasoning was based on a fixed-pie bias—that the only way to win something is for the other to lose something. This assumption may be true in some situations, but integrative thinking often can produce greater satisfaction and a higher profit to both parties.

The Camp David Talks (1978). Egypt and Israel were at odds over control of the Sinai Peninsula. Israel, which had occupied the Sinai since the Middle East War of 1967, refused to return any of it. Egypt demanded its immediate return in full. A compromise, which would have allowed each to retain half of the Sinai, was not acceptable to either party.

The difficulty was that the Sinai dispute was defined in terms of how much land each side would control. But when it was realized that what Israel really wanted was the security the land offered and only Egypt really wanted full sovereignty over it, the impasse was overcome. This integrative solution resolved the stalemate: In exchange for surrendering the land, Israel would receive assurances of a demilitarized zone and would have air bases on the Sinai.

Selecting a movie and a restaurant. You and your date or spouse have planned an evening of a cinema and dinner, but you have different tastes in movies and restaurants. A distributive, fixed-pie solution would entail haggling over each entertainment item separately. An integrative, win-win solution would be to check and see who cares more about the restaurant than the movie. When this is known, one party selects the movie, the other the restaurant. This allows each party to get what is more important to him with adequately high satisfaction for both.

We might add another example involving Beverly and Gordon who, like many marrieds, continually battle over money. Intermittently, Gordon explodes over his spouse's spending patterns. Their arguments typically end with Beverly stating defiantly: "I am working, it's my money, and I'm not going to allow a penny pincher to tell me what I can and can't buy."

Their conflict reached the stage where it was threatening their marriage, so they decided to see a counselor. With careful probing, the latter discovered that the issue was essentially one of power. That is to say, the problem was not how much was spent nor what the spending was on, but who had control over the spending. The win-win solution was to a) allow both parties to have large amounts of control via separate bank accounts, separate credit cards, and separate investment plans, and b) set up a joint budget, with planned contributions by both parties, for common purposes such as food, house and garden, entertainment, vacations, and the like.

Collaboration, obviously, takes a high degree of skill in communicating, relating, and joint problem solving. But with an attitude of mutuality (win-win), the skill is certainly learnable.

Guidelines for Collaboration

It undoubtedly is apparent to the reader that the author favors resolving differences on a constructive, win-win basis—collaboration. Here, then, are a number of procedures and guidelines to help to make such an approach work.

Attitudinal input. Your own attitude will be a key factor in how you approach and ultimately resolve the conflict. Do you believe that the other party ("the opposition") is unreasonable, unyielding, stupid, narrow-minded, detached from reality, selfish, disloyal, "on the side of the devil"? Whereas you are "the fountain of all wisdom and truth" and thus "on the side of the angels"? If so, your behavior in the negotiation room will reflect those feelings.

Conversely, if you can tell yourself (self-talk) that the other person is sincere and sees the issue differently simply because he is coming from another perspective, you will have a better mindset to help establish a true problem-solving atmosphere.

Also, if you resent the fact that you have to spend time "on something like this," this attitude will come through and poison the negotiation process.

Finally, conflict resolution involves risk. Hopefully, the process will produce high-quality solutions for your differences. Conversely, it is possible that nothing may be resolved and relations aggravated. However, if you can tell yourself (more self-talk) that this is an opportunity to make a worthwhile breakthrough on a festering difficulty and thus is a challenge rather than a headache, it is quite likely that things will work out well for both parties. The best mindset, then, is buoyancy, good cheer, and optimism as opposed to self-defeating dread, gloom, and doom.

In sum, we should be aware that we are creating a self-fulfilling prophecy—positive outlooks are likely to produce positive results and negative attitudes are almost certain to provide unfavorable outcomes. But you *are* free to make the choice.

Scheduling/timing. Try to set a time for the negotiation session that meets your needs. If you are under pressure to work on a dozen "must-do" projects, this may well affect your attitude and behavior in the meeting. Also, consider your mood. Select a time when things are going well for you and avoid scheduling a meeting when you are somewhat on the "down" side. Anticipate, too, that there may have to be more than one meeting. In fact, the first meeting may well be a "climate setter" and an "issue definer," not a reach-the-solution-stage.

Location. A neutral location such as a conference room or a vacant office may be the best site for the meeting. On the other hand, if you wish to show that you are willing to meet the other person more than half way, swallow your pride and meet on his turf. But be certain that the location will be free of interruptions like phone calls, visitors, and staff members.

Using an intermediary. If you intend to bring a third party along, even if it is only for informational inputs, inform the other party in advance of this. The latter probably won't appreciate such surprises. ("How come he is here?" or "I thought you were coming alone.") Don't use the added representation as a means of augmenting your clout, but rather as a means of clarifying issues and helping to set a true problem-solving atmosphere.

Goal exploration. At the outset try to establish whether your differences relate to goals, values, or methods. If there are common goals and the dispute relates to methods or procedures, you are well on the road to resolving the conflict. If the problem revolves around goals or values, it will probably take a great deal of discussion before a consensus is reached. In either case, post on separate flipcharts the areas of agreement and disagreement. With the disagreements highlighted, you are then in a position to explore mutually how each item can be minimized or overcome.

Identifying issues. If more than one issue underlies the conflict, it is only common sense to avoid trying to resolve multiple differences in 90 minutes. List all the issues, but try to prioritize them. Securing agreement on the various areas of conflict and their relative importance is a major step toward conflict resolution. ("Well, at least we can agree on what our problems are and how important they are to both of us.") If the issues are numerous and quite complex, more than one meeting would certainly seem to be in order.

Soft-pedaling history. In a meeting over a conflict, there often is a tendency to dredge up a great deal of ancient history—old grudges and grievances, wrongs (real or imagined), past mistakes, and other longstanding irritations and resentments. It will be more productive, however, if both parties downplay the past, take a positive and constructive stance, and look to the future instead. In fact, a guideline for the meeting might be that dwelling on the past is taboo.

Maintaining a professional manner. Even if the other party is a bit stubborn, sarcastic, or otherwise abrasive or obnoxious, be sure to "keep your cool." Don't fall in to the trap of responding in kind. The odds are that if you treat the other person with dignity and respect, your considerate behavior will be reciprocated. A good way to keep things at a high level is to have a flipchart pad and easel at the meeting. If both parties have a chance to present their data on the large sheets and post them on the wall, the discussion is more likely to be confined to facts and issues as opposed to blaming, complaining, name calling, and the like.

Use active listening. In this mode you try to understand things from the other person's viewpoint. You should restate and paraphrase from time to time ("You are saying that..."). This will convince both of you that you did pick up what was stated. **Note:** In active listening, you show that you are tuning in to the *feelings* associated with the statement ("I gather that you feel that..."). Also, it is helpful if you summarize intermittently the gist of what was said. Read on for more skill pointers on listening.

Lowering defenses. In a conflict negotiation meeting, people often raise their defenses above their usual levels. Thus the confrontation may be marked by attitudes of suspicion and low trust and such behaviors as attacking, bickering, blaming, dredging up the past, and selective listening.

What is needed, then, are ways to lower defensiveness. This would include active listening, the use of "I messages" as described in Chapter 1, looking for good points in the other party's ideas and offering praise about them, seeking ways to adapt or build on the other party's proposals as opposed to rejecting them outright, letting the other person spot the shortcoming(s) in his own proposal, and generally allowing the other party to keep face rather than lose it.

As has been indicated, not all interactions in the negotiation room will represent "Sunday school" behavior. Thus, Dr. Roger Fisher, a Harvard Law School professor and authority on negotiation, offers this helpful advice which he terms negotiation "jujitsu": If the other party pushes, don't push back, and if he attacks, don't engage in counterattack. Instead, regard attacks as attacks on mutual problems and do these two things to defuse the situation: 1) ask questions rather than make statements of your own, and 2) use a long silence when presented with unreasonable statements (John Huey, "Our Group Finds That Negotiating Means Agreeing to Disagree," *The Wall Street Journal*, Dec. 24, 1985).

Pneuman and Bruehl, authors of *Managing Conflict*, suggest concern with high-trust *initiating* and *responsive* behavior to move the climate of interaction toward a cooperative direction. *Initiating* behaviors include:

- ☐ **Authenticity.** Try to keep words and actions in sync to build trust. Behaviors contrary to your statements will undermine trust. **Example:** A plea for cooperation, followed by a sarcastic statement, is hardly authentic behavior.
- ☐ **Consistency.** Carry through on commitments and promises. Avoid secretive behaviors or those that produce surprises.
- ☐ **Openness.** Don't be afraid to level. Be honest about your values, motivations, attitudes, and feelings.
- ☐ **Relationship building.** Conduct yourself in a way that shows your integrity and respect for the other party. These elements are essential to a collaborative relationship.
- ☐ **Flexibility.** Don't cast your position in concrete. Be open to the contributions of the other party for a balanced position on the issues.

Responsive behaviors include the following:

- ☐ **Listen actively to the other's needs.** Check, as necessary, whether you heard what you should have and whether you were understood. ("May I check with you whether my last statements were picked up? Would you please summarize what you heard me say?")
- ☐ **Assume both parties have legitimate needs.** Respond in ways that indicate you see all needs and wants as valid and real. To do otherwise is to contribute to a hostile relationship.

- ☐ **Recognize the other's resources.** If you can openly acknowledge the skills and resources of the other party, you are moving well toward a problem-solving endeavor.
- ☐ **Accept and legitimatize feelings.** Not only are facts facts, but so are feelings. That is to say, try to accept the other's feelings rather than to deny or downgrade them. By "acceptance" we mean *understanding* of his motivations, concerns, needs, etc. **Note:** Acceptance doesn't necessarily mean "agreement with."

Avoid the temptation to play psychoanalyst and look for deep-seated motives behind statements. Even if you were to "analyze" correctly, and this is hardly a certainty, your "unveiling" of a hidden motive is a certain way to raise defenses.

- ☐ **Clarify assumptions about motives and the meaning of behaviors.** Unchecked perceptions may lead to faulty conceptualizations. It is all too easy to fall into the trap of misperceiving statements and actions, thereby augmenting defenses.
- ☐ **Assume collaboration is desired by the other party.** Recognize that the other party could enter into things with a competitive stance but has opted for a collaborative, win-win outcome. Thus both parties are looking for superordinate goals (commonalities that will best serve the total organization).
- ☐ **Accept the other's goals and position statements as legitimate.** Assume that the other is stating his goals/positions accurately. If you have any doubts about them, ask for a clarification. But don't assume or cast doubt about the other person's integrity.

How to Deal with an Impasse

If I had refused to institute a negotiation or had I not persevered in it, I should have been degraded in my own estimation as a man of honor.

—John Adams (1735–1826), lawyer, leader in the American Revolution, and second president of the U.S. (1797–1801)

Negotiation between conflicting parties is not always akin to a seat in the rose garden's gazebo. Rather, it often is hard work generating a gamut of negative emotions (irritation, frustration, anger, disappointment) and stressful behaviors (disagreement, repetition of arguments, quoting higher authority, long silences, long speeches, digressions, tuning out of facts and suggestions).

And most annoying of all is to reach an impasse. Things seem to be totally stuck. No one is able to rise above the collective immobility. However, an impasse does not signify that it is the end of the world. Rather, it to be expected as part of the negotiation process. Here are some behaviors you may engage in to break the deadlock:

Suggest: taking a break, adjourning, summarizing the views/ideas expressed so far, engaging in a short period of silence and reflection, changing the meeting location, calling in a third party, or critiquing negotiator behavior.

Ask: about feelings, what seems to be going on here, what seems to have produced the deadlock, why the silence, if new rules should be developed to guide the discussion.

Describe: how you feel, what the mood seems to be at this point.

Engage in constructive behaviors: admit to a behavior that has turned off the other party, offer praise on what has transpired so far (patience, listening, ideating), redirect the conversation to another issue ("let's table this item for now"), draw a 7- or 10-point rating scale of and secure two separate ratings of progress and satisfaction.

Ending the First Session

If one or more meetings seem to be in order to close things out, point to any progress made and summarize where you agree. Thank the other party for joining in the discussion. Stress the need for continued cooperation. Try to schedule the next meeting in the immediate future while the momentum for action is favorable.

Achieving Resolution

Your task as a negotiator is to resolve the divisive issue in a high quality way. This means two things:

1) searching for mutual interests, for both sides need to claim victory to save face, and
2) avoiding the temptation to wrap things up before all options have been considered.

There is little point in coming to agreement on a problem that will not produce a durable solution or, worse still, create new problems in the future. If time is a factor, an interim solution may have to be accepted. But be sure to recognize that that's all that has been achieved, and more hard work is in the offing.

Depending on the nature of the problem, a written agreement may be appropriate. Also, it may be wise to meet again at a later date to see how well the mutually agreed-upon decisions have worked out; e.g., have both parties lived up to the agreement? If things have not gone as well as expected, a post-mortem critique is in order to find out where and why there was a breakdown.

You may wish to regard the agreement as worthy of a special celebration. If so, a particularly nice restaurant may be the locale to toast the triumph.

Should Collaboration Fail

It is always possible that despite your most professional and sincere attempts at collaboration, a climate of mistrust prevails and collaboration is patently unrealistic. Management consultant Dr. H. B. Karp, ("The Art of Creative Fighting," *The 1983 Annual for Facilitators, Trainers, and Consultants,* San Diego: University Associates, 1983) suggests that conditions precluding collaboration are severe time constraints or deadlines, poor interpersonal relations between the parties, extremely limited resources, and highly divergent values. So what do you do? All you can do, short of aborting the attempt at negotiation, is to fall back on another mode of conflict resolution, possibly compromise, competition, or even accommodation. Other options are using a third party as mediator or resolving with the aid of a person in higher authority.

ADDED CONCEPTS FOR CLASH CONTROL

It's a tough little exercise, though, of getting the conflicts out and getting them settled. But after you've survived it, people begin to feel good with each other. Absolutely straightforward. Until you've done that, all you're doing is playing games.

—A quote from a manager successful in confronting and resolving a conflict, per John J. Gabarro, *The Dynamics of Taking Charge* (Boston: Harvard Business School, 1987, p. 86)

If you want to succeed in conflict resolution, as did the manager quoted above, here are some added guidelines. Successful negotiators have found that these precepts and techniques helped them to move to win-win conclusions.

Before the Negotiation Meeting

☐ Try to minimize or eliminate conflict by building and maintaining healthy relations with peers and colleagues. Your "tools" for this are clarifying and defining responsibilities, functioning cooperatively wherever possible, maintaining close contact, communicating authentically, possibly maintaining some informal social contact, and generally behaving in ways to augment rather than diminish trust.

☐ Start with a mindset that conflict is neither abnormal, shameful, or sinful. People in any relationship are bound to have disagreements. In fact, surfacing of a conflict is likely to benefit both parties, since a) it can put them on the road to overcoming the difference, and b) it can strengthen the relationship once the difficulty is candidly faced and resolved to the satisfaction of both parties.

☐ Recognize that conflict is basically *evolutionary*. It is not something that erupts without any prior warning. So keep your antenna up to sense the early warning signs. Some serious signals: communication is typically formal, memos are written to avoid direct contact, complaints are vented from time to time and may be increasing in frequency, agreement on problems is hard to achieve, and the like. And be certain to assess your own contribution to the coming explosion.

☐ Ready your mindset for your conflict resolution meeting by clearing your thinking of all the negative, non-productive things you've heard about such meetings, e.g., "It's a no-win situation," "somebody has to lose," "every game has a winner and a loser," "I'm sure the blood will flow," etc.

☐ Think beforehand about possible mutual interests, "common ground," as opposed to "how can I rebut the expected arguments he is likely to toss at me?" Common ground may include overall company goals, past success based on joint action, common adversaries (e.g., the competition, the economy, new legislation), a better bottom line, new opportunities for the outfit, etc.

☐ If the other party does not have access to the same information that you do, share it with him or advise how to obtain it.

☐ Try to unload your "cultural baggage" before you enter your meeting, e.g., as social/literary critic Russell Baker put it in *About Men* (1987), you were exhorted from the cradle to "be like a man," "act like a man," "take it like a man" which means to be totally fearless, relish combat, and to nobly disregard pain. Obviously, such macho attitudes and behaviors may well help rule out working cooperatively and expressing gentler emotions when they might be very appropriate and useful.

Women, too, may have to temper or drop some of their culturally acquired taboos such as "never get into a disagreement with anybody," "don't say anything which may hurt someone's feelings," "always be nice." These admonitions by themselves are OK, but if they serve to inhibit confrontation, i.e., make one culturally reluctant to face up to candid dialog, they certainly merit re-thinking.

☐ If you have a conflict with another person, the worst thing you can do is write a memo about it. Also, asking for a meeting in writing is too cold and formal and, as is often the case with the written word, it runs the risk of misinterpretation. So deal personally.

☐ In negotiation over a conflict, as in any other negotiation, perception of one's power (or lack of it) is often as significant as its actuality. For example, as many financial people will attest to, if you owe someone $1,000, the other party obviously has greater control of the relationship. Conversely, if you owe $1 million dollars you have the greater control!

☐ Conflict can lead to creativity or to hard feelings. It all depends on how it's managed. Particularly important is whether we communicate attitudes of respect. You can't expect progress in a dispute if one or both parties enters the negotiation with a "I'm OK, but you're not" attitude.

☐ Regarding attitude: a) Think "win-win" throughout your dialog. b) Think in terms of being against the problem, not "you vs. me." You don't need the usual non-productive, inflammatory baggage of who is totally right and who is totally off base. c) Try to turn both positions upside down, i.e., agree at the outset that both parties are right! Recognize that both parties have healthy intentions based on their needs as they see the situation. d) Most importantly, think in terms of *outcomes* that allow both parties to win. Finally, heed the words of Winston Churchill:

Never give in.
Never give in.
Never, never, never, never
—in nothing great or small,
large or petty—
Never give in except to convictions
of honor and good sense.

☐ Give your fellow negotiator the benefit of the doubt that he is not evil. Assume that he causes you "pain" because a) he is acting to meet his legitimate needs as he sees them and b) he is not aware how his behavior is impacting on you.

☐ Maintain a resolve to communicate on an "adult-to-adult" basis. Regardless of the other person's behavior, don't fall into the trap of communicating on a "parent-child" basis (i.e., talking down to someone), or worse, on a "child-child" basis (e.g., shouting, blaming, name calling, whining, etc.). In other words, be your own person. Don't let anyone else determine your behavior.

☐ Try to avoid making attributions, either in your mind or stated openly, about the other party's motives, feelings, and attitudes. Better leave such speculation to the real psychologists.

☐ In your negotiation, try to follow this simple (paradoxical) rule: The best way to win is to forget about winning!

In the Negotiation Session

☐ If the conflict is of an inter-group nature, try to secure agreement at the outset on guidelines to make the meeting proceed well and be productive. **Examples:** agree to talk about the present, not a lot of old history; agree to cite specific cases, behaviors, circumstances, rather than broad, undefined generalities; agree to close the discussion temporarily when emotionality is taking over; only seek solutions best for the whole organization, not just one side or the other. Post the agreed-upon guidelines on a prominently displayed flipchart.

☐ Aim for dialog, not debate. Remember that your task is to produce a solution that both parties will respect, not to score points.

☐ Try to understand where the other party is coming from. You have your views, perceptions, and possibly "vested interests" in the problem, and so does the other party, which means that he, like yourself, is not necessarily negative or stubborn. He is mere-

ly responding to the principle of "where you stand is where you sit."

☐ A good way to begin the discussion is to ask the other party how he sees the situation/problem/difference. This approach has these merits: a) it shows that you are a fair-minded person and want to enter his world, b) you may learn something of his position you did not understand, and c) you help to set the tone for a true problem-solving session rather than a debate or a duel.

☐ Try to get clarification, if needed, whether the disagreement is based on facts, goals, methods, values, or possibly ancient history.

☐ Avoid the accusatory approach—that differences are due to the other party's needs for power, prestige, or possibly a personality quirk. So strive to handle differences/disagreements without resorting to behaviors that are demanding, debating, directing, downgrading, deafening, digit-pointing, devaluing, defending, destroying/devastating, diminishing, or depreciating. Accepting/appreciating differences is basic to communication effectiveness as well as personal growth. In short, your job in negotiation is to look for answers, not victims or victories and to move from *who* is right to *what* is right.

☐ Acknowledge constructive behaviors wherever you can. Even in a strained relationship, the other party in all likelihood isn't all wrong or totally beyond redemption.

☐ Give yourself the benefit of the skilled mediator's rule, namely, shift from "when I talk, people listen" to "when I listen, people talk." Good listening is essential to overcome what has been termed "the dialog of the deaf." Effective negotiators find that listening may be more persuasive than talking. Consider, then, the various "levels" of listening.

Levels of Listening

In any attempt at conflict resolution, it is essential that listening proceed in flawless fashion. Otherwise, the disagreement may not only remain unresolved, but may become aggravated. It thus behooves negotiators to sharpen their listening skills. One way to do this is to acquire a fuller understanding of the various levels of listening. Management consultant Gary Copeland ("Levels of Dialog: Analyzing Communications in Conflict," *The 1995 Annual: Vol. 1, Training,* San Diego: Pfeiffer & Co., 1995) suggests that whether we are aware of it or not, there are seven levels of listening. They are:

Level −1: Unaware. This is the level of the classic non-listener. He is so concerned with his thoughts, rebuttals, etc., that he is very likely to miss what the other party has to offer.

Level 0: Avoiding. Here the listener is very much aware of the speaker, but prefers to tune him out.

Level 1: "No, you are . . ." This style entails a deflection back to the person providing the message. **The result:** emotions are escalated and real communication/understanding is stymied.

Level 2: "You shouldn't feel that way." This person is intent on depriving the speaker of his feelings. Why? Because those feelings make him uncomfortable. **The result:** communication is aborted, neither party understanding the other very well. Conversely, tuning in to the speaker's feelings is an essential way to improve communication.

Level 3: "Let me tell you." Here the listener has a king-sized need to get his own story out, so he frequently interrupts. The story may be used to top that of the other person's, to correct the facts being supplied, or to solve the problem of the presenter. **The result:** a strain on the relationship.

Note: None of the above listening styles serve to strengthen or move the relationship forward. In fact, they are more likely to derail it.

Level 4: "Tell me more." This is the understanding response, the mark of a good listener for one is stating loud and clear that added explanation, examples, and expression of feelings are wanted. **The result:** the speaker feels that caring and understanding is the name of the game.

Level 5: "What I hear you saying is . . ." This entails the use of the paraphrase, a hallmark of the effective listener. **The result:** the speaker appreciates that he has been understood. (Understanding, of course, does not mean agreement, but that real listening took place.)

☐ Watch your language in your negotiation session. Use "I messages" ("I feel frustrated when . . .") freely as opposed to accusatory words and phrases ("You're wrong!" or "You have failed to . . ."). Also, avoid all encompassing words like "always" or "never," for they are certain to trigger a response of

denial ("Oh yes I did. For example, last week I . . ."). A skill worth cultivating is how to disagree without launching an argument, e.g., "May I present another point of view on this?" "I understand what you're saying" or "I know where you're coming from . . ." "Permit me, please, to suggest another alternative."

Your language can also be used to show that you have a helpful attitude, e.g., "Pat, you've felt for a long time that we've been getting all the travel money. Let me suggest a way to do something about that."

☐ Serve as a trainer or coach in your negotiation meeting by modeling a positive tone. If you speak slowly, listen carefully, and restate from time to time what the other party said, you are setting a high standard for the other party to emulate.

☐ Direct the dialog to new behaviors, that is, what you might do differently and what the other person might do differently.

☐ When dealing with peers, you obviously don't have command authority to insist on the other party's cooperation, e.g., to secure data from another department. Says organization development consultant Karen Massoni ("How to Develop Influence," *Supervisory Management,* July 1994), "Using influence you work through alliance rather than compliance."

☐ If a peer is irate because of an act of commission or omission on your part (or that of your staff), admit to the error and ask, "What can I (we) do to make it right for you?"

☐ Strive to focus on shared needs—the good of the organization—not on unshared hostilities. Remember that only lawyers are paid to argue—you never will be.

☐ Use *empathy* to assess the validity/reasonableness of any of your proposals. Ask yourself: "If I were in the other party's shoes, would I be likely to accept my offer?" Or, if you intend to ask for something from the other person, query yourself whether the other person is in a position or of a mind to respond favorably to your request. And when you make such a request, will the other party feel that by meeting your need he is furthering overall corporate goals/success/accomplishment?

☐ If you propose a solution and the response is a quick or sharp "It won't work," simply say, in response, "Do you have another alternative?" If one is forthcoming, then suggest putting these two options on a flipchart, seeking out other possibilities, and then weighing the pros and cons of each proposal in light of *joint* (or organization-wide) needs.

☐ If your discussion reaches an obvious impasse, you may wish to stop things at this point and suggest doing what the Quakers do to promote harmony—call for five minutes of silence before returning to the discussion. And if things do not improve, say, "I'm sorry, but the climate isn't helpful right now. Why don't we reschedule this? When would you like to meet again?" Obviously, putting negotiations on hold or bowing out entirely takes a lot of fine judgment and sensitivity. As the Kenny Rogers' song, *The Gambler,* puts it:

Know when to hold them,
Know when to fold them,
Know when to walk away,
And know when to run.

☐ If in the course of the negotiation you become upset with the other party, try to assess what style of speaking he is using that caused your negative reaction. Says linguistics professor Deborah Tannen, author of *That's Not What I Meant: How Communication Style Makes or Breaks Relationships* (New York: William Morrow & Co., 1986):

"Once you identify his or her style, you will be in better control of yourself.

"Metacommunication is discussing the other person's ways of talking and how it affects you. It is talking about the argument during the argument. It is often very effective to draw attention to the way the other person is speaking."

Adds Tannen, "A classic metacommunication is 'You seem angry. What made you angry?' or 'It upsets me when you raise your voice.'"

☐ Inject humor into the discussion wherever possible; e.g., after yesterday's "rough" opening meeting, you might say something like, "Shall we spend the first 15 minutes in mutual recriminations?"

☐ So be cool, be loose, be flexible. Don't let your status, authority or ego get in the way of being rational, reasonable and human. If you strive too hard to win, disappointment or disaster may bedevil you as the anecdote below suggests.

Story: One night at sea the captain saw what looked like the lights of another ship heading toward him. He told his signalman to blink to the other ship: "Change

your course 10 degrees north." The reply came back: "Change your course 10 degrees south." The ship's captain answered: "I am a captain. Change your course north." To which the reply was, "Well, I am a seaman. Change your course south."

This response infuriated the captain so he signalled back, "Dammit, I say change your course. I am on a battleship!" To which the reply came back: "And I say change your course south. I'm in a lighthouse."

After the Negotiating Meeting

If agreement on one or more issues was reached, arrange at meeting's end for a follow-up session to review progress on fulfilling the terms of the agreement. It also may be desirable at this time to assess the status of the relationship between the two parties.

Resolution with the Aid of Third Party

Sometimes a conflict situation can be facilitated via a neutral third party. The intermediary is particularly useful if those in conflict lack the requisite skills to negotiate collaboratively. Such an individual, if adequately skilled, can help to define issues and goals, facilitate the communication process, and create a problem solving atmosphere. The mediator would not have the authority to render a final decision. However, he should have enough expertise and prestige so that he would be listened to insofar as the *process* of negotiation is concerned.

A merit of this approach is that some obstinate/overly aggressive negotiators are likely to behave in a more reasonable and cooperative manner if a third party is present to provide and monitor negotiation guidelines. This method does have some limitations. If the organizational culture regards conflict as a "no-no," few will admit publicly to having a disagreement with someone else. Also, those in dispute may not wish to admit that they cannot resolve their disagreements without outside help. ("Who says I can't fight my own battles?") **Other considerations:** a skilled mediator may be hard to find; it may be hard to get agreement as to who the third party should be; it may be difficult to secure such a person when needed, particularly if a series of meetings is in order; the mediator, consciously or below the level of awareness, may not be fully neutral.

If the mediator does begin to side with one of the parties in conflict, his usefulness is at an end for he has become part of the disagreement. In fact, over the long term, this person will not only have his reputation tarnished as a possible mediator, but he is likely to be regarded generally as a person of limited trust. And most seriously, if an agreement is reached, the party who "lost out" may feel that the decision was imposed on him. In this circumstance, the latter may support the agreement only in a tepid way.

Should a win-win decision be reached, satisfaction, learning, and personal growth should be high.

Resolution by or with the Aid of a Higher Authority

In instances when those in conflict do not feel that they can work together successfully toward an agreement, when the nature (subject matter) of the conflict is such that it cannot be resolved appropriately by the parties involved, or when a deadlock is reached after an attempt at negotiation, resolution by or with the aid of a higher authority may be essential.

In some instances, one or both of the conflicting parties may feel that "a fair shake" is likely only from the top person. Some may even hope for preferential treatment based on an "in" with the top official or "foreknowledge" as to his thinking on the issues in conflict.

The technique for the higher-level manager asked to help resolve the difference, per management professor Dr. Daniel C. Feldman, may involve imposing a solution or employing conflict diffusion strategies such as "smoothing" or appealing to "superordinate" goals ("A Taxonomy of Intergroup Conflict-Resolution Strategies," *The 1985 Annual: Developing Human Resources,* San Diego: University Associates, Inc., 1985).

Imposing or forcing a solution may be appropriate when quick, decisive action is needed or when the parties involved are so far apart that it is unlikely that they will ever reach a decision. However, since the conflicting parties are not likely to have the chance to air their grievances fully and to work their differences through collectively, the "peace" achieved may well be short-lived. And if the underlying issues or causes for the conflict are not addressed, the conflict may surface later in other forms and situations.

Smoothing involves a playing down of the extent or importance of the difference(s). Thus, the top executive may try to smooth things over by persuading the warring parties that "you're not as far apart as you think" by highlighting similarities in their positions or by "stroking" hurt feelings. Although smoothing may help to calm people down and regain their perspective, it generally is ineffective because it fails to address the basis for the conflict.

Appealing to superordinate or higher goals of the organization, e.g., survival, is a good way to defuse hostility and bring things into a higher level focus. If common interests can be found— "We're all trying to win this war, aren't we?"—parochial interests can be subordinated.

The top person may also be in a position to expand resources—money, space, authority, equipment, personnel, etc.—so that both contestants achieve a gain of some sort.

If the top manager is uncomfortable with conflict ("We're just one big happy family here"), he may stress the need for cooperation, loyalty, and teamwork, and politely scuttle attempts "to let the sparks fly," even though this might well be the way to produce a high-quality solution. Conversely, if the authority recognizes the importance of facing up to conflict, as opposed to allowing the two parties to engage in endless squabbling, he may "force" a collaborative problem solving effort. Thus, in one instance, a top manager told his two managers who were at loggerheads for many weeks over an authority issue: "I'm going to listen to both sides of this dispute very carefully, but I'm not going to decide who is right and who is wrong. Instead, I'm going to decide who is bullheaded and who will not listen to the other and I will get rid of him." Needless to say, both "gladiators" got the message and quickly decided to try again to work things out on their own.

To sum up, a higher authority can, indeed, settle two-party disputes and at times must. Nevertheless, the shortcomings of this approach are that the basis for the conflict may not be fully aired and it may not resolve strained relations. Nor will it necessarily provide the shared experience of having worked through differences in a mutually supportive and caring way. These limitations are analogous to the situation discussed under compromise.

Furthermore, some warring parties may not wish to admit to someone up the line that they can't work out their own difference or, more basically, that they actually are in dispute with someone. Instead, they are more likely to resort to non-collaborative approaches such as compromise or competition to resolve their disagreement.

In general, the most helpful role of the high-level manager is to encourage the two parties to enter into a problem-solving mode as opposed to forcing or imposing his own solution on them.

Comparing Conflict Resolution Approaches

Table 2-1 (pages 58–59) compares the various approaches to conflict resolution.

MANAGING INTER-GROUP CONFLICT

Thus far we have discussed the management of conflict with another person. There are times, also, when one unit or group may be in conflict with another—sales vs. production, manufacturing vs. quality control, line vs. staff, headquarters vs. field, program offices vs. the comptroller, and so on.

A helpful way to resolve the conflict is to meet jointly—all staff members or the chiefs and their key assistants, depending on the size of the units involved. Each side develops "images" (perceptions) of themselves and the other group. The idea is to get into the open data concerning the perceptions and feelings about the relationships, for how we regard ourselves and the other group typically is the root of the conflict. The procedure is as follows:

1. Each group prepares on three flipchart sheets stating perceptions (adjectives will suffice) as to a) how we see ourselves, b) how we see the other group and c) how we think the other group sees us. The flipcharts are posted on the walls for easy scanning.

2. A discussion is then held to examine the statements. Attempts are made to clarify possible misconceptions.

3. To develop specific action plans for the improvement of relationships, the "Role Negotiation Model" is employed. Both groups should list, on three separate flipchart sheets, the kinds of needs the other group must try to meet if relations are to be improved. More specifically, each flipchart has the following headings:

   ☐ The things we need *more* of that we are now *not* getting are:

   ☐ The things that we *are* now getting and need *less* of are:

   ☐ The things that we *are* now getting and wish them to *continue* are:

4. The needs data sheets are posted on the walls and become the basis for discussion and negotiation.

Note: A facilitator or trainer skilled in conflict resolution techniques should be used to help set guidelines, build a supportive climate, defuse arguments, and develop concrete plans for new, cooperative behaviors.

SEVERAL PROBLEM-SOLVING MODELS

Underlying all that has been stated above is the need to resolve differences in a systematic, rational, problem-solving manner as opposed to reliance on power or Machiavellian tactics. Four problem-solving models are presented below.

Scientific Problem Solving

The first model is the classic scientific problem-solving method. It has these steps:

1) define the problem
2) generate possible solutions to the problem
3) evaluate each option or possible solution
4) select the highest-quality solution
5) plan for implementation, and
6) follow up for purposes of evaluation.

The Win-Win Model

The second model is specifically geared toward conflict resolution. It was developed by Drs. Roger Fisher and William Ury, Director and Associate Director, respectively, of The Harvard Negotiation Project. The model, described in their book *Getting To Yes: Negotiating Agreement Without Giving In* (Boston: Houghton Mifflin Co., 1981), includes these guidelines:

Separate the People from the Problem

The aim is to have the vying parties attack the problem, not one another. Strong emotions and widely different perceptions are to be expected, but they must be recognized as barriers to focusing objectively on the problem.

Focus on Interests, Not Positions

If each party begins with a staunch negotiating position, the real interests tend to become lost. So the focus has to shift to needs as opposed to endless wrangling and bargaining over-stated, frozen positions.

Invent Options for Mutual Gain Before Trying to Reach Agreement

Instead of searching for the single "right" solution, generate a variety of possibilities. The pressure of being in the presence of an adversary and having a lot at stake

Table 2-1
Conflict Approaches/Styles—A Comparative Summary

Approaches/ Styles	Major Elements	Strengths	Limitations
Avoidance	□ Flight (as opposed to "fight") supported by various rationalizations/denials. □ Behavior: unassertive and uncooperative. □ Since problem not addressed mutually, both parties should experience a "lose-lose" situation.	May be appropriate if other party is highly powerful, negotiation skills are lacking, time is not available for negotiation, the timing is not right, or the issue is a minor one or may be resolved by waiting.	The opportunity to seek a creative, "win-win" solution is lost; the source of the conflict remains and may even worsen.
Accommodation	□ Defer to presumed superior needs of other party, even if one's own needs are strong. □ Behavior: unassertive and cooperative (one cooperates to let other win). □ Again, a likely "lose-lose" situation.	May be a means of relationship building, climate setting, and confrontation avoidance. May be worthwhile if achieving harmony is very important or when other party has the greater power.	Opportunity to achieve a creative "win-win" solution is lost; growth through conflict is also lost.
Compromise	□ Entails "splitting the difference"; essentially a lose-lose approach since a creative solution was not sought and both parties gave up some of their needs. □ Behavior: assertive and cooperative (in the sense that both parties assent to work on the problem to some degree).	Both parties experience some gain; saves time and may keep relationships from deteriorating.	Since a creative solution is not sought, the agreement may be only a "quick fix." Commitment to the decision may be weak since some needs were not met. Hurt feelings may remain or develop.
Competition	□ Entails use of power to have one's way, the classic "win-lose" mode. □ Behavior: assertive and uncooperative.	Brings about a needed decision, especially if time is of the essence.	Decision may be viable only in short run since one party was forced to yield and a creative solution was not sought. Future relations may be damaged since one party was a loser.
Collaboration	□ Entails a search for mutual goals and gains, a creative "win-win" solution. □ Behavior: assertive and highly cooperative.	Taps wisdom of both parties and thus has potential to produce a creative solution and strengthen future relations.	Takes skill, patience and motivation to cooperate and problem solve, attributes not all negotiators may have. The process may be time-consuming.
Use of a Third Party	□ In the absence of negotiating skill by one or both parties, a third party may be called in to help define issues and to provide guidance on joint problem solving.	A neutral, experienced and skilled mediator can be useful to help set a climate and provide guidance for mutual problem solving.	There may be a reluctance to admit that one needs outside help, and a "suitable" outsider may be hard to find. The mediator may not be totally objective or impartial.
Resolution by or With the Aid of a Higher Authority	□ The prestige and/or authority of the higher-echelon figure can help mediate or decide the conflict. The approach: use of "forcing" or diffusion strategies (such as smoothing over differences or appealing to superordinate goals).	Helpful to encourage a decision, especially if time is a factor. May provide added resources to overcome deadlock. Can encourage looking at the big picture as opposed to parochial interests alone.	If the authority figure makes the decision, neither party benefits from a worthwhile "give-and-take," "working-through" experience. The cause for the conflict may remain unresolved.

Negotiatior Satisfaction	Growth Potential	Impact on Trust Level and Future Relations
Low; feelings of self-doubt and self-blame (guilt) may arise for failure to confront the issue.	None at all, since conflict was side-stepped and there was no opportunity to learn from a negotiation experience.	Improvement not likely; may even worsen.
Fairly high if decision to accommodate was truly altruistic; less so if decision was more political.	Ditto.	Improvement possible since the "winner" may feel more kindly toward the "loser."
Low to moderate, depending on how "hard and dirty" the bargaining was and what the gains and losses were.	Some learning is possible since a confrontation did take place and an agreement was worked through.	Probably unchanged; lower if the bargaining was "dirty" and "bloody."
High for the winner; low for the loser.	A learning experience for the winner, but he is probably learning the wrong things.	Probably worsened, due to power plays and ploys of the winner.
Very high, for both parties were equals and were involved on a caring, sharing and intimate basis.	Very high, since both parties worked actively and mutually in a creative interactive learning experience.	Strengthened, due to the joint efforts of the two negotiators.
High, if a collaborative win-win effort takes place.	High, if both parties have full opportunity to work things through jointly.	High, if both parties are fully involved and a win-win solution is achieved.
Low, if a decision is imposed from on high. Moderately high if the decision is based on expanded resources or deferral to super-ordinate goals. Very high if a collaborative experience ensues.	Depends upon the degree to which the conflicting parties had the opportunity to work things through.	Ditto.

tends to shrink your creative potential. Nevertheless, a search for shared interests and mutually beneficial solutions can overcome these constraints.

Insist on Objective Criteria

Try to identify a fair standard such as expert professional opinion, custom or practice, law, market value, etc., as a basis for agreement, as opposed to the power position each side may be tempted to rely on. In effect, both parties abandon subjective approaches and defer to a fair, rational, objective, criteria-based solution.

STP Model

A third model, to aid discussants to move directly to real rather than to phony or peripheral issues, is the STP model (Steven R. Phillips and William B. Berquist, "Focusing Problem Management," *Training and Development Journal,* March 1987). STP stands for Situation, Target, and Proposal.

Situation refers to the information pertaining to the current state of affairs. This is the starting point, where the parties are at the moment. Included are both facts and opinions about the current state of affairs, including predictions about change possibilities. Research may be needed to secure relevant data.

Target represents the desired outcome or end point. Here, participants to the negotiation talk about objectives, goals, ends, aims, purposes, and most importantly, *values,* both personal and organizational.

Proposal relates to actual action proposals to move the parties from the current state to the desired one. This, of course, is the "sticky" area, the one most likely to generate conflict. But if steps one and two (the "S" and the "T") have been worked through fully, conflict is likely to be reduced.

Note: By using this model, the problem-solving action is slowed down so that premature attempts at considering proposals are not likely to occur.

Added Value Negotiating (AVN)

In the fourth model, management consultants Karl and Steve Albrecht provide a systematic approach designed to facilitate win-win outcomes ("Added Value Negotiating," *Training,* April 1993). It has the following five steps:

Step 1—Clarify Interests

Start with a search for the interests of both parties. Why? Because you can't construct a deal or solution before you know what each person wants from the negotiation. Interests can be slotted into two categories: *subjective* and *objective*. The former are judgmental, i.e., intangible, personal, and perception-based. **Example:** to achieve good relations with the other person. *Objective* interests are concrete—measurable, observable, tangible. **Example:** assets such as a truck or access to a computer.

Step 2—Identifying Options

With interests defined, you are now ready to assess elements of value in the negotiating, tangible and intangible. Pose these questions to yourself:

a) What can I give that the other party needs?
b) What can he give that I need?
c) How can we jointly add value to the deal?

By elements of value we mean money, property, actions (agree to do or quit doing), rights, risks. That last element relates to risks in the deal, either open or hidden, that either party can take.

Step 3—Design Alternative Design Packages

Note that unlike other models, the aim is to create several deals or offers so no one is forced to only consider a single option. Procedurally, each deal encompasses options in the five value categories (money, property, actions, rights, risks). With a choice of solutions, agreement on a deal that satisfies the needs of both parties is more likely to emerge.

Step 4—Select a Deal

With two or three deals on the table, they now are ready to be analyzed. Use these criteria:

Value. What (how much) value is offered to each party? What value is created for all concerned?

Balance. Is equal or comparable value available to both parties?

Overall approach. In its totality, do the elements of the deal meet well the interests of all?

Appeal. Is there at least one deal all parties can salute?

If the answer to the last question is "no," you have to retrace your steps, go back to Step 1, and try a new tack. Then come up with new designs (solutions).

Hopefully, one acceptable deal will be on the table. If so, you can go to the final step.

Step 5—Perfect the Deal

Here everything is reviewed to be certain that a mutually satisfactory deal has been carved out. Is it balanced in total value and are both parties comfortable with it?

Summary Point

The AVN model stresses openness, flexibility and a fair exchange of value. It helps build healthy relationships over time and, say the Albrechts, "better deals than could be gotten by any other method."

TABOO APPROACHES

Conflict resolution proceeds best when we do things in an open, straightforward, aboveboard, win-win manner. Thus, ploys such as the following are to be discouraged:

End Runs

At times we may be tempted to deal with the other person's boss (boss two) rather than with the person (boss one) with whom we have a difference. But going over the other party's head by contacting his boss (boss two) directly is likely to backfire. Conceivably, boss two may take a broader view of the issue in dispute. But the odds are that boss two may feel that his subordinate (boss one) must be "protected" and thus, as a minimum, will ask: "Have you taken this up with Velma at all?" or "Can't you work this out with her?"

Threats

Another temptation may be to use a threat of some sort: "I'll just have to tell the VP that I couldn't get this project done because you simply won't cooperate." A more rewarding and less threatening way to get the needed cooperation might be to make a statement such as this: "Branch X really needs this data. In fact, they told me that you're really *the* expert on this and are the only one who has the background to help out on it."

Connections

Real or implied ties with a high-authority person(s) may be used to hint that organizational power is on our side. There may even be an implication in our statement that our position already has been cleared and supported by such a high-status figure. ("I was talking to the Director of Operations the other day and he seemed to think . . .") Name-dropping, to imply intimacy with someone on high, may also be part of the scam.

All of these tactics are patently Machiavellian in character. They are designed to achieve a goal by outfoxing the other party rather than by resolving the issue on its merits. Thus, they are certain to reduce trust and weaken, if not destroy, future relationships.

APPLICATION (SKILL-BUILDING) ACTIVITIES

Now that you have perused the text on conflict management, you can capitalize on your reading by completing the "Worksheet 2-1: Conflict Management Approach Assessment" (page 66). In this skill-building activity you will have the opportunity to assess your approach to coping with a prior conflict situation and to consider how you might handle the situation today.

After you have completed the Worksheet, it will be helpful to study the "Worksheet 2-2: Planning For A Conflict Resolution Meeting" (page 67). It should be of considerable help in preparing for a discussion with another party to resolve a disagreement should one arise at a future date.

You also may wish to review the self-quiz you have already taken, "How I Deal With Conflict—A Self-Quiz." It will provide the opportunity to check your current approach to conflict resolution in relation to the ideas contained in this chapter.

Finally, as added practical work, you may wish to tackle the problems presented in the section on "Questions and Problems for Discussion in Management Training Workshops and College/University Courses in Management and Supervision." You may not necessarily agree with the "school solution" (the author's answers) every time, but you will sharpen your approach to resolving conflict-laden problems on a win-win basis.

KEY SKILL POINTERS

The Winning Manager:

- ☐ Works actively at building and maintaining relations with peers/colleagues.
- ☐ Manages these relations by defining respective responsibilities, functioning cooperatively, keeping in close contact, communicating actively, and building trust.
- ☐ Confronts conflict when it arises.
- ☐ Recognizes conflict as a creative force.
- ☐ Knows his primary and backup styles of conflict resolution.
- ☐ Endeavors to resolve conflicts in a collaborative, problem-solving (win-win) manner.
- ☐ Strives to resolve inter-group conflict via development and sharing of perceptions of images (self and other group), and role negotiation.

EXERCISES, QUESTIONS, AND PROBLEMS FOR INDIVIDUAL OR GROUP WORK AT MANAGEMENT TRAINING WORKSHOPS AND COLLEGE/ UNIVERSITY COURSES IN MANAGEMENT AND SUPERVISION

1. To start things off, ask participants what the term "conflict" connotes. List responses on a flipchart and then categorize them as positive or negative. Discuss significance of responses.
2. Take a vote of your participant group in response to these questions: How much conflict do you experience each day? None? Little? A moderate amount? A great deal? After your tally, discuss the results and relate it to the session/course's goals.
3. Organizations today are marked by greater diversity, a workforce with different cultures, values, and drives. How does this trend relate to conflict in today's organizations? Is diversity the road to creativity or conflict?
4. Recall a conflict you had with another person in the last year or so. What was it about? How was it

resolved, or does it still exist? In hindsight, could it have been handled better? If so, how?

5. What are "superordinate" goals? How important are they to conflict resolution?
6. What kinds of "common ground" can be appealed to minimize conflict?
7. Comment on the seven levels of listening given in the text. How do they compare with your own practice and experience in dealing with others, particularly in areas of disagreement?
8. **Role plays.** Provide skill practice using the "I message" approach. Express how you feel, describe the offending or irritating behavior, and state how that behavior impacted on you and your work. Working in pairs, have the participants propose a problem, real or possible, to practice delivery of an I message. (**Examples:** Your boss ribs you unnecessarily at staff meetings. A car pool member is often late, causing you to arrive late for your staff meetings. Your neighbor's dog decorates your lawn with growing frequency.) Both members of the pair should have the opportunity to present a problem.
9. **Role negotiation exercise.** Working in pairs, have participants develop/describe a difficulty with another person using the role negotiation approach/ technique (I want/need more of . . .; I want/need less of . . .; I appreciate receiving . . . so please continue doing it).
10. The following problems for discussion are designed to provide practice in resolving conflict situations along collaborative (win-win) lines. Possible solutions appear after the problems.

A. **The Delinquent Loan.*** A credit union had loaned money to a member, Jenny Frieze, to buy a truck to set up her own trucking business. Jenny kept up her payments conscientiously until she was stricken with a debilitating illness and could not work or make payments on the loan. Some credit union board members favored foreclosing the loan and taking over the truck for resale; others favored taking a chance on Jenny's possible recovery and waiting things out. In effect, the board was polarized over two possibilities: to foreclose now or to wait.

What interests are at stake here? Is another alternative possible so that both Jenny and the board are winners?

B. **The Church Construction Project.** A board of the local church was polarized for nearly a year over who should build its new church. Several board members favored hiring a contractor to do the job; others preferred that the church do the job, relying on the skills of the parishioners.

The arguments for using a contractor were these: assurance of fully professional work; guarantees as to quality and a completion date; a fixed price; and more efficient worker supervision. (How do you supervise friends?)

The rationale for a church-directed operation were as follows: it would provide a feeling of achievement to church members; it would give emotional meaning and personal investment in the church; it would provide for a community activity by having meals for the craftsmen prepared by church members; it would permit construction at lower cost because the church could buy materials and equipment from church members and friends; the money to build the church could go to church members (the craftsmen) rather than to the contractor.

Can this conflict be resolved along collaborative lines? Is (are) there another alternative(s)?

C. **The Homework Hassle.** Pat and Kim were doing their homework at a long work table in their very comfortable family room. Soon a dispute developed: Pat wanted an open window, but Kim wanted it closed. They wrangled over the issue until their mother arrived on the scene and queried them as to the "why" (need) of their respective positions. Pat favored an open window because the room was stuffy. Kim opposed the open window because it produced a big draft, ruffled her papers, and disturbed her studying.

Assume you are Pat and Kim's mother. Can you help produce a creative win-win solution, i.e., one that meets the needs for both ventilation and quiet? (**Note:** for a variety of reasons—the size of the table, the ample light in the room, the availability of reference books, library-type chairs, etc.—the family room was deemed the ideal study locale.)

D. **Kiddie Conflict.** Two small children are fighting over who should play with the wagon. Each says vigorously: "The wagon is mine." You are their parent. What might you do to help mediate the conflict and produce a collaborative result?

E. **Using Fragmenting.** One approach to overcoming conflict is to use the technique of fragmenting the problem: to break issues down into a series of little ones to get some leverage. In this way, areas of agreement can be identified. With these signs of visible progress, the remaining area(s) of disagreement can be tackled with more confidence and, hopefully, less rancor. **Note:** In conflict situations, the parties involved often are deadlocked on one point when they could, instead, move on to other more promising areas of discussion.

Your task: A married couple engages in an annual shouting match over their forthcoming summer vacation. Assume you are a good friend and they have asked you to intervene and help mediate the dispute. Can you break the big holiday issue down into a series of more manageable concerns along different dimensions? One obvious concern is location (the mountains vs. the sea; going to the northwest vs. the southwest). What concerns might you identify to help unfreeze the impasse?

F. **The Hapless Hotel Guest.** On the second day of her week's stay, a hotel guest discovered a leak in the ceiling above her shower stall. The ceiling had a small but noticeable hole in it. The leak was a bit noisy, but not otherwise annoying. The guest spoke to the hotel manager, who indicated that he would be glad to provide another room if one became available. The manager was not too certain about a possible switch of rooms, however, because the conference group had booked the entire hotel and vacancies were not likely to be available. The guest agreed to the manager's offer but later, upon further reflection, decided to "stay put" because she didn't care for the inconvenience of moving to another room. Besides, the drip was not that noisy. Also, a room switch would mean a loss of revenue to the hotel until the ceiling of her room was repaired. She then thought of a "win-win" solution. What was it?

G. **Conflict Over Customers.** A large, active women's clothing store was faced with constant conflict among the sales force. The sales personnel, who were paid on a commission basis, fought over customers and were reluctant to do the necessary stock work in the back of the store. (The minimal amount of stock work didn't require a regular stock clerk. The clerks resisted the stocking chore because it kept them off the sales floor where their money was to be made.) The manager, having tried "everything" to secure "peace" and efficiency, finally decided to let the sales staff meet as a group to resolve their problems. If you were in the sales staff meeting, what would you propose to achieve a "win-win" resolution of the longstanding conflict?

H. **Pie Split.** You are a parent of two small children. They are wrangling over who gets to split a piece of pie. Why the conflict? Each wishes to be certain to get a "proper" piece. Can you bring about peace and harmony via a win-win solution?

I. **The Heated Air Conditioner Conflict.** Two apartment mates had a continuing disagreement about the extent of use of their air conditioner in the hot summer months. One wanted to use it minimally (only on extremely hot, steamy days and nights) to reduce their electric bill. The other favored total summer comfort and wanted to run the cooling unit continuously. What might you advise to cool the argument and achieve a mutually satisfactory solution to both roommates?

J. **The Illegally Parked Commuters.** The manager of the Prince George's Plaza Shopping Mall in Hyattsville, Maryland, and the merchants in it were happy to see the opening of a long-awaited Metro station nearby. Sales rose smartly, but so did the Plaza's parking woes. It seems that commuters in large numbers were now parking at the mall to avoid paying the daily Metro parking charge of $1.75.

The manager considered these options: He could install fences and gates around the mall's parking lot, but that would inconvenience true shoppers and the merchants. He could charge for the parking. He could chain off the section most likely to be used by the commuters, but that would mean closing the parking area leading to the food court. He could tow cars aggressively, but that would anger the commuters he hoped would become shoppers.

All of the above ideas were rejected because they were not customer friendly. What did the manager finally decide to do that wouldn't alienate the commuters and produce a win-win effect?

Possible Solutions

A. **The Delinquent Loan.** A creative, win-win solution might be to adopt this alternative: Hire some-

one to operate the truck for Jenny while she is ill. This would provide income to pay both the truck driver's wages and Jenny's payments on her loan. This would eliminate the need for foreclosing on the loan, the credit union would continue to receive its monthly payments and the board would garner the reputation as a financial institution that is empathic and helpful. (**Note:** A compromise solution, certainly one less desirable than the one suggested above, might be to "carry" Jenny for an added but fixed period of time—say, 3 to 6 months.)

B. **The Church Construction Project.** Instead of thinking solely in terms of *who* might build the church, the board might consider what *needs* must be met. If this is done, it could produce this win-win result: Hire a contractor who would agree to give priority in his hiring to members of the church who have the requisite building skills. The church would thus have the best of both possible results—the services of a professional contractor and the use of the skills of church members.

C. **The Homework Hassle.** Once the needs of both parties to the dispute are clearly defined—adequate ventilation and the prevention of the rustling of papers from the wind—a simple, win-win solution is possible: Open a window in an adjacent room. Another possibility: if available, place a self-standing screen or other partitioning object in front of the open window.

Note: A compromise solution, such as opening the window partially, could have produced a situation where both parties win to a degree and both lose to an extent. A move to another room by one party would be resolution by accommodation, which would mean a loss for that party.

D. **Kiddie Conflict.** A win-win solution would be to encourage one child to pull the other for a while and then to reverse the procedure. Both would get to ride in the wagon and both would get to pull it. By taking turns at both operations, the children have the opportunity to play *together*. They also learn something about *sharing*. (**Note:** The children in dispute, like many adults, were stuck on an either-or, win-lose solution, i.e., each must have the wagon to himself. A compromise, which would have been less desirable than the solution suggested, would be to rotate the use of the wagon on a time basis. A more expensive and less desirable solution would be to provide both tots with their own wagons!)

E. **Using Fragmenting.** Some travel concerns, in addition to location, might be:

Dates: Before or after Labor Day.

Trip length: 5, 8, or 12 days.

Participants: He wants to invite another couple along, and she wants to take her mother.

Transportation: Driving vs. flying and then renting a car.

Accommodations: Camping vs. use of one or more motels.

Budget: Low, medium or high.

Outside advice: To use or not to use a travel agent.

Nature of holiday (pace): "Active" events vs. a lot of relaxing.

Meals: Do-it-yourself, eat out entirely, or some mix of the two.

Clothes: Use of current clothes vs. procurement of new outfits.

Side visits to friends/relatives: One visit, several visits, or no visits at all.

F. **The Hapless Hotel Guest.** A win-win solution for both parties would entail keeping the guest in her assigned room and simultaneously reducing her unhappiness. How to do this? The hotel manager could reduce the hotel rate substantially, say by 25%. After all, the room was noisy but basically acceptable. The guest's real concern related to paying full price for a room that was below standard.

G. **Conflict Over Customers.** The group came up with two major recommendations the manager readily accepted. One related to a change in the compensation plan—earnings from commissions were to be pooled. Secondly, a system of rotation was introduced both as to waiting on customers and doing the stock work. The latter chore was no longer perceived as a commission-robbing nuisance because commissions were shared.

H. **Pie Split.** A workable proposal to the kiddies would be to let one child divide the pie and let the other have first choice of the two cuts. The guaranteed result: The most carefully cut piece of pie you'll ever see!

I. **The Heated Air Conditioner Conflict.** After considerable discussion, with the guidance of a close mutual friend, a collaborative decision was reached. One roommate agreed to pay the extra cost incurred in running the air conditioner full time during the summer months. The satisfactory decision was possible by meeting the needs of both parties—one achieved comfort and the other avoided added out-of-pocket cost.

J. **The Illegally Parked Commuters.** The manager developed a plan combining the carrot and the stick. He allowed commuter parking at no charge if each month they would present $75 in sales receipts from the mall. He also hired a tow truck one day per week to tour the parking lot. He attached his own car to it to introduce a heavy image of law enforcement. (This procedure reduced illegal parking promptly, and office workers from a nearby office building hastily retrieved their cars.)

The net effect of the plan: 100–150 commuters used the $75 parking plan. The manager called it "a win-win" situation. Those who took advantage of the program save money on parking, and for us, it encourages shoppers at Prince George's Plaza and increases revenue for our merchants."

---

*Problems A–D are based on situations described by John Wallen, in "Creative Conflict," Personnel Panorama, January–February 1957, pp. 12–18. Problem E is based on an article by Derek Sheane, "When and How To Intervene in Conflict," Personnel Journal, June 1980, pp. 515–518. (The article originally appeared in Personnel Management, November 1979.) Problem J is drawn from Kirstin D. Grimsley, "The Mall With a Frequent-Shopper Parking Plan," Washington Business, Dec. 26, 1994.

Worksheet 2-1
Conflict Management Approach Assessment

This worksheet is intended to help you augment your skill in dealing with conflict situations by letting you examine how you handled a prior disagreement. Answer the questions below carefully and candidly for maximum benefit from this exercise.

1. A recent conflict that I had was with (cite person):

   _____

   _____

2. The cause of the conflict was (check one or more items):
   [   ] An informational misunderstanding (our data were different, incomplete, or totally lacking).
   [   ] Difference in perception of *same* data.
   [   ] Role-related factors.
   [   ] Values.
   [   ] Goals.
   [   ] Personality differences.
   [   ] Communication bottlenecks/barriers (channels, physical location, absence of face-to-face contact, etc.).
   [   ] Too-frequent interaction or contact.
   [   ] Methods and or procedures.
   [   ] Responsibility and authority issues.
   [   ] Resources (money, space, equipment, personnel, etc.).
   [   ] Friction over power and prestige.
   [   ] A long-standing history of disagreement.
   [   ] Economic conditions (e.g., the stress resulting from business/economic conditions).
   [   ] Climate in the organization.
   [   ] Career advancement.
   [   ] Ambiguity (in organizational structure, goals, roles, authority, etc.).

3. In more specific terms, the problem related to (cite problem):

   _____

   _____

4. My timing when I decided to resolve the conflict was:
   [   ] Premature   [   ] Somewhat tardy   [   ] About right

5. The approach I used to resolve the conflict was:
   [   ] Avoidance/Withdrawal   [   ] Competition   [   ] Collaboration
   [   ] Accommodation   [   ] Compromise   [   ] Use of a third party
                                                        [   ] By or with the aid of higher authority

5. My satisfaction with the outcome was:

   /_____/_____/_____/_____/_____/_____/
   1   2   3   4   5   6   7
   Low   High

6. The reason for the above rating is:

   _____

   _____

7. After reading this text, my future approach to a similar problem would be:
   [   ] Avoidance/Withdrawal   [   ] Compromise   [   ] Collaboration
   [   ] Accommodation   [   ] Competition   [   ] Use of a third party
                                                        [   ] By or with the aid of a third party

8. The reason for answer 7 is:

   _____

   _____

Worksheet 2-2
Planning for a Conflict Resolution Meeting

1. The conflict involves (cite person or group):

   _____

   _____

   _____

2. The issue relates to (check one or more):
   - [ ] Informational misunderstanding
   - [ ] Perceptual factors
   - [ ] Role-related factors
   - [ ] Goals
   - [ ] Values
   - [ ] Personality differences
   - [ ] Methods/procedures
   - [ ] Ambiguity (role, goals, authority, organizational structure)

   - [ ] Resources
   - [ ] Longstanding history of conflict
   - [ ] Economy/business
   - [ ] Organizational climate
   - [ ] Lack of contact
   - [ ] Communication bottlenecks/barriers
   - [ ] Career advancement
   - [ ] Power/prestige
   - [ ] Responsibility/authority

3. In more specific terms, the dispute relates to:

   _____

   _____

   _____

4. I see the issue in these terms:

   _____

   _____

   _____

5. The other party sees the issue in these terms:

   _____

   _____

   _____

6. If I had complete power to resolve the issue I would:

   _____

   _____

   _____

7. If the other party had complete power to resolve the issue he would:

   _____

   _____

   _____

8. Because neither of us has power over the other, we should approach the issue via (check one):
   - [ ] Avoidance/Withdrawal
   - [ ] Accommodation
   - [ ] Compromise
   - [ ] Competition

   - [ ] Collaboration
   - [ ] Use of a third party
   - [ ] By or with the aid of higher authority

9. If I were to operate in the collaborative mode and sought a win-win solution based upon mutual interests and/or a superordinate goal (overall organizational benefits), I would favor:

   _____

   _____

   _____

3

The Manager as a Communicator: How to Secure Understanding on the Job

Great Spirit, help me never to judge another until I have walked in his moccasins for two weeks.

—Sioux Indian Prayer

I know you believe you understand
What you think I said,
But I am not sure you realize that
What you heard is not what I meant."

—Anonymous

THIS chapter is concerned with a number of key communication skills plus basic principles and concepts—theory, if you will. Its purpose—the theory—is to provide a foundation for the more meaningful understanding of the practical, skill-oriented (how-to-do-it) materials of this chapter. As has been observed, to know practice without knowing theory is to not know practice. In essence, there is nothing as practical as good theory.

Our overall objective, then, is to provide general communication ideas to the acquisition and improvement of interpersonal communication skills, e.g., the areas of listening, nonverbal communication, giving feedback, and so on.

In more specific terms, your reading of the text and completion of the accompanying worksheets and self-quizzes should:

☐ Assist you in becoming more sensitive to the communication process.

☐ Help you recognize and understand blocks and barriers to communication and listening effectiveness.

☐ Provide you with a high degree of familiarity with key skill approaches basic to sound interpersonal communication and interpersonal relations.

☐ Provide you with an opportunity for *introspection* of your current interpersonal skills. (Introspection entails an inward look at your ongoing attitudes, beliefs, values, skill levels. It is essentially a process of self-inquiry and self-assessment.)

☐ Provide you with an opportunity for *reflection* on your current skill as a communicator/listener. (Reflection is allied to and follows introspection. It is a process of giving meaning to the material developed/discovered through introspection.)

This chapter treats the following skill areas to help improve your capabilities in interpersonal communication and relations:

☐ How to Listen Effectively.

☐ How to Manage One-way vs. Two-way Communication.

☐ How to Manage Gender Differences in Communication.

☐ How to Prevent the Defensive Response.

☐ How to Recognize and Use Nonverbal Communication.

☐ How to Provide Negative Feedback.

☐ How to Deal with the Angry Person.

☐ How to Deliver the Bad News.

☐ How to Engage in Creative Contact.

☐ How to Ask Questions.

☐ How to Increase Upward Communication.

☐ How to Communicate New Policies and Procedures.

☐ How to Manage the Grapevine.

Each of these skill areas is accompanied by either a self-quiz or a skill-development worksheet. These practical activities are designed to encourage introspection and reflection about your current communication and listening prowess, key routes to realistic skill development. They are intended to enrich your learning. They will also help you apply the concepts and skills to your own needs and situation.

Notes: Although our emphasis is on improvement of interpersonal communication with subordinates, many of the concepts and skill approaches apply to communication with your boss, colleagues (peers) and others such as family members.

Communication, in the full sense of the term, obviously includes listening. We have made a distinction between the two processes to highlight the importance of listening from a skill acquisition standpoint.

This chapter also has an Action Plan for overall, long-range planning to improve your communication/listening capabilities.

Finally, if you are concerned with the planning and organizing of a communication skills workshop or teaching college/university classes in communication, the questions, problems, and exercises at chapter's end should be of help.

Communication Myths and Fallacies

Managers, typically, are not paid to be "good" communicators. At least few managers would complain that their bosses—top management—constantly jump on them for failing to share information or to listen empathically to their people. Rather, top management's prods relate to end results such as meeting deadlines, costs, customer satisfaction, and the all-important bottom line.

Interestingly enough, however, communication miscues or breakdowns can have bottom-line impacts—sales may be lost, important orders botched, shipments mishandled, accidents triggered, employee relations aggravated, letters and reports re-done, and so on.

In any case, regardless of the kinds of admonitions managers may or may not receive from their bosses, the sophisticated and able ones know that they have to be A-1 information transmitters and listeners to meet the challenge of the bottom line. They may also be aware that they may spend as much as 70% of their working day trying to communicate and listen.

If we were to tune in to the on-going communication in any organization, we would probably hear statements such as the following:

"It's just a communication problem."

"Just tell her what's what. You're the boss, aren't you?"

A: "Boy, was that meeting a waste of time." **B:** "So why didn't you speak up about it?" **A:** "Who, me? You must be kidding!"

"I wonder if she really meant that?"

"How come it isn't done when I told you two days ago that we needed it today?"

"I can't figure out where he's coming from."

"Sometimes I think no one listens."

"Trust management to tell the truth? Come on!"

"Yeah, John's the great stone face, all right. Silent as a clam. You never know how he feels about anything."

Despite the above indicators that all may not be well on the communication front, few managers take time out to reflect on their communication style and how well communication is going in their organization, let alone work at its improvement. Or if there are conscious endeavors to improve their communication skill and on-going communication activities, most of these efforts are doomed to failure because of erroneous assumptions about the communication process. Some of these myths and fallacies follow.

The Meaning is in the Message

Oh, that this simplistic view of communication were true. Unfortunately, what bedevils our communication efforts is that the meaning is *in the receiver* rather than in the message. Thus people's perceptions, their "world view," will determine what they really hear and understand. This, of course, is a natural and expected phenomenon. People are what they are based on their experiences, attitudes, values, beliefs, and physical and emotional states at the time the message is sent. Hence, their filters or mental sets may not permit them to hear what the sender wants them to. Instead, they only hear what they are programmed to hear. Communication—perception, really—indeed lies in the eyes of the beholder. And the message is not somewhere out there, but "in here," in the listener's head.

Story: Jane was dating a young man for three months. She said little about him at home. Finally, her mother could restrain herself no longer and said to Jane: "Tell me, what sort of a fellow is Fred?"

"Oh, he's nice enough, I guess," came the reply.

"You guess? Is there anything about him that bothers you?"

"As a matter of fact, yes, mother," replied Jane.

"What's that?" asked Jane's mother anticipatorily.

"Well, it's all those naughty songs he knows."

"You mean he sings them to you?"

"No," replied Jane, "but he whistles them."

Skill Pointer

You can reduce your frustration level and augment your communication capability if you assume that communication is inherently distorted. Don't operate on the premise that people will hear what you intend. Instead, assume that people, being a product of their experience, will "organize their world" in ways which make sense *to them*. This necessitates that you "check out" your message (get feedback) to find out what was really heard and understood. For in the final analysis, the listener determines the precise nature of the message.

The Meaning is in the Words

Also known as the "one-definition syndrome," this is a serious misconception, for the same words all too often mean different things to different people. *Examples:* The manager who innocently says at the end of an employee meeting: "OK, let's get back to our duty stations" may turn people off because the words "duty stations" may have heavy military connotations. Or the manager who makes a casual reference to a "weak" third quarter (actually an expected seasonal phenomenon) without any historical (comparative) reference or other clarifying data, may cause the newer employees to feel that the whole operation is about to close down and to begin to look for jobs elsewhere.

Even a common word like "noise" depends on one's perception of it. Talking about noise pollution, industrial sound consultant Tony Schwartz said: "Noise is an editorial word. When you talk about noise, you are talking about sound that is bothering you. There's no party so noisy as the one you're not invited to. A fire engine may be noise when you're trying to sleep, but music when our house is burning." (Quoted by Alan L. Otten in "Politics and People," *The Wall Street Journal,* May 31, 1973.)

So don't be trapped by the one-definition syndrome. As one communication authority has pointed out, there are more than 14,000 dictionary definitions for the 500 most-commonly used words. That's an average of 28 different meanings per word!

Story: An elderly widow had some corporate bonds nearing maturation. She dialed her bank to get some advice about cashing them in. Widow: "I have some bonds I want to dispose of."

Bank person: "For conversion or redemption?"

Widow (long pause and then finally): "Is this the First National Bank or the First Methodist Church?"

Words also take on special significance depending on the feeling tone which accompanies them. This is known as "the music of communication." For example, I knew a G.I. in the army who could call a fellow soldier an SOB and it was perceived as a term of endearment. A mother who soothes a hurt child or a wife an irritated spouse does so by the tone used, not the words. So people communicate at both *word levels* and *feeling levels*.

Managers as authority figures run large risks as communicators. Why? Because those below may interpret messages from them literally and implement them without questioning what the words really mean. Although such "blind loyalty" may be ego building, the end result may be something other than that which is expected or required. For example, the late J. Edgar Hoover, the FBI's first and longest-term Director (1924–1972), once dictated a letter to his top agents, which his secretary typed up with unnecessarily wide margins. Mr. Hoover wrote an admonishing note to his secretary on the bottom of the letter: "Watch the borders." Over the next couple of weeks FBI agents were put on special alert along the U.S.–Mexican and Canadian borders! (Cited by Roger T. O'Brien, "Using Jung More [And Etching Him In Stone Less]," *Training,* May 1985.)

If we can understand that just as a map is not the territory and the value of an object is not in the object (but in the would-be buyer or owner), so, too, the meaning is not in the words but in the sender and the receiver. Messages are given meaning by the history (background, world view, frame of reference) of speakers and listeners, not by the words employed.

Skill Pointer

Words are tools that require careful selection. They may be emotionally laden and turn people on or off, they may be subject to more than one interpretation, or they may be a form of jargon that can't be understood by those not technically versed in the subject at hand. So try to anticipate the impact your words may have on the other person(s).

Communication is an Intended Process

Certainly we plan our message and state what we think will be picked up by the receiver. But what we say—the words—are only a small part of the communication. More important are the nonverbal behaviors that accompany and define the words. Also, even if we don't communicate formally, we are constantly emitting messages. *Examples:* The boss walks rapidly into her office, doesn't say "good morning" to anyone, and closes her door for the next two and one-half hours. Or the manager ceases to hold his customary weekly staff meetings without any explanation for the new routine. Or the hyperactive, somewhat autocratic manager returns from a course on "Communication Principles" and immediately announces via memorandum (!) that he now has an "open door" policy. Several weeks later he wonders why no one tried the open door.

What is at work in these situations? People will interpret the manager's behavior if they have a need to, irrespective of the presence or absence of formal messages. In fact, it's not unusual for a manager to ask: "I wonder what gave those people that idea? I didn't say anything like that to them."

Skill Pointer

Recognize that you, as a manager, are constantly sending messages regardless of the presence or absence of any formal communication on your part. It's akin to a faucet that has no controls and just flows. We can choose not to send messages, but we cannot choose not to affect people. In fact, *affecting* others is what communication is all about. Good communicators coordinate their verbal and nonverbal communication. This requires empathy, which is the ability to perceive ourselves as others do, to enter momentarily into the other person's world.

The Tell and Sell Theory

Many managers operate on the assumption that it is their job to get the word out, to persuade, to influence. How else do you get the job done or ensure compliance? But overlooked in this sales approach to communication is that people are not mere passive sponges. They still have to process the messages coming their way. That is to say, they have to tune in, pick up, understand, reflect upon, and interpret what has been said. If your listener has not contributed to the communication (instruction, plan, order), his acceptance of the communication may be slow, or not forthcoming at all. Hence, delays, resistance, misinterpretations, and the like may arise.

Quite often people rank themselves as effective communicators because they "tell it like it is." However, the facts of communication life are that it is no simple feat to so communicate. Rather, the best we can do is to tell it as *we* see it. And the listener, in turn, will understand it as he sees it, not necessarily as we tell it.

Skill Pointer

Selling, persuading, telling, etc., are essentially unilateral efforts at message delivery. One-way communication may be appropriate or even essential at times, e.g., if there is a fire we don't have time to call a staff meeting to discuss the event. But if a message has an element of complexity to it and thus may be misunderstood, or if the message is possessed of novelty or controversy and thus may be resisted, two-way communication is a must. Recognize that "selling" and "buying" are discrete functions that don't necessarily operate in tandem. Don't be lulled into a false sense of communication security that as long as there is a message flow we have communication.

The Minimal Need to Know Assumption

Adopted from the military model, managers often make several unwarranted and hazardous assumptions about communication:

a) There is no need to communicate any more than employees have to know.

b) Besides, people aren't really interested in much more than their paychecks.

c) We don't have the time to communicate on "every little thing."

d) Over-communication will only "stir up the animals needlessly."

Underlying these premises is a somewhat paternalistic "big daddy knows best" outlook. In fact, managers may even say: "Of course we know what employees need to know. After all, we were subordinates once ourselves, weren't we?" But a new managerial role is accompanied by new experiences, changed values, different outlooks, and new expectations. Thus, relying on recollections of bygone days as a subordinate has little reality for operating in the vastly different managerial world.

Thus, what is being overlooked is that management in its wisdom can hardly anticipate all employee needs for and interest in information. In the absence of full communication, the very likely result is a great deal of dissatisfaction along with a flourishing grapevine.

Story: Employee A: "I feel like we're just a bunch of mushrooms."

Employee B: "Mushrooms? What do you mean mushrooms?"

Employee A: "Yeah, mushrooms. They always keep us in the dark and just dump a lot of manure on us."

Skill Pointer

Don't assume employees have limited needs to know. Instead, take active measures to find out what people are really interested in and then share such information fully. So keep in touch, confer, ask, and listen before you communicate.

The Increased Volume Approach

Just as we may communicate when we don't intend to, we may also *not* communicate when we really wish to. If we view communication simply as a process of sending messages, we may all too easily assume that if we send something more often or say it louder, it will affect the receiver more. But ask any teacher, parent, clergyman, or lecturer how easy it is for receivers to tune out senders. Visualize the irate parent who says repeatedly to her youngster: "Do I always have to yell at you before you come to the dinner table?" Or the manager who says to his assistant in frustration: "I guess we'd better send out another memo about starting and quitting on time. And we'd better make it a lot stronger, too."

Skill Pointer

If the message isn't getting through, why keep flogging the dead horse? Turning the volume up or increasing the frequency of transmission has little bearing on the message's worth insofar as the listener is concerned. Certainly the better approach is to analyze the undesirable behavior and try to learn the possible cause(s) for its persistence. The solution to the problem may lie in many directions other than via communication approaches, all of which can be easily resisted, distorted, or ignored. Coaching, counseling, or group problem-solving approaches may be more appropriate.

The Non-emotionalism Approach

Growing up in our culture typically involves learning to deny feelings or emotions. For example, we learn very early on from parents, relatives and teachers such protocols as: "Big boys don't cry." Or: "If you can't say anything nice, don't say anything at all." Or: "Now you be real polite to your Aunt Dorinda."

Later on we are taught to avoid expressing our feelings lest we offend or engage in "conflict" with someone: "I wouldn't make an issue over that if I were you." Or: "Just keep your cool and everything will be all right." Or: "You can't be that candid about it." Or: "Better leave your feelings at home."

But all these well-meaning bits of advice—to engage in phony politeness, to avoid asserting ourselves, to shun necessary confrontation, to avoid leveling or to be candid—add up in time to a denial of the feeling side of ourselves. They also set a self-model for the "managing" (manipulation) of our communication efforts, which creates a feeling of distrust by the receivers. ("I wonder what she *really* thinks about the new program?")

Underlying all these "shouldn'ts" and "mustn'ts" is an assumption that we are a product of reason, logic, rationality, and intellect, that we should only deal in knowledge, facts, formulae, and figures. Actually, man is very much a feeling person. He has pleasures and angers, joys and sorrows, loves and hates, hopes and fears. This follows because he experiences victories and defeats with ensuing highs and lows, all of which have emotional impacts. These feelings determine whether he will turn on or turn off, tune in or tune out, cooperate or resist, engage or disengage. So emotions should hardly be regarded as a "no-no," a naughty burden. Emotions are normal, inevitable, and everpresent. Their expression thus should be encouraged.

When we enter into the communication process as either senders or receivers, we do so with both emotion and intellect, feeling as well as fact. So if we try to eliminate feeling from our communication, we can't communicate authentically. We know that people bring their feelings to the workplace, but typically emotions are discouraged. ("Now let's not get excited over this . . ." Or: "I wouldn't bother her with such a trifle . . . But it *is* a trifle.")

But what if at a staff meeting someone actually said: "I'm feeling totally uncomfortable and frustrated. We've been here two hours and we've been skirting the real issues all that time." How often does that happen? And what would the chairperson be likely to say if it did? Wouldn't our communication be more authentic and healthier if expression of feelings were encouraged rather than stifled?

You can augment your communication skill and success many fold by including your feelings, both positive and negative, in the messages you send.

Examples:
"I'm feeling uncomfortable, Janet, about the time we're spending on this procedure." "I was really pleased by your active participation at this morning's meeting." "I feel good about the way you've taken charge of that new unit, Tom." "Let me see if I understand your feeling on this. Your concern is that . . ." "I was quite upset, Joan, when you spoke harshly to Mary about her leave." *Skill Pointers*

Recognize that our whole person communicates, not just the words we send. Be yourself. Try expressing your feelings if you are not already doing so. You will feel awkward on your first tries, but you'll become more comfortable doing this as you do more of it. And the rewards from this approach will be tremendous—you will achieve greater credibility as you develop trust with the receiver. Remember, too, that listeners hear with their hearts as well as their heads. Their emotional side may thus produce messages different from the ones you intended. Use your antenna to pick up such responses. Also, look and listen for the emotional side of messages others are sending your way.

The Fallacy of Learned Techniques

Much of our education and training in communication emphasizes methods and techniques—writing, reading, public speaking, briefing techniques, conference leadership, and the like. All of these skills are certainly important. But to learn the techniques without understanding both ourselves (including our feelings and our motivations) and the communication process with its pitfalls is to fall into the trap of merely transmitting words, symbols, and messages and hoping for the best.

Basically, knowledge of those communication techniques does little to ensure that our communication attempts become *shared* experiences; that is, that they take into account the relationship between the parties involved and the effect each has on the other.

Skill Pointer

For effective communication, keep the total relationship in mind—support, intimacy, trust, mutual interests, sharing, caring. In the absence of these elements, communication is a tough, up-hill task. Actually, managers don't necessarily have communication problems. Stated more accurately, they have *relationship* problems.

The Fallacy of Knowledge Possession

Even if a message gets through fully, there still is no assurance that people will act on the basis of that knowledge. For example, despite their being taught or told how to work safely, we can't assume that workers will behave in a safe way. Or visualize the manager who complains to her boss: "I don't know how many times I've told Betsy about those letters." Knowledge, indeed, does not guarantee the proper behavior/performance. Ask any smoker, overweight person, heavy drinker, gambler, or chronic violator of traffic rules. Obviously, other needs are motivating the patently undesirable behavior.

Story: A child psychologist had spent all of a hot summer's day laying down a new concrete driveway. As he was taking his well-earned shower at project's end, he heard the sloshing of little feet in the newly laid concrete. The psychologist, in disbelief and chagrin, grabbed a towel, wrapped it around his midriff, ran out the front door, and began to berate the small fry. His wife, hearing the shouts, came quickly to the drive, began pulling her irate, be-toweled husband into the house, and said: "John, why are you screaming at those children? You're a child psychologist, don't you like children?" His reply: "Of course I like children. But I like them in the abstract, not in the concrete."

Skill Pointer

Communication/information per se will not ensure the performance of a desired behavior. Other actions or strategies may be necessary in support of or in lieu of that communication.

The Single Communication Function Fallacy

Managers typically regard communication as a means of giving instructions and influencing attitudes and behavior. Obviously, people do require instructions to get their jobs done and to function properly. Psychologists call information transmitted to produce some action *instrumental* communication, e.g., "Lock the file cabinet" or "Here's what I want you to do this morning." However, there are three other communication needs that all too often are overlooked. These are *cognitive, expressive,* and *supportive* needs.

Cognitive needs relate to the need to know. People require information to give them a feeling of structure, order, predictability, control of their lives. But what happens if the formal communication system is slow, spotty, not to be trusted, or inadequate in other ways? Because people have a need to know, they will fill the information vacuum by creating their own information. Hence the phenomena of rumor, gossip, and the grapevine.

Expressive communication relates to the need people have to express themselves, particularly when they are disappointed, upset, angry, frustrated, or in some other stressful emotional state. In other words, they need an opportunity to ventilate their feelings, to have a catharsis. Quite often "talking it out" will cause the "pain" to disappear. Obviously, this need cannot be met by having people write memoranda about how they feel. Managers all too often, however, are either too busy to listen or are unskilled or uncomfortable with people who have a need to get their feelings out. Also, some managers feel that the role of expressive communicator or empathic listener is incompatible with their job: "My job is to get the work out, not to run a clinic." Hence expressive needs are not too likely to be met.

Interestingly enough, sometimes managers will say: "It's sure hard to get people to say what they think." Actually, the problem is not to turn people on but to turn them off. As one psychologist put it: "Give them half a chance and they'll really spill their guts."

Supportive communication relates to the need for people to feel that there is an interest or concern in them as persons, that they are much more than a name on the payroll printout. A caring attitude is, of course, basic to the development of a feeling of trust by subordinates. Supportive communication behaviors may range from a pleasant smile and a friendly "good morning" to politeness ("Would you please help me find that Z-42 file?") to appreciation ("I really appreciated the extra work you did to get that report in two days before the deadline") to encouragement.

Skill Pointer

Regard communication as more than a means to give orders or to influence behavior. Recognize that cognitive, expressive, and supportive needs may exist, too. Learn about those needs and act conscientiously and promptly to meet them.

The Communication Changes Attitudes Fallacy

Many managers assume that giving people information will readily change their attitudes, and the way they see things. ("Give them the facts and they'll do what we want them to.") Unfortunately, the change process is not that simple. Actually, only lightly held attitudes will be susceptible to new information. These are essentially "fragile" attitudes. But attitudes with a strong emotional component will resist change.

Note that politicians and advertisers don't expect to successfully convert people who already have deep-seated convictions on politics or products. Instead, they concentrate on the undecideds or those whose attitudes are not solidified. For in advertising as in politics, a few percentage points of change determine success, so there is no need "to win 'em all over." Management communication, contrariwise, is typically concerned with *all* the work force, a group, or a particular individual.

Skill Pointers

If it is essential to change attitudes of a group, consider the use of group meetings. This approach takes time, of course, but the potential for acceptance of change is much greater. If the change effort is directed at a single person, consider the use of coaching, counseling, training, or involvement in the planning and decision-making processes.

The Fallacy of Good Intentions

Managers typically see themselves as responsible, highly motivated, well-intentioned people. But this outlook, which may be hard to fault in the abstract, may be of limited value in the real world. Why? Simply because other managers (and non-managers) with whom they interact may be equally well-intentioned, but have different needs and values, and thus operate under entirely different assumptions. So when two well-meaning managers proceed along unilateral lines of communication, unintended conflict may develop.

> **Example:** One summer my secretary was to be gone for 13 work days on summer leave. Her absence was certain to delay a number of key projects. As I saw it, the secretary in a nearby office would make the ideal vacation replacement, for she had worked in my office previously and knew our work quite well. Surely someone else could pinch-hit for her. I thus wrote a memo to my boss on this replacement need, a very normal procedure. You have a "critical" problem, you take it up

with your boss, right? My boss agreed with my reasoning and approved the request for the replacement secretary. But the chap who was to lose his secretary to me exploded when he learned of our boss' decision. He, too, had important work, his secretary was indispensable, and why hadn't I checked this out with him first?

Of course my irate colleague was right and I, as a well-intentioned but self-centered communicator, was wrong. My office secured some other help and struggled along the best it could for that part of the summer.

While the Golden Rule ("do unto others as you would have others do unto you") may be a helpful guide in managerial communication, the "platinum rule" may be of even greater value in communicating with others: "Do unto others as *they* would want to be done unto them."

Skill Pointer

Don't allow yourself to be carried away by the righteousness of your cause. Avoid being "The Lone Ranger" and try instead to think in terms of collaboration with and the needs of others. Even a worthy objective requires careful communication to avoid unwanted conflict with others.

The Is, All, and Because Assumptions

The difference between the right word
And the almost right word
Is the difference between
The lightning and the lightning bug.

—Mark Twain (1835–1910), U.S. author and humorist

Semantacists are people who study the meaning of words and symbols in relation to behavior. They tell us that many of us create difficulties in our communication endeavors because of three "diseases" or tendencies: "isness," "allness," and "becauseness."

The Disease of "Isness"

The "is" implies that we are giving meaning to something "out there" when the assigned meaning is actually in us, i.e., based on our own experience, our world view, our frame of reference. As Humpty Dumpty said to Alice: "When I use a word, it means just what I choose it to mean, neither more nor less." (Lewis Carroll, *Through The Looking Glass*). The implication of the "is" is that everyone else must accept the meaning we have provided. Overlooked is the reality that every word or phrase creates a different thought or image in the minds of others.

Examples: "Betty is totally lazy." "Stan is a nice guy." "The organization is too old hat." ("Lazy?" "Nice?" "Old hat?")

If we are dealing with words at a low level of abstraction, that is, the meanings are concrete and crystal-clear to everyone, there is no problem for the receivers of such messages, e.g., "the notebook is blue," "John is late," "Mary is our senior steno." But as we move up the level of abstraction, we obviously run into difficulty, say, when we use words like "demagogue," "conscientious," "initiative," "creative," "power hungry." The answer? Credit the definition you are communicating solely to yourself: "I think she's too conservative for that job," "As I would see it, the regional office simply is not pulling its weight," or "It looks to me like she's afraid to delegate."

The Disease of "Allness"

This entails a tendency to make assertions or express beliefs that are so ironclad, positive, and all-encompassing, that no one is his right mind would dare question them—or at least so the communicator imagines. Examples of these generalizations are: "Senator X said it, so it must be true." "I read it in *Time* magazine." "I studied it in graduate school." "I worked in the field for 13 years, so I know those people." "I had no other course of action."

Story: The tale of the six blind men and the elephant illustrates the concept particularly well. Each developed his overview—his generalization, really—by patting or touching only one portion of the animal. Thus, the man who touched the tail perceived it as a snake; to another, the trunk became a long, flexible pipe; to the third man, the tusk was a smooth, curved club; a fourth man equated the large ear to a fan; the last two men assumed the heavy legs were sturdy, massive pillars.

Allness also encourages stereotypical thinking: "Politicians are out for themselves." "Jocks are not too bright." "Salespersons will make any promise to close the deal." "Promotions go to the apple polishers in the outfit." "My boss has it in for me." "I'm really a washout. I'll never get what I should out of life."

Psychologically speaking, the allness victim, with these overwhelming generalizations, is striving for a world in which everything is secure and certain. Ambiguities and exceptions are too painful to cope with. Indulging in the allness game is also ego-building, for it provides a feeling that we alone have "the big picture," "the answer," the corner on "truth." Unfortunately, allness closes our minds to other possibilities, to the thoughts or approaches others may have.

To overcome possible allness tendencies, consider the following:

☐ Recognize that each person, situation, or experience is truly unique.

☐ Withhold judgment as to the totality or all-inclusiveness of things, persons, or "truths."

☐ Check out your view with that of others.

☐ Add measurement concepts to your assertions so that you and your listener won't be trapped by confusing, all-inclusive words like "great," "high," "low," "always," "never," "everyone," "no one." Drop all "all" and "all-type" words, phrases and concepts from your vocabulary. Add, instead, open-ended words like "sometimes" and "etc."

☐ Try thinking in terms of plurals: the possibility of their being *multiple* solutions to a problem, *alternate* goals, *various* procedures, *numerous* candidates, and the like. Thus if one approach doesn't work well, another might. Why restrict yourself to being a "Johnny (or Janey) one-note"?

The Disease of "Becauseness"

This entails a tendency to jump to a conclusion, probably a wrong one, and justify it on the basis of "the facts," which are typically very limited or carefully selected. It entails being solution-minded ("solutionitis") rather than problem-minded. ("Don't bother me with the facts, my mind's already made up.") It may also entail confusing symptoms with causes. For example, one complaint or even a few scattered ones about a product or service doesn't mean that everything that has been done must be scrapped.

Jumping to conclusions and shooting from the "lip" are poor forms of problem solving and communicating. More realistic problem solving accrues from patiently and objectively employing the journalist's six questions: Who? What? Where? When? Why? How? If your data are based on a sample, make certain it is statistically sound—large enough and representative.

Avoid hasty assumptions of cause and effect before communicating them. Instead, look for quantitative trends in relation to production, sales, costs, turnover, and waste.

In dealing with others, recognize that a single behavior may have several causes. For example, an employee staring out the window isn't necessarily loafing or daydreaming. He may be collecting his thoughts, pondering a complex situation, rehearsing a talk, or resting his eyes. Communicating first impression of the behavior is a certain way to alienate the receiver of such a message.

Or, apparent causes may camouflage underlying ones. For example, an employee complaint on a particular issue like pay may conceal dissatisfaction with the job per se, career opportunities, or supervision. In your dialog, try to ferret out the real causes by careful questioning (see the section on "How To Ask Questions," later in this chapter).

Skill Pointer

"Isness" ignores the wisdom of the old song line that "It ain't necessarily so": Even the fact that you, the boss, says so, doesn't *make* it so. The real world couldn't care less about our definitions, our labels, our documentations, our cherished opinions. So, *the word is not the thing.* "Allness" is the servant of the person who knows everything. This type of person has seen it all, heard it all and thus knows it all, except knowing one important thing—that *he has a closed mind.* "Becauseness" bespeaks of an analysis that is surface, shallow, and sloppy. What it lacks in depth and logic it makes up in speed. It ignores the fact that *jumping to a conclusion and exercising the mind are not like operations.*

Recognize that users of isness, allness, and becauseness traffic in absolutes. They make statements that are neither fair nor accurate. They are quite certain to confuse, irritate, or overwhelm the listener. They may create defensiveness and possibly discourage two-way communication, and *who needs that?*

Overcoming Myths and Fallacies

The previous subsection outlined a good number of myths and erroneous assumptions about the communication process. Any of these, if adopted and acted upon, are certain to make the manager a less-effective communicator than he would like to be. A more useful way of looking at the communication process is to draw on the concepts developed by communications authority Dean C. Barnlund ("Toward A Meaning-Centered Philosophy of Communication," *Journal of Communication,* December 1962).

Communication is not a thing, but a dynamic process. In any act of communication, the sender, the receiver, and the message do not remain the same. To assume that communication is an automatic, static phenomenon is erroneous. Change, which is virtually certain, in any of those three forces will affect the communication process and the intended message.

Communication is circular, not linear. If we accept the notion that communication is a process, it is also appropriate to state that communication is not an event. The process does *not* entail A affecting B, B affecting C, and so on, akin to cascading dominoes where the motion stops after the last one falls. It is *not* a simplistic, short-lived activity involving a sender, a message and an interpreter, all operating in isolation. Rather, the process is one of mutual dependence or interdependence with interactions of a *continuing* nature.

Communication is complex. When a single communication transaction takes place between A and B, there are *six* people present:

A
• The person you think yourself to be
• The person your partner thinks you are
• The person you believe your partner thinks you are

B
• The person you think yourself to be
• The person your partner thinks you are
• The person you believe your partner thinks you are

Any one of these six variables affects not only what is said, but what is actually received and interpreted.

Communication is irreversible and unrepeatable. Communication is *not* a mechanistic and deterministic system. Rather, it is spontaneous and evolutionary. For example, you can saw a log, starch a shirt, or carve a turkey and that's it. But, says Barnlund, you can't make someone start to think, scold your secretary, or return a compliment with the same final consequence. Visualize the words of a manager to a subordinate or peer—they may lead to new insights and new possibilities or to increased anxiety or total boredom. Similarly, a moment of indifference or a possible put-down will have permanent impacts. Just like you can't put squeezed toothpaste back into the tube, so, too, you can't readily retrieve or erase a delivered message. ("Gee, I wish I hadn't said that.")

Communication involves the total personality. Although we often like to make sharp distinctions between mind and body, reason and emotion, and thought and action, meanings continue to be generated by the whole person. So every fact, conclusion, decision, shame, guilt, anxiety, and joy requires accommodation by the entire personality. Thus, the more profound the involvement produced by a given message, the sooner and more serious its effects will be upon the other person's behavior.

To avoid being trapped by these communication myths and assumptions, the manager needs to develop skill in the areas listed at the outset of this chapter. Each of these vital skill areas is treated in detail below.

HOW TO LISTEN EFFECTIVELY ("THAT ISN'T WHAT I MEANT")

Know how to listen and you will profit even from those who talk badly.

—Plutarch (circa 46–120), Greek biographer and moralist

Nature has given to man one tongue, but two ears, that we may hear from others twice as much as we speak.
—Epictetus (1st–2nd century A.D.),
Greek Stoic philosopher

He knew the precise psychological moment to say nothing.

—A comment about a friend by Oscar Wilde (1854–1900), British dramatist, poet, novelist essayist, and critic

How many times have you heard or possibly made statements such as these:

"Oh, that isn't what you said?" "You haven't heard a word that I've said." "That isn't what I meant." "You never listen to me." "I guess I wasn't paying attention." "I didn't mean to cut you off." "It's getting harder and harder to get through to people."

If you have experienced these or similar statements, you're hardly alone. They simply reflect the difficulty most of us encounter daily as we endeavor to listen accurately to others and others to us. Interestingly enough, listening is one of the more critical skills a manager can possess as it is vital to securing information from others.

Also, listening is a tremendous means of developing strong interpersonal relations with others. Why? Because people have a need to feel good about themselves, to feel important. By listening attentively we help to meet that need.

Most people are quite candid about their somewhat mediocre listening skill. For example, Dr. Lyman K. Steil, an authority on listening, asks people to rate themselves on their listening effectiveness ("Secrets of Being a Better Listener," *U.S. News and World Report*, May 1980). Most give themselves a 55 or so on a scale of 0–100. None say they are superior or poor. When he asks them whether they believe a 55 is good enough, most reply: "Of course not."

Listening is never an easy task. Why not? Because the phenomena at work to reduce our listening effectiveness are many. Here are the key factors (blocks and barriers) psychologists and educators commonly describe.

Blocks and Barriers to Listening Effectiveness

Psychological/Perceptual

A prime psychological factor is speaking and hearing rates. Speakers deliver words at a rather slow rate of speed—about 125–140 words per minute. Listeners can absorb at two or three times that rate. The result? A great deal of free time for daydreaming (mental downtime) and thus tuning out the speaker. Many of us use that free time to prepare a response to what is being said before the speaker has completed his message.

Other psychological factors are ignoring or overreacting to the nonverbal aspects of the message: listening only for facts and thus ignoring the very important emotional side of the message.

Key perceptual factors include our personal history (family, education, and work influence), expectations, attitudes, values, and prejudices that may predispose us to distort or block out what is said. Thus, a presumed "dull" subject may cause us to tune out, or a line official may lower his antenna as he listens to a staff person.

Other perceptual factors at work may be our animosity toward certain individuals or groups the speaker represents or possibly reminds us of; dislike of or disagreement with the speaker's ideas; dislike of the sender's vocabulary (too sophisticated or too colloquial), dress, grooming, accent, skin color, sex, age, mannerisms, posture, voice quality, or weight. Of course, an overly favorable attitude toward a person and his ideas may produce distortions, too, in the form of presumptions, preconceptions, and exaggerations.

Emotional

Problems of tune out or distortion may arise due to such states as depression, anxiety, anger, sorrow, grief, stress (health, job, family), or receipt of bad news. Temporary positive moods such as exhilaration, joy, or exuberance may inhibit accurate listening, too. ("I was so elated about the promotion that I missed most of what was said at the meeting.")

Cultural

The American organizational culture tends to reinforce and reward telling and selling rather than listening. For example, a supervisor who has a difficult problem with an employee may mention it to his boss in the hope of getting some advice about "reaching" (motivating) that person. Instead, the likely response is: "Look, you're the boss, aren't you? Just straighten him out and tell him what's what."

Research shows that men dominate women at professional meetings by interrupting. When men and women talk with one another, almost all interruptions are made by male members. Men also tend to interrupt women more than they do men. Men also achieve dominance by answering questions not addressed to them. When women are interrupted, they tend to write rather than regain the floor (Judy Mann, "It's a Boy's World," *The Washington Post,* April 23, 1986.)

In general, because most organizations are male dominated it is to be expected that values such as being decisive, taking charge, giving orders, looking confident, moving ahead, minimizing debates, and wrapping things up will take precedence over less-masculine values such as listening, supporting, caring, encouraging, and exercising patience.

Semantics

The words we hear may convey different meanings than the speaker intends. In fact, certain emotionally laden words (radical, hippie, capitalist, feminist, politician, atheist, foreigner, racist, jock, vegetarian, Moslem, Catholic, Baptist, welfare, etc.) may cause a total tune out.

Time and Timing

We may neither have the time to listen nor wish to give the time it may require to listen attentively. (How many subordinates would actually say to an impatient boss: "Would you please hear me out?") Also, our daily clocks—some of us are morning people, others afternoon or evening people—may limit our overall effectiveness, including our listening capability.

Education and Training

Lack of familiarity with certain words may limit attention, reduce overall listening activity, and thus reduce comprehension. The lack of formal training in listening skills may produce such undesirable behaviors as interrupting, premature preparation of a response to the speaker ("shooting from the lip"), jumping to conclusions as to what will be said, or faking listening.

Physical State

Listening may be affected by fatigue, drowsiness, hangovers, overeating, headaches and colds, thirst, hunger, or hearing disabilities.

Environmental Factors

This might include such factors as distance from the speaker; aural and visual distractions such as noise, scenery, room color, or movement of people or objects; odors; room temperature and humidity; uncomfortable seating.

Skill Pointers: Listening "Do's" and "Don'ts"

Listening authorities offer these suggestions to improve your listening skills.

Do's:

1. Start with two assumptions: a) as with most people, you probably need to improve your listening skills, and b) listening is a learnable skill.
2. Look for areas of interest in a subject you perceive to be dull and old hat.

3. Become an "active" listener. Use encouraging head nods and inviting phrases such as "uh huh," "I understand," "I see," "tell me more." Lean forward to show interest. Maintain good eye contact. Position yourself closely to the other person. Paraphrase (restate) what is said from time to time to show understanding and interest in both the person and the message.

4. Check for understanding, as necessary, by restating what was said: "You're saying that . . ." "What I hear you saying is . . ." "Let me see if I picked up what you said . . ." "You are proposing . . ." "You feel (or believe) . . ." "Your perception of the problem is . . ."

5. Pay attention to the nonverbal aspects of the message. Because words per se may carry only a small portion of the message (10% to 20%), it is essential to work with a high antenna.

6. Recognize that just as a speaker *presents* a message through his particular set of filters, you, too, are *receiving* through your particular set, which may create distortions for you.

7. Be patient and empathic. Not everyone can deliver a message in an interesting and appealing way.

8. Listen to the full message before coming to a conclusion as to what was said and its full significance. This may take time, but what is the alternative to hearing the other person out?

9. Be aware of your own nonverbal behavior as a listener. Your cues may show interest or indifference, warmth or coldness, closeness or distance, any of which may affect the communicator favorably or unfavorably.

10. Use downtime before the speaker gets his thoughts out to: a) anticipate what may be coming, b) review and summarize, and c) relate a) and b) to the main trend of thought coming your way.

Don'ts:

1. Avoid interruptions. They are not only impolite and annoying, but may distract the speaker and direct him into a train of thought you may not even intend. Male listeners should work at subduing their culturally induced tendencies to interrupt women.

2. Avoid argumentation and one-upmanship. Good listening is anything but a debate, a chance to best the other person. If you are trying to win, it will be hard to listen to another point of view.

3. Avoid selective listening. Listen for *all* the facts, ideas, and opinions being presented, not only those you expect, are comfortable with, and would like to hear more of.

4. Don't get hung up on how something is said—poor delivery, weak voice, different accent, halting style, or extreme gestures. As a good listener you will want to zero in on the message. Period!

5. Don't ignore feelings. Facts can't be assimilated without appraising the emotional context in which they are delivered. Good listeners tune in to feelings as well as facts.

6. Don't fake attention. This kind of activity certainly won't help you to hear and its phoniness is very likely to be perceived by the other person.

7. Don't overreact to the speaker, either negatively or positively. Instead, try to concentrate on what is being said.

8. Don't get derailed by words with emotional significance to you. I recall an official in the national office of a large organization who would go berserk when anyone made reference to a "policy" set by a field office: "Only we at headquarters establish policy; the field sets up *procedures.*" Some pertinent verse:

> *To the extent that we become frantic*
> *Over the antics of semantics,*
> *We will see a lot of red*
> *And hear much less of what is said.*

9. Don't tune out because the material coming your way is novel, controversial, somewhat complex, or generally not what you anticipated. Instead, concentrate harder, or consider posing clarifying questions or asking for a restatement. ("I'm sorry but I lost you on that last point. Could you give me another go at that?") Also, regard the "tougher" or newer information or ideas as a challenge and a mind sharpener instead of a headache.

10. Don't distract the communicator. Avoid discourteous habits as fidgeting, rocking on your heels, watching your computer screen, cleaning or polishing fingernails, etc.

Establishing Rapport

The meaning of your communication is in the response you get. If you notice that you are not getting what you want, change what you are doing.

—Richard Bandler and John Grinder, *Frogs Into Princes,* 1977

All of us have a basic language pattern that reflects our individual speaking style. The more we can match our language with that of another person, the more we can increase our rapport (establish a relationship based on commonalities). The way we can begin to reduce the difference in our speaking styles is via good listening. What do we listen for? We listen for the particular speaking style the speaker uses:

1. **Visual.** This refers to people who speak with references to *seeing*. They typically use words such as:

look	brilliant	hide
picture	bright	focus
show	portray	diagram
horizon	scan	neat
shine	inspect	foggy
hazy	clear	pretty
dull	appear	vague

They use visual words in sentences such as these: "It *looks clear* to me." "Do you get the *picture?*" "Let's get some *light* on the subject." "Well, from my *perspective* . . ." "I *see* it this way . . ."

2. **Auditory.** This refers to people who have a frame of reference which is essentially *sound* based. Typical hearing-related words they may use are:

buzz	hear	purr
bell	squawk	call
ring	utter	whine
noisy	say	tone
sound	shriek	talk
echo	clang	yell
hiss	scream	chime

They use auditory words in sentences such as these: "I *hear* you *loud* and *clear.*" "Boy, does that ever *ring* a *bell* with me." "I can't make *rhyme* or reason out of her statements." "*Sounds* good to me." "That idea has been *rattling* around in my mind since day one."

3. **Kinesthetic.** This refers to people who speak in terms of *feelings,* both internal and external. Typical touch-related and feeling-type words are:

support	play	balance
attack	cut	resist
warm	vibes	smooth
cold	dig	rough
electric	press	sturdy
tickle	grasp	shape
poke	fumble	stress

They use feeling-type words in sentences such as these: "I'm *comfortable* with that approach." "Of course I'll *support* you on that." "That proposal really *feels* right to me." "You hit the *hammer* on the *head.*" "He's a *soft touch.*" "We're up against the *wall* (or in a *bind* or in a *box.*)"

The procedure, then, is to listen for words and phrases that are visual, auditory, or kinesthetic. When you have determined the primary pattern being used, begin to use a similar pattern to match the other person's speaking style. This will let the other person perceive that you are on his wavelength, and rapport should be augmented or accelerated.

Note: These concepts and techniques are drawn from the field of "Neurolinguistic Programming" (NLP), presented by Gustave J. Rath and Karen S. Stoyanoff, "Understanding and Improving Communication Effectiveness," in *The 1982 Annual for Facilitators, Trainers and Consultants,* editors J. William Pfeiffer and Leonard D. Goodskin, University Associates, Inc., San Diego, CA, pp. 166–173.

Check Your Listening Skills

It is a way of calling a man a fool when no attention is given to what he says.

—Sir Roger L'Estrange (1616–1704), English journalist and translator

Check your listening prowess with "My Skill as a Listener—A Self-Test," (page 121). The quiz will not only help you to gauge your listening capability, but will point out various key factors that help or hinder the listening process. It is suggested you take the test now.

Listening—A Summary of Requisite Skills

If we analyze and reflect on the list of blocks and barriers to effective listening presented above, the list of "Do's" and "Don'ts," and the items in the self-test, we can see that our overall listening capability requires three basic listening skills:

Empathic Listening

This entails letting people present their view of the world, express themselves, and ventilate their feelings. To be avoided are listening ploys that attempt to deny or downgrade the feelings of others: "You shouldn't feel that way." "Everybody has problems like that." "That's hardly a reason to be so upset." Instead, a simple "I understand" will allow the other person to talk it out and have his say. Empathic listening is a powerful means of establishing rapport and building good relations.

At times an employee may be obviously agitated but reluctant or possibly unable to speak freely. If so, you may wish to use this simple statement to encourage the person to talk about his concern: "Sometimes it helps to talk about it." Then engage in a patient pause and the conversation should begin.

Analytical Listening

This refers to the ability to distinguish between factual data vs. judgments, opinions, perceptions, and biases. Obviously, our skill as a problem solver and decision maker will be undermined if we can't separate fact from fantasy, enthusiasm from evidence, and lofty language from logic. Recognizing major ideas and separating them from minor ones are also vital. Finally, skill is required to avoid being sidetracked by details, digressions and repetitions. This means listening holistically, that is, for *patterns* of ideas and central themes.

Integrative Listening

This entails utilizing accurately and fully the ideas presented by others in one-on-one and team situations. This is essential to achieve innovation, invention, and creativity in developing policies, programs, plans, products, and services, and resolving operating difficulties and other problems. The process is one of adapting and adopting what others have suggested, and blending these possibilities with your own perceptions and approaches. The result is a new, enriched, and dynamic end product. If you have a mindset that assumes people can and wish to contribute to organizational improvement and success, the necessary integrative skills will be readily on tap.

HOW TO MANAGE ONE-WAY VS. TWO-WAY COMMUNICATION

Providing a message to another individual, group, or organization may proceed as intended—or it may not. So we may get these everyday responses to mixed messages:

"I had assumed that you said to contact . . ."

"Oh, did you mean *today,* boss?"

"But I thought you said it should go to *all* field offices."

"If I had known that you wanted . . ."

"Hey, we sent the same set of instructions to all eight plants, and can you imagine that *four* came up with different interpretations?"

What is going on here? Why can't sincere, conscientious managers get their communication through successfully? The following communication models should help managers better understand why one-way communication is imperfect at best and highly hazardous at worst (but more likely).

Let's call our first model the "naive" model:

Naive Model

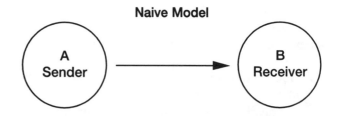

In this model, **A** communicates to **B** and **B** hears and understands accurately not only what **A** said, but also what **A** *meant* to say! **B** is successful as a receiver because he is both a "sponge" and a "mind reader."

But since this model is not very readily found in actual practice, we need a more realistic and helpful model.

Incisive (Realistic) Model

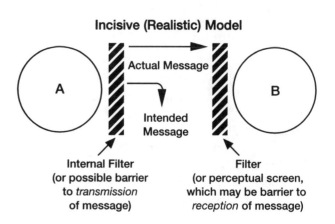

In the previous model, we introduce more realism into the communication process. We point out that **A** is not only communicating to **B** with words, but with:

☐ Semantic preference (choice of words which may be neutral, turn **B** on, or turn **B** off).

☐ Kinesics (or body language such as eye contact, facial expression, distance from **B,** the receiver).

☐ Paralanguage (voice tone, inflection, speed, volume, stops, hesitations).

☐ Attitudinal system (values, expectations, self-concept).

☐ Prior history (past relationship with **B,** especially how open or satisfying it has been).

☐ Congruence (do words support the behavior, both past and present?).

☐ Feelings about **B** (like/dislike, trust/distrust, high/low regard).

☐ Feelings about message (Important? Willing to share them? Responsible for their full reception?).

☐ Personality (warm/cold, low-key/exuberant, friendly/reserved, calm/anxious).

☐ Needs system (for security, affiliation, appreciation, accomplishment, domination).

☐ Role (plus perception of your own role).

☐ Status and authority.

☐ Reputation (credibility, trustworthiness).

☐ Emotional state (anxious, elated, neutral, agitated).

☐ Physical state (fatigue, cold symptoms, etc.).

☐ Background (technical expertise, subject familiarity).

☐ Timing.

☐ Other factors.

One or more of the above elements, which comprise **A's** *internal* filter, may well influence (distort) what **A** actually *transmits* to **B.** And a further complication: **B** may receive **A's** message imperfectly or not at all because of his own filter (perceptual screen), which is comprised of:

☐ Semantic preference (blocks).

☐ Attitudinal system.

☐ Prior history with **A.**

☐ Feelings about **A.**

☐ Feelings about the message (important/unimportant).

☐ Personality.

☐ Needs system.

☐ Role (plus perception of role, e.g., "that's not in my job description").

☐ Status and authority.

☐ Job pressures.

☐ Emotional state.

☐ Physical state.

☐ Background.

☐ Listening ability (attention span).

☐ Empathy (listening with understanding, interest, etc.).

☐ Other factors.

Lest we forget, we should recognize that **A** and **B** are communicating in a particular environment, so we should add that factor to our second (realistic) model:

By environment we mean one or more of these vital, influencing factors:

☐ Availability (sufficiency) of information.

☐ Available time.

☐ Time of day.

☐ Workload.

☐ Problem complexity.

☐ Medium of communication (phone, voice mail, personal contact, written memo).

☐ Location.

☐ Physical factors (light, temperature, color, clutter, etc.).

☐ Interruptions.

☐ Acoustics.

☐ Distractions (noise, weather, movement of people and objects).

☐ Possible audience (observers or added participants).

☐ Organizational factors (culture, policies, etc.).

☐ Other factors.

Note: In the above discussion, we only described the pitfalls which might bedevil **A's** attempts to communicate with **B.** A similar process occurs when **B** endeavors to communicate with **A.**

The bottom line? Communication—sending and receiving (understanding) messages—is *seldom* easy and and can never be taken for granted. It also means that:

1) **A** has to have a good interpersonal relationship with **B** so that they are more likely to be on the same wavelength.
2) There must be a heavy use of *feedback* by **A** to check out what is actually being received by **B,** or two-way communication. **Example:** "I wish to be certain that I communicated clearly. Would you please tell me what your understanding is of what I said?"

Does all this mean that you should never use one-way communication? Not at all. If time is of the essence, such as in an emergency situation, there obviously is no choice. Or if a message is very simple rather than complex and has little serious consequence, e.g., "Turn off the lights when you close the storeroom door," the one-way procedure is OK. Of course, communicating in writing, which is one-way communication, may be unavoidable.

But to ensure that your communication produces true understanding, the savvy manager will rely on two-way communication to the greatest extent possible. This is particularly important if the message is not a simple one and serious consequences will ensue if the message is misunderstood or distorted by the receiver. (See Worksheet 3-1, "Building Skill in the Use of Two-Way Communication," page 122.)

HOW TO MANAGE GENDER DIFFERENCES IN COMMUNICATION

Why can't a woman be more like a man?

—The question posed by Professor Henry Higgins in the musical, *My Fair Lady*

Nobody will ever win the battle of the sexes. There is too much fraternizing with the enemy.

—Dr. Henry Kissinger, former U.S. Secretary of State and National Security Adviser

If you encounter difficulty, occasionally or frequently, in communicating with the opposite sex, be assured that you are hardly alone. Georgetown University linguistics professor Dr. Deborah Tannen, author of the best-seller *You Just Don't Understand: Women and Men in Conversation* (New York: Morrow, 1990) asserts that the difficulty is due to differences in communication style. How different? Vastly. Women communicate to establish rapport, men to report, to give information. So women talk to develop relationships, men to tell what they know.

Tannen found men use language to "achieve and maintain the upper hand if they can, and protect themselves from other's attempts to put them down and push them around." Conversely, women typically use language to "seek and give confirmation and support, and to reach consensus."

So Tannen's thesis is that men predominantly are concerned with achieving and maintaining *status* whereas women are primarily concerned with winning and maintaining *intimacy.* The male fixation on status gets translated into lifelong concerns about independence and rank in the male hierarchy. Men also see life as series of problems that demand clever solutions. Conversely, the feminine focus is on achieving intimacy and a lifelong quest for acceptance, understanding, connection, and consensus.

How does all this come about? Why the acute differences in communicating styles? According to Tannen, boys are socialized to play in groups having a leader and followers: "It is by giving orders and making them stick that high status is negotiated. Another way boys achieve status is to take center stage by telling stories and jokes.

"Girls, on the other hand, play in small groups or in pairs; the center of a girl's social life is a best friend. Within the group, intimacy is key."

An illustration of the consequence of this early development is the way men react to a woman's discussing trouble. The man's immediate reaction: giving a solution. But the woman doesn't want a solution. Says Tannen, "A lot of men go back to saying, well, why does she ask for my advice when she doesn't want it? It's hard for them to grasp the idea that a woman would want to simply talk—that talking is what she's after."

The result: Women find themselves in a super double bind. To quote Tannen: "Our expectations for how a person in authority should behave are at odds with our expectations for how a woman should behave. Everything she does to enhance her assertiveness risks undercutting her femininity, in the eyes of others. And everything she does to fit expectations of how a woman should talk risks undercutting the impression of competence that she makes."

Tannen, in a more recent book dealing with the corporate world—*Talking from 9 to 5: How Women's and Men's Conversational Styles Affect Who Gets Heard, Who Gets Credit, and What Gets Done at Work* (New York: Morrow, 1994)—presents the premise that women's socialization makes the climb up the corporate ladder more difficult. Her research in hundreds of workplace conversations found that women engage in these communication behaviors: They apologize more frequently, downplay their accomplishments and ideas, and soften criticisms with compliments. Men, as you would expect, see these traits and behaviors as professional weaknesses.

According to communication research, women may be "verbally disadvantaged" in a male-dominated organizational culture. Thus, in a research study at Hood College, Maryland ("What's in a Word? A Job, Hood Senior's Study Says," *The Washington Post,* June 6, 1991) personnel officers of 24 companies listened to tapes of a prospective employee, 12 hearing a version using what are considered four characteristically unassertive female speech features (described below) and 12 hearing a tape using the same words but without those features. As might be expected, the employee who spoke without the "female" speech features was rated far more favorably, i.e, described as more likely to succeed and more likely to be respected by co-workers.

This study cited four examples of powerless language (also cited in various other studies):

Tag questions. This refers to questions at the end of a sentence asking the listener for confirmation of what is being presented. **Example:** "John is strong in statistics, isn't he?" "We should send this to all field offices, shouldn't we?" Of course, this is polite speech, but it is less direct and powerful. To male managers it may make the speaker appear to be seeking approval or lacking in authority.

Hedges. These are qualifiers that may make the speaker appear indecisive, tentative, and unassertive. **Examples:** "I hope I'm right about this," "I'd kind of like to go," "I guess you could say."

Hesitations. These can make the speaker appear submissive, ineffective and without authority. **Examples:** "uh," "um," "well."

Intensifiers. These are emphasizing words, usually adverbs. **Examples:** "so," "such," "really," "awfully friendly," "really neat." Again, the speaker may be perceived to lack authority.

Although the Hood study related to a job applicant interview, there may be a similar carryover to actual on-the-job situations.

As reported by management consultants Arlette C. Ballew and Pamela Adams-Regan ("Sexual Differences in the Workplace: The Need for Training," in *The 1993 Annual—Developing Human Resources,* San Diego: Pfeiffer and Co., 1993), a number of significant differences between men and women were perceived by management training groups:

Task orientation. Men have a strong orientation toward the task. Women have a high orientation toward *maintenance of relations* with people and environment that affect the task.

Competition. Men, because of early orientations toward team sports, accept or even prefer competition. Women are less comfortable with even friendly competition.

Kidding/teasing. Men see and use kidding as ways to develop and maintain relationships. Women take kidding more seriously, especially if it reflects on their job competency.

Emotion. Other than showing emotion about sports and other male-oriented topics, men tend to shy away from open displays of emotion. They are likely to be confused when it is shown regarding tasks and teamwork.

People issues. Women tend to be superior in treating personnel issues because of their high listening skills and attention to maintaining interpersonal relationships.

Feelings of isolation. Women may feel isolated from core business concerns because men exclude them from mentoring and bonding activities.

Rewards. Women grow up without being rewarded for use of confrontation to resolve difficulties with others, so women tend to get their rewards for serving as peacemakers. They have a need to learn confrontation skills essential to keep tasks on track.

Sharing skills and strategies. Men can learn to share their more aggressive skills, management strategies, and teamwork capabilities to make a better work environment. Women can learn to share their listening and relationship skills and their detail orientation. Women can learn to express emotion in ways that zero in on task-related issues; men can learn to focus more on implementation, not just the big picture.

Training consultant Judith A. Starkey ("Women in Business: A Cultural Change," *Managing Diversity* newsletter, 1995) found in one of her workshops that a group of women defined "women as a cultural group" as "sensitive, adaptable, determined, having fortitude and emotional strength, doers with a high work ethic, nurturing and caring, open, communicative, confrontive in a positive sense, and having integrity."

Men, conversely, defined "men as a cultural group," as "confident, aggressive, head of the family (including finances), open to change, involved in sports, a hero, we 'fix' things, run the company and the country, are leaders, decision makers, successful, and bond with other males."

In a presentation ("Gendertendo—The Games Men and Women Play") before the 1993 National Conference of the American Society for Training and Development by trainers/consultants Karen Grote, Myrna Marofsky, and Kirk Millhone, these 10 male/female differences affecting communication style were highlighted:

People focus: Men tend to be self-focused, women other focused.

Competition: Men are likely to be competitive, women cooperative.

Authority: Men are apt to be directing, women nurturing.

Emotions: Men generally control them, women express them.

Speaking style: Men make statements, women ask why?

Action orientation. Men prefer to act, women prefer to discuss.

Overall language style: Men speak and hear a language of status and importance; women speak and hear a language of connection and acceptance.

Confrontation: Men enjoy confrontation whereas women tend to avoid it.

Practical approaches to improve communication between men and women, per management consultants/trainers George Simons and Sue Cornwall ("Managing Gender Differences," *Supervisory Management,* August 1989) are:

Recognize that communication mix-ups can (and do) occur. If we are fully sensitive to this possibility, we will be better armed to prevent problems from arising.

Clarify expectations. It can help greatly if both genders spell out their expectations. **Examples:** "She shouldn't bother me with such a trivial question," or "He should acknowledge my contribution to the project." Little is gained by blaming the other person or getting upset if we have failed to communicate our expectations or get a clear-cut agreement on them.

Use questions that encourage communication. The idea is to employ questions that have the power to elicit more of what is really meant. **Examples:** "What does . . . mean to you?" "How do you picture the situation?" "What do you see as the pros and cons of . . .?" Obviously, if you don't probe when necessary, you will remain in the dark. So use questions to get the other party to better express what he is trying to communicate.

Provide fuller pictures. We can't afford to assume that the other party knows that we are only sharing our opinion, our experiences, our view of things. In effect, that we are not presenting the whole or only truth. To do this we should use personalized, low-key statements that are not likely to produce unwanted defensive reactions. **Example:** "Here's how I see the problem." "What led me to assume that is . . ." "I believe that if . . ." "Given what is now known, I think that we should consider. . . ."

Secure clear agreement. Develop an agreement with the other person (1) that both parties will strive for greater clarity, to secure better information from one another so that communication foul-ups don't occur;

and 2) to mend matters should communication break down at some point.

Note: By actually working candidly on a plan for communication strengthening, relationships will be improved and the likelihood of communication disasters occurring will be minimized.

If you discern a clash of "conversational styles" in any of your close relationships, there are some helpful steps you can take, says Dr. Deborah Tannen (in "Talk, Talk, Talk," *The Washington Post,* January 20, 1986):

☐ Step one is to become aware of the other person's style as well as your own. You might tape several conversations. Listen to yourself. How do you affect others when you speak? Do you dominate the conversation or are you usually cut off?

☐ If you feel uncomfortable in a conversation, try altering your style a bit. If someone asks too many questions, ask more yourself. If you get cut out of the conversation, speed up your talking pace. If you sense you're monopolizing the conversation, opt for longer pauses. Note how your changes alter the style of the others.

☐ If small adjustments in style don't help much, try talking about the communication itself. Some examples: "Slow down...give me a chance to say something," or "I feel as if we're in a shouting match," or "What did you expect me to say?"

☐ You might try "reframing" the conversation by defining the context and limitations for everyone. **Example:** A statement of "But that's not what we're discussing here" can help redirect the conversation.

Concludes Tannen, the way to solve conversational style problems is stepping back to observe interaction rather than accepting emotional reactions as givens—inevitable and unavoidable.

As to improving and changing your overall communication behavior, you may wish to consider the suggestions made by communication authorities Blaine Goss and Dan O'Hair, in *Communicating Interpersonal Relationships* (New York: MacMillan, 1988).

Suggestions for Women

1. Use less passive language and adopt stronger, more action-oriented language.
2. If you smile a lot, you may want to employ a more neutral facial expression when the situation calls for it.
3. Speak up more in professional settings. Your ideas and comments are as important as those of your male colleagues.
4. Don't hesitate to touch males when it is situationally appropriate.
5. Assume a more relaxed, open posture in your male interactions.

Suggestions for Men

1. Avoid invading others' personal space.
2. Avoid touching females when they suspect it's situationally inappropriate.
3. Don't interrupt women when they are talking.
4. Be more sensitive to female nonverbal behavior.
5. React to female speakers as you would to male speakers—be positive and supportive.

Summary Points

Progressive organizations and managers are moving toward communication styles that emphasize listening rather than telling and selling, relationship building rather than creating distance or defensiveness, and sharing rather than monopolizing the available air time. Thus, there is a recognition that greater attention should be paid to adopting "feminine" communicating traits such as establishing rapport, giving confirmation and support, encouraging negotiation, striving for consensus, seeking cooperative (win-win) solutions, downplaying your own status and authority, discussing matters patiently as opposed to acting on an obsessive need to "get on with it."

While women may occupy relatively few upper-level management slots, there's increasing evidence that they may be superior leaders ("Working Life: Hardball versus Softball," *Training and Development,* May 1991). Female managers often are found to be more democratic than male managers, better negotiators, and more adept at bringing people together. A key to developing these traits is to be a good listener, a skill at which women tend to be very good.

In respect to women's listening capabilities, the above-cited article reported on a Cornell University research study (per a *Behavioral Sciences Newsletter* report) which queried 144 managers and 827 of their staffers in six hospitality organizations. The survey had this finding: Whereas women comprised only 37% of those polled, they accounted for 58% of those rated as the best listeners. (See Worksheet 3-2, "Improving My Skill in Cross-Gender Communication," page 123.)

Note: Much of today's management literature and management training advocates reliance on "feminine" leadership and communication skills, as described in this section.

HOW TO PREVENT THE DEFENSIVE RESPONSE ("HOW COME YOU WERE LATE AGAIN WITH THAT REPORT?")

George: But boss, I wasn't even at work that day.
Boss: OK, but why are you getting so defensive?

Although we aren't privy to the start of the above conversation, it's a safe bet that George became defensive because of his supervisor's communication approach.

Why do people become defensive and how does it affect communication between people? Defensiveness arises when a person feels that he is subject to an attack, threat, or some possible harm. Not physical injury, of course, but damage to his pride, self-esteem, or personhood. So attacks upon or questions about one's ability, trustworthiness, integrity, fidelity, loyalty—characteristics with extremely high value to oneself as a person—are likely to provoke anxiety and make one see red and look for ways to defend oneself. The "attack" may be mild or even unintended, but the receiver's perception of the message may still produce anxiety and an accompanying defensive reaction.

People differ, of course, in their ability to tolerate attacks upon their self-worth. The person with a "fragile" ego will be more vulnerable to perceived attacks and thus more likely to respond defensively.

When defensiveness arises, the attacked person is very likely to be impaired as a communicator. He may not be able to listen properly and may magnify or distort in other ways what is said. In fact, the whole message may be blocked out if it is too "painful" to hear. The response to the perceived threat may entail a verbal counterattack. The net effect? Communication chaos.

Certainly, if the receiver is not objective, his ability to engage in a rational exchange of ideas and solve problems is reduced significantly.

How can we communicate so that defensiveness is unlikely to arise? Fortunately, behavioral scientists have researched the area of defensive communication. They thus have provided us with skill pointers to keep our interpersonal communication from bogging down in the morass of defensiveness. Psychologist Jack Gibb, in particular, has devoted his career to help people in education and business to develop a closeness, a "withness," and a climate for meaningful listening and learning. Dr. Gibb, in his now-classic article on "Defensive Communication" (*Journal of Communication,* September 1961) has identified six pairs of behaviors that can trigger either defensiveness or feelings of rapport, mutuality, and support. The behavioral categories are:

- ☐ Evaluation vs. Description.
- ☐ Control vs. Problem Orientation.
- ☐ Strategy vs. Spontaneity.
- ☐ Neutrality vs. Empathy.
- ☐ Superiority vs. Equality.
- ☐ Certainty vs. Provisionalism.

The behaviors on the left typically produce a defensive climate. The behaviors on the right encourage a supportive, non-threatening atmosphere. Let's look at these behaviors in more detail and see how they affect communication between and among people.

Evaluation vs. Description

Communication that evaluates or judges us tends to put us, as listeners, on guard. **Examples:** "How come you were late again with that report?" "I thought you could handle that customer better than that." "I don't think you listen at all to what I tell you." Conversely, descriptive communication keeps anxieties from mounting. **Examples:** "I would like to talk to you about the A-64 report, Midge. I think we have a problem there." "Mary, could we review our procedures concerning our handling of out-of-town customers?" Notice the latter statements, which are reasonable requests to handle a problem, are neutral in tone rather than accusatory. They do not imply that the worker has goofed, is stupid, or needs to change her egregious attitudes or behavior.

A very useful form of descriptive communication, particularly helpful to prevent defensive responses and to secure cooperative behavior, is the "I message." The "I message" lets others know where you are, where you're coming from, how you feel. The "I message" has three parts: (1) "When . . .," (2) "I become . . ." and (3) "Because . . ."

The *when* relates to the problem, behavior, or situation you are experiencing or being confronted with. It is descriptive (non-judgmental).

The *I become* communicates your true feeling or reaction to the problem.

The *because* outlines the cost, impact, or consequence of the other person's behavior.

Example (off the job): Your neighbor's dog often visits your yard and leaves reminders of his visit on your lawn. You wish to maintain good relations with your neighbor, but change his indifferent behavior to a more "caring" one. Also, you don't want to go to the expense of installing a fence. Here's how you might communicate with your neighbor on the problem: "May I get your help on a problem we're having? When your dog leaves a deposit on our lawn I become upset because my kids track it into the house, mess up the rug, create a smell, and require us to clean the rug at considerable trouble and expense."

Example (work oriented): Your carpool mate is often late in picking you up in the morning. You speak to him as follows: "When I'm late for work, because of a delayed pickup on your part, I feel angry because I can't start my staff meeting on time and my people are just sitting around wasting their time. Our meeting then has to be cut short because the staff has other commitments at 10 a.m."

Notes:

1. In the "I message" you are engaging in self-disclosure: You are describing how you feel. Communicating a feeling, as opposed to blaming, finger-pointing, or engaging in a put-down, defuses possible hostility on the part of the person receiving the feedback. Most listeners will respect and accept a feeling, whereas they are quite likely to bristle at lectures or accusations.

2. The procedure may be diagrammed this way:

"Doormat" (Non-assertive)	Cooperative ◄— (Assertive) —►	Angry, autocratic (Aggressive)

3. Words to use to express your feelings are: I become/ feel (upset, fearful, frustrated, furious, angry, irritated, anxious, embarrassed, attacked, ridiculed, overwhelmed).

4. "I messages" can be used to communicate with peers and bosses as well as employees. In the latter instance, for example, you may state to your boss: "When you joke about my performance at the staff meeting, I feel ashamed because everyone else picks up on your remarks and they have a big laugh at my expense."

Control vs. Problem Orientation

Messages that state or imply a need for us to change in some way because we are inept, unsophisticated, ignorant, or immature are surefire devices to make us bristle. Why? Because they are perceived as attempts to control us, to do something about our "unworthiness," to "straighten us out." The problem orientation, conversely, sends us an entirely different message. It communicates a flexible, open-end approach to a problem without an attempt to impose a solution upon us from on high. Since the latter approach is mutual and collaborative, rather than unilateral and hence controlling, it encourages receptiveness rather than defensiveness. For the sagacious manager, then, the "let's discuss this problem" approach, as opposed to "here's what you have to do about this," is basic to the avoidance of possible negative reactions by the listener.

Strategy vs. Spontaneity

An important element in our self-worth is that no one will think so little of us that he believes he can use cheap tricks and ploys to manipulate or deceive us. Who relishes the humiliating feeling of being taken in by a con man? So most of us are on guard for tricks or gimmicks intended to take advantage of us. Visualize the subordinate's defensive reaction to his tricky boss' latest communication attempt: "I wonder what he's up to now? Did he really think we'd believe that?" On the other hand, communication behavior perceived as natural, clean, clear, uncomplicated, integrity-based, or spontaneous will attract our ear and not unleash any defensive feelings.

At a management development workshop I conducted, the group was debating the techniques and merits of participative management, with particular emphasis on group decision making. One patently manipulative manager, after listening to the heated discussion, finally entered into the fray. He presented his views as follows: "I don't have any problem with participative management. I just let the staff talk until they come around to my point of view and then we make our group decision." (!!)

Neutrality vs. Empathy

As human beings we possess feelings about our importance and self-worth. We thus find it difficult to communicate with a person who is neutral or disinterested in us as a person. ("She comes across to me as a cold fish.") Conversely, we find it easier to listen to and relate to a person who reacts warmly to us and shows that he appreciates, respects, and cares about us. If we're "in pain," the least we can expect from the other person is a statement to the effect that: "I understand how you feel" as opposed to an indifferent: "You will have to fill out another form."

Also, we resent it when someone tries to take our feelings away from us: "You really shouldn't feel that way" or "Don't you think you're making too big a deal out of this?" And worse still is the king-sized insensitive retort: "I don't care how you feel."

All we want, in many situations, is an indication that the other person is able to walk in our moccasins, that he has tried to see things from our point of view. In short, to give us a caring, empathic message.

Superiority vs. Equality

To the extent that the communicator stresses his superiority, wisdom, appearance, power, or status, he again raises doubts about our self-worth. This type of behavior thus runs the risk of triggering a defensive reaction. We may become so busy mentally appraising the "attacker" and defending ourself against him that we may tune him out immediately and fail to zero in on the message.

The more effective behavior for the communicator who wishes his message to get through is to create an atmosphere of equality and mutual respect. Remember, you and I may, in fact, be superior to the person listening to us. But if we want him to tune in to our wavelength, we had better downplay our superiority. Authority figures (bosses, teachers, parents, the cop on the beat) who have the power to control and punish us have a "built-in" communication problem. The sensitive ones who wish to be effective communicators work assiduously at minimizing their obvious status and power.

In this connection I recall a manager I knew quite well. Tom was 6'5" in height and had a large frame. Fortunately, Tom knew that he presented a formidable figure. In fact, he once told me that when he first started out as a manager he literally frightened people because he was not only large physically, but quite direct in his style of communicating. He thus worked very diligently to cultivate an image of a person who was gentle, empathic, supportive, candid, and really quite approachable.

Certainty vs. Provisionalism

Who has not been turned off by the person who knows it all, who comes on "too strong," who is constantly telling and selling? Why our negative reaction to such a communicator? Because the person who is steam-rollering us is obviously trying to control us, to make us less of what we really are. Conversely, we can lower our defenses and listen more willingly to a person who is low key, who brings tentativeness and inquiry rather than finality and certainty to the communication endeavor. In effect, a joint problem-solving attitude rather than a "here it is" approach will open up the well-springs of communication and keep the defensive hackles down.

Regarding the use of tentativeness in communication, I recall a colleague of mine, Gordon, who could express the most outlandish ideas and raise few hackles, if any, in the process. How? His style of introducing ideas. In his low-key, tentative way, Gordon would start out with: "I have an hypothesis that . . ." (to a fairly sophisticated individual or group) or "I've got the feeling (or hunch) that . . ." (to a more pedestrian individual or group). After all, who could take umbrage at someone half-apologetically advancing a mere *possibility?*

Interestingly enough, the prevailing organizational culture advises managers to "look positive," "show determination and decisiveness," "stand tall and tough." Advisories such as these may serve a leader well if he has to encourage his reluctant troops to take HILL 906. But the facts of interpersonal relations and communication, given the workforce in today's organizations, are that these kinds of macho postures all too often are prescriptions for the creation of defensiveness. For presenting an image of of being tough, staunch, and totally certain only emphasizes the manager's status, authority, and power, attributes which hardly encourage free and easy communication. (See Worksheet 3-3, "Upgrading My Skill to Prevent the Defensive Response," page 124.)

How To Recognize and Use Nonverbal Communication ("But I Didn't Say a Thing")

There was speech in their dumbness, language in their very gesture.

—William Shakespeare in *The Winter's Tale*

When a player thinks they can win, they start to strut around a little. When they don't really believe in themselves, you can see them hang their heads a little on big points. You have to learn to read it.

—Chris Evert Lloyd, former world-class tennis player

A business acquaintance is said to have asked famous financier J.P. Morgan for a million-dollar loan to finance a special project. Morgan's reply: "I won't lend you the million. But I'll walk across the trading floor with my arm around your shoulder, and then anyone will lend you the million." Obviously, Mr. Morgan understood well the importance of nonverbal communication and the adage: "Tell me what company thou keepest, and I'll tell thee what thou art."

Presented below is a situation described in six paragraphs, each of which exemplifies a form of nonverbal communication. How many types can you identify and what might their significance be from a communication standpoint?

1. Employee Bob Henton enters the office of his boss, Frank Korb. He walks in slowly, head bent and shoulders slumped. Bob is here to talk about a serious marital problem that will prevent him from making a highly important field trip. The trip had been planned carefully over the prior three-month period. We notice that Bob speaks rapidly and gesticulates animatedly. Frank is leaning toward Bob, has his eyes fixed on his face and nods his head from time to time. Bob appears to be doing all of the talking without any interruptions from Frank. Bob sits somewhat stiffly in his chair as he talks.

2. In the above meeting the two men are seated at a coffee table well away from Frank's desk. Frank's chair is positioned closely to Bob's. An easel and a flipchart pad stand nearby.

3. The conversation continues for some 45 minutes. As we tune in on the tail end of it, we note that both men are now speaking at the same rate of speed and in the same calm tone. This is in contrast to the rate and tone Bob used in the early part of the interview. Bob seems to be more relaxed and is leaning toward Frank, rather than speaking from his earlier stiff and erect position.

4. An added bit of background about the meeting: Bob knew Frank to be a busy manager so he phoned for permission to see him sometime during the day for some 15–20 minutes. Frank stated that he would be glad to see Bob immediately if he wished. Bob came over at once. As we observe the conversation it is apparent that Frank is letting Bob talk about his problem in detail and makes no attempt to hurry him along. In fact, as the conversation draws to a close, Bob rather than Frank checks his watch and apologizes for having taken so much of Frank's time. Frank responds with hand movements and facial gestures which state, in effect, "I'm glad to help out." A final conversation, very relaxed, ensues at the door as Bob is leaving.

5. In the early part of the conversation, Bob spoke rapidly and loudly and, at times, gave strong emphasis to his words.

6. When the conversation ends, both men rise and engage in a long, vigorous handshake. As they walk to the door, Frank puts his arm around Bob's shoulder and gives it an encouraging squeeze. They shake hands warmly again at the door as Bob leaves. Frank watches Bob walk down the hall and notices that he is walking briskly and his shoulders are erect.

Analysis

Have you identified the forms of nonverbal communication that took place and analyzed their significance? If so, compare your analysis with the author's, which follows.

1. Kinesics

In step #1 above, Bob's slow walk and droopy body posture indicated an uncertainty, even a feeling of shyness and shame. Bob's stiff sitting posture and extreme gestures while he talked indicated that he was in anything but a relaxed state. Frank was endeavoring to be the good counselor—he leaned forward to show his interest in Bob's story, he used head nods intermittently to indicate "I understand," he maintained steady eye contact with Bob to show that he was listening and to maintain rapport, and he let Bob talk freely so that he could ventilate his feelings.

Both parties were clearly exhibiting elements of "kinesics" (from the Greek word *kinema* or motion) or body movement, popularly called "body language." Although not apparent in the Bob-Frank interview, kinesics may take these added forms: facial movements such as glances, smiles, frowns, winks, yawns, sighs; finger taps; doodling; staring up, down, or vacantly into space; various arm and leg movements such as arm and knee folds; self-touching of hair, knees, forehead; chin and cheek rubs, head scratching, fist clenching, beard stroking; posture; stride or pace while walking; blushing; perspiring.

Note: Some body movements are easier to interpret than others. Any possible interpretation has to be made in context, in relation to the total conversation. As a minimum, one should observe that they are taking place, as opposed to ignoring them totally.

2. Proxemics

Note that Frank had a coffee table in his office, which he used for the meeting. He obviously wanted to get away from his desk. He did this to communicate informality, to reduce his status as a boss, and to help put Bob, who was very agitated, at ease. Frank sat very close to Bob communicating a desire to establish rapport, to show caring and closeness. The flipchart and easel, although not used in the interview, connotes Frank's leadership style—a group problem-solving orientation. We noted that Frank sat close to Bob to augment rapport and to show his interest. At meeting's end, they walked toward the door in a close physical position.

Proxemics is essentially *territoriality*. It relates to how we use the space around us as an extension of our personalities. In our culture most of us guard our turf zealously and frown on people "moving in" on us too closely. Visualize the crowded elevator and how uncomfortable everyone is, no one daring to communicate with anyone else.

Some examples of proxemics in the workplace are these: how we structure the office environment, particularly furniture selection (visualize, for example, heavy furniture, providing a cold, formal, impersonal, status-oriented environment, all of which operates against free and easy communication); how people are positioned in the work environment (e.g., few managers prefer to have their secretary located in their own office despite

its outstanding communication advantages; or visualize the manager who holds his staff meeting from behind his desk while his staff members are squeezed in uncomfortably in front of him); how we position ourselves in relation to others as we sit, walk or stand (note how careful we are to avoid any touching).

Despite our cultural influences that stress distance, we should recognize that physical closeness communicates warmth and interest in the other person and aids the communication process. Physical distance, especially where a boss and a subordinate are involved, highlights status differences, and often inhibits communication. Visualize the performance appraisal session with the boss behind his massive desk and the subordinate quite a few feet away, possibly with his back against the wall!

3. Synchrony

As the conversation was winding down, both parties were speaking at the same normal pace and level and had the same body posture (leaning forward), too. Frank had modeled a calm voice level and pace and used forward body leans, to which Bob responded in time. These behaviors encouraged rapport and intimacy. **Note:** These voice and body positions, ultimately exercised in concert, were very different from those we observed in the early part of the conversation.

When a rhythmical relationship evolves between receivers and senders, we call this *synchrony*. As a general rule, communication is helped as both parties begin to use the same kinesics (body movements) and vocalics (voice aspects such as volume, pitch, tone quality, rate). The mirroring of one another's physical movements and voice qualities in a conversation, which tends to achieve empathy and rapport, is a subtle process. One or both of the parties involved may be unaware of the changes taking place.

Note: In the section on establishing rapport via *mirroring* (matching) the other party's language pattern, we are talking about communicating with a person in a normal emotional state. In the example above, Frank had to deal with a person in an agitated state. He thus *modeled* a different style of communicating (one of calmness), rather than copying the other person's agitated style.

4. Chronemics

Frank showed Bob his sincere interest in his problem by asking him to come right over and by letting Bob have his full say, even if it resulted in a long talk (45 minutes). They even chatted leisurely at the door as Bob was leaving.

Chronemics entails the use of time in relation to its impact on the communication process. In other words, our use of time communicates our attitudes and values towards people, situations, and events. **Examples:** When we start and end a meeting indicates how we value our time and that of others; the frequency and nature of staff meetings signals how we value group input; the amount of time we allot to an interpersonal transaction evidences how we value the other person and possibly his concerns; allowing a visitor to cool his heels outside our office vs. permitting a prompt entry communicates how we feel about our visitor, his problem, his time, etc.; the staff member who is frequently late to staff meetings is communicating the value he places on them (or possibly has a need to challenge authority, secure attention, show how busy he is, etc.).

A lack of understanding of how time is regarded in other cultures can create problems for us. It therefore is essential that we be to sensitive to local outlooks and practices. For example, according to Drs. Edward T. Hall and William F. Whyte ("Intercultural Communication: A Guide to Men of Action," *Human Organization,* Spring 1960), researchists on intercultural communication, there typically are differences in appointment time (a 45 minute wait may occur in Latin America); discussion time (the American "hit-and-run" business meeting will not go over in many other cultures); acquaintance time (how long must we know a person before we can do business with him?); visiting time (who sets the time for the visit?); time schedules (we worship them, whereas other cultures are often very relaxed about deadlines, schedules, time tables, and priorities).

5. *Paralanguage*

Bob was communicating with more than words. At the outset, he spoke rapidly and at times raised his voice. He obviously was upset. These behaviors changed to "normal" as the conversation drew to a close. Frank's supportive manner contributed to a return to normal vocalics.

Paralanguage (literally, more than language) entails the use of extra-verbal speech elements. It represents the *how* of what is said—tone and voice quality, pitch (how high or lowness of sound), speech rate and volume, plus assorted grunts, sighs and sounds such as "ah" and "er," choking and crying, etc. Pauses and silence as well as pacing of speech are also significant elements of paralan-

guage. Some examples of paralanguage and their possible meaning are: an even or moderate pitch, rate and tone of voice may indicate boredom; a loud voice at a rapid rate in a high pitch shows anger; joy is expressed by loudness, high pitch, fast rate, upward inflection, and regular rhythm; sadness, contrariwise, uses soft volume, slow rate, low pitch, downward inflection, poor enunciation.

Exercise: Say aloud, "Hello, how are you?" to the following individuals:

1. Your spouse or fiancé who has been away for 10 days to visit his ailing mother.
2. The fancy restaurant's headwaiter, with whom you have conversed with before.
3. The first arrival to a party you are holding on a cold, snowy and icy evening.
4. Your boss, who is an aloof cold fish, whom you run into in a shopping mall.
5. Your neighbor, who is a bubbling comedian, totally extroverted.
6. Your secretary, who has just returned from maternity leave after having had twins.
7. The trash collector.
8. Your dentist.

What kind of tone did you use in each case? If they differed, why the difference?

6. *Haptics*

At conversation's end, Frank and Bob had two handshakes, and Frank put his arm around Bob's shoulder. These gestures indicate warmth, support, and intimacy, and are examples of touching behavior that influences communication and relationship building. But notice that Frank, as the higher status person, put his arm around Bob but not vice versa. Very few bosses receive or encourage such gestures.

Haptics (from the Greek "haptesthai," meaning to touch) is the study of touching behavior. Most of us do little of it (tactile communication) except possibly at weddings and funerals. Athletes, as a privileged class in our society, are permitted to engage in "high fives" and pat one another on their bottoms if someone makes a crucial basket, scores a touchdown or hits a home run. And if a championship is won, group hugs are OK, too.

Obviously, our culture sets firm limits on our touching behavior. Status, age, and gender are certainly restraining factors. Nevertheless, to the extent that we can add haptics (touch) to our total communication repertoire, we will be better communicators and people relaters for it.

In addition to the six major aspects of nonverbal communication, which encompass a lot more than "body language," we should also add a seventh—*surface language*. This is also known as "the psychology of first impressions" or the symbols with which people surround themselves. Included in this concept are such observable elements as dress (size, texture, shape, pattern, color, currentness); grooming (cut, style, and neatness of hair, mustache, or beard; neatness of shoes and clothes; use of perfumes, deodorants and lotions).

Our names communicate for us, too. To make the concept come alive, one keen observer of the non-verbal communication process, facetiously advises: "Never eat at a place called 'Mom's,' don't play poker with a guy named 'Doc,' and don't get involved with anyone who has more problems than you do."

The significance of the above paragraphs is that we can hardly understand and use the communication process fully if we pay little attention to its nonverbal aspects. In fact, communication authorities believe that as much as 90% of our interpersonal communication is nonverbal. Dr. Ken Cooper, author of *Non-Verbal Communication for Business Success* (New York: AMACOM, 1979), breaks down our normal communication skills as:

Body 60%
Voice 30%
Words 10%

Two well-known sayings seem to confirm these figures: "Actions speak louder than words," and "It's not what you do but the way that you do it." So if you only listen to the words people emit, the odds are that you won't receive their messages very accurately.

Skill Pointers

Here are some skill pointers in the nonverbal area to boost your overall communication capabilities:

1. When communicating—and we always are whether we intend to or not—try to keep your nonverbal signals congruent with the verbal message. **Examples:** The manager who is engaged in a conversation and starts to shuffle papers or sign letters is obviously only feigning interest; the manager at a staff meeting who says he wants everyone's ideas, but as soon as he receives one he goes on quickly to another agenda item or may say dubiously, "We'll have to think about that one"; the colleague who tells us that she has all the time in the world to listen to our problem, but shortly thereafter begins to drum her fingers impatiently on her desk and steals furtive glances at her watch, too; or the classic example of the manager who is excitedly raising his voice, but denies his emotional outburst and says loudly: "Excited? Who's excited?"

2. Many people are able to "read" a fair amount of nonverbal communication unconsciously transmitted to them. We, too, are interpreting "the vibes" others are giving us all the time. So be aware that a) you are sending such signals and b) these signals will provoke a positive or negative reaction in return. Keep your antenna up so you will pick them up and then be in a position to evaluate the reactions of others.

3. On the other hand, it is very easy to misinterpret nonverbal behavior. For example, I once worked for a personnel director who never said "Hello" to anyone or acknowledged their presence as he walked down the hall. Many individuals mentioned this to me: "Your boss is awfully stuffy, especially for a personnel man. He doesn't even say 'Hi' when I wave to him." When I assured the "snubbed" person that my boss had very limited eyesight and could rarely recognize someone in our wide hallways, he was very surprised.

4. No single message (gesture, symbol, word) says it all, and that message can signify many things, including opposites. Therefore, when others are communicating look for the *gestalt,* the total pattern or big picture, which is a combination of the verbal and nonverbal messages.

5. Although we can't readily "fake" our nonverbal behavior, such as in our use of body language, we can be sensitive to it and thereby achieve greater congruity and impact. For example, if you are trying to sell a proposal to your boss, you should maintain good eye contact to communicate your confidence in it. Enthusiasm is essential, too. Conversely, looking down and speaking lethargically will communicate doubt. In essence, it's not just the words the listener receives, but the vibes that go with it.

A classic instance of the premeditated use of nonverbal behavior—surface language in this instance—entailed the stratagems employed by a contract negotiator. He always scheduled the negotiation sessions in a hotel where he also rented a sleeping room for himself. To communicate to the other side that that they could not tire him out, he took special measures to always present a neat, crisp appearance. He achieved his fresh look by shaving during the breaks and changing to fresh shirts as necessary!

Check Your Skill

One way to sharpen your appreciation of nonverbal communication, especially kinesics (body movement), is to watch TV with the sound off. Also, listening to audiotapes should help you increase your sensitivity to paralanguage.

You may also wish to tape your own voice to to test its tone, pitch, pace, or other qualities. You may be able to make some changes, but major alterations will probably require the help of a trained speech pathologist. (See also Worksheet 3-4, "Augmenting My Skill in Nonverbal Communication," page 125.)

Check Your Knowledge

The above paragraphs presented seven forms of non-verbal communication:

1. Kinesics.
2. Proxemics.
3. Synchrony.
4. Chronemics.
5. Paralanguage.
6. Haptics.
7. Surface language.

Listed below are 15 statements, each of which describes a form of nonverbal behavior. Identify each behavior by assigning a number to it from the above list.

[   ] a. In the company cafeteria, people are very careful to avoid sitting at an occupied table if one or more empty ones are available.

[   ] b. In a very friendly and supportive office, hugs are commonly given and received.

[   ] c. The boss' secretary invariably exceeds her lunch hour by 10 to 25 minutes.

[   ] d. The pilot gives the ground crew a triumphant signal by forming a circle with the thumb and adjacent finger.

[   ] e. In one office, button-down shirts and Brooks Bros. three-piece suits are the uniform of the day.

[   ] f. Employee Bill Ray is late again and delivers his alibi in a halting manner.

[   ] g. The autocratic boss surprises everyone by asking for suggestions on a policy matter. A long silence ensues.

[   ] h. "I'd never hire a secretary with a name like Bertha."

[   ] i. At the end of an intensive three-day team-building session, it is apparent that the total group is speaking in the same calm, carefully modulated tone of voice.

[   ] j. The young attorney changes his surname from Grabowski to Graves.

[   ] k. An enthusiastic handshake is accompanied by a staunch arm grasp by one of the parties.

[   ] l. The holiday party was loud and everyone was caught up in it.

[   ] m. Staff member Jones is late to the staff meeting and tiptoes in very carefully; his face registers guilt.

[   ] n. As people sit down for the committee meeting, everyone shuffles chairs to avoid offending anyone by sitting too closely.

[   ] o. Manager Toms holds a weekly staff meeting which runs for exactly 20 minutes.

Answers:

a. 2	f. 5	k. 6
b. 6	g. 5	l. 3
c. 4	h. 7	m. 1
d. 1	i. 3	n. 2
e. 7	j. 7	o. 4

HOW TO PROVIDE NEGATIVE FEEDBACK ("YOU REALLY GOOFED THAT ORDER UP")

We do not really see ourselves. All mirrors are in fact quite useless except the living, human mirrors who reflect us: They do not lie.

—Francois Mauriac (1885–1970), French novelist and winner of Nobel Prize for Literature (1952)

Feedback is a means of providing information essential to correct a given behavior. Some everyday examples:

☐ Position data to guide a missile in flight.
☐ Temperature data to the thermostat to control the furnace in our home.

☐ Data from the golf pro concerning our stance and swing at the ball.

☐ Information from the parent to the small child about crossing the street safely.

☐ A red-penciled theme paper from the English teacher to the high school student.

☐ A set of charts from our doctor about our physical state.

☐ A batch of stats from the coach to the athlete.

Compare the above list with the following one:

☐ Mrs. Brown informs her husband about the sorry state of the bathroom sink after he has completed his morning routine.

☐ Mr. Jones informs his spouse that the last three pairs of shoes she has purchased brings the total of unworn shoes to eleven.

☐ George informs Helen, his fiancee of three years, that all her slacks seem noticeably tighter.

☐ Supervisor Jo Ann White tells employee Monte Burr that four of his last reports were late and three of those were below standard.

☐ Manager Entwhistle advises subordinate Carston that he will not receive his much sought-after promotion because other managers perceive him to be "too aggressive."

☐ Personnel Manager Tom Bronson tells Training Specialist Ellen Fixx that her last workshop on interpersonal relations was marked by three trainee complaints.

Question: Which of the two lists of feedback items is more likely to be accepted "as is" by the feedback recipient and which set is more likely to produce defensiveness, rebuttals and/or counter charges? If you recognized the explosive potential of the second list, you are on target. You are aware that feedback is not always welcome and may have negative effects. Hence the need to explore the nature of feedback to see if we can identify and use strategies that 1) will not produce defensiveness, 2) will increase the likelihood of the feedback being listened to and accepted, and 3) will help keep relationships intact.

Although we used a missile and a thermostat as examples of the feedback process, it is obvious that providing feedback to people is much more complicated in nature. Why? Because people have to process the data through their attitudinal and value systems before they can be internalized and accepted. Thus, quite often there is a wide gap in perception about the significance of a particular behavior between the feedback giver and the feedback receiver. For example, a colleague of mine, who is a trainer and conducts management development workshops, was told by his boss that a workshop participant had complained that he was "too low key." My colleague responded to his boss in this fashion: "If only one participant in 26 felt that way, I don't think we have to give that comment much weight. Besides, as a workshop trainer, I regard 'low key' as a compliment. And being low key, I would say, helped to win the other 25 trainees over."

So while "facts" may, indeed, be facts, people's perceptions or filters—attitudes, values, feelings, biases—about the facts cannot be ignored. Hence, the need for a discussion to share perceptions about the facts and to seek agreement as to their meaning, utility, and possible plans for corrective action, if warranted.

It should be apparent, then, that the feedback process has a *dual* aspect and function:

1) To reconcile the gap or variance in perception concerning how the feedback recipient thinks he behaves and how the feedback giver sees the behavior.

2) To provide data and help so that the feedback recipient can consider the nature of his behavior and then decide whether it merits any possible alteration.

In essence, feedback is more than a "here it is" kind of thing. Rather, it has to be really heard, understood, digested, believed, and assessed before any acceptance will take place.

Judgmental vs. Descriptive Feedback

One source of difficulty with feedback giving is that all too often we present it in a *judgmental* (evaluative) fashion rather than in a descriptive (non-evaluative) way. By judgmental we mean assessing, appraising, or being critical of the performer as a person. **Examples:** "You really goofed that order up." "You never think of anyone but yourself." "You're a loudmouth." "You have a bad habit of . . ."

Descriptive feedback, on the other hand, entails the rendering of data that describe the other person's behavior objectively and how we feel about it. By keeping our focus descriptive rather than evaluative, we reduce the risk of defensiveness arising and possible rejection of the feedback.

Consider this example. Henrietta Adams, your subordinate, missed her 7 a.m. plane to attend an important conference of yours on the West Coast. (You had arrived the night before the meeting.) Unfortunately, Henrietta was to bring some of the key handouts for the early sessions. A *judgmental* form of feedback to Henrietta might be: "I'm sure that your late date with John made it impossible for you to get up early enough to catch your plane. If you had flown out with me yesterday as I asked you to, we wouldn't have had this problem." Note the heavy focus on the person, the blaming approach, particularly Henrietta's apparent meeting of her personal needs before business needs, her poor judgment concerning the workability of the early departure time, and her inconsideration of the needs of the conferees.

A *descriptive* statement to Henrietta might take this form: "I'm sorry you arrived late to our meeting. We missed your input at the early sessions. And, of course, I was embarrassed and inconvenienced by the absence of the handout materials." Note the focus on the actual behavior and the expression by her boss of her feelings about the impact of that behavior. Also, the supervisor kept her cool, didn't unload on Henrietta, and even paid her a compliment which was a good relationship builder.

If we were privileged to listen to Henrietta's response to the evaluative feedback, it would be a safe bet that it might well be defensive, alibi-laden and, at best, received sullenly. And her performance during the balance of the conference might be affected adversely.

Judgmental or evaluative feedback entails reactions to and opinions about the person and his behavior. Descriptive feedback is data-based (objective) and also describes how you feel about the behavior. The former approach is not very helpful and is very likely to trigger defensiveness. The latter technique is more likely to produce data that are listened to and acted upon. Note the examples of judgmental feedback in the boxed item on page 98. The purely judgmental statements appear in column one. The descriptive feedback is presented in columns two and three. Column two presents totally objective or factual data; column three presents data regarding the boss' feelings about the specific behavior of the subordinate. A combination of objective and feeling-type data is generally more effective. Why? Because all of us have feelings about someone's behavior. It thus helps the the performer if he she knows clearly how the other person feels about

it. For purposes of balance, the boxed items contain several positive as well as negative feedback statements.

Guidelines for Feedback

There are a number of important guidelines that merit observance if you wish to be effective as a provider of feedback. These principles are given below in the form of a question list. Study the list now to ensure your understanding of key feedback-giving concepts. Review the list carefully again when you are about to give someone feedback.

Providing Feedback to Others—Some Questions to Ask Myself

My Attitude

- ☐ What is my "philosophy" about providing feedback? Do I regard feedback as a process of *sharing* data rather than giving information from "on high"?
- ☐ How important is candor, leveling about performance or behavior?
- ☐ Do I regard feedback as an opportunity to provide help toward job improvement? Or do I shy away from it for fear of "hurt" feelings, confrontation, or mutual embarrassment?
- ☐ Do I recognize that feedback is a motivating force—that it can create and unleash energy as well as correct behavior?

My Motivation

- ☐ Why am I giving feedback? To help? To punish? To psychoanalyze? To ridicule? To put someone down? To feel superior? To show who's boss? To "win"? Whose needs are being met?

The Behavior

- ☐ Is it one over which the feedback recipient has adequate control (modifiable vs. non-modifiable behavior)?
- ☐ Is it reasonable to expect that he can change his behavior (high vs. low likelihood of improvability)?

Specificity of the Feedback

- ☐ Is my feedback specific (as opposed to being tentative, general or vague) so that one can act on it? **Note:** A target is not a target if it can't be hit.

Feedback Language—Some No-Nos and OKs		
Judgmental/Evaluative Feedback (No-Nos)	**Descriptive Feedback (OKs)**	
	Objective (Data-based)	**Subjective (Expression of Feelings)**
You really goofed up on that Watt order.	The Watts order left here last Friday and was 8 days later than it should have been.	I was really angry when I learned that the Watts shipment was 8 days late.
You certainly behaved in an inconsiderate and selfish way at today's meeting.	You interrupted people 6 times at today's meeting.	I felt embarrassed when you cut those people off at the planning meeting.
Sometimes I wonder how you can find anything in your office, let alone work in such a mess.	Your desk, the two work tables, the top of your filing cabinet, and one of your two chairs are covered with loose papers and booklets.	I am disappointed that you have made no attempt to put your papers and pamphlets in the file cabinet and on the book shelves, despite your agreement to do so.
Boy, you really unloaded on Joan this morning.	Joan left your office abruptly and went to the ladies' room in tears when you were talking to her about her appraisal.	Frankly, I was very concerned at the sudden ending of your appraisal session with Joan.
Your recent letters show good PR sense.*	The written response you gave the supplier on price was factually stated. The final note on financing was particularly helpful.	I feel good about the letters you are sending out because they are factual and friendly at the same time.
The patients really relate to you very well.*	When you use patients' first names and chat with them a bit you get great cooperation from them.	I'm pleased to see that you are showing our patients interest and concern.
You're doing everything right that a salesperson should do.*	Records show that since you took over that new territory, sales are up 22% for the 3rd period.	I'm very happy to learn of your contribution to our sales effort for the prior period.

NOTE: These general statements, while good to hear, are not related to any specific behavior and thus are not as effective as statements containing specific references to the given behavior. If the statements in columns two and three were added to those in column one, they would be OK.

☐ Have I provided representative examples of the undesirable behavior?

☐ Do I recognize that current or recent examples are more meaningful than old ones?

☐ Do I avoid comparisons with the "better" behavior of others? **Note:** References to *standards* of behavior or performance will reduce the risk of provoking defensiveness.

Verifiability of the Feedback

☐ Is the feedback valid—experience-based—so that there is no room for debate about the data per se? Or am I passing on my impressions, perceptions, assumptions, or inferences, or even secondhand information or gossip?

Trust

☐ Does our relationship have enough trust so that the data will be listened to?

☐ How will the feedback affect our future relationship? Will it be stronger, weaker or unchanged?

Locale/Setting

☐ Will the feedback be given in private? In public? Which will work best?

☐ Should it be done in the subordinate's workplace to reduce the possible impact of my status? Would a neutral location be more effective (library, cafeteria, empty office)?

Style

☐ When I give feedback is it typically negative? Do I ever give positive feedback? If it is rarely positive, why is this so? **Note:** A discussion of giving positive feedback (praise) is presented in the chapter on "Motivation."

☐ Do I provide feedback in a way that is supportive, caring, friendly, considerate? Or is it hard-hitting, rude, or even crude?

Medium

☐ Do I give feedback in oral or written form? Which method is more likely to involve the other person? Which is likely to be more effective? If I tend to do it on a written basis, is it because I wish to avoid a face-to-face confrontation with the other person? What is the likely reaction of someone who typically receives written feedback? ("He doesn't even have the guts to tell me about it to my face.")

Volume

☐ How much do I give at one time? Do I limit my feedback to significant, key, or critical behaviors or do I try to cover "everything"? If it is the latter, do I run the risk of "overloading the intake valves" and thus having the feedback misunderstood or ignored?

How Given

☐ Is it evaluative (of the person or his personality) or descriptive (of the behavior and my feelings about it)?

☐ Is the tone one of sharing information as opposed to "here's what you must do to straighten yourself out"?

☐ Is the language used encouraging rather than threatening (e.g., not "this is the worst job . . ." but "what can we do to improve . . .")?

Timing

☐ Is the feedback given as soon as possible in relation to the behavioral event to ensure its recollection?

☐ Is the receiver ready, interested, and thus likely to be receptive? Or is he burdened with or preoccupied by other details, events, activities, or personal problems?

☐ Is this the best time (of day or week) to give it? **Note:** Feedback given early in the day and early in the week affords an opportunity for "the pain," if any, to be worked through with the aid of one's normal work activities as opposed to brooding about it at home. It also provides opportunities for the feedback deliverer to have casual contact with the feedback recipient to permit working on the relationship. Conversely, feedback late in the day or week provides little time for the "wounds" to heal and may mean sending the employee home concerned about his job.

☐ What about my own mood or physical state? Am I calm or relaxed enough to be helpful?

☐ Have I allowed enough time to do the task properly or will I be rushed because of other job demands? Which procedure will be more effective?

Possible Impact on the Receiver

☐ How well do I know the receiver? Is he receptive to ideas for improvement?

☐ Is the feedback likely to be understood as I intend it? Will it be regarded as reality-based? Will it produce defensiveness? If so, what can be done to defuse that possible reaction?

☐ Is the feedback likely to serve as an impetus for change?

☐ Have I asked the feedback recipient for a restatement of what was delivered to ensure that the feedback was truly heard? **Note:** If a person perceives himself to be "under attack," the potential for full listening and understanding is likely to be severely reduced.

The Relationship

☐ Will giving feedback improve it (build bridges) or injure it (erect walls)? If there is a possibility of damaging the existing relationship, what might I do to prevent this from happening?

☐ If I wish to improve the relationship, do I try to offer feedback with an attitude of sharing, caring, interest in the other party, warmth, empathy, support?

The Risk

☐ Will I be perceived as a wise guy, a know-it-all, a punisher? Or as a concerned friend, helper, peer, support giver?

Awareness

☐ Do I know how the other person feels about being the recipient of feedback? Do I care?

☐ Do I recognize that people want to preserve or even enhance their self-concept? Does my approach to feedback giving recognize this principle?

Action Planning

☐ Do I present the advantages (gains, benefits) of the change in behavior to enhance the likelihood of the acceptance of the feedback?

☐ If the feedback is understood and accepted, is the other person encouraged to develop a plan of action to overcome the undesirable behavior? **Note:** A plan developed by the feedback recipient, at least in part, is more likely to be implemented than one developed solely by the feedback giver.

☐ Are alternate courses of action explored as opposed to hurriedly latching on to a single remedy?

☐ Have I expressed my willingness to work with the other person to facilitate the implementation of the change?

Two-way Flow

☐ Before giving feedback, do I try to get the other person's view of the problem and his feelings about it?

☐ Do I recognize and admit my own faults and that in some way and to some degree I may have contributed to the problem?

☐ Do I occasionally try to elicit feedback from others on my own behavior? Or is feedback essentially a one-way flow to others?

☐ Do I recognize that my own growth as a manager is dependent upon feedback from others (subordinates, peers, bosses, family members, and possibly clients, customers, suppliers, outside professional acquaintances)?

Skill Pointers

Dr. Bruce A. Baldwin, a counselor, trainer, and psychologist, points out ten pitfalls to avoid when giving negative feedback. Otherwise, you will be sending messages perceived as attacks on self-esteem and thus generate defensive behavior ("Critical Communication: Giving Negative Feedback With Positive Results," *Pace,* Nov./Dec. 1982):

1. Avoid Historical, All-encompassing References

Examples: "You always miss the deadline." "You never treat the customers right." The use of "always" and "never" are surefire ways to evoke negative reactions such as defensiveness, argumentation, and denials as to who did what and when to whom.

Preferred skill behavior: Present data based on "here and now" (as opposed to "there and then") performance and offer help as to the more effective behavior. **Example:** "Your last two reports have been late. Also, data on the current period are absent. To get your reporting up to standard, these procedures are essential . . ."

2. Avoid Giving Public Feedback

Example: Giving negative feedback while subordinates are present. Most people are willing to take their "licks," if deserved. But having their shortcomings shouted to the world from the rooftops only adds humiliation to the obvious miscue or weakness.

Preferred skill behavior: Follow the well-established rule of "criticize in private and praise in public." It makes good sense because it recognizes the importance of preserving people's self-esteem. It will also show that you possess a good deal of humanity.

3. Avoid Undue Emotionality

Example: "There you go again. How many times have I told you . . ." "Of all the thoughtless mistakes I've ever seen . . ." Obviously, your ability to objectively point out someone's inept behavior is weakened when you lose your cool or patience. (This prayer may provide a calming chuckle when you are ready to lower the boom: "God, grant me patience; and I want it right now!") Again, over-reacting will produce alibis, defensiveness or counterattacks instead of listening to and accepting the feedback.

Preferred skill behavior: Talk to the errant one only when you are fully in control of your temper. Then explain and describe the nature of the unwanted behavior, its impact on the operation or even the organization, and what should be done to prevent its recurrence.

4. Avoid Phony Praise

Example: "You're one of our favorite people, Bob; however, we simply must stop . . ." False compliments will be transparent to its recipient. He will readily anticipate a lowering of the boom and begin to react defensively. Insincere messages will only undermine any trust in your relationship.

Preferred skill behavior: Describe the unwanted behavior, provide corrective procedures, and exhibit optimism as to the person's capability to accomplish the necessary changes.

5. Avoid Rejecting the "Offender"

Example: "You just can't get things right, can you?" "I was never sure of you when you were transferred here from shipping and this confirms my feeling . . . " Esteem-lowering put-downs as opposed to a behaviorial focus may relieve one's own frustrations. But they will do little to bolster the will to redirect one's energies toward the desired behavior. And they certainly won't help the relationship essential to provide the support for change.

Preferred skill behavior: Focus on the behavior, not the person. Support the errant one's self-image while offering constructive criticism. ("I would like to offer some help which will make you a better performer . . .")

6. Avoid Communication Overload

Example: "You failed to complete two of the last four projects, your weekly reports have not been coming in for I don't know how long and, to top it all, your lunch periods are getting longer and longer." A broadside of this sort can only make the accused see red. Dr. Baldwin calls this "garbage dumping" and suggests that the bigger sinner may be the supervisor who has permitted all

these derelictions to continue without acting on them when they became evident.

Preferred skill behavior: Focus on a single behavior or issue. Both parties will find this to be a much more manageable procedure. Feedback should define rather than overwhelm.

7. Avoid Amateur Psychoanalysis

Example: "I think you have a hard time accepting me as your boss because you never learned to deal with authority figures when you were younger." "I don't know, maybe you're doing all these things because your mother didn't give you enough attention when you were a kid." It may be a temptation to draw upon one's presumed knowledge of Dr. Freud's work. But it is is patently out of place and unproductive in a feedback session.

Preferred skill behavior: Stick to the facts—the observed, here and now behavior—and offer job-oriented but not therapeutic remedies.

8. Avoid Premature Judgments

Example: "I see no reason at all for going over your budget. We had talked all this through before the project began, and I expected you to follow through on it." The "accused" may be totally derelict in his duty, but it's still only fair to provide a chance for that person to state his side of things. It's always possible that extenuating circumstances may have arisen.

Preferred skill behavior: Patience and listening rather than a preconceived mindset are in order. This approach will not only produce a more rational conclusion, but will keep intact your image as a fair and reasonable supervisor.

9. Avoid Buck Passing

Example: "The people upstairs expect it to be done in this way." Giving negative feedback is neither a simple nor a pleasant task. Nevertheless, blaming someone above you for setting a particular requirement only communicates that you are just a message-transmitter and not a bona fide member of the management group. Managers are paid to handle unpleasant tasks, not to get off the hook by blaming their bosses.

Preferred skill behavior: Assume full responsibility for your operation, including any feedback you have to give to employees.

10. *Avoid Trafficking in Threats*

Example: "I've had it up to here with your excuses. Either you get those people of yours in line or I'll get someone who can." If a statement such as this is a repeated one, it won't be taken very seriously. The probable reaction: "She'll cool down and forget as previously." Unenforced threats—usually those made in a moment of anger—are a good way to reduce your credibility.

Preferred skill behavior: Deal with the problem on its merits. Provide feedback in the most constructive way possible. If the undesirable behavior truly merits discharge, take such action promptly.

Note: Although the above paragraphs have focused on the use of negative feedback (constructive criticism) to change behavior or improve performance, there are other important functions of feedback, too:

1. To provide a reward for proper or above-average performance. This relates to the use of "positive reinforcement" or the sharing of positive data. This is discussed in Chapter 4, "Motivation."
2. To improve one's behavior as a boss and overall team functioning. These uses are discussed in Chapter 9, "Team Leadership."
3. To improve relations with another person. See Chapter 2, "How To Work With Peers/Colleagues."

(See also Worksheet 3-5, "Building Skill in Giving Negative Feedback," page 126.)

HOW TO COMMUNICATE WITH THE ANGRY PERSON ("I UNDERSTAND HOW YOU FEEL")

If you wish to make a man your enemy, tell him simply, "You are wrong." This method works every time.

—Henry C. Link (1889–1952),
U.S. psychologist and author

If you are patient in one moment of anger, you will escape a hundred days of sorrow.

—Chinese proverb

Rare is the manager who has not encountered an angry person—employees, peers, customers, family members. Dealing with people who are angry, upset, or demanding is a given of the managerial world. Whether the cause for the emotional onslaught is valid has no bearing on how such people feel. Their feeling is real to them and thus must be dealt with in some way so the "pain" is alleviated.

Here are some skill pointers to deal with the angry person:

1. Try to regard anger as a normal expression of a deep-seated feeling. It is an emotion that arises from time to time in all of us. And it is healthier that the emotion be expressed than bottled up. If we understand this side of human nature, we won't try to deny the other person's emotion and we will avoid such unhelpful statements as: "You shouldn't be so upset." "Why are you so angry—can't you control yourself?" "There's really no reason to feel that way." In sum, your attitude at the outset should be that it's OK to exhibit anger.

2. Approach the incident as a problem-solving situation. This means that you must treat (deal with) the emotion *before* you can work on the person's problem. Why? Because angry or defensive behavior precludes effective problem solving. If one is upset or busy defending oneself, one can hardly attempt to solve a problem rationally. Certainly the inflamed person will hear little of the information you may wish to provide.

3. Treat the aggrieved person in a fully polite and courteous way. If the incident takes place in your office, ask the person to be seated and sit away from your desk so that your status doesn't hamper the discussion. Try to keep things private and interruption-free. Avoid incoming calls and visits from others. If the outburst has occurred in a work area, ask the angry person to join you in a more private location. An audience may encourage an exaggeration of the flare-up. Finally, smiling and small talk are inappropriate and are to be avoided.

4. Work on your own emotions, too. It's certainly not pleasant to be under attack. But don't fall into the trap of responding in an irate way. Losing your cool will only escalate the emotionality of the situation (Mark Silber, "Dissolving Defensiveness," *Supervisory Management,* June 1985). You will then have a dual problem—how to deal with another person's anger along with your own. It may help your own emotional state if you can engage in "self-talk"—tell yourself that the attacking person is not necessarily angry at you, but at an unfair sit-

uation, a mixup of some sort, an irritating regulation or procedure, possibly at another person, and that you just happen to be the best available target for the emotional discharge. Another way to avoid being pushed into an angry state is to also tell yourself: "I am not going to let another person determine my behavior. My aim is to keep cool and no one can make me act otherwise." Even though you may be correct in feeling that you are being assaulted unfairly, try to remember that your own calmness will, in time, help quiet the other person.

5. Your job at this point, then, is to drain off some of the emotionality, to serve as a sponge to absorb the hostility with which the other person is burdened. You do this by permitting the other person to ventilate his feelings, to talk them out. So open the conversation with a disarming, low-key comment or question: "How can I help you?" "You seem to be concerned about . . ." Your friendly, encouraging opener will produce a flood of response such as: "I'm upset because . . . And in addition . . . Furthermore, I don't think it's fair for . . ."

6. "Stress listening"—coping with angry confrontations—requires that you use your active listening skills to encourage the free flow of information. This means that you show real interest, maintain continuous eye contact, lean toward the other person, and respond with brief, neutral, low-key statements such as: "I understand," "I see," "Uh huh," and the like. Head nods will help, too. An occasional "I understand how you feel" will go a long way to defuse the initial hostile state. People appreciate that their feelings are respected. If the problem is somewhat complex, it may help to take some notes. This communicates your interest and objectivity.

7. When the verbal torrent is over, try to restate what you heard: "Your concern is that . . ." "You believe that . . ." "Your feeling is that . . . ." By restating accurately what you were told, you evidence that a) you have listened (sometimes that is all that is wanted), b) you have accepted the complainant as a person, and c) you have understood the feeling that the agitated person was trying to communicate. Restatement does not mean that you agree with what you were told. Rather, it signifies that you have been able to enter into the other person's world and now are able to see things from his frame of reference.

8. Secure agreement (feedback) that your restatement mirrors what was said. ("Have I stated your concern correctly?")

9. If you passed the above test, you are now ready to ask questions to secure clarification or possibly additional information to round out the complainant's story. Some helpful questions are: "Could you tell me more about . . .?" "I'm afraid I missed your point about . . ." "It would be helpful to me if you could expand upon your thought that . . ." **Note:** Don't pepper the upset person at the outset with questions—you may run the risk of drawing an angry response. Also, you might steer the speaker's communication in a direction other than in the more natural one which should ensue. Finally, if questions are asked, they are posed in a gentle way, for what the aggrieved needs least of all is a police-type interrogation.

10. Anticipate, too, that at times the *stated* complaint may not be the underlying cause for the anger. The real problem may relate to another event, situation, person, etc. Your questions should help to ferret out what is triggering the irate behavior.

11. Avoid rebuttals, arguments, and observations or questions that may create defensiveness or other added emotionality. Put-downs or any other comments that may produce feelings of inferiority, embarrassment, or anxiety are equally taboo. Also, don't state or even intimate that the complainer expressed something poorly ("You were hardly clear about . . ."). Instead, put the monkey on your own back: "I'm sorry, but I didn't really understand your comment about . . ."

12. Try to bring closure to the meeting when the angry one seems to have had his full say and is satisfied that you have gotten the message. A question such as this may help: "OK, I think I understand what your concern is. Now what would you feel is the best (or fair) way to resolve this situation?" **Note:** Sometimes the irate one merely had a need to let off some steam. Thus, action on your part may not be necessary. If so, you may close things out by simply saying: "Thanks for coming in to talk to me about your concern. Don't hesitate to see me again if you think I can help."

13. If the problem is such that you have to secure additional information about it or need to secure clearance or approval from another office, advise the aggrieved of this: "I don't have the authority to accede to your request. But I'll look into it for you and get back to you tomorrow, OK?"

14. Conversely, if you do have the authority or discretion to act on the need of the angry person, by all means do so. If the complaint is a valid one, so advise the complainant. If the change or action required to satisfy the person will be long-term in nature, so advise. In either case, thank your visitor for calling the problem to your attention.

15. If the complaint is invalid or unreasonable and you need to outline your reasons for a negative response, you may wish to state: "I understand your problem (concern, position) and I can understand why you feel as you do." You may then ask for "permission" to state your position (or your organization's point of view): "May I share with you how I (or the organization) see the problem you have presented? As I said, I can understand why you have expressed your concern about . . . But here is the way I (or the organization) have to look at the situation . . ." After your explanation, be sure to ask the other person for feedback concerning what you have stated. In this way you can be certain that he has grasped your point of view. A possible statement for this: "I think it would be helpful to both of us if we are in sync on my (or our) position. Would you please restate what I presented to you?"

16. Throughout the discussion be mindful of your future relations with the distressed person. After this meeting, you may still have to "live" with him. So try to keep things on a positive, friendly, helpful, and fully professional level.

17. If appropriate, you may wish to wrap things up by mutually exploring how vexing incidents of this sort may be prevented in the future.

(See Worksheet 3-6, "Building Skill in Communicating with the Angry Person," page 127.)

HOW TO DELIVER THE BAD NEWS ("I SURE HATE TO 'DROP THE BOMB' ")

In the medical world, doctors often find that they must level with their patients and deliver the "bad news." What may happen, if the blow is severe enough, is that the patient stops listening. The doctor goes on talking, but the patient has engaged in what is known as "shutdown." Psychologists call it "selective denial" and "selective listening (or hearing)." The phenomenon is one of people screening out information that they simply cannot bear to hear.

Managers, too, find that one of their less-attractive chores is that, at times, "bad news" must be given to people—a much sought-after field trip must be cancelled, an opportunity to attend a long-awaited workshop deferred, office space reduced, a "pet" project eliminated, or a promotion denied. While no one likes to be the messenger who bears bad tidings, listening can be encouraged and the blow softened by using appropriate communication skills. Training consultants Richard W. Leatherman and Dennis M. La Mountain offer these practical skill pointers ("How To Break Bad News Without Bad Results," *Training,* July 1985) to help communicate the bad news effectively:

☐ Clarify your own attitude toward denials and setbacks in organizational life. They *do* go with the territory. Feeling guilty about a "takeback" of one sort or another is totally counterproductive.

☐ Anticipate negative reactions when you "drop the bomb." To the extent that you do so, you will be in better control of the situation.

☐ Communicate the denial or loss promptly. Why run the risk of having the affected person learn the bad news from someone else? Your task is to ensure that the bad news is accompanied by the correct reasons for the action taken. You are the best person to provide such information, *distortion free.* Also, any delay may be interpreted as guilt for delivering an unnecessary message or simply cowardice on your part.

☐ Communicate on a face-to-face basis. Hiding behind a memorandum—or an intermediary—may well aggravate the situation.

☐ If it is a matter that affects the total group, communicate it in a group meeting. Otherwise, inform only the one(s) affected.

☐ Directness rather than verbal pussyfooting is to be preferred. An "Oh, by the way, your budget has been cut 15%" will most certainly raise the consternation level.

☐ Don't pass the blame on to someone else. As a manager, you are expected to make decisions, including unpopular ones, and take the consequences.

☐ Encourage the affected person to express his feelings about the blow. Better that the possible emotionality is vented with (or even toward) you, than with someone else. An "I understand how you feel" in response to the emotionality always helps.

☐ Avoid defensive reactions. The denial or cutback simply had to take place. It was a business matter, not a personal action against anyone.

☐ After the ventilation of feelings, you may wish to provide some positive reinforcement to the employee. ("I know you would have done a terrific job on that field visit had it taken place . . .").

It may help, too, to touch base with the employee later in the day. This would be a casual contact, not an opportunity to rehash the unhappy event. Such an action signals that you wish to maintain a good relationship as existed previously and that "life must go on." (See Worksheet 3-7, "Building Skill in 'Delivering the Bad News'," page 128.)

HOW TO ENGAGE IN CREATIVE CONTACT ("LET'S MEET IN YOUR OFFICE")

There are many techniques managers can use to give and receive communication from subordinates. The more effective procedures are informal rather than formal ones. They entail showing a genuine interest in the employees. I call the use of these devices "creative contact." Some examples: empathic listening; acting promptly on suggestions; "going to bat" for employees when they are in trouble; joining subordinates for coffee or lunch; maintaining a true open door; and so on.

One of the most effective of these techniques is MBWA—Management By Walking Around. This approach to create contact is hardly new. Insightful managers have long practiced this technique. Japanese managers, who spend a lot of time on the shop floor, are artists in employing MBWA. Top-level military commanders also deem it important to spend time in the field with the troops. What is new about MBWA is the prominence it has achieved recently because of the emphasis given it by Tom Peters and Robert Waterman in their best-selling book, *In Search of Excellence* (New York: Harper and Row, 1983).

Basically, the Peters-Waterman thesis is that the effective manager maintains a high degree of contact with his people. This is done by getting away from your desk and talking with people at *their* work site. I still have a mental picture of one of my better bosses who, despite his full schedule, frequently would pop into my office, sit on a chair in a reverse position so that he could lean forward and drape his arms over the chair's back, and then begin to chat informally about a current project or problem. Sometimes he would turn my wastebasket upside down (if empty) and use it for a chair. These visits varied in length, but were long enough so that the contact was meaningful.

What are some of the psycho-dynamics of MBWA? They include the following:

☐ **Reducing the "psychological size" of the manager**—not his authority or power, but de-emphasizing the words on the manager's badge which boldly states: "I am your boss." Remember, the manager's status is one of the greatest deterrents to free, easy, and authentic communication between bosses and their subordinates. After all, who wants to argue with a ten-foot-tall giant or give him the "bad news?" But by spending time with subordinates on their turf, the manager can encourage much-needed leveling—being open, candid, honest—despite his being the authority figure. Behavioral scientists call this process one of "status reduction" or "reducing psychological distance."

☐ **Keeping in touch with your people.** How else can a manager show interest in his subordinates, to learn of their needs, to offer help and advice, to gather valid information for better problem solving and decision making? If you wish good relations and vital information, you have to work to accomplish such results. And intimacy, sharing and caring, rather than aloofness and distance, are the keys to such ends.

☐ **Building teamness.** Think of the athletic mode of managing. Can a basketball or baseball coach develop a team by working primarily in his office?

☐ **Building trust.** Because authentic (free, open) communication is essential to the willingness of employees to impart information, trust must be developed to ensure that genuineness. MBWA is a basic trust-building device. People will share information with someone they know, respect, and trust. Conversely, they will be reluctant to communicate with a mystery man or woman.

Some skill factors in the use of MBWA are these:

☐ **Use "naive listening,"** that is, ask a question and remain silent (a tough task for many of us) until a full response has been given.

☐ **Keep the time assigned to MBWA at a high level.** Peters and Waterman believe that managers who operate from their office more than 25% of their time are ineffective.

☐ **Practice makes for comfort.** The first few times MBWA is tried may prove to be awkward and uncomfortable for both parties. Employees may be quite skeptical of this new and sudden attempt at closeness. ("What is he up to now?") Some workers may even expect the usual "reading out" when such a visit occurs. ("When the boss hits our turf you know he's got a bug in his craw.") But despite possible mixed reactions at the outset, the best course of action is to stay with it until employees see it as being "for real." As you become more comfortable with this way of managing and mutual trust develops, people will accept you and your visits and may even look forward to them. And best of all, both parties will profit enormously from them.

How to Reduce Status to Encourage Communication

Mention has been made of the role of status as an inhibitor of communication. Obviously, bosses have status, power, and prestige and can't readily divest themselves of their authority and its symbols. However, they can reduce the impact of their status in various ways. I asked a group of managers in a leadership workshop to brainstorm ways of reducing their status. They came up with more than 30 of them (listed below). Obviously, not all these ideas will be applicable to every managerial situation. The ones that might work will depend on your own leadership style, personality, and mission, and the character of your group. The point is, however, that effective communicators do work at status reduction. You may wish to do the same, using the following ideas or your own.

Ways of Reducing Managerial Status

Don't sit behind your desk when meeting with a subordinate.

Make certain your body language doesn't say "PARENT."

Don't sit at the head of table during staff meetings.

Hold staff meetings away from your office.

Get out of your office into theirs ("Let's meet in your office.").

Let another staff member lead a group discussion on occasion.

Rotate chairmanship at staff meetings.

Share concerns freely (as opposed to keeping them bottled up).

Increase frequency of contacts with staff.

Be honest about your superior's instructions or policies (express feelings freely even if they may entail disagreement with your own boss).

Ask for individual's opinion in his workplace.

Encourage free discussion (greater frequency).

Listen, understand, assist.

Try to learn more about and understand employees' jobs and their *real* problems.

Exercise fairness—no double standards.

Rely on delegation of authority to the maximum.

Create a friendly atmosphere.

Share information freely.

Engage in self-examination re status problems. (We all have them!)

Show a genuine interest in personal needs of workers.

Respect the judgment of subordinates.

Make time available for the staff to see you as needed.

Go to bat for subordinates.

Use group and team action to a large degree.

Increase the frequency of social occasions (birthdays, holidays, any special successes by the group or individuals).

Ask for individual's opinion in *your* office.

Reduce status symbols.

Reject managerial perks (e.g., executive parking or dining room).

Work the same hours as employees.

Take people along on trips and meetings.

Remove your coat, loosen your tie when appropriate.

Use blackboard or flipchart at meetings.

Have coffee or lunch with staff on occasion.

Hold a brown-bag lunch with staff from time to time.

Practice participative management.

(See Worksheet 3-8, "Building Skill in Engaging in Creative Contact," page 129.)

HOW TO ASK QUESTIONS ("YOU DON'T REALLY NEED A BOSS, DO YOU?")

In any communication with subordinates, and others, too, there will be a need to elicit information and encourage thought. But how the query is posed will determine:

☐ The feelings generated by it, and thus
☐ The possible nature of the response,

☐ The direction which the conversation may take, and

☐ The impact upon the relationship with the other person (that is, whether it is strengthened, weakened, or unchanged).

Questions may be presented in a variety of ways. Their formats and respective merits are discussed below.

Closed-ended Questions

Closed-ended questions typically produce a "yes" or "no" answer. They generally begin with the words such as "do," "are," "did," or "is." **Examples:** "Do you understand?" "Are you ready for another flood of inquiries?" "Did you consider calling the regional office?" "Is this the last batch of yellow folders?" This type of question has the value of producing a terse response, either positive or negative. However, it is hardly as inviting as the open-ended question and is not likely to generate an in-depth response.

Open-ended Questions

Open-ended questions encourage people to think, to respond, to "open up." The journalist's six questions are particularly useful for this purpose: Who? What? Where? Why? and How? (Sherod Miller, et. al., *Straight Talk*, New York: Signet, 1982.) **Examples:** "How do you think we should go about it?" "What do you see as a reasonable goal for the third quarter?" "What might be done to improve our safety meetings?" "How would you apply the limitation to our field offices?" "What do you think?"

Questions of this sort—hypothetical and vision-driven questions—encourage involvement, unfettered thinking, and a freer expression of attitudes and values. They are particularly useful when someone should be encouraged to have his full say, e.g., when someone is frustrated or angry and wishes to offer a suggestion or recommendation. To deal with an upset person, a useful question at an appropriate point in the discussion is, "What might I (or we) do to give you the satisfaction you seek?"

Information-seeking Questions

Information-seeking questions are essential in most discussions. Proper timing in their use is vital. For example, one must have a definition of a problem before one seeks factual data about it. Similarly, a problem must be explored in depth before one can ask for possible solutions to it.

Follow-up Questions

Follow-up questions are logical devices to secure added or clarifying data. They are used to keep the dialog moving forward. **Examples:** "Can you tell me more about why you feel that way?" "How would you define (or prescribe, predict, assess, etc.) it?" "Could you please give me an example or illustration so I can understand what you mean by...?" These questions work best when they are neutral, judgment-free, and non-threatening.

Feedback-type Questions

Feedback-type questions are designed to explore the other person's understanding of an issue, concept, or instruction without creating any possible defensiveness. **Examples:** "I'm not sure that I expressed myself on this as well as I should have. Could you restate (or feedback to me) what I said?" "OK, could you tell me what your understanding is about what has to be done?" "I want to be sure that we are both on the same wavelength (or in the same ballpark). Could you tell me how you intend to go about it?"

Follow-up questions may also be necessary to ensure the listener's full understanding. **Note:** In contrast to the above examples, a "Did I state this clearly?" is a close-ended question. It thus may only draw a polite "yes" response and not provide the certainty you need concerning the other person's true understanding.

Partial Verbalization

Questions may also be asked to overcome partial verbalizations. Quite often we may ask a question, receive a response, and content ourselves with the answer when it has not responded meaningfully to our query. We can overcome this shortcoming in response by:

1) Having a prepared set of questions to help the employee (or other respondent) verbalize at a much more profound (and often specific) level.

2) Repeating a question to secure a fuller and/or deeper response.

For example, assume you are engaged in a dialog with an employee concerning the setting and reaching of career goals. The key concern, of course, is the *outcome,* i.e., what will be achieved when the goal is actually reached. Questions such as the following may be used:

1) What do you want? (Answer: "A new job.")

2) What will that do for you? (Answer: "I'll get some new learning experiences.")

2) What will that do for you? (Answer: "It will give me more personal growth.")

2) What will that do for you? (Answer: "It will give me a warm feeling inside.")

2) What will that do for you? (Answer: "It will strengthen my feelings about myself, my self image.")

2) What will that do for you? (Answer: "It will give me the confidence I need to....")

3) What criteria will you use to tell yourself that you have reached your goal? (Possible answers: "Be exposed to a different group of people." "Perform higher-level tasks." "Be able to help others in deeper ways.")

4) What resources do you already have and what added help will you need to reach your goal?

5) What are the things that are holding you back?

6) What is the first step you can take to reach your goal?

Note: Questions such as the above have the power to force critical thinking (introspection) about what the employee is really trying to do and how to go about it. They help the individual get away from the generalizations, cliches, and other assorted forms of fuzzy thinking. They help to zero in on expectations or *outcomes*.

Another way to force a meaningful "internal dialog" is to ask questions which focus on values, standards, and/or criteria.

Examples:

☐ What would you say is the value of . . .?

☐ What benefits will . . . provide you?

☐ How important is . . . to you (or to your career, your work, your satisfaction)?

☐ Does it (or will it) get you what you really want?

☐ If you could attain (or reach) . . . what would that do for you?

☐ Imagine that you reached your goal. What would things be like for you?

☐ Is it worth what it would take to reach that goal?

Ambiguous Questions

Ambiguous questions, that is, those with fuzzy or multiple meanings, should be avoided. **Example:** A company president calls his personnel director and asks:

"What is our policy on employing summer help?" The personnel chief explains the policy fully to his boss who thanks him for the information. After he hangs up the phone, the personnel head begins to wonder about the call. Is there something wrong with their policy or procedures? Certainly the big boss had never posed that question before. He thereupon called a meeting with his key staff to discuss the president's call and the adequacy of the current policy, procedures, and practices. The group decided to 1) check policies and practices of companies in the area, 2) review the personnel management literature, and 3) present the president a comprehensive report on the subject, including recommendations for such changes in policy and procedure as seemed appropriate. Several days after the report is submitted, the president calls the personnel director and asks why the elaborate report on summer employment policy was prepared. The personnel chief replies that the president's question triggered the study, whereupon his boss says: "Fred, all I wanted to know is how we hire summer help. A neighbor of mine is interested in having his kid, a bright math major, work for us this summer."

Evaluative, "Leading" Questions

Evaluative or "leading" questions contain a built-in bias, preference, or evaluation. They are intended to slant the listener's response in a desired direction. **Examples:** "Don't you think that we can do this with a lot less staffing?" "Would you not agree that a three-week time frame is more than adequate for this project?" Questions stated in an evaluative way are likely to pose a threat to the listener and thus create defensiveness. Why? Because they give the subordinate *two* problems simultaneously—the problem related to the question *plus* how to cope with the boss' strong feelings on the issue involved. It thus is desirable to phrase such questions in an open-ended way. This suggestion assumes that one is sincerely interested in gathering information as opposed to generating a preferred response.

Manipulative, "Loaded" Questions

Manipulative or "loaded" questions are posed as questions, but are really statements reflecting a decision or a feeling. **Examples:** "Since you know company policy, why would you . . .?" means "You should have known better than that." "Have you talked to Pat about it yet?" is translatable to "Speak to her, and *now!*"

"Your budget is under control?" probably signifies "I'm concerned about overspending on your part." "Would you care to stay late tonight and get those letters out?" really means "I want you to get the work done *before* you leave." The skill pointer in this area is to recognize when you have a feeling or preference and present it directly *as a statement*. This approach will create a warmer and more intimate climate for full, free discussion. Conversely, statements disguised as questions may produce a resentful reaction such as: "If she feels that way, why doesn't she come right out with it and say it?"

Note: While both evaluative and manipulative questions are forms of game playing (non-authentic communication) and are likely ways to trigger defensiveness, they differ in that the former seeks a particular response, whereas the latter presents a feeling or even an order or instruction.

"Holier Than Thou" Questions

"Holier than thou" questions are designed to show the other person our superiority, rather than to elicit information. As put-downs, they are quite likely to "GAS" the other person; that is, produce guilt, anxiety or shame. **Examples:** "You don't really need a boss, do you?" "Don't you know better than that?" "Would you mind telling me why you did that?" "Is that the way you were trained to do the job?" "What makes you think you can . . ." "Is this the best you can do?" Better ways of posing questions such as these are: "It would help me if I understood a little more about how you arrived at your decision. Could you tell me about that?" "May I offer a suggestion on that task?" "I think it would be helpful to review the procedure. May we do so?"

Story: To illustrate the importance of posing a question properly, this brief story merits citation. It seems that a tourist was happily exploring the picturesque backcountry roads in Vermont. Late in the afternoon, however, he realized with some concern that his meanderings had caused him to drift from his intended destination. He had reached a crossroads which, unfortunately, no longer had any signposts. He thought he was in luck, however, when he spotted a farmer leaning on his fence. Said the tourist to the farmer: "Does it make any difference which road I take to Rutland?" Replied the farmer: "Not to me it doesn't."

Skill Pointers

Skill Pointers in asking questions are these:

1. Keep the question short to avoid possible confusion.
2. Keep the question pointed. Limit it to a single thought.
3. Try to use the language of the receiver. Small words help, too. In communicating, "small is beautiful."
4. Be honest. Don't cover up your feeling or desire with an oblique question. Use a direct question instead.
5. If there is any doubt about understanding on the part of the other party, rephrase the question.
6. Use a friendly, non-threatening tone.
7. Be patient. Provide enough time for the other to reply.
8. Don't "GAS" anyone, i.e., don't phrase your questions so that they are likely to produce guilt, anxiety or shame.
9. Don't react negatively if you receive a question in return. A counter-question shows that the listener is trying to think through the question received.
10. It helps, at times, if you indicate to the listener why you are asking the question.

(See Worksheet 3-9, "Improving My Skill in Presenting Questions," page 130.)

HOW TO INCREASE UPWARD COMMUNICATION ("THEY THINK; WE WORK")

"Hey, man, what makes you think that they want *our* ideas? Peons don't have any ideas."

"I tried it once. Told the boss why his new procedure wouldn't work. Would you believe he wouldn't speak to me for three weeks?"

"OK, so I'm a 'yes, man.' You start bombarding the boss with red-hot ideas and you'll be labelled a 'smart ass.' And what will that get you?"

Do the above statements have any ring of verity to them? If so, they indicate that managers all too often behave in ways that communicate a disinterest in ideas and suggestions from those they supervise. Someone observing the managerial scene from Mars might perceive such a situation to be highly anomalous. After all, doesn't management want to solve problems and make decisions that are the most effective? And doesn't wise decision making depend upon the maximum rather than the minimum amount of information brought to bear on a problem? Since the answers to the above questions are "yes," irrational, self-defeating behavior should hardly occur.

Yet the facts of life in today's organizations are that soliciting and listening to ideas from subordinates are hardly the norm. Hence, top management grafts onto the normal, informal communication system such formal communication mechanisms as suggestion systems, attitude surveys, and quality circle programs. It may also issue periodic proclamations concerning its "open-door" policies.

Note: Suggestion systems and attitude surveys are useful communication tools for organizations that are basically non-participative and low-trust in character. Observe that these systems depend on *anonymity* for their success. Suggestion systems assume that managers can't be trusted to accept or review objectively employee suggestions. Hence the requirement to send the suggestion anonymously to a separate committee for an objective, unprejudiced appraisal. Attitude surveys assume that 1) managers are not likely to ask employees how they feel about practices in their organization; 2) if managers did ask for such data, employees would be reluctant to respond candidly for fear of punishment; and 3) if the manager concerned tallied the data he might manipulate it in some way, hence its removal to the personnel office or an outside consulting firm.

Quality circles (employee problem-solving units) are worthwhile tools if fully supported by the managers concerned. However, if managers ran their units on a participative, team basis, they would not be essential. Instead, soliciting ideas from employees would be part of the normal business routine.

As for the "open-door" policy, a *true* open door is so perceived and requires no formal statement concerning such an opportunity.

Few managers would admit, of course, to not wishing input from below, let alone that their behavior discourages it. In any case, employee reluctance to communicate upward fully is a common phenomenon. It occurs because of factors such as these:

Perceived Role Definition

The whole system is regarded as being comprised of the idea creators (management) and the idea implementors (the employees). As an employee on one occasion put it to me: "They think; we work. They plan; we execute. They're the smarties; we're the dummies."

Power and Status

People in authority are perceived as having great power to punish those below for any undesirable behavior. So why risk giving information or ideas to someone who may regard you as a "wiseguy" or a "troublemaker" and thereafter hold it against you? Status is emphasized in organizations in many ways, of course: the private office, a secretary, fancy furniture and furnishings, parking and dining room privileges, travel, extended lunch periods, control over funds, etc. And the greater the status, the greater the separation from the rank and file, and the greater the reluctance to attempt upward communication.

The Reward and Punishment System

People may learn over time that in their very real employee world "meddlers" (idea bringers and challengers) get punished; e.g., at a staff meeting the boss may "jump" on the employee who tries to "second guess" him once too often. The bearer of bad news (errors, mistakes, oversights) may also receive a cold or angry reception. And the promotions tend to go to those who smile at the boss and "go along" rather than "push" for change or improvement. As one employee said to me: "Frankness is like smoking; it's hazardous to your health."

Looking at the reward system in broader terms, it is safe to say that very few managers have been denied a merit pay increase or downgraded in their annual performance review for failure to listen to subordinates' ideas or to aggressively seek information from them. The message to the manager, then, is that listening to employees is very much an optional extra rather than an important job requirement.

Historical Events

Employees may remember the time they got "shot down in flames" for proposing a new idea or leveling with the boss about a current shortcoming in procedure or practice. ("I once tried to tell the boss that....") Experiences entailing rejection of ideas tend to be communicated to others who learn rightly or wrongly that "only fools rush in" with bad news or challenges to the status quo. Also, employees may have offered suggestions for improvement, but no feedback (response) was forthcoming concerning the worth of the idea. The obvious message to the idea sender is that your help is not really wanted in the idea department.

Full Schedule

The boss' active life—a full schedule entailing early arrivals and late departures, numerous visitors and phone calls, field trips, extended meetings, the take-home brief case—may discourage people from trying to enter what is perceived as the "throne room." As one employee put it, "Yeah, it's the 'throne room' alright; if you try to take up his time with your stuff you'll get *thrown* out."

The "Empty Job" Syndrome

In the absence of praise or recognition for job accomplishment, employees may feel that their jobs are not very important to the organization. Under such circumstances, why bother to communicate information to the boss about the work?

Management professor Dr. Phyllis Thomas ("Plugging the Upward Communication Channel—How Managers Stop Upward Communication," *Supervisory Management,* April 1985) finds that managers unwittingly stop the flow of upward communication by behaviors such as these:

Revealing Sources

Employees who discuss a controversial topic with their bosses expect their input to be confidential. Yet disclosure may take place when the boss discusses the problem with another supervisor, revealing information that few employees, if any, were supposed to know. By providing the details, the boss identifies the source.

Public Confrontation

If a manager "dresses down" an employee in public for having expressed disagreement to someone else about a plan, policy, or procedure, the employee is not likely to open up again to either the boss or co-workers. Other workers who observe the "chewing out" will be frozen out, too, for fear that they may suffer a similar embarrassment.

Discrimination

If penalties are provided to those who disagree or voice criticism, e.g., "being shipped to Siberia" (an undesirable lateral transfer), the information channels will become clogged. What is needed, obviously, are clear-cut, fully publicized standards as to how people are given task assignments, promoted, or retained. The criteria should be followed religiously lest people feel that discriminatory actions may be taken against those who speak up.

False Promises

Appearing to agree to a suggestion and then doing nothing about it as a certain way to erode confidence in a manager. And if such a behavior is chronic, employees will no longer trust the boss with their suggestions, ideas, or complaints.

Clouded Judgments

Managers should take special care when trying to mediate a conflict when one of the parties involved is a personal friend. If the employee is told that "there's really no problem here" because the other party "could not have acted in the fashion you have described," it is only natural that a bias toward the other party is suspected. The better procedure is to call in both parties, listen to both sides of the conflict, and then try to resolve the difficulty on an objective basis. By having both parties present, exaggeration and buck passing can be avoided. After all, where does the employee go with his problem if the boss denies the possibility that a problem may exist?

Opening Meetings

Starting a meeting requested by employees by saying something like: "All of us are much too busy to spend a lot of time on this, but we'll do the best we can" will most certainly stem the possibility of free flow of ideas. The ensuing silence may surprise the insensitive manager, particularly if the manager asked for the meeting! As a colleague of mine put it: "Calling a meeting is like engaging in love making. Don't start it if you're rushed!"

Management consultant Melville Hensey ("Consulting Patterns of Successful Managers," *Supervisory Management,* May 1986) believes that managers are reluctant to consult with staff due to:

- **Fear of being perceived as being weak.** A "strong" manager doesn't need help from anyone!

- **Fear of being shown to be in error.** If one has a strong need to be right, "my way or no way" is certainly the route to follow.
- **A compulsion toward immediate action.** If you are impatient and the need to act now is stronger than the need to act with care and wisdom, obviously you can't wait for the staff to contribute.

The behaviors described by Thomas and Hensey are certain, over time, to dampen employee enthusiasm to contribute and produce a self-fulfilling prophecy: a) because ideas are not forthcoming, employees are perceived to be limited in their capabilities or disinterested in organizational betterment; b) hence the need to "go it alone"; and c) by going it alone, employees see little need to contribute. Thus, the non-participative cycle continues relentlessly.

Finally, we should note that managers cannot be any more effective as encouragers of upward communication than the organization itself is. That is to say, managers typically labor in organizations that provide far too little in the way of good communication practice (models) for them to emulate. For example, *The Wall Street Journal's* "Ear to the Ground," bar chart (July 21, 1986, p. 19), using as sources the Wyatt Co. and Opinion Research Corporation, cited these 1986 figures concerning how corporations use their communication programs:

☐ Just to keep in touch with the work force: 47% (but this was an improvement over the 1981 figure which was a high 69%).

☐ As input to aid in major policy development: only 19% (but this was a modest improvement over the 1981 figure of only 6%).

☐ As input to aid in implementation of major policies: only 27% (but up from the low 1981 figure of 13%).

Note: The first figure—47%—is considered an improvement over the 69% because it means that somewhat more organizations were involving employees in policy development and implementation; hence a rise in the latter two figures (19% and 27%, respectively) and a corresponding decline in the first figure (to 47%).

Skill Pointers

For the manager who sincerely wishes to encourage upward communication, these procedures should provide helpful:

1. Communicate loud, clear, and often that everyone in the organization is a resource, has ideas, and has valuable information, all of which are essential to solve problems.
2. Act on the above pronouncement so that your actual behavior supports your statement about the desired participation.
3. Work actively at creating an atmosphere that communicates that "we're all in this together" rather than "it's me versus them."
4. Try to use the "what do you think" approach regularly as opposed to "here's what I want you to do."
5. Listen fully when ideas come your way. Show respect to the idea presenter.
6. Reward good ideas via positive strokes (praise).
7. Act on ideas and suggestions promptly to show that you place high value on them.
8. Implement team management procedures. Hold group meetings frequently as the normal way of conducting business. Quality circles may help, too, if you support them fully.
9. Work actively on status reduction, detailed earlier in this chapter.
10. Make yourself readily available to subordinates. The "open door" is such an overworked term that it is almost meaningless. Nevertheless, your behavior can create a true open door without talking about it.
11. Avoid the trap of shooting the messenger. Painful data must be expected and faced up to.
12. Install and use a flipchart in your office to capture ideas from people. The chart itself communicates that gathering ideas is what management is all about.
13. Get out of your office and use MBWA—Management by Walking Around.

(See Worksheet 3-10, "Improving My Skill in Encouraging Upward Communication," page 131.)

HOW TO COMMUNICATE NEW POLICIES AND PROCEDURES ("BOSS, DO YOU AGREE WITH THIS NEW DIRECTIVE?")

It is better to deal by speech than by letter.

—Francis Bacon (1561–1626), English philosopher, statesman and essayist

Every organization has to inform its employees, from time to time, of new or revised policies, rules, regulations, and procedures. The goal of such communication, obviously, is their full understanding *and* acceptance.

However, anyone who has worked in an organization knows that it is a lot easier to get the word out than to ensure that it will be comprehended and followed. Hence the need to think through very carefully how the new requirements are developed and disseminated. The following skill pointers should help minimize possible misunderstandings or resistance to the new directives.

1. To the extent practical, hold a group meeting(s) to involve those affected by the new policy or procedure *during its development.* People are more likely to support a new requirement they helped create than even the wisest policy designed by someone else.

2. As an alternative to a group meeting, ask for *ideas* about the change in requirement(s) in writing. This procedure may be necessary when it is not practical to assemble people for a meeting (due to shiftwork or people who work away from the main office). Depending upon the nature of the new policy or procedure, it may also be desirable to submit a draft of the proposal for comment.

3. When announcing the new policy, pay careful attention to the medium of communication. As a general rule, an oral message (group meeting) followed by a written reinforcing one is good procedure. Employees of limited education or language facility will be more comfortable with the spoken word. The group meeting is particularly essential if the new plan or procedure may be misunderstood or if resistance is expected. The questions you receive and the facial expressions you observe will indicate the degree of employee understanding and acceptance. Be sure to allow enough time for people to verbalize doubts and ask questions.

4. Be careful about the phraseology, symbols, and images you use. For example, one manager I knew used the military phrase "duty station" while explaining the new time employees were to be at their desks in the morning. Employees thereafter used the term derogatorily when they wished to joke about their boss's somewhat military style.

5. Anticipate messages to fade out over time. Consider intermittent reinforcing reminders to counteract this phenomenon.

6. Consider carefully how you transmit policies promulgated by echelons above you. While you wish to indicate clearly that you support such policies because you are a part of management, anticipate a problem if there may be any doubts by employees about the wisdom of a given policy. Why the prob-

lem? Simply because you may be asked: "Boss, do you agree with this directive?"

Your dilemma arises because of your desire to show support, yet you don't want to be untruthful to your staff if you have certain doubts yourself. In fact, if you have a doubt, they may sense it. You hardly wish to undermine your credibility with your staff, so it may be desirable, on the few occasions when you disagree with a policy from above, to be candid about the matter. A statement such as this may help: "This policy was developed after much thought and discussion. Obviously there is more than one way to look at it. I don't happen to see it the way it came down from the front office. However, as a manager I know that you can't have everything your way. So I'm going to support the policy fully and I expect you to do the same. Is that a fair answer to your question?" (See Worksheet 3-11, "Improving My Skill in Communicating New Policies and Procedures," page 132.)

HOW TO MANAGE THE GRAPEVINE ("THE MORE YOU CUT THE VINE, THE BIGGER THE GRAPES BECOME")

Rumors without a leg to stand on still have a way of getting around.

—Anonymous

Survey figures of the Hay Research for Management Data Base (reported in "Word from Above," table in *The Wall Street Journal,* August 13, 1986, p. 25) indicate that satisfaction among employees with the *amount* of information they receive is hardly what organizations would hope for. The satisfaction rates were as follows: clerical—60%, professional—54%, hourly—47%. Middle management was a bit more satisfied than the rank and file: 68%. High satisfaction rates would produce figures at the 90%-plus level. Credibility of information fared somewhat better: clerical—80%, professional—75%, hourly—61%, and middle management—86%.

Information, of course, is basic to a full understanding of the organization's policies and procedures. This is illustrated by an attitude survey of Hewitt Associates (reported in "Perceptions of Pay," table in *The Wall Street Journal,* July 7, 1986, p.15) which found that the better employees understood the company pay system, the fairer they regarded it. Thus, those who said they understood the system "very well" gave it a fairness rating of 72% ("very fair"—21%; "pretty fair"—51%);

those who understood it "pretty well" gave it a fairness rating of 73% ("very fair"—11%; "pretty fair"—62%); those who said their understanding was "not very well" gave it a fairness rating of 50% ("very fair"—3%; "pretty fair"—47%); and those who said their understanding was "not well" gave it a fairness rating of only 36% ("very fair"—5%; "pretty fair"—31%).

In any case, it is quite understandable that if people do not receive information they need or are fuzzy about what they do receive, they are quite likely to use the grapevine to help fill in their informational void. But as might be expected, rumor and the grapevine are regarded by most managers as an unnecessary irritant if not a total abomination: "If people would just wait until we give them the facts . . ." "There's no good reason why they should have all those details anyway." "No matter what we tell them they'd rather listen to the rumormongers." And so on. But as we will see, the indefatigable grapevine serves a number of constructive purposes.

The conventional view of the grapevine, then, is that it is essentially anti-organizational in character—an evil rumor mill. Why this belief? Because the grapevine may spread false, imagined, inaccurate, or distorted information, create unfounded suspicions, distract people from their work, and thus impair morale and productivity. There is also the feeling that rumor is spread by a few organizational gossips, which becomes a grist for the mill of those who are idle, bored, or hostile to the organization. Underlying management's antipathy toward the rumor mill is the feeling that it unfairly competes with the authorized communication system, that it undermines management's rightful power to control the flow of information to the workforce.

More accurately speaking, however, the grapevine exists because people have a need to know what is going on: Will automation create a loss of jobs? Are the new products "bombing" in the marketplace? Will the bonus be off again this year? Is the new VP coming in to "clean house?" In the absence of any formal or official communication, the grapevine moves in to satisfy that need to know.

What is significant from a communication standpoint, then, is that if management fails to provide information, people invent it. They may even take two disparate facts, put them together or enlarge upon them, and then become paranoid. Also, if employees are doubtful about the credibility of management's information, they may well create their own.

Managers, of course, become frustrated and angry over the grapevine's rich life and constantly think in terms of choking or cutting it off. Unfortunately, the more you cut the vine, the bigger the grapes become. Actually, the only way to choke the grapevine is to feed it more fully.

Behavioral scientists who have studied the role of rumor and the grapevine state that in times of economic slowdown or retrenchment, an *absence* of rumor is a signal of serious demoralization and that rumor is essential to maintain organizational health. This is akin to military officers asserting that "when the troops stop 'bitching,' then you're really in trouble." In other words, the total absence of complaint or rumor is a sign that people have become too apathetic to have any interest in what may ail them.

So the most realistic and useful way to regard rumor is as a tool to provide vital clues as to what is going on in the organization, as a safety valve for the release of employee anxieties and tensions and, of course, as a supplement to the typically inadequate formal communication system. In fact, rumor, because of its unfettered and swift character, may helpfully spread the word well in advance of the formal system.

Certainly, false rumors may well be destructive at times. But *useful* rumors have these vital functions, says communications professor Donald B. Simmons ("The Nature of the Organizational Grapevine," *Supervisory Management,* November 1985):

Providing Structure to Reduce Anxiety

People have a basic psychological need to be in the know—to have their *cognitive* needs met, as the psychologists put it. They need a *specific* focus to cope with vagueness and uncertainty, and the resultant uneasiness and anxiety. When people can team up with others to share *focused* information, even if it is only rumor, they can overcome feelings of isolation and ignorance. **Example:** Job anxiety over a possible plant move or downsizing can be eased by chitchat about a specific "decision" (a rumored one, of course) as to what might take place. So rumor provides a structure, something to latch on to, by focusing employee concern on a specific possibility or decision.

Filling in Information Gaps Regarding a Specific Situation

People have a need to make sense of partial, limited or fragmented information. They want a *unified* picture, a fuller perspective of the total situation of which they are a part. They thus scan their environment avidly in an attempt to predict the nature or a forthcoming (possible or actual) change. Since management has not filled in obvious information gaps, people use rumor to help clarify and predict management's possible actions. Typically, the void is created by management adopting a military approach to dissemination of information—i.e., "on a need to know basis only"—as opposed to sharing it freely. Examples of a need to know more fully may relate to a change in procedures, organization, equipment, budget, leadership, product design, product mix, etc.

Helping People to Organize a Strategic Stance

Unlike the situations above, people may also be coping with a specific, known problem. They are trying to assess the *consequences* of an impending decision. They are attempting to meet the need to control their destiny and feel that they do have power to influence outcomes. There thus may be an attempt to influence others and to organize people into supporting subgroups. This circumstance arises when there are ambiguous lines of authority and opportunities for influence appear to be highly available. Healthy ambition motivates people to try to be in on the decision-making process. Typical concerns may relate to reorganization; closing plants, offices, or stores; mergers, etc.

Communicating Status and Power

Rumor can help people feel important, powerful, or valuable and to be regarded as "insiders." Information is power, and the rumor disseminator is trading what he knows for others' willingness to listen to him. The rumor distributor's mantra is: "I can put you in the know."

Skill Pointers

Here are some ways to "control," or more accurately, live with the grapevine:

1. **Regard the grapevine as inevitable.** Certainly management cannot anticipate employees' every need to know. Nor can the formal communication system move as fast as the informal one. So devel-

op a sense of humor about it. Some of the more effective top managers that I have met do just that.

2. **Regard the grapevine as a useful tool,** rather than as competition, a threat, or a nasty conspiracy. By tuning in to rumors, management can learn where new or added information must be provided. The adage "if you can't beat 'em, join 'em" is a good guideline to follow. In essence, the grapevine is a supplement to the formal system of communication and may as well be used to the extent possible.

3. When a rumor hits your desk (or more likely your ear), check with others to **learn how far it has spread.** Then act to fill the obvious information void.

4. **Rethink your communication philosophy and practice.** If it is one of "on a need-to-know-only basis," you're in deep trouble. A more realistic outlook is that people have an on-going, profound need to know. If that need is ignored, anticipate that gossip and rumor will try to meet it.

5. **Build trust with people.** If there is a serious credibility gap, only the grapevine will be listened to. Bad news should be communicated fully and promptly, rather than sugar-coated or delayed. Candor in such matters will build trust.

6. **Strengthen and utilize to the maximum the formal communication system,** particularly in periods of rapid change, hard times, budget cuts, reorganization, leadership changes, etc.

7. Also **latch onto the informal communication system.** Use MBWA (Management by Walking Around). Talk to informal leaders to get their opinion on possible alterations in policies or procedures. Hold group meetings to secure employee inputs about current problems and to learn of their concerns and informational needs, as well as to share information.

(See Worksheet 3-12, "Improving My Skills in Using the Grapevine," page 133.)

KEY SKILLS AND CONCEPTS

The Winning Manager:

1. Avoids taking the communication process for granted. Instead, he operates on the more realistic assumption that is is difficult to communicate effectively at all times, with all persons, on all

problems and situations. Accordingly, he proceeds carefully in all communication endeavors and works constantly on upgrading his communication skill.

2. Recognizes that *relations* with people are a critical determinant in how effective communications outcomes will be, that managers typically don't have communication problems but *relationship* problems.

3. Understands that strong relations with others require a high degree of concern with building trust (via intimacy, openness, sharing, caring, support giving).

4. Avoids managing or manipulating the communication process. Rather, strives for open, honest, candid, and fully authentic communication.

5. Operates on the assumption that the meaning is in the receiver, not in the message. Understands that the receiver processes the message through his particular set of filters (experience, values, attitudes, personality) and thus is not likely to receive "objectively," for few of us, as receivers, engage in "immaculate perception."

6. Recognizes that messages have both explicit and implicit meanings. Of the two, the latter are more important, that is, what is *not* said may be more significant to the receiver than what is. People *do* pay attention to what may not be said or written.

7. Anticipates that much of what he does as a manager may be interpreted in ways that are not intended. The phenomenon is akin to reading tea leaves—people will see what they want to see (or are "programmed" to see).

8. Accepts the notion that the meaning of the communication is determined by its consequences (i.e., the impact on the receiver), not by the communicator's intent.

9. Endeavors to keep in phase his verbal and non-verbal communication. (An "I'm very upset" accompanied by a big smile provides a confused message.)

10. Recognizes that people pay attention to what you do, not just what you say. And no one cares for a hypocrite.

11. Understands the merits of two-way communication and the serious limitations of one-way communication. (A message without feedback built into it is hardly a message.)

12. Recognizes that listening by the manager may be more useful than telling and selling.

13. Avoids "GASing" people in his communication endeavors. (GAS: Guilt, Anxiety, Shame.) Instead, he so behaves that trusting, sharing, and caring are regularly communicated. The latter behaviors prevent defensiveness.

14. Encourages people to express their feelings openly so as to "have the whole person." This avoids losing out on a lot of what a subordinate can bring to the job if his feelings are ignored—namely, information, ideas, suggestions, insights, challenges to the status quo.

15. Works actively at encouraging upward communication.

16. Keeps in touch with people—creative contact—to reduce perceived status and thus learn how people see their world.

17. Appreciates that good communication means not having to say: "I'm sorry"

"I'm sorry I cut you off (interrupted) . . ."

"I'm sorry I hurt your feelings. I really didn't mean to . . ."

"I'm sorry, but I wasn't really listening . . ."

"I'm sorry I was a bit sharp (or abrupt, or argumentative, or impatient, or stubborn, etc.) the other day . . ."

(And so on. Once the toothpaste is out of the tube, it's irreversible.)

OVERALL SKILL CHECK AND ACTION PLANNING

Now that you have read the text on communication, it will be helpful to check your skill as a communicator with other people. The self-test on page 134, "My Skill as a Communicator—a Self-Quiz," is designed for this purpose. Take the quiz now and use it as a basis for discussion with a friend or colleague.

It is hoped that you now have acquired new insights and stimulated your interest in communication. To capitalize on this interest and to improve your skill as a communicator and listener, the development of an Action Plan will be of real value to you. Worksheet 3-13 (page 136), "My Action Plan for Improved Communication and Listening Skills," is available for this purpose. Draw on the various in-text worksheets and the self-tests for ideas for your Action Plan.

But don't merely complete this form and file it away. Instead, do two things:

1. "Reality test" your Action Plan with someone you respect and trust—a colleague, your spouse, a professional acquaintance, a key assistant, possibly your boss. You're certain to get some helpful feedback about your Plan.
2. Review your Action Plan with your confidante at three-month intervals over the next year. Check to see what you have accomplished and what changes may be necessary in the Plan to ensure that it is realistic.

These procedures may seem like a lot of difficult, time-consuming work. Possibly so. But how else can you ensure that you have identified your communication and listening skill needs and actively worked at their improvement?

PROBLEMS, DISCUSSION QUESTIONS AND EXERCISES FOR COMMUNICATION SKILL WORKSHOPS AND COLLEGE/UNIVERSITY CLASSES IN MANAGEMENT

1. **Brainstorming.** Have the group brainstorm topics such as:
   a. How the manager can minimize or reduce his status so as to encourage communication.
   b. How to encourage vertical (upward) communication by employees.
   c. How the manager can improve communication with his own boss.
   d. How to improve communication with peers and colleagues.
   e. How to make staff meetings both interesting and effective.
2. In small groups, have participants compose "I messages" in relation to these difficult situations:
   a. You are the head of the Budget Committee. One of your members is very negative about most things. You decide to talk to him about this tendency.
   b. A subordinate of yours is typically late to your staff meetings. You decide to level with him on this.
   c. Your boss made several unnecessary interruptions in your presentation to the safety committee which got you "off track." Because this has happened before, you decide to speak to him about it.
   d. A fellow section chief frequently visits your section to engage in long conversations with several subordinates of yours, people with whom he has worked with previously. The conversations typically relate to an athletic event of the prior day. You decide to speak to him about this.
   e. You are Mary Larson, supervisor of the Mail, Files and Records Branch. Your boss, Chief of Administrative Services, has been engaging in what you consider to be sexual harassment—comments about the physical characteristics of some of your more attractive female subordinates, creating sexual innuendos out of ordinary conversation, hinting about having dinner or an end-of-the-day cocktail, narrating an occasional off-color joke. You decide to confront him about his behavior.
3. Assign to trios or quartets one or more of the questions below for discussion. Post the answers of the small groups on flipchart sheets for comparative review and analysis.
   a. What criteria would you use to assess how well communication is faring in your organization?
   b. What criteria would you use to assess how well communication is faring in your own unit?
   c. What is the relationship between communication and motivation?
   d. To what degree and in what way is the delegation process related to or dependent upon communication?
   e. What are some of the causes of communication breakdown?
   f. Assume trust is basic to authentic communication. How can a manager go about building it?
   g. You find that a new subordinate of yours is botching her assignments. It is obvious that she is not picking up what you tell her. What can you do to ensure that she "gets it right" in the future?
   h. You have to communicate to your staff a decision from *your* boss that you strongly oppose.
      What are the risks and benefits of these two approaches:
      a. Being candid about your feeling to your staff.
      b. Just passing the decision along as if you agreed fully with it.
4. Have each participant rate the communication prowess of himself, his boss and his spouse (or equivalent) on the scale below. Use the letters M (for me), B (for boss), and S (for spouse). Then discuss the ratings in small groups.

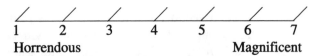

1   2   3   4   5   6   7
Horrendous   Magnificent

5. Ask group members to develop a mental image about a woman named Bertha and a man named Oswald. (Or substitute other names that evoke certain images as appropriate for your group.) Then have them rate on the scale below how they feel about Bertha and Oswald.

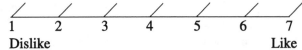

1   2   3   4   5   6   7
Dislike   Like

   Secure ratings from the group and post on flipchart. If there are few strongly positive ratings, ask "why?" Do names communicate something to us? Why? How? How does this relate to our use of nicknames and short forms of names? What about the use of first names in the office?

6. Have your group rate the words and phrases below as follows: L (like), D (dislike), and N (neutral).

   Then ask for a show of hands to tally the three ratings (L, D, and N) on all items from all group members.

   Discussion questions: Why did we rate certain words differently? How do our emotions and per-

ceptions relate to the words? Are the meanings in the words or ourselves?

7. Divide the total group into pairs. Have each pair come up with two examples (in either job, home, school, community) where failure to listen had significant consequences.

8. Divide the total group into small groups. Instruct one or more of the small groups to take this position: "Communicating openly (no secrets) about people's salaries and pay increases is hazardous for the organization's health." Instruct one or more small groups to take this position: "Communicating openly (no secrets) about people's salaries and pay increases is a healthy thing for organizations to do."

   Secure reports from the small groups. **Note:** Try to secure a focus on how open vs. closed communication policies affect morale, relationships, trust, etc.

9. Working in small groups, have members in the groups *agree* on whether they would use the formal or informal communication system to resolve the following situations:

   a. A difficulty with a manager in another part of the organization.

   b. A difficulty with a manager who reports to your boss.

	Rating		
	L	D	N
bistro			
ballpark			
alarm clock			
Democrats			
Republicans			
non-voters			
reactionary			
radical			
racist			
snow			
rabbi			
Bible Belt			
terrorism			
school prayer			

	Rating		
	L	D	N
hot cereal			
hippie			
boondocks			
marijuana			
living together			
bestseller			
chicken livers			
priest			
Mercedes-Benz			
Congressman			
nuclear energy			
X-rated flicks			
abortion			
key lime pie			

c. You accidentally discover an employee in another office is conducting a "small business" on company time and premises.

d. It is common knowledge that two employees in the stock room are operating a betting ring. You wish to stop this activity, especially because your organization has just come out with a new set of guidelines on employee conduct banning such behavior on the premises. Besides, some of your employees are spending time there to place bets, discuss past and forthcoming athletic events, gossip with friends, etc.

f. You are all set to send out some new instructions to the field. Your assistant suggests you show these materials to a knowledgeable colleague in another office to play "devil's advocate" before showing the final product to the "big boss." The big boss likes to keep these kinds of matters within the division lest there be a "leak" of some sort before the material hits the field.

g. You have an unusually large typing bottleneck. You could get a temp to do the work, but the hiring procedures are quite complex. A long-time friend of yours in another office would gladly let you use one of his versatile typists to help reduce this huge backlog.

10. Have each participant complete the following worksheet and then a) discuss it in trios, and b) hold a general discussion re learnings in the small groups. (**Note:** Rank order relates to the seriousness of the problem, i.e., 1 is the most serious and 7 is the least serious.)

Blocks/Barriers to Communication With My Subordinates

Difficulty	Rank order	Remedial procedure
1.		a.
		b.
2.		a.
		b.
3.		a.
		b.
4.		a.
		b.
5.		a.
		b.

11. A. Secure data from the total group and post on flipchart responses to the following questions:
   a. What do managers do which causes others to "tune them in?"
   b. What do managers do which causes others to "tune them out?"
   B. Working in trios, have each participant respond to these questions:
   a. What are my behaviors when I am at my communication best and thus cause others to tune me in?
   b. What I am not at my communication best, what might I do which causes others to tune me out?
   c. Why do I communicate in a manner that causes tune-out?
   d. What might I do to overcome practices that cause tune-out? (Secure help from the other trio members.)
   C. Conclude the exercise by holding a general discussion regarding what was learned from the activity.

12. The following questions relate to two-way communication. Assign one or more of the questions to small groups.
   a. How can it be developed between the boss and individual staff members (one-on-one relationships)?
   b. How can it be enhanced in *group* situations?
   c. How can it be enhanced *between units* in an organization?
   d. When may two-way communication be inappropriate?

13. Role Play: Communicating Negative Information (Instructions for Role Play)

Fred Damper—Supervisor

You are Chief Auditor for the All Too Easy Home Finance Corporation, with corporate headquarters in Buffalo, New York.

An audit is required of the San Francisco branch office and you had hoped to send John Eager since he had been there before. However, sometime after his trip out west you received some negative feedback—some subtle, some direct—that John was officious and abrasive and had a couple of "run-ins" with people there.

You would like to send John again because his report last time was top-notch. You know he would like to go since he has a brother there. But you don't think it is a good idea to send someone to an office where he is *persona non grata,* especially because other auditors are available and would relish the trip. You have the task of communicating the "bad news" to John.

John Eager—Subordinate

You are an auditor with the All Too Easy Finance Corporation, located in Buffalo, New York, corporate headquarters. Although most of your work is performed in the office, on occasion you go to the field to audit the accounts of branch offices. You are looking forward to another trip to San Francisco: You had an enjoyable trip the last time you were there, and you have a brother who lives in Oakland and would like to spend some time with him. Your boss, Fred Damper, Chief Auditor, has called you in to talk about the trip. You know that Fred was pleased with your last report.

My Skill as a Listener—A Self-Test

For each of the 25 statements below, circle the number that best describes your perception of your skill as a listener: 1 = never or almost never; 2 = seldom or rarely; 3 = sometimes or occasionally; 4 = usually or most of the time; 5 = always or almost always. *Be as candid as you can* to learn of your true skill and what added work or goals may be in order to upgrade your listening effectiveness.

1. I listen for the actual message, not just to the words presented to me.	1	2	3	4	5
2. I try to distinguish between facts vs. judgments, opinions, assumptions, perceptions.	1	2	3	4	5
3. I try to listen for the feeling expressed as well as the message itself.	1	2	3	4	5
4. I listen for the tone of voice as an aid to understanding the message.	1	2	3	4	5
5. I observe body language (position, tenseness, facial expression, movements, etc.) as an aid to understanding the sender's message.	1	2	3	4	5
6. I try to "get into his shoes" to ensure that I understand his frame of reference, value or belief system, "world view."	1	2	3	4	5
7. I try to minimize the impact of my own expectations about the message, that is, to avoid hearing what I expect, need, or want to hear.	1	2	3	4	5
8. I try to listen with my "third ear"—to what is *not* said as well as to what is said.	1	2	3	4	5
9. When I am in doubt about the significance of a message, I restate or summarize it so that both I and the message sender can check my understanding of it.	1	2	3	4	5
10. I try to keep in mind that words may have more than one meaning; hence the need to to check with the sender to ensure that I understood what was *meant,* not just said.	1	2	3	4	5
11. I may ask relevant questions to aid my understanding and/or to show my interest.	1	2	3	4	5
12. When I listen to someone in a location with distractions (noise, movement of people or objects, low or high temperature, etc.), I try all the harder to zero in on the speaker's message.	1	2	3	4	5
13. I try to be an "active" listener—I use eye contact, head nods, smiles, "uh huhs," relevant comments or restatements, positive body posture such as leaning forward.	1	2	3	4	5
14. I recognize that time pressures may limit my listening capability and act appropriately to prevent listening disasters.	1	2	3	4	5
15. I listen patiently and empathically to an angry or frustrated person to permit ventilatio of feelings. I thus recognize the need to "treat" the emotion before I can work effectively on the problem.	1	2	3	4	5
16. I recognize that my own values, beliefs, perceptions, and feelings may cloud the message I am trying to receive.	1	2	3	4	5
17. I avoid making judgments about the speaker, particularly when he is presenting ideas I may not favor.	1	2	3	4	5
18. I avoid "listening traps"—letting myself be turned off by the speaker's delivery, voice quality, dress, physical appearance, pace or energy level, name, affiliation, skin color, sex.	1	2	3	4	5
19. I recognize that my receiving rate as a listener may be three or four times greater than the rate at which the message is sent. I thus work at overcoming possible tune-out practices—daydreaming, unrelated thinking, preparing a response to what is said.	1	2	3	4	5
20. When I listen to someone at my desk I avoid doodling, signing, reviewing or shuffling papers, making notes on unrelated matters, etc.	1	2	3	4	5
21. I avoid interrupting a speaker at all costs.	1	2	3	4	5
22. I avoid faking interest in or understanding the other person's message.	1	2	3	4	5
23. I am conscious of and try to minimize the impact of my own emotional state (expectations, needs, attitudes, values, preferences, prejudices, motivations, etc.) when I receive messages, for it may influence what I hear.	1	2	3	4	5
24. I recognize that by listening fully to people, I help meet certain basic needs—namely, to feel important and to feel good about themselves.	1	2	3	4	5
25. I am aware that my own body language may be communicating messages to the message sender, e.g., interest/disinterest, agreement/disagreement, like/dislike of the other person.	1	2	3	4	5

Scoring

1. Tally your responses according to the number you assigned to them. Enter your totals below:

　　1s × 1 = _____
　　2s × 2 = _____
　　3s × 3 = _____
　　4s × 4 = _____
　　5s × 5 = _____
　　Grand Total _____

2. Multiply each total by the weight provided in each line.
3. Add your scores on each line to arrive at a summary score (grand total).

　　Your score can range from a high of 125 to a low of 25. If your point total is at or near 125, you probably have the potential to function in an occupation where a high premium is placed on listening—counselor, personnel interviewer, social worker, psychiatrist, bartender, etc. If you scored somewhere in the 25 to 75 range, you're probably in trouble in many or most of your interactions with others. A score of around 100 would indicate that you're probably a pretty good listener.

　　In any case, you now know where you stand. Use this rating form as a guide to strengthening your listening skills.

Note: As an aid to upgrading your listening skill, you may wish to check your self-ratings with others who know you well—your spouse, boss, colleagues, friends, subordinates. The employee check is a particularly helpful one. However, a trusting relationship must exist before candid feedback will be given to you.

Worksheet 3-1
Building Skill in the Use of Two-way Communication

1. I would rate my concern with two-way as opposed to one-way communication *prior* to reading this text as follows (circle one):

1	2	3	4	5	6	7
Low						High

2. The most important ideas I have received from this section of the chapter so far are:

a. _____

b. _____

c. _____

d. _____

e. _____

3. The behaviors I should do *less* of to improve my skill in the area of two-way communication are:

a. _____

b. _____

c. _____

d. _____

e. _____

4. The behaviors I intend to engage in to improve my skill in two-way communication are:

a. _____

b. _____

c. _____

d. _____

e. _____

Worksheet 3-2
Improving My Skill in Cross-Gender Communication

1. My effectiveness in communicating with members of the opposite sex is:

_____ Low

_____ Moderately Effective

_____ Highly Effective

2. The communication behaviors I now engage in with the members of the opposite sex which I find effective are:

_____

_____

_____

_____

_____

_____

_____

3. The communication behaviors I now engage in with members of the opposite sex which are less than effective and should be discontinued are:

_____

_____

_____

_____

_____

_____

_____

4. The communication behaviors I should adopt to improve my communication and relations with members of the opposite sex are:

_____

_____

_____

_____

_____

_____

Worksheet 3-3
Upgrading My Skill to Prevent the Defensive Response

Do you recall an incident (interviewing, coaching, counseling, a peer meeting) wherein the person with whom you were communicating became defensive? If so, completion of the responses to the questions below will help to assess and augment your skill in the area of defensive communications.

1. I recall _____ becoming defensive on the problem relating to

   _____

   _____

   _____

   _____

2. What seemed to trigger his defensiveness was

   _____

   _____

   _____

   _____

3. As a communicator, my impact on him was:

```
     /           /           /           /           /           /           /
   1           2           3           4           5           6           7
Produced                                                          Produced High
Low Defensiveness                                                 Defensiveness
```

4. If I were to conduct the interview or meeting again, I would

   _____

   _____

   _____

   _____

5. The skill elements I plan to use in the future to avoid any defensiveness from arising in communication situations are:

   a. _____

   b. _____

   c. _____

   d. _____

   e. _____

Worksheet 3-4
Augmenting My Skill in Nonverbal Communication

Reflect on your learning about and possible improvement in your recognition and use of nonverbal communication. Then answer the questions which follow.

1. The most important ideas which I received from this section are:

    a. _____

    b. _____

    c. _____

    d. _____

    e. _____

2. The behaviors I should do less of to improve my skill in the area of nonverbal communication are:

    a. _____

    b. _____

    c. _____

    d. _____

    e. _____

3. The behaviors I intend to engage in to improve my skill in the nonverbal area are:

    a. _____

    b. _____

    c. _____

    d. _____

    e. _____

Worksheet 3-5
Building Skill in Giving Negative Feedback

How conscious are you of the interpersonal side of giving constructive criticism (negative feedback)? Your candid responses to the questions below should help to sharpen your sensitivity in this skill area.

1. Feedback from the boss.

a) The last negative feedback I received from my boss related to _____
_____

b) My boss' concern for my feelings was:

```
   /        /        /        /        /        /        /
   1        2        3        4        5        6        7
little                                                  great
concern                                                 concern
```

c) My feelings about my boss after I received the feedback was that he was a:

```
   /        /        /        /        /        /        /
   1        2        3        4        5        6        7
lousy                                                   top-notch
supervisor                                              supervisor
```

d) What my boss might have done differently was:
_____
_____

2. Feedback to a subordinate.

a) I recently provided negative feedback to _____ about
_____
_____

b) My concern about the subordinate's feelings was:

```
   /        /        /        /        /        /        /
   1        2        3        4        5        6        7
little                                                  great
concern                                                 concern
```

c) If I had the chance to communicate the feedback again, I probably would
_____
_____

3. Future feedback. In the future when I have to give negative feedback I intend to pay attention to these skill elements:

a. _____
b. _____
c. _____
d. _____
e. _____
f. _____
g. _____

Worksheet 3-6
Building Skill in Communicating with the Angry Person

Now that you have read this section on communicating with the angry person, it may be helpful to you to review your own experience in this skill area. Your analysis of a recent incident of this sort should help to sharpen your skill.

1. I recently had to deal with _____ who was very upset about

_____

_____

2. As I recall, the things I did well in that situation were:

    a) _____

    b) _____

    c) _____

    d) _____

3. The things I could have done better were:

    a) _____

    b) _____

    c) _____

    d) _____

4. I would say my handling of this incident was marked by:

```
   /        /         /          /          /          /          /
   1        2         3          4          5          6          7
Low Skill                                                   High Skill
("I really blew it")                                   ("I acted like a pro")
```

5. Should a future incident arise, I will exercise these skills:

    a) _____

    b) _____

    c) _____

    d) _____

Worksheet 3-7
Building Skill in "Delivering the Bad News"

Have you had to deliver "bad news" to anyone recently? If so, review what you did as a means of "upping" your skill quotient in this area.

1. I recently delivered bad news to _____ about

_____

_____

_____

2. The impact on _____ was:

_____ quite negative ("shook him up").

_____ slightly negative.

_____ imperceptible (no noticeable effect).

3. In this incident what I did well was

_____

_____

_____

4. In this incident what I could have done better was

_____

_____

_____

5. If I have to deliver the bad news in the future, the skilled elements I shall pay attention to are:

a) _____

b) _____

c) _____

d) _____

e) _____

Worksheet 3-8
Building Skill in Engaging in Creative Contact

1. I would rate my current interest in the area of "creative contact" as:

```
  /        /        /        /        /        /        /
 1        2        3        4        5        6        7
Very little                                    Great deal of
interest/concern                               interest/concern
```

2. The things I now do to ensure creative contact with subordinates are:

a) _____

b) _____

c) _____

d) _____

e) _____

f) _____

g) _____

h) _____

i) _____

j) _____

3. The things I intend to do in the future to ensure creative contact with subordinates are:

a) _____

b) _____

c) _____

d) _____

e) _____

f) _____

g) _____

h) _____

i) _____

j) _____

Worksheet 3-9
Improving My Skill in Presenting Questions

1. My current approach to asking the types of questions below:

Type	Frequency of Use		
	Seldom	Fairly often	A great deal
Open-ended			
Feedback			
Partial verbalization			

2. My current approach to asking the types of questions below:

Type	Frequency of Use		
	Seldom	Fairly often	A great deal
Closed-ended			
Evaluative			
Manipulative			
"Holier than thou"			

3. The concepts I appreciated most from the text are:

a)_____

b)_____

c)_____

d)_____

e)_____

4. To improve my skill in asking questions I should:

a)_____

b)_____

c)_____

d)_____

e)_____

Worksheet 3-10
Improving My Skill in Encouraging Upward Communication

1. I would rate my *interest* in upward communication as:

/	/	/	/	/	/	/
1	2	3	4	5	6	7
Low						High

2. I would rate my *skill* in upward communication as:

/	/	/	/	/	/	/
1	2	3	4	5	6	7
Low						High

3. The things that I do now that *encourage* upward communication are:

a) _____

b) _____

c) _____

d) _____

e) _____

4. The things that I do now that probably *discourage* upward communication are:

a) _____

b) _____

c) _____

d) _____

e) _____

5. The things that I intend to do in the future to encourage upward communication are:

a) _____

b) _____

c) _____

d) _____

e) _____

Worksheet 3-11
Improving My Skill in Communicating New Policies and Procedures

1. I would rate my skill in the area of communicating new policies and procedures as:

```
  /        /         /         /         /         /         /
  1        2         3         4         5         6         7
Highly                                                    Highly
Limited                                                   Effective
```

2. The things that I do now in communicating policies and procedures that work well are:

a) _____

b) _____

c) _____

d) _____

e) _____

3. The things that I do now that are less effective are:

a) _____

b) _____

c) _____

d) _____

e) _____

4. What I intend to do in the future to improve my skill in this area are:

a) _____

b) _____

c) _____

d) _____

e) _____

Worksheet 3-12
Improving My Skill in Using the Grapevine

1. I would rate my feelings about the grapevine as follows: (**Note:** Provide two ratings: Use a B to indicate your feeling about the grapevine *before* you read the text; use an A to indicate your feelings *after* you read the text.)

```
   /        /        /        /        /        /        /
  1        2        3        4        5        6        7
Really                   No Special              Regard It as
Ticks                     Concern                a Valuable
Me Off                                                Tool
```

2. What bothers me about the grapevine is (are):

a) _____

b) _____

c) _____

d) _____

3. As a result of my reading of the text, I intend to do the following in respect to the grapevine:

a) _____

b) _____

c) _____

d) _____

My Skill as a Communicator—a Self-Quiz

For each of the 40 statements below, circle the number that best describes your perception of your skill as a communicator: 1 = never or almost never; 2 = seldom or rarely; 3 =sometimes or occasionally; 4 = usually or most of the time; 5 = always or almost always. *Be as candid as you can.* In this way you will learn of your true skill and what added work or goals may be in order to upgrade your communication effectiveness.

Note: If you have taken the self-test on listening, you will find that this quiz does not treat listening skills per se. The two quizzes, in combination, cover the interpersonal communication skill area comprehensively.

1. I provide full information about policies and procedures so that people can do their work properly.   1 2 3 4 5
2. I communicate fully to employees so that rumor and the grapevine are not a problem in my operation. 1 2 3 4 5
3. I present the "why" of a decision before I announce it.   1 2 3 4 5
4. I use face-to-face communication rather than the written word wherever possible.   1 2 3 4 5
5. I operate on the assumption that frequent group meetings, regular and special, are essential to solve problems, not only to pass along information.   1 2 3 4 5
6. I operate on the assumption that confrontation and conflict are natural and to be expected, for they provide stimuli basic to creativity and effective problem solving.   1 2 3 4 5
7. When I have to deliver the "bad news" to an employee, I try to do it promptly, candidly, on a face-to-face basis, and with concern for the best time of day or week for the message delivery.   1 2 3 4 5
8. I try to minimize or reduce my status so that people will not regard me as a "10-foot giant" and b afraid to communicate openly with me.   1 2 3 4 5
9. I try to visit my employees in *their* work locations to discuss a problem.   1 2 3 4 5
10. I make it a point to have lunch or coffee with subordinates often enough so that they can get to know me as a person and thus trust me more.   1 2 3 4 5
11. I try to communicate my interest in and caring of people. I see this as means of developing trust and open communication.   1 2 3 4 5
12. In my dealings with my employees I try to be open/honest/authentic and expect them to be the same way with me.   1 2 3 4 5
13. I try to ensure my credibility as a communicator by using candor, keeping promises, admitting error, and sharing information freely.   1 2 3 4 5
14. I try to communicate confidence and credibility by keeping my head up and maintaining eye contact, and by a willingness to get physically and emotionally close to people.   1 2 3 4 5
15. I try to recognize that every communication with someone affects our relationship—that is, it can strengthen or weaken it.   1 2 3 4 5
16. I use communication as a tool to help people feel better about themselves, e.g., by listening to them and giving earned praise as often as I can.   1 2 3 4 5
17. I act on the principle that by communicating to my employees the good things they do—positive feedback—I develop a closeness and trust in my relations with them.   1 2 3 4 5
18. I operate on the assumption that when I communicate it is based on my "world view" (frame of reference) which may differ from that of the receiver.   1 2 3 4 5
19. I thus recognize that my messages may result in unanticipated results—distortion, disinterest, disagreement. I therefore try to learn how well my message was received by checking for understanding.   1 2 3 4 5
20. I recognize that messages may have emotional meaning to people which may influence what they really hear and understand.   1 2 3 4 5
21. I try to recognize that the message I send is in the receiver and not in the message itself.   1 2 3 4 5
22. I am conscious of the words and phrases I use because certain ones may raise "red flags" and thus cause distortion or tuneout by the receiver.   1 2 3 4 5
23. As a communicator I try to ensure that my verbal message is in "sync" with my nonverbal behavior.   1 2 3 4 5
24. I recognize that involving the listener fully—two-way communication—is the best way to get a message through.   1 2 3 4 5

My Skill as a Communicator—a Self-Quiz (Continued)

25. I avoid the trap of "isness" (my view is *the* correct and only view) by making it clear that I am presenting *my* opinion, *my* perception, or *my* bias.	1	2	3	4	5
26. I avoid the trap of "allness" (tendency to generalize rather than to deal in particular situations), as it overwhelms people and turns them off.	1	2	3	4	5
27. When giving criticism I describe specific behaviors and avoid assumptions, generalizations, put-downs, name-calling, or references to personal characteristics.	1	2	3	4	5
28. I follow the rule of "praise in public and correct (criticize) in private."	1	2	3	4	5
29. I am aware and act on the assumption that the knowledge or information I give will not necessarily result in the desired behavior by the listener.	1	2	3	4	5
30. I operate on the premise that if the employee hasn't understood I haven't communicated properly, i.e., I have failed to secure feedback regarding his real understanding.	1	2	3	4	5
31. I act on the assumption that communication is a means of learning from the other person as well as to inform or persuade the listener.	1	2	3	4	5
32. I provide opportunities for people to "blow off steam," to ventilate their feelings about things that bother them.	1	2	3	4	5
33. I operate on the assumption that listening to people is just as important as getting the work out.	1	2	3	4	5
34. I utilize annual performance reviews (employee appraisal) to strengthen relations and thus improve communication.	1	2	3	4	5
35. I find that employees are willing to talk to me about anything of concern to them.	1	2	3	4	5
36. My employees are willing to communicate to me the bad news (problems, mistakes, delays) as well as the good.	1	2	3	4	5
37. I periodically try to secure feedback from my staff concerning my communication behavior.	1	2	3	4	5
38. I take pains to keep my boss informed about accomplishments, progress, and problems so that he will not be subject to surprises.	1	2	3	4	5
39. As an upward communicator, I respect channels and avoid "end runs."	1	2	3	4	5
40. I keep in close touch with peers and colleagues to develop strong relations with them.	1	2	3	4	5

Scoring

1. Tally your responses according to the number you assigned them. Enter your totals below:

    1s × 1 = _____
    2s × 2 = _____
    3s × 3 = _____
    4s × 4 = _____
    5s × 5 = _____
    Grand Total: _____

2. Multiply each total by the weight provided in each line.
3. Add your scores on each line to arrive at a summary score (grand total).

Your score can range from a high of 200 (40 items × 5 points each) to a low of 40 (40 × 1). If your score is in the 180–200 range, you're a good bet to be president or chief of your organization, if you're not already! If your score is closer to the minimum (40 points), you're probably in hot water, communication-wise, much of the time. If you scored somewhere in the middle range—160 to 180—you're probably communicating well much of the time. In any case, use this quiz as a guide to upgrade your communication skills in the months ahead.

Worksheet 3-13
My Action Plan for Improved Communication and Listening Skills

Overall Communication Skills and Behaviors

A. My needs for improvement as a communicator are:

1. _____

2. _____

3. _____

4. _____

5. _____

B. My plans to improve my communication skills and behavior are:

1. _____

2. _____

3. _____

4. _____

5. _____

C. Possible barriers or blocks to improvement are:

1. _____

2. _____

3. _____

4. _____

5. _____

D. I can overcome such obstacles by:

1. _____

2. _____

3. _____

4. _____

5. _____

Worksheet 3-13
My Action Plan for Improved Communication and Listening Skills (Continued)

Listening Skills and Behaviors

A. My needs for improvement as a listener are:

1. _____

2. _____

3. _____

4. _____

5. _____

B. My plans to improve my listening skills are:

1. _____

2. _____

3. _____

4. _____

5. _____

C. Possible barriers or blocks to improvement are:

1. _____

2. _____

3. _____

4. _____

5. _____

D. I can overcome such obstacles by:

1. _____

2. _____

3. _____

4. _____

5. _____

4 Motivation: The Manager as a Motivator of People

Hence an unexpected development in the history of leisure: for many people weekend free time has become not a chance to escape work but a chance to create work that is more meaningful—to work at recreation—in order to realize the personal satisfactions that the workplace no longer offers.

> —Witold Rybcznski, "Waiting for the Weekend," *The Atlantic Monthly,* August 1991

Journalist to plant manager: *"How many people work at your plant?"*
Plant Manager: *"About half."*

I'm in no hurry. I'm on my way to work.

> —Spotted on a bumper sticker

The floggings will continue until morale improves.

> —Wall poster spotted in a Massachusetts computer firm

Is it Friday yet?

> —Sign posted on front rim of desk in an automotive insurance claims office

Every morning I get up and look through the Forbes' *list of the richest people in America. If I'm not there, I go to work.*

> —Robert Orben, U.S. humorist

A bad day fishing beats a good day at the office.

> —Spotted on a bumper sticker

90% of life is showing up.

> —Woody Allen, film producer, director, actor, and humorist

When people don't want to come, nothing in the world will stop them.

> —Sol Hurok (1888–1974), ballet and opera impresario

INTRODUCTION

You and I regularly encounter a variety of motivational phenomena as expressed in *everyday* statements such as these:

"I'm not up to it."

"He's his own worst enemy."

"Go for broke."

"You have to have fire in the belly."

"He's an oddball, isn't he?"

"She is a real competitor."

"He really turns me off (or on)."

"You only go around once."

"I wonder what makes him tick."

"I can't take it any more."

"Better to wear away than rust away."

And in *organizations* we typically hear motivational reactions and expressions such as the following:

"He'll do it, but he'll sure take his own sweet time."

"How do you reach a person like that?"

"She just isn't motivated."

"That's old Joe for you."

"TGIF (Thank God It's Friday)."

"People don't work like they used to."

"They simply won't accept change."

"I've got to light a fire under him."

"A real self-starter."

"It's not a matter of money."

"You can never predict what he'll do next."

"She's nice to know socially, but she's a bear at her desk."

Obviously, a number of these statements reflect confusion and consternation about people and their presumed lack of motivation. Do you feel that there is a serious "commitment gap" in U.S. organizations? If so, you certainly are not alone. Consider the following data found in a study by Daniel Yankelovich and John Immerwahr (*Putting the Work Ethic to Work: A Public Agenda Report on Restoring America's Competitive Vitality,* Public Agenda Foundation, 1983):

☐ Only 23% of workers in the survey said they are performing at full capacity.

☐ Nearly half (44%) stated that they expend only a minimum effort to get by on their jobs.

☐ 62% of managers, workers, and union officials believe people aren't working as hard as they used to.

☐ Some one-half of the surveyed managers questioned the effectiveness of the reward system—there was no relationship between a job done well and pay.

Although this is an older study, there is little reason to believe that the need for managers to "recapture" worker commitment no longer exists, what with the considerable emphasis in the past decade or more on restructuring, re-engineering, mergers and acquisitions, downsizing, and the like. However, for organizations that have gone in seriously for Total Quality Management (TQM), employee involvement teams, team building, self-directed teams, empowerment programs, and other efforts to unleash potential and tap creativity, workers certainly are responding in a more committed/motivated way.

A Thought-Sharpening Exercise

To stimulate your own thinking further about motivation, respond to the following worksheets.

Checksheet: General Motivating Factors

Check the items below which you feel aid materially to "turn on" or motivate employees to perform more productively or creatively.

_____ 1. Year-end bonus

_____ 2. Good pension plan

_____ 3. Parking privileges

_____ 4. Company cafeteria

_____ 5. Opportunity to buy company stock

_____ 6. Training at company expense

_____ 7. Job challenge

_____ 8. Realistic travel allowance

_____ 9. Comprehensive medical-dental plan

_____10. Cost-of-living pay adjustments

_____11. Job evaluation plan

_____12. Annual leave plan recognizing length of service

_____13. Comfortable, modern offices

_____14. Growth on the job

_____15. Pleasant, cooperative associates

_____16. Recreation sponsored by company

_____17. Piped-in music

_____18. Company-sponsored events (Christmas party; annual picnic)

_____19. Capable supervisors

_____20. Recognition and praise for a job done well

Checksheet: What Motivates Me?

1) Check the following items which are motivators for *you*. By a motivator we mean a force or influence that causes you to work harder, more productively, or more creatively.

2) After you have checked the items which are important to you as motivators, rank the 5 items with the most motivational significance.

Keep these two checksheets handy for analysis of their significance, motivation-wise.

___ Good working conditions	___ Continuing growth on the job
___ Friendly associates	___ Recognition by peers
___ Full delegation	___ Special assignments
___ The paycheck	___ Hospital and medical plan
___ An understanding boss	
___ Clear-cut goals	___ Vacation policy
___ Pension plan	___ Recognition by the boss
___ A job well done	
___ Well-furnished office	___ Annual bonus
___ More responsibility	___ Involvement in important decisions
___ New, challenging assignments	
	___ Field trips
___ Job security	___ Advancement
___ Periodic pay increases	___ Training courses

As you read this chapter, consider the questions below. They loom very importantly to anyone who is trying to get a "handle" on this business of motivation. Some key questions:

1a. What triggers people's behavior? 1b. Why do they behave in certain ways at certain times and yet so differently at other times?

2. How do I go about getting my people to perform the way I want them to?

3. Why do people, at times, seem to act in ways not in their self-interest?

4. How can motivation be sustained once it's kindled?

5. What is the significance of money as a motivator?

6. Can people ever be fully satisfied with their circumstances?

7. How can you get someone to achieve their potential?

8. How can I understand myself more fully? Is this important to an understanding of the motivation of others?

Answers to these questions appear on pages 249–250. Defer reading these answers until you have worked your way through the entire chapter.

What's In This Chapter

Here's what comes next:

☐ Some background (theories) about motivation—a brief look at what an early and several more recent writers (behavioral science researchers) have to say about it.

☐ We then move from motivational theory to practice. We present 30 plus practical ways to help you "turn on" your people.

☐ In Chapter 5 we become even more specific and present motivational strategies for particular classes of workers such as women, older workers, people with disabilities, people with diverse cultural backgrounds, high achievers, and others.

☐ We discuss the significance of the two check sheets you completed at the start of this chapter (pages 139–140).

☐ We provide some answers to the eight questions about motivation presented at the outset (pages 249–250).

☐ We set forth some brief, summary concepts about Chapters 4 and 5 (pages 251–252).

☐ We provide a series of questions and problems for discussion which may be used in in-house management development workshops and college/university classes in management (pages 252–254).

THEORIES OF MOTIVATION

We as managers have already developed our own "theories" of motivation. We may not have gotten them from a systematic collection of data or controlled experiments, nor reduced them neatly to writing. Nevertheless, from our experience we have developed some assumptions about people and their behavior. We use these guides in our day-to-day actions.

Some of our theories also may have been acquired from our bosses. For example, if we tell our supervisors that we have a difficult subordinate and don't quite know what to do about it, we may well get a prompt, direct, and impatient response such as: "Just tell him what's what. Lay it on the line. You're the boss, aren't you?" So our boss' theory with a problem employee is to be direct, firm, use your authority as a supervisor, and don't spend a lot of time listening, fact gathering, counseling, supporting, or discussing alternatives.

In any case, a more helpful way to understand motivation is to review what several leading theorists on motivation have been telling us. By theory we don't mean "arm-chair" philosophizing or speculating. Rather, we mean a body of concepts developed systematically from planned observation, research, and specialized professional experience.

A common reaction to theory by many "practical" managers is: "Don't give me all that ivory tower malarky; just give me the practical stuff, what really works." Yet, as the late, great social psychologist Dr. Kurt Lewin observed, "There is nothing so practical as a good theory."

Frank G. Goble, a successful business executive and management consultant, in a report for the American Management Association on *Motivation and Effectiveness* (1971), believes that an understanding of motivation theory is important for these reasons:

1. Managers who understand the "why" as well as the "how" will know the "how" better.

2. Theorists typically are ahead of the pragmatists. If we follow theory, we are in a better position to learn about new ideas.

3. If you understand theory you are better able to teach ideas about motivation to others, particularly those just starting to supervise people.

4. Scientific progress typically is based on theoretical breakthroughs, not just blind trial and error.

5. Motivational theory has broad application. In addition to its use in organizations, it has bearing on child training, family relations, education, economics, political science, etc.

As you will see, the various theorists have approached motivation differently. Nevertheless, their ideas do have some significant common threads we will bring together after our discussion of their theories.

As you read, compare the theorists' ideas with your own hunches, guesses, and assumptions. You may find that they have insights into human behavior that have eluded you in your managerial career thus far.

Scientific Management ("Jump for the Jelly Beans")

Up until the late 1930s, organizations and managers operated on the theory that money was the prime motivator of people who worked: Pay them more and they will be more hard working, more loyal, and more obedient. The major ideas underlying this thinking were developed formally by a mechanical engineer named Frederick W. Taylor in his work *Principles of Scientific Management* (New York: Harper & Brothers, 1911).

Taylor, the father of scientific management, emphasized the performance of specialized tasks to bring about efficiency. He and others at that time also stressed: a) the use of time and motion studies and work analysis to help design efficient jobs, plus b) reliance upon a piecework system of compensation. In Taylor's scheme of things, managers planned all activities and the employees executed them. Management's job was to set job standards, train workers to perform their tasks, and monitor performance closely for conformance to standards.

In Taylorism or efficiency engineering, all workers were assumed to possess similar needs, and boredom as a result of high job specialization was of no concern. Recruitment was to be accomplished carefully in relation to job standards, and those who could not perform to the standards could seek employment elsewhere. Taylor was particularly concerned with achieving a system that counteracted "natural" tendencies to "soldiering" (or loafing).

Taylor's ideas ran into difficulty with organized labor, which saw them as designed to produce a "speed-up." In 1915, Army and Navy appropriation bills forbade the use of funds for time studies or payment of bonuses. In 1916, anti-efficiency riders were added to the Fortifications, Army, Navy, Post Office, and sundry civil bills.

To put Taylorism into proper perspective, it should be recognized that in Taylor's era, most people had limited education and literally worked just to put bread on the table. Understandably, they could be expected to "jump for the jelly beans" like well-trained seals. Notions of human relations, employee involvement and participation, enriched jobs, morale and job satisfaction, individual differences, and group decision making were not developed until the late 1930s and into the '40s and '50s. Ideas of the latter sort were espoused by various behavioral science theorists, several of which are discussed below.

The Personality Approach ("People don't have any initiative around here.")

Social psychologist Chris Argyris, a prolific management writer and researcher formerly of Yale and now at Harvard, studied the relationship of worker functioning and needs in relation to organizational life. He concluded that organizations tend to stifle basic personality needs—for growth, accomplishment, contribution, assumption of responsibility. That is to say, he saw a basic incongruity between the needs of a mature, healthy adult personality and the harsh, ongoing requirements of the formal organization.

Dr. Argyris stated in *Personality and Organization—The Conflict Between System and the Individual* (New York: Harper and Brothers, 1957) that if managers used their people along classic or traditional management lines, employees will necessarily work in an environment where five things occur:

1) They will be given minimal control over their workaday world.
2) Their behavior is expected to be subordinate, passive, dependent.
3) They need only have a short-time perspective.
4) They need only use a few skin-surface, shallow abilities.
5) They are expected to produce under job and organizational conditions that can only lead to psychological failure.

In short, management receives normal, healthy adults who are responsible, self-reliant, and independent, and confines them into roles that require little responsibility, self-reliance, or independence.

The result: The production of infantile behavior, with a heavy set of submissive, dependent, and frustrated responses. Thus, when management observes this regressive behavior, it is convinced that its initial assumptions about limited capacities of individuals were correct. ("People don't have any initiative around here.") It then imposes more restraints and controls, and a cycle that crushes motivation starts anew.

In general, Argyris' thesis is that organizations have a need for low-level, low-aspiring people. And because there are not enough of them to go around, the organization works very hard at creating them.

Guidelines for the Manager

Argyris' thesis, developed in the 1950s, is certainly a gloomy one. But the manager can do many things to rise above the kind of management he described. Certainly the ideas of McGregor, Herzberg, and Likert, discussed below, can be tapped to manage in a more empowering and thus more motivating way.

Hierarchy of Needs ("What a man can be, he must be.")

Clinical psychologist Abraham H. Maslow developed in the 1950s a widely referenced theory of motivation which he termed "The Hierarchy of Needs." (See Figure 4-1.)

The hierarchy (in *Motivation and Personality*, New York: Harper & Row, 1954) covered five levels of needs:

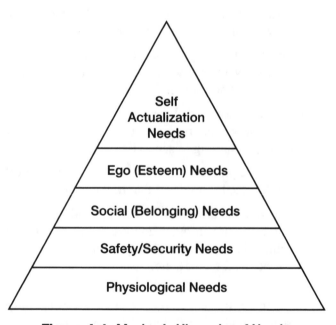

Figure 4-1. Maslow's Hierarchy of Needs.

1. **Physiological:** includes such survival needs as oxygen, water, food, warmth, sleep, exercise, etc.
2. **Safety/security:** includes physical safety plus economic security and freedom from threats, arbitrariness, and discrimination.
3. **Social/belonging:** includes acceptance, to be part of a group, to give and receive affection, identification with a successful team.
4. **Ego needs:** includes needs for self-esteem, recognition from others, status, prestige.
5. **Self-actualization:** the need for self-fulfillment or self-realization, to create at a high level, challenge.

Note: While ego needs relate to doing what you are capable of achieving—tapping your competency—self-actualization relates to a reaching out for your fullest possible potential. To quote Dr. Maslow: "What a man *can* be, he *must* be."

In his theory, Maslow saw people moving from lower-order needs to higher-level ones—a sequential movement—but only as those below became satisfied. Thus, if a person were suffering from hunger (level one), that individual would not be eager to write poetry (level five). There is an adage that man does not live by bread alone, which is very true. Man *may* live by bread alone, but only as long as there is no bread, that is, bread is an item of scarcity.

Maslow also believed that a need once satisfied can no longer serve as a motivator. Thus, once an organization—and the manager—meet lower-order needs via adequate pay, money can no longer serve as a motivator. Of course, people are always glad to get more money, but it won't necessarily provide added motivation. Conversely, higher-order needs, such as the need for recognition or the opportunity to function creatively, are *insatiable*—people simply can't get enough of that wonderful stuff.

It should be noted that:

1) Personality, education, training, and social and cultural factors inhibit many persons from functioning at the two upper-need levels. They thus may be satisfied to have only their lower-order needs met. These same factors may also produce movement along the hierarchy in a non-sequential fashion. For example, an individual may have strong needs for self-actualization but very few social needs.
2) The more basic needs are simple and satisfied quickly, like eating a meal. Conversely, each higher-level need is more complex than the preceding one and takes much longer for its satisfaction: Self-actualization ordinarily takes many years to achieve.
3) A particular need does not require total satisfaction before a new one is triggered. In fact, most of us can be at least partially satisfied in all of our basic needs somewhat simultaneously, e.g., modest income is adequate to encourage movement up the hierarchy.
4) Movement in the hierarchy is not always upward; shifts both up and down are possible. Thus a person may reach a particular level in the hierarchy and move downward as his situation or status changes: a recession, a downsizing, or a merger may push one down the hierarchy, and lower-order needs would re-emerge.
5) People obviously differ in their methods of satisfying a given need: A person may meet his higher-order needs by working in the community or in professional or trade organizations. This may be essential if such opportunities are not available on the job.

Guides for the Manager

The Hierarchy of Needs is a useful way of providing motivation based on the meeting of *individual* needs or differences. Thus, if an employee is group-oriented (strong social needs), the boss should try to provide opportunities for group activity. Similarly, the employee who has strong ego or esteem needs should be afforded plenty of praise, recognition, and possibly visibility. And the one who is attuned to self-fulfillment needs should be given opportunities to be creative, to solve special problems, to innovate, etc.

To maximize your understanding of and benefit from Maslow's concepts, you should complete the worksheet in Figure 4-2. It will give you the opportunity to apply meaningfully what you have learned. Simply (1) list the names of your staffers in the left-hand column, and (2) place an x in one of the five columns on the right. This procedure will identify clearly for you the location of staff members on The Hierarchy of Needs.

Note: You may wish to re-read the ideas about the hierarchy to ensure a fuller understanding of it.

Name of staff member	Stage				
	1	2	3	4	5
1.					
2.					
3.					
4.					
5.					
6.					
7.					
8.					

Figure 4-2. Worksheet to apply the Hierarchy of Needs to staff members.

Theory X and Theory Y: The Self-Fulfilling Prophecy ("They only need to know no more than the job requires.")

In the widely quoted work *The Human Side of Enterprise* (New York: McGraw-Hill, 1961), behavioral scientist Douglas McGregor of Massachusetts Institute of Technology presented two classifications of assumptions managers may make about people and work. He labelled these assumptions Theory X and Theory Y.

Theory X Has These Assumptions:

1. The average person dislikes work and will avoid it if at all possible.

2. Thus, the manager must coerce, control, direct, and threaten his people with punishment to secure their effort toward organizational objectives.

3. The average person prefers to be directed, tries to avoid responsibility, has little ambition, and primarily wants security.

Theory Y Has These Quite Opposite Assumptions:

1. Work is a natural activity for people.

2. People will work willingly without external controls and threats of punishment.

3. Given the right rewards to meet their needs for satisfaction and self-actualization, people will commit themselves to organizational objectives.

4. People seek rather than shun responsibility.

5. The ability to use one's imagination, ingenuity and creativity in organizational problem solving is *widely* distributed in the population.

6. In today's organizations, people's intellectual capacities are used only partially.

Obviously, Theory X is a pessimistic, low-trust way of looking at people whereas Theory Y is totally upbeat, optimistic, and high trust.

McGregor was not saying that these are the only ways of looking at people in the world of work. But that they are simply two ways. His central thesis was that the way the manager goes about trying to influence people's behavior is determined by the set of assumptions he carries around in his head. Thus, a self-fulfilling prophecy becomes operative.

If you believe that people are inherently lazy, motivated only by money, selfish, dependent, resist change, short-sighted, irresponsible, respond only to being pushed or threatened, you will act on that assumption. Conversely, if you believe that people are active, possess many motives (money is only one), wish to achieve goals, are mature and responsible, are capable of self-direction, are ever learning, are innovative, seek meaning, are self-actualizing, and possess far vision, you will act on that assumption.

Story: I had a workman replace a couple of old drafty, wooden windows with new, modern, vinyl-clad, well-insulated ones of the tilt-in type for easy cleaning. As he was finishing up, doing a very careful job of caulking around the windows, I complimented him on his neat, painstaking performance. He said in reply: "You have a nice house here and you take care of it. So I want to give you a really good job, even if it takes longer. When I come into a run-down neighborhood where no one cares, I do the job quickly. They don't care and I don't care. Why should I?" What triggered the difference in his behavior? Clearly the assumptions he made about his clients!

And a bit of added evidence concerning the role of our expectations in motivation. In various experiments, schoolteachers, who had average students, were told (falsely) that their students were outstanding, exceptionally gifted. **The result:** The teachers really pitched in and at course's end both grade levels and IQs were elevated. Previous teachers had underestimated the students' competence and unconsciously encouraged the students to expect less of themselves.

Guidelines for the Manager

You have your choice in your use of motivational strategies. If you look at your people as static, limited, unimprovable, and disinterested in organizational goals, you will be consistently thinking in terms of strategies that emphasize surveillance, bribes, threats, discipline, and limited flow of information. ("They only need to know no more than the job requires.") If you see your people as able, creative, and teachable, you will be utilizing motivational strategies that emphasize involvement, participation, trust, increased responsibility, opportunities for growth and creativity, sharing information freely, and the use of praise and recognition. And remember, your assumptions will be communicated by your voice tone and body language, not just your words, and certainly by your actual behavior toward your people.

Employee-Centered Supervision ("I've got to keep the pressure on for production.")

The Institute for Social Research of the University of Michigan has conducted many studies since 1947 in industry and government concerning productivity in relation to group member satisfaction and leadership. The head of that research group was Dr. Rensis Likert, who also taught sociology and psychology at the University.

Basically, Dr. Likert found that supervisors with the best productivity records focused on the human aspects of worker problems in an effort to build effective work groups with high performance goals. Likert called such supervisors "employee-centered." Supervisors who operated along more traditional lines of management—scientific management or Theory X style, if you will—had lower-producing work units. Likert called these supervisors "job-centered." As one of those latter group supervisors put it, "This interest-in-people approach is all right, but it's a luxury. I've got to keep pressure on for production, and when I get production up, then I can afford to take time to show an interest in my employees and their problems." (Rensis Likert, *New Patterns of Management,* New York: McGraw-Hill, 1961, p. 7.)

In general, Likert found that supervisors of high-producing units operated along these lines:

1. They were employee oriented rather than production oriented. (This might even include counseling on personal problems.)
2. They provided general rather than close supervision to their workers.

3. They tended to spend more time with their workers.
4. They had high standards (high performance goals).
5. They used group methods of supervision, i.e., when problems arose they called the work group together to resolve their difficulties in a collegial fashion.
6. They seemed to apply less pressure to their people (per attitude survey reports as to how the workers felt).
7. They were able "to go to bat" for their people to a higher degree because they had acquired greater influence with their bosses.
8. They received greater confidence and trust from their workers.
9. They tended to avoid dwelling on workers' mistakes because they believed the workers learned from those unsatisfactory experiences. (Conversely, foremen in low-producing sections tended to be critical and punitive when miscues occurred.)
10. They spent more time on worker training.
11. They integrated themselves more into the work group and thus were perceived as "really part of the group."
12. They were more interested in employees' ideas.
13. They created units that tended to have greater pride in their capacity to produce or with greater loyalty and attraction to the group (high peer-group loyalty). The workers thus tended to cooperate with one another more.

Guidelines for the Manager

People who come to work ordinarily bring their motivation—the will to do—with them. However, the operating style of the manager will determine whether that motivation will be unleashed or stifled. The 13 points above—essentially team building and team management—are helpful skill factors in tapping and maintaining high employee motivation. Much of it depends on your willingness as a manager to think and act in terms of "empowering" people, i.e., recognizing that they do have needs to contribute and require the freedom to do so. Alternatively, operating in traditional management styles can only get your people to work for the paycheck alone.

Remember, as a manager you can, indeed, get people to work. You have enough power and authority to do that. But you can't necessarily get them to work hard, enthusiastically, imaginatively, or creatively. Only your workers can decide how much of their available energy they should expend in a positive way.

The Motivation-Hygiene Theory ("Few of us are satisfied with our paychecks.")

Research in the 1960s among engineers and accountants in the Pittsburgh area, and replicated later in studies in other occupational groups, produced a "two-factor" theory of motivation. The researcher, who was based at Case Western Reserve University at the time of his investigation, is internationally known psychologist Frederick Herzberg.

Dr. Herzberg and his staff interviewed their subjects to learn about work experiences that produced favorable vs. unfavorable reactions. They found this duality: Job experiences producing good reactions typically related to job *content* —the tasks being worked on—and those incidents leading to bad reactions related to job *context* —experiences *surrounding* the work.

Herzberg called the work-related factors causing favorable experiences and reactions satisfiers or *motivators*. They are ("One More Time: How Do You Motivate Employees?" *Harvard Business Review,* January-February 1968):

☐ **Achievement**—a chance to engage in independent problem solving, complete tasks, see final results.

☐ **Recognition**—acknowledgement of accomplishment.

☐ **The Work Itself**—job content providing challenge, interest, and variety as opposed to dull, boring activities.

☐ **Responsibility**—having full responsibility and accountability for results, including freedom to act, control, decide.

☐ **Advancement**—movement to a higher-level task or activity.

☐ **Growth**—growing, learning, expanding on the job.

The factors producing dissatisfaction he termed *hygiene* factors. They arose from job *context,* the environment or surroundings, rather than from the task itself. Hygiene (or maintenance) factors, said Herzberg, don't serve as motivators, but are useful for "pain avoidance." They reduce unhappiness. These preventive factors are:

☐ **Company policies and administration**—red tape or a reorganization may produce a lot of negative feelings.

☐ **Supervision**—the supervisor's technical ability does not bear on the worker's motivation. While oppressive supervision may even lead to extreme behavior such as sabotage, pleasant, helpful supervision won't augment motivation for anyone in an impoverished job.

☐ **Working conditions**—good ones prevent unhappiness, but don't bear on motivation.

☐ **Money, status, seniority**—all of us need these to survive.

Hygiene is very necessary, says Herzberg, for it keeps the body from becoming sick. But it doesn't provide motivation, the will to perform. Only satisfaction from the work provides that.

The significance of Herzberg's investigations is that motivation is not to be viewed as one-dimensional as had been previously supposed. That is to say, motivation does not operate on a continuum with dissatisfaction on one end and satisfaction on the other, one being the opposite of the other, so if you change one factor you necessarily affect the other. Rather, because the factors leading to job satisfaction (motivation) are so different and distinct from those leading to dissatisfaction (hygiene), satisfaction and dissatisfaction have to be examined, understood, and administered *separately.* Herzberg called motivation and hygiene "unipolar traits."

As summed up succinctly by management professors E. Dennis Middlemist and Michael A. Hitt in their *Organizational Behavior—Managerial Strategies for Performance* (West Publishing Co., St. Paul, Minnesota, 1988), ". . . satisfaction and dissatisfaction are not merely opposite ends of one attitude but are separate and distinct attitudes. In other words, the opposite of high job satisfaction is not high dissatisfaction but, rather, is low job satisfaction. Alternatively, the opposite of high dissatisfaction is simply low dissatisfaction."

Note: A good way to distinguish between the two factors is as follows:

Motivation: Am I *used* well?

Hygiene: Am I *treated* well?

Herzberg's emphasis on the work itself as a potential motivator led him to develop the concept of the enriched job. In fact, he has been credited with being "the father of job enrichment." An enriched, well-designed job, per

Herzberg, has these empowering qualities or characteristics (described in Frederick Herzberg, *The Managerial Choice,* Salt Lake City: Olympus Pub. Co., 1982):

Direct feedback: Have it come to the worker, unfiltered through the boss; and it should be objective (i.e., work oriented rather than person oriented).

Client relationship: Permit the worker to deal directly with the in-house client or outside customer.

New learning: People require constant growth, challenge, stimulation, new experiences.

Scheduling: The one doing the job can best decide pace, timing, sequencing, prioritizing.

Unique expertise: Give people an opportunity to apply their uniqueness, to do their own thing.

Control our resources: To the extent possible, let people assume responsibility for cost control, requisitioning materials, etc.; encourage creation of cost and profit centers.

Direct communication authority: Don't insist on clearing everything "through channels"; give full freedom to contact others and for them to contact your workers.

Personal accountability: Provide maximum freedom and minimum controls, and checks and reviews along with full accountability for results.

Note: Job enlargement is not the same as job enrichment. The former only adds like tasks to the job, whereas the latter upgrades the job and is thus a motivator. **Example:** giving the janitor six restrooms to maintain as opposed to four makes the job structurally larger, but is hardly enriching or empowering.

Guidelines for the Manager

Herzberg presents a powerful set of motivational ideas to you, as a manager. Most important is the notion that the work itself—not money and all the other expensive, limited goodies—which you control, must provide opportunities to achieve, accomplish, imagine, initiate, innovate, and grow. You thus should think continually in terms of enriching jobs and empowering your people to

turn them on and thus to discharge better their duties and responsibilities. Roadblocks to effectiveness in the areas of policy, procedure, relationships—hygiene factors—should be identified and removed to keep people "well."

In general, Herzberg tells us, as managers, to so manage that we meet peoples' *dual* needs:

1) to avoid pain or unhappiness (hygiene).
2) to grow psychologically—to expand, to create, to contribute (motivation).

Note: Motivators maintain satisfaction/motivation for long time periods. They don't require constant supervisory attention, for they are self-sustaining. Conversely, hygiene or maintenance needs are never satisfied completely and require constant replenishment, that is, few of us are satisfied with our paychecks and we need a good physical environment all the time or we get "sick" or unhappy.

While both needs must be met, we can't expect motivation to take place until the hygiene need is satisfied. Nor can we be creative while cold, hungry, thirsty, or harassed in unwanted ways. So hygiene eliminates deficits, but doesn't create gains (motivation). And motivation per se comes from the individual worker, not the manager. The latter can only set up conditions (e.g., challenging work assignments) so that it takes place.

The careful reader will note the close relationship of Herzberg's ideas to those of Maslow. Recall that Maslow distinguished between lower-level needs—physiological, safety—essentially hygiene—vs. higher-order needs—esteem, self-actualization—which turn out to be Herzberg's true motivators.

Expectancy Theory ("Why knock yourself out?")

An interesting and practical theory of motivation, developed by industrial psychologist Victor Vroom (*Work and Motivation,* New York: John Wiley & Sons, 1964) tells us that motivation is a function of the expectation of a reward and the importance placed on that reward. More specifically, as stated by management professor Dr. Edward E. Lawler (*Motivation in Work Organizations,* Monterey, CA: Brooks/Cole 1973), four conditions must be met before the worker will be motivated to perform:

1. **Reward value.** The employee must value the reward/outcome/end result related to a given per-

formance level. Obviously, if there is no value of the reward or no fear of punishment, no motivation will occur.

2. **Capability.** The worker must believe he can do the task, if he engages in the effort, and execute it well enough to merit the reward. This is a personal confidence element, of course.

3. **Confidence in the rewards system.** The performer also must believe that proper performance will net him the valued reward. This means the system works and thus can be trusted fully.

4. **No unwanted costs/outcomes.** The worker is certain that his effort will not produce negative outcomes or unacceptable costs. **Example:** A potential rate-buster is likely to shun the opportunity to make more money and sticks to the group-established production standard to remain one of the group. Being at odds with the group is hardly a reward.

Note: Expectancy is based on past history or experience. For example, you may have learned that working much harder produces no better results. ("Why knock yourself out? Things are so screwed up around here we can never get those shipments right.")

Or, worse still, if better results were produced, high performance may not have had any relationship to the available rewards. ("All the promotions either go to the 'apple polishers' or to those who've been here 50 years.") And the rewards themselves may not have been worthwhile or may even have had negative value. ("Yeah, you can get a promotion all right, but who wants to end up in the boondocks?" or "It's a good deal, if you can take all the headaches and hassles that go with it.")

Guides for the Manager

As indicated, employees must have a high expectation about their effort and their resultant enhanced performance. It thus is the supervisor's job to ensure that there are no barriers or roadblocks to high performance in the system or environment, like lack of authority to accompany responsibility, low-quality materials or cumbersome procedures. Also, the supervisor must identify on an individualized basis the rewards employees value highly. For example, a highly paid, able employee is not likely to be turned on by more money. Rather, that individual is more likely to respond to more job challenge, more involvement, greater responsibility, or opportunities for innovating and pioneering. Other employees may respond favorably to a reward of time

off, a pat on the back, a chance to participate in a quality improvement group, an opportunity to attend a prestigious training program, or a chance to conduct a field visit or inspection.

To implement expectancy theory, management writer Thomas L. Quick offers these five steps ("Expectancy Theory in Five Simple Steps," *Training and Development Journal,* July 1988):

1. **Define expectations.** Although this would seem to be an obvious advisory, the facts of organizational life are that all too many managers don't take the time to spell out vital goals—day-to-day, long-term (12–18 months), problem solving (working on what's "bugging" us), innovative (seeking new, creative approaches), personal (worker development and growth). All these goals can readily be tied into the regular performance review system. Says Quick, "Expectancy theory can help shift appraisal systems from a subjective, input orientation to a more objective, results-oriented orientation."

2. **Make work valuable.** All employees have personal goals—money, accomplishment, professional development, challenge, self-esteem, meeting social needs. The manager's job is to blend and complement personal goals with those of the organization. Obviously, greater commitment will ensue when people feel that their personal goals are in line with, rather than in opposition to, organizational goals and expectations. But you, as a manager, must know what people value. So for best results, tailor the work and assignments to workers' drives, needs, and preferences.

3. **Make work doable.** The manager can't afford to assume that the employee can go ahead on the assignment without a concern whether it can be done successfully. Uncertainty about accomplishment is a road to demotivation. So the manager should:

   ☐ **Make assignments realistic.** Check out employee perceptions about the task assignment. They may be as important as your own.

   ☐ **Monitor progress.** Know what is and isn't being done and provide help if needed.

   ☐ **Negotiate assignments.** Don't hesitate to alter an assignment if it will use employee skills better. Also, adopt a flexible work schedule as appropriate. And a mutually agreed upon evaluation method will avoid later conflicts and hard feelings.

4. **Provide regular feedback.** Don't wait for the year-end job review to do this. The worst kind of appraisal at year's end is "appraisal by surprise." So regularly provide constructive criticism and positive reinforcement (praise). And the best (most meaningful and motivating) feedback is marked by giving it as close to the event as possible, being specific, skipping past grievances, and keeping it task rather than person oriented. ("You don't have the right attitude.")

5. **Provide rewards when expectations are met.** Make it clear that a good job will be recognized. Think in terms of praise rather than dollars, for the former is more lasting and meaningful. Financial rewards typically are too small and too late to impact a lot.

Summary Points on the Various Theorists' Ideas

A common thread running through the motivational ideas of our several behavioral science theorists is the importance of the work itself, and all its attributes, as a motivational force. This is understandable, for what we are is what we do. Work gives us our identity, our feelings of self-worth, and our status in both the organization and in society at large.

Note: In earlier times people identified so closely with their work that they adopted surnames based on their occupations: Baker, Barber, Butcher, Carpenter, Cook, Draper, Farmer, Fisher, Hunter, Mason, Tanner, Shepherd, Shoemaker, Stockman, Tailor, Wainwright, Weaver, etc.

In recessionary periods the loss of jobs creates an increase in depression. This is not only because of its obvious financial effect, but as Joseph Cassius, a Memphis, Tennessee, clinical psychologist sees it, "People lose their jobs. They tie in their sense of self-worth with the work they do, so not having a job means they're not okay. This then hooks into the basic sense of inadequacy that we all have," (Don Oldenburg, "Feeling Signs of Better Times," *The Washington Post,* May 19, 1992).

How the work itself can be utilized as a powerful motivator is the substance of this chapter.

MOTIVATIONAL TECHNIQUES AND CONCEPTS

If you are truly interested in unleashing potential and increasing creativity and commitment, here are a good number of helpful motivational tools and concepts. And the best part is that they don't require any special cash outlays or even approvals from your boss.

But they do take a bit of courage and trust in your people. Are you ready to rise to that challenge?

ORGANIZATIONAL CLIMATE: THE CULTURE WE ACTUALLY LIVE (WORK) IN

Many organizations choose to direct their energies toward protecting individuals (and itself) from failure. This philosophical orientation has the outcome of providing a 'safety' net for individuals in the organization, and to guarantee a risk-free experience: an experience in which failure is prevented but success is not assured.

—Drs. Cheryl K. Duvall and Roy H. Autry, "Empowering for Success: Developing an Individual's Freedom to Act," a paper prepared for the 1991 Annual Conference of the American Society for Training and Development, San Francisco.

Every organization and every segment of it has a distinctive climate or atmosphere. It is not something that has been prescribed in any manual or policy statement, but it is there. People who work in those shops or offices are aware of it, feel it, talk about it, assess it, and respond and react to it.

Climate, obviously, takes many forms, ranging from the highly encouraging to the highly discouraging, concerned with assuring success vs. designed to prevent failure. Much-quoted management authority Peter Drucker sees it typically as less than encouraging: "So much of what we call management consists in making it difficult for people to work." And: "I'm convinced we know everything about quenching motivation in a person but nothing about kindling it."

Drucker, at times, does tend to overstate things for effect, to provide a bit of shock to get managers to think. But whether or not we accept his rather gloomy views of what goes on in organizations, we probably can agree that organizational climate can be better—more success oriented—than it often is.

A negative climate results when employees are subject to management behaviors they perceive as controlling, fear inducing, punishing, shaming, blaming, and judging. A positive climate results when managerial responses are involving, informing, rewarding, encouraging, supporting, trusting, sharing, caring, listening, and growth-inducing. In the latter type of climate, risk taking is favored and failures aren't punished. Team-work and creativity are encouraged.

If the climate is highly negative, people may well become defensive and fearful. The fear response, per management consultant Hugo Barucco ("Fear and Productivity: More Closely Related Than We Think?," *The Management Review,* January 1981), produces a protective "fight/flight/freeze" reaction. More specifically, *fight* results in responses such as these: anger, hostility, resentment, antagonism, opposition, annoyance, irritation, disrespect, discounting, and inconsideration. Barucco didn't specifically state that these feelings might result in various forms of acting out behavior such as acts of sabotage—recall the placement of soft-drink bottles in sealed fender wells of cars by disgruntled auto workers some years back—but the intense reactions he lists certainly imply such behavior. Pilfering may also be a form of worker strike-back or anti-organizational behavior.

Flight reactions, according to Barucco, might take these forms: withdrawal, avoidance, evasion, absenteeism, regression, retreat, neglect, thoughtlessness, absence, termination.

Freeze responses might include inactivity, apathy, idleness, passivity, laziness, stagnation, procrastination, lethargy, insensibility, dullness.

The point should be made that no single manager can alleviate all the ills that large, modern organizations create to form a less-than-healthy climate, such as bureaucracy, impersonality, conformity, status quoism, super specialization, overmanagement, exploitation. But the individual manager can do quite a bit to recognize individuality, encourage creativity, and unleash potential. This section presents a number of practical suggestions toward such objectives.

INTRINSIC REWARDS

Rewards and motivators fall into two categories: *intrinsic* (or internal) and *extrinsic* (or external). While people do respond to external rewards (threats or pressure from the boss, money, benefits, etc.), the carrot-and-stick approach, you will be far ahead of the game if you can find ways to provide internal rewards. One of the most significant motivators, then, is to provide tasks and other work activities which are *autotelic* in nature, i.e., having a purpose in itself. This is the way you engender self-propulsion. People who are really intrigued or challenged by a novel, exciting task attack

it with relish. They may even stay after 5 p.m. to work on it, take it home, or come early the next day.

Extrinsic rewards can get people to perform, to do enough to meet the minimum standards. But such rewards won't necessarily spark enthusiastic, innovative, and creative performance.

One way to appreciate the distinction between intrinsic vs. extrinsic rewards is to regard them as existing on a continuum, extending from fear, threats, punishment, and financial incentives and benefits on one side to challenging work, involvement, and high standards on the other side:

| Extrinsic | Intrinsic |
| Rewards | Rewards |

Research by sociologist Clifford J. Mottaz supports this view ("Not Everybody Wants to Climb The Ladder," *Changing Times,* June 1986). He states that intrinsic rewards provide greater satisfaction than social rewards (friendly, helpful, supportive colleagues and bosses) or organizational rewards (pay, promotion, security, and fringes).

Incidentally, one extrinsic reward—praise, which recognizes accomplishment—is a powerful motivator. This factor is discussed later in this chapter.

Consulting psychologist Gary Schuman has pointed out ("New Motivational Strategies to Pursue," *Management Solutions,* January 1987) that the traditional motivational "currencies" of work such as pay and promotion are convenient for managers to use because they are tangible, concrete rewards. Conversely, intrinsic motivators are harder to identify, understand, and distribute. But in light of today's more educated workforce plus reduced opportunities for advancement due to downsizing, Dr. Schuman advocates intrinsic motivators. He buttresses his position by citing a Gallup Poll that asked workers to rank a list of 46 possible motivators, including money. The top 10 selections were: working with peers who provide respect, interesting work, recognition for accomplishment, a chance to develop skills and abilities, opportunities to be creative, having ideas listened to, seeing an end result, working for an effective boss, a job that isn't too easy, and having a mentor. Money was not in the top ten. (Money and motivation is addressed in a later section.)

Incidentally, research on creativity at Brandeis University by psychologist Teresa Amabile suggests that work on creative tasks can be hindered by external rewards (reported by Alfie Kohn, "Art for Art's Sake," *Psychology Today,* September 1987). Why? When people are working for a reward, they are less likely to find that work interesting in itself and thus not worth pursuing voluntarily. Dr. Amabile has come up with what she calls the Intrinsic Motivation Principle of Creativity: "People will be creative when they feel motivated primarily by the interest, enjoyment, satisfaction and challenge of the work itself—and not by external pressures." Dr. Amabile finds that a reward encourages us to focus only on the task, to do it rapidly, and not to risk too much. So we produce satisfactorily, but not creatively. Amabile believes, too, that when we work for a reward we often see ourselves as controlled. This lack of autonomy restrains creativity. Other restrainers are surveillance, deadlines, and evaluation. And the more complex the activity the more likely it is to be set back by extrinsic rewards. Why? If we expect a reward we may work faster and produce more, but the products may not be very imaginative.

Dr. Amabile states that the early periods of preparation for a creative task—information gathering and learning techniques—can be helped by conventional rewards. So can the later process of validation and communication of one's idea. But the in-between phases—dreaming up something novel—takes the motivation of love, not money.

Note: The best motivational approaches recognize that motivation is internal—that the desire and will to do something springs from the needs within us. People always will try to satisfy their needs in one way or another. If their needs can't be satisfied on the job, they may try to do it off the job—via community work, volunteer activity, work in professional societies, teaching, writing, home projects, etc. The question for you, as manager, is this: If there is that motivational force within, am I tapping it, ignoring it, or even stifling it? Do I want my people to exercise their individual initiative? Or am I content to permit them to expect others to assume responsibility and just react to events, never taking charge of them?

INDIVIDUAL DIFFERENCES, NEEDS, AND INTERESTS

Some managers operate on the unrealistic assumption that there are universal motivators, typically tangible, to which *everyone* will respond. Or, worse still, that the things which motivate *us* will motivate our employees.

But the facts of organizational life are that each of our staffers is an individual. He thus has his own particular interests. For example, Mildred likes to dabble in PR and "wheel and deal" as your liaison to other organizations. George likes to write. Mary likes to talk to groups. Pat likes to travel. And so on.

Why not use their special skills and interests above and beyond their regular duties? These opportunities are surefire ways to provide recognition, unleash energy and enthusiasm, and encourage self-expansion. In effect, the best motivational approach begins with a consideration of the needs of individuals.

Maslow's Hierarchy of Needs supports a multi- rather than a mono-motivational approach. That is to say, at different stages of their careers, people are likely to be at different need levels of the hierarchy, or have stronger needs than other people in relation to any one Maslowian level, e.g., strong support from one's teammates.

Also worth considering, when making work assignments, is *when* people are at their best. Some of us are morning people and relish an early start. Others are the opposite and get into high gear in the p.m.

What we are saying, then, is to recognize the principle of individual differences. Of course, it is one thing to accept this principle as a "nice" theory. It is quite another to apply it to the need systems of your staff members. Part of the difficulty lies in learning what turns on each staffer.

How can the manager learn of people's needs? Fortunately, there is a simple and effective way: Ask your subordinates! By "ask" we don't necessarily mean posing a direct question about needs. Rather, by being in frequent contact with your staff in both work and social situations, by getting to know them *as individuals,* you will automatically learn of their special needs. The adage "One man's meat is another man's poison" is still operative.

One way to keep the concept of individual differences in mind is to consider (and use) the formula, $B = f(E \times P)$. This means that behavior is a function of not one, but two elements: environment (situation) and personality. Thus, George may be a terror-producing bear in the office, but given another situation, e.g., a party, he may become a real pussycat. So a change in the situation results in a change in how the person perceives it, thereby producing another kind of behavior. **The principle:** Change the E factor and you may alter the behavior of the person.

This chapter has been designed to give you the grounding needed to understand and to apply a variety of motivational concepts to your employees. Use the "Guidesheet to Aid in Planning for Employee Motivation" (Figure 4-3, page 207) to plan different motivational approaches for your work group members. ("Different strokes for different folks.")

When working with a diverse workforce, you should consider a principle of motivation that educators, psychologists and successful managers have long recognized: namely, all people are motivated, but not necessarily to do what your or I may want them to do or to regard things as we do.

Story: The superintendent of a large western national park was showing a group of VIPs from the national office in Washington, D.C., around the park. They stopped at a construction project and the superintendent, wishing to demonstrate to visitors how mission-oriented and motivated his employees were, stopped to chat with several bricklayers at work. This conversation ensued:

Superintendent: "What are you doing here?"

Worker #1: "I'm earning a big bundle of cash each day so I can have a big weekend in Vegas."

The superintendent, disappointed by the obviously narrow response, posed his query to another bricklayer.

Worker #2: "I'm laying brick."

Although this was a slightly better answer, it still didn't show the superintendent the motivation he was seeking. So he quizzed a third worker with the same question.

Worker #3: "I'm putting up a wall."

A fairly good reply, certainly more purposeful than the prior ones, but still not quite a satisfactory one to the superintendent. So he made another try.

Worker #4: "I'm building a cathedral!"

So the superintendent had to fire the craftsman, for they were only building a comfort station!

To Sum Up

People can't be lumped together into one category and treated alike. Rather, motivational strategies have to be tailored to the individual. *You begin with where the worker is.* The old saying, "If the mountain won't come to Mohamed, Mohamed must go to the mountain" is still applicable.

While you, as a manager, want to recognize diversity, there still are certain commonalities that cut across all

these groupings—everyone has a need to feel important, respected, and valued; to be challenged; to be part of things, particularly something important; to be informed and to be heard; and to be treated according to the "Platinum Rule."

The Golden Rule asks that *we* treat others as *we* would want to be treated. Conversely, the Platinum Rule asks that we treat others as *they* would want to be treated. The Golden Rule, then, assumes that we know how others want to be treated, using our own needs and values as a guide. The Platinum Rule, conversely, asks of us that we be more empathic and sensitive, dig deeper and try to learn (not assume) how the others really want to be treated.

COMPETENCY/MASTERY

By way of definition, performance technologist Tim Newby states ("Increasing Intrinsic Motivational Change Within Organizations," *Performance and Instruction,* July 1989) "competence is the feeling of confidence and satisfaction gained through using one's learned abilities and skills to attain a goal." When given a choice between easy or challenging problems, says Newby, people select the one that maximizes their feelings of competence even though greater investment of effort is required.

People in every culture engage in activities to demonstrate their competency. In our culture, we show our mastery primarily through our work. Work serves as a mechanism of defining ourselves, giving us identity. And, as we indicated earlier, people are so closely integrated into their work that, in centuries past, they adopted surnames based on their occupations.

Sigmund Freud saw the successful, well-adjusted person as one capable of love and work. In like vein, former President Calvin Coolidge once stated: "All growth depends on activity. It is not development physically or intellectually without effort, and effort means work. Work is not a curse, it is the prerogative of intelligence, the only means to manhood and the measure of civilization."

Our language is rich with statements and phrases that show all of us have a need to be competent: "I wonder if I really can pull it off." "Rise to the challenge." "Look at it as a challenge, not a problem" (or a headache). "Burned the midnight oil." "Nothing succeeds like success." "He's a workaholic." "Burnout." "I don't want to make an ass out of myself" (looking incompetent). "It was a learning experience." "It's a man's job." "It's a Mickey Mouse job." "Trial and error." "Sink or swim." "On track." "In the groove." "Zeroing in."

Competency, per psychologist Dr. Abraham Maslow, relates to the need for esteem—self-esteem and esteem from others (status, prestige, recognition). If we have doubts about our competency, we begin to doubt our self-worth.

One way to recognize that the need for competency exists is to observe that people are constantly trying to assess their competency: "Did I do a good job?" "Could I have done it better?" "Have I learned from the experience to do it better next time?"

Competency is both a feeling—a sense of awareness—and a fact. Sometimes people do well but don't feel certain of their competency. Or they may feel competent but don't really do well. In either case, the need for feedback is essential—the reality-based person is in tune with his feelings and the facts about his competency.

We said that in our culture competency, i.e., our feelings about it, derives primarily from our work. However, if our work doesn't provide that opportunity, people may do various things off the job in a quest for competency; e.g., engaging in do-it-yourself projects around the house, teaching, writing, and participating in community, civic and/or professional society affairs. In the latter area, almost anyone who is interested can become a member of a committee and with a bit if extra effort become a committee chairperson—actually be be in charge of something and thus show one's competency to all.

Note: People may be motivated to engage in these extra-curricular activities for reasons other than the lack of opportunity to show their competency on the job, e.g., satisfying contacts with other professionals, networking to secure a better job, community service, etc. But these off-the-job activities always provide opportunities to demonstrate one's competency.

How can the manager contribute to the employee's need for competency? This can be done in a variety of ways: create opportunities to experience success via the establishment of short-term, achievable goals; encourage risk taking; let people be their own bosses by not second-guessing and double-checking the decisions they make; allow people to set their own goals; provide "stretch" in relation to goals; involve subordinates in new or start-up activities; give the staff a large piece of the action (decision making); provide a chance to make things happen, to be proactive rather than merely reactive; grant the opportunity to accomplish what one feels capable of achieving, and possibly even more than what one thought was possible (self-actualization); give people a

chance to grapple with and master new skills. In general, the growth-oriented ideas of Maslow and Herzberg are very pertinent to the competency/mastery concept.

Final point: When people feel competent in their activities, says management professor John R. Schermerhorn, Jr. ("Team Development for High Performance Management," *Training and Development Journal,* November 1986), you can expect that they'll work harder at it. So competency is truly a natural turn-on. It's an internal, self-renewing force that motivates and energizes without external help. If a worker in a freewheeling critique session with management feels competent, he is unlikely to state what one General Electric worker did about his tenure: "For 25 years, you've only paid for my hands when you could have had my brain for free" (quoted in *Training and Development Journal,* April 1991).

The motivational importance and respect for competency is illustrated by the following anecdote.

Story: The head of the Accounting and Financial Branch was extremely able. Everyone admired his ability to resolve perplexing problems with perspicacity and creativeness. Everyone also noted that each morning when he sat down at his desk he would unlock the middle drawer and carefully retrieve a small card and glance at it penetratingly for a minute or two. He would then return the card to its resting place and lock the drawer.

The head accountant worked at his job for some 40 years. He finally succumbed to various illnesses in his later years and after a very long hospital stay he passed away. Everyone was saddened for he was the mainstay of the accounting function, Mr. Competence himself.

Of course, his desk had to be cleared out on his demise. Naturally, everyone was curious as to what was on that small card that he read each morning. Surely it had some religious quality which gave him the sustenance to tackle each day's problems with such vigor and aplomb. So the middle drawer of his desk was unlocked and his assistant read the card aloud. It said: "Debits on the left, Credits on the right."

GOAL SETTING: GEARING UP FOR COMMITMENT

To the extent practicable, i.e., depending on the nature of the work, experience level, or job interest, a major motivational approach is to allow your people to set their own goals. Or, as a minimum, allow them to join with you or your team to establish goals via a process of joint negotiation. If people have a real say in setting goals, they automatically become committed to their execution. Remember, people support what they create.

Goal accomplishment obviously is a great source of satisfaction ("I said I would do it and indeed I did," exalts Professor Henry Higgins after teaching Eliza Doolittle to speak like a lady in George Bernard Shaw's *Pygmalion)*. It is also a great motivator. Why? Because success in reaching one's goal encourages movement toward another. *Success breeds success.*

Business school professor Edwin A. Locke studied the effects of goal setting on performance as reported in more than 100 published articles. He concluded: "In 90% of the studies, goal setting was found to be effective in improving task performance. This makes it one of the most effective and reliable motivational techniques known. The average goal-setting program in an organization achieves a 16% improvement in task performance; some achieve much more. In combination with money incentives, goal setting has been found to achieve performance improvements in excess of 40% ("Goal Setting," *The Encyclopedia of Management,* 3rd edition, New York: Van Nostrand Reinhold, 1982).

Goal selection, goal negotiation, and goal prosecution are true motivators. They enliven people and keep them from occupying a rut (which has been defined as a "grave with both ends open"). They are a sure-fire way to secure commitment.

An added motivational aspect of goal setting is the concept/technique of "stretch," discussed below.

STRETCH: SEEKING NEW TARGETS

As people learn their jobs it is not unreasonable to expect them to perform more productively, i.e, to produce more, to increase quality, to accomplish results in shorter time frames, to produce at lesser cost, and to innovate more. One way to encourage more productive behavior is to encourage "creative dissatisfaction"—to point out the need to rise above the status quo. An effective way to do this is to use the concept of "stretch." That is to say, you challenge the performer to contribute to a greater degree based on his prior stellar accomplishment. You ask him to compete with himself. **Example:** "Jenny, you have been one of our more steady field sales reps in terms of gross sales. You do a great job identifying and satisfying new customers. Your repeat business is also

very commendable. But I note that most of your sales come from a very limited range of our broad product line. This is OK, but I think that there are more opportunities out there for you if you were to encourage some of your very satisfied clients to consider our other very helpful products. Could you work up a six-month sales plan with some small targets for several other products which might also be pushed a bit?"

Note: The concept of stretch is designed to appeal to the performer's sense of pride, interest, capability, competitiveness, and creativity. It is not an attempt to exert unreasonable or improper pressure or manipulation to accomplish more. Stretch works best when it is perceived as a worthwhile challenge, not the old-fashioned "get off your duff and do more because I say so" kind of thing. You certainly don't want to trigger a negative reaction such as: "I work my butt off to get the job done, and he wants still more. How do you satisfy a guy like that?"

Stretch entails encouragement to strive for a goal that is *attainable* as well as worthwhile and pride inducing. The operative concept is that a good target is one that can be reached. "Dangling the carrot just beyond the donkey's reach" will only produce frustration and bitterness, not motivation.

Stretch carries no guarantees that the agreed-upon higher goal will be reached.

MEASURING GOAL ACCOMPLISHMENT

The most meaningful goals are those relating to a specific measurable standard: quality, quantity, time (meeting deadlines), budget, cost. For example, emergency room personnel at one hospital are expected to see new patients within one minute after their arrival. And they do! (Cited in "Tips on Customer Service," *Exceletter,* U.S. Learning Inc., Winter 1987).

The principle: What gets measured gets done. Measurement ensures accomplishment because employees respond to clearcut expectations by the boss. Also, people will strive (be challenged) to reach to known, agreed-upon targets. Athletic coaches know this principle and may set goals such as five sacks per game, commission of no more than x number of turnovers, or completion of x percent of free throws. Sales managers, in like fashion, may establish a goal of x number of new customers per quarter.

Two rules for your guidance:

1. If a task is done more than once, it can be measured.
2. Employees produce what management counts.

Inspection of Results/Goals Accomplishment

Quite often managers unintentionally curb high motivational potential by ignoring the need to follow-up on assigned goals. This is one of the major reasons why goal-setting programs sputter and ultimately die. Goals may be established (hopefully agreed-upon mutually), but then the boss becomes highly involved in other activities. He may thus skip the agreed-upon quarterly review. **The result:** In the absence of a review (inspection) of progress toward goal accomplishment, employee interest may well lag. Why bother if no one really cares? The principle for the manager, then, is this: People may do what you expect; they are very much more certain to do what you *inspect*.

Moral: There are many ways a manager can ensure the demise of a program or activity he started. A simple and certain way is to abandon inspection of what is being done or expected to be done.

TAKING RISKS: FOCUSING ON POSITIVE OUTCOMES

Our greatest glory consists not in never falling, but in rising every time we fall.

—Oliver Goldsmith (1728–74, British poet, novelist and dramatist)

I'd rather you ask for forgiveness than permission.

—advisory to staff of Dun and Bradstreet's Information Systems product group by Executive V.P. George Martin, quoted by Joseph Conlin, "Simple, But Effective," *Successful Meetings,* May 1994

It is not unusual for managers to complain: "I just can't get my people to show initiative. They just won't take any risks." Not everyone, of course, is a risk taker. Low risk-takers usually lack self-confidence. Management consultant Suzanne Sisson ("Managerial Risk Taking," *Supervisory Management,* January 1986), drawing on *The Guide to Personal Risk Taking* by Richard E. Byrd, identifies these fears which are tied to risk taking:

Fear of Failure

People who fail may blame themselves for their inadequacies. ("There I go again." Or: "How could I be so stupid?") They may also set unattainable high standards that guarantee failure. Their "answer" to their problem, then, is to play it safe.

Fear of Success

Some people are reluctant to move up to better jobs. Why? Because of a fear of being visible as a failure, plus the fact that they will have left behind people they know, colleagues who could support them if and when needed. ("If I succeed I'll be alone at the top.") "Practical" ways to avoid promotion may be to do a lot of job hopping or career changing or simply to withdraw and claim burnout.

Fear of What Others May Think

Some employees are so "other directed" that they won't risk doing anything which is not run of the mill. Favorable opinion of others is more important than following their own preferred directions. ("If they don't think well of me, they'll leave.") Conformity, getting along with everyone at all costs, commands a high personal value. Hence, "wave-making" becomes a non-preferred activity.

Fear of the Unknown

No one wants to be out of control. It can bring about high anxiety, loss of confidence, and/or depression. Hence the need for order, certainty, and predictability as opposed to new adventure and ambiguity. The resultant behavior is to avoid risks, to shun outcomes that are uncertain, ambiguous, or unpredictable.

Underlying all of the concerns is the fear of abandonment and rejection—being alone without resources or support.

To overcome these fears, managers can do these things:

☐ Encourage your employees to do a thorough job of *fact gathering*. Having the right kind and amount of information is a tremendous confidence builder.
☐ Focus on possible *positive results* that might come from taking a "risky" course of action.

☐ Encourage your people to *visualize success.* By converting negative images in one's mind to positive ones, employees can see possibilities for positive outcomes more clearly.

☐ Encourage your people to engage in *"self-talk"* that gives encouragement, as opposed to that which predicts disaster, e.g., "I *can* handle that assignment. I know I'm as good as those guys. In fact, I'm looking forward to showing everyone I can pull it off successfully."

☐ Provide *support* for the undertaking. Show them that you (and possibly others) are available to help underwrite success. Keep in close touch with the performer as he progresses. Render praise for each bit of accomplishment, i.e., provide praise for effort as well as for the final result.

☐ *Model* risk-taking behavior. Show consistent risk-taking behavior and a courageous attitude that tolerates and accepts personal failures and mistakes. Provide a *non-punitive environment.* Applaud attempts at accomplishment and don't dwell on and bemoan failure. Equate risk-taking with *growth.* Point out the obvious fact that all of us grow and have grown by the risks we have taken. This is true whether we are talking about learning to drive a car, going to college, seeking a new job, switching careers, selecting a date or a mate, and so on. In general, risk-taking tests us, measures us, and helps us to understand better what we *can* do.

Early in 1994, the U.S. Bureau of Reclamation in its interest of promoting innovation and risk taking, issued its subordinate managers in the field a risk-taking coupon booklet. Each of the booklet's two "forgiveness coupons" is good for one "screw-up" without fear of punishment. The coupons read "It is easier to get forgiveness than permission." The bureau chief told his managers, "If you do something bold and innovative and it's controversial and people start yelling at you, then you whip this sucker out and wave it, and then they have to shut up." (Stephen Barr, "Bureau Concedes Downsizing Pain," *The Washington Post,* April 14, 1944.)

The Bottom Line

People need to hear that "It's OK to make mistakes." The traditional management advisory of "Do it right the first time, or else . . ." is a certain means of getting people to pull in their horns rather than to expand their vision.

COMPLEXITY

Per available research, if we have a choice between a variety of tasks or duties we are likely to be most interested in those that are moderately complex. Why is this so? Per performance technologist Tim Newby ("Increasing Intrinsic Motivational Change Within Organizations," *Performance and Instruction,* July 1989), that type of "interest is generated because ultimate comprehension requires the focusing and maintenance of attention and then, the recall and use of previously learned skills."

Example: If we were charged to study a change in the pay structure at the corporate level, the work demands attention to all pertinent details and information, plus the ability to figure out all the ramifications and relationships of specific critical segments. Conversely, investigating a like change in a small department would generate much less interest and effort.

Note: If a task is regarded as too complex, interest is rapidly lost because ultimate comprehension seems impossible or takes too large an investment of effort. And a trivial task will not be a motivator, either. So to generate maximum interest, a task must be perceived as "optimally complex" for anyone involved in it.

VARIETY: THE SPICE OF (WORK) LIFE

A practical energizer for most people is variety. People are stimulated by diverse tasks (job enrichment), new goals, different schedules, job rotation, special assignments, implementing new policies and/or procedures, new approaches. For example, why not let a staffer of yours be the chairperson for a weekly meeting and let the group provide feedback regarding his skill in that role? Or why not hold an occasional meeting in a nearby Chinese (or ethnic) restaurant? If the organization is located in a suburban, industrial park, why not hold some of the meetings outdoors, under a shade tree? Why not occasionally invite your boss or other operating officials to the meetings?

Expanded/enriched assignments are possible even for those in lowly jobs. For example, management authority Tom Peters ("Management's Greatest Crime—Ignoring Worker's Talent," *The Washington Business Journal,* October 5, 1987) points out that one of the secrets of the highly successful Chaparral Steel Corporation is that they turn nearly every one of their 1,000 team members into a "valued and value-adding resource." He quotes the company president as follows regarding their innovative use of night watchmen and guards:

It's really amazing what people do when you let them. Normally when you think of security guards at four o'clock in the morning they're doing everything they can just to stay awake. Well, ours also enter data into our computer—order entry, things like that. They put the day's quality results into the computer system each night. We upgraded the job and made a very clear decision not to hire some sleepy old guy to sit and stare at the factory gate all night. Our guards are paramedics; they run the ambulance; they fill up the fire extinguishers; they do the checks on the plant; now we're even considering some accounting functions.

To give the concept of variety practical meaning, jot down in the space below concrete, cost-free actions one or more of your bosses (past or present) could take (or could have taken) to enrich your job.

Job Enrichment for Me

Action 1 _____

Action 2 _____

Action 3 _____

Action 4 _____

Action 5 _____

Action 6 _____

Note: In the management training workshops I conduct, I often present the above exercise to the group. Here are some of the responses I get:

☐ Freedom to act.
☐ Act as liaison to Dept. X.
☐ Greater responsibility.
☐ Act for the boss when she's away.
☐ Make field visits.
☐ Head up a project team.
☐ Serve on a safety committee.
☐ Handle PR work.
☐ Work on our long-range planning activity.

Note that in my list above, and probably in yours, too, all these actions are 1) within the scope of the boss' power (authority) and 2) they don't necessitate expenditure of money at all.

An obvious question to ask yourself is this: To what extent am I enriching the jobs of my subordinates? If not, why not? Accept this challenge and begin to plan job enrichment for at least some of your staffers.

In general, look for opportunities to break routine, established ways of operating and substitute new, even novel procedures and job opportunities. Variety is still the spice of life. It may give your outfit that extra vitality you seek.

CHOICE ("DON'T FENCE ME IN.")

You and I are likely to feel uneasy, maybe even bristle a bit when we are told by our superiors in no uncertain terms to "Do it this way." (Or worse, "My way or the highway.") We would feel a lot better if we are given options, wherever possible, to execute a task.

So if you wish to provide motivation and commitment for a job, you'll be ahead of the game if you allow your people to choose freely among alternatives. Insisting on one approach, out-and-out compliance, with no leeway to choose among possibilities, is a likely vehicle to disgruntlement and demotivation.

Remember, youngsters need a lot of structure. ("Finish your homework and then you can watch TV.") Adults, conversely, require freedom, more "wiggle room" (discussed later in this chapter).

W. Mathew Juechter, Chief Executive Officer of ARC International, Englewood, Colorado, put it this way (Patricia Galagan, "An Interview with W. Mathew Juechter," *Training and Development,* September 1988):

. . . When you are in an environment in which you are taken care of, the blade of choice grows very dull. When people tell you what to do, and you don't have any decisions to make, being accountable for what happens in your life just gets to be a smaller and smaller thing.

Learning to choose is important because it's the start of empowerment. No one can give you empowerment. It can only come from inside, and when you feel empowered then you will be willing to commit.

People are good at making choices about their lives in terms of what they like or where they want to live or what kind of car to drive. But I'm talking about choice in the workplace—the feeling that what they do makes a difference, that it is worthwhile, that they will be held accountable. . . .

Choice is a powerful concept and people's readiness to

be in charge of their own lives varies greatly. But the payoff for the organization that can risk teaching people to choose what they really want is the ability to create a different kind of culture—one with a lot more flexibility and more power to create.

So shed the managerial approach that deals primarily in pre-determined solutions, ultimatums, and directives. Let employees enter the world of options and alternatives with opportunities to choose among them. Remember, people grow and get turned on when they have to weigh the choices before them. Conversely, they stagnate, become passive, lethargic and generally turned off when choice disappears.

What we are saying, then, is that each person wants to be his own person. Freedom to choose is basic to maintaining self-esteem. The following story illustrates this concept:

A mother and her 10-year old son were ordering lunch in a restaurant. This conversation ensued:

Waitress to the boy: What will you have, young man?

Boy: A big, juicy hamburger.

Mother: *He'll* have roast beef.

Waitress (still talking to the boy): And what will you have with the burger?

Boy: Lots of ketchup, mustard and onions and french fries.

Mother: *He'll* have green beans.

Waitress to boy: And what to drink?

Boy: A giant chocolate milkshake.

Mother: *Plain milk!*

The waitress returns several minutes later with the food, all of it as the boy had ordered: hamburger, ketchup, mustard, etc.

Boy: Hey, look, mom. I'm for real!

JOB ENRICHMENT

Enriching or broadening the job is a well-established technique to provide workers with autonomy, challenge, and variety. To the extent that people are encouraged to become self-directing, they have the opportunity to be innovative in their area of responsibility.

Job enrichment is not to be confused with job rotation (to other routine tasks) or job enlargement (adding more routine tasks). As management authority Dr. Edward Glassman points out ("Creative Problem Solving: Your Role As a Leader," *Supervisory Management,* April

1989), true job enrichment occurs when these conditions are in effect:

☐ You assign a complete unit of work.

☐ You provide full responsibility for task accomplishment.

☐ You provide adequate authority to discharge that responsibility.

☐ You remove controls/reviews to ensure full independence.

☐ You introduce more difficult tasks or assign unique roles.

☐ You build into the operation a feedback system for self-correction.

Note: A distinction should be made between job enrichment and job empowerment. Job enrichment entails full responsibility for a complete operation. Empowerment means giving people responsibility in their jobs to take whatever action is necessary to satisfy a customer or ensure a quality product. Empowerment is applicable to people in all sorts of jobs, even limited or narrow ones—a checker in a supermarket, a teller in a bank, a mechanic in an auto repair shop.

OWNERSHIP ("DO I HAVE A PIECE OF THE ACTION?")

People need (and want) to feel that the jobs they are doing are their own, that they can legitimately feel a sense of personal responsibility and proprietorship. Sure, there is always a segment of the workforce who reports to work primarily for the paycheck. That is as far as their ownership goes. But most workers are autonomous individuals who are willing to work if the job—*their* job—is (or can become) a tremendous source of self-esteem, achievement, self-fulfillment, and an opportunity for growth.

So whether you are designing jobs, assigning duties and delegating, or reviewing and checking work, think in terms of ownership: "Will my action cause a greater or lesser feeling on the part of the employee that "This job *is* mine?" And as indicated above (also see "Closure," below), responsibility for the whole job provides that feeling of *ownership.*

One way to tell whether people feel that they have ownership about their work is to listen to their language, particularly their pronouns and adjectives. Do they speak in terms of "we," "us," and "our," or "they," "them," and "their"?

A practical way to provide ownership is through the establishment of Performance Measurement Teams (Rick L. Lansing, "Cost-Cutting Profit Making Ideas," *Supervisory Management,* July 1989). One company (Martin Marietta Missile Systems, Orlando, Florida) found that it dramatically improved production and cut costs greatly. The success of the PMTs resulted in their adoption in the company's divisions and other locations.

These PMTs are comprised of 15–25 people, all the production workers and technical support people in a work area. The team meets for one hour per week to review the prior week's performance, measuring all aspects of output—yield, rework, scrap, unit-cost reduction, schedule performance, overtime, and lost time. Action items are assigned to a specific technical support employee for corrective action.

According to a key official of Martin Marietta, the program's success is based on the fact that it gives work group members more accountability and ownership of their work. This in turn fosters teamwork and communication. In a sense, the official said, "What we did was make 70 little companies . . . The meetings generate a sense of ownership in the weekly results, with each member of the team pulling for each other. Even the technical support groups, such as production and industrial engineering, which are not part of the work group, are concerned with the performance of the team."

An anecdote to illustrate worker attitudes about their outfit, their work, and their involvement in it—ownership—is this:

Story: The sea had been rough for two days. A sailor smoking a cigarette, was leaning calmly on the deck rail, well accustomed to the action of the ocean waves. A fellow sailor suddenly popped his head through a nearby hatch and said excitedly, "Hey, Mac, the ship is sinking."

Mac inhaled deeply on his cigarette, shrugged his shoulders, and replied matter-of-factly, "So what? It's not *my* ship."

COMMITMENT: WHAT MONEY OR THREATS CAN'T PRODUCE

Managers typically have an awareness that employee commitment to the work is important. They may not always know how to bring it about, but they do know that it's highly essential. If commitment is not forthcoming, we're likely to hear managerial statements such as "They're only here for the paycheck," or "Yeah, they'll do what they're asked to do, but not a heck of a lot more."

Over the years various surveys have found that U.S. workers have limited enthusiasm for their jobs. One poll by the Wyatt Company ("Well, It Beats The Unemployment Line," *Training and Development Journal,* September 1990) indicated that only 36% of working Americans consider their firms anything more than "just a place to work." Pollster John Parkington asserts that the poll evidences that worker interest and commitment tends to peter out over time: "People enter new jobs with high levels of enthusiasm and dedication. But the novelty soon wears off and so does the enthusiasm. As the saying goes, the honeymoon is over."

Among first-year employees, 43% state they are highly committed, but by years two and three the percentage begins to drop. After service of four years, commitment falls to a level of 34%, where it stays even for employees who have more than 20 years with the same outfit.

One way to understand commitment is to consider the potential commitment to work using a model developed by management consultant Ken Macher ("Empowerment and the Bureaucracy," *Training and Development Journal,* September 1988). He presents a seven-degree continuum ranging from hostile on the left to truly committed on the right. Here's what his continuum covers:

1. **Actively hostile.** People work subtly but vigorously in an anti-management or anti-organizational way.
2. **Alienated.** A large degree of mistrust exists about organizational motives toward the workforce and/or the customers.
3. **Retirement on the job.** People dodge work and responsibility. Getting by, goofing off, and making excuses for low or non-performance are typical behaviors.
4. **Formal commitment.** People do what's required, but no more than that. (Visualize the waiter or waitress who won't remove a dish, give you a glass of water, or tell you the correct time because "It's not my table.")
5. **Concerned but limited sense of power.** People performing at this level of commitment are technically competent, have a concern for quality, but feel victimized by the system. Hence, they tend to hold back.

6. **Personal ambition.** These people work hard at meeting their own goals and know how to work within the system.

7. **Deep commitment.** Here we find a sense of meaning and purpose above and beyond personal ambition. The people at this level exert themselves in many ways to make a real difference.

So if we truly wish "deep commitment," how do we go about getting it? One likely-to-be-successful answer lies in making work meaningful. Management consultant Ken Macher ("Creating Commitment," *Training and Development Journal,* April 1991) draws on the work of psychologists F.E. Emery and E. Thorsud and suggests that we ensure that jobs be designed so that they are rich in the several attributes that make work inherently rewarding:

☐ **Meaning.** People need work that they care about and can believe in. High standards, integrity, and concern with customers and quality are key.

☐ **Contribution.** If people are slotted into "dumb" jobs—those that are easily learned, simple, and repetitive—they won't feel valued. Opportunities to express initiative or creativity, as opposed to feeling automated and replaceable, are "musts."

☐ **Community.** People need to feel connected to the outfit, to believe that a worthwhile sense of purpose exists. If that is the case, we can expect ready alignment by employees with business objectives.

☐ **Growth.** To avoid letting people retire on their jobs, they need to feel and experience movement, progress, interest, and challenge. Note that growth still is possible even if traditional advancement opportunities are limited by a "lean and mean" operation.

☐ **Influence.** Everyone wants a say ("A piece of the action") about decisions that they are knowledgeable about and may affect them. The concept of "localness," that is, letting people closest to the customer make decisions that affect customers, is a way to provide influence. So management has to "let go," to be less controlling and more trusting.

What the above paragraphs signify is that commitment isn't something that has to be instilled in people, but rather something that has to be evoked from them. It can't be commanded, it can only emerge if the climate is right.

Management consultant Kenneth M. Schatz suggests using this exercise with your people if you want to begin to achieve commitment ("Viewpoint," *Training,* October 1986):

1. Ask staffers to rate anonymously the level of commitment the outfit shows to them, using a scale of one to ten.
2. Then ask them where on the scale it should be.
3. Ask them to rate the level of commitment people show the organization, again using a one-to-10 scale.
4. Then ask how high it should be.
5. Ask them what they believe accounts for the (very likely) differences.

It may take a fair amount of courage to undertake the above polling and then to engage in an open discussion of the polling results. But it is one way to clear the air and show your interest in upping the organization's current degree of commitment to people.

EMPOWERMENT: LETTING COMPETENT PEOPLE LEAD/ACT/DECIDE

Stated simply, empowerment is getting workers to do what needs to be done rather than what they're told. In both the manufacturing and service industries, it means giving workers the competence and confidence to take actions not covered by the firm's rules.

—"Basics of Employee Empowerment," *Info-Line,* American Society for Training and Development, May 1991

Eliminating boss control is at the core of empowerment . . . (Employees) need proficiency: Disney doesn't give its street sweepers four days of training because street sweeping is complex; Disney wants sweepers who are able to answer guests' questions about the park.

—Management consultant/trainer Chip R. Bell, in *Training,* December 1991

Efforts toward continuous improvement take hold only when employees feel a sense of pride and ownership in their jobs. And pride and ownership are the heart of empowerment efforts. Empowered individuals take initiative to find better ways to accomplish their everyday tasks.

—Dr. William C. Byham, President and CEO, Development Dimensions International, Pittsburg, in *PEPI Update,* August 1991, Positive Employees Practices Institute, Clemson, South Carolina.

To appreciate how empowerment might (or might not) work in actual practice, consider these four incidents or practices:

☐ A panicked customer called the Saturn Pohanka dealership in the Washington, D.C., area. Her problem? She had locked herself out of her car while the motor was still running. The receptionist, recognizing that the dealership was short-staffed, quickly climbed into her own car and hand-delivered a new set of keys. Owner Jack Pohanka commented on this customer service act as follows: "The phone operator didn't hesitate. She didn't look for approval. She felt empowered to handle the situation on her own because of what she's been hearing during the training. She thought she was doing what was best for the customer" (reported in *Selling,* March 1994).

☐ At Atlanta's Kudzu Cafe, which features Southern cuisine, serving personnel have the discretion to offer customers a free dessert or even a meal if they have to wait too long for their food. The manager states that the employees have the authority and flexibility to resolve a problem promptly without the need to request permission to do so (reported in *The Wall Street Journal,* June 7, 1993).

☐ At the Hampton Inn hotels (headquarters in Memphis, Tennessee), all employees are authorized to take whatever action is necessary to keep the customer satisfied, says Ray Schultz, President and CEO ("Satisfaction Guaranteed for Customers and Crew," *The Wall Street Journal,* January 28, 1991). For example, a housekeeper notices a guest is getting frustrated because the key won't unlock the door to his room. But instead of simply calling the front desk or the maintenance department, the housekeeper assumes responsibility for getting a new key, changing the lock, or arranging for a different room. And if the guest still isn't happy, the housekeeper may offer to refund the room charge for the night without clearing it with the hotel manager.

☐ A waitress, who had spilled red wine on a customer's tie, called for her boss, the restaurant manager. The customer stated that the stain will never come out of the tie he had just bought for $45. The customer lived out of town and had a flight leaving in the morning. The boss decided to give the customer the $45. When he proudly told his supervisor, the district manager, about the incident, he got chewed out for not filling out insurance forms. And the corporate insurance coordinator phoned to remind the restaurant manager of company regulations regarding loss and damage procedure. He stated: "After all, what if the customer takes the tie to another of our restaurants claiming that they spilled wine on him?" (Cited by corporate trainer Jay Cone, "The Empowered Employee," *Training and Development Journal,* June 1989).

Questions: Which of the incidents cited above will encourage employees to continue to act in an empowered way, and which will discourage it? What risks does an employee face if he places the customer's interest above long-established company procedures?

Perhaps at this point we should explain empowerment more fully. It is a formal attempt by the organization to please the customer, to put him first. It is done by enabling or allowing the person serving the customer to take the initiative to meet customer needs fully. The assumption is that the employee who is closest to the customer is in the best position to keep the customer happy and thereby increase the likelihood of much-wanted repeat business plus favorable word-of-mouth advertising.

From an employee standpoint, empowerment encourages employees to participate actively in the decision-making process. It provides them with opportunities to be innovative, to receive recognition, and to garner increased pride in their work.

From an organizational standpoint, it leads to a better company image, better quality products and services, increased employee satisfaction, and reduced employee turnover. The watchwords are total quality, customer satisfaction, and continuous improvement.

How does the organization produce a coherent plan for empowerment? Per Marian J. Thier ("In Practice: The Path to Empowerment," *Training and Development,* October 1993 based on an article by Thier in the *Journal for Quality and Participation),* the following principles should be used:

☐ **The goal:** To achieve interdependence (as opposed to dependence or independence).

☐ **The culture:** The culture is subject to both evolutionary and revolutionary change. It occurs over time, in stages, and yet extreme measures are taken to radically alter the status quo.

☐ **The levels:** All levels of the organization must become involved in the change process. No one can empower another or be empowered without full participation.

☐ **Cooperation:** Everyone must work together toward like goals to give and take the benefits of empowerment.

☐ **Communication:** Everyone has to be posted on what is to happen and what is happening, how the new push is working. These communication skills are needed: Giving and receiving feedback, facilitating meetings, using conflict creatively, and understanding cultural differences.

☐ **Framework:** A structure (plan, design) is needed to allow creativity; but traditional control—the opposite of vitally needed freedom—is an unwanted inhibitor.

☐ **Quality:** The goal of continuously improved products and services requires involvement of all employees.

Conditions for empowerment, per management consultant John H. Dobbs ("The Empowerment Environment," *Training and Development,* February 1993), are these:

☐ **Participation:** Employees have to be interested in and willing to improve work processes and work relationships. However, the organization has to encourage that involvement. Training employees to use total-quality tools is an effective mechanism to provide the interest and know-how, and to build the confidence essential to take the initiative needed when problems arise.

☐ **Innovation:** Empowerment can't take place if innovation is ignored, stifled or discouraged. The organization can't expect its employees to perform in the same controlled way as previously. Innovation is most likely to come from those in "the trenches"—employees who have direct contact with manufacturing processes or who deliver service to customers.

☐ **Access to information:** On the assumption that information is power, managers must provide (not hoard) information to employees at all levels in the organization. This is the only certain route to intelligent decision making at the worker level.

☐ **Accountability.** Some managers may be fearful of the possible excesses of too much freedom for their employees—poor judgment will produce wrong and terrible results. **The Answer:** Increase employee accountability. Employees should be held responsible for:
—Responsible behavior toward others.
—Operating in a positive manner.
—Producing agreed-upon results.
—Keeping their word, thereby ensuring their credibility.

The key to empowerment is to feel a sense of control rather than feeling helpless, say management writers Edward Betof and Frederic Harwood ("Raising Personal Empowerment," *Training and Development,* September 1992). This means that organization leaders must engender the following concepts:

☐ Everyone is part of management and all can improve things.

☐ Worthwhile ideas and suggestions are wanted, appreciated, and may be implemented.

☐ All suggestions will be appreciated and rewarded even if not accepted.

☐ We can trust everyone with responsibility.

☐ People are respected for their ideas and their judgment.

Empowerment is not an easy concept to implement, for it means shedding traditional ways of operating and establishing a radically altered enabling culture. Can it work? Apparently so, if there is the will to make it work. Consider the following data:

An American Society for Training and Development fax survey of professional personnel (reported in *Training and Development,* April 1993) indicated that 67% of the companies surveyed are encouraging empowerment via:

☐ Creating self-directed work teams and providing training for self-management.

☐ Encouraging employee flexibility in thought and action.

☐ Establishing autonomous teams, i.e., without managers at all.

☐ Requiring managers to delegate more to their people.

☐ Encouraging employees to assume more ownership of their own work areas.

☐ Fostering open communication and shared values among managers and staff.

Some survey respondents, however, had negative comments: "My organization talks about empowerment, then punishes people who practice it"; "My boss doesn't understand or support empowerment"; "With the new management, there's been a lot of yelling, scapegoating, and fear."

Note: A fax survey is not a scientifically conducted poll or survey. Rather, only certain readers of the periodical take the time to respond.

Key Learning Points for the Manager

If you are sincerely interested in motivating your workforce, try to think in terms of empowerment. This means to cut down on all the standard controls and procedures which inhibit independence, freedom, initiative, risk-taking, assuming responsibility, self-control, and exercising judgment. One might say that empowerment is a "Zen concept": You must release control to gain control(!).

Secondly, heed the helpful counsel of management consultant Robert Barner ("Enablement: The Key to Empowerment," *Training and Development,* June 1994) who asks us, as managers, to also think in terms of *enablement.* He states, "Enablement involves helping people to develop the necessary competencies to manage their own empowerment effectively. When enablement isn't part of an empowerment effort, the effort is likely to fail." So giving people power and autonomy is great. But it must be accompanied by a sincere and solid effort to provide the skill and knowledge—the competencies—to make it really happen.

One way to get on the road to full empowerment is to assess your current empowerment prowess. The self-quiz on page 208 should prove helpful for this purpose.

"WIGGLE ROOM": PREVENTING FAILURE OR ASSURING SUCCESS?

People are more likely to respond to approaches to their work of their own choosing than to the methods you decree. They want the independence and freedom—"wiggle room"—to decide their own style, pace, who to contact, modus operandi, and sequence of operating. Think of the leeway your boss undoubtedly gives you to decide many things, e.g., whether and when to hold staff meetings or problem solving meetings, what the agenda should be, the length of the meetings, who to invite from your staff or elsewhere in the firm, whether subgroups are to be formed, and so on. So how would you feel if your boss made one or more of those decisions for you, or even told you to skip the meetings and solve the problems yourself?

Wiggle room, or control of various aspects of one's job, say management professors Patricia L. Perreive and Frank A. Vickory ("Combatting Job Stress," *Training and Development Journal,* April 1988) may take these three forms:

Work process. The workers might determine the order in which tasks are completed, select the method of accomplishing the tasks, or determine their own work pace.

Work schedule. Employees might have the freedom to schedule their lunch and break periods, using flex-time to choose their working hours, and possibly choose the work shift and vacation time they favor.

Work decisions. More control over work decisions might be given by including employees in meetings on organizational policies and objectives and departmental procedures. Other choices might relate to work space or their office decor.

Another facet of the wiggle room concept is to recognize that your employees may need to bend certain rules to do their own thing properly. Slavish adherence to "the book" will stifle rather than unleash the energy and enthusiasm in them that you desire.

Story: Management authority Dr. Kenneth Blanchard ("Ideas From Experts," *The Service Edge,* sample issue, 1989) relates the incident concerning a colleague who went to an ice cream shop. While mulling over the flavors, he noticed the clerk's supervisor whisper something to the clerk. This dialog then ensued:

Clerk: Please take a number.

Colleague: Why? There's no one in the store.

Clerk: It's our policy.

Colleague: But I'm the only one here.

Clerk: Please don't get me in trouble. My boss is over there.

Colleague (takes number 30).

Clerk (shouting dutifully): 27, 28, 29, 30.

Colleague to clerk's supervisor: Do you realize what you're doing? You're taking away a person's pride and self-esteem.

Supervisor (angrily): If you can't get people to follow the policies when there's nobody here, how can we expect them to do it when it is crowded?

What we are saying, then, is that you, as a manager, cannot automatically create people who are innovative or creative, or automatically turn them on. But by granting them the maximum amount of leeway (wiggle room) in their work, you can help them to discover the creativity and potential that exists within them.

A caution: If people aren't performing well, don't automatically fall into the trap of adding more controls: People dislike being controlled, and their performance may deteriorate further. Instead, diagnose carefully before you slap on those added controls. It just may be that what is needed is more rather than less wiggle room. One way to bring this about is through training. So wherever possible, teach your people to do something rather than do it for them. Steer clear of the old philosophy of "If you want a job done well, do it yourself." The key advisory for you is this: Stay out of the way of your people so that they can get the job done for you.

CLOSURE: THE ECSTASY OF DOING THE TOTAL JOB

He who trusts men will make fewer mistakes.

—Camillo Di Cavour (1810–1861), Italian statesman and architect of Italian unification

Traditional management styles regarded work as something that must be checked, reviewed, controlled, and rechecked. Employees were not allowed (trusted) to have full and final responsibility for the work, to "sign off" on anything. Only those at the managerial level could close something out.

Psychologists have long pointed out that people need closure in respect to their undertakings, be it playing a game, mowing the lawn, finishing a piece of furniture, or conducting an activity on the job. An often-used example by psychologists is the strong anxiety one experiences about an unmailed letter residing in a purse or coat pocket left inadvertently at home. Late German psychologist Dr. Bluma Zeigarnik found in her research that uncompleted tasks are better remembered than completed ones. Only when the task is completed is the tension of motivation discharged. But when the activity is subject to interruption, the continuing tension keeps the memory live. The phenomenon, the need for closure, has been named the "Zeigarnik effect."

Closure is important to people whether the tasks they perform are highly professional, technical, or very mundane. For example, *Washington Post* columnist Courtland Milloy, writing about trash collectors in Washington, D.C., ("Finding Dignity Amid Garbage," April 5, 1988), quotes a supervisory trash collector as follows:

> *You go into an alley and see a whole gang of cans lined up. Then you get to the end, and look back and they're all empty. You say to yourself, "I moved something. I got the job done. That's nice.*

A splendid way to meet the need for closure is to provide opportunities for people to perform holistically, i.e., to do the total job. For example, how can an assembly line worker get excited about an electrical product he is working on when all he does all day is solder five or six connections on a single part? The job of the manager, then, is to design jobs and assign tasks on the basis of job enrichment—the total job—rather than job fragmentation.

Another aspect of the total job closure concept relates to people's full understanding of what they are doing. It is obvious that people are enabled to function with more job interest and enthusiasm when they can appreciate the significance of what they do. Thus, it is essential for you as manager to stress the totality of a task or job—its purpose, worth, and impact. Lisa Carlson of the Professional Managers Association (at a meeting of the National Society for Performance and Instruction, Washington, D.C., January 1985) cites the examples of three New York City employees who regard their operations in broad, holistic (and human) terms:

☐ The worker in charge of 3,200 elevators in public housing sees his job as one having "Quality of Life" impact. He appreciates keenly that if the elevators aren't working, the tenants understandably will get hostile.

☐ The person in charge of subway engineering and repair (tunnel fixing) knows that it is his job to help people to get to work on time.

□ The woman who supervises morgue autopsies regards her job with a truly high-level perspective. It is not just a matter of getting forms filled out by visitors, but to deal with the concerns of bereaved people—those who wish to see a body, someone they may care about.

The Bottom Line

Recent developments in the management field have stressed the importance of responsibility for the whole job as a means of securing worker commitment, enthusiasm, and innovation. In the latter respect, how much can you innovate if all you have to do is tighten a single bolt on the rear bumper of a Chevrolet? But by seeing (and overseeing) the total job/task/operation, a manager is in a good position to see the need for changes and improvements.

Examples of newer management programs and activities with closure built into them are job enrichment, MBO (Management by Objectives), self-directed teams, performance improvement teams, empowerment, and profit centers. Delegation and decentralization, while not recent developments, might be added to the array of techniques available to us to let people take charge and close things out.

Remember, for most people responsibility is sought because it conveys the feelings of importance and power as well as the satisfaction that accrues when you can see a job through to its final completion.

WORK AS FUN

We do not take humor seriously enough.

—Konrad Lorenz (1903–1989), Austrian zoologist and Nobel Prize winner in physiology of medicine (1973)

Is work a turn-on? If not, do something about it. Now. Dull products and dull services usually come from dull companies. Use your colleagues' imagination to perk up your 25 or 2,500 square feet. Beware the operation devoid of laughter.

—Management guru Tom Peters in his syndicated newspaper column of January 10, 1994

It is my belief, you cannot deal with the most serious things in the world unless you understand the most amusing.

—Winston Churchill (1874–1965), British statesman, author and soldier, and Nobel Prize winner in literature

The world will never be happy until all men have the souls of artists—I mean when they take pleasure in their jobs.

—Auguste Rodin (1840–1917), world-class French sculptor

He who laughs, lasts.

—spotted on a bumper sticker

Part of the folklore regarding work is that it is a necessary but distasteful activity. Mark Twain puckishly put it this way: "Work is what you do when you'd rather be doing something else." I once spotted a sign on a wall in a publishing firm which stated: "I love my job. It's the work that I hate." And a standard quip among the retired has it that "The worst thing about retirement is having to drink coffee on your own time."

That the workplace is typically a grim locale is evidenced by an *Industry Week* survey of middle managers and first line supervisors. Here's what these managers said ("Work Is No Fun," *Personnel Journal, May 1991):*

□ Two of three managers say work isn't fun anymore.
□ Nearly half blame the absence of teamwork and their firms' dog-eat-dog environments.
□ 39% assert that paperwork, meetings, and other bureaucratic nightmares stifle their initiative.
□ 30% complain their efforts are not acknowledged or appreciated.
□ Others point to personnel cutbacks, poor communication or weak or inept management.
□ How to get fun back for employees? Abolish stuffy titles, encourage teamwork, provide recognition for good work, and have a boss who cares.

Actually, work can be fun or at least have fun elements integrated into it, and thus provide a great deal of natural motivation. Thus, a Gallup Poll (*Nation's Restaurant News,* July 27, 1987) reporting on morale in the fast-food industry found that teenagers liked their jobs for these reasons: they gain job experience for use later in their careers, they learn responsibility, and they "are having a good time." Similarly, the VP for personnel of Pizza Hut found that what their young employees (ages 16–24) liked most about their work were the flexible hours and the teamwork that made working in the restaurant "fun" (David Zemelman, "Climbing the Ladder of Success With A Spatula," *The Wall Street Journal,* February 4, 1988).

A growing number of companies are recognizing the importance of fun in the workplace. In "Workweek," *The Wall Street Journal* (March 22, 1994) reported that "laughter is big business, as companies seek ways to break office tension." It stated that companies are increasingly hiring "humor consultants" to help reduce employee stress and burnout. It quotes humor consultant Joel Goodman, director of the Humor Project, Saratoga Springs, New York, who says, "Everyone uses the expression 'Some day we'll laugh about this.' Why wait?" Goodman suggests employees might pretend that they're Allen Funt of Candid Camera fame and find humor in stressful situations each day for five minutes.

Psychologists and humor consultants believe that employees who are allowed and encouraged to have fun at work generally score high marks in job satisfaction, productivity, and creativity. Jerry Greenfield, president of Ben and Jerry's Homemade Ice Cream, Inc., in Vermont, subscribes to this view, believing that if something isn't fun, why do it? His firm created a committee, the "Joy Gang," charged with distributing joy grants (worth up to $500 each) to work units that produce creative ideas to bring long-term joy to the workplace. Some of their ideas to date: purchase a hot chocolate machine and company roller skates, and recognize Elvis' and Barry Manilow's birthdays (Shari Caudron, "Humor Is Healthy in the Workplace," *Personnel Journal,* June 1992). Greenfield himself is the self-proclaimed "Minister of Joy" (Craig Cox, "Are We Having Fun Yet?", *Business Ethics,* July-August 1992).

Silliness at work may look just like that, but it tends to loosen people up, all of which can facilitate camaraderie, teamwork and creativity. So some managers may wear fun-type buttons that say, "Save Time: See It My Way." Or workers may have medicine bottles on their desks labeled, "Extra Strength Screw-It-All." One CEO arrived at work to find his office turned into a one-hole, par-four miniature golf course complete with two sand traps and a bird bath.

And in lean and mean times, when job security is a lost benefit, companies need to offer something to employees that will make them want to come to work each day. So by creating a workplace that "allows playfulness and values a sense of joy," Shari Caudron says the firm can take a major step to reach that objective.

Note, too, that a growing number of companies are allowing employees to dress for comfort rather than "success" ("Employees Dress for Comfort, Not Success," *Personnel Journal,* October 1992). So instead of "dress to impress," employees are trading in suits for jeans and skirts for sundresses. A nationwide poll of 500 human resource managers found that two-thirds agree that there is a trend toward more casual dress. Thus, 67% of the firms allow professional, management, and administrative staffers to wear casual clothes either regularly or on special occasions (14% allow informal dress each day).

Informal dress also helps to blur the traditional lines between white and blue collar workers. At the Saturn auto plant in Tennessee everyone, from execs down, may dress casually daily—no ties, jackets, dresses, pantyhose. Saturn's dress policy, per spokesman Bill Betts, is part of the company philosophy of all workers being partners without distinction among employment levels, and a desired general informal atmosphere throughout the facility as well.

Ben and Jerry's encourages employees to arrive at work in truly tacky toggery—mismatched plaids, paisleys, and polyester. High-tech robotics firm Odetics of California sponsors fun events such as Hula-Hoop events and bubble-blowing contests during the regular work day (Ann E. LaForge, "Know Any Good Jokes Lately?", *Successful Meetings,* May 1989).

The key point to the fun fest idea at work (Craig Cox, "Are We Having Fun Yet?", *Business Ethics,* July/August 1992) is this:

> *Though isolated events and activities can work wonders on employee morale, it's the sense that the company—and its managers—are putting work in its proper perspective every day that makes them happy to come to work. To do that, managers need to examine their own priorities, explore what it is about their own jobs that makes them happy, and discuss with their co-workers ways in which tension can best be relieved on the job.*

One way to appreciate the possibility of enhancing employee satisfaction and motivation is to analyze popular games like golf and bowling. After all, why would anyone want to lift and throw a large, heavy, cumbersome object like a bowling ball or to trudge around a golf course, possibly in the hot sun, just to smack a little white ball and then have to chase after it?

Organizational psychologist William H. Mobley has analyzed the motivational components of the game of golf. He breaks it down thusly ("Where Have All the Golfers Gone?" *Personnel Journal,* July 1977):

Clarity of goals. You can see the pin (the staff of the flag at the hole) awaiting your driven ball; you have the par for each hole clearly in mind and you know it has been set fairly—not too easy or impossible to reach; you know your usual results (score); and there are competitive goals with par, your prior scores, and with the other member of your golfing party. All in all, the goals provide a lot of challenge.

Feedback. There is a lot of it to keep you on track: after every hole, after nine holes, and after the full 18 holes. Note that the feedback comes directly, not through someone else, just as Dr. Herzberg of Motivation-Hygiene fame recommends. And note that *you* keep score. Feedback, it is to be observed, serves to provide both *instruction* and *motivation*. The best feedback is direct to the performer, immediate, and goal related. Golf meets all these requirements handsomely.

Completeness. You are totally responsible for all aspects of the operation (game)—from the tee to the far-off green and from the very first to the last stroke at the 18th hole (or the 19th, if you decide to have some added camaraderie). Note that the activity is structured so that there are intermediate goals (18 of them) and intermediate feedback. In all these steps, no one second guesses you, criticizes you, or nags or can complain about your performance. It's your deal. PERIOD. You get what the psychologists call "closure"—there is a beginning and an end that you strive to reach and control completely.

Skill-variety. Each hole is different in terms of distance and conditions (including terrain, hazards, wind). You are required to use different clubs to perform properly. The activity requires physical effort and mental output, too, to plan your strategies as you go along the course.

Judgment. It's your task to judge distances; read or estimate the nature of the greens; select the appropriate club; and put the ball in play by selecting and adjusting critical elements such as stance, grip, and swing. You have to decide on the best strategies to meet the varying conditions of the game.

But what if a scientific management person like Fred Taylor came along and wanted to simplify the game for you so you could get through it more easily and quickly? If so, he might let you play just one hole, or even a part of it, decide you only need one club, and simplify all operating conditions so that judgment and decisions would be minimized. Would there be any fun left? Do we, as managers, do this when we design jobs or supervise the performance of others?

Management consultant George Truell has dissected the game of bowling in a way similar to the golf analysis, to see what is so motivating about it. His findings about the bowler in action are ("Where Have All the Achievers Gone?", *Personnel,* Nov.-Dec. 1973):

Decision making. The bowler decides to engage in the sport. It is his decision to spend the required time, energy and money. Note that the time bowling takes place is generally *after* a full day's work.

Involvement. The bowler alone picks up the ball and sends it down the lane toward the pins.

Goal complexity. The lane has been designed in length and width so that the desired accomplishment is neither too easy nor too hard—challenging but attainable goals. Thus, the bowler can get a strike, a spare, hit some of the pins, or miss totally. Strikes are hard to get, but doable. So the bowler feels good when he makes one.

Feedback. Feedback is clear and immediate, enabling adjustment on the next throw of the ball. The feedback also permits the bowler to improve his performance while the game is taking place.

Rewards and recognition. The reward system is logical and fair. Points are awarded on the basis of actual accomplishment. A strike gets more points than a spare and so on. In essence, performance is recognized with appropriate rewards.

Support and encouragement. Teammates encourage and cheer the bowlers on. They may offer helpful tips to assist one's efforts toward the end result. The bowler is totally free to accept or reject the advice.

One element of satisfaction that is derived from the two games (or any other game) is that of *closure*. That is, the performer is totally responsible for the full operation and has the satisfaction of overseeing all aspects of it to its final conclusion. Visualize the pain that would ensue if the players were only permitted to play a segment of the game. Note, too, that the bowler is part of a *team* and thus can receive encouragement from team members, whereas the golfer is in competition with fellow players. But both games meet important social needs, although in somewhat different ways.

The challenge for the manager is to study these two games and observe the strong motivating elements in them. It just may be that these factors can be applied to the jobs one supervises, and thereby upgrade the capacity of people to achieve and also to have fun while performing.

The bottom line of work and play in a motivational context was probably best stated by Sigmund Freud: "We never do anything unless we would rather."

Story: A group of middle-aged army officers was having a couple of pre-dinner drinks in the officer's club. Their imbibing and camaraderie ignited a friendly discussion about whether sex was work or play. They couldn't agree and thus decided to ask a young GI, who was passing by the club, for his opinion. Presumably a younger person might have some thoughtful insights to help resolve the issue. So one of the officers posed the question in dispute to the young soldier who replied, "Well, sir, I believe it's all fun."

Officer: And why do you say that?

Soldier: Because if there were any work attached to it, sir, you officers would have us GIs doing it for you.

HIGHLIGHTING MISSION: "WE HAVE AN IMPORTANT JOB TO DO."

Many organizations attract people to their workforce because of their service-oriented mission. **Examples:** hospitals, the Peace Corps, the FBI, the National Park Service, the VA, the Food and Drug Administration, police and fire departments, volunteer agencies, churches, schools and colleges, newspapers, and so on. People in these organizations typically are very dedicated to the lofty goal of helping others in various ways. This is true, at least, for those who are in direct contact with the clientele served by those organizations, i.e., nurses, social workers, teachers, park rangers, etc. It may be less true of support personnel such as maintenance workers, cooks, clerical and administrative staff, printers, etc.

Other organizations may not have "natural," "exciting" missions to which people may "rally" as those cited above. Nevertheless, practically all organizations exist to provide vital products or services, to assist people in various ways, or to enrich their lives. Visualize a world without firms that produce food, shelter, medicines, cars, clothing, household goods, books and magazines; or companies that provide transportation, communication, insurance, banking services, entertainment, and recreation.

Admittedly, when workers operate on a fragment of a product, e.g., producing boxes for shoes, assembling the handlebars of a lawn mower, operating a machine that folds paper napkins, or routinely billing anonymous customers for purchases made in a department store, the all-important mission may become somewhat distant and foggy.

To the extent, then, that the mission becomes lost in the daily routine of producing goods and providing services, the work's true importance, understandably, may become less of a motivator to those so involved. Hence the need for managers to provide ongoing reminders of organizational purpose: "Our customers are counting on those car batteries to hold up for five full years. When a mother has to pick up her kid at school at 3 p.m., she wants to be sure her car will start when she leaves the house." Or: "It's our job to be sure that our customers' bills are correct in all respects or we may lose them as customers. Customers in the store are what gives us our jobs."

What we are saying, then, is that it is the manager's role to constantly help workers to visualize that there is an actual end-user (customer, client, citizen) out there, a real person with important needs who is depending on us, as performers, for what we produce or provide. Thus, orientation sessions, plant tours, regular staff meetings, and work reviews should be used actively to keep the all-important mission out front: "Every job in the plant (or store or office) contributes to quality and customer satisfaction. We don't have any unimportant jobs here at all."

Keep the following items in mind:

1. Even highly dedicated nurses, teachers, pilots, and park rangers need reminders from time to time that they are in their jobs to provide critical services to their publics.

2. There are certain jobs that create end results that don't necessarily get rave notices from those affected by them, e.g., tax assessors and collectors, police officers who dole out traffic tickets, claims

examiners, morticians, referees and umpires, mechanics, and various other repair people. Nevertheless, they still have vital functions to perform. They thus require periodic reminders about their significant roles.

3. People in routine, boring, and splintered jobs may be so mad at their bosses and the organization that they may be hard to reach with the usual pep talks about quality, excellence, customer service, repeat business, and the like. Hence the need to (a) involve them in the work in more meaningful ways, e.g., via employee involvement teams, (b) to treat them with dignity, and (c) to provide praise frequently for quality performance. These actions should help to reduce feelings of frustration and anger, thereby paving the way for actual listening to our customer-oriented messages.

Management professors Ken Matejka and Audrey G. Federouch ("Uniting Employees Around a Mission," *Supervisory Management,* September 1990) say that most workers (some 80%) want more challenge in their jobs. Motivational devices toward this goal are these:

Enrich jobs. Allow employees to eliminate their boring jobs and swap them for more difficult ones. The Japanese have used this approach successfully.

Rewards. Provide rewards that relate to their value systems. Don't err by assuming your goals and theirs necessarily mesh. For example, a promotion requiring long hours may not be regarded as a true, worthwhile promotion.

Freedom. Provide maximum freedom possible for self-management. This may relate to control of work, setting of production goals, or scheduling their own purchasing.

Flexibility. Provide maximum flexibility, e.g., permit job sharing and cross training.

Team involvement. Seek out opportunities for team functioning, such as in joint problem solving.

Career planning. This is a highly desirable motivator because it entails long-term commitment.

Praise. Everyone wants to feel good about themselves, to be well regarded by others and by themselves as winners.

Feedback. Make it frequent and specific.

THE PYGMALION EFFECT: THE POWER OF EXPECTATIONS

I've always had people doubt me. Supposedly, I didn't throw hard enough to even make it to the major leagues. I accomplished more than anyone ever thought I would the day I played in my first big league game. You just have to stop listening, stop hanging around the negative people. When you're around negative people all the time, you start believing it . . . and pretty soon, you're so low you can't rebound.

—Jamie Moyer, one-time Baltimore Orioles pitcher, quoted in *The Washington Post,* March 29, 1994

The Roman poet Ovid (43 B.C.–A.D. 17?), in the tenth book of his *Metamorphoses,* narrates the tale of sculptor Pygmalion, a prince of Cyprus, who wished to create a statue in ivory of the ideal woman. The finished artwork was so beautiful that Pygmalion fell in love with it. He thereupon secured the aid of Venus, the Goddess of Love, to bring the statue to life, which she did and the couple lived happily ever after.

Irish dramatist George Bernard Shaw returned to the theme of transformation in the form of a play, *Pygmalion* (1912). The drama, later made into the famous musical comedy *My Fair Lady* (1964), tells how Professor Henry Higgins' strong will and full confidence transformed a Cockney flower girl, Eliza Doolittle, into a beautiful, sophisticated, properly speaking London lady. Higgins even succeeds in passing her off as a duchess. Eliza explains the true significance of her transformation—the power of expectation or the self-fulfilling prophecy—to Higgins' friend Pickering as follows: "You see, really and truly, apart from the things anyone can pick up (the dressing and the proper way of speaking; and so on), the difference between a lady and a flower girl is not how she behaves, but how she's treated. I shall always be a flower girl to Professor Higgins, because he always treats me as a flower girl, and always will; but I know I can be a lady to you, because you always treat me as a lady, and always will."

There have been more than 3,200 studies of the impact of expectations on performance—in the classroom, in business and in industry. A classic classroom study (*Pygmalion in the Classroom* (New York: Holt, Rinehart and Winston, 1968) by Harvard social psychologists Robert Rosenthal and Lenore Jacobson showed how a teacher's expectation of her pupils' intellectual competence can become an educational self-fulfilling prophecy. The two researchers, working with elementary-level students, chose children from 18 classrooms. They randomly selected one-fifth of the students from each room and advised their teachers that they were "intellectual bloomers," and that the children could be expected to show remarkable academic gains. The result—children in the experimental groups averaged these gains in their IQs: verbal ability up two points, reasoning ability up four points, and overall score up four points.

The teachers, interestingly, didn't spend more time with their "special" charges. But apparently there was a significant difference in the quality of their interactions. The teachers' body language (facial expressions, posture, touch) evidently communicated to the children that they expected higher performance. The teachers undoubtedly increased the students' confidence level (stronger self-concept) and their own expectations of themselves. The study also stated that the teachers found these children to be more appealing.

The concept of the self-fulfilling prophecy is summed up by human relations director Len Sandler in these five principles ("Self-Fulfilling Prophecy: Better Management by Magic," *Training,* February 1986):

1. All of us form expectations of people, events, situations.
2. We communicate our expectations directly or indirectly (transmit cues).
3. The receivers adjust their behavior in response to our cues.
4. The end result: Our expectation is converted into like behavior.
5. A cycle of self-fulfilling prophecies ensues.

Sandler develops several corollaries based on these principles:

1. High expectations lead to higher performance and lower ones to reduced performance.
2. The resultant better performance, due to the high expectation, causes us to like the performer more; lower performance, a result of lower expectations, causes us to like the person less.

3. We tend to be comfortable with those who meet our expectations, whether high or low; we tend not to be comfortable, again whether high or low, with those who don't meet our expectations.
4. Forming expectations is a natural, unavoidable phenomenon.
5. Once expectations about people are formed, they become self-sustaining.
6. Good managers produce workers who feel good about themselves and perform well; bad (ineffective) managers affect their employees in the opposite directions.
7. Performance ratings are more than summaries of the past year's performance—they help to determine *future* performance.
8. The best managers enjoy high confidence levels in themselves and are confident in their ability to hire, train, develop, and motivate their performers. Their high self-confidence tends to communicate high expectations to others.

The interpersonal dynamics of the relations between managers and their subordinates, from whom they have high expectations, take these forms (just as the teachers reacted), per social psychologist Robert Rosanthal (cited in "Self-Fulfilling Prophecy: Better Management by Magic," *Training,* February 1986):

Climate. A warmer socio-emotional climate is created—more smiles, approving head nods, more eye contact. Their overall attitude is one of offering more support, encouragement, and warmth.

Input. They give their high expectation performers more projects, and these assignments are more challenging and provide higher visibility.

Output. Managers provide their high-expectation performers with more air time at meetings and pay closer attention to what they say, be they statements of agreement or disagreement. They also help them more to come up with solutions to problems.

Feedback. High-expectation employees tend to get more positive reinforcement—more praise, less criticism. The result: a growth in employee self-confidence.

How can the Pygmalion Effect be utilized for good management practices? Management writer Robert W.

Goddard offers these suggestions ("The Pygmalion Effect," *Personnel Journal*, June 1985):

Assume universal improvability. Everyone can upgrade his performance. Consider that (a) most people use only a small portion of their mental and physical capabilities, and (b) people "bloom" at different rates. It may be a slow process in some cases, but it is doable.

Demonstrate confidence. Show your staff that you think they can. How to do this? Via greater delegation, more challenging assignments, more freedom, more one-on-one coaching, more involvement in planning and decisions, etc. All of these activities on your part will show your interest in them and that you expect big things of them.

Engage in on-going dialog. Be a truly great communicator. Have an open door, listen, provide full information to do the work properly, and provide feedback on performance.

Set high standards. Setting high expectations shows that you trust your staff to do well. Your trust, which will show that you have high expectations of them, will encourage your people "to rise to the occasion."

Offer praise regularly. Offer praise liberally, even if the job isn't totally perfect. People need praise to bolster their self-image. This recognition will encourage greater effort for the next "big push."

Criticize the work, not the person. A job done imperfectly merits constructive criticism. That is, zero in on the performance, not the performer. This will show you're on the side of the worker.

Encourage self- and career-development. By helping people to strengthen their performance, capabilities and career progress, you demonstrate that you have confidence in their ability to do more, to assume greater responsibility.

Integrate new staffers into your unit in a positive way. Introduce the new subordinate as a person of potential. If you believe the newcomer is a person of high quality, your staff will show more interest and devote more time to him.

Watch personal biases. If you show strong preferences (likes, dislikes) to those with particular dress, personalities, political views, etc., the expectations phenomenon will kick-in in a particular way, that is, either negatively or positively. Your personal prejudices may well set up counterproductive expectations. You certainly don't want to doom someone to failure because you are communicating that the employee's tastes, opinions, or style are incompatible with success.

Watch incongruent nonverbal messages. Remember it's not so much what you say, but what you do. If your nonverbal behavior communicates low confidence, that message will be picked up. You certainly don't want to clobber high potential people with messages that assert low confidence in them.

A novel and dramatic illustration of how a top manager's expectations can ignite the behavior of subordinate managers is exemplified by the approach taken to keeping the washrooms clean at Greyhound bus terminals. Company research evidenced that dirty washrooms made a bad impression on customers. So the VP for marketing and operations launched a program of surprise visits to the firm's 570 terminals, featuring a working, gourmet lunch or dinner with the local manager—in the restroom! Soon, managers who had not been visited, sent the VP photos of themselves eating in their restrooms, hoping to show that he need not drop in. The VP said that half of the managers thought he was crazy; the other half thought he was totally committed to customer service. But the end result was that with crystal-clear communication of expectations, station managers began to really attack their washrooms (Gary Lamphier, "Suddenly, Our Local Greasy Spoon Is Taking On an Aura of Luxury," *The Wall Street Journal*, October 5, 1990).

An interesting form of self-fulfilling prophecy is that of the language we use. Thus, as Jefferey Pfeffer points out in *Competitive Advantage Through People: Unleashing the Power of the Workforce* (Boston: Harvard Business School Press, 1994), Disney in its theme parks uses the language of show business to help its employees deliver high-quality service. **Examples:** The personnel department becomes "central casting"; people work "on stage"; those coming to the park are neither visitors nor tourists, but "guests."

And persons with disabilities are referred to as persons with disabilities as opposed to "the handicapped," "physically disabled," "cripples," and the like.

Summary point: The important thing to remember about the Pygmalion effect is that you have the power to determine whether the self-fulfilling prophecy is one of success or failure. So you can upgrade marginal performers by your expectations, and you can cause high-potential people to fail if they feel you don't have confidence in them. What you expect is what you get!

Story: The aerodynamic limitations/imperfections of the bumble bee were under discussion by two aeronautical engineers:

Engineer A: Aerodynamically speaking, it's impossible for the bumble bee to fly. The wings are much too short and the body is too bulky to even get off the ground. How do you imagine he does it?

Engineer B (with a smile): Maybe no one ever told the bee that he couldn't fly.

MODELING: WHAT YOU DO IS WHAT YOU GET BACK

Few things are harder for people to put up with than the annoyance of a good example.

—Mark Twain (1835–1910), U.S. novelist and humorist

Vigor is contagious, and whatever makes us either think or feel strongly adds to our power and enlarges our field of action.

—Ralph Waldo Emerson (1803–82), a leading U.S. author

You can also develop the climate you favor *by the behavior you exhibit,* by setting the appropriate examples. As the boss, you automatically become the role model for your people (at least for most of them). Management consultant Dr. Steward R. Segall ("Reflections of Your Management Style," *Supervisory Management,* February 1991) poses these questions to you, as your team's model:

☐ How do you respond to emergencies? What is your reaction to a "crisis"? Do you lose your cool, which certainly affects everyone's confidence in you? If the unexpected event was due to someone's "boo-boo," do you zero in on the problem or do you dress down the error maker?

☐ How do you deal with outside pressures? If those above you make unreasonable demands on you, do you respond in kind, possibly screaming at your staffers? Or do you try to absorb some of that pressure, letting the brunt of the impact fall on yourself?

☐ How do you respond to change? Do you regard it as unfair, the end of the world? Or do you accept it and present it to your staff in the best light possible, as "a given" in today's dynamic world? And do you present the issues openly and honestly, answering everyone's questions about the change?

And some added questions: Do you listen to new ideas? Are you consistent in your dealings with staff? Do people regard you as predictable, inconsistent, or unfathomable? Do you provide challenge or do you hoard the more significant work for yourself or pass it on only to one or two select individuals? And the author, would add, how do people see you in the vital areas of ethics, quality, and customer service?

To illustrate the potent influence of managerial modeling, management guru Tom Peters suggests a highly informal program along these lines to get people to climb aboard the all-important quality ship ("Quality of Work Can Improve Even Without Agenda," *Washington Business Journal,* November 16, 1987):

The Book Gambit

Go to your bookstore or order a batch of books on quality improvement. Just stack them on your desk; no need to read them. Soon the grapevine will let everyone know what the boss is up to: "It looks like he means business." "Yeah, he must have 15 books or more on the stuff on his desk!"

The Outside Course Ploy

Take off five days to attend a course on quality. You don't even have to go to class. Just return with a big, fat notebook that the instructor gave you and listen for staff reactions: "A whole week. This is really different." "Looks like this is high-priority stuff."

The Reading Circulation Device

Feed your staff newspaper clippings and journal articles dealing with quality. Attach to them slips with an "FYI" note or such queries as "what might we do with this? Please advise in 10 days." Regardless of whether or not you have any specific answers, you can be certain your staff will put their thinking caps on ("Hey, I guess the boss thinks we're not doing as well as we might.") and get some ideas to you, posthaste.

The Meeting Alert

Start all your meetings with a short "quality update." Agenda items should have a quality tie-in, too. Also review quality each quarter. **The results:** Anticipate a rush by staff to respond positively in various ways.

Performance Reviews

Be sure to include quality as a key element on the annual performance appraisal. This stance will communicate loud and clear that quality is hardly a lip-service kind of thing.

Work Place Visits

At visits to people's desks, pointedly ask: "What progress are you making in the quality area?" Word will get around that one had better be prepared to provide a meaningful response.

The Celebration Approach

Schedule a three-day quality summit six to nine months from now to celebrate progress and accomplishments. Appoint a live wire to spearhead things, including facilitating the shindig. Anticipate a hefty agenda with much involvement by staff.

Supplier/Customer Meetings

Set up one-hour biweekly meetings with suppliers and customers to probe quality status and new needs. Anticipate a lot of healthy scurrying around by staff to be prepared for these meetings.

According to Peters: when your staff starts to say, "He's darn near obsessed with this quality thing," you know that you have modeled and communicated the message clearly. Note that the activity and interest you created was done without constructing a specific, precise agenda. In fact, that might have stifled the process. What you did was to release people's energies and creativities by keeping things informal, but totally focused (on quality).

Note: The eight behaviors engaged in by the boss obviously exhibited a personal interest in the area of quality. Most of them could serve as models for the staff to engage in, too.

Research has evidenced that a make-or-break factor in successful EEO/Affirmative Action programs is the perception by staff that they are supported by top management. Obviously, senior managers have to demonstrate (model) their interest and support. Thus, psychology professor Dr. John Dovido cites the case of a CEO in a large firm who merely requested his key senior staffers discuss their progress in equal opportunity for minorities and women. The results were quick and profound: By the next quarter there were significant increases in both the hiring and promotion of the groups in question ("The Subtlety of Racism," *Training and Development,* April 1993).

Summary Points

First, modeling, or leadership by example, offers all too many opportunities for cynicism, say management consultants Irwin Rubin and Robert Inguagiato ("Changing the Work Culture," *Training and Development,* July 1991). For example, the manager may sponsor an important change-type training program, but fail to attend. Or, the manager may attend, but such comments as this one may be made later by staffers: "He sang a good tune during the program, but Monday morning was business as usual." In other words, you can't say one thing and practice another. The advisory "practice what you preach" still rings true.

Second, character is taught by example. As this adage phrases it, "The apple doesn't fall far from the tree." Educator Joseph W. Gauld ("Character Development: A School's Primary Task," *The Wall Street Journal,* April 1, 1992) strongly supports the notion that parental modeling of desired behavior is the key to proper behavior by young people. Gauld states: "When Dad becomes open and less defensive, so will Junior; when Mom accepts a new challenge, so will Suzie; and so on." Substitute the word "manager" for "Mom and Dad" and you've got the key to development of proper style, behavior, or performance by the staff.

The Bottom Line

When you model you are leading by example. So when you practice what you preach—"walk the talk" in today's jargon—you encourage like behavior (mimicry) by staff. If your behavior is not in sync with your preachment, your staffers will regard the preachment as mere mockery. Mimicry can produce the payoffs you wish; mockery is counterproductive, only creating distrust.

Note: Modeling, a form of expectation setting, entails engaging personally in *a desired behavior* for all to see and emulate, e.g., limiting one's lunch period to prescribed time limits. In contrast, expectation setting (The Pygmalion Effect) typically takes various forms of *communication,* sometimes novel, to indicate the expected behavior.

THE POWER OF FEEDBACK

The manager of a telephone answering center for a major telephone company said, "We don't pay much attention to the percentage of 'fairs' and 'poors' we get from customer phone surveys. But we study the dickens out of the percentage of 'excellents' we get. Our staff meetings are almost entirely devoted to what we can do to get more."

—Management consultants Chip R. Bell and Ron Zemke in *Personnel Journal,* September 1988

Feedback or knowledge of results is basic to our everyday needs to maintain, or improve, or change our performance. It can let us know in specific terms about our health (via various blood and other tests, x-rays, professional observations), financial conditions (via bank or credit card statements), learning prowess (via test scores and grades), athletic ability (via various scores, averages, coaches' comments), and performance on the job (via production data and comments by bosses and peers). Our interpersonal relations, too, are strengthened by feedback data from others, which helps us "to see ourselves as others see us."

In simple terms, feedback is an energizer. It augments our will to do, to change, to improve.

That feedback can have tremendous motivating effects is illustrated by the following research reports.

1. One study found that training improved sanitation practices (hand washing behavior of kitchen workers) by 21.7%. But by adding feedback to the training, the required handwashing soared to 203.1% (Mortimer R. Feinberg and Aaron Levenstein, "Developing and Making the Most of the Slight Edge," *The Wall Street Journal,* July 9, 1984).

2. An electronics firm in Scotland developed a computer-controlled device to provide immediate feedback on machine operator performance, measuring how much and how fast an operator is working. For example, a visual display mechanism shows the number of units produced hourly. In one company, the feedback device had this result: Completed components per hour went up from 65 to 130–140. The device also enabled the operators to better pace themselves. Thus one female operator who previously "made a fortune" in the morning, would collapse in the afternoon. With pacing, she produced at a steady rate throughout the day and actually made more money in the long run (*Behavior Improvement News,* February 1980).

Motivational vs. Developmental Feedback

Management consultant Donald T. Tosti ("Formative Feedback," *Performance and Instruction,* March 1987) makes a helpful distinction between motivational and developmental feedback. The former type affects primarily the quantity of performance, that is, a specific performance is likely to be increased or decreased. We can say, then, that motivational feedback affects the frequency of response/performance. **Examples:** A supervisor compliments a habitual latecomer on his arrivals to work whenever he appears early or on schedule. In time, the late arrivals decrease very significantly. Or a boss may punish an employee for violation of a company policy. Violations thereby no longer occur.

Developmental feedback, on the other hand, operates to alter the form or quality of performance; that is, it corrects, guides or improves it. Tosti calls this **formative** feedback. Note that in everyday life actors and athletes, among others, regularly receive correcting cues from their directors or coaches and adjust their performance appropriately.

Motivational feedback is the basis for **contingency management,** that is, "if this, then . . ." It entails providing the performer with reinforcement (reward) when the preferred behavior occurs. (Or negative reinforcement—punishment may be provided to discourage an unwanted behavior.) In formative feedback, the supervisor initiates a developmental or **corrective approach** to bring about change. Let's assume that George, an engine tune-up mechanic, functions below standard. George's boss, Sam, using formative feedback, could operate in this manner:

1. Describe the problem to George: "Our standard is nine tune-ups per day. The data on this graph shows that you reached this requirement only once in the last 10 work days."
2. Sam may then ask George if he has any thoughts or suggestions as to how he can get back on track.
3. Alternative routes (suggested by both parties) to a return to standard are discussed, and the pros and cons of each approach are evaluated.
4. Agreement is reached as to appropriate measures to follow to reach the standard again.

Note that Sam took corrective action rather than waiting for the right behavior to occur for which he might provide reinforcement (praise).

Tosti also points out that motivational feedback should be immediately given; formative feedback should be immediately useful. For example, Tosti found that telephone sales people, whose performance was monitored by the sales manager, were helped very significantly when they received performance feedback at the start of each day as opposed to receiving it at day's end.

Tosti also recommends against mixing the two types of feedback, for they don't enhance one another. In fact, the effectiveness of both may be lost. Praise in one breath (motivational feedback) and correction in the other (formative feedback) only produces dissatisfaction with both.

When do you use formative/developmental feedback?

☐ When training or coaching is required to increase proficiency. This may be for a new job, new duties or to correct bad work habits.
☐ To bring performance in line with new or changed systems, new procedures, or new standards or expectations.
☐ To bring behavior back to standard. "Drift" from standard may occur for reasons ranging from chance events to elements in the system.
☐ To reconcile priorities. If new duties have been added, there is an obvious need to resolve any conflicts that interfere with basic task performance.

How does the manager actually give formative feedback? Stephanie F. Jackson and Donald Tosti provide these 10 guides ("Ten Rules for Formative/Developmental Feedback," *Performance and Instruction Journal,* December 1984):

1. **Use appropriate sized steps.** Break the task down into workable, digestible elements as opposed to doling it out in its entirety.
2. **Tailor information to the performer's needs.** Everyone requires different bits of skill or knowledge.
3. **Use the performer's language.** Communication-wise, you must move to the understanding level of the performer. Shop workers will only be frustrated by graduate school jargon.
4. **Concentrate on behavior, not the person.** This is essential to avoid defensiveness. Listening is not likely to occur if one is being attacked.
5. **Avoid mixed messages.** For example, don't weaken your message by combining praise and criticism.
6. **Avoid overload.** Performers can only absorb a limited amount of data. So zero in on the big need, and save the other data for another feedback session.
7. **Be specific.** Your job as a giver of feedback is to provide clearcut, pinpointed data about the need for improvement. The performer must be clear about the needed change before he can possibly execute it.
8. **Check receptivity.** Provide feedback when the performer is best able to hear you. Then check for actual understanding rather than assume the message got through.
9. **Give feedback when it is most useful.** If the new data cannot be applied immediately, they are very likely to be lost.
10. **Give feedback often enough to prevent major errors.** Anticipate the performer's needs. "Better late than never" is not a workable rule at all in the feedback-giving process.

To sum up Tosti's approach to giving of feedback:

Task Performance

If it meets your standard, use motivational feedback (praise) to maintain it. If it is below, use formative/developmental feedback to correct or upgrade it.

Timing

Give feedback immediately after performance if the concern is motivational. If the concern is correctional, give it when immediately useful—that is, just before an opportunity for actual practice.

Feedback Cues

The cue (stimulus) should be adequate and appropriate to the feedback purpose, i.e., you should be certain that the performer will understand whether he is to engage in the preferred activity (maintenance of the behavior) or in a correcting one.

Feedback Activities

The nature of the behavior evoked by the feedback cue must be clear—whether it is reinforcing (motivational feedback) or serves as a correctant (formative feedback) the performer is actually able to act upon (has the requisite repertoire of skills and knowledges) and watch for unwanted, incompatible responses triggered by the feedback (anxiety, anger, frustration).

Effects on Performance

You can decide whether the frequency of the behavior is to be maintained or increased (via motivational feedback) or the form of behavior is to be changed (via formative/developmental feedback).

Feedback Systems

A truly effective feedback system, per performance technologist John Staelin, has these characteristics ("Using Feedback to Change Behavior," *Bulletin on Training*, May-June 1979):

1. Performance data are based on **objective** criteria (standards), not guesses or subjective opinions such as "everyone works hard" or "not hard enough."
2. Data pinpoint **specific** and **meaningful** aspects of performance. For example, in a restaurant situation: "You were very polite to the customer, but could you give her a big, happy smile, too?" is more useful than a terse "You're not friendly."
3. Data should go to the people who do the work; not just to a "correction specialist"; e.g., if an airline counter clerk misroutes a bag and only someone at the other end gets the data, the feedback is improperly directed.

4. Data accurately reflect **current** performance. Resurrecting history—old incidents, events, trends—is akin to flogging the dead horse.
5. Data are reported **regularly,** not temporarily or intermittently. Good feedback is not a "sometimes kind of thing."
6. Data go to the performer immediately or as soon as possible—the feedback about the lack of a smile for the customer is most meaningful when the customer leaves, not at the end of a very busy day. Delayed data runs the risk of being doubted, debated, or disregarded.
7. Data relate to **individual** performance (unless a true team operation is used).
8. Data are measured against fully understood, agreed-upon performance standards, against a reachable goal or baseline. People need to learn of their progress toward goals.
9. Data are quantified wherever possible.
10. The format and the numbers are easy to follow.
11. Trends in performance are made clear. The very legitimate and normal "How am I doing?" question should be answered on the basis of what has been happening over meaningful time periods.
12. Data are expressed in positive terms. Talk about accomplishment, not just errors. Dr. Thomas K. Connellan, a pioneer in applied behavioral technology, gives this example in (*How to Improve Human Performance*, New York: Harper & Row, 1978): Instead of complaining to the maintenance mechanic about a 13% downtime factor, the manager would do much better to inform the worker that there is 87% "uptime." Thus, instead of discussing with the mechanic what has produced the 13% situation, it would be much more helpful to talk about how the very good record of 87% can be increased to say, 92%.
13. To the extent practical, the data should be self-administered—collected and summarized by the worker. This approach provides involvement, encourages responsibility and makes the data fully credible. It encourages the employee to become his own supervisor. (Obviously, data to our non-smiling waitress can only come from the supervisor.)

Two additional points, suggested by Dr. Connellan, are:

1. Relevant feedback should go to all levels in the organization. In this way, managers can recognize

employee progress and use it as a basis for reinforcing performance.

2. Feedback in graphic form is to be preferred. People can understand graphs more readily than a lot of numbers and words.

To set up or improve a feedback system, you, as manager, must respond to these issues: What is to be measured (new sales, renewals, etc.)? What is your index (e.g., output per hour)? When should the measurement be made (for immediacy or fuller impact)? Who should collect the data (the worker, the boss, or the two together)? How should the data be collected (video, worker ticket sheets, graphs)? Who should receive the feedback (others besides the performer may have a need to know)?

Conditions Affecting Feedback Effectiveness

When we talk about feedback, we should recognize that presentation of data is only half the definition. The other portion relates to how the performer will perceive and respond to the information. Quite often, then, ineffective feedback is a result of elements in the recipient. Some of these factors, per education professor George L. Geis ("Formative Feedback: The Receiving Side," *Performance and Instruction Journal,* June/July 1986) are:

The Performer's Mood or Emotional State

If the performer is upset, deferral is wiser than following the rule of immediacy. An emotionally besieged person is not very likely to hear the feedback as intended. He thus may distort, deny or otherwise block it.

The Performer's Perception of the Value of the Task

"Big deal, so the report which never gets read was a day and a half late." Obviously, the performer must appreciate the value of a task if the feedback relating to it is to be effective. It thus may be wise to deal with the "What's in it for me?" issue before delivering any feedback.

The Performer's Perception of the Value of the Proposed Change

"Sure, I could get here on time, but things never get going until everybody has had that extra cup of coffee anyhow." Thus, there is a need for early agreement in the feedback session as to the importance of the new,

desired or changed behavior, or the "performance gap" may be subject to an unwanted debate.

The "Messenger"

If the advice-giver has been helpful previously, the advice is likely to be given full attention. ("Charlie knows what's what. I always pick up some practical ideas from him. So I make it a point to listen to what he has to say.")

Timing

"Better late than never" is not a useful guide in giving feedback. The "now he tells me" or "how was I supposed to know?" response is to be expected if the supervisor is late or lax in providing information to facilitate proper performance.

Language

Technical jargon or too little context will reduce understanding. ("He must have gone on for 30 minutes; but, you know, I never could figure out what he was driving at.")

Knowledge Limitations

If the performer doesn't have the background to see that the advice can be implemented or doesn't have the resources to do what is requested, appropriate action cannot be expected. ("I'm sure it's a great idea, but I've only been here three weeks." Or: "Sure, we could get out all the orders the day they come in, but not if customer services sends us them at 4 p.m. and half the crew has already gone home.")

Past History of Success

If the performer has previously succeeded with prior changes or ideas, the new ones are more likely to be listened to than if there is a history of the reverse. ("I've tried a dozen different ways to sell customers on the new widget, but nothing seems to work.")

Competing Behaviors

If the performer is engaged in a particular task or concerned about others which require attention, receptivity is likely to be reduced. ("Here I'm chewing my nails over those eight unhappy customers I've got to call back and she goes into her long song and dance about the changes in the weekly progress report.")

And if there is any doubt at all as to whether the message did get through to the feedback recipient, it is wise to ask a question such as this: "Could you give me an example of how this suggested change could have been applied to the problem you faced yesterday?"

Feedback Dynamics

As managers, we know that feedback has educational and motivational value. But do we know how it changes behavior? In other words, what is the mechanism or the dynamics underlying this very powerful process?

Dr. David Nadler, an organizational psychologist, provides us with these insights in *Feedback and Organization Development—Using Data Based Methods* (Reading, Mass.: Addison-Wesley, 1977):

Disconfirmation. Feedback can motivate and thus change behavior by giving data inconsistent with prevailing perceptions. The disconfirming data create anxiety basic to any change in behavior and learning. People don't change if they are satisfied with the status quo. Of course, the data must be seen as valid and accurate. If they are not believed, the inconsistent perception will not serve as a motivator. Also, the feedback process itself must be non-threatening, ensuring psychological safety. If one perceives oneself to be under threat, defensiveness will arise and the feedback recipient will distort or belittle the significance of the data. **Example:** As a result of a coaching practices survey, a manager learns that most of his staff feels that his delegation practices are wanting.

External reward expectations. Feedback can work—if it provides successfully the perception that a new activity will lead to the new outcomes (rewards). But for feedback to succeed as an external motivator, these conditions must be present:

a) The level of performance needed to obtain favorable feedback and rewards must be attainable

b) The link or relationship between receiving feedback and receiving rewards must be clear, and

c) The outcome must have value for the performer.

Thus, telling the shipping clerk to work hard, stay out of trouble, and some day he may head up the company, will hardly be feedback data to serve as an effective external motivator.

Internal reward expectations. In addition to external rewards, feedback may be perceived as a reward in itself. Why? Because it tells the performer that his behavior is good quality. For the feedback process to work, however, the desired level of behavior must be attainable. If the expected level is too high, it will be frustrating. But it must be high enough to provide challenge and resultant positive feelings upon task accomplishment and receipt of the feedback. **Example:** Encourage goal setting that has some "stretch" built into it.

Cueing. The above three mechanisms related to motivation or the creation of energy. But assuming that energy already exists, feedback can serve as a guide, an error-correcting device. **Example:** The truck driver receives visual cues that his vehicle is moving out of its lane and onto the shoulder. He responds to the feedback cue by turning the wheel, which quickly corrects the problem, at the same time receiving feedback cues that he's back in the correct lane.

For feedback to serve as an effective cueing device for behavior change, these conditions must be present: the feedback must be specific, and the performer must know what the desired behavior is so he knows that the correction worked. In the absence of these two conditions, cueing feedback can lead to frustration, inappropriate responses and failure to make needed corrections.

Learning. As you can see, changing behavior through cueing is a relatively simple process, particularly when compared to the learning interaction. In the latter case, the correction routine is not known or obvious. In relation to learning, feedback only highlights the problem; it doesn't provide the solution. It triggers "search activity," which means securing more information about the nature of the problem and its possible solutions. This means trial-and-error behavior, with feedback ultimately advising that all is OK or that more trial behaviors are needed. Once a correct routine is learned, feedback can operate as a cueing device. **Example:** The young manager who is seeking to develop a pattern or style for the conduct of successful meetings.

Diagnosing Feedback Systems

Every manager, whether he is aware of it or not, has a feedback system. It may be effective or ineffective, but it exists, nevertheless.

When a feedback system doesn't work, consider troubleshooting it. Management consultants Chip Bell and Ron Zemke ("On-Target Feedback," *Training,* June 1992), drawing on the work of performance technologist Karen Brethower, suggest using these six questions to diagnose an ailing feedback system:

1. Is the feedback punitive in character—that is, is it used primarily to put down, embarrass, or lecture people in a parental way? **Example:** Assume the boss blows his top over the error rate—"I don't want to catch you with an error rate over 3%." The employees most certainly will see that they're not "caught" again by simply falsifying their error rate. Accidents and small fires also may go unreported if there are penalties attached to reporting such data.

2. Are the data collected relevant to the needs of the performers? Is there evident payoff for those receiving it? Another way of stating this situation is that the feedback is about variable A, but the payoff relates to variable B. **Example:** quality is given a lot of lip service, but the payoffs go to sheer volume of work. Or, in a situation where the boss says he wants effective quality circles, but if the meetings run past the allotted time because the participants are so involved, he raises the roof, complaining about loss of production by several circle members who are telemarketing people.

3. Do the data arrive too late to be acted on? **Example:** quality control reports may be essential to control excessive scrap, rework or rejects. But if the reports come 2–6 weeks late, little can be done to trace through the variable involved at the time of the undesirable performance.

4. Does the feedback relate to something the performers cannot change? **Example:** Customers complain about "poor service," the problem being that there are not enough telephones to keep the lines open.

5. Is it about the wrong things? **Example:** Sales personnel can do little about an inconveniently located store.

6. Are the data hard to collect and record? A burdensome collection system will cause an inevitable reaction of "This is much more trouble than it's worth."

Guidelines for the Manager

1. Recognize that your feedback system is a tremendous means to influence behavior/performance/ change.

2. The best feedback system relies on a combination of correctional/developmental/formative feedback and consequence/motivational feedback (to confirm or maintain the desired performance or decrease the likelihood of its repetition).

3. When giving feedback, try to make it objective (standards based or goal oriented), specific, direct to the performer, current, recurring (or regular), immediate, quantified, easy to digest (avoid feedback overload), and most importantly, *positive.*

4. If practicable, let employees administer their own feedback system.

5. When giving feedback, consider the performer's readiness to receive it, the possible impact on the performer, and the effect on your future relationship with the recipient.

6. When giving criticism (formative feedback), critique the behavior, not the person. Most of us can alter our behavior, but hardly our personalities.

Notes:

1. Chapter 5 relates directly to this chapter by providing motivational concepts and techniques applicable to particular segments of the workforce—women, the older worker, etc.

2. Summary concepts about motivation, relating to Chapters 4 and 5, appear at the end of Chapter 5.

3. Problems, exercises, and questions for discussion, for use in management training workshops and university classes in management, appear at the end of Chapter 5.

PRAISE: THE NO-COST EGO MASSAGE

Every child is an honored student at Sandy Springs Friends School (Sandy Springs, Md.)

—spotted on a bumper sticker

The deepest principle of human nature is the craving to be appreciated.

—U.S. psychologist/philosopher William James (1842–1910)

I can live for two months on a good compliment.

—Mark Twain (1835–1910), U.S. novelist and humorist

Napoleon is said to have stated that his troops as a reward would rather have the Legion of Honor, a scrap of colored cloth, than a fat French farm.

—quoted by Andre Nelson, a freelance writer, in *Supervisory Management,* May 1989.

Most managers have developed a rather definite style or philosophy about providing subordinates with praise. This philosophy may never have been reduced to writing, but it exists nevertheless. What is *your* style and philosophy? Might it be helpful to re-examine your attitudes and behaviors respecting praise? If so, complete the self-quiz on page 209 to receive a reading concerning your style as a giver of praise.

The quiz should not only give you a "fix" on your praise-giving style, but, hopefully, also make you aware of the importance of praise as a motivator. In my own case, I became more aware of people's acute need for praise some years back when I saw this sign on the wall behind the work table of a shipping clerk:

"When I do something right no one remembers. When I do something wrong no one ever forgets."

If you are committed to giving praise as a matter of good supervision and want to make certain that the praise you provide has the positive effect your really wish, try to follow these guides offered by management consultant Robert A. Luke, Jr. ("Meaningful Praise Makes a Difference," *Supervisory Management,* February 1991) to maximize results from this motivational tool:

Preparation. Know the behaviors you deem important. When giving praise cite examples and their *positive consequences:* greater sales, reduced complaints, better quality. Note that these precise outcomes are not related to intelligence, character (dependability), or personality (warm, friendly, likable).

Specificity. The greater the specificity the more it will impact on the receiver. **Example:** "You developed the background data on the X4R contract so fully that it gave us an edge on our bid. We now know the kind of bids we have to submit in the future." Praise related to a particular behavior is more meaningful than a general dose of the same.

Realism. Avoid phony praise. Only give credit where it is earned.

Timing. Not only should praise be given often, but it should follow the event as soon as possible. This will give it the greatest impact. It also lets people know immediately that they're on the right track.

Discernment. Inform the performer promptly if improvement in performance is in order. Corrective feedback not only helps the employee to improve, but it increases the sincerity of the praise you give. All praise and no criticism might lead to skepticism of your intentions.

Creativity. Increase the impact of your verbal praise by adding to it tangible rewards—trips, raises, bonuses, jewelry, cash awards, gift certificates, a day off, training. Two cautions: The reward should be valued by the employee, and he should know why the praise is being rendered.

And says Robert Luke, the worst thing you can do in the area of praise is to withhold it. No news is likely to be interpreted as bad news. Meaningful, earned praise clears the air. It communicates without doubt that they're doing OK.

Several added pointers re the giving of praise are given by management authority George S. Odiorne (in *The George Odiorne Letter,* September 1980):

Location. Give praise and recognition in public or private. Criticism should only be given in private.

Quantity. If earned, provide as big chunks of praise as possible.

Modeling. If you have subordinate supervisors, serve as a good model for them. A modeling posture you don't want is that of being quick to criticize, but slow to provide praise.

Time expenditure. Taking the time to give earned praise is good supervision. It is not a waste of time, for praise giving has strong, positive effects.

Added opportunities. Use regular meetings and special ones such as luncheons and dinners to provide praise and recognition. These opportunities are particularly helpful if you missed the chance to give praise in the course of the regular work day.

It is also a good idea to vary your praise. There is a likelihood of resentment if you only give praise for the same behaviors. Also, some praise recipients may tend to discount praise. This indicates a lack of self-confidence so proceed cautiously. Try to bolster employees self-image in as many ways as you can, expressing confidence in their ability to carry through on an assignment when it is assigned. For some employees it may also be good practice to praise *effort* as well as results.

Added criteria for proper recognition of your staffers' contributions, per management consultant Karen Larson ("How to Recognize Your Staffers' Contribution," *Supervisory Management,* August 1991) are:

Criteria. Be certain your standards are fair and reasonable. This means that the majority of your people should be able to earn recognition.

Staff perceptions of criteria. Additionally, you want the criteria you use to be perceived as fair. This issue is not how you regard its fairness, but how do your subordinates feel about it?

Frequency. Because you want to provide recognition as often as possible, consider this guideline when giving gifts: smaller gifts, given more often for more people, are likely to have more impact.

Interests. Tailor recognition to the special interests of the individuals involved. **Example:** Someone who is heavily into sports might well appreciate two tickets to a sporting event.

Novelty. Look for new ways to provide recognition. This may range from giving an individual (or a team) a chance to do a special project or asking a staffer to serve as a mentor for a newcomer, to inviting your boss to a meeting where you provide a special recognition or having your honored staffer join you and your boss for a special lunch.

Note, too, that in giving praise there are several things to be avoided, says management professor and communications authority Walter D. St. John ("Plain Speaking," *Personnel Journal,* June 1985):

☐ When providing a commendation, don't patronize or act superior. This type of behavior will destroy the value of the praise and have a boomerang or negative effect.

☐ Don't dole out phony praise or flattery. People know when they did or didn't earn a compliment.

☐ Don't use praise as a put down or ridicule: "Nice job. It's about time you did it right." Or: "I would

like to praise you on your work. When are you going to give me that opportunity?"

☐ Don't embarrass anyone when rendering the deserved praise. Low-key it when praising people who are less sure of themselves.

☐ Don't act uncomfortable or embarrassed when giving praise, for it will make the praise recipient ill at ease.

☐ Don't rush the compliment as if your big need is to get the nasty business over with. You want a positive rather than a puzzled or even a negative reaction.

☐ Don't give praise grudgingly. Either give it with enthusiasm or skip it entirely.

The author would provide this added "don't": Don't weaken the potential impact of the praise you may give by engaging in what has been termed "pimple management," that is, by saying "Great job, but you should have . . ." and then proceed to list (or even highlight) all the nasty "blemishes."

There is another growing "don't" about praise; that is, about celebrating Secretary's Day. Staff reporter of *The Wall Street Journal,* Christina Duff, in her article "Secretaries Say This Is a Day to Forget" (April 21, 1993), points out that many secretaries don't look forward to this day at all. They believe it trivializes their job and that good work should be rewarded by a bonus, raise, time off or educational seminars. They feel that their so-called special day has become too commercialized, what with all the predictable chocolates and flowers. To quote one secretary, "It belittles us. The message is: Let's keep those little girls happy. Give them some flowers."

Another secretary phrased it this way: "A day set aside for posies or lunch is tantamount to saying: 'Hey, I'm so insignificant and valueless, there's a day set aside to remind you I exist.'" So she told her boss she would rather not celebrate the day.

The answer to the above-described secretarial reactions? Treat them well year-round. To show your appreciation, give them increasingly more responsible work, make them a member of the team, and provide them the same treatment, praise-wise, as any other staffer. Being singled out for "special recognition" once a year is hardly a compliment when no one else is treated that way.

Note: Judith Waldrop ("More Than a Typist," *American Demographics,* April 1994), points out a survey by Professional Secretaries International (PSI) which found that 60% are involved with computer equipment purchases; 80% buy desk and filing supplies; 64% make travel arrangements; over 33% are involved in decisions to buy office furniture, hire temporary employees, and choose courier services. So, among other things, they wield considerable buying power.

In respect to how managers acknowledge accomplishment, management consultant Andrew E. Schwartz ("Managing to Be a Leader," *Training News,* May 1985) draws on the work of Ken Blanchard, author of the mega-bestseller, *The One Minute Manager* (1982), who observes that managers respond to performance in one of three ways. First, there is the "seagull manager" who flies in quickly, makes a great deal of noise, and then dumps on everyone. The result: lowered productivity. Second, there is the "let alone zap manager." He is seldom seen except when something is done wrong and, you guessed it, zap! Again, productivity drops because the Zapper never reinforces (praises) employee performance. The third type is the "positive regard manager" who provides positive feedback as frequently as possible. In fact, he actually spends time looking for work done well!

To round out our discussion of praise, you should recognize that there are several media or methods of praise giving. They are:

Verbal: "You did a very prompt and accurate job on Project R-4, Mary." Or: "You exceeded our expectations on that last assignment. You developed a new way . . ."

Written. This includes formal letters of commendation and complimentary notes on a report, memo, or project turned in by a staffer: "Good job. Keep it up." Or: "I intend to send a copy of your report to the regional offices as a guide for their future submissions."

Non-verbal: Use appreciative head nods, smiles, laughs, touching (pat on the arm or the back), use of the hand, e.g., the circular "OK" sign, the thumbs up gesture, fist projected forward vigorously, exchange of "high fives," etc.

Work assignment: Delegate more challenging tasks.

Positive outlook: Show high regard for and confidence in others—"I know you can do it for us even though this is a new activity for you." Praise givers have been referred to as the "inverse paranoid," i.e., they believe everyone is out to do them good.

Regardless of the method you employ to express appreciation, your rendering of praise has one solid objective:

You want your people to feel like winners. And you certainly don't want to manage your praise-giving behavior in a way that causes employees to say, "The only way to get noticed around here is to make a mistake."

If you wish to capitalize on the motivational potential of giving praise, a good way to start is to collect data on your actual praise-giving vs. criticism-giving behavior. But you must do this conscientiously over a several-week period. Why go to all the hassle of data collection? Two reasons: (1) Because you can't shift to a new style of behaving, assuming a change is appropriate and desired by yourself, without knowing from what to shift; and (2) self-monitoring of your behavior (self-feedback) will inform you of progress over time (3–4 weeks) toward your new goal. The Praise/Criticism Tally Sheet on page 211 will help you in your check for progress.

CONNECTION

We are very much social beings with needs for and value friendships with colleagues, to work with people who respect and support us, and to be associated with people with whom we share a common purpose. In short, much of our day-to-day gratification comes from the people with whom we are "connected." Sociologist Robert Schrank believes people like jobs primarily because they need other people—they need them to gossip with, to hang out with, to "schmooze." To quote Schrank: "The workplace performs the function of community" (reported by Lance Marrow, in *Time* magazine's Essay, "What Is the Point of Working?" May 11, 1981).

It thus suggests to you, as manager, to think in terms of how you can encourage natural tendencies toward "groupness." What comes to mind obviously, is to develop a team of people who enjoy working with one another and, secondly, putting staffers into other team situations wherever possible—task forces, survey teams, special project groups, study teams, and permanent and ad hoc committees.

TEAM EFFORT AND INFLUENCE

As stated above, most of us are gregarious folk. We like to rub shoulders with people who share our concerns, interests, and values. We like to interact with people we respect, listen to us, and challenge us in constructive ways. In short, a major source of our on-the-job gratification results from the contacts we have with our peers. Tap this natural preference, then, and provide the fullest possible opportunities for peer interaction. For example, in addition to conducting group-at-large problem solving meetings, put people to work on unit problems in pairs, trios, or quartets.

A Cautionary Reminder

When you involve your people (the team) fully in planning, problem solving and decision making, don't count on these approaches for fast results. Rather, regard them as the best way to secure successful results. Initial "losses" in discussion time have their ultimate payoffs, particularly in ease of implementation. Why? Because people who have helped to create the idea, who have "argued it through" in terms of pros and cons and benefits and possible disadvantages, are automatically ready to support it. Remember, people support what *they* create, not necessarily what *you* create.

A useful form of team management is decision making by consensus. Note that this doesn't mean routine voting. All too often voting creates winners and losers, which doesn't contribute at all to "teamness." Consensus means letting everyone concerned have a chance to have his say about the issue or problem. When the issue has been well "talked through," people are ready to decide (choose, not vote) on a course of action. Although not every participant may be fully in favor of the final decision, he will still support it because of full involvement in the discussion process. Participation leads to understanding and ownership of the decision which, in turn, leads to commitment to it.

A team that works well together can influence motivation and productivity greatly. Members who are lukewarm in decisions of the group or "out of line" in other respects, can be brought back into the fold via peer pressure. The manager doesn't have to do all the motivating personally.

It is not unusual for managers to hope that everyone in the operation will share a common vision of the mission, objectives and goals. However, the commonality is not very likely to come about via decree or fiat. It can come about through full involvement and participation of staff, giving people "a piece of the action." In this connection, any of the current programs for quality improvement are doomed to achieve only minimum results because they fail to involve people. To quote organization psychologist Dr. David Nadler, president of Delta Consulting Group, New York, the programs that fail "are the ones where the top tells the middle what to do at the bottom" (reported in *The Washington Post,* October 28, 1987). Nadler adds: "Talk is cheap. The real question is whether there is a true commitment to spend time, to commit resources and to really examine a different way of doing business."

A final thought: Management is often defined as "getting things done through the efforts of others." I would add "through and with" others, which is the team concept.

Particulars concerning team development and team management are discussed in more detail in Chapter 9.

SELF-ESTEEM: HOW TO BUILD AND MAINTAIN IT

Of all the judgments we make in life none are more important than the ones we make about ourselves.

—Dr. Nathaniel Branden, psychotherapist, management consultant, author, authority on self-esteem in the *Bottom Line,* June 1, 1994

Building Self-Esteem

As managers we have considerable power to raise or lower our workers' self-esteem, i.e., how they value themselves. (Other terms used to examine what people think of themselves are self-worth, self-confidence and ego strength.) Five key behaviors by managers (per Roy J. Blitzer, Colleen Peterson and Linda Rogers in "How to Build Self-Esteem," *Training and Development,* February 1993) can help people build their self-esteem and thus improve their performance on the job:

1. **Help staffers to feel uniquely valuable.** People with high self-esteem have a clear picture of the contributions they can make to their organizations. They also believe strongly that those contributions merit praise. Thus, you would compliment individual accomplishments and abilities to promote that special feeling of self-worth. These skill factors can contribute to that feeling:
   □ Recognize and capitalize on individual differences.
   □ Ensure that people feel free and easy to express their feelings and attitudes.
   □ Reward ideas and contributions of individuals.
   □ Reinforce people's accurate pictures of their capabilities.
2. **Help people to feel competent.** High-esteem individuals regard themselves as highly able. Besides

knowing their strengths, they recognize their weaknesses and learn from non-success experiences. Additional qualities are sharing of their thoughts, showing initiative, seeking solutions, and opting totally for quality. Their feelings of competence accrue when they perform valuable work and take responsibility for their own decisions. To develop that sense of competence in others, recognize positive results and provide helpful feedback on improvement efforts. Here's how to do that:

☐ Support responsible risk taking.

☐ Highlight strengths and skills.

☐ Encourage monitoring of progress toward goals.

☐ Assist learning from errors.

☐ Ensure needed training occurs.

☐ Encourage individuals to blow their own horns occasionally.

3. **Help team members feel secure.** High-esteem types feel secure for various reasons, an important one being clarity about what you as their boss expect of them. They don't favor being kept in the dark or game playing. These skill pointers are pertinent:

☐ Tell it like it is, even the bad news.

☐ Provide long-term plans and forecasts.

☐ Specify limits and standards for a given mission.

☐ Set and refine established procedures.

☐ Keep your commitments.

4. **Help your people to feel empowered.** A key form of empowerment is to let people choose among alternatives to meet their goals. Also vital are clear expectations, true ownership of their jobs and considering staffers' ideas seriously. Key skills for this are:

☐ Establish challenging but realistic goals.

☐ Develop a questioning spirit among staff.

☐ Tap employee interest and experience in the decision-making process.

☐ Offer choices, not directives.

☐ Show empathy toward interests and concerns of your people.

5. **Help team members feel "connected."** People feel better about themselves when they feel valued by colleagues and participate in a true team operation. But don't ignore individual worth as well. To promote connectedness, do the following:

☐ Foster group acceptance and cooperation.

☐ Recognize individual contributions to the team.

☐ Provide opportunities for team members to learn of and use other team members' skills, knowledge, and experience.

Maintaining Self-Esteem

"Impostors," described below, are extreme cases of low self-esteem. Nevertheless, all employees can have their self-esteem lowered if supervisors behave in ways that limit employees' ability to feel good about their accomplishments and thus themselves. Robert Cyr, manager of training and development, Underwriters Laboratories, Northbrook, Illinois, points out (in "Maintaining Self-Esteem," *Supervisory Management,* June 1992) a number of esteem-damaging behaviors which supervisors should guard against:

Verbal Affronts to Self-Esteem

This includes such behaviors as:

Posing questions that indicate lack of employee competence. Frequent questions, implying error or dumb mistakes, signal supervisory doubt about an employee's capabilities. It's akin to parental nagging of the kids ("You're sure you have your lunch money?"), so be more trusting. Don't look for miscues when they probably aren't there.

Talking down to employee in lower grades. Watch your communication with clerical or service personnel. As a manager or a professional worker, protect rather than destroy employee dignity by inferring that those at lower job levels are second-class citizens.

Prescribing choices. While most employees appreciate guidance from their bosses, they do like to feel that they can choose freely among alternatives in their area of responsibility. Being told what to do unnecessarily diminishes worker self-importance. The better tack is to pose questions like "What do you think?" "How do you see it?" "What course of action do you recommend?" all of which provides a feeling of empowerment.

Finding fault. Suggestions for improvement certainly are appropriate. But petty criticism and nitpicking are destructive of feelings of self-worth. Building people up with praise is more effective than tearing people down with negatives.

Criticizing in presence of peers. Public criticism provides a double whammy: reduction of self-esteem and lowering of one's status in the eyes of one's colleagues. The old rule of praise in public and criticize in private is still a sensible guideline.

Things Left Unsaid

Ineffective, esteem-reducing behaviors are:

Failing to request input. Not consulting with the employee who is responsible for a project or has a special expertise is a major insult. No one likes to be ignored when they have a solid contribution to make and have an opportunity to demonstrate their know how.

Neglecting to praise sufficiently. All of us need and crave recognition for our accomplishments. Overlooking opportunities to render praise is a lost opportunity to build self-esteem.

Failing to listen. The supervisory error here entails both not listening to what is said and not eliciting employee opinions frequently.

Actions that Damage Self-Esteem

Belittling task importance. Our jobs are part of us. We identify with them strongly. So if we are told our work is minor, unimportant, or insignificant, our self-esteem takes a nosedive. So the manager must bestow respect on all jobs, regardless of their hourly rates, criticality, or status level.

Holding a grudge. Employees will goof up now and again. But to keep reminding the worker of a former boo-boo is counterproductive. After all, committing the error was punishment in itself. So get past that old stage of your annoyance and disappointment and move on to the present. No one likes to be reminded (punished) of long-gone mistakes.

Assigning work fairly. No one should be subject to repeated assignment of the less-desirable tasks. So make it a practice to let all concerned share in the "dirty," unwanted jobs.

Doing What Should Be Done

Overlooking people. No one likes to be excluded when inclusion is appropriate. This may relate to meetings, celebrations, luncheons, etc. Being left out signals that one doesn't belong or is unworthy, a certain way to lower self-esteem.

Ignoring people. All of us like to feel that we are worthy enough to merit a hello, a smile, eye contact, possibly a bit of chit chat at the water cooler. In the absence of social contact, we may feel that the unfriendliness means that we are not as important as others.

Inadequate work space. A work area which is marked by minuteness and poor maintenance signals that a not very significant person is parked there. It is the supervisor's job, then, to be certain that people have office areas which are painted, that furniture is well above the discard stage, that cabinets are available to provide for orderly storage, and that decent lighting is assured. People can hardly feel good about themselves if they are required to perform in a slum-type set up.

Lack of formal recognition. Work that is well done merits recognition in the form of letters of appreciation sent to the home, complimentary memos for the personnel jacket, and public award ceremonies. This should be done for all employees, regardless of level.

"Impostors"

Many work groups contain one or more people who exhibit what management consultant Dr. Valerie Young calls "the impostor syndrome" ("What Others Are Saying: The Imposter Syndrome," *Management Solutions,* August 1986): People who have low self-esteem see themselves as "impostors," that is, less qualified or able than others see them. These "impostors" tend to discount the validity of positive feedback and good performance appraisals. They explain these accomplishments away as "luck," generosity by the appraiser, or circumstances other than merit.

Impostors, says Dr. Young, can affect productivity adversely due to such factors as:

Procrastination. Excessive fear of doing something or not doing it well enough results in delays in production.

The untapped labor pool. Doubts about their abilities cause a rigid self-classification of "unqualified for promotion." They want to be seen as experts so they are very satisfied to continue doing only what they feel comfortable doing. They deny having outgrown their jobs because of the fear of traveling over new, uncharted waters.

Risk avoidance. For fear of looking ridiculous or ignorant, they hesitate to offer their insights and ideas about problems.

Fear of success. While most of us thrive on success, impostors find success stressful. So the response to a well-done job may be a harried, "Phew, I got through that one." So instead of success feeding on itself to create more of it, opportunities for success become something to be shunned—who wants to be subject to "an empty experience?" In like fashion, opportunities for visibility, a chance to shine, are regarded as a threat, a potentially anxiety-producing experience.

Impostors are easily spotted. Clues to holding back are:

☐ Clamming up at a meeting when you know the impostor has an idea. You may know this for a fact because the idea was mentioned to you before the meeting.

☐ Endless delays and alibis for them.

☐ Difficulty accepting a mistake and moving on. Instead, they brood over errors for long time periods.

☐ Difficulty in accepting reasonable and necessary criticism. Their strong self-doubts about their capabilities tend to block out helpful comments about their work—they see such feedback as proof of their low abilities.

☐ Rejection or discounting of praise. ("That wasn't anything that anybody else couldn't do.")

☐ Using disclaimers such as "This is probably a dumb question" or "I probably goofed this up . . ."

Once you have identified an impostor, your motivational strategy should encompass these approaches:

☐ Praise good work as often as you can.

☐ Assist them to feel comfortable in discussing their feelings of inadequacy.

☐ Stress in your work assignment and review contacts that job ability is a matter of acquired skill, not innate ability. Show that you have confidence in their improvability.

☐ Point out the learning value of errors. Few of us are so perfect that we never commit a mistake.

☐ Provide feedback on a constructive, hopeful note as opposed to impatiently blaming or criticizing performance.

☐ Encourage letting go of details to move ahead toward goal accomplishment.

☐ Encourage risk taking. Assure them that they have the capabilities for doing, that they will be rewarded for trying, that no punishment will ensue for conscientious attempts at performance.

Personal Involvement for Empathy

Trying to "move" people toward our goals, however reasonable, often encounters resistance. The resistance is not necessarily of the clearly announced "I'm not going to do it" type. Rather, it takes the form of lip service, foot dragging, forgetting partial or intermittent compliance, and other subtle demurring ploys.

A reason for reluctance to perform is that people may not fully appreciate the importance of their duties and responsibilities. This may be due to a lack of exposure to the consequences of their indifferent behavior. For example, in the airlines only the pilots, flight attendants, and gate agents are on the "front line." Mechanics, air traffic controllers, baggage handlers, and executives are not involved with air travelers to the same degree.

Syndicated columnist Ellen Goodman ("For Airlines: A Taste of Their Own Medicine," *The Washington Post,* November 28, 1987) reminds us that during World War II those who packed parachutes were occasionally asked to take a test drop with their own finished products. This intermittent possibility obviously provided added empathy and sensitivity to their work.

Hitchhiking on the parachute packing experience, Goodman provides added ideas for personal involvement: Randomly select airline mechanics to take rides on planes they worked on; let midlevel airline executives explain the ticket-price system to harried, frustrated passengers; require baggage handlers to periodically check-in their grandmother's china or other prize possessions. In respect to the stressed air controller, she has this suggestion: "Why not send them for a nice relaxing trip over Chicago during peak hours? They could pass the time by reading the identifying letters on the planes surrounding them. They could feel what it's like to be a mere blip on a radar screen. And airline CEOs should serve annually as troubleshooters to deal with the cancellation of a jumbo jet on a Friday night."

What Goodman is saying, and what sophisticated managers already know, is that people will be at their empathic best to the degree that they have been exposed to or involved in a situation on a truly personal basis. The expressions "I've been there" and "I've paid my dues" sum it up meaningfully.

To improve customer service, The Holiday Inn Crowne Plaza Hotel, New York City, invited its employees to experience the hotel as a guest, accompanied by a relative or friend. The employees received a free room, in-room breakfast, use of the health club, soft drinks at the bar, and dinner at the hotel restaurant. At the end of their visit, they were asked to complete an evaluation questionnaire as critically as possible. The overnight stay helped the concierge respond better to daily complaints. For example, he learned that they were providing complimentary bottles of water in the rooms but not openers to open them; the TV's remote control had to be pointed at the pay-per-view box instead of the TV screen ("Service Journal: Science Improves When Workers Become Customers," *The Service Edge,* February 1992).

COMMITMENT TO QUALITY AND CONTINUING IMPROVEMENT: "CONTINUE TO QUESTION WHAT YOU DO AND WHY"

It is quality rather than quantity that matters.

—Seneca (circa 3 B.C.– A.D. 65),
Roman philosopher, dramatist and statesman

. . . to go in search of quality is to go in search of your customer, for there is where value is determined and the definition of quality begins.

—F. W. Nichols, Chief of Staff, Operations,
Educational Testing Service, Princeton, New Jersey (in *Performance and Instruction,* February 1944)

Thinking always of trying to do more brings a state of mind in which nothing seems impossible.

—Henry Ford, American Industrialist (1863–1947)

. . . quality affects morale because poor quality tends to create rework and people get upset over having to do a job over again. Quality affects productivity because it eliminates scrap and rework. Quality reduces costs because doing something right the first time is cheaper than doing it over. So instead of telling your employees they must increase productivity or reduce costs, for example, you make quality your stated goal. This goal is not only less threatening to people, but it also appeals to their pride in running out a better product—and it works.

—Peter C. Reid, *Well Made in America: Lesson from Harley-Davidson Being the Best* (1990)

In recent years much has been said and written about the need to deliver quality service and produce quality products. Foreign competition has made it crystal clear that American firms must opt for quality or perish. In consequence, management increasingly rejects the antiquated notion that higher quality means higher costs. Actually, doing it right at the outset reduces costs in terms of reduced warranty expenses, service costs, and waste, and helps ensure repeat business. This message, obviously, needs to be communicated to employees at all levels in the organization over and over again. Interestingly, stressing quality of product or service is a management demand that is not likely to be perceived as pressure or hassling. Rather, most employees will readily respond to requests for adherence to high quality standards. People like to be part of an effort that "tries to be the best." In short, the opportunity to perform at a high standard—pride in accomplishment—is a natural motivator.

Note that one of the "secrets" of Japanese industrial success is that of *kaizen,* or the never-ending quest for perfection. Continuous improvement is a basic tenet of their organizational value system. The fact that something is done well doesn't mean that it can't be done better. Employees readily relate to an organization that prides itself on providing the customer with better products or service, as opposed to one which has a stagnant, outdated philosophy of "If it ain't broke, don't fix it," "leave well enough alone," or "don't mess with success."

From a skill-development standpoint for constant improvement, supervisors must work with their employees to learn and use the following skills, says quality improvement authority Lawrence Holpp ("Achievement, Motivation and Kaizen," *Training and Development Journal,* October 1989):

☐ Look systematically at their jobs to determine effective vs. ineffective behaviors.

☐ Take individual and/or team action to upgrade quality, productivity or customer satisfaction.

☐ Use an action-planning process to ensure that agreed-upon actions are implemented successfully.

To foster a spirit of constant improvement requires that employees do the following, says Holpp:

☐ Develop an action philosophy by adopting action orientations toward both their lives and work.

☐ Overcome any and all obstacles to action.

☐ Apply a series of action steps to solve usual work-related problems.

☐ Install/implement action plans.

☐ Monitor action strategies to ensure their full accomplishment.

And as employees learn how to take a broader, innovative view of their jobs, they need to learn how to do the following:

☐ Identify the key resources used in producing products/services.

☐ Working as a team, identify improper inputs and outputs of their jobs.

☐ Zero in on areas of opportunity to correct those unwanted inputs and outputs.

The above program for continuing improvement is based on the very logical assumption that no one is in a better position to improve a job than the guy who works with it every day. The search for improvement is a true motivator.

Management professor William I. Gordon believes that the supervisor can upgrade quality significantly if he uses these motivational devices ("Gaining Employee Commitment to Quality," *Supervisory Management,* November 1985):

Encourage commitment to the organization's mission. Define it and define it again and again so everyone understands its importance.

Assist employees to see the "big picture." Supervisors should help their people to see quality as a concern in everything the organization does.

Encourage "thinking up." This means conveying a commitment to do things better, e.g., achieving zero defects.

Talk excellence. Quality is an important message and the least a supervisor can do is to latch on to every opportunity to talk it up. One way to do this is to use catch slogans. Make one up if the organization doesn't already have one. **Example:** "I make the difference" (the Rockefeller Group). Also consider the use of sports talk: "You scored." "That's a homer." "Between the uprights." "All net." A third way is to give people work-influencing names such as "cheerleader" or "pacesetter."

Praise quality performance. The praise may be verbal, short notes of appreciation or more formal in nature, entailing written awards and ceremonies. Think, too, in terms of *unit* recognition.

Added pointers for the manager to build quality awareness, per manager David W. Cross ("Building Quality Awareness in Staffers," *Supervisory Management,* June 1991), are:

Stress quality each day. Insist on top quality from your staff. Remind them of the benefits from quality and the negatives that ensue from sloppy work.

Keep tuned. Listen to employee complaints and suggestions. Complaints about worn or defective equipment must be responded to if quality is truly wanted. Employee ideas may reduce cumbersome procedures and reduce costs.

Encourage double checking of work. A second check of completed work may ensure quality. Also, encourage employees to inspect each other's work to get the benefit of a second pair of eyes.

Expect mistakes. Don't overreact to errors. Instead, work with the error-maker to find a corrective solution. You want to so behave that people aren't afraid to come forth with bad news. Errors can't be corrected if they are covered up.

Build your team around the goal of quality. High standards, well-trained people and searching continually for improvement should be the hallmarks of your operation.

Of course, managers' talk must be supported by managers' personal behavior—modeling for quality. In other words, a sign on the wall insisting "Quality Isn't An Option" will take on credence only if all managerial actions are in consonance with it. Although ideally managers should "walk the talk," two surveys cited below illustrate the all-too-often gap between management preachment and management action.

A survey at 12 companies by consultant Brooks International found that (reported in "Labor Letter," *The Wall Street Journal,* July 10, 1990):

☐ Most of the workers insist they are personally committed to meeting quality standards and that their fellow workers also try hard. But two-thirds say that work quality "is not an important measure of performance in my group."

☐ Only one-fourth believe that management does an excellent job of rewarding work groups who make quality improvement recommendations.

☐ Middle managers also share the disenchantment. Although 78% of top execs declare "management is committed to achieving and maintaining highest quality levels possible," only 52% of midlevel managers, 46% of first-line supervisors and 43% of workers share that view.

☐ One company pushed for quality improvements but based rewards solely on the number of units turned out.

A survey on quality issues conducted by the Gallup Organization for the American Society for Quality Control (ASQC) found that ("Facts and Figures: Workers Judge Their Companies' Quality Efforts," *Training,* January 1991):

☐ Some 80% of all workers polled said that their firms offer at least one type of quality improvement activity.

☐ But 36% of employees in the firms offering quality improvement activities stated that they don't participate.

☐ Of those who do participate in quality improvement programs, they have two main complaints: (1) There is a gap between talk and action on quality principles; (2) they are unhappy with the rate of quality improvement to date. 54% of respondents gave their firms a "10" on their desire to achieve quality objectives. But only 36% gave their companies a "10" on their performance in achieving those goals. Most (75%) respondents were content with the company progress on quality, but 25% were not.

One helpful way for managers to be alert to what their customers and employees think about their operation and service is to actually get out on the frontline where the action and the customers are. Executives at Hyatt Hotels Corporation do just that. They close their corporate offices in Chicago one day each year and visit a particular hotel. The execs and their aides from the Chicago and regional offices take jobs at the various hotels and resorts. They carry bags, park cars, make beds, wait on tables, fix toilets, and work at other frontline service jobs.

The Hyatt program, called In Touch, reminds the headquarters staff what it takes to be truly focused. It also reinforces respect for each employee's contribution to the firm's customer service efforts. One of the reasons for the program is to avoid being out of touch with workers' problems. Hyatt is responding to a 1990 consulting firm's national survey which found that 55% of American workers believe that their managers don't understand employee problems ("Training Today: Getting In Touch," *Training,* March 1991).

Similarly, the general manager at a Weyerhaeuser sawmill in Cottage Grove, Oregon, had a cross-section of the workforce—from general manager to forklift operators—spend a week as "employees" of their customers: the shipping manager worked on the receiving dock of a California distribution center, customer service reps worked as sales assistants at Builders Emporium and Home Depot stores.

The payoff: They returned with insights that allowed them to distinguish their mill. The mill now wraps its lumber in plastic and paints the ends in a distinctive color. They also load lumber onto railway cars so that unloading is easier. And their customers find that sales reps understand their problems and even anticipate them ("Service Journal: Spend a Day as an 'Employee' of Your Customers," *The Service Edge,* February 1994 based on a *Harvard Business Review* article).

Another key behavioral factor which can influence employee performance regarding quality and service toward the customer is the health of the relationship between the manager and his subordinates. Industrial psychologist Harry Levinson (in a letter to the editor of *The Wall Street Journal,* January 8, 1991) puts it this way:

The single most important factor in the attitude of the employee toward the customer is the experience the employee has with his own boss. You can always tell when you walk into a restaurant or department store what is going on psychologically among higher management. Most often hostility to the customer is a direct displacement from the kind of hostility that the subordinate experiences either directly or as a consequence of conflict among superiors.

No amount of training will overcome the anger of people who feel they have been overcontrolled, manipulated, unsupported, ignored or treated contemptuously by their bosses. True, some people occasionally 'have had their toast burned' that morning, and some may be sick or in pain, but by and large in too many business organizations from top management on down there is a failure to understand the emotional atmosphere of a company starts at the top and cascades.

The Bottom Line

Try to keep these two vital messages in front of your employees:

(1) Don't blow it for the customer. Remember, it's easier and cheaper to satisfy customers than to replace them.

(2) Keep questioning what you do and why you do it.

And for you as manager, consider keeping this message at your eye level: "How I act will determine how my staff reacts and thus acts toward product quality, continuing improvement and customer service." Also, as the Hyatt and Weyerhaeuser experience suggests, you can't apply motivational forces meaningfully unless you know where your people are coming from.

And a brief anecdote to highlight the importance of top-flight employee performance on "the frontline":

Story: Airline traveler to ticket agent: Route this large brown bag to Chicago, this medium-sized gray one to New Orleans, and the small one to Philly.

Ticket agent: Oh, we can't do that.

Traveler: Oh, you can't? Why not? You did it last Monday!

Employee Involvement Teams for Continuous Improvement

An integral aspect of many TQM (Total Quality Management) programs is the use of employee involvement teams (EI teams) for continuous process improvement. A survey reported in "The 10 Dimensions of Employee Involvement," *Training and Development,* April 1993, by management professor Richard J. Magjuka of Indiana University of 703 manufacturing firms identified 10 themes that influence EI team effectiveness and maximize employee motivation:

1. Range of problem content. EIP (Employee Involvement Program) administrators believe that the EIPs are more effective when employees tackle problems concerning areas of process improvement—sequencing operations, reducing production cycle length and developing quicker setup techniques—as opposed to addressing a wide array of problems and issues.

2. Team staffing policies. The respondents favored a heterogeneous and multi-functional membership. This means inclusion of staff as well as line workers for broader input. Multi-functional teams are especially effective when these objectives are paramount:

☐ To improve customer service continuously.

☐ To reduce production cycle time, i.e., between the time of receipt of an order and its final delivery.

☐ To improve capacity to deal effectively with organizational product or market changes.

3. Team-membership status. The respondents favored required rather than voluntary membership (as in Quality Circles). Their reason? Employees typically see required activities as those that the firm values. Conversely, volunteer activities are seen as peripheral and unimportant to their outfits.

4. EIP team resources. EIP teams must meet about one hour weekly to make a significant contribution to the continuous-improvement process. Meetings must be held regularly to attain constancy of purpose. EIP teams should be permanent rather than temporary, that is, they shouldn't be disbanded at the end of a designated project.

5. EIP training practices. Issues relate to:

☐ How to use information to improve processes.

☐ How to perform in a team setting.

☐ How to use problem solving techniques.

☐ How to provide education and technical training to cover areas such as cost accounting, statistics, marketing, production, and finance. Orientation training is also essential to secure uniform understanding of what EI is all about.

6. Information access for team members. Although not all firms wish to share information broadly, EI teams can't be effective without information on product lines, sources of profit, cost of quality, cost of losing a customer, trends, and forecasts.

7. EIP financial rewards. Financial rewards are not common (only 10% link such rewards to TQM outcome). While overtime (for EI work) is likely to be compensated, bonus systems are felt to be unnecessary. Instead, EI administrators favor tying EI efforts into the firm's ongoing performance management system. This approach is deemed to be more motivating than providing financial rewards.

8. **Links to performance—management systems.** Most EIP administrators believe EIP performance must be explicitly included within such a framework to ensure that EIPs continue to occupy an increasingly more central position in continuous-improvement strategies.

9. **Goal setting practices.** Because goal setting (using numerical target) improves motivation and task performance, it is believed that it should be adapted to EIP operations. But only 54% reported using goal setting to improve EIP participant performance. Another reason to use goal setting is that employees interpret it as a signal of organizational importance, that participation on EIP teams is not a waste of time.

10. **Supervisory roles.** While some self-directed teams may not have a supervisor, most EIP teams do have one. This latter procedure is favored by the administrators. An advantage with a supervisor is that it permits more ready access to plant information. Some respondents favored rotational leadership and having non-supervisors occupy leadership roles for developmental reasons.

USING CAREER PLANNING TOOLS FOR MOTIVATION

One of the traditional givens in the organizational world is that to make your mark, career-wise, you must move into the management ranks. Only a managerial position can provide the desired prestige, power, authority, salary, and other trappings of success (a fancy job title, a carpeted office, a group of eager subordinates).

However, moving into management is something not everyone is qualified for, personality-wise, or seeks. And in recent years all the reorganizations, restructurings, delayerings, re-engineerings, and downsizings have reduced the number of available managerial jobs to which technical, professional, and administrative personnel can aspire.

Certainly moving into and up the management ladder has strong motivational appeal. But if a managerial career is neither available nor appropriate, how can organizations provide vertical movement and prestige without moving people into management? One good answer is the dual-career ladder.

A dual-career ladder is a two-track career system, one for management people and the other for people who are not and may not care to be bosses. In the non-managerial or technical track there may be several job leads so that a firm's best scientists, engineers, researchers, and others (sales, customer service, information systems) may advance by gaining top salaries and special titles such as "fellow," "senior scientist," and "service consultant II." Pay and prestige are comparable to those in management without the corresponding authority, says reporter Gilbert Fuchsberg ("Parallel Lines: Companies Create New Ways to Promote Employees—Without Making Them Bosses," *The Wall Street Journal,* April 21, 1993).

Of course, a dual-career ladder has to be administered and explained properly lest it be perceived as a minor consolation prize. It is to be noted that while 67% of companies surveyed by consultants Hewett Associates said their dual-career ladder policies had achieved desired results, 13% said they hadn't, and another 20% said it was too early to tell. The problems with dual-career ladders, per the Hewitt Associates' survey (reported in *The Wall Street Journal,* April 21, 1993) were these: Level of responsibility not clearly defined between levels on the non-managerial ladder (77%); career paths poorly defined (62%); purpose not clear to employees (38%); management uses the technical ladder of the two-ladder system as a dumping ground (23%); employees don't like to decide which ladder to pursue (23%); unequal responsibility exists between ladders (23%); lack of salary comparability exists between ladders (15%).

Another useful motivational tool is the lateral transfer, wherein employees are shifted sideways rather than up. The idea, says staff reporter Joan E. Rigdon ("Using Lateral Moves to Spur Employees, *The Wall Street Journal,* May 26, 1992) is "to light a fire under workers at a time when few promotions or pay raises are on the horizon."

In years past, lateral movers were regarded by many as a demotion because they derailed what seemed like certain promotions. Today, laterals make more sense now that there is greater competition for fewer rungs on the corporate ladder, says Rigdon.

Of course, not any lateral move is good strategy. Rigdon cites the view of Marilyn Moats Kennedy, editor of the newsletter *Kennedy's Career Strategist,* that the right lateral move puts one into a core business, provides closer contact with customers or teaches new skills to increase one's marketability in case one should be pink-slipped.

Lateral moves are part of current career trends to make workers responsible for determining their own training and career needs. Rigdon quotes one corporate executive who states, "We're trying to get through to people that they have to be self-managed."

So for the manager who is interested in sparking his career or helping staffers to jump start theirs, the lateral may be the best form of career action. As one top executive put it (Steve Painter, "Middle-Management Spread Hits Corporate America," *The Washington Post,* May 26, 1991), "If it's for job enrichment or enhancement . . . lateral moves are not frowned upon," a practice once considered a sign that a manager was headed nowhere.

ENVIRONMENTAL FOCUS

Protecting the environment is not only good for the bottom line, but it can serve as a "green flag" around which employees can enthusiastically rally. Seattle-based environmental consultant Sheila Kelly cites these examples (in *Training and Development,* November 1992):

☐ 3M has a successful "Pollution Prevention Pays" program. The firm has learned that the best way to prevent pollution is to avoid generating it in the first place. 3M encourages its employees to identify pollution-prevention opportunities. Since the program's inception in 1975, more than 3,000 projects have eliminated over a billion pounds of emissions, saving more than $500 million.

☐ Xerox Corporation encourages employees to eliminate waste before it's generated and to save the costs of materials and disposal fees. The firm provides customers with options to recycle cartridges and waste paper. Xerox states that it is "committed to the protection of the environment and the health and safety of its employees, customers, and neighbors."

☐ Weyerhaeuser Company has a policy that favors being "viewed by our customers, neighbors, and other key audiences as the environmental leader in each locale." Its environmental awareness came from the top, but it can also come from the ranks (described below).

☐ At USAIR, flight attendants and other employees pressured the firm to recycle the 11 million beverage cans it carries yearly and to donate the proceeds to environmental causes.

☐ Kodak has linked some managers' pay, in part, to their performance in preventing chemical spills. The payoff: a 47% drop in spills.

☐ The Xerox cafeteria offers free coffee refills to those who provide their own mugs instead of using polystyrene cups, which often contain ozone-damaging compounds.

Summary Point: Involving people in and stressing the importance of preserving the environment is a natural, built-in motivator. It appeals to a better side of us, our idealistic self. It's akin to our responding to appeals that stress high standards, quality of product, A-1 customer service, ethics, helping others, and the like.

PAYOFFS FOR EFFORT

People will perform to the extent that their effort is rewarded. A corollary of this concept is "the principle of least effort." That is, people will expend the least effort necessary to get satisfactory results. So if there are roadblocks to performance, effort will most likely taper off. ("Why knock yourself out when all you get back is a lot of nothing for trying?")

Roadblocks come in many forms: Impossible jobs; responsibility without authority; cumbersome procedures; antiquated, irrelevant policies; lack of support, guidance or reinforcement; lack of trust. It is your job, then, to manage effort properly, to remove barriers to effectiveness. Otherwise, effort may fade out despite its potential to create and contribute.

COMPLAINT CONVERSION

When employees come to you with complaints or defeatist attitudes, don't get caught up in their malaise. Instead, get to the nub of things by shifting quickly to constructive thinking. Challenge them by asking "What can we do about this problem?" "What would you like me to do about it?" "What would you do if you were in my chair?"

Also, turn their thinking around, if less than positive, by asking them to focus on *possibilities:* "OK, we know what all the bad points are, but what do we have going for us? What are the strengths in the situation?"

A third motivational approach is to use visualization techniques. More specifically, ask employees to think in terms of desired end-results or outcomes as opposed to the current miserable state of affairs: "If we could resolve this difficulty, if we could reduce the pain, what would the new situation look like?" and then: "What can we do *together* to get that desired end-result?"

Note: A lot of energy resides in your staff. Identifying and bringing a complaint forward is good evidence of it. It is your job to turn that energy from its random, unfocused, somewhat defective state to a hard-hitting, problem-solving mode. In effect, by challenging staff to become problem solvers, you are providing them with the motivation to act rather than to merely whine.

WHAT ABOUT COMPETITION?

One of the cliches of management is that competition is a sure-fire motivator. However, the facts of the managerial world are that the end result may not be what you, as a manager, really wanted. Why not? Because encouraging competition among individuals or units may well produce a concern with beating others at all costs, as opposed to getting the job done properly for the benefit of the whole unit or the entire organization. For example, there may be a reluctance to report mistakes or to share information lest one's competitors look as good or succeed to the same degree. Visualize competition between units to achieve the best company safety record. An obvious means of winning is to conceal accidents and thus fudge the stats in one's favor.

Or, says management writer Bob Flipczak ("Why No One Likes Your Incentive Program," *Training,* August 1993), assume sales personnel are in competition for a trip to Europe. So they start promising products the shipping people simply can't deliver. Shipping may hurriedly pass this need onto production, but the frenzy only produces subpar products and disenchanted customers. Concludes Flipczak, "At best, a competitive reward system won't produce cooperation among people striving for a limited supply of rewards. At worst, it could undermine your company's efforts to foster teamwork, improve the 'handoffs' of work between different departments and so on."

Also to be considered is that competition necessarily not only creates winners which we do want, but it also creates losers which we don't. Losers tend to feel less good about themselves and, in time, may slacken or even give up. For the manager, then, the challenge is to use competition only when it is certain to be healthy or constructive. Examples of healthy competition are these:

- ☐ A manager encourages his staffers to compete with *themselves* to achieve a better productivity record compared to the prior quarter or year. The motivational approach he uses is "stretch," discussed in conjunction with goal setting (page 154).
- ☐ A biochemist is encouraged to become the most well-known professional worker in her field. She thus embarks on a program to write more professional journal articles than anyone else.
- ☐ A scientist is given the support and resources so that he can become the *first* researcher to lick the AIDS virus.

In essence, competition that challenges people is very desirable. Consider this statement at halftime by Quarterback 1 to Quarterback 2: "You had a very good performance in that first quarter. Keep it up. When you're sharp it makes me work harder. It improves my game."

Certain types of competition among or between groups may be healthy. (Recall the competition between two crews working on the first transcontinental railroad.) Group competitive activity, based on group-developed goals, will encourage camaraderie and cohesion and result in collaborative behaviors within the group—sharing, supporting, communicating, helping, pinch-hitting when someone is absent or away, etc. Some examples of useful intergroup competition:

- ☐ A human resources management office at a field location of a large government agency decided that it wanted to be regarded as having the best HRM program in the agency. It plans and implements its program accordingly.
- ☐ An auto dealership established an objective of having the best service facility (highest quality, fewest complaints) in the community. It thus increases employee training and adjusts the reward system to support the new goal.
- ☐ A producer and distributor of training films decides that it wants to be the best single source for such products. It then changes its basic procedures to upgrade the quality of its products.
- ☐ An employee-involvement team decides to assess its safety procedures so that it can develop the best safety record of all units in the company. **Note:** The decision is made by the group on its own, without reference to a competitive prize offered by the firm.

We should also mention that certain types of group competition are natural, to be expected and are not necessarily destructive; e.g., all divisions in the organization compete for available dollars at budget time, for the best space, personnel, and so on. Ideally, organizational units should be in competition to achieve a reputation of having the best developers of people, or being the most innovative or cost effective.

It is not unusual for managers to try to use competition as a challenging force when other motivators are more appropriate. For example, I worked for a personnel director who always urged the staff to contribute generously to the annual charity fund so that we would have the best record of all the divisions in the organization. I always wondered if it would not have been more meaningful to appeal to our sense of community and altruism as opposed to our presumed "need" to out-distance everyone else. As adults, couldn't we rally to support high-level purposes, or can we only "do good" if we top others?

An obvious danger of competition among and between groups is that it may get out of hand. We call this destructive form of competition rivalry. **Examples:** sales vs. production, manufacturing vs. R&D, line vs. staff, headquarters vs. field, Division A vs. Division B, union vs. management, men vs. women, newcomers vs. old timers, and so on.

Finally, in a psychological sense the shortcoming of competition is that it is based on extrinsic rather than intrinsic motivation. Alfie Kohn, author of *No Contest: The Case Against Competition* (Boston: Houghton Mifflin, 1986), puts it this way:

> *Anytime you give a reward for doing something, you are sending a message that the task must not be worthwhile in its own right, because otherwise, you wouldn't have to bribe people to do it.*

> *According to massive research in social psychology, intrinsic motivation is much more powerful than extrinsic rewards, those that lie outside of the task—it can be a paycheck, a grade in school, a bonus, even the extra hour of TV we offer our children—as reward to get someone to do something, and you belittle the task. End result: poorer performance. In contrast, someone who is intrinsically motivated likes what he does and finds it fulfilling within itself. No one does a better job than someone who likes that job.*

> *If someone feels controlled by a reward, they feel less autonomous, and this interferes with performance. Research has shown that people do their best work*

when they enjoy a sense of autonomy and ownership over their efforts."

—from an interview by Jenifer Juergens with Alfie Kohn in "The Competition Quandary," *Meetings and Conventions—Incentive Supplement,* September 1990.

WHAT ABOUT MONEY? AN ENTITLEMENT OR A MOTIVATOR?

The love of money is the root of all evil.

—New Testament, 1 Timothy

The lack of money is the root of all evil.

—George Bernard Shaw (1856–1950),
Irish playwright and critic

I've had a lot of money and I've had no money. It's better to have a lot.

—syndicated radio shock jock John Donald Imus, quoted in *Smart Money,* February 1994

Money does not buy happiness. But it surrounds you with the goods and services to make misery more tolerable.

—Author unknown

Money is better than poverty, if only for financial reasons.

—Woody Allen, U.S. comedian, author, actor, and filmmaker

Whoever said money couldn't buy happiness didn't know where to shop.

—Author unknown

Pecunia omnia vincit. (Money conquers all.)

—Anonymous

Love may make the world go round, but money buys the ring.

—Anonymous

If you don't pay people enough to live on, they don't feel much loyalty. There's real anger.

—Stephen Lerner, director of the Service Employees International's Justice for Janitors Campaign (quoted in *The Wall Street Journal,* May 9, 1989)

Financial incentives are not the way to get better employee performance; good management is.

—Management consultant Robert H. Schaffer, author of *The Breakthrough Strategy* (quoted in *Business Month,* April 1989)

An often-used gag, guaranteed to evoke a chuckle, goes like this: "Money isn't everything, but it sure beats whatever is in second place." But does this quip really reflect how all of us regard money?

There is no question that in our culture, as in others, money is a strong motivator. People will do many things for it: rush to stores for sales, mail in boxtops, collect and use grocery coupons, switch bank accounts for a higher interest rate, subscribe to magazines on a multiyear basis, dive for buried treasure, hire a wily accountant to save on taxes, pay bills early to avoid late charges, work for years for a college degree in anticipation of a high-salaried career, etc. And on the job individuals will sell goods or services for commissions only, work on a piece-work basis, be a high-producing "rate buster," try to lose weight or quit smoking to receive bonuses offered by management, voluntarily work for paid overtime, switch to better-paying jobs in other communities, and so on.

Additionally, the world has always had individuals whose total life seems to revolve around the pursuit of money. Thus we find such money-oriented people as mercenaries, spies, traitors, gamblers, pimps, smugglers, tax evaders, forgers, counterfeiters. (Of course, these people may have other non-financial needs met by their activities, too.)

Money may even be desired when it has little intrinsic value. For example, I know an executive who was earning over $130,000 annually, but enthusiastically took a like job with another firm in another state for an added $15,000. I suggested to him that the increase did not seem too significant monetarily after taxes and relocation. So why take it? His reply: "I want it because I'm worth it." He was saying, then, that in our society money is a way we measure our worth.

On the other hand, we know that there are many people who do things which have little or no financial pay off: teachers who put in long, unpaid hours for the kids; volunteer workers of all sorts in community, civic, political, and professional groups; retirees and lottery winners who return to work "just to keep busy"; volunteer firefighters and rescue workers; Peace Corps workers; highly paid business executives who leave for government jobs; doctors and lawyers who provide free services to the poor; highly paid professional athletes who are not content to warm the bench and demand: "Play me or trade me"; piece-rate workers who work at "standard" (because of peer pressure) when they could easily exceed it and make more money.

A survey of 298 owners of small businesses by Cicco & Associates, Inc., a management consulting firm in Pennsylvania, found that pride in product/service ranked first among 12 possible sources of satisfaction. The other five non-financial motivators after pride were ranked in this order: control, freedom, flexibility, self-reliance, and customer contact. Income was only number seven.

Does size of income have a bearing on happiness? Surveys by the National Opinion Research Center at the University of Chicago asked respondents whether they are "very happy," "pretty happy," or "not too happy." As reported by economics writer Robert J. Samuelson ("It's Not the Economy, Stupid," *The Washington Post,* January 7, 1994), except at the lowest and highest income levels, the differences in happiness aren't big at all. Here are the NORC figures:

Income	Very Happy	Pretty Happy	Not Too Happy
$0–14,999	21%	58%	21%
$15–24,999	32%	56%	13%
$25–34,999	32%	60%	8%
$35–49,999	36%	59%	5%
$50–74,999	34%	60%	6%
$75,000 +	45%	49%	6%

Among many older people, says Robert Menchin, financial executive and author of *New Work Opportunities for Older Americans* (Englewood Cliffs, N.J.: Prentice Hall, 1993), "Money is the Number 1 factor motivating many older people to stay on the job or go back to work. For many, the added income makes the difference between thriving and just surviving." But there are other reasons, too, says Menchin: "Often, the psychological and social benefits to work far outweigh monetary considerations. Work allows mature people to stay active and involved and to maintain their esteem and self-respect in the community" (quoted in "Odd Jobs," *The Washington Post,* December 19, 1993).

For many people time is more valuable than money. A Time Values Survey conducted by the Hilton Hotel Corporation (reported in "Time: More Valuable Than Money?", *Personnel Journal,* October 1991) posed this question: "If given the choice, would you sacrifice a day's pay for an extra day off from work?" At least one-half of the survey participants responded affirmatively.

The survey found that 70% of the respondents earning $300,000 yearly or more would make the swap. Of those earning $20,000 a year or less, 48% would also take that extra day off. So people in all segments of the work force, regardless of marital status, geographical location or educational level, would favor time over money. According to John P. Robinson of the University of Maryland who analyzed the survey for Hilton, this would equate pay cuts of 20–40% for a week's pay to get that extra day off. Interestingly, these attitudes prevailed in a year of economic uncertainty (1991).

When those surveyed were given a choice of eight goals, 77% selected "spending time with family and friends as their Number 1 priority. "Making money" got a Number 5 ranking and "spending money on material possessions" ranked last, with only 29% ranking this a Number 1 priority.

The following story illustrates the not-surprising limited power of money, at least for some people:

A wealthy rancher, walking along the shore of a marina, was attracted to the work of an artist who was painting a sleek-looking boat on his canvas. Intrigued by his artistic style, the rancher approached the painter and this conversation ensued:

Rancher: That's good work. I like your style.

Artist: Thank you.

Rancher: I raise horses and have a favorite horse. A really fine animal. I would pay you a good sum to paint my horse.

Artist: That's very kind. But I only paint boats.

Rancher: I'd be glad to raise the ante. (He did so several times, but each time the artist said he only liked to paint boats. Finally, the proposed price got so high that the artist could no longer turn it down.)

Artist: OK, mister. I'll paint your horse for you. But he's still going to look like a boat.

What about merit pay, profit sharing and "gain-sharing" as incentive pay systems? Merit pay is hardly a motivator. Charles Peck, compensation specialist with The Conference Board, New York City, finds that these increases are an across-the-board euphemism for annual pay increases. Most people end up with about the same increase irrespective of their individual performance. Also, says Peck, it is not clear whether the merit increases reinforce existing behavior or serve as a spur to better performance ("Merit Pay: An Unbalanced Approach to Pay-For-Performance," *Personnel Journal,* April 1992).

Profit sharing is another incentive program subject to debate regarding its effectiveness as a motivator. Critics of these plans state that they overlook more important variables such as providing positive feedback or an adequate amount of freedom. Management consultant Alfie Kohn states "When employers dangle goodies in front of employees, they may work harder for the short term, but they undermine creativity and interest in the job" (quoted in Neela Banerjee, "Rebounding Earnings Stir Old Debate on Productivity's Tie to Profit Sharing," *The Wall Street Journal,* April 12, 1984).

Defenders of profit sharing do concede this to its critics: When it works, it's typically because the plan is part of a broader management strategy to reduce hierarchy and boost employee involvement. Says David Wray, president of the Profit Sharing Council of America, "To maximize the value of profit-sharing, you need to empower employees. If you have an authoritarian type of management and employees can't bring something to the table, then the plan can't perform at its best" (quoted by staff reporter Neela Banerjee in *The Wall Street Journal,* April 12, 1994).

"Gain-sharing" is a form of profit-sharing that shares cost and efficiency savings with workers who are operating in an empowered environment, typically in teams. Gains are shared on a unit basis per a single, predetermined target. A good example is the success of Rowe Furniture Corporation, headquartered in Arlington, Virginia. A one-time traditionally run company, complete with a hierarchical management structure and time clocks, it now employs workers in teams who can challenge any corporate practice. These empowering approaches have had these effects: From 1991 to early 1994 furniture shipments have climbed some 40%, three times the industry average increase. The gross profit margin has increased to 25% of sales from 19%, without raising prices. In fiscal year 1993 sales rose 21% to $88.9 million, while its profits soared 264% to $5.1 million (reported by Kara Swisher "The Fabric of a Company; How Rowe Furniture Turned a Disgruntled Workforce Into Its Biggest Asset," in *The Washington Post,* March 21, 1994).

Rowe's high profitability is attributable to elimination of traditional piecework, where workers were paid for each piece of furniture produced. This is a method valuing speed and quantity over quality. A new compensation system entails offering bonuses based on performance in relation to cost. Work is now produced in teams. The group benefits if they can boost group productivity via cost cutting and more efficient ways to do their work. Employees' ideas have saved millions of dollars, annual turnover has dropped from 26% to 2%, and the absentee rate is down from 10% to 1%.

Some examples of cost-cutting suggestions at Rowe: loading dock workers suggested purchase of slightly bigger trailers so that more sofas can fit on the trucks, thereby reducing shipping costs. The order-entry department revised an outdated order form which cuts down errors and saved money. In the credit department, the workers suggested elimination of their "hovering" middle managers, so now three people do the work of seven.

What we are saying, then, is that money has different functions. It serves people in different ways, depending upon their needs, their life goals or aspirations, and their personalities generally. Some of these functions are:

To meet survival needs. Money pays the bills. This quip is pertinent: "I don't have to do this for a living; I could starve to death."

To meet security needs. We don't have to worry about the landlord, grocer, or our comfort in old age if we can count on a steady flow of the green.

To provide feelings of independence or freedom. This may range from the freedom of living high on the hog ("I can fly to Paris anytime I'm in the mood for a good time") to quitting an irritating or demeaning job ("Take this job and shove it," or "I'm mad as hell and I'm not going to take it any more").

To serve as as a status symbol. It tells others who we are, that we have power, authority, or "smarts." In essence, it is an affirmation of our competence. As Tevye observed in the musical *Fiddler on the Roof,* "When you're rich, everyone thinks you're wise."

To serve as a personal badge of honor. It tells us how others feel about us.

To serve as a score card. It permits us to compare our worth, success, or progress over time as well as to compare our status and accomplishment with others. ("Is that all they're paying you? I make a dollar more per hour than that.")

But money takes on varying meanings for us, depending on our:

Current financial standing. For example, the person who earns only $500 per year will do almost anything for $5.00. Of course, the person who earns $100,000 or more and gets excited over $2.00 is probably in need of a mental health checkup.

Career level. The beginning careerist will place a much higher value on money than the mid- or late-careerist who enjoys a greater salary and may have socked away a sizable nest egg.

Personal circumstances. Various individuals have high money needs at different times, e.g., to finance a mortgage, to pay abnormal medical bills, to send several kids to college, to keep up with the Joneses, etc.

What does all this mean to you, as a manager?

1. Money is, indeed, a motivator. But it is hardly the only motivator. For some people and under some circumstances it may provide little or even zero motivation. University of Chicago psychologist Mihaly Csikzentmihalyi finds that it is useful to remember that different situations produce different motivational needs. He states, "Under the right conditions, material incentives can add to the intrinsic rewards, but sometimes they don't make a difference and sometimes they detract from the intrinsic rewards" (quoted by Jay Matthews in "For Love or Money? Behaviorists Debate What Really Makes People Work Hard," *The Washington Post,* December 5, 1993).

2. Money, if used as a motivator, is both expensive and limited in nature. Thus you must seek out other motivators as incentives and rewards. Fortunately, there are many others.

3. Money requires continual renewal to be effective as a motivator. Once given, it puts you in the "what have you done for me lately" trap. As Ray H. Rannfeldt, facility engineer, John Deere Product Engineering Center, Reinbeck, Iowa, commenting on the fadeout effect of money, stated ("Approach Tendencies in Business: Employees That Like Their Jobs," *Supervisory Management,* June 1990),

"The differences between a monetary reward and a verbal reward . . . are significant. One is a traditional attempt at motivation that can almost be assured of diminishing in effectiveness from the outset, while the other is a much more humanistic approach that will live on in John's memory."

4. Not everyone perceives money as important as other motivators; e.g., the 54-year professional or administrative employee on a permanent plateau is more likely to respond to the chance to head up an important task force than to a minor addition to his paycheck.

5. Certain financial rewards are assumed or expected—annual "merit" raises, profit sharing, Christmas bonus, product discounts, stock purchases. To an extent they are taken for granted, so they no longer serve as motivators. They will inspire little in the way of added effort or creativity.

6. Rewards intended for everyone such as a special across-the-board pay increase of 3% or 6%, or the items mentioned in item 5 above, are not motivators. Why not? Because they are non-differentiating, non-individualized, non-job related. Also, because the payoff typically comes long after the performance has occurred, it is not perceived as contingent upon performance.

7. And, of course, major financial benefits such as medical and health plans have no bearing at all on the daily work. In Herzbergian terms, these goodies are essentially hygiene (see Fred Herzberg's Motivation-Hygiene Theory presented earlier in this chapter).

8. As this chapter has been emphasizing, financial incentives are hardly strong motivators for many workers. The rewards they expect from their jobs have radically changed since the Scientific Management days of Fred Taylor. People expect and actively seek personal fulfillment in one or more forms—challenging work, including continuing opportunities for growth, recognition, involvement and participation, innovation and creativity, contribution, commitment, wholeness, ownership of results, and a lot of "wiggle room."

9. The best use of money is as a supplementary reinforcer, that is, to combine it with other non-financial rewards. For example, praise is an effective motivator. But if managers constantly give praise and never a raise, praise may lose its punch as a motivator. (Certainly some—but not necessarily all—will expect you to put your money where your mouth is, for money talks.) And as stated earlier, empowered workers, especially those working in teams, will be motivated by bonuses based on their productivity, efficiency, and cost cutting.

Note: Broad-gauged, far-seeing managers regard money and other forms of compensation, such as benefits, as single elements in the ongoing total reward system. It thus is much more helpful to you to think constantly about the overall reward system in operation. Note, particularly, those aspects of the reward system that may be rewarding unwanted behaviors.

For example, an educator/consultant tried to sell a super interactive video system, to build the basic skills of sub-literate adults, to the adult education unit of a large urban public school district. He pointed out that the system would nearly pay for itself via a productivity increase of 30% or more, that students could move through the course of study with better results about one-third more rapidly. The adult education director's reply was astounding: "You don't understand. The district pays us for attendance, not achievement. There's no reward for getting students through here faster; if anything my ADA (average daily attendance) might go down and my budget could get cut."

Similarly, an offer to an official in another school district to expand computer-based instruction netted this reply: "Why should I do anything different next year from what I did last year? Who cares?" (reported and quoted in Lewis J. Perelman, "Luddite Schools Wage A Wasteful War," *The Wall Street Journal*, September 10, 1990).

YOUR REWARD SYSTEM: HOW TO MAKE IT PAY OFF

Usually the things that get rewarded are the ones that get done.

—Ron H. Cassell, director of quality systems at ITT Higbie Baylock, a 14-plant automotive supplier firm (in *Quality Digest*, June 1994)

The whole thrust of this chapter is to get you, as a manager of people, to think about rewards, incentives, and motivators that really turn people on, which shift them from an "OK, I'll do it because you're paying me to do it" to an "I'll do it because I'm excited, curious, and I want to contribute." In other words, we want you to get past the carrot-and-stick approach to motivation because, as management professor C. Brookly Derr puts it ("What Value Is Your Management Style?" *Personnel Journal*, June 1987), "Managers who have only carrots and sticks in their repertoire of rewards and sanctions are going to be less successful at motivating people who do not really want carrots or who are not afraid of sticks."

And to quote management writer John Case ("Why Work?" *INC*, June 1988):

Traditional punishments and rewards can get people to show up for work and do what they have to do to look good in the boss's eyes. But what companies need today is employees who want their performance to be good, not just look good. For that, conventional approaches to motivation are usually too blunt. No amount of supervision, for instance, can force an employee to smile at a customer and be helpful when the boss isn't looking. And no bonus system yet invented can reward someone who sees a little problem in the mail room, solves it on the spot, and never tells anyone that the problem even came up.

So how best can you provide incentives that ignite the spirit of the subordinate and make him truly productive? Management writer Jana Dovgan ("Managing the Workforce—Reward: Incentive for Employee Satisfaction," *Laborwatch*, December 1989) offers these guidelines to make rewards truly effective:

Individualize rewards. Because people are different, it is imperative to tailor-make your rewards system. Get to know your people so that you can adapt rewards to their individual needs. **Example:** A day off to a young mother with three children is likely to be more valuable to her than theater tickets to a new musical in town. Or a bonus may be welcomed by one employee and regarded cynically by another. Also, because employee needs change, you must adjust their rewards over time accordingly. Consider an employee at his three career stages: early, middle, and late. For the new careerist, field trips and training are likely to be big turn ons; for the careerist in his 50's, much less likely.)

Relate the reward to the performance. Make certain rewards correlate to the work performed. **Example:** Consider the reward you might give to a new approach to procurement versus the development of a new procedure to schedule leave.

Ensure fairness of rewards. Provide rewards based on employee perceptions of what is fair and just, and in relation to what their peers are receiving. Fair rewards are the most motivating.

Distribute carefully. Consider timing. Schedule the receipt of rewards close to the occasions for which they are given. Also, show enthusiasm for the reward you pass out. If you, yourself, don't value a reward, its motivational value is diminished.

Pay attention to presentation aspects. Words of praise have the most meaning when they come from co-workers who actually are in a position to judge. Also, company service rewards possess more value when they come from the company president as opposed to peers. Present rewards before an audience whenever possible, particularly one of peers.

Ensure rewards are performance based. Rewards have the most meaning when they are fully earned. For example, an automatic promotion, one based on length of service, has less meaning than one based on real accomplishment.

Relate rewards on a situational basis. Circumstances should determine the type of reward. Match rewards to the employee's values, lest they be perceived as of low value. For example, one with a need for status and esteem should be rewarded on the basis of these factors: How others have been rewarded previously, personal preferences, and his likely future in the firm. This type of employee might be rewarded with a better office location, as opposed to a write-up in the company house organ, because of its superior motivational value.

Keep rewards exclusive. Rewards have greater meaning when they are doled out on a truly limited basis. If nearly everyone is "outstanding," the reward loses its meaning.

The author would add these three points:

Regarding reinforcement of a negative behavior. Don't reward undesirable, unwanted behavior: **Example:** John is invariably late to staff meetings and other meetings as well. So meetings don't start until John arrives. What has John learned? That it's OK to be late to meetings. So John's behavior, although annoying, is rewarded and thus remains unchanged. Your desirable action, then, is to *withhold* rewards for undesirable behavior. This approach should help to change behavior from the unwanted to the preferred. In this case, starting meetings on time and letting group members provide punishing glances or comments will probably do it for you. If not, coaching is your next obvious tactic.

Regarding punishment of a desired behavior. Tellers in a bank are told to smile, be friendly, and chat with the customers. However, their performance is evaluated strictly on a production basis: the number of customers serviced each day. So a behavior that is presumed to be wanted—friendliness—is actually punished. For if one is friendly with the customers one's production will suffer. **The result:** The dictum of being friendly to the customers, to management's surprise, is ignored by the tellers.

Positive Reinforcers

A reward system that works well typically will be based on its capability to provide consequences or rewards to provoke and maintain desired behavior. We should note, however, that too many supervisors have been conditioned to think primarily in terms of financial rewards as motivators. Actually there are many other possibilities, as the listing below indicates. You may be able to add some others based on your own experience.

Tangibles

(non-financial)
Use of company car
Parking space (if a "rare" item)
Special or upgraded equipment
Prizes (a paid vacation or assorted "goodies")
Trophies
Lunch in an upscale restaurant with the boss
Chance to participate in a lottery
Office with a window or a larger office
New furniture for office
Free tickets to musical or sporting events
Points (backed by prizes; e.g., for good attendance, safety, sales)
Suggestions submitted
Use of company equipment/facilities for personal projects

Feedback

Self-monitoring data
Specific data from boss about performance ("Your reject rate in May was 15% below the plant average")
Information about new, forthcoming activities
Wall charts on production, quality, accidents

Job-related activities (preferred tasks)

Extra time off for a well-done job
Birthday off for special performance
Participation in special projects, task forces, study groups
Responsibility for a total activity or project
Chance to orient or train others on the job
Chance to mentor others
Chance to serve as an instructor in a formal training program
Membership in a standing committee (e.g., safety)
Chairpersonship of a committee
Acting for the boss
Conducting a meeting/conference
Field trip
Attendance at a convention or important conference
Chance to develop job aids, charts, new forms
Group decision making
Set own goals (subject to discussion with boss)
Job rotation
Job enrichment
Added delegation
Visibility (accompany boss to a "big" meeting)
Chance to handle a larger/more prestigious account
Serving as a representative for the office, either inside the organization or outside of it
Being asked for opinions ("What do you think?")
Status augmentation ("Only you can do this job, Pat")

Social Approval (Reaction of others)

Oral praise from boss, peers, customers, suppliers
Written commendations
Letters of appreciation
A write-up in house newsletter
Picture in local newspaper
Request to join an "elite" group, e.g., the Friday night poker club
Friendly greetings
Smiles
Appreciative head nods
Special job title
Invitations to coffee/lunch/athletic events

Approval of requests for:

Training
Special or added equipment
Added space, personnel, or funds
Change in policy, procedure, system
Field trip

Financial Rewards

Individualized bonus or pay increase based on special performance

Promotion

Overtime (if truly desired)

Stock bonus

HOW TO DECREASE OR ELIMINATE AN UNDESIRED BEHAVIOR

When someone is doing something that you would like to diminish or cut out totally, i.e., extinguish the behavior, you can accomplish this in several ways: remove all reinforcement, replace the undesired behavior with a preferred one, or punish the undesired behavior.

Remove all reinforcement. You can do this by providing neutral or no consequences for the undesired behavior. In this way, the performer will perceive that it matters not at all whether he engages in that behavior or not for the other person's (non-reinforcing) response is always the same. **Example:** Manager Tom Brown finds that a colleague, Joe Horne, likes to come into his office and just talk—politics, sports, his non-tranquil domestic life, etc. Brown doesn't wish to be rude so he politely listens (reinforcement). **The result:** Horne enthusiastically continues his time-wasting behavior. Finally, Brown realizes that Horne's prattle must stop for he really is too busy for aimless chit-chat. Gradually, Brown tends to find ways to listen less—he allows his secretary to interrupt (Mr. Brown, I've got to see you on Project K4," or "Your boss wants to see you right away"); he takes phone calls; he frequently tells Horne that he has to take off for a meeting in a few minutes; he says: "Joe, can we pick this up at lunch? I've got to get these letters out by noon." **The result:** Horne receives no favorable consequences (reinforcement) from Brown as a listener so he departs and seeks out a new victim for his chatter, hopefully one who will be very kind and listen endlessly.

Replace the undesired behavior with a substitute (preferred) behavior This is essentially a "crowding out" of the unwanted behavior by allowing a new one to enter. You do this by reinforcing the desired behavior which should, in time, replace the undesired behavior.

a) A subordinate tends to interrupt speakers at meetings. Your procedure is to reinforce the desirable behavior—

i.e., not talking—and ignore the interrupting behavior. **Example:** "I really thought you did a good job today, Helen, in listening to Charlie totally before you expressed your own view. He appreciated it, too."

b) A subordinate tends to miss deadlines for the weekly production report. You provide positive reinforcement (praise) when the report does come in on time and you ignore the "misses": "I appreciated your submission of your report on time. I know you had to work hard to do that. It helped me tremendously to get all the figures together for today's planning meeting with the front office."

The same principles apply where employees are late (you reward prompt arrivals and ignore lateness), absent (you reward presenteeism and ignore absenteeism), or working below standard (you reward good work and don't comment on the bad). And be sure you reinforce even the slightest improvement in performance.

Punish the undesired behavior. Punishment (aversive behavior) is a consequence (negative reinforcement) that can decrease or even eliminate an unwanted behavior. **Examples:** feedback overload; harsh criticism; fault finding; nitpicking; labeling someone in a negative way ("How could you do such a stupid thing?"); threats; the "silent" treatment; isolation (coventry); put downs; rambling, endless lecturing; off-the-cuff, top-of-the-head negative comments; "on-the-run," somewhat cryptic evaluations without a chance for the accused to respond or to learn from what is said ("You know that you loused up that Endicott order, don't you?"); plus any and all salvos which create anxiety and tend to lower self-esteem.

As you will see, punishment may have various unintended, negative effects. Yet, we know that punishment—called the "captious complex" by some observers—is used widely by those who manage others. Why? One clearcut reason is that they know of no alternative: the behavior is obviously bad so you simply lower the boom. Training in the use of more effective, positive reinforcement procedures (described above) has not occurred.

A second reason is that they (the bosses) may not be aware that they are engaging in punishing behaviors. **Example:** I once had a boss who was extremely pleasant and friendly on a face-to-face basis in both work and social situations. But once he found himself behind his desk and encountered behavior he didn't like, he became a master (monster?) at penning hard-hitting, highly critical notes or memos to his "errant" staffers. In more than one instance in which I felt the criticism was totally unfair, I summoned up my courage, walked into his office and politely challenged him about his captious note. Embarrassed and flustered, he would back off and say, "Did I write that? Forget it." He then rapidly drew several large Xs through his nasty note, dramatically tore it up, chucked it into the waste basket, smiled broadly at me, and would say, "I guess I should have checked with you on all the circumstances before I gave you this."

A third reason for delivering punishment is that it does work. The unwanted behavior will cease. (But there may be drawbacks, as we'll see later.)

Reason four is that it is quite easy to apply. Little imagination or creativity is required to unload on someone—a subordinate—who can't hit back.

A fifth reason is that by clobbering someone, either orally or in writing, there may be a worthwhile "psychological gain": it may help the punisher feel good (get rid of frustration or anger) when he can "dump" on an inept, irritating person.

A sixth reason is that much of management emphasis often is a concern with seeking the exception—errors, defects, deviations from standard or expected performance. The hunt for exceptions conditions managers to think about performance in negative terms. So when employees fall below standard—the exception—they are very likely to hear about it, loud and clear, in negative terms. ("Holy mackerel. You loused up in that Pacific Coast order again. Didn't I tell you that when we send something to . . .")

Finally, our cultural managerial stereotypes tend to support the strong, aggressive, tough, hard-to-please manager who relies heavily on criticism when he encounters miscues or low performance. The manager's boss often supports this behavior: "You got a problem in shipping? Straighten 'em out. Let 'em know who's boss. You *are* the boss, aren't you?" Opposite behaviors—being friendly, patient, supportive, encouraging, complimentary—are not likely to be encouraged by the stereotype of the "successful" manager.

However, if you are the deliverer of punishment you hardly have a certain road to success. You are quite likely to encounter serious problems such as the following:

1. Punishment may stop an undesirable behavior, but it may produce a less desirable one. **Example:** A supervisor chews out an employee for repeated tar-

diness. The employee shapes up and arrives on time. But the employee is now angry at his boss and the company. So he "drops out" (performs somewhat indifferently or complains to his colleagues about the tyrannical boss and lousy company), or increases his absentee rate, or even engages in minor sabotage. The boss now has a new problem. Does he provide punishment again? So the difficulty is that while people may learn what not to do, they are not necessarily helped to do what they should. Punishment has limited or even no power to correct. And people are certainly not encouraged to perform creatively via this mechanism. In fact, the likelihood is that they will perform only at the level required to avoid future negative feedback.

2. Subordinates may learn that the boss, as punisher, is a "tough cookie," a real S.O.B. Is this the real learning that the boss wants to pass on to his subordinates? And because of the fear of the boss, they thus may try to avoid him and communicate less with him. **The result:** a lose-lose situation for both parties.

3. The boss may unwittingly establish himself as an undesirable role model for others: A manager who has subordinate supervisors may bawl them out regularly and thus communicate that harsh criticism is the way to deal with errant workers.

4. For some employees, punishment may be perceived as a reward. Why? Because now they are getting attention, something they crave and wouldn't ordinarily receive. Any attention may be deemed to be better than none at all, even if there is a high price-tag attached to it. And as management professor Dr. Gene Milbourn, Jr., points out ("The Case Against Employee Punishment," *Management Solutions,* November 1986), if the entire work team is at odds with the boss, punishment may be a positive reinforcer as the individual is rewarded by his teammates for irritating management ("Hey, man, you really got to the boss that time. I thought he'd get a heart attack when you . . .").

5. Punishment may lead to anxiety, tension, or stress, which in turn may lead to anger, a desire for revenge, lowered output, new mistakes, or absenteeism. So, again, you may be encouraging behavior which you can't predict or control.

6. Punishment may have to be increased to maintain a continued suppression of the unwanted behav-

ior. ("I'll just have to crack down harder on those who get a customer complaint until they get the message.")

7. The undesirable behavior may be suppressed, but it may require constant surveillance to ensure its suppression. In other words, the effect is temporary because there is no built-in mechanism to ensure self-management or self-control when the boss is away.
8. The punisher is quite likely to be rewarded for its instant effects—cessation of the undesirable behavior—and thus he may learn that "This is the way to go." The consequence: New learning to modify employee behavior is not very likely to enter into the manager's motivational toolkit.

Despite the above admonitions against the use of punishment, there are times when it may be used appropriately. Typically it relates to the need for an immediate cessation of the behavior in these kinds of situations (per Paul L. Brown, *Managing Behavior on the Job,* New York: John Wiley and Sons, 1982):

1. When danger is quite likely to affect a performer. For example, if an employee is committing or is about to commit an unsafe act such as operating a grinder without goggles or wearing clothing which may get caught in a machine, there is not time to employ polite, reasoned coaching. In these cases the boss has to act immediately, even if his act is perceived as punishing in nature. In addition to safety considerations, punishment may be in order if a significant cost is involved, e.g., wasting valuable materials for misusing expensive equipment.
2. When a behavior is disruptive or highly distracting to *others,* e.g., gambling; serious (hazardous) horseplay, especially in a customer service area; sexual harassment. ("Using language like that again to female employees, Fred, will mean that your job is on the line.")
3. When the performance of one worker may have a dangerous or other harmful effect upon others; e.g., speeding in a "go slow" area, using gasoline to clean tools, smoking in a non-smoking zone, handling food unhygienically, etc.
4. When customers clearly may be mistreated or alienated, an intervention by the boss is essential even though the employee concerned is angered by the boss's behavior.
5. Confidentiality may require a quick action to safeguard sensitive data.

To employ punishment properly, you should:

1. Use it only as a last resort kind of thing. It should be contingent on an actual (improper) behavior, not on a whim.
2. To the extent practicable, people should know what the criteria are for punishment and the expected penalties related thereto. Of course, you can't predict every behavior that may require some form of punishment.
3. Punish only the person who acted improperly. The whole team should not pay for the faults of a single performer.
4. When the punished person does perform properly following the administered punishment, be certain to provide positive reinforcement to maintain the new, proper behavior. This also is a form of "welcome back to the fold" greeting after the offender has paid his debt. This procedure will show that you don't hold grudges, that the miscue is forgotten.
5. Just as in the case of positive reinforcement, the punishment should be rendered as close to the performance of the act as possible. This procedure will ensure maximum learning from the unhappy event.
6. Choose your punishment carefully. There is no need to lecture, berate, embarrass, or ridicule people when one can alter behavior with a frown, the raising of a disapproving eyebrow, the shaking of the head, or other similar body language to express disapproval, disappointment or even disgust. Silence can also be punishing. You can also withdraw privileges, withhold raises, and use other standard, aversive devices such as oral warnings and reprimands, a memo for the record, reassignment, transfer, suspension, or demotion.
7. Just as in the case of punishing a child, try to communicate that you are punishing the behavior, not the person. You certainly don't want a "Is it me or the performance you're upset about?" response. Your past strong relations with the performer will help to communicate a caring attitude should you have a need to criticize. An example of a statement stressing concern about an unwanted behavior is the following: "You're a fine workman, George, and everyone here knows it. But taking tools home without permission is against the rules and something we simply can't tolerate."

8. Be aware of your own emotional state when punishment seems to be in order. You certainly don't want to overreact to an improper behavior. ("I miss one staff meeting and it becomes a federal offense.")

9. Punishment should always fit the crime. Minor infractions of rules don't warrant supreme penalties. In their operetta *The Mikado,* Sir W.S. Gilbert and Sir Arthur Sullivan put it this way: "My object all sublime, I hope to achieve in time/To let the punishment fit the crime, the punishment fit the crime."

10. Be consistent. Treat all "offenders" alike. Because punishment is rarely appreciated, the least the administrator of the punishment can do is to dole it out to everyone in like fashion.

11. Be predictable. Don't "lower the boom" for a given behavior at certain times or occasions, but not at others. ("I did it that way last time and there was no problem. I must have caught her in a bad mood.")

12. Be clear in your own mind how the punishment will affect the relationship with the receiver. Will it strengthen, weaken, or leave the relationship unaffected? And which effect do you favor? Managers who pen punishing memos to subordinates may feel better after the act, but the impact on the recipient may be more than is wanted or anticipated. ("Gosh, I didn't realize Charlie would take it so hard.")

13. Reprimand in private rather than in public. Your objective is to communicate displeasure with a behavior, not to humiliate anyone before his colleagues.

In general, a commonsensical guideline for the would-be punisher is this: Punishment should educate, not devastate.

Anecdote: That punishment, or even the threat of it, can influence behavior is illustrated by this story: A fully loaded station wagon pulled up to a campsite in Yellowstone National Park, and five children and their parents promptly piled out and began hastily to set up for the night. The boys quickly unloaded all the camping gear, set up the tent with Dad, and then took off for firewood. The girls helped Mom set up the campstove and organize the cooking utensils.

A camper at the adjacent campsite looked on with envy and said to Dad: "I've never seen teamwork like that. Amazing."

Said Dad: "It's my system. No one leaves for the comfort station until everything is set up."

Note: The above discussion has focused on punishment administered by the manager—verbal criticism, disapproving looks, extended silence, avoidance (non-contact), threats, etc. But punishment may also come from:

The work itself, e.g., ambiguous or inconsistent instructions; a lower-order, demeaning task; unwanted overtime; excessive travel; a distasteful activity; working with a person(s) one dislikes; work perceived as "busy" work; a highly routine, monotonous job; unreasonable deadlines; an overly demanding pace ("a widow maker"); constant re-work.

The environment or system: improper or outdated tools, equipment or materials; frustrating, time-consuming procedures; antiquated, inconsistent or absent policies; unrealistic standards or none at all; harassing physical factors such as heat, cold, poor ventilation, noise, odors, potential hazards, light (too much or too little), distractions.

It thus is your job, as manager, to ascertain whether your employees are experiencing unintended punishing consequences from the work or the environment and to take corrective action wherever indicated.

Prompting and Shaping to Influence Behavior

Two additional ways to influence behavior are via prompting and shaping. Prompting is a simple concept. It is anything you do to get a behavior started. It thus takes place before the behavior occurs. *Examples:* oral or written instructions; handbooks; signs; a schedule to be followed; the yellow guidelines on a warehouse floor; arrows in a parking lot; training programs; rules and regulations; goal-directed, non-verbal as well as verbal communication, etc. (Listed by Paul L. Brown, *Managing Behavior on the Job,* New York: John Wiley and Sons, 1982).

Some benefits of prompting, per management writer Tom Roth ("Design a Performance Improvement System: Prompt Desired Behavior," *Performance Improvement,* December 1976), are:

1. You can prevent an undesired behavior (or no response) from occurring and thus avoid having to deal with deficient performance after the fact. (A

good diet is more sensible than repeatedly taking aspirin for the headache.)

2. You can encourage the performer to make the desired response which you can then reward.
3. You encourage the desired response faster.

Example: You have scheduled a special 10 a.m. meeting. You have a full agenda and you thus want everyone to arrive on time. You can provide prompts in several ways:

1. Have a copy of the agenda on your subordinates' desks at 8:30 a.m. so that it will be the first thing they see.
2. Alternately, you can have your secretary visit each subordinate at 8:30–8:45 and pass out the agenda with a "strong" oral request to arrive on time.
3. You can call your subordinates at 8:30 to remind them to arrive on time.
4. You or your secretary can phone 15 minutes before the meeting. When your people do arrive on time, you could reinforce their behavior with an appreciative comment, a smile, etc.

Note: If similar meetings take place in the future, prompting, over time, can be reduced in frequency, in strength or in its immediacy. The procedure may be used to ensure that reports are submitted on time.

Prompting is a good tool to help a new worker experience success rather than improper performance. A senior employee on a new task can also profit from prompting.

Shaping relates to the manager's efforts to mold, develop or upgrade a subordinate's capabilities in a gradual, sequential way. Procedurally, you would take a large, complex task, break it into small components, and teach each component in logical sequence. As each step is mastered, you provide positive reinforcement. **Examples:** learning to fly an airplane, tune an engine, operate a computer, develop a budget, etc. (described by Paul L. Brown, *Managing Behavior on the Job,* New York: John Wiley and Sons, 1982).

The same procedures may be used to help people to reach a somewhat difficult goal. You would reinforce "successive approximations" to the goal, even if the goal is not yet attained. Once the goal is reached, your external support (positive reinforcement) can be faded out and "natural" reinforcers can take over. This procedure would be useful to control lateness and absenteeism, to reach a new production or quality standard, or

to encourage any other behavior which may entail some form of "stretch" (reaching a higher-level goal).

To illustrate the relationship and dynamics of reinforcement and shaping, let's take the prior example of auto mechanic George Watts, who specializes in tuning car engines. George's boss has set a standard of nine tune-ups per day which George ordinarily meets very well.

In recent weeks, however, George has been averaging only six tune-ups in his 8-hour day. George's boss, Spark Phlugg, has heard about behavior modification techniques (management by consequences) and would like to provide positive reinforcement when George hits the nine tune-up level again. But Sparky is under pressure from his boss to get results, so he can't wait until that event happens. So he decides to use the "shaping" procedure instead.

Recall that in shaping you can reinforce (reward) any approximation to the desired behavior, which is what Sparky does. When George produces seven tune-ups, he praises him for his improvement in production. When George gets his output up to eight, he provides further praise. On the days when there is no improvement, Sparky says nothing at all. When George hits the standard and stays on it, Sparky is very complimentary and provides praise each day. When he feels that George is really back on track, he may skip the daily dose of positive reinforcement and only do it intermittently.

MOTIVATION AND MORALE

The work of the behavioral science theorists in the area of motivation does not support the notion—really a misconception—that a goal of management is to make workers "happy." There certainly is nothing wrong with having your workers happy (high morale), but the facts of organizational life are that happy workers are not necessarily motivated to work harder or more creatively. Similarly, highly motivated and productive people are not mere happiness seekers. They want joy and satisfaction from their work, but they know that only comes from working hard at it. Accomplishment, while satisfying when a task is completed successfully, typically entails sober thought and perseverance along with risk-taking, pressure, frustration, headaches, and often even set-backs and conflict.

Business writer Walter Kiechell III quotes Frank Landy, Pennsylvania State University psychology professor ("How Important Is Morale, Really?", *Fortune,*

February 13, 1989) as follows: "Positive emotions don't cause productivity. It seems more likely that high productivity causes morale. If you look at firehouses in a community, the slowest houses have the lowest morale. There's a lot of bickering. The happiest house is the busiest, its inhabitants merrily racing off to put out one conflagration after another."

Military commanders know that their best troops are those who "bitch a little." Their biggest fear is the prevalence of too much happiness, for it produces complacency. In fact, I once had a commanding officer in a combat zone who said in reference to the troops: "When they start building foot lockers, that's the time to move on." He was referring, of course, to the undesirability of the troops "settling in" at a given location, seeking extra comforts, developing local social or romantic ties, and generally becoming fat and happy. That kind of "country club" happiness he deemed to be anti-motivational.

Economics writer Robert J. Samuelson sees the issue this way ("Corporate Loyalty Is Not Dead," *The Washington Post,* September 20, 1989): "Everyone assumes that a satisfied worker is always a more productive worker. Not so. Of course, some people love their jobs, work hard, do well and feel appreciated. And others detest their work, hate their bosses, and work poorly. But some workers are satisfied precisely because they aren't working hard. They have cushy, well-paid, and secure jobs. And some productive workers are dissatisfied precisely because they are working hard. Their jobs are demanding and stressful."

In general, there is no reason why organizations and managers should not favor happiness or high morale. But this should not be an end in itself and be traded off for motivation. High motivation (based on high accomplishment) typically produces high morale, but not necessarily the other way around.

Professor Murray Barrick, University of Iowa, puts the issue this way, "You have to do specific things to increase productivity, and separate things to improve satisfaction and the things may not be all that related" (quoted by Walter Kiechel III, "How Important Is Morale, Really?", *Fortune,* February 13, 1989). This observation would certainly fit in with Fred Herzberg's Motivation-Hygiene Theory discussed earlier.

The bottom line. The relationship between contentment and productivity turns out to be a researcher's nightmare. Certainly we can measure morale (job satisfaction) via attitude/climate surveys. But what does it mean? Happiness on the job? Real commitment/motivation? Does it affect business results? Morale is a squishy concept and psychologists tend to stay away from it. They prefer, instead, to think in motivational terms, i.e., is there the will to do, and if it's lacking what can we do to bring it about? So opt for motivation, for highly motivated people are likely to be quite happy (high morale), too—at least most of the time.

Figure 4-3
Guidesheet to Aid in Planning for Employee Motivation

Listed below are seven motivational approaches. You may wish to add some others based on your experience. Drawing upon the needs of your team members, plan the application of these motivational concepts to them:
1. Recognition/praise. 2. Challenging work. 3. Independence/freedom (empowerment). 4. Added responsibility.
5. Leadership opportunities. 6. Contacts with others. 7. Job enrichment (greater variety).

Examples:

Staff Member (enter name)	Motivational Approach	Implementation Procedure
Mary Scott	1. Praise	"I intend to comment on her work at staff meetings whenever she turns in a very good operations analysis."
Phil George	4. Added responsibility	"I plan to delegate full responsibility for Project WR29 immediately."

Staff Member (enter name)	Motivational Approach	Implementation Procedure

My Empowerment Behaviors—A Self-Quiz

The survey below is designed to measure your performance/skill in empowering your staff. Be candid to provide an accurate reading of your usual performance. Assess each statement on a 1–5 basis:

1. Represents a very low practice or agreement; practically none.
2. Minor agreement or practice.
3. Moderate agreement or practice.
4. A high degree of practice/agreement.
5. An extremely high degree of practice or agreement; very much your typical behavior.

Place your ratings in the space provided to the left of each quiz item. Scoring and interpretation procedures follow the quiz.

_____ 1. I operate with a minimum amount of controls on and reviews over what my people do.

_____ 2. I provide my employees with full freedom to resolve the problems they encounter each day so that they will have high job interest/ concern/commitment to our operation.

_____ 3. As manager, I ensure that my subordinates have the resources—information, equipment, material—to do their jobs independently.

_____ 4. I provide in-depth training so that my people can have the competencies to function independently and effectively.

_____ 5. I encourage my employees to feel that their jobs belong to them rather than to me.

_____ 6. It is important for my people to assume "ownership" of their jobs without my second-guessing what they do.

_____ 7. I expect my people to develop and apply their own procedures rather than wait for me to tell them how to do things.

_____ 8. I expect my staff to determine their own pace, style, schedule, sequence of operating, etc.

_____ 9. I give my people full opportunity to make decisions about matters within their own expertise and delegated authority, so that they will take pride in what they do and try their best to perform properly.

_____10. I expect my people to go beyond the rules, if necessary, rather than "go by the book" without thinking about the best result for the organization and the customer.

_____11. Because my employees are most effective when feedback concerning their operation comes *directly* to them rather than through me, I operate in that manner.

_____12. I try to make my people more effective by encouraging a team operation wherever practicable.

_____13. I allow those who are closest to the customer—my employees—to make decisions that affect the customer.

_____14. I encourage my people to satisfy the customer so as to earn their confidence and trust, and thus their repeat business.

_____15. I encourage my people to think in terms of continuous improvement. I thus support their new ideas wherever I can.

_____16. I try to create a climate wherein people are respected for their ideas and their judgment.

_____17. I allow my people to function in an innovative, risk-taking way, rather than to control what they do.

_____18. I operate in a manner that recognizes it is more important to reward risk-taking than to punish mistakes.

_____19. I encourage my people to question any policy, process, system, standard, or procedure that we have.

_____20. I recognize and praise good work to secure the benefit of my people's self-propulsion.

Scoring and Interpretation

Scoring: Tally your scores for all the quiz items. Enter your total points here _____.

Interpretation:

90–100. You trust and rely on your staff to operate independently and to do what it takes to solve problems, satisfy the customer, and improve operations. You are an empowering manager. Keep up your empowering practices!

80–89. You are quite in tune with the concept/skill of empowerment. But you should review your operating style to ensure that your staff has the maximum amount of freedom to operate effectively.

70–79. You are striving to be an empowering manager, but you have a lot of work to do to reach that goal. Review your operating procedures to see what is required to further the goal of full staff empowerment.

Below 70. You are a long way from having an empowered staff. Until you alter your management philosophy, style and practices, you are losing out on the benefits to your operation empowerment can bring.

Note: Your final score above obviously is a *self-rating*. You thus may wish to corroborate its accuracy by getting added ratings from your staff. A simple way to do this is to reproduce the quiz and let your people rate your empowerment practices on an *anonymous basis.* Let one of your employees consolidate all the final scores, also indicating the range of final scores. Then discuss results with your staff.

Another helpful procedure is to secure an average team score for each of the 20 quiz items. Then compare team scores with your own. Discuss differences in perception should they exist.

Praise Reappraised: A Self-Quiz

This instrument is designed to stimulate your thinking about giving praise. Circle one answer. In some cases you may have difficulty deciding between the two statements; if so, select the one that you can agree with more readily. Please recognize that there are no right or wrong answers in the quiz. The statements merely represent points of view about working with praise in our dealings with people.

1. **Praise and leadership philosophy**
    a) Effective leadership means running a tight ship—high, clearcut standards, discipline, and financial rewards to those who produce.
    b). Leadership today requires attitudes and behaviors marked by clear goals and high standards plus mutual support, sharing, communicating, caring, and encouraging.
2. **Praise and the leadership role**
    a) A strong leader is very careful about doling out praise since it may be misinterpreted by the receiver.
    b) Effective leadership includes rewarding people for their accomplishment through praise.
3. **Praise and the strong leader**
    a) Strong leaders lay it on the line and straighten people out as often as necessary.
    b) Strong leaders think in terms of turning people on via positive strokes.
4. **Praise and time management**
    a) Administrative chores must be accomplished and take a much higher priority than praise giving.
    b) Taking the time to give praise to subordinates is very worthwhile regardless of other considerations.
5. **Praise and work results**
    a) Workers need and expect high standards, clearcut instructions and prompt feedback if they goof things up in any way.
    b) Praise is a lubricant—a motivating force—to increase productivity and help relationships to go smoother.
6. **Good news/bad news and productivity**
    a) Bad news about performance is a key to improved performance.
    b) Good news about work accomplishment will produce higher performance.
7. **The new worker and praise**
    a) The new worker has to meet the standard. If he makes it, that is the best reward he can receive.
    b) Praise at each step of the way will help to solidify improvements as they are made.
8. **Praise and the weak achiever**
    a) The weak performer should be praised sparingly lest he gets some wrong ideas about his real performance.
    b) Low achievers can be helped by an ego boost such as praise.
9. **Praise and the average worker**
    a) Praise for the average worker will backfire—he will expect pay increases, possibly other rewards, and just get a swelled head.
    b) One way to elevate his performance is to provide praise for accomplishment.
10. **Praise and the strong achiever**
    a) These workers have self-propulsion. They know they're good and need little outside stimuli such as praise to perform well.
    b) Strong achievers profit from recognition from the boss. It helps to maintain that drive.
11. **Internal motivation and praise**
    a) Because most motivation is internal, the wise manager will supervise closely to be sure that that motivation is in force.
    b) Motivation is internal, but it can be augmented by the power of praise.
12. **Performance, pay and praise**
    a) Because people basically come to work for the paycheck, praise for performance doesn't have any special meaning to the worker.
    b) People come to work for various reasons, including feeling good about themselves. Hence, praise for performance is basic.
13. **Positive vs. negative feedback**
    a) Most people accept and can profit from constructive criticism, even if it hurts a little.
    b) It is more important to acknowledge people's strengths than to dwell on weaknesses.

Praise Reappraised (Continued)

14. **Praise and deserved criticism**
    a) When someone needs to be told they have slipped or goofed, it's no time to confuse the message with praise.
    b) It's a good idea to look for the good in people even when criticism may be necessary.
15. **Praise and added expectations**
    a) Once you start praising people they'll expect it all the time, even if there's no special reason for it.
    b) The purpose of praise is to help people feel good about themselves. Hence the need to give it as often as we can.
16. **Improvement incentives and praise**
    a) When you tell people they are doing a good job already, it eliminates the incentive to do better.
    b) Telling people they are doing a good job is a tremendous motivator to do better.
17. **Praise and success**
    a) A little success causes people to slow down and rest on their laurels. Praise is not desirable for it would contribute to that slowdown.
    b) A little success causes people to want to keep having such experiences. Praise is a good way to encourage continuing success.
18. **Self-assessment and praise**
    a) People know when they're doing well without anyone having to tell them about it.
    b) Self-awareness about results should be accompanied by a pat on the back by the boss.
19. **Praise and support**
    a) Because people know when they are doing a good job, there's little need to tell them what they already know.
    b) An excellent way to show interest in and support of my people is through frequent praise.
20. **Praise and communication**
    a) Once you start to praise people, it may open up communication links that you don't need or want.
    b) Praise is a good way of reducing distance with others and thus can open up important communication channels.
21. **Praise and interpersonal relations**
    a) Praise is a high-risk activity for such reasons as they'll want it all the time, they'll start getting too friendly, it'll go to their heads, etc.
    b) Praise is a good way to get closer to people and to build strong relations with them.
22. **Frequency of praise**
    a) I may give praise, but very carefully and sparingly. It's not a routine thing with me.
    b) I look for opportunities to give praise as frequently as possible.
23. **Sincerity of praise**
    a) Praise is a tool and at times may be used whether it's deserved or not.
    b) Praise is meaningful only if earned.
24. **One's comfort level and praise**
    a) It's often uncomfortable for me to give others praise.
    b) I find giving praise very satisfying because most people respond to it enthusiastically.
25. **Expectations of praise**
    a) I work hard, do my job well and don't expect to be praised for it. I believe my subordinates feel the same way about it.
    b) I like praise, I expect it if I do my job well, and I am liberal in giving it.

SCORING: Count the number of a) and b) answers.

If your answers are mostly a), you tend to be cautious in your use of praise and see little value in its use as a management tool. If your answers are mostly b), you see it as a motivator of a considerable importance and a builder of closer relations as well. If your answers are divided somewhat equally between a) and b), you probably have not developed a clearcut philosophy about the use of praise.

Praise/Criticism Tally Sheet

To assist you in securing a good reading on your praise (P) vs. criticism (CR) practices, make appropriate daily entries (tally marks) on the form below. Compare results for a 3–4 week period, noting trends, if any, in your behavior.

Note: You should include in the praise column statements that are encouraging, supporting, and complimentary.

	Mon.		Tues.		Wed.		Thurs.		Fri.		Total	
	P	CR	P	CR	P	CR	P	CR	P	CR	P	CR
Mary	///	///		//		/		///	/		4	9
George												
Kim												
Totals												

5 Managing a Changing (Diverse) Workforce

Motivational Strategies For Particular Categories of Workers

The future of America 'in a globalized economy without a cold war will rest with people who can think and act with informed grace across ethnic, cultural, and linguistic lines. And the first step lies in acknowledging that we are not one big world family, or ever likely to be . . . In the world that is coming, if you can't navigate differences, you've had it.'

— Robert Hughes, Time, February 1992

Building a new, more diverse workforce and making it tick will be one of corporate America's biggest challenges in the decade ahead.

— *Business Week*

Instituting diversity interventions is not risky, it's essential. Those who fail to do so underutilize the majority of their workers; and a human resource is an expensive asset to waste.

— Kate Butler, The American Humanagement Association

A basic principle to aid in understanding and supervising your staff is that *people are different.* They have different values, perceptions, needs, hopes, dreams, expectations, joys, fears, and tolerances for "pain" which may rise in the work environment. You will want to recognize, then, that there may be different "types" or categories of workers in your workforce. Some of the more common groupings are young or new workers, high achievers, "plateaued" persons or other non-promotables, temporary workers, hourly workers, support personnel, survivors after a downsizing, women workers, and the status-deprived employees. We thus will discuss: (1) the characteristics of several of these worker types, (2) their needs, and (3) what motivational approaches might best tap their power, energy, and creativity.

But a word of caution. Even though we are lumping together certain types of workers, you should still recognize that there are quite likely to be broad differences of personality and need within any single grouping. For example, certain plateaued performers may require a great deal of special attention whereas others at the same stage in their careers may require no special motivational strategy at all.

Similarly, as Harvard Business School professor Quinn Mills points out in his book *Not Like Our Parents* (New York: Morrow, 1987), the "Baby Boomers" are hardly a homogenous group. He categorizes them into five classifications:

The Competitors—These are the much-talked-about high-striving "yuppies," actually a minority.

The Pleasure Seekers—Both highly motivated and highly unconventional, they strongly favor personal freedom and individualism. They thus give "success" a new definition.

The Trapped—This group feels that circumstances have trapped them in dead-end jobs or failed relationships.

The Contented—Nearly half of the boomers are quite content with most things in their lives.

The Get Highs—These are the few boomers who are struggling to survive. They cope via drugs, booze, or religious fanaticism.

Note, too, that underpinning the motivational suggested strategies are the ideas and concepts advanced by behavioral scientists Maslow, Herzberg, Likert, et al., which were discussed earlier.

THE WOMAN WORKER

Our best hope for the future are women who don't see the ceiling but the sky.

—Dr. Claudia Golin, professor of economics, Harvard University, in *BNAC Communicator,* Rockville, MD, Winter 1993

Women today are an increased presence in the U.S. workforce. Per the Labor Department's stats, some 47% of all workers are women. Most (two-thirds) are in clerical, food service, sales, nursing, teaching, and child care, with 80% earning less than $25,000 per year. Their earnings are about 75% of what men in like jobs receive (Kara Swisher, "Giving Women a Voice," *The Washington Post*, May 4, 1994).

For organizations and the managers in them, it is essential to understand better the personal characteristics of the female worker; on-the-job problems facing women workers, including the gender bias that blocks their advancement (the "glass ceiling"); sexual harassment; lesser pay than men; and family vs. career concerns. Initial hiring may also be subject to discrimination, says Mary Mattis, V.P. of Catalyst, a New York consulting firm concerned with women's issues (Peggy Stuart, "What Does the Glass Ceiling Cost You?", *Personnel Journal,* November 1992), because male managers assume women will have a lower career commitment than men, for they're likely to have children and leave.

In respect to female characteristics, management consultant Stephanie Allen, head of the Athens Group, Denver, states that research shows very little difference in male vs. female traits—that is, in I.Q., ability to stick with a task, intuition, verbal ability, and so on. Even certain physical tasks, traditionally assumed to be too demanding for women, can be handled by physically fit women. For example, a St. Louis packaging firm changed its ban on hiring women after they found that women could move packages weighing more than 20 pounds without incurring back injuries. Male workers in those positions commonly experienced back injuries (Peggy Stuart, *Personnel Journal,* November 1992).

Besides the above-stated capabilities, women offer "a different perspective of the world," says Allen. When entering a room she is more likely to observe the interaction between people, whether harmony and concern exists. Conversely, men are more interested in the task and their locale in the hierarchy. Of course, some women are more task-oriented and some men are more concerned with cooperative relationships. The more effective staffers are the "bridge people," those who can deal with people of both genders.

Another significant difference, says Kathy Doyle Thomas, marketing V.P. for Half-Price Books in Dallas, is that "A woman is more apt to see several points of view; men are more likely to see things as either black or white and miss the shades of gray." While this should be an advantage, it may be a disadvantage because male staffers often seem to feel they must have the answers (Peggy Stuart, *Personnel Journal,* November 1992).

The differences of women and men can be of real value to the organization moving toward a more collaborative management style.

Also, per human relations consultant Carolyn Kenner-Varner, "Women tend to be more intuitive and visionary—at least they don't have to work as hard at it as men do. Women often produce a good working product with less effort than men have to make" (quoted in Peggy Stuart, *Personnel Journal,* November 1992).

A problem facing women is the kind and amount of feedback given female workers. For example, an inappropriately dressed female saleswoman may be talked about, rather than talked to. A male salesperson would learn of his sartorial inadequacy directly. Asserts Kate Butler, American Humanagement Association, Flemington, N.J., a consulting/training firm concerned with strategic gender issues, women have been deprived of feedback all their lives. She says, "I've found that feedback given to men is two-and-a-half to three times lengthier than that given to women" (quoted by Peggy Stuart in *Personnel Journal,* November 1992).

Another concern for women is that many men feel uncomfortable mentoring women. So the woman seeking a helpful mentor should endeavor to locate one who has related well to women—good relations with his mother, sisters, spouse, daughters—and understands the problems arising from lack of feedback and job challenge. Male mentors often may be reluctant to give feedback to women for fear that they'll cry. Nevertheless, women want and need the feedback essential to upgrade their performance.

An added problem facing women is their "invisibility." Says Allen, "Women often don't get credit for their ideas." Male cohorts may simply take the credit for the ideas after their presentation to them. If she brings up an idea at a meeting, it may well be overridden or ignored. One woman found that the only way to get listened to was to stand up when she had something to say. Within a year, the stand-up procedure was no longer necessary.

Kathy Doyle Thomas also finds a double standard regarding objectionable behavior. She says, "A woman is hardly ever accused of being hard-nosed. Instead, she's a bitch. She isn't lacking consistency, she's scatterbrained. She isn't overworked, she's too weak to handle it."

Women may also sabotage their own success by failing to network; selecting staff jobs (as opposed to line jobs) where it may be difficult to prove one's contribution; trying to do everything because of low self-esteem; engaging in perfectionism, which may mean missing deadlines; a reluctance to point out unfair practices and behaviors; and being feedback-deficient, they may be less likely to offer it to others.

The bottom line for women workers is that they comprise a significant segment of most organizations today. This resource should be utilized fully, both from the standpoints of economics and good spirit in a democratic culture.

Leonard H. Chusmir and Douglas E. Durand have studied the role of women in the workplace. Their advice to those who manage women is to take these four action steps ("The Female Factor," *Training and Development Journal,* August 1987):

Increase job satisfaction. How? Match aspirations and rewards. Learn what rewards are significant to your female workers and try to match them appropriately. Drs. Chusmir and Durand state that this is more important with women than men. Why? Because research strongly ties job satisfaction with job commitment for female workers, but not necessarily for men.

Increase the meaning of work. Tap a variety of skills and stress task meaning. Expand jobs (job enrichment) to overcome narrow, dull, and boring work. Increased job satisfaction may not always increase production, but it should improve work quality and reduce absenteeism and turnover. Dedication and loyalty should also be augmented.

Use skills fully. No one relishes work below her skill level. Think in terms of full utilization of skill repertories as opposed to categorizing certain preferred tasks to be only a "man's job."

Involve in decision making. Women, as do men, require autonomy, feedback, and opportunities for participation in decision making. This will increase job satisfaction, self-esteem, and job commitment. Per available research, there is a strong correlation between need satisfaction, job satisfaction, and job involvement.

Drs. Chusmir and Durand offer some added ideas to help women to be successful and fulfilled:

Support women's decision to work. Women have enough off-the-job problems without questioning their job and career motives, thereby raising feelings of self-doubt, fear, and guilt.

Develop in employees a sense of loyalty to their total work team. This is particularly essential if the overall corporate climate is one with which women understandably are in conflict.

Help women cope with personal and work role conflicts. This may or may not entail counseling by the manager personally. The personnel office or a female manager elsewhere in the firm may be helpful for this purpose.

Use flex-time if needed. Understanding of family demands should be translated into flexible work hours. Job sharing, four-day work weeks, and early daily departures are also helpful practices. This will reduce unwanted pressure and stress on the female worker and the work unit.

Interpret rules realistically. Family demands, emergencies, etc., may require "bending" the rules a bit.

Provide for social contact. Integrate female workers fully into the work team. Involve them in social activities, too, as may be practical. No one wants to be "put in a corner" and excluded from closer contact with others.

Additional advice to the manager of women, per Deborah J. Cornwall, ("Managing Women for Success," *Supervisory Management,* January 1985), is to:

Provide support, encouragement, and counsel in areas requiring improvement. Don't let unresolved situations fester for fear of hurting someone's feelings.

Ensure equal pay for equal work. Managers need "to put the company's money where its rhetoric is and pay for performance."

Overcome the usual stereotypes about women. Women are people. Don't assume they are "sweet," "sensitive," "ladylike," or "bitchy," "castrating," and "aggressive." Women may have their quirks and faults, but men are rarely without them, too.

Don't make assumptions about career goals. Women may or may not be interested in better jobs. But don't make assumptions about their aspirations. Instead, discuss possible job opportunities as you would with male staffers.

Believe in your women employees and they will have confidence in themselves. Encourage them to strive for better job opportunities.

Encourage women to be both tough and direct and sensitive and diplomatic as well.

Coach them about the politics of the organization. This will help them, you, and the total enterprise.

Note that the above recommendations were made by the writer in 1985. Certainly since that time a growing number of organizations have adopted a number of those suggestions, and the status of their female workforce has thereby improved. However, note the 1992 study by Rose Mary Wentling, professor of business education, Illinois State University, of 30 women in midlevel management jobs at 15 Fortune 500 Midwest firms. She zeroed in on factors that assisted or hindered career development, career goals and aspirations, perceived barriers to attaining desired jobs, and actions thought necessary to reach such jobs. Her study indicates that many women are still finding the road to career success is a rocky one.

Dr. Wentling found that the four barriers to career development most frequently encountered by female managers she interviewed include:

Supervisory guidance. This was very limited. Male bosses frequently are unable to give women candid feedback about their performance. (So how does one improve if one doesn't know in what to improve?)

Gender bias. Women have to work harder to prove themselves, aren't taken seriously, are banned from certain jobs, and don't receive equal pay for equal work. (Sex discrimination doesn't die easily.)

Political savvy. Women typically lack this because they don't have access to information on informal power structures and don't fit into organizations run by men. (If you're an outsider how can you act like an insider?)

Career Planning. Women lack a career strategy; which is to say, they don't think early enough about their careers, don't acquire the needed training, fail to seek individual recognition and status, and don't make informed career decisions (summarized in "Reaching Past the Glass Ceiling," the BNAC *Communicator,* Winter 1993 from *Business Horizons,* January–February 1992).

Key point: Women are an important human resource and will be more so as their numbers increase in organizations. Few organizations can afford to ignore or sabotage this important asset. Obvious motivators are opportunities for advancement, being involved in decisions, being listened to, and flexible work schedules: flex-time or part-time employment, job sharing, working at home (telecommuting), and compressed work schedules (e.g., squeezing a 40-hour week into a four-day schedule).

VALUING WORK FORCE DIVERSITY: MOTIVATION AND MANAGEMENT OF INDIVIDUALS WITH DIVERSE CULTURAL BACKGROUNDS

Diversity management is more than managing those with different backgrounds. A better definition: "The process by which a company (or manager, or human resource department, or any individual) incorporates the dissimilarities of its workforce into the decision-making process in order to motivate, direct, lead, organize, plan, and staff more efficiently" (per David Gold, Senior Information Specialist with the Society for Human Resource Management, in "Diversity Means Considering More Than Demographics, in *PEPI UPDATE,* Positive Employee Practices Institute, Minneapolis, MN, April/May 1992).

In a growing number of organizations, the workplace is marked by people who differ from one another in a variety of ways. Marilyn Loden and Judy P. Rosener suggest in their *Workforce America! Managing Employee Diversity as a Vital Resource* (Homewood, IL: Business One Irwin, 1991) that there are two dimensions of diversity: *primary,* which includes age, race, ethnicity, gender, physical abilities/qualities, sexual/affectional orientation, and *secondary,* which encompasses work background, communication style, socio-economic status, marital status, native born/non-native, military experience, commuter, religious beliefs, cognitive style, geographic location, parental status, education, smoker/non-smoker.

With the changes in the composition of the U.S. workforce, as human resources writer Carol Kleiman points out ("Can a Non-Diverse Crowd Push Diversity on the Corporate Ladder?", *The Washington Post,* May 8, 1994), by the year 2000 white males will comprise only 15% of new hires.

Kleiman cites a study of 785 human resource executives, sponsored by the Society for Human Resource Management and the Commerce Clearing House, Inc., which evidenced the following:

☐ From 1983–1993, the number of women in their work forces increased an average of 69.1%; African Americans, 59.1%; Hispanics, 49.4%; Asians, 44.4%.
☐ The number of white men in the workforce increased only 10.4%.

So if the multicultural workforce will be our reality in the 21st century, how do we react to it? Do we shake our heads in despair or chagrin or do we look forward to it as an opportunity to use and profit from the new talent pool of culturally diverse workers?

A survey of 44 human resource professionals saw significant gains from managing diversity effectively. Management consultants Kathleen Whiteside and Julie O'Mara said their perspectives were these ("Diversity in Our Changing World," *Performance and Instruction,* February 1993):

☐ From a moral and ethical standpoint, it's the right thing to do.
☐ It aids our global competiveness because the organization has a diverse workforce that understands other cultures and customs.
☐ People become more loyal, productive, and committed when they feel their differences are valued.
☐ The atmosphere becomes more open and trusting.
☐ A future competitive edge will emerge as we learn to manage diversity now.
☐ The author would add another value: Creativity is enhanced because diverse, possibly less-conventional views are added to problem solving and decision making.

When working with culturally diverse individuals, it is all too easy to create problems in the workplace because of our traditional assumptions about people. Management consultant Selma Myers, in a presentation at the national conference of the American Society for Training and Development, May 10, 1993, pointed out that we should guard against falling into these culture-bound traps:

Our values: We assume that getting the task accomplished is more essential than engaging in small talk and building interpersonal relations. As Americans, we also assume that taking initiative is vital (but those from other cultures may prefer to be asked to do so).

Our perceptions: We are likely to assume that everyone thinks alike, seeing is equal to believing, commitments are certain to be honored, and recognizing people publicly is favored by everyone.

Our beliefs about communication: Communicating directly ("tell it like it is") is preferred; body language is a universal, cutting across all cultures; "yes" equals an affirmative; silence is unwanted because it produces frustration.

Our beliefs about motivation: Competition is a good way to improve results. For a positive environment, emphasize informality. Everybody favors upward mobility.

To be successful today, managers must acquire and use a new set of awareness, sensitivity, knowledge, and skill to manage and motivate our increasingly diverse workforce. One area of major importance is that of cross-cultural communication skills. Educator Martha Meacham ("The Multicultural Work Environment: Are You Ready?" *Performance and Instruction,* April 1994) asserts that the biggest error we can make is to assume that there is only one correct way to listen, talk, or have a conversation.

The core of cross-cultural interpersonal communication skills is *perception.* That is to say, things aren't always as they seem. Rarely is there agreement among us on the intended message. Miscommunication even occurs often among those speaking the same language. And the problem gets compounded when a different set of cultural values exists. The problem is one of communication style.

But, says Meacham, neither style is right or wrong. Understanding the different views can help the situation so that both parties to the conversation adjust. **Note:** Mutual acceptance and respect for another's mode of speaking is a lot easier than to alter someone's long-programmed cultural communication habits. If conversational style differences are not recognized and appreciated, we can all too easily draw false conclusions about communicative intent.

To understand the communication dynamics with culturally diverse employees, Meacham suggests we take an anthropological approach and consider the communication model developed by cultural anthropologist Edward T. Hall. This is the concept of "high-context" versus "low context" cultures.

High-context cultures, e.g., the Hispanic culture, are more sensitive to the surrounding circumstances (context) of an event. This means that nonverbal cues play a big part in the interpersonal intervention. Communication is for social interaction, not merely for exchange of information. Thus, the social setting, phrasing gestures and voice tone, one's status, and posture are taken into consideration.

In medium/low context cultures, such as the Anglo-American culture, we tend to rely on words alone to vary our meaning.

We can anticipate problems, then, if the new entrants into the labor force are high context, but their bosses are mostly medium/low context. Some of these problems are:

☐ Those in high-context cultures may regard others as unfriendly if personal matters and social amenities are not brought into the conversation by the totally business-like communicator. High-context persons approach the world as a network of connections where conversation solidifies a relationship and builds trust. Without understanding of a differing cultural style, a conflict is quite likely.

☐ Eye contact and handshakes are another source of cultural difference. The Anglo business culture considers them essential to good communication. But among Hispanics avoidance of eye contact signifies deference to authority and respect. In Mexico direct eye contact in a conversation is deemed to be rude. And women are not expected to shake hands at all.

☐ Gestures also may create difficulty; e.g., the OK finger signal used by Anglo-Americans is interpreted differently by Mexicans. Pointing with the index finger is regarded as a rude gesture by some Hispanics.

In summary, the assets and liabilities for intercultural communication, per educators Valerie Eastmond and Rebecca Smith ("Linking Culture and Instruction," *Performance and Instruction,* January 1991) are as follows:

Assets: Flexibility/adaptability; knowledge of cultural values; respect for other points of view; sensitivity to cultural differences; awareness of potential difficulties; interactive listening skills; previous intercultural experience.

Liabilities: Ethnocentrism (assuming one's own cultural values are the only valid beliefs); use of stereotypes; critical/judgmental attitude; fear of foreigners; inability to cope with unfamiliar situations; rigid expectations; lack of familiarity with the host culture.

A worthy goal for managers is to stress those characteristics that are assets among workers.

As far as motivating the culturally diverse workforce is concerned, there obviously are effective and less effective ways to do so. Dr. Sondra Thiederman, an authority on inter-cultural communication and cultural diversity in general, suggests that we can up our success rate by following this seven-point approach ("Managing and Motivating the Culturally Diverse Work Force," *The 1993 Annual, Developing Human Resources,* San Diego: Pfeiffer and Co.):

1. **Counteracting resistance to change.** We have to start with the understanding that those from other cultures expect to act/perform/behave on the basis of their learned culture. Their culture is part of their identity. So for such a person to feel comfortable engaging in a behavior at odds with his culture is a monumental event.

   Examples: Asians being asked to praise themselves in front of a group; Hispanics encouraged to seek promotions over fellow Hispanics who are their seniors (a source of shame, not pride); Asians or Hispanics being asked to take initiative on a task when their preference is to be asked; expecting an Asian worker to inform the boss of problems in the work place or to complain about something.

   Motivational Strategy: Provide employees with the maximum amount of power, that is, to include them in the decision to change. Don't tell them what to do, but query them as to how far they're prepared to go to alter their behavior. This approach is key to reduce anxiety and defensiveness. Having been asked for comments is a form of empowerment to the employees.

2. **Assessing behavior accurately.** We want to understand why someone is behaving as he does for these reasons: trying to understand the worker is a form of respect and caring and will reduce defensiveness; incorrectly interpreting the behavior will frustrate your attempts to change it.

3. **Communicating your expectations.** When dealing with those from other cultures, it is not easy to explain expectations. Differing values impede such transactions. **Examples:** Getting employees to admit lack of understanding of a task when making such an admission is deemed rude and disrespectful in other cultures; praising onself is in opposition to a desire to maintain social harmony and balance.

   Motivational strategies: Admitting lack of understanding can be overcome by pointing out that this means the employee is more enthusiastic, committed, and concerned with correct performance than one who won't confess to a lack of understanding. Also, pretending to understand is actually dishonest and may result in mistakes that create problems for others. In respect to the praise problem, one might explain, for example, that stating one's qualifications in an interview enables the manager to make better decisions in initial hires as well as promotions.

4. **Showing a willingness to compromise.** This shows respect and encourages cooperation and change. **Examples:** reluctance to complain; admitting lack of understanding.

   Motivational strategies: Regarding complaint hesitation, let complaints be presented on a group or team basis. This procedure avoids putting any one worker in the limelight and recognizes that group opinion is valued. Or complaints might be presented by the informal group leader or given in a suggestion box. Also, accepting complaints in private and preserving the anonymity of the complainant may help.

   In respect to admitting non-understanding, let the worker present it in private so he won't appear foolish to his peers. Or, request that questions about a task be presented in writing, thereby reducing possible embarrassment.

   Another form of compromise is to reassign the worker to better utilize his skills. Dr. Thiederman cites this example: In a hotel restaurant an Asian female worker was reluctant to ask customers if anything else was needed. Rather than nag this gracious and hardworking employee about that task, the management reassigned her to the concierge desk where her formality and graciousness would be responded to favorably and the guests would come to her!

5. **Using the employee's "cultural language."** For example, one good way to reach the worker on failure to take initiative, to complain or to confess to

lack of task understanding, is to present rationales based on the possibility of the manager losing face. **Examples:** If initiative isn't taken and the job doesn't get done, it reflects on the manager's ability to do his job properly; if the manager is not aware of problems, he can't solve them and may look to his bosses and others as incompetent; if the manager doesn't know his instructions were not comprehended, errors will occur and both parties will be embarrassed; if workers don't highlight their qualifications, poor staffing decisions will ensure and the manager will lose face with his bosses.

Another way to show respect for people's culture is to stress group benefits from behaviors deemed by the worker to be "anti-cultural." For example, workers may be reluctant to seek promotions because it calls attention to the individual at the expense of the group and thus creates alienation from peers. Or engaging in self-praise disrupts group harmony. **Strategy:** Point out that promotions and achievement help the group as well as the individual to look good. Similarly, taking the initiative will help the group to be more effective.

6. **Meeting culture-specific needs.** It is all too easy for U.S. managers to fall into the trap of assuming that the motivators (rewards) of people from other cultures are the same as ours. But we can't work on the motivation of culturally diverse workers if we don't know what they really are. Keep in mind that universal motivators are very rare. One that is universal is "social needs," that is, the desire for contact with others, comfort, and companionship. But the point is that we can't assume that the needs deemed important in Western industrialized societies—advancement, competition, autonomy, opportunity to contribute ideas, recognition, money—are sought after by those from other cultures.

Other cultures also place great value on the family or group. So you might motivate some Hispanic or Asian employees by giving them time off to return to their prior country for family events and other special occasions. Company picnics and other company-sponsored "family gatherings" will show that their needs are being considered.

Overtime may also be favored to enable the worker to send money back home or to bring family members to this country. Permitting of celebrations of their national holidays provides for family time and shows respect for their group traditions.

Key point: Knowing that one's needs are recognized will help to encourage cooperation and overcome resistance to change. **Example:** Recognizing needs for relaxation, companionship, and identity, says Dr. Thiederman, may well diminish one's desire to speak a foreign language on the job.

7. **Using positive reinforcement to reinforce the wanted behavior.** Although positive reinforcement such as praise is a strong motivator, it has to be administered with respect to cultural differences. Many workers of other cultures may not want to be praised publicly because it draws attention to them as individuals (the group aspect, of course); they have a deep concern for maintaining harmony and balance; and they have a high regard for social hierarchy and seniority. And praise by the manager may be interpreted that he is surprised that the employee has performed so well!

So if praise is important, how can it be rendered in terms of the other's culture? Be discreet—use a third party or word of mouth. Or praise the total group or put an appreciative note in the person's personnel file. And don't overpraise.

And what about criticism when a boo-boo has been committed? Errors inevitably will occur if we encourage the taking of initiative. The best procedure to avoid discouraging future independent action: Point out the mistake but indicate pleasure at the worker having taken the initiative.

Summary Point on Cultural Diversity

While the Golden Rule may serve as a useful guide in many interpersonal situations, doing unto others as *you* would have them do unto *you* is not likely to work in culturally diverse situations. A better guide is the **Platinum Rule:** "Do unto others as *they* would have had done unto them." In other words, exercise a lot of sensitivity and empathy as to how others see things and what their needs, wants, and expectations are. So look for cues as to how comfortable the other party seems to be—silence, confusion, uneasiness, or evasiveness may signal that they have encountered information, requests, or behavior that violates their cultural norms.

THE OLDER WORKER

40 isn't old if you're a tree.

—spotted on a bumper sticker

After rising less than 3% between 1979 and 1992, the number of U.S. workers 55 and older will increase 38% by 2005, more than either blacks or women, the Labor Department predicts.

—*The Wall Street Journal,* June 13, 1994

The demographic realities of our time are that the workforce will soon have a greater proportion of women, minorities, and older workers. But are we, as managers, psychologically ready to accept them, to work with them so that we can capitalize on their strengths, to do what it takes to ensure their indoctrination, training, and continuing motivation?

Many organizations today like to see themselves as young and vibrant. The older worker thus is seen as "not being with it." The headline of a *Wall Street Journal* article (June 19, 1994) by Sue Shellenberger and Carol Hymowitz on the older worker reported this view thusly: "Over the Hill? As Population Ages, Older Workers Clash With Younger Bosses. Employees, at 50, Are Seen As Rigid, Expendable."

This article cites the case of a 42-year old manager at Macy's in San Francisco with 22 years of service who had risen in the ranks to store superintendent. A 31 year-old store manager began to exclude him from memos and weekly management meetings. He noticed that soon other managers began to come to work in T-shirts and jeans. He was totally "out of it" with his suit and tie. When an irate customer appeared, his casually dressed colleagues would call on him to meet the complainant since he was the only one dressed for it!

In respect to our aging workforce—some writers refer to it as "the graying of America"—even the early baby boomers (born 1946–1964) can look forward in the not-too-distant future to becoming senior citizens themselves. One estimate has it that by 2015, 25% of the workforce will be 55 years of age or older ("Training 101: Cultivating the Potential of All Workers," *Training and Development Journal,* April 1991).

In any case, older workers are and will be a significant manpower resource, so managers must learn to manage them for maximum accomplishment.

Many myths and stereotypes have grown up about the capabilities of the older worker. But research studies (Robert W. Goddard, "Viewpoint: How to Harness America's Gray Power," *Personnel Journal,* May 1987) show these antiquated views are hardly supportable. Consider these findings:

Productivity levels. Changes in physical ability, cognitive (thinking) performance and personality don't affect older workers' output. Of course, the most demanding physical tasks will produce a difference.

Creative and intellectual achievement. Again, there is no decline with age. **Example:** Musicians' abilities rise up to their mid-60s and decline at 85 or more.

Absenteeism. It tends to decline with older workers.

Loyalty. Anticipate this factor to be stronger with the older worker compared to the younger employee. This means less turnover can be expected among the older group.

Work ethic. The edge here, again, goes to the older worker, although all age groups pride themselves on hard work and doing the best job possible.

Job satisfaction. This element is likely to be stronger with older personnel than with the younger workers. **The reasons:** They appreciate the opportunity to work and have learned over the years how to adjust to the work environment.

Less significant tasks. Expect the older worker to respond more favorably than his more youthful counterpart to jobs seen as "meaningless." Seniors work to remain active and engaged, to enhance meaningful life experiences, to have social contact, and to ease depression. So they are more able to accept tasks of varied quality.

Learning. Older workers can be trained or retrained as well as anyone. Physical and mental changes influencing ability to learn are minor.

Work characteristics. If treated with respect and dignity, older personnel show greater critical judgment, insight and patience, and produce more workable ideas than their younger associates.

In general, their more extensive experience and wisdom will compensate for any possible declining speed in mental or physical effort.

Our concern as managers, of course, is how to best manage older workers so that they function in the most motivated and productive way. Management authority George S. Odiorne ("Managing Grampies," *Training*, June 1988) offers these suggestions:

Health and safety. As older persons, expect that they will be health conscious and less likely to accept hazardous conditions of work than younger workers. Also, they may be less able to cope with stressful jobs. But aside from those more demanding work conditions, they should be solid contributors based on their experience, excellent work habits, and ability to work without close supervision.

Information. Older workers want to know the future of their jobs, job expectations, and how well they are doing. They don't require much information about careers, but expect advice about maintaining their status and their functioning in the work unit. So don't shy away from offering them candid feedback about their performance.

Team membership. Given their strong attitudes toward loyalty, anticipate that they will want to be fully integrated into the team. Try to include them in special activities such as employee involvement groups.

Recognition. Some older workers may have doubts about their true acceptance and appreciation in the organization. Thus it is sensible to recognize them as frequently and in as many ways as possible—verbal praise, employee-of-the-month awards, pins, plaques, serving as an instructor in a training program.

Poor performance. If slippage in performance occurs, be as candid about it as you would with anyone else. Sometimes a new assignment may be in order. But in any case don't ignore below-standard performance.

Dignity and respect. Don't snub the older worker by not inviting him to meetings, socials, lunches, etc. If health problems arise, be understanding and provide leaves of absence or possible less stressful or demanding assignments.

Termination. When the older worker reaches the end of the road due to health or performance reasons, work with him to achieve a normal retirement. If the senior person is inconsiderately put out on the street, middle-aged workers in the organization will notice it and wonder if they, too, will get the same harsh treatment. At their retirement, hold a dignified retirement ceremony or luncheon to show appreciation and thanks for their long or significant performance. At the ceremony, consider having a top official on hand to provide a formal thanks and good-bye.

In respect to the perceived problem of the young manager managing someone who may be a lot older than he is, "older than my parent" as one manager put it, here are some guidelines offered by business writer Minda Zetlin ("Young Managers Force a Generation Gap," *Management Review,* January 1992):

Introduce changes slowly. Get to know your staff first, solicit their input, and communicate how the changes would help the operation. Don't be the proverbial bull in the china shop.

Develop trust with your staff. (You already have it with your bosses or they wouldn't have put you in the job you're in.) You need to prove that you value and respect your staffers, *all* of them regardless of age.

Manage by listening. Hold frequent one-on-one meetings with your staffers. You want to communicate that in respect to the open door, you do "walk the talk."

Show that you care about your people as individuals. Try to get to know them as people, not just as hired hands.

Communicate that you don't have all the answers. Avoid what has been termed the "over-educated smart-aleck syndrome." Don't pretend to know what you don't, for this is the quickest way to lose respect.

Use older workers as trainers. Tap their knowledge and experience for this will serve as great motivators for them.

Recognize differences in motivation. As a young manager you undoubtedly are motivated by status, success, advancement, competition, money, and recognition. The senior worker is driven by security, camaraderie (peer contact and support), a sense of belonging, comfort, and pride, plus success and recognition. He also may focus on job security and benefits (pension, medical insurance).

Relative to differences in learning by the older worker, Catherine D. Fyock, author of *America's Work Force Is Coming of Age: What Every Business Needs to Know to Recruit, Train, Manage and Retain An Aging Work Force* (Lexington Books, 1990) states that there actually are more similarities than differences in training older vs. younger adults. Both want:

☐ A supportive, friendly learning environment.
☐ To be able to apply new learning.
☐ To build new learning on past experiences.

As to differences, Fyock states that aging may require longer time to store and retrieve data. This may slow down the learning process as well as recall. So some older adults may learn new tasks or skills at a slower rate; but for most people mental functioning isn't affected until about age 70. But once the new tasks are learned, they tend to make fewer mistakes than their younger counterparts.

Vision, of course, is likely to be affected by aging. The answers: In training materials try to avoid small print, glossy materials, and low contrast colors such as blues paired with greens, and pastels.

For some older people, hearing soft, high-pitched sounds may present a problem.

As to learning how to use hi-tech equipment, including computers, research indicated that that is no problem.

The best training procedures of older learners are these:

Provide self-paced learning. This is a sensible procedure because everyone learns at a different pace. This approach will build self-esteem and self-confidence. Learning new subject matter and equipment will best be accomplished on a self-paced basis.

Provide easy-to-read materials. This means using high-contrast colors and bold typefaces, and avoiding high-gloss items.

Post training materials at eye level. Use of bifocals may make it difficult to look up to read above-eye level training posters.

Make adjustments for hearing difficulties. Clear, distinct speech is a must. Remove distracting noises. Front-row seating may be desired for hearing-impaired people.

Adopt adult learning principles. Assuming new skills will be learned more slowly, break skills into small tasks and then build upon mastery of the new knowledge.

Eliminate jargon. This creates walls between those who know and those who don't. Assuming every organization has some or more of it, explain it on the first duty day.

Use a variety of training methods. All adults learn best when methods are varied, older workers in particular. So besides short lectures, use case studies, exercises, videos, demonstrations, job aids, handouts.

Use older adults to train older adults. This approach will make older adults feel more comfortable. The older trainers are likely to be more sensitive to the learning needs of their older trainees. Also, this feeling is likely to arise: "If they can do it, I can do it."

Peer learning. If practical, group older learners together. This, again, will be a confidence builder for there is comfort in seeing other workers who are "just like me."

Tie learning to rewards. For example, if successful completion of a training module provides eligibility for a pay increase, be certain to communicate it.

Some additional do's and don'ts in training the older worker are offered by education/trainer J. J. Johnson ("Cognition and Aging: A Practical Analysis," *Performance and Instruction,* January 1994):

The Don'ts

Don't regard old biases about age and memory. Research studies on memory and aging are contradictory. So don't assume a true relationship between the two is valid.

Don't provide meaningless materials or tasks. If older adults can't relate to it, they won't absorb it. As you might expect, the research shows a strong correlation between applicable pertinent information and its retention.

Don't pressure older people with timed tests or exercises. Sure it may take a bit longer, but older adults will, in time, retrieve the information.

Don't tell older adults unnecessarily what to do. Just indicate the task and let them work it out. Creativity in older adults doesn't decline enough to be significant towards their actual contribution. **Note:** George Bernard Shaw wrote several plays in his 90s.

The Do's

Treat them as individuals. Like the rest of us, some are smarter, sharper, faster, or more practical than others.

Present one idea at a time. This is termed "chunking" by educators. **Example:** it's a lot easier to remember a phone number (or a Social Security number) when written 372-8419 than 3728419.

Use memory aids. This procedure helps the learner to organize information better.

Use teams, as appropriate, to solve problems. Group thinking and sharing are great confidence builders.

Summarize frequently. This will help to consolidate learnings.

Learn from the older worker. What they may lack in information—your information, that is—they may make up in maturity and wisdom.

Also consider using this set of training strategies, as provided by performance technologist Susan K. Clark ("Training Implications for Our Graying Work Force," *Performance and Instruction,* January 1994):

Regarding hearing. Hold classes in a room with sound-absorbing materials, e.g., carpeting and drapes. Arrange chairs so participants can see one another and the trainer to facilitate lip reading. Allow enough time for receipt and interpretation of information. Stand close to trainees, face them, and speak clearly. With a large group, use a public address system.

Regarding reaction time. Encourage older learners to be attentive, exercise care, and stress accuracy. Foster a risk-taking atmosphere to reduce worries about making errors. Avoid unnecessary time-pressured activities. Let people know in advance what's coming to avoid unnecessary surprises. Give clear instructions and encourage questions. Give plenty of positive reinforcement (praise).

Regarding memory. Use summaries to close a session as well as to start one. Adjust pace to facilitate mastery. Use displays for better retention. Most importantly, base training on need, build on life experiences, and point out issues of concern to the participants. It's easier to absorb and retain that which relates to our lives and experiences.

Finally, if you have to evaluate the many programs and products in the marketplace aimed at providing instruction for older workers, adult educators Dr. James L. Mosely and Dr. Joan C. Dessinger suggest you assess the use of these essential instructional strategies ("Criteria for Evaluating Products and Programs for Older Adult Learners," *Performance and Instruction,* March 1994):

- ☐ The learner's attention is secured before providing information.
- ☐ Sufficient practice for mastery is provided.
- ☐ The program provides constructive feedback.
- ☐ The material is broken into short modules: 10–20 minutes each.
- ☐ Session time is limited to two hours or less.
- ☐ Frequent breaks and opportunities for walking, talking and sharing are provided.
- ☐ If physical activities are involved, the program works into them gradually.
- ☐ Activities, such as writing assignments, don't involve extended physical exertion.
- ☐ Directions for the physical activities are flexible and adaptable to changes in learners' energy and enthusiasm levels.
- ☐ Time is provided learners to review, reflect and apply a new task before another is introduced.
- ☐ The climate is supportive and non-threatening.
- ☐ New concepts are introduced gradually (time is allowed for discussion) to minimize conflict with prior knowledge.
- ☐ Learners are allowed to control time (self-paced instruction).
- ☐ Fear of failure is minimized in all instruction.
- ☐ Participation is rewarded and the reward is instant.
- ☐ Auditory and visual modalities are combined to enhance learning: The auditory modality is stressed for information to be stored in short-term

memory. The visual modality is emphasized for information to be stored and retrieved from long-term memory.

☐ Learners take an active part in the learning process.

☐ Positive over negative feedback is stressed.

☐ To avoid error by learners, appropriate support mechanisms are included.

To close our discussion of training and motivation of the older worker, a pointed summary observation by Catherine Fycock merits citation. She states that General Electric has found that it's cheaper to retrain veteran engineers in the latest technology than to hire new ones!

THE BABY BOOMER

This is the group of workers born after World War II. Their expectations in the workplace differ markedly from their much more traditional, older colleagues. The differences relate to areas of control, compensation, and component. In more detailed terms, says personnel consultant Richard Chanick ("Career Growth for Baby Boomers," *Personnel Journal,* January 1992), consider:

Control. Baby Boomers desire more control over their work environment. They have a need to participate in decisions, previously an area of concern only of upper management. They want to be consulted on issues such as work schedules, the kinds of benefits offered, and when and how and if a new product should be developed and sold.

Compensation. Those born before 1946 favor a compensation that provides a "fair" amount of money. Baby Boomers tend to use the word "more" when describing their pay expectations. They regard their paycheck as their report card, so more is better. Baby Boomers also stress "linkage" in pay, that is, they want their pay to be linked to their productivity, not just to seniority. A certain gripe-triggering event is pay comparable to colleagues who hardly perform as well as they do.

Component. Baby Boomers are big on quality of life. A job, therefore, is only one component of their lives. For true job satisfaction, another life must be recognized, that is, one with family, friends, and recreation. Anticipate, then, that in a social setting they will define themselves in well-rounded terms: "I live in Oak Hill.

I'm married now for over 10 years and have two kids, 7 and 4. I work for Acme Electric Motors." The traditionalist, pre-Baby Boomer, conversely, is likely to simply say, "I'm a systems analyst with Quality Foods."

So the Baby Boomer is a complete person, not just one into his job and nothing more.

THE BABY BUSTER

This is a term to describe the generation—some 50 million strong—that is the newest addition to the labor force. Lawrence J. Bradford and Clarie Raines, authors of *Twenty something: Managing and Motivating Today's New Work Force* (New York: Master Media, Ltd., 1992) help us to locate them in the generational chronology by describing the three generations that comprise our work force thusly:

Traditionalists (the "Silent Generation"): Born 1925–1945).

Baby Boomers: Born 1946–1964.

Baby Busters: ("Generation X"): the generation waiting to be defined): Born 1965–1975.

To manage the Baby Busters, managers have to recognize that traditional rewards such as rapid promotions and quick salary increases are limited due to all the downsizing, restructuring and reengineering that took place in the '80s and '90s. So other rewards have to be used.

All of us, regardless of our particular generation, have "turn-ons" (motivators) and "turn-offs" (demotivators). What sparks or turns on the Baby Busters? Per Bradford and Raines, the following:

☐ Recognition and praise.

☐ Time spent with their boss (you, the manager). This is particularly vital for the Baby Buster entering his first job.

☐ A need to learn how they're performing *now* so as to make them more marketable.

☐ Fun at work: structured play, mild practical jokes, cartoons, moderate competition, and surprises.

☐ Small and unexpected rewards for work assignments done well.

Note: While upward mobility is still desired, it may not be deemed an unshakeable goal if it takes an 80-hour week to climb the success ladder.

Baby Busters are turned off by:

☐ Hearing about the past—particularly yours.

☐ Inflexibility or rigidity about time.

☐ Workaholism. (**Note:** They favor the well-balanced life style.)

☐ Being watched and scrutinized.

☐ Being pressured to convert to traditionalist behavior.

☐ Negative comments about their generation's values, tastes and styles.

☐ Feeling disrespected ("dissed," as they are likely to say).

A secret of success in managing Baby Busters is to provide a free and loose work environment. For example, the Patagonia Company, maker of products for outdoor enthusiasts, Ventura, CA, has no offices; employees work, instead, in open spaces. It not only has a flexible work hours policy (come as early as 6 a.m. and leave as late as 6 p.m.), but there also is an option to work at the office for five hours a day and at home for the other three. Personal leaves of absence, unpaid, may be taken for as much as four months each year. This provides for a long summer break and is a good burnout preventer. Empowerment via deep delegation and involvement in decision making is the norm. Creativity is strongly encouraged (reported by management writer Charlene M. Solmon, "Managing the Baby Busters," *Personnel Journal,* March 1992).

Other firms rely heavily on education and training as significant aspects of their reward system. Rapidly changing technology, experienced by such firms as Texas Instruments, makes for frequently changing jobs. So new education and training are musts to adjust to the changes.

In summing up, then, what is the best recipe to manage these workers? A Generation X female consultant with a marketing firm puts it this way: "Manage me by teaching me things. Manage me by showing me how to do my job. Manage me by getting me better tools. Don't manage me by sitting on me and giving me demerits because I'm five minutes late. Don't manage me by saying I can't be trusted to give the customer a 35-cent credit. Don't manage me by telling me that you know better than I do and, if there's information that's critical to my job, you will be the judge of when it's appropriate to tell me" (quoted by management writer Bob Filp-

szak, in "It's Just A Job—Generation X at Work," *Training,* April 1994).

The bottom line. Keep in mind that they will respond to a management style that trusts, empowers, shares, and supports them. They have a significant need to be respected, and valued, to feel important.

PEAK PERFORMERS

Money alone won't attract, hold, or motivate talented creative people. To be sure, they appreciate money. But in the end, the good ones choose a place to work based on pride—in their work, their colleagues, their clients, the standing of the agency. And they want a supportive environment where their skills can flourish. Provide that environment, and you'll attract talented people.

—Kevin O'Neill, creative director of the ad agency Lord Einstein O'Neill and Partners, New York City, in *The Wall Street Journal,* August 30, 1990

Although "peak performers" comprise only a small portion of an organization's workforce, they provide much of the energy that propels it. Hence every organization has to be concerned with the opportunities these workers have to perform to their maximum capacity.

What precisely is a peak performer? Charles A. Garfield, author of *Peak Performers: The New Heroes of American Business* (New York: Morrow, 1986), found in his study of 1,500 peak performers over a period of nearly two decades, that they have six salient characteristics (described in "Peak Performance—It Can Be Learned and Taught," *Management Solutions,* June 1986):

1. They are driven by a *strong sense of mission.* They know where they want to go. And once they have a clear image of an end result, they commit themselves fully to it. This sense of mission entails a total alignment with the company—the two move in the same direction.

2. They are *results oriented.* They don't waste time on activities not related to the desired result. They acquire new or expanded skills for their goal. They believe strongly in training. (Parenthetically, we should note that workaholics are committed to activity; these people are committed to results.)

3. They are *self-managers and self-starters* as well. They know their capabilities and strengths and capitalize on them. They are strongly committed to per-

sonal growth and work assiduously at developing the skills of self-mastery. They have self-confidence, cultivating it in themselves and others around them.

4. They are both *team players and team builders.* They empower others to produce for peak performance. They delegate to multiply their capabilities.

5. They can make *course corrections* as plans don't fully materialize. They can make necessary adjustments and get back on track without trauma. They regard setbacks as useful information and use such data to change course.

6. They are skilled in *change management.* They are not overwhelmed by accelerating rates of change. Their success in adapting to change is based on these four attributes: being a student forever, expecting to succeed, mapping out alternative futures, and updating their missions as necessary.

In sum, these performers are not hyperactive types, workaholics, creative geniuses, or performance superstars. Rather, they are people at all levels who consistently deliver peak performance—people contributing at extraordinary levels.

Other "secrets" of peak performers, per Dr. Gerald Kushel, President, the Institute for Effective Thinking, New York are these (presented in *Bottom Line,* March 15, 1994):

Performance responsibility. Peak performers are neither interested in blaming others nor creating alibis for less-than-excellent results. Rather, they willingly take responsibility for their own accomplishments.

Effective thinking. These people are *effective* thinkers (not to be confused with positive thinking). This means that there is a strong internal drive toward achievement of results. They pursue excellence, but not perfection. They don't have a *need* to do well; rather they have a *preference* to do so. **Note:** One who is driven to do well will be immobilized when success is evasive.

Self-motivation. They look for reasons to keep delivering. If a reason for self-motivation becomes old hat, they seek a new way to become motivated.

Help seeking. Their goal is to constantly do better. Hence, they seek help from others, particularly mentors for both career guidance and technical help. Even when at the top of their careers they seek guidance and counsel from others.

Team player. They try to inspire others by their stellar examples. Cooperating to increase one another's performance creates a peak performance zone. **Example:** They may join self-help groups such as weight control groups or divorced parent groups.

Rich personal life. Peak performers enjoy their work and their family lives. They know what is important to them and work enthusiastically at it. What they do is what they want to do, not what others expect them to do.

To round out the unmistakable earmarks of the peak performer's success, management writer Michael Rozek, drawing on Dr. Garfield's research, lists these additional characteristics ("Can You Spot A Peak Performer?", *Personnel Journal,* June 1991): strategic planning ability for both careers and projects; risk taking in the pursuit of excellence; high self-confidence and self-esteem; need for responsibility and control; ownership of their own good ideas; ability to prepare psychologically for key situations; A-1 time management capabilities; capacity to learn from past miscues; belief in one's creativity regardless of the limited understanding of their ideas by others; a positive work environment, which they may create if lacking; concern for others, permitting them to work well jointly; decisiveness when opportunity calls; foresight to detect both possible setbacks as well as opportunities; a need to check to see whether they are on course; an insatiable quest for new ideas, knowledge and experiences.

To build a department of peak performers, Dr. Garfield advises the supervisor to become a role model for his unit. You must become a peak performer yourself before you can inspire others to do the same. Second, you must communicate that average performance is not enough. Excellence becomes the new norm. Third, excellence must become a team goal.

Dr. Garfield believes that peak performers are made (trained) not born. His training approach, then, has these six steps ("Peak Performance—It Can Be Learned and Taught," *Management Solutions,* June 1986):

1. Develop a mission statement for each subordinate which answers this query: "Why do I work as hard as I do?"

2. Identify key result areas in the job. "How does my job contribute to overall objectives?"

3. Allow for self-management via a system to measure one's performance.

4. Encourage team performance. "How can I best help the team?"

5. Recognize when course corrections are needed and thus be able to get back on track.

6. Manage for change. "What changes are occurring in and out of the firm and how do I ready myself for them?"

While the peak performer is a high-powered contributor who has already been identified and unleashed, there is another related group which should be of managerial concern. These are the "high potential/high achievers." Management consultant J. Alan Ofner finds that organizations concerned with the potential of such personnel have organized selection and training programs which have these goals ("Keeping Your High Achievers Motivated," *Management Solutions,* July 1987):

1. Identify such personnel, not just the top performers in an organizational segment.

2. Develop "doers" (not learners) who are held accountable for end results.

3. Provide special training.

4. Provide opportunities for work in task forces.

5. Train the supervisors of high potential/high achievers.

Once in the program, these individuals need constant feedback about their performance; counseling about their work progress and next milestones in a career path; job enrichment to make assignments more challenging and to improve skills; job rotation; special assignments outside the organization, e.g., to a local government.

Ofner offers one major caveat: Don't assign people to artificially created jobs or to token projects that only create a learning experience at the expense of a true doing experience.

Summary points. The oldest and brightest performers will be the next generation of organizational leaders. It thus is essential to provide these individuals with opportunities to develop and to perform, including opportunities for them to take risks. Risk-taking equates with growth. As the adage has it, "No risk, no gain, no glory."

THE TECHNICAL PROFESSIONS

These people are the "knowledge workers," the independent, creative employees most likely to be found in R&D (Research and Development). In more specific occupational terms, they are the engineers, the scientists, the designers of computer hardware and software, etc., who make our splendid scientific and technological world possible.

As a high-achieving group, they bring unique values and expectations to their world of work. A leading behavioral scientist, Dr. Bernard Rosenbaum, Chairman of MOHR Development, Stamford, CT, has studied the special needs of technical professionals. He finds the following issues to be pertinent ("Leading Today's Technical Professional," *Training and Development,* October 1991):

Autonomy. As achievement-oriented workers, they seek motivation from their work. They want to be able to decide the conditions, pace, and content of their work. This means that they want a large voice and role in goal setting and decision making. Freedom from close direction and control is a must to obtain and retain their motivation.

Sense of achievement. They prefer to work on activities that necessitate high levels of skill and challenge. Exciting and meaningful work provokes their commitment. Of great importance to them is support and recognition from bosses and peers, coupled with acceptance and recognition of their quality results by their organizations and their professions.

Fear of burnout. Limited accomplishment, emotional exhaustion, and inability to influence change are the conditions that produce burnout. A related fear is that of obsolescence, as are personal problems, demotivation, under-utilization, and downhill performance.

Loyalty. Technical professionals' first loyalty is to their profession. The second is to their firm. So if professional goals are not in sync with departmental and organizational goals, conflict is likely.

Company missions. Because control over one's work is the hallmark of the technical professional, there may be a resistance to participating in the firm's missions. Their need, then, is to participate fully in the goal-setting process, otherwise their motivation and job satisfaction will suffer. But once committed, they will set high performance standards and even experience anxiety over meeting them. **A hazard:** The attachment to the agreed-upon goals and standards may become so strong that any change may produce demotivation.

Collegial support, stimulation, and sharing. These elements are vital for high performance. Professional competition is a motivator; but unproductive competition is not, for it may impact negatively on sharing information and team cohesion and effectiveness. So for the leader of these professionals, he must manage a productive balance between interpersonal competition vs. collegial support, and teamwork vs. individual creativity.

To meet these needs of technical professionals, the leader of these people must have a super combination of technological expertise, interpersonal skills, and leadership abilities, says Dr. Rosenbaum. The leadership role is a difficult one to assume even if one has these capabilities. But it becomes even more so for many managers if these people are selected for their technical capabilities rather than their interpersonal skills. In fact, their backgrounds and personalities are more oriented toward things than people.

In a comprehensive survey of the leadership of technical professionals (in 19 companies, with more than 300 leaders and professionals), Dr. Rosenbaum found that 80% of the technical leaders said that preparation for their managerial role was limited or non-existent. But 91% said training to manage technical professionals would be valuable.

The skills needed to manage such personnel effectively, as pointed out by Dr. Rosenbaum's leadership survey, are coaching, providing organizational interference, ensuring staff development, encouraging teamwork, and promoting self-management. Each of these five managerial skill areas is discussed below.

Employ Coaching

Because technical professionals are so self-directed, traditional (command) management styles are demotivating. What is needed, instead, is to coach for peak performance. This means that the manager listens, asks questions, facilitates, integrates, and renders support. Ideas and goals are developed rather than dictated. He reinforces discussion, and networks and shares information fully. In short, the aim is to encourage self-management, not dependency.

Note that in an area where the right answer often is unknown, the coach serves best when he functions as a sounding board for ideas, as a supportive critic, even as a devil's advocate.

Consider, then, three possible leadership styles:

Focus on organizational goals. But if individual needs are ignored, short-term project goals, at best, may be accomplished. The cost, however, is lost commitment, resulting in apathy or turnover.

Laissez-faire. This style is the reverse of the above: exclusive attention to the technical professional without much focus on organizational goals and requirements. This type of leader may receive a lot of affection from his charges, but innovation slides as the outfit's competitive position deteriorates. In some cases little attention may be paid to either staff or projects that cause problems.

The blend. The most successful leaders merge individual and organizational goals through a strong coaching approach. They use technology to serve market needs while being sensitive to the needs of their people.

A key skill of successful technical managers is to use their logical and critical thinking to analyze performance problems and deficiencies such as missed deadlines and cost overruns.

Another hallmark is anticipating and communicating change. In the high-tech outfit, change, of course, is a way of life. But how the leader handles it will determine whether it is accepted or resisted. The key for the successful coach: Communicate the reasons for the change and involve personnel extensively in its implementation.

Provide Organizational Interference

In this role, the manager teaches his professional staffers to advantage themselves of organizational opportunities, e.g., getting involved in a high visibility project that could resolve a major quality problem. Also, the manager works actively to eliminate organizational barriers and bottlenecks to innovation by doing these things:

☐ Provide resources to aid creative efforts.

☐ Keep the organizational bureaucracy from obstructing the professional's activities.

☐ Gain management support of a worthwhile proposal initiated by a professional.

Also, the professional staffers appreciate the support they receive that may take these forms:

- ☐ Publicizing successes and explaining less-than successes.
- ☐ Hacking away at red tape so that their work on projects can proceed without the distractions of "administrivia."
- ☐ Working within the organization's structure by advising whom to inform, how to time a request, and how to develop reciprocal assistance networks.
- ☐ Conserve professional time and concentration by screening out non-essential requests.

Encourage/Ensure Professional Growth

Technical professionals grow via achievement, recognition, challenging assignments, and freedom to perform. Enriched, varied jobs, and a stress on performance over process are essential to ensure motivation and prevent under-utilization. Narrow, highly controlled jobs are certain routes to apathy, burnout and alienation. Managers can best orchestrate professional development via:

- ☐ Providing a business perspective, including a vision of where the firm is heading. Understandably, technical professionals may not have insights into marketing, the competition, and the business climate.
- ☐ Championing professionals' ideas and protecting them from bureaucratic stifling and trampling. Innovation is regarded as the only name of the game, which even includes encouraging "intelligent failure."
- ☐ Encouraging and facilitating career planning and development. "Stretch" assignments and networking opportunities are basic tools to encourage growth and maintain commitment. **Note:** Networking includes professional societies and associations. Attending conferences, delivering papers and serving on committees are highly pertinent to secure new ideas and for professional growth as well.

Encourage Teamwork

Science and technology are too complex for people to function in isolation from their colleagues. Inspiration and breakthrough, big and small, only come about through group collaboration. Teamwork expands individual productivity. It is the way to shorten product development cycles, stimulate innovation and respond to the marketplace in a timely manner.

Effective group leadership requires these skills:

- ☐ Setting goals marked by clarity, achievability, mutuality, realistic timing, and, hopefully, stability.
- ☐ Clarifying roles of all concerned.
- ☐ Identifying and securing necessary resources.
- ☐ Providing an information exchange system.

Additionally, to kick off a project and to resolve problems as the project develops, call for group meetings at which the leader should be group-centered rather than manager-centered. Note that informational-type meetings can be conducted in a manager-centered style, but planning and problem-solving meetings require a group-centered facilitatory style. Assumption of inappropriate roles are certain time wasters, demotivators, and creativity stiflers.

Empower Staff (Self-Management)

As stated above, technical professionals need and want autonomy, achievement, growth, and challenge. The route to this is the maximum of freedom or self-management. These leadership functions are basic to real empowerment.

Information sharing. If information is hoarded or doled out reluctantly, people will feel manipulated. Alternatively, information about a project has a motivational effect.

Delegation. Worthwhile tasks and responsibilities, assigned on a delegated basis, have enriching and empowering impacts. Delegation gives insights into the outfit's big picture, reduces dependency, and meets needs for achievement. Delegation is a key to maintenance of a highly motivated project team.

Upward communication. Two-way (up and down) communication contributes to self-management. Encouraging the sharing of information builds trust and a sense of ownership in projects.

In addition to the highly perceptive pointers of Dr. Rosenbaum, the reader will be interested in these added guidelines to supervise technical personnel provided by management consultant Larry L. Axline ("When You're Supervising Technical Personnel," *Supervisory Management,* September 1990):

1. Treat each professional as an individual, for there are differences in style, preference, and interest, even within the same technical field.

2. Ensure the clarity of the information you receive before taking a position. So probe carefully for it.

3. Build a reputation as a person who technical and professional personnel wish to seek out for advice and guidance on their problems involving interpersonal relationships.

4. Ask yourself and staff this question repeatedly: "How are we meeting our goals?" This query will keep the big picture before them.

5. Be the bridge builder between your professional staff and the overall organization. Help them to keep in proper perspective issues such as quality, safety, scheduling, customer service, and ethics.

The author would add another goal in working with professionals is to try to create a work atmosphere where work is regarded as fun. Note that an *Industry Week* survey (reported in "FYI: Work Is No Fun," *Personnel Journal,* May 1991), found that a high state of unhappiness is prevalent among engineering staffs—75% of those surveyed said that they have no fun at work. The manager should ask himself: Which set of work conditions is more likely to provide curiosity and creativity, one marked by fun and excitement or one that resembles the traditional, formal tight ship?

THE PLATEAUED WORKER: COUNTERING CAREER GRIDLOCK

A fact of organizational life is that the organizations people work in are pyramidal in form. There thus are a limited number of desirable positions at the upper levels of the organizational structure. In consequence, there is a harsh process of selection at work, "natural" or otherwise—a limited number of people move into the bigger and better jobs and the others stay behind and sadly watch those who advance.

Today, the problem is compounded because of downsizing, mergers, outsourcing, and delayering (reducing the number of levels in the organization). And for those who might in years past have had a shot at better jobs, the opportunity is further shrunk by essential endeavors to move long-overlooked women and minority members upward in the organization.

Career planning and development authorities Zandy B. Leibowitz, Beverly L. Kaye and Caela Farren ("What To Do About Career Gridlock" *Training and Development Journal,* April 1990) refer to and build on Dr. Judith Bardwick's *The Plateauing Trap,* New York: AMACOM (1986), which makes an important distinction between *structural* plateauing and *content* plateauing. The former type, described above, is natural, inevitable and has no relationship to a person's skills or inherent value. The latter type, however, is avoidable. It relates to the end of a job's challenge, that is, one has mastered the tasks to the point where things become stagnant and repetitive.

Plateaued performers are hardly a homogeneous lot. Rather, point out Liebowitz, Kaye and Farren, they fall into four categories:

Productively plateaued. These people and their bosses take a lot of action to keep them motivated and challenged. They are content with their challenging duties and high-quality performance and most likely to not see themselves as plateaued or "dead-ended." They are doers, they seek out possibilities and they take risks. Their colleagues and bosses appreciate their enthusiastic contributions. They have a degree of organizational loyalty and feel indispensible in their jobs. The only caution one must raise about these A-1 performers is that they need constant challenge to keep them motivated. Baseball afficionados would say, "You don't keep your Cy Young Award pitchers out of the pitching rotation."

Partially plateaued. Although the organization does very little for these employees, they do have a special interest or project that keeps them turned on about their work. These people have reputations as experts in their field. They make presentations at professional conferences, are active in their professional organizations, and have strong personal networks. The organization values their contribution, but for these performers it seems routine. **Caution:** They'll head for burnout should their excitement vanish. What they need most are new opportunities to provide strong payoffs.

Pleasantly plateaued. Despite offers of training and mobility opportunities, they don't respond. Deep contentment has set in—"They are happy doing what they are doing" and resist change in their jobs or their lives. These happy campers seem to feel that they have already made it and thus value their comfort zone and the routine accompanying it. They are not interested in leaving their outfits, value their connections and belongingness, and even feel that their organizations care. Promotion is hardly a motivator for them. Their motto seems to be: "Give me no pain and I'll live with no gain." The caution for the organization is this: If you accumulate too many of these types, your much-wanted innovation and creativity will be imperiled.

Passively plateaued. These types are likely to be depressed, passive, in a rut, and feel impotent to alter their glum situations. They may have held the same job for over five years, and any new learning is not likely to eventuate. They care little about added training for new skill development, even if it were made available to them. Curiosity, creativity, or initiation of change are hardly their hallmarks. Their apathy is likely to be reflected in passive statements such as "it's not my job" or "it's not going to make a difference anyway" (a reference to the value of a pending change). Although not totally hopeless, these are the toughest cases for employee developers.

The thrust behind the above four-part breakdown of the plateaued population is that we can't assume that "they're all alike"; and that if we are going to take any action regarding them, our strategies have to take into account their specific, individual characteristics and related "need systems."

Also, a distinction has to be made between the strategies that might be employed by employees themselves, the strategies managers might utilize with and for their employees, and the broader strategies which the organization itself might pursue.

Strategies for Employees

Employees who are not content with their plateaued circumstance can exercise initiative and take responsibility to manage their careers better. With encouragement and counseling by their bosses, here are some of the things they might do, per Leibowitz, Kaye and Farren:

Reputation. They might develop a strong reputation for being an expert in their work so they can demonstrate their special talents or skills; e.g., making presentations on important completed projects so as to let others know of their capabilities.

Feedback. Because feedback is not always forthcoming automatically, they might ask those they respect for help by posing these questions: "As you see me, what are my strongest skills?" and "What are my greatest needs for development?"

Visibility. It's all too easy to get buried or lost in a big organization. So they must push themselves a bit—seek out special assignments or committee slots.

Job change. Quite often one's job can be expanded or enriched by the person in it. Because no one knows the job better than the incumbent, that person can work actively at augmenting its responsibilities and value.

Training. New skills and assorted forms of upgrading one's job often are possible by seeking out training opportunities. New learning is a challenge in itself.

Networking. Networks lead to new contacts, any one of which can open new doors and new stimulations.

Strategies for Managers

Managers have a key role to play in upending the plateau trap for subordinates. They can do the following, say Liebowitz, Kaye, and Farren:

Job redesign. By "reworking" the work, stretch can be introduced. Development and job challenge can ensue when jobs are broadened and made more exciting and responsible.

Job improvement. Work with employees to improve their jobs. Give them a start on possible task improvement and let their natural motivation go on from there.

Job learning. Development of people is a top managerial priority, something that can't wait until tomorrow. As Leibowitz, Kaye, and Farren put it, "short-term thinking can lead to long-term plateauing."

Job feedback. People can't upgrade their performance without candid, pin-pointed feedback, both positive and negative. Feedback is a key motivator in the manager's motivational repertoire.

Peer coaching. Let employees coach their colleagues in areas in which they are particularly strong. Interaction with associates is a real stimulator and a source of growth for both parties.

Training and skill upgrading. Ask employees how their skills could be used better, now and in the future. A good motivational statement, per Leibowitz, Kaye, and Farren, is: "Tell me what you want to do and figure out how it can be done, and I'll work with you to see if it can be done."

Exposure. Make visible all your employees, not just the star performers. Regard everyone as valuable contributors.

Non-monetary rewards. Provide non-financial incentives. Promotions and money are hardly the only motivators.

Networks. Build networks throughout the organization so doors are open to your staffers. Let them build their own networks, too.

Project teams. Use such teams more extensively. Such teams have many benefits including involvement, stimulation, colleague interaction, exposure to change, and improved team work.

The author would suggest these added strategies:

Consultant. Provide opportunities to function as a consultant to other segments in the organization, for example, to field units.

Liaison. Provide opportunities to serve as a representative or liaison to other segments in the firm or to outside organizations—vendors, suppliers, contractors, unions, the media, educational institutions, etc.

Devil's advocate. Use them as a source of criticism to ensure that new plans and ideas are examined fully from all possible points of view.

Trainer. Use the plateaued person to train new workers or to bring others up to standard.

Lateral transfer. Consider a lateral to another department as a device to reinvigorate the dead-ended worker. Conceivably, one's special skill may be valued elsewhere.

Project responsibility. Show the plateaued person that you do value his talents by assigning him full responsibility for the shepherding of an important project.

Strategies for Organizations

Although the organization itself may have to be the initiator and sponsor of the strategies listed below, managers themselves may be able to initiate such actions or possibly recommend that they take place. The strategies, per Leibowitz, Kaye, and Farren, are:

Create generalists. An overload of specialists may create plateaued people because of their limited mobility. Today's organizations need more fluidity.

Pay for performance and growth of skills. A reward system that recognizes accomplishment and personal development is a great motivator.

Encourage skill mastery. Consider basing career paths on skill and mastery instead of on pay-related promotion. **The procedure:** Provide a series of job sequences where certain sets of skills must be mastered. One could start at the bottom, master the skill set, and then start a new job sequence as opposed to being promoted.

Sponsor job rotation programs. Lateral movement can broaden skills and revitalize the performers. It is also a practical and realistic way to help people move away from declining areas and to move into growing ones.

Sponsor mentoring programs. Senior employees can enrich their jobs by mentoring new arrivals.

Reward experience. Recognition programs should reward accomplishment and skill as opposed to time on the job.

Utilize line instructors. Use instructors from the line in in-house training programs. **Advantages:** job enrichment for the instructor and upgrading of the training program by tapping the experience and knowledge of the expert.

Use task forces. Special committees or study groups can review the current plateau problem and recommend ways of dealing with it.

An issue that arrives with plateaued persons is the degree of awareness of their plateaued state. Some may not know it's happened, some may have some awareness of it, and others may have seen clearly the large print lettered on the wall. Dr. Judith M. Bardwick ("Counseling a Plateaued Employee," *Management Solutions,* December 1986) advises to level with people if you are asked by them of their status. Candidly describe their future prospects in the organization.

Conversely, if they seem to be functioning well and appear involved and satisfied, say nothing. If there is apparent dissatisfaction or stress, you should raise the issue and discuss the situation in all its aspects. Part of the counseling technique is not only to indicate that promotional opportunities are essentially small, but to call attention to the work satisfactions and achievements they will be able to secure. Try to create a positive, optimistic, and constructive mood. Indicate that you intend to tap their expertise and that you feel that they have a lot to offer the organization.

Actually, there is no need at all to tuck people away on a shelf in a corner to let them brood over their fate until their retirement, for they are an important resource and should be used properly. Recognize that the plateaued worker typically has a lot of knowledge and experience under his belt. He knows his job and his way around the organization. He knows the organization's policies and programs, what has and hasn't worked in the past, who the influential people are, and so on. Management consultant Dr. Edward Roseman, author of *Confronting Non-Promotability: How to Manage a Stalled Career* (New York: AMACOM, 1977), also points out that the plateaued person's lack of upward mobility may actually be an asset. Why? Because there is no longer a need to compete for advancement. Because the pressure is off to "look good," this person can concentrate on getting on with the job and help others to succeed in their endeavors.

Problem behaviors, resulting from one's plateaued situation, will require special motivational strategies. Dr. Roseman offers these suggestions:

☐ The employee is *winding down* due to feelings of disappointment, frustration, or exclusion. **Motivational strategy:** Meet unsatisfied needs by providing added responsibility and more opportunity for achievement.

☐ The employee is *withdrawing* because he feels that he has been pushed aside. **Motivational strategy:** There are feelings of alienation, neglect, and rejection. To overcome these feelings, provide *psychological closeness* via warmth, support, consideration, and showing of genuine interest in the person. Also provide opportunities for affiliation—build a strong work team and put him in the middle of things by assignment to worthwhile work projects with compatible peers.

☐ The employee is *wandering*: he is bored, indifferent, uncommitted. **Motivational strategy:** Providing heavy doses of involvement via shared problem solving and decision making, self-control, independence, and freedom, signifying high trust, can put people back on track.

☐ The employee is *wailing*. He feels hurt, unappreciated and/or envious. **Motivational strategy:** Provide a lot of recognition to bolster needs for augmented self-esteem.

☐ The employee is *warring*. He is hostile, vindictive, and feels cheated. **Motivational strategies:** Don't argue or defend, but listen instead. Also interact positively with that person on a highly frequent basis to show caring, trust and a desire to help. Look for mutual problem-solving situations to involve him fully and actively.

☐ The employee is *worrying*. The person feels obsolete, unimportant, intimidated. **Motivational strategy:** Overcome these insecurities by providing growth and learning opportunities. People who have a chance to grow and become "updated" will feel better about themselves.

The bottom line. Allowing people to reach senility with dignity (the happy camper type) is not worthwhile motivational strategy. Nor is permitting people to merely become "PO-POS" (passed over and put on the shelf) or, worse, "PO-PO" (passed over and pissed off).

Rather, there is a need to work actively on the plateauing problem on all fronts—employee, managerial, and organizational. This, we would maintain, is not a form of "do-goodism," but a key element of any organization's effort to utilize and motivate its all-important human resource. The alternative effect? An inevitable loss in organizational productivity, morale, motivation, and even reputation.

THE SUPPORT STAFF

Customer service in many organizations is receiving a greater emphasis today than previously. But the customer is well served not only by those who deal directly with him, but also by those who lend support behind the scenes—secretaries, credit reps, receivers and shippers, data-entry people, accounting clerks, and various technicians. Manpower-wise, more jobs of this sort are being created each year.

The picture is further complicated by these factors:

☐ The growing complexity of office technology that places higher demands on the support staff, e.g., to use computers fluently.

☐ Most of the output from the support job is intangible and thus is subject more to employee discretion than managerial direction and oversight, i.e., the workers can set their own pace and decide work details or neglect them, all of which may deeply affect the customer.

☐ Today's young workforce is motivated by opportunities for decision making and growth, not just pay. They may also expect (unrealistically) rapid career advancement which, if not forthcoming, may lead to frustration.

☐ In the absence of frequent promotions, they may leave, resulting in a constant training and exit phenomenon; or they may tune out and "play dead," not exercising initiative or accepting responsibility.

What motivational emphasis, then, is needed to overcome the inertia that may affect customer service? Management consultant Buck Blessing ("Support Your Support Staff," *Training and Development Journal,* November 1986) recommends that management build into support jobs these four elements:

Mastery. People need to master the skills that are personally and professionally important to them in their jobs. This means a chance to acquire and build upon personal strengths and to use them to achieve and to grow.

Autonomy. People need to feel that they are in charge of their work life. They want to make a contribution and feel that they are truly a part of something significant. The strategy, then, is to so organize and manage that secretaries, technicians and others become autonomous "managers" of their own work.

Relationship. People need a relationship with their bosses that allows for full communication and a high concern for development of their skills and abilities.

Change. People require opportunities to clarify what makes work satisfying to them—their personal goals, values, motivations, and talents in relation to job needs.

In sum, the four factors of mastery, autonomy, relationship, and change can make a difference in how the support staff is motivated and how well customer service is delivered.

PEOPLE WITH DISABILITIES

To introduce yourself to this special human resource, you should find it interesting and helpful to take the short quiz below prepared by the Davis Memorial Goodwill Industries unit of Washington, D.C. (in *Goodwill Works,* Third Quarter, 1993).

Disability Awareness

Can you separate fact from fiction? Many powerful perceptions surround people with disabilities, creating attitudes and perceptions difficult to erase. The following are some thought-provoking statements. See if you can separate fact from fiction.

1. T F Most people who are blind can read Braille.
2. T F Public rest room signs marked "ladies" or "gentlemen" may pose barriers for people who are mentally retarded.
3. T F People with mental illness are dangerous.
4. T F If a door is wider than 32″, it is accessible to people in wheelchairs.
5. T F Most people with disabilities live with their families or in institutions.
6. T F People with mental retardation cannot read and write.
7. T F People who are deaf can read lips.
8. T F People should never ask people about their disabilities.
9. T F Placing people who are deaf into noisy work environments is a good job match.
10. T F Most people with disabilities prefer to interact with other individuals with disabilities.
11. T F People with disabilities are brave and courageous.
12. T F Most people with disabilities need accommodation on the job.
13. T F Most people with disabilities prefer low stress, repetitive work.
14. T F The average income for a working person with a disability is less than $15,000 per year.

15. T F People with disabilities are more accident prone.

16. T F People with disabilities will cost the employer more in workers' compensation and health care insurance.

17. T F Consulting with the applicant about job accommodations will often reduce the cost of solutions.

18. T F Working adults with disabilities are undervalued and underutilized.

19. T F Expecting people with disabilities to perform a little less than employees who are not disabled is considerate and helpful.

20. T F People who are not disabled should avoid using words that relate to disability such as "see you later" to a blind person or "let's go for a walk" to a person in a wheelchair.

Answers:
1F, 2T, 3F, 4T, 5–13F, 14T, 15–16F, 17–18T, 19–20F

Many organizations in years past have found it practical and profitable to hire, train, and utilize those with disabilities. There now are legal requirements not to discriminate against people with disabilities (The Americans with Disabilites Act of August 1990), which means that those with physical and mental limitations must be given the chance to work. But aside from statutory mandates, are there not moral and humanitarian considerations to treat people with limitations fairly? After all, we're all limited or disabled in one way or another. The people who are termed disabled are merely limited to a greater degree. But their limitations do not mean that given the right job (one of proper design), adequate training, and accommodation they can't find a productive niche in the working world.

Since July 1994, the ADA applies to all employers with 15 or more employees. The disability can be a physical or mental impairment. Employers must hire qualified job applicants who can do their jobs with the aid of a "reasonable accommodation" that will not cause an undue burden to the organization.

Notes:

1. The law does not require anyone who is not qualified to be hired.
2. We are talking about *people with disabilities*—differently able—not people who are disabled or handicapped. For example, a person who is totally blind or legally blind is likely to object to being termed "visually handicapped." He would favor being called "visually impaired." This supportive language is extremely important, for it can help to create a more positive mindset toward those who are willing and otherwise able people. Goodwill Industries of America Inc., Bethesda, MD, frowns on the use of such phrases as "confined to a wheelchair," "crippled," "afflicted," or "suffers from a disorder."
3. The goal for you and your staff should be to recognize people for their abilities, not their disabilities or limitations. Employers can benefit from their skills, knowledge, abilities, and positive attitudes.
4. Many employers find that employees with disabilities are strong on job performance, have excellent attendance records, and are likely to be dedicated, cooperative, and loyal.

A number of myths keep managers from tapping the resources offered by people with disabilities. Here are some of the most prevalent myths per Dr. Hugh McDonough, who counsels and assists such individuals in job placement ("Hiring People with Disabilities," *Supervisory Management,* February 1992):

They are fit only for menial or entry-level jobs. But the fact is that there are people with disabilities who work at nearly all professional levels in most professional fields.

A disability is a continuing, frustrating tragedy. Actually, from a job standpoint a disability is only an inconvenience. One good answer is the accommodation approach (discussed below).

Those with disabilities don't want to work. Fact: two-thirds of the 43 million people with disabilities currently try to find work, although only some 17% are at work. A Lou Harris and Associates 1994 survey reported that two out of three people with disabilities aren't working, a figure unchanged since a similar 1986 survey. But 79% said they would rather have a job (reported in *The Wall Street Journal,* June 7, 1994).

They are more accident prone. This is a major misconception for, per many surveys, they actually have lower accident rates than their non-disabled colleagues.

Expect insurance rates to rise when those with disabilities are hired. Some health rates may go up. But for the most part insurance rates are based on the type of hazards in the work and the company's accident record, not anyone's physical state.

Expect high absentee rates. Actually, their attendance records are equal to or better than their non-disabled colleagues.

One aspect of the ADA that may frighten some employers or managers is the concept of "reasonable accommodation." There is a fear of costly expenditures for physical changes to plant, office, or store or for new, special equipment. But a 1987 evaluation by the Job Accommodation Network found that most accommodations are inexpensive—30% of them are cost-free, half cost less than $50, and 70% cost less than $500. Actually, given a reasonable amount of concern and cogitation, it is very practical to install simple, inexpensive accommodations.

Example: Having reserved parking spaces close to doors; placing a string on the door of a bathroom stall so that a female worker in a wheelchair could enter and exit more readily; providing maps to employees with disabilities to point up the shortest way to get from one spot to another in all the buildings of a large complex; using automatic doors; providing a step stool for a dwarf to file papers in a top drawer of a file cabinet ("The Disabled: Ready, Willing and Able," Beverly Geber, *Training,* December 1990).

Certain cost-free accommodations may be made via policy and administrative changes. Some examples, per Charlene S. Solomon ("What the ADA Means to the Non-disabled," *Personnel Journal,* June 1992), are these: If a firm uses a public address system to transmit messages, a buddy system can be used to help a hearing impaired person receive the message. If a mail slot is a long way from a wheel-chaired worker, a co-worker might get that person's mail when he picks up his own. Or flextime might be used for intermittent leave for someone who has a psychiatric disability or needs to see a doctor on a scheduled basis. Or to accommodate disabled persons who wish to visit the employment office, the interview room might be located at the building's entrance.

How should the manager supervise persons with disabilities? Aside from possibly providing a reasonable accommodation, the best advice is to treat them like everyone else. Keep them in line for promotion; provide them with training opportunities; encourage them to stretch; stay in touch (communicate) with them; permit them to travel and attend meetings; encourage them to join in on social activities.

Individuals with Mental Disabilities

A number of myths or misconceptions exist about those termed "mentally retarded." (Actually, today the preferred term is the "mentally challenged.") Included are the following, per the Association for Retarded Citizens (ARC) and the President's Committee on Mental Retardation (reported in William E. Smart's "Workers with Something Extra," *The Washington Post,* January 20, 1987):

Nature of illness: An individual with mental retardation is not the same as one with a mental illness. The former relates only to learning ability. The mentally retarded merely learn less rapidly than "normals." But both the retarded and the normals are subject to mental illness.

Trainability: Some 90% of the six million persons with mental retardation in the U.S. are classified as "mildly" retarded and with proper training and education can learn to perform responsible, productive jobs.

Productiveness: Once hired (and trained if necessary), they are likely to outproduce normals in terms of job performance, fatigue, resistance, motivation, and job satisfaction.

Absenteeism: Personnel with mental retardation have A-1 attendance and low tardiness.

Degree of supervision: Supervisors are not likely to have any more problems with those with mental retardation than with the regular work force.

Safety consciousness: No problem. Marriott, for example, has found that their records are equal to or better than non-disabled workers.

Once a person with a mental disability is hired, per industrial psychologist Dr. John Lawrie ("Supervising the Mentally Retarded: Do's and Don'ts," *Supervisory Management,* August 1993), you should do the following to provide a success experience for both the organization and the worker:

Gather facts. Talk to the new hires to learn as much as you can about their strengths. There's little point in concentrating on capabilities or skills they don't have. Rather, focus on the abilities they do have or can be developed into usable skills.

Create a job that is a "good fit." After you have learned what the person can and might do, and recognize his limitations, do what is necessary to help overcome obstacles to performance.

Check out feelings often. Make it a point to learn from the new worker his feelings about things. Ask: "How are things going?" "Is anything giving you trouble?"

Anticipate slumps. While all of us may have slumps, these individuals are more likely to experience learning and doing slumps more often. They may also be more pronounced.

Secure group support. Be certain to encourage your team to provide all the help these individuals need.

Encourage questions. Remind the worker that problems will arise. He thus should feel free to ask you or anyone else for help about the work or other concerns.

Allow for reaching goals in stages. As a confidence-building procedure, set goals and standards on an interim basis. You can't expect a person with limitations to reach standard immediately.

Design the job to reduce anxiety. You want a success experience to ensue. One helpful way to do this is to organize or reorganize the job so that the tasks are easier to learn, more doable and less threatening.

Training, obviously, is a major key to job success for the person with mental disabilities. Basically, the training should (a) provide the right type and amount of assistance, (b) stress measurement of learning to assess progress and where more emphasis is needed, and (c) reinforce learning to solidify accomplishment. Each of these points is developed by management professor David Mank, et al. ("Accommodating Workers with Mental Disabilities," *Training and Development*, January 1992) more fully below:

Assistance. Training help may range from physical guidance and gestural prompts to verbal instruction and pictorial prompts. There also may be natural aids such as a wall clock to ensure completion of tasks on time or an assembly-line prompt as material passes from one station to another.

The best training occurs when the learner can do the tasks without being dependent on the trainer. With the completion of formal training, the trainee is enabled to respond to either the natural cues or the prompts in the job setting.

Assistance must be strong enough to ensure that error-free performance occurs and inappropriate learning does not.

Measurement. Four features are required to ensure that proper learning occurs:

1. Preparation by the trainer so the he understands what training elements ("a map") need to be mastered by the trainee.
2. The job must be broken down into learnable chunks for easy learning. The more complex the learning, the more specific and precise the map must be.
3. Measurement of the degree to which a task is performed properly is basic. Learning pace can be assessed via documented changes as the learning occurs during the training phase.
4. Precise identification of learning and independent performance is essential. Gaps or weaknesses in learning can then be overcome by a more precise job analysis, more help and possibly more feedback.

Reinforcement. Rewards (praise, etc.) are essential to strengthen performance. By definition, reinforcement is that which increases the likelihood that, given like conditions, the same behavior will recur. For an effective response, the reinforcement must follow the desired behavior.

In addition to accommodating the non-traditional worker with careful, patient training, other accommodations may be essential to increase productivity, tenure, and job satisfaction. These may range from flexible hours to family counseling.

THE REHABILITATED MENTALLY ILL PERSON

Working with mentally rehabilitated (or emotionally restored) persons is not significantly different from working with anyone else. They are anxious to "fit in" again and most do. Once hired, these guidelines should be of help, per Dr. Jeffrey R. Solomon ("How to Work with the Rehabilitated Mentally Ill," *Supervisory Management,* January 1986):

☐ Watch new situations for they may be stressful. Explain new responsibilities and changes carefully.

☐ Be consistent. Inconsistent behavior on your part will provide unwanted, added pressure.

☐ Deal with performance problems promptly. Communicate your concern if performance slips below agreed-upon standards.

☐ Level with the employee. Don't soft-pedal criticism. But as with anyone else, distinguish the behavior being criticized from the worker. State this: "We expect everyone to provide A-1 care for our equipment," not: "You always leave your job area in disarray. Do you have to be so messy?"

☐ Provide praise for good performance. But don't give unwarranted "strokes" to build morale.

☐ Keep the employee's illness confidential. Let him decide whether he wishes to share it with others.

☐ Don't weaken the job to favor the employee. Instead, expect the employee to perform to normal requirements.

CUSTODIAL WORKERS AND OTHERS IN BORING JOBS

People in these positions typically are at the bottom of the vocational ladder in terms of job interest, job challenge, and social standing. Their jobs, unfortunately, are tedious, repetitive, boring, and often dirty. So what motivational measures can the manager take to overcome, at least in part, the depressing character of their work? Consider these possibilities:

Career advancement. Use the job as a stepping stone to better positions.

Re-engineering. The jobs might be automated in part or possibly redesigned to make them easier and safer. For example, the materials on floors and walls might be replaced for easier maintenance.

Training. Jobs can be made less stressful via instruction as to easier ways of operating. For example, the

person mopping the floor can be trained to stand erect, for bending over produces fatigue.

Listen to and act on their problems. At Syracuse University the custodial staff grumbled for years about sunflower seeds. Sunflower seeds? Yes, indeed. It seems that campus vending machines sold the seeds with zebra-striped hulls. The inevitable result: The hulls ended up on classroom floors, which made for a sloppy learning environment, damaged cleaning equipment, and caused cleaning delays. The problem was resolved when the university's first quality improvement pilot team, part of the Total Quality Management (TQM) effort at the university, had a meeting with the custodians and the bosses. The solution: Simply stock pre-hulled sunflower seeds! **The results:** cleaner classrooms and happier custodians, bosses, faculty, and students (Bob Hill, "TQM Comes to Campus," in *Syracuse University Magazine,* Winter 1993).

Praise. Work well done should be recognized both privately and publicly. If the work impacts on customer or visitor satisfaction, prime performance should be praised on that basis. Behavioral scientist Dr. Louis Tagliaferri ("Plain Talk About Motivation," *Training Ideas:* Resource Guide and Product Catalogue, Talico Inc., Summer 1988) cites this situation: While having breakfast at the counter of a national chain restaurant, the server, Ann, noticed that she was out of coffee cups. She called to Charlie to bring some out. Charlie quickly brought out one rack of clean cups and then another. As he was placing the third rack on the other two, Ann said aloud to everyone at the counter, "Well, all of you can be sure you're going to get a nice clean cup because Charlie is the best dishwasher around."

Charlie grinned broadly, stood erect, beamed with pride and returned to his post in the kitchen. So Charlie got the kind of applause that some people never receive in a lifetime of work. And Ann wasn't even his boss!

Highlighting mission. Even people in mundane jobs can identify with the organization's purposes if they are trained properly. For example, management consultant and author Ron Zemke, ("Rewards and Recognition: Yes, They Really Work," *Training,* November 1988) states that he asked a young groundskeeper at Walt Disney World, "How do you like being a street sweeper in a theme park?" The custodial worker stepped back, straightened up, looked his questioner in the eye, and forcibly replied, "I'm not a street sweeper. I'm in show business. I'm part of the Act." Concludes Zemke, "To front-line workers in any organization with ambitions of providing distinctive service to its customers, the feeling of being a part of something important may be the most important motivational principle of all."

Focus on output/value. Related to the above, is pointing up of the value of what is done (the output), as opposed to merely a stress on task execution. The idea, then, in the initial orientation and in later contacts, is to encourage the worker to think and verbalize about his job in this fashion: "My job is to impress people with how clean and sparkling our floors are," as opposed to "My job is floor cleaner."

Dignity and pride. Preserve and enhance self-esteem via natty uniforms, a social room for lunch and breaks, a comfortable locker room, etc. Occasional write-ups and photos pertaining to custodial work should be included in the company house organ.

While driving in heavy traffic, manager Jerry Wilson noted this luminescent lettering on a large truck: "The Professional Operator of This Motor Vehicle Is James Smith." It triggered a number of thoughts about motivation and encouraged him to write a brief article for *The Washington Post* ("A 'Professional' Society," February 28, 1975) which expressed these pointed thoughts about motivation and the truck driver:

No doubt the trucking company is seeking, by fashioning its drivers 'professionals,' to instill in them a sense of pride in their job and their work. That is a commendable objective, but I wish they would just stress quality without the euphemism. What's wrong with stressing competence, safe driving, delivery of goods undamaged, courteous service, high productivity, for non-professional working people. The company made a start at that simply by painting the driver's name on the truck. Maybe it might also furnish him a supply of business cards to leave with customers. Putting the driver's signature, figuratively and literally, on the work produced goes far toward instilling competence and pride.

Procurement. Consider allowing custodial employees to select their own equipment. John Handlery, vice-president and general manager, the Handlery Union Square Hotel, San Francisco, allows the maids to choose which new brand of vacuum cleaner to buy. He says, "They're the ones vacuuming the rooms. My only requirement is that they pick a vacuum that will do the job" (Quoted by Gregg Lieberman, "Service Picks Up," in *Meetings and Conventions,* September 1989).

Job rotation. In an overall operation with a number of routine jobs, such as in a cafeteria where there are clean-up people, dishwashers, food preparers, etc., why not rotate personnel between the various jobs? Some may prefer to stick with the same task. But for those who opt for variety and an intermittent opportunity to tackle a higher-level task, it can bring about greater job interest.

THE "TEMP" WORKER: USING THE "JUST-IN-TIME" INVENTORY CONCEPT

In today's world of downsizing, restructuring, and re-engineering, organizations are relying on temporary and part-time workers to a greater degree. Economists refer to them as "contingent" employees—the "flexible workforce"—which includes short term/temporary, part-time, sub-contracted and leased workers, and consultants. Sociologists are likely to refer to them as "nomads" or "the throw-away worker," people without organizational identification, organizational status, company-paid training programs, promotions, a career future (let alone job security), paid vacations, sick pay, medical benefits, profit sharing, or pension possibilities. Organizations refer to the procedure of hiring temps as "outsourcing." Management may also prefer to refer to the just-in-time people as "supplementary" or "complementary" workers, terms that help to play down the idea that the temps will replace the regulars.

Pay for temps is likely to be lower than that of their full-time counterparts, and they may not be eligible for unemployment insurance. *The Wall Street Journal* (Clare Ansberry, "Hired Out: Workers Are Forced to Take More Jobs with Fewer Benefits," March 11, 1993) reported that contingent workers cost an estimated 20% to 40% less than core employees.

As to numbers in the U.S., there are an estimated 35 million contingent workers, or one out of four of those in the civilian workforce (Frank Swoboda, "For Growing Ranks of Part-time Workers, More Burdens and Fewer Benefits," *The Washington Post*, September 5, 1993). The Washington-based Employee Benefit Research Institute found that between 1969 and 1992, part-time workers in the U.S. grew to 20.4 million from 10.8 million, an 88.9% increase ("Odd Jobs," *The Washington Post*, February 6, 1994).

For the organization, temps provide these benefits:

☐ There is a chance to recruit workers at lesser cost. Pay rates may be lower, fewer employment hours may be involved, and the usual benefits package need not be offered. The Work in America Institute, Scarsdale, New York, states that fringe benefits now account for 30% to 40% of payroll (Beverly Geber, "The Flexible Workforce," *Training,* December 1993).

☐ There is a capability of avoiding massive layoffs, thereby offering the "leaner," permanent workforce stable employment and conditions. People can be hired for special projects and then dropped "painlessly" at project's end.

☐ There is a chance to hire professional and technical personnel at "bargain" rates because such temps may work very efficiently, skipping long lunches, extended coffee klatches, water cooler chit-chat, personal phone calling, and the like. Also, professional-type temps are quite likely to put in extra hours because of work interest and a desire to create a favorable impression on their employer, which may result in full-time employment or produce a favorable reference.

☐ It allows ready replacement of full-time workers who are absent due to sickness, injury, or vacations.

☐ It permits the hiring of needed personnel for seasonal workloads or special production workloads.

☐ There is a chance to observe the skills and habits of workers prior to offering them full-time employment.

☐ A new business may find it more practical to hire temps rather than to commit to full-time employment.

☐ If a major military call-up occurs, temporary workers can easily replace the "lost" reservists.

☐ Temps do not count against head count, which may allow some firms off the hook insofar as their inclusion or exclusion goes under various labor laws.

☐ Temps allow organizations to adjust readily to changing economic conditions. In good times, expansion can be met by adding them to the workforce. In bad times, the temps can be lopped off with ease and recalled if and when needed.

☐ Termination costs (severance pay and vested pension benefits) can be avoided totally with contingent workers. Note that senior regular workers with the firm may be expensive to lay off because of their long-accumulated end-of-employment benefits.

☐ Temps are usually not involved in office politics, which can be a great "productivity robber" says human relations consultant Audrey Freedman (quoted in Shari Caudron, "Contingent Workforce Spurs HR Planning," *Personnel Journal,* July 1994).

Some negatives exist for the organization, too:

☐ Those in part-time or temporary jobs can't be held accountable in the same way as full-timers; nor can the same job interest, devotion and commitment be expected. As a temp, it's hard to have the same interest in the success of the business as do the core people.

☐ Temporaries may be prone to sudden departure, particularly in a competitive labor market.

☐ The core workforce may get a bit jittery if there is a sudden switch to temps. They may assume that their jobs are next to be farmed out, points out management writer Beverly Geber ("The Flexible Work Force," *Training,* December 1993).

☐ If temps are retained for long periods of time they may begin to perceive themselves as regulars and feel they are doing their jobs as well or better than the full-time people, points out Human Resource Representative Karen S. Roberts in a letter to the editor of *Personnel Journal,* February 1991. This can result in the building up of resentment against the firm and erode any productivity gains.

☐ They may be subject to more accidents because they receive less safety training. Shari Caudron ("Contingent Workforce Spurs HR Planning," *Per-*

sonnel Journal, July 1994) cites the 1992 Massachusetts Institute of Technology study of contract workers in the petrochemical industry which showed that just-in-time workers experienced more accidents due to less training.

And looking at management of the workforce in broad terms, Jerome Rosow, President of the Work in America Institute, Scarsdale, New York, believes contingent workers are an unstable and unsatisfactory way to manage a business. He states, "Employees are not a commodity. People have an emotional and psychological reference point to their place of employment. Once you put them in the contingent category, you're saying they're expendable and not part of the business. Over time, there will be diminishing returns because you lose company loyalty. Contingent workers are good from an emergency staffing standpoint, but they shouldn't form the basis of a company's long-term strategy" (quoted by Shari Caudron in *Personnel Journal,* July 1994).

Despite the negative aspects of temporary work, various temps do find these benefits for themselves:

☐ For the "cautious" job seeker, it's a chance to "test" an organization or type of work to see if it is a locale or operation with which to hook up more permanently. **Note:** Per Sam Sacco, Executive V.P. of the National Association of Temporary Services (NATS), Arlington, VA, 38% of temporary workers in the U.S. are offered full-time jobs because of their temporary assignments (Sheryl Silver, "An Evolution in Temporary Service," *The Washington Post,* April 17, 1994).

☐ For the mother who is about to enter (or re-enter) the workforce and may not wish full-time work, temp work is a worthy convenience.

☐ For the "free spirit," who does not wish to become wedded to an overbearing boss or an insensitive bureaucracy, he can freely choose his job location, employer, type of work, and vacation time. In fact, one survey indicated that 39% of the respondents wanted to remain temps indefinitely (reported by Shari Caudron, *Personnel Journal,* July 1994). Some 38% prefer to remain a temp even after an offering of a full-time position.

☐ For the college student who needs to weave paid employment into his college schedule, it's a

chance to assist with many high costs of a college education.

☐ For the first-time job aspirant, e.g., the "hamburger flippers," it provides a chance to develop good work habits and to pick up a few bucks in the process.

☐ For the downsized worker, it can provide a locale to put down an anchor with pay (reduced, of course) while one is between jobs. With a paycheck coming in, one can choose a new employer with a bit less panic.

☐ For the moonlighter, it provides a chance to garner an extra paycheck.

☐ For a person seeking a new or second career, it can provide an opportunity to acquire new skills without abandoning one's regular full-time job.

☐ A person ready to "taper off" before moving into retirement may negotiate a part-time arrangement with his employer.

☐ Members of various special groups may appreciate the temporary or part-time job opportunity, too, e.g., the emotionally restored, the senior worker who is bored at home or may need the extra compensation to augment his limited income.

Recognizing that the temp may not be as committed and motivated as the regular or core worker is likely to be, how, then, does the manager supervise the contingent worker so that greater motivation is likely to ensue? These suggestions should help:

1. Plan ahead for the arrival of the temporary worker, says management consultant J. E. Osborne ("Using Temps to Get Through the Rough Times," *Supervisory Management,* June 1992). Make certain that the assignment is defined clearly, that reasonable standards have been established, that proper tools, equipment, and supplies are available, that the full-timers who will be working with the temp are identified, and that all staffers are alerted to the temp's arrival and know what support they are to provide.

2. Get to know the new worker well—his needs, interests, values, family circumstances. And do it early on lest the temp is ready to depart before you have acquired this fund of information. By knowing the temp better, you can meet his needs

more readily and generally do a better job of supervising him. Remember that people take temporary jobs for diverse reasons so their expectations and attitudes on the job will differ.

3. Treat the temp as a regular staff member to the extent practicable. Provide adequate desk space and a nameplate. Involve him in staff meetings and other team functions. By integrating the new hire into ongoing activities, the worker is more likely to feel part of the group and thus become more productive. Conversely, tucking the individual away in a corner "to do the job as hired for," is hardly a motivator.

4. Keep the temp well-informed. Make certain he understands the importance of the organization's mission and how the unit he is in contributes to its fulfillment. Provide him regularly with pertinent in-house news. Make certain he knows who to turn to for answers to questions which are certain to arise. Attention to these details should serve to unleash the temp's capabilities more fully and help his morale as well.

5. Don't hesitate to provide the training needed to make the temp fully productive. In the absence of training, anticipate indifference and mistakes. For example, L.L. Bean Inc., the Freeport, Maine mail order firm, uses training to stress customer service to temps hired for the Christmas rush. Its one-week training for order-takers who work only six weeks has real payoffs (Michael J. McCarthy, "Managers Face Dilemma with 'Temps'," *The Wall Street Journal,* April 5, 1988).

6. Meet frequently with the temp to find out what needs are not being fully met, to learn of the existence of any special problem, to offer encouragement and support, and generally to show that you appreciate both the temp's work and the temp as a person. **Note:** Consider offering the temp special assignments that would recognize his special talents and thus are likely to turn that person on. You may want to ask about special interests, which, if utilized, would excite the worker.

7. Don't give the temp all the "dirty" jobs. That's a certain mechanism to build resentment.

8. Involve the person in social activities—lunch, breaks, and after-hours events such as in-house athletic teams, picnics, etc.

9. Provide the fullest possible praise and recognition for accomplishment. Don't store up your compliments for delivery at departure time.

10. When the temp gets ready to leave, make it a special social occasion, such as a special luncheon with the staff at a nice restaurant. This friendly gesture may produce future dividends, too—the temp may return at a later date or recommend others for employment.

11. Meet with the departing temp to learn of satisfactions and possible dissatisfactions. This data will strengthen your ability to supervise other such hires in the future.

12. Assure the high-producing, departing temp that he will get good references if and when needed.

If practicable, offer qualified temps opportunities for full-time jobs. Why not tap the experience they have acquired with you?

A final note on the maximum utilization of temps. Joseph D. O'Brian ("Let Temps, Interns, and Others Give You Management Pointers," *Supervisory Management,* July 1994) suggests tapping their prior knowledge and experience and current observations about your operation to aid you in making possible improvements. Specifically, they can be helpful in these areas:

☐ Securing comparative data about management practices here vs. other places the temp may have worked. Ask: Is management here better or worse? What practices or conditions might be changed?

☐ Assessing your training programs. Ask: How can our methods be improved?

☐ Identifying talent in various employees. Ask: Who has been particularly helpful? Who do you admire?

☐ Changing rules, procedures and priorities.

O'Brian points out that you have to gain the temp's confidence before you can elicit feedback from him. Thus, asking for feedback before an appraisal interview is not likely to be too productive. It also may be more productive to seek out feedback in a group meeting. Leveling may come easier if there are colleagues to back up one's observations and suggestions.

SURVIVORS OF DOWNSIZING AND MERGERS

What happens to the downsized and the merged—those who survive restructurings, reorganizings, re-engineerings, downsizings, mergers, acquisitions, outsourcings, and other cutbacks? Does life go on as previously or do the survivors experience assorted trauma in the form of anxiety, guilt, anger? Are attitudes necessarily negative? Is motivation decreased, increased, or unaffected? Is performance hindered, helped, or unchanged?

People, of course, are different, and we thus may expect different reactions after the dust settles. Dr. Joel Bruckner, who has researched the impact of layoffs on survivors, finds ("The Impact of Layoffs on the Survivors," *Supervisory Management,* February 1986) a mixed effect. Layoffs may cause some workers to work harder, others tend to be demotivated and some continue to work unaffected.

Attitudes, too, may assume a mixed reaction. Reactions of survivors typically assume these forms:

Anxiety." Will I be next?" Possible effects: This may lead to increased or decreased work performance.

Guilt. This is a surprising reaction because the survivors certainly didn't trigger the calamity. A possible effect: increased motivation and performance so as to show the organization that its decision not to fire them was correct.

Anger. This may reflect a feeling that the layoff was unnecessary or the process of doing it was flawed or unfair. A possible effect: a witholding of effort, possibly as retaliation against the organization.

Relief. Survivors may have one or both of these reactions: elated that they were not axed or pleased that the "dead wood" was finally removed.

Obviously, the manager has to learn how people feel after the change and design appropriate motivational strategies, including showing of support, patience, listening, sharing of information, and so on.

Part of the manager's action, per Dr. Bruckner, should be based on the factors that impact on the survivors:

Nature of work. People who were in jobs that were stressful, or had little variety, or were ambiguous, or participated little in determining how to do their jobs, are likely to be dissatisfied and show reduced motivation.

Formal organization. How the organization conducted the layoff—seniority, merit, or random selection—affects reactions. Dr. Bruckner's research evidenced that random survivors increased their efforts on an assigned task whereas most survivors, probably figuring they "deserved to stay on," exhibited no motivational increase. Also, the post-cutback aid received by separated employees affects the attitudes of survivors—they are less likely to feel guilty or anxious if those dismissed were helped in generous ways.

Informal organization. If an organization has developed a family-type culture as opposed to an authoritarian one, more anger and anxiety are likely to occur among survivors. Why? Because layoffs are perceived as a threat to the informal organization.

Individual differences. Rank, work attitudes and personality factors will produce varying reactions.

Environment. If cutbacks are the norm in the industry, they are more likely to attach legitimacy to it. But if those who survive know that those dismissed will have a hard time finding comparable work, anxiety, guilt or anger will arise.

In a study of the impact of a merger ("Helping Employees Cope with Merger Trauma," *Training,* January 1986), Julia H. Dull, a bank vice-president and director of development and training, found that acquisition means major trauma to those in the acquired outfit. Once the shock of the merger news subsides, people develop their own perceptions of the new situation, based on their beliefs, values, past experience, and "stress information" about other mergers—which is usually negative. Typical reactions are: anger, fear, denial, frustration, and depression. This is understandable because those acquired face general fear and uncertainty, fear of stymied careers, possible job loss, assignment to a lesser job, the possibility of having to move to another city, and the demise of the firm to which they had strong loyalties.

The results of the emotional reactions to these uncertainties may be changed behavior, lowered production, stress, illness, accidents, conflict, and lack of commitment to the merger. Managers need to operate cautiously to reduce anxieties. This includes providing accurate information to dispel rumors, counseling employees to understand that loss of control is temporary, and generally trying to keep people productive and challenged. Team building becomes especially important to re-establish goals, communication, and good interpersonal relations.

As has been indicated, severe organizational change affects people differently. Management consultants Joan Alevras and Arnold Frigeri see the survivors (employees) of a downsizing fall into these four categories ("Picking Up the Pieces After Downsizing," *Training and Development Journal,* September 1987):

Leaders. These are the positive people. They wield power and focus on the organization. They sense the organization's new direction and plan and urge others to move towards it.

Followers. They decide consciously to follow the leader. They support their bosses to achieve organization goals. They feel loyalty is best for them in the long run. In a large department, followers may be leaders in their own sections.

Victims. They feel powerless. They feel helpless, and are concerned only with themselves. They obediently follow orders from above, but no longer take initiatives. They carefully say the right things at the right time. They obviously have been traumatized out of real thought into blind organizational allegiance.

Avengers. They want to get even for their pain and perceived loss of status. They have power, but it is narrowly and personally focused. To rebuild themselves, they must tear down "the others." They may strike overtly or covertly.

Sometimes people move from avenger to victim. ("I'll wait my three years to retirement.") Avengers rarely become followers because their anger is too strong to permit cooperation with others. In fact, their ploy may be to try to infect others with their animosity. ("How can we work in a terrible place like this?")

One way to cope with the avenger is to capitalize on his high energy by placing him in a leadership role—e.g., to head up a task force.

Victims can be moved to the follower role by clear definition of the new role, recognition and gradually increasing their responsibility.

If downsizing, operating on a lean and mean basis, and reduced opportunities for advancement are now the norms in today's organizations, how do you, as a manager, keep your people challenged? Management writer Joseph O'Brian ("Motivating When Times Are Slow," *Supervisory Management,* September 1993) offers these suggestions:

Prevent panic. Sure, the recent cutbacks have made your employees anxious. But you can provide a calming influence by assuring them that the outfit will soon stabilize; and that if everyone gives it their best shot and works as a team, the new, leaner setup should be stronger.

Avoid bitterness. Even if your unit got clobbered unfairly, don't exhibit dissatisfaction. Developing an "us vs. them" attitude is hardly the best form of modeling for your survivors.

Operate on a high profile basis. You want your bosses to know of your department and its value to the firm. So let them know of your staffers' good work. Also, try to involve yourself in high-visibility projects so that your reputation as a live wire will be evident to top-level decision makers. If people at the top think well of you, your department may well benefit by having more resources allocated to it.

Help staffers sell themselves. If you've taken over a merged or acquired unit, explain the new culture to your new staffers. They want to know how to impress top management and to learn about possible opportunities elsewhere in their new firm.

Provide career guidance. If promotions are limited in your own setup, provide help to your employees in securing advancement in other departments. A lateral move may be one of your recommendations.

Sponsor cross-training. By broadening your people, you can aid them to make a career comeback based on a new set of skills and knowledge. The cross-training may be internal or, if practicable, accomplish it by working with managers in other departments.

Restructure teams. Provide team members with new tasks with different partners. A team reshuffle will help to spark motivation and creativity.

Provide more time and contact with your less confident people. While everyone is likely to experience the downsizing blues, low self-esteem people are particularly vulnerable. So identify them and work on their self-confidence by providing added support, encouragement, and more responsibility.

Meet individually with your staffers. Discuss their jobs, possible career opportunities and what they might do to reach their career goals. Develop specific action plans with them.

Create a fun and exciting workplace. Bolster morale and *espirit de corps* (teamness) by letting enough diversion and laughter into daily activities. People who feel "relaxed" will respond better to new demands and challenges. And it will certainly help to ease the pain of the downsizing or mergers.

Added suggestions (per Thomas A. Mahan, "In Practice: Surviving Survival," *Training and Development,* April 1992) are these:

Insight. Be certain your survivors understand that their feelings of loss, guilt, and fear are totally normal and that, in time, they will resolve them. Communicate that going through major (negative) changes entails experiencing these stages: denial, anxiety, anger, depression, and finally acceptance. If they know this, they will do a better job of coping with the big, unwanted change.

Participation. To ensure employee commitment, involve them in important decisions. Let them help to plan the new organization.

Goal setting. Develop new, realistic, attainable goals, working jointly with staffers on them. Then reward goal accomplishment. The thrust is to evidence to the surviving employees that they are still productive and can provide worthwhile contributions.

Communication. Disseminate information fully and truthfully. The alternative: the negative, inaccurate rumor mill will take over. And who needs that?

Stress management. Think in terms of stress management. Watch out for overwork due to staff reductions. Institute stress-reducing activities such as softball teams, bowling leagues, post-work barbecues, and stress-management training.

Certainly most managers and employees know that the old "psychological contract," based on an exchange of loyalty to the firm for a job as long as one wanted it, plus regular pay increases and promotions for hard work, no longer exists. Downsizing has clearly voided that implied contract. But there still is a need to reward productive employees. How might it be done? Management consultants Frances Patch, Dan Rice and Craig Dreillinger suggest these non-financial incentives ("A Contract for Commitment," *Training and Development,* November 1992):

Pet projects. Allow the worker to use the time and resources to further a preferred or favored activity. While not a formal portion of one's job, the project may still be of value to the unit or the overall organization.

New responsibilities. Added responsibilities may be provided which the worker is willing to assume. A broadened job is a sincere form of recognition.

Additional authority. Consider assigning the staffer to head up a committee, special project, or work group.

Training. Encourage the employee to add to his skill repertoire by taking advantage of training opportunities. Support him in securing training opportunities.

Job rotation. An employee can be loaned to another unit or exchanged with an employee in another department to expand his fund of knowledge and to augment his skill repertoire. Multi-skilled employees will be in better shape to resist future downsizing and possibly advance their careers.

Advocate for employee ideas. The manager can support the employee by presenting his ideas up the line. Good ideas don't necessarily sell by themselves. If you can run interference for them, they have a better chance of moving forward.

Competition. A competitive employee may value opportunities to "win." He thus may wish to enter contests within or between work units.

Awards. In-unit programs of awards for special accomplishment may strike a favorable chord with employees. **Examples:** checker of the month; top producer of the period.

Recognition. The company newsletter can be used to tout the special accomplishments of one or more employees or that of a work team.

Other prescriptions to help bond employees to common goals, per Carol K. Goman, author of *The Loyalty Factor: Building Trust in Today's Workplace,* New York: MasterMedia, Limited "Books," (summarized in "Books," *Training and Development,* November 1991) are:

☐ Conduct employee openness surveys and feedback results.
☐ Provide accurate expectations and feedback.
☐ Explain the rationale for decisions and policies.
☐ Always be candid.
☐ Explain how individual employee contributions underpin the goals of the organization.
☐ Communicate clearly the mission, philosophy, and values of the firm.
☐ Present communications early on to prevent "surprises."
☐ Conduct exit interviews.

It also may be anticipated that the downsizing will have increased everyone's workload. To help overworked employees reduce stress, Northwestern National Life offers these pointers (presented by management writer Charlene M. Solomon in *Personnel Journal,* June 1993):

Permit free communication among employees. In an outfit where people can talk freely with one another, productivity and problem solving is likely to increase.

Lessen personal conflicts. Use these procedures: train everyone to resolve conflicts via communication, negotiation and respect; treat everyone fairly; spell out job requirements clearly.

Job control. Give people the fullest possible control over their work. People are more productive and less susceptible to stress if they have control over and flexibility in how they do their jobs.

Relate budgets to new projects. Before new projects are undertaken, be certain staffing and funding are adequate. Adding to existing heavy workloads may increase turnover, accidents, illnesses, and reduce overall productivity.

Talk openly to staff. This includes presenting both good and bad news, and providing opportunities for employees to vent their concerns to management.

Be supportive. Coping with heavy workloads will be eased if management provides sympathy, understanding, and encouragement.

Address procedural needs. By reducing red tape, frustration and possible burnout can be prevented. Conscientious workers don't relish wasting their time on unnecessary paperwork and procedures.

Reward accomplishment. Ignoring employee contributions in a high-workload period are certain routes to reduced morale and unnecessary departures of capable people.

Self-assistance. The above paragraphs have suggested primarily what the manager might to do bolster survivor morale and motivation. But he, as a fellow survivor, should not overlook his own needs and well-being. This means, say management consultants Dan Rice and Craig Dreillinger ("After the Downsizing," *Training and Development,* May 1991), that you should recognize that your statements and behaviors communicate, intentionally or otherwise, your attitudes about what is going on, and how staffers should react to what is going on. You certainly don't want to communicate resentment, fear of making mistakes or taking risks, or that you don't trust your bosses.

Don't hesitate to seek out information that you need to answer your own questions or to reduce possible anxieties. Talk to peers, your boss and family about your feelings about the downsizing. Try to learn what the organization has in mind for you, what it expects, why you were retained.

Be frank about your own feelings, doubts, grief. Expect that it may take a while for healing to take place. Secure support from others.

And above all, says J. E. Osborne ("Combatting the Consequences of Cutbacks," *Supervisory Management,* July 1990), resist the temptation to combat the consequences of cutbacks by taking on all the unit responsibilities yourself. That's what your survivor group needs to engage in. The better use of your skills is to guide your people through the troubled waters. All of which means that (1) you should identify the problems you do and do not control, (2) zero in on the situations you can change, and (3) find ways to work around the ones over which you have little or no power.

To sum up. For the manager faced with severe organizational changes, as described above, positive steps must and can be taken to bolster morale and keep motivation from eroding badly. Recognize your people may be demoralized, suspicious, self-absorbed, and most likely less productive. Dr. Dorri Jacobs offers these skill pointers ("Maintaining Morale During and After Downsizing," *Management Solutions,* April 1988):

☐ Try to understand everyone's feelings, including your own.

☐ Meet with staff to discuss feelings and concerns.

☐ Help people to regain control of the situation.

☐ Reduce emphasis on your managerial status so people will feel you are fully accessible and want to listen and help.

☐ Work on improving communication—up, down, and across.

☐ Set a positive, patient tone. Praise effort and results. Be supportive.

☐ Recognize the need for an adequate time period for "mourning" losses and adapting to change.

☐ Plan at all phases of the change—before, during, and afterward. Communicate your plans.

☐ Keep your own humor on an upbeat note.

☐ Assess progress frequently.

The above steps won't guarantee total success, motivation-wise. But what is likely to happen if you don't take them at all and passively hope for the best?

MANAGING VOLUNTEERS

In decades past, the typical volunteer was a homemaker with considerable time on her hands. Typically, these volunteers had little workplace skill and were content to engage in unskilled tasks such as envelope stuffing, collecting donations or possibly driving meals around town.

However, per management writer Beverly Geber, ("Managing Volunteers," *Training,* June 1991), the world of volunteering has changed radically. According to Gallup Poll data, nearly 100 million adults were volunteers in 1990, a big boost over the 80 million in 1980. Volunteers average four hours weekly for their causes. Young adults and baby boomers are big volunteer groups—people who have full-time jobs, have significant job skills, and are not content to perform routine, unskilled chores.

Volunteers, says Beverly Geber, give up some of their valuable free time for one or more reasons:

The charitable impulse. Some people want to do something worthwhile for society. Altruism is a real motivator.

Skill sharpener. Some volunteers are seeking opportunities to expand their job skills.

Career search. Others are interested in entering a new field of work. Volunteer work may be an effective way to develop a résumé and get good recommendations from a superior to impress an employer.

Social. Most volunteer organizations are great locales to meet new people. Latching on to new friends is facilitated by the common interests the volunteers bring to the volunteer organization.

Power and influence. Volunteer organizations are always looking for willing leaders. Thus leadership roles are easy to fill. Being a volunteer leader offers splendid opportunity to develop and exercise leadership and managerial skills, opportunities which may not be available back on the job.

What do volunteers expect when they climb aboard? Says Beverly Geber, they expect to work on carefully defined projects with a clear beginning and end. They don't just wish to volunteer for something "every Saturday."

They also expect to use their regular job skills that might be in the areas of training, computer programming, finance, etc. They also are likely to insist on tasks that interest and challenge them.

Volunteer organizations today are very likely to ask their volunteers to sign contracts outlining what they have agreed to do. Job descriptions, too, are included in the "contractual" arrangement. This forces the managers to define crucial job elements and job requirements and clarifies the ground rules and expectations for the volunteer.

Another change non-profit organizations have instituted is to cut down on the number of meetings volunteers are asked to attend. This is essential, for busy volunteers resent and resist time wasting.

Full orientation and training are a must for today's volunteers. If you don't indoctrinate and train them properly, you won't keep them very long.

Many volunteer organizations, in their efforts to practice good personnel management, not only set high standards, but provide volunteers with performance appraisals. In effect, although unpaid, the volunteers are treated as professionals are in any organization. Interestingly, volunteers may demand appraisals. Understandably, if their interest is to build skills for private sector work, they wish to be able to show that they did a good job, not only that they volunteered.

Non-profits, says Beverly Geber, stress rewards and recognition of their volunteers. This is essential since pay, as a motivator, obviously is not in the picture. Frequent verbal praise, thank-you letters, pins, plaques, birthday cards, and annual dinners are devices to provide appreciation and recognition. Of course, the reward has to be tailored to the needs of the individual volunteer.

To sum up. According to performance technologist Nancy Snow, who has been active in several volunteer organizations, attend to the following management principles ("Optimizing Performance in Volunteer Organizations," *Performance and Instruction*, September 1993):

1. **Recruitment.** Locating the right people is basic to your success. Use a live-wire volunteer for this. Part of the job is to encourage current volunteers to do more, but this must not entail overloading anyone.

2. **Align skills and qualifications to jobs.** Get to know your volunteers. Learn of their special skills. If possible, let them select their tasks. Share unpleasant tasks among many volunteers.

3. **Prescribe performance standards.** Communicate your job standards. Use job descriptions and give feedback on performance. Cut those who don't meet standards. And be certain all standards are realistic and reflect what's really important to the operation.

4. **Training.** While people can learn their jobs via osmosis, planned and organized instruction will be many times more effective. Use job aids wherever possible, especially for seasonal or occasional workers.

5. **Communication.** Keep your communication two-way. Listen to complaints and for negative attitudes. Keep everyone posted about meetings, events and deadlines. Involve people in decisions. Their input may be critical to a sound approach to a problem. Encourage inter-volunteer communication.

6. **Rewards.** Because money is not in your bag of rewards, use feedback, praise, write-ups in local papers. Provide progress reports. Help volunteers document their work for résumés. Provide thanks often.

7. **Support.** Try to meet volunteer needs. This may include locating baby-sitters for parents with

youngsters. Provide transportation if needed. Keep them involved, as opposed to letting them drift off by themselves.

8. **Reward attendance.** Manage meetings well by starting and ending on time; having an agenda; keeping meetings business-like, yet relaxed, friendly, and positive in tone. Provide for socializing after the meeting for those who can stay.

9. **Build on success.** Train your first group of volunteers carefully. They will draw others. Let potential recruits know that they will work with others who are "seasoned" and will offer help.

10. **Evaluation.** Measure performance based on your goals. Secure feedback from the public you serve. Critique major events and activities with the volunteers.

Eight Questions About Motivation

1a. What triggers people's behavior? Why do they respond/perform/behave as they do?

Typical reactions/expressions: "I wonder what makes her tick?" "He's an odd one, isn't he?" "She's hard to reach." "Nothing seems to turn him on." "He'll do it, but he'll take his own sweet time doing it."

People act in ways that best meet *their* needs. That behavior, of course, may not always be what we would like it to be. But we can reduce our frustration over the "errant" or "weird" behavior of others if we can understand that *all behavior is caused.* Behavior doesn't originate or operate in a vacuum. Nor is it necessarily a product of people's evil or contrary nature. Rather, it exists because some need is met by it. It thus is your job, as manager, to try to understand what triggers it (causation). Obviously, you can't alter the result if you don't understand its cause. **Note:** Everyone is motivated. Of course, they may not share the the motivation you hope for because their needs are different.

One helpful way to get a "fix" on people is to consider their attitudinal system—that is, what values do they hold, what is their self-concept (how they see themselves), and what are their expectations?

1b. Why are people so unpredictable? Why do they respond/perform/behave in certain ways at certain times and yet so differently at others?

Typical reactions/expressions: "You never know what Mary will do next." "He's only consistent in his inconsistencies." "She's nice socially, but a real bear in the office."

People respond in "unpredictable" ways or, for that matter, in "predictable" ways to best meet their needs. If they respond differently at different times, it is because their needs or the situations are different. Human beings are very "complex" because of the shifting character of their needs system. We can hardly expect people to be as predictable as the behavior of your car or a household appliance.

Remember the formula $B = f(P \times E)$ which tells us that behavior is a function of both personality (which includes one's needs system) and the environment or situation.

2. How can I get people to respond to me the way I want them to?

Typical reactions/expressions: "I just don't seem able to reach John." "All I get is a bunch of alibis and excuses." "She'll do it, but it takes an extra 30 minutes of debate before she will."

This is probably a "poor" question for it is framed solely in terms of your needs as manager rather than that of the performer. A better question: "Knowing the needs and the attitudinal system (values, self-concept, expectations) of my subordinates, what can I do to tap into those needs and values?" The use of the latter question is more likely to trigger the desired behavior.

Key point. Don't expect people to salute your every command. Think instead of where they are, where they're coming from, and use that data as your starting point. "If the mountain won't come to Mohammed, Mohammed must go to the mountain" is still a profound and useful proverb.

3. Why do people, at times, seem to act in ways that are not in their self-interests?

Typical reactions/expressions: "You know, Marge actually turned down that promotion," "He's his own worst enemy." "She must have a death wish."

What may not appear to be in someone's "best self-interest" is a matter of perception rather than a clearcut finding. For example, employee A may turn down a promotion—something which we cannot understand and we would never do—because his needs or values so dictate. And his needs or values obviously are dissimilar to our own.

4. How can motivation be sustained once it's kindled?

Typical reactions. "He'll do it, but you have to keep after him or nothing will happen." "People don't seem to be with it in the holiday period." "You would think that big bonus would make a difference."

To keep motivation going, give it the attention it needs. If we assume it's totally self-sustaining, we may well be in error. **Example:** Even the high achiever needs continuing opportunities to perform at a high level. So keep the challenges coming as well as the praise/recognition for the accomplishments. Letting people set (or at least, recommend) their own goals is a good way to encourage their self-propulsion.

5. What is the significance of money as a motivator? Aren't all people motivated by money?

Typical reactions: "He'll do anything to make a buck." "She said it wasn't the money that matters; she just wanted a job she enjoyed."

A discussion of money as a motivator begins on page 194.

6. Can people ever be satisfied with their lot/situation/circumstances?

Typical reactions/expressions: "Give me the boss' job and I'll be in seventh heaven." "These kids expect a promotion as soon as we've completed the paper work on their last one."

People are never satisfied with their lot. **Example:** If I have a tasty dinner tonight, I will also want one tomorrow night. Similarly, if I have the opportunity to perform exciting work this week, I'll have a like need next week and thereafter. This ongoing dissatisfaction is a positive good, for it keeps people constantly striving to perform, to achieve, to excel.

The facts of life are that there is no readily available paradise or heaven on earth. A colleague of mine jokes about this and says: "If my wife ever got to heaven she'd immediately start to redecorate." So man is a wanting creature who has needs which are rarely and not easily satisfied.

7. How can you get someone to achieve their potential?

Typical reactions: "She's got the stuff but she seems to run away from real opportunities." "What he needs is a lot of counseling." "He could have the world in his hands if he ever made his mind up to do it."

This is probably another one of those questions based on a set of misconceptions. The reality is that you can't get anyone to do anything which is not in accord with his needs, values, self-concept, etc. Of course, you can encourage, support, remove roadblocks, give feedback, and so forth, but the desire has to come from within. No one ever made a great surgeon, a great writer, or a great baseball player by pushing that person into it. Motivation is very much an *internal* kind of thing.

8. How can I understand myself more fully? Is this the key to understanding others?

Typical reactions: "I guess the Devil made me do it." "I'm not sure that I know what I really want." "Imagine it's a turnon for me. But I'm not sure about anyone else."

Greek philosopher Socrates advised "Know thyself" and the Scottish poet Bobby Burns lamented: "Oh that we could see ourselves as others do." Both of these lofty literary figures felt that man should engage in a lot of introspection to acquire the insight to get a good fix on who we really are, what we're up to, even what's bugging us. Various counselors and therapists make their living offering help to open the windows to ourselves.

If we can really understand our own needs system—what turns us off and on—we will be in a better position to understand the needs or "hot buttons" of others. The point is that just as we have needs, be it for responsibility, power, achievement, money or whatever, so do others. The managerial task is to try to learn as much as possible of our own needs and that of others as well.

A FEW THOUGHTS ON THE TWO CHECKSHEETS (PP. 139–140) CONCERNED WITH MOTIVATION

The first checklist, "How to Get Employee Motivation," lists primarily fringe benefits and pleasant conditions in the workplace, what Dr. Herzberg would call "hygiene" factors rather than true motivators, i.e., those which relate directly to the work itself: challenge, growth, achievement, recognition, advancement.

Items #7, job challenge; #13, growth on the job; and #19, recognition/praise are true motivators.

Item #6, training, may have motivational value, although for those who are "pushed" into it, it obviously would not. Training as a motivator might be so perceived if it provides an opportunity to learn new things so as to grow in one's job. A training opportunity may also be a form of recognition, an acknowledgement that one has done well and merits further support to continue to excel.

Item #13, pleasant, cooperative associates, may also serve as a motivator if it relates to the opportunity to be a member of a prestigious, knowledgeable, hard-hitting team. If it only relates to having nice buddies to hook up with for coffee and lunch, it is a doubtful motivator. The key, then, is whether there is a significant relationship to the work itself.

Item #17, capable supervisors, typically is a hygiene factor, per Dr. Herzberg, since it is an external rather than an internal force. Of course, some workers may bust a gut to perform well for a boss they identify with totally and fully respect. However, they are still doing it because the work itself is motivating.

Which items on the Employee Motivation Checklist did you check? Hygiene Factors or Motivation Factors? If you checked Hygiene Factors primarily or totally and ignored the Motivators (Items 7, 13 and 19), is there a possibility that you have not been thinking in the best motivational terms, something which Chapters 4 and 5 suggest?

The second check sheet, "What Motivates Me?", has both hygiene and motivational factors. Which did you rank as the five most significant to you? Did you state that you felt motivational factors or hygiene factors were most important to you?

Looking at both sheets in relation to one another, did you assume that you were motivated by work-related items (responsibility, challenge, growth, recognition, involvement in decision making, etc.), but that your staffers were motivated primarily by hygiene factors? If so, why? Is there a possibility that this exercise points up the need to re-think your approach to motivation?

KEY SUMMARY CONCEPTS

A. The manager, as a motivator, *assumes* that:

1. People want to do a good job—they *are* motivated! (You can make this into a self-fulfilling prophecy. If you think they can do it, they most likely will.)
2. People are capable of doing a good job.
3. People may require added help—coaching, counseling, training, giving of encouragement, support, and recognition—to enable their basic motivation to be fully unleashed and capitalized upon.

B. The manager, as a motivator, *recognizes* that:

1. Everyone is motivated. They may not be motivated to do what you or I want, in whole or in part, but they are motivated. They do have their "hot buttons."
2. The challenge is to identify those hot buttons and thereby unleash the desired motivation. This is another way of recognizing the need to respect individual differences.
3. People act in their own self-interest. This means you must help subordinates to see why it is in *their* best interest to perform as you and the organizations wish them to. "We have an important job to do here."
4. In respect to people's behavior, consider these two principles, per performance technologist Clay Carr, "How Performance Happens (and How to Help It Happen Better)—1: What This Is and Why," *Performance and Instruction,* November/December 1990):

   a) An individual does what makes sense to him in the situation.

   b) People act in ways that enable them to control their environment.

   So there's little point in getting upset or disappointed over other people's behavior. It may seem ludicrous or irrational to us, but it makes a lot of sense to them.

   A corollary to principle a) above, is that a person will shift from the old behavior to a new behavior when it makes sense to him. So it's our job, is it not, to help make the wanted behavior look sensible, most likely by rewarding its performance.
5. By empowering people, you demonstrate that you trust them to do their best for the organization.

6. People respond best to your application of the "Platinum Rule"—Do unto others as they would have done unto *them*. (Recall that the Golden Rule asks that you do unto others as you would have done unto you. With the former rule you enter into their world. You recognize their needs and perceptions. With the latter rule you are "governed" only by your own world, your needs and your perceptions.)

C. The manager, as a motivator, *ensures* that:

☐ The overall mission is understood and deemed to be important.

☐ Goals and standards in relation to the mission are clear. Quantity, quality, cost, and time (deadlines) are significant motivators and measuring rods.

☐ People have a say in setting up these goals and standards. (Remember, people support what *they* create).

☐ Goals are reasonable and reachable.

☐ Goals, to the extent practicable, contain "stretch" (challenge).

☐ People are enabled to perform by having proper tools, equipment, instructions, procedures, standards, policies, and other resources to do the job.

☐ People are empowered to discharge their responsibilities *independently*.

☐ Feedback is provided regularly about performance.

☐ Motivational concepts relating to the work—mastery, risk taking, complexity, variety, choice, ownership, job enrichment, wiggle room, closure, high expectations, feedback, praise, fun, excitement, involvement—are kept in mind when planning, assigning, discussing, and reviewing tasks.

☐ The reward system empowers rather than inhibits or punishes people.

☐ People are treated as individuals, providing "different strokes for different folks."

☐ People are organized into self-directed teams whenever practicable, so that teamness becomes a motivator.

☐ Money is used as a motivator, but primarily in conjunction with non-financial rewards such as job responsibility, job challenge, job empowerment, job accomplishment, job growth, and job recognition.

PROBLEMS, EXERCISES AND QUESTIONS FOR DISCUSSION

Note: Most of the items listed below can be treated by your participant group on either a team, paired, or individual basis. For greater participant interest, vary your approach. The author recommends that small groups be used primarily.

1. As an opener, ask participants to come up with a definition of motivation.
2. Another possible opener: Turn to your neighbor and discuss "Why should we, as managers, worry about motivation? Why devote these class hours to it?"
3. Working with a T-column, ask the group to list in the left column motivators which are *commonly used* by managers and organizations and in the right-hand column the motivators that are *less commonly used*. Is there a difference? If so, what is significant about this difference?
4. What is the difference between intrinsic and extrinsic rewards? Can you cite examples of each? Which might work better with rocket scientists, accountants, nurse's aides, sales personnel, clerk typists, cooks, teachers?
5. What were the motivations of people who came to work in our kind of industry 10–15 years ago? Have they changed? How? Why?
6. Discuss this statement: "For most people money is a certain motivator much of the time."
7. We know that motivation bears significantly on performance. But is this the only factor? Are there other factors which are more or possibly equally important? **Note to Discussion Leader:** The purpose of this question is to point up that other factors influence performance such as skill repertoire, personality, off-the-job problems, stage in one's career, etc.
8. What is the relationship of motivation to self-esteem?
9. How would you characterize company loyalty by employees in this decade? Is it greater or less than a decade or two ago? Why? If it is less, should it be worked on to increase it? If so, how? If not, why not?
10. Can you identify any behaviors or practices American personnel take for granted, but those from other cultures may be uncomfortable with?

Example: U.S. workers are very quick to learn and use brainstorming; people from cultures which are more "reserved," may be less likely to respond to it.

11. What is a "self-starter?" How can you spot one? What kind of motivational strategy is needed to maintain that self-starting? What kind of feedback would you give this person and would it differ from that you would give anyone else?

12. How does Herzberg's Motivation-Hygiene Theory square with your own experience?

13. What are the motivational implications of Theory X and Theory Y?

14. In some organizations, the threat of being fired is ever present. In others, the culture is such that no one ever gets fired. What are the pros and cons of these practices from a motivational standpoint?

15. What is meant by "anti-organizational behavior?" Why would employees who are paid adequately engage in such behavior?

16. Secure comments on the motivational aspects of the following programs:
    - ☐ Job enlargement
    - ☐ Job enrichment
    - ☐ Job empowerment
    - ☐ Self-directed teams
    - ☐ Employee involvement teams
    - ☐ Employee suggestion systems
    - ☐ Employee training
    - ☐ Total Quality Management (TQM)

Do they work? Is so, why? If not, why not?

17. Assign one of the topics below to pairs for analysis and presentation of their conclusions to the total group. What are the motivational attributes of one of the following?

☐ Empowerment	☐ Competition
☐ Closure	☐ Goal Setting
☐ Job Enrichment	☐ Wiggle Room
☐ Variety	☐ Ownership
☐ Risk taking	☐ Competency/mastery
☐ Choice	☐ Complexity
☐ Feedback	☐ Commitment
☐ Modeling	☐ The Pygmalion Effect
☐ Praise	☐ Fun on the job
☐ Teamness	☐ Quality

18. In pairs or small groups, identify and discuss the principal motivational needs of the following categories of workers:

☐ Temporaries	☐ The X generation (Baby Busters)
☐ Volunteers	
☐ Women	☐ Minorities
☐ Older workers	☐ People with disabilities
☐ People with low self-esteem	
	☐ Plateaued people
☐ Peak performers	☐ Professional/technical personnel

Report your conclusions to the class.

19. Working in pairs, take a job in your unit. Assume it should and can be enriched. What responsibilities might be added?

20. Other than job enrichment, what are some ways to deal with dull, dirty, boring, monotonous jobs?

21. Divide your class into two types of small groups:
    a) In one or more small groups, have participants come up with terms to describe managers they have known who supervised using the principle of high expectations as a means of motivation of their subordinates. (**Examples:** inspirer, praise giver, cheerleader.)
    b) In one or more small groups, have participants come up with terms to describe managers they have known who supervised staff using the principle of *low expectations.*

22. The shipping unit frequently finds that they have to work overtime to handle late outgoing shipments. There have been a large number of complaints concerning this. What might the foreman do to minimize the gripes about this? (**One answer:** Meet with all concerned to see what can be done to reduce "the pain.")

23. You are the manager of a very socially-oriented group. Togetherness is stressed via lunches, picnics, a bowling team, swim parties, barbecues, after-hours cocktails, card parties, etc. But Marie, an unmarried senior customer service rep in her mid-30s, typically avoids all this extracurricular group activity. Occasionally a team member mentions this to you. Is this a problem for you? For the team? Should you take any action on this? If so, what?

24. What motivational strategies might you use to get your people to do their best work and take pride in what they do?

25. You are a new manager on the job. Your people seem to be reluctant to accept new ideas, new methods, change of almost any sort. What might you do to turn things around?

26. You have been told by a top management official to "Go down to (X) plant (or office) and bring things in line, but don't upset people down there." Is it possible to change an organization without upsetting people?

27. You find that Pat gets defensive whenever you offer suggestions for work improvement. What might be done to reduce her defensiveness?

28. **Role play activities.** The problems cited below may be used as role plays. The manager's task in his role play is to alter the behavior of the particular employee via a new motivational strategy.

    a) Kim, a salesperson, does great on the "easy" money makers, but tends to ignore the rest of the product line.

    b) Tom, a grizzled 30-year veteran who is a strong producer, seems to have difficulty adapting to the new Hispanic and Asian workers now being hired for his shop.

    c) May does an excellent job securing new accounts, but gives them little attention once they are on board. You're concerned that these new customers may go elsewhere for "better treatment."

    d) Jane Jones is a 30-year veteran, age 49, who seems to be coasting toward early retirement. Jane always had a lot to offer, but now seems content to let others carry the ball.

29. On an individual basis, check the appropriate boxes in the following table for the motivators which relate to people at the three career levels (early, middle and late). Then compare and discuss your results in trios.

Career Stages and Motivation

Motivator	Early Stage	Mid Career	Late Stage
1. Team feeling (being part of a successful operation; receiving gratification from peers in work unit)			
2. Earned praise from someone you respect			
3. Making progress toward goals which one feels are important			
4. Recognition as the expert (via special assignments, task force membership, seeking his/her counsel on tough problems, etc.)			
5. Advancement; professional progress			

The Manager as a Delegator: The Art of "Letting Go"

Delegation consists of giving subordinates plenty of rope, but being certain that they don't hang themselves.

> —Anon.

There are now more than 5 billion people in the world. So much for indispensability.

> —*Modern Maturity,* Dec. 1986–Jan. 1987

Getting an entrepreneur to let go has to be like water torture; you do it drop by drop.

> —W. Hardie Shephard, New York financial consultant, quoted in *INC,* April 1979

Higgins, we've decided to let you go before you become irreplaceable.

> —caption for a cartoon in *The Wall Street Journal*

IN this chapter, we'll operate on the experienced-based assumption that delegation is very much a learnable art/skill. Toward this end, then, we hope to accomplish three things:

☐ Help you acquire a solid conceptual or philosophical base concerning the delegation process.
☐ Strengthen and expand your repertoire of delegation skills.
☐ Assist you in planning for more effective delegation on the job.

Thematically speaking, we have organized the chapter into the following topics:

☐ Why Delegate?
☐ Some Logical Reasons For Non-Delegation.
☐ Barriers to Delegation.
☐ R$_x$ For Effective Delegation: Requisite Attitudes.
☐ R$_x$ For Effective Delegation: Requisite Techniques.
☐ Delegation and Control.
☐ Delegation Taboos.
☐ What Our Delegation Practices Communicate.
☐ Your Delegation Quotient: A Self-Appraisal.
☐ Key Points: The Manager as Delegator.

WHY DELEGATE?

All of us who work in organizations are subject to the delegation process, either as delegators, delegatees, or both. Reactions to and comments about how delegation actually fares are therefore legion:

"He's overloaded, but he doesn't know how to let go."

"George? A real one-man band."

"How can I delegate when no one has my background and experience?"

"If I only had 10 more hours in the day!"

"If she delegated the job to me, why does she check with me every other day to learn where I am on the project?"

"How can you expect Mary to delegate when she wants all the credit for everything that gets done here?"

"Gee, look at that in-box. I better start delegating more."

"Dave surrounds himself with second-raters so that he doesn't have to delegate to them."

As the above comments suggest, delegation is not an easy tool to apply to the managerial job. Nevertheless, it is one of the most helpful devices the manager can employ to achieve the requisite results. Here are the benefits it can provide you, as a manager:

1. It can free you from unnecessary detail, allowing time for concentration on the more responsible portions of your job—setting goals, planning, measuring results, developing and maintaining external contacts, spending more time with staff to build relationships and resolve knotty problems, conducting field trips, going away for training, working on your own critical projects, taking on special assignments for your boss, and so on.

2. It can permit your subordinates to discharge duties and make on-the-spot decisions based on a more intimate knowledge of relevant data, conditions, circumstances, or needs relating to the work. The alternative is for you to second-guess your employees in subject-matter areas in which you may not be as knowledgeable or competent as they are. This fact of life may be hard to accept, but rare is the boss who knows it all!

3. Related to (2). above, decisions and actions taken by employees may not only be "wiser," but they may be executed more speedily and possibly with better timing because the delegatees may be more cognizant of actual operating needs, customer preferences, and the like.

4. It can encourage more rapid and fuller development of people. By letting your employees have the maximum of wiggle room and allowing them to carve out their own destinies, growth can be facilitated and expedited. **Note:** Although not always stressed by bosses at higher levels, the manager's role as a developer of people is a key one.

5. It can increase the rate of innovation in your organization. If you insist on doing things yourself, the odds are that they will be accomplished as before. (This isn't necessarily bad, but the point is that you are quite likely to do things as you have been doing them.) Conversely, if you allow delegation to take place, the odds are that the duties will be executed differently. Therefore, you should look at delegation as an opportunity for innovation, invention and creativity.

6. It can augment your reputation as a true manager, including being a developer of people, as opposed to being known as a bottleneck, nitpicker, comma chaser, grandstander, workaholic, or perfectionist. Do you really want the image of "Harried Hannah (or Harry)"?

7. It can reduce the stress that might accrue if you have to do it all, including carting home that stuffed, heavy briefcase evenings and weekends. Subordinates are *aids* to the extent that they are so utilized. They can help immensely to make the managerial life less pressure-laden and stressful.

8. Delegation may lead to a promotion for you. If you are embroiled in the day-to-day, the mundane, and thus are not on top of your job, upper management may feel that you "simply aren't ready." On the other hand, if you train your people properly and delegate fully to them, you can ask for more challenging tasks ("I've really got the operation clicking on all six cylinders, boss. The staff hardly

needs me down there."), and provide prima facie evidence that you are now available for greater responsibility.

9. It can improve relations with your employees. People like to feel that they are capable, worthy of being given full authority to act, and can be trusted to act reasonably, promptly, and accurately. By placing trust in your people—via delegation—you can get closer to them. This intimacy is basic to good relations and to open, two-way communication. And to the extent that people become more self-confident, their job satisfaction and organizational commitment will increase, too.

A summary point about delegation: The interesting thing about it is that it is a process which you, as a manager, ordinarily can control quite fully. For example, no one at upper levels of management will tell you how rapidly and thoroughly you should develop your people via delegation. Similarly, no one will tell you how much innovation you should extract from full or deep delegation. So you, as a manager, typically, have the authority and power to delegate as much as you wish. Rarely will someone second-guess you on such behavior. Figure 6-1 illustrates this concept graphically.

In the above paragraphs, I have endeavored to demonstrate that delegation is a highly significant and irrefutable principle of management. In fact, top officials in a few progressive, management-oriented organizations may even remind their subordinate managers, on occasion, that "you've got to start delegating more." Yet the facts of organizational life are that the delegation principle may not be applied as extensively as it should. The reasons for non-delegation are many and quite varied. Generally, they fall into two distinct categories:

☐ Logical or "legitimate" reasons, i.e., based on sound, well-thought-out management principles.
☐ Less-than-rational reasons, which we shall call "barriers" to delegation.

These reasons for non-delegation are discussed in the following two sections.

SOME LOGICAL REASONS FOR NON-DELEGATION

Reasonable and responsible non-delegation may occur for purposes or reasons such as these:

Delegation—Two Quality By-products

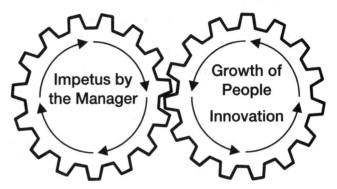

Figure 6-1. The manager has the power to accelerate the development of people and the rate of innovation.

☐ The organization may expect its managers alone to execute certain responsibilities, e.g., interpret and explain organization policies to staff (and to do this with the fullest possible clarity and conviction), and coordinate actions with other organizational units (because the top person is in the best position to understand, appraise, and reconcile the divergent interests involved).

☐ The tasks or activities may be those which, by their very nature, should be performed by the managers themselves—highly sensitive tasks having strong PR implications; certain ceremonial and/or representing tasks; resolving a conflict with another office; field visits where the manager is expected to appear personally; various personnel management responsibilities such as selection for promotion, compensation, rating of efficiency, discipline, firing someone, and the like.

☐ The managers may be able to accomplish a vital task more quickly or ably because of their position, personal contacts, power, or prestige in the organization.

☐ Employees may not have the necessary information or other resources to perform well.

☐ Employees may not be adequately qualified or properly trained to accept the delegated responsibility. This may be particularly true of new and possibly marginal workers.

☐ Employees may not wish to accept a delegation due to their disinterest in the task or low commitment to the organization and its mission.

☐ The organization may be subject to numerous organizational changes and other instabilities that generate anxieties and uncertainties. In such a climate, delegation may be understandably difficult to pass on. As one section chief once said to me in a period of frequent policy and top personnel changes: "When they get their act together and get their objectives straight, I'll take on the added responsibility and not a minute sooner."

☐ Proper performance is so critical that a miscue in any form or to any degree cannot be tolerated. Obviously, this should be a rare event, for presumably people are being trained to avoid the creation of indispensible and irreplaceable managers

☐ Delegation may not be possible due to statutory reasons; e.g., a doctor cannot delegate certain professional duties to a nurse nor can a licensed supervisory nurse delegate all of his responsibilities to non-licensed hospital attendants or aids.

James Jenks and John Kelly, authors of *Don't Do. Delegate! (The Secret Power of Successful Managers),* New York: Alexander Hamilton Institute (1985), found in their research of delegation at the chief executive officer level, that delegation is inappropriate in the following five situations ("When A Manager Is Duty -Bound Not To Pass The Buck," *The Wall Street Journal,* July 1, 1985):

1. **Fielding the repercussions of sudden changes. Example:** An organization, which had been a long-time payer of dividends, took action that eliminated its dividend. Complaints and questions poured into the firm. The company president took every phone call himself because he felt that it was his job to explain the new, unprecedented action.

2. **Performing rituals when power and prestige are critical. Examples:** testifying before a legislative group to show the president's concern about the pending legislation; attending the retirement dinner of a valued employee.

3. **Reprimands, praise, resolution of disputes and discharges.** "Nasty" jobs often are best done by the top person. Similarly, praise or recognition means more when it comes from "the top."

4. **Policy-making decisions. Example:** To avoid irritating and possibly losing major customers by requiring advance payment of bills before shipment of high-tech reports, the company president decided to make the billing decisions himself.

5. **Final, win or lose decisions. Example:** The coach of a pro basketball team always decided the details of the last play when the game was on the line—who was to receive the ball, who was to pass for the final shot, who was to shoot, etc.

BARRIERS TO DELEGATION

Although delegation is a logical and beneficial process, there are many forces at work that may bedevil it. These forces reside in:

☐ The manager
☐ The manager's boss
☐ The manager's subordinates
☐ The organization

Each of these forces is discussed in turn.

Forces in The Manager

There are many reasons why managers are reluctant to delegate. Here are the most common ones:

Lack of a Sound Philosophical Base

Many managers have had little or no management training nor have they read much of the available management literature. Worse still, their superiors may have been poor delegation models. In the absence of even a modicum of educational stimulus, it is understandable that they have not developed a progressive philosophy about delegation. In fact, their perceptions and beliefs about it may be a bundle of misconceptions, as we shall see.

For example, many managers look at delegation in "less-less" rather than "more-more" terms. That is to say, they regard the delegation process as akin to a pie. Specifically, there is only so much responsibility and authority available to the manager; and if one gives any of it away, less of it, obviously, remains. Actually, the reverse is true—the more the manager gives up responsibility, the more he gets back in return: greater self-propulsion of employees, more time to perform higher level tasks, and so on.

The challenge, then, for any organization is to convert its managers from their "less-less" philosophy to one of "more-more."

Lack of Skill

Delegation, like communication or planning, is a learnable skill. But in the absence of management training and concerned coaching by superiors on delegation, the manager may not have the motivation and know-how to "pull it off" properly.

Example: Bob White, Purchasing Head, has not learned to assess the importance of the decisions he has to make each day. All of them are considered crucial and urgent. Given Bob's assessment of his operating responsibility, it is inevitable that he will have to make all (or nearly all) the decisions himself. Bob's bosses are not unhappy with his style of operating, of which they actually know little, for the work always gets out. Of course, turnover is high and morale trends in the opposite direction. But things do get done, so what else matters? Oh, yes. Bob rarely has a vacation and has serious family problems because his work (nights, weekends) gets the No. 1 priority.

Example: Cynthia Bell, payroll supervisor, has been "stung" by her attempts at delegation because she didn't understand the role of communication and control in the delegation process. She failed to tell her subordinates about her expectations about the delegated work and she made no provisions for follow-up. Cynthia will be very cautious about delegating important work for some time to come.

Lack of Time

Managers are busy people. They thus may find little time to train others to do what they themselves do so well and so quickly. ("I simply can't spend the time to explain all the ins and outs of the work, so I'll just have to do it myself.") This approach to delegation and time management is certainly a rationalization for non-delegation. For while training does take time, it is an excellent investment over the long haul.

Lack of Confidence in Subordinates

The manager who operates on the assumption that "if you want something done well, do it yourself," is really asserting that he doesn't trust his people to perform well. ("Delegate? Do you know the kind of clods I've got in my unit?") This type of manager may also feel that if the subordinate "goofs things up," much time will be lost to straighten out the mess.

Example: In a large tool and die factory, operated by a father and son, the father insists on personally attending to the maintenance and repair of the machines. The father also resists taking vacations, even though the son, who knew the operation well, frequently urges him to do so. On one of the many occasions when the son urged his dad to delegate the responsibility for machine maintenance, this conversation ensued:

Son: Aren't there some people here who could attend to the machines?

Father: Sure there are. But how do I know they'll do it right?

After much badgering, the son managed to send his father off for a vacation in the north woods, something the latter hadn't done for some 25 years. This conversation took place upon his Dad's return:

Son: Well, Dad, things seemed to go pretty well while you were away. At least no one pushed the panic button and called you up for advice.

Father: That's true. But, then, they didn't have my phone number, did they?

Lack of Personal Security

If the manager has doubts about himself, these anxieties can be readily converted to excessive needs for power, prestige, activity, visibility, and control. The insecure manager may thus see delegation as a minus proposition, a mechanism to lose opportunities for accomplishment, involvement, recognition, and satisfaction.

By hoarding all (or nearly all) of his responsibilities, the manager can convince himself that he is strong and important. Evidence of this is readily apparent to the non-delegator because of the full in-basket, the long work day, plus the constant flow of visitors seeking information, clearances, approvals, confirmations, and the like. Hence the tragic phenomenon of the "indispensible" and "irreplaceable" boss. ("You better see Baxter on that. She's the only one who's checked out on those procedures." Or: "The place really can't function while she's away.")

The key learning required for such a manager is that dependency relationships frustrate people, stunt their growth, and actually reduce productivity rather than increase it.

The Daily High

If Manager Jones does it all, the day is likely to wind up with a feeling of high satisfaction. And why not? For work can be satisfying, even if done alone. But this compulsive behavior is likely to have this by-product: The staff may spend large amounts of time at extended lunch and coffee breaks while the boss toils away at his and everyone else's chores. Resentments and indifference may also build up. A typical reaction to Jones' hyperactivity: "Jones is the busiest guy in this building; why, man, he wouldn't leave his desk unless the place were on fire." Jones, of course, has made himself too busy to be cognizant of his over-managing style and resultant staff under-utilization and frustration.

Lack of Commitment

The five "lacks" described above are certain to produce a sixth one—a lack of true commitment to the delegation process. Sure, the manager may have heard the "good managers delegate" advisory, but he has not really internalized the need for it. Hence, the manager may give the delegation principle a certain amount of lip service. For example, I used to work for a man who always had an overflowing in-basket on his desk. Practically all documents, in and out, had to clear through him. (A standing joke was that if paper sold for a dollar a pound, old Vince would be a millionaire.) Every so often when I would be in his office discussing a problem with him, he would break away from our discussion, point to the sagging in-box, and say to me very seriously: "You know, I've simply got to start delegating more." Unfortunately, his rather general awareness of his problem was never followed by any concrete, corrective action, delegation-wise.

A common form of limited commitment is for the delegator to delegate in the formal sense, but to withdraw much of the delegation by personally making the major decisions. **Example:** Hilda Braun was carefully selected from a large pool of applicants to be director of marketing and sales to promote a new line of video software. But Hilda soon discovered that the more significant activities were being undertaken by the company president who had hired her. First, her boss insisted on interviewing and selecting all members of the new sales force. Then her boss began to develop the training plan for the new recruits. And the training itself, which was to be conducted solely by Hilda, began to be "shared" with the boss. In time Hilda was primarily dictating routine correspondence, which produced this reaction of dismay: "I've got the title, the salary, and the plush office. But everyone knows who the real marketing director is." She left, after six months on the job, when she learned from a colleague that her non-delegat-

ing, insensitive boss was unhappy with her performance because "she wasn't bringing ideas into the company." Hilda's post was occupied by five people during a three-year period, all of whom were promised a great deal of autonomy but never experienced it.

Another form of wishy-washy commitment takes place when the manager delegates formally, but vitiates the delegation by constantly checking up on the subordinate's progress. The result of such over-managing is a typically frustrated subordinate: "Does he want me to implement the plan for the move to the new building or doesn't he? If he doesn't trust me to pull it off properly, why didn't he say so at the outset?"

Or the manager may delegate formally, again, but intervene in ways that patently undermine the delegation—a "suggestion" here, a "contribution" there, and so on. And the not surprising employee reaction: "I thought *I* was writing the manual for new supervisors. But the way she keeps popping in with added suggestions and new instructions, it won't really be my product when it hits the supervisors' desks."

Phony delegation hardly fools anyone, of course. Only the ersatz delegator believes he has delegated. One response I encountered to such flimflammery was for the employees to refer to their boss' deceptive behavior in this jocular vein: "Don't make a move without calling Smith," a quote borrowed from the final line of a radio commercial touting the services of a large furniture moving company.

The Experience Trap

Some managers may enjoy and insist on doing particular tasks themselves because of their prior experience. For example, an industrial relations director in a large firm, who had moved up to her position via the job evaluation route, insisted on being involved in many of the details of salary and wage surveys. Needless to say, this meddling into minutiae drove her Chief of Compensation up the proverbial wall: "If I can't be trusted to do the job, why doesn't she get someone she can trust?" Of course, the boss not only felt that her expertise was indispensible to the success of the job evaluation survey, but could rationalize her involvement further: "I want to keep a hand in it lest I lose touch."

Added motivations for not letting go of familiar tasks are these: They provide a secure and comfortable feeling to perform duties one knows well plus a splendid opportunity to demonstrate one's expertise. The latter motivation is particularly important to the managerial ego because the other duties that one is responsible for may be new and one is not likely to be expert in them.

Monopoly on Wisdom

An added barrier to delegation may be the feeling by the manager that there is only one way to solve a problem, only one answer to a difficulty. And, unfortunately for the organization, the manager sincerely believes that he alone possesses the requisite wisdom to respond to that challenge. Under these circumstance, the "best" response can only come from the manager and delegation to subordinates is not only unnecessary but "high risk."

Perfectionism

Some managers may discourage acceptance of delegation because of their acute need for a "flawless" end result. But if the boss is too hard to please, subordinates may conclude that the nitpicking resulting from the "poorly" completed task simply isn't worth it: "Why knock yourself out doing something for Kim when all you get are endless requests to revise it, improve it, rework it? It's one thing to 'take another crack at it' when the added try or two will really make a difference. But when all we're doing is trying to placate a very anxious person . . ."

Punitive Behaviors

Every act of delegation entails an element of risk. Certainly a subordinate may, on occasion, botch things badly and embarrass you, cause the loss of a valued customer, and so on. But the possibility of error is the price you must pay to secure all the worthwhile benefits of delegation. It is not unusual, unfortunately, for employee "goofs" to be accompanied by verbal onslaughts by their bosses. If so, those who have been "chewed out" will react predictably in the following ways:

1) Reduced Risk Taking

Because no one wishes to be punished for unintentional mistakes, one response by subordinates is likely to be reduced initiative: "Why stick your neck out on projects like that when you run the risk of getting a king-sized kick in the pants if things don't work out?"

2) Frustration

Employees who try their hardest to do a job well resent a torrent of criticism that may follow an error. A typical reaction: "I did my best. No one's perfect. I ask myself: 'Is all this verbal abuse worth my sticking around here?'"

3) Cover-Up

If an employee is certain to be "reamed out" for a mistake, a likely response is to downplay it or even conceal it, if at all possible. Why be the messenger bringing the monarch the bad news? **The result:** An opportunity is lost to discuss the mistake, to learn mutually from it.

Of course, not all bosses overreact to a miscue. I worked for a man who had learned wisely, in his managerial career, to resist doling out punishment when things went awry. He seemed to understand that the very experience of the mistake, if committed by a responsible, conscientious employee, was punishment in itself. For example, our marketing people procured a special, free access telephone line to our office for an important promotional campaign. Unfortunately, the printed promotional material carried a transposed telephone number. As a consequence, the intended incoming phone calls by potential customers went to a private residence instead of to our office. When my boss received the news of this gaffe at our weekly staff meeting he smiled, shook his head gently and said to our group in a quiet but sad tone: "We sure make it hard for our customers to reach us, don't we?" All of us appreciated that the boss didn't engage in any recriminations ("Who goofed this one up?") and simply asked what was being done to salvage the botched promotion.

Fear of Competition

Along with all the other doubts, concerns, and anxieties the manager may have about delegation, there may be his fear, conscious or otherwise, that a subordinate may be able to perform the job as well or even better than the boss. So why delegate and risk being "shown up" by an underling?" Obviously, managers of this type need to learn that:

1) good management includes development of people,
2) delegation is a key tool for such development and
3) effective managers strive to acquire unblemished reputations for being sincere delegators and strong people developers.

Fear of Resentment or Dislike

Some supervisors are afraid that their delegations may be perceived by employees as an effort to "dump" things on the staff to avoid work for themselves. At work is the supervisors' misguided feeling that people will not like them for being "too tough" a boss. The primary route to employee affection, then, is to *do* rather than to delegate. Obviously, an excessive need for affection—to be liked at all costs—is hardly compatible with being a good manager. In fact, employees respect a boss who does his job properly, whether it relates to assigning work, setting standards, expecting a full effort and quality results, and so forth.

Forces in the Manager's Boss

While the manager is the major block to greater delegation, the manager's boss may, at times, be an added obstacle. The latter may unwittingly block delegation by behaviors such as these:

Deciding on What is Delegatable

The manager's boss may insist that certain projects/problems/assignments are to be handled by the subordinate manager alone. But if some or many of the not-to-be-delegated tasks *are* delegatable, the manager's freedom to assign work is being undermined. And the net result is that the overall operation is likely to be less rather than more effective.

Demanding Minutiae

The boss may insist that the subordinate manager be immersed in detail so that the latter can respond immediately to all and any queries from the boss about the ongoing work. Consider this very common conversation:

Boss: Fran, how is that response coming to that complaint from Omaha?

Subordinate manager: I'm not sure, Boss. I'll have to check with Chris on that and get back to you.

Boss: You mean you're not handling that yourself? The message the subordinate manager gets from his boss is loud and clear: "I better start handling these kinds of problems myself since the boss expects me to be up on all aspects of them."

Poor Modeling

Bosses, whether they are aware of it or not, serve as models for subordinates. Thus, if the boss engages in over-control, he sets a poor example for other would-be delegators. Failure to let go all too often breeds like behavior down the line. Ideally, one's boss should not only serve as a model delegator, but should systematically quiz subordinate supervisors concerning their hopes and plans for added delegation to staff.

Climate for JIC/CYA

Managers may not always plan as well as they are actually capable of doing. But one area in which they often do plan well relates to that of "protecting one's flanks" in case something goes wrong with a given operation. These defensive maneuvers are deemed essential to ward off possible future criticism from superiors who are short on empathic behaviors, but long on castigating ones. The terms "JIC" and "CYA," now part of our management jargon, are commonly used to describe such defensive activities—the "Just In Case" file and "Cover Your Anatomy" (translated loosely) management.

The point of it all is that managers who are operating in what they perceive to be a highly defensive climate are hardly going to be great risk-takers and broad and deep delegators. (Remember, every delegation entails risk.) Instead, they will be content to play it safe and delegate no more than seems prudent, given the prevailing atmosphere.

Forces in the Subordinates

While delegation to subordinates may be a worthy goal, inadequate subordinate responses to delegation may frustrate the process. For example:

Poor or Partial Accomplishment

The subordinate may not perform well or complete the task on time. Employee errors may indeed be costly, e.g., a PR oversight. Yet the manager is held accountable by his superiors for the end result. If these circumstances arise frequently enough, the supervisor may be reluctant to delegate further and may even withdraw what has been delegated. In many cases, however, patient coaching can overcome this difficulty.

Low Commitment

Performers who are weak or poorly motivated obviously won't rise to the challenge of new or added responsibility. ("Gosh, I'm in deep water already.") Although encouraging coaching and training may help to overcome a certain amount of timidity, the delegator can only go as far as the delegatee will allow.

Delegation vs. Dumping

Some subordinates may perceive the delegation process as a "dumping operation." That is to say, the employees' perception of work assignment is that the boss is determined to divest himself of the "dirty" jobs—the highly routine, the mundane, the "Mickey Mouse," the uninteresting tasks—and consistently hoards the attractive, enjoyable, challenging, and fulfilling work for himself. This perception may or may not be correct. But if it persists, the workers will act on that premise, i.e., they will resist attempts at further delegation. ("I'd like to, boss, but I'm overloaded already.") If the employees' perception is erroneous, the situation can be turned around by greater concern with communication, augmenting intimacy and thereby building trust. A heavier emphasis on coaching and team building should help, too.

Dubious Delegation

Some subordinates may resist delegation because they feel that the boss already has "the answer." That is to say, the boss' behavior pattern is one of asking for solutions to a problem but rarely adopting employee recommendations. ("She knows what she wants. Why bother to ask for a 'fresh look' at the matter?") Again, there is a need to build trust so that authentic interpersonal communication and relations are possible, assuming that the employees' perception of their boss' behavior is not on target. If the employees' assessment is correct, the boss, obviously, has a real problem, resolvable only by altering one's behavior.

Upward Delegation

A trap for the unwary manager is to allow subordinates to unload some of their responsibilities on him. An employee may approach the all too cooperative boss with this scam: "Boss, I'm stuck on this part of the F-4Z project. Can you help out on it? You've encountered this bug before and worked it out." The supervisor, his ego assuaged, rushes in to respond to the request for assistance: "Sure, let me work on it this morning and I'll get back to you later today." **The result:** the employee takes an extended coffee break and the boss spends the day doing the employee's work. The more sophisticated, delegation-conscious manager would avoid this pitfall by putting the responsibility back where it belongs: "Yeah, it's a tough one, all right. But how would *you* debug it? Not sure? I think you're savvy enough to work it out on your own. Why not give it some more thought, come up with some options, and we'll talk about it some more tomorrow. I'll be real surprised if you don't come up with a better approach than I could. OK?"

Other Factors

Subordinates may resist attempts at delegation due to lack of training ("Gee, I've never done this before"); lack of interest in the particular project or task; lack of apparent rewards ("No one appreciates what you do here. Why do more?"); work overload (real or imagined); or feelings of inadequacy ("I wonder if I'm really qualified to pull this off?"). Conscientious, empathic coaching should be able to overcome these resistances most of the time.

Forces in the Organization

The organization itself may be a prime inhibitor of good delegation practices. Policies and procedures such as these may have a discouraging impact:

Low-trust Atmosphere

Is the organization obsessed with checks, controls, reviews, audits, avoidance of mistakes, or multiple reviews and approvals? If so, the climate for delegation is hardly a salutary one. How can the manager learn to let go if the observable models operate in a low trust or non-trusting way?

Reward System

Who gets the promotions and the desired job assignments, the supervisors/managers who are super-technicians, those who know every jot and tittle of their jobs and tend to hoard responsibility, or the conscientious delegators and people developers? The question is a basic one for organizations all too often promote individuals primarily on the basis of their job knowledge and technical skill. The assumption underlying such promotional criteria is that if one has certain expertise, he can readily instruct and supervise others to do such tasks properly. Overlooked, of course, is the fact that the technician may derive his real job satisfaction from *personally doing* what he has been long engaged in, as opposed to teaching others how to do it, and then stepping back and proudly watching them grow from their new assignments.

Performance Review

How likely is an upper-level manager to quiz a subordinate manager about his delegation practices at annual performance review time? You could make yourself a bundle betting against such a likelihood. For the facts of organizational life are that the annual review is work oriented (results, goal accomplishment) and is rarely utilized for such a management purpose. The net result: existing delegation practices—good, bad, or indifferent—are presumed to be the desired ones and are thus reinforced (rewarded by default).

R$_x$ FOR EFFECTIVE DELEGATION: REQUISITE ATTITUDES

The prior sections have outlined the values ("the why") of delegation and the many reasons—both rational and often less than rational ("the barriers")—why it may not occur. But what about "the how?" Are there not better ways (skills and techniques) of delegating? Indeed there are.

But delegating properly requires a combination of *both* skill factors and attitudinal elements. The latter aspect is particularly important because delegating is far more than routinely following a set of prescribed procedures and mechanics. Rather, it depends heavily on the kinds of outlooks, beliefs, and values that you, as a manager, hold about people. These attitudes are discussed below.

Delegation is more likely to work well if you possess and exhibit these feelings and attitudes about your subordinates:

☐ Employees can be trusted fully to execute their assignments within your prescribed guidelines.
☐ Employees wish to do a good job for you, their boss, and the overall organization. They know that their livelihood depends on the success of the firm and that they have an obligation to contribute fully to that success.
☐ Employees require the fullest possible wiggle room to execute their responsibilities properly. Conversely, no one can operate effectively with you, their boss, constantly hovering over their shoulder, second-guessing each and every action.
☐ Employees want to grow and develop. And it is your job, via delegation, to help accomplish this result. Try to use this concept as a guide to better

delegation: If you give your people little jobs, you will develop little people; if you give them truly significant jobs, you will create true adults. The operative concept is that of *empowering* people, to help them to become bigger than they are; and for some, even bigger than they, themselves, thought they could become.

☐ Employees expect to be challenged and stimulated to the extent that their work allows. Added or enriched duties and responsibilities—more delegation on your part—are a means to that end. So try to think in terms of job enrichment, of what else a subordinate might do.
☐ Employees will take more pride in their work and be more highly motivated to the extent that you "engineer" their jobs for the fullest possible delegation to them. A manager can't escape the role of "motivator." You can fulfill that role via delegation.
☐ Employees have to be allowed a certain margin for error in exchange for their self-propulsion. They have to operate without fear that their efforts will be rewarded with blame and second-guessing. One of the biggest compliments you can receive occurs when a subordinate tells someone: "My boss supports my decisions, even when I muff one."

Fairmont Hotels' CEO Robert Small approaches the area of employee goofs in this fashion (quoted in "The Indomitable Mr. Small," *Meeting News,* September 1992):

. . . And don't worry about making mistakes. If you start doing something and it's wrong, it's okay to change.

. . . Did you ever hear of the bell in my office? On the bell it says, Mistakes are great moments. And when they (employees) make a mistake, they can come in and ring the bell and it's over. If you freeze your people when they make a mistake, they're never going to try to do something. They're not going to be curious and they're not going to be creative and they're not going to be innovative, because if you spank them when they make a mistake, what is the reward for taking risks?

☐ Employees, as delegatees, may require training, either on or off the job, to function to their fullest potential. However, this investment in your people will pay off in terms of their increased motivation and higher quality and productivity in general. Remember, if you don't train and develop them, you'll have to "carry" them. The choice is yours.

☐ Employees who operate on a fully delegated basis are quite likely to come up with approaches which are different than yours. But that's what delegation and good management is all about. So if you reject new ideas and approaches because of the NIH factor ("Not Invented Here"), you will have found a sure-fire way to discourage initiative and creativity. Your best guideline as a delegator is to let people "do what comes naturally."

☐ Employees are your best ally to help you look good. You will look good if your employees are empowered to produce for you. So try to always think in terms of the freedom people need to perform well.

☐ Employees are entitled to all the credit they can get from you for work accomplished well. So praise in both public and private, and do it as often and as sincerely as you can.

☐ Employees achieve job satisfaction by the opportunities they have for growth on the job. Their satisfaction means that you are truly a manager, not just an assigner and reviewer of work. You can (and should) take pride in their feelings of achievement, their successes, their progress. These are some of your most significant rewards as a manager. They should replace the satisfactions you formerly had when you turned out a good job yourself. New role, new satisfactions. Just like the proud parent is elated when his youngster enters college, receives a degree, or gets his first job and first promotion.

Besides your sincere belief in the capabilities and positive attitudes of your staff, you, as a delegator, should have a strong faith in the dynamics of the delegation process itself. Once you have delegated, you are no longer *the* prime motivator. The objectives, the tasks, become "the boss." The need to do, to complete the job, to show his stuff, are the real motivators. Delegation, then, once you have unleashed the process, becomes a powerful, self-propelling force.

Part of the dynamics of delegation is generated by a self-fulfilling prophecy. If you believe people can do well, they typically will do well. Conversely, if you have a lot of doubts about their ability or willingness to do well, and you thus act on that assumption, they probably won't do well. In short, trust begets the will to do. Distrust and doubt begets the opposite.

The manager who has difficulty accepting the realities of the delegation process requires a radical shift in his thinking about modern, progressive management.

Psychologists call this readjustment of thought processes "reframing." In respect to delegation this means that there is a need to reframe the role of the manager from that of doer to director, from player to coach. And a shift in one's expectation of rewards is also in order—from personal gratification for one's own task accomplishment to joy and pride in the results others are able to achieve under their own direction.

To wrap up our discussion of attitudes, CEO of Mackay Envelope Corp. and best-selling author Harvey Mackay credits a former super successful CEO colleague with these four rules to build a successful business (cited in *Successful Meetings,* November 1993): 1) find the capital, 2) find a favorable environment in which to employ it, 3) hire key people, and he paused and said: "Number four is the important one. You've got to know when to get the hell out of the way. That's the hardest part, but that's the one that will make you rich."

In like vein, popular speaker Bob Basso updates MBWA (Management By Walking Around) with these three simple empowering principles (cited in the *Pryor Report,* Vol 9. No. 1A, 1993):

1. Give your people something important to do.
2. Give them the authority to do it.
3. Back off and let them do it.

Basso calls his philosophy MBGOOTW (Management By Getting Out Of The Way).

R_X FOR EFFECTIVE DELEGATION: REQUISITE TECHNIQUES

While the philosophy of delegation may be understood in general terms, i.e., the purposes and the benefits to be gained therefrom, the *skill* aspects may not be fully integrated into the manager's repertoire of techniques. Or, putting it more bluntly, good intentions are not enough. Hence the need to outline how delegation should proceed to make successful.

Basically, delegation requires these behaviors by you as the manager/delegator:

1. Appraise your own job carefully to consider which tasks can be delegated to others. To do this in a serious and methodical way, you should keep a precise and detailed log of your daily activities for two weeks. Include *everything* that you do. Enlist the aid of your secretary to assist in the mainte-

nance of your log. Then transfer that data to the "Guidesheet to Delegate Realistically," Figure 6-2 (page 278), as an aid to begin your planning for delegation to your team.

2. Develop performance standards for the proper performance of delegated tasks.

3. Assess staff capabilities to ascertain who has the qualifications, interest, and motivation to assume the delegations. Workload of subordinates should also be taken into account lest an overload be created.

4. Provide delegated authority in relatively small doses to personnel who are new in their jobs. In this way you will prevent a possible feeling of "panic" in the newcomer ("Does she really think I can do all of this by myself so soon?"). Also, miscues, if any, can be corrected before the situation gets beyond repair. As competency develops, you can—and should—increase the delegated load accordingly.

5. Establish control procedures, either alone or preferably with the delegatees, to ensure that duties are performed in relation to all performance standards, including time frames. (See "Delegation and Control" in the following section.)

6. Meet with your subordinates to provide a clear communication as to what is to be delegated, the importance of the tasks, and how much *authority* you are providing to discharge all duties and responsibilities. **Example:** A subordinate may be delegated authority to contract for printing work for a sum of no more than $2,500.00. **Note:** Two serious oversights in the delegation process are a) the absence of clear-cut guidelines or limits concerning authority to execute responsibilities, and b) inadequate granting of authority to carry out delegated tasks. ("How does he expect me to do the job if I have to check back with him every time I need to reach for a Kleenex?")

7. Define precisely at your meeting the parameters or limits of the delegation—quantity, quality, deadlines, budget, etc. If you are dealing with experienced personnel, you should do this on a "negotiated" basis. Input from the delegatees will help to ensure that the items of delegation are subject to the fullest possible realism; ensure full understanding of the what and why of the delegation; and remove possible conflicts later on about your intentions and expectations. ("Oh, did you want me to clear those brochures with you, boss, *before* I sent them to the printer?") In any case, your delegation meeting should leave no doubt in the delegatee's mind of the purposes, scope and time frames of the delegations, and the control measures to be used to monitor them.

Depending on the complexity of the tasks involved and the capabilities and personalities of the delegatees, you may wish to "button things down" a bit more firmly via the aid of a written statement. If so, be certain to spell out objectives/goals; required resources, including budget; authority; priorities; reporting procedures.

8. Wherever possible, try to delegate a single task to one person rather than splitting it up among several people. Total responsibility for the task is a great motivator. Also, by fixing responsibility for results on one individual you obviously have more control over the delegation.

9. But use the team approach when delegations are better served by joint effort or when one person's work may impinge on that of others. In the latter instance, you provide your team with necessary coordination. Also, if an activity is too large for for one person to handle within the requisite time limits, subdivide the job into several components and delegate them to several staffers.

10. Specify and secure full understanding and agreement about the areas where delegation is *not* to take place. ("I will personally handle all contacts with Branch X because . . .") Indicate, too, which items must be cleared with you before anyone goes ahead with the job. Of course, you should keep these clearances to a minimum lest your staffers feel that they are enmeshed in a phony delegation.

11. Indicate your availability to discuss problems that may arise after work begins on the delegated tasks. You certainly wish to be seen by the delegatees as a coach and helper, not as an aloof assigner of work. ("This is your worry now.")

If you have read and digested the above guidelines, it should be apparent that delegation is a process, a systematic way of managing. It would not mean, for example, that you provide the file containing a current problem to the first subordinate you meet as you walk down the hall. Rather, you would consider carefully capabilities, interests, and workload before you assigned any special task. (Parenthetically, I might mention that I worked for a boss who was notorious for buttonholing staffers for ad hoc assignments. Needless to say, we learned quite rapidly that when we saw the boss in the hall, armed with a manila folder, we reversed our course lest we got saddled with an assignment we didn't particularly want or have time for.)

There will be times when you have doubts about the delegatability of a particular task or are uncertain how well a subordinate can execute properly a delegated task. If so, these procedures may help:

The "Double Check" Method

Delegate the task *and* perform the task yourself, as you may have done before. Then, on task completion, objectively compare the two results. It may well be that the delegated result may be equal in quality or even exceed your own effort. In either circumstance, delegation would become a "no-risk" matter in the future.

The "Carbon Copy" Technique

Assume you are bogged down with a lot of correspondence. You are not sure, however, whether your secretary or other staffer can make the proper written responses if this chore were delegated. A workable procedure is to coach a potential delegatee on the fine points of the activity, delegate the task, and then review copies of the outgoing correspondence. You may wish to make marginal notes on the copies for the benefit of the preparer where you feel particular responses could have been handled more properly. ("Good factual reply. But could you 'sweeten up' the last paragraph on these kinds of cases?") Gradually, your written comments should become less frequent and, in time, you may decide to abandon your review of the copies entirely.

From time to time, you should secure some candid feedback from your delegatees concerning their view of your delegations. For example, you may feel that you have delegated the right tasks with the right amounts of authority to execute them. And you may be correct in your perception. Or you may not be. In any case, it is good procedure to check out their perceptions about the delegation process as it actually impacts on them. By learning how they see your delegations, you may forestall considerable trouble—misconceptions, irritations, frustrations, disenchantments, bad-mouthing you to others, and more.

Finally, to ensure that you pull off your delegations effectively, you should understand the difference between three terms which befuddle many delegators:

☐ **Responsibility** relates to any and all work you have been given formally (see your job description) and you decide to let others perform for you. You can authorize others to perform many or even most of your responsibilities, if you are so inclined.

☐ **Authority** is the power you give to a delagatee to carry out the responsibilities you have assigned. This may be the power to spend, contact people, collect information, travel, write letters, hold meetings, or make certain decisions. No doubt you have heard the statement: "Authority should be commensurate with responsibility." If you follow this principle none of your subordinates will complain that: "Yeah, she gave me the responsibility, all right, but I didn't have half the authority I needed to carry it out."

☐ **Accountability** is your obligation to account and report for the responsibility and authority you and your subordinates have had available for the execution of assigned tasks. So you can delegate responsibility and authority; but your boss and the organization will expect you to recognize that you are accountable for end results, be they good, bad, or indifferent. In common parlance, you are operating with the understanding that "the buck stops here." This means that you can't palm off on your boss alibis blaming others, such as: "What could I do? George held up the shipment and never told me word one about it." "Sure, Katie had the wrong VCR for the meeting. But how was I supposed to know that she had never operated a VCR before and could hardly be expected to know a Beta videotape from a VHS?"

One of the first and somewhat paradoxical learnings for the delegator is that he must give credit generously to those who do well and selfishly hoard the blame when things go awry. But that's probably one of the reasons why managers are paid more, have more information, power, authority, and prestige, and have the opportunity to meet (and eat) with a wider and higher level of associates.

DELEGATION AND CONTROL

Delegation is a vital tool to enable you, as a manager, to multiply your capabilities. It accomplishes this by letting you deputize others to perform for you. But sharing responsibility with others does not mean abandoning interest or control in what has been delegated. Delegators cannot afford to be helpless spectators of work being accomplished by others. If they so behaved, they would be engaging in abdication, not delegation.

What we are saying, then, is that there are two sides to the delegation coin—one is assignment of responsibility and authority and the other is control. The concept of control relates to staying on top of your delegations. It does not mean over-managing (some people call it "micro-managing") via such suffocating behaviors as perfectionism, nit-picking, second-guessing, or needless intervening (taking over). Rather, control is a sophisticated, professional managerial tool to ascertain conformance with agreed-upon goals, to check the extent of progress, to offer such help as may be needed, and to intervene, if truly necessary, to correct any serious deviations from plans and standards.

In sum, control is essential because delegation of responsibility does not relieve you of accountability for final results. As we have said, the buck stops with you and you alone.

Reasons for Control

Control may be essential for a variety of reasons, other than to ascertain how well and to what degree a task is being accomplished by your delegatees:

1. You may need to know of progress or task completion so as to coordinate that task with other operations, activities or projects. Other jobs may not be able to start unless the delegated one reaches a certain stage of completion.
2. External needs also may require data about accomplishment or progress, e.g., a customer may be waiting for delivery of a product or service.
3. The delegatee may have been given too much freedom or, possibly, not enough latitude to do the assigned job properly. By checking on accomplishment, appropriate adjustments can be made.
4. New, inexperienced or "weak" performers may require more frequent contacts for help or encouragement. In fact, minimum contact on your part

may produce a feeling of abandonment. ("I guess the boss doesn't care whether I sink or swim on this thing.")
5. Conditions may change, necessitating added information from the delegatee. For example, your boss may suddenly deem Project X to be "hot" and thus request that you keep him posted more frequently on progress than had been agreed upon at the time of your delegation.
6. The changed conditions may require a totally new direction for a given project or activity. For example, a project may have been authorized considerable funds. But if the organization is undergoing a sudden budget crunch, the project may have to be reappraised in terms of possible "downsizing."

Nature of Controls

Typically, controls are implemented on a *post-assignment* basis. That is to say, the delegatee embarks on the project and at appropriate stages, you, as the delegator, conduct your checks or reviews to ascertain the degree and nature of accomplishment. These controls may be looked at as a continuum, ranging from the highly informal to the highly formal.

Informal progress/accomplishment checks may be executed in the course of:

☐ One-on-one conversations about other matters: "Oh, by the way, Pat, how is Project M-4 coming along. Please let me know if you hit any snags and need some help."
☐ Lunch or coffee breaks.
☐ Regular staff meetings: "Any problems or bottlenecks on the Wichita activity? Do you need any help from anyone here?"

Of course, your informal, somewhat casual inquiries as to progress should be conducted minimally lest your subordinates feel that you are intervening unnecessarily.

Formal checks or follow-ups may be accomplished via:

☐ Meetings scheduled at the outset of the delegation to review progress, e.g., a six-month project may require a progress check at 30- or 60-day intervals.
☐ Planned inspections of results (if the project is a physical one).

☐ Periodic written reports to review progress.

☐ The "milestone" approach, i.e., work is reviewed at logical accomplishment points—an eight-part manual may be reviewed at the end of each part.

☐ The budgetary approach; e.g., a progress meeting may be held when 20% of the budget is spent and the next step or stage is ready for discussion.

☐ Interventions by you, as the delegator, when there are indications that things are not going well; e.g., exceeding the budget, quality lapses, departures from the agreed-upon schedule.

Pre-assignment Control Procedures

At times you may wish to institute controls when a project is being assigned (as opposed to doing it on a post-assignment basis):

1. Ask the subordinate for a written plan of attack to meet the agreed-upon or prescribed goal. When the action plan is reviewed and approved, the delegatee begins to carry out the goal. This procedure assures you that the performer knows fully what is expected and how to execute the project. **Note:** This procedure is best applied to the new or weak performer or possibly when the project is so novel or complex that it is simply good business to know beforehand how things will be done. Also, although you discuss the subordinate's plan with him/her, make certain it remains his plan. If you do all the planning, you are hardly delegating. A weak or skimpy plan should be reworked by the employee. Or,

2. Set a clearcut deadline for final accomplishment of the activity. This scheduling procedure ensures that your delegatee's work has a beginning as well as an end. (A review at other intervals was mentioned above.) The accomplishment date serves as a basis for control and as a motivator as well.

Control: Skill Pointers

Some skill pointers for effective control are:

1. It is good practice to indicate the nature and frequency of your controls, be they reviews of work, inspections, reports, or whatever, when the work is assigned. If reasonable and necessary control procedures are communicated at the outset of the delegation process, misunderstandings about their nature and purpose will be eliminated. It is impor-

tant from a morale and motivational standpoint that your subordinates not feel that they are being harassed by picayune and overly frequent interventions by you, the delegator.

2. To the extent practical, involve the delegatee in setting controls. This is a particularly workable procedure when you are using the milestone procedure, i.e., checking interim results at logical accomplishment points.

3. Once the ground rules for control have been mutually set, you should exercise the necessary self-discipline to observe them strictly. Resist the temptation to make surprise inspections or other reviews. Your subordinates don't relish surprises any more than you do.

4. Strive for reasonableness when you set your controls. A new or weak performer will require more checks and follow-ups than a seasoned, able one. And as been indicated, new or complex projects or activities require more monitoring than established tasks.

5. Although we are using the term control in this text to indicate the overall process involved of keeping on top of things, you should use less directive and possibly threatening terminology with your staff. For example, after goals are agreed upon, you may wish to state something like the following: "Betty, I'd like to review with you your progress in say, 30 days. At that time you and I can see how things are going and I can offer some help should you need it, OK?" (Other low-key, non-threatening terms are discuss, review, follow-up, talk over, chat about, compare notes, exchange views.)

6. Indicate that your door is open should a contingency arise. Delegation certainly does not mean that all communication about the assignment ceases once your delegatee begins the job. If you have made a point of developing easy and open relations with your staff, they will not hesitate to go to you for help. Nor will they be afraid to deliver any "bad news" you should have about the delegation.

7. Look at the control process as a means of knowing the approximate status of the work under way. It is *not* akin to the data the baseball manager requires about his pitcher—the number of balls and strikes thrown per inning, whether the pitcher falls behind the batter in terms of balls and

strikes, as well as how many walks, hits, strike-outs, and runs have been allowed.

8. Try to select controls that are least expensive in character, relate well to the nature of the project and the capabilities of the performer, meet the acid test of "a real need to know," and won't injure relations with the delegatee because of their burdensome character. It may also be desirable to think in terms of a greater emphasis on informal as opposed to formal controls.

9. Insist on strict adherence to agreed-upon deadlines. If the deadline is a reasonable one, it is certainly fair to expect compliance. So be sure to follow up if a deadline is not observed. If you are prompt in your follow-ups, you will encourage future promptness by the delegatees. Conversely, if you are lax about them, you are communicating that deadlines are not important and you will reap indifferent behavior thereafter. **Note:** The best deadlines, whether at interim or final points, are marked by realism. They are not set hastily or arbitrarily. They are thought out carefully with inputs from both parties to the delegation contract. Also, they are flexible, recognizing that delays, unanticipated problems and assorted crises may require readjustment in the agreed-upon time frames.

10. You should use intervention as a control mechanism only as a last resort measure. Use it when the delegatee is in real difficulty for one reason or another. Of course, poor delegators tend to intervene prematurely and unnecessarily. In effect, they nullify the agreed-upon delegation. So heed this big caution: Don't rush in to take over unless it is crystal clear that you must. In fact, the whole idea of control is to be up on things so that you can offer help via good coaching before matters get out of hand.

11. Develop and apply a strong, clearcut, consistent, and realistic philosophy about control. Be clear about why, where and how much of it you really need. For example, Mobil Corp. Chairman Lucio A. Noto said in reference to a major downsizing at its Fairfax, VA, headquarters that the company had commissioned a number of studies that show it has "too many checkers checking the checkers" (Daniel Southerland and David S. Hilzenrath, "Mobil to Cut 1,250 Jobs in Fairfax," *The Washington Post,* May 2, 1995).

DELEGATION TABOOS

Delegation is a basic key to your effectiveness as a manager. Of course, the process probably never will be a totally easy or comfortable one. But if you understand it fully, it can become an adequately straightforward, logical and "doable" skill. A significant part of that understanding is to recognize that there are certain pitfalls or no-no's that can entrap the untrained, unwary, or overzealous delegator. A score of these cautions are listed below. You probably can add some others to this list based on your own experience as either a delegator, delegatee or both.

1. Don't delegate tasks that are highly confidential, sensitive or have been mandated by your boss for you to perform. To ignore your boss' preferences, even if the latter is patently overcautious, risks an unnecessary confrontation and possible added second-guessing on his part as to the character of all your delegations.

2. Similarly, don't delegate tasks that are totally your responsibility as the manager. For example, certain external relations such as resolving a difference with a difficult colleague (a peer) are essentially non-delegatable. Similarly, the annual performance review and discipline are solely your tasks.

3. Don't delegate tasks to people who report to other superiors. If you wish an employee in another unit to execute a job for you, you can avoid violating the sensitive chain of command principle by first talking to that employee's boss about the proposed assignment. The same caution applies if you have subordinate supervisors: Contact them rather than approaching the employee directly.

4. Don't delegate tasks up the line. Your bosses won't appreciate it one bit. If your rationale is that you are overloaded, secure their help to locate added staff (via loans, temporary hires) if you can't get the added temporary staffing on your own. In any case, it is hardly a wise procedure to tell your bosses that you can't handle a given responsibility. The odds are that they will feel that it is your job "to work it out," current workload and all.

5. Don't delegate to people who are already overloaded. It is your job to know the nature and extent of your subordinates' workloads. Delegating to overworked staffers risks the performance of a poor job, possible delays on other assigned tasks,

and generally strained relations with subordinates. ("Why is the boss punishing me with the added project when he knows I'm already up to my ears in work?") One obvious answer to the need to begin a new activity is to renegotiate existing priorities and deadlines with the performer.

6. Try not to delegate regularly to only one or two capable people. Others may want to get into the act and may feel that they are slighted, overlooked or forgotten purposely. Also, this practice is quite likely to overload the high achievers and stunt the growth of the others. **Note:** This is a *suggested* caution. There may not be any alternatives if one or two people are far superior to the others.

7. Don't assign the *same* responsibility to two or three employees as a device to ensure that the job gets done by *someone*. Such a procedure is an unnecessarily expensive use of staff and will hardly build trust when those affected learn of your ploy. In a similar vein, don't delegate to another employee the task of "spying" on the delegatee. The best approach to reduce your anxieties about the proper performance of a delegated task is to either assign it to your truly best performer or to set stringent guidelines and controls for its accomplishment. Of course, if no one is trained to do the job, delegation is not practical at all. In the latter instance you may have to do the work yourself.

8. Don't create a no-man's land wherein important duties and responsibilities are left in limbo—unclaimed, unattached, unassigned, and thus unperformed. If you haven't farmed them out to someone in a timely, professional way, you may end up doing them yourself or risk censure for their non-performance. Delegating is a form of decision making. Delaying decisions of importance can only work to the decision maker's detriment.

9. Don't be a backseat driver. You shouldn't expect that your delegatee will rely on the same methods to achieve the goal that you would. Because people have different personalities, styles, and experience, their routes to task accomplishment will necessarily vary. Part of the price you pay for the many benefits of delegation is a tolerance for departures from your own modus operandi. And as we have said earlier, there is always the possibility—and this thought may pain a bit—that someone else may do things in a fashion superior to the way you have been doing it. As a speaker at

a management conference that I attended sagely put it: "If you always do what you've always done, you only get what you've always got."

10. Don't delegate responsibility without providing adequate authority to execute that responsibility. For example, regional or district sales managers can hardly discharge their responsibilities if they do not have the authority to arrange for training sessions, to purchase necessary training materials, to travel to the field, etc.

11. Don't fall victim to the "80/20" principle, which tells us, in reference to delegation, that we as managers may well be spending 80% of our time on activities that have only a 20% payoff. Avoid the 80/20 trap by concentrating on the "big picture," the highly productive tasks, and shed most or all of the others. Management consultant Dr. Tom McDonald suggests we ask ourselves how much of what is on our plate is strategic and how much is tactical. He says ("So Little Time," *Successful Meetings*," July 1994):

> *To decide, remember this guideline: Anything tactical you're doing that someone else can do is ripe for delegation; anything strategic that only you can do should not be delegated to anyone. The 80/20 Rule works well here: 80 percent of what's on your plate probably could be done by someone else; 20 percent can't. Examine your plate carefully—you'll be surprised what's available to delegate.*

The old economist's query: "If you were the best lawyer in town and also the best typist, would you do your own typing?", is fully pertinent as a reminder to work smarter, not harder. And you do this by focusing personally only on the major tasks or problems.

12. But don't only delegate the "stinkers"—the routine, nasty or "dirty" jobs—or those you don't personally care about. Instead, consider delegation as a means of providing "stretch." Delegate, then, tasks that are demanding, growth-inducing, challenging, reputation building, visibility augmenting, and the like. Your employees will respond favorably to such treatment and certainly avoid tabbing you as a "dumper" rather than a delegator.

13. Don't arbitrarily withdraw a responsibility from one subordinate and assign it to someone else without adequate feedback to the original performer. People are entitled to know fully why their responsibilities are being removed or dimin-

ished. If the initial performer has goofed or is not producing to standard, that information should be provided. If the changeover is intended to get a "new look" at the task, advise the subordinate of that desire on your part. Alterations in what has been delegated require as much attention, communication-wise, as do the initial delegation.

14. Don't succumb to the temptation of "post-delegation hovering." That is, don't keep looking over the delegatee's shoulder to check if things are going as planned. If you insist on breathing down people's necks, expect a reaction such as: "Am I responsible for this job or aren't I? One more question from the boss about how I'm doing on SV-4 and I'll ask her if she wants to finish the job herself." Remember, the operative concepts in delegation are "trust" and "self-restraint." Instead of worrying hourly about how things are going, rely on the control procedures or system you have established to learn how well the delegation is proceeding.

15. Don't delegate a problem accompanied by a solution. That is to say, don't ask a subordinate to resolve a problem or difficulty and simultaneously imply an answer—or worse still, *the* answer. Why not? Because if you provide a possible solution you are compounding things by giving the would-be problem solver two problems: the stated problem, and what to do about your feelings regarding your proposed solution to the problem.

I recall a situation of this sort when I was directing training for a large organization. We had an intensive, six-month management development program for six to eight carefully selected young supervisors who were brought in to Washington from the field. After six months of getting "the big picture," they typically returned to the field. They generally received promotions and reassignments sometime after their return to the field, but not immediately. One group of graduate trainees, feeling that they might get lost in the shuffle, wrote a joint letter to our director asking for refresher training to keep "alive" the things they had learned in their Washington training experience. The organization chief wrote this note on their memo: "Why not work up some kind of correspondence course for them?" The director felt that he was responding to their request for more training and at a low cost, too. Of course, the ex-trainees were really seeking visibility, rather than just some more training. In any case, I had the awkward task

of not only responding to the trainee's concerns, but how "to rebut" the approach that the director seemed to favor.

16. Don't permit your delegatees to delegate their responsibilities upward—"reverse delegation" as it is often called. Their job is to implement the agreed-upon delegation to the fullest extent possible. In the military this is known as "completed staff work." So if employees bring their relatively routine problems to you for resolution, insist that they develop some options (alternate solutions) before you engage in discussions about them. You may wish to ask them questions such as these: "What do *you* think should be done?" "What are the barriers that keep you from resolving this on your own?" "What action would you take if I were away on a field trip?" In this connection, management consultant Peter Yensen states that it is the manager's job "to manage others and manage situations, not solve every problem that pops up" ("The Manager Who Didn't," *Training News,* August 1986).

Management authority George Odiorne (in the *George Odiorne Letter,* Aug. 19, 1983) cites the following incident involving a superintendent and his boss, the manufacturing manager:

Supt.: I screwed up, Chief.
Boss: Can you unscrew it?
Supt.: (Nods assent)
Boss: Then unscrew it.

While the terse dialog may indicate a certain gruffness on the part of the boss, the more significant aspect of the brief conversation is that the latter had full confidence in the ability of his subordinate to correct his own mistake. He was certainly not inclined to intervene or take over. Note, too, that the boss exercised considerable self-restraint and resisted the all-too-frequent managerial temptation to pepper the errant subordinate with a lot of questions about the why, how, and what of the goof.

17. Don't overlook the need to communicate to interested and potentially affected parties that you have delegated certain responsibilities to a given subordinate. They may have a need to know of such assignments early on and shouldn't be alerted to the event on a surprise basis. ("No one told me that Janice now makes all the travel arrangements.")

18. Don't unload your disappointments and frustrations on a subordinate who occasionally goofs.

("How could you do this to me?") Expect certain miscues and use them as an opportunity for work review and added coaching. After all, errors are often a result of inadequate training or ambiguous instructions. So punishing the errant one via harsh words ("Didn't you know better?") or disgusted body language will only deter future risk taking.

19. Don't overlook the need to give credit and recognition for a delegated job well done. Progressive supervisors seek out such opportunities and subordinates appreciate the boss' supportiveness.

20. Don't embark on a "crash" program of delegation if you have been holding the reins tightly for a long time. Why not? For one thing, people may be highly suspicious of your newfound "religion" and leadership style. ("The boss is really doing a 180. I wonder what he's up to now?") For another, subordinates may not be ready—technically as well as psychologically—to assume heavy doses of new responsibility. The best strategy is to alter your delegating style gradually. People will be much more comfortable with that approach.

WHAT OUR DELEGATION PRACTICES COMMUNICATE

Our delegation practices are much more than abstract, formal acts that automatically put our staffers into motion on their jobs. Rather, whether we know it or not, or intend it or not, they communicate loud and clear to staff various things about our self-image, how we may feel about staff, and the values we place on the work itself. Management professor Dr. Rita T. Noel points up a number of communication implications of our approaches to delegation as follows ("What You Say to Your Employees When You Delegate," *Supervisory Management,* December 1993):

Values Placed on Particular Workers

Assignments to our staffers indicate whom we regard as most dependable. If we continue to lean on the same people because they are very capable and dependable, an inference may be drawn by those not so chosen that the chosen ones are the boss' pets.

Continued delegation of a majority of tasks to the same staffers may communicate that these people have little else to do or that their own work should take a

backseat to the assigned tasks. Both of these messages are potential motivation squelchers. And if we delegate few meaningful tasks, the staffer's perception is likely to be that he is not regarded highly by the boss.

Value Placed on Tasks

If the glory tasks are restricted to a select few or only to ourselves, we communicate that we have a closed autocratic environment.

The manager may also err in assuming that the employee will regard a particular task to be of considerable value, e.g., taking a customer to the airport may provide one with a bit of a breather. But the employee's perception of the task may be that it's a means of dumping an undesirable, low-order job on someone. The answer? Work hard at ferreting out staffers' perceptions of tasks prior to making the assignments.

Value Placed on Style

New managers may operate in different ways. One may wish to hit the ground running and delegate at a super-rapid speed. Another may study his staff to learn of their capabilities regarding particular tasks. The point is that one's approach to task assignment communicates one's managerial style.

Similarly, delegation presented formally via memo vs. on a an informal, verbal basis communicates other style and personality characteristics: cold vs. warm, aloof vs. friendly, disinterested vs. supportive.

The answer to these unintended consequences of one's delegation practices? Get to know your staffers more intimately and seek feedback as to their feelings and values about particular tasks.

YOUR DELEGATION QUOTIENT: A SELF-ASSESSMENT

Now that you have read the text on delegation concepts and techniques, you undoubtedly are curious as to your own skill as a delegator. If so, you will want to take the self-quiz (inventory) which follows. The quiz contains instructions for scoring and has a worksheet for self-analysis and improvement planning.

MDQ (My Delegation Quotient) Inventory

The MDQ Inventory is designed to give you a reading concerning your delegation practices and attitudes. Please read all quiz items carefully and respond to them as candidly as you can. Honest responses on your part will make this self-quiz a meaningful and helpful tool for you.

If you are a new or future delegator, you may have a little difficulty responding to some of the items. If so, answer them as you think you would if you were a seasoned manager.

Procedure: Enter an A next to the quiz items with which you agree. Enter a D next to all quiz items with which you disagree. Scoring instructions are provided at the end of the inventory.

1____I am careful to avoid doing things my subordinates could do in lieu of me.

2____Because it is highly important to be in control of things, I prefer to do many tasks myself.

3____When I delegate responsibility, I ensure that subordinates have full authority to do the job properly.

4____If it is essential to get a job done right, I simply do it myself.

5____When I delegate tasks, my subordinates are clear about standards of performance—quantity, quality, time frames, cost.

6____It is frequently easier and quicker to do a job myself than to explain to a subordinate what needs to be done.

7____Even though it is time-consuming, I explain complex tasks to subordinates to avoid doing them myself.

8____I tend to delegate tasks I don't care to do and personally perform those I enjoy doing.

9____I coach my staff in depth if they lack the qualifications/background/experience that I have. I thus avoid doing many tasks myself.

10____To ensure that a job gets done well, I specify the methods (the "how" of the job) to be used to accomplish the task.

11____I delegate with the thought that my subordinates' approaches to a job, which may be unlike mine, may produce new, creative ways of doing things.

12____I tend to check closely on tasks in progress to ensure their proper performance.

13____I delegate with the thought that it is a good way to help people to grow to their fullest potential.

14____I spend more time on work details than I do on planning.

15____When delegating I consider whether the subordinate will like the assigned task.

16____I find that I spend much more time on my job than my employees do on theirs. But that is OK because I am the boss.

17____I am able to take errors committed by my staff in stride, for I don't want to destroy their motivation or enthusiasm, or our relationship.

18____I tend to check closely on the work in progress to be certain that errors are kept to a minimum.

19____I provide the fullest possible training so that my employees can work out their own problems thereafter.

20____To speed up a job or problem that my people are working on, I tend to draw on my greater experience and simply provide them with the right answers.

21____I avoid spending time on the details of jobs because others could handle them as well as I can.

22____To keep up with my workload, I find it necessary to take work home evenings and weekends.

23____I encourage other supervisors to deal directly with my staff on matters with which they (the supervisors) are concerned.

24____I expect good work and pay properly for it. I thus don't see the need to give people a lot of pats on the back for work they are paid to do.

25____I have enough time to meet with my subordinates on any and all of their problems or concerns.

26____When my people make mistakes that they should not, I let them know "loud and clear" how I feel.

27____I find that I have adequate time for planning, meetings, training sessions, handling contingencies, and special problems.

28____I find that I have to be very careful about delegating because the work may not get done the way I like it.

29____I review my job periodically (every 3 to 6 months) to see whether I can increase my delegations to my staff.

30____I check regularly (every 3 to 6 months) to learn whether my staff members have enough authority to do their delegated tasks properly.

31___I check regularly (every 3 to 6 months) with my people to see whether they feel I should delegate added duties or responsibilities.

32___I am regarded by my boss as a good delegator.

33___I am regarded by my employees as a good delegator.

Scoring

Step 1

a) In the first two columns below, enter all of your A responses. Do not enter any D responses in these two columns.

b) In the last two columns, enter all of your D responses. Do not enter any A responses in these two columns.

"A" responses		"D" responses	
1___	21___	2___	16___
3___	23___	4___	18___
5___	25___	6___	20___
7___	27___	8___	22___
9___	29___	10___	24___
11___	30___	12___	26___
13___	31___	14___	28___
15___	32___		
17___	33___		
19___			

Step 2

Count the number of As and Ds in the above columns and enter the totals here:

As___ Ds___

Step 3

a) Give yourself 3 points for all items you marked A (Agree). Total points (number of As times 3).

b) Give yourself 3 points for all items you marked D (for Disagree). Total points (number of Ds times 3).

Step 4

Combine your A and D scores. Total points___. This is your MDQ.

Step 5: Interpretation of scores

The items in the first two columns represent *desirable* delegating practices and attitudes. The items in the last two columns represent *undesirable* practices and attitudes. If your total points are:

90–99. Congratulations! You are an A-1 delegator. Your delegation attitudes and behaviors undoubtedly please your staff and possibly your boss as well.

75–87. You are doing a fair job of delegating now. However, there is room for a strengthening of some of your delegation habits and outlooks. See Steps 5 and 6 for help on this.

72 and below. Your delegation practices would seem to require considerable improvement. Be sure to do the tasks given in Steps 5 and 6. After scoring, go back to the items for which you have received no points and do two things:

1. Ask yourself: Why do I behave or feel this way?
2. Respond in writing to this statement: "I could improve my behavior/attitude as a delegator" by:

A. _____
B. _____
C. _____
D. _____
E. _____
F. _____
G. _____

Step 6

Set up a plan to follow up on your plans for improvement at 3- to 6-month intervals. Feedback from your staff will help on this.

KEY POINTS: THE MANAGER AS DELEGATOR

☐ Believes firmly in the value and benefits of delegation.

☐ Supports his beliefs by delegating, to the extent practicable, broadly (to all staffers) and deeply (as opposed to partial delegation).

☐ Involves subordinates in the delegation process to be certain that delegations are realistic, understood, and accepted.

☐ Employs proper control procedures in support of all delegations.

☐ Utilizes delegation consciously as a tool to develop people and to encourage innovation.

☐ Secures feedback from staff periodically to assess (1) how well delegations are proceeding (e.g., Do people have enough authority to discharge their responsibilities?) and (2) whether added delegations are feasible.

☐ Encourages subordinate supervisors, if any, to delegate as broadly and fully as possible and reviews periodically their delegation practices.

☐ Recognizes that one's delegation practices communicate to staff values placed on particular staffers, values placed on particular tasks, and the nature of one's managerial style.

QUESTIONS, EXERCISES AND PROBLEMS FOR DISCUSSION IN MANAGEMENT TRAINING WORKSHOPS AND COLLEGE/UNIVERSITY CLASSES IN MANAGEMENT AND SUPERVISION

The following situations and problems are designed to stimulate thinking and discussion about typical problems and situations in the area of delegation. They may be discussed in small groups or in the group at large. A number of the situations lend themselves to the role-playing technique, particularly Nos. 1, 2, 4, 5, 6, 7, 8, 9, 10.

1. You have delegated a project you estimate for completion in six weeks. A week after the assignment you realize that your subordinate can't handle it properly. What do you do and when?

2. A delegated task is completed. Unfortunately, it is poorly done. What do you do?

3. Mgr. Joe Browne has attended a management development workshop and shortly thereafter he begins to delegate with a great deal of enthusiasm. Several weeks later he feels that he has overdelegated and is in danger of losing control. Two questions: a) What indicators might Joe have used to get a reading about his possible over-delegation? and b) If widespread over-delegation has taken place, what can Joe do about it?

4. Mgr. Mae Forbes finds that one-half of her eight employees are reluctant to take on added responsibilities. What can Mae do about it?

5. You believe strongly in delegation. Your boss, however, expects you to know everything about your operation. He is dismayed when you tell him: "I'll have to check that detail out and get back to you." What might you do to get your boss to support your enlightened delegation practices?

6. Subordinate June Ames wishes to take on more responsibility as a means of securing a promotion. You feel June is barely holding her own on her regularly assigned work. What do you do?

7. Subordinate Tom White keeps trying to get you to fall for his reverse delegation ploys. What might you do to stop Tom's attempts at upward delegation once and for all?

8. You are fairly new on your job. You find that your boss, who knows your subordinates quite well, frequently delegates tasks directly to some of your senior people. (Your boss was in your job for several years before you came to it.) You are unhappy with this situation. What are your options to try to change your boss' delegation practice? Select one option and develop in detail how you would implement it.

9. You feel that you know your job well and could handle more responsibility. Your boss shows no signs of "letting go." What do you do?

10. You are in charge of the Legislative Liasion Division for the County Government. You have a subordinate who has the responsibility of contacting State legislators in the State capitol, which is located some 45 miles away from the County Government Office. The contacts may be made day or night, depending on when your subordinate is able to "corral" a particular legislator. The contacts are very important because they provide a chance to explain the county's viewpoint on issues which may affect the county. Your subordinate, who is a woman, has the authority to decide whether she will stay overnight in a hotel if she gets delayed. Her stayovers are quite frequent in the three-month period when the State Legislature is in session. But you have some doubts about the need to stay over on numerous other occasions when the legislature does not meet. What should you do, if anything?

11. Set up a four-column chart and enter the following data:

a) The kinds of responsibilities which you find you can delegate easily.

b) The kinds of responsibilities you rarely delegate.

c) The kinds of responsibilities your boss always delegates.

d) The kinds of responsibilities your boss rarely delegates.

Note: You are to list *kinds* or *types* of tasks, not the tasks themselves.

Compare the data in the four columns for similarities, differences, possible rational/irrational behaviors.

12. What is the relationship of communication to delegation. When should it take place? Why?

13. What attitudes facilitate the delegation process?

14. What skills should a manager have to be an effective delegator?

15. Division Chief Barnes has 6 branches under him. Each branch has different functions. Barnes is new on the job and expects to delegate to the same degree to all branches. Is Barnes on the right track. Why or why not?

16. You have a problem you wish to delegate to a subordinate for resolution. You can delegate the problem-solving task in two ways:

    Full delegation: Let the subordinate tackle it entirely on his own, on an open-ended basis.

    Partial delegation: Suggest one or two possible approaches for resolution of the problem. What are the pros and cons of each approach? Which approach do you favor in light of your current style and philosophy of delegation? How would your boss respond to the latter question?

17. Assume you have been asked to explain to a group of new supervisors the best procedures to make delegation effective. What pointers or principles would you pass along to them? Would your presentation differ if the supervisors were much more experienced? If so, how?

18. What kinds of duties or responsibilities might a supervisor justifiably *not* delegate?

19. Assume every delegation has an element of risk. What might you do to reduce it and still keep it a genuine act of delegation?

20. A principle of communication is that the meaning of messages is in the nervous systems of the receiver and the sender, not in the message itself. Thus, in the area of delegation, it is not unusual for the supervisor to perceive his act of delegation to be one of deep or full delegation; however, the delegatee may perceive it differently. What measures can the supervisor take to ensure that both parties perceive the delegation similarly?

21. Where delegation has not worked—or where you encountered problems with delegation—what were the reasons?

22. Under what conditions does delegation work best?

Figure 6-2.
Guidesheet to Delegate Realistically

Tasks/Responsibilities That I *Must* Perform (1)	Tasks/Responsibilities That I Can Delegate *Now* (2)	Tasks/Responsibilities That I Can Delegate With Added Training (3)	Name of Delegatee (Indicate Whether Task/ Responsibility Relates to Column No. (2) or (3)) (4)
1. _____	1. _____	1. _____	1. _____
2. _____	2. _____	2. _____	2. _____
3. _____	3. _____	3. _____	3. _____
4. _____	4. _____	4. _____	4. _____
5. _____	5. _____	5. _____	5. _____
6. _____	6. _____	6. _____	6. _____
7. _____	7. _____	7. _____	7. _____
8. _____	8. _____	8. _____	8. _____
9. _____	9. _____	9. _____	9. _____
10. _____	10. _____	10. _____	10. _____
11. _____	11. _____	11. _____	11. _____
12. _____	12. _____	12. _____	12. _____
13. _____	13. _____	13. _____	13. _____
14. _____	14. _____	14. _____	14. _____
15. _____	15. _____	15. _____	15. _____

The Manager as a Coach: How to Upgrade Performance and Develop Your Staff

Very few are wise by their own counsel: or learned by their own teaching. For he that was only taught by himself, had a fool for his master.

> —Ben Jonson (1572–1637), English dramatist,
> poet, satirist, and moralist

Learning teacheth more in one year than experience in twenty.

> —Roger Ascham (1516–68), English scholar, writer, humanist and
> tutor to Queen Elizabeth in the classics

I am not a teacher. I am an AWAKENER.

> —Mark Twain (1835–1910), U.S. author and humorist

As a field, management has evolved in a hierarchical model of organization. Coaching requires a more interrelated and dynamic vision of organization based more on relationship, commitment, purpose, and results than on role, hierarchical position, prescribed order, and authority.

> —Roger D. Evered and James C. Selman, "Coaching and the Art
> of Management," *Organizational Dynamics,*
> Autumn 1989

I focus on their progress, not their failures.

> —Paul "Bear" Bryant, coach at the University of Alabama for 25
> years and the most successful coach in major college football (six
> national championships, 323 victories). Quoted in *Training,*
> August 1988

People need information that supports their positive self images, eases their consciences, and refuels them psychologically.

—Harry Levinson, *Harvard Business Review,*
May–June 1981

The terms "coaching" and "counseling" are typically used interchangeably in the workplace. However, from the standpoint of your skill development, it will be more helpful to you if you regard them as separate activities requiring different objectives and different approaches (skills) as well.

Let's define our terms. Coaching, as I'll treat it here, relates to ongoing, day-to-day efforts by the manager/supervisor to upgrade performance and develop people more fully. The objective is to empower people—tap their potential and unleash their creativity—to secure their fullest possible commitment to organizational objectives and their own jobs.

Counseling, which is discussed in the next chapter, is concerned with these two areas:

☐ The giving of guidance and advice on careers. This, typically, is done with and for one's own staff or, in other cases, with others, in one's capacity as a mentor.

☐ Dealing with "difficult" employees and those who are experiencing emotional problems of varying degrees.

In more specific terms, this chapter is concerned with the variety of skill areas shown in Figure 7-1, "Coaching Skills Sequence." Each of them will be discussed in turn. Delegation, which is part of the coaching sequence, was discussed in detail in Chapter 6.

The chapter closes with:

☐ A self-quiz to provide you with an opportunity to check your prowess as a coach.

☐ A rating form—"Coaching Practices Review"—which can be used by yourself, optionally, to get some feedback from your staff concerning how they see you as a coach.

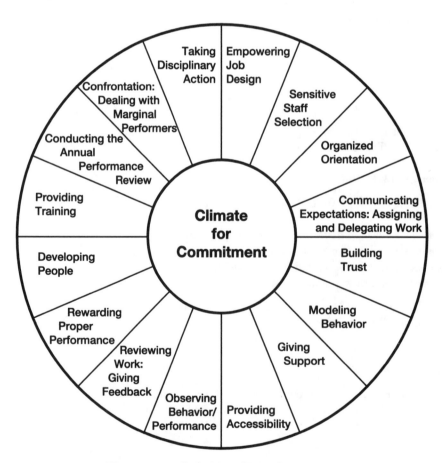

Figure 7-1. Coaching Skills Sequence.

USING JOB DESIGN FOR EMPOWERMENT AND WORK IMPROVEMENT

Insightful coaches think constantly in terms of empowering their staffs. That is, they are actively concerned about getting commitment of staff via jobs that provide opportunities for self-management, offer challenge, tap potential, and encourage growth on the job.

Unfortunately, many jobs are designed in such a way that they produce boredom and low sense of self-esteem. And this often is true not only of routine, assembly-line jobs, but of higher level positions as well. A major source of the problem is the antiquated notion that we can get greater efficiency by splitting jobs into small, specialized bits. But what is overlooked is that narrow, limited, impoverished jobs produce boredom, diminished job interest, reduced sense of responsibility, and stagnation rather than job growth.

So what can the manager do in the way of job design so that people will become turned on rather than turned off as a result of their daily efforts? Performance technologist Jay Huntington Hume ("Can We 'Go with the Flow' at Work?", *Performance and Instruction,* February 1992) cites these characteristics of jobs that can empower people:

The Job Itself

First, people require jobs that are so organized that they have a clear, worthwhile goal. They need to know that what they are doing is important and what success on their part will look like. Second, workers require immediate feedback about their accomplishments. They don't want to do a lot of wheel spinning and worrying about whether they are on the right track or whether they hit the target. Successful performance in itself is a tremendous empowerer. Third, employees want to know when a job is complete. They very much need a sense of closure on their activities. And lastly, the work should be organized so that concentration on the required task is certain. Conversely, jobs that are fragmented or subject to many interruptions don't allow for full concentration and high performance.

The Fit Between the Job and the Performer

The work should be so organized that it demands of the performer that a significant skill be exercised. Note that this is a means of producing challenge based on work that is neither too simple, so that only skin-surface abilities are tapped, nor too complex so that it asks for skills the performer doesn't have. In the latter circumstance, frustration rather than challenge will result. The operative concept, then, is a proper fit or match in skill requirements between the work and worker. A second condition of it relates to control by the worker over the work flow. (Visualize the frustration of a pharmacist if he were told which steps to take, how to do them, and their sequence when filling all his prescriptions.) Autonomy or independence is a powerful empowerer of performers.

The Performer

Empowered performers are deeply involved in their tasks. There may be problems, but they are regarded as highly interesting rather than merely frustrating. The usual anxieties on the job are replaced by a deep involvement of the worker in the task. People in this state are so engrossed that they lose concern for self; the task and the performer are blended into a single entity. And finally, the job is so worthwhile and involving that the performer experiences an altered sense of time. Time moves so swiftly that the performer has no awareness of it.

The bottom line, then, is that jobs and tasks that are properly organized and designed—enriched (varied) rather than impoverished, involving rather than disengaging, feedback-giving rather than silent as to outcomes, self-managing rather than controlling, and liberating rather than frustrating—will be empowering (i.e., enabling and challenging) rather than diminishing of one's sense of self-worth. Work is more likely to have a "fun" component to it, too.

Note: Obviously there will be a small percentage of employees, depending on the particular type of work, who are not "self-starters" and who do not have strong needs for self-management. They, of course, will require more structure, more direction, more control. However, the supportive coach will operate on the assumption that most people crave opportunities for self-direction and will so organize the work until proven otherwise.

Another approach to job design is offered by performance technologist Dr. Dean Spitzer ("Performance Improvement Ideas-4," *Performance and Instruction,* April 1988). He has identified 14 job design issues which, if addressed properly, can have a positive effect on work improvement. The design issues are:

1. **Effectiveness:** Is the task accomplishing what it is supposed to?
2. **Unnecessary steps:** Could any steps in established procedures be dropped or combined?
3. **Delays and bottlenecks:** Are there any holdups in the work process causing people to wait for a prior step to be completed?
4. **Closure:** Can the worker see the results of his accomplishment before starting a new task?
5. **Pacing:** Is the task being executed at the appropriate pace for both the workers and the system?
6. **Worker control/input:** Do workers have an adequate degree of control and say on how the work is done (work process)?
7. **Meaningfulness:** Are the purpose and context of the task/activity operation clear?
8. **Variety:** Is there enough variety in the work process to encourage motivation?
10. **Work distribution:** Is there an even distribution of work among the workers?
11. **Feedback:** Is feedback being provided as a motivator?
12. **Man-machine interface:** To what degree are mechanized work systems designed to facilitate effective use by the operators?
13. **Documentation:** Is documentation (procedural information) to help workers do the job right the first time adequate?
14. **Training:** Is the training provided meeting identified needs?

A third approach to job design is, to the extent practicable, to design the job around the employee's strength. Rick L. Lansing ("Training New Employees," *Supervisory Management,* January 1989) advises making a "knowledge/skills analysis" of the new employee's capacities. That is, ascertain (develop a list) of what the employee needs to know or do and compare it to what he knows and can do now (a second list). On the basis of the two lists, a set of objectives can be developed to provide maximum challenge for the worker. Lansing quotes Arthur Schwartz, president of a business training and consulting firm who states: "Many organizations and managers are increasingly designing jobs to make use of their employees' strengths."

To sum up: Empowering jobs are the route to motivation and commitment. But they do not occur by themselves. Careful thought and work are required to make them happen. Use of the above ideas are mechanisms to achieve this goal.

SELECTING STAFFERS SENSITIVELY

Managing performance, as every athletic coach knows extremely well, begins with the raw material with which one has to work. Coaches, of course, are paid to produce and inspire high performing athletes. But coaches are not miracle workers. They can capitalize on their coaching skills only to the extent that their recruits have the potential and will to learn and perform.

Thus, the coaching cycle begins with recruitment and selection of those candidates with the most promising talents in relation to the *needs* of the team. All of which means that the selection process has to be approached with a maximum degree of sophistication and care. For no one wants to be saddled with people who can't or won't perform in the fashion necessary to get the job done well.

Although there are no sure-fire rules to pick "winners" every time, there are better ways to go about the task of selecting people for hire. Richard Pinsker advises how to avoid "the seven deadly sins" in hiring ("Training Today: Seven Deadly Sins in Hiring," *Training,* May 1992). Mr. Pinsker is the author of *Hiring Winners* (New York: AMACOM, 1991). These hiring mistakes are:

Defining the Job too Broadly

Job requirements must be pinpointed to the results you expect. If your requirements are not stated with specificity, you won't screen out those who can't perform as well as you wish. If you are specific in your requirements, you can develop a candidate pool with the kind of accomplishments for which you are looking. So keep your job specifications very precise.

Example: If you are a housing contractor and require someone who is highly skilled in aluminum siding work, you can't settle for a general building craftsman who is great on porches and rec rooms but who had done siding work only on occasion.

Restricting Candidate Sources

A common error is to limit possible sources of recruitment. In fact, a highly worthwhile recruiting source, says Pinsker, is your own workforce. He recommends building the recruitment function into everyone's job description. Some companies even pay bonuses to their employees for every referral they make that ends up as an actual hire.

Conducting Ineffective Interviews

Although many managers believe they know how to interview job applicants properly, all too often interviews produce little in the way of essential information. To overcome this deficiency, the manager in his recruiting effort should (a) begin with a full knowledge of job requirements; (b) ask probing questions about education and job history; (c) keep the applicant talking some 80% of the interviewing time; (d) pose real problems to test ability to think and respond quickly and meaningfully; and (e) take notes to show your interest in the person, as well as for reference purposes later when you have to compare the several applicants you have interviewed. Recognize that memory can be an unreliable tool.

Succumbing to the "Halo Effect"

Don't make the assumption that quality performance in one function will carry over to another one. Thus, an outstanding electronics engineer isn't automatically the best selection for a *managing* engineer post. Much more probing and assessing is essential prior to the making of that all-important final decision.

Hiring in Desperation

If you are badly in need of hiring someone, you can fall victim to hasty hiring decisions, including being trapped by the "Halo Effect." The cost of selecting a poor candidate is too great to engage in wishful thinking and taking hiring shortcuts. Poor selections may not only impact internally (e.g., produce lowered morale), but externally as well (e.g., create customer irritation).

Overlooking Intuition

The above points relate to the logic of candidate review and selection. But intuition has an important role to play, too. So listen with your "third ear," heed your inner voice, don't disregard your gut feelings. If there was something about a candidate's remark or style that bothered you, that seemed to penetrate and stick in your subconscious mind, regard it as a big, red flag. So Pinsker advises: "When in doubt, don't."

Don't Disregard Reference Checking

Sure, some people won't respond candidly on a reference check due to fear of being sued for having provided a negative comment about an ex-employee. But reference checks still can be productive, says Pinsker, if you observe these two rules: (a) ask every reference for another person you can check with, and (b) observe good interviewing procedures when talking to the reference. This means posing interview-like questions and zeroing in on actual candidate accomplishments. Your reference checks should be conducted only with people who supervised or worked closely with the candidate. Don't expect much help from human resource professionals in the personnel office who can only provide second-hand, filtered information.

ORIENTATION: GETTING THE NEW GUY OFF TO A GOOD START

"No one knew that I was to start today."

"The boss gave me so much information the first two hours . . ."

"If my first day is typical of how they're organized . . ."

"The job doesn't seem to be what I thought it was."

"I thought someone would volunteer to take me to lunch, but . . ."

"By the end of the day I wasn't sure that I would return the next day."

Do the above statements of frustration and disappointment of new workers ring familiar? If so, it would not be surprising, for orientation of the new worker is an aspect of the coaching process that all too often is done on a somewhat casual, indifferent basis.

On-the-job orientation by the manager, irrespective of what the personnel or training office may or may not do, has these worthwhile purposes:

☐ To reduce the new worker's anxieties.

☐ To make him feel welcome, that he is important to the unit.

☐ To get him into production as soon as possible.

☐ To help develop a positive attitude about the job, the unit, the total organization.

☐ To communicate the boss's expectations about the work.

☐ To create a positive first impression of the shop or office.

☐ To integrate the new worker into the established work team.

☐ To provide guidance concerning office values, norms, protocols, procedures, objectives.

□ To learn of the new worker's concerns, if any, encouraging him to ask questions.

□ To remove possible misconceptions about duties and responsibilities, standards, conduct, etc.

□ To reduce turnover by reducing first-day anxieties, frustrations, disappointments.

What the above objectives suggest are two basic principles of effective orientation:

1. "Failing to plan is planning to fail." A cliché? Yes, but also a very sound concept.
2. "You pay for a good orientation program, whether you have one or not" (stated by Howard Schwartz, president of Video Genesis, Inc., Cleveland, in *Audio Visual Communications,* March 1991).

As we indicated, a major objective of the orientation process is to help the new worker "fit in" to the established organization. Linda J. Segall ("Integrating Your New Employee into the Organization," *Supervisory Management,* February 1986), offers these guidelines to speed up the individual's integration into the organization:

□ Watch for and then counsel the new worker to de-emphasize "newness" behaviors. **Example:** a heavy use of "we/you," i.e., the use of "we" to refer to the new employee's prior employer and "you" to the new firm or unit; offering numerous incidents/anecdotes of the prior job; comparisons to policies and facilities of the previous employer; "I-can-do-it-ness": a too-eager willingness to do things before he is fully accepted. The understanding manager will discourage "newness" behaviors, for they are very likely to discourage his colleagues' acceptance of the new hire.

□ Define the new worker's role clearly to both the new worker and the staff.

□ Establish the frequency to which the new person is to "check in" with you; spell out authority levels; indicate how independently he is to operate, etc.

□ Make a point of holding regular and frequent one-on-one meetings with the new person. Provide praise when things go well; show concern and give support when they don't.

□ Provide insight into the ongoing culture: key authority figures, protocols, procedures, politics, where channels must be observed and where they can be short-circuited a bit, etc.

□ Include the new worker in meetings, advising whether his role is that of full participant or observer.

□ Provide opportunities for "visibility." You want your new worker to become recognized as quickly as possible as a regular, valued staffer.

The best way to ensure that the orientation process goes smoothly on Day One is to develop and use a checklist, such as the one on page 324, of the points you plan to cover and the actions you intend to take. You may wish to add other items to the list.

Note: The above discussion relates to the emphasis to be placed on orientation on Day One. However, this does not mean that the new employee is to be "abandoned" thereafter. Make a point, then, to touch base frequently with the new worker in the early days and weeks after entrance on duty. The added contacts are necessary to answer questions, to show interest in him as a person, to give encouragement and support, to build confidence, to learn of possible dissatisfactions, to learn of possible training needs, etc.

COMMUNICATING EXPECTATIONS: ASSIGNING AND DELEGATING WORK FOR MOTIVATION AND COMMUNICATION

"The boss never really spells out what he wants me to do and then he gets mad if I goof it up."

"If my supervisor would only take enough time to outline my assignments . . ."

"Sometimes I think the boss doesn't know herself what she wants."

Have you ever heard an employee voice these concerns? You probably have. Certainly as a manager you have your expectations about what is wanted from a particular assignment. The challenge is to communicate fully so that your expectations become your subordinate's expectations. The suggestions that follow should help to ensure that there is mutual understanding of the "parameters"—goals, standards, tools and resources, boundaries, priorities, reporting requirements—for a given task.

1. Recognize at the outset that people are different. They have different needs for accomplishment, different degrees of ability to understand what is wanted, different styles of execution of a task.

2. Thus, plan your presentation of an assignment in relation to the capacities, interests, and style of the employee.

3. Highlight the key elements of the task—the "make or break" factors of a job done well. Obviously, some aspects of the job to be done are more important than others.

4. Pass along key points to make the job easier or certain to succeed. Also point out pitfalls that may arise as the task progresses. As appropriate, stress safety requirements, too.

5. Advise as to who to see for information or help as the project proceeds. Candidly admit that you may not have all the answers.

6. Allow time for the employee to ask questions about the assignment. But don't fall into the trap of assuming that the absence of questions equates with full understanding. Instead, ask the worker to restate in his own words what he has been asked to do. Phrase your request so that it does not produce irritation or defensiveness. **Not:** "OK, tell me what I told you so there won't be any slip up." **Better:** "Could you sum up what you see the job to be so you and I can be sure that we're on the same wavelength?"

7. Watch assignments that are marked by role conflict and role ambiguity. Karl Krayer ("Using Training to Reduce Role Conflict and Ambiguity," *Training and Development Journal,* November 1986) refers to role conflict as a situation in which two or more pressures—incompatible task instructions—exist simultaneously and make it difficult to execute the assignment properly. **Example:** A manager assigns a project to be executed on a fully delegated basis. ("It's your baby, Kim. Give it your best shot.") But Kim soon finds that his boss engages in constant informal checks to ensure that "everything is going according to plan" and insists on providing procedural advice. Or nurses in hospital settings may receive conflicting demands from their supervisors vs. the physicians.

   Role ambiguity occurs when instructions are vague, incomplete, or contradictory. **Example:** A sales clerk is advised to be very cooperative in accepting returned merchandise; but he may not be told that if the customer wants a refund rather than an exchange, that a lengthy form has to be completed, a supervisor's signature is required on the form, and the refund can only be made by

check, which the customer will receive from corporate headquarters in 10–15 days.

8. If an assignment is multi-faceted, consider giving both oral *and* written instructions. The latter will reinforce the former and eliminate later hassles about what was really wanted. As a tool to guide your assignment of work, the form given in Figure 7-2, "Worksheet for Task Assignment" (page 325), should be considered. Prepare the form in duplicate, giving one copy to the employee and retain the second copy for your own use.

9. If you have your doubts about the employee's ability to get going on the assignment, work closely with him on it in the initial stages. Your investment of coaching time at the outset may save time in the long run.

10. Don't treat every assignment as "an emergency" or "totally unique." You can cry wolf only a limited number of times.

11. A significant aspect of the task assignment process is to develop employee interest in it. Explain the "why" of it, i.e., what makes it important to the unit or even the total organization. Employees will be more fired up if they are in on the "big picture." Management professors Barry L. Wisdom and D. Keith Denton ("Manager as Teacher," *Training and Development,* December 1991) see the manager in broad terms as a teacher. They state: "When a manager tells a worker to do a task, he or she discharges the responsibilities of the moment. When a manager teaches the worker the elements, logic, and interrelationships inherent in a system, he makes a downpayment on the future of the organization."

12. Consider timing, too. Give the assignment when both you and the assignee are adequately relaxed. Poor timing would be just before lunch or quitting time.

13. Look for body language that indicates indifference (e.g., not paying full attention), irritation (e.g., tenseness), confusion (e.g., a puzzled look), doubt (e.g., a frown), enthusiasm (forward leans, smiles, head nods, more rapid speech), and so on. Based on the non-verbal feedback you receive, you can adjust the delivery of your instructions accordingly, possibly restating or rephrasing them as necessary.

14. When an employee comes to you for help after he has gotten started on his assignment, ask yourself afterward whether this visit was really necessary. It

may be that with clearer and fuller instructions, a request for help may not have been needed. What we are suggesting, then, is to think continually in terms of how well you are functioning as an assigner of work and what you can do to upgrade your prowess in this aspect of the coaching job.

15. Use the work assignment process as a means of developing your staff. Specifically, think in terms of stretch, i.e., provide assignments that provide opportunities for greater challenge, new experiences, acquiring broader understanding, added productivity, etc.

16. A final skill pointer, which is really an opener: If possible start your assignment sessions with a reference to a prior task that was completed well: "I was pleased with your handling of the last customer complaint problem. I thought that you really went out of your way to satisfy her." Praise in respect to a recently completed task, which thus is *task specific* rather than merely global in nature, is a good way to set a positive, friendly, and supportive tone for the work assignment meeting.

In assigning work, you should also define the nature of the delegation that goes with it. In view of the importance of delegation plus the various ramifications of it, we have treated it separately in Chapter 7.

BUILDING TRUST

Be sincere—even if you don't really mean it.

—Slogan on a bumper sticker

Note that we say *building* trust since it is an element in an interpersonal and group relationship that develops gradually. A trusting relationship implies a high degree of confidence between/among the parties which, obviously, cannot materialize by issuing a directive or waving a magic wand. Trust has to be earned over time.

In everyday parlance, trust means that we can count on someone to keep his word, to do what he has promised, to meet commitments, to act ethically. But in interpersonal relationships involving an authority figure (the boss) and a subordinate, trust also relates to the feeling by the subordinate that he can communicate upward freely without any fear of penalty or recrimination. The communication may relate to technical matters, both good and bad news, and sharing feelings

freely about what is going on. In essence, employees want to know whether it is appropriate (safe) to speak up, to criticize, to report bad tidings, to advance new ideas, to share feelings (concerns, anxieties, hopes, fears, ambitions)—to do all these things without having one's head chopped off or living in fear that it may be.

In specific terms, then, how does the boss develop trust? He must engage in these kinds of behaviors:

Intimacy. There must be an attempt to get close to people, to let others know how you think and feel and who you really are. After all, how can one trust someone one doesn't really know? Intimacy permits one to feel comfortable with the other party which can lead to honest communication.

Giving Support and Encouragement. People like to feel that the boss is on their side, that there is a partnership rather than an uncertain and even an adversarial relationship. Thus, the boss shows confidence in the subordinate and takes pains to say positive things about the work performed.

Sharing information freely. The boss who expects full information from the staff is more likely to get it if he shares freely the information he has. It is a phenomenon akin to an ever-widening versus an ever-restricting circle. The more you give, the more you get back. Conversely the less you give, the less you will receive in return.

Championing the team. The boss has to show that he is really in there working for the team's betterment. This means, among other things, going to bat for the team with his superior to help the team thrive and succeed in its mission. And, incidentally, authentic team leaders talk about "our" team rather than "my" team.

Approachability. Intimacy can produce approachability. But the boss must work at this because his higher status tends to interfere with his approachability. But the boss has a choice—he can encourage perceptions that make him approachable or those which cause him to appear aloof and distant. Approachability can be developed via MBWA (Management by Walking Around): visits to subordinates' turf to discuss problems; foregoing some of the usual perks such as the large private office, executive parking, executive dining room, long social lunches, etc.; permitting one to be called by one's given name; joining the staff for lunch and/or coffee on occasion; admitting error ("Boy, I really goofed on that one").

Listening non-punitively. It also helps to have both open ears and an open mind. While not every idea advanced by a staffer need be accepted, people do expect that some of them will. And those that don't get a fair hearing and a full explanation of why they are short of the mark.

Tolerance of error. People who work actively at their jobs inevitably will commit an occasional error. No one likes mistakes, but they do occur. Lowering the boom because of a boo-boo will discourage initiative and creativity, and reduce approachability. So the wisest course of action is understanding and tolerance. After all, no one commits mistakes willfully. If anything, the error maker needs encouragement since he undoubtedly feels terrible for his dereliction. The commission of error is punishment in itself. Comments like: "You did your best," "It's hardly the end of the world," "Forget it. That's the way the ball bounces sometimes," can help to restore employee confidence and simultaneously build trust.

Story: In an important baseball game the center fielder dropped two fly balls in a row. In disgust, the manager substituted another player who promptly lost the ball in the sun on his first chance. So the manager made another substitution with, again, disastrous results. In a rage, the manager decided to take over the center field position himself. But he dropped an easy pop fly himself, which produced a torrent of runs thereafter. When the long inning finally ended, he came storming into the dugout, threw his glove down and exclaimed in disgust: "You guys have got center field so screwed up that no one can handle it out there!"

MODELING: MANAGEMENT BY EXAMPLE

People learn how to behave in a variety of ways. One way is to adopt the behavior of others. Behavioral scientists use the term "role model" to explain the adoption of behavior from persons with whom one identifies very strongly. Some examples of role models: parents, relatives, older brothers and sisters, teachers, top-flight athletes, TV and film stars, and bosses. One top-notch college football player told his TV audience that he has seen the Humphrey Bogart film classic "Casablanca" over 60

times, and that he watched the film before each game to help him get "psyched up" (ABC News, November 1987).

Humorist Mark Twain probably described the power of modeling best when he facetiously observed: "Few things are harder for people to put up with than the annoyance of a good example."

In organizations, the most logical source of modeling is the boss's behavior. But bosses may unwittingly encourage mediocre or even less than desirable behavior as well as the good.

People in organizations, as elsewhere, are constantly seeking cues and clues as to proper behavior. Seeking cues, you may ask? Aren't there tons of policies, procedures, rules, and regulations intended to prescribe behavior clearly? Of course. But what employees are really asking for are assurances that all the formal prescriptions mean what they say.

The search for cues may not necessarily proceed at the conscious level, but it goes on nevertheless. Your behavior, as the key person in your unit—authority figure, if you will—is a natural model for others. People (not necessarily everyone) thus will try to emulate your behavior.

This means you not only have to set and observe high standards in everything that you do, but that you have to be consistent in their application. People will do what you practice, not what you preach. **Examples:** You can't consistently take long lunch hours and expect others to adhere to the stated time requirements. Or you can't expect people to perform ethically in all respects, if you seem to be looking for sharp ways to skirt established environmental or ethical standards. Or you can't constantly criticize or gossip about people without expecting like behavior by your subordinates.

Or, as management authority George Odiorne put it, "Don't call in from the golf course to see if everyone has his or her nose to the grindstone. You can't expect everyone else to slave away if you don't show some commitment yourself" (*The George Odiorne Letter*, September 1980.

Management consultant Alan Jay Weiss asserts that the manager must enforce policies totally or not at all. "Whether it's accepting lunch from prospective vendors, flying first class, arriving on time for meetings or dealing with customer complaints, ignoring transgressions will inevitably create disrespect for *all* policies" ("Coping with Promotion," *Training News*, December 1987).

Management authority and best-selling author Tom Peters offers a unique eight-suggestion "program" for managers who want to demonstrate or model clearly that they sincerely are for quality. See Peters' creative example given in Chapter 4, Motivation, "Modeling: What You Do Is What You Get Back," page 172.

Peters also cites the approach to quality of Phil Bressler, the top Domino's Pizza francisee. Bressler's "secret":

At the crew meetings, I get the team together and ask each member, 'What have you done for the customer today?' We put up all the stories, what they've done, and then we vote. I give the manager (of one of his 18 franchises) who has done the best deed for the customer an award. And then I tell each manager to go give a similar award to one of their people. So they hold the same contest at their store. That gets your people to think about what the customer is.

(Quoted in Tom Peters' "Simple Solutions Often Solve Complex Problems," *Washington Business Journal,* November 23, 1987)

That the boss sets the tone by his behavior is illustrated by this example: Employers in a hospital were lax about wearing their name badges until the top administrators began to wear theirs all the time. Their modeling behavior was more effective than their usual lectures and memoranda.

To sum up: The concept/skill of modeling essentially has two aspects to it: 1) promulgating the high standard for subordinates to emulate and 2) personally living up to that standard to avoid assuming a "do-as-I-say, not as-I've-done" posture. Hypocrisy is not an aid to good modeling.

GIVING SUPPORT

As a manager you undoubtedly have heard about the importance of "being supportive" or "giving support." But what, in specific terms, does the supporting role comprise? Listed below are some indicators that support giving can become a reality. They are based on a coaching study conducted in a major national service organization with units in most states ("Coaching: A Commitment to Leadership," *Training and Development Journal,* June 1988). The study's author, Steven J. Stowell, co-founder of the Center for Management and Organization Effectiveness, Salt Lake City, asserts that the study "suggests that support is the centerpiece of coaching." In fact, "The most significant difference between effective leaders in successful encounters and less effective leaders in unsuccessful encounters is the frequency of supportive behaviors used in the coaching sessions."

Here are the most significant supportive behaviors found in Stowell's study:

☐ **Collaboration** regarding solutions to problems. Highly effective coaches view their employees as *partners* in the unit or operation.

☐ **Provision of help,** assistance, guidance. This included training, resources and the like.

☐ Concern about employee's **needs and goals.**

☐ **Empathy** shown the employee with attention to obstacles and his concerns and problems.

☐ Expression about the **value** of the employee, including his contribution to the work.

☐ **Acceptance of some responsibility** for the situation.

☐ **Interaction** that allows air time for the employee to express his feelings. **Note:** In our chapter on communication we refer to the need for "expressive communication."

☐ **Encouragement and recognition** for work done well.

In general, per the study, the leader's words and actions communicated consideration, concern, and acceptance of the workers. And these behaviors tended to reduce tension and encouraged open, authentic communication.

The author would add these behaviors as other indicators of support giving:

☐ The boss listens carefully to another point of view or aspect of a problem and, as appropriate, accepts and acts on it.

☐ The boss "goes to bat" for his people. He thus will try to influence higher authority in respect to new ideas, policies, budgets, space, added personnel, etc., and generally has a high batting average in doing so.

☐ The boss takes some risks on new proposals advanced by staff. Nothing is sweeter to employees than the words: "I will support you on this." The opposite behavior—nit-picking new proposals to death—is a prime way to turn people off.

☐ The boss shows his willingness to trust his people. This is done via soliciting ideas from staff, group decision making, deep delegation, sharing information freely, and minimizing irritating controls, checks, and reviews.

☐ The boss de-emphasizes his status to get closer (greater intimacy) to staff.

☐ The boss provides contact and support to all his staffers. He is aware that the employees who typically receive most of the boss's attention are either top or bottom-level performers. People in the middle—the average performers—need a lot of contact, support, praise, and encouragement, too. No one wants to be abandoned!

☐ The boss exercises patience with new people and those whose performance is not equal to "the stars." Not everyone is a home run hitter.

☐ The boss always communicates in positive terms. **Example:** As opposed to a negative "you've got a long way to go to get this assignment right," he states positively "you've made real progress on this assignment."

The following story illustrates the latter two points.

Story: Fran, a young highway engineer, had labored intensively over his first assignment—a design for a 12-mile stretch of road in hilly country, one segment of an overall plan for the reconstruction of a major artery. With a combination of pride and trepidation, Fran presented his design materials for review to his boss, a no-nonsense, supervising highway engineer of the old school.

Boss (after considerable thought): You might recheck those cuts and fills. This is pretty hilly country, you know.

Fran: I can do that, sir. Anything else?

Boss: Glad you asked. I would go back over the drainage plans while you're at it; a lot of rainfall there in the spring.

Fran: I'll be glad to check that. Everything else OK?

Boss: Well, not entirely. Some of those curves are a bit too pronounced for a modern thruway.

Fran (desperately seeking any support he could get): I can see how my design doesn't meet the standards on the cuts and fills, the drainage and those curves. But how is she for length, sir?

PROVIDING ACCESSIBILITY

While employees cannot expect their bosses to be available every minute of the workday, the coaching relationship is most helpful if workers can get help when they need it. Obviously, bosses have many demands on their own time—meetings; phone calls; "rush" assignments from the boss; possibly travel; individual management tasks such as budget preparation, public relations, personnel management responsibilities (e.g., interviewing, performance reviews, etc.); negotiating matters with other departments; and so on.

Thus, the challenge for the coach is to so arrange his work, to the extent possible, that employees don't feel timid or guilty about invading the boss's already overloaded schedule. We know, of course, that in any organization some bosses are totally relaxed and accessible while others seem to be as busy as a general ready to launch an armed invasion the next day.

Ideally, the manager should be in full control of his job so that he appears relaxed as evidenced, for example, by engaging in MBWA. Coaching can take place at the worker's desk or bench just as well as it can in the boss's office.

If the manager is well-schooled in time management, with particular emphasis on delegation, the use of one's secretary, managing phone calls, meetings, visitors, and paper flow, he should be available to staff as needed. If one is very busy, it may help to schedule time to meet with each staffer on a one-on-one basis once or twice a week.

Note:

1. When we talk about accessibility we mean being available to help the worker who has "legitimate" needs for guidance. You certainly want the worker to solve his own problems without leaning on you unnecessarily. On the other hand, you don't want your staffers to feel that they have been abandoned.

2. Not all employees have the same need for frequent contact with the boss. Obviously, some people's needs for guidance, support, restatement of instructions, etc., are greater than are others. (The author has a colleague who likes to work independently to the point that meeting with his boss was done by him primarily for "courtesy" reasons. In fact, his boss, irked by my colleague's infrequent contacts, once said to him in irritation: "You don't really need a boss, do you?" So my associate has tried to internalize the feedback and now makes a point of not abandoning his boss!)

OBSERVING BEHAVIOR/PERFORMANCE

The effective coach is concerned with employee performance and how it can be upgraded as may be necessary. A good deal of that behavior is *observable,* which means that the manager has to be a conscious observer of what his staffers are actually doing.

Example of ongoing observable behaviors are:

☐ How a bank teller, customer or sales representative interacts with customers—smiles, posture, positioning (distance from other party), eye contact, voice tone, distracting mannerisms, small talk, etc.
☐ How staffers communicate, interact, and listen at staff meetings. Do they participate actively, argue, give support, provide praise, monopolize the available air time, waste time?
☐ Telephone style—manner, voice tone, length of calls, conducting personal business.
☐ Time management—respect for office hours including lunch and break time.
☐ Traffic patterns may indicate that frequent visiting points are improperly located—copy machine, fax machine, supply cabinet, library, file cabinets, bulletin boards, time clock, etc.
☐ Social patterns—who hob nobs with whom? Who is "in" and who is "left out"? This information has a bearing on team development, possible work assignment, etc.

MBWA (Management by Walking Around) is a logical method to check visually on employee behavior. If done often enough, employees will accept his procedure as normal rather than as a form of spying. Dr. Linda Stoneall, an authority on managerial observational techniques, advises ("Open Your Eyes: Observation End Skills," *Personnel Journal,* October 1988) to be careful about intruding in work situations and taking notes too obviously. She points out that if the observer is too conspicuous it may interfere with the work, that is, it may irritate workers or cause them to alter (upgrade) their behavior only while being observed.

The data collected via observation may be used to:

☐ Provide feedback about improper performance.
☐ Provide positive reinforcement about activities done very well.
☐ Be placed on the agenda for the next staff meeting, assuming the item for discussion is one of concern to the total team.

Learning from the Best Performers

An important aspect of work review is capitalizing on what is learned from stellar performers. In most operations, average performers are exceeded in performance by best performers. If we can identify the differences

between the two, it may be possible to upgrade the performance of the average workers.

Dr. Dean Spitzer, an authority on performance improvement, states ("Best Performer Analysis," *Performance and Instruction,* May/June 1989) that "In many cases, this analysis has identified creative job improvements that have been initiated by best performers. Based on this information, jobs have been re-engineered, resulting in significant productivity improvements."

The nine factors used by Dr. Spitzer to distinguish between the two types of performers are these: Expectations, Capacity, Knowledge, Skills, Attitudes, Job Design, Incentives, Feedback, and Tools and Resources. To facilitate your analysis, prepare a worksheet listing these nine factors in a vertical column (on the left of the sheet) and compare the two types of performers (Best and Average) in two adjoining vertical columns. Label the latter two columns, "Best" and "Average." As a final step, fill in the vertical columns. You are now ready to analyze the data.

REVIEWING WORK AND GIVING FEEDBACK

The work review phase of the coaching process, if properly understood and executed, is a proactive, forward-looking activity designed to induce a new, constructive, growth-oriented outcome on the part of the employee. To illustrate, if an employee of yours writes a windy or impolite letter, you have these options:

a) You can accept it as is, possibly because of time pressures, a reluctance to deal with an employee who may become defensive, and so on.
b) You can rewrite it yourself.
c) You can let another staffer redo it.
d) You can return it with a note with a brief suggestion or two for improvement.
e) You can discuss it with the subordinate on a face-to-face basis, detailing where improvement in style should be accomplished, the possible effect of the negative tone on the reader, and so on.

If you take approach e) you are actively endeavoring to bring about a change in quality of workmanship and growth of the performer. This is coaching. Conversely, approaches a), b), c), and d) are merely forms of routine, day-to-day supervision.

Let's also look at a shop situation in which genuine coaching might take place. Assume a worker backs his truck into a large refuse can and damages badly a rear light. Many supervisors would be tempted to respond with a "Hey, Mac, can't you see what you're doing? Let's be more careful with that truck." A more effective coaching approach with the employee would be to sit down and discuss the incident helpfully and calmly as to its future avoidance. At this time, an endeavor also would be made to broaden out the discussion to include general care in operating the vehicle, the initial cost of the vehicle, as well as repairs, possible costs in damage to other property, the desirability of having a reputation as an accident-free driver, possible injury to oneself in an accident, and the like.

Giving Ongoing Feedback

Feedback is a double-barreled device. For the manager, it is an indispensable, motivational tool to maintain and improve performance *and* to encourage growth. For the worker, it answers the all-important, anxiety-reducing question: "How am I doing?" and, if positive in nature, it can build the worker's self-esteem and confidence.

Because feedback is so important (see the detailed section on feedback in the chapter on Motivation), it is not something that can be stored up and given to the employee once a year at performance review time. Rather, it must be given on a prompt and continuing basis.

Human resource manager Michael Smith ("Feedback As a Performance Management Technique," *Management Solutions,* April 1987) provides these five pointers for effective feedback:

1. **Keep it descriptive, not evaluative.** That is, describe the behavior/performance and its impact as opposed to evaluating the performer. An example in respect to late submission of reports would be to state: "Pat, your reports have been late the last four weeks. This means we have not been able to determine our costs promptly for headquarters." This approach is preferable to this statement: "Pat, your poor attitude about our weekly reports is causing everyone a lot of headaches." Actually, as a manager, your concern is with behavior and *results,* not attitude.

2. **Give feedback only for controllable elements.** There is little point in providing a critique about something the worker has no control over, e.g., his personality. Thus, the teller or waiter who has a somewhat uptight personality and rarely exhibits smiles, can hardly be expected to smile on demand

at the customer. We can, of course, expect politeness, interest, concern, possibly friendly chitchat. But to ask for smiles may be expecting too much.

3. **Watch timing.** The best feedback is immediate. It is most meaningful when it is presented as close as possible to the execution of the behavior. Dredging up an event that took place last quarter is likely to be rebutted or downgraded by the performer for the event now lacks vividness. The principle of immediacy applies to both positive and negative behavior.

4. **Keep it constructive.** Think in terms of how the data will be perceived by the performer. Information presented in a way that causes defensiveness or denial is to be avoided. Rather, present the data in terms of their having value as a learning experience. So avoid the "How could you?" or "Why did you?" approaches. Rather, talk about the incident in terms of what happened, what can be learned from it, what might be done to prevent future like occurrences, and so on.

Note: More material on providing constructive criticism is given below.

5. **Give feedback to meet employee needs.** People have different needs and tolerances for feedback. Some employees will internalize the negative feedback only if it is given very deliberately. Others can be given it very quickly and it "sinks in." Some employees can handle a lot of criticism at one time. To others, with more fragile egos, it must be doled out very gingerly. Some workers need a great deal of positive feedback, others may require very little. Even high performers may expect a great deal of positive feedback.

Although most managers know that they are supposed to provide feedback, some may be reluctant to do so, says Michael Smith, for these reasons:

☐ They don't believe it is necessary. They may feel that people know how they stand.
☐ They doubt their ability to judge others.
☐ They fear a negative reaction if they give negative feedback.
☐ They are not comfortable giving positive feedback (praise recognition).
☐ They fear that their statements, especially positive ones made during the year, may be used against them at the annual performance review session.

Correcting Without Discouraging the Performer

Undoubtedly, there is an art to giving effective feedback. Two skill pointers:

1. **Use a lot of empathy.** That is to say, before giving feedback to anyone ask yourself this question: "If I were the recipient of this information, how would I feel and how would I be likely to respond?"
2. **Consider future relationships.** Ask yourself this added question: "After I have given the feedback, how will the other person feel about himself, myself, and the task subject to the feedback? Will our future relationships be stronger, weaker, or unchanged?"

Two examples of feedback to a performer, which are marked by sensitivity to his feelings of self worth, are these:

Use the "I" statement. Weak form: "If you do it as you have outlined, you will most certainly experience failure." Better form: "I have some questions about how it will work out. May I share them with you?" The latter statement is tentative, less threatening, and simply expresses your own sincere, very legitimate feeling, as opposed to pointing an adult-to-child, warning finger at the performer.

Recognize effort. Weak form: "Without full documentation of your second recommendation, your overall report loses its effectiveness." Better form: "Your recommendations show a lot of work and thought and, overall, make a lot of good sense. I wonder, though, if you would have a stronger report if you were to cite added examples on recommendation #2?" The latter statement praises the good side of the accomplishment and gently raises a question about more work on one segment of it.

Providing Constructive Criticism

Reference was made above to giving constructive feedback. Certainly, as managers, we want to provide data about performance that will not discourage the performer but, instead, will increase a person's value to the organization. But what if the recipient of our "constructive criticism," our well-intentioned help, does not perceive it as helpful or useful. Because such a response will not result in a sincere motivation to change nor pro-

duce desired growth in the performer, we have to look for orientations or approaches to nurture the helping relationship.

Psychologist Jack Gibb, in his now classic article "Is Help Helpful?" (*Association Forum and Section Journals,* February 1964), suggests that there are various orientations that can help or, conversely, hinder the relationship. They are:

Reciprocal Trust vs. Distrust

Help is most helpful when given in an atmosphere marked by mutual feelings of confidence, warmth, and acceptance. In such an atmosphere, a person feels valued and thus is psychologically ready to receive help. Conversely, when fear and distrust exist and people sense they are being punished, put in a dependent position, or that the other party (the critic) is asserting his superiority or power, well-intended help will be resisted and resented.

Cooperative Learning vs. Indoctrinating

If the learning atmosphere is one of joint inquiry and exploration, an opportunity for both parties to learn and grow, help is likely to be appreciated. Conversely, if the perception is that one party is determinedly out to indoctrinate, persuade, or give iron-clad advice, learning will be reduced. To quote Gibb: "People cannot be taught. People must learn . . . The most deeply helpful relationship is one of common inquiry and quest, a relationship between co-learners . . . in which each is equally dependent upon the other for significant help and in which each sees and accepts this relationship."

Mutual Growth vs. Evaluating

The most significant help occurs in a relationship wherein both parties continually seek growth and fulfillment. Fundamentally, one can only help himself. The helper can only participate with another to establish a climate in which growth can take place. Conversely, growth is hindered when one party is determined to appraise or remedy the "defects" of the other. The best help occurs when it is perceived as a force for growth rather than an effort to remove gaps, remedy defects, or merely bring another up to a standard criterion.

Reciprocal Openness vs. Manipulation

The best opportunity for learning occurs when the person being helped is exposed to behavior of spontaneity, candor, and honesty. Conversely, if the feeling is that genuineness is lacking, that one is being subject to strategizing, gamesmanship, or maneuvering, one will draw back and reject or, at best, accept the help in a half-hearted manner.

Shared Problem Solving vs. Unilateral Expertise Giving

Mutual problem solving entails a joint definition of the problem, joint redefinition as new insights are developed, joint focus on alternate solutions, and joint reality testing of those alternatives. Conversely, if the offered help is perceived as that which comes from on high, that the problem solving process is unidirectional, the results are most likely to be increased dependency and limited growth.

Autonomy vs. Control

Ideally, the relationship between the helper and the helpee is one of interdependency, that there is an exchange of equals. Each party preserves his freedom and his autonomous responsibility for guiding himself toward his freedom and his own learnings, growth, and problem solving. Conversely, the helper in the role as "expert" endeavors to mold, steer, or control the behavior of the other. Securing help in organizations is hardly the same as receiving help or training from the tennis pro who provides advice and guidance that won't be questioned or challenged in any way. But the tennis coach's job is merely to help the learner gain skill, not to grow as a person.

Experimentation vs. Patterning

The best learning climate ensues when there is a sense of tentativeness and innovative experimentation. A sense of play, excitement, and fun arise in the common search for new solutions to continually changing problems. Errors can be committed and expected. Finding creative solutions keeps the fun-filled, zestful game going. Conversely, help is limited when the process is seen as an effort by one party to help another meet a totally prescribed standard, a unilaterally developed, rigidly specified goal. Ideally, helping is a creative synthesis of growth and an ongoing search for new forms.

To sum up. What Dr. Gibb is telling coaches is to not communicate *ex cathedra,* "from the chair." This is a term used widely in Catholicism. When a high church official, such as a bishop, speaks *ex cathedra* on issues of dogma, such as faith or morals, that is it. Debate, dissent, discussion are totally out of order. Hopefully, few managers will see themselves as bishops.

CONFRONTING UNDESIRABLE PERFORMANCE/BEHAVIOR

Confrontation is a managerial skill entailing the ability to give feedback in a helpful way regarding the need for a change in behavior, e.g., lowered performance, departures from standards or policies, inappropriate practices, and so on. The major skill factor is that of securing cooperation rather than generating resistance such as denial, argumentation, blaming others, sulking, etc. In essence, it should become a form of mutual problem solving.

For the manager, confrontation means, attitudinally, facing up to the problem as opposed to living with it or postponing it, and thus allowing it to become more serious. It means "laying it on the line," certainly in a polite and constructive way, but nevertheless making it clear that a behavior or practice is below prescribed expectations and thus requires a significant change in behavior of some sort.

Confronting the marginal performer is discussed in detail below.

Feedbacking via Graphs

Graphs are an excellent performance improvement tool. They communicate one's performance clearly, quickly, irrefutably, and inexpensively. A graph, as a nagging, ever-present reminder, serves as a challenge to do better. Graphing works best when it is tied into specific productivity goals. Mark G. Brown ("Extending Performance Technology: Part 5 Improving Performance Using Graphs," *Performance and Instruction,* December 1988) presents 10 simple rules for effective graphing. He advises to rely on line graphs (as opposed to bar graphs, pie charts) as they communicate ongoing performance results in the clearest fashion. Brown's rules are as follow:

1. In using the line graph, show performance along the vertical axis and time along the horizontal one, as in Figure 7-3..

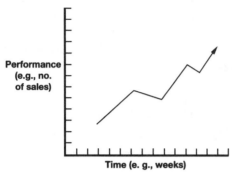

Figure 7-3. Line graph.

2. Label both axes appropriately, as above.
3. To show maximum variances in performance, don't label the vertical axis (performance) on a 0 to 100 percentage basis. Instead, compress the scale to only cover the 70 to 100 percentage range. In this way, the peaks and valleys in performance changes will stand out more vividly. (Conversely, with the full 0–100 percentage scale performance changes will be harder to notice.)
4. Graph desired performance so improvements appear as an ascending line. **Example:** Show percent accuracy as going up rather than error rate declining.
5. Graphs should depict individual performance rather than unit or total department performance. Obviously, they mean more to the individual worker. On the other hand, if you also are emphasizing team accomplishment, an additional group graph is appropriate.
6. Limit lines on the graph to two to ensure ease of interpretation. If you want to show more trends, use another graph.
7. Always show goals (or standard) on the graph. If the goal is absent, the feedback potential of the graph is only minimal. If performance is a long way from the goal, simply set subgoals as motivational steps toward the major goal.
8. The graph should show baseline data, that is, the starting point at which performance measures are being taken. Obviously, performance data are most meaningful when compared to the beginning point (e.g., May 1 or Week 1).

9. If the data on the graph are marked by much variability, a trend line rather than an average line is to be preferred. The problem with the average line is that because it only shows ups and downs, it fails to show direction—that is, if performance is getting better or worse. By using the trend line, you can show the general direction of the data.
10. Be sure to label graphs clearly and specifically. Specify the specific performance (e.g., number of widgets) and time (e.g., number of weeks) indices being used. Also show baseline, subgoals and goals so that performance data are clearly highlighted.

A worthwhile use of the graph is to measure improved performance as a result of a particular coaching effort or formal (classroom) training. The baseline to be taken would be immediately before the coaching or training program began and subsequent measures would relate to that baseline.

Checking an Ailing Feedback System

If the feedback system now in operation seems to be sputtering, use the six questions presented in Chapter 4, Motivation, "Diagnosing Feedback Systems," page 178.

Rewarding Proper Performance

A reward doesn't necessarily mean providing monetary or other tangible benefits. Rather, keep in mind primarily the granting of sincere praise or recognition: a show of appreciation; public acknowledgment of extra accomplishment; possibly assignment of added, challenging responsibility ("Mary, how would you like to tackle the new, M-7 project?").

Rewards should be considered in relation to the needs of employees. Some may appreciate a simple, verbal "well done" or a pat on the back. Others may favor a written expression of their significant accomplishment. Some with other cultural backgrounds may not favor public recognition. All of which means that the manager has to get close to his people to know them well enough to be able to recognize individual differences insofar as their needs for rewards go.

It is worth noting that in a survey of 20,000 employees by a large manufacturing company, the least-used but most highly valued reward was the boss' verbal praise and recognition (Craig E. Schneier, et al., "Unlocking Employee Potential; Managing Performance," *Management Solutions,* January 1988).

The motivational aspects of reward are discussed in more detail in Chapter 4, Motivation.

THE COACH AS DEVELOPER OF PEOPLE

It is a fine thing to have ability, but the ability to discover ability in others is the true test.

—Elbert Hubbard (1856–1915), American writer and author of the inspirational essay "A Message to Garcia" (1899)

I enjoy hiring a new person and watching them blossom, helping a representative who is not doing too well and seeing them turn around due to my efforts, and motivating the more senior representatives.

—Tom Caso, Southeastern Region Sales Manager, Bureau of National Affairs Inc., quoted in *BNA Field Reporter,* June 17, 1988

A vital asset in every organization is its human resources. Maximum return from this asset is only possible if you, as a manager, work actively to develop it fully, thereby tapping potential and unleashing creativity. Development of people is too important to be left to chance, to be conducted intermittently or indifferently.

The primary purpose of a sound staff development effort on your part is to improve the performance of all personnel in their present assignments. In addition, it is designed to identify those people who have potential for greater responsibilities and to focus attention on some of the ways and means by which they can be prepared to assume such responsibilities in the future. (See the section on "Counseling for Careers" in the following chapter on counseling.) In essence, you should be concerned with both short-range and long-range improvement and development.

An effective leader is one who has a sincere and strong desire to help his staff grow and advance, and who enthusiastically works at it, too. The manager who achieves a real satisfaction from serving as a coach will have little difficulty in "finding time" for this responsibility. The time required to work with subordinates on their development should be regarded as an investment. If it is done enthusiastically and thoroughly, you can expect payoffs in terms of higher performance, improved operations, increased quality, better communication, better customer service, and the like. All of which will save time in the long run.

Also, the matter of expenditure of time is a personal kind of thing and has to be resolved for each manager in relation to questions such as these: Am I really satisfied with the quality and quantity of work of my subordinates? Are they entirely clear about my expectations regarding their work? Are they doing all they can to improve quality and customer service? Am I doing everything I should to encourage their creativity and unleash their potential? Am I effective as I should be as a developer of staff? What are the alternatives to a planned approach to staff development?

Basic to the development of the staff is an ongoing system that provides for:

☐ A passing on to subordinates, in a systematic way, the knowledge and skills you already have acquired. This is essentially a responsibility to function as an enthusiastic coach.
☐ A plan for the individual's development worked up on a mutual basis by him and you, the boss.
☐ The fullest possible encouragement and help to your subordinates to see that such development actually takes place.

Guidelines for staff development. If you understand the importance of developing your people and are sincerely committed to working at it actively, you will find it useful to operate from the guidelines which follow. These principles may not meet all your needs as a developer of people, but they should prove superior to a total "flying by the seat of one's pants" approach.

Development Proceeds Best When it is Based on Self-Appraisal

Why? Simply because a person can accept criticism from himself more readily than from anyone else. If you can encourage the worker to reflect upon his own accomplishments, progress, shortcomings and weaknesses, you avoid putting him in a position where he has to accept criticism and advice solely from you.

Development Must Provide for "Feedback" from Others, Principally Yourself, Regarding Your Subordinate's Performance

If you are operating on a team management basis, development needs may be pointed up by other team members as well. An individual must have adequate data regarding how his performance is perceived by someone else before he can change or improve it. The assumption that most people don't want or can't take feedback about their performance is a rationalization set forth by timid managers. Adults want to know how they are doing.

Provide Your Staff with High Expectations and Standards

If they are content with operations as they are, improvement in their work and their own development is not possible. Provide challenge with a dynamic environment, new and higher goals ("stretch"), and a constant search for better ways of doing the job. You should appreciate that the old saw "We grow as long as we're green" applies to both their work and their development.

Development is the Responsibility of the Individual

You, as the supervisor, can provide the stimulation, encouragement, active interest, support, and organization resources; in short, the proper climate. But the individual must possess and use the energy, the drive and the initiative required to develop his talents. The key idea here is self-development as opposed to total "spoon-feeding" by the organization. Encourage your subordinates to participate in outside activities already mentioned, educational courses, and professional and community affairs. Taking the "risk" of a lateral transfer is also a worthwhile form of self-development.

Provide for Individualized, Tailor-Made Development Plans

Because all individuals have different strong points and weaknesses, their training needs will vary. It is good business to put the development in writing and to review it periodically (quarterly) with the employee to learn of progress being made and to offer additional guidance as indicated.

Development is Best Approached From the Standpoint of Doing One's Present Job Better

This may be developing greater skill in planning, scheduling, organizing work, problem solving, communicating, working with others, improving procedures, increasing quality, satisfying customers/clients to a greater degree, etc.

Developing People is a Continuous, Ever-Present Task

It is not something that is done in six days, six weeks, or six months. For example, learning to speak well before groups is not accomplished simply by taking a short course in public speaking. If anything, that course is just a motivator to keep one in a constant state of development after the course is over, e.g., by joining a Toastmaster's Club.

People Learn From People

The examples you set will determine the way subordinates approach their problems. This is particularly true in such vital areas as communication, human relations, customer relations, ethics, etc. High quality performance can't be learned in a poorly managed outfit. A worthwhile example you should set relates to your own development. Your staff should perceive you as a person very much interested in personal growth and development. If you do nothing or little about your own self-development, which is to say that you see yourself as having "arrived," it may be difficult to expect others to do what you don't do yourself.

We Learn Best by Doing

The training, therefore, should emphasize active participation and performance, and provide opportunities for the solving of real problems. Formal courses are useful, but the real learning comes from what people actually do and experience.

Experiences Acquired on the Job and Within the Organization Are Most Meaningful and Useful

To the extent that training is based on internal situations and problems, development will be most effective. Organizations have enough know-how to make people more effective. The real challenge is to provide planned opportunities for the necessary learning and growth.

Let Your Subordinates Get Away Now and Then to Get a New Look at Their Jobs and the Organization

It will keep them fresh and help them understand better the purpose of their work. Outside contacts will enlarge their horizons. Tools for this are college courses, participation in community affairs and professional and trade organizations, networking, plant visits, field trips, etc.

Delegation is a Basic Tool to Encourage Motivation, Creativity, and Development

Don't be afraid to "give people enough rope." The alternative is to encourage dependence upon you.

People Need Broadened Outlooks

Unless you work at this diligently, specialization and resultant narrow outlooks are inevitable. Therefore, you should think in terms of "job enrichment" as opposed to job specialization and job fractionalization. If you operate your organization on the basis of watertight compartments, the by-products will be these: creation of "experts" who know little and care less of anyone else's activities; limited interaction among staff; limited cooperation among staff; creation of "stars" rather than a team. Specialists have their place in every organization, of course; but specialization has to be tempered with concern for motivation, growth, development, and teamwork. Tools for broadening people's perspectives include job rotation, cross training, special assignments, field trips, etc.

Keep Your Development Efforts Job-Oriented as Opposed to Concern With Personality Traits

We as managers are interested in such personality traits as initiative, neatness, enthusiasm, loyalty, integrity, dependability, and decisiveness, and we certainly hope that all our staff rank high on these qualities. But these traits are all-too-often abstract items that are hard to define, hard to reach agreement on meaning and importance, and harder to bring about any real improvement in them. Therefore, why not discuss the job and standards, which are tangible things, and the situations where progress was not made or where problems arose? Develop plans jointly to see that the difficulties do not arise again.

In general, personality is viewed differently by different people, whereas performance is perceived with greater reliability and consistency. People know how to improve their results on the job; they seldom know how to change their personalities. There are tremendous opportunities for improvement in such areas as work planning, quality improvement, communication, problem-solving approaches, participation in staff meetings, customer relations and service, etc., without getting into the quicksand of personality analysis.

As a summation, see Figure 7-4, "Basic Elements of a Staff Development Program." It outlines your role—particularly as a climate setter—and that of your subordinates.

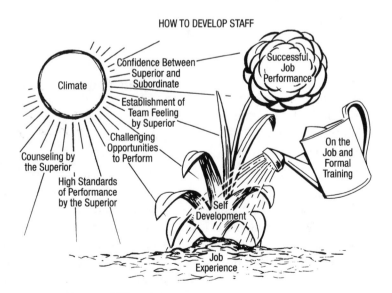

Figure 7-4. Basic Elements of a Staff Development Program.

The "How" of Staff Development

Managers will consciously develop their subordinates to become more effective in their jobs to the extent that (1) they hold strong convictions concerning the need for people to grow and develop, and (2) they are familiar with the know-how to make development happen. On the assumption that the motivation to develop others does exist, the chart given in Figure 7-5, "Chart for Staff Development" (page 326), should provide managers with the tools to do the job. Of course, the best use of the chart will eventuate if an *individualized plan for development* is prepared for and with the subordinate concerned on the basis of need and interest. Note, too, that a plan for development does not necessarily mean a plan for promotion, for everyone has a potential for improvement, strengthening, growth in one's current job. This is essential to keep people alive, vibrant, challenged, and creative. Or in the jargon of the day, "tuned in and turned on." Conversely, to ignore growth needs is to ensure apathy, stagnation, obsolescence, status quo-ism, bureaucracy, and dissatisfaction of all sorts.

For an example of an individual development plan, see Figure 7-6 (page 327).

In reviewing Figure 7-5, you will note that the process of people development encompasses much more than training per se. It covers growth experiences of many sorts, on and off the job, organization sponsored and self-developed. It thus may be useful to distinguish more precisely between training and development. William Fitzgerald ("Training Versus Development," *Training and Development,* May 1992) defines training as the acquisition of knowledge and skills for present tasks, a tool to help people contribute to the firm and to succeed in their current jobs.

Development, says Fitzgerald, relates to knowledge/skill acquisition used now or in the future, preparation of people to enrich the outfit in the future, and involvement in a variety of training and growth-inducing activities.

As to time frames, it may help to think of training as having a short-term focus or impact, a year or less. Development has a long-term focus, possibly one to three years. Fitzgerald also points out that development is not a training class-bound activity. Rather, it is what happens after the class that causes real development to occur.

THE COACH AS TRAINER

Coaching, at times, takes on a more formal aspect to it; that is, by providing training to overcome a performance deficiency or possibly to teach a new skill. We define training as planned activities, either formal (in a classroom setting, conference room, or private area) or informal (on the job), which are designed to help employees acquire new or refresher skills or knowledge. The training activities may be group or individual, internal (in-house), or external (off-site), brief (one or two hours), or extensive (several or more days). The paragraphs following discuss the training role along these lines:

☐ Is Training the Answer to a Performance Problem?
☐ Job Aids as a Tool for Learning
☐ Identifying Training/Coaching Needs
☐ Guides to On-the-Job Training
☐ Prescriptions for a Motivated Learner
☐ Training on a One-on-One Basis
☐ Maximizing the Return from Training Workshops

Is Training the Answer to a Performance Problem?

Before considering the need for training to remedy a performance problem, it may be more appropriate to take a broader, more inclusive view of the total work situation. Consider that people may already know how to perform properly but still may not do things right. Paradoxical? Not at all. Improper execution of tasks may be due to a variety of other (non-training-related) factors:

☐ **Poor job design.**
☐ **An unfriendly environment,** e.g., physical problems relating to lighting, temperature, ventilation, distance (to receive or deliver items), noise, hazards.
☐ **Faulty systems,** e.g., cumbersome or unclear policies or procedures, haphazard or inconsistent scheduling, improper methods, information delays or mix-ups, equipment/tool shortcomings, material delays or defects, and so on.
☐ **Unclear performance goals.** For example, in the sales area are sales personnel expected to maximize their sales (secure a large revenue) or to sell products across the board (the total product line) regardless of total revenue?

☐ **Inconsistent reward system** that may provide punishment even though the job is accomplished properly, e.g., a customer service representative may be complimented for effective customer service, but gets chewed out for spending too much time on the telephone with customers.

☐ **Inadequate feedback about performance.** People may not know that their performance is not up to standard.

☐ **Rewards (praise, compliments) for proper performance may not be forthcoming,** leading to the ultimate demise of the effort to perform properly; e.g., safety procedures are followed regularly but no supportive comments are received about them, leading to the conclusion that adherence to the procedures is not that important.

Note: As a point of clarification, feedback relates to people being told that what they did was right and proper. Reinforcement or reward follows the feedback.

☐ **Team impediments.** Cooperation may be lacking, personality conflicts may hinder or delay accomplishment, coordinating actions may be slow or late, etc.

☐ **Weak motivation.** If motivation is lacking, training is not the answer to a performance problem. Rather, the supervisor must provide feedback about performance or attach rewards (positive reinforcement) to proper performance.

If all of the above performance-hindering factors can be ruled out and a true skill or knowledge deficiency exists—i.e., "can't do" as opposed to "won't do" or "not permitted to do"—training is very much in order.

But once we begin to think in terms of *performance* problems as opposed to training solutions, new approaches to meeting needs become possible. Dr. Robert Mager of performance objectives fame (Robert F. Mager and Peter Pipe, *Analyzing Performance Problems or 'You Really Oughta Wanna,'* Belmont, CA: Fearon Publishers, 1970) suggests that a good term to use is *discrepancy* in performance as opposed to deficiency. The former term implies that there may be a fault in the system, the latter implies that the fault is essentially with the performer, that he "has to be fixed" in some way.

We should recognize, then, that performance problems are either internal or external to the person. The

internal ones—those relating to skill, knowledge, ability, capacity, and the will to perform (motivation)—are, of course, amenable to change efforts such as coaching, training, or counseling. But it is not always an easy or certain process because individual differences are at work. Conversely, *external* causes for performance discrepancies—those relating to the system, information, equipment, incentives, etc.—are often changed more easily, economically, and even permanently: also, such changes are likely to "take" for everyone. On this latter point, see "Changing the Situation for Better Solutions" in Chapter 10, The Manager As a Problem Solver and Decision Maker: What Managers Get Paid For."

Performance should be regarded as a chain with various links in it. If one or more links are weak or missing, performance will probably be less than required. Performance technologists James F. Bolt and Geary A. Rummler ("How to Close the Gap in Human Performance," *Management Review,* January 1982) describe the performance chain as an integrated process comprising these five links:

1. **Job/task clarity:** Performance standards exist prescribing what is expected and when; the worker sees the work as important and challenging, and the work standards as reasonable and attainable; other tasks don't interfere or compete with the required task.

2. **Resources:** Adequate money, person-power, equipment, materials, information, and time are available to do a quality job.

3. **The worker:** Has the skills, knowledge, and willingness (motivation) to perform.

4. **Feedback:** The worker receives immediate, frequent data about his performance in relation to job expectations.

5. **Consequences:** Rewards, which the worker views as appropriate, follow successful performance.

If we understand the above-described performance chain, we can see that a) any weak link must be corrected to close a performance gap, and b) training as a solution to a performance problem only makes sense if there truly is a deficit in worker skill or knowledge (link #3).

Job Aids as a Tool for Learning

In the above paragraphs, we suggested that training to overcome a performance deficiency may not necessarily be the proper answer, that other avenues should be explored first. Another alternative to training is to provide the worker with a *job aid.*

A job aid is an instructional aid or tool that guides the worker by specifying when, where, how much, and how to go about accomplishing the task. With a job aid, the worker need not rely on memory, what he learned in training, nor need he seek help from the boss, who may not even be available. In effect, the employee proceeds independently (a self-esteem builder), at his own pace, using the aid until it is no longer needed. And if the task is only performed intermittently and the steps to accomplish it are forgotten, the aid is readily available to refresh one's memory. (No need to say, "Stupid me. How could I forget that last step?")

Some everyday examples of job aids: a recipe in a cookbook; procedures to operate your microwave oven; how to program your VCR; how to pump gas at a self-service pump; a guide to changing a wheel on your car; the IRS tax form to speed delivery of your taxes to the collector; procedural information to enter, play back, and change a message on your answering machine; instructions to wash a pair of slacks.

Common, at-work job aids include instructions on a fire extinguisher; a checklist of points to cover in a job interview or in orienting the new worker; a set of procedures to process a sale in a department store.

Performance technologist Allison Rossett ("Job Aids in a Performance Technology World," *Performance and Instruction,* May/June 1991) cites a light-hearted job aid, in the form of a poster on the wall in a crowded university registration office, which said very briefly, "As you know, you all are going to be standing here for a long time. Rather than getting upset, why not say hello to the people all around you???"

As to format, the do-it-yourself aid may be written, use pictures (photos or drawings), or combine words and pictures. Color coding, flowcharts, or diagrams may also be used. Formats may vary, e.g., all instructions may be a on a single plastic card or a sheet of paper, on a decal posted on a machine, in a spiral notebook, on a label in a piece of washable clothing, or on an audiotape if the operator is in a dark area or he should not take his eyes off an instrument panel.

Job aids are not certain to be effective unless they are user friendly or "ergonomically designed," i.e., the relationship between the user and the aid is in sync so that usability and utility are assured. According to performance technologists Nancy A. Snow and Timothy J. Newby ("Ergonomically Designed Job Aids," *Performance and Instruction,* March 1989) ergonomically designed job aids are marked by these four key factors: accessibility, convenience of use, ease of perception, and task focus.

Accessibility

If job operations have an emergency aspect to them— if an equipment operator must monitor a situation constantly—then the aid must be immediately accessible. There is no time to conduct a search to locate the aid in a drawer in another room or to flip through a hefty manual for answers. So the more severe the consequences and the likelihood of error, the greater the need to build accessibility into the job aid. Accessibility means continuing the task *without* interruption.

Convenience of Use

If several job aids are to be used, each must be clearly labeled to avoid confusion with the others. If there is a possible difficulty in making such a distinction, valuable time may be lost and even worse impacts may occur. Second, the aid must be usable while the worker is performing the tasks. **Example:** Changing a wheel on a car should not require working with a tightly bound manual that requires two hands to keep it open. Or instructions to develop a film in a darkroom would be more helpful if presented on an audiocassette rather than via a visual job aid. Third, the aid should not divide attention between the task and the aid itself. And lastly, the aid should be designed with the user in mind—simple language, few words, avoidance of complex documentation that requires back-and-forth reference to several pages, etc.

Ease of Perception

Aligned closely with convenience and accessibility, is the ease with which a job aid can be perceived by the performer. If it's too hard to read or perceive, it will be ineffective. **Examples:** a chart of fuse types and positions not legible by flashlight; an auditory signal that can't be heard reliably above shop noise.

Focus to Task

Proper focus for usability by the operator depends on simplicity. Surplus information defeats the goal of simplicity. Unneeded or poorly organized information of either a verbal, visual, or auditory sort adds to effort and time required for interpretation of the job aid's instructions. The problem is particularly aggravated if the aid is to be used in a stressful situation. To ensure simplicity and proper focus, color, type size or increased volume are helpful devices.

It is a good idea to pretest a job aid to be certain that it is user friendly, meeting the key conditions described above. Susan Zaforski adds ("The Job Aid as Zen Art," *Performance and Instruction,* November/December 1989) that a good job aid should look like "Zen Art." That is, it should look like it was created in an hour, that anyone could have designed it, and be marked by understated simplicity. And, like the potter who sweated over the creation of a simple tea bowl, the mammoth struggle can't be observed at all. Says Zaforski, "The job aid designer sweats too, and if his efforts are successful, his job aid is elegantly simple."

Identifying Training/Coaching Needs

Training/coaching has the potential for maximum payoff when it is based on *actual need.* Needs are readily determinable since the manager has been observing behavior and reviewing completed work. If end results are less than satisfactory and one has been able to ascertain the reasons therefore, training needs will clearly emerge. In some cases, the worker himself may point out the need for added training. Training needs may also arise due to new requirements resulting from a change in mission or a new emphasis on the existing mission.

A systematic way to zero in on and monitor need is to utilize a chart such as given in Figure 7-7, "Manager's Guide to Coaching and/or Training Needs" (page 328). It simply asks the manager to list the major elements of the job and to rate the proficiency or skill level of staff members in relation to those job elements. Elements that receive poor ratings should be remedied by either coaching or training. Most performance deficiencies or needs for upgrading or updating of skills will probably be met via informal, on-the-job, day-to-day coaching. Conversely, major deficiencies and new skills of a significant sort will require a more formal effort—training.

Note:

1. As has been indicated, training is a structured endeavor to teach new skills or upgrade performance. Coaching, in the literal, traditional sense, relates to informal, work-related actions the boss takes to change a behavior, broad-en an understanding, or alter an attitude. A coaching opportunity may arise from observing, say, an improper behavior or reviewing completed work. In any case, it is the manager's job to decide whether a performance or skill deficiency is to be treated on a coaching or a training basis.

2. Training is designed to teach particular skills and knowledge, whereas coaching is an ongoing process covering the whole job. Training is given within prescribed time restraints; coaching is not subject to any established time limits.

Guides to On-the-Job Training

The manager's role in training his staff is an ongoing one rather than a one-time or an intermittent endeavor. Also, training is essential for both new and more experienced workers. Here are nine tips for more effective training, as recommended by training consultant Vernon Magnessen ("Training Today: A Manager's Guide to Training," *Training,* January 1990):

1. Don't Train Without a Plan

Instead, develop and use a simple, workable training plan for new employees and a "refresher" plan for the experienced people. The plan is your recognition that the needed training certainly won't occur properly by itself. A plan will ensure full coverage of what has to be covered and will reduce your anxieties about the training when you provide it.

2. Don't Overestimate the Value of "Experience"

Because people can acquire bad habits from their experience, even experienced workers require training from time to time. Also, a senior or veteran employee, new to your unit, requires full orientation as to your standards on production, quality, deadlines, cooperation with others, etc.

3. Don't assume an experienced worker may be the best person to break in a new hire

Why not? He may not have all the skills needed to make the buddy system work. Also, being "experienced" runs the risk of skipping information one knows so well, leaving the trainee less than fully trained. Other possible difficulties are being too busy to answer questions, this being particularly a problem if the new worker is a bit timid to "intrude"; teaching "shortcuts" around important rules, and passing along his own biases that may tend to reduce trust in bosses and reduce cooperation with the team.

4. Don't Forget that New Workers Need the "Big Picture"

It may take time to provide it, but in the long run it will pay off in terms of better understanding of the *why* of objectives, policies, standards, and rules. The alternative? A feeling that one is a mere bit player and thus not much of a contributor to the overall mission.

5. Don't Overlook Handouts

These materials help the new learning to "glue in," overcome memory lapses, and are useful for future reference and review. Handouts are your recognition that people can't be expected to remember everything they hear.

6. Don't Overlook Opportunities to Provide Positive Reinforcement

Jobs executed well, especially in the early weeks following entrance on duty or after training is given, should be reinforced with praise. Remember, people want to know how well they are doing.

7. Supplement Your Expectation With Inspections

This means that the behavior you actually check and measure is very certain to get done by the staff. You want to send clear messages about the behaviors you feel are critical. Do this via frequent reminders about standards, feedback about performance, and praise for tasks done in accordance with standards and requirements.

8. Your Examples Influence Behavior

How you behave/perform sets the tone for your staff. People look to you as a model for their behavior. So you can't talk one way on the job or in the training situation—e.g., regarding customer service, quality, ethics—and act in opposite ways and expect people to do what's right.

9. Don't Overlook the Need for Refresher Training

People, despite experience and good intentions, over time can overlook requirements, cut necessary corners and get lax in a variety of ways. As the coaches say in athletics, "we have to get back to basics."

Prescriptions for a Motivated Learner

If the learner is not motivated to learn, no matter how well-planned and developed the training may be, little learning will take place. Thus, for the manager as trainer, he must be concerned about the motivational state of the trainee and have proper "tools" to elevate and sustain motivation. Philip C. Grant, a management consultant and professor of management ("Employee Motivation: Key to Training," June 1989) offers five strategies to kindle high learner motivation. They are:

1. Ensure That the Learner Perceives the Training as Highly Valuable

If the trainee feels the training effort will be a waste of time, he will resist it. Here are some ways to communicate the worth of the training:

Impact on Performance and Job Satisfaction

Communicate that the new learning is a route to possible promotion, pay increases, more interesting work, and greater freedom to make decisions. Point out, too, that boredom, fatigue, stress, and injury are much less likely via the training.

Support for the Training

Stress that the training is supported up and down the line—by management and the trainee's associates.

Granting Rewards

Give the trainee rewards for his participation in and completion of the training. The rewards may range from the intangible—recognition—to the tangible—bonuses and prizes. Try to individualize the rewards for people have different needs and interests. But rewards should be granted on an equitable basis so there is no perception of unfairness, e.g., a bonus to one trainee should be equal to what others receive as a bonus.

Scheduling Rewards

Rather than provide a lump sum bonus at training's end, greater motivation will accrue if several smaller bonuses are passed out at critical points during the whole training period.

Determining Reward Size

Regardless of when the reward is given, it must be large enough to be perceived as significant. Reward size should not be treated lightly.

2. Integrate the Rewards With What is Learned

As the trainer, you want your trainee not only to regard the rewards as having real value, but also to recognize that the rewards are dependent on *the degree of learning*. To implement this concept, you, as trainer, must take these actions:

☐ Assess learning progress and distribute rewards in relation to actual accomplishments. Test scores may be used as a basis for evaluation.

☐ Provide learners with a reward schedule to correspond with learning progress. The higher rewards go to the higher scores, of course.

☐ Assure learners that the person distributing the rewards will do so on a totally equitable basis.

☐ Point out that the system used to evaluate learning is totally valid. You don't want the trainee to feel that the rewards given are not related to what is learned. If so, why work hard at it?

Note: While the rewards referred to in Point 2 above are financial, rewards may also be less tangible as stated in Point 1.

3. Communicate to the Trainee That His Hard Work as a Learner Will Not Have Negative Effects

By negative effect or costs we mean boredom, stress, fatigue, frustration, or time wasted. To prevent these punishing effects from arising, take these actions:

The Environment

The training facility itself should be pleasant and comfortable.

Length of Sessions

Avoid overly long training periods. Be sure to provide frequent breaks.

Relaxation Opportunities

Build exercise and relaxation periods into the agenda.

Methods

Vary training methods to prevent boredom. Consider case studies, quizzes for discussion purposes, small group work, role plays, activities with worksheets and check sheets, etc.

Objectives

Establish objectives for the training that relate clearly to the job.

Presentations

Pep up lectures with problems and questions to the group, question and answer periods, use of worksheets, short quizzes to check for understanding, etc.

4. Establish Clearly That the Amount of Learning is Dependent on the Effort Made to Learn

To ensure understanding of this concept take these actions:

Objectives

They must be totally realistic and clear to the learner. The learner must feel that what is to be learned can be mastered. A target is a target only to the extent that it can be hit.

Learning Plan

If you have a well-thought-out plan for learning, you can do an effective job at it. The plan will assure that proper pace is considered in the teaching process.

Feedback

Learners need to know how well they are doing, what progress is being made. If slippage is taking place, they need to know it to take corrective action.

Trainee's Needs

Trainees need to have opportunities for practice, to ask questions, and to receive help as appropriate.

Resources

If equipment, materials, and aids are of high quality, trainees will feel that learning is related to effort and that their effort can pay off. Consider using other instructional resources—subject matter experts—to add to the perception of the effort to learning relationship.

Trainee Capabilities

Check in advance of the training to be given that the learners know how to learn. That is, that they can listen, observe, take notes, ask questions, etc. If they, as learners, don't do these things, you may have to work with them on these skills.

5. Ensure That the Learning is Not Subject to Competitive, Learning-Interfering Systems

You don't want the trainee distracted by non-supportive influences. To prevent possible competition take these actions:

Time of Training

Don't hold sessions outside of the normal workday.

Job Responsibilities

Reduce responsibilities while in training. Trainees should not feel that the training is punishing them by having their regular work pile up while they are away.

Distractions

Keep the training environment free of noise and sights that compete with the training.

Personal Problems

If the trainee has personal, off-the-job problems he should be excused from the training. Learners can't concentrate if they have anxieties due to other non-job concerns.

Association

Try to make the learning as closely related as possible to normal work activities. The training should correspond to the job rather than conflict with it.

Philip C. Grant labels the above five strategies as the "Effort-Net Return" model of motivation.

Training on a One-on-One Basis

Although at times you may provide training to your total work team, or possibly have a staff member or someone from the training department provide the train-

ing, for the most part your training is likely to be conducted with and for one employee. This training may be for a new hire, a worker who needs strengthening or updating on a particular skill, or an employee who has returned from a lengthy illness and needs to catch up on changes in the work.

In any case, to train effectively, you should follow these broad instructional strategies, per training consultant Carolyn Nilson ("How to Train Employees One-On-One," *Supervisory Management,* May 1991):

1. Provide a Global Overview, the "Big Picture"

For motivational purposes, your trainee needs to see how his role fits into the total operation.

2. Clarify Learning Goals

The trainee should be presented with a clear view of what requirements are to be mastered to reach the desired standard of performance. The trainee needs to know the Whys, not just the Hows.

3. Close the Gaps

Provide the learner with basic information to overcome any knowledge deficiency. If you don't have the information yourself, route the learner to the one who does or provide appropriate printed material.

4. Build on Prior Experience

Capitalize on what the employee already knows or can do. Use the employee's knowledge/skill base as a bridge to the new material. Remember that little pieces presented slowly are much easier to digest than huge chunks offered at one time. These approaches will avoid feelings of inundation with totally new requirement.

5. Use the Problem Solving Approach

Present a problem as a challenge, allowing the learner to draw on his prior experience.

6. Point Up Training Outcomes

Training is not an end in itself. Benefits, results or outcomes should ensue. By stressing these end-products, the training will take on real meaning.

7. Follow-Up

Don't assume the trainee can apply totally or properly everything that was learned. Check to offer added help as needed.

8. Provide an Outline

To facilitate application, provide an outline of key points. Allow for space between items so that the trainee can enter his notes in relation to your major ideas covered in the training.

To ensure that the instruction is fully meaningful, apply these four guidelines, says Carolyn Nilson:

1. Keep it Job-Related

Try to duplicate actual job conditions as much as possible. Use the same tools or equipment that will be used on the job. Also, use the same on-the-job terminology required to perform the task properly.

The following story illustrates the pertinence of keeping training reality-based as opposed to theoretical and abstract.

Story. The grizzled, old naval captain, who was assessing the progress of a young student, posed this query: What action would you take if a storm suddenly appeared on the starboard side of the ship?

Naval student: I would have to throw out an anchor, sir.

Captain: And if another storm hit the ship aft?

Naval student: I'd toss out an anchor again, sir.

Captain: And if another storm hit forward?

Naval student: I'd throw out an anchor, sir.

Captain: Hold on there, lad. I must ask you where are obtaining all these anchors?

Naval student: Pretty much the same place where you're getting all those storms, sir.

2. Avoid Interruptions

If the training is worth doing, do it where there are not interruptions and there is enough quiet. It may be wise to limit each training session to one or two hours to avoid learner fatigue.

3. Use a Comfortable Room

The training area should be neat and comfortable to avoid unnecessary distractions. Provide coffee or a soft drink to make the atmosphere a relaxed one. Comfortable chairs, good lighting, and ventilation are essential.

4. Provide Properly Prepared Training Aids and Materials

Regard the one-on-one experience as worthy of your best effort, just as if it were a group training experience.

And as far as the actual instruction goes, these guidelines should help the trainee learn more effectively, per Rick L. Lansing ("Training New Employees," *Supervisory Management,* January 1989):

1. Involve the Learner

People learn more effectively from what they experience, rather than from what they only hear. So make the training live, participative, active.

2. Avoid the Telling Trap

Passing along information is not training. So use methods that avoid lectures, and have the trainee do something.

3. Use Repetition

Unless the learner has a chance to repeat what was learned, fadeout and forgetting are all too likely.

4. Avoid Information Overload

Instead, provide the new learning in small doses. Simple, small steps make for digestibility. Large, massive chunks of new material can only overload the intake valves.

5. Move from the Simple to the Complex

Start with easy-to-learn tasks to build confidence and to provide a base for added, more difficult material or tasks.

6. Use Visual and Audio Aids

They will help to reinforce ("glue in") what was heard.

7. Expect Learner Fatigue

Learning takes place one chunk at a time, and then a natural weariness may set in. So expect this phenomenon and be persistent in your instruction, and don't give up if the trainee seems weary. Instead, return to the training task, for the learner is certain to recover his interest once "digestion" has taken place.

Maximizing the Return from Training Workshops

Sending an employee to training in an in-house or an outside facility may seem to be a "painless" way to upgrade an employee's skill and knowledge. After all, someone else is doing the job for you, isn't he? But real payoffs are possible only if:

☐ The objectives of the training being offered are very clear and pertinent to the employee's needs.

☐ You meet with the employee in advance of the training course to state clearly what you expect to be gained from the training in relation to the employee's needs. As an added incentive to learn, you may wish to indicate that the participant will be expected to train others in the new learning acquired in the outside workshop.

Note: The fact that you have taken the time to meet with your employee and discuss the course shows that you are interested in and support the training. Conversely, just "sending" someone to a course without any discussion of it is much less likely to produce a perception that the training is indeed worthwhile.

☐ You hold a discussion with the employee at training's end to determine what was learned and how it can be plowed back into the job, and what obstacles exist which might prevent implementation of the new training on the job. The key concept is transfer of what was learned in the classroom to what is needed on the job for better performance.

☐ You reward use of the newly acquired and implemented skill or knowledge: "I'm glad to see that you're applying what you learned in that workshop, Pat. It really is making a difference here. Please keep it up."

Note: It should be clear to the employee whether he is being sent off to training as a reward, as a form of punishment or, as described above, to meet a real need for new or better performance. Of course, a comment by the manager when training is being offered as a reward will be appreciated and serve as a motivator for learning: "You have been performing well in the accounts function and I think a broad course in financial management will be helpful to your career." Conversely, if being sent to training is perceived as a form of punish-

ment ("Why don't they just tell me what they want me to do, instead of just shipping me off to that dull customer relations training course?"), whether real learning will take place or be implemented is problematical.

In connection with the use of training as punishment, management professors Dan Costley and Faye A. Moore ("The Subliminal Impact and Hidden Agendas of Training," *Personnel Journal,* March 1986) cite an instance of management's hidden agenda being to "teach employees a lesson," by showing them that continued customer complaints would result in more forced attendance of training programs on their own time and to report their implementation of the training to management.

Some organizations use training essentially to help present a positive public image. Costley and Moore cite the instance of a company conducting a "women in management seminar." A consultant, who asked what benefits were to be expected, received this reply: to project an image of equal rights for women and "to get the women's groups off our back."

In passing, we might mention that tuition-reimbursement programs can cause significant reductions of employee turnover. For example, in the restaurant industry 50% of all new workers leave within their first 30 days. But at Carl's Jr. restaurants (based in Anaheim, CA), the use of prepaid education benefits encourages employees to stay on the job as long as 30 months, or three-and-one-half times longer than employees not participating in the educational program. Also, whereas tuition costs came to $90,000, turnover costs were reduced by $145,000 (Diane Filipowski, "For Your Information: Education Benefits Reduce Turnover Costs," *Personnel Journal,* January 1992).

CONDUCTING THE ANNUAL PERFORMANCE REVIEW

"What a waste of time!" "Do I have to go through that again?" "Kim gets so defensive when I tell her what went wrong in the past year." "I'm not sure that there's that much to talk about." "Boy, another starry-eyed program cooked up by those Human Resources people in their ivory tower." "I'll just rate the elements on the form on the high side and it'll all be over and done within 10 minutes."

Do any of these managerial comments seem familiar? You may have made one or more of them yourself. These laments reflect, of course, managerial attitudes and anxieties about the annual performance review process. To many managers it is regarded as a headache, a threat and/or a monstrous time waster.

And for that matter, your employee may not be looking forward to a "white knuckle" session either—visualize the employee clutching the rating sheet in great despair! ("I'd just as soon go for root canal work.")

In any case, to stimulate your thinking about the issues involved in the annual review of performance, please complete the short quiz that follows. Then check your responses with those provided by the author.

Performance Appraisal: A Short Quiz

Indicate whether each statement below is T (true) or F (false).

_____ 1. An effective annual performance review discusses salary and performance at the same time.

_____ 2. An in-depth annual performance review discusses promotional possibilities (career planning) at the same time.

_____ 3. In a comprehensive annual performance review, the manager should discuss personality traits as well as job-related issues.

_____ 4. "Star" employees should be exempt from the annual appraisal review process because they are already doing an outstanding job.

_____ 5. One effective way to assess performance is to compare the employee's performance with one or more other employees performing like work.

_____ 6. The key objective of the annual performance review process is the completion of the appraisal form with the employee's signature on it so that there is no confusion about what was communicated.

_____ 7. If the annual performance review is accomplished properly, other periodic coaching and review sessions can be eliminated.

_____ 8. In the annual performance review, it is more important to overcome deficiencies than it is to comment on accomplishments.

_____ 9. The annual performance review should stress the results of the year just completed and focus minimally, if at all, on the year ahead.

_____10. A realistic communication ratio in the annual performance review is 70–30, with the manager providing 70% of the input and the employee providing the balance.

Author's Answers to Quiz

1. **False.** Most authorities in this area favor conducting the salary discussion and the annual performance review separately. Their reasoning is as follows: The annual performance review should be a meaningful and constructive experience in itself. It thus is too risky to merge discussions of pay or salary, often an emotionally laden and anxiety-producing topic, with annual performance. Actually, the key objectives of the annual performance review are:
   a) To learn all we (the manager and the subordinate) can about the past year's performance—what went well, what went less than well, and what can be learned from it so as:
   b) To plan and organize better next year's work—new goals, objectives, plans, added resources, etc.—on a mutual basis, and
   c) To prepare jointly a development plan for the subordinate.

So if we take the annual performance review seriously, it is apparent that there is enough to talk about without muddying the waters by adding or including pay in the discussion. Also, a progressive performance or appraisal review system should favor more rather than fewer opportunities for boss-subordinate meetings. So why not discuss pay in a later meeting?

Note: The employee is certain to be more relaxed and "centered" on the performance review if he is not also thinking about "what kind of pay raise will I get?"

2. **False.** Both topics are too important to be discussed in a combined session. The better approach is to hold a separate meeting to discuss career planning. Actually, career planning discussions are not necessarily held with or for every employee. Some may have already reached the peak of their career ladder; others may be determined specialists who are not interested in moving to new or broader fields; some may be approaching retirement age; still others may not have exhibited enough success on the job to merit such discussions.

3. **False.** Avoid the quagmire of personality traits, which are subjective as to meaning and typically not easy to relate to actual performance. So stick to performance, which is observable, measurable, and a lot easier to get agreement on regarding its

relationship to actual job requirements. **Note:** If the official performance review form asks you to rate traits such as creativity, conscientiousness, initiative, and the like, you obviously have no choice but to do so. But don't confuse rating of traits with the assessment of actual accomplishment for the past year.

4. **False.** All employees, regardless of their degree of proficiency and/or performance, can profit from a work review at year's end. How else can the next year's work be planned and targets set if this is not done? Also, even outstanding performers need recognition, support, and encouragement for work done well.

5. **False.** Comparing one worker with another in the annual performance review session is courting trouble. The best approach is to discuss performance in relation to known, agreed-upon standards and objectives. Most performers don't mind a review of their accomplishments in relation to established standards, job requirements, or agreed-upon targets. They don't relish being compared to someone else. Little is to be gained by stating that "You didn't do nearly as well as Pat did."

6. **False.** The key objective is not to complete a form but to assess what was done (actual accomplishment) as a basis for planning next year's work better.

7. **False.** Coaching is an ongoing, day-to-day process. It entails frequent discussions about the work. Giving feedback about the work can hardly wait for December 30 to arrive if we want ongoing improvement.

8. **False.** People need frequent positive reinforcement to sustain them. This means recognizing and rewarding work done well. Dwelling on shortcomings is hardly *the way* to instill confidence and encourage motivation.

9. **False.** As I have been indicating, the emphasis is to plan ahead, to improve what is done each year. Our concern with last year is to extract what we can from that learning experience to move on to greater accomplishment in the new year.

10. **False.** The annual performance review session is for the employee. It provides him with a chance to present what he did well, what might have been done better, and how he sees his work in the immediate future. It may also be an opportunity to ask the boss for greater help (coaching time, more

resources, etc.). You want to ascertain how the employee sees himself and his prospects for greater achievement and personal development. If you monopolize the session's available air time, you won't learn as much as you could by listening more.

The Annual Performance Review: Skill Pointers

If you have taken the above self-test as suggested and reviewed the author's "answers," you may now feel that the annual performance review can be a worthwhile, highly productive experience. Use of the following guidelines should help to make it so.

1. **Preparation.** Be certain to prepare in advance for the performance review session. Think in terms of: a) what was accomplished and what was not, b) what you would like to see done in the following year (goals, objectives), and c) the major development needs (personal growth/improvement) of your subordinate.

Ideally, you should have been making notes about these issues throughout the year.

2. **Mind-set.** You want this session to be an experience that is positive, strengthens your relationship with your staffer, and lays the groundwork for high accomplishment in the coming year. So think of the forthcoming meeting as a joint planning session, one in which you avoid dominating it. You want to take advantage of your subordinate's motivation, which is possible only if you involve him fully in the planning of next year's work.

You also want to avoid dwelling on past mistakes. Blaming, fault-finding and petty criticisms are hardly routes to building self-confidence and self-esteem. Regard possible miscues only as opportunities to create learning experiences. Further, you don't want to fall into the trap of "appraisal by surprise," that is, dredging up negative events that were never discussed previously with the employee. The inevitable reaction: "Gee, boss, I didn't know you felt that way about that. If you had told me when it happened . . ."

3. **Coaching impacts.** If you have functioned as the "good" coach the past year—open, frequent dis-

cussions on daily problems, and quarterly reviews of previously agreed-upon goals—the performance review at year's end should be a "piece of cake." Since most matters will have been previously discussed, there should be no surprises and, for the most part, both of you should be on the same wavelength on key aspects of the work.

4. **Time allotment.** Don't treat the session as something akin to an appointment with your dentist—to get in and out as quickly as possible. So allot enough time for the meeting so that matters of mutual concern can be discussed thoroughly and meaningfully in a relaxed way. And be sure to have your secretary protect you from telephonic and other interruptions.

5. **Communication pattern.** As indicated above, you want your subordinate to do most of the talking in the meeting because, basically, it is his opportunity to discuss his progress and to present his plans for the next year. So use your good listening skills and resist any possible temptation to "take over." Careful listening is the only way you can be certain you know where your staffer is coming from. You know *your* point of view, but you don't necessarily know his.

6. **Purposes.** We have indicated that the annual performance review relates to work accomplishment, with past results serving as a guide to planning for the future. So the prime purpose has little to do with completing a rating or evaluation form. If the human resources people want a "report card" to be prepared, do so. But making check marks on an evaluation form that is personality-trait oriented is hardly the same as conducting a genuine, in-depth discussion of work plans for next year.

7. **Praise for performance.** Use the session to express your appreciation for work done well. Everyone appreciates praise and recognition from his boss. So don't overlook opportunities to provide positive reinforcement to the extent possible. Communication of earned praise will serve both as a motivator and as a means of getting closer to your staffer.

8. **Development.** Use the session to work with your subordinate on his personal growth and development. Rare is the employee who is so perfect that he no longer needs to improve in some respect. So while setting *work* goals for the next year, also think in terms of specific *personal development* needs and goals. **Note:** Our reference here is personal develop-

ment for better work accomplishment. It is not necessarily tied into career development, which should be subject to a separate meeting.

Management consultants Z. B. Leibowitz, J. E. Shore, and G. M. Schuman, in a study of managerial roles in people development ("Managers Can Be Developers Too," *Training and Development,* March 1992), report that a growing number of companies are having managers' performance appraisals include consideration of their efforts to develop people. For example, at Gannett Co., executive compensation bonuses are based in part on their effectiveness in employee development. Similarly, Lotus Development Corporation's incentives and bonus plan for managers is based on both people management and business goals.

9. **Closing the session.** You want to end the session on a high plane. You want your subordinate to feel good about what he accomplished in the prior year and to look forward to the next year's agenda. So thank the employee for his past efforts and achievements. Set a date to discuss progress on the agreed-upon goals and plans for the new year. Typically, a quarterly review should suffice. At that time you can review progress, offer added help as needed and amend or update plans and goals as new circumstances may require.

CONFRONTATION: DEALING WITH MARGINAL PERFORMERS

"Where does personnel find these people?" "Old George just isn't up to what we need now." "Pat could do a lot better if she really wanted to." "I guess we can live with Kim until she decides to 'pull the plug' (retire)." "We've tried everything here at headquarters. Maybe it's the field's turn to see what they can do with the guy."

As the above statements indicate, supervising less-than-competent people is a real source of managerial pain. Of course, workers who are clearly incompetent or ineffective—the "deadwood"—are easier cases to act on. If the duties and responsibilities and performance standards are very clear, and work results are patently below those requirements, the obvious course of action is to remove the person from the job. An appropriate personnel transaction—reassignment, transfer, demotion, or possibly discharge—should (and normally would) take place.

However, the marginal or borderline worker presents another type of headache, for he is not totally unqualified or incompetent. He can perform, but with serious limitations. He thus borders on the ineffective.

Causes

What are the causative factors for lukewarm performance? A pedestrian and thus surface analysis would tell us that, obviously, it's lack of ability, i.e., deficits in skill or knowledge, or possibly "attitude." But a more profound and realistic assessment of causation would recognize that there may be one or more of a whole host of causative factors at work, which include:

Inept Recruitment/Placement

The selection process itself may have been flawed due to preparation of fuzzy job requirements, misunderstanding of job requirements by recruiters, poor appraisal of the candidate's educational and/or experiential background, inadequate reference checking, and possibly a shortage of qualified candidates and a resultant surface-type evaluation of the applicant.

Faulty Orientation/Training

The new recruit may be subject to a "sink or swim" job experience. The worker is not given the proper guidance to get off to a good start, and his performance is all downhill thereafter.

Lack of Clear-Cut Responsibilities, Goals, Objectives, Standards, or Priorities

A target which can't be discerned can't be hit. If one is operating in a sea of ambiguity, a less-than-successful job experience is inevitable.

Lack of Feedback About Performance

Procedures for vital feedback to the worker may be absent, or the boss may be reluctant or too busy to provide indispensible, constructive criticism. Under these circumstances, performance cannot be corrected. The months go by and the manager then wonders why he has a "problem child" on his hands.

Negative Balance of Consequences

In connection with the above factor, management consultant Gilda Dangot-Simpkin ("Getting Your Staff to Do What You Want," *Supervisory Management,* January 1991) points out that the consequences are more favorable when employees don't perform than when they do.

Example: Employees may perform poorly in various ways such as late arrivals, half-hearted cooperation with others, sloppy work, skipped deadlines, etc. What are the consequences? Poor work, for example, may be assigned to someone else to complete or "clean up," or the boss may do it himself. If nothing of a negative sort happens (no consequences), then there is little incentive to improve.

Coaching authority Ferdinand F. Fournies, in *Why Employees Don't Do What They're Supposed to Do (and What to Do About It)* (New York: McGraw-Hill, 1991), states that managers unconsciously reward and influence poor performance. Some examples:

☐ If difficult tasks are performed poorly, employees receive only easy tasks.
☐ If employees are difficult to control, they receive job assignments giving them a lot of freedom.
☐ If employees complain repeatedly about certain work assignments, they get them less often.
☐ If employees perform badly, their reward is to receive a lot of attention from the boss, who adopts the role of amateur psychologist.
☐ If employees produce errors in their work, the boss very kindly corrects them.

What is overlooked by well-intentioned managers is that *performance that is rewarded will increase in frequency.* This rule applies whether the behavior/performance is or is not desirable.

An Impossible Job

Some jobs are certain prescriptions for failure or, at best, marginal success. Visualize the secretary who works for several managers, is severely overloaded, receives conflicting instructions about procedures and standards, is subject to ambiguous or shifting priorities, is not cued into program developments, and so on. Replacing the worker is hardly an appropriate response. The only answer, of course, is some form of job redesign. At higher levels in the organization, jobs may be marked by so great an overload—constant pressure, changing demands, inordinate amounts of travel, etc.—that burnout and even greater damage may result. Management writers have long referred to such punishing jobs as "widow makers."

Systemic Weaknesses

The system or environment itself may be flawed; e.g., cumbersome procedures or processes, murky policies, missing guidelines, inadequate equipment, etc., may be root causes for the marginal performance.

Uncooperative/Indifferent Associates

Fellow workers may not accept the newcomer to the "team" due to age, sex, race, nationality, appearance, or physical limitation. Without peer understanding, support, and cooperation, the new worker may find it difficult to function to his full potential. This is particularly likely if there is a high need for interdependency in the job situation.

A Major Change in Job Requirements

A capable worker may be caught up in a reorganization, new goals or new programs for which he has limited background. **Example:** A well-established film-producing company, which made training films, "suddenly" found itself besieged by numerous competitors producing much higher-quality and more exciting products. The film director, who was primarily a capable maker of documentary films, could not readily meet the new requirement for more creative, fast-paced, all-dramatic productions, with a Hollywood-TV flair.

A Personality Conflict

The boss and the new worker may simply not "hit it off." Different backgrounds, outlooks, values, work styles, philosophies, and so on may bedevil the relationship. In such a hostile climate, with each party trying to prove the other to be misguided, success on the job is hard to obtain. Also, if a manager is trying to direct someone he doesn't like, in all likelihood the result will be minimal contact by the boss. This will mean less rendering of praise, appreciation, interest, support, and encouragement, which will, in turn, aggravate the relationship and impact on an unfavorable performance. Behaviors to be anticipated are reduced effort, less-than-

quality work, and even subtle attempts to "sabotage" the boss' operations.

Management consultant Barry Willis has studied the causes for poor performance. He has worked with more than 30,000 people tagged as poor performers. Lack of know-how and lack of skills were two obvious causes. But the biggest complaint by their bosses was "style or manner in carrying out the work" rather than technical ability to perform properly. Willis cites these specific failure factors (in "On Strategy: HR Skills Help Managers Turn Around Poor Performers," *Personnel Journal,* May 1991): interpersonal difficulties with bosses, peers or subordinates; confused job expectations due to poor communication or changes in structure, or both; a basic disagreement in values, i.e., how the work should be accomplished or what is important in the position; low job interest due to a feeling by the employee that one is doing less meaningful work; lowered future expectations of the employee, leading to a lack of motivation to do well; lack of discipline and control to get the work done; a communication/relationship "space" between the boss and the failing worker, i.e., since the employee doesn't listen, the boss spends less time with the person, the space widens, and poor performance results.

Personal/Domestic Problems

The worker may bring a great deal of personal baggage to the job—at-home problems with spouses, teenagers, finances, illnesses, an imminent or completed separation or divorce, death of a loved one, and the like. **The result:** enough job distractions to prevent the performance desired by either the boss or the worker.

An Uninvited Transferee

At times, due to reorganizations, mission changes or downsizings, a manager may be required to "take on" an employee from another part of the organization who is generally capable and willing, but is not suited for high-quality work in the receiving organizational segment. Typical managerial reactions? "Live" with the person or try to "unload" the worker at a later date on to someone else. The author worked in an organization where the boss was very glad to receive a transferee because it would add another position to the unit. Even though the transferee was generally known to be somewhat of a misfit, his hope was that he could divest himself of that person in time and then have the extra slot to recruit whomever the wished! Unfortunately, the marginal transferee had enough "organizational smarts," including connections, to manage to stay on.

The "Puny" Promotee

In a hierarchy, every individual tends to rise to his level of incompetence."

—Lawrence J. Peter, *The Peter Principle*

At times individuals may be promoted to a job that is simply beyond them. The manager, who may have had high hopes for the incoming person, finds to his dismay that his judgment in selecting the person was flawed. Few managers, of course, like to admit that they are not expert judges of people. So the manager has to do considerable soul-searching: Do I admit error in my selection and take action to remedy the mistake, or do I "sit tight" and hope that time, somehow, will remedy the situation?

The On-the-Job-Retiree

From time to time managers may find that they have an employee on their hands who is able but not totally willing. The person may be a senior worker who has been "through the wringer." He has experienced all the usual changes, reorganizations, downsizings, new and abandoned programs; been passed over for promotion several times; and has watched numerous bosses come and go. He has "seen it all" and has now reached the stage of "it ain't worth fighting about anymore." His newfound "contentment" is based on a philosophy of "it really doesn't matter too much what I do around here, so I'll just put out enough to get by until I'm ready to cash in on the retirement plan." For this person's boss, who may be loaded with vim and vigor, it is indeed a tough challenge to face, for "Old Jane (or Joe)" is not easy to ignite, displace, or unload on other managers.

The "Savior Syndrome"

This is a super-optimistic managerial outlook that he can succeed in transforming the weak performer where others have not. Based on the delusional belief that he can make a difference, the manager utilizes a wide gamut of defenses—denial, rationalization, etc.—to justify his toleration of a performer whom others see as beyond redemption. So we might expect glowing statements—self-talk or talk to others—such as these: "He needs a little more time, that's all," "Given the right kind of treatment, she'll come around," "As a manager, it's my job to give everyone a fair shake," "I don't think anyone under-stands what it takes to motivate an employee like that," and so on. The net result: The outfit is saddled with the borderline performer for the long haul.

Barriers to Acting

Although managers know intellectually that they have to deal with ineffective performers, there may be a number of barriers to taking action (per Vicki Paulik and Dr. Brian H. Kleinger, "Communication—On-the-Job Employee Counseling: Focus on Performance," *Personnel Journal,* November 1986):

Time Pressures

Other needs—programs, operations—may loom more importantly. As they would see it, the time to do the job properly just isn't there. So it can be deferred until a "true" crisis arises.

Intimidation

A reluctance to act may be based on the manager's fear of an aggressive employee or of a close associate(s) of the employee, particularly if the latter is (are) in powerful positions.

Pity

There may be a tendency to feel sorry for the poor performer, particularly if the latter is trying very hard to perform to standards. The result is to "go easy" on the person.

Friendship

If the poor performer has a personal tie with the manager, the latter may be very cautious in acting as he would with other weak producers. **The result:** a delay of action.

Legal Fears

Minority or disadvantaged employees performing below standard may create fears of possible legal ramifications if definite action were taken. Thus, "more time to work things out" or living with the problem may be the decision.

Lack of Skills

Some managers may feel that they are neither trained nor experienced to confront performance difficulties. As they would see it, the annual performance review is enough of a headache, so why do it more often?

Seniority Considerations

With "good" intentions, the manager may feel that it is not "fair" to ride roughshod on someone who has risen from the ranks or has been on board a long time. So there may be a tendency to go easy on such long-time workers.

Cures

If you or I have a borderline worker on our hands, we should ask ourselves these four key questions:

1. Have I fallen into the trap of accepting alibis for the substandard performance? If so, consider the import of the old army infantry saying: "Don't tell me why your rifle isn't working. Tell me why you didn't hit the target." Sure, there may be legitimate reasons for weak performance. But those reasons are to be differentiated from mere excuses. The manager's job is to insist on *results*. So the skill factor for the manager who is presented with excuses is to deal with them on a gentle, but *positive* basis. **Example:** In response to a subordinate's lament that the people in certain departments are "hard to deal with," the skilled manager responds thusly: "I know those people are not easy to deal with. But what can we do to get our job done?" In effect, the manager functions as a coach/teacher by communicating that he will listen to explanations and excuses. "But we still have to think in terms of how to overcome them."
2. Have I fallen into the added trap of reducing the standards either with or without my awareness of it and learning to "live" with the marginal performer? "Lowering the goalposts" is hardly an answer to a performance problem.
3. Am I, in any other way, a contributing factor? Or, as it is phrased these days, "Am I part of the solution or part of the problem?" If you have nurtured or tolerated the problem to one degree or another, obviously you have a special obligation to try to get the employee back on track. If you are not a contributor, as an ethical, professional manager you still should feel that it its your job to help the employee as opposed to arbitrarily "writing him/her off."
4. What is the best way to "salvage" the worker? Recognize that everyone has some good qualities (knowledge, skill, attitude) that may be tapped in one form or another.

In response to the all-critical question #4, here, then, are some ways to cope with the employee "on the brink":

Coaching

Make a needs/performance analysis to learn what the mediocre employee can and cannot do (skill or knowledge deficiency). In the weak areas, consider whether he can be bolstered via

a) clarifying responsibilities; defining goals more precisely and realistically; re-stating standards, priorities and deadlines, and the like; b) assigning work very carefully, i.e., providing a full explanation of requirements and expectations; c) reviewing promptly all completed work, in conjunction with the worker (feedback), to upgrade quality.

Note:

1. Coaching, at the outset, may entail confronting the employee about his performance, for some workers may not be aware that their work actually is below standard.
2. When confronting the marginal performer formally, it is a good idea to begin the coaching session by asking the employee to assess his own performance. If the worker can recognize and admit to significant weaknesses, the likelihood of defensiveness arising is reduced. And if the employee can see his shortcomings, it may also help to have him offer suggestions to overcome performance deficiencies.
3. Regardless of who initiates and offers suggestions to upgrade performance, the coaching session should end on a specific and firm note: "These are the things that have to be done to achieve at standard." In effect, an action plan must be developed, mutually agreed upon, as a basis for a new start.

Training

Formal training, either in-house or at an outside facility, may be another way to upgrade capabilities. These training courses should be attended with the objective of overcoming identified skill deficiencies, not to overcome amorphous "bad" attitudes, to "broaden outlooks," or to provide "added motivation," the latter goals being too general to produce worthwhile, realistic, measurable pay-offs.

Reassignment

If one understands fully the marginal worker's capabilities, and he simply cannot "cut the mustard" in the unit to which now assigned, an earnest effort should be made to place the person elsewhere. This should not be an attempt to dump off one's problem on someone else, but a good-faith effort to place the person in a job for which he is actually qualified. There is little point in repeating the "round peg in the square hole" mistake.

Demotion

At times we may encounter an employee who is hard-working, eager, and cooperative, but simply finds that he is over his head in the current job. Placing the worker in a more manageable job, even if it may mean a reduction in responsibility and even rank, is a very appropriate solution. In fact, the employee may welcome the removal of the pressure to succeed in a situation where he clearly cannot. Keys to a "successful" demotion are supportive counseling and, if possible, reassignment to a new, different location where the worker now can operate within a "stigma-free" atmosphere.

Departure Counseling

One way to resolve the difficulty is to level with the marginal worker about his below-par performance, his likely future in the outfit, and to suggest a voluntary departure. To sweeten the pot, the proposal may be accompanied with an offer to help him to relocate elsewhere. The assumption here is that the boss has tried conscientiously to upgrade performance, but to no avail. In some cases, the worker may be relieved at hearing the proposal, for "being in over one's head" is an anxiety-producing circumstance. Not many of us like to struggle constantly in an impossible job situation. If the employee does decide to leave voluntarily, both parties can breathe a heavy sigh of relief.

Of course, the well-intentioned offer may be bitterly declined. ("It's not my fault that things didn't work out," or "I don't think I'm doing any more poorly than anyone else here," or "I've been with the outfit for 19 years, I'm 48 years old and I don't see anyone hiring me at my age.") In that case, courage is called for and a discharge is the only remaining alternative.

Early Retirement

In dealing with the senior marginal worker, early retirement may be another possible option. With sensitive counseling, the worker can be helped to think through the merits of staying on in an uncomfortable situation vs. leaving the organization and the new, rewarding freedom it can bring. Of course, economic needs and other considerations (e.g., "I can't just sit at home and do nothing") may militate against such a choice.

Discharge

Even though managers understand that firing someone "goes with the territory," it still is one of the toughest tasks a manager has to face. (One senior manager told the author that in his career, he has had to remove employees from their jobs a number of times. Each time, his stomach would act up and he would have to go to the restroom for some 30 minutes before delivering the bad news.) Few of us enjoy putting anyone on the street, even if the employee is "in over his head," job-wise.

But firing someone is not necessarily the end of the world for the person. In fact, many such workers admit they have seen it coming for some time. Also, discharged personnel do survive and go on to other jobs.

An additional rationale for taking such an action is that the marginal person, in all likelihood, is a thorn in the side of other staffers. Taking the bold action is a means of improving the overall work climate and work relationships.

In any case, if termination is the only remaining course of action—the last-resort kind of thing—three requirements must be met:

1. The action being taken should be based solely on performance, and every possible opportunity—coaching, training, feedback, etc.—has been provided the employee to improve his work. Also, every attempt should have been made to accomplish a transfer or reassignment once it was established performance was below par.
2. There has been a full documentation of the worker's inability to meet clearcut job requirements. The personnel office should be contacted and worked with to ensure that the case is not likely to be rebutted by any appellate body (arbitrators, the EEOC, the courts, etc.).
3. The manager must draw on his reserve of courage. Firing someone is not for the faint of heart. A supportive procedure for the manager contemplating

or in the throes of removing someone from the job is to read (and reread) the well-known poem "Invictus" written by the English poet William E. Henly (1849–1903) while in a TB hospital:

Out of the night that covers me,
Black as the pitch from pole to pole,
I thank whatever gods may be
For my unconquerable soul.
In the fell clutch of circumstance
I have not winced nor cried aloud.
Under bludgeonings of chance,
My head is bloodied but unbowed.

Firing Someone Artfully

As we have said, firing someone when necessary is a distasteful and even a stressful job. But there are better as opposed to poorer ways to do it. Dr. W. A. Recker, professor of supervision, formerly at Northern Kentucky University, helpfully offers "The Ten Commandments of Firing" (*Management Solutions,* May 1987):

Thou Shalt Not Fire in Anger

Firing someone is a decision-making event. It thus should be approached carefully in a problem-solving manner.

Thou Shalt not Fire on the Spot

Observing a bad behavior meriting dismissal does not mean you have to act immediately. A more appropriate procedure is to institute a suspension without pay, possibly for three days. This will give you time to investigate things and allow you to re-think your thoughts about termination. If your study of the matter proves firing is in order, you have given yourself adequate time to plan for the termination session. If your decision is not to discharge the worker, the lost salary can be restored.

Honor Thy Manager's Opinion

Seek out your boss' advice before you act. He may be able to be of help, especially if he has encountered this problem before.

Thou Shalt Not Ignore Precedents

Touch base with the personnel people lest there has been a like infraction that was resolved *without* a firing.

Thou Will Document Everything

Button down the who, what, where, and why of the case, for you never know when you may have to defend your decision in court.

Thou Shalt Look at Previous Performance Appraisals

On the assumption that the basis for the proposed termination has been developing over time, refer back to prior performance evaluations for useful data.

Thou Shalt Terminate with a Positive Attitude

To reduce the stress a bit in the termination interview, present as many tangible benefits or entitlements as you can—back pay; severance pay, if applicable; extent of unemployment benefits; the status of any insurance plans, etc. Then give the worker a written statement about them to ensure that what was said was understood. The odds are that the stress of the message—"You are being released"—will cause a tune out of what has been said about his benefits.

Thou Shalt Not Fire in Your Office

If available, a quiet, telephone-free, neutral location is to be preferred. The change of location will communicate loud and clear that the meeting is of a special order and is to be a short one, not to be prolonged by a pointless debate.

Thou shalt not fire on Friday

The worst time to fire anyone is at the close of the week's business. This gives the worker a large amount of grieving time, at home, on Saturday and Sunday. It also means that you have to worry over your weekend how he's handling it at home. Dr. Recker advises to fire on Monday so that the worker can begin his job hunt on Tuesday. This should give the person the full week to check with buddies on possible job leads. The prompt start of the job search is a healthy way for the worker to deal with his loss.

I would provide these added commandments:

Thou Shalt Not Terminate Someone Who has Just Returned from an Extended Illness, Experienced a Personal Tragedy, or Been Away on Vacation

The experience of a discharge is punishment enough without communicating it in a time frame that is quite certain to augment the shock.

Thou Shalt Plan the Termination Meeting Carefully

This means being sure of your facts, knowing what you intend to say (reasons, examples of deficient performance), anticipating possible defensiveness, and knowing how you intend to close the session.

Thou Must Allow for Ventilation of Feelings

Since you have anticipated an emotional response—tears, anger, raised voice, denial, disbelief, complaint of unfairness or discrimination—do let the worker get his feelings out as necessary. Your job is to listen politely and not fall into the trap of responding with anger or argument. Simply assure the worker that the decision has been thought through carefully and is firm.

Thou Must Provide for a Departure with Dignity

You want the worker to leave the organization with the feeling that he is certainly a worthy human being. Your action is being taken for only one reason—the person's skills/abilities simply did not match key requirements of the job. Stay away from patronizing and less than-sincere comments about the person, e.g., "You probably saw this action coming," "This may turn out to be the best thing for you in the long run," or "I'm sure your next employer will find that you have a lot to offer."

Thou Shalt Close the Meeting in a Professional Way

Keep the meeting short—15–30 minutes should do it. You may wish to express your regrets that things didn't work out and that you hope that the experience gained here will be useful in future positions elsewhere. Be sure to ask the worker to clear his desk or locker of personal belongings and to turn in keys, identification badges and the like. A final handshake and a "Good Luck" can serve as the close-out procedure.

Thou Shalt Meet with Staff Afterward

Your staff is entitled to know of the action taken and the reasons for it, how it will affect the responsibilities of everyone else, and what plans, if any, are contemplated to replace the discharged worker. Express your feelings about the unpleasant nature of the removal action, indicating that it was done for the good of the organization.

Solutions of a Less-Common Kind

As we have indicated, when we are faced with a marginal performer, we typically tend to think in terms of coaching, training, reassignment, transfer, demotion, and even discharge. And these are the proper approaches. However, if those are our only approaches, we may overlook other powerful possibilities. Three of these less traditional approaches are *restructuring the situation, using visual graphic feedback,* and *altering the reward procedures.*

Restructuring the Situation

A tomato-processing plant was faced with worker productivity that was low and becoming lower. A performance analyst observed that workers looking at the moving belt saw only a constant movement of red tomatoes all day long. But when they looked up at the white walls of the building they still saw a moving belt of red tomatoes! This was a stressful situation, indeed. **The solution:** no lectures, pep talks, training and the like, but simply to transform the white wall to blue and the tomatoes on the wall quickly disappeared (reported in *News and Notes, National Society for Performance and Instruction,* November/December 1988).

Visual/Graphic Feedback on Performance

A manufacturing firm, producing 67 million industrial fasteners monthly, wanted greater output. Although initial thinking for increased production related to a large-scale redesign and retraining program, this approach was dropped for an alternate solution recommended by a performance analyst. **The solution:** simply put a graph by each employee's workstation. Provide visual data regarding the production standard and the worker's performance. **The result:** In three months, worker productivity soared by 27% (reported in *News and Notes, National Society for Performance and Instruction,* November/December 1988).

Note: While the above two examples relate to augmenting plantwide productivity, the strategies involved obviously apply to *individual worker* situations as well.

Altering the Reward Procedures

As stated above, performance problems arise for a variety of reasons, everything from a lack of skill or knowledge to questionable supervisory practices and impediments in the system/environment. All of which adds up to "can't do." However, in some instances the worker may have a motivational/attitudinal block, or "won't do."

So what can the conscientious manager do? He should think in terms of changing the reward procedures, i.e., locating the employee's "hot button" and altering the rewards accordingly. **Example:** Assume you have a "plateaued" worker in your unit, someone who has very clearly reached the high point in his career, possibly having been passed over for promotion a number of times. He is now "coasting" toward the "happy days" of retirement. Trying to "light a fire" under the worker who has retired on the job via lectures, pep talks, threats and the like, is equivalent to pushing an army tank up hill.

The better approach is to identify and use rewards with "turn-on" value. In the case of the plateaued worker, treat him as "an expert," tapping his accumulated, unique experience in a variety of special ways—to serve on a special study group, head up a task force, serve as a special liaison or representative of the office, assume a major instructional role in a training program, develop new procedures or manuals, conduct field evaluations, etc. In general, the idea is to show respect for the person's prior successes by showering him with a variety of ego-inflating, special assignments. Praise for quality results is also very much in order. Also, seek out his opinion regularly—"What do you think of this?"—as problems come up.

Note:

1. In all of the above proposed solutions, we have not suggested applying a lot of pressure on the below-standard performer—via lectures, pep talks, threats, ostracizing, shaming (e.g., via put-downs) personalized pleas ("How can you do this to me?"), etc.
2. Also, we have *not* suggested reducing the standards. We do expect the shallow performer to per-

form a legitimate day's work in one capacity or another, either with us or with someone else in our organization.

GUIDELINES FOR EFFECTIVE DISCIPLINE

At times, managers are faced with employee behavior that may merit some form of disciplinary action—oral or written reprimands, suspension, demotion, and discharge (discussed above). The behavior may relate to violation of safety rules, gambling on company property, insubordination, falsifying documents, fighting, dishonesty, sexual harassment, and so on.

Management professor Robert N. Lussier prescribes "16 Guidelines for Effective Discipline," *Supervisory Management,* March 1990:

1. **Understand your authority.** How far can you act on your own in giving warnings, or suspending or firing someone? If there is a union, what procedures must you follow?
2. **Know the rules and the reasoning behind them.** In this way you can speak for management to employees about them.
3. **Communicate rules accurately.** Those who work for you should be clear about applicable rules.
4. **Support the rules in your communication with employees.** Your job is to support the rules, not to raise doubts about them.
5. **Be a role model.** You can't expect employees to follow the rules if you are lax about them.
6. **Don't discipline anyone on hearsay information.** Collect your own evidence before you act.
7. **Get the facts before you act.** Give the accused a chance to state his case.
8. **If rules are broken, you must act.** Trying to be "the good guy" will only lose respect for you and the rules.
9. **Discipline in private and wait until day's end to do it.** By waiting until the end of the day, emotions will have subsided, the employee will have had a chance to reflect on his infraction, and work disruption will be minimized. Also, if the worker is disciplined, he won't have to go back to work to face his associates.
10. **Disciplinary action should be documented.** Have the employee sign the document, and give

him a copy. If the employee balks at providing his signature, involve your boss in the case. The latter can sign it, certifying that the employee did receive the written warning.

The following six rules, known as Douglas McGregor's "hot stove rules," relate to the disciplinary *process* itself:

11. **Discipline should be immediate.** The longer the delay, the less effective it is. Just as the touched hot stove gives immediate feedback, so should the boss' discipline. The best discipline has clarity between the cause-and-effect relationship.

12. **Discipline should provide advance warning.** Prior warning, rather than unexpected discipline, is the best and fairest educational tool. Again, just as the hot stove gives warning—heat and color—employees should be informed of the rules and the penalties for breaking them.

13. **Discipline should be marked by consistency.** Just as the hot stove burns everyone alike, so should the supervisor treat everyone alike when discipline is involved. Also, the stove burns everyone every time it is touched. This means not only applying the same penalties, but acting uniformly when violations arise. Favoritism has no place in a consistent disciplinary system.

14. **Discipline on an impersonal basis.** The boss must focus on the behavior, not on the person. Remember that the hot stove punishes the behavior alone, burning people for what they do, not for who they are.

15. **Use appropriate punishment only.** The old maxim of "the punishment should fit the crime" holds sway. Light punishment for a heavy offense will be ignored. Too heavy punishment may produce anxiety and reduce employee productivity. So tailor the punishment to the offense. Again, the hot stove, if touched, gets one's attention without disabling anyone.

16. **Discipline with regard to future relations.** Treat the offender with grace, as a one-time errant person not as a lifelong rules violator. Don't hold grudges, and welcome the employee back into the fold. Your attitude is that it was a one-time mistake, so let's forget the event and get on with things.

HOW TO SEE YOURSELF AS YOUR STAFF DOES: A PROCEDURE FOR A COACHING PRACTICES REVIEW

(A survey form is given on pages 332–334.)

Story: The late Hollywood movie mogul Samuel Goldwyn is said to have made this request of his key staff: "I want you to tell me exactly what's wrong with me; even if it means losing your job" (quoted in *Supervisory Management*, August 1992, p.5).

As a manager, you have a coaching style that you have developed over the years. Undoubtedly, your style works for you. But have you ever wondered:

☐ How your subordinates see your style?
☐ Is there any possibility that with some feedback from your group you might improve certain aspects of your coaching style?

Because managers often express concern about their own development, which could be aided by seeing themselves through the eyes of their subordinates, a growing number of companies have adopted upward feedback systems to improve managerial coaching skills. Of course, entering into these systems is *voluntary* on the part of the manager.

In universities and colleges, it is a common practice for students to give feedback to their instructors on their teaching capabilities via questionnaires. Generally, the questionnaires are routed to the department head, who then shares the results with the instructor concerned.

Feedback systems are always anonymous insofar as the participants are concerned. To protect anonymity fully, employee assessments (ratings) should be provided only if the unit has a moderately sized employee staff, about five or more. Also, to ensure objectivity and credibility of the process, the tallying of the team member's ratings should be accomplished by an "outside" source, e.g., the personnel, training, or human resources office, or possibly an external consulting firm.

To ensure that the upward feedback system accomplishes what it is supposed to, the manager who is rated by his staff should a) study the final results given to him, b) take time (two or three days) to think about the feedback, and then c) meet with the staff to discuss the feedback.

How does the conscientious, progressive manager implement such an activity? To start the ball rolling, the manager, along with a member of the personnel or training office, should meet with his staff and explain that he is very interested in his development and that he believes that feedback about his coaching skills would be helpful toward this end. Therefore, he is working with the human resources office to administer a coaching practices survey, via questionnaires, to be completed by the staff. The responses on these forms are to be totally anonymous, and everyone's participation in the feedback program is strictly *voluntary.*

The manager should provide further assurances about his sincerity since he doesn't want an "I wonder what he is really up to" response. He thus should make it clear that he has no interest in what any *one* person said on his questionnaire, that he is only interested in total *group* responses. Also, no matter how negative any feedback might be, he has no intention to find out "who said that." And finally, when all the data have been tallied by the human resources (or training) office, he will study it and meet with the staff to discuss it. Wherever possible, he will try to respond to employee suggestions: "Rest assured, I do not intend to ignore your feedback. I am not entering into this just to produce a paper exercise."

After providing the above assurances about his objectives and sincerity, the manager should then turn the meeting over to the personnel or training representative to explain the survey procedures fully and to respond to further questions. It is a good idea for the manager to leave the meeting at that point so the discussion can proceed with the fullest possible candor.

Notes:

1. The feedback data go only to the manager immediately concerned. They are not shared with his boss nor with the human resource office. This is the only sensible procedure because the feedback is intended strictly as a developmental tool, not as a "report card" on the manager to become part of his "file."
2. Employees who give feedback to a manager must work directly for him. There is no point in eliciting feedback on coaching practices from a worker who is not in a clearcut, boss subordinate relationship. Also, the subordinates should have worked for their boss one year or more.
3. The information to be collected should relate only to on-the-job, managerial coaching *behavior,* practices that can have serious impact on employee relations and productivity. It is *not* a rating of the manager's personality traits.
4. The upward feedback system is not practical for every manager. It is a useful tool only for those

managers who are able to tolerate feedback, whether positive or negative, and who have a sincere desire to use the feedback for self-improvement. If a manager sees the process not as an opportunity but as a threat, that his staff will use the feedback opportunity to "get even" or "to nail him to the wall," he obviously should not enter into it. Actually, employees already have many long-standing, significant perceptions and feelings about the boss as a coach. In effect, they have been "rating" their bosses right along. The only pertinent issue for the manager is this: Will the data my subordinates now have help me to see my coaching practices more realistically and thereby allow me to make such changes in them as are worthwhile?
5. If one decides to take advantage of the feedback opportunity, it is a good idea to repeat the survey process a year or so later. This will enable the manager to see if his attempts at improvement/change have been successful.
6. Entering into the process is a good way to begin a team-building program. Eliciting feedback from staff is a good indicator that the boss is sincere in improving staff relations, communication, etc.

See "How I See Myself as a Coach" (page 329) and "Coaching Practices Survey" (page 332).

KEY POINTS: THE MANAGER AS A COACH

1. Successful coaching encompasses two components—skill and attitude. While the skill aspects are very learnable, the attitudinal aspects often are harder to acquire and implement. Why? Because they can only come from one's personal philosophy about people. The most meaningful people-type philosophy has two tenets:
   - ☐ A strong and sincere conviction that people want to do a good job.
   - ☐ Helping conscientious people to do their jobs better and encouraging their growth.
2. The coaching process is a *circular* one. It has various stages and never ends. Each stage is critical to successful coaching. (See Figure 7-1.)
3. The effective coach looks for people's strengths and builds on them.
4. Coaching proceeds best when employees not only have the know-how to do their jobs, but when they are given the confidence, support and resources—

empowerment—to execute their assignments properly.

5. When making assignments, check the current workload of staffers; make your expectations clear; check for employee understanding of them; operate in a relaxed rather than harried manner; indicate your availability, for added help as may be needed; delegate adequate authority to execute assigned responsibilities; and indicate how (and possibly when) progress will be checked.

6. Part of the coaching process is to maintain contact with staff. The tools for this are group and one-on-one meetings plus a lot of MBWA (Management By Walking Around).

7. Effective coaches readily distinguish between helpful review of work vs. mindless micromanaging.

8. Feedback to the performer is a powerful device to upgrade performance. When thinking about feedback, think in 360-degree terms, i.e., securing feedback not only from you, but also from co-workers and possibly customers and suppliers, too.

9. When giving feedback, think in terms of praise as well as constructive criticism.

10. Improve your own coaching prowess by getting 360-degree feedback, i.e., from your boss, your staff, peers, internal clients, and customers and suppliers.

11. Good coaching entails establishing high standards and insisting that they are met. Most people prefer to work for an organization and a boss who take pride in what they do.

EXERCISES, QUESTIONS, AND PROBLEMS FOR DISCUSSION

The following questions and problems may be used in management training workshops or college/university classes in management.

1. Small group assignment: What did a prior boss, teacher, scoutmaster, neighbor, athletic coach, or minister, etc., do to you, for you, or with you which impacted favorably on your growth, development and self-esteem? Secure reports from each group and post on a flipchart sheet. (Or let each team complete its own flipchart sheet and tape to wall with masking tape.)

2. Hold small group discussions on these questions: What skill points can you recommend to give feedback to employees? What approaches seem to help, what seem to hinder? Is there such a thing as being too candid with subordinates when discussing performance?

3. Supervisors are frequently told in supervisory training workshops to get "close" to their people. Is it possible to get appropriately close and still keep one's "professional" distance?

4. What is the best physical location to deal with an employee who has a serious performance problem?

5. Exercise Sheet: Developing Skill in Confrontation

In the situations described below, you have decided to confront the employee about his performance. Enter the substantive statement you would make after having made a friendly, opening comment designed to put the subordinate at ease.

a. **Problem:** A reports analyst has been late in completing the weekly report to the national office. There have been four late reports in the last nine submissions. On two occasions, the headquarters has called about these delayed reports.

Your confrontation statement:

_____

_____

_____

b. **Problem:** In the course of your MBWA, you note that the receptionist typically uses the first hour of work to get through the morning newspaper.

Your confrontation statement:

_____

_____

_____

c. **Problem:** One of your crew chiefs, a very productive supervisor, seems to "ride" the new workers rather severely. It's almost as if he feels he has to let them know who's boss. Several other crew members often "join in" on the "fun."

Your confrontation statement:

_____

_____

_____

d. **Problem:** Machine operators seem to be lax about wearing their safety goggles. You decided to talk to your shop foreman about this.

Your confrontation statement:

_____

_____

_____

e. **Problem:** Your administrative officer, who is very close to her staff, frequently takes off with them for lunch, leaving only one worker to tend to the very active phones over the noon hour.

Your confrontation statement:

_____

_____

_____

Share results in trios; close with a class discussion on what was learned about the technique/skill of confrontation.

6. Here are several suggested role plays involving coaching-type discussions between the boss and a subordinate on these problems:
   a) An employee of yours is capable, but is extremely shy and quiet, and interacts little with the rest of the staff.
   b) The performance of one of your better people has drifted downward noticeably. (Your secretary, who is in this employee's carpool, mentioned casually to you that the employee has been doing a lot of moonlighting of late, has been making a lot of money from that work and just bought a fancy car with leather upholstery.)
   c) You have just met with three members of your staff to give them special assignments. As the trio are leaving your office, you overhear one of them remark to another staffer: "I don't think the boss knows the workload I already have."
   d) Two of your staffers are at one another's throats with regularity. Their conflict comes out often at your staff meetings.

e) You are planning a coaching session with a subordinate regarding a performance problem. You are concerned that the employee may not see the problem as you do, if at all.

f) You are about to have a one-on-one meeting with an overly sensitive employee on a behavior which resulted in a lost customer.

7. A Coaching Quiz

The items below fall into two categories: either true coaching behaviors or merely examples of day-to-day supervision. Place a C before the coaching examples and an SA before the more routine supervisory actions.

_____ a. A section chief is at the over-budget point after only 8 months into the business year. You decide to review her authorization practices and procedures with her and develop, on a mutual basis, plans for strong financial controls.

_____ b. A typist overlooks procedural details with annoying regularity. You know she is careless so you decide to give her a good talking-to about the need for accuracy in the office.

_____ c. A worker is spending an undue amount of time on the phone on personal business. You decide to level with the employee about this, with particular emphasis on the need to keep all lines open for customer calls.

_____ d. One of your section chiefs has been tardy a good deal of late. You meet with her about this. You cite specific data (dates and arrival time) regarding her latenesses, explain how they affect operations, secure agreement regarding her adherence to the established work schedule, and provide praise thereafter when the proper arrival time is followed.

_____ e. You explain to a new worker the rules and procedures regarding requesting annual leave.

_____ f. You are a sales manager. One of your more promising new hires is floundering. After a lengthy telephone conversation with him, you decide to visit him in the field to assist in territory planning, interviewing methods and closing the sale.

_____ g. Your weakest worker turns in the required weekly report two days late. You send it back with a note explaining that it came in too late to be consolidated with the others.

___ h. Two of your employees are at the water cooler engaging in a heated argument which doesn't seem to be getting anywhere. You decide to intervene, advising them that "There's a lot of work to be done around here."

___ i. A subordinate submits a requisite form which requests tuition aid for an evening college course of interest to him. Following organization policy, you sign off on the request. No discussion is held on the request.

___ j. You decide to use your weekly staff meeting as a vehicle to check up on action items to which your staffers have committed themselves.

(Scoring key: Items a, c, d, and f are examples of coaching, for they involve positive actions to upgrade performance and/or change an attitude or behavior. The other items merely entail routine, day-to-day supervision.)

8. List 5 things you do, as a supervisor/manager, which seem to help to orient a new worker effectively.
   a. _____
   b. _____
   c. _____
   d. _____
   e. _____

9. List two things in your orientation activities that are not done now and should be and/or are not done as well as they should.
   a. _____
   b. _____

10. On an individual basis, have participants develop an orientation checklist for their own unit. Then have them meet in small groups to compare and critique their checklists.

11. On a total group basis, brainstorm elements to be included in a check list for employee orientation.

12. The following case may be discussed either in small groups, with reports to the total group, or by the total group.

The Toastmaster's Membership Case

You are Pat Kirby, Operations Manager. You have six supervisors who report to you. One of them, young Kim Goodell, approaches you about possible attendance at a Toastmaster's Club meeting during office hours. You have no objection to the Toastmaster idea, but Kim's club holds its luncheon meeting every other Friday at noon and Kim has to leave early (around 11:15 a.m.) to get to the meeting.

Kim has been very active in Toastmaster's and is now president of the newly formed club. Thus the need to arrive early enough to ensure that all arrangements at the restaurant are in order, to greet arriving members, to welcome guests from other clubs, etc.

The difficulty that arises for you is this: Your weekly staff meeting takes place on Fridays from 10:00 a.m. to about noon. You like this period for these reasons:

a. Your boss holds her staff meeting on Friday from 8:30 a.m. until 9:30 a.m. You thus like to relay the events of that meeting to your staff at your meeting while the information or action items are "hot."

b. You generally go to lunch with your staff at a nearby restaurant at meeting's end. You have found that going to lunch with the team once a week helps maintain rapport and good communication with all concerned.

c. You like to use your staff meeting time not only to review the week's work, but also to plan and coordinate certain things for the following week.

How do you respond to Kim's request to leave the staff meeting early to attend the Toastmaster's Club meeting? What are your options?

13. Small Group Activity: Annual Performance Review
   a. Discuss the annual performance review program in your organization, including the current performance rating form in use related to it. (You were asked to bring a copy of the form to class.)
   b. Agree on the elements of the various programs that 1) make for *effectiveness* and 2) those

which make for *ineffectiveness.* (The form should be treated as one element.)

c. Summarize your conclusions regarding 1) and 2) above on a flipchart sheet, using a two-column format.

d. Now try to visualize an ideal annual performance system. What would its attributes be like? Summarize on a separate flipchart sheet.

e. A member of your team will report your findings/conclusions to the total class.

14. Pass out copies of the worksheet on page 335 to all participants. Have them complete the form individually, and then meet in trios to share experiences. Then secure reports from each team as to what was significant in their discussions.

Checklist for Orientation of the New Worker

Yes	No	Planning Activities
___	___	I have allotted enough time to do it properly without any interruption.
___	___	I have informed my staff of the new person's arrival.
___	___	I have provided a workspace (office, desk) for the new hire.
___	___	I have assembled necessary supplies, files, etc., for the new hire.
___	___	I have reviewed and updated the job description.
___	___	I have assembled all the explanatory materials I will need (e.g., job description, manuals, organization chart, job aids, etc.).

Yes	No	Preliminary Activities
___	___	Provide an enthusiastic welcome.
___	___	Introduce to fellow staffers.
___	___	Introduce to your boss (optional).
___	___	Provide tour of building, office, or shop.
___	___	Point out facilities/location for lunch and breaks, the restrooms, first aid room, copy machines, etc.
___	___	Assign locker (if appropriate).

Yes	No	One-on-One Sessions
___	___	Provide information about company philosophy, objectives, history, etc.
___	___	Provide background of the unit's functions.
___	___	Provide and discuss job description.
___	___	Point out major units with whom there is cooperation/interaction.
___	___	Describe a typical workday, including time of breaks, lunch, etc.
___	___	Spell out expectations: teamwork, standards of production, quality, deadlines, etc.
___	___	Specify dress code (as appropriate).
___	___	Specify security procedures (as appropriate).
___	___	Explain role of union, union contract, union representative (as appropriate).
___	___	Explain safety considerations (as appropriate).
___	___	Explain office/shop policy on personal calls, calling in if sick or late, etc. (as appropriate).
___	___	Advise whether you or someone else will join the new worker for lunch today (as appropriate).
___	___	Allow time for employee to ask questions.
___	___	Explain your availability ("open door"), whether total or partial.
___	___	Assign the new worker to a senior, experienced staffer (the "buddy system") for "break in" purposes (as appropriate).
___	___	Meet with worker at end of day to learn how Day One went.

Figure 7-2.
Worksheet for Task Assignment

The Task:

_____

_____

_____

Desired Outcomes/Results:

_____

_____

_____

Quantity Requirements:

_____

_____

_____

Quality Requirements:

_____

_____

_____

Cost (Budget Limitations):

_____

_____

_____

Interim Progress Reports (Dates):

_____

_____

_____

Expected Deadline for Project Completion:

_____

_____

_____

Resources/Tools/Equipment Needed:

_____

_____

_____

Safety Factors to Be Observed:

_____

_____

_____

Figure 7-5

Chart for Staff Development

Job Experience		Formal Training (in-house and in outside facilities)	Self-Development	
Regular Job Activities	**Broadened Experience**		**Professional and Civic Activities**	**Educational Activities**
☐ Guided Experience or Coaching by Superior ☐ Discussing Performance ☐ Try-out Experience ☐ Unavailability—Forced Decision Making ☐ Staff Meeting Participation ☐ Discussing Key Work Problems ☐ Goal Setting ☐ High Standards (including "stretch") ☐ Feedback (from boss and team members) ☐ Early Assumption of Responsibility for a Cost or Profit Center ☐ Consultation with "Experts"	☐ Job Enrichment ☐ Job Rotation ☐ Cross-Training ☐ Lateral Transfer ☐ Foreign Visits and Assignments ☐ Participation in Policy Development ☐ Speaking Opportunities ☐ Instructor in a Training Course ☐ Special Work Assignments and Special Projects ☐ Temporary Duty Assignments ☐ Acting Assignments for Boss or those on Sick or Annual Leave ☐ Asst. to Chief Position ☐ Understudy Post ☐ Committee Assignments ☐ Task Force Work ☐ Field Trips ☐ Tours, Visits, Inspections ☐ "Sending Upstairs" Technique ☐ Observational Assignments ☐ Mgt. Trainee Approach ☐ Mentoring ☐ "Buddy" System (breaking in a new worker) ☐ Guided Reading ☐ Serving as a Representative or Liasion to other offices or departments	☐ Workships and Seminars ☐ Case Study Discussions ☐ Public Speaking Course ☐ Attendance at Meetings and Conferences on Technical and/or Mgt. Subjects ☐ Team Building ☐ Group Discussion of a Book or Article ☐ Luncheon Meetings With a Speaker	☐ Participation in Community Affairs ☐ Holding Office in Civic Organizations, Professional Societies and Service Clubs ☐ Attending and Participating in and Organizing of Conferences, Conventions, Workshops, Symposia, and Institutes ☐ Writing Articles ☐ Teaching ☐ Toastmasters Club ☐ Networking	☐ University Courses in: Mgt. Subjects Liberal Arts, Writing, Public Speaking, Reading Improvement Technical Subjects ☐ Correspondence Courses ☐ Great Books Club ☐ Planned Reading in Business and News Magazines ☐ Foreign Travel and Study ☐ Sabbaticals ☐ Personal Growth Experiences (e.g., Sensitivity Training, Encounter Groups, Assertiveness Training, Stress Mgt.) ☐ Leave of Absence for Advanced Academic Work

Figure 7-6
Plan for Development

Engineer Jane Grove and I met on Nov. 1 to discuss her development needs. We agreed on these points:

Development Need	Action to Meet the Need
1. Technical a. Hydraulic problems are becoming pressing. Jane has not had any formal training in this area.	1a. Jane will attend Local University at night and take Hydraulic Engineering I and II in the next two semesters. We will pay for this under the firm's tuition reimbursement plan.
b. Our safety matters are requiring closer coordination and direction. Jane has not worked much in this area before.	b. Jane will spend ⅕ of her time with the Safety Engineer in the next six months. This will be primarily in the afternoon, although in some weeks it may be for a full day or two.
2. Management a. We expect Jane to speak before outside groups. She now finds this embarrassing.	2a. Jane has agreed to join Toastmaster's Club No. 682 which meets in town, every Thursday at noon.
b. Jane can use a broad picture of the administrative process, for she is new to her job which is essentially management.	b. In the next 24 months, Jane will enroll in a two-week management program at a major university, based on a recommendation of the Training Dept. We have agreed that a summer might be the best time for this.

(Signed) <u>Jane Grove</u>

(Signed) <u>Leslie Lawton</u>

Figure 7-7

Manager's Guide to Coaching and/or Training Needs

Job Title: Telemarketing Specialist

Name of Employer	Product Knowledge: Features and Benefits	Knowledge of Competitor's Products/ Services	Plans and Organizes Daily Work— Time Mgt.	Calling on "Qualified" Prospects	Cold Calling (Prospecting)	Handling "Call-ins"	Solution Selling (Ascertaining and meeting needs)	Sells Full Product Line	Securing Repeat Business	Building a Client List	Closing Effectively	Handling Customer Problems and Complaints
Pat	A	C	B	A	B	A	B	A	A	A	B	B
Kim	B	C	B	B	B	A	B	B	C	A	A	B
Sandy	C	B	B	A	C	B	A	C	B	A	C	B
Fran	C	C	C	B	C	A	A	C	B	C	B	C
B.J.	B	C	C	B	B	A	B	B	B	B	A	C
Billy	A	B	A	B	C	B	A	A	A	C	C	A

Key: A—Outstanding skill/knowledge
B—Acceptable skill/knowledge
C—Coaching and/or training needed

How I See Myself as a Coach: A Self-Quiz

Now that you have read the text, you know that coaching is a managerial skill concerned with job accomplishment and job improvement. It not only entails assigning and reviewing work, but also upgrading individual performance, ensuring growth of people, and building strong individual motivation and group cohesion.

The following statements are designed to help you assess your skill as a coach. Try to be as candid as you can in your responses so that you can identify clearly your opportunities for growth as a coach.

Procedure: Rate each statement by placing a dot in the appropriate box. When you have rated all of them, take a straight edge or ruler and draw lines to connect the dots. This will provide you with a profile of your capabilities as a coach. The more your profile leans toward the right, the more capable a coach you are. If your profile is skewed to the left or is in the middle, you probably are less effective as a coach. In any case, you now should have a good picture of your coaching prowess and see where your needs for growth and development lie.

Element	Never	Seldom	Occasionally	Frequently	Always
1. My subordinates know clearly what their jobs require them to do.					
2. I make priorities and deadlines clear when I assign work.					
3. I ensure that all projects and activities are subject to clear-cut standards as to what is a well-done job.					
4. I set high standards because they encourage people to do their best.					
5. I let my staff have full control over their work so that they can perform better.					
6. I am concerned with end-results, rather than the activities my subordinates may engage in to produce those results.					
7. I try to deal in goals and results rather than orders and instructions.					
8. As a means of influencing proper behavior by my subordinates, I try to serve as a good model in my behavior. I ensure that there is no gap between what I say and what I do.					
9. I encourage my staff to approach problem solving in terms of creative alternatives rather than limited solutions, that there is no such thing as "only one way" to accomplish things.					
10. I use the annual performance review primarily as a basis for planning next year's work.					
11. I operate so that I tend to ask questions rather than give answers.					
12. I encourage my people to think in terms of doing the right things as well as doing things right.					

Element	Never	Seldom	Occasionally	Frequently	Always
13. I use discussions of everyday work problems as opportunities to alter attitudes, change behavior, and upgrade performance.					
14. I give new employees the attention they need until they feel comfortable with their work, their colleagues and myself.					
15. I try to train my people to think in terms of handling contingencies (unforseen events, emergencies) that may arise.					
16. I try to manage so that people are helped to experience increasing responsibility and growth on the job.					
17. All of my employees have a development plan, either job-related, career-oriented or both, which was worked up on a mutual basis.					
18. The above-mentioned development plans are discussed quarterly with each employee.					
19. I use the work team to set realistic standards and goals for the group.					
20. I secure group thinking before moving ahead on important matters.					
21. I use the total group to help solve problems of above-average difficulty.					
22. I conduct meetings to develop creative solutions *and* to produce strong group feeling as well.					
23. I hold group meetings often enough so that people feel they are part of a vibrant team.					
24. I regard conflict (differences) in my group as a means of achieving higher-quality solutions to problems.					
25. I use our group meetings to get feedback on my skill as a coach—communicating, listening, assigning and reviewing work, delegating, supporting, etc.					
26. I am in frequent contact with my subordinates. They find me very approachable concerning any concerns, needs, problems, etc. they may have.					

Element	Never	Seldom	Occasionally	Frequently	Always
27. I try to discuss my subordinates' problems away from my desk or work area, for people are more comfortable on their own turf.					
28. I rely on face-to-face discussions concerning problems, as opposed to sending my people little notes and memos about the problems.					
29. I try to influence my superiors to get the things my people need to be effective.					
30. I inform my people of their accomplishments and successes as opposed to giving repeated reminders of their mistakes.					
31. I treat my subordinates as individuals because they have different needs.					
32. I operate on the assumption that people come to work for more than the paycheck—namely, accomplishment, challenge, growth, recognition, social interaction, even fun.					
33. I try to establish a climate that helps creativity, job interest, and group pride and cohesion.					
34. I place as much stress on the needs and concerns of people as I do on results—i.e., getting the work out.					
35. I try to manage so that people feel they are valued.					
36. I work closely with my staff so that there is a high degree of trust among us.					
37. I advise my people in advance of any changes that may affect them.					
38. I try to operate so that I communicate my interest in sharing, caring, and supporting, as well as informing, instructing, and implementing.					
39. A criteria I use to assess the success of my coaching opportunities is to ask myself: "Will he now feel better about himself as a result of our discussion?"					
40. I try to manage so that all employees feel good about themselves, their peers, their boss, our goals, and the total operation.					

Coaching Practices Survey

You and your fellow staff members are being asked by your supervisor to assess how well he is functioning in his capacity as a coach. The information you provide will help him to consider possible changes to be made in any of his coaching practices.

Please try to be as candid and objective as you can. In this way, your information, in combination with that of your colleagues, will be of maximum value to your superior.

Procedure: Simply check the degree (never, seldom, occasionally, frequently, or always) that best describes your feeling about the various coaching practices given on the evaluation form.

Note: Do *not* sign your name on this form, for the survey is fully anonymous. Turn your completed form in to the Human Resources Office for tallying of results. They will give your supervisor a consolidated tabulation of results for his services.

Coaching Practices	Never	Seldom	Occasionally	Frequently	Always
Work Assignment					
1. Assignments (work to be done) are clearly stated by my superior.					
2. The purposes (goals or end results) are clearly presented by the boss.					
3. New assignments to me take into account my current workload.					
4. My supervisor insists on high standards as to quantity, quality, cost, deadlines, customer service, etc.					
5. Work is assigned fairly to the staff.					
6. Assignments are given with the expectation that they will be approached creatively.					
7. My boss tries to use my skills and abilities.					
Delegation					
8. My responsibilities and authority to act are clearly stated.					
9. I am given enough authority to carry out my assignments.					
10. I am permitted to work out details of assignments in my own way.					
11. Delegation is genuine, not just a "paper" commitment.					
12. The boss avoids getting into petty details.					
Work Review					
13. When I have a problem with my work, the boss helps me out.					

Coaching Practices	Never	Seldom	Occasionally	Frequently	Always
14. My completed work is reviewed promptly.					
15. Work review is given the time it deserves.					
16. Criticism of my work is fair and constructive.					
17. I am fully informed as to how well I am doing.					
Decision Making					
18. I am able to get clearcut decisions when I need them.					
19. Decisions are not subject to unnecessary delay.					
20. I am involved fully in decisions in which I have special knowledge or expertise.					
21. Decisions are made objectively and logically without any "fence straddling."					
22. Ethical aspects are considered fully when decisions are made.					
23. A full range of options/alternatives is considered when a decision is made.					
24. The boss readily admits mistakes or errors he has made.					
Communication					
25. The boss shares information I need to do my job properly.					
26. We (the staff) are kept informed fully of business plans and operations.					
27. Changes that may affect me and/or my job are communicated early (in a timely fashion).					
28. The boss listens to my ideas and suggestions.					
29. I can talk freely to my boss about my work and problems.					
Interpersonal Relationships					
30. I can trust my boss to do what is right and proper.					
31. I get the support and encouragement I need.					

(*table continued on next page*)

Coaching Practices	Never	Seldom	Occasionally	Frequently	Always
32. I can count on my boss to stand behind me as needed.					
33. My boss is approachable on matters of my concern or interest.					
34. My boss is available to discuss work problems.					
35. When I do a good job, I receive praise/recognition for it.					
36. I am treated with respect.					
37. I feel the boss is interested in me as a person.					
38. Everyone here is treated fairly so as to avoid feelings of favoritism.					
39. The boss brings out the best in people.					
40. The boss interacts actively (keeps in contact) with the staff.					
Team Development/Team Relationships					
41. Group meetings are used to plan operations so as to avoid crises.					
42. The team is used to solve problems wherever the staff can make a helpful input.					
43. The team, working together, makes significant decisions.					
44. Group meetings are held often enough to help everyone do their jobs better.					
45. Group meetings are used to critique ongoing operations.					
46. The boss tries to resolve disagreements between/among staff members.					
47. We hold sessions to assess how well we work as a team.					
Training and Development					
48. I receive the training I need to do my job properly.					
49. My boss is interested in my growth and development.					
50. I am encouraged to take advantage of all possible training opportunities, either within or outside the organization.					

My Experience in Giving and Receiving Feedback About Performance

As a Giver		As a Receiver	
This Helped	This Hindered	This Helped	This Hindered

8

The Manager as Counselor: How to Provide Guidance on Personal and Personality-Type Problems and Career Planning

The worst sin towards our fellow creatures is not to hate them, but to be indifferent to them; that's the essence of inhumanity.

> —George Bernard Shaw (1856–1950), British dramatist, in *The Devil's Disciple* (1896)

The biggest block to personal communication is man's inability to listen intelligently, understandingly, and skillfully to another person. This deficiency in the modern world is widespread and appalling.

> —Carl R. Rogers (1902–1987), U.S psychologist, leading exponent of non-directive counseling, in *Harvard Business Review*, "Barriers and Gateways to Communication," July–August 1952

Of course we have an open-door policy. It means that if you don't like the way we do things around here, management will be glad to show you the door.

—common employee joke cited by Rosabeth M. Kanter, in *The Change Masters* (1983), p. 69.

Whereas coaching is concerned with *job-related* performance improvement, the need for counseling arises when the worker's personal (off-the-job) or *personality-type* problems interfere with his job performance. In fact, the employee may not be aware that his behavior/performance is interfering with his productivity. Hence the need for the counseling intervention.

And a second distinction: In addition to upgrading performance, coaching, as discussed in the prior chapter, is also concerned with employee *growth and development* in relation to the *present* job. But it is *not* necessarily concerned with advising about the employee's career as is the case with the counseling function. Mentoring is also part of the career planning and development activity.

Finally, coaching is a *daily* activity. Just as in the case of the athletic coach, it goes on all the time. Conversely, counseling is or should be accomplished when a particular need arises, e.g., to provide emotional support and understanding for employees who are experiencing emotional setbacks of various sorts.

The manager as a counselor is concerned with:

1) Working with (advising, guiding, referring) the employee on *personal* (off-the-job) and *personality-type* problems which affect performance adversely.
2) Guiding the employee on his *career* planning and *career* development.

The following chart shows the relationship between the coaching and counseling functions:

This chapter, then, will treat these major areas:

☐ Coping with "Difficult" People
☐ Working with the Troubled Employee
☐ Counseling Staff Members on Their Careers
☐ Mentoring: Getting the "Big Picture" the "Hands-on" Way
☐ Directive vs. Nondirective Counseling

The chapter also includes a self-assessment instrument to evaluate one's current counseling skills. Questions and problems for discussion in management training workshops and college classes comprise the final portion of the chapter.

CLOSE ENCOUNTERS OF THE "IMPOSSIBLE KIND": HOW TO WORK WITH DIFFICULT PEOPLE

You must look into people, as well as at them.

—Lord Chesterfield (1694–1773),
English statesman and author

The greatest discovery in our generation is that human beings, by changing the inner attitudes of their minds can change the outer aspects of their lives.

—William James (1842–1910),
U.S. psychologist and philosopher

Sign on a bulletin board near the boss' office:

LONESOME?
LIKE TO MEET NEW PEOPLE?
NEED A CHANGE?
LIKE EXCITEMENT?
LIKE A NEW JOB?
JUST SCREW UP ONE MORE TIME.

As a manager, you undoubtedly have found that most if not all of your staff can be referred to as good employees. They arrive for work when they are sup-

Distinguishing Element	Coaching	Counseling
Source of performance problems	Job performance alone	Personal (off-the-job)/personality factors
Frequence of concern with performance problems	Daily	Intermittent (when problems arise)
Developmental focus	For growth/strengthening in present job	For future positions: career advancement and mentoring

posed to, attend to business fully, meet deadlines, cooperate, take suggestions for improvement in a responsible way, and some of them may even show a creative flair from time to time.

On the other hand, occasionally you may encounter a bad apple—someone who you might describe as a problem employee, a difficult person, one who is a misfit or out-of-step with the organization. This is the person who engages in behaviors that really give you Excedrin-size headaches. These behaviors may range from goofing-off, chronic complaining, and not showing up for work, to procrastination and gossiping. Psychologists call these behaviors acting out, i.e., demonstrating their conflicts ("hang ups") via some form of overt behavior as opposed to controlling them via suppression or other defenses.

Management consultant David Gouthro ("Dealing With Difficult People," *Performance and Instruction,* May/June 1991) defines a difficult person as one who:

☐ Has a concern solely with his own best interests.
☐ Won't accept logical reasoning.
☐ Won't listen to your viewpoint.
☐ Disagrees with your viewpoint.
☐ Objects to how you do things.
☐ Presents an aura of intentional obnoxiousness.
☐ Can't relate well to anyone.
☐ Is an obstacle to the achievement of your goals.

Of course, not all problem people are overly aggressive or insensitive. Some of them may also suffer from a lack of assertiveness or a reluctance to participate fully in group activities.

Note that when we talk about difficult employees we are not talking about people who are different—mavericks, non-conformists, independent types, people who may even adopt a lifestyle on the outside which varies from the norm. As long as these people are productive and even creative, we certainly can accept their somewhat different personalities and styles. Also, our concern with difficult people is not their attitude—we can live with that—but their actual behavior or performance which impacts negatively on productivity, cooperation, communication, etc.

And a final cautionary note. We must make a distinction between inappropriate behavior (the mark of the difficult worker) versus unproductive behavior, for they are dealt with differently. As organization psychologist H. B. Karp ("The ABCs [Appropriate Behavior Change] of Effective Management," *Training and Development Journal,* Jan. 1985) puts it:

Some inappropriate behaviors are dealt with easily through policies regarding safety regulations, lateness or attendance at meetings. Inappropriate dress or abusive behavior are more difficult to confront. In behavior situations there is an element of personalization that does not exist in productivity issues; the issue is always, to some degree, subjective. Second, in behavior situations, the manager deals with personal issues before confronting the offending party. Should I call it to the person's attention now, or hope that the individual will catch it? Won't this person be offended if I raise this issue? What really constitutes an infraction? Is this particular issue any of my business?

In the pages that follow, I present descriptions of a number of difficult people, their personality dynamics, and possible treatment for their maladies. The types discussed are fairly common in organizations and include:

☐ The Constant Complainer
☐ The Pleaser
☐ The Know-It-All
☐ The Procrastinator
☐ The Social Butterfly
☐ The Naysayer
☐ The Goof-Off Artist
☐ The Gregarious Gossip
☐ The Clutter Champ
☐ The Personal Needs Devotee
☐ The Vendor
☐ The Lone Wolf
☐ The Put-Down Artist
☐ The Silent One
☐ The On-the-Job Romancer
☐ The Determined Dresser
☐ The Externalizer
☐ The Late Comer
☐ The Absentee

The Constant Complainer

These individuals seem to thrive on identifying irksome situations that, to most of us, are of little concern. But to them, they are constant and major sources of irritation. Their complaints may range from room temperature, lighting, and available space, to ill-operating equipment, obnoxious fellow workers and customers, and impossible work assignments. There may even be attempts to enlist allies about their complaints.

Personality Dynamics

Constant Complainers feel inadequate and powerless, and thus crave attention and recognition. They want to be regarded as people who can point out the inadequacies of things and situations and the shortcomings of others. By complaining to anyone who will listen, they believe they achieve recognition as astute, perceptive observers. Unfortunately, these super-critics hardly see themselves as others do. What others see are persons engaged in magnification of total minor or irrelevant happenings. Because their nitpicking and whining turns others off, they don't get the warm response they crave. **The result:** They intensify their complaining behavior, which, of course, reinforces people's negative feelings about them. In general, those who complain about others and "bad" situations are really complaining about themselves. Their problem is not with other people, but with their low self-image.

Possible Treatment

Sometimes merely listening, nodding one's head and responding with an "I see" or "Oh, is that the case?" will meet The Constant Complainer's need for a brief contact and a chance to blow off a little steam. A simple restatement or paraphrasing ("You feel that . . .") of what the complainer said may help, too. This procedure will show that he was heard. If the complainer persists it may help to do one or more of the following:

☐ Ask for a memo outlining the particulars of the complaint: "I'm a little rushed now, can you give this to me in writing and I'll look into it." The Constant Complainer wants personal contact, someone to listen to him, so the odds are that the memo will never be written.
☐ Advise to bring it up at the next team meeting for group discussion.
☐ If the complaint is global and vague, be certain to ask for specifics: "Can you give me two or three examples where Charlie failed to cooperate with you?" This approach may cause a "cooling off" of the alleged irritation.
☐ Ask problem-solving-type questions: "What do you see as the solution? How widespread is this? Has this happened before? Who else is involved? What expenditures would it take to correct it? What action do you want me to take to deal with this situation?"

☐ If the complaint relates to matters beyond your control, point that out: "We would have to get Congress to amend the law on that, wouldn't we?"
☐ Try to dilute the merit of the complaint by introducing a note of realism into the conversation: "Have you ever encountered a perfect machine?" "Is it realistic to expect that all customers will be happy with us?" "Since that is headquarters' policy, shouldn't we try to live with it and get on with our job?" "Is our cafeteria worse than others you know of?"
☐ Provide an added assignment when the complainer approaches you with his complaint. It may be that he isn't fully occupied and thus has free time to discover and brood about allegedly irksome matters. Also, if the complainer learns that approaching you produces an extra assignment—negative reinforcement—the unwanted behavior will probably taper off or cease.
☐ Because the complainer is a person with a low self-image, try to build his self-confidence by asking for his opinion on work problems, by assignment of added responsibility, and by providing earned praise.
☐ At times complaints may reflect little job interest due to minimum job challenge. If so, some form of job reassignment may be in order.
☐ In any attempt at counseling to change the behavior, it may help to point out that by offering complaints constantly the complaints tend to be taken lightly. In other words, if The Constant Complainer wants to be effective and to be regarded highly, it is far wiser to select his areas for complaint carefully. An occasional, well-thought-out complaint will be regarded with more seriousness.
☐ Depending on the personality of the complainer and his "irritant quotient," it may be desirable to hint that he may wish to consider a search for greener pastures: "If things are as bad as you say, would you be happier in another department (or company)?" "If your staff is as hard to manage as you say it is, can you give me a name or two of persons who might be willing to take over your job?"

The Pleaser

This employee has these concerns: to get along, to please everyone, not to ruffle anyone's feathers. He will only tell you what he thinks you want to hear. Disagreement with anyone, particularly the boss, is a cardinal sin. Unfortunately, the reactions of others typically is that "He's unreal"; "I wonder what she really thinks"; "I don't mind heavy syrup on my waffles, but here . . ."

A problem with The Pleaser is that he may agree all-too readily to any request, e.g., a deadline, yet won't deliver on that commitment. **The result:** You can't count on what he says or promises. Of course, you may get a lot of apologies for non-performance, but what value are they?

Personality Dynamics

At a very early age, The Pleaser learned that the only way people will like (love) you is to be super nice to them. Obviously, parental advice and admonishments to be polite, be nice, be kind, say only nice things, etc., really took. Syrupy behavior produced the reward of the much-wanted love.

Possible Treatment

Because The Pleaser's totally deferential behavior is both an annoyance and unproductive, its concern and cure would seem to lie in the hands of the team. At team-building sessions, the pleaser needs candid but support-ive feedback along these lines: "We think you have a lot to offer, but you are not helping us to solve problems if you don't tell us what you really think. Actually, we will respect and like you more if you level with us, speak up, disagree with us." And if and when The Pleaser does pre-sent a candid response, it should be rewarded/reinforced with praise: "We really appreciate your sharing your feelings on this. It's important to us to know how you see things, where you stand. We can't become a team if any-one holds back on his ideas and feelings."

The Know-It-All

This individual presents himself as an invincible, indefatigable authority on many, if not all topics. Refer-ring regularly to his prior experience in the field, at headquarters, at Company X, or in another department, plus his extensive reading, etc., The Know-It-All wish-es everyone to understand that he is drawing on his unique background to support his many inputs. Part of his stock in trade is to one-up others with his superior knowledge ("Let me tell you how it really works.") In sum, he knows everything, everyone else knows very little. An obvious problem with The Know-It-All is that since he possesses all the wisdom and all the answers, there is little need to listen to anyone else.

Personality Dynamics

The Know-It-All operates on the assumption that his high volume of input into discussions will produce high regard from others. High knowledge equates with high power and control. Possessed of low self-esteem, he has a need to assure others that he is a very knowledgeable and capable person, indeed, and thus should garner their grateful admiration for his frequent, sage inputs.

Possible Treatment

Probing for specifics is one way to deflate the world's foremost authority's pompousness. Another is simply to say: "You have an interesting point of view. Would you care to entertain another?" Or: "You have a point there. As a knowledgeable person, can you think of some arguments on the *other* side?"

Also, in team meetings the group may wish to point out politely to The Know-It-All that:

1) They are glad to receive his bountiful, learned con-tributions, but that they might be received better if he didn't present them so often and so self-assuredly. ("You know, anyone of us could be wrong *some* of the time."), and

2) The self-announced expert may learn more by lis-tening to others on the team, as opposed to pellet-ing the group with his torrent of ideas.

The Procrastinator

Comic writer Bob Orben defines procrastination as spending Labor Day opening Christmas cards. Procras-tinators are past masters at "awfulizing," convincing themselves that a task is too distasteful, too complicat-ed, too unpleasant, too demanding, too boring, and the like. They have perfected their anti-action behavior by developing their self-talk into a humongous art form. That is to say, they are masters at trotting out alibis and rationalizations to justify to themselves the need to delay things. Here are some of the excuses they excel at employing: "Not yet." "Too complex." "Too routine." "Can't do it." "Can't make it." "Can't afford it." "Wish I could." "Out of the question." "Not a chance." "It's out of my hands." "Maybe next time." "Maybe next sum-mer." "If I only had more time." "I'll get to it." "Let me think about it. I'll get back to you."

Personality Dynamics

One cause for procrastination is that it is a defense against reality. It is a means of defying and denying the real world fact that there is a task to be done. It provides a way out of doing what has to be done, particularly a task that is too complex or too routine, via the simple act of deferment. Unfortunately, the task doesn't tend to disappear and, in time, it may produce guilt, anxiety, and even shame. Procrastinators may have learned their bad habit while growing up—if one didn't do something when required someone else would, which essentially rewarded the delaying behavior. Parents who decide everything for their children create a procrastinator reluctant to make decisions/choices.

Another cause or dynamic is perfectionism, the feeling that what we have done is not good enough for others to see. If we release it too early, with all its faults, people will think poorly of us, we will be regarded as failures. Perfectionism also may have been learned in childhood—parents set high expectations and the youngster felt it was wiser to wait and see if a task was good enough to let go rather than to say "done" spontaneously. Constant parental criticism of mistakes is a builder of perfectionist behavior.

Psychologist Joseph R. Ferrari (at the 1992 Conference of the American Psychological Association, reported in "Science," *The Washington Post*, Aug. 17, 1992) says that people procrastinate not because they are lazy or poor time managers, but because they are afraid of looking "bad." People who persistently put off tasks tend to be those who assess their self-esteem on how well they perform in the eyes of other people. He states: "By never completing the tasks, they are never judged on their ability, thus allowing them to maintain an illusion of competence."

With respect to decision making, perfectionism encourages deferment. The operative self-slogan is that "*No* decision is decidedly better than the wrong decision."

Procrastinators are masters at rewarding themselves for their delays—get a cup of coffee, secure another soft drink, call a friend, walk to the fountain, visit a fellow worker, take care of another pleasant task, and the like. **The result:** non-completion of the main job.

Possible Treatment

The main learnings for The Procrastinator, if the habit is to be overcome, are:

a) If a task is to be completed, it has to be started, and
b) If it is done, it's OK to let go. It need not be totally perfect; instead, it only has to be accomplished.

Obviously, the manager has to set realistic, logical targets and deadlines for this new behavior to happen.

Management consultant William Hennefrund ("Dealing With Procrastinators—Today," *Supervisory Management,* July 1992) suggests that reforming The Procrastinator totally is unrealistic because he has had a long personal and work life perfecting "tactics of delay." So a more realistic goal is to help The Procrastinator meet his deadlines on a project-by-project basis. Hennefrund offers these procedures to get the work done when required:

Reduce Some of Your Control Over the Project

Recognize that procrastinators frequently use delay as a means of getting added control. So give him more control at the outset. Rather than saying: "Give me your portion of the report by Thursday P.M.," say: "I must hand in my report on Friday P.M.; when can you give me your part?"

Provide Help with Budgeting of Time

Recognize that procrastinators tend to overestimate the time needed to finish a job. If they feel that too little time is available to do the job right, they may get anxious and frustrated and not start at all. So point out that there is enough time to do the job well if the work has been subject to proper organization. Your job, then, is to break the job down into smaller steps, thereby demonstrating its manageability. But don't agree to a new deadline. Instead, make changes in the assignment so that more time is freed up.

Offer Added Backup Help

If more time has to be spent tracking resources and collecting information than anticipated, The Procrastinator can become easily frustrated. He may also be shy about asking for help lest one appear incompetent. So when The Procrastinator has hit a roadblock, offer backup help as may be needed.

Counsel Further if the Problem Continues

Try to learn why deadlines are being missed. If you can help on any of the uncovered reasons, make the adjustment.

Be a Good Model

Don't be a procrastinator yourself. A good practice to follow is to avoid delaying review of turned-in work. If staffers see you as doing last-minute, frenzied reviewing, you'll lose your own credibility as a good time manager.

As indicated above, the understanding, patient manager will attempt to ease The Procrastinator into new work habits that have the potential to produce real payoffs. As added tools for this, the manager can offer The Procrastinator the helpful guides developed by Charles R. Hobbes, author of *Time Power* (New York: Harper & Row, 1987):

☐ Have a *daily* action plan. But build flexibility into it. Recognize that legitimate interruptions may well arise. (But they must be legitimate.)

☐ Stick with one activity to ensure its completion. Flitting from one task to another is a self-defeating no-no.

☐ Think in terms of one step at a time, rather than global goals.

☐ Tackle the tough tasks of a project first.

☐ Tie yourself to your desk, mentally. Do the job and give yourself a reward on task completion.

☐ Know your personal clock. Do the job at the time of day which is best for you, considering the nature of the job.

☐ Establish a deadline and vow to keep it. A goal sans a deadline is only a dream.

☐ If you get bogged down or fatigued, take an earned break and return with new gusto.

☐ At day's end, create a sense of urgency for the next day. How? Put your No. 1 priority in the center of a clear desk.

Improved behaviors by The Procrastinator, no matter how small, merit praise. Positive reinforcement will trigger more of the desired behavior. Small successes should lead to this key insight:

It is far better (more rewarding) to get work done than to sit around worrying about getting it done.

The Social Butterfly

This person loves to regale others with the accomplishments and tribulations of the last weekend, the prior evening's TV movie, the spouse's peccadillos, the children's successes, the plight of the family garden, and so on and on. There is never a shortage of topics to present. Once or twice each day, he may visit one worker and then another, until the rounds have been completed. The visiting, it seems, looms more importantly than does the work.

Personality Dynamics

The Butterfly obviously has a tremendous need to be in contact with others, to be loved, to show that he is a real person with many outside activities, interests and even victories. He feels that it is extremely important to be in touch with people, for that is how one wins their respect and even admiration. Conversely, being aloof will cause others to think less well of you.

Possible Treatment

Quite often these individuals are hard workers and do get their own work done properly. The problem, of course, is that their visiting disrupts the thoughts and work of others. It also sets a bad example for the office. Accordingly, if action is deemed necessary, the manager should confront the heavy socializer on the basis of the impact the lengthy visiting has on others' productivity. If The Social Butterfly is touching base with everyone because of a light workload, the solution is obvious— simply add more work to his existing assignments.

The Naysayer

Naysayers or negative personalities specialize in seeing the hole in the doughnut, the half-empty glass. As predictable wet blankets, they are quick to point out why a proposed plan or project won't work. If there are any flaws in a proposal, they will ferret them out before the ink is dry on it. They may also find flaws where none exist. Cynicism and bountiful skepticism are their basic approaches to life.

Personality Dynamics

Because of their basic insecurity and low self-esteem, The Naysayers have a need to one-up everyone else and their ideas. Their confidence is shored up by deflating the ideas of others. It's almost as if they are saying, "If I can show how everything is bad, I will really look good."

Possible Treatment

When a negative idea is expressed by The Naysayer, it may be helpful to say: "OK, that's the downside. But as a perceptive analyst can you see any positive values at all?" If one positive statement is forthcoming, you may wish to say: "Good point. Anything else on the positive side?" The idea is to communicate that there are positives as well as negatives in any proposal or plan and that our job, as objective analysts, is to seek out the good and the bad. A useful tool, to trigger and record both positive and negative comments, is to use a T-column on a flipchart sheet.

If the negativism is disruptive to the work group, it may merit candid discussion in a team-building session. Typically, The Naysayer is not aware of the extent of his negative remarks, and the impact of his style or pattern on others who have to work with him. Consequently, candid but supportive feedback should be provided to The Naysayers.

Example: "Kim, you have a lot of good ideas and have a great ability to analyze what is going on. But I find you more attractive as a person when you present positive ideas as well as negative ones." Or: "It really makes me uncomfortable when you only offer negative comments on things. I think you are a broad-gauged person and can see positive sides as well as negative ones. Can we get more of the positive from you?"

The Goof-Off Artist

This person specializes in avoiding work, dodging responsibility and alibing about the reasons for delay or non-accomplishment of assigned tasks—equipment is down, materials arrive late, others didn't cooperate as they should have, and so on. At times, this person may disappear entirely, no one knowing of his whereabouts. Faking illness, taking long lunches and breaks, and leaving early may be part of the behavior pattern. Two obvious problems may arise if the behavior is permitted to continue—1) It may rub off on others, and 2) The rest of the crew may wonder about the guts of the boss: "It looks like he's either afraid to tackle that goldbricker or he doesn't care." Doubt about the boss' willingness or ability to do his disciplinary job when necessary can hardly help his image.

Personality Dynamics

The "goldbrick" is essentially a con man. He achieves gratification by outwitting the boss and the system. He values his independence and thus will do things on his own sweet time. Cooperation with others is far less impor-

tant than seeing how far he can best others. In a sense, this person is creative. Unfortunately, he uses that creativity to meet personal rather than organizational needs.

Possible Treatment

Confrontation rather than delay is very much in order. In your counseling session, establish clearcut goals and standards as to what is expected and when. Advise that you expect results and will not accept excuses for non-performance. Document his performance fully. When the data indicate clearly that goldbricking still is taking place, advise The Goof-Off Artist that you intend to take disciplinary action unless there is a change in his behavior. If there is any noticeable improvement, compliment him on that performance. Positive reinforcement (earned praise) may help to alter his egregious behavior.

Note: Don't overlook the possibility that this person is underworked and underchallenged. Truly busy people don't have time to goof off.

The Gregarious Gossip

Information, real or imagined, harmless or harmful, is the lifeblood of The Gossip. He excels in corralling the latest and juiciest about what is happening by, to and with whom in the office at large—divorces, promotions, reassignments, transfers, conflicts, dressings down, foulups, etc., are all grist for The Gossip's mill.

Personality Dynamics

The motivation for The Gossip's behavior is a combined need to know and an even greater need to tell. By telling, one automatically evidences his importance and thus power, for, in effect, "I know something that you don't." Another motivation, like that of The Social Butterfly, is to develop and maintain contact/rapport with people.

Possible Treatment

The best defense against The Gossip's attacks is to make certain that much of the information that is being peddled reaches everyone early on through regular communication channels. This is particularly possible in respect to personnel transactions, often a major element of The Gossip's material. Also, strategically placed personnel such as secretaries, who often are the source of The Gossip's confidential information, should be reminded frequently to keep a well-buttoned lip. If The Gossip, like The Social Butterfly, has large amounts of time to share his information, additional assignments would seem to be in order.

The Clutter Champ

This person conducts a career of creating, collecting, and coveting clutter. Not only does The Clutter Champ's desk look like it just has been vandalized, but there are stacks of materials behind the desk and on the window sill. Other mountains of paper may be on worktables and piles of yellowing materials reside on top of file cabinets. The Clutter Champ has no awareness of how his behavior is perceived by others. Fellow workers make little jokes among themselves about "file phobia," "pilomania," "desk stress," and "the information explosion must have started and stopped right here."

Personality Dynamics

Because a totally cluttered office is an affront to most people, The Clutter Champ obviously must gain something, psychologically speaking, from the mountains of mess. Here are some possible significant benefits:

- ☐ Image of *indispensibility:* "Only I can give them what they need."
- ☐ Image of *power:* "They will get it when I am ready to give it to them."
- ☐ Image of *invincibility:* "I can best defy the system by keeping my turf the way I want it."
- ☐ Image of *responsibility:* "I've got so much to do that I just can't find time to do the filing." Message to self: "If I were to clean things up I'd look as if I have nothing to do." (**Note:** The Clutter Champ equates a high volume of visible materials with high responsibility.)
- ☐ Image of *importance:* "Everybody sends me their stuff. They must think I have nothing better to do than to plow through all their paper."
- ☐ Image of *superiority:* "I've got a lot more important things to do than all this Mickey Mouse filing."
- ☐ Image of *independence.* Ordinary norms of order and neatness are for "all the conformists, apple polishers, and little people around here."

Possible Treatment

Can The Clutter Champ be converted to engage in normal, neat behaviors? Is clutter containment very likely?

Probably, if the conversion effort is conducted on a high-level, professional plane. Here are some possible counseling-type approaches to deal with "Clutter Carrie":

- ☐ "Carrie, you have a lot of important papers in your office. But when you are away and someone else needs to find something, it is very difficult for them to do so. I know you want to be helpful to others, so can you arrange all your papers so that others, in your absence, may find things readily?"
- ☐ "Carrie, you're an intelligent person. You know that not every document is of equal value. Some age and outlive their usefulness. So it's OK to let some of them go. In fact it's the wise thing to do. Do you agree?"
- ☐ Assuming that Carrie agrees, you may wish to add: "I'll be glad to have my secretary assist you in purging and rearranging your files, if you wish." (This offer of help may be a bit threatening, so Carrie may opt to do the cleanup job on her own.) **Note:** You also may wish to offer to help produce a more appealing office by contributing pictures for the walls and sculpture, pottery, or plants for the table and window sills.
- ☐ On the assumption that a fair amount of the loosely strewn documents does merit retention, you may wish to add: "Carrie, you have a lot of material that is begging for helpful storage. I will be glad to requisition another file cabinet or two for you and possibly a bookcase, too. Do you want them?"
- ☐ "Carrie, all of us have our style of operating. But how we operate communicates an image to others. I don't know whether you are aware of this, but I must level with you and tell you that your image is one of a pack rat. People make jokes about you and your office—'The Paper Palace,' 'Junk Junction,' 'The Trash Treasury,' and so on. Do you want an image like that?" **Note:** If Carrie has a very low self-image, reference to a pig sty, a trash heap or that "people are afraid to enter because of the clutter" should be avoided because such statements may well be perceived as personal attacks and merely produce defensiveness. Your aim is to change the behavior in a gentle way via confidence building, not to provide a counterattack or a sulking withdrawal.
- ☐ "Carrie, the best help I can offer you is to work with you to set a new goal for yourself: Your desk should be used only for papers that are being

worked on. I know this may require you to operate differently than you have. But I see you as a flexible person and I think you can adjust to such a procedure. Can you do this?"

Of course, a direct order may work, too. "Carrie, I expect all that paper to be cleared up over the weekend. So when I come in Monday morning you will have a neat desk and these tons of paper will have been filed or discarded. Is that clear?" But why strain the relationship with a tough edict? After all, you will have to live and work with Carrie after she "flies right" and gets her office tidied up a bit. You not only want compliance, you also want to kindle or maintain her enthusiasm, not to build resentments that may lower her job interest.

A final note. Remember that a Clutter Champ like Carrie typically has one of two fears: that a new system may not work or, possibly worse, that it will!

The Personal Needs Devotee

All of us have an occasional off-the-job problem. But personal needs and problems of all sorts demand the time and attention of this type of employee to an abnormal degree. The needs may range from care of young children and elderly parents to heavy concern with the car, the broker, home repairers, etc. **The result:** much time is spent on the telephone on non-office business accompanied by frequent late arrivals, early departures, extensive use of sick leave, and the rest. Other staff members may even complain to you about the person's unavailability when needed.

Personality Dynamics

While everyone has a personal problem on occasion, this person seems to be inundated with them. In fact, it is his lifestyle. Much of the problem revolves around poor planning coupled with a relatively low concern for the needs of others—the boss, colleagues. There also may be a misconception that being harassed by problems signifies that one is a very important person, indeed.

Possible Treatment

If the behavior is truly disruptive, not only annoying, a serious confrontation—on a documented basis—is in order. The manager needs to level with the employee concerning the impact his personal activities is having on the job and the needs of other people. There is little need

to explore all the reasons for the behavior. Rather, a legitimate demand must be made to put office needs first. Period. If any improvement does occur after the frank talk, provide praise to reinforce the new behavior. Point out in your discussion, however, that there is no objection to very short, check-in calls from the kids for peace of mind, and certainly emergency calls are OK, too.

The Vendor

A nuisance in any shop or office is the person who is constantly trying to sell things to others—eggs from the farm, greeting cards for the next holiday, perfumes, costume jewelry, insurance, tickets for the church raffle, orders for Girl Scout cookies, and the like.

Personality dynamics

The person who tries to sell things to others is likely to be a gregarious, friendly person who may sincerely believe that he is providing a service to his fellow workers. However, this high gregariousness is accompanied by an acute insensitivity—an unawareness that the vending may be perceived as pressure selling, and thus make others uncomfortable, and that he may be consuming unfairly some of their job time.

Possible Treatment

A policy should be placed in effect that selling in the shop or office is a no-no and will be a cause for disciplinary action. The taboo should extend to any and all selling, however well-intentioned, such as for a charity. If the ban relates to all selling on company premises, it will obviate the problem of selling during lunch hour or breaks. **Note:** This type of problem is one that could be handled via group discussion and group decision. The odds are that most employees will favor a selling ban because it is embarrassing to turn down a colleague vending Girl Scout cookies or to tell The Vendor that he has work to do and is too busy to discuss the sale. If a no-selling policy already exists, The Vendor may need a gentle reminder of it.

The Lone Wolf

Any office may have an individual who prefers going it alone. The loner makes it very clear to others that there is a psychological moat or Chinese Wall surrounding his persona. So this person strenuously shuns the usual social contacts and chitchat in the office, and avoids working on projects with others. Contacts, if needed, are strictly brief and very businesslike, much of it by memo. Opportunities to get to know others informally, such as at coffee breaks, lunches, organization parties and picnics, are not pursued. Everyone learns to live with The Lone Wolf's "do not disturb" personality, although, at times, projects could be accomplished more smoothly if there were more informal contact and looser communication.

Personality Dynamics

The hermit-like behavior of The Lone Wolf reflects a fear of getting too close to others. It's almost as if he is saying, "If you really knew me, you wouldn't respect or like me." Hence, the only solution is to keep others at arm's length. He has learned to live successfully in isolation, the maintenance of the protective shell being more important than receiving warmth and camaraderie from others.

Possible Treatment

Because the manager is concerned with results rather than therapy for others, he certainly can live with The Lone Wolf's withdrawal. However, if the isolationist tendencies result in reduced cooperation and communication and thus impact on the work in a serious way, confrontation may be in order. It also may be possible to use certain work assignments as a means of encouraging more contact with others so that in time the wall may be breached a bit. The manager may make a point of having friendly chats with the recluse, initially on the loner's turf and from time to time in the manager's office. The idea is to continually ask his opinion about current problems as a means of confidence building. Team members might be encouraged to go out of their way to exhibit behavior which can help to bring the loner out of his sturdy shell.

The Put-Down Artist

This individual specializes in snide remarks, one-upmanship, and generally besting someone in a variety of verbal ways. It's almost as if the person believes that "The only way I can look good is to make you appear bad."

Personality Dynamics

This person has a low self-image and craves desperately to be well-regarded. His assumption is that by exhibiting superiority he will gain respect, appreciation,

and admiration. But his lack of sensitivity prevents him from knowing that his "system" isn't working. If anything, it produces an opposite effect.

Possible Treatment

The best cure is group feedback to let The Put-Down Artist know how others feel about his behavior.

Example: "When you make jokes about my slow speaking style at our staff meetings, I feel very ashamed and embarrassed. I like you as a person for you are very bright and verbal, but I would like you a lot more if you could say some kind things to me instead of putting me down."

The Silent One

This person takes a backseat in discussions until someone insists on knowing what he sees, feels, believes, thinks. He is glad to go along with others, just so he doesn't have to present or debate a particular point of view. Of course, his more verbal colleagues may find no problem with such reticence, for it gives them more air time at meetings.

Personality Dynamics

The Silent One suffers from a low self-confidence level and thus is doubtful of the value of his own opinions. He is reluctant to offer them because they are "not too valuable" or they may be shot down by a more knowledgeable person. The Silent One thus handicaps himself by his feelings of low self-worth.

Possible Treatment

The need for the leader and the team is to bolster this person's low self-esteem. How?

1) Ask for his opinions and ideas: "We haven't heard from Kim yet on this."
2) Provide praise when an idea is presented. The praise may be in reference to the worth of the idea or the fact that a contribution was made. ("That gives us another angle on the problem.") Outside training in such organizations as the Toastmaster's Club may be a valuable confidence-building endeavor.

The On-the-Job Romancer

People of the opposite sex who work closely together and have like interests can, understandably, become romantically involved with one another. The romance may be open—a dating relationship—or clandestine, particularly if one or both parties already have marital partners.

The objective and practical supervisor is not concerned about romantic relationships as long as they do not affect productivity. But as management professors R. Wayne Mondy and Shane R. Premeaux point out ("People Problems: The Workplace Affair," *Management Solutions,* November 1986), the lovebirds may spend an abnormally large amount of work time together, and their colleagues may devote added work time analyzing and speculating on their behavior and intentions. And if the romance ultimately produces a divorce, further lowered productivity may be anticipated—loss of time from the job, numerous phone calls, increased anxiety as the divorce process evolves, and so on.

Possible Action

The manager has to be certain of two elements—the facts concerning the romantic behavior and its impact on productivity. If he can meet both conditions, it is appropriate to meet with each party individually and state the problem candidly, secure a response, and then agree upon what future action/behavior must take place to return productivity (possibly decorum, too) to the prior, pre-romantic state. In some cases, a reassignment or transfer may be a graceful way out of the messy situation. **A caution:** In the counseling session, the manager must take pains to avoid passing judgment on the behavior, for the only legitimate concern is with productivity. Romance is a very personal thing, and the astute supervisor will avoid presenting himself as a judge, busybody, killjoy, censor, or prude.

The Determined Dresser

Most employees do not look at the workplace as a locale to demonstrate or shock others with their favored costuming. However, occasionally the manager may encounter an employee who wishes to substitute his concept of attire for the established corporate dress code. The outlandish dress may range from that reflecting one's particular lifestyle to (in the case of a female employee) the sexually revealing and provocative.

Personality Dynamics

In some cases, of course, the far-out dress may reflect an unawareness of what is acceptable in an office. In other cases, it may be designed to draw attention, to define oneself ("to make a statement"), to shock others, even to challenge the power structure. Some employees, too, may feel that highly individualized dress is a means of self-expression.

Possible Treatment

The manager's concern with dress is not to stifle individuality, but to ensure that it does not create a distraction, an unfavorable impact on productivity, or, in the case of persons in contact with the public, produce an inappropriate image. The manager's role is to counsel the employee as to what is appropriate in light of the aforementioned, impacting factors. Appropriateness, either in reference to the written code or the office's needs and circumstances or both, is the basis for the manager's intervention.

Improvement in dress practices by the counseled employee, like any other change toward a desired behavior, merits praise: "I like your outfit today, Kim. You look great in it." Disregard of repeated "fatherly (or motherly) advice" as to dress is a cause for disciplinary action.

If the problem is one that involves more than one worker, it is wise to make it a team problem. In the group meeting, ask what is appropriate dress behavior in light of office circumstances. By letting the group set standards that they feel are reasonable, group commitment is very certain.

A caution: In today's world of cultural diversity, the manager may encounter different attire that is culturally based, not necessarily hostile or shocking in intent. For example, a woman from India may wish to wear her sari in the bank on occasion. If the dress is neat, merely native to the person's home country, and probably not likely to offend customers, why not? Use of the rule of reasonableness will avoid unnecessary confrontation.

The Externalizer

If you have employees who dodge responsibility with alibis such as "nobody told me," "it's not my fault," "I just got here," you are dealing with what Jerry Conrath ("Teaching Responsibility to Poor Performers," *Supervisory Management,* October 1988) terms The Externalizer. These are low-esteem people who see life happenings—good or bad—as out of their control. Luck is what determines results for them.

Possible Treatment

You, like most supervisors, are an internalizer, i.e., you see life as well within your control. You naturally take personal responsibility for your department's performance without even having to reflect on it. It thus may be hard for you to deal with The Externalizer. Conrath, author of *Our Other Youth*, a handbook on how to deal with youthful externalizers, advises that the usual supervisory actions such as threatening discipline, putting The Externalizer into a sink-or-swim situation, using external rewards, and reasoning with the employee simply won't work.

But there are ways to get them to assume responsibility. Conrath advises these approaches:

☐ Insist externalizers take personal responsibility for their successes as well as their mistakes. With a lot of patient explaining, they will see that they accomplished their successes.

☐ Help them to understand that all achievement is a result of effort and skills, as well as luck. Luck is helpful, at times, but only if it accompanies effort. Your objective is to build self-pride in the performer. Tell the externalizer "You should feel pride in . . ." as opposed to "I feel proud of you for . . ." But only praise real effort and accomplishment.

☐ Assign tasks for which the externalizers are qualified. Since simply telling the person that effort pays off won't be accepted, they have to learn from experience that success ensues from their own effort, that they can be successful.

☐ Emphasize skills over smarts. Externalizers look at smarts as a genetic element and thus something they can't control. But as long as they can see that skills are learnable, it matters little whether smarts are at work or not.

☐ Stress behavior over attitude. They probably have heard many times that they were born with a bad attitude, so it is wise to forget the fuzzy concept of attitude. Behavior, performance, and like skills are much more tangible concepts and lend themselves to easier discussion in relation to their internal responsibility. People can understand and relate to behavior rather than the will-o'-the-wisp and even negative concept of attitude.

☐ Reinforce the message to be internalized. Give positive feedback as soon as the desired behavior occurs. This will reinforce the behavior. Don't accept claims that the good result was luck. Insist that it was his effort that really did it.

Again, the key to squashing the luck concept is to patiently insist over and over that his effort produced the result.

The Late Comer

A dillar, a dollar
A ten o'clock scholar,
What makes you come so soon?
You used to come at ten o'clock,
But now you come at noon.

—Mother Goose

Most employees respect the maxims the early bird gets the worm, time and tide wait for no man, punctuality is the politeness of kings, and time is money. But inevitably, there are a few workers who behave as if they never encountered these adages. The chronically tardy ones typically possess an inexhaustible supply of alibis: "my alarm clock didn't go off," "my bus was late," "my car pool had car trouble,' "my sitter didn't make it," and so on. (I worked in an office with a colleague whose secretary was frequently late. He finally confronted her about her derelictions, whereupon she replied very frankly, "You see, my husband works the late shift and he doesn't want me to get out of bed in the morning." My colleague nearly fell out of his teeth!)

Tardiness is not the gravest of employee sins. But it is disruptive if the late person is expected to perform a particular operation upon which others depend. Also, lateness, if unchallenged, may well create a bad example and have a serious contagious effect.

Problems allied to a.m. tardiness are late returns from breaks and lunch and early p.m. departures.

Personality Dynamics

Psychologically speaking, the chronic latecomer, in challenging the boss as an authority figure, may be rebelling against his parents. It thus may be a way to act out one's residual feelings of hostility. A late arrival, particularly an ostentatious one, also may be a means of drawing attention to oneself. The author has worked in offices where a particular manager frequently would arrive late to staff meetings as a ploy to stress his heavy workload and importance ("I was tied up with a client"; "I had to get the bid on the 4RTX project procurement"; "Department X needed some advice on their new marketing plan").

Possible Treatment

As managers, few of us wish to be picky about minor and infrequent instances of tardiness. We know that everyone may have such a problem on occasion. So our real concern is with the chronic offender. Also, we want to act early on lest the infractions become the norm. And we certainly don't want to harass our good workers and de-motivate them.

In any case, the first step is to collect data about the behavior. There is little point in counseling someone about a bad habit if one can't deal in specifics. ("In the last two months you have been late for work six times. The late periods have been as follows: 5 minutes on one occasion, 12 minutes on two others, 15 minutes once, 18 minutes once and 22 minutes this morning. In addition, you have extended your lunch period by over 20 minutes on three occasions.")

After presenting the data, an explanation (most likely a reminder) should be presented concerning the importance of observing the formal schedule of arrival and departure time. (Why arrive on time if it doesn't really matter?) An offer to help then may be made: "Do you have any suggestions as to what I can do to help you meet the office starting time requirements?" The meeting should end with a request for cooperation and a few words of encouragement: "I am confident that you can arrive on time if you make a firm decision to do so."

Note: A practical suggestion to the counselee might be to set a target of arriving 15 minutes early! This would help to deal with late buses, alarm clocks that don't perform as expected, slow-moving schoolchildren, and the like. This will give The Late Comer a better chance to accomplish a more certain and on-time arrival, provide an opportunity to relax a bit with that second cup of coffee, and show one's interest in the job.

Assuming the counseling effort takes and cooperation is forthcoming, the new performance should be monitored and, if improvement occurs, rewarded via praise. "I appreciate your adherence to the starting hours. Keep it up."

But what if there is a backslide? Positive reinforcement may still be in order. "You were a bit late today, but I know you are trying to arrive on time. I sincerely appreciate your effort to do this. Please stay with it, which I'm sure you can do."

Incidentally, if the problem is more widespread, it may be discussed at one of the regular team meetings. The objectives might be to:

a) Ascertain that the arrival and departure time schedule is appropriate in light of both employee and organizational needs,

b) Check whether flextime, if not now in effect, might be adopted,

c) Decide the obligations of the latecomer, e.g., to call in so that people have an idea as to when his arrival may occur. If a strong feeling of teamness has been developed, peer pressure and feelings of obligation to the team will be the forces to discourage indifference to established time schedules.

And you must set a good example yourself. If you are modeling inappropriate behavior—late arrivals, long lunches, etc.—you can hardly expect others to hew to the line totally. In fact, it is a good idea to arrive before the others show up.

In passing, we might mention that a research study (*Changing Times,* December 1986) by University of Iowa communication professors Nancy Harper and Randy Hirokawa indicted that male and female bosses tend to deal differently with late comers. They asked 46 female and 30 male managers how they would handle the problem. Their findings were:

Men were inclined to use punishment-based techniques such as warnings: "Unless you stop arriving late for work, disciplinary action will be taken" or ultimatums: "Shape up or find yourself another job." Some two-thirds of the male managers would take this tack, whereas only one third of the female bosses would.

What approaches were most of the female bosses likely to take? They favored altruistic or rationale-based techniques such as:

☐ **Counseling:** "Is there anything I can do to help overcome the problems that are preventing you from arriving on time?"

☐ **Duty:** "It is your obligation to report to work on time."

☐ **Explanations:** "You need to be at work on time because . . ."

In respect to the gender-biased differences in taking a course of action, Harper observed: "There is a lot of opinion that women are more emotional and wouldn't be as rational in handling these kinds of situations, but this study indicates that if anyone would get emotional and shout, it would be the man."

The Absentee

Absenteeism negatively affects the organization. First, it may add directly to the cost of the operation by the need to hire replacement workers or to pay overtime to workers who fill in. Second, it may make for various inefficiencies, e.g., work gets delayed or customers may be inconvenienced. Third, replacement or "switched" (reassigned) workers may not have the background or skill to prevent a deterioration of quality of production or service.

A Research Institute of America study (*The Wall Street Journal,* July 29, 1986) estimated a clerical worker's one-day absence can cost up to $100 in reduced efficiency, and the total productivity drain on the U.S. economy approaches $40 billion annually.

What can the manager/supervisor do if absentees or absenteeism are deemed to be a problem? These procedures can help:

☐ Think in terms of prevention. A safe, supportive, friendly, stress-free atmosphere, proper assignment of worker to jobs to prevent boredom, and team management should serve to limit unwanted absenteeism. If the worker feels that he is part of a team, he will strive very hard to come to work rather than let his co-workers down. Careful selection and orientation of new workers also are preventive measures.

☐ Maintain good records of absenteeism. Are certain units, certain occupations, certain age groups, or certain shifts more derelict than others? Are individual absences related to a pattern, e.g., before or after the weekend or a holiday or after pay day? Is Pareto's Law at work, i.e., 80% of the absences are caused by 20% of the work force? How does your absentee rate compare with other departments?

☐ Watch for excessive absenteeism, for it may signal a troubled employee is at hand.

☐ Stress regularly the importance of "presenteeism." People need reminders that their absence may affect cost and cause inefficiencies and inconveniences to staff and customers.

☐ Consider flexible work hours as a means of preventing no-shows. **Example:** At a large San Francisco corporation, employees have a compressed work-week program that provides them with 26 three-day weekends. All employees work nine hours, Monday through Thursday. On Friday about half of them work eight hours; the others get the day off. On the following Friday, the schedule switches. Over a two-week period, everyone works 80 hours in nine days. The firm finds that this program increases productivity because there is less need to take time off for medical visits, haircuts, and so on, personal business being taken care of on the employee's Friday off day. Other benefits accrue, too: fewer commutes to downtown San Francisco, meaning less freeway congestion, and recruitment of new employees is facilitated.

☐ Meet with the sick leave abuser to learn whether there is a medical, family or other problem. Accept no excuses for not showing up to work. Remember, that no one is entitled to paid sick leave for it is a specifically designed benefit, not a general fringe benefit or a right. Home responsibilities and personal business should be accomplished via annual leave, not sick leave. (Absenteeism frequently expands to equal the number of sick days authorized.) End the counseling session with a commitment from the employee to alter his behavior and meet organizational requirements and standards.

☐ Ask for a doctor's sick note if the abuse is serious.

☐ Use the disciplinary system for true sick leave abusers—oral and written warnings, suspension, and ultimately termination. Morale is not helped when conscientious, reliable employees feel that "some people can get away with murder."

☐ Employ an Employee Assistance Program for chronic absentees.

☐ Reward/recognize excellent attendance, e.g., make a special point of it at your staff meetings.

Note: If you work actively on your absentee problem, you won't be like the British executive who frustratingly said, "We do not mind whether our workers come in three, four, or five days a week but we really would like to know which days they will be."

Guidelines to Cope with "Difficult" Behavior

Most of the above-suggested approaches should help you to cope constructively with people who seem determined to give you king-sized headaches. But no guarantees, of course. As a minimum, they should serve to trigger added, worthwhile ideas of your own.

Undoubtedly, you may have already developed some practical coping methods. But if everything you have tried has not changed the undesirable behavior, why not give one or more of these techniques a whirl?

Also presented below are a number of more specific guidelines to help you in the coping process. Of course, when dealing with difficult people you always can "lay down the law" or "read the riot act." Your boss may even advise you: "You're the boss, aren't you? So why pussyfoot?" But in today's world, managers are paid to solve people-type problems with understanding and finesse, without alienating otherwise competent, loyal workers and destroying collaborative relationships based on mutual trust and respect. Also, your staff will respect you more for acting in a caring, sensitive and professional way. Hence the need to assemble facts, try to analyze what is going on, and possibly to develop an action plan via counseling with the person involved. The guidelines follow.

Check Perceptions

Do your impressions/feelings/reactions about the behavior and its impact on your unit's work coincide with those of others? Check them out. It may be that you are responding to a personality quirk to which you are overly sensitive.

If you do have a truly difficult person on your hands, he falls into one of two categories: reachable or unreachable. Of course, you won't know which category the hard-to-manage person falls into until after you have attempted to change his behavior.

Take Action

If there is a problem with a difficult person, it is generally agreed that it will affect productivity, cooperation, communication, and the like, so act on it. The odds are that the behavior will not change by itself without constructive confrontation on your part.

Capitalize on Their Better Qualities and Skills

Even difficult people can make worthwhile contributions to the unit's work. So while trying to hone their rough edges, make a point of profiting from what they can do well. The manager's job is to utilize the best in people and accept some of their less attractive sides as well.

Recognize the Rewards at Work

In dealing with the difficult person, remember that while his behavior may annoy you and possibly the rest of your team, it undoubtedly makes a lot of sense to him. That is to say, it meets real needs for such rewards as recognition, importance, control, power, contact, concealment of inadequacies, expression of hostility, and the like.

So if the behavior is providing real benefits/gains/rewards, it won't go away very readily. This means you need to develop profound rather than simple strategies to alter the behavior. And the best strategies are those that are *confidence building* in character. The difficult person typically is one who has low self-esteem. Helping that person to feel better about himself is the route to abandonment of attention-seeking and related self-destructive behaviors.

Focus on Behavior

While you may feel that the difficult person has a bad attitude, it will only inflame him to approach the problem along that line. Attitudes are hard to define and harder to agree on. Behavior, which is observable and even measurable, is much less subject to debate. For example, a person who is consistently late to staff meetings is engaging in clearcut, tardy behavior. Whether that person has a nasty attitude, is hostile, disinterested, or is trying to draw attention to himself, is harder to talk about and is really irrelevant. What counts is the performance or the behavior. As a manager, you always are on solid ground when you express concern about behavior or performance as it relates to productivity, cooperation, and communication.

Note: A confidence-building form of feedback to the late-comer to staff meetings is the following: "Kim, I know you try very hard to come to the meetings on time. But when you are late, we lose out on your input. We can't capitalize on your ideas if you're not here to give them to us."

Involve the Team

To the extent possible, consider using your team to help resolve the difficulty. If the person's behavior impacts others, they have a collective responsibility to let the offender know how his behavior is impacting on them. Also, group feedback and group pressure to shape up will have a stronger bearing than one person's opinion, even if that one person is the boss. Besides, why go it alone, why bear the brunt of the task when you have a team able and willing to help out?

Use Feedback Appropriately

In giving feedback, remember that your goal is to change the behavior, not to provide punishment. Recognize, too, that difficult people typically aren't aware that their behavior is perceived by others as unwanted or obnoxious. Also, think in terms of how your feedback will affect future relationships. Keep it high-level and professional—behavior-oriented and supportive. When giving feedback about behavior, it helps the recipient to learn how you feel about it. **Example:** "When you present total agreement with everything I and the others have to say, I feel that you are holding back, not leveling with us, denying us from having your more valuable thinking."

Prepare for the Meeting

You may decide to have a one-on-one meeting. If so, don't go into the counseling session unprepared or rushed. Set aside enough time for it so that the session can proceed in a relaxed, totally professional way. Think through carefully and rehearse what you intend to say. Anticipate possible negative or defensive reactions.

One way to prepare yourself psychologically is to try to visualize a successful outcome. This will help to overcome negative feelings you may have about the other person.

A process to deal with difficult people, says management consultant David Gouthro ("Dealing With Difficult People," *Performance and Instruction,* May/June 1991), is to think in terms of difficult situations rather than merely difficult people. This means to do whatever you can to ensure that you are not responsible for the difficult situation and apply the CURE (care, understand, respect, empathize) approach:

☐ **Care about:** The difficult performer as a human being. If you communicate, intentionally or unintentionally, that you don't care about the person, you are likely to increase the intensity of the conflict.

☐ **Understand:** The interests and wanted outcomes of both parties involved. By trying to understand all the factors and nuances of a difficult situation, you can increase the likelihood of a positive outcome. This means trying to see things from the other person's perspective as well as from your own.

☐ **Respect:** The person, as opposed to judging him. If we are to drop the judgmental mode, the skill needed is to avoid seeing what we believe as opposed to seeing what is really there. Obviously, if negative opinions about the other party have already

accumulated, it's very difficult to respect the judged person, to appreciate possible strengths and to capture his point of view.

☐ **Empathize:** Try to feel what the other person does, to "walk in his moccasins." Of course, as human beings we have our own emotions to deal with. And these emotions, of course, can distort what is being communicated to us. **The result:** miscommunication leading to misunderstanding. So try to enter into the other person's world and thereby cut down on or eliminate the unhelpful "emotional clouding" you may bring to the situation.

As a practical tool to plan for the interview, you may wish to use the Pre-Interview Planning Work Sheet, Figure 8-1. Use it only as a guide to your discussion, for as the interview proceeds you may wish to make adjustments in your strategy.

Develop an Action Plan Jointly

Helping to shape a new behavior may be done, in some situations, on an informal basis. But it probably will be more effective to sit down with the difficult person in a counseling session to develop an Action Plan on a collaborative basis.

Organization psychologist H.B. Karp ("The ABCs [Appropriate Behavior Changes] of Effective Management, *Training and Development Journal,* January 1985) suggests that the manager has two choices in dealing with the difficult person. They are the *judicial* approach and the *collaborative* approach. In the judicial approach, the goal is to protect rules or standards via a disciplinary strategy. Visualize the manager ending the session with a warning: "Don't ever let me catch you doing this again." The staffer learns, then, that the payoff is *not* appropriate behavior, but *not to be caught* engaging in inappropriate behavior.

In the collaborative approach, one utilizes a problem-solving methodology with the manager supporting the expected, appropriate behavior. How the offending person interacts with the organization is the key concern.

The distinctions between the two approaches, per Dr. Karp, are as follows: "In the *judicial* approach: the manager relies on authority; the working relationship is adversarial in nature; rules are often arbitrary; subordinates submit; compliance increases resistance to the rule; the result is temporary; and compliance is minimal. In the *collaborative* approach: the manager relies on the ability to influence; the working relationship is cooperative; rules reflect reality; subordinates make choices; compliance reduces resistance to rules; the result is permanent; and compliance is optimal."

Set High-Level Goals

In your attempt to change the unwanted behavior, either individually or with the team, try to get agreement that there is a new, and better way to go. Presumably the old, unwanted behavior provided certain psychological benefits to the difficult person. The new behavior, which replaces the old, should be seen as rewarding, too. For example, removing clutter from the person's office should give The Clutter Champ an image of being a true professional worker, one who is fully organized and is on top of the job rather than buried by it, and one who is interested in operating in a much more efficient and cooperative manner. Or The Constant Complainer can achieve a much higher regard from his colleagues by zeroing in on a limited number of real problems. By over-complaining, he loses his effectiveness as a problem identifier.

What we are suggesting, then, is that the "Law of Replacement" is to be observed. That is, if you remove a particular role (e.g., The "Office Clown") or behavior, you need to provide a new, satisfying one in its stead. This may mean you have to teach new skills and new approaches to substitute for the taboo, less effective ones. People want to be successful, so it is your job to give them the new tools with which to move forward.

Closing the Counseling Session

Close the session on a positive note: "I don't believe I am asking you to do something you cannot do. I am fully confident that you are fully able to make the change and that you will feel better about yourself, and so will others, too."

Be sure to ask the other party if he can now carry through on the new goals/expectations. Indicate your future availability to discuss them further at any time.

Lower Expectations

Don't expect miracles in the way of behavior change. Settle for small, gradual improvements. Anticipate "backsliding," too. For example, the person who has been putting others down for 17 years is not likely to abandon that shabby behavior overnight, even if he receives some stern feedback about it. Reminders (continuing feedback) probably will be necessary from time to time. Added support, in general, to increase self

esteem, will help to eliminate the need to engage in his usual self-defeating behavior.

Provide Continuing Rewards

Be certain to reinforce the new behavior, whenever possible, with praise. Compliments, even for small improvements, will provide encouragement to perform along the new path and will help to maintain the new behavior.

WORKING WITH THE TROUBLED EMPLOYEE

Managers/supervisors may have to deal not only with difficult employees—those who are a pain in the neck (or elsewhere)—but with employees who have more deep-seated emotional problems they bring to work. This includes such troubled workers as the following:

- ☐ The Depressed Employee
- ☐ The Grieving Employee
- ☐ The Status-Deprived Employee
- ☐ The Workaholic
- ☐ The Drug Abuser
- ☐ The Alcohol Abuser
- ☐ The Compulsive Gambler
- ☐ The Worker with Marital Problems
- ☐ The Employee Undergoing Therapy
- ☐ The Rehabilitated Mentally Ill Person
- ☐ The Thief

Description of the behavior and general recommendations as to coping procedures follow.

The Depressed Employee

Depression, a psychological phenomenon, can strike anyone for any one of a number of reasons—a loss of a loved one, a prolonged illness, family problems, financial concerns, burnout, etc. Depression is a common problem, affecting 20% of all Americans at various times. Symptoms include some or all of the following (M. G. Pryor and M. K. Golden, "The Depressed Employee," *Supervisory Management,* October 1984): reduced interest in life events and people interactions, e.g., family, work, community, hobbies, sex; irritability and hostility; tearfulness; unexplainable anxiety, worry, guilt; difficulty in concentrating; difficulty in sleeping; feeling tired; changes (up or down) in eating habits (and consequent weight changes up or down); physical pain which can't be diagnosed as to cause; feelings of help-lessness; possible memory lapses; low self-esteem. **The result:** Their overwhelming character causes withdrawal from people or situations, all of which serves to aggravate the condition.

On the job, the sufferer has difficulty concentrating, and contacts with others are reduced. This produces greater feeling of inadequacy and helplessness, and a full-fledged depression may ensue.

Role of the Boss

What can the boss do? A perceptive boss will recognize and understand the symptoms. Recognition is not difficult because the new behavior is so different from the prior, healthful, and zestful behavior pattern. The depressed person should not be treated as a disciplinary case. Rather, attempts should be made to be supportive, e.g, give assignments that have a high probability of success and display a great deal of caring and concern. By maintaining rapport, the supervisor will be perceived as a credible person, and a referral by him for medical help is more likely to be accepted by the depressed employee.

One hundred percent recovery is not guaranteed. However, the supervisor who has provided help as described above need not blame himself if full recovery does not develop.

The Grieving Employee

Caring for a terminally ill person and dealing with the death of that loved one—the mourning period—produces a serious grieving reaction per Employee Assistance Program therapist Sally A. Johnston ("Dealing With A Grieving Employee," *Supervisory Management,* July 1987). In the former case, the period before the ill person dies—anticipatory grief—can wreak considerable emotional havoc on the employee who has the concern.

Anticipatory grief can last weeks, months, or even years. The emotional impact may affect work habits and work quality. If the person dealing with anticipatory grief is the primary caregiver, there may be a whole gamut of personal problems—time demands, financial details, caretaking, etc. These problems, in turn, can create on-the-job problems: preoccupation, telephoning, added leave taking to take the dying person to the doctor and the hospital, plus added stress and fatigue.

If the ailing person is not in the immediate vicinity, a natural reaction would be feelings of detachment and despair over the separation. **The result:** interrupted sleep,

telephoning, traveling to visit the patient, stress, worry, fear, etc. In this period the stressed-out primary or secondary caregivers may even receive medication or resort to alcohol or drugs to cope with the attendant stress.

In light of all the harassing circumstances affecting the employee, the manager may find that his worker is angry, resentful, highly emotional, totally apathetic, ready to quit the job, and so on. The role of the boss, says Johnston, is to be very supportive, flexible, and available to listen to the grieving worker. Specifically, the manager should:

☐ Recognize that the employee is going through one of the most difficult periods in his life.

☐ Brainstorm with the employee necessary accommodations.

☐ Ask the employee for ideas on how the expected level of performance can be maintained while he is attending to all the personal details.

☐ Discuss reduced performance frankly to get mutual agreement as to what might be done about it. But be careful how any negative feedback is presented.

☐ Advise that you are available to help if the situation becomes unmanageable.

☐ If the anticipatory grief is reaching a crisis stage, suggest a referral to organizational or community counseling services.

☐ Review leave policies with the employee if it is apparent there is a drain on his leave allotment.

☐ Don't hesitate to ask from time to time how the dying patient is doing—and be prepared to listen to the response.

The payoffs for your concern, empathy, and support should be a good feeling about yourself for your understanding and help; other employees will see you as a compassionate human being; the grieving worker's performance will probably be maintained, the likelihood of the employee quitting is reduced, and after the mourning period the employee will long remember your supportive efforts.

The Status-Deprived Employee

All of us have needs for self- esteem or self-worth. A key element in that is our status, which is derived from our position, grade, rank, and/or salary. It is to be noted that in our culture, work "defines" us, it tells us who we really are. So any work-related event that causes us to experience loss or deprivation in our status may produce feelings of dissatisfaction.

The feeling of loss may arise because of an actual reduction in status, such as in the case of a downgrading or, says management consultant Dr. Paul O. Radde ("Dealing With Employee Status Deprivation," *Training and Development Journal,* January 1986), due to:

☐ Being passed over for promotion.

☐ Being "underemployed"—i.e., one's skills are not used with resultant lack of challenge or even boredom.

☐ Lack of proper pay for performance of additional work or assumption of extra responsibility.

☐ A managerial expectation that the employee acquire added skills just to keep the same position or status.

For many employees, a loss of status may result in only temporary disappointment or hurt. For others, the event may be perceived as a grave insult and injury and linger on. **The result:** possible depression, lowered productivity, and even vindictiveness, a need "to get even." Getting even may take the form of spreading rumors and petty griping about the boss, the boss' boss, and/or company policies, practices, and programs. Radde states that following the actual or perceived loss of status, the employee goes through the usual phases of the process of loss and grieving before adjustment to the new facts of life can take place. For example, if one is passed over for promotion, the phases are:

Shock

There is disappointment accompanied by sadness and depression. One feels numb: "I thought it was in the bag." This stage has to be "worked through," which leads to stage two:

Anger

There is a variety of confused feelings, anger mixed with sadness: "Why didn't they appreciate all I have done here?" "How could they choose him over me?" "How could they ignore my potential?" After venting one's anger, the employee can move on to a realization that this is the way things are for now and thus can move on to stage three:

Neutral or "Limbo" Stage

The new reality is accepted generally, with most of the "healing" having taken place.

"Restructuring"

One's energy is now invested in the new circumstances. New roles, relationships and activities are adopted. One's feelings of status deprivation are overcome.

If the employee can move through the four stages properly, usually in about six weeks, there is no major problem. The boss need only show empathy and give support during the healing process. But if there is great disappointment and the employee undertakes a personal vendetta or undergoes deeper despondency and depression, and productivity is affected, intervention by the boss is essential.

Actions by the manager/supervisor to deal with more serious, unresolved feelings of status deprivation are as follows, says Radde:

☐ Recognize that there is pain, but the employee did make it to work. So a reasonable managerial expectation is that the employee perform according to standard.

☐ Provide counseling, which may include a reference to the probable career consequences of lowered performance. The annual performance report may have to reflect lowered performance and other negative behavioral data, e.g., "bad mouthing" the big boss.

☐ In extreme cases, references may be made to possible termination. This may cause the employee to shift his performance and behavior.

☐ If an employee is highly upset and is ready to leave, you should tell the employee you will work with him to help accomplish a promotion or transfer.

☐ Be candid about future promotional opportunities. If you "inherited" the passed-over employee and have prior negative data about him, share it with the employee. That is the fair and helpful thing to do. The employee can't overcome unwanted, unhelpful behaviors if no one ever communicated them to him.

What about prevention of status deprivation? The boss should be conscious of the possibility of status deprivation when an event with such potential is looming. Use your knowledge of this phenomenon to counsel with employees likely to be affected in an untoward way by the denial of a promotion or a downgrading. The early communication may help the potentially affected employees to weather the storm.

The Workaholic

While some managers may like to joke about workaholism—"Workaholics? I wish I had a few in my department!"—it, nevertheless is a serious emotional problem. The workaholics are only comfortable with their work. They are driven performers and care little about the 9-to-5 concept or a "big, fun weekend." In our current era of downsizing, obviously the remaining workers have to do more. But for the workaholic, staff reductions will spur an even greater urge to compete with the "normals."

Personality Dynamics

According to industrial psychologist Dr. Ruth Haas ("Strategies to Cope With a Cultural Phenomenon—Workaholism," *Supervisory Management,* November 1991), the personality of the workaholic is comprised of four types of behaviors existing simultaneously in the person: obsessive-compulsive, addictive, workaholism, and the Type A behavior pattern. These traits, in combination, produce the tremendous abnormal need to perform, achieve and accomplish.

Possible Treatment

Managers who supervise workaholics have a responsibility to help them to alter their frenzied behavior. Haas offers an eight-point framework to bring about change:

1. The employee must recognize that he has a problem, a strong tendency to overwork.
2. Because workaholism is a disease stemming from a dysfunctional family background, a referral to an EAP (Employee Assistance Program) or a recovery program is to be accomplished.
3. Provide the workaholic with direction to establish a priority list and related time frames, long- and short-term.
4. Encourage the workaholic to delegate to others.
5. Meet daily at day's end to check accomplishments and to plan the next day's work.
6. Encourage him to make a daily work plan with a time component attached to each activity. This is for the next day's work and must be done. **Note:** A

supportive plan with time limits is a route to limiting endless work routines.
7. Set specific times for breaks and when to end the day.
8. Encourage the employee to pick up a hobby or team sport that can be shared with friends or family.

The Drug Abuser

The drug abuser is a concern to the manager because of his impact on productivity. Ideally, the manager should be sensitive to a growing addiction before it reaches out-of-control proportions and thus affects work results adversely. In extreme cases, the user may steal supplies and equipment from the company to support the habit, or he may become the in-house vendor of drugs to others.

What are the signals that the manager has a user on his hands? According to drug abuse expert Charles R. Carroll ("Drug Proofing the Workplace: A Guide for Supervisors," *Supervisory Management,* October 1989), the supervisor may expect mood swings and irritability, including overreactions to minor criticisms, above average number of visits to and more time spent in the bathroom, lateness, increase in and/or missed deadlines, a decline in personal appearance and grooming such as being unshaven, and red eyes and/or shaking hands.

Possible Action

First, be certain your own understanding of drug addiction is not contaminated by man-on-the-street myths and prejudices. Recognize that drug addiction is an illness and may impact on anyone, not just irresponsible pleasure-seekers. For example, the addiction may have arisen due to the use of painkillers for a bad back or to avoid job stress. Or an employee, who is an evening student, may have become physically addicted by using amphetamines for late-evening study.

Second, be aware that there are several things you should *not* do, such as attempt to diagnose the problem, discuss it with people who have no reason to know about it, and getting personally involved in the employee's situation. What *should* be done, says Carroll, are the following:

1. **Maintain accurate records** on a) production and b) related data such as appearance, bloodshot eyes, shaking hands on particular days. The productivity records should cover prior and current performance and, of course, relate to performance standards.

2. **Measure performance regularly,** i.e., on a weekly or monthly basis.
3. **Act on poor performance.** Call in the employee to discuss his *performance* only. You may ask why the slump, but, in any case, you have to insist on a return to normal, expected performance by a particular date. Alibis and excuses are not to be accepted.
4. **Follow-up.** If improvement does not occur, meet again. Include another person in the conference—your boss, a representative from the personnel office, and a union representative, if appropriate. This time the employee is warned that he faces suspension or even termination if improvement does not take place.
5. **Watch work assignments.** The user should be reassigned to less dangerous work if it is quite apparent the the employee is "high."
6. **Anticipate an occasional admission.** If a confession is forthcoming, be prepared to offer proper referral—to the Employee Assistance Program (EAP) if there is one in-house, or to an outside organization that deals with drug rehabilitation problems.

Points to remember:

1. If drugs are discovered accidentally, you must report it to your front office because such possession is a crime.
2. Your prime purpose in dealing with the user is to provide help, not punishment.
3. You have a lot of leverage over the user—more so than the user's spouse—since you control that person's livelihood. You (or someone else in the firm) thus must insist on the securing of professional help, as indicated.

The Alcohol Abuser

The alcohol abuser may be blue or white collar, managerial or rank and file, male or female, young or more mature. Symptoms include heavy absences, particularly Monday or Friday; tardiness; lowered productivity; alcohol on the breath; possibly an above average involvement in accidents.

It is important to distinguish between heavy or problem drinkers vs. true alcoholics. Andre Nelson ("I won't be able to come to work today . . .," *Supervisory Management,* May 1985) points out that the former have problems with their self-esteem, with others, or adjusting to society. The alcoholic may have these problems, too, but in addition he can't function normally in society. In fact, drinking becomes the alcoholic's "central activity." The manager's concern typically is with the problem drinker.

As in the case of the drug abuser, fact collection on productivity—not apparent symptoms of heavy drinking—and early confrontation on it are essential. Because the problem drinker's job is at risk if he doesn't shape up, the manager, with organizational support, has strong leverage to insist that he enter a corrective program such as AA (Alcoholics Anonymous).

A point to recognize: The problem won't go away by itself. If anything, it will get worse before it gets better. So the proper thing to do in the best interests of the employee and the organization is to face up to what is going on and act decisively. Experts in this field point out that getting the alcoholic into treatment may be more difficult than the treatment itself. In any case, an early referral to the firm's EAP (Employee Assistance Program) is an effective way to get the ball rolling. If there is no EAP, a referral to a community corrective center is appropriate.

And a final point: addictive behavior, whether drug or alcohol related, doesn't mean the person is "bad" or "immoral" It simply means that the worker has a tough problem that must be faced up to and worked on.

The Compulsive Gambler

Gambling in its compulsive form is a drugless addiction. The American Psychiatric Association regards it as a progressive behavioral disorder. Typically, this medical condition is either underdiagnosed or misdiagnosed. Peggy Stuart, assistant editor of *Personnel Journal,* "The Hidden Addiction," November 1991, points out that the malady has nothing to do with "willpower." She quotes Dr. Thomas Blocker, medical director of New Spirit Chemical Dependency Treatment Program in Houston who says that people ". . . think the problem is one of moral decrepitude. It isn't that these people are morally impaired. They tend to be a little self-centered, but turn out to be excellent employees." Unfortunately, public awareness of the problem is at the same stage alcohol addiction was 30 years ago.

As to the extent of the problem in the US, the Council of Compulsive Gambling of New Jersey, Inc., estimates that there are some 12 million compulsive gamblers, with an average gambling debt of $43,158. Three-fourths commit felonies because of gambling. If they are "bailed out" (i.e., have their debts paid off), 91% continue gambling. But the good news is that 80% can be treated successfully.

How does the manager identify the compulsive gambler? Unlike chemical addictions, says Stuart, there is no physical evidence—no smell of alcohol or drug paraphenalia to be found. Also, the gambler, who typically is of above average IQ (120 or better), uses his intelligence to be a super con artist. Adept at fooling himself, he is thus skilled in fooling others. But there are indicators that should merit a referral to the EAP. They are reduced productivity; excessive phone use; ups and downs in mood; borrowing money, including hitting up colleagues for loans; considerable absences, often for only a few hours; ostentatious behavior such as heavy spending and generosity; bragging of his gambling; home problems. Sometimes the gambler may seek help on a debt problem, which is easier to talk about than gambling.

The debt problem may result in turning to selling drugs or stealing from the firm. Multiple addictions may also occur, involving alcoholism and/or compulsive overeating.

In any case, because the gambler is a troubled employee, a referral to seek professional help is essential. The supervisor/manager, as with chemical dependency, must focus only on job performance and not try to be a therapist. If the discussions about the reduced job results are not productive, a referral to EAP or community resources is very much in order.

After professional help or self-help (via a Gamblers' Anonymous group) and the employee is restored to duty, he should not be given responsibility to handle large sums of money. (This is similar to not allowing an alcoholic to become a bartender!)

The Worker with Marital Problems

Employees who are experiencing problems of a marital sort—divorce, separation or serious discord—are increasing in frequency in the US. A study by management professor Clinton O. Longenecker and Dennis M. Kale, a counselor at the Discovery of Life Counseling Center ("When Marital Problems Come to Work," *Supervisory Management,* November 1991) surveyed 21 managers in ten large manufacturing and service organizations:

- ☐ 69% had one or more employees with marital problems in the past three years.
- ☐ 73% said that those problems had a negative impact on performance—absenteeism, accidents, inept decision making, bending of work rules, interpersonal conflicts, and loss of valuable customers.
- ☐ 76% were less than confident to approach employees whose work had deteriorated because of marital difficulties.

Instead of hoping that the problem will go away, Longenecker and Kale advise using an intervention strategy with these steps:

- ☐ Observe carefully the employee's behavior and evaluate its impact on the workplace as well as the work.
- ☐ Provide an opportunity for the troubled worker to talk about his problem. It may be embarrassing to discuss one's personal problem, but with an atmosphere of trust and concern, the employee is very likely to "open up."
- ☐ Meet, preferably after hours, in a private, comfortable, and interruption-free location and present your concern about changes in his work behavior. Your willingness to meet after hours is one way to show your concern and support.
- ☐ Make a point of really *listening*. The idea is for the employee to talk (ventilate feelings) about what is bothering him. Use head nods, "uh huhs," and an occasional restatement of what is said as opposed to interrupting, questioning, evaluating, and advising. Listen to learn how emotionally concerned the worker is.
- ☐ Try to assess whether the employee requires a referral for professional help. The indicator is how well the person is coping with the problem.
- ☐ The meeting should lead to a decision by the employee to take some action such as seeking outside help, if necessary, and personal "regrouping" to overcome current performance problems. In the latter connection, an action plan to reduce the impact of lowered performance should be developed. The plan should address the specific areas of reduced job effectiveness you have pointed out.
- ☐ At meeting's end, assure the worker of the confidentiality of your discussion, and indicate that you

are available to talk further and to help in any way that you can.

☐ Follow up with a later meeting to restore normalcy to the relationship. Use small talk to ease into a discussion of performance. Avoid the marital issues discussed at the prior meeting, unless the employee wishes to talk further about them. Provide feedback about job accomplishment and provide appropriate praise and support.

The Employee Undergoing Therapy

In today's stress-laden world, it is not unusual for a manager to have an employee who currently is receiving therapy from a psychologist or psychiatrist. The employee may have sought professional counseling help on his own, or you may have encouraged it via your referral of him to the EAP (Employee Assistance Program) counselor. In either case, the question arises concerning the way you now supervise him.

Guidance counselor Adrienne Lampert ("Supervising an Employee in Therapy," *Supervisory Management,* February 1985) offers the following guidance:

Consider Your Attitude

Your mindset toward therapy in general and the employee in particular is key. The fact that your staff member is trying to deal with his problem head on is a big plus. You should thus feel positive about the person and act in a supportive way toward him. More specifically:

Keep Assignments "Normal"

That is to say, don't try to ease the workload. The last thing the person in therapy needs is for someone to be a "Big Uncle" to him. Treat the person as you would anyone else and as you did previously. If you tamper with the person's regular workload by lightening it, you are communicating that you feel that there now is something wrong with him, that he can't handle the job, and that special treatment thus is required.

Provide Support

Certainly the person in therapy needs all the encouragement and understanding possible. So give praise as warranted for A-1 work, express appreciation for job assistance, etc.

Co-worker Relationships

Since therapy is a personal and private concern, there is no need to inform the staff of it. If the person in therapy wishes to tell his colleagues about it, that's his decision.

The Rehabilitated Mentally Ill Person

Persons returning from a mental illness can prove to be valuable employees. Mentally restored workers are eager to succeed and, given a fair shake, will work hard to prove their new-found "normalcy." Industry statistics of such employees evidence a high success probability. The work itself is therapeutic for the recovering worker.

The Boss' Role

Dr. J. R. Soloman, a specialist in placing such persons, advises ("How to Work With the Rehabilitated Mentally Ill," *Supervisory Management,* January 1986) that the best approach to supervision is to treat them like everyone else. There is no need at all to try to play "therapist." If a problem does develop, simply contact the referring agency for advice. Soloman offers these suggestions to ease the transition back to work:

☐ Explain job responsibilities clearly so that if criticism should be required, misunderstandings will be be prevented.

☐ Be consistent.

☐ Communicate freely and candidly if performance is below standard. Criticize the performance, but not the person.

☐ Provide praise for a well-done job.

☐ Let the employee decide whether he will share his medical history with co-workers.

☐ Don't try to reduce job responsibilities on the assumption that this will reduce stress. Presumably the nature of the job was considered by the placement agency when the initial contact was made.

☐ Give yourself a pat on the back for demonstrating community and corporate responsibility.

The Thief

Employee thievery and dishonesty take various forms; converting office/shop supplies to personal use; "borrowing" equipment for at-home use sans authorization; dipping into the till; manipulating the expense account for personal gain; letting friends receive free or "mispriced" merchandise (as in a retail store); reselling pilfered goods; approving phony "refunds" of merchandise; winking at shortages of delivered goods; etc. An American Management Association study reported a loss to US business of $40 billion (Elliot D. Lasson, "How Good Are Integrity Tests?" *Personnel Journal,* April 1992).

Personality Dynamics

Motivations of the thief are diverse. They may range from hostility toward the boss or company ("getting even") to out-and-out sociopathic (conscienceless) behavior. Employees into drugs or gambling may steal to support their habit. Some employees may feel that minor pilfering is OK because the company "can afford it," "my pay is too low" and/or "everybody does it." Still others may look at it as "a challenge" to pilfer without getting caught.

Possible Treatment

First, there should be enough controls, checks, and audits in place so that theft is readily ascertained. Second, selection methods, including psychological testing and reference checking, should be fine enough to screen out a good number of potentially at-risk employees. Third, supervision should be employee-centered (supportive) so that there is no need to "settle a score" with the boss or the company. Praise good work regularly so that people feel rewarded for their effort.

Fourth, manage on a team basis. Employees who feel that they are part of a team are less likely to commit a hostile act such as thievery. Maintain close contact with your people, e.g. MBWA (Management by Walking Around). Fifth, stress cost consciousness in every way possible, emphasizing how it relates to profitability and survival. Point out, too, that because assets and income are so important to financial soundness, that the firm (or the unit) has a number of protective measures and penalties in place as defenses against theft or fraud. This point—cost consciousness, profitability, and existing measures against dishonesty—should be stressed in the orientation of new employees.

Sixth, if your operation is such that it produces nonsaleable products such as damaged, returned, or discontinued goods, consider giving away such merchandise. Discounts on company products should be offered, too. Seventh, provide a model for an ethical and honest operation. Indifferent standards as to ethics on your part can

invite irresponsible employee behavior. Ethics relates to all aspects of the operation, including treatment of customers, suppliers, competitors, other departments, employees, advertising, the environment, etc.

Note that the "treatment" described above relates to high-quality management and supervision, rather than actual counseling, as in the case of the previously described troubled employees. And, of course, any employee caught stealing should be punished immediately in accord with previously established organization guidelines.

For information on psychological testing as an aid to improving selection decisions, the reader may wish to refer to the article by Scott L. Martin and Loren P. Lehnen, "Select the Right Employees Through Testing," *Personnel Journal,* June 1992, pp. 46–51.

Guidelines to Cope with the Troubled Employee

Managers have a vital role to play in identifying the troubled employee and taking appropriate action on his problem. However, there may be a reluctance by managers to do so, per management writers Mark Ralfs and John Morley ("Turning Employee Problems Into Triumphs," *Training and Development Journal,* November 1990), for these reasons:

- ☐ There may be a greater identification with their employees than with management.
- ☐ They don't want their employees to lose their jobs.
- ☐ They are reluctant to confront an employee about sensitive, personal matters.
- ☐ They don't want their staff to feel that they are on a "witch hunt."
- ☐ It's a lot easier to close one's eyes to the problem, to live with it, possibly to put the worker on lower-grade work.
- ☐ They may not be aware that with proper professional treatment (therapy), troubled employees can be restored to their former level of productivity.
- ☐ They may not be aware of the extent of troubled employee problems in the US: almost one in 10 workers abuses drugs or alcohol; a substance abuser, compared to the "normal" worker, is three times more apt to be late to work, four times more likely to be in a job accident, and 16 times more likely to be an absentee.
- ☐ They may not be informed about the cost of troubled employees to organizations; e.g., in North

America it totals some $100 billion annually in worker's compensation, health insurance, and benefit costs. Also, poor decisions, equipment damage, safety violations, and lowered morale typically result from these problems.

The manager/supervisor who is willing and able to act on the problem of the troubled employee should do the following, per Ralfs and Morley:

Know When to Act

A basic step is to monitor the employee's performance and work habits. Telltale signs to point up concern are unexplained absences, withdrawal, blaming others for weak performance, frequent accidents, or reduced productivity.

Document Behavior

Specific data about changes in work patterns are essential to be certain of the existence of a problem. Also, should disciplinary action ultimately be taken, the employee and/or his representative may insist on seeing the records.

Maintain Self-esteem

With the aid of full documentation, the supervisor is in a better position to confront the employee to show his desire to help. This may encourage the worker to share his problems and to deal constructively with them. (For suggestions on how to start the first meeting off, see "Approaching the Troubled Worker" below.)

Discuss Work Habits and/or Performance

In any discussion designed to secure a commitment to attack his problem, the focus should be strictly on job results. Express your concern about the employee's difficulty and provide assurance that you are committed to help the worker find a solution. Assure the employee that you appreciate the employee's contributions and value to the unit, and that you want to do everything you can to ensure that they continue. In this meeting give the employee plenty of time to present his side of the difficulty.

Secure an Agreement as to Possible Action

The discussion about performance should lead to a mutually agreed-upon plan to take corrective action. Try to show how the employee will benefit from the changed behavior. Be certain that the plan deals only in achievable targets.

Close the meeting on an appreciative note: "I'm glad that we had a chance to talk about your situation and I appreciate your candor in filling me in on it."

Follow Up

If the action plan fails, added meetings are necessary; e.g., to determine an alternative course of action, even including a disciplinary action or to take disciplinary or other corrective action, which may include a referral to the Employee Assistance Program (EAP).

Immediate EAP referrals are to be made if a) there is an admission of substance abuse or a personal problem or b) a discovery is made of possession of an illegal drug.

Ongoing Support

If the employee begins to "shape up," meet with him to solidify your relationship. Provide feedback and praise as warranted.

One of the problems that may arise in dealing with employees who have personal and personality problems is the tendency to go overboard in providing support. Thus, one may shift from a supportive, nurturing manager into a "patsy," says business writer Sharon Sullivan ("Are You Too Nurturing a Manager?", *Supervisory Management,* August 1992). She advises the manager who finds himself in the counseling role to be guided by these signposts of overnurturing:

Getting Overly Involved

If one begins to ask oneself: "Am I doing too much?", it's a good idea to get another opinion from either the EAP representative or the personnel officer. There is a strong possibility that you are taking on more than you should.

Making Allowances

Another trap may be in prospect when the "Am I making allowances?" question arises. Being "kind" instead of taking positive action is of little value. Again, an appropriate referral for professional counseling and proper documentation is in order in case things don't get any better.

Feeling Angry

This is a signal that you probably have tried too hard and feel that you have been taken advantage of. Again, this nagging question: "Do I feel angry?" is a potent indicator that action is now called for.

Assuming the Professional Counselor Role

When the employee starts to share loads of highly personal data, it's time to ask "Am I acting like a professional counselor or the manager?" At this stage it is wise to recognize that professional help is called for. Advise the employee: "I appreciate your sharing your problem with me. But it would be better for you if you talked with a professional counselor who can really help on these kinds of problems."

Grumbling Co-workers

If the troubled employee's behavior continues and begins to impact on his colleagues, anticipate anger and jealousy on their part. Why? They may feel that they are being taken advantage of. And since they are not up on the cause of the irritating behavior, they may even begin to pass unkind jokes about the troubled employee. So added signposts to monitor are these: "Are staffers getting angry or jealous?" and "Is the troubled worker becoming an object of daily conversation?" Affirmative answers to either question should serve as a motivator to act, lest your employees begin to appraise you negatively.

Approaching the Troubled Worker

With your usual observational skills, you readily can become aware of new behaviors, those that are now clearly different—late arrivals, longer lunch periods, tenseness, irritability, missing deadlines, sloppy work, badmouthing authority figures, and the like. So how does one make contact, communication-wise, with a person in an obviously troubled state?

Guidance counselor Adrienne Lampert offers these ways to broach the subject ("Supervising an Employee in Therapy," *Supervisory Management,* February 1985):

Be Direct

A good, general, simple opener is to ask: "How are things going for you?"

Be Specific

State clearly which behaviors are causing problems. If you feel that you need to discuss a new specific behavior, e.g., late arrivals, late returns from lunch, etc., you may say: "I've noticed that you are late a lot lately and you seem to need long lunch periods. I may be able to help you get back on your regular schedule. Let's discuss it, OK?" Or: "I notice that you seem to be tense of late. Is there something troubling you that I can help out on?"

Make Referrals

If the troubled person asks about getting professional help, you can suggest contacting the EAP (Employee Assistance Program) counselor, someone in the personnel office, his family physician or clergyman, the community mental health service, or the like. Of course, depending on the circumstances and the gravity of the situation, you may wish to make a referral yourself, even if not asked to do so. If so, simply state: "If there are personal problems which are not letting you do as well as you would like to, you may wish to see the EAP people. They are experienced in situations of a personal sort."

As the conversation proceeds, be certain to show and state your concern for the troubled person. Give the other party full opportunity to "open up." Listen, nod your head, say "uh huh," and use phrases like "I understand," "I see," and "Tell me more." Avoid interruptions lest you inhibit the conversation or channel it into another unwanted direction.

To Sum Up: The manager's/supervisor's critical role in respect to troubled individuals is to have cognizance of their troubled state and to take appropriate action. If this is done, many of these workers can be restored to their normal condition and made fully productive again.

The signal for the manager to intervene fully is *falling productivity,* not merely behavioral changes. If one tries to upgrade or restore productivity via encouraging and sympathetic comments and they do not accomplish any change, then a direct and frank discussion with the troubled employee is in order. The objective at this point is a referral to the EAP or a professional source for counseling or therapy.

The big advisory to the manager, when identifying the troubled worker, is this: Whatever is ailing him, in all likelihood, won't go away by itself. If anything, the condition is more likely to become aggravated if left untreated. An added caution is to avoid assuming roles that are inappropriate for a manager: therapist, physician, legal advisor, or financial planner.

Finally, try to regard and use your counseling session with the employee as *his* meeting. Your aim is to encourage him to open up, to talk about his concerns, to achieve a realistic recognition (insight) as to what his current behavior/performance is, and to arrive on his own at a decision which will embark him on to the road of normalcy insofar as the job is concerned. Your job in the meeting is to put the worker at ease, to establish rapport, to encourage free and full communication, to set a businesslike but supportive tone, to show that you appreciate the other's good qualities, to listen, to communicate that you have full confidence in the other party's ability to make a sound decision to resolve the current problem or setback, and that you want to be as helpful as you possibly can.

COUNSELING EMPLOYEES ON THEIR CAREERS

The bulk of the manager's responsibility for developing subordinates relates to the *current* job: better performance, identifying and overcoming weaknesses, making more progress, meeting deadlines, improving customer service and/or product quality, solving problems more effectively, etc. This is logical since at any one time not all employees are being readied for advancement. For example, a person may have just come on the job; or a subordinate may be a specialist who now needs broadening, stimulation or challenge but not necessarily promotion; some employees may have reached the top of their career ladder—they may no longer be promotable because they may be determined specialists who want to stay in their own field, they are at the top of the grade or career ladder for their particular kind of work, they are approaching retirement, etc.

However, for employees who are at the bottom or midpoint of the career ladder and have some or consid-

erable potential ("the comers" and the "late bloomers"), as a progressive manager you have an obligation to counsel them about their future careers.

Employees today typically expect their bosses to be interested in their careers. They may expect, as a minimum, advice and guidance on how to move up in the immediate organizational unit. They may also expect counsel on how to advance elsewhere in the organization and even desire active assistance in furthering their careers, e.g., obtaining a worthwhile lateral transfer, a short-term assignment in another segment of the organization or special training in an outside facility. Some employees may expect their manager to give them feedback on their strengths and weaknesses, including advice on how to capitalize on the former and how to overcome the latter.

Although a growing number of organizations are encouraging managers to work with their subordinates on their careers, many others take little interest in counseling employees on careers. As a result, career counseling by managers is hardly a universally accepted role.

Managerial reluctance to assume the career counseling role is based on a combination of misconceptions, fears, and anxieties. They include the following:

Being Overextended

Managers may feel that with current downsizing, organizational restructuring, reduction of administrative support, and intense pressures for results, they are "over-stretched already." A typical reaction: "Hey, man, do you know my schedule? If I have to sit down with all my people and take a lot of time to get into the nitty-gritty of their future careers . . ."

Absence of Personal Experience

Another reason for reluctance to assume the counseling role is that "it never happened to me." Managers may not have received any career guidance or help themselves, achieving what they have "entirely on my own." It thus is understandable that they may shy away from embarking on an activity with which they are totally unfamiliar and may even look to them like a "lot of spoon feeding."

Being Untrained

Another concern is that one simply does not have the skills to do what employees may expect of them. But in reality, counseling a person about his career doesn't require a Ph.D. in psychology. All it takes is:

☐ An interest in the employee.

☐ A desire to be helpful.

☐ A recognition that it is our obligation, as managers, to help people to move themselves along in a planned and positive way.

☐ A knowledge of the questions to ask in such an interview (see box). Additional questions to pose to the career-oriented person appear on the following page under "Classic Employee Career Concerns."

☐ Use of your good active listening skills (see Chapter 3).

☐ Practice—you'll probably do a better job the second time.

☐ Assigning time to do it.

☐ Completion of a plan emphasizing career development which you and the employee feel is reasonable and attainable. Pinpoint both short- and long-range goals, and plans to meet such goals.

Some Suggested Questions to Open a Discussion for Career Advancement

1. What satisfactions do you get from your job?
2. Do you feel that your present type of work is the one in which you want to continue your career?
3. What would you like to be doing five years from now? Ten years?
4. What have you been doing to ready yourself for the career you favor?
5. How do you use your leisure time? Is this the best use, careerwise?
6. Can the organization and I help you to reach your career goals? If so, how?
7. Have you considered lateral transfer? Degree programs? Special courses? Job rotations? Toastmaster's? Participation in civic, community, and/or professional society affairs?
8. What do you see as your strengths? Do you feel you have any weaknesses which you need to overcome to help your career?

☐ Follow up to see that progress on the plan is being accomplished, offering such added help as may be indicated and practical.

Encouraging Job Dissatisfaction

A common fear is that concern with career planning will result in the creating of "false expectations" and "job restlessness." It thus will engender major urges to move on to better opportunities, either within the organization or outside of it. Actually, job change is a fact of organizational life. People will seek better career opportunities whether there is a planned effort to help them or not. Rest assured that the "American dream" of upward mobility is alive and well. And to the extent that people do have a chance to think and talk through their career possibilities, they are more likely to stay with their own outfit. This follows, because decisions to leave will be based on greater realism as opposed to impetuous career adventuring into presumed "greener pastures."

And is this not the real issue: What kind of image and relationship do we, as managers, wish to project—aloof, cold, disinterested, and totally production-centered or warm, friendly, and employee-oriented? And which image and relationship will have greater impact on job satisfaction and productivity?

Career Counseling Phases/Roles

To bring out the best in people, says Tod White, chairman of Blessing/White, a New Jersey-based training and development company ("Career Coaching: A Whole New Ball Game," in "Training Today," *Training,* June 1991), managers will have to be active career counselors. Their five specific roles are these:

1. **Communication.** To encourage their people to talk freely about their career concerns and aspirations, managers will have to develop a high degree of trust and rapport with them.
2. **Information sharing.** Even in periods of downsizing and organizational turbulence, managers have information they should share with staff. Managers may feel that they are in the dark about things, but in reality they do have a good fix on what is going on. It is better to err on the side of "over-communicating" than the opposite. What may seem irrelevant may have real meaning to staff.
3. **Identify career alternatives.** Work (brainstorm) with each employee regarding possible career

options. Reduce these possibilities to writing. **Note:** As indicated earlier (see boxed item, page 364), the employee should be encouraged to engage in adequate introspection about strengths and weaknesses before setting career goals.

4. **Develop a plan.** Several days later, based on the above brainstorming, sit down with the employee to choose a direction to travel. Provide (enumerate) worthwhile developmental steps to take to implement a reality-based plan.

5. **Monitor the plan.** Don't let the plan gather dust. Review it periodically (possibly quarterly). Keep employees posted about any changes that might affect their plans.

Various personnel management authorities feel that employees should receive early feedback on career prospects with their firm. For example, Terry Slater, chief of personnel policy for the International Labour Office, Geneva, Switzerland ("Viewpoint," *Personnel Journal,* September 1991), states employees should get such information whether or not it is part of the firm's regular performance appraisal program. Managers should advise on company policy on training and development; explain the usual career path or career ladders within the occupational group, division or company; provide an indication of the employee's next job or type of job which may be given; identify required training; and provide an early assessment of the new worker's potential. In the latter connection, says Slater, "even if these are provisional or negative assessments, if given in a constructive way, they will result either in a change in behavior and improved performance, or lead more quickly (and painlessly) to breaking the employment relationship, if that's the inevitable outcome of the circumstances."

Classic Employee Career Concerns

For the manager who understands the importance of his career counseling role and wishes to work actively at it, he should be aware of the concerns their staffers may have. Per human resource consultants Barbara Moses and B. J. Chakiris ("The Manager as Career Counselor," *Training and Development Journal,* July 1989), these concerns include the following career issues:

"I'm Bored and Dissatisfied"

Step one is to zero in on what is really bothering the worker. Is it lack of job challenge, greater challenge due to increased work load, a desire for greater or lesser visibility to upper management, an uncomfortable feeling that those in other jobs are having more fun, or what? The best course of action for the manager is to insist on adequate introspection and self-assessment by the employee before any meaningful discussion of causes for his distress can take place. And, of course, there is always the possibility that the real source of dissatisfaction may lie in something that is or isn't happening in his off-the-job life.

"What Should I Be When I Grow Up?"

A misconception about career planning is that it is only concerned with how to advance from job A to job B. But the real purpose is to help staffers see who they really are and what they are actually accomplishing on the job. They should be encouraged to look at the broader context of their work, say Moses and Chakiris, and ask these kinds of questions:

☐ *Why* do I work? Do I understand the purpose and importance of my work and how it ties to overall organizational goals?

☐ *Where* should I work? Given my work style, what kind of work setting would permit me to achieve/perform most effectively?

☐ *How* do I prefer to work? Do I favor working on a good number of tasks at one time or prefer one or two at a time? Do I see myself more of a contributor in a specialist, generalist, or managerial role?

☐ *Whom* do I prefer to work with? Given my personality, what degree of interaction with colleagues do I require?

In sum, the manager should encourage employee introspection along the above lines. If this is done, realistic career and life goals can, in time, be plotted by the employee. It is not the manager's job to chart appropriate career courses for the staff members. Counseling means helping people reach informed, pragmatic decisions on their own. It is not about making decisions for people. The counselee must assume responsibility for making his own decisions.

"I'm Stuck"

As organizations strive to become "lean and mean," fewer opportunities inevitably become available. So more people will find themselves on plateaus. But this is not the end of the world insofar as job challenge and job contribution are concerned. The manager can use various techniques—e.g., job enrichment, lateral transfer, task force work—to keep people alive, growing, and contributing.

"I've Been in This Job a Year. When is My Next Move?"

High achievers understandably will become "restless." But the manager must not make promises to these high-potential people that he can't deliver. Certainly, some of these very good people will be lost. But so be it. The manager's job is to:

a) Provide the maximum amount of challenge possible to the high achievers so that they can enlarge their skill repertoires, and
b) Provide heavy psychological rewards (status, prestige) that accrue from responsibility for projects giving them high visibility to upper management.

There also is the possibility that investing more time in the organization may produce a higher degree of skill development. And as one acquires greater recognition and tenure, broader, more diversified and more challenging assignments may come one's way, too. The would-be job hopper should be encouraged to think through carefully immediate vs. long-term career gains.

"I'm Ready for Promotion. Don't You Agree?"

What does the manager do when an employee feels he is "ready" to move up, but the manager hardly sees it that way? Explanations have been given by the manager as to the worker's limitations, but the employee still believes what he wishes to about his capabilities. The only answer to the person who won't accept the "You aren't ready yet" response is to give and repeat, if necessary, honest feedback. No one can do a "selling job" on someone who is not reality-based about his abilities and/or potential. ("A person convinced against his will, is of the same opinion still," as the old couplet has it.)

"I Need a Coach, Not a Fortune Teller."

Managers can provide a lot of assistance to their people in planning their careers—giving information about career opportunities, encouraging introspection about strengths and weaknesses, actively broadening people out with challenging job assignments and training, etc. But managers are neither psychiatrists, fortune tellers, nor magicians. Their job is to coach and counsel in a empathetic, reasonable, and reality-based way, no more no less. If employees have been informed about and understand the proper managerial role as a counselor, they can shed their possible flights of fancy about the manager's possible magical powers.

Story: The Great Writer delivered a brilliant lecture on the American novel which produced a standing ovation by the audience. After the lecture, a young member of the audience approached The Great Writer and offered him a bound manuscript of some 200 pages. This conversation ensued:

Audience member: "Would you please look at this manuscript and advise me whether or not I should become a writer?"

The Great Writer skimmed through the manuscript and said: "Definitely not."

Audience member: "Why not. You became a writer, didn't you?"

Great Writer: "Yes, but I didn't have to ask."

MENTORING: GETTING THE "BIG PICTURE" THE "HANDS-ON" WAY

Moving up in the organization entails "learning the ropes," acquiring the necessary savvy ("accumulated wisdom") so that one can function adroitly at higher levels. As managers, most of us learn the appropriate skills and protocols the hard way, that is, via the school of hard knocks, sink or swim, trial and error, or osmosis. But a better way is for managers at upper levels—the "old hands"— to provide promising individuals with special help—guidance, counsel, tutoring, individual attention, support, encouragement, opportunities for growth experiences, and visibility. We call this planned counseling, development, and support "mentoring."

As a manager you should be interested in the mentoring area, for, depending on your needs and interests, you may wish to be on either the delivery or receiving end of the process.

To appreciate the workings of the mentoring process, visualize the protégé (also known as "mentee" and "mentoree") observing and interacting with his mentor in a "freeze frame" situation—i.e., the learner can stop the mentor while at work and discuss the "whys" and "hows" of critical actions taken or about to be taken. Mentees can also accompany their mentors to important meetings, conferences, and hearings to observe how higher-level problems are tackled, decisions made, and policies developed "at the top." Mentors also give their protégés feedback about their performance and needs for training and development.

Mentoring is an ancient process. The term comes from Greek mythology. Mentor, the friend of the Greek King Odysseus, was entrusted with the care and tutoring of the King's son Telemachus, while the King departed to fight in the Trojan War. Thus, a mentor is deemed to be a wise and trusted counselor and educational nurturer.

A more modern example of "super" mentoring occurs in George Bernard Shaw's play *Pygmalion* (1913), which was the basis for the sprightly musical *My Fair Lady* (1956). Recall that speech Professor Higgins, with the power of high expectations and patient tutoring, transforms Liza, the Cockney urchin and flower girl, into a superbly well-spoken and polished society lady.

Mentoring provides significant benefits to the organization and the mentor, as well as to the mentee, per management professor Dr. Michael G. Zey, ("A Mentor for All Reasons," *Personnel Journal,* January 1988). For the organization it helps to transmit the "corporate culture," philosophy, values, norms, politics, and priorities. It can accelerate the development of a pool of individuals who can move up to more important positions as the need may arise. It can aid recruitment, reduce turnover, and help to meet EEO objectives. It can augment morale. It can encourage innovation via the interchange of ideas between individuals who are in different stages in their careers. It can show that the organization is a progressive employer, providing broader developmental opportunities as opposed to sole reliance on "the old boy's network."

For the mentor, says Zey, the intimate exchange with younger personnel can help to keep him "alive." It can help to keep in touch with the thinking of lower-echelon personnel. It can serve as a "sounding board" on which the mentor can bounce ideas off the mentee. It can provide added person-power to launch or complete projects.

Obviously, mentoring has been taking place formally and informally in modern organizations for a long time in the form of understudies, assistant chiefs, special assistants, management trainees, and the like. In more recent years, mentoring has been used in some organizations to help women and minority group members move more rapidly up career ladders.

Mentoring succeeds best when:

☐ The mentor is a top performer who is regarded very highly in the organization.

☐ The mentor has a high interest in development of people. The more effective mentors are those who act by conviction, not obligation or duty, or for personal, selfish reasons.

☐ There is a close, trusting relationship between the mentor and the protégé. Communication is free and easy, and thus status barriers are minimal.

☐ The mentor is able to assume, at appropriate times, the multiple roles of friend, colleague, guide, advisor, sounding board, challenger, counselor, consultant, tutor, role model, feedback giver, encourager, standard setter. **Note:** The mentor need not assume all of these roles, only those with which he feels comfortable. For example, some mentors may prefer to help in the area of career counseling; others may prefer to concentrate on the tutorial side of things.

☐ There is a training plan so both parties know what the mentoring goals are.

☐ There is organizational support for the program.

Mentoring is hardly a "sure-fire" activity. As management consultants Beverly J. Bernstein and Beverly L. Kaye have learned from their research ("Teacher, Tutor, Colleague, Coach," *Personnel Journal,* November 1986), typical problems relate to excessive time and energy demands placed on the mentors, inappropriate matching of mentors and mentees from a personality standpoint, jealousy by those not involved in a mentoring arrangement, and conflict between the mentee's manager and the mentor. In the latter case, conflict may arise because the mentee takes problems to the mentor which are more appropriately addressed by the manager of the mentee. Another problem is that mentors may feel that they are not recognized by the organization for the effort put into the relationship.

There are other problems, too, says management professor Dianne D. Horgan ("Multiple Mentoring: All of the Gain; None of the Pain," *Performance and Instruction,* July 1992):

☐ Mentoring programs may unwittingly give protégés the message that their success is the responsibility of the mentor rather than themselves.

☐ Mentors may interfere with what managers/supervisors are trying to get done in their units.

☐ The protégé's experience is not subject to consistency or quality control.

☐ The demand for mentors is greater than the supply, so a significant number of would-be mentees are left out.

☐ If the mentoring program is restricted to women and minorities, white male workers may be resentful. This may create a hostile work environment for those that the outfit is earnestly trying to make more comfortable.

☐ The program may create unrealistic, high expectations that may lead to frustration, resentment, and disappointment among the mentorees.

☐ Mentors may provide bad advice; others may become sexually involved with their protégés.

Researchers Dianne D. Horgan and Rebecca J. Simeon ("The Downside of Mentoring, *Performance and Instruction,* January 1991) point out another pitfall. They report "a most disturbing finding": *female* managers were more likely to mentor others if they were *dissatisfied* on the job, whereas satisfied males tend to mentor. **Significance**: protégés having female mentors may receive a vastly different mentoring experience because their learning comes from disgruntled managers. Female mentors, possibly reflecting their own experience, may feel it essential to build learning around avoiding obstacles and means to rise above such barriers. Women subordinates conceivably may thus require *two* mentors: a female mentor to learn of possible obstacles facing women in the outfit and a male mentor to provide the good news, that the world is full of opportunities. So any organization interested in mentoring women workers needs to think through carefully what learning might come from their mentors.

The above research finding suggests that it may be highly desirable for the protégé to be exposed to more than one mentor. As human resources manager Jack J. Phillips suggests in respect to supervisors who are mentees ("Training Supervisors Outside the Classroom," *Training and Development Journal,* February 1986), "Supervisors learn from poor role models as well as good ones. Therefore, the supervisor with a variety of mentors holds an advantage over the supervisor with a single mentor, regardless of the competence of the mentor. In practice, most successful managers have worked for several memorable bosses and have learned what not to do from role models almost as often as they have learned what to do."

In respect to the possibility that mentees may learn the wrong things from their mentors, the following story is pertinent.

Story: A father took his 12-year-old son into a bar and said: "Son, I have something important to teach you today."

Father: "I'm going to order a half-glass of gin and a full glass of water and watch what I do with them."

Son: "OK, Dad."

Father, removing a plastic pouch from his coat pocket, took out several earthworms from the pouch and dropped them in the water glass. "See how they wriggle around and are having a great time?"

Son: "That's right, Dad."

Father: "Now I'll put several other earthworms in the gin glass." The worms took one gulp and immediately descended to the bottom of the glass, totally dead.

Son: "So what do I learn from that, Dad?"

Father: "Simply this, son. If you drink enough gin you'll never have worms."

Management professor Dianne D. Horgan ("Multiple Mentoring: All of the Gain; None of the Pain," *Performance and Instruction,* July 1992) favors group rather than traditional one-on-one mentoring for these added reasons:

☐ Mentoring programs rarely produce the close emotional attachment between mentor and mentee which makes for maximum learning. This follows, since the pairing of mentor and mentee is an arranged, formal affair, something akin to an arranged marriage. So it is more desirable to focus on what protégés learn, rather than on their relationship. Note that in group or multiple mentoring the mentee is provided with a diverse team of knowledgeable, experienced mentors. This procedure serves to provide a broader network that can offer greater support, more information, and wider contacts. So the emphasis is not on the mentor-mentee relationship, but on the functions of that relationship.

☐ Mentors are not "pressured" to promote their protégés so as to enhance their own prestige as successful mentors. Nor would protégés expect such favors since they are not working with several mentors.

☐ Because multiple mentoring makes for functioning in a more "public" way, mentorees don't have the same intimacy expectations. So intense, detrimental personal relationships should not develop and "get in the way" of a pure coaching relationship.

☐ Rather than have the mentor be the total source of knowledge, guidance, and help to the mentee, in multiple mentoring each mentor can function in the areas in which he is strongest. Protégés can maximize their learning about the firm, garner different perspectives, realize different experiences, and generally broaden their horizons because of their more varied contacts.

☐ Rather than place responsibility for protégé success on one mentor, successful development now becomes the responsibility of the mentee. Since the protégés work with several mentors and the locale for their learning is more diffuse, they can no longer expect their mentors to "make them successful." Obviously, this makes for a more "healthy" approach.

☐ Bad advice from a single mentor is more easily overcome because of exposure/involvement to and with multiple mentors.

☐ The limitation of one role model, which may provide a style which is inappropriate for a particular protégé, is overcome with the group format. Proteges have a chance to see how different people deal with problems, issues, organizational complexities, and decisions. Also, protégés are more likely to find a mentor (role model) who shares their style.

☐ Because mentors differ in effectiveness, in the one-on-one mentoring format some protégés inevitably receive higher quality coaching than others. With group mentoring, the overall learning experience of the *mentees* is more likely to be uniform.

☐ On the assumption that one goal of the protégé's learning process is to experience "cultural diversity," the protégés can learn more readily from the perspectives of a broader range of mentors plus their contacts with a wide range of personnel in several departments. Mentors themselves also learn to appreciate diversity via their interaction with diverse protégés.

Mentoring authority Gordon Shea (author of *Mentoring: A Trainer's Workbook,* 1991) reports that there is a newer emphasis in the mentor-mentee relationship. It is not to groom one for a particular position; rather, the emphasis is on empowerment and developing the over-

all potential of the protégé. If the right kind of relationship develops and the development is meaningful, mentees will move upward by demonstrating the skills and knowledge they have acquired.

Mentoring organizations have begun to take on new forms. Gordon Shea (writing in *Human Resources Forum,* American Management Association, June 1991) spells out the characteristics of the "new" mentoring approaches:

Broader Participation

Mentoring opportunities are not limited to senior executives and managers. Rather, training courses in the mentoring art are offered to all personnel who are strongly motivated to help others. Mentoring thus should take place more widely in organizations.

Greater Sophistication

Mentors are now being trained in such key developmental skills as active listening, creative problem solving, and rendering effective counsel. The assumption is that the acquisition of vital mentoring skills is too important to be left to chance.

Individual Focus

There is a shift from preparing people for specific positions (position power) to helping them develop their inner selves (personal power).

Greater Honesty

The operative concept is "networking for knowledge" rather than for "position power and influence." Learning rather than promotion is the primary objective.

Greater Demands

Higher standards of mentoring performance are expected. Consequently, they (mentors) are being trained to integrate ethical, cultural, and societal responsibilities in addition to concern only with business skills.

Greater Versatility

Training programs now emphasize development of a variety of mentors for different purposes and, possibly, at different states of career development. This approach is a departure from the traditional idea of creating a single relationship.

Life-long Experience

Rather than regard mentoring as a relationship marked by specially established time constraints, the newer concept is to have it continue as long as it is satisfying, rewarding, and useful. **The reason:** People are capable of growth and development throughout their organizational lives.

Abandonment of the Constraints of Organizational or Geographic Boundaries for Learning

In this age of globalization, learning can come from many rather than limited sources.

Organizational Unity

Although offered a broader set of global relationships, mentors also learn via their training in the art of cooperation, at least internal to the organization.

Greater Introspection

Mentors are being trained and are expected to be consistent role models, that is, there should be a higher congruity between their actual behavior and their stated ideals. Keen, continuing reflection and self-analysis in this area are essential.

Greater Use of Intuition

Guidelines for mentoring in unexpected situations cannot be laid out neatly in a manual. Rather, mentors must learn to sense the situation, to "intuit," and free-wheel as the situation calls for.

DIRECTIVE VS. NON-DIRECTIVE COUNSELING

For the person who is only peripherally familiar with the goals and techniques of counseling, he is likely to assume that it simply entails giving "good advice" or a stern lecture to someone who is having (or possibly causing) a problem. We thus may hear a statement like this: "Why don't you counsel him on it?" The implication is that one person (the boss) has the answers and he only need communicate them to the person (the employee) experiencing the difficulty. The counseling presumably should "clean things up once and for all."

Actually, counseling is a much more complex form of interpersonal communication and may have these diverse purposes:

Information Dissemination

The counselor (manager) presents data to the counselee (employee) to prevent problems from arising or to limit inappropriate behavior. **Examples:** information and advice regarding preferred safety practices; reminders of important office rules and policies on sexual harassment.

Problem Resolution

Data are developed and exchanged between the counselor (the boss) and the counselee (the worker) to resolve a personal problem. **Example:** A very able employee who resides in the inner city is carless and is experiencing difficulty with her transportation to her job in outer suburbia.

Attitude and/or Behavior Change

A meeting is held to help the employee to understand better himself, his concern(s), his goals. The result is the making of better (more reality-based) decisions by the worker. The type of counseling is considered to be *developmental* in nature.

Support

An employee is experiencing emotional problems off the job and desperately needs to talk to someone about them. **Example:** A female worker, a single parent, has two teenagers who are into drugs and, she fears, intermittent shoplifting.

Basically, from a skill standpoint we can divide counseling into three major categories:

1. Directive Counseling

In this approach to counseling, the purpose is corrective or remedial. It is *counselor centered.* There is a heavy emphasis by the counselor on either presenting or diagnosing the problem, supplying a solution, and/or giving advice. The counselor's style emphasizes telling and selling behavior. **Example:** A supervisor meets with a foreman to advise in no uncertain terms that his sexual harassment activities must cease *now* or he will face discharge.

2. Non-directive Counseling

In this approach, known as *client-centered* counseling, the counselor operates on the assumption that the counselee (client or employee) is fundamentally responsible for himself and is fully capable of solving his problems and making his own reality-based decisions. The counselee is given every possible opportunity and full assistance to become mature and independent. The primary skills used by the counselor are *active listening* and *reflecting feelings.*

In the active listening mode, the counseler is trying to show that he understands—not necessarily agrees, but has received what has been transmitted. Everyone appreciates someone who is really willing to listen to us. By showing an attempt at understanding, you communicate that you accept the other party as a worthy person. So the non-directive counselor refrains from disagreeing, criticizing, arguing, judging, and interrupting, as well as offering sympathy or agreement. Typical *neutral* comments, designed to keep the communication going in an unimpeded way, are "I understand," "Uh, huh, "I see," "Uh huh." Head nods are also used freely. Questions are not of the probing sort, but are designed to encourage "opening up" the counselee: "Would you wish to tell me about that?" "Could you tell me more?"

Reflecting feelings means responding to the other's feelings by summarizing and re-stating them. The counselor, in mirroring feelings, does not pick up the content (what has been said) of the statement(s), but the feeling tone underlying it. The counselor is after the meaning of the emotions at work, not the words used to present the feelings. **Example:** The employee presents a long, windy, somewhat bitter complaint about her fellow team members—they don't want her ideas, they don't socialize with her, they don't help her when she needs assistance, and so on. The counselor does not pick up (comment upon) any of her specific complaints, but reflects her feeling: "You feel that your team members are not treating you fairly."

To reflect feelings properly, the following points, per industrial psychologist Norman R. F. Maier (*Psychology in Industry,* Boston: Houghton Mifflin Co., 1965) should be observed:

1. Use your own words to restate feelings. A *restatement* rather than a parroting is proof that you really heard.
2. Your initial reflected comments should use the "You believe . . .," "You feel . . .," "On occasion you find . . ." Later, these prefatory phrases can be dropped.
3. Offer statements, not questions. Try to speak in a quiet, emotion-free tone.

4. Take advantage of pauses by waiting them out. The counselee may be having difficulty expressing his feelings, hence the pause to "regroup" his thoughts. The silence will probably seem longer than it really is.
5. If many feelings are expressed in a long statement, only pick up the last one.
6. Your reflections of feeling must be based only on what is said, not what you may infer.
7. Anticipate contradictory statements when high emotionality is present. But merely reflect each feeling when given, without trying to point out inconsistencies.
8. If the counselee cries, it is OK to refer to it, providing there was no attempt to hide the tears.
9. Note and reflect mixed feelings; e.g., a conflict between what he wants to do vs. what he feels one should do; or his values and those of society at large.
10. You can reflect decisions and solutions when they predominate over non-constructive feelings such as confusion, hostility, fear, rejection, etc. But the reflection should not be premature, i.e., before the counselee is ready to act on his own suggested possibilities.
11. Reflection should avoid approval as well as disapproval. Avoid these responses: probing, blaming, advising, persuading, reassuring, sympathizing. Reflection is a totally *neutral* response.
12. Avoid diagnosis, i.e., why the counselee feels as he does. This behavior only leads to biased listening.
13. Operate on the assumption that for the most part the initially presented problem is not likely to be the real one. Hence the need to keep the counselee expressing his feelings.
14. Don't seek solutions. They must come only from the counselee's own insight into his problem.

One also should be wary of such dependency-creating traps as: "What would you do if you were in this situation?" The appropriate response to the counselee is: "You feel that I should tell you what to decide?"

In general, the counselor's role is to foster growth and maturity, to encourage independence rather than dependence, and to encourage the making of one's own decisions and assumption of responsibility for them.

3. Combined Approach

Many counseling sessions may require the counselor to use both his directive as well as non-directive counseling skills. This follows, since the manager is often the initiator of the counseling session, e.g., in the case of the marginal performer, the difficult person, and the troubled employee. The common thread in these situations is the manager's concern about performance. Hence, he initiates the interview and describes his concern and tries to reach the point where some sort of action planning takes place. These counseling actions are essentially directive in nature. But in the course of the discussion, the effective counselor uses non-directive approaches, too, particularly active listening and reflection of feelings.

The mentor, at different stages in the mentor-mentee relationship, is likely to use both directive and non-directive approaches. Conversely, the manager as career counselor is concerned primarily with helping the counselee think through his career objectives and to make his decisions about them. He thus functions essentially in the non-directive mode.

Similarly, if an employee comes to the boss with a back-home problem—e.g., an errant spouse, financial difficulties, a rebellious teenager, a daughter in a big city who is facing an unwanted pregnancy, a child who has left home, a kidnapped grandson as a result of a messy divorce, etc.—the boss can only respond non-directively, that is, let the worker drain off the emotion by talking about the problem and ultimately making his decision to either seek further (more professional) counseling or to identify the possible courses of action which are available. Obviously, the boss cannot provide answers (directive counseling) regarding an employee's personal problems which clearly are not related to the job.

Listening and Responding

In every counseling situation, the counselor has to *listen* and to *respond*. What may not always be appreciated, however, is that how we, as listeners, respond to the counselee's statements (a) affects the relationship and (b) can influence the nature—direction, quality, and quantity—of the counselee's communication to us.

Behavioral scientists who have studied the skill factors involved in listening and responding point out that when we respond we have several options—or response categories—that we can use. They are:

Probing. Here we attempt to secure more information by asking questions.

Interpretive. With this response, we try to uncover what lies behind a particular statement (motives), what it really means, what the counselee is telling (or trying to tell) us. In effect, we are assessing the personality of the counselee and using it to explain the meaning of the communication.

Evaluative. In this case, we make a judgment about a counselee's statement—wise or unwise, desirable or undesirable, considered or impulsive, acceptable or unacceptable. In making our assessment, we rely on our value system, our standards, our preferences, our biases.

Supportive. Here we try to provide help, advice, comfort, assurance ("You're on the right track"), all of which can help to reduce the counselee's anxieties about his understanding of the problem or the taking of a particular course of action.

Understanding. This is the "mirror response." Here we simply reflect back (restate) what was said, either the content or the feeling underlying it, or possibly both. This is a totally neutral, non-judgmental response statement on our part, as counselors.

To illustrate how these five responses might apply in an actual counseling interview, let's assume a very able employee of yours comes to you and says: "I feel I should get another job because the transportation to this place here is too much for me."

Using the five possible response styles described above, you might respond in these ways:

Probing: "Could you tell me more about how you arrived at this decision? How long has this problem existed?"

Interpretive: "Is that the only or real source of your dissatisfaction?" "Do you like your work, your work station, your colleagues?"

Evaluative: "I wonder if that's the only factor to consider in making a decision on something as important as a career?" "Have you considered a carpool at all?"

Supportive: "I can see that your long trip to and from the plant is a real headache. Good transportation is certainly basic to any job."

Understanding: "You feel that your bus transportation is inadequate to the point where you feel you should relocate, is that right?"

Any one of the five responses might be appropriate in the course of the total interview. But the understanding response certainly would be preferable at the outset because it merely reflects what was said by the counselee. It thus would encourage further communication by the counselee, possibly resulting in a "Yes, I feel that . . . etc., etc."

Effective listeners use the understanding response a great deal in their counseling at the outset and an other times, too. Who are these good listeners? Psychologists, social workers, clergymen, personnel interviewers, various counselors. Bartenders and possibly even janitors in an apartment building also may use this response with their "clients"(!).

Why is the understanding response recommended?

1. It encourages people to talk, to open up. So if that's what you want, use it. If not, don't use it.

2. It helps people to feel that they, as persons, are being accepted, that someone cares about them, that they are approved of.

3. Also, they appreciate that their ideas, sentiments, concerns are understood, i.e., listened to—not necessarily agreed with, but heard. In effect, the counselor is saying: "I hear you."

4. By letting the other party "talk it out," it may serve to drain off emotion or strong feelings.

5. If you disagree, quibble, or ask a lot of questions, you may discourage the hoped-for free flow of communication by the counselee. The latter may clam up or, worse still, proceed in another direction.

To provide an understanding, non-judgmental response, you can use introductory phrases such as these:

"What I hear you saying is . . ."

"My sense of your concern is that . . ."

"My understanding of your situation is that . . ."

"I believe you are saying that . . ."

"You are telling me that . . ."

Typical restatements to show your understanding of particular counselee statements are these:

"The promotion would enable you to get that mortgage." (solution or course of action)

"You require more responsibility to have a truly worthwhile career." (need)

"You are very disappointed in B.J." (feeling)

"An office with a window is very important to you." (value)

"So, this is a totally irritating situation." (feeling plus problem)

In addition to restatement, it is also possible to show that you understand via head nods, simple "Uh huhs" or comments like "I see," "I follow," "I know what you're saying," "I know where you're coming from," or "Yeah, I hear you."

To sum up. In responding to the other party you have a fairly large toolkit of responses to draw upon—probing, interpreting, evaluating, supporting, and understanding. All of them may be useful, but be aware that the one you choose to use has the potential to influence the course of the conversation. By using the very neutral understanding response, you allow the counselee to open up and traverse the communication path he really favors.

How one responds (e.g., via a probing question) can make a difference, as illustrated by the following story:

Story: A woman visits her lawyer to seek a divorce.

Lawyer: "Do you have any grounds?"

Woman: "Oh, yes, nearly three acres."

Lawyer: "I guess I'm not being very clear. Do you have a grudge?"

Woman: "No, we only have a double carport."

Lawyer: "Let me approach this differently. Does your husband beat you?"

Woman: "Oh, no. I always get up before he does."

Lawyer (a bit frustrated): "Madam, are you certain that you really wish a divorce?"

Woman: "I don't care for one at all, but my husband does. He claims we have difficulty communicating."

YOUR COUNSELING SKILL: A SELF-ASSESSMENT

You now have read the text on various aspects of the counseling process and your role in it. You thus may wish to know how your current skill level matches up with the counseling concepts presented in this chapter. Accordingly, I have provided the following self-assessment instrument you can use for that purpose.

My Skill as a Counselor

Rate the counseling skill factors listed below as you believe they apply to you. Try to be as frank as you can.

The quiz will give you a good reading on your current counseling skill and possible opportunities for added growth. Scoring procedures are given at the the end of the quiz.

Skill factors	Never (1)	Seldom (2)	Occasionally (3)	Frequently (4)	Always (5)
1. **Preparation:** I obtain and organize in advance data necessary for our meeting.					
2. **Strategy:** I develop a strategy for the session based on the needs and personality of the other party.					
3. **Time allotment:** I look at a counseling session as of major significance to the employee and an important part of my job. I thus schedule it so that no one is rushed.					
4. **Location:** I arrange for a meeting room that is quiet, free of interruptions, and private. I do not use my office because of its status implications and influences.					
5. **Tone:** I put the counselee at ease and try to set a relaxed, warm and friendly tone for our meeting.					
6. **My demeanor:** I try to behave in a genuine, candid, and non-manipulative way.					
7. **Emotional state:** If the counselee is obviously upset, I try to deal with the emotion before dealing with the problem per se.					
8. **Total regard:** I try to communicate that I regard and accept the other person as a worthy human being, regardless of his problem or emotional state.					
9. **Employee value:** At the outset, I try to communicate that I appreciate the worth of the employee and his value to the unit.					
10. **Opening:** If I have initiated the session, I start it by being direct and specific about my concern.					
11. **Perception check:** I check my perceptions of the situation with those of the counselee during the session.					
12. **Listening:** I try to function as an active listener (good eye contact, positive body posture, use of restatement, etc.).					
13. **Participation:** I regard the counseling session as belonging to the counselee, so I encourage his fullest possible participation.					

(continued on next page)

Skill factors	Never (1)	Seldom (2)	Occasionally (3)	Frequently (4)	Always (5)
14. **Values:** I listen to understand fully where the counselee "is coming from," his values, beliefs, attitudes, perceptions.					
15. **Technique:** I use the "uh huh" or understanding response to encourage the counselee to "open up" fully.					
16. **Restatement:** I try to state in my own words the feelings underlying the counselee's statements.					
17. **Neutrality:** When I reflect the other's feeling, I avoid any indication of approval or disapproval of them.					
18. **My value system:** I recognize that my values, beliefs, prejudices may influence the counselee so I try to keep them in check.					
19. **Silence:** I respect pauses in communication so that the counselee can better assemble his thoughts.					
20. **Agenda:** I try to ensure that the conversation focuses on job performance.					
21. **Pace:** I allow the interview to proceed gradually rather than to force or rush it.					
22. **Insight:** I try to help the counselee to understand better his values and attitudes as they relate to the problem.					
23. **Decision making:** I encourage the counselee to think in terms of alternate courses of action.					
24. **Consequences:** I encourage the counselee to explore the possible consequences of each alternative.					
25. **Responsibility:** I ensure that any decision made is one that the counselee fully understands and for which he alone claims ownership.					
26. **Confidentiality:** I assure the counselee of the confidentiality of our discussion.					
27. **Session close:** I try to close the session on a positive, encouraging note.					
28. **Follow-up:** I conduct added sessions as may be necessary to fully resolve the problem.					
29. **Results:** If there is an improvement in performance/behavior following the counseling, I grant praise for it.					

SCORING

Now that you have completed the quiz, total the number of points for each of the five columns where you have made entries. **Example:** Assume you checked column three 6 times. This will give you 18 points (6 × 3 = 18) for column three. Make similar additions for the other columns and total all columns for total points.

130–140 points: Congratulations! You are a top-notch counselor, for you are sensitive to the needs and feelings of people. (I and many others would seek you out if we had a problem to discuss!)

119–129 points: You show very good insight into the counseling process. You have the potential to become an A-1 counselor.

109–118 points: You have a fair repertoire of skills and knowledge in respect to the counseling process. You now know what it takes to upgrade your capabilities to become a more fully skilled counselor.

108 and below: You now are at the level where you need to sharpen a number of your counseling skills and strive for greater consistency in what you already can do well.

QUESTIONS AND PROBLEMS FOR DISCUSSION

The following questions and problems may be used in in-house management development workshops and/or in college/university classes in management. Most of them lend themselves to small group work and/or total group discussion.

1. How does coaching differ from counseling in respect to a) objectives and b) skills needed?
2. To develop counseling skill, provide your participants with role-playing opportunities. A good, easy-to-manage design is to set up the role players in teams of three: counselor, counselee, and observer. Let the role players work for 25–30 minutes. Then secure feedback from the observers along these lines: "What went well" and "what went less than well" (or "what I liked" or "what I'm not sure about"). Post observer reports to flipcharts using a T-column. Wrap up the session with a discussion of learnings from it. **Note:** If time allows, repeat the above procedures with a new problem, and reversing (or rotating) of the counselor, counselee, and observer roles. Typical problems situations which may be role played:

   a. A highly capable young engineer who would be on his way "up," except for tendencies to be abrupt and abrasive with people.
   b. The senior worker who has been a great contributor and stellar performer in prior years but now seems to have "run out of gas."
   c. The technically able computer specialist who wishes to get into management. You feel that this is a very much premature career objective for this person.
   d. Any of the "difficult" people described in the chapter, such as "The Social Butterfly" or "The Put-Down Artist."
   e. Any of the troubled employees such as "The Alcohol Abuser" or "The Workaholic."
3. At the outset of a counseling session with a troubled employee, the counselee begins to cry. What do you do?
4. Have the participants individually complete the instrument "My Skill As a Counselor" and discuss in pairs or trios.
5. What are the skill components of an active listener?
6. Have participants meet in small groups to discuss this issue: What skills of an effective counselor are the most difficult to learn and "pull off" effectively?
7. You are meeting with a troubled employee. He seems very reluctant to speak freely. What do you do?
8. You give feedback to a difficult person about his (negative) behavior. He/she rejects it with a scornful laugh: "Hey, that's a bunch of stuff. I don't buy any of that at all." What do you do?
9. In a counseling session, the counselee frequently downgrades himself, questioning his capabilities. What do you do?
10. At the close of a career counseling session, a decision is about to be made. The counselee says to you: "What would you do if you were in my shoes?"
11. In a counseling session the counselee prematurely wishes to decide on a course of action. What do you do?
12. In a career counseling session, the counselee seems to be ready to embark on a course of action (career goal) which you are certain is inappropriate (neither realistic nor achievable). What do you do?
13. What are the ethical responsibilities of a good counselor?
14. What would be some indicators that your counseling session appears to be fruitless? What do you do?

15. In a counseling session, the counselee makes some derogatory inferences regarding your "good" intentions. What do you do?

16. Can you think of any counselor responses/behaviors which would inhibit free and full communication in a counseling session? (**Examples:** putting down a counselee; looking at one's watch; the counseling session is held in your office and your secretary pops in every six minutes about information she just has received over the phone; asking unnecessarily personal questions).

17. You have an outstanding performer in your unit. She is certainly ready for promotion, but your organizational setup doesn't have such an opportunity at this time. What can you do to keep her satisfied?

18. One of your better staffers recently has become quiet, withdrawn, and overly sensitive about minor feedback. What do you do?

19. Your immediate assistant has just lost her spouse in an auto crash with an emergency vehicle. What do you do?

20. A shop employee comes to your home at night with a highly personal problem: his daughter, an airline flight attendant based in another city, has become pregnant by a pilot. He is very concerned. What do you, as a counselor, do in your meeting with him?

Pre-Interview Planning Worksheet

A. I am about to have an interview with _____

B. My feelings about him (her) are these (consider work accomplishments, qualifications, personal characteristics, inter-personal relationships, etc.):

_____
_____
_____
_____
_____
_____

C. I hope to accomplish the following in the interview:

1. _____
_____

2. _____
_____

3. _____
_____

D. My strategy for achieving my objectives is:

_____
_____
_____
_____
_____

Figure 8-1. Guide to prepare for an interview with the "difficult" employee.

9

How to Build and Manage Your Team: Overcoming "The Lone Ranger Syndrome"

There is nothing good or bad about a group. A group can be a road block to progress, enforcing 'group think' and conformity on its individual initiative. Under the other conditions, a group can be a powerful synergism of talents, strengthening its members, speeding up the decision-making process, and enhancing individual and personal growth.

> —Dr. Rensis Likert (1903–1981), director of the Institute of Social Research, University of Michigan

The question before us is how to become one in spirit, not necessarily in opinion.

> —William Rainey Harper (1856–1906), U.S. educator and first president of the University of Chicago (1891), at the first meeting of the University's faculty

It only works for each of us when it works for all of us.

> —Author unknown

None of us is as smart as all of us.

> —From a wall poster

The concept of a team—unselfishness—goes counter to what I assume human nature really is. My life as a coach has been battling with human nature trying to overcome it.

> —Joe Gibbs, former coach of the Washington Redskins football team

It's easy to get the players. Getting them to play together, that's the hard part.

—Charles Dillon "Casey Stengel" (1891–1976), manager of the New York Yankees, who guided them to 10 American League championships and seven World Series championships in 12 seasons

Effective teamwork will not take the place of knowing how to do the job or how to manage the work. Poor teamwork, however, can prevent effective final performance. And it can also prevent team members from gaining satisfaction in being a member of the team and the organization.

—Group dynamics authority Robert F. Bales, Harvard University

The concept of a *team* is very much a part of our everyday management vocabulary. However, verbal references to it don't necessarily mean that managers really understand it or are comfortable with the concept. Thus, some managers may talk abstractly of "*the* team." (**Question:** Whose team is it? The manager's? The staff's? Everyone's? No one's?) Others, autocratic but candid, are likely to refer to "*my* team" ("and make no mistake about it!").

Story: In a job interview at a major firm, a hotshot project manager was asked if he was a team player. "You bet," he replied, "team captain."

More sophisticated managers may speak of "*our* team," which, of course, doesn't necessarily mean that true teamness exists.

A more realistic test of the existence of teamness is whether *subordinates* consistently talk of *our* team. Also, whether the staff refers to policies and decisions in "we" or "us" terms, rather than "he/she" or "they" and "them" terms. ("*They* want it that way." "It's up to *them*.") Former Secretary of Labor Robert B. Reich refers to this phenomenon as the "pronoun test." He states in "The 'Pronoun Test' for Success," *The Washington Post,* July 28, 1993):

. . . I've been visiting the workplaces of America administering a simple test. I call it the 'pronoun test.' I ask front-line workers a few general questions about the company. If the answers I get back describe the company in terms like 'they,' or 'them,' I know it's one kind of company. If the answers are put in terms like 'we' or 'us,' I know it's a different kind of company. It doesn't much matter what's said about the company. Even a statement like 'they aim for high quality here' suggests a workplace that hasn't yet made the leap into true high performance. It isn't yet achieving ever higher levels for quality, productivity and service. Only 'we' companies can do this.

Note, too, that even in team sports, which are often used as the model for teams in organizations, there is a great emphasis (recognition) on *individual* accomplishment: The most valuable player, "the franchise," the highest scorer, being nominated to all-star games, the highest-paid player, the coach of the year, Hall of Fame awards, etc.

That support by management for team functioning often is only half-hearted is evidenced by a study by the Wilson Learning Company of more than 4,500 teams in more than 500 organizations. Two important findings (reported in "News Briefs," *Healthy Companies,* September 1993):

☐ Per 80% of the survey participants, incentive-based compensations plans rewarded individual as opposed to team performance. In the yearly job review, team performance was a factor reported by only 10% to 20% of the survey respondents.

☐ A most critical survey result: Pertinent information is not made available to teams. Why not? Apparently, management assumes the information isn't vital to team functioning. So although management may sponsor team operations, it frequently remains unconvinced that they're really able to perform the task.

Also, a 1993 survey conducted by the Gallup Organization for the American Society for Quality Control suggests that the goals of team activities are not communicated by management as well as they might be. Employee understanding of those goals is not likely to be universally understood. Thus, in the Gallup survey, 1,300 employed adults were asked about quality improvements at their companies. Consider the responses to this question: "If team activities are in place at your firm, what are the team's major goals?" Most (75%) saw team activities having clearcut goals—quality, efficiency/productivity, profitability, or cost reduction. But a significant 25% said that they "don't know" (reported by Shigehiko Togo, "The Scratch Team's Quality Lesson," in *The Washington Post,* January 27, 1994).

WHAT MAKES AN EFFECTIVE TEAM

Obviously, there are all sorts of teams. Some may work well; others may not. Consider this example of an organization beset by less-than-excellent team functioning.

A subsidiary of a medium-sized company had been floundering for the past six years—a poor bottom line in most of these years; turnover of several key personnel; high employee turnover and absenteeism; and a not-surprising set of low scores on an employee "climate" survey, initiated by the parent company (but conducted by an outside consulting firm).

The parent company, finally recognizing that things would not get better by themselves, asked a management consultant to visit the troubled subsidiary to "check things out." The consultant began his review of operations by sitting in on meetings, talking to key staffers and employees, and observing interactions among the key staff. The consultant informally jotted down his observations about the management team, which pointed out the following:

1. The boss tends to ask the key staff what they think of his new proposals. Everyone readily agrees with them, for it is apparent that he already has his mind made up.
2. So-called "problem solving" meetings frequently end with the scheduling of more meetings, nothing concrete being developed.
3. The true reactions/feelings to problem-solving sessions are exchanged *after* the meetings, typically in the restroom or at the coffee bar.
4. At meetings and at one-on-one discussions, staff members take great pains to avoid disagreeing with the boss.
5. Staff members tend to blame one another for various miscues and lapses rather than own up to their inadvertencies.
6. Goals for the year are established by the boss rather than set jointly by the management group.
7. Existing policies are seldom questioned by anyone.
8. New policies proposed by the boss get a quick "amen" when a lot of doubt about them actually exists.
9. The adequacy or quality of current products/services are never questioned or criticized by anyone. Rather, there seems to be an implicit understanding that "what we have and what we're doing is great" and that critics are not good team members.

10. Obvious interpersonal problems between/among team members are never addressed.
11. Staff meetings are used by the boss primarily to pass along routine information rather than to solve pressing problems.
12. Staff members engage in a lot of "CYA" (cover your a-s) management.
13. Solutions to problems typically are the result of compromise and past precedent, real debate and discussion to secure creativity not being called for.

Quiz: Regarding the above team management behaviors, which of the following three statements is *most* significant:

A. The subsidiary is beset by many problems.
B. The subsidiary could use a strong leader.
C. The behaviors are key signs that the team is not really a team.

If you chose answer C, you merit a big fat A on the quiz. Obviously, these behaviors are symptoms of a poor functioning management team. Let's look, then, at the characteristics of a well-functioning, hard-hitting, high-performance team, one that is marked by true teamness rather than lip service.

What makes for an effective team? The author sees it as a matter of having a lot of "Vitamin C." Consider the following C-type characteristics:

Clarity of Goals, Expectations, and Roles

Everyone knows (full agreement) what business we're in, why we're here, where we're trying to go, and how we plan to get there. High agreement exists in this *results-driven structure* because everyone on the team was involved in and contributed actively to the development of goals and plans to reach them.

Commitment

Team members identify fully with objectives (overall purposes) and goals (annual targets) of the team. They recognize that only through their staunch commitment is goal accomplishment possible. Convictions about the worthwhileness of targets, directions, priorities, and mechanisms to accomplish things are never in doubt. True *team ownership* exists.

Congruence

There is high agreement between formally stated objectives and goals, and the policies and procedures essential to carry them out. No one finds himself in a position where a response to a query about a policy is only a lame, "I know it doesn't make sense, but it's a company policy." Or worse still, "I don't make these stupid policies. I only have to carry them out."

Clarity of Individual and Group Assignments

Goals may be agreed upon, but their actual implementation depends upon specific assignment to team members of necessary plans, tasks, projects, programs, and the like. Obviously, these assignments have to be marked by clarity and specificity, rather than by ambiguity and generality.

If the team is truly functioning as a team, post-meeting queries and comments such as the following should not arise: "Does she really mean next week?" "That budget figure is flexible, I hope." "We can do it in stages, can't we?" "Why is she giving me all that work. I'm not the only one here, you know?" "So what happens if the computer people can't help us on it?"

Collective Trust

The most significant adhesive binding team members together is that of collective or mutual trust. Note that in everyday parlance we speak of (and think of) trust primarily in terms of:

(a) honesty: do we have confidence that the other person will perform properly in a monetary sense (pay his bills; handle money or other valuables with integrity), and
(b) reliability: can this person carry through on assignments, commitments, promises ("If Jan says she'll do it, I know I can count on her word." Or: "I trust her to follow through on it.")

Note, too, that in the culture at large young people learn early about trust and are very conscious of it: "Dad, but you promised me . . ." As adults we form impressions about various groups and cultures based on our perceptions of their trustworthiness. Some of these feelings may be based on a fair degree of fact. Other impressions, based on prejudice, may take the form of rigid, all-encompassing stereotypes. So who, in society at large, do we trust more or less? Advertisers? Politicians? Lawyers? Teachers? Surgeons? Bureaucrats? Park Rangers? Car dealers? Arabs? Canadians? Orientals? Blacks? Hispanics? Swedes? Englishmen?

In respect to a team operation in an organization, the concept of trust has an added, broader, and more profound meaning than honesty and reliability. In the team context, trust relates to my confidence that the leader or team members will not advantage themselves at my expense. This means, for example, that if I convey an opposing or unpopular view to my boss or provide him with "bad news," I can be certain that I won't be punished in any way. Thus, I can trust the team leader (and team members) to listen to my ideas without fear of attack, put down, or other forms of disapproval, either now or in the future.

A second concept of trust in the team setting relates to authenticity. This means that I can count on others to be themselves, to be genuine, to express feelings freely, to say what they mean as well as mean what they say. The team leader and team members, then, are not playing games, manipulating others, playing favorites, engaging in any flimflammery. Thus, when a meeting ends, a team member need not ask a colleague, "I wonder what the boss really meant by saying . . .?" If one doubts what the boss means in a high-trust team operation, one would simply ask the leader for a clarification of what he had said.

A significant aspect of trust is that it hard to build, but easy to lose. Building trust takes time and hard work, hence the need for the manager's concern with *team building*. Methods and procedures to build trust are presented below under team-building techniques.

Customer Concern/Focus

Team members understand the importance of high customer satisfaction. If customers feel they are receiving poor product quality or mediocre service, they won't hesitate to take their business elsewhere. They agree with Henry Ford, who said, "It is not the employer who pays wages—he only handles the money. It is the customer who pays the wages."

Candid Communication

Team members communicate freely and fully with their team leader and with other team members as well.

Feelings and ideas are fully expressed, people listen to one another, and no one hesitates to raise questions about things that bother him. Descriptors for this highly effective communication are leveling, candor, authentic, open, timely, honest, truth telling.

A team's functioning can be no better than the communication it receives from and provides to all team members. The team leader, by virtue of his position in the team's structure, plays a key role in the team communication process. He provides a strong model for authentic communication and works vigorously to get team members to communicate helpfully. In *Teamwork: We Have Met the Enemy and They Are Us* (Bartlesville, OK: The Center for Management and Organization Effectiveness, 1989), Matt M. Starcevich and Steven J. Stowell advise team leaders to employ the following behaviors to achieve team-oriented, win-win communication:

☐ Be descriptive, not accusing. This means to rely on non-evaluative "I messages" when communicating your feelings about a particular behavior to a team member.

☐ Communicate a desire to collaborate in seeking a solution on what you perceive to be mutual problems.

☐ Be empathic and supportive. Show full, genuine interest and concern.

☐ Communicate conjecturally/tentatively, as opposed to presenting ideas in black-or-white, take-it-or-leave-it terms.

☐ Rely on appeals—request ideas from staffers.

☐ Facilitate team meetings in a manner so that team members are discouraged from emotional attachment to issues confronting the team.

Collaboration/Cooperation

Team members enthusiastically work with one another on team functions, for they recognize that the purpose of a team is to take advantage of the *synergy* it creates: that is, the whole, through group action, becomes greater than the sum of its individual parts. Thus, team members perform in unison on the basis of mutual interests, mutual concerns, mutual support, mutual loyalty, and mutual trust. There is a recognition that team problems can be best tackled and new programs best designed when team members operate on the basis of the *interrelatedness* of their functions, activities, and programs (see Figure 9.1, page 392).

Also understood is that dysfunctional behaviors such as credit seeking, grandstanding, finger pointing, nitpicking, cliquing, competing, protecting turf, foot dragging, and harboring hidden agendas and resentments are anathema to the healthy team. To underline what team work is not, you may be familiar with the well-quoted statement by Gail Goodrich, team leader of the L.A. Lakers basketball team in the early 1970s. He stated in an interview, "Sure I'm a team player, that is, after I score my first 30 points" (quoted by management consultant Robert Bookman in "Igniting Team Spirit," *Personnel Administrator,* April 1989).

Team members not only work with other team members in an interrelated way, but they also are eager to cooperate with one another. No person is an island, and everyone can profit from a helping hand from someone else. People thus are willing to substitute for someone who has to be away, to share (rather than hoard) information fully, to review and critique someone else's completed work, to loan a staffer to another manager as the workload may dictate, and the like.

In general, team members unhesitatingly provide backup and support without the team leader having to intervene.

Concern/Caring

Members of the team and the leader identify strongly with one another. There thus is a genuine caring, a demonstration of warmth and affection toward fellow team members. This strong feeling of concern carries over into actual behaviors that provide help and support to those who may need it.

There are three issues that determine whether a group that needs to be a team will become one, said the late Mike Blansfield, a widely regarded trainer/consultant (reported by Marvin R. Weisbard, "Team Effectiveness Theory," *Training and Development Journal,* January 1985):

1. Am I In or Out?

This is the issue of membership, and most people want to be valued and to belong. The more "in" any of us feel, the more likely we will cooperate. Team member/leader attitudes toward us will determine whether we feel that we belong.

2. Do I Have Any Power or Control?

If you or I have to face something we can't handle very readily, we're likely "to come apart a little." All of us want to feel powerful and in charge of our lives. Again, team member/leader attitudes and behaviors of support and caring can contribute to our feelings of being in control.

3. Will I Have a Chance to Use and/or Develop the Needed Skills and Resources?

Few of us want to leave our brains home when we come to work each day. Growth, involvement, and contribution are goals of truly healthy people. True team membership, involvement, and support can contribute positively to one's skill development and utilization.

Challenge

Team members are given a constant challenge via high standards; stretch (increasingly higher goals); a search for high-quality decisions, products, and services; and continuing opportunities for innovation. Problems are not regarded as harrassers or headaches, but as opportunities to exercise one's creativity and possibly to grow in the process, too.

Note: High standards and increasingly higher goals are arrived at on a team basis. This approach is essential to secure acceptance. Imposition by the boss of higher requirements is very likely to run into debates about their "reasonableness," foot dragging, and disgruntlement.

Climate

The effective team becomes that because it operates in an atmosphere marked by high standards, freedom, informality, *esprit de corps,* friendliness, trust, even fun. People work hard, yet they feel relaxed and comfortable rather than that they are operating in a pressure cooker or laboring on a treadmill.

The team leader is very conscious of the need to set an informal climate. He tries to get closer to his team by MBWA (managing by walking around), by reducing his status (e.g., by dressing informally), by facilitating meetings rather than dominating them, and by sharing the leadership role (e.g., rotating the chairperson function at staff meetings), etc.

A key component of the climate is the reward system in effect. The aim is to recognize and reward team members for excellence and results as opposed to only "unloading" on (punishing) them when mistakes and errors occur.

In general, the total team—leader and members—pay full attention to the need to create and nurture an atmosphere and culture that stresses the respect and dignity of everyone, high standards (excellence and quality output), risk taking, and opportunities for innovation/creativity/discovery.

Creativity

The high-performing team is very much concerned with unleashing the latent creativity of its team members. It operates on the assumption that there is a real potential in everyone to produce new approaches, inventions, innovations. Thus, the team atmosphere is such that there is maximum freedom to function in a creative way.

New ideas are given full respect rather than depressing reactions such as "It'll never work," "The big boss won't go for it," "It'll break the bank," or "We tried that two years ago."

An aspect of creativity that the team takes pride in is that it is highly concerned with experimentation and risk-taking. A search for new and better ways of doing things is standard operating procedure. The dictum of "if it ain't broke don't fix it," is not a hallmark of the effective, high-performing team.

Continuous Improvement

A hard-hitting team does not content itself with pride in past accomplishment. Rather, it works actively on (1) constant improvement/updating of product quality and service, and (2) an ongoing review of its own functioning. In the latter connection, it uses the athletic model, asking how can we learn from what we did or are doing so that we can perform better next week, next month, next year. (Additional comments regarding review of team effectiveness are given on page 386 under "Candid Critique of Team Functioning.")

In general, high standards, excellence, and moving forward are terms that are not tossed around loosely. For, in actuality, there is an attitude/concern/focus on excellence, quality, and the future that is encouraged and rewarded. Harvey Mackay, president and CEO of Mackay Envelope

Corporation, Minneapolis, an exponent of using teams for creativity as opposed to worshiping the status quo, says (in "Teamwork," *Successful Meetings,* March 1992), "Remember, you'll never stub your toe if you walk backwards, but you won't get very far either."

Cohesiveness

This term refers to the strength of team members' wishes to remain group members. As individuals become more attracted to and identified with the team, they want to be involved more in the ongoing work of the team. As cohesiveness develops, we can anticipate these behaviors by group members (per Alvin Zander in *Making Groups Effective,* San Francisco: Jossey-Boss, 1982): They talk more readily, listen better, have a greater likelihood of influencing one another, volunteer more frequently, and observe groups standards more fully.

We can also anticipate that cohesive groups will work energetically on team activities; have high morale, loyalty, and *esprit de corps*; have high attendance rates; and work hard at maintaining their relationships with other team members.

Confrontation

This means a facing up to problems and situations requiring remedial action, as opposed to allowing things to fester—or worse, sweeping them under the rug entirely. So there's no dodging or deferring of a problem presented by a less-than-able employee, another department, another echelon, or a supplier. Similarly, problems that arise from faulty equipment, systems, policies, or procedures are dealt with in timely fashion. Phraseology such as "we're not ready for it," "all in due time," or "it's really not that bad" are not likely to be encountered in the alert and active team.

To quote management professor Robert Cunningham ("Confront and Engage for Organizational Development," *Training and Development Journal,* February 1989), "To confront is to speak the truth face-to-face, to vigorously invite comparisons, and to enter into open, healthy conflict. The confronter does not claim to possess absolute truth, but challenges others in pursuit of such truth, based on personal perceptions and understanding."

Cunningham also points out that we should not confuse confrontation with aggressiveness. In fact, communicating the needed message requires sensitivity to those affected. So confrontation "may be as gentle as a suggestion or as strong as a transfer or dismissal."

Conflict

The effective team recognizes that conflict can be beneficial or destructive. Disagreement is healthy, helpful, and inevitable, for it reflects the naturally diverse perceptions, attitudes, and feelings team members bring to their problem-solving activities. In fact, only from this diversity of ideas can the best solutions emerge.

Disagreement is unhealthy and a hindrance when team players are primarily interested in protecting their own views and scoring points (win-lose behavior), as opposed to seeking win-win results.

So the best type of problem solving takes place when there is passion rather than lethargy, when everyone's ideas are subject to full debate, when the sparks fly, and when team thinking is channeled to advance team objectives and goals.

Note: The worst thing a team leader can tell his group is "Now, let's not get excited. Calm down." For what is wanted is excitement, introduction of opposing views, full expression of feelings, and open, candid dialogue. Suppressing conflict/disagreement will only deprive the group of potentially high-quality solutions.

A hard-hitting group concerned with innovative problem solving welcomes conflict and looks at it as "creative tension," not as something to smother because some group members may be uncomfortable with it. The question for the team is this: Do we want contented, cautious colleagues or "irritating," inventive iconoclasts?

Change

The high-performing team expects change, welcomes it, and is very willing to initiate it. There is recognition that we are living in a dynamic world and that team thinking and team behavior must be in sync with it. So the concept of "resistance to change" is foreign to the effective team. In fact, change is regarded not as a headache but as an opportunity.

In respect to the initiation of change, the team is very likely, among other approaches, to employ the long-range planning acronym, SWOT. It thus will think in terms of identifying team Strengths and Weaknesses, as well as team Opportunities and Threats, and plan accordingly to deal with these elements.

A key factor in anticipating, coping with, and implementing change is the team leader. It is his task to provide team members with the skills, attitudes, and thinking tools to act in new different, forward-looking, and positive ways.

Consensus Decisions

Decisions are made by the team by talking things through. Everyone gets a chance to get his ideas, views, and feelings into the hopper. Everyone thus feels that he has had a fair opportunity to participate in and influence decisions. By talking things through, the team ultimately reaches agreement. There is no need for voting. In fact, effective teams don't vote. Rather, they deliberate, define, discuss, debate, encourage dissent, develop scenarios, describe alternatives, and depict consequences. Then, and only then, do they decide.

Of course, group meetings to reach consensus take time. But the end results are:

(1) well-considered, high-quality decisions because of broad input and full deliberation;
(2) full understanding and support for decisions because of total team member participation;
(3) rapid implementation of decisions for all hazy elements and doubts have been removed, everyone understanding the importance and implications of what was agreed upon.

Note:

1. Consensus means securing general or substantial agreement on decisions, not necessarily 100% agreement. Also, in consensus the search is for the best solution, not one that is acceptable via bargaining, negotiation, compromise, "coin flipping," or accommodating the unrelenting clock.
2. One way to "close out" any group decision, says training coordinator Bill Williams ("Ten Commandments for Group Leaders," *Supervisory Management,* September 1992), is to do what a manager in his organization does, namely, to ask each team member which of these three statements best defines his opinion on the pending decision:
   a. "I fully support the decision."
   b. "I have some reservations about it, but I can live with it and will support it."
   c. "You may take this decision and stick it . . ."

If someone picks item c, then the team has yet to reach consensus.

3. While consensus is a key element in group decision making, it should not be assumed that all decisions of the team are group decisions. Rather, the leader and team members will make individual decisions where total group action (input, commitment) are not necessary. And if at least half the team has reservations, the decision obviously is not a strong one. What is needed, then, is a decision that all the team can live with, and one that a majority will support fully, says Williams.

Continuous Learning

Problems, difficulties, errors, and successful work experiences are used routinely as learning tools and opportunities. ("What can we learn from Project XY4Z, now that it's over?")

Because effective teams are not content to rest on their laurels, they are interested in continuing growth of all team members. Training opportunities, both on and off the job, thus are sought vigorously by team members and are encouraged by the team. The training may be designed to cover gaps in experience, to update or upgrade skills, or to help one to launch another career. Competency development is indeed the name of the game.

Training is looked at as an important investment, not as a costly expense. Thus, time away from the job is not viewed as "lost time," but as an opportunity for personal growth, revitalization, and team betterment over time. The training philosophy of the team, then, is that "if it will keep our team members alert, alive, and growing, we'll support it."

Clock Conscious

The successful team understands the importance of timing, or "waiting for the moment," as trainer/educator Michael A. Berger terms it (in "The Technical Approach to Teamwork," *Training and Development Journal,* March 1985). To quote Berger,

A team leader must be able to determine the right time to introduce a new rule, identify a new problem, or propose a new solution. Acting too quickly or not soon enough will send everyone into a panic. However, if the leader understands the natural rhythm of events and is able to wait until the very last moment, he or she will increase the probability that the intervention will achieve the intended goal.

Collective or Mutual Accountability

Jon R. Katzenbach and Douglas K. Smith, authors of "The Wisdom of Teams: Creating the High Performance Organization" (1993), state (in *The Harvard Business Review,* March-April 1993):

No group ever becomes a team until it can hold itself accountable as a team. Like common purpose and approach, mutual accountability is a stiff test. Think, for example, about the subtle but critical difference between 'the boss holds me accountable' and 'we hold ourselves accountable.' The first case can lead to the second; but without the second there can be no team.

Team members have to feel that "we're in this boat together." They can't be coerced into collective or mutual accountability. But when a team shares a common purpose, goals, and approach, say Katzenback and Smith, mutual accountability grows naturally. It arises because of the time, energy, and action the team invests in figuring out what it is trying to accomplish and how to achieve it most effectively.

A hallmark of teamwork, then, is the willingness of all team members to assume responsibility for their actions/behavior. Thus, there is no need to blame others for what isn't done or what goes wrong. Also, there is no need to protect one's self from blame (CYA management). Thus, team members are not likely to emit defensive statements such as "I wasn't even there. I was off on Tuesday." "No one told me about it." "Those were the instructions, so that's what I did." "You can't pin that one on me."

The team's sense of mutual accountability also produces the gratifying rewards of mutual achievement in which all of the team shares.

Celebration of Diversity

Team effectiveness depends in large part on the full use and mutual support of its human resources. Thus, all team members, regardless of seniority, age, sex, race, ethnicity, national origin, or physical status are welcomed, respected, and, yes, celebrated as worthwhile contributors. In fact, diversity is celebrated because it provides an added dimension for creativity. Diversity, with its unique ability to provide a greater mix of viewpoints/perception, strengthens the team's overall processes of ideation and creativity.

In general, celebrating diversity gives the team the chance to capitalize on the unique strengths of individual members and to respect their dignity in the process. And by so doing the team transforms itself from a collection of unrelated individuals to a close-knit, cohesive community.

Charting Progress

The importance of measurement can't be overemphasized. If you can't measure it, you can't understand it. If you can't understand it, you can't control it. If you can't control it, you can't improve it.

—Quality consultant James Harrington, quoted in "Viewpoint," *Personnel Journal,* February 1994

High-performing teams look forward to growth, improvement, accomplishment, and results that go beyond what was done previously. Consequently, they need data to chart their progress: Are we ahead of schedule? Are we ahead of last month or last year? Are we ahead of the competition? Has our quality gone up? Is our waste and scrap down? Are customer complaints down? Are accidents down? Are costs down? As indicated by the new data, new goals are set and/or corrective action is taken promptly.

Bulletin boards or particularized scoreboards (e.g., on sales or accidents) are very useful to provide specific data regarding "where we are." Effective teams want to rise above the status quo. Quantitative feedback is the tool to let people know if the team is on target. The data also can serve as a real motivator to team members. ("Hey, we cut the scrap rate 12% this year. We should be able to do better next year.")

In general, by charting progress, particularly in measurable terms, all team members know when it has achieved success. Measurement also permits meaningful communication to others in the organization.

Candid Critique of Team Functioning

An effective team is no better than its effort at systematic evaluation of itself. In effect, the team takes time out from time to time to ask itself how are we doing as a team—what are we doing well together and what are we doing less than well? Particular areas for team inquiry relate to communication, cooperation, decision making, problem solving, opportunities for creativity, clarity of goals and task assignments, opportunities for personal growth/training, etc.

The team leader and the team members understand the importance of giving and receiving helpful feedback about one's behavior and thus practice it without hidden agendas, pussyfooting, shilly-shallying, or acting punitively. The goal is to help, not to hurt.

Collective Leadership

While a team may have a designated leader, many leadership roles can and should be shared. For example, consider *task*-oriented roles in group meetings such as giving information, seeking information, clarifying, elaborating, summarizing, reality testing; and *maintenance* roles such as gate keeping ("We haven't heard from Sue yet"), harmonizing, encouraging, mediating, tension breaking, consensus testing. Obviously, any of these roles/functions can be assumed by any team member as well as by the leader. Roles may well require a shift among members, depending on the particular expertise required.

Questions: Why should the leader, who has a willing and able team, assume responsibility for all of the above functions? How can team members grow if they are not given opportunities to exercise their potential? Is the formal leader not a stronger leader by modeling desirable and appropriate behavior, by getting everyone into the act, by asking such questions as "What's the best way to do this?", by stimulating creativity and risk taking, by encouraging the growth and development of people, by so behaving that the team achieves consensus and full commitment in its decisions? Is not the supervisor who has the most people coming up with ideas the most powerful?

Note, too, that no one really "likes" a boss or a supervisor because they are higher-status people who are in a position to control, limit, or punish us. Rather, most of us prefer to work with someone who is a *person,* someone who thinks so well of us that he treats us as colleagues, peers, or equals. Not pals or buddies, but as professional associates.

Finally, far-seeing, strong leaders work hard at building leadership skills in and of the total group. In this manner, team accomplishment does not depend on the prowess of one individual, be it the boss or anyone else. Certainly, then, crisis situations can be responded to effectively without total dependence on one person.

Celebration of Events

High-powered teams understand the importance of having the team feel good about itself, of drawing team members closer together. In consequence, social/fun opportunities are capitalized on for such purposes.

Besides the usual national holidays, the team may celebrate the launching of a new product or service, the meeting of a tough goal, the achievement of superior results for a month or a quarter, or having a banner year. Birthdays and other special days (e.g., a member of the engineering staff receives his long-sought-after MBA) also merit celebration.

These gala activities aid in establishing high camaraderie, morale, and teamness. Team members will thus go all out to avoid letting other teammates down.

Continuity

The characteristics described in the above paragraphs are attainable only if team members have the opportunity to establish their identity, develop intimacy and trust with one another, and work together for adequately long time frames in meeting goals and resolving problems. Conversely, team membership that is subject to a revolving door can be seriously disruptive to team cohesion and team accomplishment.

BARRIERS TO TEAMWORK: ARE WE ALERT TO THEM?

Dr. Robert E. Lefton, President, Psychological Associates, Inc., St. Louis, has worked with many top management teams in major U.S. companies. He finds that eight problems prevent the desired synergism of teamwork. Described in "The Eight Barriers to Teamwork," *Personnel Journal,* January 1988, they are:

1. Poor Probing

Probing is a key skill to elicit needed information. But Dr. Lefton finds that top executives do an ineffective job of probing. At meetings there is a tendency to rely on three probes that produce the least information:

- ☐ **Closed-end probes,** e.g., "Do you buy that?", which only evokes a yes or no response. Obviously, this ploy only encourages ready agreement rather than meaningful dialog (exploration of the issue).
- ☐ **Leading questions,** e.g., "Do you want the big boss to think we don't know what we're trying to do?", which only answer themselves but don't generate new information.
- ☐ **Brief assertions,** e.g., "Go on," which tells nothing of consequence.

Five other, more useful probes are open-ended and neutral probes, pauses, summaries, and reflective (mirroring) statements. Dr. Lefton finds that only some 10% of managers regularly use these superior five probes, all essential for reaching the central point of things. Synergistic, creative problem solving is hardly possible if the team can't get to the heart of the issue.

2. Manipulative Leadership

If the leader subtly or unwittingly reveals his own preference for a solution to a problem, the team is likely to cease to offer other solutions. Candor and full debate are certain to be abandoned if the boss enters into the discussion with a statement such as "I'm leaning toward the Springton site, but I'd like your thoughts before we finalize it."

3. Team Conflict

Full, candid debate, discussion and argumentation are the only route to a synergistic solution to a problem. But if team members push their own agendas, *de*synergism is the end result. Private agendas will displace team goals, eliminate candor, encourage dissension and one-upmanship, and scuttle true teamwork.

4. Ignoring Alternatives

Too many teams hasten to decide, when only by generating alternatives and exploring all those options can a high-quality decision be reached. Brainstorming ideas may be a messy, noisy, time-consuming process, but there is hardly any other alternative.

5. Lack of Leveling

Synergistic teams are consistently candid. Only by leveling can true (valid, accurate) information be placed into the problem-solving hopper. What interferes with truth telling? Two things:

(1) People have personal agendas for avoiding honesty, such as an unwillingness to put someone on the spot, possibly hurting their feelings;

(2) Intra-team politics may cause holding back or even distorting information. There may be a feeling "it's the safe thing to do." Says Dr. Lefton, "It may be safe, but it won't be synergistic."

6. Useless Meetings

Meetings with no objectives, or fuzzy goals at best, defeat efforts to tell whether a meeting is or isn't synergistic.

7. No Self-Examination

In the absence of regular, systematic self-critique, teams limit their ability to build on strengths and to overcome weaknesses. Effective teams build post-session assessment into all problem-solving discussions and other meetings.

8. Failure to Explain Decisions

Teams at the top may make worthwhile decisions. But in their failure to pass down the rationale for them to lower levels—that is, to those who are to implement them—the ideas may simply die rather than take root. Executives thus may state in their frustration and disappointment, "We had a worthwhile idea. But no one saluted it. What went wrong?"

Added reasons for team ineffectiveness are offered by management consultant and team development authority Glenn M. Parker, author of *Team Players and Teamwork: The New Competitive Business Strategy* (San Francisco: Jossey-Boss, 1990). They are:

- ☐ **"You cannot easily describe the team's mission."** This may be a problem for a new team, but a well-established one may lose its focus over time.
- ☐ **"The meetings are formal, stuffy, or tense."** In the absence of an informal climate, essential to get people to loosen up, team members are not enabled to do their best work.
- ☐ **"There is a great deal of participation but little accomplishment."** High involvement by itself cannot guarantee real results, progress, or output.
- ☐ **"There is talk but not much communication."** People may do a lot of talking but little listening to others' contributions. In the absence of listening, real planning, problem solving, decision making, and conflict resolution are not possible.
- ☐ **"Disagreements are aired in private conversations after the meeting."** If the team is healthy and truly synergistic, differences are aired publicly at the meeting. Again, leveling and truth-telling are something that can't be dodged.

☐ **"Decisions tend to be made by the formal leader with little meaningful involvement of other team members."** Leaders today have many devices to involve team members in decision making such as meetings and surveys. But the bottom line is this: Are member inputs utilized to reach a true consensus?

☐ **"There is confusion or disagreement about roles or work assignments."** While conflicts over interpersonal and emotional issues do surface and thus are visible, role conflicts are less likely to be spotted. Hence there is a need to explore candidly such possibilities with team members.

☐ **"The team has been in existence for at least three months and has never assessed its functioning."** Evaluation at two levels is needed: 1) progress toward goals, and 2) team process, that is, how well are we functioning as a team?

Team Development vs. Team Building

The effective team, per the above-listed characteristics, does not come about by itself. Much patience and know-how are necessary to accomplish it, which means there has to be a heavy investment in developing and building the team. We say "developing" and "building" because the two concepts entail different processes.

Team development is an ongoing process essential to upgrade team performance. It may entail activities ranging from improving the quality of staff meetings and problem-solving approaches, to developing feedback systems and conflict-resolution procedures. Generally, improvements are made by the team using its own resources, as opposed to utilizing an outside trained facilitator/consultant as in the case of *team building*. Team development work may build on the foundations laid in team building.

In **team building** the group has one or more deep-seated and possibly urgent needs to get the team on track. Typically, as we will see, the team gets away from the office for two or three days to work on its goals, policies and problems. It is aided by a trained facilitator who assists in climate setting and monitoring the communication, interpersonal, and problem-solving processes.

TEAM BUILDING: WHY DO IT?

Typically, a manager may become interested in team building in a formal way when he becomes aware of or is altered (jolted?) to conditions such as these:

☐ a marginal or shrinking bottom line
☐ decreased productivity
☐ a stagnant product line
☐ problems with customers
☐ problems with suppliers
☐ problems with other departments (or work teams)
☐ lack of cooperation among staff members
☐ interpersonal conflict among team members
☐ misunderstanding of objectives and policies
☐ unclear or unmet goals
☐ low trust in the group
☐ mounting costs
☐ confusion about assigned responsibilities
☐ decisions implemented in a hit or miss way
☐ cumbersome systems/procedures
☐ unclear, unrealistic, outdated, or non-existent policies
☐ communication among team members in need of repair
☐ apathy rather than creativity seems to be the order of the day
☐ low marks on a climate/attitude/communication survey sponsored by the front office or headquarters

Besides getting into team building when vexing problems such as those enumerated above are plaguing the outfit, team building may loom importantly, too, when:

☐ A merger or acquisition has occurred and there thus is a need to get everyone on the same wavelength.
☐ A new team leader (manager) is about to come aboard; a "transition team building" effort thus is highly desirable. (See the more detailed discussion of this type of session below).
☐ A major reorganization and/or a downsizing has taken place.
☐ A new product development team, project team, task force, study group, production team, etc., needs help to get started—and to get started "right" and rapidly as well.
☐ New responsibilities have been added, a major change in mission has occurred, or new programs are being launched.

☐ Dramatically increased workloads have occurred.

☐ It is desired to set objectives and goals (targets) for the next year.

If the need is to engage in team building because of deep-seated problems and/or concerns, such as those cited above, it is strongly recommended that these two procedures be utilized:

1. Conduct the team building sessions on a "cultural island"—that is, go off site and get away from the daily routine of business.

2. Use a trainer/consultant to serve as facilitator at the team-building sessions.

Both of these approaches are discussed below.

Note: If those reporting to a single boss have little or no working relationships with one another, a true team does not exist. The individuals may comprise a unit that is so identified on an organizational chart. But it is not a team in the sense that (a) they are working toward a common vision, and (b) they share responsibility to operate as a team to move forward toward that vision. In these circumstances, a retreat for team building is inappropriate.

The Management Retreat: A Vital Tool to Help the Team Stop, Listen, and Jolt its Thinking

While a work group may be able to work on its major problems in its staff meetings and in other problem-solving meetings, it can do a more in-depth, comprehensive, and meaningful job by conducting it off site. Getting away from the office—the two- or three-day "management retreat" for team building—is becoming an increasingly popular tool in American management. Consider these advantages of the management retreat:

☐ It permits the team to get away from the pressures of daily operations, interruptions, and assorted crises, and to focus fully on its concerns in a more relaxed, leisurely, collegial atmosphere.

☐ It ensures that all team members are in attendance to work on team problems/needs. (The team-building session is announced sufficiently in advance so that possible conflicts arising from outside meetings, conferences, and travel do not occur.) Also, it goes without saying that the team leader must attend full time. To do otherwise is to communicate

that the team-building session is not very important.

☐ The elongated time span (two or three days) allows for interpersonal contacts that are not possible on site, particularly having three meals and breaks together, engaging jointly in recreational activities, etc.

☐ The fuller time span allows for in-depth discussions without the need to abort intense problem-solving sessions because time has run out. Evening sessions are also possible.

☐ Most importantly, by allotting a large block of time (two or three days) to the retreat, doing it away from the office, and even incurring costs for motel rooms, meals, and the outside facilitator, the manager in charge communicates loud and clear that team building is, indeed, serious business.

Using an External Facilitator for the Management Retreat

Typically, a management retreat uses a trained facilitator, someone who is well-versed in group dynamics, climate building, communication processes, giving and receiving feedback, conflict resolution techniques, problem-solving and decision-making procedures, and the like. The use of an outside facilitator also gives the team-building session an aura of professionalism and objectivity. He thus can intervene helpfully in instances of reluctance to confront issues, interpersonal conflict, non-participation, over-dependence on the formal leader, moving too rapidly to decide things, and so on. He can also help, at the outset, to set standards and guidelines to facilitate the deliberations.

While a small number of managers may function successfully in the facilitator role, most would not have the skills or training to "pull it off" properly. Also, if the manager is unable or unwilling to share the leadership role and develop an open communication climate, something that is essential in an effective team-building session, the team-building effort is likely to be only marginally effective.

How might the facilitator proceed if he is to work with the staff in the team building effort? Typically, he will interview the manager and team members in advance of the management retreat. His rationale:

1. To get acquainted with the team members, to get some "feel" for the group. It also allows team members to work a bit with the facilitator.

2. To gather data to understand better team problems and attitudes. Some of this data may be introduced in the team-building sessions in a catalytic way, that is, to surface data that team members may not feel comfortable to share.

In the course of the interviews, the facilitator will collect data that falls into these broad categories:

☐ general questions
☐ task (work) elements
☐ interpersonal factors
☐ process factors
☐ systems influences

General questions may follow these lines: What are the group's key problems? What are the group's major strengths? Its major weaknesses? Its opportunities? What one thing would make the group more effective than it is? How do you feel about being a member of this group? What, if anything, would make you more effective? What are your major satisfactions/dissatisfactions on the job? What would you like to see happen in the team-building session that would make it a worthwhile venture for you?

Task- or work-related questions may assume these forms: What are the goals of the team? Are they clear? Logical? Current? Attainable? Are any goals absent as you see it? Are there any policies, either current or absent, that affect team effectiveness? Is the team planning-minded? Are priorities clear? Are there any procedures that are hindering effectiveness? Is your own job clearly defined? How do you know when you've done a good job?

Interpersonal factors may be probed with questions like these: How do you relate to the team? Do you feel you are part of it? How would you describe each team member? Who is the most influential? Are there any members who produce conflict? If so, how do they get resolved? Who do you work with the most? How sound is this relationship? How is your relationship with your superior? What one thing would strengthen it (or make it even stronger)? How would you describe your boss as a leader? What is your boss' influence up the line?

Process factors relate to how the group goes about doing its work. These kinds of questions should illuminate this area: How are decisions made? What is the nature of your input in decisions? Are problems faced up to? How would you characterize communication in your team? Do people level with one another? Do people trust one another? Is this a creative or a conforming group? How effective are staff meetings? How effective are other problem solving meetings? How is conflict handled? Is it welcomed or smothered? In what kind of climate does the team operate?

Systems influences relate to broader aspects of the group's culture that influence behavior. Questions worth asking are these: What is the nature of the reward, measurement, and feedback systems? Does real accomplishment get rewarded? What would you say about the nature/adequacy of the pay system? The training system (growth opportunities)? The career development/promotion system?

Note: Some facilitators may use questionnaires rather than interviews to gather advance data about team functioning, problems, needs, hopes, relationships. Others may use both tools. Instruments such as those at chapter's end also may be used.

As indicated, the retreat should be planned to last two or three days. It is a good idea to begin things with a social or cocktail party the first evening. This should be followed by dinner and an opening session of two hours or so.

The first session is a crucial one. For at this time, team members are eager to learn answers to questions such as these:

☐ Is this going to be a serious effort or are we just going to go through the motions?
☐ Will I be put on the spot in any way?
☐ How candid can I be? Or should I just "play it safe?"
☐ What is the facilitator like? Is he the boss' stooge?
☐ Will he take sides? How useful will he really be?
☐ How eager are the boss and others to learn about their own shortcomings?
☐ Can this group really be helped?

To put the team-building effort into proper perspective, we should recognize that it is not a panacea. It cannot overcome problems that relate to the larger system, such as insufficient resources, an ineffective reward system, poor leadership at the level above the work team, an ineffective organizational communication system, or lack of cooperation by other work units.

A Saga of Support and Cooperation

A group of five hunters and their guide, while walking in the woods, fell into a deep pit.

At first they wept and bemoaned their fate.

Then they blamed themselves . . .

. . . and blamed one another . . .

. . . and then their guide.

Then they tried prayer . . .

. . . and climbing the wall . . .

. . . and jumping off the ground.

Days passed; gloom settled on the group and none tried anything anymore . . .

. . . until one day, a farmer came by, peered into the pit, saw their plight and said, "Why don't you help one another out?"

So they discussed this suggestion and decided to try it out. And, lo and behold, it worked. And they went on their way.

Moral:
If your group finds itself in a hole, try cooperating.

Figure 9-1. Example of Team Problem Solving.

The Transition Team-Building Session: Clearing the Air

When a new manager comes aboard there is a good deal of uncertainty, curiosity, and possibly anxiety on the part of both the manager and the team as well. Management consultant Dr. James Looram ("The Transition Meeting: Taking Over a New Management Team," *Supervisory Management,* September 1985), points out the new manager lacks much of the information he needs to be effective. He may garner it gradually in the next few months, but to hit the ground running, he needs much of that data now.

What information is needed?

☐ The strengths and weaknesses of the organization and that of individual staffers as well.
☐ Existing interpersonal issues and how they impact the team.
☐ Team history.
☐ Major operating problems of the component units comprising the team.
☐ Assumptions and perceptions staffers have about his management style, philosophy, and reputation.
☐ Problems that exist and opportunities to be taken advantage of.
☐ Values, goals, and priorities—are they clear and realistic?
☐ Who to see to get things done.
☐ What are the rewards people get and how are results measured?
☐ What is the character of the team's planning, cooperation, and coordination?
☐ Are job assignments clear, or are there overlaps?
☐ As a team, what should we do more of and less of; what should we stop, start, and keep doing?
☐ Possible concerns/anxieties of staff about the new team leader.

Added questions to the staff, per management consultant Frank Petrock ("Clearing the Air During Transitions," *Training,* April 1991) are these:

☐ What hampers your progress now and what can I do about it?
☐ What is your biggest immediate concern?
☐ What should I "move in on" right now?
☐ What are the unit's top five priorities?
☐ Are there any unique policies or procedures?

☐ What do you do best and what less well?
☐ What are your personal goals?

If new managers feel they have a lot to learn about their new organization and the team as well, employees are likely to have even more questions they wish to pose to their new boss. Typically, they want to know the following, says Dr. Looram:

☐ What is the extent of your knowledge and your perception of our outfit? What assumptions have you already made? And what more information can we provide?
☐ What should we know about you?
☐ What is your role and management style, and your perception of it?
☐ What might we do that would "bug" you?
☐ What feedback have you gotten about your strengths and weaknesses as a manager?
☐ In this transition meeting, what outcomes would you hope for and what would you like to avoid?

Dr. Petrock adds these "life and death" questions that employees may have:

What do you see as our goals?

What might you expect of me and what would make me a top performer?

Will I know loud and clear if my performance is below par?

Are you a risk taker? How do you respond to new ideas?

What is your philosophy about delegation and decision making at our level?

Can we level with you about any possible errors/oversights on your part?

What guidelines can you give us about what you regard as important?

What is your need to know about what I'm doing? How much and how often do you want to know?

What is your approach to conflict? Face up to it or smother it?

Can I call you at home if I have a real need to do it? When or when not to call?

If you lose your temper what do I do?

Are there any moral or ethical issues which you feel are important?

Do you accept rough drafts or must written work (reports, letters, memos) be in final form?

What is your need to know about a problem? How much is enough?

Are you an a.m. or a p.m. person?

Can you share with us your number one priority?

Can you share with us your career goals?

How much interaction of a social sort do you favor?

Note: The questions that employees may have, as cited above, represent their real concerns. However, all of them may not necessarily be presented to the new team leader at the first team-building session or stated in the form stated above. Why not? Because trust has to be established before people will feel free to level about their needs and anxieties. However, a good start on those questions/concerns will be made at the transition team building.

Longtime team-building authority Glenn Parker presents these steps and procedures to make the transition team build pay off well (reported in "Passing the Reins, Smoothly," *Training,* October 1990):

1. The facilitator/consultant interviews the new manager/team leader to learn of his concerns regarding the new assignment. He asks what the employees, other managers and the departing manager can do to ease the transition.
2. The outgoing manager is interviewed to learn of his concerns about leaving, goals achieved, and goals remaining.
3. Employees are interviewed to learn of unit strengths and weaknesses, what they liked about the former manager's style, and what they might do to help the new team leader.
4. The transition meeting is conducted with the new and old bosses and full staff in attendance.
5. Both managers describe briefly their management styles. The new team leader is asked to summarize his work experience.
6. Staffers present a summary of current projects and responsibilities.
7. A question and answer period is conducted.
8. The facilitator summarizes the data collected in his interviews with the managers and the staff. This can lead to more group discussion or it can be used to create an agenda for later meetings.
9. The outgoing manager now leaves and the new manager and staff set goals, establish priorities for current projects, and air any concerns they may have.

It should be apparent from the above paragraphs that effective transition team building is a key tool in building relationships, trust, openness, and morale. The alternative? A slow, hit-or-miss process of adjustment for all parties involved. The staff and the new manager inevitably have a lot of unanswered questions about one another. The sooner an earnest attempt is made to learn of expectations and questions, the better off the productivity effort will be.

Team Building After Downsizing

Staffing cutbacks affect not only those laid off, but also those who remain. Team-building consultant George M. Smart, Jr., cites these problems the retained employees may have ("Building On Downsizing," *Training and Development,* August 1991):

☐ significantly greater workloads

☐ guilt feelings about being retained, whereas their co-workers are now out on the street

☐ anger at the firm for the downsizing, even if it was necessary

☐ fear of later added cutbacks

Says consultant Smart about team building as a means of helping the retained staff to adjust to the downsizing:

Team building—which addresses the norms, values, and culture of a group and then helps that group improve its own communication—gets at these issues through interactive training in consensus, evaluation, clarifying goals, and getting ownership or 'buy-in' before proceeding with decisions.

Team building has traditionally focused on the realm of developing management skills or assessing interpersonal issues in work groups, but now companies have a way to back up those hard choices about layoffs with the proper training for the team that's left to carry the ball.

Team Building After a Merger

A merger is certain to disrupt established team structures, team processes, team relationships, and team *esprit de corps.* All of which means that organizational productivity will take a severe blow. Hence the need to take positive action to cushion the inevitable trauma. Team building is a key tool to take positive action after people have been rearranged into new work groups. And if the acquisition had been resisted strongly by those in the merged firm, and the greater the amalgamation/integration of the workforces, the more vital the team-building role is.

What are the goals of team building in the stressful aftermath of the merger? They are designed to do the following, per Pritchett and Associates, Inc., a Dallas,

Texas management consulting firm that specializes in management consultations on mergers and acquisitions (per an undated brochure describing its professional services):

☐ establish/clarify each person's role and responsibilities
☐ secure agreement on objectives and goals (targets)
☐ provide priorities on agreed-upon goals
☐ upgrade communication by encouraging openness, speaking the truth
☐ make a solid start toward cooperative functioning
☐ overcome interpersonal conflict
☐ increase trust and support
☐ identify barriers to full team functioning
☐ reduce resistance to change
☐ pinpoint team and individual strengths and demonstrate how to capitalize on them.

Note: Team members will bring a whole host of doubts, anxieties, insecurities, resentments, and possibly misconceptions to the team-building session. The question, with an obvious answer, is this: Which is preferable: to let people merely harbor their strong negative feelings inward or to ventilate them, to get them out of their systems, to share them with their colleagues, and possibly to "test them" in the reality of their new world? Much of the answer lies in such everyday expressions as "misery loves company," "we're all in the same boat," "if you can't beat 'em, join 'em," and "it's hardly the end of the world."

Team Building—What Results Might Ensue?

If a trained team-building consultant/facilitator is used to guide the off-site retreat, we can anticipate a productive two or three days. More specifically, we can expect the following:

☐ At the retreat, team problems are identified, defined precisely, prioritized, and assigned to individuals or subgroups for in-depth study and specific recommendations for corrective action.
☐ The team is now equipped to do a better job of problem solving—the group has learned to treat causes rather than get fixated on symptoms.
☐ The team functions more effectively as a decision-making unit. Many decisions will be resolved in the future on a group consensus rather than on a directive basis by the boss.

☐ Policies and procedures are clarified, revised, or issued as necessary.
☐ Goals are defined and agreed upon.
☐ The leader's role may be altered, shifting from a more or less command style to more of a team-oriented one. The team's climate is more open, with an emphasis on sharing, mutual trust, and respect.
☐ The team returns to work with a resolve to be more open, caring, trusting, cooperative, and supporting.
☐ Conflicts between team members may have been brought out in the open and now are either resolved or a start has been made to resolve them. Agreements for changes in behavior and improved relationships should be posted on a flipchart and taken back to the office as a permanent record. A sample agreement between a manager and his staff is given on page 396.
☐ A decision may be made by the team to meet again at a later date, possibly in three to six months, to assess progress and deal with any unresolved issues. The follow-up session may or may not use the facilitator, depending on how the group feels about its new-found powers to work together as an open, hard-hitting, problem-solving unit.

THE MANAGEMENT TEAM: VARIOUS TECHNIQUES TO UPGRADE ITS EFFECTIVENESS

Previously, we discussed team building, with particular emphasis on the management retreat, as a formal, all-out effort to get the team on track and to keep it there. However, there are a number of other things the manager can do, short of the comprehensive team-building approach, to stimulate greater teamness and to make his team more productive.

The management team is the key to successful functioning of any organization. This concept would also apply to the top management team as well as to the units that comprise it. Hence it is essential for the manager of any size unit to (a) take an in-depth look periodically at how well his team is functioning, and (b) as indicated, work actively at its upgrading.

The management team may be composed of all managers or supervisors (unit, branch, or section heads), a mix of managers and key specialists, or the manager and his key, non-supervisory staff.

The management team, regardless of its composition and the level at which it functions, is the force that

Manager-Team Agreements
June 23, Three Pines Inn

Manager agrees to:	Manager requests team to:
☐ Use staff meetings to discuss and solve problems, in addition to usual routine in formation dissemination. ☐ Talk directly with a staffer on an "annoyance," as opposed to sending "nasty" notes and memos about them. ☐ Make performance reviews a two-way communication process, not just a "here's your rating for the year" procedure.	☐ Tell him when he fails to give a staffer full attention in a one-on-one meeting. ☐ Review currently required reports and make recommendations for simplification or abandonment. ☐ Provide a complete justification when requesting attendance at an outside training course. ☐ Discuss with him individually existing delegations of authority—is there enough clarity and freedom to do the job properly?

makes things happen. For it is concerned with such basic management functions as visioning, planning, budgeting, organizing, staffing, coordinating, directing, evaluating, and reporting its accomplishments.

The techniques described below are intended primarily for *team development,* that is, to *improve* team functioning. However, they may also be used to *build* a team that is newly organized or is already established but is not on target or is even floundering.

Set Goals With and For the Team

In an effective team, members participate actively in setting group goals relating to their situation/function/operation. Hammering out goals collectively not only taps the wisdom of the group, but is the only certain mechanism to secure individual loyalty, ownership, and commitment to group goals. People are more likely to support that to which they have contributed and created, as opposed to having to accept something autocratically handed down from on high.

So statements like "Hey, man, I was never for it in the first place," "I didn't think it would really work" or "That's what the boss wanted so I signed off on it," are unlikely to surface later on should certain goals run into difficulty.

Note:

1. Goals or targets for the group generally are established for a one-year period, although some may require shorter or longer time frames.
2. Team goal-setting, as opposed to one-on-one goal-setting, is a key mechanism to avoid establishing goals for one person that may be in conflict with someone else's.
3. Team goal-setting is also a means to allow all team members to assess opportunities and threats that may be embedded in one individual's proposed set of goals.
4. Priorities for the team can be adjusted and established more logically when the team has the opportunity to make an "across-the-board" review of the goals of all team members.

Pin Down Who is Responsible for What

Your team may find itself with problems such as overlapping responsibility or even unassigned responsibility, a confusion over delegated authority, inadequate coordination between functions, and the like. These problems may arise due to a merger, assumption of new responsibilities, loss of certain functions, contraction of staff due to downsizing, changes in key staff, establishment of new positions, reorganization, etc. Regardless of the cause(s), however, it is essential for high-performing teams to clarify responsibilities and expectations for all concerned. This can best be accomplished via one or more *team responsibility planning sessions* because all team members have a stake in the clarification of team responsibilities. The necessary clarification can be accomplished via the preparation of a team responsibility chart (page 397). When completed, it will show who the major "players" are and the responsibilities each is to assume.

A responsibility chart can be prepared quite readily by listing key functions on the vertical axis of the chart and the team members who have particular responsibilities on the horizontal axis. A sample responsibility is given in the following chart. It depicts the responsibilities of various team members in a company engaged in

Example of a Responsibility Chart

Responsibility	Company President	Planning Unit	Production Unit	Quality Control	Marketing/ Sales Unit	Training Unit
Creation of ideas for film/video projects		R	I		I	I
Approval of new projects	D				I	I
Script (story) development	D	C	R		I	I
Selection of cast, location, film crew			R			
Technical quality assurance of audio-video			C	R		
Development of trainer's user guide	D				I	R
Editing of film/video work		C	R	C	I	I
Plan and develop public workshops in support of project	D				C	R
Development of promotional materials	D				R	I

Key: R = Primary responsibility
C = Coordination
I = Provide added advisory input
D = Final decision

the production and marketing of training film/videos for business, industry and government.

Note:

1. Separate charts may be needed for each major project, function or activity.
2. Because the responsibility analysis is accomplished in a team setting, each manager can assess how his work (major responsibility) impacts the work of other managers. Charting also can show who can provide input and coordination necessary to secure a high-quality, on-schedule project.
3. The charting process, although invaluable, may take considerable time. However, by avoiding confusion over responsibilities and expectations, time will be saved in the long run, and smooth working relations among team members will be assured.
4. Although job descriptions may have some of the necessary data regarding responsibility, they hardly have the rich fund of information generated by team meetings on responsibility charting. Also, job descriptions tend to become dated quickly in today's fast-moving work environment.

Identify Key Roles Essential for Team Effectiveness

Team members play dual roles: 1) a *functional* role based on one's job expertise, e.g., accountant, salesperson, human resource specialist, etc., and 2) a *team* role, which provides the lubrication essential to keep the team vehicle in high gear. Management consultant Tom Noonan draws on the work of British researcher Dr. Meredith Belbin, who studied 120 management teams for more than 20 years and identified nine vital roles essential to develop high-performance teams.

The nine roles are as follows (Tom Noonan "The Search for Balance: Team Effectiveness," *The 1995 Annual, Vol. 2 Consulting,* J. William Pfeiffer, editor, San Diego: Pfeiffer & Co., 1995):

1. **Plant:** Typically comes up with the bright ideas, the creative solutions to the team's problems.
2. **Coordinator:** Exercises traditional leadership functions such as interpreting objectives, encouraging final action (decisions) and facilitating appropriate resources.

3. **Resource Investigator:** Locates helpful contacts and resources external to the team.
4. **Monitor Evaluator:** Points out alternatives and provides penetrating judgments and observations.
5. **Implementer:** Converts team ideas into action and organizes the machinery for it.
6. **Team Worker:** Smooths ruffled feathers so that disagreements don't impede team progress; essentially the team diplomat.
7. **Completer-Finisher:** Mends mistakes, checks on task completion and ensures that deadlines are observed.
8. **Specialist:** Provides special know-how that no one else possesses.
9. **Shaper:** Provides challenge to the team when it encounters difficulties or setbacks.

Note:

1. The mix of team roles provides the special chemistry needed for effective team action.
2. When team roles are clearly identified, tasks can be assigned based on individual talents and skills.
3. No one team member is broad enough to assume all nine roles. So if needed roles are lacking, teams have to select individuals who can provide roles essential for team balance.
4. The nine-role concept means that the functional (formally designated) leader doesn't have to do it all.

The importance of role clarity is illustrated by the following anecdote.

Story: The airplane ride over the Rockies was extremely bumpy. An elderly woman, seated next to a priest, was very uncomfortable and concerned. She turned to her clerical seatmate and, somewhat apologetically, she said, "Father, I'm getting anxious about our roller-coaster ride. May I be so bold as to ask whether you might be able to do something about it?" Replied the priest empathically, "I really would like to help, dear lady, but unfortunately my role is that of sales, not management."

Build Trust

We indicated above that collective or mutual trust is a key characteristic of an effective team. Every organization, big or small, necessarily operates with a degree of trust. Thus some organizations—and their segments such as teams—may be perceived and described as "high trust." Others may be regarded as "low trust."

Assuming that you recognize the importance of a trusting relationship with your team, here are a number of techniques and approaches that you can use to develop trust:

☐ Behavior which is consistent and thus predictable builds trust; unpredictable behavior breeds anxiety and mistrust. (Visualize the employee who repeatedly and anxiously asserts: "I hope this is what the boss wants.")

☐ A congenial, supportive atmosphere/climate builds trust.

☐ Feelings that are expressed freely build intimacy and thus trust. Conversely, feelings that are withheld make for distance and mistrust.

☐ "Gassing" someone or others makes for mistrust. (GAS refers to punishing behaviors such as censoring, blaming, belittling and nit-picking that produce guilt, anxiety, or shame.) Conversely, supportive behaviors such as sharing, clarifying, and giving praise encourage trust.

☐ Helping behaviors—e.g., in coaching and counseling—produce trust.

☐ Behaviors perceived as fair, equitable, and just build trust.

☐ Listening to all team members is a lubricant for building trusting interpersonal relationships. (Consider the reverse: "The boss never listens to what I have to say.")

☐ Status reduction by the boss builds trust; conversely, a superior attitude and acting as "The Big Boss" reduce it.

☐ The encouragement of questioning attitudes by team members builds trust.

☐ Spontaneous as opposed to devious or manipulative behavior encourages trust.

☐ Well-manneredness—being polite, courteous, considerate—impacts favorably on trust.

☐ Energetic, enthusiastic, zestful behavior encourages trust, just as disinterested, flabby behavior works the other way. (Who can trust a half-awake, lethargic leader to act wisely or to carry through on agreements and commitments?)

☐ Opportunities for experimentation and risk-taking build trust.

☐ Being accessible or available for help, guidance, and direction encourages trust.

☐ Providing reliable, accurate, and consistent information freely builds trust. Conversely, sending mixed messages makes for mistrust.

☐ Championing the team to higher authority, e.g., regarding the securing of budget, personnel, space, a change in policy or procedure, etc., builds trust.

☐ Being calm under stress builds trust, whereas overreacting, "blowing one's top," discourages trust.

☐ Taking miscues in stride, as opposed to stressing errors and shortcomings, builds trust. ("He's making a federal case out of this!")

☐ Using "win-win" problem-solving approaches, as opposed to making points or winning over others, makes for trust.

☐ Using "I messages" makes for a trusting relationship.

☐ Using consensual decision making to seek the best decision builds trust. Conversely, decisions based on fiat, coercion, emotional appeals, rushing to vote, railroading, etc., reduce trust.

☐ Insisting on only face-to-face criticism of a team member, as opposed to backstabbing, which is likely to divide team members, builds and maintains trust.

☐ Treating all ideas generated in brainstorming with respect builds trust. **Example:** Not this, "Let's review these items and discard the far-out, silly, or impractical ones," but this: "Let's review all of our ideas and select those on which we can get full agreement." (Note that the latter approach avoids a reference to discarding or discounting anyone's ideas. It simply avoids debating ideas which have little support in the group.)

Final, key points: Trust is a circular phenomenon—trust builds trust and mistrust begets mistrust. The more you give the more you get back and vice versa. It thus is essential to use techniques that are certain to build, increase, and maintain trust. And as the list above indicates, there are many available techniques with that to build trust. There is nothing vague or mysterious about it. What it comes down to are values, beliefs, and attitudes. So if we feel it's worth having, we can have it by exercising the behaviors that produce it.

Elicit Feedback

You and I can learn about our behavior/performance in relation to others in only two ways: Either we determine it ourself because of our sensitivity and percep-

---

A Note On Effective Group Work

Recalling the days of the 1962 Cuban missile crisis,* the late Senator Robert Kennedy described the tension and disagreement among the men meeting for recommend an action that might "affect the future of all mankind." Finally they split into groups that wrote recommendations, submitted them to the other groups for criticism, then reworked their original ideas. "Gradually," Kennedy write, "from all this came the outline of definitive plans. . . .

"During all these deliberations, we all spoke as equals. There was no rank and, in fact, we did not even have a chairman . . . As a result, the conversations were completely uninhibited and unrestricted. It was a tremendously advantageous procedure that does not frequently occur within the Executive Branch of the Government, where rank is often so important."

*Robert F. Kennedy. The 13 days of crisis. The Washington Post, *November 3, 1968. Pp. B1-B3.*

---

tiveness (introspection), or we receive data about it from others (feedback). Introspection, unfortunately, can help us but only up to a point. Why? Because it is difficult to see ourselves totally as others do. Hence the need for feedback from the team.

Dr. William Dyer, early, long-time authority on team building, states ("Feedback: Making a Tough Process Easier," *Bulletin on Training,* Sept./Oct. 1978) that he has asked hundreds of managers this question: "If you engage in behaviors that create problems for the people who work with you and for you, would you like to know what these behaviors are?" Their response? Hardly a surprise: Over 90% say they'd like such information. Dyer then asks a second question: "How many of you have a method you feel good about for finding out such data?" Sad to relate, less than 25% say that they have a process to get such feedback.

So the need for feedback certainly exists, but few of us have as yet developed mechanisms to get it. Obviously, feedback from others is a scary, possibly painful kind of thing. Who really wants "constructive" criticism. (One wag has stated that of all the kinds of criticism, the constructive kind is the worst!)

But if we can recognize its importance—visualize an airplane pilot without instruments to tell him how well he is performing—we can agree that it's worth seeking out, even if it may bruise our egos a bit. Dyer suggests that we can get feedback via these devices (*Insight to Impact: Strategies for Interpersonal and Organizational Change,* Brigham Young University Press: 1976):

Individual Direct Request

Give a staffer a note inviting him to a one-on-one session to secure feedback about your managerial performance: "Do I create problems for others? How might I upgrade my effectiveness?" The meeting should be held in the staffer's office so that your status as a manager is not emphasized. Obviously, this method has potential only if your relations with this subordinate are very open. For many employees would regard leveling with the boss equivalent to a form of hari-kari. ("Tell the boss what I really think? You must be kidding. Don't forget I have a wife and three very hungry kids.")

Written Feedback

Instead of asking for a face-to-face meeting, you might ask for helpful data on a written basis. Indicate that you are trying to improve your managerial effectiveness and would welcome information in writing on how you impact others, positive or negative, or both. Again, your subordinates may be reluctant to engage in such candor and you may not get back what you hoped for.

Priming the Pump

This is a technique to stimulate the flow of data by providing some data already known or observed. **Example:** "I have been told that I turn people off by signing letters and glancing at the mail when someone is talking to me. Have you observed this? Is there anything else that I do that bothers you? What might I do to strengthen my management style?"

The merit of this technique obviously is that by sharing/admitting known data, one is indicating one's earnestness in receiving feedback. A partial "confession" is certainly a means of uncorking feedback that has been long bottled up.

Sub-group Feedback

For greater anonymity, divide the staff at a staff meeting into sub-groups of three or four persons. They should meet for 30–45 minutes to discuss behaviors they have experienced/observed that reduce the effectiveness of the operation. Your instruction: "Jot down (type) your ideas on a sheet of paper and give them to my secretary. Don't sign it, for I'm interested in what is said, not who said it. I won't be at your meetings, of course. If you want to meet with me directly, we could do that, too, or you could skip the written statement entirely."

This procedure, aside from its anonymity, has these added merits: It elicits feedback from the group rather than one person, which has the potential to increase its validity; people are more likely to be candid in a group situation, for they have the support of their colleagues at their subgroup meeting; by involving the total group, you as the team leader are stating that eliciting feedback to strengthen the leader's performance is a total team concern.

After the data is received, you as the team leader should review it carefully and try to internalize it. If the feedback makes sense, accept it rather that discount it or get angry. Then meet with the staff to share your reactions, to ask for clarification as necessary, to indicate where you believe you can make changes, and to thank them for their help.

Total Group

You may wish to put your interest in securing feedback on the agenda of your next staff meeting: "I would appreciate it if you would give thought to how I as your team leader can improve my effectiveness. We'll devote our next meeting to this topic. Try to be as candid as you can and I'll try to be as receptive as I can to what you come up with."

It is obvious that there has to be a climate of trust and openness for the feedback session to be a meaningful one. If such a climate exists, you can learn a lot about your impact on others, and the total operation as well.

Note: It may be desirable to have an outside consultant/facilitator to conduct this session.

Instrumented Feedback

You can use one or more questionnaires to gauge group feelings about such management areas as goal setting, communication, climate, opportunities for creativity, etc. You can circulate the questionnaires yourself, your secretary can pass them out, or you can have the human resources office circulate them and tally the results for you.

The advantages of the questionnaire method are that you can get data from a large group; everyone responds to the same questions so you have a total group response on the questions; you receive data in quantitative form (e.g., "5% of the group feel that . . ."); the questionnaires can be distributed again at a later date to note if there is a change in subordinates' attitudes; and anonymity for the respondents is assured.

Sample instruments appear at chapter's end. **A caution:** Only use the instruments which are most pertinent. If you used them all, people would most likely be totally exhausted.

Shared Assessment

In this approach you write down your assessment of your performance as you see it. Your staff is asked to confirm or deny your observations. In your write-up, list (a) the things you believe you do well, and (b) the things in which you probably could improve. Space should be made available for staffers to make comments to the right of each statement in your memo.

Outside Consultant

An objective, "outside" person—either an internal trainer or an external consultant—can be used to observe and gather data about your performance. He can sit in on staff meetings, observe you as you go through your work day, interview peers and staffers, and administer instruments. The big advantage to a trained outside consultant is that he can see behaviors that insiders may have learned to live with and thus not even report.

Some Final Cautions

When you receive feedback, you should:

Listen, Don't Explain or Justify

You asked for it, so try to understand it rather than discount it. Remember, defensive behavior on your part will dry up the flow of communication to you about your performance.

Ask for More

Say "That's very helpful. Is there more that I should know?" This will keep the flow coming, if that's what you want.

Express an Honest Reaction

You asked for feedback. You were given it. So now the feedback giver(s) is (are) entitled to know how you feel about it. If the feedback is off base, say so, of course. Not all feedback is totally valid.

Express Appreciation and Plan for the Future

Thank the feedback givers. It was hard to do, and you appreciate the risks they took. Indicate you hope to do this again, possibly make it a "normal" way of leading the team.

Use the Team Appropriately

A team-oriented management style does not mean that all problems that arise require group action. In fact, many problems can best be solved via individual problem-solving approaches, i.e., by the manager himself. Here, then, are several criteria to guide you when to involve the team in the search for a high-quality solution/decision:

☐ The problem is quite complex, having several parts and many ramifications.

☐ The problem's solution requires a number of steps or stages. (For example, Step 2 cannot be undertaken until Step 1 is completed or implemented.)

☐ Diverse information is required to attack the problem, and no one team member is likely to have all the pertinent data.

☐ A number of staffers are interested in the problem; some even have a "vested interest" in its resolution.

☐ It is essential to secure a good number of high-quality options/alternatives before a decision is made. The team must be careful (for PR or other reasons, e.g., interest in the problem by higher authority) to exhibit the soundness of its deliberations.

☐ Commitment of the team to support the decision/solution is essential.

☐ All or most team members will have specific responsibility for implementing a particular phase of the solution.

☐ There is enough time to involve the group; that is, there is no need to act quickly.

Note: The degree or extent of team responsibility for making decisions is less important than clarity about which decisions the team is to make and the amount of support the team leader will provide for those decisions.

Provide Opportunities to Do Things Together

Team building and maintenance can be encouraged by having team members engage in various joint activities from time to time. **Examples:** field trips, plant inspections, study of competitors' operations, and training. The latter activity is discussed in more detail below.

Having contacts with colleagues in different situations provides new, added insights into their personalities, capabilities, interests, and styles. It thus can augment appreciation (and possibly tolerance) of their differences, goals and needs.

Provide for Team Training

Much of management training is ordinarily accomplished on a one-manager-at-a-time basis. Thus, one manager may attend a workshop on time management, another on long-range planning, a third on decision making, a fourth on stress management, and so on. While the individual manager may profit by virtue of his attendance, it generally is difficult for the returning manager to transfer his new learning to his colleagues. Thus the opportunity to make a real impact in one's unit by implementing the new learning is generally lost. In fact, trainers typically report that participants in their workshops are likely to lament, "This is very helpful stuff, but I wish my boss (or my team members) were here. I can't really change my operation unless everyone I work with understands why the change is essential."

A remedy for this difficulty is for certain types of training to be provided to the entire team. The team, after its immersion in the training, can return "back home" to discuss (a) the implications of the training for the total team, and (b) what applications can be made of the training to team needs and circumstances.

A good example of the benefits accruing to the team from training the entire team is apparent in the area of time management training. Thus, attempts at curbing interruptions, reducing wasted time at meetings, and instituting a "quiet hour" are more likely to occur if all concerned have been recipients of the same training message and skill development.

Similarly, if the team undergoes stress training together, team members may learn how their behaviors, or team practices in general, serve as stressors for team members. And as a result of the training, the team can plan how to manage the team operation better so that stress is kept under control.

Another worthwhile area of team training is in the area of diversity training. The idea is to help the team come to terms with people's differences, to develop empathy for others regardless of their backgrounds. The learning objectives are awareness building, knowledge acquisition and skill development.

Note:

1. Added payoff from training is more likely if a training-needs analysis is conducted prior to the training by the workshop facilitator or the team itself. This approach should permit the training program to be designed on a "tailor-made" basis— that is, to cover performance issues identified by the analysis, thereby meeting the needs of the participant group more precisely.

2. Team learning can produce a "synergistic" effect, i.e., the benefits from the training can multiply many fold. The reason? All team members return to the workplace with the same mindset, understandings, and goals. They also may have learned to work together in the training program and thus can work together better on the job, communicate better, and give one another greater support.

3. Real team development does not occur in the training session, but in the interactions between team members and their environment back on the job. As industrial and organizational psychologist Gregory H. Huszczo put it ("Training for Team Building," *Training and Development Journal*, February 1990): "The real progress toward developing a more effective team occurs as team members attempt to work together, to get their jobs done, and to provide each other with the satisfying experiences of being on an effective team."

Help Newcomers Become Bona Fide Team Members Rapidly and Painlessly

The manager has these options in respect to integrating new hires into the team:

☐ He can let nature take its course and hope that things will work out for the best over time. Or,

☐ He can work actively at ensuring that the new person bridges the gap from outsider to team member in a rapid, non-traumatic way.

For the manager who wishes to make the newcomer an effective team member quickly, these things might be done:

Let the Team Assume Final Responsibility for the Selection

This will expose the team to the new person early on, and team members will feel responsible to help the new hire to become one of the group in the best sense of the term. After all, it *is* their own selection. Note that as a result of their work on selection, the team will have a good fix on the new team member's strengths and personality characteristics, and thus will be able to relate to him more readily.

Encourage the Team to Give the New Arrival a Warm, Enthusiastic Welcome

Team members can help the new person adjust to the new environment in a myriad of ways. Certainly as a minimum they should invite him to their coffee and lunch breaks.

Recognize That Most of Us Have Needs for Inclusion.

To have membership in a group can provide gratification, support, encouragement, respect, and congeniality. Of course, not everyone has the same degree of need to be in contact with people. Nevertheless, most people prefer to be "in" rather than "out." It thus is essential that the team leader and the team members learn early on the degree of inclusion the newcomer really favors.

These added procedures will help the orientation and adjustment process, too, says Joseph D. O'Brian ("Making New Hires Members of the Team," *Supervisory Management,* May 1992):

At the Outset, Stress to the New Team Member That He is Now Associating Himself With an Elite Corps—Talented People, High Achievers, Positive Thinkers, Winners

He will be very pleased to be part of such a stellar group.

Assign a Mentor to the Newcomer for the First Few Weeks, One Who is Popular, Affable and Knowledgeable

In this way, he will feel very welcome and that his joining up is certain to be a pleasurable experience.

Maintain a High Profile and Point Up Actual Team Accomplishments

This will aid in building *esprit de corps.*

Assign Confidence-Building Tasks in the Early Stages

Pick assignments of moderate complexity and for which the new team member has the background to accomplish readily.

Meet with the New Person on a One-On-One Basis in Two Weeks or so After His Entrance on the Job

Ask questions such as these: How does the team operate? What are its strengths? What might be done to improve its functioning? Is the team using your strengths fully? What might we do to upgrade/update your capabilities?

Tap the Newcomer's Ideas

As an outsider with more of a detached view, he may observe things about the operation that seasoned team members, functioning in the team for long periods of time, may not be able to pick up very readily. (An analogy is the doting mother who is so enthralled with her offspring that she is unable to notice their shortcomings and peculiarities.)

Manage Disagreement Constructively

If two people always agree, one of them is unnecessary.

—Robert Frost (1874–1963), U.S. poet and four-time winner of the Pulitzer Prize for poetry

Creativity in groups is dependent on discussion, debate, and, yes, disagreement. A group that is placid, lethargic, and totally congenial will not ignite the flow of ideas essential to high quality problem solving and decision making. So the effective team will relish having the sparks fly, for that is the only route to true, bountiful "imagineering."

The team leader's interest certainly is not to produce chaotic communication in the group, but to stimulate constructive controversy. Phony politeness, smoothing over differences, suppressing honest feelings about issues, and postponing meetings to avoid controversy are ways of managing—actually soft-pedaling—controversy. But for the manager who really understands the importance of managing disagreement/conflict/controversy to ensure creativity, he will employ two key problem-solving tasks/skills, per management authority Dean Tjosvold ("Constructive Controversy: A Key Strategy for Groups," *Personnel*, April 1986): (1) stimulation of controversy by encouraging team members to express and discuss divergent views, and (2) creation of conditions that encourage/enable participants to treat controversy constructively. Each of these facilitating skills is discussed below.

How to Stimulate Controversy

This can be done via these techniques:

Opt for a diverse member group

Team members who have different backgrounds, experience, expertise, and thus varying frames of reference and perceptions can provide the needed grist for the problem-solving mill. However, diverse views alone are not enough—there also must be a strong commitment to team and organization-wide interests. Not everyone need have a different approach to the problem. But certainly there should be enough diversity and disagreement and, yes, even unpopular views to enrich the discussion and thus challenge the team's thinking.

Allow Free Debate

The best discussion takes place when debate is encouraged and time is made available to allow it to happen. Pressure for quick agreement without generating and discussing a good variety of options stifles the much-needed controversy. So several meetings may be needed to explore and understand the differing positions. Also, time between meetings can help team members to gather added data and to formulate their positions.

Recognize Divergent Viewpoints

The team leader should encourage broad participation and the offering of tentative ideas that can be used by all concerned to develop new positions. Self-censorship should be discouraged, for what is wanted are new solutions, not a shift to traditional positions. **Note:** The manager should facilitate (manage) the discussion rather than present, let alone advocate, a particular point of view. This will avoid possible tendencies for team members to be pressured subtly to go along with the boss' ideas.

Assign Conflicting Viewpoints

To keep the healthy discussion/debate going, the team leader may establish subgroups to defend opposing views or solutions. Also, individual team members may be asked to evaluate a subgroup's position. And if there is an overabundance of agreement, a "devil's advocate" could be appointed to take an "anti-position." Assignments to the different positions are vital aids to recognize new viewpoints and to broaden perspectives.

How to Ensure Constructive Controversy

Controversy, debate, and argument are essential, but in a way that augments participation and "imagineering" as opposed to stifling discussion because "hard feelings" have developed. These techniques can help to achieve that objective:

Stress Group Goals

Everyone inevitably brings his particular set of lenses to the discussion table through which he sees the issues. Yet, if decisions/solutions are to be arrived at that best reflect team and organization needs and interests, individual, parochial positions have to be subordinated. Thus, the team leader and its members must constantly pose to the team at large this question: "Yes, but is it really good for our group and/or the organization?"

Spell Out "Effectiveness"

Everyone should understand that there are no evaluations of and rewards for how well one's ideas are received; nor is one's competence challenged because one's position is "attacked." High-quality performance in problem-solving sessions simply means contributing, exploring, and integrating divergent viewpoints rather than rigidly sticking to one's position and pushing one's own interests.

Monitor Sequencing of the Discussion

Initially, each team member should present and argue for his viewpoint. Then there is a need to move to integrating the various ideas to arrive at a consensus. But opposing views merit a full and fair hearing before that integration is possible.

Develop Interpersonal Skills

The ability to engage in constructive controversy requires an abundance of "social competence." This means team members must express their ideas and feelings freely and encourage others to do the same. A key element or skill is to critique ideas, not to criticize people. Also, disagreement by others with one's ideas has no relation to one's competence nor does it signify a personal rejection. Finally, free-wheeling (controversial) discussions are very likely to provoke emotions, so everyone has to learn to manage them—not to smother the emotions, but to control them so they don't "turn off" anyone else. Skills of these sorts will require training, coaching, practice, and feedback about performance.

Note: The author suggests heavy use of flipcharts in managing disagreement. By putting the ideas where everyone can see them, they are easier to assess. Also, once on the flipchart they become "group property:" Intermingled with all the other ideas, they are less likely to be overprotected by the initiators.

Use Teams in Negotiation

Are two heads better than one at the negotiation table? Management Researcher Susan Brodt (University of Virginia) and Leigh Thompson (University of Washington, Seattle) believe so (reported in "Negotiations: Are Two Heads Better Than One?", *Harvard Business Review,* November–December 1993). This is so not because the team "outmuscles" their one-person opponents, but because they increase the value of the deal subject to negotiation. In fact, *only one of the two negotiating parties needs be a team.* Having at least one team engaged in the negotiations improves the outcomes for both parties.

The research found that team negotiations are more accurate than solo ones in detecting the other party's interests. They thus are better able to find common interests and create win-win circumstances from which both parties can profit. **Example:** While nearly a third of the one-on-one negotiations surveyed failed to identify a single issue both parties had in common, all of the two-on-two negotiations unearthed at least one area of agreement. This result occurred regardless of whether or not the teammates worked closely together.

Some Other Strengths of Team Negotiators

They were better at logrolling, finding issues for which the negotiators had different priorities and accomplishing tradeoffs (each party gives concessions on what it cares about least in exchange for outcomes it values more highly).

In another study, the researchers found that moderately cohesive negotiating teams could out bargain solos and gain an average 60% of the resources. However, the solos weren't necessarily losers. Because a larger pie was created, the solos ended up with the same amount they would have gained if facing off another solo.

Brodt's conclusion: "Teams improve the overall quality of negotiations by finding creative solutions that work for both sides."

Stress "Orderly" Problem-Solving Methodologies

In the chapter on problem solving and decision making (Chapter 10), I stressed the importance of logical, orderly, sequential problem solving; that is, the team should proceed from Step 1 to Step 2 and so on without skipping any steps. Each step should be fully explored before the team moves to the next one. In this manner, high-quality decision making is more likely. The seven steps are:

Step 1: Identifying and defining/formulating the problem

Step 2: Gathering information about the problem

Step 3: Developing/generating alternate solutions

Step 4: Assessing alternate solutions

Step 5: Choosing (deciding) among alternatives

Step 6: Implementation—converting hope into reality

Step 7: Evaluation: Did your solution work?

By following the seven steps in the logical order, the problem-solving process is slowed down. This is highly essential, for groups often get into difficulty because they are too eager to get on to later steps, such as Steps 5 and 6, without adequately completing the preliminary work toward choosing and implementing a decision.

Manage Team Meetings Efficiently

Meetings that are poorly run or even unnecessary are ailments common to many organizations. Visualize these irksome phenomena:

- ☐ There is no agenda or there is disagreement on what the agenda should encompass.
- ☐ Meetings resemble a hockey game—there is much competitiveness, everyone trying to make points for himself.
- ☐ Decisions are rushed, and possible options or alternative solutions are not considered. (In fact, decisions may be made only because of frustration or time pressures.)
- ☐ Meetings run overtime.
- ☐ Vital experts/specialists are not brought in.
- ☐ Voting rather than consensus is the basis for decisions.
- ☐ Some participants arrive late; others leave early.
- ☐ Proceedings are hardly helped by the presence of traditional dysfunctional meeting types such as the monopolizer, the clown, the non-participant, the arguer, and the put-down artist.
- ☐ At meeting's end, there is considerable confusion about what was really agreed upon.

At the team level, properly conducted meetings are a basic ingredient of effective, high-order team work. Obviously, the meeting maladies cited above, if in existence, should be corrected. Additionally, however, certain techniques can be employed to augment meeting quality and also to contribute to feelings of teamness by staff members. Consider the following:

Rotate the chairmanship

This will not only involve the total team in meeting management, but will also provide team members with the opportunity to develop skills in facilitating meetings. This procedure will help demonstrate your commitment to shared leadership.

Appoint a Progress Monitor

At 20-minute-or-so intervals, have this team member report to the group how he sees group action: Are we moving toward our goal, or are we wheel-spinning? Do people seem interested and energized, or do they seem lethargic or frustrated? Are there any behaviors that block progress?

Appoint a "Plop" Counter

A plop occurs when a group member makes a statement, or offers a suggestion or a solution, but no one responds to it. The group ignores it and goes on to something else. In effect, the statement plops to the ground without any acknowledgment. This phenomenon happens quite often in groups. It is indicative of:

- ☐ Poor listening.
- ☐ Unwillingness or inability to treat or deal with an unpopular or minority view.
- ☐ Poor group cohesiveness, e.g., ideas presented by "low status" group members are generally ignored (allowed to plop).
- ☐ Insensitivity to the feelings and self-esteem of the person making the statement. **A possible result:** Withdrawal from the group. ("If they don't want my ideas, I just won't give them any.")

Appoint a Communication Process Evaluator

Have this person monitor team communication. He can report back to the group his observations at meeting's end. To assist the evaluator in his task, the Guidesheet to Monitor Communication at Team Meetings might be used (page 434).

Pin Down Responsibilities and Assignments

Don't adjourn the meeting without making certain that actions to be taken have been specifically assigned to individuals or subgroups. Effective groups don't let important matters "fall between the cracks."

Assess Progress/Satisfaction at Meeting's End

Have participants rate their satisfaction with the meeting. Use a 10-point scale, with 1 meaning low or little satisfaction and 10 meaning high or total satisfaction. The ratings may be made on slips of paper or given orally to the facilitator, who records them on a flipchart or blackboard and secures comments about the ratings.

This evaluative aspect of the meeting may be conducted in a 10-minute time frame.

Note: Appointments of a progress monitor, plop counter, and communication process evaluator need not be made for every meeting. Use these techniques whenever it seems appropriate—that is, when help seems to be needed. Also, evaluate meeting effectiveness regularly only as long as it seems to pay off.

Use "Storyboards" to Focus Attention and Streamline Discussion

Storyboards (described by Barbara A. Langham, "Drawing It Out," *Successful Meetings,* January 1994) are four-foot-square foam boards with index cards pinned to them that boil down the group's/team's ideas and decisions. They are intended to achieve focus, creativity, and productivity. They can be used for generating new ideas on any program or problem. They also serve to keep "troublemakers" and "windbags" focused on the issue rather than on their emotions, gripes, pet peeves, and the like.

The problem-solving session begins with the meeting coordinator or facilitator providing background on the topic with the aid of the displayed index cards. Group members then provide ideas, which are written on cards and displayed to the boards. As in brainstorming, ideation (creating of ideas) proceeds first and evaluation (idea analysis) is deferred. It's a good idea to have a formal break between the two processes.

If executed properly, storyboarding can be a great time saver at meetings. Sometimes it helps meeting objectives to describe a "non-purpose," or issues that are *not* to be discussed. By offering a non-purpose at the outset, people are alerted to avoid being sidetracked by dated or irrelevant issues.

A helpful ground rule is that no one is to offer speeches, but to simply state an idea in 15–20 seconds. The rule overcomes tendencies to drift off the topic and prevents windy speakers from dominating the session.

The value of the posted cards is that not only are the team's ideas visible to all, but that people shed protectiveness of their ideas once they become "group property." Also, ideas can be readily grouped, prioritized, and, as agreed upon, discarded.

At meeting's end, the cards can be collected and filed for reference or left up as a visual display of team collaboration and accomplishment.

Upgrade Team Decisions via "Social Judgment Analysis" (SJA)

Groups frequently are able to make better decisions than their average member would, but not as good as their best member would. So how can groups take advantage of the best judgment and ideas the best member can produce? Behavioral scientist John Rohrbaugh favors a technique he calls "social judgment analysis" (reported in *The Pryor Report,* March 1986, based on an article written for *Organizational Behavior and Human Performance*). His approach: Instead of individuals presenting their judgments per se, they explore in-depth the *differences in the logic* underpinning their judgments.

Rohrbaugh tested his theory thusly: First, a number of persons were asked to handicap horses based on data contained in a racing form. Thus, each rated the diverse factors involved—prior record, jockey, weather—and then weighed the importance of each factor in predicting the winner.

Then, Rohrbaugh put into groups those who made differing predictions. These were termed SJA groups, and they were then asked to work together to develop a system for handicapping, to agree on the factors that might predict a winner.

The SJA participant groups were asked to offer the logic behind the reasoning they gave for the various factors. **The salutary results:**

1. The SJA groups came up with results as good as their most able or proficient members, and far superior to those produced by the non-SJA groups that only discussed their judgments but not the reason (logic) for them.

2. SJA group members were more satisfied with the SJA group process, and they believed that the logical system they developed was superior to (of higher quality than) those developed by members of the other (non-SJA) groups.

The Pryor Report's conclusion: If a group is only producing surface-type compromises, add the SJA approach. Ask all group participants to explain the factors taken into account and the underlying reasoning. This should enable the group to produce higher-quality decisions and to be more satisfied in the process, too.

Watch for Indicators of Work Overload

The team leader has many responsibilities. One of the most important is his concern for the mental health of the group, particularly impairment by work overload. Indicators of such work stress are:

☐ Difficulty in meeting usual deadlines
☐ People taking work home regularly, evenings, and weekends
☐ Reduced cooperation among staffers
☐ People being "on edge," exhibiting considerable irritation at minor annoyances
☐ Griping, whining, complaining
☐ Overlooking important details with noticeable frequency
☐ Committing errors in above-"normal" quantities
☐ Increasing customer complaints

Use the Team to Generate Cost-Cutting Ideas

When there is an urgent or compelling need to slash costs, you may wish to leave the office and go into a "retreat" situation with your team. By leaving the work site, you communicate unequivocally that cost-cutting is high-priority business.

One way to stimulate interest in the cost-reduction activity is to divide the total group into sub-groups (3–4 persons). Each small team then brainstorms ideas to cut or reduce costs. The idea of the subgrouping is to set up a competition as to which small team can generate a greater number of ideas. A prize may be offered to the winning team.

Each team then returns for a session-at-large, with brainstormed ideas on flipcharts. The ideas are then evaluated by the total group.

Conduct a SWOT Analysis

Assume your unit has reached a critical point where long-range thinking and planning are imperative. You thus may wish to join with your team in a retreat or retreat-type situation for a "SWOT review"—i.e., to examine team *Strengths, Weaknesses, Opportunities,* and *Threats.* By a scan of the environment to identify the opportunities and threats that are "out there," the team is better able to develop and launch plans to take advantage of opportunities and to cope with threats.

Regard the retreat session as a first step in your long-range planning process. Identify areas of concern and opportunity and set up subgroups to develop specific plans for them. The small groups may be given 15–30 days to come up with specifics to be presented at a later, second retreat session. Note that we say 15–30 days, which is a fairly short time-frame. But if things are permitted to coast along lackadaisically, the momentum (high interest and motivation) garnered in the initial retreat will be lost. So the best tactic is "to strike while the iron is hot," as the old saying has it.

Improve Morale

A practical way to upgrade morale, per training supervisor Robert Buckham, is to conduct a modified "force field analysis" (reported in "May the Force Be With You," *Training,* January 1987). The idea is to involve the team in assessing problems and looking for ways to solve them. The team examines all positive and negative forces influencing morale, and then implements and follows up on an action plan to overcome the negative morale determinants. The specific procedures are:

1. Call a team meeting and have everyone rate morale on a scale of one to ten.
2. Ask the team to decide where morale *could be* in the not-too-distant future, say six months from now. (Allow a time frame that allows for results to be "visible," yet long enough to change things.)
3. Have the team list current and potential events that reduce or keep morale down, e.g., conditions of work, cumbersome policies or procedures, pay cuts, etc.
4. Use the team to brainstorm everything that might reverse the unwanted conditions, e.g., training, improved communication via a newsletter, etc.
5. Request the team to identify the most powerful forces from both sides of the list. The team votes on priorities, totals the scores for each force, and ranks them in order.
6. Have the team plan countermeasures for each of the most powerful negative (restrainers) forces. Ask: "How can we reduce or neutralize the impact of the negative forces?" and have the team draw from the list of positive (building) forces.
7. Ask the team to set target dates to ensure responsibility and accountability. Use subgroups to follow through on the plans agreed upon.

8. Measure morale when the due date arrives.

The attractive aspect to the whole process, says Buckham, is that those who need a morale uplift become part of the answers/solutions/remedies.

Conduct Team Building the "Natural" Way

Paul S. George, professor of education and human resource development ("Team Building Without Tears," *Personnel Journal,* November 1987), suggests that people who work in groups or teams can be brought closer together—team development—via a good number of strategies that are very native and natural to the daily work. His suggestions include:

Provide for Opportunities to Have Fun Together So as to Enjoy Those Activities and Very Likely One Another

Examples: Sharing meals together, both on regular and special occasions; rotating responsibility to bring in the morning donuts or Danish; team picnics.

Encourage Laughter to Build Empathy and Understanding

Examples: Share humorous stories, incidents and/or jokes; post cartoons and quips on the bulletin board; hold rituals, reward ceremonies, possibly "roasts." Says Dr. George, "Shared laughter is a sign that bridges are building between persons and that communication is possible within all ranks of the hierarchy."

Capitalize on Parties

Examples: Exchange inexpensive gifts at Christmas; recognize team members' birthdays and weddings; "exploit" other holidays as well, or (per my suggestion) make up a holiday, e.g., why not celebrate the first day of Spring, the Boston Tea Party, President Millard Fillmore's birthday, or the invention of the electric can opener?

Highlight Physical Symbols

The team may have one or more identifiers which provide a sense of unity and thus bring team members closer together. **Examples:** Trademarks, logos, mottos, coats-of-arms, banners, indicators of company products. Some organizations may use T-shirts, neckties, or jew-elry to point out team aspirations. **Note:** If your team doesn't have a symbol, have them create one.

Don't Overlook Social Symbols

Various group activities can identify and build group unity. **Examples:** Award banquets, plus various rituals, ceremonies, and recognitions. Launching a new product/service or celebrating a very successful month or quarter are logical opportunities for a group festival.

Use Pictoral Displays

Use the walls to highlight achievements, products, early history. Keep a team scrapbook.

Organize for Teamness

Try to locate people (work team members) so that they are in close proximity to one another. Provide a lounge, a refrigerator, and/or a coffee station to encourage frequent close contact. Encourage (sponsor) multiple memberships in professional or trade associations. Sponsor athletic events such as bowling, volleyball, softball—all group-oriented devices to encourage team bonding. Use the team to select new members. Bring family members into various activities.

Model Team Interest

Set a good example, engaging in such activities as self-disclosure (reveal feelings and important information) and de-emphasizing one's status.

Celebrate Team Accomplishment

Celebration is an easy-to-do device to keep the high-accomplishing team "all revved up." Management professors Ken Matejka and Dick Dinsing (in *Training and Development Journal,* March 1989) suggest these advantages of celebration: It fulfills people's needs such as for individual recognition, accomplishment, affiliation, and self-esteem. It also provides a diversion and a release, providing time for re-energizing before the next "big push." Finally, it builds respect among the team players.

Yet, despite its worthwhile values, all too often celebration may not take place. Why not? Matejka and Dinsing suggest these barriers may exist:

Urgency. Everyone is on a treadmill. So we rush from one project to the next, only saying hurriedly "we did it."

Jealousy. Competition may produce reluctance to acknowledge the good works of another. Presumably a victory for Pat means a defeat for the rest of us.

Perfection. We assume "there's always room for improvement." So unless what is done is "perfect," a pat on the back is inappropriate.

Praise impairment. Managers themselves are often compliment-shy, so people are cheated of their earned praise.

But these self-defeating attitudes can be overcome if these strategies are used:

Frequent praise. Think praise. Resolve to praise often. Locate good works and comment on them. And why not start each (or most) staff meetings with some positive strokes?

Learn to accept praise yourself. Overcome possible tendencies to discount praise. ("Not much, really") or to get embarrassed by it ("Aw, shucks"). Instead, practice saying meaningful things in return for praise such as "That's good to hear" or a simple "Thank you."

Create meaningful, attainable rewards. People who do well merit an appreciative response or action on our part.

Celebrate the families, too. Invite them to training classes, certain retreats and social events. Give the "we're all one big, happy family" slogan real life.

An example of a unique celebration of half-year accomplishment was that conducted by the editors and staff of *The Personnel Journal* (reported in "Letter to Readers," September 1992). The staff gathered in the lobby to play some 20 percussion instruments from Africa, South America, and the Caribbean. The music was a chance to have fun and to stimulate everyone's creativity as well. The *Journal*'s publisher brought in a group that specializes in making tribal/native musical presentations, typically to school children. The musical group quickly demonstrated the instruments and then had everyone join in on the conga drums, Tibetan bells, a rain stick, the maracas, and the rest of the exotic instruments.

The *Journal* staff was impressed by how quickly they could learn new things and how rapidly new knowledge can be applied creatively. The event provided a vivid reminder of teamwork—each instrument sounded good on its own, but things really came alive when everyone was playing.

Select New Team Members via Consensus

A worthwhile, but not common use of the team, is that of final selection of new team members. In effect, the team *decides* collegially on (a) the merits of the candidate's qualifications and (b) his suitability, how well the applicant will "fit in."

Team consensus on selection makes sense from these standpoints:

☐ Multiple review of qualifications (technical/professional ability, track record, personality) is more likely to zero in on shortcomings, as well as strengths, than is a single review. Also, different slants on qualifications can enrich the assessment process.

☐ Multiple review has the potential to acknowledge and accept diversity needs; that is to say, a larger or broader group of evaluators is more likely to opt for candidates who may have been routinely rejected previously. This should enable minorities and women to receive fuller and more earnest consideration. (Of course, if the mindset of the total selection team is cast in the traditional mold, points of view favorable to non-traditional candidates are hardly likely to emerge.)

☐ Team involvement in the selection process, particularly if it entails responsibility for *final selection*, not merely making a recommendation, is likely to engender greater interest, concern and seriousness in its deliberations.

☐ Team responsibility for selection is very appropriate because team members are the ones who will actually have to work with the selectee.

Use Instruments ("Quizzes") to Measure Team Functioning

As the team leader, you may wish to measure your group's overall effectiveness—identify team strengths and weaknesses, particularly if you are ready (or getting ready) to move into a more complete form of team management. And at various stages of your group's life, you may wish to learn more about particular aspects of its functioning, e.g., how your team feels about its capabilities in communication, problem solving/creativity, goal setting, climate, teamwork, leadership.

Team members may also wish to assess their individual prowess as team players.

To assist you and your team in making any one of the above assessments, I have provided the following instruments, which appear at chapter's end:

☐ Team leadership quiz (page 427)
☐ Our team—how effective is it? (page 436)
☐ A rating scale to assess effectiveness of our team's goal setting (page 437)
☐ A rating scale to assess our team's problem-solving/creativity competencies (page 438)
☐ A rating scale to assess our team's communication (page 440)
☐ How our team manages its meetings: a self-quiz (page 441)
☐ Team membership—are you on track? (page 442)

You may wish to take any one of the quizzes yourself and then compare your scores with that of the team. Then hold a discussion with the group about the two sets of ratings. Try to learn from the discussion the reason for the difference in perception, if it exists, and what can be done to improve team functioning wherever indicated. A feedback session of this type will communicate to team members that they have been heard and that you are sincere in your willingness to respond.

Note:

1. To assure your group that their ratings will be tallied professionally and objectively, have another person—someone from the Human Resources Department or an outside facilitator—collect the papers and rate them. Have the outside tallyer produce team scores (an average) for each of the quiz items and a composite score for the team on all items combined.
2. Or you may wish to discuss team ratings with the team, each team member holding on to his own paper. This procedure assumes that enough trust exists for you to hold such a free and open discussion with your group.
3. Regardless of whether scores are or are not tallied by an outside party, do the following in your feedback session:

☐ Admit to your need for improvement in certain areas. Candor on your part will help to set the right climate and encourage more open discussion.
☐ If people do "open up," *try to listen.*
☐ Don't be defensive. This is a sure way to cause the discussion to dry up.
☐ One way to communicate that you are serious about the team critique is to use a flipchart to record major suggestions from team members. Advise the team that you will take the sheet back to the office for further study and to serve as a reminder of team ideas.
☐ Consider using an outside facilitator to conduct the session. This may be someone from the HRD or an outside consultant/facilitator.

TYPES OF TEAMS

We have already discussed the management team, including ways to improve its functioning. Other teams that merit our serious attention are:

☐ Self-directed work teams
☐ The project team (includes cross-functional teams)
☐ Concurrent engineering teams
☐ The selling team

These teams, it is to be noted, are playing greater roles in today's organizations as the quest for greater productivity, quality, and improved customer service is pursued.

SELF-DIRECTED TEAMS: HOW TO ORGANIZE AND MANAGE THEM

The action teams of the 1990s will be groups of multi-skilled workers who freely rotate jobs in order to produce an entire product or service. Supervision will be minimal and bureaucratic barriers between departments will disappear.

The result will be changes in employee knowledge and commitment. Productivity gains will exceed expectations, quality will improve, and fewer accidents will occur. Once again, people will enjoy their work and participating in their firms.

—Lee E. Christensen, in *Training and Development,* February 1991

What Are Self-Directed Teams?

An SDT is a group or team of employees (5–15) who have daily responsibility to manage their work (a whole product, a whole sub-assembly process or service) and themselves as well. This means that operating independently, they plan, budget, organize, schedule, control, and evaluate their own work (calculate their productivity). They thus handle their own job assignments and respond to problems that may arise. In essence, they assume many, if not all, of the responsibilities of the supervisor. The teams may or may not have a formal leader. (See a discussion of the leadership role below).

Note that SDTs are permanent, operating, decision-making units with full responsibility for business results. They meet and work together regularly rather than intermittently. They thus are to be distinguished from such other groups within organizations such as quality circles (which can only make recommendations and have no operating responsibility), task forces, certain project teams, product development groups, committees, etc.

In sum, SDTs engage in a relentless focus on improving productivity/profitability and competiveness. Empowering employees as a team—giving them full responsibility for their task/activity/operation—is the key to achieving the high-quality results the team and the organization as a whole hope for.

Why Self-Directed Teams?

SDTs, because of their empowerment/autonomy plus the synergy that accrues from group action, have the capability of benefiting the organization, customers, and employees. More specifically, they can make significant accomplishments in the areas of quality of product or service, productivity, cost reduction, customer satisfaction, continuous improvement, supporting change, empowerment of team members, and increased innovation and creativity.

Additional benefits, per management consultant Darcy Hitchcock ("Self-Directed Work Teams and Performance Technology: A Good Marriage," *Performance and Instruction,* September 1991), are better work methods, greater safety, increased flexibility, fewer organizational layers and supervisory staff, fewer grievances, broader (multi-skilled) personnel, and higher job satisfaction.

How Do SDTs Compare With Traditionally Managed Units?

Drawing on a presentation by Dr. Glenn Varney, president, Management Advisory Associates, Inc., Bowling Green, Ohio, at the 1991 Annual Conference of the American Society for Training and Development, the table on page 435 highlights the differences in the philosophy and operation of traditional ways of managing organizations and the SDT approach:

Career Track, Inc., Boulder, Colorado, the largest producer of professional development programs in North America, provides added characteristics (page 435) of traditional departments vs. SDTs (based on and adopted from its seminar brochure, *Implementing Self-Directed Work Teams,* 1993):

What Are the Growth Rates of Self-Directed Work Teams?

In the quest for higher quality and productivity, the more alert and progressive American organizations, both manufacturing and service, are moving rapidly into team-oriented operations. Consider the following data on the growth in the United States of self-directed work teams (also known as self-managed teams, autonomous work groups, high-performance teams, empowered work groups, high-involvement work force, self-reliant work groups, and leaderless work groups):

☐ An early survey of 476 *Fortune* 1,000 companies published by the American Productivity and Quality Center, Houston, found that only 7% of the workforce was organized in self-directed teams. But half the firms said they would rely on them more significantly in the years ahead (reported in *Fortune,* May 7, 1990).

☐ A later (1990) survey conducted by the consulting/training firm Development Dimensions International (DDI), Pittsburgh, in conjunction with *Industry Week* magazine and the Association for Quality and Participation (AQP), found that some 25% of the surveyed companies were implementing SDTs somewhere in their organization (Richard S. Wellins, "Building a Self-Directed Work Team," *Training and Development,* December 1992).

☐ A *Training* magazine survey of training trends (October 1994) found that 28% of all U.S. organizations stated that some of their teams were self-directed or self-managing. This figure had dropped from 35% reported two years earlier.

What is the Role of Training in the SDT Concept?

Training is a major key to SDT success. In the aforementioned DDI, AQP, and *Industry Week* magazine survey, respondents listed these barriers to self-directed teams: insufficient training (54%); supervisor resistance (47%); incompatible systems (47%); lack of planning—too fast implementation (40%); lack of management support (31%); lack of union support (24%). Note that lack of training was at the top of the list.

DDI consultants Richard Wellins and Jill George, who provided the above figures in "The Key To Self Directed Teams," *Training and Development Journal,* April 1991, quote several officials on the importance of training:

Don't underestimate training or you'll always be playing catch up"

—a plant manager at Rohm and Haas

Training and organizational growth are so woven together that you can't accomplish your objectives without training, both technical and interpersonal.

—a human resource representative at GE Aircraft

Without extensive training, teams aren't effective. Period. I have employees who say they can't believe the positive difference our team training has had on their work.

—a Tennessee Eastern Company training representative

Working in a self-directed team obviously requires many diverse skills and using them in a mature, sophisticated way. The acquisition of team-oriented skills is in addition to learning the many technical (work) tasks of the team so as to become "multi-skilled."

The DDI, AQP, and *Industry Week* magazine survey found that the responding companies offered these types of team training (listed by Wellins and George in *Training and Development Journal,* April 1991): problem solving (83%); meeting skills (65%); communication skills (62%); dealing with conflict (61%); SDT roles/responsibilities (58%); tools/concepts for quality (56%); evaluating team performance (39%); work flow and process analysis (36%); selecting team members

(35%); presentation skills (35%); influencing others (29%); budgeting (14%).

Wellins and George quote trainer Lori Campbell at Schreiber Foods in Arizona on the importance of training in team and interactive skills: "In a team environment, it's critical to know how to talk constructively with peers. That's something employees haven't had to do in the past. Our job is to give them the skills and the interaction opportunities."

Several principles of training SDT members are these, per DDI consultants Wellins and George:

- ☐ A training plan should be developed prior to team implementation.
- ☐ It is essential to involve the team in deciding its own training program.
- ☐ Team members can learn best from one another.
- ☐ It is essential to guard against the sidetracking of training when there are equipment breakdowns, production problems, or quotas unmet.
- ☐ Appropriate steering committees should be set up to assume responsibility for guiding the training process. Committee members should be trained in team concepts to model and reinforce skills of team members on the job.
- ☐ Training makes the most sense when it develops skills that will be used close to the time when they are needed on the job.
- ☐ Training for self-directed teams never ends. There is an on-going need for growth and development.

What Specific Skills are Needed for Team Members to Be Effective?

The following skills are essential.

- ☐ Interpersonal: Listening, communicating, giving and receiving feedback, resolving conflicts, giving praise and support, valuing diversity.
- ☐ Problem solving: Using brainstorming, Pareto analysis, cause-and-effect analysis; using a problem-solving model; striving toward consensus in decisions.
- ☐ Meeting management: Participating in and/or conducting meetings; keeping the team on target; applying task and maintenance roles appropriately.
- ☐ Information sharing
- ☐ Management and administration: Set goals and standards; assign and schedule work; set and meet deadlines; requisition and/or purchase materials

and equipment; control costs; cross-train other team members (to acquire multiple technical skills); improve work methods; coordinate with other shifts; coordinate with external units, both within the organization and outside such as with clients, customers and suppliers; communicate vertically (with the boss); hire new team members; discipline and appraise team members.

Also, management writer Shari Caudron (in "Teamwork Takes Work," *Personnel Journal,* February 1994), stressing that good team members are trained, not born, draws on the incisive work of Michael Leimbach, research director for Wilson Learning Corporation, and recommends that team members receive training in:

Advocating: Learning how to convince others to adopt their point of view.

Inquiring: Listening to and eliciting needed information from teammates.

Tension management: Using and encouraging disagreement/conflict for greater ideation, as opposed to smothering it.

Sharing responsibility: Aligning one's goals with team objectives; functioning in one's role to achieve shared outcomes.

Leadership: Each team member has to adopt leadership roles, as needed, to ensure team success.

Appreciating diversity: Only by valuing team members' differences does synergy (making the whole greater than the sum of its parts) become possible.

Self-awareness: Being self-critical and willing and able to accept constructive feedback from colleagues

Note:

1. Team members obviously would not have all of these skills at the outset, but via continuing training and experience, they will acquire them.
2. Responsibilities assigned to SDTs will vary among organizations; e.g., selection of team members may or may not be delegated to the SDTs.

What Benefits Accrue to Team Members by Acquiring One Another's Skills (Multiple Technical Skills)?

Meeting/training consultants Bob and Ann Harper, authorities on SDTs and co-authors of *Succeeding as a Self-Directed Work Team* (Croton-on-Hudson: MW Corp., 1991), point out these significant benefits:

Replacement capability: There is an ability to pinch-hit for another team member when he is absent.

Staff augmentation: There is an ability to provide added person power when a deadline has to be met.

Enriched problem solving: There is an improved problem-solving capability since all team members share the needed information.

Greater empathy: There is an increased insight/understanding into other team members' problems because each has done the other's job.

Greater creativity: Increased team creativity is possible because each team member has knowledge of all aspects of the team's work.

Growth and career development: As a multi-skilled worker, team members have greater opportunities for personal growth and career development. Why? Because the added skills give them greater value and marketability.

Job challenge: Diverse job functioning provides greater opportunities to engage in more interesting work. Monotony and boredom are eliminated.

Rewards: A climate that recognizes accomplishment readily provides praise and recognition. Team accomplishment is also likely to be rewarded financially by the organization.

Problem identification: By using team problem-solving tools (e.g., Pareto Diagram, cause-and-effect analysis, sampling, etc.), team members understand the total system better and thus have greater capability to make improvements.

Are SDTs for All Work Settings?

Not necessarily. They make sense and can work well if there is a need for high dependency among people engaged in a common, fairly complex process in a shop or office. Conversely, if people are on an assembly line where each worker does a simplified, individualized task (e.g., putting a walnut on a chocolate square), there is no need for an SDT.

SDTs probably would not work well in authoritarian or command-type organizations such as the military or in prisons. Similarly, if the work is highly disciplined or regulation bound, it would be difficult to give this type group real authority to manage itself.

What is the Role of the Leader in an SDT?

While some groups may function without a formally designated leader, most SDTs have one. The leader may be assigned by management or selected by the SDT. However, the role of the leader in an SDT is very different from that of the one in the traditional work unit. He thus is hardly the usual controlling, decision-making boss. Rather, the new role requires functioning as a coach, trainer, tutor, guide, counselor, advisor, listener, facilitator, empowerer, empathizer, coordinator, cheerleader, roadblock remover, and external liaison (with the above level, other departments, and possibly key customers and suppliers).

His new leadership role, then, requires an emphasis upon shared rather than directive leadership. He is not merely concerned with securing compliance, as in traditional work groups, but with tapping potential and unleashing creativity, initiative, and risk-taking.

Added concerns/roles for the effective SDT leader are modeling proper behaviors and attitudes; mediating difficulties and differences among team members; discouraging undesirable behaviors such as buck passing, turf protecting, putting others downs, scapegoating, assignment dodging, foot dragging, showboating; celebrating team progress and accomplishment; valuing the uniqueness of people (appreciation of diversity).

Note:

1. If there is no formally designated leader, the leadership role would be rotated on the basis of the particular expertise required at any one time, e.g., in matters of finance, safety, statistical quality control, presenting data up the line, etc. Management consultant Harlan R. Jessup ("New Roles in Team Leadership," *Training and Development Journal,* November 1990) states that rotation through at least one of the designated leadership roles becomes a condition of team membership. In the "everybody's a leader" approach, typical leadership assignments are these:
   - ☐ **Moderator:** Conducts the team's meetings
   - ☐ **Schedule coordinator:** Relays schedule requirements from production meetings; may provide work assignments
   - ☐ **Recorder:** Keeps minutes of meetings, attendance records, vacation schedules, and overtime records

   Less common roles are these:

   - ☐ **Goal tracker:** Evaluates and posts team performance results
   - ☐ **Training coordinator:** Schedules needed training to upgrade group process skills and multiple (job) skills
   - ☐ **Cheerleader:** schedules celebrations and prompts recognition from managers.

2. The leader's role at the outset of the team's life would not be as broad gauged as described above. Rather, it would only take on all the broadly described dimensions over time, i.e., as the team grows, develops and matures. The leader's role would shift, then, from one of power over and dependence by subordinates to that of influence and interdependence. The diagram on page 416 illustrates this concept.

3. Not all managers can make the transition from traditional controlling management to the facilitating/empowering role. Thus, Northern Telecom found that some 25% of its first-line supervisors left after team direction was adopted (Jana Schilder, "WorkTeams Boost Productivity," *Personnel Journal,* February 1992).

4. Of the many attributes the effective team leader must have, one of the most important is optimism. He must be optimistic about the capability of the work group to transform itself into a true team, of the team's ability to solve whatever problems it may encounter, of the team's capability to grow, broaden, and mature, and of upper management's willingness to support the team whenever support is needed. The optimism shouldn't be a sometime kind of thing as the story below indicates.

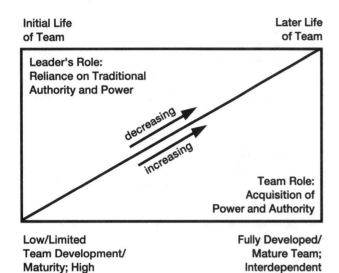

Initial Life of Team — **Later Life of Team**

Leader's Role: Reliance on Traditional Authority and Power

decreasing

increasing

Team Role: Acquisition of Power and Authority

Low/Limited Team Development/ Maturity; High Dependence on Boss — Fully Developed/ Mature Team; Interdependent Functioning

Relationship of leader and group power as the SDT matures.

Story: An executive once asked a friend who worked on Wall Street, "Are you optimistic?" His friend responded, "Why yes. Of course." So the executive asked, "Then why do you look so worried?" Replied the Wall Streeter, "I'm not sure that my optimism is justified."

Is it Easier to Build an SDT Into a New Function or an Ongoing One?

Experience to date indicates that it is easier to do it in a start-up operation because people can be recruited anew, i.e., those who have the all-important capacity for team functioning. Conversely, converting individual players to team players means that one has to provide a lot of training and coaching to remove or temper old work habits. This is not to say that training won't be successful with an established group. Rather, what we're saying is that training takes thought, time, effort, and patience. But the reality is that most SDTs are comprised of people who have been "retrofitted" (trained) to become team members. This means that they have been trained to acquire and apply effectively interpersonal, team, and problem-solving and other business skills as required.

If you were to find yourself involved with self-directed teams, either as a coordinator, sponsor, leader, or facilitator, it is helpful to understand that the well-functioning SDT doesn't become that way by the issuance of a directive or the snap of one's fingers. Rather, it is likely to occur only via gradual, often painful, development

through four states. Trainers/consultants John H. Zenger, Ed Musselwhite, Kathleen Hurson, and Craig Perron, in *Leading Teams: Mastering the New Role* (Homewood, IL: 1994), cite these four phases of team development:

1. **Forming.** Group members are groping with questions such as these: What's expected of me? How do I fit in? What are we supposed to do? What are our rules? People play it safe, no one feels secure enough to be "real," so little conflict emerges. As the leader, you'll have to help the team develop the ground rules governing the interaction among members and the leader.

2. **Storming:** Early enthusiasm is likely to give way to frustration and anger. People are struggling to work together. There is mindless resistance, hostility, wrangling, subgrouping, jealousy, and disgust with the whole process. Ground rules may be attacked and splintered. But all this means that the process of synergy is underway.

3. **Norming:** In this tranquil phase, balance enters into group life. Standard routines, helpful to accomplishment, emerge. Negative behaviors—grandstanding, powerplays—are dropped. Team members are trying hard to be cooperative, but even to the point where good ideas may be held back to avoid conflict. As a sensitive leader, your job is to aid the team to overcome this unhelpful reticence, doing this by augmenting their responsibility and authority.

4. **Performing:** Things are now ready to roll. The team has acquired the proper degree of self-confidence. Disagreement is handled constructively. People take measured risks and apply their enthusiasm and energy to the challenges they face. Because there is now a high level of mutual trust, the leader steps back to let the team do its thing.

Note: Although the team has worked itself through the four phases of development, there may be relapses to an earlier stage such as forming, particularly if team members are added or lost, or other unusual pressures arise. As the leader, you may have to assume a more active role to help the team find its balance and resume its normal productive role.

How Does the Reward System Differ for People in SDTs?

On the financial side, team members may be compensated (a) individually for the acquisition and use of

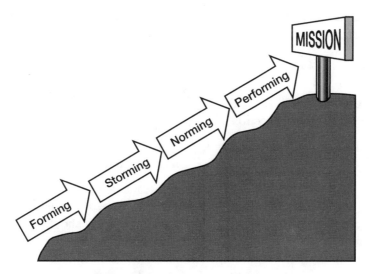

Four-stage development of new groups.

skills, and (b) for team accomplishment via profit sharing. The teams (previously paid hourly) may also be paid on a regular *salary* basis and time clocks eliminated. **Note:** The formal reward systems typically are skill- or team-based, as opposed to seniority-based.

However, the most significant rewards—the real turn-ons for people—are non-financial: identification with the team; pride in the team; work variety (use of multiple skills); growth on the job; career growth; involvement in planning, problem solving, and decision making; pride in the quality of work produced; functioning (intermittently) in a leadership capacity; being "in the know," i.e., having information shared freely with one; helping one's teammates functioning in a work culture marked by autonomy, trust, openness, cooperation, support, respect, encouragement of innovation, and high standards. Plus, there's a spirit of inquiry: There are no taboos about questioning existing policies, procedures, goals, standards, programs, or products.

An interesting non-financial rewards program was developed by U.S. West Communication's Seattle Small Business Services office in conjunction with management, the union, and employees (reported in *Quality Assurance Bulletin,* Section 2, August 25, 1991, Bureau of Business Practice): time off with and without pay; staffers are given the chance to do their favorite work; opportunities are provided to advance employee skills via internal and external courses and conferences; use of flex time; participation in "team-building days" to improve team functioning.

At General Motors Saturn Corporation Plant in Spring Hill, Tennessee, any Saturn team member can call a meeting on any topic that bears on improving the company or its product (reported in *Meetings and Conventions,* March 1991). Empowerment of this sort is, indeed, a strong psychological reward.

Organizational psychologist Dr. Judith Mower, who has studied team rewards, believes that rewards should be given throughout a project's life, not just at project's end. Because some projects may continue over several years, it is essential that team members receive positive feedback well in advance of the completion date. Mower sees the three-fourths mark as a time when the team needs a morale-building uplift. Says Mower, "That's when morale typically declines, when the team leader is likely to get the most criticism, and when people begin to grieve because they sense their project is coming to an end" (reported by Virginia Johnson, Manager, 3M Meeting Management Institute, Austin, Texas, in "Total Quality Management," *Successful Meetings,* May 1992).

Adds Mower, other psychologically appropriate times to provide rewards are at the start of the project, at the start or end of a team meeting, when a milestone is reached, when the team weathers a crisis or solves a tough problem, and at the end of the project to celebrate it. But the strongest reward is one the team informally invents itself, e.g., meeting for lunch every Friday.

What problems may the team encounter?

Dr. Glenn Varney of Management Advisory Associates, Inc., Bowling Green, Ohio, points out the following difficulties that beset the SDT:

☐ **Expectations:** They may be set too high, creating frustration and disappointment.

☐ **Facilitator or supervisory role:** This new role may be hard for traditionally oriented managers to accept and/or execute.

☐ **Human resource office responsibility:** The HR office may feel a loss of power, e.g., in selection, setting compensation, etc.

☐ **Measurement:** This is a difficult task, but it is vital, for management wants to know what the payoffs, if any, are.

☐ **Regression:** Problems and disappointments may encourage a feeling that "we're in over our heads." But the team can't abandon ship when the going gets tough.

☐ **Pace:** Don't expect too rapid results. Launching an SDT effectively may take months, even years.

☐ **Interfacing:** The SDT can't operate in isolation from other departments. It must stay in close contact with them to learn of their needs and thinking.

☐ **Costs:** Expect management to ask critical questions. Anticipate this and collect data to show worthwhile results.

What Are the Pointers to Observe in Making a Transition to SDTs?

Management consultant Bob Hughes offers these suggestions (reported in "Tips for Teams," *Training,* February 1994):

1. Baseline Performance Data

To be certain that changes in performance can be ascertained, establish baseline performance data prior to training any teams. Otherwise, performance gains will be hard to track. Decide on how to keep score, the current status, the hoped-for future status, and how you should proceed to get there.

2. Decision Boundaries

Make clear what level of decisions the teams can make and what decisions are to be left to others in the organization. In other words, what they can do and what they can't.

3. Implementation Time Lines

Spell out clearly to everyone when the team action begins for particular work units. This allows those who continue in traditional work units to know when their conversion to SDTs may begin.

4. Rewards

Rewards should accrue in three ways: individual contribution, team-performance bonuses, and organizational bonuses (gain-sharing).

5. Business Education

If the teams are to make business and management decisions, they need appropriate business and management training. Teams should learn everything from balance sheets to scheduling to inventory turns.

6. Team Climate

The work environment in the SDT is one of high expectations. Team members are responsible to one another, so those who may have been successful at goofing off under a single boss will be in for a shock. Games, excuses, delays, and the like won't be tolerated by one's hard-working, performance-oriented, serious peers.

Additional pointers are presented by management consultant Lawrence Holpp ("Applied Empowerment," *Training,* February 1994):

☐ In respect to the aforementioned "decision boundaries," it is prudent to phase in added responsibilities on a specific time basis. **Example:** An assembly team may already be conducting meetings, conducting safety checks, and performing general housekeeping duties. So the plan may call for the team to take over responsibility for the following in the first three months: responsibility for inventory control, daily quality checks, and handling production changeovers. In the following three months, the team may begin to order supplies, maintain budgets, and meet with customers. A longer-range goal—in 12–18 months—might be to participate in sales presentations, job redesign, and team-leader rotation.

☐ Appropriate training must be provided each step of the way. Teams can't be expected to assume new tasks until the proper groundwork has been established.

☐ Don't overlook quality. Check with customers to be certain that quality of goods or services is as high as or higher than previously.

☐ The measurement system should cover how people feel about the new process; their success in broadening their jobs; whether bottom-line results are being delivered in terms of cost, quality, and productivity.

HOW TO MANAGE THE PROJECT TEAM

To an increasing degree, organizations today are creating project teams for such purposes as new product development or quality improvement, or to solve an important organizational problem. Typically, management is interested in an innovative solution or approach that is not likely to be secured in a regular operating department. In contrast, the project team has greater flexibility in staffing, being free to tap the human resources of a number of departments. Also, it can concentrate its attention on the assigned, innovative task without being concerned with the usual operating responsibilities of a given department.

So if you were asked by top management to head up a special project team, how would you go about it to ensure that your team produced a triple-A end result? Here are some suggestions to help you get your project team off to a good start and to produce top quality accomplishments.

Be Certain That You Understand What is Really Expected

It is not unusual for project teams to flounder around and produce very little because their missions were quite murky. I recall a CEO who was extremely unhappy with the conduct of the training function, particularly the head of training. He established a project team to study the training operation. Project members were brought in to the national office from six field locations. The Project Team deliberated full time for seven work days and developed an elaborate report that recommended many new training courses. The Project Team had assumed that the CEO wanted an overall assessment of the training needs, including an expanded training program, which was not the case. When the CEO saw the report he angrily slammed it to his desk and said, "This isn't what I wanted at all."

In general, it's a good idea to get a written statement of the assigned mission, including anticipated outcomes of the study. If there is any fuzziness in the statement, be certain to get a clarification.

Based on Your Understanding of the Mission, Recruit Project Team Members

Take into account their reputations and capabilities, securing a diverse group so that inputs from a variety of perspectives will be certain to come forth in team deliberations. **Note:** A good guideline for selection is to think in terms of the stakeholders involved, that is, those who have a stake or interest in seeing the problem solved properly.

Try to Secure a Comfortable Working Room, One That Will Be the Group's for the Life of the Project

In this manner, the walls can be used permanently for bulletin boards and flipcharts. This will provide the project team with a sense of ownership and permanence. Members will be able to refer to it as "our team project room."

Send a Memo to Project Team Members

Welcome team members to the project, stating the nature of the project mission, indicating when and where the first session will be held. Advise them of materials, if any, they should bring to session one.

Plan the First Session Carefully

This is your opportunity to set the proper tone and tempo for the project team's work. By tone we mean a climate that encourages mutual respect, camaraderie, full opportunities for communication, participation, and openness. Creativity/innovation rather than traditional thinking is wanted. Be sure to provide food and beverages to emphasize the relaxed atmosphere.

If team members do not know one another well or at all, have them introduce themselves to the team, indicating how their particular competencies will move the group toward mission accomplishment. Let the team know of your own strengths, too.

Discuss the assigned mission to be certain that there is full understanding and support for it. Also, indicate clearly when the team has to complete its work.

Note:

1. Consider having a top official, one who instituted the project, meet with the group to explain the mission and to respond to possible questions about it.

2. If practicable, set target dates (milestones) for the accomplishment of the various stages of the project.
3. Indicate what is now known about the topic—what background has been developed, if any, and what recommendations/decisions already have been made.
4. Advise what resources now are available to the project to ensure that it goes well. Discuss with the group the adequacy of the resource commitment based on the team's understanding of the project.

Have the group develop guidelines for project team operation such as rotation of the chairperson, when meetings are to be held, minute taking and distribution, that team decisions will be made on the basis of consensus rather than voting, etc. **Note:** This is essentially the first opportunity for the team to work together on a task. There may be some awkwardness in this first try. Nevertheless, it will provide an opportunity for joint action and to produce a concrete end product.

In conjunction with development of the ground rules, it may be desirable to have the team first list on a flipchart factors—procedures, behaviors, attitudes—that (a) make for successful project teams and (b) hinder high-level accomplishment. **Note:** Contributions to the two lists need not necessarily be made on the basis of personal experience. Rather, members' ideas may be based on their assumptions about effective team operation. The rationale for this exercise is threefold:

1. To stimulate thinking about team effectiveness,
2. To give the group an early chance to work together on a task, and
3. To demonstrate that you, as project leader, are very much interested in quality team performance as the vehicle to quality mission accomplishment.

Although You Are the Designated Project Leader, You Will be More Effective in That Role if You De-emphasize Your Formal Status

Strive for intimacy rather than distance with the team. Rotate the chairperson role at meetings. As project leader you have many things to do besides formally chairing all the meetings, e.g., serving as liaison to key personnel in the organization including reporting on progress; building team *esprit de corps;* giving praise and support; calling meetings; attending to the minutes of the meetings, etc. **Note:** Because you are not the actual supervisor of project members, you will be most effective if you think in terms of influence rather than authority, power, and control.

Stay in Touch With "Those on the Outside" Who Have a Keen Interest in What the Project Team Produces

So keep stakeholders, top management, and your boss informed regularly about progress. Of course, you can't release information that is not firmed up or is in a confidential state.

If You Are Project Leader in Addition to Your Regular Duties, You May Have to Work Harder or Perform Overtime to Keep Current in Your Regular Job

Secure your boss' expectations in advance as to how he sees your added responsibility in relation to your regular role.

Encourage the project team to think in terms of evaluation. Assessment should take these forms:

Content evaluation: How are we progressing toward mission accomplishment? What is our progress in relation to our deadline? If we are behind, what can we do to forge ahead? Do we need added resources/help from the organization?

Session evaluation: How each session proceeded; what went well, what went less than well; what can be done to strengthen future sessions. Conduct such an evaluation after session one to set the tone for assessment of future sessions.

Process evaluation: How well is the team working as a team; what needs improvement; what should the team do more of, less of, and keep doing.

Management consultant Beverly Kaye ("Advisory Groups on the High Cs," *Training and Development,* January 1992) lists seven components (seven Cs) of successful advisory groups that might serve as a guide to team project evaluation. They are:

1. **Clout:** The group must have enough of a high "clout quotient" to get things done, to do more than just talk. This includes having access to the top management of the organization, being able to tap the human and physical resources of the outfit,

conducting pilot projects, collecting data via surveys, arranging for focus groups, etc.

2. **Compensation:** People want (and need) to know that their contributions are valued; they want their good efforts to be recognized. Of course, the collegial associations, the work of the group, and learning from it are worthwhile rewards.

3. **Contemplation:** Thinking to get team members' creative juices flowing is a must. The team atmosphere must be such as to support that new thinking.

4. **Conviction:** The team must feel that there are some significant tenets to which the team subscribes. Without principles or beliefs, the team is essentially rudderless. The team also needs courage to stay with its convictions. Taking a stand is a great team unifier. The old saying, "If you don't stand for something, you'll fall for anything," still makes a lot of sense.

5. **Conversion:** By virtue of its work, the team converges toward conversion. That is to say, they develop a common vision of what they are trying to accomplish. As they buy into it, they begin to educate others (non-team members) about its importance. The above four Cs contributed to the conversion process. The end result: a set of new and renewed beliefs centered in team members, possibly extending to other key personnel in the outfit.

6. **Competencies:** Experience in the work of the team produces new concepts and skills for team members. For example, meeting in the numerous sessions of the project team provides opportunities to learn about group dynamics, group leadership and followership, conflict management, planning, meeting facilitation, and the like.

7. **Closure:** Celebrating closure gives everyone a sense of contribution and completion. The team's successes over the life of the project are now recognized by the organization as well as by the team.

Don't Overlook the Importance of the Fun and Social Side of Group Life

Bring in food and beverages to sessions; meet for lunch or dinner; have a weekend swim party or barbecue. Look for opportunities to introduce fun into the group.

Anticipate That the Life of the Project Will Come to an End

By project's end, team members will have learned to appreciate one another, and an element of sadness, possibly "separation anxiety," may well arise because the team must now disband. As team leader, you may wish to let everyone verbalize how they feel about the group, its members, its significant moments, its accomplishments, and the inevitable separation. Ask if there is an interest in keeping in touch, possibly meeting together six or twelve months from now, if practicable. Certainly team members can now network on a one-on-one basis. Let the group decide the kind of closure ceremony or celebration they wish to have for their adjournment.

CONCURRENT ENGINEERING: USING TEAM COLLABORATION FOR PRODUCT DEVELOPMENT

Traditional product design, per management consultant Richard E. Anderson ("HRD's Role in Concurrent Engineering," *Training and Development,* June 1993), encourages a kind of "hands-off" policy between product designers and manufacturing engineers. The former group often works in isolation in an off-site design center or in secured areas on site. Also, the designers see themselves as an elite group, reluctant to rub elbows with the manufacturing engineers in their plant environments. To add to the existing status barriers, shop people without college degrees may be promoted from the shop floor to engineers.

Manufacturing engineers see the designers as "ivory tower techies" who throw elegant designs at them and then say, "Build them," but offer no help for this.

In any case, if manufacturing firms are to maintain their competitiveness today, the isolation and status problems between the two groups have to be overcome. How to do this? Via concurrent engineering—a team-oriented approach to product development in which designers and engineers work on design and manufacturability simultaneously. The aim of concurrent engineering is to reduce time-to-market and improve quality in the process.

Overall objectives of concurrent engineering, then, are to:

☐ Speed up product development
☐ Identify problems early on

☐ Reduce the possibility of having to make costly engineering changes later in the process

☐ Reduce costs due to last-minute delays in the production cycle

☐ Reduce time-to-market

It thus is essential to merge the two units of design and manufacturing into a single design-production team. And if the actual manufacturing is done outside the plant, the external suppliers should be included in the early stages of the product's design so that they can provide both design services and production know-how.

Experience to date indicates that merely creating a cross-functional team is not a certain road to success. Conflicts may arise and reduce team cohesiveness. Or this new diversity may impede innovative problem solving because team members may opt for harmony as a means of reducing disagreement. **The answer:** team development via training.

For example, in Deere's Harvester Works, the concurrent engineering effort involved training of the groups in "soft skills"—team building, problem solving, and conflict resolution. Also, to break down the functional barriers, the designers and engineers formed teams that included personnel in purchasing, supply, and service areas as well as employees from the shop floor.

Additionally, managers at upper levels now give teams information that in the past was treated as confidential. The goal is to make certain that team members understand their roles in the context of business goals, market needs and the firm's bottom line.

At Ingersoll-Rand, per Richard Anderson, team members created innovative ways to resolve their conflicts and to develop trust. They went to horse races and hockey games together and went to the team leader's home for swimming, basketball, and outdoor cooking. The team asserts that barbecues are basic to their team-building effort and the key to project success.

Cadillac Motor Division's teams introduced "jeans days" to further team building, abandoning their suits and ties for jeans and workshirts. They also joined assemblers on the plant floor. By working side by side with shop floor employees, engineers garnered first-hand information on design glitches. They received coaching in assembly practices from line operators. They also developed a real-world appreciation of their primary in-house customer—the car assemblers.

Also essential to breaking down barriers between/among departments are these added strategies: cross training, rotation of engineers between functions, and career flexibility as opposed to promotion only in a single functional area. At Xerox Corporation and Apple Computers, new design engineers must spend at least six months in manufacturing prior to formal entry into their design jobs.

Japanese firms stress cross-functional career development for their engineer and research staffs. In fact, they develop generalist engineers with capabilities in both manufacturing and design.

The bottom line, per Richard Anderson: The design phase of product development typically represents some 5% of a product's cost. But design decisions affect at least 70% of overall production cost. So *getting it right the first time* depends on the staffs and their organization more than on technology.

TEAM SELLING: HOW TO MAKE IT WORK

Team selling is a response to today's competitive world economy. Customers are not only buying a product or service. They also expect their suppliers to help them solve their business problems. Marketing authority Jay M. Orlin ("Selling in Teams," *Training and Development,* December 1993) quotes one computer company executive as follows: "To be successful in the future, the marketplace is demanding that we join in consultancy partnerships to deliver business solutions. The consultancy relationship will be what we sell first, followed by hardware technology."

Team selling, per management consultant Mark Blessington, "Five Ways to Make Team Selling Work (Really)" *Business Month,* August 1989), means selling with the aid of other sales and nonsales personnel, those who know much more about a product or industry than any single salesperson possibly could. They form a team with a leader who serves as both strategist and information pipeline, plus a supporting group that may include top executives, engineers, product planners, technicians, sales reps, and sales personnel from other locations.

In concert, they thus are enabled to launch an all-out, coordinated effort to secure and maintain a given account. So when the team meets with a prospect or customer, they can develop precise product specs and manufacturing schedules, meeting customer needs better.

Consultative team selling is neither fast-talking the customer nor rendering slick product demonstrations, says Orlin. Rather, it is the art of developing long-term relationships, including acting with integrity, honesty and professionalism. It requires delivering bad news as readily as good news. It means being a committed team salesperson that the client/customer can trust. Sales personnel need to become highly knowledgeable about the customer's business and problems. They must also become A-1 listeners and communicators.

As a team, sales personnel can obtain customer information more quickly and accurately than an individual salesperson can. This high-quality information permits the team to make quicker, more effective decisions. The team can decide better where to put its efforts and what to defer. The team knows when it is selling its company's strong points and where the customer sits in the buying circle. Collectively, team members can use their creativity to isolate customer needs/problems and come up with innovative answers related thereto.

Finally, says Orlin, because team players are likely to serve on other teams, now or at a later date, there is a built-in, healthy cross-fertilization of experience and information, all of which augments the supplier's institutional knowledge base.

Per Mark Blessington, the firm entering into team selling should recognize that there are obstacles to overcome in team selling:

Customer Expectations

Customers may assume that because several people are assigned to them, they will receive double or triple the usual attention. So to avoid disappointing the customer, the sales team must decide in advance and communicate to the customer how far the firm can go to fulfill likely requests in anticipated situations.

Leadership

The effective sales team needs a strong leader, one who can provide the needed direction, motivation, and coordination. The emphasis on selection is to seek non-technical traits, particularly the ability to influence as opposed to coerce, and to plan rather than to react.

Team Integration

Team selling is not likely to work if the firm places the sales team outside the regular sales organization. The sales team thus should be integrated into the sales organization, being viewed as a critical addition to the overall sales efforts. In the absence of integration, there may be a reluctance to use the new program. Why?

Because salespeople are apt to fear they would lose control and their incentive income.

Motivation

Managers may fear that sales personnel will lose their motivation if they sell in teams. Why? Because their individual contribution can't be recognized. Also, there may be a fear that a weak performer will drag down the overall team productivity. To overcome these possibilities, these things should be done: Remind team personnel often why team selling is critical; measure both individual and team performance and provide the team with such data; establish the norm that performance problems are team problems; seek out ideas to improve team success; and celebrate team as opposed to individual accomplishment.

Sales Credit

The problem: How do you provide sales credit and set quotas with a mix of individual and team selling? **The answer:** Use the double-credit approach on national accounts. National account managers receive credit and so do those working on the same account on a local basis. Split sales credit when a few peers work on the same accounts. If it is impossible to determine who sold what, it may be essential to use a combination of double and split credits.

To make certain that team selling pays off, Allen S. Boress, author of *I Hate Selling* (New York: AMACOM, 1995), offers these guidelines to prepare for the sales meeting and the conduct of the meeting itself ("Ten Rules of Effective Team Selling," *Supervisory Management,* February 1995):

1. **Choose group members with care.** If the chemistry among the team isn't right, the client will readily pick it up.
2. **Provide a capable team leader.** The leadership role is to maintain control of the sales meeting, ask most of the questions and route the client's questions to the most knowledgeable team member for the best reply.
3. **Provide for advance preparation.** In advance of the sales meeting, a pre-briefing is essential to discuss the agenda and to develop an action plan.
4. **Use team member questions for agenda preparation.** At the pre-briefing, each team member brings along three questions for discussion as an aid to mold the agenda.

5. **Keep the team small.** Only have the essential reps attend the the sales meeting to avoid possible problems.

6. **Respond precisely and briefly to client questions.** The sales meeting is not an educational forum, says Boress. So brief, pointed responses to client questions are essential. This will ensure that enough time is available to respond to the customer's most important concerns.

7. **Plan a flexible agenda.** The aim of the meeting is to meet client needs. The team, therefore, must be adaptable enough to shift gears in line with the particular direction the meeting takes.

8. **Team thinking must be unified.** Those on the selling team must present a united front, all differences having been settled previously.

9. **Produce a result, even if small.** The team should expect to return with some selling success, regardless of size. The team should be committed to this goal.

10. **Evaluate results.** Critique the meeting—what went well, what went less than well. Assign follow-up responsibilities to team members.

The bottom line: If there are real gains to be garnered by improving relationships with customers, team selling may well be the answer. Problems which may arise are surmountable, given the right degree of commitment and thought.

GEARING UP THE TEAM FOR QUALITY

The team can be a tremendous force for quality, a goal most organizations today are avidly seeking. Particularly significant are two factors: (1) the synergistic capabilities of the team and (2) peer pressure. The latter force ensures that everyone gets aboard the quality train without foot-dragging and continues to perform at the level the team expects.

But the unleashing of the team's latent capabilities won't occur by itself. Rather, leadership to build momentum for quality is essential. Dr. Eberhard E. Scheuing, professor of marketing at St. John's University, New York, suggests ("How to Build a Quality Conscious Team," *Supervisory Management,* January 1990) that these steps be followed:

Hold a Freewheeling Meeting. Functioning as a facilitator, meet with the group to discuss in depth the goal of quality. The aim at this "kick-off" meeting is to secure agreement that quality is a worthy goal, not to impose it on the group. Group ownership of the quality vision is imperative if the idea is to really take root.

Identify Team Capabilities. Current strengths and weaknesses of the team in the quality area should be flipcharted. "Let it all hang out" so that existing competencies can be assessed.

Discuss the Value/Significance of Quality. Quality should be defined so that full understanding of it exists. **Key points:** Do it right the first time so that rework is eliminated. Then expect these gains: lowered cost; increased productivity; better profitability; greater pride in product/service.

Build a Passion for Quality. What is needed is full commitment, not passive lip service. This applies to the total team.

Establish Goals for Quality. The team should set challenging but reachable goals for quality. Improvement, to be realistic, should be incremental, not sought for in giant steps. Unreasonable goals will only dampen team ardor for quality.

Identify and Remove Inhibitors. The team must put its collective finger on those barriers that now exist, be they policies, procedures, equipment, workflow, or environmental factors such as poor lighting or excessive noise.

Support Quality Efforts. As better things begin to happen, people need praise, recognition and encouragement. In their absence, the all-out effort is likely to falter.

Prevent Defects. Work processes must be controlled so that defects are eliminated while work is in process. End-of-the line inspection for quality is "old hat" and is no longer workable. The only acceptable standard today is zero defects. Finding defects should be subject to praise, not blame. Quality will suffer if team members feel they have to please the boss rather than the customer.

Measure Results. Quality must be measured, not assessed at an abstract global level. Customer satisfaction, as well as team outputs, are the basic measuring rods.

Institute a motivating reward system. The goal should be to reward progress and to correct weaknesses. Bonuses should be shared equitably among team members.

Review Progress and Establish New Goals. Quality, as a process rather than a program, means setting new, higher goals—"stretch," if you will. Continuous improvement is the only name of the game.

Rekindle the Flame. Obviously, once major changes are made in processes and quality mounts, future gains will be less spectacular. Nevertheless, it is the team leader's job to reawaken interest, to keep the ball rolling, to avoid any complacency from setting in.

RESOLVING INTER-GROUP CONFLICT

Don't push your opponent against a locked door.

—John F. Kennedy (1917–1963), 35th president of the U.S. (1961–1963)

Teams not only have their internal problems to deal with, but they may have disagreements with other units. Some of these differences may be minor, others major. Some may be short-lived. Others may continue and fester for long periods of time.

The effective team tries to prevent, if possible, such conflict situations. Or, if they do arise, it tries conscientiously to resolve them. In our chapter "How to Work with Peers/Colleagues and Manage Conflict" we present a number of helpful strategies to resolve inter-group differences. These include image development, role negotiation, and the use of two problem-solving models. Underlying these several approaches is the need to identify and support *superordinate* goals—i.e., what is best for the total organization, not just for us or them.

Of course, resolution of conflict depends on both parties recognizing and rising above these two attitudinal ailments:

☐ "A dialog of the deaf"—agreement is impossible if one side doesn't listen to the other.

☐ "Immaculate perception"—conflict resolution can't succeed if either or both parties to the conflict assume that "The way we see it is the way it really is." What is essential, then, is *truth seeking* not "truth" presenting.

So both parties have to think in terms of "breakthrough" rather than "breakup." This means that there must be a lot of broad-gauged thinking, i.e., seeking a win-win solution rather than merely a compromise, which one wag defined as "a solution that combines the worst features of all the alternatives."

Note: There are some 5,000 "peer mediation" programs in U.S. public and private schools (both elementary and high school levels) designed to solve student conflict amicably. Student mediators are trained to spot assorted spats, skirmishes, and more serious violence, and then to intervene in a mediating peacekeeper role. The first step for the student diplomat is to draw on his training and recite the four rules basic to resolving the disagreement between/among the belligerents:

1. Each combatant (or would-be combatant) restates the problem.
2. Each of the heated students agrees not to interrupt one another.
3. Each agrees to solve the problem.
4. Feelings may be freely talked about.

If a fight still erupts, teachers are alerted.

The results: Student violence and suspensions have been reduced dramatically. Also, a San Francisco high school finds an improvement in behavior and less acting out in class. Says the dean, "They now have a place to go to talk before fighting" (Sharon Massey, "Schools Find Pupil Mediators Cuts Violence," *The Wall Street Journal,* February 24, 1994).

Hopefully, if schoolkids can resolve their differences, teams in organizations should be able to do as well.

OVERCOMING THE "GROUP THINK" TRAP

The thrust of this chapter is that a team can be a powerful influence on productivity, innovation, control, improvement of quality, and upgrading of customer service. The flipside of the coin, however, is that a group can impose conformity on team members—"group think"—thereby stifling its potential for creativity and original thought.

In a 3M study conducted by its Meeting Management Institute, 37% of meeting participants "felt pressure to express an opinion with which they did not agree," per 3M Institute Manager Virginia Johnson (reported in "The

Group Think Trap," *Successful Meetings,* September 1992). That dissent can be readily stiffled by a group is a concern of which any manager should be acutely aware.

Johnson cites the work of social psychologist Dr. Irving Janis who, in his now classic *Victims of Group Think* (Boston: Houghton-Mifflin, 1972), listed several major U.S. political events that were subject to group think and thus produced highly inadequate problem solving: the Vietnam War, Cambodian bombing, Bay of Pigs, Watergate, and, earlier, the decimation of our fleet at Pearl Harbor in 1941. The list could be updated by adding the space shuttle *Challenger* disaster in 1986, wherein decision makers launched the shuttle despite the misgivings of key engineers.

Drawing on Dr. Janis' provocative book, Virginia Johnson outlines eight symptoms of group think:

1. **Illusions of invulnerability by the group.** People erroneously believe that they are immune from mistakes.
2. **Illusions of the group's inherent morality.** A strong, unquestioned faith exits in the "rightness" of its decisions.
3. **Closed-mindedness.** Team members discount new or opposing data. They focus grandly instead on past accomplishments.
4. **Negative stereotyping of those outside the group.** Stereotyping "the enemy" as evil, they reject criticism from others. There is essentially an "us-against-them" outlook, with a paranoid feeling that these outsiders are "out to get us." ("Who is not with us is against us.")
5. **Self-censorship of deviant behavior by individual members.** The pressures begin to build on dissenters and, in time, they may start to devalue their own opinions.
6. **Direct pressure on deviant group members.** Dissenting team members are subject to out-and-out ridicule. **The message:** Adopting an opposing view is not only unacceptable, but downright disloyal.
7. **Mindguarding to ensure conformity.** The mindguarding phenomenon protects the group from new, threatening ideas. (This is akin to a bodyguard protecting one from physical hurt.) Expression of non-conforming beliefs/ideas are discouraged; even documents that go against group thinking may be suppressed.
8. **An illusion of unanimity by the group.** The obvious norm that gets established is that total agreement by the group is essential. The resultant behavior, based essentially on a false sense of group unity, is a high eagerness to arrive at a decision.

What these symptoms add up to is that if one is surrounded by "yes men" (or women) who fail to challenge assumptions and act creatively, unwanted setbacks or even disasters are certain to be created.

How can group think be overcome? Virginia Johnson suggests we consider the work of psychologist Dr. James K. Esser, Lamar University, Beaumont, Texas, a leading group think researcher who offers these strategies to avoid the group think trap:

Set an Open Climate. The manager should encourage a totally free, open atmosphere for group discussion and problem solving. He should stress that (a) everyone's views are wanted and (b) differing approaches to the problem are essential to reach a high-quality solution.

Don't Overcontrol. Avoid behaviors that communicate that you're in charge and that the group should go in a certain direction. Consider using an outside group facilitator to resolve conflict.

Use a Problem-Solving Model. Train and insist that the group use a logical, sequential problem-solving model. This will ensure proper problem definition and generation of a number of solution alternatives for evaluation by the team.

Seek Dissent. Several techniques for this are to appoint a devil's advocate, have everyone serve as a critical evaluator, and break the total group into subgroups to assess/critique the possible solutions to the problem.

Watch Group Silence. Silence doesn't mean consent. It may mean a reluctance to speak up for fear of being "unpopular" or "looking stupid."

Get Outside Feedback. Don't assume all the wisdom resides in the group. That may or may not be true. It thus may be wiser to secure feedback from knowledgeable outsiders. Sheltering the group from external, objective critique does the group a disservice.

Allow Enough Time. Rushing to a decision may well do the group in, insofar as a high-quality decision is concerned. In fact, it may be good business to adjourn, let everyone sleep on things and come back later for a second go at the possible solution.

Are You an Effective Team Leader? A Self-Quiz

Now that you have worked your way through the pages on team work and team building, you may wish to see what your own orientation is toward this leadership skill area. The self-quiz that follows should serve to give you a reading along this line.

Team Leadership Quiz

Select the one best decision, as you see it, to resolve each of the 10 problems below. Enter your choice in the blank answer line after each problem. Scoring instructions follow the quiz.

1. You have a relatively new secretary (four months on the job). She recently has been making requests of you to attend outside workshops, the brochures for which claim will improve her skills. You are not so sure of the claims in the brochures, the courses cost considerable money, and, besides, she's only been here a short time.
   a) You tell her that she is a relatively new employee, the course costs a fair amount of money and when you, yourself, see a worthwhile course you'll simply send her. You want to make it clear that any decision about training is yours, not hers.
   b) You don't really see the need for this, but finesse the situation by telling her to keep looking at the brochures; to save them for comparison purposes; and when the right course comes along, that might be the time to do something about it. You avoid any specific promises, however, and hope that this whim will pass as she gets more seasoning on the job.
   c) You sit down with her to discuss her capabilities, career objectives, training needs, etc., and mutually agree on the best training course she should take. Both of you will watch the incoming brochures for such a course and you will support her on this.
   d) This seems to be premature, so you decide not to act. You don't tell her that you don't intend to do anything about her interest, but assume that if you don't respond she'll get the message. As you see it, this seems to be a case where the less said the better.

   My decision is _____ (enter a, b, c, or d).

2. You are the head of a small company which reports to a successful parent company. Your subsidiary has begun to face severe competition. **The result:** Your once quite-profitable firm is barely in the black, and prospects for turning things around are bleak. The parent company hasn't gotten tough about things, but you wonder how long that will last.
   a) You call your key managerial group together and give them what you feel is a complete and realistic new productivity and efficiency program. This entails higher production goals for everyone, plus considerable cost-cutting programs such as on travel to outside training conferences, magazine subscriptions, advertising, new hires, etc. There are a few questions, but basically everyone now understands what the new thrust is, that "economy is the name of the game."
   b) You call your managerial group together, give them all the facts and figures as to where the company stands, remind them of and compliment them on their past successes, and request their cooperation in the difficult days ahead. You close the meeting by adding that if anyone has any ideas about these problems your door is open, as it always has been.
   c) You call a group meeting to work on the tough problems facing the company. As company president you are really the only one who has "the big picture." But there's no harm in getting a good discussion going. You have found in the past that if you let people talk long enough quite often they will come up with the programs and ideas you favor.
   d) You decide to use your team as a problem-solving and decision-making group. You tell them that "we're all in this together and that collectively we are going to hammer out a productivity, quality and improved service program that makes sense to everyone here and that all of us can commit ourselves to."

   My decision is _____ (enter a, b, c, or d).

3. You are the head of a department with seven supervisors. You meet for regular weekly staff meetings plus special problem-solving meetings as may be necessary. At times the meetings get pretty heated as people get caught up in their own strong feelings

about the issues involved. Today you are presiding at one of the "hottest" meetings ever, with outspoken disagreements popping up all over the place on a particular issue.

a) You welcome the frank and open discussion because you feel disagreement and difference are the road to creativity.

b) All this disagreement and raising of voices makes you feel uncomfortable. You finally intervene and "pour oil on the trouble waters" by saying: "OK, OK, let's not get so emotional about this. Let's just agree we can't agree and go on to our next topic."

c) You feel that things are really getting out of your control so you intervene by saying: "OK, we've kicked this one around long enough. I'm the boss so I'll just have to make a decision on it. This is what we're going to do . . ."

d) You realize that the group is split down the middle on this issue and isn't ever going to make any progress. At the same time, you don't want to take sides and there's a lot of other business to take care of at this meeting. So you set up a small study group to examine the issue further and make some recommendations at a later time, no date specified. You have found in the past that "sending it to committee" looks good, that is, it shows your interest; but it's a convenient way of getting the group to go on to some other topics.

My decision is _____ (enter a, b, c, or d).

4. You are the leader of a work group that meets frequently to solve problems. One thing that you notice is that when one of your newer members (Sally) makes a point, she frequently is interrupted or even ignored. As a result she typically clams up after that, and you wonder what action you should take, if any, about this.

a) You decide to ignore the problem because, as a newer member, Sally has to "earn her way" to be heard. Time will probably solve the problem anyhow. At least you feel that's what the group thinks.

b) You believe strongly this is a group issue. You can't have a team if one member is constantly ignored. You decide to level with the group about how you feel. So you confront them with their inconsiderate behavior toward Sally and state that the team can't afford to lose out on anyone's ideas.

c) You decide to talk to Sally the next morning about her feelings about the previous day's meeting and her participation in it. You don't intend to do anything about it, but passing along a little sympathy can't hurt. So you tell her that you recognize that she's not getting her share of the available "air time," but "to hang in there." You make a vague promise about doing something about it "when the right opportunity comes along."

d) You decide not to take any positive action because Sally is a "big girl" and it's up to her to enter into things. But you decide to call on Sally occasionally, just to let everyone know that you're the boss and that you're in charge of the meeting. You call on her toward meeting's end, when things are pretty well decided upon. ("Anything to add, Sally?")

My decision is _____ (enter a, b, c, or d).

5. As a manager, you have recently attended a leadership workshop which was very "group oriented." A point the leader kept stressing was for the manager to provide praise, support, and encouragement to the group and that group members should do this to one another, too.

a) You are not sure you want to get into this. If you do decide to do this, you will do it very carefully and selectively, for you know that not everyone can handle praise—some get embarrassed by it, some even discount or deny it. Also, some may resent praise given to others. This seems to call for real sensitivity to people's feelings and probably a "hands-off" policy.

b) You have some grave doubts about this. In your experience sticking to the task and not getting too "palsy-walsy" with the troops works best. Production and results count, not just being nice to people.

c) You hadn't looked at group work this way before and you decide to serve as a model to the group and give them earned praise frequently.

d) If honey gets the results you want better than does vinegar, you'll certainly apply the honey, really spread it on. As a former salesperson, you think you can pull this off successfully. You certainly know how to give compliments which flatter people.

My decision is _____ (enter a, b, c, or d).

6. You recently had the opportunity to attend a staff meeting of a plant manager on a visit to the field.

You noticed two things that surprised you: (1) Everyone sat in a circle on chairs, but there was no table; (2) The leadership role seemed to be shared or rotated among the group with Al, the manager, who seemed to reduce his status as the formal leader.

a) You like the way the group operated and you resolve to try a sharing of the leadership tasks (initiating, clarifying, summarizing, etc.), instead of doing all of it yourself.

b) This might not be a bad way to operate if it can help bring the group around to your way of thinking on issues you favor.

c) This seems to be a pretty "far out" way to run a group. People respect firm leadership and that's what you intend to practice as you have all along.

d) You conclude that the leader was trying to respect the feelings of the group, which you would certainly go along with. However, there's no reason why people's feelings can't be treated properly using more conventional ways of managing. So you decide to wait and see.

My decision is _____ (enter a, b, c, or d).

7. You are the manager of large procurement office in City Hospital. You find that your new boss, the hospital director, is "hepped" on team building. You want to be on good relations with your boss, but are not too sure what this (team building) might lead to.

a) You see this as really "opening a whole can of worms." A group can go too far in looking at itself and just create a lot of trouble for everyone. Besides, your group, for the most part, seems to be working OK. But you decide to play along, but being careful so that you don't alienate the boss. "Lip service" on a questionable idea—telling the boss what he wants to hear—is as good a way to handle this as any.

b) You decide to attend an outside workshop on this subject to learn more about it. If it makes sense from a productivity/quality/service standpoint, why not?

c) You are not sure you want to get into this. But you gather that the boss wants his subordinate managers to be more "groupy." So you tell him you'll look into this and give him more specifics as to what, when and where as soon as you can. You pride yourself that as a manager you have

learned, over time, two things: (a) starry ideas like this die a natural death, and (b) quite often no decision (or action) is the best decision.

d) Team building, what's that? Who needs it? But you follow orders just as you expect your people to follow your orders so you just salute and say: "Yes, sir." Your real hope is that your boss will "wise up" and back off on any fancy program that could undermine a manager's authority. But if that's what the boss wants, you'll go through the motions and do it, but end up managing as you always have—being in command and control of things.

My decision is _____ (enter a, b, c, or d).

8. You have been on the job four years now as department chief. Lately, you have been getting some feedback that your weekly staff meetings are not too productive. The meetings are either "gripe sessions" or "brag fests," the staff seems to be saying.

a) Because they are not meeting your needs, you simply decide to abolish these meetings and save valuable time. This action would seem to tie in with the ideas that come out of the time management course you recently attended.

b) You have your assistant prepare a questionnaire to give to all your staffers to find out what's all this fuss about the meetings. You don't commit to doing anything about the ideas which might be on the questionnaires. You'll just wait and see and let nature take its course. Things like this are likely to blow over if you don't overreact to them.

c) At the next meeting you tell the group that you want to pep up the staff meetings. You will let each staffer present something about his program for about half the meeting time and then conduct the usual general business the balance of the time. This tack should show the group that you're responding to the criticism without changing things too much.

d) You candidly present the problem to the group and ask them to brainstorm ways of "pepping up" and improving the staff meetings.

My decision is _____ (enter a, b, c, or d).

9. A group member proposes that each staff meeting, and possibly other meetings, too, have an observer from the Human Resources Office. This person would not participate, but would observe what goes on in the group. At meeting's end the observ-

er would report back on such aspects of group functioning as proper sequence in problem solving, the nature of participation, use of candor, listening, praise and support giving, pace, sticking to the issue, etc.

a) You see this as a means of improving overall group functioning, so you're for it. You introduce the idea to the group and propose it be tried on a pilot-run basis.

b) You don't know whether this is a good idea or not. So you decide to take a "hands-off" policy. Just let the group talk about it at the next staff meeting and see what happens.

c) You don't see the need for an observer when there already is a formally designated leader. If things are off kilter, as the boss, you'll correct them.

d) You let the group respond to this proposal. You don't favor it yourself, but you don't want to go on record as being negative about it. You hope that enough "negatives" about it will arise in the discussion so that you can tactfully table it.

My decision is _____ (enter a, b, c, or d).

10. An employee down the line proposes that a Productivity/Quality Committee be established composed of non-managerial personnel. The committee would meet weekly and make recommendations to management.

a) You accept the idea, but carefully appoint people to the Committee whom you know "won't rock the boat."

b) You go along with the idea enthusiastically, because you feel that employees should be treated properly and this idea fits in with your thinking about participative management and empowering the work force.

c) You appoint a special study group to look into the matter and make some recommendations. If the report is favorable, it can be tried out. If it's unfavorable, that's OK, too. But you're not going to get excited about something you don't know too much about.

d) This you don't need. You call the suggestor in and explain to her in very clear terms that (1) this would undermine the authority of your branch chiefs, (2) your branch chiefs are already paid to do this, and (3) more meetings would work in the opposite direction—lower productivity.

My decision is _____ (enter a, b, c, or d).

Self-Scoring Sheet

For each of the 10 items in the quiz, circle the one letter that represents your choice as to the best course of action. Then add up the number of circled responses in each column. For example, if you circled 6 items in the first column, enter 6 in the bottom line. Then do the same for the other three columns.

Problem	D/D	T	M	T/LF
1	a	c	b	d
2	a	d	c	b
3	c	a	d	b
4	d	b	c	a
5	b	c	d	a
6	c	a	b	d
7	d	b	a	c
8	a	d	c	b
9	c	a	d	b
10	d	b	a	c
Column Totals				

Interpretation of Scores: The column with the most responses represents your primary leadership style. You may also have a secondary style (represented by a significant number of responses in a second column). Or you may have a totally mixed style, that is, a roughly even distribution of scores in all four columns.

Definitions of the four styles are given below.

Now that you know your style, or at least your tendency toward it, you may wish to consider whether you need to alter or strengthen it. The hope of the author is that you would wish to work toward a true Team Leader style, should you not have one already.

Definition of Leadership Styles

D/D is your tendency to lay it on the line in a Direct/Directive way. No nonsense, no timidity, no hesitation—"damn the torpedoes, full steam ahead" is your management philosophy and way of acting on a problem. Production and results take a higher priority than human considerations. You believe that firmness gets both respect and results.

T is your tendency to act as a true Team Leader, emphasizing high concern for involvement of team members in problem solving and decision making. You also feel that concern with growth of people via training and other developmental opportunities is a hallmark of a high performance team.

M is your tendency to endeavor to get results through manipulation of people. This is a less-than-direct approach and, at times, even a bit less than honest. By out-maneuvering people, "finessing the situation," you generally get the results you want and avoid a lot of confrontation, complaints and the like.

T/LF is your tendency to be tolerant/laissez-faire of people and situations. You don't want to confront and upset people. You believe in "letting sleeping dogs lie" because, given enough time, many situations will work themselves out.

PROBLEMS, EXERCISES AND QUESTIONS FOR DISCUSSION

Note: Because your participant group is to discuss issues that relate to teamwork and team building, you should let your class tackle the problems below on a small group basis to the extent practicable.

1. A good way to start a session on team building, teamwork and/or group dynamics is to have the participant group play the game "Auction."

   Procedures:

   a. Divide the class into small teams (3 or 4 persons per team). Try to position each team far enough apart so that they cannot hear each other's deliberations.
   b. Explain to the group: "We're going to play the game 'Auction.' Now in an auction people bid against one another to make a purchase of a very much desired object. In this case you will be bidding on a mythical $1,000 bill. (Draw a $1,00 bill on a flipchart with a green-colored marking pen.) Your objective is to acquire the $1,000 bill by bidding on it. Now I must remind you that if you bid very high you may pay more than you should. If you bid too low, you stand to lose out to a higher bidder. But that's the way an auction goes.

   "OK, go ahead, decide on your bid and I'll call time in 5 or 6 minutes."
   c. When time is up, ask the teams to enter their bids on a slip of paper. Collect the bids and have

a participant read them off to you. Enter the bids on a flipchart or blackboard as follows: Team A: $900; Team B: $70; Team C: $750; Team D: $400; Team E: $990. Then declare the winner—Team E, which had the highest bid.

   d. Ask the group what the game as played tells us.
   e. Then make observations of this sort:
      i. Team E is the winner, but they only gain $10. Hardly worth the effort, about $2 per participant.
      ii. Now consider this approach to winning the $1,000 bill: What if all the teams had gotten together and jointly agreed to a very low bid, say $10 or $15. Then all of you would be winners and would win a large number of bucks at that.
      iii. So I have this question: Why didn't you do that?
      iv. The answer: we generally tend to think in terms of competition, beating the other guy (or team in this case), rather than in terms of cooperation, everyone thereby getting a big piece of the pie by joint action.

2. Another icebreaker to start a discussion on team building is as follows:
   a) Give the class this assignment: "Assume you are marooned on a South Pacific island. Select the 5 most useful items you would like to have with you."
   b) Divide the class into teams of 3–5 participants to discuss and *agree* on the 5 most significant items.
   c) Secure reports from the small groups and post to flipchart.
   (**Note:** The objective is to "loosen" people up, to give them an appreciation of others' values and to let them experience working on a team problem without a leader.)

3. As a possible opener, ask the class (preferably in small groups) to come up with a definition of a team. (Note: Be certain stress in the definition is placed on *interdependence*. So a team is a group of people who share a common vision/mission/objective/goal, are committed to it and function interdependently to accomplish it. Also, a team reports and is responsible to a larger organizational component.

4. How would you distinguish between "team development" and "team building?"

5. Assume you have been newly promoted to the position of operations manager. You have eight

subordinate supervisors who report directly to you. You have heard that a "transition team build" is a good way to get to know the team and vice versa and to get off to a good start in short order. You debate the merits of bringing an outside facilitator aboard for this. What might the pros and cons be of this approach?

6. What are the major limitations to team building? (**Answer:** Team building cannot neutralize totally the rigorous effects of external forces, e.g., a recession, the market, the competition, new legislation, lifestyle changes, population changes, etc. Also, it cannot overcome the influence of management direction and policies at the top of the organization. And it cannot succeed if the team leader is unwilling or unable to shift from a directive, controlling type of management style to one of shared leadership.)

7. Through what four phases or stages are newly formed work groups likely to go through? (**Answer:** forming, storming, norming, and performing.)

8. In the culture at large, we hear statements such as "birds of a feather flock together" vs. "opposites attract." How do these two apparently contradictory ideas or concepts relate to team building? (**A possible answer:** The latter phrase relates to diversity, which is essential for high-quality team decision making.)

9. How important is "truth telling" (leveling, openness, candor) to the health of a cohesive team? Can a team be effective if truth telling is not a norm for the group? Are there any issues the team should not bring up?

10. If you were to predict that a particular work team, just being formed, would work well together, have a hard-hitting team, what criteria would you use to make your forecast?

11. You are the head of operations. Pat is invariably late to your staff meetings. What might you do about it? Bring it up at the meeting? Confront Pat with the problem privately? Make it a team problem? Live with it? Encourage another team member to bring it up at the meeting or, alternately, do it privately?

12. You are a member of a work group that is very congenial, friendly to the point that your meetings are great "gabfests," even social affairs. What might you do to get the group to be more productive at its meetings?

13. Your boss' staff meetings are real bores. The boss drones on, just passing along information from his boss's staff meetings or talking about his last field trip, etc. What might you do about it? What are your options?

14. At your boss' staff meeting two branch heads—purchasing and operations—are constantly in conflict. No one likes it, but the boss merely sits back and smiles. You would like to alter this situation, end this personality clash, for it is disruptive to good team functioning. What might you do? What are your options?

15. To everyone's annoyance at team meetings, George invariably gets one or two phone calls and excuses himself to take the calls. What might be done to curb this inconsiderate, self-centered behavior?

16. Assume you have a "negative" team member. She engages in sarcasm, put-downs, disagreement for the sake of disagreement. You decide to give her some feedback about her behavior. What guidelines should be used in this kind of interaction with a team member?

17. Assume that you are a member of a work team of seven people. You are irritated with your group, for they very carefully avoid conflict. You feel that this results in a lot of lost creativity. What might you do about it? What might happen if you offered to play "the devil's advocate?" Is this a good idea? What else might be done to get some sparks flying?

18. Your team has developed two factions in the last 18 months. What might be done to overcome this unwanted rivalry?

19. How can you, as team leader, ensure that a decision, not agreed to unanimously, is supported by everyone? You are particularly concerned because two "dissenters" of your team of eight have been very reluctant to go along with the rest of the group.

20. Assume you are an outside trainer/consultant, specializing in team building. You have been working with a manager for several weeks now, making preparations to hold an off-site, two-and-one-half day team-building session. Several days before the event, the manager says to you: "I don't think I'll be able to make it the first day. But I definitely will be there for the second and third

days. You just go ahead with the group, get things warmed up and I'll join you for cocktails and dinner the first evening. You can brief me later about what took place." What is your response to the manager? (**Answer:** Simply postpone it. You can't build a team without the 100% commitment of the team leader. Being absent is not a commitment.)

21. Which type of organization works best for SDTs, the *functional* or *process-oriented* approach? (**Answer:** the process orientation. **Example:** Sales activities are integrated to include the processes of generating, selling, servicing, and billing a customer. This results in the sales-management process becoming part of the total order-fulfillment process, including technical support and billing.)

22. How does "benchmarking" relate to the launching of a SDT program? (**Answer:** In benchmarking, we study the best practices of other organizations, competitors, and non-competitors, regarding their products, services, and processes. Benchmarking as a continuing practice can ensure constantly improving processes.)

23. At GM's Saturn plant, SDTs reach decisions on the basis of the "70% comfortable" rule of consensus (Charlene M. Solomon, "Behind the Wheel at Saturn," *Personnel Journal,* June 1991). How do you see this approach to decision making in a group? How would you compare it to voting? A unilateral decision by the boss?

24. An organization is considering letting the SDTs assume responsibility for the making of the annual performance appraisals of its team members. What might some of the pros and cons of this approach be? (**Note:** For a full discussion of this approach at Digital Equipment Corporation, you may wish to see Carol A. Norman and Robert A. Zawacki, ("Team Appraisals—Team Approach," *Personnel Journal,* September 1991).

25. Assume you are a member of a self-directed team (SDT) with this problem: A hard-working team member has been observed engaging in a serious violation of organization safety rules. What major, overall considerations should guide the team in its deliberations as to what action to take? **Note:** The team has been given responsibility to act on individual performance problems that interfere with its goals of production, quality, cost, etc. (**Answer:** The team in its discussion should outline, first of all, the mutual obligations that exist among the organization, the team, and the team member with the problem. **Note:** For a detailed discussion of this type of problem, you may wish to see Donald F. Barkman, ("Team Discipline: Put Performance On The Line," *Personnel Journal,* March 1987).

26. The inventories or quizzes included at chapter's end may be used by the participant group to provide added insight into team leadership and team functioning. Here is a procedure to follow:
    a. Distribute copies of the quiz for individual member completion.
    b. Assign participants to small groups (3–5 members). Have them compare and discuss their work on the instrument.
    c. Secure feedback from the teams as to possible learnings from the instrument and their discussion of it.

Guidesheet to Monitor Team Communication

You have been asked to observe the communication process at this team meeting. You will report back at meeting's end how well the team members communicated with one another. Here are some criteria you may wish to use to assess team communication.

Aids to Effective Communication

Gatekeeping: Drawing less active team members into the conversation ("We haven't heard from Pat as yet on this.")

Supporting: Giving support and encouragement to one another ("I think Kim has a very workable idea. I really like it." Or: "I think we're really on a roll now.")

Mediating: Acting as a force to reconcile differences to get agreement ("I don't think you and Gene are that far apart. For example, . . .")

Harmonizing: Ensuring cohesion by smoothing "ruffled" feathers ("Barry, you and Sue both favor a direct mail approach. Your only difference is when to kick it off, right?")

Summarizing: Bringing together all ideas that have been generated. ("Up to this point we have pointed up these problems . . .")

Confronting: Facing up openly to a problem/difficulty/issue ("I think we have to recognize that in the last 18 months our marketing effort has stood still. This is because . . .")

Listening

Restating content: Rephrasing and repeating what was said

Reflecting feelings: Stating the emotional underpinning of what was said ("I think you are frustrated with the operation because you feel that the help you got was too little and too late.")

Barriers to effective communication:

Holding back opinions	Non-participating
Interrupting	Not listening
Putting others down	Acting negatively
Acting defensively	Not stating feelings frankly
Sulking (withdrawing)	Subgrouping
Allowing plops	

Non-verbal communication

If behaviors such as the following were exhibited, what did they seem to mean (communicate):
Head nods, smiles, shoulder shrugs, winks, other body movements (of arms, legs, hands); fiddling with papers, pens, or other objects; sighs; glances at watch.

A Comparison of SDTs and Traditionally Managed Units

Element	Traditional Unit	SDT
Decision making	From above	By the team
Provision of information	Limited to "on a need to know only" basis	Open sharing and discussion of information
Job anxiety	Fear of layoff	Job/career continuity because of increased skill/knowledge
Attitude toward change	Favors status quo; slow to change	Continuous improvement
Policies	Used for control purposes	Used to inspire/improve
Supplier relationships	Suppliers compete for favor	Work with suppliers
Customer/client relationships	Formal, not close	Very close
Specialization	Many specializations	Use of generalists
Organizational layers	Many	Few

(per Dr. Glenn Varney, President, Management Advisory Associates), Bowling Green, Ohio)

Additional Comparative Characteristics

Element	Traditional Department	SDT
Directions	Follow	Initiate
Rewards	Individual focus	Team focus
Relationships	Compete	Cooperate
Problem-solving attitudes	A blame focus	A solution focus
Goal outlook	Work only to reach goal	Continual improvement
Resource outlook	Demand more	Accept what's given
Contingency behavior	React to emergencies	Plan to prevent emergencies
Spending money for quality	Improve quality by spending money	Improve quality to save money

(per Career Track, Inc., Boulder, Colorado)

Our Team—How Effective Is It?

Listed below are 27 characteristics of team effectiveness. Please give candid responses (ratings on a 7-point scale) for each of these key characteristics. Circle the number that best expresses your feeling about the characteristic, considering the behavior and attitude of both your team members and your team leader. Scoring instructions appear at the end of the quiz.

Note: Please do **not** sign your name to the quiz.

1. Clarity of goals, expectations, roles	Vague	1	2	3	4	5	6	7	Explicit
2. Commitment of team members to objectives/goals	Limited	1	2	3	4	5	6	7	All-out
3. Congruence (policy and procedures are in line with goals)	In conflict	1	2	3	4	5	6	7	In agreement
4. Clarity of assignments	Obscure	1	2	3	4	5	6	7	Definite
5. Collective trust	Negative (suspicious)	1	2	3	4	5	6	7	Positive (confident in others)
6. Customer concern/focus	Minor	1	2	3	4	5	6	7	Major
7. Communication	Unreliable, phony	1	2	3	4	5	6	7	Authentic, open, 2-way
8. Collaboration/cooperation	Divisive	1	2	3	4	5	6	7	Unified
9. Concern/caring	Distant	1	2	3	4	5	6	7	Supportive
10. Challenge, opportunities for	Rare	1	2	3	4	5	6	7	Frequent
11. Climate	Autocratic	1	2	3	4	5	6	7	Participative
12. Creativity, opportunities for	Insignificant	1	2	3	4	5	6	7	Diverse
13. Continuous improvement	Indifferent	1	2	3	4	5	6	7	Emphatic
14. Cohesiveness (identification with team)	Individual players	1	2	3	4	5	6	7	A tight-knit group
15. Confrontation (face up to problems)	Uncertain	1	2	3	4	5	6	7	Clear
16. Conflict (to stimulate ideas)	Avoided	1	2	3	4	5	6	7	Encouraged
17. Change (mindset for)	Play-it-safe	1	2	3	4	5	6	7	Forward looking
18. Consensus (in decision making)	Not used	1	2	3	4	5	6	7	Emphasized
19. Continuous learning	Unimportant	1	2	3	4	5	6	7	Stressed
20. Clock conscious (timing)	Apathetic	1	2	3	4	5	6	7	Aware
21. Collective or mutual responsibility	Blaming	1	2	3	4	5	6	7	Shared accountability
22. Celebration of diversity	Ignored	1	2	3	4	5	6	7	Stressed
23. Charting progress	Minor emphasis	1	2	3	4	5	6	7	Highly important
24. Critique of team functioning	Never	1	2	3	4	5	6	7	Frequent
25. Collective leadership	Boss dominated	1	2	3	4	5	6	7	Shared by team
26. Celebration of events	Rare	1	2	3	4	5	6	7	Frequent
27. Continuity (of membership)	Fragile	1	2	3	4	5	6	7	Stable

Scoring Instructions

Tally all your individual scores to get a total score. For example, if you had all 1 ratings, your total score would be 27; if you had all 7 ratings, your total score would be 27 × 7 = 189.

You will be given the opportunity to discuss your scores, both total and individual ratings, with your teammates. In your discussion, try to accomplish two things: (a) explore why differences in ratings exist (assuming they do) and (b) what might be done (or what it would take) to move any of the ratings to a 7.

Interpretation: A score based on mostly 1s, 2s, and 3s would provide a low score, meaning a limited degree of teamness. Conversely, a score based on mostly 5s, 6s, and 7s would give you a high score, meaning a high degree of teamness.

A Rating Scale to Assess Effectiveness of Our Team's Goal Setting

Procedure:

1. Enter a dot in the appropriate box for each of 12 items below.
2. Using a ruler or straight edge, connect the dots. This will give you a profile of how you see the team's communication prowess.
3. **Note:** Try to be as candid as you can in your responses.
4. Do not sign your name to the profile.
5. Profiles may be collected and tallied for a team profile.
6. A team discussion will be held about the team profile results when they are returned. If the profiles are not sent away for scoring, a discussion will be held by the leader and team members on the basis of the individual scoring.
7. In the team discussion try to do two things: (a) explore why differences in ratings exist, and (b) what might be done (or what it would take) to improve the ratings.

Criteria	Strongly Agree	Agree	Undecided	Disagree	Strongly Disagree
1. Team members work as a group to set goals that pertain to the total group.					
2. Individual goals are worked through on a mutual basis between the team leader and the appropriate team member.					
3. Our goals are marked by clarity.					
4. Our goals are marked by reasonableness.					
5. We try to introduce a "stretch" element into our goals so that we are constantly upgrading our performance.					
6. We set goals for personal growth and development as well as for the work.					
7. Our goals are revised as new circumstances arise, on a joint basis (leader/ group; leader/team member).					
8. Once goals are agreed upon, everyone concerned is given full authority to execute them (deep delegation).					
9. Progress on established goals is reviewed at least quarterly.					
10. Non-accomplishment of goals is subject to discussion/critique, not punishment.					
11. Goals are assigned and reviewed for results/accomplishment rather than for details of execution.					
12. Goals are reviewed at year's end to plan better the next year's work as well as to learn what was done.					

A Rating Scale to Assess Our Team's Problem-Solving/Creativity Competencies

Procedure:

1. Enter a dot in the appropriate box for each of the 19 items below.
2. Using a ruler or straight edge, connect the dots. This will give you a profile of how you see the team's capabilities in the areas of problem solving and creativity.
3. Try to be as candid as you can in your responses.
4. Do not sign your name to the profile.
5. Profiles may be collected and tallied by an outside source for a team profile.
6. A team discussion will be held about the team profile results. If the profiles are not sent away for scoring, a discussion will be held by the leader and team members on the basis of individual scoring.
7. In the team discussion, zero in on two things: (a) explore why differences in ratings exist, and (b) what should be done to improve the ratings.

Criteria	Never	Rarely	Occasionally	Frequently	Always
1. Problems are met head on rather than "swept under the rug."					
2. Problems are regarded as challenges and opportunities rather than headaches.					
3. Broad participation is a basic tool of team problem solving.					
4. The team leader regards the team as a constructive problem-solving force.					
5. As appropriate, problems are solved with the total team on a consensus basis.					
6. Group members present and discuss their ideas rather than defend them.					
7. Problems are defined, discussed, and acted upon in accordance with a logical, sequential problem-solving model.					
8. A striving for innovation/creativity is a part of the team's way of life.					
9. The team's climate is concerned with the big picture rather than nit-picking new ideas to death.					
10. Conflict/disagreement are utilized for purposes of creativity and ideation.					
11. Delegation is regarded as a tool for innovation.					
12. When we brainstorm, we separate phase one, *ideation* (generating ideas) from phase two, *evaluation*.					
13. Risk taking and experimentation are encouraged and rewarded rather than discouraged and punished.					

(continued on next page)

Criteria	Never	Rarely	Occasionally	Frequently	Always
14. Team members are encouraged to interact with others outside the team.					
15. We have a daily "quiet period" to encourage individual creative thinking.					
16. Our climate is marked by "being loose" (informality), congeniality, fun, freedom to do one's own thing.					
17. The team thinks in terms of barriers to creativity, and when identified we work at overcoming them.					
18. Our team uses analogies, fantasy and/or guided imagery to encourage creativity.					

You will be given the opportunity to discuss your scores, both total and individual ratings, with your teammates. In your discussion, try to accomplish two things: (a) explore why differences in ratings exist (assuming they do) and (b) what might be done (or what it would take) to move any of the ratings to a 7.

Scoring Procedure

1. Use a straight edge or a ruler to connect the dots in all the boxes. This will give you a profile of your ratings.
2. If your profile encompasses "Frequently" and "Always" primarily, you see yourself as a strong, cooperative team member.
3. If your profile encompasses "Never" and "Rarely" primarily, you have a lot of doubts about your team, its members, and team operations.
4. If your ratings do not form an obvious pattern, as described in items 2 and 3, your feelings about your team membership are of a mixed sort.
5. In your discussion with team members about your ratings and theirs, try to accomplish two things: (a) explore why differences in ratings exist (assuming they do); and (b) what it would take to improve upon any of the ratings.

A Rating Scale to Assess Our Team's Communication

Procedure:

1. Enter a dot in the appropriate box for each of the 13 items below.
2. Using a ruler or straight edge, connect the dots. This will give you a profile of how you see the team's communication prowess.
3. **Note:** Try to be as candid as you can in your responses.
4. Do not sign your name to your profile.
5. Profiles may be collected and tallied by an outside source for a team profile.
6. A team discussion will be held about the team profile results when they are returned. If the profiles are not sent away for scoring, a discussion will be held by the leader and team members on the basis of individual scoring.
7. In the team discussion, zero in on two things: (a) explore why there are differences in the ratings among team members and (b) what should be done to improve the ratings.
8. Ideally, ratings should be of the "strongly agree" and "agree" type for these are the positive responses.

Criteria	Strongly Agree	Agree	Undecided	Disagree	Strongly Disagree
1. Team members listen to each other.					
2. The team leader listens to all group members.					
3. Everyone feels free to level and to be candid with everyone else.					
4. All team members "check things out" with all concerned before action is taken.					
5. Constructive feedback is given freely to group members to improve their functioning.					
6. Broad participation is strongly encouraged at all group meetings.					
7. No one uses a disproportionate amount of the available "air time" at group meetings.					
8. People are available to secure information needed.					
9. Information is shared willingly and no one hoards information.					
10. Information of interest to team members, such as information on new policies, new projects, and pay, is not categorized as "secret."					
11. Information about one's performance is communicated regularly and candidly by the team leader so that there are no surprises at performance review time.					
12. Team members are not afraid to give the boss the "bad news."					
13. We communicate well with other groups in the organization.					

How Our Team Manages Its Meetings: A Self-quiz

Circle the appropriate degree for each statement as you have experienced it. Be as candid as you can.

1. Objectives of our meetings are:	Fuzzy	1	2	3	4	5	6	7	Clear
2. Meeting objectives are reduced to writing wherever helpful:	Rarely	1	2	3	4	5	6	7	Regularly
3. Meeting objectives are disseminated in advance:	Never	1	2	3	4	5	6	7	Regularly
4. Meetings start on time:	Rarely	1	2	3	4	5	6	7	Always
5. Meetings finish on time:	Rarely	1	2	3	4	5	6	7	Always
6. Time at our meetings is used:	Poorly	1	2	3	4	5	6	7	Extremely well
7. Participation at our meetings is:	Narrow	1	2	3	4	5	6	7	Broad
8. The way members listen to one another is:	Casual	1	2	3	4	5	6	7	Intense
9. Plops (ignoring a member's idea, hence it "plops" to the floor) are rare:	Strongly Disagree	1	2	3	4	5	6	7	Strongly Agree
10. The atmosphere, in so far as it encourages ideation/creativity, is:	Dull	1	2	3	4	5	6	7	Exciting
11. Support/encouragement/praise recognition of member contributions are:	Miserly	1	2	3	4	5	6	7	Generous
12. In our meetings we search for solutions, not scapegoats:	Rarely	1	2	3	4	5	6	7	Regularly
13. Meetings produce decisions:	Rarely	1	2	3	4	5	6	7	Regularly
14. Decisions made at meetings are subject to follow-up:	Uncertain	1	2	3	4	5	6	7	Rigorous
15. At our meetings we try to have fun as well as solve problems:	Never	1	2	3	4	5	6	7	Usually
16. Evaluation (critique) of how we conduct our meetings is undertaken:	Never	1	2	3	4	5	6	7	Frequently

Scoring For Group Discussion

Total the scores for each item and secure a group average for the item. **Example:** If there are 7 team members and the scores on item one are 5, 6, 6, 6, 7, 4 and 3, the total score is 37 and the average is 5 (37 divided by 7 = 5).

The discussion should be geared to ascertain why there is not a perfect score ($7 \times 7 = 49$) and what might be done to bring about improvement.

Team Membership—Are You on Track?

This quiz is designed to give you a reading on your skills, behavior, and attitudes as a member of your work team. Please be as candid as you can in your responses. Simply enter an "x" in the appropriate box for each statement. Do not sign your name to this quiz. The scoring procedure follows the quiz. You will be given the opportunity to discuss your quiz results with your fellow team members.

A. My feelings about our team	Never	Rarely	Occasionally	Frequently	Always
1. I get all the information I need from my teammates.					
2. My teammates listen to what I have to say.					
3. I get a lot of help from team members.					
4. I appreciate my teammates' work styles, contributions, and attitudes.					
5. Cooperation rather than competition/rivalry is the hallmark of our team.					
6. I trust my teammates to always be honest, to do their best work and to treat me fairly.					
7. No one on the team will take advantage of me or anyone else for we have a high-trust group.					
8. Team members are very approachable and friendly.					
9. I receive affection, warmth, recognition, and support from team members.					
10. I feel that I am treated as a full member of the group and feel very much a part of it.					
11. I can be myself in our team.					
12. Team members avoid negative, irritating behaviors such as finger-pointing, disrespect, nit-picking, bickering, foot-dragging or stonewalling.					
13. My teammates demonstrate that they have a high personal opinion of me.					
14. My relations with team members are such that if I were to leave, I believe the team would miss me.					
15. I so operate that I don't let anyone on the team down.					
16. I try to help my teammates to resolve their problems in any way that I can.					
17. I pitch in to give help as needed, for I see myself as a team player.					

B. My Role In The Team	Never	Rarely	Occasionally	Frequently	Always
18. My behavior in the group is interdependent, rather than independent or dependent.					
19. I help my teammates to work through disagreement/conflicts with others.					
20. I am patient with my team members.					
21. It is more important to me to get good results than to worry about who on the team gets the credit for them.					
22. If we miss a target or a boo-boo occurs, my concern is to find out why rather than to blame anyone for the unwanted result.					
23. I am open to new approaches, procedures, and ideas advanced by my teammates.					
24. I try to consider what other team members have said before I firm up my own opinion and express it.					
25. I pay close attention to what team members say, for I want to be a good listener.					
26. I do not interrupt when team members speak.					
27. I treat my team members with respect.					
28. I avoid defensiveness when I am subject to negative feedback feedback (constructive criticism) or questioned about a behavior or attitude of mine.					
29. If the facts so warrant, I can alter my opinion/position.					
30. I am willing to tell others how I feel about issues, problems, progress, policies.					
31. I discuss and give feedback on our group process, that is, how well we are working as a team.					
32. All of us, including myself, can (and do) "tell it like it is."					
33. I give earned praise (compliments, recognition) to my teammates.					
34. At meetings and problem-solving sessions, I feel my influence is high.					

10 What Managers Get Paid For: Problem Solving and Decision Making

If you don't know where you're going, any place will do.

> —Lewis Carroll (1832–1898), in *Alice in Wonderland*

It's what you know after you know it all that counts.

> —Harry S Truman (1884–1972), 33rd U.S. President

No problem is so large that it can't be run away from.

> —Charlie Brown, character in *Peanuts* cartoon strip

Don't make the wrong mistakes.

> —attributed to Yogi Berra, the much-quoted former New York Yankees baseball player and coach

We're all ignorant, just about different things.

> —Mark Twain (1835–1910), U.S. writer

Get your facts first, then you can distort them as you please.

> —Mark Twain

TO stimulate your thinking about the skill area of problem solving and decision making, take a few minutes to complete the short quiz on page 508. Try to answer the quiz items as candidly as you can to learn how you measure up in this skill area. Your responses should serve as a guide to the portions of this chapter that merit fuller concentration.

THE WORLD OF THE PROBLEM SOLVER

If we were to plot the extent of our problems in today's business/management world, we might well produce a graph of this sort:

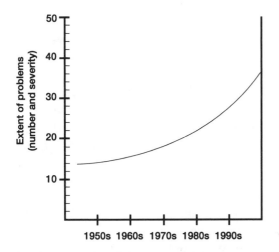

What the graph would tell us is that everything that should not be going up is going up: rate of change, costs, debts, competition, customer demands, uncertainty, confusion, frustration. It is akin to chaos becoming the norm. Murphy, author of Murphy's Law ("If anything can go wrong, it will"), if anything, probably should be regarded as an optimist.

So if our problems are accelerating in number and severity, it would seem to be a good idea to learn all we can about problem-solving and decision-making techniques. Because the problems most certainly won't disappear on their own, the only practical alternative is to upgrade our capacity (skill development) to deal with them. And as for Murphy and his rule, well, some rules are made to be broken, aren't they?

Top-level managers see their subordinate managers and supervisors as individuals who are hired and paid to solve problems and make decisions. Of course, they may use other language, e.g., "stay on top of things," "keep within budget," but basically they regard problem solving and decision making as key roles to be discharged.

Top management, to be sure, not only expects that problems are to be solved, but that they are solved with wisdom or high quality; that is to say, that they meet the need/difficulty totally and possibly creatively, too. In addition, there is an expectation that solutions take into account their possible future consequences. Certainly,

solutions to problems that create new or added problems are not wise decisions.

Globally speaking, a problem is a gap or discrepancy between *where we are*—the current state of affairs—and *where we want to be*:

current state;   desired state;
level of   level of
performance/   performance/
results   results

In effect, in "gap analysis" we are identifying concrete differences between the status quo (sometimes referred to "as the mess we're in") and a preferred state. Some management authorities refer to this approach as "Discrepancy Theory": decide what you want/need, determine what's what (what exists), assess the difference between the two, and develop some plan of action to eliminate the gap or difference.

This concept can be applied to individual, group, and organizational performance. The challenge, as an ancient Chinese proverb has it, can be stated as follows: "If we don't change our direction, we'll end up exactly where we are headed."

Problems don't necessarily arrive with a large, boldly stamped message: "Warning! This problem requires your urgent/immediate attention." So part of the problem-solving process entails recognizing that a difficulty—or possibly an opportunity—exists, identifying precisely what it is and getting a good feel for its magnitude and direction.

Few problems or performance discrepancies resolve themselves. In fact, like the leaky roof or noisy engine, they can only get worse. So an intervention of one type or another is imperative to get things back on track or possibly to move in a new direction.

However, before we apply remedies or interventions, we have to be certain of three things:

1. What the problem is or, perhaps, we should say what the problem *really* is. For if we don't know what's broken, how can we know whether its fixed or not? This is Step 1 of our problem-solving model, Identifying and Defining/Formulating The Problem (Figure 1, page 448).
2. We have gathered appropriate data about the problem, particularly, what are the nature and dimensions of the problem and what brought the problem about, or cause and effect. Causative factors may range from people's performance (or non-performance) or a deficiency in the system to faulty sup-

plies/equipment or an external event (the market, the economy, the competition, consumer attitudes/lifestyles). In any case, problems don't occur in the abstract. Something concrete triggered the event. This is Step 2 of our model, Gathering Information/Data About Our Problem.

3. We understand that effective problem solving is not about solutions. It is about *different routes* to solutions, which means we need to choose carefully the path that will provide the best return/payoff/result. This relates to Step 3 of the model, Developing/Generating Alternate Solutions; Step 4, Assessing Alternate Solutions; and Step 5, Choosing (Deciding) Among Alternate Solutions.

THE MIND OF THE PROBLEM SOLVER

The frame of mind—mindset, world view, or outlook—of the problem solver has a vital bearing on how energetically and creatively he will tackle a problem. If a problem is perceived as a headache or a harasser, obviously only limited enthusiasm and optimism will be applied to it. Conversely, if the problem is regarded as a challenge, that is, an opportunity for innovation, personal/group stimulation, growth, recognition, or special accomplishment, beating the competition, etc., a super effort will be unleashed to master it.

That one's mindset will determine one's approach to a problem is exemplified by this anecdote.

Story: An American shoe salesman wired his company from a remote, primitive spot in Africa as follows: "No one here wears shoes. I'm coming home on the next available transport." A Japanese salesman, who was in the same location, wired back in a different mode: "No one here wears shoes or even sandals. Send 1 million of each at once."

In a similar vein, some people offer this advice: "If life tosses you a bag of lemons, make lemonade out of it." Which is what a marketing group in a West Coast cannery finally did. They had been stewing for days over what to do about a batch of gray salmon, which, because of its dingy color, was of doubtful marketability. Just as they were about to give up on the dismal-appearing seafood, a young management intern galvanized the group into action by suggesting a promotional campaign based on this slogan: "Uniquely colored gray salmon. Guaranteed not to turn red."

Certainly, we can't be responsible for the problems, traumas, and setbacks daily work and living may bring us. But we should feel responsible for *our reactions* to these events, for we can control those reactions.

Viewing problems as hassles, headaches, and harassers is basically a copout. It is essentially an argument to self for limited effort. Do we really want that response?

The best advice anyone can give to a problem solver is to expect adversity, not serenity. Although we might like the world to be neat, tidy, orderly, and very predictable, the realities are that it is more likely to be murky, askew, pitfall-laden, and neither friendly nor controllable.

I recall a problem-solving meeting with my boss and his boss. My superior was complaining about the resources he felt were vital to complete a project, but which were lacking. His boss listened carefully to his lament, looked him in the eye, smiled, and said: "Look, George, if you had all the tools you need to get the job done, why would we need you?"

So when the going gets tough and the headaches mount, it's a good idea to engage in a bit of self-talk along this line: "Hey, man, my job is to solve problems. That's what they hired me for and why they pay me more than the staff. If there were no problems, they wouldn't need me, would they? So it's hi, hi, ho, and back to the mat we go."

And if for some unforeseen reason, the problem-solving effort becomes a cropper—that is, you're clearly beaten—a real-world philosophy to adopt is this: Don't waste your time and energy stewing over it. Grieve shortly and get on with it. There are more problems and challenges waiting for you, most of which will give you a chance to "knock 'em dead!"

Finally, because, as a manager, wrestling with problems is the heart of our job, we have to accept them as they come—easy or hard, fun or irritating, new or old, of our own doing or someone else's. In respect to the latter point about problem "ownership," try to live with the adage that says: "Maybe it's not your fault, but it's still your problem."

Effective and rewarding problem solving is possible to achieve. But we have to go about it in the right direction.

Story: A somewhat uncertain driver up in Maine stopped his car and asked a farmer leaning on his fence for help: "How far is it to Rumford?" The farmer surveyed the traveler and advised: "The way you're going at it I'd say about 24,892 miles."

A Problem-Solving Model

Problems may be tackled randomly, that is, "as the spirit moves one," or they may be approached via a system or model. Much has been learned and written about problem solving in recent decades so that "flying by the seat of one's pants" is hardly a primary method of attack. Our approach, therefore, is to work with (or perhaps from) a model. A model has these advantages for the problem solver:

1. It encourages a rational, orderly, and sequential approach so that key steps in the total process are not overlooked. Problem solving is a linear process so that a later step should not be taken before an earlier stage is worked through thoroughly. As an obvious example, there is little point in developing a sophisticated action plan before we are totally clear about the nature and scope of our problem.

2. It facilitates learning about the process of problem solving and decision making. Learning proceeds more meaningfully when it proceeds from an overall plan or design.

3. It allows work teams (and individuals) to critique their prowess as problem solvers for it provides standards/criteria for evaluation. In the absence of a model, an assessment would be totally subjective, random, unstructured. Would you want to evaluate a marketing plan, a vacation plan or a marriage without any criteria to go by?

In short, the model provides the rigor problem solvers need to keep them in touch with their "game plan."

There are various problem-solving models in the management literature. Some have three or four steps; others have five or more stages. The one I have developed has seven steps. My assumption is that a fully developed model—seven steps—because of its explicitness should serve as an extremely helpful tool for problem solving and decision making. It ensures that "all bases are touched," that one or more key steps are not overlooked.

The model (Figure 1) is presented in circular fashion. This configuration is designed to point out that the problem-solving process is a dynamic, continuing process. As conditions change or new needs develop, the search for new and better answers begins again.

Step 1: Identifying and Defining/Formulating Our Problem

The most common source of mistakes in management decisions is the emphasis on finding the right answer rather than the right question.

—Management authority Peter Drucker in The Practice of Management (1954)

The formulation of a problem is far more often essential than its solution, which may be merely a matter of mathematical or experimental skill.

—Albert Einstein (1879–1955), American (German born) Nobel Prize (1921) winning theoretical physicist

A problem well-stated is already half-solved.

—John Dewey (1859–1952), American philosopher and educator

It is better to ask some of the questions than to know all the answers.

—James Thurber (1894–1961), American humorist

It is all too easy to make assumptions and thus draw improper conclusions about the exact nature and cause(s) of a problem. But do we wish to spend a lot of time, energy, and money to take corrective action when we are not working on the real problem or its root causes? (If the roof is leaking near our chimney, new copper guttering is hardly an answer.) And worse still, an unsolved real problem will certainly come back to haunt us—in an aggravated state, too.

Hence the need to be certain that the problem is *identified* and *defined* properly in all its dimensions. Producing an accurate and adequately detailed description of the problem helps us in two ways: It forces us to have a better understanding of the total problem situation and thus creates possibilities for producing realistic solutions.

Identifying Our Problem

It is obvious that we can't solve a problem if we haven't identified it properly—what is *really* bugging us? Yet we know that in managers' haste to solve a problem, or for a variety of other reasons, careful diagnosis may not take place. For example, if the problem in marketing our product (or service) is that it is not sufficiently current or of high enough quality to attract the

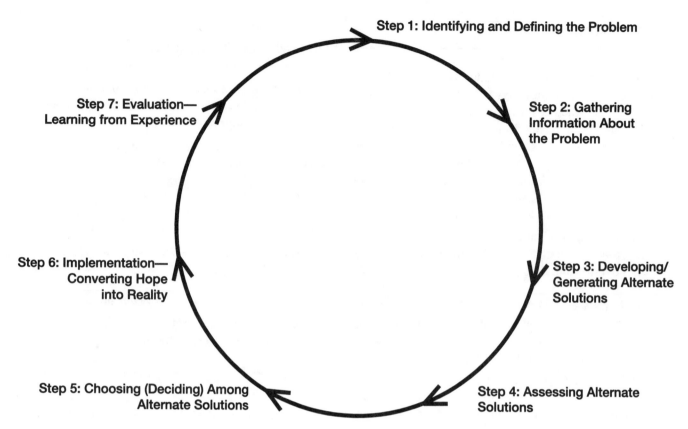

Figure 10-1. Seven-step model for problem solving and decision making.

desired customer/client interest, there is little point in launching additional aggressive, expensive promotional programs to gain consumer acceptance.

Of course, it may be hard on our egos to face the fact that we have a nondescript product/service on our hands. Yet, facing reality—what the problem really is—is an essential part of the problem identification process at all levels of the organization. It may range from Pat's productivity (or lack thereof) to "what business are we really in?" In the latter connection, airlines have learned in recent years that they are as much in the business of selling seats as they are in flying airplanes. Similarly, marketing guru Theodore Levitt of Harvard University has pointed out that if we are in the cosmetics business we are not selling perfume, but hope (!).

Asking the Right Questions

At one time, I worked in a rapidly changing organization in which one of the key officials frequently expressed doubts about the value of organizational personnel who had a lot of "smarts" and presumably knew "all the answers." Thus, when the issue of knowledgeable personnel arose, he would invariably present this response: "We don't need people who know all the answers. We already have a lot of those. What we need are people who can ask the questions." (Or to be more precise, the *right* questions.)

Management authority Peter Drucker (in one of his classic works, *The Practice of Management,* New York: Harper & Row, 1954), states that ". . . there are few things as useless—if not as dangerous—as the right answer to the wrong question."

Enumerated below are a number of pertinent questions to aid in identifying the problem properly—that is, to help us to do so clearly and realistically.

General question: What is going on that tells you that a problem exists? Which end results are sources of "pain"?

Problem ownership: Is it your problem? Why? If it is not your problem, why not? If it is your problem, who else—the stakeholders—is involved? Individuals? Your group? Other groups? The total organization? Suppliers? The community? **Note 1:** Some of these persons or groups may be able to provide assistance/support in identifying the problem. **Note 2:** It is essential to identify early on all parties who have a key (and keen) interest in the problem's resolution. If they are ignored, you run the risk of creating unwanted "post-solution after-effects": "We didn't know that you intended to upgrade the standards." Or: "You didn't tell us that you were going to consolidate the local operations." Or, visualize the bank customer blasting the cowering bank manager with: "You never told us orally, or in writing, that there now would be a per envelope charge for depositing these municipal bond coupons. If you had given us an early warning, we could have made other arrangements."

Severity—Cost: What is the cost (dollar amount) of not solving the problem? Is the cost small enough to merit not solving the problem?

Severity—Frequency: How often does the problem occur? Daily? A.M.? P.M.? Evening? On a particular shift? On any particular day of the week? Weekly? Monthly? Seasonally? Is there a significant trend line?

Severity—Location: Where does the problem take place? Shop? Office? Lab? Warehouse? Headquarters? Field? Is it widespread or isolated?

Severity—System: Is there any relation to particular policies, procedures, rules, procedure, forms, processes?

Severity—Equipment: Is equipment proper? Is there an obsolescence factor or maintenance need? Are hazards or fatigue factors at work?

Action to date: What remedial action, if any, has been considered? What actions, if any, have been actually applied? With what results?

Outcomes: What end result(s) would you want to happen? Would the preferred accomplishment(s) involve a fundamental or major change in what is now being done? A slight to moderate change?

ARE WE SOLVING THE RIGHT PROBLEM?

Most of us, as managers, not only feel that we can solve problems, but that we know better than to work on the wrong problem. But what makes a problem "right"?

Consulting psychologist Jane E. Allen (How to Solve the Right Problem," *Training,* February 1987) has conducted research in identifying what are "right" problems. She advances these criteria:

☐ It is one in which the *organization,* as a cultural entity, will recognize as a problem—that is, one compatible with its norms (standards, values). So it is "safe" to say that there is some kind of disturbance and it's appropriate to act on it. **Note:** a problem in IBM may not be perceived as a problem in General Motors and vice versa.

☐ The *stakeholders* in the situation accept it as a problem. **Note:** A problem may be festering, but without ownership it is hardly likely to be tackled vigorously or at all.

☐ Possible solutions that will remove the perception of a trouble-some situation are in evidence. **Note:** Organizations not only want to solve a problem, but they want all concerned to know that it happened.

☐ It leads to solutions that impact favorably or at least neutrally on profits and costs. **Note:** No one wants solutions that will break the bank!

Allen also states that we have to go further than to assert that we have latched onto something that causes unease. That is to say, we should recognize that problems fall into two vastly different categories: *causality based* and *meaning based.*

Causality-based situations are marked by clear-cut boundaries, connected by **cause and effect.** This allows us to isolate clearly the elements that are part of the problem and which aren't. Also, the elements are related in a linear or logical way. **Example:** an office intercom that isn't working; or, at home, a leaky faucet.

Meaning-based situations are more complex because the boundaries are poorly defined—i.e., we can't tell which elements are contributing to the problem and which aren't. Instead of a cause-and-effect linkage, the nature of the connection depends on the meaning we provide each element. **Example:** Assume a particular sales program is in grave difficulty. What factors are at work? The overall marketing plan? The selection of sales personnel? The training provided? The supervision of the sales force? The product itself? So the elements involved are not givens, but must be analyzed first and then corrected. The interrelations among the elements are not determinable on a cause-and-effect basis, but rather on the *meaning and values* we attach to them. **Example:** the elements which led up to an unsuccessful marriage and ultimately a messy divorce.

What all this points up, says Allen, is that if we don't know whether we are focusing on a causality-based vs. a meaning-based situation, we may choose and solve the wrong problem! This is inevitable because the type of situation determines the type of problem and thus demands a different mode of attack. Specifically, a causality-based situation, which generates problems arising from breaks in cause-and-effect linkages, asks that we analyze the facts in the situation and find those breaks. Conversely, in meaning-based situations, which generate problems arising from differences in assumptions, values, perceptions, we engage in an analysis of process and context as well as facts and try to decide/construct a picture of the possible interconnections. So in the former instance we identify the problem quite clearly; in the latter we have to formulate it.

Allen, then, advises us, as managers, to recognize when we need to use *problem-identification* techniques and when to apply *problem-formulation* approaches. If we can't differentiate between the two, we are very likely to identify and attack the wrong problem. Once we are certain we are in a meaning-based situation, here is the strategy we use, not to find a problem, but to construct it:

1. Ensure organizational interest, concern, and support of the situation. Recognize that every organizational culture has its limits, taboos, pride(s), blind spots. I once worked in an organization where all company products were totally sacrosanct so that it was not wise even to imply that a product that was doing poorly might be a lousy product. A critique of a newly launched product was even a greater heresy.
2. Establish clearly the identity of the stakeholders in the situation and their views (values, perceptions, assumptions, biases) related to the problem. Because these individuals have ownership of the situation, their "world view" about the situation is basic to any acceptable formulation of the nature of the problem. And the emphasis on involving stakeholders must be very broad. That is, we must capture as many of them as we possibly can for their perceptual inputs—whether wise, wooly, wacky, or

otherwise—in combination, will make for the most valid formulation of what the problem really is.

3. Include in the gathering of information not only the *content* of the problem, but the *context* and *process* as well. The latter two areas relate to the culture of the organization—norms, values, attitudes, perceptions, unstated as well as stated assumptions, including any discrepancies between those assumptions. Inconsistencies between actual and espoused (formal, adopted) policies need to be pointed out, for they may well be the source of the sore spot in the system.

4. Avoid creating "winners and losers" by building consensus among the stakeholders. The consensus process involves a "talking through" to get agreement on what seems to be going on, i.e., the troubled state. If all differing views as to the disturbance are not reconciled, we will not have authentic information on the formulation of our problem. Allen points out that managers may have learned in their experience to seek consensus on *selecting a decision* or solution regarding a problem. But much less common is the tendency to seek consensus in *defining the problem* at the outset. More typical is unilateral problem definition, followed by attempts by the manager to sell or persuade the stakeholders on that definition. This nonconsensual approach, if bought by the stakeholders, is certain to force a lot of time and thought on the wrong problem.

If we ask enough questions and the right ones, it may well turn out that a different problem is involved than the one we had identified initially, or possibly that we don't have a problem.

Anecdote: To illustrate the importance of knowing whether or not we have a problem (problem identification), the story of the six-year-old boy, apparently mute, is pertinent. It seems that Junior had never spoken a word until one morning he cried out: "There are lumps in my G—d D—n oatmeal." His parents, taken aback by his choice of language, but elated at his sudden, clear-cut speech, asked their son in wonder: "Junior, how come you haven't spoken until now?" Replied the six-year-old: "I never had a problem before!"

Defining/Formulating Our Problem

A proper formulation of a problem is indispensible to its resolution. Yet, as clinical psychologists tell us, people often formulate or frame a problem in ways that make resolving it extremely difficult if not impossible. This occurs in both organizational and personal/individual life. **Examples:** "The market isn't what it used to be." "We've already organized three times in the last two years, and we're still in the same box." "We simply can't match their product line." "Sell the boss on my idea? No way. He only listens to the apple polishers." "If I had the (education, know-how, track record, experience, time, energy, smarts, connections, influence), it would be different." "How can I soar like the eagles when I have to work with a bunch of turkeys?"

What is at work here is the formulation (definition) of a problem in terms (frames) that are instantly and totally self-defeating. The statements are framed on the basis of blame of others, self-blame, resignation, creation of imaginary, mile-high barriers, repeating of a patently unsuccessful course of action, and the like.

In respect to framing, the good news is that we can frame or reframe the problem in positive terms so that psychologically we can look on our problem as a challenge or even an opportunity, instead of looking at it as an impossible headache. So rather than saying despairingly to ourselves or, worse, to the staff, "We really have a tough problem here," we can reframe it in more positive terms: "Hey, here's one that we can really sink our teeth into."

Visualize the relief pitcher who comes into the ballgame in the ninth inning, the score is tied, there are three men on base, and no one is out. How should *he* frame the problem?

And if a project or activity results in a *less-than-success* result (note that we didn't say failure), our reframing should cause us to say something like this: "I (we) didn't fail, I (we) learned."

A useful opportunity for reframing lies in the concepts of disappointment vs. frustration. In the former, we did not get what we thought we would. In the latter, we didn't get it, but "we're still going after it," psychologically speaking, when we should "let go" of it. So it's up to us to shift (reframe) from frustration—a pointless, irritating frame—to disappointment, which, as a frame, is much easier to tolerate and to leave behind.

Note that when we are talking about "reframing," we mean changing the significance of a behavior/interaction/event by either reinterpreting it or placing it in a different or more helpful context.

Management consultant Judy Springer (in a workshop of the National Society of Performance and Instruction, January 1988), asserts that all of us have a choice about how we think, how we see things, how we sort out and make sense of all the data constantly coming at us. The manager's job is to provide frames for the followers, preferably to help them glimpse some higher vision, a worthwhile *outcome,* not just a vexing problem. The reality is that it takes more energy out of us to focus on a problem than through the lens of a desired outcome. So if we, as managers, want to point out worthwhile directions and set a challenging mission, we must offer people a different frame to find an outcome that we (and they) strongly want.

Empowering people, says Springer, involves providing them with an "as if" frame, creating visually the wanted outcome as if it were at hand, unfettered by the usual perceived limitations and road-blocks; then moving out of the first frame into a second one in which we think back on what we did to get "there" (frame one) and "beyond" (frame two). But, note, all this visualization for reframing is not just reaching for a standard dose of optimism; rather, real effort and follow-through are essential, too.

The frame of reference we adopt, including the label we apply to it (e.g., "it's a cost problem" or "a morale problem"), will determine which route our inquiry will take, and this will be for the better or worse. At times by reformulating or reframing our problem—e.g., recognizing realistically that a product the market won't accept is not a promotional problem, but one, possibly, of acceptance (need or benefit), or quality, or convenience, or cost, etc., we are in a better position to resolve our real difficulty.

Or take the problem of ensuring production of quality products. The U.S. approach (problem formulation), traditionally, was to ask: "How can we structure things so that we don't have faulty products leaving the plant?" The response thus was to cover the plant with a layer of inspectors. But the Japanese after World War II, adopting the quality control ideas of management guru William Deming, saw the problem in totally different terms. In their framing of the problem they saw it as an *individual worker problem.* They thus got each worker to take responsibility for all the quality aspects of his own job, including stopping the assembly line if needed. As they say (in Detroit), the rest was history.

Anecdote: The importance of proper formulation of a problem, and reframing it as may be necessary, is illustrated by an incident involving a seven-year-old boy who had a bat and a baseball. He said: "I'm the world's greatest batter," threw the ball in the air, and swung the bat vigorously, but missed. He repeated the procedure two more times, missing the ball each time. On his fourth try he reframed the problem as he missed the ball and said: "I'm the world's greatest pitcher."

Pitfalls and Perils in Problem Solving

There are many traps that may bedevil us as problem identifiers and formulators. A number of them are presented in Chapter 11 (The Manager as a Problem Solver and Decision Maker: Key Issues and Guidelines for Effectiveness).

A common difficulty is that of *denial,* a process of not facing up to things that are taking place in the real world. For example, when competitors clearly have a leg up on us, we may emit dubious and less-than-helpful declarations such as: "Yeah, but how long will *they* last?" "We're still number one." "There are a lot of factors beyond our control." "Look at the wages they pay," and so on. These denials are essentially defenses against reality. They are a means of coping with the bad news. But they are not helpful ways of confronting the problem head on, as painful as reality may be.

Other traps in defining the problem may include overreacting due to:

☐ **The amplifier effect**—responding to overly loud complaints. Does the "squeaky wheel gets the grease" phenomenon define the severity of the problem and get our excited response?

☐ **The one-postcard effect**—allied to the above pitfall is the reality that one complaint from a customer, scribbled hastily on a postcard, doesn't mean that our new product/service is in serious trouble and that we better get a new advertising agency to bail us out.

One of the added traps that bedevil many would-be problem identifiers is to reach for a solution before a careful diagnosis (see Figure 1) is made of the problem in all its dimensions. A typically common, quickie response, when confronted with a performance problem, is to decide that we have a "training" problem. Is production low? Set up a training course. Are accidents up?

Let's get some training going. Are customers complaining about service? Let's get the service reps back in class. And so on.

Certainly, quite often training may be the way we should define our problem. But a more sophisticated problem diagnosis may indicate that other causative factors—other than a lack of skill or knowledge—account for the ineffective performance. **Examples:**

The environment. Your investigation may indicate that there is a lack of space, poor lighting, lack of privacy (for interviewing and telephone work), excess heat from the sun in the afternoon, etc.

The system. Problems may develop due to improper or dated policies, procedures, rules, processes, delays in getting needed materials, inadequate feedback, equipment failures, etc.

Motivation. People may not be performing because of improper incentives, which may indicate a need to alter the reward system. An illustration of the relation of motivation to performance occurred in a large grocery warehouse plagued by increasing back injuries due to improper lifting. The warehouse superintendent came to the training department and asked for a training program on proper lifting for the warehouse crew. Fortunately, the training people knew the history of the warehouse, safety and training-wise. They recalled that they had provided training on proper lifting two ago. As they saw the problem, it was not that the workers did not know how to lift properly, but that they had become lackadaisical in their lifting practices. So instead of training, the trainers proposed a short meeting with the foremen regarding the use of positive reinforcement. Their idea was for the foremen to praise each worker when he lifted properly or used a buddy to help on heavy loads: "Hey, that's the way to do it, George. Good show. That'll save your back." Did the praise-giving approach work? Yes indeed. Injuries due to improper lifting plummeted dramatically.

Also, there are numerous other alternatives to training, including use of job aids, altering selection methods, restructuring/redesigning/enriching jobs, modeling by the boss, team building, revamping the physical layout, better maintenance of equipment, and so on.

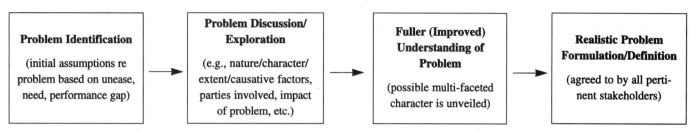

Figure 10-2. Securing a reality-based definition/formulation of our problem.

Reality Testing

The final step in the process of problem definition/formulation is to pose these questions to ourselves:

☐ Have we distinguished between what is essential and what is desirable?

☐ Have we distinguished between what is possible and what is beyond our capabilities?

☐ Have we distinguished between efficiency and effectiveness? Management guru Peter Drucker makes a significant distinction between *efficient* and *effective*. The former relates to doing a job right, the latter to doing the right thing. Thus, we may be very efficient (high productivity, high quality, low cost) at manufacturing buggy whips, but very few people are likely to buy them. So the question for any manager and/or his work team to ask repeatedly is: Are we doing the right things? Staff units (personnel, office management services, finance, etc.) in particular, which are created solely to serve line operations, should periodically pose that question to themselves.

As part of our reality testing, it may be desirable to corroborate our responses to these questions with others who are in close touch with the problem—peers, colleagues, clients, bosses, suppliers, customers, community members, etc. Remember, good ideas come from exchange opportunities. What is needed, then, is someone (one or more persons) off of whom we can bounce our ideas.

Another aspect of reality assurance in our problem statements is to guard against "simplistic" thinking. Undoubtedly you have encountered perceptive individuals who have labeled problem formulations as simplistic. What do they mean? Taking a problem of considerable complexity and reducing it to a false unidimensionality. Essentially what is being done is to ignore or downplay significant, ramified, complicating factors. **Example:** Ascribing high turnover to compensation practices when employee departures may be due more realistically to such causative factors as poor working conditions, mediocre (or worse) supervision, lack of job challenge, being dead-ended, job stress, etc.

Simplistic thinking or surface-deep analysis typically is pursued for reasons such as these:

☐ A quest for a "quick fix," an easy-to-understand solution. Time pressures also may contribute to this "easy way out" approach.

☐ A bias as to the best course of action relative to a given problem—"standard" rather than creative thinking is applied. This might be termed the "Johnny One Note" approach.

☐ An unwillingness to face up to a more complex reality, for it may demand a painful process of adjustment.

☐ "Tunnel vision"—use of provincial rather than global thinking entailing an inability to cope with multiple causation. But as we know, problems often are subject to many factors rather than one.

Anecdote: It seems that there was a chap who was run over by the Labor Day Parade in downtown Chicago. His friend visited him in the hospital and asked: "What went wrong?" The unfortunate victim responded realistically: "It was a combination of things."

A recap of Step 1, Identifying and Defining/Formulating Our Problem, is given in Figure 2.

A number of practical tools to help you, as a conscientious and perceptive manager, identify problems realistically are presented in the following section.

A guide sheet to assist you in defining/formulating the problem is given in Figure 3, page 509. It should help you to get on track and to stay on it.

Tools for Effective Problem Solving

Problem solving is a leadership skill underpinned by a good number of philosophical, conceptual, and research-based approaches. It also is an area buttressed by a variety of tools or techniques "to make it happen." Consistent use of these devices will upgrade your problem-solving skills and increase the likelihood of achieving high-quality solutions to problems. The techniques described below are particularly helpful in identifying problems.

☐ Pareto Analysis
☐ Brainstorming
☐ Rolestorming
☐ Scatter Diagram
☐ Check Sheet
☐ Problem Identification—ABC Approach
☐ Numerical Indicators of Problems
☐ Priority Setting
☐ Consultants—When It Makes Sense to Use Them

Pareto Analysis

Vilfredo Pareto (1848–1943), an Italian mathematician, economist, and sociologist, researched the distribution of wealth in Italy. He found that 80% of his country's wealth was controlled by 20% of the population. From this finding, he postulated his famous "Law of Disproportionate Distribution," known commonly as the 80/20 rule or the principle of "the vital few and the trivial many."

Examples (hypothetical, but not atypical) of Pareto's Law abound:

☐ 80% of the sales may come from 20% of the product line.
☐ 80% of the sales may come from 20% of the sales reps.
☐ 80% of the complaints may come from 20% of the employees (or the customers).
☐ 80% of the accidents may be experienced by 20% of the employees.
☐ 80% of a politician's exposure came from 20% of his speeches.
☐ 80% of the turnover may come from a small percentage (15% to 20%) of the job classifications.

☐ 80% of the revenue in brokerage houses may come from 20% of the account executives.

Two actual examples of the "maldistribution rule" are as follows:

☐ In Washington, D.C. (reported by *The Washington Post,* August 12, 1991), less than 1% of the 4,800 police officers are the subject of nearly 25% of the complaints pending before the Civilian Complaint Review Board. Forty-four officers had three or more complaints pending against them for harassment, verbal abuse, or excessive force.
☐ Tests in Chicago, Los Angeles and other cities evidenced that 50% of all carbon monoxide emissions came from only 10% of moving vehicles. Similarly, 14% of the cars account for half of the emitted hydrocarbons (reported in *The Wall Street Journal,* September 27, 1991).

Pareto's analysis is a practical, easy-to-use tool to identify our graver problems, those which merit our expenditure of significant resources. We can't work on every problem, so we need to learn which ones have the greater payoff possibilities.

Here is an example of how we might apply Pareto Analysis to a company problem. Let's assume the Rickety and Howe Toy Service, Inc., manufactures, markets, and ships toys to retailers in the U.S. and 15 foreign countries. Complaints about goods received by retailers seem to be increasing. The operations manager thus decided to give the problem to one of the Employee Productivity/Quality Teams for study. The team studied the complaint letters for August and September, a heavy shipping period, and listed the complaints in a table (see Table 1). The Team then grouped (consolidated) the complaints into a small number of categories (see Table 2).

The team put the data into a bar chart—The Pareto Diagram (see Figure 4). The chart shows each category of complaint on *both* a numerical and percentage basis. The 100% figure (right vertical line of diagram) relates to the total number of complaints (left vertical line of diagram). By segregating or scaling the percentage line downward (from 100 to 0) we can readily see how the percentages for each category relate to the numerical data. The cumulative or "cum" line, which goes from 0% on the left to 100% on the right, shows the accumulated total of complaints as we go from the far left bar to the bars on the right.

Table 10-1
Complaints from Retailers Concerning Toy Shipments
(Months of August and September)

Complaint	Number of Complaints
Broken parts	120
Missing parts	85
Non-functioning toys	50
Incomplete shipments (some items missing)	25
Damaged shipments	18
Erroneous shipments (totally wrong items)	12
Missing instruction sheets	30
Late shipments	20
Wrong colors shipped	4
Wrong sized items shipped	6
Over shipments (right item, but extra amounts)	16
Missing shipments	4
Billing problems	10
Total complaints	**400**

Table 10-2
Grouping (Consolidation) of Retailer Complaints

Complaint	Number of Complaints
Parts problems (broken or missing)	205
Shipping problems	105
Non-functioning toys	50
Missing instruction sheets	30
Billing	10
Total complaints	**400**

The chart shows that the first two bars—parts and shipping problems, respectively—account for the main sources of the complaints. This gives the team a clear indication of what the major problems are and thus sets priorities for further problem solving. In the absence of such an analysis, problem solving could hardly proceed in a very orderly way.

Pareto Analysis ensures that large bundles of data are sorted out and put into workable perspective for the manager and the team. An anecdote about a wealthy lawyer and his accountant makes the point about the horrors of

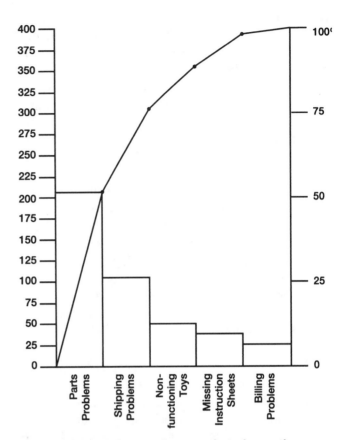

Figure 10-4. A Pareto diagram that shows the number and corresponding percentage of complaints presented by retailing to a top manufacturing compa-

a limited perspective: It seems that the lawyer asked his accountant to check out a particular horse in which he was interested. In the course of their phone conversation from the stable, the accountant provided a ton of data: height, weight, age, condition of teeth, hide and hair, prior owner, and so on. Finally, exasperated, the lawyer asked: "But what does the horse look like?" To which the accountant, constricted by a short phone line, replied,

"Well, sir, on this side it's brown."

To sum up the 80/20 rule or Pareto's Principle: It tells us that there is a mismatch between cause and effect—80% of the important results (e.g., gross sales) come from 20% of the programs/activities responsible for those key results (e.g., 20% of the products or 20% of the sales staff). Thus the "vital few" produce the biggest payoff.

Brainstorming

Brainstorming, an "invention" of the 1950s, is a remarkably effective tool to identify problems, to suggest causes for problems, and to produce solutions to resolve a problem. As a means of generating ideas, albeit for these different purposes, it has become integrated into the manager's everyday vocabulary: "Why don't we brainstorm it?"

However, it is often more valuable to use brainstorming in its original and more structured form. Procedurally, then, a brainstorming session works best if conducted along these lines:

1. If possible, inform participants of the problem in advance of the brainstorming session. Encourage them to think about the problem. Of course, it is also effective to conduct a session as the need arises, without advance notice, e.g., in a staff meeting.

2. Present your problem in highly limited terms—not "How can we improve operations?", but "What can we do to satisfy our customers better?" A narrow, finite problem is easier for people to sink their teeth into as opposed to a broad, global, or open-ended one.

3. Limit the group to six or 10 people. A large group makes for an unwieldy operation.

4. Keep things informal and fun-oriented. Set up chairs in a circle. Participants get "turned on" if they can see their colleagues in action. Refreshments help to make for a relaxed atmosphere.

5. Appoint a moderator to explain the several, simple ground rules (see "Rules for Brainstorming," below); to start things off; "to encourage "ideation," particularly if there's a lag in it ("We've got two flipchart sheets full of ideas; let's see if we can fill up another one.") **Note:** An added round of contributions is very likely to produce higher quality ideas because participants have had their thinking on the topic well provoked.

6. Join the brainstorming group as a participant, assuming you have delegated the moderator role to someone else, as above.

7. Appoint a recorder to capture the group's ideas. Recording them on a flipchart is preferred because eyeballing the posted ideas is a means of stimulating added ones. If you don't have a flipchart, an ordinary writing pad will do.

8. You can conduct the brainstorming session in one of two ways:
   a) **"Round Robin"**: Go around the circle several times, and have each participant submit an idea when his turn comes. **Advantages:** It is orderly, it is easier for the recorder to jot down the

generated ideas, and it encourages everyone to join in on an equal basis.
   b) **"Free form"**: All participants submit ideas as rapidly and as often as they can. **Advantages:** It becomes a fun-filled, exciting, involving, and active experience. The spirited, fast-paced process is likely to produce a "contagious" effect, with each participant's idea stimulating the others to create and contribute added ideas. This format obviously makes for harder work for the recorder because the ideas come fast and furious. Another "negative" is that the more reticent people may take a "backseat" to their more verbal colleagues. **Suggestion:** Try both methods. The personality of your group will determine which style works better for you.

9. When ideas seem to lag, the moderator should call time, have the recorder count the number of ideas generated by the group, and say something encouraging like this: ""We have produced 27 ideas in six minutes. That's very good. Let's stand up now, stretch a bit, and then we'll conduct a second round."

10. The moderator, and the participants as well, are not to comment on ideas, either positively or negatively. Negative comments may "turn off" potential contributors ("They don't seem to want my ideas.") Complimentary comments about a particular idea may imply that the other ideas are not as as "great." This, again, may discourage ideation. **Note:** At this stage of the process, our concern is to *generate* ideas, not evaluate them. Evaluation is a later, second process.

11. If the group is new to brainstorming, as described herein, a warm-up topic may be used to give participants a quick feel for the process. **Suggested topics:** "What uses can we make of this brick?" (or this paper clip or ball of cord). Or: "My dog has a terrible case of fleas. How might he have gotten them?"

12. After the ideation phase is completed, another session should be held to evaluate the ideas. This may be done immediately after ideation, later in the day, or the next day. **Note:** The evaluation session is a more deliberate, calm, and orderly one than the idea-generating one.

Rules for Brainstorming

A brainstorming session has five key ground rules:

1. **"Free wheeling" is wanted.** In the ideation stage we don't worry about how wild, wooly, or wacky the ideas may be. "Wild" ideas can be "tamed down" later. And allegedly far-out ideas may prove to be the breakthroughs the group is seeking. Actually, "wild" ideas are part of the fun and can stimulate others to think freely (and thus creatively) rather than cautiously.

2. **"Hitchhiking" is OK,** That is, one can "piggyback" or build on someone else's idea, combine ideas, add to an idea, etc.

3. **Quantity is wanted.** Out of quantity will come quality. The greater the pool of ideas, the more likely a number of "gems" will be produced. This is why we stress such concepts as encouraging "contagion," avoiding positive or negative comments and conducting a second round.

4. **Critical remarks are taboo, for we want all the ideas we can get.** Negative comments like "We tried that before," "The big boss won't go for it," "What about the cost?" are certain to dampen the ardor of contributors. So try to keep the process upbeat. One way to deal with negatives is to have the moderator blow a loud whistle or ring a bell when they are given. Remember, the basic principle of brainstorming is to separate idea generation from idea evaluation—the principle of deferred judgment—because the intermingling of the two decreases ideation.

5. **Conduct an evaluation session after the ideation session.** At this point, participants weigh, sift, assess, judge, recast, and discard ideas.

Rolestorming

Rolestorming is a cousin to and offshoot of brainstorming, according to management consultant Richard E. Griggs who gives it high marks for creativity, openness, originality, and implementation success ("Training Today," *Training,* November 1985).

Here's how it works. Each group member assumes the role of another person, someone not in the group such as a peer, subordinate, boss. He then brainstorms ideas based on how the other person, given the other's attitudes, values and/or predelictions, would propose them.

The rolestorming follows the usual brainstorming procedures. Griggs asserts that the second-go-around in rolestorming increases group ideation by 60% to 70%. Why does it work so well? Because people, liberated from being themselves, are free to attribute ideas to

someone else! Says Griggs: ". . . anyone with a really crazy idea can say it without anyone knowing that it was really their own."

The Scatter Diagram

A scatter diagram is a graph showing the relationship between two variables, e.g., errors and time of day; accidents and months on the job; rejects and hours of overtime.

The data on the graph may suggest a straight-line relationship, as determined by an "eye inspection." This may show that "Y" (the vertical axis) increases as "X" (the horizontal axis) increases. This signifies a positive, linear relationship. The reverse, a negative relationship, may also occur: Y increases as X decreases, e.g., accidents increase as positive reinforcement by supervisors decrease. Figure 5 illustrates a scatter diagram presenting a positive relationship between the variables of sales and and hours of training.

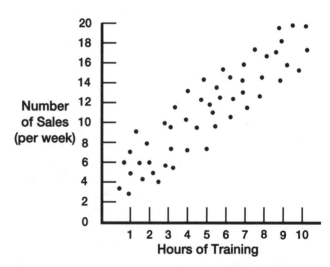

Figure 10-5. A scatter diagram showing a positive relationship between number of sales per week and hours of training received.

Check Sheet

A helpful way to identify problems your employees are having before those problems become chronic is to use a check sheet to monitor their performance. In Figure 6 (page 510), we show the productivity (number of written inquiries handled) of a customer relations staff. The idea is to locate trends or patterns of an unwanted sort. The data are used as a means of zeroing in on problem performers and to develop a plan to remedy their performance deficits.

By visual inspection of Figure 6, we can tell quickly that Pat and Sandy are the top performers; Jean and Kim are the weakest; and Al started well, but after returning from leave (week 4), his production slumped steadily.

As managers, we can use a check sheet to assess skill/capability of our subordinate supervisors, possibly averting serious problems before they occur. In Figure 7 (page 510), the manager of a large independent supermarket has ranked the capabilities of his department heads on a 5-point scale, 1 being low and 5 being high. Ratings of 3 or less are circled, and appropriate counseling is given or performance improvement plans are developed jointly with the problem-type department heads.

Check sheets may be used for a whole host of purposes: accident trends; tardiness and absenteeism; and quality and cost indicators such as waste, re-work, rejects, returns, customer complaints.

Problem Identification—A B C Approach

One way to "jump-start" your work team's thinking about unit problems is to have them review the multi-faceted question list given in Figure 8 (page 511). The idea is that working from this list makes problem identification "as easy as A B C."

Numerical Indicators of Problems (and Opportunities)

Many problems can be identified readily by zeroing in on various quantitative indicators—everything from sales expense and turnover to customer complaints and employee suggestions. See Table 3, Various Quantitative Indicators To Identify Problems/Opportunities.

Note, however, that we are only talking about *indicators* of problems. The *causes* for a given indicator typically will require further digging.

Priority Setting

If at any one time you and your work team do a comprehensive job of identifying problems, e.g., at a team building session, you undoubtedly will encounter a greater number of problems than can be tackled at one time. Hence, the need to sort out or prioritize them.

Specific criteria, of course, are needed to help set those priorities. Possible factors to serve as criteria are the following:

Frequency: What is the predominance, prevalence, widespread character, or frequency of the problem?

Severity: How serious, critical or severe is the problem?

Solvability: How amenable or vulnerable is the problem to possible resolution (success likelihood)?

Some groups may wish to add other criteria such as cost, time factors, customer impact (likelihood of customer acceptance), and so on.

Figure 9 (page 512) provides an illustration of priority ranking of various problems identified by a work team. The criteria (frequency, severity, solvability) used to set the priorities are assessed on a 5-point scale, with 1 being low and 5 being high. Note that the rankings are subject to a weighting process. This is accomplished by *multiplying* the rankings from left to right (e.g., $2 \times 3 \times 3 = 18$). If we only added those numbers (rankings), the differences among the totals for the four problems would not receive the same prominence.

Consultants—When It Makes Sense to Use Them

Although managers and employees undoubtedly know their organization best, consultants can bring a perspective to bear on problem identification and resolution that often goes beyond in-house knowledge. More specifically, consultants can be helpful in organizational problem solving when the following elements are needed:

Objectivity

An "outsider" can bring to the organization a view, approach, or style that is not influenced by in-house policies, politics, programs, traditions, values, or experience.

Special Expertise

Based on their broad experience and special skills, consultants often can learn better about organization problems from customers, suppliers, and competitors as well as from the in-house staff.

Breadth of Experience

The consultant typically works in a variety of organizational settings. He may thus bring a broad-gauged, more realistic view of the "real world" to the in-house effort to identify or to deal with a given problem.

Special Qualifications

An outside consultant may be more prepared professionally, often with an advanced degree in his field.

Table 10-3

Various Quantitative Indicators to Identify Problems/Opportunities

Ratios (miscellaneous)	Time factors	Money factors	Other miscellaneous numerical factors
Employee turnover	Response time to fill orders (average)	Unit production cost	Sales (no. of units)
Inventory turnover	Response time to complaints (average)	Sales volume	New accounts
Accidents	Unit production time	Sales expense	Accounts closed
Absenteeism	Setup time	Maintenance costs	Customer complaints
Grievances	Down time	Repair costs	Errors
Employee suggestions received (in relation to total work force)	Rework time	Salary expense	Waste
		Materials costs	Rejects
Employee Suggestions adopted (in relation to those received)		Utilities costs	Rework (no. of units)
		Overtime costs	No. of employees:
Overtime		Bad debts	a) full time
		Equipment rental costs suggestions received	b) part time
			No. of employee
		Savings from suggestion plan	No. of returns (of good/product)

Such a person is likely to have a deep grasp of the subject, be very current in it, and add an element of prestige and support to the problem-solving effort.

Risk Taking

An outsider may be able to take "risks" and offer fresh, innovative approaches that an inside person may not be able to do. The "outsider" is not bound, of course, by the prevailing culture, norms, or traditions as is the in-house staff.

A Second Opinion

At times, in-house ideas may merit corroboration or reinforcement by tapping the experience and prestige of the outside consultant.

In general, the question to ask when considering the use of consulting services is this: Who is the most qualified to aid in the problem-solving effort? For to always rely exclusively on internal resources, regardless of the situation/problem, may mean depriving the problem-solving effort of an important resource.

To aid in choosing a consultant properly, see Figure 10, Do We Need a Consultant? (page 512).

STEP 2: GATHERING INFORMATION ABOUT THE PROBLEM

The best way to have a good idea is to have a LOT of ideas.

—Linus Pauling, (1901–1994), American chemist, two-time Nobel prize winner (chemistry in 1954, and peace in 1962) and guru of vitamin C.

It's not what we don't know that gives us trouble. It's what we know that ain't so.

—Will Rogers (1879–1935), American humorist and actor

If we wish high-quality solutions to our problems, the solutions must be data-based. Unfortunately, a heavy investment in collecting facts and information for problem identification, analysis, and definition before we decide is not always an approach followed by managers. As Dr. Thomas C. Tuttle of the Maryland Center for Quality and Productivity, University of Maryland, puts it, "This approach is not natural for managers and specialists. Our training and much of our reinforcement comes from 'putting out fires.' The idea that we should collect data before action, while logical, is unnatural for action-oriented American managers" (*The Maryland Workplace,* Newsletter of the Maryland Center for Quality and Productivity, Winter 1989).

The aim of Step 2 in our logical and orderly problem-solving process is to avoid the trap of the "fire-fighting mode," that is, moving into action (decision making) at the sound of the fire-house bell. What is needed, instead, is to slow the action down and attempt to learn all we can about the difficulty—background information, historical material, cause and effect data, the forces at work in the situation.

The information we collect typically is referred to as a "database." A good database (Stephen L. Cohen, "Information, Please," *Training and Development Journal,* July 1989) has these characteristics:

Usefulness (or relevancy): Can it be applied readily to a decision that you need to make?

Validity: Is it accurate—that is, does it reflect or measure what it is supposed to reflect or measure?

Reliability: Can your data be reproduced over time by other data collectors?

Measurable: Is it quantifiable? German philosopher Immanuel Kant has observed: "When you can measure what you're talking about and express it in numbers, you know what you're talking about." If your data are not measurable, are they at least observable?

One of the many myths of problem solving is that to solve a problem successfully, our main job is "to get the facts." Certainly effective problem solving is dependent on good data collection. But to assume that gathering facts is a certain route to resolving a problem is quite simplistic. For when we talk about getting the facts, we have to recognize that people have different value systems, backgrounds, and perceptions, and thus have different *assumptions* about what facts to collect and accept.

So we have to deal with questions such as these: Whose facts? What facts? What is and is not relevant? How "hard" (quantifiable) or "soft" (qualitative) should these facts be? To what degree do we accept opinion and judgment in lieu of or in relation to facts? How current or recent must the data be? Which sources are acceptable and which are not? When is enough data enough?

Data Can Be Dangerous

While this chapter stresses the importance of data collection as a vital tool in problem solving, data may be collected (and worshiped) when it is inappropriate to do so. For example, management guru Peter Drucker ("Marketing 101 for a Fast-Changing Decade," *The Wall Street Journal,* November 20, 1990) points out the debacle that occurred in the U.S. regarding the marketing (or non-marketing) of the fax machine.

Would you believe that the fax is American in all respects—invention, technology, design, and development? In fact, U.S. manufacturers had produced them and were ready to sell them, but decided against it due to negative data from the marketplace. As a result, all fax machines used in the U.S. are imports. What happened?

As Drucker explains it, the U.S. manufacturers didn't put the machines on the market because market research said convincingly that there was no demand for the product. But the flaw in this reasoning, says Drucker, is that we cannot conduct market research on a product not now in the market. So if in our data collection we were to ask potential users if they would buy a $1,500 telephone accessory gadget to transmit for $1 a page the same letter the Postal Service delivers for a small portion of that amount, we can anticipate a resounding negative response.

The Japanese, however, looked at the *market,* rather than market research. They learned that economics (cost) are a poor guide to the information and communication markets. All the other technological successes—mainframe computers, PCs, copy machines, car phones, VCRs—were marketed on a non-economic basis, for none reduces costs or increases profits, says Drucker. More important, the Japanese, instead of asking: "What is the market for this machine?", asked: "What is the market for what it does?" They thus saw the huge demand for courier services (e.g., Federal Express) and realized that the market for the fax was already there.

Tapping Ideas of Staff

A given in today's management culture is that managers are supposed to elicit ideas from their staff to help solve unit problems. Yet all too often employees are reluctant to advance their ideas, even when specifically asked for them. An "Anyone have any ideas what might be done about this?" may produce only blank stares. Dr. Darrell W. Ray and Barbara L. Wiley ("How To Generate New Ideas," *Supervisory Management,* November 1985) suggest that such employee reluctance is a result of unintentional discouragement of employee ideation by the boss. The latter does this by trying to be too protective of his own ideas. Ray and Wiley call this phenomenon "ideanarcissism." Recall the handsome youth, Narcissus, in Greek mythology who became highly enamored with his physical beauty. Similarly, bosses may become mesmerized by the value of their own ideas. The unfortunate result: creativity of others is smothered—"Why bother to suggest anything? The boss has all the answers."

To overcome ideanarcissism, Ray and Wiley suggest that managers should do the following:

1. Recognize that one's ideas, even though worthwhile, are still based on prior and allied thinking by others. No one develops ideas in total isolation from others. To quote Issac Newton, "If I have seen further, it is by standing upon the shoulders of giants." Hence, egotism in reference to the uniqueness of one's ideas is hardly warranted. (An analogy in the field of athletics is the statement of humility by a superstar about "the talents I have been given," as opposed to self-congratulation for his accomplishments.

2. Create an operating climate whereby employees are encouraged to think constantly in terms of creativity, innovation, new approaches. Conversely, allowing people to become slaves to the tried and true, the established routine, can only produce rigid, non-innovative behavior. New ideas should be fully rewarded, preferably in "public," whenever possible: "Great idea, Pat. Your approach will really make a difference on the R-4W project."

3. Treat your own ideas as group property. What is important is that good ideas, regardless of the source, are created, submitted unhesitatingly, and fully implemented. So don't insist on labeling ideas as yours. Your main concern is fostering an environment friendly to creative thinking, not insisting on idea ownership. In fact, an idea billed as the boss' may discourage others from trying to improve on it. Status (the boss') *is* a fact of organizational life.

If a major role of the supervisor/manager in the area of creativity is that of idea generator by staff, Ray and Wiley recommend that he engage in the following behaviors:

☐ Serve as a resource for ideas. From time to time, pass out helpful articles on subjects of unit concern. The idea is to communicate that everyone is to think continually about work improvement and to offer aids for that purpose.

☐ Drop ideas informally to others. If the other party responds favorably, possibly with an added twist, compliment him for his good thinking on the idea. Provide added support for the "new" idea over time. Ideas typically take time to be fully digested.

☐ Present ideas you like, proposed by outside experts, to the staff. Point out the fact that the idea comes from a key figure in the field. Again, this shows that you are seeking ideas from multiple sources and are not "tooting your own horn."

☐ Present new assignments on a "come back and let's talk further" basis. This approach gives the subordinate time to mull it over and possibly develop some new angles for the conduct of the project.

☐ When introducing a fairly complex problem, ask people to think about it. Then bring it up on a later occasion such as at a staff meeting, discuss it a bit, and let it gestate further. At a later meeting or two, further inputs should be elicited. The merit to this gradual approach, say Ray and Wiley, is to encourage thought over time, to let resistances melt gradually, and to gain collective agreement ultimately as to the best course of action based upon unhurried involvement by all concerned. An approach of this nature is a sensible way to overcome resistance to change and all the anxieties typically associated with the introduction of "the new."

Another technique to elicit ideas is to ask staff members to put themselves mentally in charge of the unit and to respond to this question: "If I were the head of this department, I would . . ."

MBWA

Still another way for the manager to gather information is to use the Japanese technique of MBWA—management by walking around. Liberating yourself from the isolation and insulation of the desk in your office and developing rapport with the workforce on the shop or office floor is a good way to collect information. However, simply walking on employee turf is not enough. There must be a sincere effort to raise your antenna very high and to really listen. Employees can differentiate very quickly gimmickry from sincerity, artificiality from authenticity. Phoniness will merely produce a "What's the boss up to now?" reaction. One employee, subject to patently insincere inquiries, put it this way: "Management is like a flock of starlings. They drift in, make a lot of noise, mess up the place, and then take off."

Even better than MBWA, if one is sincerely interested in developing rapport with the rank and file, is MBSA—management by *sitting* around. That is, taking the time to sit down with people to learn how they see the world—their problems, their concerns, their ideas.

Lunch with the boss each week is another practical way to keep in touch with employees, says CEO Paul Bullinger. In fact, since Bullinger likes to cook, he prepares a gourmet meal for six to eight employees. His rationale: "In order to find out what's going on in the company, you have to spend time with people one-on-one." The lunches "give us all a chance to find out what people are doing and give me an opportunity to talk about what I can do to make their jobs easier" ("If That's What the Boss Wants," *The Wall Street Journal*, November 22, 1991).

Depending on your operation, it also may be desirable to walk around *outside* your plant or office. For example, in the retail field the manager might spend a Saturday or Sunday in competitors' stores, watching and possibly interacting with customers and salespeople. Visits to suppliers may also be illuminating from the standpoint of upgrading quality of parts and materials that are purchased.

Management professor Dr. D. Keith Denton recommends ("The Service Imperative," *Personnel Journal*, March 1990) that management use the quality *audit* approach to learn what is going on in the marketplace. This means buying the product or using the service to compare your product/service with the competition. **Example:** A Domino's Pizza quality audit entails store managers going to a friend's house, calling for a pizza, and then assessing the product and the service related to it.

Meeting Information Needs of Employees

Managers know that their workers need adequate information to do their problem-solving activities properly. But they may not be aware that those information needs, particularly for professional and scientific people, may be more profound than what is ordinarily assumed. Dr. Albert Shapiro (*Managing Professional People: Understanding Creative Performance* New York: The Free Press, 1985), points out that knowledge workers in particular need two kinds of information: **Logistical** and **nutrient.**

A *logistical need* arises when the information desired is known and we know how to use it, but the precise content of the information is not known. **Examples:** we want to know the names and titles of our counterparts in five competing companies. Or we want to know the trade balances of the leading European countries in the past decade. Sources for such logistical data are easily identifiable: the library, government reports, information services, and the like.

A *nutrient need,* however, is vastly different. It is information whose use is not yet known. It relates to future use and is important for the all-important growth of the professional or knowledge worker. Thus, there is a need for storage of large amounts of information in the professional worker's memory bank, of which pertinent bits may be tapped when a new, unique, unforeseen need arises. These data become grist for the creation of exciting, tailor-made, high quality solutions—"breakthroughs"—as demanded by the challenging situation.

How does the knowledge worker acquire the needed nutrient information? In many subtle and informal ways: something read in a professional journal or heard at a professional workshop or institute, a conversation over lunch with a colleague, an encounter with equipment on a summer job in years past, and so on. And if the information is deposited in the memory bank, it may be retrieved in both conscious and unconscious ways to form the "grand design."

For the manager supervising such personnel, the significance of nutrient learning or information is quite clear: He must strongly support continuing opportunities for the acquisition of new inputs, whether informally, such as exchange of ideas on the job, or more formally via conferences, courses, wide reading, and the like.

Thus, old attitudes as expressed in the traditional question: "Can we afford such expenditures?" (e.g., to attend a professional meeting or conference), must give way to a more realistic assertion that: "We cannot afford *not* to send our people for growth experiences."

Problems vs. Symptoms

If the leaves on my azalea plants are turning a sickly yellow, I can't merely fixate on the yellowing process, for that is only a symptom of the problem. What I have to do is look for the *causes* underlying the problem, which might be lack of water, air, nutrients, light, or maybe some infestation in the root system. So my need is to look for causes, not manifestations (symptoms) of the problem.

Similarly, at the workplace, instead of diagnosing for causes we may fall into the trap of making causative assumptions and thus confuse symptoms with causes. For example, "low morale" is not the cause of a work problem, but a symptom or indicator of it. Similarly, high turnover, excessive lateness, absenteeism, or grievances are *indicators* of problems but are not the problems themselves. In fact, low morale, high turnover, and absenteeism and the like may have one or more causes.

The task, then, is to dig (diagnose) more deeply to learn of the precise cause(s). If we can learn the cause, like the physician, we then can apply an appropriate treatment.

In respect to turnover, our "natural" response to why people are leaving us is likely to be inadequate pay. But a more careful diagnosis may indicate a range of causative factors, everything from poor supervision and lack of career opportunities to inadequate attention to young parents who have a need for child care.

Consultants at Monsanto's Pensacola plant learned, through careful diagnosis, that if a worker slipped on an oil spot on the floor, the basic cause wasn't the oil at all, but a set of interacting events. Specifically, an understaffed maintenance crew caused machine maintenance deferral which, in turn, allowed a machine to leak and thus caused the oil spill on the floor ("Companies Turn to Peer Pressure To Cut Injuries As Psychologists Join the Battle," *The Wall Street Journal,* March 29, 1991).

The bottom line for the manager, as problem solver, is to see himself as a diagnostician and to function as one. This means avoiding the trap of attacking symptoms, for such an approach won't solve problems. It will merely serve to gloss over the real difficulties. Worthy diagnostic role models are medical doctors, auto mechanics and athletic coaches. They look for causes before they try to fix things.

Cause-and-Effect Diagram

Once we have identified and defined our problem (the effect) clearly, we are ready to seek out *causes* for it. A helpful way to do this is to use the cause-and-effect or Ishikawa fishbone diagram (see Figure 11). The diagram is named after Dr. Kaoru Ishikawa, an engineering professor at Tokyo University, who studied the work of U.S. management writers and researchers and adapted their ideas to Japanese needs. His diagram was adopted for and used extensively in quality circle work in Japan and many foreign countries.

The fishbone diagram can be structured with the various M's of management, as in Figure 11, or we may take major categories of causes we have identified and

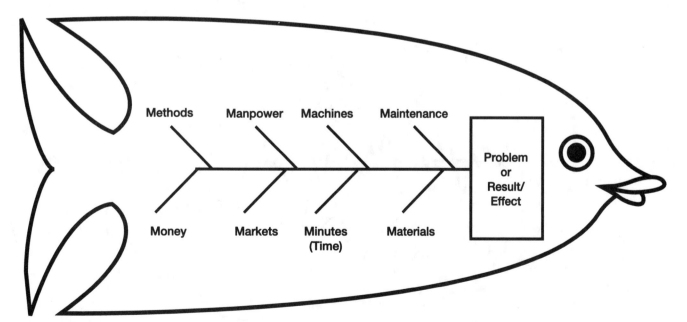

Figure 10-11. Example of a cause-and-effect fishbone diagram using the various "M's" of management. (Team members use this framework to brainstorm causes for each "M".)

list subordinate causative factors related to those broad categories. For example, if we are dealing with defects in an automobile, our major categories might be engine, electrical system, heating and cooling system, transmission, brakes, body, etc., and we would list specific problems or complaints for each major category.

In sum, the idea behind the fishbone diagram is to encourage us to break down each major cause into smaller, more workable elements.

Brainstorming and Rolestorming

We previously presented brainstorming and rolestorming as techniques to aid groups in identifying their problems. In the context of Step 2 of our problem-solving model, these two techniques again can be useful.

For example, the group may be asked to brainstorm the *causes* for problems with illumination in a machine shop. Here's what a productivity improvement team that brainstormed the problem identified as causes: burned-out light bulbs stay put instead of being replaced promptly; smaller-intensity bulbs often are used as replacements; machine dust drifts upward to cover bulbs; bulbs are not cleaned regularly; no planned maintenance (replacement) program; bad bulbs removed but not replaced; larger-size bulbs often out of stock; lights too

high up on ceiling; staffing cuts of maintenance crews; new (added) machines positioned away from established ceiling lights; inadequate number of light fixtures.

Brainstorming and rolestorming obviously can be used by groups to fill in the spaces in the Ishikawa fishbone diagram, cited above.

Problem Diagnosis Using Force Field Analysis

Based on the research of the late Kurt Lewin, a world-renowned social psychologist and pioneer in the field of group dynamics, we can look at any problem situation metaphorically as a "force field," a sea of forces in motion, yet stable (see Figures 12 and 13). That is to say, while the forces are in constant motion, their competing pressures and counterpressures produce a level of equilibrium or stability (a steady-state condition) at any particular point in time. Lewin called this situation "quasi-stationary equilibrium."

We thus can look at any organizational phenomenon—production level, sales, error rate, costs, absenteeism, scrap, accident rate, rework, degree of employee satisfaction—and identify the forces at work that are keeping it at a particular level. The forces may be looked at as being of two sorts: Favorable—encouraging, facilitating, or pushing toward the desired level, and

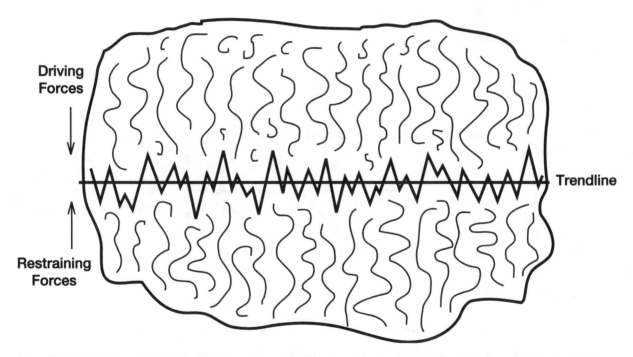

Figure 10-12. Despite the fluctuations, the forces at work produce a steady, discernable trend line.

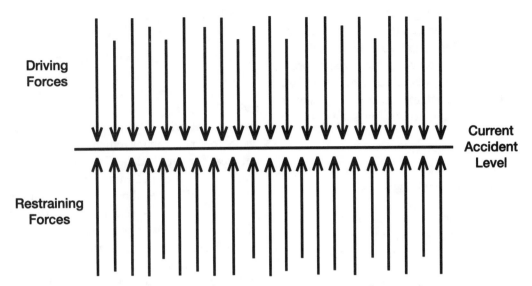

Figure 10-13. A force field analysis showing the various factors influencing the level of equilibrium.

unfavorable—discouraging or resisting movement toward the desired level. We call the former forces the *driving* forces and the latter the *restraining* forces.

To illustrate the two opposing forces, let's take the accident level at the XYZ plant. Let's visualize the driving and restraining forces at work, the former serving to change or lower the accident level and the latter exerting pressure to increase the accident level or possibly to maintain it at its current level (see Figure 14).

The point of the above diagrams, and the logic behind them, is that by developing a detailed listing of positive and negative forces influencing the situation—knowing what is actually going on—we can be more effective problem solvers. By donning our diagnostician hat we can identify the causative forces at work—either helping or hindering—and thereby assess their relative influence.

When we have a good fix on the nature of the force field, we then can develop an appropriate strategy to influence the power of either set of forces. We thus can do the following:

1). Increase the power of the driving forces.
2). Decrease the power of the restraining forces.
3). Do both of the above in some combined form.

Social psychologists believe that the greater emphasis should be placed on weakening or removing the restraining forces as opposed to increasing the driving forces. Their reasoning is that by reducing the restraining forces, the driving forces are permitted to move in or take over. Also, if we increase the driving forces considerably—that is, add more pressure—we run the risk of triggering an unwanted reaction—*resistance* to that added pressure.

For example, in our accident situation, we could turn on the pressure (working on the driving forces) by

Figure 10-14
A Force Field Analysis in an Accident Situation

Driving Forces	Restraining Forces
Cost of injuries	Employee work behavior (haste, carelessness)
Safety signs	Horseplay
Provision of safety equipment	Supervisory pressures for production
Safety meetings	Poor lighting
Training	Messy housekeeping
Lectures, pep talks	Turnover resulting in new hires.
	Safety equipment cumbersome in actual use.

adding more safety signs, giving more pep talks and the like. Conversely, we could weaken the restraining forces by providing better lighting, improving the housekeeping, reducing turnover, and reducing supervisory pressures to produce. Note, too, that all driving forces are not necessarily effective in nature, e.g., safety signs over time blend into the wall and lectures are subject to the usual tuneout.

A skill pointer: To launch a force field diagnosis with your work team, do three things:

1. Explain the force field concept, as above.
2. Brainstorm the driving (positive) forces.
3. Brainstorm the restraining (negative) forces.

Securing Facts From Literature Searches and Organizational Surveys

It goes without saying that it is a lot easier to jump to conclusions (often a favorite managerial exercise) than it is to dig for data in a systematic way, that is, doing one or both of the following:

☐ Conducting a literature review to learn how other organizations are dealing with a similar problem.
☐ Collecting data via questionnaires (field survey approach) to determine accurately—rather than with assumptions—how people in the organization view a problem area.

In respect to the literature review, if, for example, we are about to launch a TQM (Total Quality Management) Program, it makes a lot of sense to first learn all we can about other organizational experience with this technique. A literature review can help you to avoid repeating the mistakes others have already made. Today, literature search with the aid of a computer is an-easy-to-accomplish activity. College libraries and their computers can be of real help in locating the background data on your problem area.

Organizational surveys also are essential in taking a factual approach to a problem as opposed to following hunches, suppositions, guestimates, and even personal biases. For example, the Marriott Corporation (Charlene M. Solomon, "Marriott's Family Matters," *Personnel Journal,* October 1991), one of the nation's largest corporate employers, has some 206,000 employees, of which more than half are women. A large percentage of them work part-time and many have youngsters below

age 12. Most of Marriott's labor force comes from metropolitan areas, typically very competitive in nature.

Marriott learned anecdotally that employees were having difficulty meeting conflicting job and home demands. This resulted in turnover and lowered productivity. To get a good fix on the nature and extent of the problem, Marriot targeted 1,600 employees (two-thirds wage, the others management) in five major metropolitan areas for survey data. Considerable new information emerged: 35% had children below age 12 and 15% had children under five; those with children under 12 were absent four days per year and tardy five times because of child-care needs. Also, within a one-year period some 33% of these working parents take at least two days off because of inability to find a suitable substitute when child-care plans had to be altered. Twenty percent left a previous employer because of work and family issues.

The survey produced these conclusions:

☐ Personal life impacts on job efficiency.

☐ Time is the key element in balancing work with family requirements.

☐ Both male and female workers, in equal numbers, reported on these work/family role difficulties.

☐ Child-care arrangement problems are stress producers and limit ability to work certain schedules or overtime.

☐ Care of elders is a growing issue.

As a result of this survey data, Marriot developed a variety of far-sighted family and child-care programs administered by its Department of Work and Family Life, established in 1989. Specific programs: Resource and Referral to locate affordable child care; Child Care Discount Program; Family Care Spending Account; Elder Care; Work and Family seminars; a newsletter that presents information on dependent care issues; a Child Development Center at corporate headquarters (1990).

Marriott recognizes that this serious attempt to deal with family issues represents a cultural change. These issues are now included in supervisory training courses.

As indicated above, the research process, whether literature- or survey-based or both in combination, provides for an in-depth and objective analysis of a problem facing an organization.

Systems Thinking As a Guide to Information Collection

A highly useful way to understand what is going on in an organization and how it relates to data collection is to look at it holistically, as a total system. That is to say, we should recognize that it has a number of interdependent components (organizational units), each impacting on the other, which are linked by such subsystems as communication, information, authority, control, influence, reward and punishment, and so on. These subsystems may be formal (enunciated and recognized by the organization) or informal (implied). Helpful metaphors to understand the interrelated workings of a system are a clock or watch, the human body, a football team, your car, or your rose bush.

The interrelationship of organizational components can be readily understood if we think of such common units as production and sales. The former will not produce what the latter cannot dispose of, nor will the latter try to market what the former cannot manufacture. The activities of each, then, are clearly dependent on the needs and capabilities of the other. Or visualize the changes/impacts throughout the organization when a computer system is introduced to replace a manual system.

Looking at systems more broadly, they can be categorized simply as either *open* or *closed*. A closed system endeavors to operate on a self-contained basis, relying minimally on outside resources, including information. **Examples:** a prison or a monastery. An open system tries to engage the outside environment actively on the assumption that external information is basic to survival and growth.

A good metaphor for the open system is an umbrella with slits in it. The slits permit needed light (new ideas) to enter, but the umbrella, overall, provides protection from the outside world. In effect, the open system functions as a semi-permeable membrane—it takes needed things in, but not everything that is out there. Most organizations are open systems, differing in the degree to which they are open.

A key concept in systems thinking is *synergy,* that is, the whole is greater (more effective) than the sum of its parts. Greater effectiveness is achieved through cooperation, interaction, and sharing of information rather than functioning in isolation and hoarding information.

The organization that sees itself as an open system is constantly scanning the environment for data regarding new legislation, new technology, and the many changing forces in society such as economics, demographics, markets, lifestyles, politics, the competition, and the culture at large.

Management consultant Dr. Roger D. Chevalier ("Analyzing Performance Discrepancies With Line Managers," *Performance and Instruction,* December 1990), looks at performance discrepancies from a systems standpoint. He helpfully categorizes potential problem areas into four major subsystems: Human/Social, Technical, Information/Decision Making, and Structural. More specifically, the ingredients of each subsystem are:

1. **Human/Social:** Deficits in employee knowledge, skill, or motivation; counterproductive reward systems, group norms, informal leaders, and the organization's political climate.
2. **Technical:** Poor job design; lack of tools, equipment, or standardized procedures; rapidly changing technology.
3. **Information/Decision Making:** Poorly defined goals; inadequate performance measurement; information problems, that is, drowning in data but starved for information and filtered information; remoteness of decision makers from the problem source; suboptimized resources.
4. **Structural:** Unsound organizational setup; inadequate control system; operating level in need of greater flexibility; ineffective feedback/consequences; overlapping roles and responsibilities.

Dr. Chevalier's broad, systematic cataloging of potential problem areas is a tremendous guide to the problem solver, for it excites the imagination as to what data to look for in the total system. It offers a much-needed potential to alert the problem solver to think broadly rather than narrowly as to the possible origin (causative factors) of a problem. It may suggest, too, that causation may be of a multiple rather than a single sort.

Getting a Leg Up on the Competition

As stated above, in studying the outside environment, we certainly want to know what our competitors are doing in the marketplace. If we're not aware of what our competition is up to, we're flunking in CI (competitive intelligence). CI is the gathering, processing, analyzing, and disseminating of facts, data, information, and intelligence about "the other guys," our competitors, including broader, related information about the industry, products, markets, and even legal environments ("Competitive Intelligence," *Under the Dome,* The Bureau of National Affairs, Inc., October 1991).

The obvious purpose of CI is to help us to stay ahead in today's fast business race. Future success of our organization may well depend on our knowledge of competitor activities, overall industry trends, and our development of plans to take advantage of changes in current or new markets. Not getting information on the competition is equal to tying one hand behind our back in a tennis match.

Any news about our competitors is significant, whether it be a product change or a rumor about the launch of a new product. In actuality, the use of CI is wide-ranging. To illustrate, a major publisher sees these uses of such information: Top management might need data on acquisition possibilities or changes in the economy; the marketing people want to learn of competitors' activities or changes in customer markets; the purchasing department is interested in the financial condition of critical suppliers; and the sales staff seeks information about the sales activities of competitors, significant uses of existing products, and customers' unmet needs.

As to sources of information, the company library can play a major role in collecting information from many public sources: annual reports, press releases, journal articles, newsletters, etc. Employees, too, can be valuable data collectors. They must report any pertinent information they glean in the course of daily work from phone conversations, magazines, newspapers, incoming letters, and sales calls.

Sheila M. Elby ("Pssssst! [Do You Want To Know A Secret?]", *INC Magazine's Guide to Small Business,* 1987) offers these added legal and inexpensive ways to track one's competitors:

1. **Purchase competitor products.** Then test and analyze them.
2. **Stalk the competitors' territory.** Spend time where your competitors do—golf clubs, bars, restaurants. Casual conversations may produce revealing and useful information.
3. **Use print media,** e.g., trade and business journals, clipping services, computerized information services, quarterly and annual reports.
4. **Network with a securities analyst.** Financial analysts can provide information on the industry he follows, especially if you are willing to share information with him.

Are you now shopping the competition to an adequate degree? John McGonagle and Carolyn Vella, authors of

Outsmarting The Competition (Sourcebooks 1990), suggest that you may already be into CI properly if your knowledge base covers these areas:

- ☐ Ability to name your five major competitors
- ☐ Ability to name their major products/services
- ☐ What they will be doing in the next six months
- ☐ Who your counterpart is (i.e., who is doing your job)
- ☐ What your counterpart is doing now

The bottom line of CI: If we are clear about what competing organizations are doing, we can measure their experience and results against our own objectives. This can help us to think in terms of forward movement, not just basking in the comfortable glow of the status quo. German poet Johann Wolfgang von Goethe said it best: "He who does not go forward goes backward."

Shopping the competition depends in large part on our attitude about its importance. For example, a colleague of mine worked in a company that produced training films/videos for business, industry, education, and government. Although my colleague and his associates in the company's training and marketing functions tried to keep up on their competitors' work, both as to content (subject matter) and film technique (style of presentation, quality of acting), the company president and his film/video director did not. Unfortunately, they were content with their longstanding approaches. The ultimate result was that the company's once-lucrative market was lost to their very live-wire competitors.

Contrast the above self-defeating behavior with that of the Japanese. Management professor Dr. Henry Minzberg stated the following ("Mintzberg: The Insightful Manager," *The Management Review,* December 1991):

There's a famous story about a flock of Honda engineers descending on a parking lot at a Japanese golf course, looking at every BMW, Jaguar and Mercedes, measuring those cars, doing everything physically. I've also heard about a Japanese businessman traveling on a train in England, in the economy class, speaking to all the other passengers. Why was he doing that? Because his firm was thinking about building a plant in the area, and it was a good opportunity to meet the local people and find out how they work, what kind of employees they might be. Can you imagine a U.S. businessman doing that? He'd be in first class reading reports and statistics on local employees.

Benchmarking

This is a concept that moved into the management lexicon in the '80s. It entails taking a proactive rather than a reactive stance toward competitors. This is done by studying a firm's competitors, its products, services, or practices and comparing them objectively against another.

The idea is to learn which competitor is tops in the field, what makes it so, and to close the unwanted discrepancy in quality and/or service between our own firm and the leading competitor. In essence, the goal of benchmarking is to find and implement the best practices, to achieve leadership through quality, and to satisfy customer needs more effectively than do our competitors.

But the significant aspect of benchmarking is *reciprocity*. As Corning's manager of quality, William Felthousen, puts it: "You don't benchmark against companies, you benchmark with them" (quoted in "The Death of Arrogance," *Financial World,* February 17, 1991). Sharing, after all, is the best way to secure information. Charles Burke, Compaq Computer's V.P. for quality, adds, "Sharing means growth for both companies and an ability to compete on a global front."

Management consultant Mark A. Rogers ("Competitive Benchmarking: A Process for Developing A Proactive Posture to Competitors," *Performance and Instruction,* August 1991) points out that competitive benchmarking is not a "program" or a one-shot campaign. Rather, it is a broad-gauged philosophical concept that must be embedded in organizational behavior and thus become a continuous management process. It is concerned not only with what a competitor is doing now, but with its future performance as well. So the firm must ask these two key questions: Are we comparing ourselves to the standard setters of tomorrow or of yesterday? Are we making comparisons of the most important factors?

Data for competitive benchmaking, according to Rogers, is collected in five domains: Planning, Analysis, Integration, Action, and Maturation. Let's look at these phases in more detail.

Planning

The initial step entails posing and responding to these questions: What is benchmarked? Who is the strongest (most serious) competitor? How is data collected? The process is concerned with securing customer satisfaction criteria and then upgrading products and services to match that criteria, thereby pleasing and satisfying our customers.

Analysis

The goal in Step 2 is to understand our competitors' strengths and weaknesses, and to assess their performance against our own. To do this, we ask these questions: If our competitors are "better," how are they better? Why? What can we learn from them? This analysis lets us learn of gaps in our performance in relation to the field's leader. Basic questions such as "How do we obtain superiority in product reliability?" and "How do we produce quality products at low cost?" are answered, in time, in the competitive benchmarking process.

Integration

In this phase, the firm develops the resources and strengths it requires to become the leader in its market, both foreign and domestic. Obviously, the objectives of the competitive benchmarking process must be communicated to and understood by employees at all levels. Their roles in the process must also be understood and committed to fully. Two conditions are essential:

1) Everyone in the company, managers and employees alike, must internalize the results of the analysis. Facing up to the nature of the competition, rather than engaging in denials and rationalizations, is essential if the process is to be successful.
2) Strategies must be developed to implement the findings of the analysis. This may be a slow, painful process for introduction and acceptance of a major change is hardly an easy pill to swallow and digest. The new strategies are to become woven, then, into the regular business plans of the organization.

Action

In this phase, implementation of the competitive bench-marking plan takes place. Planned (periodic) evaluation and reporting are essential. A heavy emphasis on participative management must take place to ensure that all necessary talent is tapped and that commitment from all is obtained. With an energetic and conscientious effort, customer perceptions and satisfaction criteria are revised upward periodically, Again, this is a proactive stance in relation to the customers in the market.

Issues for confrontation in this phase are as follows: What new activities are being undertaken? What do the competitors' strengths and weaknesses now look like? What adjustments do we make in the competitive benchmarking process?

Maturation

The last phase, says Rogers, is reached when:

a) the firm becomes the leader in its field,
b) competitive benchmarking is integrated fully into strategic management and participative management processes.

All three processes must work in harmony to overcome possible roadblocks to becoming "No. 1," the top performer in the market.

"Big Picture" Information

Organizations generally have some sort of "strategic plan." Typically, it is long range and takes into account broad-gauged elements such as the ever-changing market, the competition, influences of new technology, political, legislative, demographic, social (lifestyle), economic factors, and the like.

Healthy and courageous organizations also pose to themselves questions such as the following:

☐ What business are we *really* in?
☐ Where are we now?
☐ Where do we want to be?
☐ What about our SWOT (strengths, weaknesses, opportunities, threats)?

To answer the above big-picture questions, information has to be unearthed continually. But note: Although these questions may apply directly to decision makers at the top, managers at lower levels also can profit from asking the same kinds of questions. Certainly almost any managerial unit should be asking itself frequently "What business are we in?" which, as a minimum, may be translated to mean:

(1) What are we trying to do?
(2) Are our objectives and policies clear to reach those goals?
(3) Are we avoiding being seduced into pursuits (fringe goals) that detract from our primary objectives?

Staff as well as line units have to be responsive to the implications of these questions.

And sound answers require collection of adequate data and serious analysis related thereto. This may mean "facing up" to what the data and analysis conclude, as opposed to machinations such as data discounting ("Oh, it's not that serious"), rationalizing ("It could happen to any outfit," "Look at the competition," "But what else would you expect in this economy?"), sweeping it under the rug ("We're really not ready for that hard a look"), appointing endless study groups, opting for timid and tepid solutions (which is akin to letting out one's belt to control obesity), or even shooting the messenger bearing the bad tidings.

In today's complex world, most organizations find that they don't have all their needed information internally. Hence, there is a need to rely on outside resources. Allan Halcrow, editor of *Personnel Journal,* describes (in a June 1991 editorial) his approach to gathering information:

One of the most important things an editor does is evaluate information. We must be avid readers and good listeners. We must take note of fresh ideas, new developments, emerging trends, passing fancies, products and services, and sage observations. From all that—and more—we must determine what is most interesting, most likely to affect something important to the reader and most useful. In many ways, determining how to present information is the easiest part of our job.

Anyone working in human resources knows it's a continually dynamic field. HR executives must respond to corporate realities, government mandate and societal values, and often must do so quickly and effectively. Keeping abreast of all the pertinent information is more than any single editor can do.

Accordingly, we depend on a variety of outside resources to help find and evaluate the information that eventually gets passed on to readers. We spend time on the telephone talking with practitioners about the day-to-day issues of HR management. We attend seminars and conferences. We read a lot of mail, manuscripts and other media.

Halcrow stated that another important resource—their "eyes and ears"—is an Editorial Advisory Board. The members pass along news of particular personnel program achievement; send in articles of interest; call in ideas for articles; and offer opinions about new personnel programs or pending legislation.

STEP 3: DEVELOPING/GENERATING ALTERNATE SOLUTIONS

If you continue to think the way
You always thought,
You will continue to get
What you always got.
Is it enough?

—Anon.

There is always an easy solution to every human
problem—neat, plausible and wrong.

—H. L. Mencken (1880–1956), American journalist, essayist, critic, and lexicographer

On the assumption that you have industriously and carefully defined your problem (Step 1) and patiently gathered data about it, (Step 2), you are now ready to generate solutions to resolve it. As we have indicated, all too many managers and groups opt for immediate solutions and are reluctant to explore fully the nature of the problem with which they are confronted. Note that we have said solutions, *plural,* because only by considering a variety of options can we find a truly high-quality answer. Again, as in Steps 1 and 2, patience is essential. Virtue may or may not have its own reward, but patience in problem solving and decision making definitely does.

Techniques for Generating Solutions to Problems

In this section, I will present several techniques useful for developing alternate solutions:

- ☐ Brainstorming and Rolestorming
- ☐ Card Posting Technique
- ☐ The Slip Method
- ☐ Ideawriting
- ☐ Problem Onslaught
- ☐ Upside-down Problem Solving
- ☐ Networking

Brainstorming and Rolestorming

As indicated previously, brainstorming and rolestorming can be used to identify problems (Step 1) and to generate data, such as causes, about those problems (Step 2).

An added format for brainstorming is to tackle a problem in a negative way, i.e., have the group list all the things that are wrong with a given product, service, policy, procedure, etc. For example, if our concern is to reduce littering in a national park, a stimulant to group thinking would be to ask the brainstormers to come up with devices to *increase* littering. Possible examples: remove trash containers from campgrounds; reduce frequency of trash collections by 50%; pepper park roads with beer cans; lighten trash containers so animals can readily tip them over; reduce size of trash containers; make trash receptacles difficult to receive trash; locate trash receptacles in non-conspicuous places.

The rationale for the above "reverse approach" is that the way to make things right is to propose or to identify first the things that are wrong. Once we have stimulated our thinking with (and about) negative solutions, we are now ready to propose positive options.

Card Posting Technique

Card posting techniques are helpful for generating ideas (solutions to problems), stimulating further ideation on the basis of ideas supplied initially by others, providing for a visual display of ideas, and facilitating the grouping and/or prioritizing of ideas. The procedures are as follows:

1. Give staff members a large batch of index cards (5″ × 8″). A large number communicates that a lot of ideas are wanted. Also provide each group member with felt-tip pen to permit writing or printing in large letters on the cards. **Note:** The large writing is essential for the visual display.

2. Ask each person to produce as many ideas as he can, writing each idea on a separate card.

3. Encourage participants to post their completed cards on the wall, using masking tape (which won't affect the paint). They may then return to their chairs for further ideation. **Note:** Considerable movement and activity will serve as an ideation stimulus to group members.

4. When all ideas have been posted, have staff members (a) identify logical (major) categories for the cards, and (b) slot the individual cards according to those categories. New cards should be made for the newly identified categories and posted to the wall. **Example:** In a team-building session, cards may be grouped into such areas as planning, communi-

cation, goal setting, policies, procedures, and coop-eration/coordination.

5. As appropriate, the cards may be re-arranged further to reflect desired priorities.

6. Further discussion should take place to modify, expand, or clarify the proposed solutions.

7. When completed, a photograph may be taken of the visual display and copies of it may be printed for team members.

The Slip Method

Another helpful technique to elicit solutions from the group is to have them write down their ideas on 3″ × 5″ slips of paper. Here are the procedures:

1. State the problem in question form: How can we improve customer service? How can we improve the quality of product XYZ? **Note:** The "how can we" approach serves as a challenge and stimulus to the problem solvers.

2. Give each person a large quantity of the 3″ × 5″ slips.

3. Instruct the group to enter only one idea on a slip. **Note:** if you have 10 people in your group and each person produced five ideas, you would have at least 50 possible solutions to the problem.

4. Keep the group working because the first few ideas are the more obvious ones. "Digging deeper" should produce ideas of higher quality, value and uniqueness.

5. When the group feels that "the well has run dry," collect their slips.

6. Ask a team of two staff members to group all the slips into logical categories. Clear-cut duplicates are to be discarded, and ambiguous items are to be reserved for clarification. (While the sorting process is under way, the rest of the group can take a break.)

7. When the ideas have been grouped, they can be presented verbally for discussion. It also is a good idea to enter the solutions on flipchart sheets, if available. In any case, a written record should be made of the ideas accepted as worthwhile.

The slip method, like brainstorming, involves everyone fully and generates many ideas in very short time frames. It differs from brainstorming in that it gives contributors anonymity, it meets the needs of those who prefer individual work to group ideation and interaction, and it favors those who are more comfortable expressing themselves in writing rather than orally.

Ideawriting

Ideawriting or "brainwriting" (presented by C. M. Moore and J. G. Coke in their *Guide for Leaders Using Ideawriting,* National Training and Development Service for State and Local Government, Washington, D.C., 1979) entails individual ideation expressed in the written mode. It works best with a large group, with limited time, and where participants have little need for group interaction. It also avoids the possibility of "status" stifling the creativity of lower-ranked members. Here are its procedures:

1. Seat 4 to 6 participants at tables.

2. Provide writing pads to all participants.

3. Assign the appropriate task for idea production.

4. Have the groups "count off"; the "ones" become "the leaders." The leader's job is to keep operations on track.

5. Ask everyone to enter his name in the upper-right corner of the top sheet of the pad and the assigned "trigger" question as well. Advise them not to remove the top sheet from the writing pad.

6. Tell participants to respond to the assigned question for the next 20–30 minutes in any form they wish.

7. Pads are then exchanged, and each team member comments in writing on the ideas of *all* their colleagues.

8. Pads are then returned to their owners. Each person now has his original ideas plus the written comments of 3 to 5 others.

Note: The above steps have been accomplished in silence.

9. Each participant summarizes the ideas on his pad for the small group on an oral basis. (Alternatively, the pads could be turned over to a monitoring team for a later reporting.)

10. The ideas of each group (table) are summarized on a flipchart sheet and then reported back by the group leader to the total group.

11. The session concludes with a group-at-large discussion of all ideas/solutions recorded on the various flipcharts.

Problem Onslaught

One way to deal with a complex or urgent problem is to launch an all-out attack on it. Ad executive Phil Dusenberry put it this way ("Phenomenal Phil," *The Wall Street Journal,* August 23, 1990):

> *When we have a problem at BBDO, we throw talent against it, put five or six teams on the same assignment. Some think that's terrible, but we think it's logical. We all know the more working hours you put against a problem, the more likely you are to come up with the best solution. So when we gang up on a problem, we're only putting the odds in our favor. The fact is, you can visit our creative department any night, and see people working on a problem. We're closer to a sweatshop than a 9-to-5 shop. But we tell our creative people to take time off when they have the chance. After all, when the work comes, they're expected to work day and night to find a solution.*

Upside-Down Problem Solving

Upside-down problem solving is a technique to move staff members away from conventional thinking. It is a means to secure real "breakthroughs" (solutions) on a problem. The stress is on departing from the tried and true, "common sense" approaches, and moving on to the totally radical and new. It is quite similar to the "reverse approach" described above under Brainstorming and Rolestorming. However, it is not done in the rapid-fire atmosphere of a brainstorming session, nor are solutions garnered necessarily reversals of what is now being done.

As an example, take the perennial problem of late-comers to work. Typically, we regale the tardy ones with lectures, warnings, or ultimatums, and circulate memos about the importance of arriving on time. We may even dock the pay or annual leave of egregious offenders. But what if we were to reverse our thinking and consider strategies to make it easier rather than harder for the late arrivers? Some possibilities: Let the employee keep a record of his arrival time, which he turns in every month; start work whenever the tardy one arrives, but put in the full eight hours; set up a special unit of late-comers; put the tardy ones on a study group to develop a policy about lateness; give the late arriver the key to the door with the responsibility to open it for everyone each morning; provide cab fare so that the tardy one need not depend on public transportation; set up coffee and Danish for immediate serving upon the late one's arrival; give the late arriver a car phone so that he can advise when his arrival might take place.

Note: As indicated, the technique is intended to get new, creative solutions into the hopper. Most of them may not be practical; some may, however. But the process, on the whole, is to encourage departures from remedies that obviously are not working too well. If something is not producing the results we want, should we continue our reliance on the same kind of thinking?

Networking

You will recall our reference to open and closed systems. We indicated that organizations profit from the new information/ideas that an open system can bring.

One means of capitalizing on the open systems concept is to develop or hook up with a network of potentially helpful individuals, either inside or outside your organization, or both. They can provide ideas or solutions to problems based on the experiences they have encountered. After all, is it worth our while to discover the Pacific Ocean all over again?

A key reason for networking is that many organizations today have developed bureaucratic barriers that create obstacles to free and easy communication with others—either internally (with other departments or echelons) or externally (with peer counterparts, clients/customers, suppliers). Networks typically can transcend these communication roadblocks.

Networking requires a careful development of relationships. It is usually accomplished with individuals who share your interests, beliefs, values, skills, and expectations. The willingness to share or exchange information is based on a high degree of trust. Obviously, trust develops slowly and has to be earned.

As a means of securing ideas for solutions, networking will not be useful until good relationships are in place. So if one has a problem, and the relationship has not been adequately developed, it is not likely to be of use. Effective networking comes about because of a long-term investment of yourself in your relations with others. It is not something one can tap with inadequate preparatory work.

Networking is often thought of primarily as a tool for job seeking. There is no question it can be helpful to engineer a job change or even a career change. But our concern from a problem solving point of view is to build channels to secure information, to secure alternate solutions our "normal" contacts are not likely to produce.

Networks can be composed of people of shared interests within an organization, e.g., all human resource managers in a large decentralized corporation or government agency. Or they can be formed on an external basis by people of the same profession or occupation e.g., school administrators, public relations people, or training managers. They may even be formed by total strangers who work closely together in a management training program and now have high rapport and empathy and are willing to serve as resources for each other. One such trainee (Paul F. Buller, "Networking: The Overlooked Benefit of Training," *Training and Development,* July 1991) stated the following about the results of his networking:

> *I now have a contact, on a first-name basis, in an area of responsibility where I previously knew no one. I have been able to work with other training participants to achieve changes and get work accomplished in a time frame that would have been impossible through the formal system.*
>
> *The first week or two, after the training, my partner and I as a team were able to influence past policy and implement changes in quality discrepancy reporting requirements that saved a total of $800,000 to $1 million.*

STEP 4: ASSESSING ALTERNATE SOLUTIONS

Grant me the courage to change the things I can change; the serenity to accept the things I cannot change; and the wisdom to know the difference.

—Reinhold Neibuhr (1892–1971),
American religious and social thinker

In Step 3 we learned how to generate a large number of possible solutions to our problem. Our task now, as sophisticated problem solvers, is to *assess* the various alternatives. Assessment is the route to selection of a high quality decision. For if we were to latch onto the first option we hit upon, the odds are that we would not choose the best possibility.

Consider this: Would you commit yourself for life to the first potential marital candidate that came down the pike? Would you buy the first house you looked at? So choice—wise choice, that is—means going through a patient process of comparative analysis, thereby ensuring that we avail ourselves of the best of all the possibilities in our universe.

As we indicate below, the assessment process takes two forms: We can use non-quantitative measures and/or more structured, quantitative procedures. We'll consider the less formal (non-quantitative) approaches first.

Non-Quantitative Measures to Assess Alternatives

Voting

One simple and quick way to choose among our options is to have the group vote on them. This may be done by a show of hands or vocally. This procedure, although commonly done, has only limited value. Why? Because people would be voting globally (hazily) rather than assessing more rigidly the elements (characteristics, pros and cons) of each possible decision. Then, too, voting is likely to lead to dissatisfaction with the decision by those who were outvoted. In effect, we run the risk of creating "winners" and "losers." And who needs that? Full discussion of each option is a much more effective means to achieve a true consensus and thus true support and commitment for the final decision.

Other voting drawbacks are that, first, it may encourage sub-grouping (factionalism) of an unhealthy sort. More specifically, the goal for the "losing" group becomes one of "how can we beat them next time?" Secondly, because winning becomes more important than producing the best decision, the meeting may degenerate into a subtle contest of "scoring points" rather than having a high-level discussion and debate on the merits of the alternatives.

Risk Analysis

Staff members should be asked to list on a flipchart sheet in a T-column (see Figure 15) the risks of or dangers in a particular decision. Quite often by ventilating feelings—"getting them out on the table" and "holding them up to the light of day for analysis"—the risks may not loom so ominously as first thought.

After listing the risks, they might be prioritized as to the degree of risk. A 7-point scale could be used for such evaluation, with 1 being low risk and 7 being high risk. By prioritizing the risks, people can learn readily that all risks are not equal in potential impact or severity.

As a final step, the various risks should be discussed as to how to overcome them.

Figure 10-15
Example of a T-column to Analyze Possible Risks in a Team-Building Session

Possible Risks	Overcoming The Risks
1. Waste of time. People won't speak up freely about real problems/issues.	Use an experienced trainer/consultant to conduct sessions.
2. Frank sharing of feelings may create permanent animosities.	Ditto
3. May open up "old wounds" as well as new ones.	Ditto
4. Puts people on spot.	Ditto
5. We'd just go through the motions, cover the same old stuff.	Ditto
6. Loss of time away from job.	Meet over a long weekend, starting Friday afternoon.

Worst Scenario

Another form of risk analysis is the "Worst Scenario" approach. Ask: "What's the worst—the most horrendous—thing that could happen if we adopted option A (or B or C)?" Again, by getting the fears and anxieties out in the open, we can look at them realistically and either decide that they are not that big a deal, or work out procedures to weaken or totally neutralize the true risks.

Living A Purpose

Fears may also be reduced or even dissolved by having staff members focus on "big picture" questions of this sort: "What are our goals?" "What are our values?" "What kind of outfit are we and what do we want to become?"

The aim is to give people empowerment by having them recognize the higher, more idealistic sides of themselves, as opposed to letting them succumb to their immediate and superficial fear impulses. Fears will go down the drain when people realize their own power to surmount fears/obstacles. They do have the capability to rise to the challenges demanded by the apparently sticky situation.

Devil's Advocate Technique

To avoid falling into the trap of "groupthink," i.e., everyone agreeing uncritically to what is proposed, ask team members to focus on hazards, roadblocks, or barriers to the workability (success potential) of a particular course of action. Ask them to pose "negative" thinking and questions to one another. The aim of this approach, of course, is to give the negatives a full airing on the assumption that they are there, so why not let them surface for full analysis? Healthy dissent is a much-needed antidote to timid agreement. Certainly if the negatives are imaginary or inconsequential, they can be disposed of as reason and logic enter into the discussion.

Another alternative is to appoint a single person—one of high analytical skill—to function as the Devil's Advocate. This person, in effect, throws "cold water" on the "hot" proposal which, in some circumstances may, indeed, need much cooling off.

Note: An important rationale for the use of this technique is to communicate to all group members that it is OK (totally legitimate) to question sternly what has been proposed. The procedure is likely to ferret out criticisms and weaknesses that might not otherwise surface. Group discussion is a powerful vehicle to dissect a proposed solution. However, it is not automatically so unless the group uses all the devices it possibly can to make that happen.

Reality Testing

To ensure that we are considering the successful working of a solution in the real world, we can ask team members to fill in the T-column below and to discuss each item in turn. Note that in this approach we are trying to smoke out real feelings, both positive and negative. As stated above under "Risk Analysis," feelings that are openly expressed are far easier to deal with than undisclosed ones.

| Solution A: Will It Fly in the Real World? | |
Expectations (Hopes)	Concerns (Fears)
1.	1.
2.	2.
3.	3.
4.	4.
5.	5.

| Consequences of Alternative #4 | |
Favorable	Unfavorable
1.	1.
2.	2.
3.	3.
4.	4.
5.	5.

In this approach, we try to discuss the pros and cons of *each* possible solution to the problem. We do this because a decision has *future* consequences—the making of a decision does not end our concern with it. Conversely, solving a problem (as opposed to making a decision), like fixing the proverbial leaky roof, does not entail a major concern for the future (unless we hired inept roofers). A quote from management authority Peter Drucker on the distinction between pure problem solving and decision making merits citation:

Well, you solve a problem so that you don't have to make a decision. Every time you solve a problem you try to "restore" the process to where you know it should be. So that you don't have to make a decision. You make a decision when you want a change, and a decision therefore creates a new set of circumstances. It is focused on the future. Solving a problem is almost, really, looking back. This is the way it should be and it no longer is. So let's go back to it. In fact, problem solving can be greatly overdone because it creates a fear of change. Managers have to see in change an opportunity; and not to ask how do we get back to where we were, but what is the new optimal stage. And so a decision has consequences; it changes the environment and the situation. It focuses on making things happen in the future. You do that when you make the most critical of all decisions, the people *decisions—how to promote somebody, to move somebody, to let someone go. You do it when you make a decision to buy a house and move out of the one you're in. And a decision therefore has a risk and an uncertainty, but it also creates an opportunity.*

—"Peter Drucker on the Manager and the Organization," *The Bulletin on Training,* March–April 1977.

In weighing the merits of our possible alternatives, it helps, as we have said, to consider the possible consequences, pro and con, of a possible decision. The use of our T-column on a flipchart can help greatly to define clearly the issues involved, viz.,

After the group has completed the above T-column, each item should be labeled M (major) or S (secondary). The use of this procedure will sharpen the focus on the possible consequences.

Several questions to ask about any course of action, per Dr. Boris Blai, Jr. ("Eight Steps to Successful Problem Solving," *Supervisory Management,* January 1986), are these:

☐ Will the situation change by this course of action?
☐ Is the action feasible, considering the apparent limitations involved?
☐ What are the possible unwanted consequences?
☐ Are those affected by the the option under consideration capable of executing it?
☐ Do we have the resources to carry out the decision being considered?

B vs. C Test

Management professor Dr. D. Keith Denton ("The Service Imperative," *Personnel Journal,* March 1990) suggests managers use the B vs. C Test as a non-statistical way to compare the effectiveness of two approaches to the same problem. (Motorola uses the technique to verify proposed quality improvements.)

Here is an illustration of how to apply the B vs. C Test: Assume poor customer service is a result of high turnover and low morale. Two possible ways to treat the problem have been identified: B policy—involve the manager and staff in a participative management program, and C policy—provide pay raises to workers.

As the second step, select six locations that have high turn-over and morale problems. Then implement B policy at three locations and C policy at the other three.

After one year, simply rank the six locations as to highest and lowest turnover reduction. If the B sites are on top and the C locations are on the bottom of the rankings, B policy would be assumed to be the better one. If the data is not as neat as described, that is, three on top and three on the bottom, statistical tests such as the T-test are essential for proper verification of results.

Suspending Reflexive Criticism

For some of us, it is almost second nature to bat down an idea or solution proposed by someone else. Performance technologist Gilbert H. Kinnunen ("On Viewing Typographical Errors As Paradigm Shifts," *Performance and Instruction,* October 1991) offers a procedure to help us keep our instinctive negative reactions under proper control. Assume the following:

☐ Person A presents a solution to the problem under review.

☐ Person B restates that solution to A's satisfaction.

☐ B, before attacking A's solution, must offer at least three reasons why A's solution will work, saying, "I like that solution because . . ."

☐ B can now unleash his "internal critic" and say: "I like that solution, but I have these concerns . . ."

In this manner, a possibly good idea/solution avoids being ground into the dust before it receives a fair hearing.

Note: The procedure is to be used, on occasion, as a "fun thing" in respect to a person who has a difficult time keeping his internal critic under wraps. It is not intended for general use for the total group on the assumption that most group members are adequately "positive" thinkers.

Quantitative Techniques to Aid in Evaluating Alternatives

Typically, managers discuss alternatives in a general way and arrive at adequately sound judgments about them. However, objectivity can be aided and a finer discrimination achieved if we use various ranking and rating devices. Note, however, that the numerical results these procedures can produce are intended to sharpen group thinking and debate. They are *not* designed to limit thought and to encourage the making of decisions hastily or arbitrarily. So the caution, then, is not to become mesmerized by the numbers and fall into the trap of following them slavishly or automatically.

The following paragraphs present these numerical or quantitative approaches:

☐ Ranking Procedures Without Using Criteria
☐ Ranking Procedures Using Criteria

Ranking Procedures Without Using Criteria

We (the group) can rank our possible solutions in the order of importance (prioritizing) with the aid of the following procedure:

1. Provide each team member with the "Individual Team Member Solution Ranking Sheet," Figure 16.

Figure 10-16
Individual Team Member Solution Ranking Sheet

Solution	Values for Ranking
	10 (most desired)
	9
	8
	7
	6
	5
	4
	3
	2
	1 (least desired)

2. Have each team member enter each proposed solution on the form, the *most desired* one receiving a 10 and the *least favored* one a 1.
3. Then transfer and consolidate the individual rankings to a flipchart sheet, using the format suggested in the Group Ranking Sheet, Figure 17. Note that we have assumed that our group has seven team members. Their individual rankings are in column two.

Another form of non-criteria ranking is to compare on a group consensus basis each proposed solution with the others. By counting the number of preferred mentions, we can get a good fix on where the predominant sentiment lies, assuming that there is one.

Assume, then, that we have produced six possible solutions to our problem. Let's label the options A, B, C, D, E, and F. We enter them into our matrix, both in the vertical and horizontal columns. See Figure 18, Matrix to Compare Possible Alternate Solutions With Each Other.

Starting with alternative solution A and working horizontally across the matrix, we (the group) compare the desirability of A with B, C, D, E, and F. If we prefer A over B we enter A. If we prefer C over A we enter C, and so on. (A solution compared with itself, e.g., A with A receives an X.) As a final step, we tally the horizontal rat-

Figure 10-17
A Completed Group Ranking Sheet that Ranks Value of Proposed Solutions to Communication Problems of the Unit

Proposed Solution to Problem	Individual Member Ranking	Total Value of Rankings	Group Ranking
Semi-monthly newsletter	7-6-7-8-8-4-3	43	7
Set up quality circles	10-8-8-6-5-9-7	53	4
Alter format of staff meetings	8-9-9-7-7-9-10	59	2
Quarterly team-building sessions	10-9-8-10-10-7-10	64	1
Include secretary in staff meetings	7-4-3-4-5-6-1	30	10
Invite Big Boss to staff meetings	7-8-8-7-6-7-9	52	5
Circulate copies of outgoing letters	7-6-5-5-4-3-4	34	9
Shift to open floor plan	8-9-8-7-7-10-8	57	3
Expand contacts with Personnel and Finance	7-7-9-8-7-5-6	49	6
Monthly luncheon meetings with total staff	6-5-9-8-7-4-3	42	8

The higher the total value of rankings of solutions the more the solutions are favored, and thus has a higher group ranking.

Figure 10-18
Matrix to Compare Possible Alternative Solutions with Each Other

Alternative	A	B	C	D	E	F	Totals
A	X	B	C	D	E	F	0 (A)
B	A	X	C	B	B	F	2 (B)
C	C	C	X	C	C	C	5 (C)
D	D	D	C	X	E	F	2 (D)
E	A	E	C	D	X	F	1 (E)
F	F	B	C	D	F	X	2 (F)

ings and enter the number of preferences in the total column. In this instance, C is the preferred solution, subject to full discussion of why that preference was registered.

Ranking Procedures Using Criteria

Rather than rely totally on individual and group rankings of a global or non-criteria-based sort, we can sharp-

en our attempts at discernment (choosing among the alternatives) by using specific criteria to aid us in our rankings. Criteria such as the following may be used:

☐ Frequency—How often, widespread, or prevalent is the problem?

☐ Severity—How critical, severe, serious, or impacting is the problem?

☐ Solvability—How certain are we that the problem is one that can be resolved readily, i.e., that there is a high likelihood of achieving success or obtaining the desired results?

Note: Other criteria could be added or substituted such as support from a higher echelon or the public, cost, impact on bottom line, time factors, etc.

An example of ranking with the aid of criteria is given in Figure 19. A work team has produced four possible solutions to a customer service problem. The scoring uses a multiplication procedure for weighting pur-

Figure 10-19
Use of Criteria and a Weighting Procedure to Assess Desirability of Poposed Solutions to a Customer Service Problem

Solutions Proposed	Predominance/ Frequency	Criticalness/ Severity	Solvability (success likelihood)	Total Weight
Expand training of customer service reps	4	4	3	48
Develop new policy re customer complaints	2	3	5	30
Reduce response time to 24 hours	3	5	5	75
Provide shirts/blouses with distinctive logo	3	3	3	27

poses. The weighting process serves to highlight the significance of a given item. An additive approach would not point out significant differences as well.

Each number, then, working horizontally, is multiplied to produce a weighted total, e.g., item 1, "expand training" has rankings of 4, 4, 3. We multiply $4 \times 4 \times 3$, which yields its total weight of 48.

In respect to item 1, "expand training," it has been given a 4 on "Predominance/Frequency," which means that the need is widespread. It also receives a 4 on "Criticalness/Severity," which means that it is badly needed. It receives a 3 on "success likelihood," meaning that the impact or possible benefit is presumed to be only moderately high.

If a large number of alternatives (courses of possible action) have been generated, it is obvious that all approaches are not of equal importance, desirability, or value. For example, a high cost of implementation may make an alternative less attractive. Also, not all possibilities are easy to implement or "pull off" successfully to the same degree. Thus, a procedure for prioritizing solutions is essential. One way to measure desirability vs. success likelihood is to secure team rankings on each alternative, considering both factors *in combination*.

As an example, let's assume a team that markets educational and training products is ready to market a major training program/package on quality and customer service. The team is considering these marketing alternatives and has ranked them as follows:

☐ Direct mail promotion—D6 and SL6 for desirability and success likelihood
☐ Recruit, select, and train field sales force—D4 and SL7

☐ Exhibit materials at professional training and personnel conferences—D3 and SL2
☐ Advertise in various business/management journals and in business sections of major newspapers—D4 and SL3
☐ Use bookstores—D4 and SL1
☐ Use existing telemarketing crew—D7 and SL7
☐ Promote product in firm's newsletter—D7 and SL5

The data regarding these combined factors then can be placed in a graph, as in Figure 20. Glancing at the

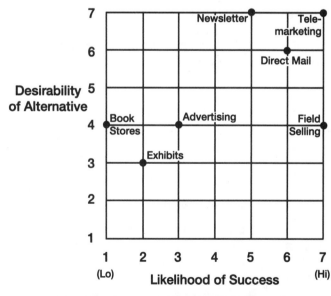

Figure 10-20. Team rankings of "desirability" and "success likelihood" of alternatives (based on a grid given by Frederica L. Geiger and John C. Wills in "Planning Strategically," *Performance and Instruction,* Sept. 1988).

graphic presentation, the team could see readily that the approaches in the upper-right portion of the graph are both desirable and likely to succeed. The others with lower rankings are thus less attractive alternatives.

Another way to evaluate alternatives is to (1) develop criteria, (2) assign values (via weights) to the criteria, (3) rank each alternative based on the criteria, (4) multiply the rankings by the weight for the criteria, and (5) add across the totals for each alternative.

In our example below, Figure 21, let's assume Elmwood Shrubb and his staff of seven professional landscapers, members of a newly formed landscaping firm, are considering selection of a company to provide them with plant materials, fertilizers, sod, seed, etc. The group developed criteria to assess the capabilities of their potential suppliers and then assigned weights as follows:

Criteria	Value/Weight: 5=Hi; 1=Lo
Product quality	5
Product variety	4
Reputation/track record	3
Realistic cost/pricing	2
Warranty/Guarantee practices	1

The group, based on its experience and related data, then identified six landscape supply companies, one of whom it would hope to hook up with on a contract basis. They entered on a flipchart sheet (1) the names of these suppliers, and (2) the criteria and their allied weights, as given above and in Figure 21 (page 513).

The group then proceeded to rank each company on the five criteria, using a 1–7 ranking (1 = lo and 7 = hi). Each numerical ranking was then multiplied by the weight assigned to the criterion. And as a final step, the scores (ranking × weight) for each company were added horizontally. As Figure 21 indicates, Perfect Plant Materials Supply, Inc., was the apparent "winner." But the group did not rely on the numbers alone for its decision. Instead, the members discussed the totals to ensure that a healthy dose of realism was cranked into the assessments.

A good procedure, to measure the possible success of our proposed solutions is illustrated in Figure 22. It is based on the practical formula of management consultant Dr. Edward Roseman, author of *Confronting Nonpromotability: How to Manage a Stalled Career* (New York: AMACOM, 1977). His formula is as follows:

Desirability (of alternative) × Probability of Success = Expected Value (of the decision)

Let's take as an example the case of Rick Shaw, who is Transportation Manager for the Totally Wayward Bus Co. Rick is young, bright, and very ambitious. He has taken an evening course at Local University and has finally received a Ph.D. in business and public administration. Rick has decided to make a career change and, using the Roseman formula, ranks his career options as given in Figure 22.

Although option #2 garnered the highest score, Rick would still study all the scores carefully lest he rely on "the numbers" alone for his eventual choice among the alternatives.

Success Prediction Matrix

Career Option	Desirability of Alternative ×	Probability of Success =	Anticipated Value of the Alternative
1. Enter public service in personnel mgt.	.25	.75	.188
2. Start a marketing career	.70	.75	.525
3. Join a mgt. consulting firm	.65	.50	.325
4. Teaching/research	.50	.75	.375
5. Set up own consulting firm	.75	.25	.188

Figure 10-22. Predicting success of alternative solutions (based on the Edward Roseman Formula in *Confronting Nonpromotability: How To Manage A Stalled Career,* New York: AMACOM, 1977, p. 235).

STEP 5: CHOOSING (DECIDING) AMONG ALTERNATIVES

We seem to be faced with an insurmountable opportunity.

—Cartoon character Pogo by Walt Kelly

If we don't change our direction, we'll end up exactly where we are headed.

—Ancient Chinese proverb

Be careful what you choose. You may get it.

—One of 13 adages to live by, as collected by General Colin L. Powell, former Chairman, Joint Chiefs of Staff (JCS)

In Step 4 of our model, we learned how to appraise the worth of alternate solutions generated in Step 3. Now "decision time" has arrived. We are ready to select one of the several choices we have carefully appraised. Following are the key elements to consider when we have to make our decision.

☐ Values
☐ A Total View for Wise Decision Making
☐ Cost and Decision Making
☐ Realizing Risk Reduction
☐ Pilot Runs
☐ "Programming" Your Decisions
☐ Intuitive Decision Making
☐ Dealing with Decision Anxiety
☐ Changing the Situation for Better Solutions
☐ Decisions Speak Louder Than Words
☐ Deciding Not to Decide

Tapping the Team's Wisdom:

☐ Group Decision Making
☐ Finalizing the Decision
☐ Loose or Rigid? A Self-Assessment Opportunity

Values

Decisions, obviously, are not made in a vacuum. Values underlie the judgment that enters into every decision. These values may not be stated or consciously recognized, but they are there.

Some key values to discuss and weigh before deciding, then, are these: customer service/relations; quality; social responsibility; possible reaction of others (stakeholders)—customers/clients, stockholders, suppliers, community, employees, the union, organized groups such as environmentalists; and the bottom line.

Taking into account the values underlying a decision certainly will slow down the urge to act, to decide, to "get on with it." But this is a healthy consequence, for it may well eliminate later complaints from any of the aforementioned groups, as well as stem regrets over a decision that ignored vital values.

A simple rating sheet (Figure 23) can be used to incorporate the importance of pertinent values. The rating procedure, providing a comparative analysis, should serve to crystallize the thinking of you and/or your staff. Time spent on this rating procedure can assist in producing a higher-quality decision than might be the case otherwise.

A Total View for Wise Decision Making

Solving a problem wisely—i.e., in a broad-gauged way—is not always an easy thing to do. For example, in recessionary times, a company seeking to boost (or even maintain) profits may decide to engage in heavy downsizing (staff reductions). But is job elimination a simple, clear-cut answer to the problem of accomplishing real cost savings? Not necessarily. For example, DuPont in the 1991 recessionary year found that it must focus on *total cost savings,* not just on a worker head count. Why? As a securities analyst familiar with the firm said: "They're not going to let managers play games and do things like hire people back as consultants ("DuPont, in Cost-Cutting Move, to Trim Thousands of Jobs, Take Big Write-Off," *The Wall Street Journal,* July 26, 1991).

In fact, DuPont decided that besides eliminating jobs through the usual routes of early-retirement incentives and dismissals, it energetically asked its managers to consider other cost-cutting alternatives such as redundant computer systems, consulting and contracting costs, and of course, travel and entertainment expenses.

As every American worker and manager knows, job cutbacks in tough times is a standard organizational procedure. But (Hugh Aaron, "Recession-Proofing a Company's Employers," *The Wall Street Journal,* March 4, 1991), a small plastics materials company in Maine was troubled by their usual layoff approach. Why? For these reasons: It's a painful thing to do to capable, reliable people you know well. When business picked up, some of these excellent well-trained workers did not return, which meant inconvenience and cost to replace them. Without

Figure 10-23
Rating Sheet to Assess Importance of Values

Values	Degrees of Importance				
	1 (Low)	2	3	4	5 (High)
Customer service					
Quality					
Urgency/Speed					
Social Responsibility					
Importance of attitudes of:					
Customers/clients					
Employees					
Community					
Stockholders					
Suppliers					
Union					
Outside groups					
The Bottom Line					

these trained workers, it was difficult to cope rapidly with the business turnaround. And those who returned were often bitter and anxious about future cutbacks.

Hugh Aaron, company CEO, decided that conventional thinking—layoffs, rehires, etc.—was not of much help as good times appeared again. So he decided to seek a solution in a condition directly opposite to the one bugging the firm. He called it "The Lesson of the Opposite." His approach: "If laying off is the problem, then people working overtime, its opposite, is the answer."

So Aaron said during a plant-wide meeting that he was not going to hire more people if the workers agreed to his proposal: Work overtime and perform other reasonable job requests, and the company would abandon its usual layoff policy. The workers readily agreed. And when sales began to lag, other work was created by expanding inventory. Also, people who were not busy were assigned to maintenance work (cleaning, painting, rebuilding worn equipment) that had been purposefully postponed for this situation; everyone was retrained to perform one or more other jobs; people were encouraged to take postponed vacations.

The results of the no-layoff policy were these: The firm achieved a reputation as a caring company; morale reached a new high; turnover became negligible; exerting extra effort became the norm; and people perceived themselves to be part of a stable, cohesive family and took pride in being part of the outfit. Also, by eliminating layoffs and reducing permanent staff, generous benefit costs were reduced. And the company's major triumph, per CEO Aaron: a dramatic financial reduction in their involuntary contributions to the Maine unemployment pool.

Two research papers reporting on the questionable effects of corporate downsizing were presented at the annual meeting of the Academy of Management (reported by Jay Matthews, "Odd Jobs," *The Washington Post,* August 13, 1995):

1. A University of North Carolina study found that many companies continue to slump after downsizing. Said management professor Patricia M. Norman, "Practitioners must be cautious of turning to downsizing before considering other alternatives. Growing evidence suggests that downsizing rarely results in increased performance."

Norman measured the financial status of 109 companies—three years before downsizing and two years thereafter. As a group, the firms did no better after their cutbacks than before. In fact, she found no difference between companies that made structural and strategic changes and those that just downsized.

2. Similarly, a University of Wisconsin-Milwaukee study found little relationship between heavy downsizing and success. Management professors Vincent L. Baker III, George C. Mueller, and Mark Mone found "no support for the proposal that quick and extensive retrenchment facilitates turnaround. How managers downsize under conditions of decline may be more important than if they downsize."

The researchers compared 34 matched pairs of companies—one group experienced a revival of financial results after three years of decline and one group didn't. Both groups added workers in year one of their decline, then reduced the workforce during the next three years.

The firms becoming successful again didn't seem to have cut back people sooner or in greater numbers than those companies that didn't. The only real difference took place during the turnaround period in years five and six, when the successful firms began to hire again while the less successful companies continued downsizing.

Cost and Decision Making

Managers, like architects and engineers, could do wonderful things if their budgets were unlimited. But the facts of organizational life are that managers are paid to use their creativity to produce decisions at the lowest possible cost.

"Elegant" solutions may appear attractive and be ego satisfying, but in today's real world managers must consider cost factors fully in every decision. **Example:** A concrete walkway in the basement of the building led to the cafeteria. It thus was well travelled. Unfortunately, a cast iron pipe crossed the walkway, protruding a bit, and thus was a constant tripping hazard. Signs and intermittent memoranda of warning did not discourage tripping mishaps. One possible solution was to rip up the concrete flooring, place the pipe below floor level, and concrete over the pipe. Fortunately, a much more economical solution was thought of—simply place a sloping wooden ramp over the offensive pipe!

At the 1,200-room Chicago Marriott, room-service personnel were on tap around the clock even though demand for such services was not always active. **A solution:** Coffee makers, irons, and ironing boards were

placed in every guest room, thereby reducing the need for costly around-the-clock service personnel. The savings didn't affect quality of service, according to the hotel manager (reported in *The Washington Post,* February 17, 1992).

Here are several employee-related problems that were solved creatively at very low cost, as reported by management professors R. Bruce McAfee and Myron Glassman ("Job Satisfaction: It's the Little Things That Count," *Management Solutions,* August 1988):

☐ Employees in one firm complained of bookcase doors that were difficult to close and open. **Solution:** Management simply removed the doors and the complaints vanished.

☐ In another company, employees complained that the parking lot was too small for everyone to park. **Solution:** Lines were drawn to guide parking, something that had not been done previously.

☐ In another instance, employees were annoyed by the ringing of their phones on *all* incoming calls, not just their own. **Solution:** A simple change in the system so that calls now ring in only two offices.

I once worked for an administrator who invariably would slow down our grand and enthusiastic proposals simply by asking: "What are the economics of this?" He, of course, wanted a much more thorough assessment of ROI (return on investment) in relation to cost. The result, not surprisingly, was that a number of those optimistic proposals did not return for further review by that top executive.

Controlling costs obviously is part of everyday decision making. Countless opportunities to control costs abound: re-work, returns, waste, scrap, inventories, oversized machines and equipment, unused space, overstaffing, accidents, absenteeism and turnover, overtime, delay of repairs, lack of preventive maintenance programs, cumbersome procedures, poor planning of projects, lack of or weak employee orientation and training programs, less-than-the-best suppliers, marginal performers, poor interdepartmental cooperation and communication, entertainment and travel, utility charges, and so on.

Besides ongoing attempts to control costs, such as in the above areas, organizations engage intermittently in various "cost-cutting" programs. Hard times usually unleash such efforts. But, typically, a number of pitfalls arise because of the decisions which relate to the structuring of such programs. They include:

The "Across-the-Board Cut"

This strategy sounds very fair for, after all, every department is being asked to sacrifice equally. But the reality is that a uniform 10% cut may ignore the varying needs of the diverse organizational units. **The result:** Complaints arise and top management may have to make special adjustments in the announced uniform policy.

A Failure to Involve the Rank-And-File Worker in the Program

In actuality, there is abundant evidence to indicate that those who do the work often know best where "the skeletons are," where money can be saved. They can spot waste in time, effort, and materials, and can suggest shortcuts to speed up operations and cut corners.

Lack of a Strong Communication Effort to Explain The Rationale for the Program

If told directly, employees can understand that their job security depends upon efficient, economical operations, that their self-interest demands cutting costs. Supportive supervisory attitudes toward the cost-cutting program are basic to the desired employee cooperation.

Cost-Cutting in Any One Department is not a One-Time Effort

The reality is that a second or third look may produce added cost-cutting benefits for (a) some possibilities may have been overlooked on the first try, (b) changes in procedures, inventory, etc., may have occurred since the first go around, and (c) with the experience gained from the first belt tightening, the team is now better armed than in the initial effort. Resting on one's laurels—complacency—is incompatible with continuing cost-reduction efforts.

Identification of Cost-Cutting Targets may Overlook the Need to Ferret Out the Causes for Fat and Waste Accumulations

For example, an unnecessarily high cost of work gloves in a plant may be due to one or more of these factors: too early discarding of used gloves, poor quality from suppliers, lack of proper controls resulting in theft and other loss, using the wrong gloves for particular tasks, unnecessarily stocking a variety of gloves, over-ordering and stocking, etc. Cutting expenditures because they are too high, without zeroing in on the reasons therefore, is a form of action taking but not problem solving.

Cost-Cutting is Regarded Soley as an In-House Activity

But what may be overlooked is the possibility that customers/clients, suppliers, and the union may contribute worthwhile ideas, too.

Realizing Risk Reduction

Every decision carries risk. Decisions relate to the future, and few of us can predict or control all possible eventualities/consequences. As a child you probably read this perceptive poem:

> For want of a nail, the shoe was lost.
> For want of a shoe, the horse was lost.
> For want of a horse, the rider was lost.
> For want of a rider, the message was lost.
> For want of the message, the battle was lost.

—Nursery Rhyme

And in the organizational world, managers typically encounter unpredictable events. **Examples:** What will be the impact of shifting to a new supplier? Will economic events support our decision to sign a 10-year lease for extra warehouse space? What are the implications of bringing in a new, hot-shot comptroller from the outside? Will the latter wear well within the company, and how will the regular staffers respond to an outsider boss?

Some decisions are reversible, which is one way of mitigating the effects of a decision gone sour. For example, the comptroller, mentioned above, can be dropped, although the hiring itself may generate enough ill will that time may erase all too slowly. Of course, we may be wedded to other decisions for longer periods than we may like and the decisions may set off shock waves that are hard to deal with.

Management guru Peter Drucker, in his book *The Practice of Management* (New York: Harper & Row, 1954), has asserted that the importance of a decision does not lie in its dollar value, but how fast the decision, if wrong, can be reversed. Recall the boo-boo Coca-Cola made in the mid '80s when it changed its long-standing formula for Coke? Fortunately, when public disapproval occurred, a reversal of the decision was quickly accomplished, and the old formula was re-instituted.

Assessing the consequences of a decision, on a pro and con basis, as discussed in Step 4 of our model, Assessing Alternate Solutions, is a basic risk-minimizing procedure. "Programming Your Decision" and

"Changing the Situation for Better Solutions," discussed below, also can help considerably.

W. H. Weiss, author of *Decision Making for First-Time Managers* (1985), in "Cutting Down the Risks in Decision Making," *Supervisory Management,* May 1985, perceptively points out that there are risks in *not* taking risks. If you are cautious to the point that you develop a no-risk stance, you will hardly make the changes and innovations essential to meet new, demanding conditions.

Because every decision entails risk, the bottom line, then, is not to avoid risk, but to decide on the risks worth taking. Decision-making clearly is managing risk.

In any case, on the assumption that risks must be taken, the best course of action is to endeavor to manage so that their possible untoward impact is minimized. Management authority Weiss offers these suggestions:

Be Goal Oriented

Take a risk only in relation to a clear-cut objective. The goal will tell you whether your risk paid off. And tie in your goal to a schedule or time table so you can make time-related measurements as to success toward that purpose.

Develop Predictions

Reduce risk by listing things that might backfire. This will alert you to possible problems and allow you to cope with them earlier rather than later.

Having Problems Means Having Risk

Deal with problems using your own management style, which will make you more comfortable in treating them. Take risks seriously, buttressed with success motivation.

Recognize that Possible Roadblocks/Obstacles will Arise

Use realism to identify barriers to goal achievement. Appreciate that some of them can be dealt with, others cannot. Also, every action entails risk; there's no easy way out of the decision-making dilemma.

Put Your Best Foot Forward

You can only do what you are able to do.

Expand Your Database

Ask others for ideas. Raise questions to avoid loose ends.

Treat Risk Seriously

Risk-taking merely to prove that you can get things done is an unnecessary risk in itself.

Allow Enough Time

Make haste slowly. Give yourself enough time to be certain that you are fully aware of what you are trying to pull off.

Recognize When Decision Time Has Arrived

Make the decision without shilly-shallying. If you did all your homework and laid the groundwork properly, there's no reason to dawdle. Do it!

Provide Praise to Your Supporters

Those who helped you reach the decision point merit full recognition for their wise counsel. Don't skimp on earned praise.

Risks may also be minimized by reliance on pilot or test runs, where appropriate. William D. Smithburg, Chairman and CEO of Quaker Oats, summarizes for us the nature of the risk concept in this quotation:

> *To innovate, you have to take risks, risks grounded in sound judgment. It's instructive to note that the word* risk *in its original form meant 'earning your daily bread.' That concept is still true today. Risk-taking is the very essence of business and management. Effective risk-taking is the hallmark of productive companies and productive managers"* (quoted in Business Month, *April 1989).*

Pilot Runs

As managers, we are not only expected to make decisions but to make them succeed when implemented. Obviously, even the most carefully researched and discussed decision has the possibility of falling below our expectations.

One effective way to reduce the possibility of a misfire, with possible injury to our standing in the organization, is to launch one or more pilot runs. Why barge forth into the real world with finality—a point-of-no-return situation—when there may be low-risk, tryout opportunities for the asking? Note, too, that the pro athletic teams, be they baseball, football or basketball—engage in pre-season exhibition games before they venture into the rigors of the cruel, unforgiving regular season.

A pilot run, if successful, can provide the support and resources needed in the way of extra staff, space, financing, equipment, etc. Your bosses will be glad to back a "winner." But if not fully successful in your pilot try, you can always go back to the drawing board and rework the idea. If all tests indicate a total bust, you can back out of the project without egg on your face.

Business writer Jacob T. Straub ("Pilot Runs: Pretest Key Decisions," *Supervisory Management,* November 1990) advises to involve your staff fully in the idea early on and to secure their frank feedback about it. He advises the following questions (which may suggest others):

☐ Have other organizations tried it?

☐ Would you favor adopting this idea permanently? Why or why not?

☐ Can we train people for the new procedures?

☐ Would the plan or project work better in another department?

One way to upgrade your success possibilities is to conduct the tests on a multiple basis. That is to say, launch the pilot runs in several places, possibly simultaneously. For example, if you run the experiment in five locales and only one bombs, you still have a strong success story to present to your superiors (assuming their support is needed to launch the project). It also is a good idea to study the lone failure situation carefully. For with a high success rate elsewhere, there are strong possibilities that there were failure factors at work peculiar to that single location.

Another form of trial run is to vary the experiment. For example, assume you are about to launch a fairly large-scale training effort and are uncertain about which training method to use. Your experimental approach, then, might be to try both methods, A and B. You then select the method which proves to be more effective.

"Programming" Your Decisions

Certain decisions can be made wisely if you know the key factors to consider, i.e., what questions to ask. And if you don't know all the pertinent questions yourself? You simply consult with others—subordinates, colleagues, bosses, suppliers, people in your network

(assuming you are hooked into one). As an example, assume that you are ready to sign a commercial lease, which potentially could cause havoc, headaches, and heartaches if one or more details were overlooked.

Property management authority Robert S. Cunningham ("Ten Questions to Ask Before You Sign a Lease," *INC Magazine's Guide to Small Business Success,* 1993) advises that you ask these 10 pointed questions before your sign your lease:

1. **Lease length.** How long? Look to the local economy for a possible answer. If you're concerned about rising rents due to inflation, you'll want to sign up for the long haul. If idle properties abound, your thinking probably will be the reverse. Also, be sure to ask: When do we move in, and what happens if a delay arises? So the lease should be specific about what happens (rent adjustments) if you can't enter on the agreed-upon date.

2. **The rent.** How much is it? Who pays for utilities, real estate taxes, insurance, repairs, maintenance? And how much *usable* space are you actually getting? Are you aware that the square footage cost may include common public space for lobbies, bathrooms, mechanical areas, cleaning closets, etc. So what are you really getting for your rental?

3. **Rent increases.** How much is likely? Is your landlord protecting himself against unpredictable costs via escalator clauses?

4. **Sub-leasing.** What if you outgrow your leased space and want to sublease? What kind of replacement tenant is suitable? And if your subtenant vanishes one night, do you realize that you're still responsible for the rent?

5. **Renewals.** Are you aware that they are not automatic? Does your contract address this issue?

6. **Bankruptcy by the landlord.** What happens now? Will the bank honor your lease as is or insist on changes like higher rent?

7. **Insurance.** Who provides the coverage? You? The landlord? Both of you? Is it adequate? Have you consulted an insurance expert on this to plug possible oversights?

8. **Services.** What do you get? Do you have separate needs for electricity? If so, who pays? What heat and AC is provided after 5 p.m. and weekends? What are the provisions for cleaning services?

9. **Other tenants.** What is your protection against undesirable tenants who may move in next to you? (Consider competitors, noisy tenants.)

10. **Improvements.** Who is responsible for what? Consider partitions, painting, carpentry, carpeting, added lighting, etc. Who retains improvements when you move?

Details, details, details. They certainly can drive you to the loony bin. But anticipation of those fine points—asking the right questions early on—will preserve your later sanity.

Intuitive Decision Making: Using Your Hunch in a Crunch

We know the truth not only by reason, but also by the heart.

—Blaise Pascal (1621–1662), mathematician

The man who insists on seeing with perfect clearness before he decides, never decides.

—Henri Frederic Amiel (1821–1881), Swiss poet and philosopher

In prior pages we placed heavy emphasis on defining the problem, collecting data and producing alternatives, and choosing objectively among the alternatives. These, of course, are all elements of a careful, logical, and rational approach to problem solving and decision making. Yet we know that rational and logical analysis may not apply to situations that are anything but neat, orderly, organized, structured, and predictable.

So if we are dealing with situations that are the opposite—totally new, complex, multi-faceted, murky, and marked by a high degree of unpredictability as to consequences—we can't use our usual hard-nosed, data-based, objective, analytical tools. Instead, we must shift to a mindset that calls for reliance on imagination, subjectivity, hunch, speculation, preferences, feelings, judgment, sixth sense—in short, intuition.

Federal Reserve Chairman Alan Greenspan has observed (reported in *The Washington Post,* September 25, 1990) that economic forecasters don't do a better job because of two key difficulties: They don't know where the economy stands even as they try to tilt its direction, and their predictions are based on past economic behavior that may have shifted without their knowing it. He said they try to deal with these problems by using data

provided by a mathematical model of the economy. But, says Greenspan, the models can't ever work because what is being measured is constantly changing. So the central bank relies on the intuition of its policy makers and economists.

All of which relates to what economist John Kenneth Galbraith said about economists: There are two kinds of economists—those who don't know and those who don't know that they don't know. Greenspan, obviously, is of a third variety—those who know when and what they don't know.

Few managers like to find themselves in situations "where they don't know" and thus must fly by the seat of their pants, engage in gut-feeling decision making. Yet, as we have indicated, there comes a time when only the intuition can be counted on to make the imaginative and courageous decision.

Research studies of U.S. executives by educator Weston H. Agor, University of Texas at El Paso ("Top Executives Disclose Use of Intuition for Strategic Decisions," *Leading Edge,* May 13, 1985), find that intuition is more widely used than was hitherto believed. He found that intuition is used best in situations of high uncertainty, few precedents, limited data. Even where all the alternate solutions to choose from appear plausible, analytical data is of little use because new trends are emerging, and time is limited, combined with pressure to be right.

Agor's executives described these feelings when they reached the critical point: "a sense of excitement, almost euphoric," "a total sense of commitment," "a feeling of total harmony," "a bolt of lightning or sudden flash that this is the solution." A possibly incorrect decision produced these feelings: "a sense of anxiety," "mixed signals," "sleepless nights or upset stomach."

Agor also identified some common sources of error in their decision making: failure to follow their intuition, allowing self deception to creep in, succumbing to time pressure, failing to be non-attached, or willing to let things be as they are.

Interestingly, due to the bias in our culture against free-form, intuitive thinking, nearly half of Agor's survey respondents keep their intuition a secret! Many are reluctant to describe their approach to others and even devote time to covering up their gut-feel strategies. They "dress up" their intuition-based decisions in "data clothes" to ensure colleague acceptance.

Agor wrote *Intuition in Organizations: Leading and Managing Productively* (Newbury Park, CA: Sage Publications, 1989) and founded the Global Intuitive Network (1986) to promote research in and application of intuition. The network conducts international conferences, produces videos and accompanying materials demonstrating the use of intuition skills, has a worldwide computer network, and publishes a newsletter (started in 1991).

A fascinating illustration of the use and power of intuition can be found in the work of Akio Morito, Chairman and Chief Executive of Sony Corporation (described in Morito's personal and business biography, *Made in Japan: Akio Morito and Sony,* New York: E. P. Dutton, 1986). Sony was an early licensee of Western Electric's new transistor technology. Ignoring the negative opinions of technical and marketing experts, Sony adapted the transistor for radios. These experts were certain that no one would buy tiny "shirt pocket" radios!

Sony never relied on market research in its quest for new customer electronic products. Morito, relying on his good judgment and risk taking, saw his role as one "to lead the public with new products rather than to ask them what kind of products they want." As an example, Morito cites Sony's successful developing and marketing of the super-successful Walkman cassette player, which would not have made it through conventional market research. In general, Sony's approach is to take a new or existing technology, apply it to a new product of high quality, and then convince the public of its benefits and value.

One way to understand the potential of intuition is to consider the differences between the left and right spheres of the brain. The left hemisphere of the brain provides our verbalizing. It gives us an organized, linear, systematic, rational, and logical approach to thinking. People who work in fields that require sequential, orderly thinking, such as in pharmacy or accounting, tend to engage in considerable left-brain thinking. They can describe and explain phenomenon with words, numbers and symbols.

The right hemisphere of the brain, conversely, cannot verbalize. This frees it to consider many facts simultaneously without the need to put them into a logical, linear sequence. Looking at data holistically (broad or total view) rather than sequentially permits the right brain to consider a broader set of relationships and experience. Also, it can tap longer-term memory, thus permitting the use of more facts and experiences in the course of thinking. From a creativity standpoint, the right brain is superior to the left brain because it can make judgments based on mental images, emotions, partial or incomplete

patterns, vague forms, and the like. Obviously, people in highly creative fields such as art, architecture, psychiatry and psychology, among others, tend to do a lot of right-brain thinking.

All of us use both sides of our brain, but some of us may use one side more than the other. Early development, personality, occupation, organizational requirements, and habit, obviously, influence our particular emphasis. But most of us have a greater potential for creativity (right-brain thinking) than we may imagine. Some ideas on how to tap our right brain more fully are provided in Chapter 13, "The Manager as a Creative Force."

In our reference above to accountants and pharmacists as predominately left-brain thinkers, we are not saying that these individuals are not bright, adaptable, intelligent, and alert. What we are saying is that their work does not require them to engage in free-form, free-flowing, creative, and imaginative thinking as does the work of, say, a Hollywood film director. In fact, I don't believe I would prefer to have my prescription filled by a "totally loose" pharmacist ("just follow the book, man, it's my life"). Nor would I want my financial records maintained and acted upon by an accountant who sees himself as a kindred soul to Picasso. (The IRS does not place a high premium on taxpayer intuition, ingenuity, and imagination!)

The problem-solving and decision-making model we have presented is essentially a left-brain one. It assumes that we can collect and analyze data in an objective, logical, and orderly manner. But we know that many decisions call for more than purely logical and orderly thinking—data may be incomplete or even murky, elements involved in the decision may be interrelated in hard-to-fathom ways, and their impact on the future certainly may not be clear. In short, what is needed is creative, innovative, and intuitive right-brain thinking.

Intuition works best for making decisions when our memory bank has in it a greater fund of experience and information, say management professors Sue Herron, Larry Jacobs, and Brian Kleiner ("Developing the Right Brain's Decision Making Potential," *Supervisory Management,* March 1985). With more ideas available to the mind (right brain), the greater the possibility of some innovation occurring based on the making of new connections or combinations. Also, a high knowledge of self—self-awareness—aids our use of intuition because our perceptions are clearer. More specifically, self-awareness means understanding realistically our own needs, values, attitudes, biases, hopes, fears, etc. To the extent that we have this much-needed clarity, we can avoid distorting (unconscious manipulation) our intuitive decisions.

To sum up, Herron, Jacobs, and Kleiner believe the right brain works best when a situation cannot be verbalized (put into words) or comprehended on a step-by-step, logical basis. This would apply when the decision maker is dealing with uncertainties, ambiguities, and murkiness of all sorts, including possible reactions of others outside the organization.

The value of intuition is described very well by management professor Russ Holloman ("The Light and Dark Sides of Decision Making," *Supervisory Management,* December 1989):

> *Intuition need not be distrusted because it lacks the sacrosanct quality of analysis. While every problem must be systematically analyzed, it's not rational to refrain from making a decision when the limitations of the analytical approach are reached.*
>
> *For effective managers, it's not a case of being analytical or intuitive but, rather, of having the ability to be analytical when it's necessary and feasible, and having the courage to be intuitive when analysis and evaluation are no longer feasible.*

A final note on intuition/hunches vs. logical/rational decision making: Dr. Herbert Simon of Carnegie-Mellon University won the Nobel Prize in Economics in 1987 for his earlier theories on decision making. The award was based on his classic work, *Administrative Behavior,* 3rd Edition (New York: Free Press, 1976) which pointed out that decision making is not the tidy, logical, rational process we may think it is. Rather, Simon's research of executive decision making found that executives performed in less than rational ways ("rationality does not determine behavior"). They used hunches, speculation, rule of thumb, personal experience; took short cuts instead of careful, detailed analysis; relied on feelings and emotion instead of reason and logic. In short, if decisions are made subjectively it's because the logical isn't always the sensible. In fact, such (subjective) decisions frequently are equal in quality to the objective ones.

That managerial backgrounds and expertise influence how managers view problems and opportunities is evidenced in a classic study by Simon with D. C. Dearborn, "Selective Perception: A Note on the Departmental Identification of Executives" (*Sociometry,* June 1958). The researchers gave executives in a manufacturing firm a business case and asked them to describe/analyze what they saw as the most important problem facing the firm, from a company-wide *perspective.* Ignoring that broad-gauged instruction, the executives zeroed in on their own areas, defining problems peculiar to their own departments.

For example, sales execs saw marketing problems as most pressing; production execs saw organization and production problems requiring the most attention. Obviously, their perceptions were influenced and biased by the perceptions acquired in their own (smaller) "world."

Simon also developed a theory of "bounded rationality," which asserts that in the real world, decision makers must cope with limited or even inadequate data, distorted perceptions of available data (as in the above research experiment), memory limitations about the data, and intelligence limitations (which alternative is really best?). **The result:** Rather than seeking the perfect decision, they inevitably settle for a decision (the first one) that seems to meet most requirements for a satisfactory resolution of the problem.

So, says Simon, they *satisfice* rather than maximize—that is, carry on a search for an optimal (ideal) decision. **Example:** Oil companies don't look interminably for the perfect drilling spot, due to time and capital limitations, so they satisfice instead. Simon and co-author James G. March, in *Organizations* (New York: Wiley, 1958), state:

> *Most decision making, whether individual or organizational, is concerned with the discovery and selection of satisfactory alternatives; only in exceptional cases is it concerned with the discovery of optimal decisions.*

To sum up: "Best" guesses, or better still, "educated" guesses—those that go to the gut or heart rather than to the rational mind (left brain)—have a genuine place in managerial decision making. But note that we are not talking about reliance on sheer spontaneous impulses. Rather, what we are saying is that when the data and the facts and numbers don't seem to be of much help, or when our gut tells us to be uneasy about the "hard stuff," reliance on assumptions and various subjective judgments (the "softer stuff") of a mature, well-thought-out sort is a worthy decision-making tool. Intuition indeed *is* here to stay!

Dealing with Decision Anxiety

Never be afraid to make a mistake.

—Soichiro Honda (1907–1991),
founder of Honda Motor Company

To be or not to be, that is the question.
Whether it be nobler in the heart to suffer
the slings and arrows of outrageous fortune
or to take up arms against a sea of troubles,
and by opposing end them? . . .
and enterprise of great pith and moment
with this regard their currents turn awry
and lose the name of action.

—From *Hamlet* Act III, Sc. 1, by William Shakespeare

He who hesitates is last.

—Mae West (1892–1980), Hollywood film actress

A mind is a terrible thing not to make up.

—Comedian Jay Leno (in reference to a prominent
politician who had difficulty deciding whether to run
for the U.S. presidency in 1992).

A given in the managerial world is that the manager
will be faced regularly with tough decisions to be
made—major expenditures, delicate personnel actions,
high-risk ventures that may well backfire, decisions that
may reflect on one's career—all of which can be worrisome and enervative. To compound matters, decision
making often produces vexing dilemmas, that is, what is
the "best" way to go, especially if one is in a "damned
if you do" and "damned if you don't" predicament.

Anxiety about a pending decision, then, is hardly surprising. I once encountered a somewhat anxious manager
who told me that he feels that there is an "Iron Law of
Unintended Consequences"—things simply don't turn
out as planned or hoped for. It's almost as if Murphy ('If
anything can go wrong, it will') now had a staff of 100
and was always on hand to see that very little went right.

On the other hand, I recently worked with a manager
who regarded decision making in a totally opposite
manner from the manager quoted above: Totally
relaxed, carefree, happy-go-lucky, he could joke about
problems of indecision. Here's what he told me: "When
I don't know what to do, I toss a coin. It if comes out
'wrong,' I go the other way (!)." On the assumption that
not all of us can be that cavalier about decisions to be
made, the paragraphs that follow provide some concrete

measures to control or at least reduce one's understandable concerns.

Management consultant Dr. Eleanor Davidson of
New York City offers these ways (in "Overcoming the
Fear of Decision Making," *Supervisory Management,*
October 1991) to overcome possible fears entailed in
decision making:

Forget the Past

Sure, you may have made mistakes (faulty decisions)
in the past. All of us have. However, that has little if any
bearing on what your decision-making ability is *today.*
No doubt you have learned a lot and grown in various
ways since you last erred.

Reversibility

Many or even most decisions can be changed or
reversed. They are not necessarily set in concrete. A key to
good decision making is to think in terms of a decision's
revocability. So before you decide, ask: "If this decision
proves to be a dud, how readily can it be reversed?"

Avoid the One-Answer Trap

Don't fall into the trap of searching endlessly for the
one right answer. If you thought through the problem
carefully, you probably produced more than one good
solution. So your task is to choose among several good
alternatives. And if they are "good," you can't really go
off the deep end, can you? Or it may be that your
approach to choosing the best alternative is simply to
select among the lesser of several "evils." **Principle:**
You can only do what you can do.

Avoid the Popularity Trap

Decisions are intended to produce worthwhile results
for the organization. They are not designed to make
everyone happy. The surest way to undermine your
image as an effective decision maker is to think primarily in terms of pleasing people.

Avoid The Equal Importance Trap

All decisions are not created equal, i.e., some decisions are more important than others. Learn to differentiate between those that may be high impacting versus
those that are more routine. For real payoffs, put your
skills, energies, and resources into the tough, important
decisions.

Reduce Risk Factors

If you do this, you can reduce any anxieties you may have, pre- and post-decision time. How do you do this? First, avoid acting impulsively, making snap judgments. Second, do a thorough job of data collection. Third, identify possible consequences. Fourth, think through how the stakeholders (concerned parties) will react to and be affected by your decision.

Added suggestions, offered by Bernard A. Deitzer and Alan G. Krigline, College of Business Administration, University of Akron (in "When Making That Decision," *Management Solutions,* November 1988), are these:

☐ First, leave certain decisions to your subconscious mind, i.e., simply sleep on them. By giving yourself some breathing room, you may gain new, deeper and more objective ways of looking at the problem. Before going to sleep or during sleep, you are more likely to be relaxed, detached, and less anxiety-laden. With a cleared mind, you may be able in the morning to deal better with the myriad facets of the problem or situation. You may even awaken in the night with an answer to your concern.

☐ Second, don't overemphasize the urgency/importance of the decision that awaits you. However you decide, will it mean the end of the world? Probably not. And if you've done your homework carefully, the odds are that you will come up with the right answer.

☐ Third, it may help to get away from it all, e.g., engage in meditation in an empty church.

I would add to the above suggestions to rely heavily on your staff and touch base with others in the organization to the extent applicable and practicable. By going it alone, you are almost certain to generate anxiety. Conversely, if you have availed yourself of the collective wisdom of your team and others, you should be able to identify a solid course of action to take.

Using the above or similar suggestions will help you to make a sound, relaxed decision. What you certainly don't want is to let natural anxieties force you into an unnatural or snap decision.

Anecdote: A father told his very worried son to leave his worries alone and they will disappear. To make his point come home he told him the following story.

A carefree bee in a pasture was partaking of the rich nectar from a flower when, to his surprise and dismay, he was gobbled up by a horse who was interested in the same blossom. The bee, initially surprised, frightened, and anxiety-laden, ultimately decided to relax and look for a good spot on the horse's stomach wall in which to lodge his stinger. But the dark and warm interior induced drowsiness instead and the bee soon fell asleep.

The father then asked his son if he could imagine what happened to the anxious bee the next morning. The son said he had no idea at all so his dad told him: "When the bee woke up, the horse was now gone and was eating flowers on the other side of the meadow." (Horses do digest and dispose of what they eat and peacefully meander on to locate newer morsels.)

An Aftermath of Decision Making: Cognitive Dissonance

This occurs when two values, attitudes, beliefs, or behaviors collide, i.e., they are in conflict, disagreement, or inconsistent with each other. To understand the concept, we should say that "cognitive" refers to cognitions or thoughts, and "dissonance" connotes a lack of harmony. Let's see, then, how cognitive dissonance relates to decision making.

Decisions, once made, may produce some or considerable anxiety in our mind. Inevitably, some of our behaviors and decisions will give us an after-the-fact feeling of inconsistency. This dissonance or imbalance comes about because of a lack of agreement (inconsistency) between our beliefs/attitudes/values or between our actions and our beliefs.

The process operates this way. Before a tough decision has to be made we may experience conflict about it. After deciding, dissonance may arise. With a simple decision, that is, one not requiring prolonged thought such as what color shirt to buy, the decision is made and there is no residual tension or anxiety. There is no need to justify the appropriateness of the decision to one's self. But if the decision has been an agonizing one because of its complex or important character, or if the alternatives have been equally attractive, or if you put a lot of mental effort into it, or if you departed from one or more of your values, you may wonder—have regrets—about how well you decided.

So if you have discomfort or dissonance after the decision, how do you go about reducing or eliminating it? Here are the possible approaches:

You Can Change the Underlying Attitude

Example: You decide to make a job change, and it is a cause for regret. In time, you can alter your attitude and begin to like the job. An early, unexpected promotion helps this changed feeling, too. **Example:** You hire a worker for summer employment from a temporary placement agency. The employee turns out to be dishonest. You simply decide not to deal with that agency again, i.e., you change your attitude about the agency.

You Can Rationalize the Inconsistency

Example: You are a firm believer in EEO and affirmative action. You sit on a promotion panel that decides not to select a well-qualified woman for an important mid-level management position. You are troubled by the panel's decision. You see it as discrimination. But you tell yourself later: "She's a capable person and will have other chances later. Besides, she probably wouldn't have enjoyed working for the guy who would have been her boss."

You Can Blame Yourself for Your Action

Example: In respect to the above EEO case, you might tell yourself: "I should never have agreed to sit on that panel. It's my own stupid fault for not expressing my views more vigorously." (**Note:** Self-blame is a response to dissonance, but not necessarily a productive one.)

You Can Blame Others

Again, in respect to the EEO case, you can tell yourself: "I did my job. I tried to talk her up, but those male chauvinists on the panel aren't ready for progressive and equitable management."

What cognitive dissonance adds up to is that decision making is a profound, personal, introspective process with a high potential for psychological "after shocks"—regrets, doubts, guilts, anxieties, and discomforts of various sorts. But if we know the phenomenon can and does arise and understand how it operates, we are in an adequately strong position to deal with it. Certainly, as a manager you can't get bogged down interminably. You have to move on to new problems, decisions, opportunities. "Moving on" is a healthy way of dealing with the phenomenon.

Anecdote: Six-year-old Betsy was in a dither, pondering her future. On the assumption that Mother knows best, she decided to consult her mom. This conversation ensued:

"If I should get married some day will I have a husband like Daddy?"

"Oh, yes," replied Mother.

"If I decide not to get married, will I be an old maid like Auntie Dorothy?"

"Yes, indeed," said Mother.

"Oh, my," said Betsy to herself, reflecting on the horns of her dilemma. "I'm really in deep trouble, aren't I?"

Changing the Situation for Better Solutions

We are all simply a product of the stimuli we get from the outside world. Specify the environment completely enough and you can exactly predict individual actions.

—B. F. Skinner (1904–1990), U.S. psychologist, guru of behaviorism, in *Beyond Freedom and Dignity* (1971)

We may not have thought about it in a conscious way, but typically when endeavoring to resolve people-type problems we have two choices—we can work on the person or work on the situation. By "working on the person" we mean employing such behaviors as giving people lectures, pep talks, admonitions, pleas, threats, memos, reminders of various sorts; posting warning signs; engaging in coaching, counseling, training. The net result of all these efforts? Unpredictable.

Conversely. we can "work on the situation," which means altering or structuring the situation/environment so that people behave in a totally uniform and predictable way. **An everyday example:** the white or yellow line road engineers draw down the middle of the road to ensure that all traffic stays right. No need for warning signs, traffic cops, or reminders of any sort. The line controls everyone's behavior—new drivers, long-time drivers, the young, the old, anyone who can discern a white or yellow line. And it does it night or day, rain or shine, summer or winter.

The several examples we cited above under "Cost and Decision Making" are also examples of altering the situation to change people's behavior. And the beauty of this approach is not only does it do it for everybody, but that it does it for all time *sans* the need for added reminders, warnings, or pleas. Several other dramatic examples of problem resolution through restructuring of the situation follow.

☐ Employees regularly using company vehicles drawn from a motor pool are likely to receive different ones each day. **The result?** Little concern by the drivers with the care and the appearance of the vehicles. But assign them a vehicle permanently and they treat it more like their own.

☐ Convenience stores such as 7-Eleven in the Pacific Northwest deal with the problem of disorderly young people "hanging out" in parking lots by providing music they can't stomach, e.g., recordings by Montavani and Perry Como ("Easy Listening," an editorial in *The Washington Post,* August 27, 1990.)

☐ Job redesign at Koehler Manufacturing Co., a battery maker, ended employee claims for backstrains. Specifically, after an employee strained his back while bending over a task, the company elevated the height of the tank to ensure easier mixing of materials ("Executive File" *Business Month,* September 1990).

☐ In the mid-'80s, baseball fan hooliganism (including a bowie knife with a five-inch blade thrown at a California Angels player) reached the point where stadium owners were forced to act. Because the rowdiness was caused in large part by the high rate of beer consumption, the owners restructured things so that the "baseball-and-beer bond" was weakened. Specifically, beer sales were cut off after the seventh inning; container size was reduced from the large 32-ounce size to an 18 ounce cup; evening games were started at 7:30 p.m, rather than at 8:00 p.m., so that less time was available to start the evening by going to the bar; the Yankees switched most of their Saturday night games to daytime (per Sportswriter Thomas Boswell, reported in *The Washington Post,* August 29, 1986).

☐ At Disneyland, visitors respond well to their experience despite high admission prices, hourlong waits for five-minute rides, high-priced, bad food. Why? One reason is that the park encourages phototaking by lending cameras at no charge, at designated photo sites. So people remember the funshot with Mickey Mouse and forget the long queue

at the comfort station. Super-tidy streets and super-friendly staff also influence people's perceptions of their park experience (reported in *The Wall Street Journal,* August 15, 1988).

☐ People who have to wait for building elevators tend to complain about the lousy elevator service. But place mirrors on the walls and the complaints practically vanish, even though the service is hardly speedier. **The reason?** The mirrors give people something to do—adjust ties, fix hair, etc. (Doctors and barbers sensed this long ago and provide assorted reading matter to those who are in a waiting status.)

☐ Research by fast-food chains has indicated that annoyances about waiting in line can be alleviated by switching to a single-serpentine line as Wendy's has done. People perceive it as fairer than the multiple-line system because there are no "slips and skips." If you are so unfortunate as to pick a slowline at McDonald's, which uses the multiple line system, someone can join a line next to you and and get through more quickly, even though you have already waited a couple of minutes ("The Line on Waiting," *The Washington Post,* November 10, 1988).

☐ Passengers disembarking from an airline at Houston complained about long delays to retrieve their bags. They walked to the baggage carousel in one minute but had to wait some seven minutes thereafter. They were irritated because they could see those with carry-on luggage leaving the airport promptly. So the airline restructured the situation: It moved the baggage pick-up point to the farthest carousel. This meant a walk of six minutes and a wait of only two minutes. So complaints disappeared because luggage at the carousel was retrieved more quickly and the passengers did not have to witness the carry-on folk leaving the airport before they did (*The Washington Post,* November 10, 1988).

In passing, we might mention that at a management development workshop, where the author presented these ideas, one participant was having difficulty with the concept. When he finally became comfortable with it, he exclaimed: "Hey, we did that with our cookie jar. We raised it to the top shelf and that ended all those raids by our four-year old!"

We said above that when dealing with people-type problems we can work on the person or the situation.

Unfortunately, in many people-type situations, our emotions (ire, frustration, etc.) may get the best of us and we end up with one choice—lowering the boom on someone. The challenge for the manager, then, is to slow down the all-too-natural emotional urge to act, and to think, instead, in terms of altering the situation to change the unwanted behavior.

Decisions Speak Louder Than Words

Decisions cannot be made in isolation. They must take into account "appearances," that is, how will they look to the rest of the organization? How will peers, subordinates, others feel about the decision? Decisions on particular issues and problems communicate the philosophy/standards which the decision maker lives by. For example, company ads that stretch the truth or are in bad taste communicate that "anything goes." Similarly, decisions and practices that show lack of concern for the environment communicate organizational policy more realistically than any written policy statement that talks up respect for the environment.

Because appearances are important, the purpose of a decision must be marked by *clarity*. Smoke and mirrors and bells and whistles are hardly aids to clarity. In effect, the manager must be able to say to all concerned: "What you see is what you get." Actually, people can distinguish quite readily symbols vs. substance, rhetoric vs. reality, images vs. ideas.

Also, it's good business to "prepare the soil" before issuing that new decision. Let the stakeholders know in advance what might be coming their way. In management, the best surprises are no surprises!

Decisions may also effect the organization's public image. For example, The Department of Veteran Affairs had conduced a longtime running battle with Vietnam War veterans over the lethal effects of the widely-used defoliant, Agent Orange. The VA had disputed veterans' claims that the chemical caused cancer, birth defects, and other ailments among the three-million-plus veterans who had served in Southeast Asia. The VA Administrator decided in May 1989 not to appeal a federal court ruling that the VA had ignored its own rules and Congressional intent. (A 1984 law had urged recognition of Agent Orange-related illnesses.) VA Secretary Edward J. Derwinski knew that his decision would be perceived by both the huge VA bureaucracy and the various veterans organizations as a symbolic action. Said

Derwinski: "I knew the perception of the VA would be seriously damaged if we appealed. . . . If we appealed, we obviously would be Scrooge." He added: "I didn't look for any scientific advice. I did look for the public perception of the agency . . . the intense feeling of the veterans and the veterans' organizations" (Bill McAlister, "A High-Risk Triumph of Politics Over Science," in *The Washington Post,* May 14, 1989).

Deciding Not to Decide

Sometimes the best decision is a decision not to make one. For example, medical doctors may rely on their experience and insight to recognize that the best decision is to require further observation, for treatment of any sort may be ill-timed, premature, or the situation may, over time, correct itself. (Note that the basic admonition to the physician is: "First, do no harm.")

Or, as organizational examples:

☐ Should a particular product that seems to be stumbling be pulled from the product line? If the key data are not available or clearcut, a proper action may be no action.

☐ Should a new store manager in a national retail chain be removed because his gross sales are below expectations? But is there a probability that that particular geographical area is facing an economic slowdown? The best decision: in all likelihood, no decision.

The late industrialist and management writer Dr. Chester L. Barnard (author of the much-quoted *The Functions of The Executive,* 1938) once said:

Consciously postponing a decision isn't the same as indecision. The fine art of executive decision making oftentimes is not in deciding questions that are not now pertinent, in not deciding prematurely, in not making decisions that others should make.

Management professors Bernard A. Deitzer and Alan A. Krigline put it this way ("When Making That Decision," *Management Solutions,* November 1988): "Sometimes situations should be allowed to accumulate, feelings to crystallize. Holding back gives complicated situations a chance to work themselves out, thus saving a lot of brainstorming work."

Management writer Leonard Silk ("On Cleaning House," *Business Month,* March 1989) cites the decision of President Lyndon B. Johnson to retain the independent, long-serving (1924–1972) and cantankerous FBI Director, J. Edgar Hoover. Johnson had little love for Hoover, but his decision not to act was based on his feeling that Hoover was less dangerous in office than out of it. Silk states that when Johnson was asked why he kept Hoover on, he replied: "Well, it's probably better to have him inside the tent pissing out than outside pissing in."

Johnson was aware, of course, of Hoover's independent power, which he had accrued over the years from his high-level connections in Congress and in the executive branch, plus his "in" with police and intelligence officials. Hoover had files on almost everyone in government, possibly including Johnson, and would use them vindictively if he were pushed hard enough.

In effect, Johnson decided to let Hoover's independent power go unchallenged. His rationale, per Silk, was that "what can't be cured must be endured."

Regarding the area of non-decision making, I like the command a Hollywood film director is said to have given to a young, perky, overly bouncy, and mobile starlet: "Don't just do something, stand there!" "Audacious inaction," as one wag termed it, may not be all bad. Unfortunately, this kind of restraint may be hard to exercise, for U.S. managers typically have been trained and lectured to about taking action, moving forward ("Damn the torpedoes, full steam ahead"), looking "strong and tall in the saddle," and so on. It's almost as if managerial role models were a combination of John Wayne and Humphrey Bogart.

The appropriate managerial philosophy, which the culture apparently forces upon managers, is that "A bad decision is better than no decision at all." **Question:** Why would we want a bad decision? Hopefully, even if the culture of the organization seems to favor action over deliberation, you, as a manager, will rise above such machismo-type imperatives.

A *Final Word of Wisdom*

Remember your mother saying to you: "If you don't have anything good to say, don't say anything at all!" Well, the concept may be applicable to decision making: "If you can't make a good one, don't make one at all."

However, we should recognize, too, that not making a decision is not only in itself a decision, but it may communicate a position, a policy or a decision. For example, if a company has a stated policy on sexual harassment, it communicates that it has decided that such behavior is decidedly off limits. Conversely, if a policy statement has not been issued, in today's world it may communicate the opposite.

Tapping the Team's Wisdom: Group Decision Making

Throughout this chapter we have alluded to the use of the group—the work team—as an aid to problem solving and decision making. The rationale for this is hardly novel or complex—multiple judgment and insight often can make for more effective decisions than if one relies solely on one's own experience, knowledge, and wisdom. As the saying goes, "All of us is smarter than one of us." The currently popular term to describe this phenomenon is "synergy," meaning that the whole actually is greater (more effective) than the sum of its parts. Visualize a football team of highly capable players that can reach greatness not by individual brilliance but by team effort.

The manager can relate to and utilize his group in a variety of ways:

- ☐ Problem solve and decide on a solo basis.
- ☐ Ask the group for some (limited) input, but decide unilaterally.
- ☐ Make a decision and then proceed to sell (persuade) your group as to its merits.
- ☐ Advise the group that you have reached a tentative decision and ask them how they feel about it. But you still decide by yourself.
- ☐ Meet with the group to discuss a problem fully, including the merits and possible demerits of the alternate courses of action. You secure their recommendations, but you alone choose among the various options and make the final decision yourself.
- ☐ Meet with the group to develop and assess the possible options and *collectively* decide on a proper course of action.
- ☐ Turn the problem over to your group for discussion and final resolution. You do not meet with the group and, in effect, you agree in advance to accept their decision regardless of what they come up with.

While both of the latter two approaches fall under the general rubric of "group decision making," the last-cited approach is the one that is probably most frightening to managers who encounter this concept for the first time. I have presented this concept/technique to many managers in numerous management development workshops, and their typical initial reactions are these: "Turn the problem over to the group? Do you know my group? No way." "What if they come up with the wrong answers?" "Do you really mean that I have to commit myself to live with *any* of their decisions, no matter what?" "I'm paid to make the decisions in my shop. They're not." And so on.

So when I begin to see the agitated hairs rising on the backs of their overwrought necks, I try to reduce the threat to their managerial prerogatives and egos in this manner:

Please understand that you don't turn *all* decision-making opportunities to the group. You sort them out. You decide the "big picture" issues yourself, those about which you have the maximum amount of wisdom and may affect the "lifeblood" of your function. On the other hand, there are a whole host of operational, administrative, and human relations-type problems that could well be decided at a lower level—by your team. As a manager and a delegator you're probably letting others decide many of these problems anyways. Let me give you several examples to indicate how the procedure works to help clarify what we're getting at.

Example: A manager had three new chairs to dole out to some 15 employees. She wanted to be fair about it, so she used the group decision approach. ("Fairness" is very important to people and group decision deals with this issue very nicely.) As a result of their discussion, the group decided to allot the chairs to the three employees who had worked the most hours, including overtime, in the prior three-month period. Had the manager made the decision herself, she would have assigned the chairs to those employees who had the most seniority. But by letting group values enter into the decision she was able to satisfy everyone, something that would not have been likely had she acted in a unilateral and arbitrary fashion.

Example: A warehouse manager needed two of his three clerical workers in his outer office to come to work on Sunday. He knew that there would be resistance to his request because all his young charges had dates on Sunday. Not wishing to alienate any of them, he let them meet as a group to select the ones who would pull the special duty. He didn't care who came in, just so two of them did and were not too upset about it.

The clerks met as a group and their discussion produced these findings: Clerk A had a date with his fiancee; Clerk B had a date with a young lady he had met at a party the prior Saturday night; and clerk C had a date with his roommate. As the young men saw these dates, something which the manager could never had fathomed because he was not a party to their values, the date with the fiancee was purely "routine." Why? Because both of them were already committed to one another. And the date with the roommate—another male—was hardly a date! But the date with the new young lady was the "hot" date. So Clerk B was selected out and the other two were "in" for the Sunday tasks.

Example: In an upscale clothing store sales personnel were paid on a commission basis and thus tended to neglect the required back-store stock and inventory work. The reasons? Money was made on the sales floor, plus the fact that the employees were hardly enthusiastic about engaging in essentially low-preference behaviors. As a result, the store manager repeatedly had to exhort his sales people to do the required back-store work.

In time, the vexing problem was resolved informally via a group meeting of the sales force. Their plan, which everyone favored wholeheartedly, was for one employee—a volunteer—to perform the stock and inventory work permanently. The others agreed to pool their commissions and share them equally with everyone, including the back-store person. The plan also had another benefit—it eliminated the unhealthy competition for one another's customers. Obviously, management could not have devised such an insightful plan because it assumed vastly different notions (values) of how its employees were motivated (reported in *The American Sociological Review,* Volume XV1, October 1951).

The significance of these examples is that it is a good idea to opt for group decision if it is important to secure *acceptance* of a decision. In fact, effective decisions have *two* components: **wisdom** (high quality) and **acceptance** by those who are to support and execute them. We can express the idea via this formula:

$$E = Q \times A$$

(E = effectiveness; Q = quality; A = acceptance)

The value of E is thus the product of the values of Q × A. Q and A can vary in degree, but if the value of either falls to zero, the value of your decision—E—will be zero.

When we talk about Q we have reference to engineering or product excellence, cost factors, A-1 customer service, high productivity, and efficiency of all sorts.

When we refer to A we have in mind social considerations, e.g., cooperation, motivation, commitment, morale, feelings of fairness, and the like.

Note, too, that the Q-factor relates to rational, logical, objective, and intellectual factors—facts, data-based material. Conversely, the A factor relates to how people feel—emotions, perceptions, attitudes, feelings. So Q and A are entirely different breeds of cats, but neither can be ignored. Both facts and feelings must be brought out and shown full respect.

Q is always wanted; it should always be high in every decision. The A factor is tremendously significant when commitment to or support of a decision is all-important. And the best way to get that commitment is to let people make their own decision, give them ownership of it. The operative principle is that *people support what they create.*

So, actually, we can have three conditions or situations as far as group vs. individual decision making goes:

1. We can opt for Q and make the decision ourself. These are the big, all-important decisions where the A factor looms less importantly; for example, PR matters, contracting for new space, selecting someone for a key job, selecting a new supplier, etc.
2. We should opt for A when acceptance is paramount, e.g. sharing or rearranging office space, developing a summer or holiday leave schedule, assigning unpleasant work ("the dirty jobs"), deciding who gets a new piece of equipment or furniture, etc. The aim is to get commitment to and satisfaction with the decision so that we don't have a lot of grumbling about it and its implementation proceeds smoothly.
3. We also can use group decision when the group can make strong contributions to the Q factor because of its maturity, experience, or possibly its identification with a particular activity or program. The boss can meet with the group or delegate decision-making in its entirety to the group. The latter approach will depend on the nature of the problem, the nature of the group, as well as the leadership style of the manager. Possible areas for group action: safety, maintenance, setting quality standards for customer service, establishing unit goals for production, quality, service, etc.

Managers who encounter this concept for the first time typically ask: "OK. So I let the group make the decision. How can I be sure that they will make a good one?" Two answers:

1. You can't be sure. So if you have real doubts about the team's capability to handle a particular decision wisely, don't turn it over to them.
2. Train your group in the process so that you will have more confidence in their capabilities. Do this by working with them on problems which the total group, including yourself, can resolve.

Group Participation: When Not to Use It

Involving your employees in problem solving and decision making can be tremendous tools to upgrade the quality of your solutions. It also can facilitate the implementation process, because with full involvement early on they will better understand the rationale for a decision and thus can be totally committed to it. Because people support what they create, it simply is good business to involve the team in the creation of the solution.

However, like any other tool, group decision must be used with proper skill and under proper conditions. Thus, you would *not* totally rely on the team under these circumstances:

Nature of Problem

Depending on the problem, there certainly are circumstances when you should make the decision yourself. Some logical situations: the situation demands immediate, urgent action and, therefore, there is no time to call the team together for discussion; the problem is one of considerable sensitivity, e.g., it has serious community or other PR implications; your boss for one reason or another expects you to handle the matter yourself; there is a high confidential aspect to the problem and the details of it cannot be shared with others; the problem is one in which the group has little experience with or knowledge of it; you already have the data to make a wise decision. (As one wag put it, when it's time to put out the lights at close of business, there's little point in calling the staff together to decide what to do.

Nature of the Group

If the group is not skilled in group discussion and decision procedures, it makes little sense to rely on them to make a wise decision. However, it's your job to bring the team along to the point where they can be involved and used effectively. **Another exception:** Your group, because of the nature of its work, may interact only intermittently with one another and thus may not have the experience to work well together. Also, if the group has little need for independent action, does not like to work in somewhat ambiguous situations, or does not identify itself closely with the outfit, the technique won't work well.

Nature of Your Leadership Style

If you always have made decisions pretty much on your own, or you are not comfortable dealing with the crossfire of group discussion, or you don't like to have your viewpoints challenged by others, particularly subordinates, you had better go it alone. Otherwise, your true reluctance to share the leadership role will be evident and not produce the energetic participation that group work calls for. In fact, people will be highly suspicious of your intentions and the lack of trust will turn people off.

Attitudinal and Behavioral Components Needed

The group decision process vis a vis the manager and his staff requires a combination of attitudinal and behavioral (skill) components:

Attitude

Your attitude should be such that you communicate loudly and clearly that you have full confidence in the team to do a thorough and conscientious job. Also, you need to exercise patience with the discussion process, which, at times, may be somewhat tortuous. And you must avoid communicating directly or indirectly that you already have a solution in mind. You don't want to be like the manager who told everyone that he favored collective decisions. His staff members, unfortunately, said that in reality "he collects himself and then decides."

Behaviors (Skills)

Identifying or locating the problem, including concern with causation. The group, of course, is used to help in this.

Stating/presenting the problem so that constructive problem-solving attitudes are encouraged. For example, the use of "How can we . . ." is a good open-ended way to begin. It avoids implying a solution. By presenting the problem pointedly and succinctly, it avoids the risk of confusing people as to what is wanted. Too much verbiage may be perceived as a lack of a belief that the group can be trusted to work on the problem. ("What's the boss getting at? Does he already have his mind made up on this?") So the best technique is to state it briefly and wait for someone to break the silence.

Leading/guiding the discussion with particular emphasis on involving everyone ("We haven't heard from Kim yet on this"), encouraging a range of views (dissent), and protecting minority or less-popular viewpoints.

Summarizing. Closure has to come ultimately so a statement like this may help: "It looks to me that we have identified these possibilities . . ."

Securing consensus. This means talking it through and stressing (reminding) that we work toward organizational goals. Compromising, bargaining and voting are to be discouraged because those approaches do not ensure high-quality decisions. Consensus means that all have had the opportunity to have their say and to be listened to fully. Through full discussion, an agreement is reached as to the best route to take. Obviously, not everyone prevailed, but they did have their chance to influence the group. With full opportunity to present ideas and to debate them, team members accept and support the decision reached.

Note:

1. Group decision is a way of developing and implementing your "Goodwill Investment Certificate." That is to say, if you have invested a lot of time, energy, confidence, and trust in building good relations (goodwill) with the staff via letting them be involved in making decisions, you can "go to the bank" and draw on that goodwill when you need it, e.g., to make unilateral, even arbitrary and painful decisions.
2. Group discussion decision takes time. Obviously, you can make a decision much quicker than the team. *But* the payoff for you in group decision is that implementation is quicker because people

have participated fully, thought it true in depth, actually created it, and they thus can readily support and implement it. Statements like "I wonder what the boss wanted?" "Did he already have his mind made up?" "If he favored that approach why didn't he just tell us that instead of calling a meeting?" are eliminated. Figure 24 depicts graphically the rapidity of implementation of a decision under group vs. individual decision-making procedures.

3. Complaints about decisions may be twofold: The decision/solution itself, and the process by which it was made. In group decision making, both complaints are automatically eliminated.

4. Group decision is a powerful mechanism to arrive at not only unified thinking (agreement), but also to produce *new* thinking as well. Figure 25 indicates the direction of thought before the discussion

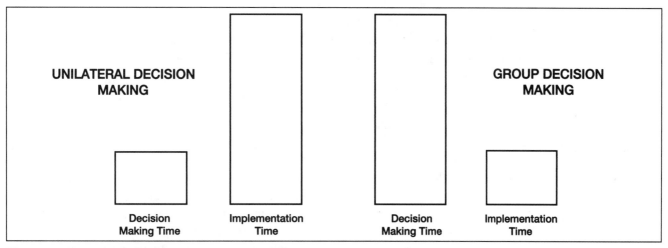

Figure 10-24. Time involved in making decisions and implementing them under conditions of individual/unilateral vs. group decision making. Decisions are made more rapidly on an individual basis, but their implementation is slower. In group decision making, the converse prevails.

Prior to Discussion and Decision

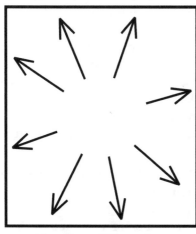

Direction of Thought
(Points of View)

After Group Discussion and Decision

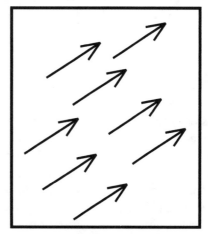

Direction of Thought
(Points of View)

Figure 10-25. Group thinking prior to and after discussion. Note that initially each group member inclined to his/her own and *different* point of view. After discussion, the thinking was not only unified, but assumed an entirely *new* direction.

(highly diverse) and the direction after the discussion—not only unified, but in a totally new and different direction.

5. Group decision does not mean a surrender of power and a corresponding weakening of your leadership role. Actually, the converse is true. You gain in terms of potentially higher quality decisions, greater goodwill, increased staff motivation, and full support for the implementation of decisions. What is at work is the "more-more" as opposed to the "less-less" phenomenon—that is, if I communicate more with others, they will share more with me. If I level more, they will so respond to me. If I trust others more, they will trust me more. And if I delegate more, I'll get more enthusiasm, job interest, and risk taking in return. So we are not faced with a "fixed pie" where if I give some away I end up with less. Rather, we are talking about drawing from a cornucopia, an inexhaustible and ever-increasing vessel, to give us a win-win rather than a win-lose *effect*.

Finalizing the Decision

A key part of the decision-making process is to think carefully through the various elements that enter into the making of an effective decision, including concern with the eventualities that might arise and thus prevent you from reaching your desired goal. To aid you in your thinking about a forthcoming, important decision, see Figure 26, Worksheet to Aid In Finalizing An Effective Decision (page 513).

Loose or Rigid? A Self-Assessment Opportunity

Effective decision making calls for maximum ability and willingness to approach problems in an open, relaxed and non-dogmatic way. The rating scale in Figure 27 should help to give you a good fix on your own degree of flexibility in the area of decision making. It should serve to point out your needs for self-development/personal growth, if so indicated, to achieve greater flexibility—and less "up-tightness"—as a decision maker. **Note:** The results of your self-assessment will be meaningful only if you provide totally candid responses to the quiz items.

STEP 6: IMPLEMENTATION—CONVERTING HOPE INTO REALITY

The great end of life is not knowledge but action.

—Thomas Henry Huxley (1825–1895), English biologist, science publicist and educator

To put one's thoughts into action is the most difficult thing in the world.

—Johann Wolfgang von Goethe (1740–1832), German poet, dramatist, novelist, and philosopher

Plans are only good intentions unless they immediately degenerate into hard work.

—Peter Drucker, management authority, consultant, writer, and educator

When we have reached the stage of implementation of our decision, we operate on the assumption that the real problem was identified and the wisest decision was chosen to implement it. As one writer put it, "Flawless execution cannot compensate for implementing the wrong solution" (Daryl Conner, President of ODR, Inc., Atlanta, quoted in *Training*, February 1990).

In any case, if we have made our decision (Step 5), we must concern ourselves with its implementation. That is, some form of action planning or policy development must take place. As has been observed, "great ideas require landing gear as well as wings."

An old adage in management has it that there are three types of managers: those who make things happen, those who watch things happen, and those who wonder what happened. Implementation of a decision is the concern for the manager who wants to make things happen, for the facts of managerial life are that implementation doesn't happen by itself, on the basis of hope. It only occurs with planning, dedication, and all-out effort. Abraham Lincoln once said: "If I had eight hours to chop down a tree, I'd spend six hours sharpening my axe."

Guidelines to Overcome Nightmares Over Implementation

Implementation of a decision can be a process that is scattered and scary, or smooth and sensible. The following guidelines can make the process an orderly and successful one.

1. Your strategy (plan of implementation) is less important than the quality of its execution. As an old popular song had it, "It ain't what you do, it's the way that you do it." Given a choice, I would opt for a less-than-perfect plan executed well than a "perfect" plan executed in a mediocre way. (Of course, if you can develop a perfect, fool-proof plan, by all means do so!)

2. Your probability of success is highly dependent on an adequate investment of time. Worthwhile implementation efforts—whether in marketing, R&D, or TQM (Total Quality Management)—are not achievable in two-hour, TV-movie time frames. So beware the search for the fabled quick-fix, the easy-to-apply Band-Aid, for in today's complex world truly profound plans are needed for real accomplishment.

3. While delegation of various aspects of the implementation plan are essential, you, as the person involved, must provide continued interest in and support of it. Your keen, visible involvement communicates your concern and expectations. Conversely, taking a back-seat, laid-back, laissez-faire approach ("leaving it to the lazy fairies," as one wag put it), communicates that the plan has lesser urgency and importance. The all-too-likely result: second-best efforts, floundering, slippage, and overall mediocre accomplishment.

So if you sincerely want to do something meaningful about a tough problem and have made a decision about it, you may have to become part of its solution. That is to say, you must invest personal time and energy in the planning of the implementation, give ongoing support and encouragement to the implementers, and engage in such follow-up as maybe needed to ensure that things don't slip through the cracks or get bottle-necked. The key idea, then, is *personal involvement* on the assumption that you have to give (possibly a lot) to get something back.

4. Plans that may encounter resistance should rely heavily on a) full involvement of those affected by the implementation, b) strong, visible leadership, as suggested above, and c) possibly altering the reward system to secure greater support. **Example:** In respect to the Affirmative Action Plan at Colgate-Palmolive Co., Reuben Mark, Chairman and CEO, stated: "Unless the leadership of a company talks about this everyday, it doesn't happen. The boss has to talk about it and back it up with money and sanctions" (quoted in Cindy Skrzycki, "Standing Up for Affirmative Action," *The Washington Post,* March 25, 1990).

Similarly, William S. Lee, Chairman and President of Duke Power Co., employs ways to quantify and reward the hiring of minorities. Lee stated: "We post progress toward the goals each month. If we make it, every single employee in the company gets a bonus" (quoted in *The Washington Post,* March 25, 1990).

5. The purpose of action planning is not only to give the implementers concrete tasks to perform, but to reduce anxieties about the difficulties entailed in its implementation. For quite often the "doability" of a task depends on its perceived difficulty. So if it looks hard, it may be approached with less/little enthusiasm, and if it looks doable it will be tackled with more confidence and energy.

Anecdote: A somewhat indolent hardware store assistant was given the choice of delivering one of two packages, a big one and a small one. He opted for the smaller one, of course, and did this without complaint. What he didn't know was that his boss understood perfectly the rule stated above and had put the item to be delivered—a blacksmith's anvil—in the smaller box!

6. Depending on the nature of the project and the time available, it often is desirable to conduct pilot or trial runs before implementing the "big plan." The idea, of course, is to get the bugs out of the plan in advance of its full and final implementation. Producers of plays to appear on Broadway have long recognized the need to take the show on the road before making the big splash in the Big Apple. In this connection, we should ask whether we heed the lament of the quality control people who say: "They never give us enough time to do it right, but we always have the time to do it over!"

As has been mentioned earlier, multiple rather than single tests are to be preferred as a form of statistical control. One bust out of five pilots is no big deal, whereas one try and one failure is. Also, it is wise to vary the approaches to learn which is most effective, e.g., before going all-out in one direction in a marketing plan, various forms of sales and advertising efforts might be tried out.

7. In developing a plan of implementation, which may have to be applied in different situations, circumstances or locations, it is essential to avoid the "one-size fits all" syndrome. What is needed, instead, is an overall plan that is flexible enough to take into account diverse or varying conditions.

8. Implementation of a plan should take into account existing programs, operations and activities. If this is done, the new plan can mesh with ongoing functions and avoid colliding with and disturbing them. (As one wag put it, "We want mesh, not mess!")

9. Part of good action planning is to develop alternate plans in case the basic or original plan encounters stormy weather, e.g., the circumstances or the environment changes. If you have a backup plan, its ease of implementation and administration can proceed without added confusion, anxiety, and delay.

10. If a proposed plan of implementation may be quite complex, e.g., have a number of subordinates phases, stages, or aspects and possibly affect a number of other departments, it may be wise to think in terms of establishing a special study group or task force to come up with an appropriate overall, detailed (multi-faceted) plan. Representatives from the affected departments should serve on the study team to a) secure the broadest possible input and b) ensure support for the plan when implemented.

11. Implementation plans should, as appropriate, provide procedures for interim evaluation of what is going on. If the assessment indicates that things are off target, adjustments should be made to ensure working toward the game plan. An analogy is in the area of athletics—visualize the coach who alters tactics or makes switches or replacements of personnel as the situation dictates.

12. Good planning does not necessarily entail the development and implementation of gigantic, long-term, blockbuster plans. Rather, small, step-by-step, short-term goals may well be the best road to an initial breakthrough. Small successes can be used as stepping stones to more ambitious projects. Psychologically speaking, greater understanding and support from superiors, peers and subordinates (the actual implementers) may be attained with smaller "victories." The operative idea is that

"nothing succeeds like success." An attention-getter in the form of small, visible successes and accomplishments can serve as a prelude to later, large-scale improvements and changes.

Management consultant and business author Robert Schaffer (*The Breakthrough Strategy: Using Short-term Successes to Build the High Performance Organization*, New York: Harper Business, 1988) advocates identifying a "breakthrough project" that is "loaded for success" and has these elements:

☐ Urgent and compelling—a true attention-getter
☐ An initial or first-step target with a potential for short-term accomplishment, i.e., in weeks rather than in months
☐ Clear-cut, measurable, bottom-line results
☐ An accomplishment that participants feel they can achieve
☐ Doable with the resources on hand and existing authority

The Action Plan

To ensure that your plan proceeds in a systematic, orderly way, you need to consider these elements:

☐ What is to be done (activities, functions) in logical order or sequence
☐ Who is to do them (assume responsibility)
☐ When each step is to be started
☐ When each step is to be completed
☐ What resources are needed for each step
☐ The indicator of successful completion of each step

An example of the first element—what is to be done—might be that of planning for a major meeting. The activities would include visiting hotel/motel facilities; studying proposals submitted by the hotels; selecting a meeting site (hotel); signing a contract; developing specific plans for meeting room layouts, audio/video needs, daily meals, refreshments, socials, evaluation, etc. A form to facilitate your planning is given in Figure 28 (page 517).

Notations or color-coded marks can be made on the chart concerning completion of particular activities. Note that the form has a column for "whom to notify or contact." This relates to the all-important stakeholders who may be affected to one degree or another by the Action Plan. Some of these persons may require very early contact for assistance; others may only require notification about the plan as it nears full implementation. In any case, these contacts are too important to delay or overlook. We certainly don't want a situation that conjures up Oscar Wilde's famous quote: "The play was a success. The audience was a failure."

Selection of Project Teams

Part of the implementation process may entail creating small work groups to plan particular aspects of the project or program. If so, a logical question is the kind of qualitative mix of personnel to serve on these teams. That is to say, should the teams have a mix of average and top performers, or should the high achievers be teamed together?

According to researchers Ahron Tziner and Dov Eden of Tel Aviv University, Israel ("Effects of Crew Composition on Crew Performance: Does the Whole Equal the Sum of the Parts?" *Journal of Applied Psychology,* February 1985), those of high ability are more effective when teamed with like performers. The research was conducted on 208 three-man tank crews on army maneuvers who were rated on their performance by their commanding officers. Greater performance gains occurred by creating totally high-ability tank crews rather than trying to upgrade lower-ability crews by adding one or two high-ability personnel. The researchers' conclusion: "Our results show that talent is used more effectively when concentrated."

Systems Planning

Depending on the nature of the decision to be implemented, the adhesive to bring things together—working on the system—may lie in the development of one or more of the following:

☐ A new or revised policy
☐ A new or revised standards and procedures handbook
☐ Job aids
☐ Expert systems

The above devices are decision-making and problem-solving tools to provide personnel with guidelines of one sort or another, either fairly broad ones (e.g., a policy guide) or quite specific (standards, procedures, expert systems, or job aids). The idea is to utilize what is known about a problem area rather than having people attempt to discover the Pacific Ocean all over again for themselves.

Policy Development

Part of the implementation process, or even all of it, may entail developing and promulgating a policy statement. This may be a new one because none exists or a revision of an existing one because it is obsolete, murky, unrealistic, or in conflict with other existing policy statements. It also may be desirable to formalize well-established, unwritten policies.

A policy statement is simply a guide for proper action. It clarifies for everyone what is to be done when certain situations or problems arise. This provides for consistency in their application. The best policy statements are those in sync with overall organizational goals, easily understood, up to date, adequately flexible to meet varying conditions, and respected by those who have to implement them. We say "respected" because if they are not, they are likely to be ignored or, possibly worse, downgraded in conversations with others. Visualize the bank teller or retail clerk who tells the frustrated customer: "I don't know why. It's just company policy."

Management trainer William J. Rothwell ("Performance Improvement Methods and Company Policy: Should the Tail Wag the Dog?" *Performance and Instruction,* November–December, 1989), states that policies are needed for these reasons:

1. To ensure consistency of operations, e.g., in administering personnel rules and procedures such as Equal Employment Opportunity (EEO).
2. To provide specific guidance for handling important issues, e.g., ethical deviations, or how to pay temporary and part-time hires, or how accurate/honest our advertising should be.
3. To provide a means to implement company plans, e.g., if an overall goal is to increase market share, and to determine if existing functional policies in sync with that goal.
4. To save time in decision making, e.g., how to deal with an employee who wishes to attend a midday Toastmaster's Club meeting every other week.

Standards and Procedures Handbook

Policies provide the organization with overall guidance as to what to do or not do when particular problems arise. Standards and procedures provide the how to or means to implement or achieve policies. **Example:** Our company may have an overall policy on sexual harassment. But a statement of standards and procedures is also needed to guide those who may wish to render a complaint, need to investigate the complaint, need to conduct a hearing on the matter, or need to take disciplinary action.

Procedures, to be effective, must be specific, presented in logical (step-by-step) fashion, and provide for little deviation. **Examples:** How to register a guest in a hotel; how a teller is to process large-amount checks; how to process a return of merchandise in a retail store; how to report a personal injury or an office fire.

Handbooks and manuals should be reviewed periodically for utility (are they helpful?), currency (are new conditions being recognized?), and necessity (have they, over time, become burdensome due to their sheer volume?).

Standards and procedures, when codified in the form of a manual or handbook, can be used for quick reference, by supervisors to train new workers, or by employees themselves as a job aid or self-study guide.

Management consultants Steven R. Baldwin and Michael McConnell ("Strategic Planning: Process and Plan Go Hand in Hand," *Management Solutions,* June 1988) suggest that in addition to new policies and procedures, other systems approaches may be necessary, namely, modifying existing information systems or creating new reporting structures. They state: "These changes help monitor progress in attaining stated goals and related interim measures, and ensure allocation of resources consistent with established goals."

Job Aids

A job aid guides a person to do a concrete task. It does this by describing in detail when, where, and how to do it. **Everyday examples:** a recipe; an instruction sheet to assemble a bike; how to operate the dishwasher. **Job examples:** how to process a check presented for payment in a bank; how to prepare a transparency slide for use on an overhead projector; how to take an order over the phone. Note that these tasks are such that they lend themselves to logical and orderly (sequential) descriptions of the steps involved to complete the tasks properly.

Job aids are not used when a problem requires special background, experience, knowledge, analytical ability, or discretion. Job aids may be verbal (one or more words) or graphic (one or more designs, illustrations, pictures), or both. To ensure that the learner or operator grasps the information to be applied to the proper

accomplishment of the task, a good job aid has these characteristics:

- ☐ Simplicity
- ☐ Clarity/specificity
- ☐ Logical flow
- ☐ Completeness of data (steps) provided
- ☐ Minimum word usage or no words at all; graphics are preferred
- ☐ No extraneous information
- ☐ Instructions for troubleshooting or a "disaster" (emergency)

The job aid is intended to serve as an individualized self-help training aid. When the task is mastered, the aid can be discarded.

Job aids can be presented in a spiral booklet so that the pages lie flat or on a handy plastic card to keep in a purse, wallet, or pocket. It may be on a large sheet of paper under a glass desktop, or on the wall or on a decal pasted on a machine.

It is a good idea to check out the usability of a job aid by testing it on several naive (inexperienced) users. If the job aid will be used in other cultures, special care must be taken regarding use of words, phrases and idioms.

Expert Systems

Also known as knowledge-based systems, expert systems consist of computer software programs to assist personnel in making decisions by asking them pertinent questions. A key function of an expert system is to ask better questions than the untrained person could. It then assesses the correctness of responses to those questions, based on a previously programmed set of rules or bits of knowledge. Essentially, it is a high-powered job aid.

Expert systems are developed by individuals who have considerable wisdom or background in a particular field. They thus know what questions to ask to lead to a proper solution. An everyday example might be a problem you or I have with our cars or bodies. We present the symptoms to the computer (as opposed to an auto service person or doctor) who can ask a series of pre-programmed questions that can lead to a sophisticated diagnosis and a proper solution. In effect, expert systems are the equivalent of "company old-timers."

Expert systems have the "right" information stored in them. Thus, the frustration of "forgetting" for the problem solver, because the particular problem may not be tackled very often, is readily overcome. Contrast this with what a learner may receive in a classroom and gradually lose some of what is learned because of non-use of such learnings.

Expert systems authority Paul Siegel ("What Expert Systems Can Do," *Training and Development Journal,* September 1989), sees expert systems as a tremendous device to get people to solve problems on their own. He cites these characteristics of an expert system:

It is Subtle

It allows people to learn effortlessly, at their own pace, with total opportunity for playback (unlike the typical classroom). People learn by doing, not by passive listening or observing. The interaction, incidentally, is in English, not computerese.

It is Flexible

Because the knowledge required for a proper decision is stored on a disk, it can be modified easily as changes in business goals, policy, or technology may require.

It is Efficient and Effective

It allows for consistent use by multiple users. Thus, a national organization can disseminate the software all over the country. And although not requiring a formal (classroom) training program, it ensures proper results. It can explain how conclusions are arrived at and deal with uncertain facts and relationships.

It is Empowering

It appeals to people because they don't see themselves as mere trainees in a classroom. Typically, they build on what they already know. Also, when a problem arises they don't need to secure help from someone else. Instead, they can haul out the expert system and diagnose and treat the problem on their own. It can free people to do more important work, e.g., a retail clerk in a department store processing a sales transaction need only respond to the computer's several specific questions and thus the clerk has more time to spend with the customer.

Cautions:

1. An expert system is capable of giving a definitive answer to the wrong problem. Unlike a human being, it may not know when it is in deep water. Unfortunately, it cannot sense that it is facing unwanted or impending trouble because of the path on which we led the expert system.

2. While expert systems can help us to make decisions or by providing advice and solutions, they don't make the decisions for us. *We* are still responsible for what *we decide* to do based on the knowledge furnished us.

STEP 7: EVALUATION—DID WHATEVER YOU DID, WORK?

Our theories determine what we measure.

—Albert Einstein

The real voyage of discovery consists not in seeking new lands, but in seeing with new eyes.

—Marcel Proust (1871–1922), French novelist

Evaluation is the all-important process of comparing results/outcomes with goals/objectives. Every decision has a hoped-for outcome, and it is our job as problem solvers to ascertain the result and the cause(s) for it.

When we think and talk about evaluation we must consider what can be measured by *results,* not merely events or activities. We must focus on measurable elements such as profitability (return on investment), market share, sales, public response/attitudes, quality, costs, quality of work life, etc. And we cannot afford to be sidetracked by a yearning for immediate payoffs. Unfortunately, the desire for quickie results often encourages managers to abort programs before they have developed enough roots and/or support to become successful.

Evaluation, our last phase in the problem-solving process, has several vital purposes. It answers these questions:

- ☐ Was the decision the proper one?
- ☐ Did we consider enough options?
- ☐ Was our implementation plan effective?
- ☐ What did we learn from this problem solving and decision-making endeavor?
- ☐ If our decision was an appropriate one, what can we learn from our success?
- ☐ Conversely, if the decision produced a less-than-successful result or experience, what can we learn from it?

Basically, evaluation of a decision takes two forms:

1. Post-mortem Critique
2. Action Research Model

Post-mortem Critique

Typically, decisions and programs/activities implemented pursuant to those decisions are evaluated when an end or measurable point is reached. Management authorities Robert R. Blake and Jane S. Mouton place great stress on the importance of the post-mortem critique. They state (*Making Experience Work: The Grid Approach to Critique,* New York: McGraw-Hill, 1978):

> *Critique introduced at the end of an activity permits participants to review and evaluate the entire experience from inception to conclusion. Interpersonal influences can be traced, critical choice points identified and evaluated, recurring patterns verified, and all these related to what actually happened. The insights gained can be significant for cause-and-effect analysis and for deciding what is and what is not the best way to carry out a comparable activity in the future.*

The process is essentially akin to the critique in athletics after the big game—what went well? What went less than well? Do we have any "second thoughts" about either the decision or its implementation? Were the resources expended well spent? Would we do anything differently, now that we have had experience with the decision/plan/program?

The alternative to a post-mortem critique? Letting things drift without an analysis, hoping that we did hit the mark somehow. Hardly an attractive alternative for the savvy and sophisticated manager. And if we are aware that we did not zero in on our target, can we afford to take a laissez-faire (hands-off) approach, i.e., skip the analysis of the failure—just shrug our shoulders and say "*C'est la vie*" (That's life)?

One of the problems in a post-mortem evaluation is that our judgments may have an all-too-limited focus. That is to say, do we rely totally on our judgment or do we utilize feedback and perceptions from others—the stakeholders—those who may see the results through a different set of lenses than our own?

And what if things turn out less well than expected? In our success-oriented culture, failure is something we don't like to dwell on. Yet, failure can be a great teacher. What is significant about failure is that it is inevitably part of our learning process. But failure and defeat are

hardly synonymous. Think of the quarterback who misses on one or more of his passes or, worse, has them caught by his opponents. What are his alternatives? He may have several, but the only one that matters is to engage in self-critique and become stronger for that kind of effort.

Think of the TV producer who launches a show that bombs; the lawyer who loses his case; the homebuilder who engenders abnormally high complaints from buyers; the manufacturer who markets a product that is rejected by the consumer; the politician who comes in second or third. All of these people have to think hard about why their efforts flopped and how they can do better next time.

Business writer Ben Stein ("Eaten Up By Failure? Turn It Into Success," *Business Month*, June 1990) puts failure into its proper perspective:

> *Repeated failures in an endeavor tell us that we are doing something wrong. We are not presenting ourselves well, are not in the right place, or maybe not connected with the right people, or maybe, God forbid, we are not doing what we do best. Certainly, failure gives us valuable data, if we only would listen.*

Stein also sees failure as a motivator:

> *Failure, and only failure, nudges us along the path of life until we get to success. Without failure, with only a kind of mediocre, mushy daily existence, we would never be prodded to do what finally we learn is best for us to do. Without failure, we would never be taught, motivated, propelled into the realm of that other great teacher—success—which tells us where to stay and what our strengths are.*

Newspaper columnist Sydney J. Harris (*Winners and Losers* Niles, Ill.: Argus Communications, 1973) divides decision makers into "winners" and "losers":

> *A winner says,*
> *'There ought to be a better way to do it';*
> *A loser says,*
> *'That's the way it's always been done here.'*
> *A winner learns from his mistakes.*
> *A loser learns only not to make mistakes by not trying anything different.*
> *A winner isn't afraid to leave the road when he doesn't agree with the direction it's taking;*
> *A loser follows the 'middle of the road' no matter where the road is going.*

And if our decision did not work out as hoped for, are we willing and able to accept responsibility for it? Simple logic tells us that we can't take credit for successes without taking the rap for an occasional failure.

Earlier we alluded to the need to learn from success as well as failure. But this kind of learning is hardly easy and thus may not take place. To quote former U.S. Senator Gary Hart, who appeared before Congress and focused on the lessons of the Persian Gulf War, "It is often much more difficult to learn from victory than from defeat. In defeat, questions are asked about what went wrong, so that those mistakes will not be made in the future. But victory seldom creates the need to inquire as to its sources" (quoted by E. J. Dionne Jr., "On War: New Ideas From A Familiar Face," *The Washington Post*, May 1, 1991).

The Action Research Model (ARM)

The ARM is an approach to evaluation while the project/activity *is in process,* rather than waiting to make adjustments at project's end. To quote Blake and Mouton again (*Making Experience Work: The Grid Approach to Critique*, 1978), the ARM is a type of critique that:

> *. . . makes it possible for those engaged in pursing a goal to interrupt their activities at various points to measure the extent to which they are moving toward or away from the goal; whether their rate of progress is as planned or faster or slower; and whether or not quality is sound. The approach being used to reach the goal can also be assessed to see if it is deficient and to what degree. Staffing to accomplish the goal can be examined to determine whether the requisite knowledge, skills, and attitudes are available. The direction (i.e., leadership or supervision) being exercised for coordinating effort can be evaluated and a decision can be reached as to whether it is too tight or too loose. Finally, the question can be asked: Are these controls providing a sound basis of relating activities with the goal?*

The ARM concept is designed to make corrections as the data (feedback) coming in indicates that things are not working out as planned. Some examples of application of the ARM are these:

☐ Department store executives examine gross dollar returns (for two days) from a heavily promoted weeklong sale and decide to add two more sales days and reduce prices an added 10% on all items in the store.

☐ Each evening, trainers in an off-site, seven-day executive development program collectively review feedback sheets from the participants. They learn that the executives feel that the class days are too long. Participants suggest a long break in the afternoon (starting at 4 p.m.) for recreational purposes followed by cocktails, dinner, and an evening session. The trainers discuss the proposal and agree to make the adjustment.

☐ The Big City College basketball team's game plan doesn't seem to be working. At the half, the coaches put their heads together and develop a new approach involving a change in the offensive strategy (more inside shooting) and switching players on defense. The new plan is implemented in the second half.

☐ Bi-weekly reading tests are conducted for all students in the Jackson Park Elementary School, an inner-city school. The quiz data are given to the school's four reading specialists, who work with classroom teachers to revise their instructional strategies for those students requiring special assistance on reading.

Of course, "mid-course corrections" are not applicable to all situations. Obviously, if one has to wait until all the data are in, the post-mortem critique, as described above, is the way to go.

Problem Solving and Decision Making—A Quiz to Encourage Reflection

	YES	NO
1. I follow a *multi-step* problem-solving and decision-making model to ensure the making of sound decisions.	☐	☐
2. I try to make decisions on the basis of facts, reason, and logic as opposed to relying on subjective factors (preconceptions, prejudices, etc.).	☐	☐
3. I search for options (alternatives) before deciding on a single course of action.	☐	☐
4. I consider the importance of values—mine and those of others—underlying a decision before deciding.	☐	☐
5. When faced with a problem, I decide early on whether to solve it alone or involve others in the problem-solving process.	☐	☐
6. I understand the role of intuition in decision making and use it when analytical methods are inadequate.	☐	☐
7. I recognize the importance of group wisdom in making decisions.	☐	☐
8. I am interested in making high-quality rather than quick decisions, so I encourage expression of divergent views (dissent) by my team.	☐	☐
9. I realize that I cannot make decisions in cocoon fashion, that I must consider how they might look to and impact on the rest of the organization.	☐	☐
10. I also consider whether my decisions might have a "ripple effect" outside the organization.	☐	☐
11. I recognize that every decision entails risk. I thus try to assess possible consequences and make plans to minimize them.	☐	☐
12. I avoid delaying decisions, hoping that something may happen to "get me off the hook."	☐	☐
13. I consider time factors (need for action) and timing (when to decide and implement) of a decision.	☐	☐
14. I try to make my decisions on a cost-effective basis.	☐	☐
15. My decision making stands the tests of organizational and societal ethics.	☐	☐
16. Our team discussions end with firm decisions, definite plans for action and fixed responsibility and procedures to follow up on implementation of our decisions.	☐	☐

Scoring

Give yourself 5 points for each "YES" answer.

70–80 points—Go to the head of the class. Or, shall we crown you "CEO"? (But don't skip this chapter: It may "hone" your skills to an even greater degree.)

59–69 points—You understand the key concepts of this skill area quite well. Your main need is to zero in on the added opportunities for growth you have identified.

Below 59 points—You have a lot of work to do—serious self-assessment and behavior change—to elevate your prowess as an effective problem solver and decision maker.

Figure 10-3
Guide Sheet for Problem Assessment

1. **Statement of Concern:** Based on your appraisal of the need/difficulty/performance deviation/ threat/opportunity, describe the problem as objectively as you can.

2. **Statement of Impact:** Based on your analysis of the problem situation, state how it impacts upon the pertinent "Ms" of management: money, manpower, motivation, marketshare, markets, machines, methods, materials, meetings, minutes (time use), MIS (management information system), meeting of quality standards, management of operations, maintenance, measurement. The impact of the problem is as follows:

3. **Statement of Seriousness:** The immediacy, frequency, severity, or widespread character of the problem is:

4. **Statement of Trend:** Is the problem increasing, decreasing, or at a constant level? How does that trend impact on the problem? The trend of the problem is:

5. **Statement Regarding Constraints:** The constraints (i.e., what keeps the problem from being solved) in the situation are:

6. **Statement Regarding Data Availability:** The information/data (what, where, when, who, how much) we now have about the problem is (are):

7. **Statement Regarding Data Unavailability:** The information/data we do *not* have, but need is (are):

8. **Statement Regarding Problem Ownership:** The stakeholders who are involved/interested/affected/concerned extends to myself, my work team, my boss, other units, the entire organization, the union suppliers, customers, the community, other, other, other. Circle the potentially interested stakeholder.

9. **Statement Regarding Organizational Support:** Is the problem which I/we have identified one to which the organizational "culture" (history, tradition, values, practices, politics, preferences, taboos) would say "amen"?

10. **Statement of Problem:** The actual problem I/we/the organization faces can be described as follows:

11. **Statement Regarding Desired Outcomes:** How will you know that the problem is solved? (What will the "world" look like when it is solved?) A resolution of the problem will give us this (these) desired situations/results/outcomes:

	Week 1	2	3	4	5	6	7	8	9	10
Pat	39	43	36	44	41	43	47	38	42	40
Chris	41	40	27	29	36	32	43	36	37	37
Kim	37	38	34	39	39	30	38	37	33	38
Sandy	40	42	41	39	46	45	44	39	44	45
Al	40	41	40	on leave	39	38	31	29	30	28
Jean	29	31	28	25	30	31	27	29	28	30

Figure 10-6. Productivity of six employees over a 10-week period presented on a check sheet.

Tasks	Produce	Meat	Seafood	Grocery	Checkers and other clerks
Concern for customer	(2)	5	4	4	4
Emphasis an quality	(3)	5	5	4	5
Training of subordinates	(2)	4	4	(3)	4
Appearance of area or display cases	4	5	4	4	4
Cost consciousness	4	4	5	(3)	4
Etc.					
Etc.					
Etc.					

Figure 10-7. Ratings (on 1–5 point scale) of Department Heads in a large supermarket on a check sheet. Circled items indicate weak areas of performance.

A Tool to Find Your Problem

A—Attitudes? Antagonisms? Apathy? Adaptability? Aesthetics? Anger? Appearance (personal, shop, office)? Authority? Action Plans? Appraisal? Absenteeism? Alcoholism? Audits? Advertising?

B—Behaviors? Burnout? Bottlenecks? Bargaining? Bureaucracy? Budgets? Backstabbing? Break-Even Analysis? Benchmarking?

C—Centralization? Chain of Command? Coaching? Counseling? Costs? Controlling? Computers? Cost Accounting? Colleagues? Competition? Creativity? Customer (focus, complaints)? Continuous Improvement? Communication? Climate? Change? Crises? Careers? Conflict? Cooperation?

D—Decision Making? Delegation? Discipline? Discrepancies? Division of Labor? Distrust? Distribution? Dual-Career Couples? Decentralization? Defects? Danger? Deviations? Difficulties? Durability? Deadlines? Down Time? Disturbances? Discrimination?

E—Environment (situation)? Efficiency? Empowerment? Economy? Ego? Ethics? Errors? Experimentation? Energy? Education? Effort? Empire? Emphasis? Endurance? EEO?

F—Feedback? Flextime? Follow Up? Forms? Facilitating? Fears? Frustration? Fantasies? Fun? Failure? Forecast? Family? Foreign (markets, personnel)?

G—Garbage (re computer inputs and outputs)? Goals? Group? Groupthink? Grapevine? Grievances?

H—Half-measures? Hierarchy? Harassment? Hazards? Help? Horrors?

I—Inputs? Indecision? Integration? Inventory? Investment? Interaction? Intentions? Influence? Innovation? Ideas? Ideals? Insensitivities? Insecurities? Improprietaries? Irregularities?

J—Jurisdiction? Job Design? Job Enrichment? Job Description? Job Rotation? Job Security?

K—Knowledge? Know-how? Kibosh?

L—Lifestyles? Layout? Layoffs? Listening? Loyalty? Leadership? Lemons? Laziness? Labor?

M—Maintenance? Motivation? Money? Manpower? Minutes? MBO? Mixups? Market Mix? Matrix Structure? Measurement? Material? Methods? Mentoring? Meetings? Misinformation?

N—Networking? Negatism? Nit-picking? Needs? Neglect? Negotiation? Nerve Center?

O—Orientation? Outputs? Ombudsman? Outcomes? Organization? Objectives? Opportunities? Obstructions? Operations?

P—Profits? Profit Center? Projects? Priorities? Pessimism? Power? Perceptions? Pilot Run? Progress? Politics? Pressures? Plans? Performance? Policies? Personnel? Procedures? Pay? Production?

Q—Quality? Quality Control? Quality of Work Life? Questionnaires? Quantity? Quotas?

R—Rapport? Records? Rules? Relationships? Resistances? Risks? Response Time? Rejects? Rewards? Responsibilities? Recognition? Revision? Revocation? Reverse Discrimination? Roles?

S—Staff Meetings? Stress? Synergy? Systems? Security? Suppliers? Stakeholders? Surveys? Safety? Standards? Scheduling? Seasonal? Sales? Secretary? Staff? Salvage? Symptoms? Search? Secrets? Storage? Sick Leave?

T—Time? Tenure? Totality? Track Record? Timing? Training? Turnover? Team Building? TQM (Total Quality Management)? Tests?

U—Underachievers? Unity? Upward Communication? Uncertainty? Union? Utilization? Unification? Urban? Understanding? Umpire? Uplift?

V—Values? Vendors? Value Engineering? Vendettas? Venom? Vigor? Variables? Visibility? Victories?

W—Workaholics? Word Processing? Work Demands? Waste? Workweek? Workday? Warehousing?

X—Excess? Extra Work? Expense? Executives?

Y—Yield? Yesterday? Youth? You-I? Yesterday's Breadwinners?

Z—Zero Defects? Zero-Based Budgeting? Zig Zags?

Figure 10-8. An alphabetically arranged question list to aid in problem identification.

Problem	Frequency	Severity	Solvability	Total Weight
1. Security problems	2	3	3	18
2. Turnover of sales staff	2	4	5	40
3. Customer complaints	5	4	3	60
4. Late reports from field offices	3	4	2	24

Figure 10-9. Priority ranking, on a weighted basis, of identified problems.

Do We Need A Consultant?

1. Yes No The decision to go "outside" recognizes that the consultant has greater expertise.
2. Yes No In deciding on a consultant, we will consider several individuals and firms before making our final decision.
3. Yes No We expect that the consultant will meet *our* needs as opposed to offering standard (or "canned") approaches to our problem.
4. Yes No We will have a clear-cut understanding with the consultant as to objectives and the time involved to work on the problem.
5. Yes No We expect the consultant's written proposal to be totally professional—pertinent and realistic in relation to our needs.
6. Yes No We expect the consultant's services to be cost-effective.
7. Yes No The consultant we select will bring strong professional *qualifications* for our particular job.
8. Yes No The consultant will have solid *experience* ("track record") in the area of our need.
9. Yes No The consultant should "wear well" in our organization and its culture.
10. Yes No The consultant will be an easy person to work with.
11. Yes No The team and I expect to learn considerably by our contacts with the consultant.
12. Yes No We intend to check the consultant's references before signing an agreement.
13. Yes No We plan to secure feedback from all persons who will have contact with our consultant.

Figure 10-10. A Checklist to Aid in Selection of a Consultant/External Resource Person

Worksheet to Aid in Finalizing the Decision

1. The decision to be made relates to the following statement of the problem:

_____

_____

2. The decision to be made is mine (I and/or my work team), not that of others.
   ☐ Not certain at all   ☐ Fairly certain
   ☐ Totally certain

   Comment:

   _____

   _____

3. I have utilized my staff (the work team) in making the decision to this degree:

   /_____/_____/_____/_____/_____/_____/
   1   2   3   4   5   6   7
   (Low)   (High)

   Comment:

   _____

   _____

4. I (we) have considered a variety of alternatives in arriving at my (our) decision:
   ☐ Not certain at all ☐ Fairly certain
   ☐ Totally certain

   Comment:

   _____

   _____

5. I (we) have considered the impact of the decision on the "stakeholders" involved (peers, bosses, subordinates, customers/clients, suppliers, community, others) to this degree:

   /_____/_____/_____/_____/_____/_____/
   1   2   3   4   5   6   7
   (Low)   (High)

   Comment:

   _____

   _____

6. I (we) have considered the ethical implications of the decision:
   ☐ Not certain at all   ☐ Fairly certain
   ☐ Totally certain

   Comment:

   _____

   _____

7. My (our) solution/decision regarding the problem is:

   _____

   _____

8. The desired/anticipated outcome(s) of the decision is(are):

   _____

   _____

(worksheet continued on next page)

9. My (our) degree of certainty that the option/alternative I (we) have chosen will remedy the identified problem is:

/	/	/	/	/	/	/
1	2	3	4	5	6	7
(Low)						(High)

10. The risks in making this decision are:

    a. _____

    b. _____

    c. _____

    d. _____

    e. _____

11. The risks in postponing or deferring this decision are:

    a. _____

    b. _____

    c. _____

    d. _____

    e. _____

12. Potential barriers/roadblocks to the desired outcome(s) is (are):

    a. _____

    b. _____

    c. _____

    d. _____

    e. _____

13. I (we) can overcome these barriers/roadblocks by:

    a. _____

    b. _____

    c. _____

    d. _____

    e. _____

14. The degree of *reversibility* of my (our) decision is:

/	/	/	/	/	/	/
1	2	3	4	5	6	7
(Low)						(High)

Comment:

_____

_____

_____

15. I (we) have considered the timing—dates of announcement and of implementation—of my (our) decision:

☐ Not certain at all   ☐ Fairly certain

☐ Totally certain

Comment:

_____

_____

_____

16. I (we) have considered carefully the adequacy of the resources needed to carry out my (our) decision:

☐ Budget   ☐ Staffing   ☐ Information   ☐ Time

☐ Space   ☐ Equipment   ☐ Materials/Supplies

☐ Other   ☐ Other   ☐ Other   ☐ Other

Figure 10-26. Worksheet to aid in finalizing an effective decision.

Loose or Rigid? A Self-assessment Rating Scale of Flexibility

Place a dot in the box which best describes your attitude or behavior on the statements below.

Element	Never	Seldom	Sometimes	Frequently	Always
1. You pride yourself on your ability to produce novel, innovative, and exciting ways to resolve problems.					
2. You recognize that you do not have all the answers to a problem.					
3. You seek out the opinions of others before making decisions.					
4. You enjoy the spirited give and take of a problem-solving session.					
5. You have no objection to having your views challenged by others.					
6. You find it easy to listen to others who have views and approaches that differ from your own.					
7. You sincerely believe that the best answer/ solution to a problem is important, even if it is not your own.					
8. You have no objection to seeing your own approach modified/amended as a result of group discussion.					
9. You do *not* enter into a problem-solving session with the idea that "there's only one way to go" and you have already found that way.					
10. When others present ideas, you refrain from picking them apart.					
11. You recognize that peoples' *values* form the basis for their opinions/approaches and thus the ideas of others are likely to differ from yours.					
12. You actually seek out divergent views on the assumption that quality solutions/decisions depend on a diversity of thought and input.					
13. You are able to assess objectively the premises that form the basis for your own conclusions/ strategies.					
14. You feel comfortable giving praise and recognition to others who present worthwhile ideas/approaches/observations and possible solutions to them.					
15. You can gracefully accept a decision that you initially "campaigned" against.					

(continued on next page)

Element	Never	Seldom	Sometimes	Frequently	Always
16. You state your views fully to your superior(s) even though they may not agree with you.					
17. You are fully willing to accept responsibility for a decision/solution even if it does not work out well.					
18. Your boss regards you as a person who is truly open to new ideas.					
19. Your colleagues/peers regard you as a person who is truly open to new ideas.					
20. Your staff regards you as a person who is truly open to new ideas.					

Figure 10-27. Loose or Rigid? A Self-Assessment Rating Scale

Scoring

Now that you have responded to all the statements in the quiz, connect the dots in the boxes with a ruler. This should provide you with a profile regarding the degree of your flexibility in the course of your daily work as a problem solver and decision maker.

If the profile is skewed to the right of the scale, you see yourself as a highly flexible problem solver/decision maker. If the profile is skewed to the left, you are less flexible as a problem solver and decision maker, probably less tolerant of the views of others. If your profile is more or less in the middle or shifts frequently between the left and right sides of the scale, your style is not clear cut. In any case, if your pattern is to the left, middle or somewhat varied, you clearly have some work to do to become a more flexible problem solver and decision maker.

Note: The profile you have developed obviously is based on your own perceptions of your skills/style. For a more accurate appraisal, you may wish to ask your staff and certain colleagues to provide you with ratings on yourself as they see you "in action."

Figure 10-28
Worksheet for Action Planning

Action Steps	Who Is Responsible	Who to Notify or Contact and When	Resources Needed	Time Frames		Indicator of Successful Completion
				Start	Completion Deadline	
1.						
2.						
3.						
4.						
5.						
6.						
7.						
8.						
9.						
10.						

Figure 10-21
Evaluation of Alternates (Suppliers) Using Weighted Criteria

Nursery Firm	Criteria and Weight					
	Reputation/ Track Record (3)	Product Quality (5)	Product Variety (4)	Cost/ Price (2)	Warranty Practices (1)	Totals
Your Plant Materials Co.	2 (× 3 = 6)	4 (× 5 = 20)	4 (× 4 = 16)	3 (× 2 = 6)	3 (× 1 = 3)	51
Super Nursery Co.	4 (× 3 = 12)	4 (× 5 = 20)	6 (× 4 = 24)	5 (× 2 = 10)	7 (× 1 = 7)	73
Perfect Plant Materials Supply, Inc.	7 (× 3 = 21)	7 (× 5 = 35)	5 (× 4 = 20)	6 (× 2 = 12)	5 (× 1 = 5)	93
Econo Plant and Seed Supply, Ltd.	3 (× 3 = 9)	7 (× 5 = 35)	6 (× 4 = 24)	6 (× 2 = 12)	6 (× 1 = 6)	86
M&L Landscape Supply Co.	6 (× 3 = 18)	5 (× 5 = 25)	7 (× 4 = 28)	7 (× 2 = 14)	6 (× 1 = 6)	91
General Nurseries, Inc.	6 (× 3 = 18)	6 (× 5 = 30)	7 (× 4 = 28)	3 (× 2 = 6)	4 (× 1 = 4)	86

(adapted from a numerical evaluation format given by Leslie W. Rue and Lloyd L. Byars in Management Theory and Application, *Fourth Edition, 1986, pp. 96 and 97.)*

The Manager as a Problem Solver and Decision Maker: Key Issues and Guidelines for Effectiveness

YOU now have read and worked your way through the Seven-Step Model for Problem Solving and Decision Making. To deepen and round out your insight into the problem solving and decision making area, you will find it helpful to focus on a number of key, related topics:

☐ Ethical Dilemmas—Decision Making in Those Gray Areas
☐ Contingency Planning—Neutralizing Murphy's Law
☐ Myths vs. Realities in Problem Solving/Decision Making
☐ Self-inflicted Wounds—Pitfalls and Perils in Problem Solving/Decision Making
☐ Guidelines and Orientations for Effective Problem Solving/Decision Making

The chapter closes with a guidesheet (action plan) for self-improvement in the skill area of problem solving and decision making (page 557) and a set of questions and problems for use in supervisory/management training workshops and/or college/university courses in management (page 552).

ETHICAL DILEMMAS: DECISION MAKING IN THOSE GRAY AREAS

The Ten Commandments are not multiple choice. Amen.

—A short, but total sermon delivered in 1945 by an army chaplain at Fort Benning, GA (quoted in a letter to the editor, in *The Cleveland Plain Dealer,* July 4, 1991)

Always do right. This will gratify some people and astonish the rest.

—Mark Twain (1835–1910), American author and humorist

If you want a friend, buy a dog.

—Statement by Gordon Gekko, the fictional corporate raider, in the 1987 movie, *Wall Street*

Don't ask whether something is legal or illegal. Ask yourself, "Is it right or wrong?"

—Business executive H. Ross Perot's advice to students of Georgetown University School of Business Administration during a convocation, November 3, 1990

The State of Ethical Behavior

In recent decades, American life has been marked by a plethora of serious ethical departures—phony body counts in the Vietnam War; the Watergate scandal; the Iran-Contra Affair (Irangate); false advertising; mislabeling of products; Salomon Bros., Inc.'s, cornering the market for Treasury securities; insider trading on Wall Street; the mammoth Savings and Loan scandals; sexual indiscretions by various religious and political figures; dirty/ugly political campaigning; political leaders who tell voters anything to secure and retain office; assorted ethical deviations in organized athletics (college athletes who are essentially hired hands, use of steroids, gambling); the NASA Challenger space shuttle disaster; Pentagon defense contracting; college student cribbing; sexual harassment; obscenely high salaries for executives who head up floundering companies; the concealment of the asbestos danger to employees of the Manville Corporation; the bizarre tale of BCCI (the Bank of Credit and Commerce International) with its prestigious clients involved in terrorism, drug vending, money laundering, and political corruption; the U.S. House of Representatives check-kiting scandal; ad nauseum.

Some survey data of ethics in organizations should help provide an overall perspective about it. Disconcerting figures of student "cribbing" (read: cheating), students who are our future managerial and professional personnel, are also presented.

☐ A Lou Harris poll found that 87% of office workers believe that their managers should deal with employees and the community in an "honest, upright, and ethical manner." But only 38% felt very confident that this really happens. And in a survey conducted by the Center for Organizational Effectiveness, 49% of *male* middle managers believe their organizations have employees' best interests in mind whereas only 19% of *female* managers felt that way (both studies reported in *Training and Development Journal,* October 1989).

☐ A *Business Month* magazine survey (December 1989) asked for responses to this statement: "It's OK to bend the rules if the survival of your job is at stake." Although 55% said they never would, a whopping 41.6% marked off "occasionally." Another 3.6% admitted a willingness to bend the rules either "always" or "often."

☐ Senior executives were asked in a survey whether people are unethical in their business dealings. Their responses: Occasionally, 66%; often, 15%; more often than not, 3%; seldom, 16% (reported in *The Wall Street Journal,* September 18, 1987).

☐ In a survey of human resource executives (*Personnel Journal,* November 1987), in which they were asked whether ethics in business was an increasing problem, 67% said "yes," 13% were "not sure" one way or another, and 19% said "no."

☐ Recent studies state that 80% of the U.S. major corporations have taken some initiative to inculcate ethical values in employees, and 44% of those firms provide ethics training for employees (Dan Rice and Craig Dreillinger, "Rights and Wrongs of Ethics Training," *Training and Development Journal,* May 1990).

☐ In an anonymous survey by Dr. Donald McCabe of Rutgers University of 6,097 students at 31 scholastically top colleges, 67% admitted to cheating at least once; 41% of the undergrads confessed to cheating on exams, and 19% admitted cribbing on four or more tests. More than 60% of future lawyers cheated once, and 12% were "regulars." The biggest cheaters plan a business career: 76% cheated once and 19% were regulars. In engineering the figures are 71% and 12%. Among future doctors: 68% and 11% (reported in *The Washington Post,* January 6, 1992).

Less than proper ethical behavior in today's business world is reflected in humorous anecdota. **Examples:**

☐ A notoriously successful crime family realized that the time had come to utilize an accounting firm in support of its illicit operations. A panel of family members interviewed representatives of some 15 accounting firms. In response to the question: "How much are three and three?" All but one replied: "Six." The remaining firm's representative parried with this question: "What would you like it to be?" and was promptly hired.

☐ A university student, enrolled in a philosophy course, encountered big theoretical ideas about values, ethics, and the like. While home for a holiday, he asked his dad, a retail clothing merchant, if the latter could share the kinds of ethical problems he encounters in his daily work. His dad was glad to give this example: "Last week we were clearing out our winter coats and suits, and an elderly, poorly dressed, obviously impoverished woman came in to purchase a marked-down winter coat. The price was $40. She took her package and left on the counter what I thought were two $20 bills. As she was exiting, I noticed a third $20 bill was attached to the other two. So my ethical question was this: Do I pocket the extra twenty or do I split it with my partner?"

☐ Two optometrists were discussing their pricing policies for glasses. One said he used the "flinch test" to set his prices. He explained his procedure as follows:

"I tell the customer that the glasses cost $100. If there is no "flinch" in response to this figure, I add: 'Plus $30 for the frames.' If the customer flinches when I first give him the $100 quote, I say: 'But that includes the frames.'"

☐ An attorney said that the motto of his profession should be this: "To you, it's a loophole. To me, it's a window of opportunity."

☐ A book featuring 158 blank pages appeared in 1987. Its title? *The Complete Book of Wall Street Business Ethics.*

You and I encounter daily situations at work or in the home, school, or community that challenge our sense of values and ethics. All of us are vulnerable to committing behaviors with ethical implications—what is right and what is not.

Most managers are fair, honest, and ethical, and want to do the right thing, at least most of the time. However, two factors often make it difficult to hew to the ethical line:

1. Internal and competitive pressures for results may encourage "cutting corners." Recessionary times certainly don't make totally ethical decision making easy. The importance of the reward system, both formal and informal, is evidenced by a survey of human resource executives (*Personnel Journal,* November 1987) wherein respondents were asked to identify the reasons for unethical behavior. Their responses: desire for more power 74%; more money 73%; more recognition 38%; faster advancement 40%. In respect to advancement, one personnel executive stated: "Advancement is limited by the economy and demographics, and common sense frequently loses to expediency. People often feel that lapses in ethics 'don't hurt anyone.'"

Psychologist Dr. Saul Gellerman ("Managing Ethics From the Top Down," *Sloan Management Review,* Winter 1989) cites the following conditions that can encourage unethical behavior:

☐ Unusually high rewards for good performance

☐ Unusually severe punishments for weak or poor performance (My Question: Is it OK to bend the rules if the survival of one's job is at stake?)

☐ Implicit sanctioning of clearly taboo actions

2. The situations themselves that managers face may not respond to clear-cut, simple right or wrong answers. **Examples:**

☐ You are the personnel manager of the XYZ Corporation. An employee comes to you with a complaint, on an agreed-upon confidential basis, about favoritism on a promotion. The conversation inadvertently reveals disturbing information about the employee's boss: On four occasions, the boss claimed reimbursement of travel expenses for trips to the field that were never made. The employee states she can document this, but reminds you of your confidentiality pledge for, she says, if the travel information gets out it could be linked directly to her. You have a tough dilemma: As a management representative, the need to alert management of this obvious fraud vs. your pledge of confidentiality to the employee.

☐ Is it OK to pay an employee in a Third World country in Asia one dollar an hour when you would pay a U.S. worker some 10 times that amount?

☐ You are a management consultant. A key official—the one who hired you—asks you to omit or delete certain data from your report.

In any case, to stimulate your thinking a bit further about ethical issues, take the quiz on page 536.

Are There "Tests" for Ethical Effectiveness?

Today's world is fast-moving and dynamic—institutions are in flux, societal values are diverse and less than stable, international and economic pressures of all sorts are the norm, and organizational needs and objectives change rapidly. It thus is all too easy to fall into the philosophical trap of "situational ethics." That is, we can rationalize/justify/explain/defend our behavior on the basis of expediency rather than from principles of what is ethically correct. So we can get ourselves "off the hook," psychologically speaking, by self-talk such as "this situation is different," "it's hardly a clear-cut situation," "ordinarily I wouldn't, but in this circumstance . . .," and so on.

We can grant that guidelines for ethical decision making may not be readily available. But there are a number of fairly solid "tests" we can employ to give us guidance and support in making our decisions. I offer 33 (!) of them and have grouped them into these four categories:

☐ How others might see us and our decision
☐ How our decision might impact on others
☐ How the decision might impact on yourself
☐ How various general considerations may influence our decision

Note: The tests that follow are *not* necessarily concerned with violations of law, government regulations, or corporate policies or regulations. We presume managers can readily identify such situations and, in all likelihood, will not involve themselves in such patently illegal and irregular behavior. Rather, we are concerned with ethical dilemmas that arise in murky situations or where choices exist in how one responds in matters impacting others.

How Others Might See Us and Our Decision

1. **The Mother Test:** Would you want your mother to know of your decision/behavior? How would she regard your action/decision?

2. **The Father Test:** Can you afford to ignore dad's repeated advice: "If you do the right thing, you don't have to worry about trying to explain it to anyone"?

3. **Boss/Colleague Test:** Would you feel comfortable telling your boss or your colleagues about the basis for your decision?

4. **The Role Model Test:** Would people you now regard or at one time looked up to as role models—teacher, athletes, authors, political leaders, neighbors, relatives—approve of your decision?

5. **The Corporate Ethicist Test:** Assuming your organization has a corporate "ethicist," a person available to advise on ethical dilemmas, what is he likely to advise about your proposed decision?

6. **The CEO Test:** If you were the CEO of a company, would you want people in it who were at best only operating on the fringes of sound ethical behavior? And how would the big boss regard this particular decision?

How Our Decision Might Impact on Others

7. **The Golden Rule Test:** Does your decision stand the test of the Golden Rule: "Do unto others as you would have them do unto you"? (A colleague of mine quips that some managers state the rule thusly: "Do unto others before they do it to you.")

8. **The "Platinum Rule" Test:** Does your decision stand the test of the Platinum Rule: "Do unto others as *they* would want done unto *them*"?

9. **The Individual Rights Test:** Am I engaging in or supporting behaviors/practices/policies that deny individuals rights to which they are entitled? **Examples:** safety, security, privacy, fair (non-discriminatory) treatment, especially in respect to pay, work assignments, promotion, avoidance of sexual harassment, and administration of workplace rules.

10. **The Affected Parties Test:** Is your proposed action such that you would have no hesitation to discuss it with those who are affected or impacted by your decision? (Consider colleagues, other departments, subordinates, stockholders, customers, suppliers, the community, etc.).

11. **Customer/Client Rule:** If I were my own customer or client, how would I see this action? Am I taking a "win-win" (all parties gain) or a "win-lose" (I win, they lose) approach?

12. **Utilitarian Test:** Does the proposed action have the potential to provide the greatest possible good for the greatest number of people? (Consider customers, employees, colleagues, stockholders, suppliers, the community.)

13. **The Five-Foci Test:** Have you tried clarifying your ethical issue by zeroing in on five foci— self, authority (the boss), work group members, the total organization, and society as a whole? A focus on multiple parties makes certain that the impact on all possible stakeholders is considered (per management consultants Dan Rice and Craig Dreillinger, "Rights and Wrongs of Ethics Training," *Training and Development Journal,* May 1990).

14. **The Instant Gratification Test:** Is there a possibility that others may see us and our behavior as having fallen victim to the "I want what I want and I want it now" syndrome.

How the Decision Might Impact on Yourself

15. **The a.m. Mirror Test:** Could you look yourself in the mirror the next morning?

16. **The Pride Test:** Now that you have decided, is your decision one in which you can take pride?

17. **The Thomas Jefferson Test:** As suggested in a letter to Peter Carr, Jefferson's nephew, "Whenever you are to do a thing tho' it can never be known but to yourself, ask yourself how you would act were all the world looking at you and act accordingly."

18. **The Media/*New York Times/60 Minutes* Test:** How would you feel if your decision/action/behavior resulted in your appearance in the newspapers, on TV or radio in negative terms?

19. **The "Inner King" Test:** Should you pay heed to the uplifting and challenging message of the Swedish proverb which tells us: "In each of us there is a king; speak to him, and he will come forth"? (Are you acting like a king or a knave?)

20. **The Inevitability Test:** Should you ignore *The Washington Post* columnist William Rasberry's rule: "If you're going to be in trouble no matter what you do, you may as well do the right thing"?

21. **The Abandonment of Principle Test:** Should you follow this pithy advice: "Sometimes you have to abandon 'principle' and do what's right"?

22. **The Career Test:** How will this and allied decisions impact on your career, over the long haul?

23. **The Cliche/Attitude Test:** Are you aware that in making your decision that you are being confronted with (a) one or both of these business *cliches*: "The end justifies the means," "Do whatever you have to do, just don't tell me about it," or (b) these harsh business *attitudes*: "Anything goes" and "Catch me if you can"?

24. **The CYA Test:** Am I doing something which requires CYA behavior? (CYA = Cover Your "Anatomy.")

25. **The 11th Commandment Test:** Is my behavior governed by the 11th Commandment, which tells me that what is paramount is that "Thou shalt not be found out"?

How Various General Considerations Might Influence Your Decision

26. **The Funeral Test:** What would you want to be said about you as a person at your funeral and who would you like to say it?

27. **The Fog Test:** When the ethical situation is foggy or murky, can you afford to ignore the maxim of "when in doubt, don't"?

28. **The Foresight Test:** What are the possible future outcomes and/or consequences as a result of this decision?

29. **The Time Test:** Do the advantages of the moment—short time frame—stand up to possible long-term disadvantages?

30. **The Distance Test:** The question "How far should I (we) go?" obviously could trigger a variety of possible answers. Would you concur that the best answer is "Don't try to find out!"?

31. **The "Fence" Test:** How would you decide if you were on the other side of the fence?

32. **The Congruity Test:** On the assumption that from time to time you have expressed your interest in and support of ethical behavior, does your decision violate the old adage: "Actions speak louder than words"?

33. **Entry/Exit Test:** Are you aware of the maxim: "It's a lot easier to get into something than out of it"?

Final Question: Assume that you had to explain your decision to someone who questioned whether you had considered the ethical values involved. Could that question have been avoided if you had applied a number of those 33 tests to your decision before you made it?

Managing Ethically—Some Skill Pointers

Your organization may or may not have a published or well-established ethical code or provided other ethical cautions or guides to decision making. However, as a manager there are a number of things you can do to ensure that your staff members operate ethically. Robert W. Goddard ("Are You Ethical?" *Personnel Journal*, March 1988) offers these suggestions:

☐ Identify ethical attitudes/behaviors peculiar and vital to your function, e.g., a high-tech firm may stress loyalty to maintain security of its professional expertise.

☐ Select employees carefully. Interviews can reveal attitudes about ethical values, e.g., feeling regarding tax compliance. Screening for "caring" personality types may help, too. Verification of resume data is important, for it may reveal dishonest behaviors or attitudes that could carry over to the job.

☐ Establish a work culture that reinforces ethical attitudes. People can readily sense what the organization's real expectations are. Is there a seriousness about ethical behavior, or does it assume a secondary role?

☐ Exhibit ethical leadership. The top person in any unit sets the tone. Thornton Bradshaw, chairman of RCA, believes it should be vital to everyone to "merge your own set of ethics and values into what you do during the day. If you have to draw a curtain down when you go to work in the morning, and spend eight hours or so doing something that you don't believe in, then you're in trouble."

Management professor Maynard M. Dolecheck ("Doing Justice to Ethics," *Supervisory Management*, July 1989) offers these added areas where supervisors can make improvements:

☐ Emphasize and discuss ethics on a continual basis. Employees should feel free to discuss relevant issues and to express their concerns and doubts about ethical considerations in their work.

☐ Devise realistic goals for employees. If goals are set mutually rather then unilaterally by the boss, they are more likely to be realistic, that is, attainable. Conversely, those set by the boss alone may produce pressure to reach goals with attendant pos-

sibilities of ethical circumventions. In fact, the ethics-conscious manager will stress that achievement of goals at the expense of ethics is not acceptable behavior.

☐ Encourage reporting of unethical activity. The obvious key to this approach is the development of a high degree of trust and an open relationship between the boss and the work team.

The Bottom Line

Organizations may provide managers with codes of conduct, require ethics training, offer ethicist and ombudsmen services, establish ethics committees, and so on. But in the last analysis, the individual manager has to decide for himself the standards of ethical conduct he will apply each day on the job, in the home, and in the community. The following quote states the case for the individual's own decision as to what his ethical behavior should be:

Rabbi Zusya was on his deathbed and sagely observed: "In the coming world, they will not ask me, 'Why were you not Moses?' They will ask me, 'Why were you not Zusya?'" (cited by marketing consultant Terry Mandel, "Marketing With Integrity," *Business Ethics,* September/October, 1990).

In making decisions, a manager also has to take into account the ethical implications. In the rush to get things done, ethical considerations may well be overlooked; for example, short-term gains/benefits in relation to possible unwanted consequences in the longer term— that is, who gains and who may be harmed. But in the last analysis, ethical decisions, as individual decisions, must be approached on a right or wrong basis. Rationalizations such as "What difference will it make?", "Just this one time," or "No one will really be hurt by this" should be rejected as guides for decision making. The following story buttresses this point.

Story: A young boy was conscientiously picking up marooned starfish along the beach and immediately tossing them back into the water. His older brother looked at him with disappointment: "Charlie, you can't throw all of them back into the ocean, can you, so why bother? What difference does it make?" Replied Charlie, tossing a sea animal into the water, "It makes a difference to *this* one."

CONTINGENCY PLANNING: NEUTRALIZING MURPHY'S LAW

Business survival depends on how well managers read trends and anticipate the problems they create.

—Robert D. Kennedy, Chairman and Chief Executive Officer of Union Carbide Corp. (in *The Wall Street Journal,* September 10, 1990)

. . . the cost of ignoring a problem is always far higher than the cost of addressing it.

—James Florio, former governor of New Jersey

Don't change with the times. Change before the times!

—Anon.

The right question to ask is not why we have crises but whether our leadership is good enough to handle the ones that we must inevitably confront.

—Business writer, Robert J. Samuelson in *The Washington Post,* September 12, 1990

Lawmaker Murphy has been telling all of us for decades that whatever can go wrong will. Old Murph even has a two-part Law of Equipment Failure: The item of equipment that has no backup will fail first. And every other item will malfunction when the technician is farthest away from it (Jim Sturdivant, "Matters of Principle," *Audio-Visual Communications,* January 1987).

So if the unexpected is the one thing you can expect, the best way to avoid or minimize crises is to try to foresee them. This means serious, continuous thinking about the unwanted, the unforeseen, the unexpected, and/or the unlikely in a truly systematic way. In fact, in the last analysis your value to your organization as a manager lies not only in your ability to solve problems, but to *anticipate* them. As columnist Haynes Johnson ("The Mideast Challenge," *The Washington Post,* August 10, 1990) put it, "The real test of leadership is not how to handle a crisis, but how to prevent one."

Also, policies and programs developed from crisis and panic are hardly to be preferred to those arising from careful, well-thought-out planning and preparation.

Columnist George F. Will ("Strike, and Baseball's Out," *The Washington Post,* March 13, 1990) has pointed out: "People do not cope with crises until crises confront them. America fundamentally altered the role of the federal government only under the duress of the Depression; Britain brought Churchill to power only after Hitler reached the English Channel." So there is a need to overcome our natural tendencies to avoid thinking of the worst, to duck facing a problem until it overwhelms us.

What we are saying, then, is that we must remove our blinders and recognize that damage prevention and damage control are part of the managerial job. For the cost of ignoring or downplaying a problem is certain to exceed the cost of tackling it head on. In connection with the cost factor, columnist William Rasberry ("When Poverty Steals a Society's Decency," *The Washington Post,* September 23, 1991) presents data from the Children's Defense Fund to indicate that certain societal spending *now* can save greater societal cost later:

. . . Childhood immunization can save 10 times their cost in future medical outlays. . . . A dollar spent to improve preschool education could save $4.75 in special education, crime, and welfare costs. An expenditure of $765 per month for homeless prevention and support services could eliminate the need to spend $3,000 a month to shelter a homeless family in a hotel. We can spend $6,700 a year on intensive community-based youth services, or $40,000 a year to keep a youngster in a juvenile detention center.

Certainly not all contingencies can be anticipated. But many can. These are the ones that we must plan for. We begin by visualizing the "worst scenario" and by asking "What if . . .?" Actually, in contingency planning, in our world of environmental uncertainty, we should think in *dual* terms:

1. In the first instance, *prevention* of problems which may ensue. *Examples:* preventive maintenance; preventive medicine; stress prevention; retirement planning; training of all sorts; environmental scanning; customer service; quality control. Obviously, preventing a problem from arising in the first instance can save time, energy and money and prevent lowered productivity.

2. Dealing effectively with unwanted events—*crisis management*—when they do arise. The operative caution is not to be lulled into complacency by the absence of the storm. As one wag put it, "If everything appears to be going well, the odds are that you've overlooked something."

Prevention of Problems

The key to item number one above, prevention of problems, is to *anticipate* those problems in all their possible impacts and ramifications. After all, other than natural events, crises don't necessarily start overnight. Today's eruption may well have been simmering for a time, but attention was not paid to the incipient signs. Or attention may not have been paid to the warnings and indicators offered by others who spotted and understood the signs.

Here are several examples of problem anticipation in industry and government:

☐ A growing number of companies are appointing environmental policy officers to advise on "curbing the environmental impact of product design, development, manufacturing, packaging and marketing" (Joann S. Lublin, "'Green' Executives Find their Mission Isn't a Natural Part of Corporate Culture," *The Wall Street Journal,* March 5, 1991). These officials also may give environmental-awareness training to the workforce. The whole thrust is to change the focus of environmental affairs "from a compliance issue to one of 'let's anticipate the future.'"

☐ A new philosophy—not just a program—is pervading an increasing number of city police departments. An article in *The Washington Post* (Laurie Goldstein, "New 'Philosophy' of Policing," December 23, 1991) states that "days are waning for police officers who drive around listening to crackling radios for the next emergency call, speed to the site with sirens blazing, take care of the job, get back in the car and, between doughnuts, do it again." As 23-year police veteran Andrew McGoey in Brooklyn put it, no more "police officer as fire extinguisher." The future is police officer as community organizer, detective, alderman, and crime fighter combined—"community policing" as the criminologists call it. McGoey states, "Running around in a radio car is not a very effective way to work. Being a good cop is knowing the community and knowing enough to be able to solve problems rather than just react to them." The concept is, at least in part, a revival of the "beat cop," someone who is visible in the community, who gets to know and interact with its citizens, who thus is regarded as a source of help as opposed to just a hard-nosed law enforcement person.

☐ Many organizations have developed anticipatory plans and programs in such areas as sexual harassment and terrorism prevention. In respect to sexual harassment, a nasty lawsuit can not only cost the firm tens of thousands of dollars in settlements, but it also can tarnish its image significantly with its female customers.

Regarding possible terrorism, security firms recommend the training of company workers to recognize suspicious persons and situations. They should be particularly watchful in airports, sports arenas, military facilities, and sites owned by targeted ethnic groups. Protective lighting, closed-circuit televisions, access controls, and sealed windows in vulnerable locations are recommended strongly. They also favor measures such as more gate guards, updating photo identification, and cutting foliage (U.S. Companies Stay On Guard Over Terrorism," *The Wall Street Journal,* March 5, 1991).

How can the manager become more of an anticipatory problem solver? Here are a number of suggestions to aid in procuring and identifying signals of impending difficulties.

1. Keep in close contact with your staff. They may be able to spot likely and emerging problems from their on-the-firing-line vantage point. Relations with them should be so open and free that they will not hesitate to bring to you all the news, good and bad. Messengers who have to bear bad tidings will not appear if they are likely to be shot down.

2. Brainstorm with your staff from time to time about problems that might arise. Ask: "What if . . .?" Then develop "contingency plans" to cope with possible difficulties.

3. Use MBWA (Management by Walking Around) to learn how people see things. You can't pick up valuable data by operating solely on your own turf. Tap the knowledge of sales people and customer relations representatives, for they are invaluable eyes and ears as to what is going on with customers, competitors, etc.

4. Develop and use key controls and indicators as "early warning systems": progress reports; statistical data; adherence to deadlines (constantly missed ones should raise a red flag); defections of sales people (they are paid for what they sell and if they

see a dismal future, they will seek greener pastures elsewhere); problems with bill collecting (which may signal inferior-quality materials, shipping delays, etc.); increase in returns of defective products and/or customer complaints. Economic indicators should be monitored closely, e.g., gold prices provide an early-warning signal on inflationary trends.

5. Study consistently the internal and external environment. Think in terms of SWOT (strengths, weaknesses, opportunities and threats).

6. Keep up with developments in your field via reading trade and professional literature, attending conferences, and maintaining personal contacts with others in your business or profession. Networking is particularly useful, for the information you gain from people with whom you are in contact may help you to:

   ☐ Spot small problems before they become monsters.

   ☐ Learn what dangers lurk via the activities of your competitors.

   ☐ Provide "leads" regarding new business opportunities (new accounts, new clients, new sources of supply, new personnel sources).

   Close contacts with suppliers can also be knowledge productive.

7. Try to avoid the cardinal sins of holding on to "yesterday's breadwinners" and "ego involvement" in products/services you created or sponsored, but are not paying off and clearly never will. The maxim of "nurture the flowers and discard the weeds" should be the operative guideline. By going with the winners and dropping the losers you will avoid many certain headaches and heartaches. This divesting concept applies not only to lackluster products/services, but also to once-productive but now lackadaisical staffers, lame programs, and limp policies and procedures. The operating concept should be "cut your losses" as opposed to continued pouring of money and other resources down the proverbial "rat hole."

8. Use manpower planning procedures to prevent people-type problems before they arise. **Example:** Cross-training of rank-and-file employees, and management development programs for upper-level personnel can prepare people to fill in for those who become unavailable without warning. **Example:** The employee who goes overseas may be out of sight, but he should not be out of mind. A position must be made available to the expatriate upon his return. And the expatriated employee should be carefully chosen and given proper orientation and training to avoid "culture shock" upon his arrival in the foreign country. The employee's family should receive appropriate orientation, too, as to what to expect in the new and "strange" environment.

In general, the idea is to keep the antenna way up. The warning signals may well be out there. If so, we hardly can afford to ignore or minimize them.

Managing the Crisis

What I am pointing out, then, is that the best philosophy regarding contingency planning is to strive for crisis *avoidance* rather than crisis management. Nevertheless, we can't prevent all problems and crises from arising, so we have to be armed to cope with them effectively should they actually arise. And arise they will: a power failure; a fire or explosion; sabotage; terrorism; a snowstorm, tornado, earthquake, or flood; a building collapse; a wildcat strike; the sudden departure, emergency illness of or accident to a key, valued employee; an unexpected rise in the cost of materials or parts; an economic downturn; a sudden shift in the market, e.g., the arrival of a new competitor; a key speaker who fails to show at our big meeting. One company barely survived when a crane knocked out the main power line to its office building and destroyed all of its computer files.

Also, preparing for problems helps prevent relatively small ones from becoming major ones. Business writer Jane Applegate ("Planning Ahead Can Speed Recovery After Catastrophe," *The Washington Post,* March 25, 1991) cites insurance industry figures to the effect that 43% of businesses shut down by a catastrophe never reopen, and 28% of them that do face financial problems three to five years after reopening.

In city government, the closing of a major plant or retail store can have serious impacts on the local economy and the city tax base. For example, in Washington, D.C., the closing of a large Sears Roebuck and Co. store caught city officials off guard. Rudolph A. Pyatt Jr. ("Sears Site Needs Supermarket Stake," *The Washington Post,* October 28, 1991) stated:

The Sears matter points up the need for the District to develop an active business outreach program or some other mechanism to monitor the pulse of business in the city. As it is, D.C. officials lack an early warning system that could help alert them to some of the problems business owners experience in the city. That's an integral part of any business retention program.

A far-seeing example of preparedness for a crisis relates to the airlines. After a plane crash, an airline usually pulls its advertising temporarily. The aim is to keep the carrier's name out of the news. The airline thus will immediately send an employee to the crash site to cover up the airline's name so that it does not appear in the media ("Joanne Lipman, "Coca-Cola Receives Unwanted Publicity," *The Wall Street Journal,* October 16, 1991).

Meeting planners are very much that—planners—because so many things can go haywire at a major meeting or conference (Margaret Vodopia, "Be Prepared for Meeting Emergencies," *Corporate Meetings and Incentives,* July 1988)—the important speaker doesn't show up; outdoor events are bedeviled by bad weather; conferees become seriously ill or injured and even die; the meeting is disrupted by outside demonstrators who are angry at the meeting's corporate sponsor; audio visual equipment fails to arrive; printed materials arrive with serious errors in them; the coffee service for 200 people has everything in place except the waiters, for they weren't specifically contracted for as a particular hotel required; the awards banquet is bedeviled by a rock band in the adjacent room, which is divided by only a thin, flexible partition; and so on.

Gearing Up for Contingencies

Preparing for crises can be accomplished via asking and responding to these questions:

1. What are my (our) goals, objectives, end results?
2. What events/problems/crises can occur that may frustrate these goals?
3. What can I (we) do to *prevent* these underminers (problems) from occurring?
4. Or, what can I (we) do to *respond* to these underminers (problems) if they do occur?

Essentially, then, what we are talking about is developing *backup* plans in support of established action plans. We also believe it essential in the back-up planning to avoid the two sins of which the military are very conscious:

☐ Underestimating the enemy (i.e., the problem)
☐ Overestimating the enemy (i.e., the problem)

Story: The importance of prevention/preparation may be highlighted by the incident involving a manager who drove by a mental institution each day. Invariably, he noticed an inmate winding up carefully and vigorously throwing an imaginary baseball. The manager frequently told a colleague about the patient's daily pitching performance. The latter then asked why the manager was so interested in the patient's routine. "Well," replied the manager, "the way things are going around here I figure I'll be catching for that guy one day soon, so I better learn how to handle his fancy curve balls."

Apparently the manager remembered the adage that "an ounce of prevention is worth a pound of cure."

MYTHS VS. REALITIES IN PROBLEM SOLVING AND DECISION MAKING

In view of the complex and ramified nature of the fields of problem solving and decision making, it is understandable that a large number of misconceptions or myths might arise. This section identifies and describes a number of myths and endeavors to put them to rest.

Myth: Efficiency is the best guide to (or goal for) performance.

Reality: Efficiency means doing a job properly, at low cost, etc. which is certainly desirable. But a more appropriate guide is *effectiveness,* or doing the *right* things—that is, things with highly worthwhile outcomes. Management guru Peter Drucker (*People and Performance: The Best of Peter Drucker on Management,* New York: Harper's College Press, 1977) states that effectiveness means focusing on opportunities to produce revenue, create markets, and change the economic characteristics of existing products and markets. **It asks:** How do we do this or that better? Which products can produce extraordinary economic results? To what results should our resources and efforts be allocated so as to produce those extraordinary results? **Some examples:** In the Persian Gulf War Saddam Hussein of Iraq devastated Kuwait's oil fields with great efficiency. But was it a worthwhile (effective) endeavor? Or: Savvy city prosecutors are not concerned with simply trying cases better, but to try better cases, that is, those that have a chance of winning.

Myth: Effective decision making involves a search for solutions.

Reality: True enough. But more significantly, it involves a concern for outcomes or consequences. A decision that does not concern itself with performance, end results, impacts, and benefits vs. deficits is not likely to yield a high-quality solution.

Myth: Managers are paid to take risks.

Reality: This is a misconception for, in actuality, managers are paid to decide which risks merit taking. Managers are expected to carefully screen the risk-taking opportunities that arise.

Myth: If a solution/decision is technically sound, it's worth a try.

Reality: Management is the art of the possible. Thus, although a solution may be deemed to be ideal or "perfect" by the decision makers, it may not be appropriate for one or more reasons—lack of support of top management, peers, subordinates; a fuzzy rationale to those who have to implement it; ill timing; perceived cost; extreme novelty, i.e., too great a departure from the status quo; possible "adverse" impact on high-status persons, organizational segments, or established programs.

Myth: Effective executives make a lot of decisions.

Reality: Not so. In actuality, they tend to concentrate on the truly important ones. As Peter Drucker says (*The Effective Executive,* New York: Harper & Row, 1966): "They try to make the few important decisions on the highest level of understanding."

Myth: The only way to improve things in organizations is to start with top management's understanding, involvement, and support.

Reality: The above approach is the *ideal* way to begin. Unfortunately, such support may not always be forthcoming. So managers at lower levels may have to adopt the philosophy that "You have to start improving somewhere." In other words, "the low-hanging fruit" approach is workable, too. Successes in lower-level segments of the organization—e.g., with quality circles or performance improvement teams—may serve as models for other units and, in time, may excite upper-level management's interest, too.

Myth: A training solution, as a means of resolving a problem, is an activity that should be treated as a cost or expense.

Reality: Not so. If the training is designed to meet a real need, has clear objectives, is properly planned, and is attended by the right people, is properly implemented, and has results of a measurable sort, it should produce worthwhile end benefits. That is to say, it should bear favorably on production, quality, customer service, etc. An expense? No, an *investment!*

Myth: If we plan the implementation of our decision, everything should work out as anticipated.

Reality: This approach ignores the "Law of Unintended Consequences." **Example:** Du Page County, outside Chicago, encouraged rapid, substantial growth with the thought that it would result in improved quality of life. How? Economic growth would so boost the tax base that the tax rate could be cut and still take in bigger revenues to finance better roads, schools, and other public services. But a planning commission study found that development, particularly commercial and industrial, burdened the infrastructure, and services were not repaid at all by increased land values. For example, malls and shopping centers required new roads and more expensive maintenance of established ones (David Bergman, "Boom County, Bust Budget," *The Wall Street Journal,* September 25, 1991).

Example: The Japanese invention of "just-in-time" inventory—maintain only the minimum inventory needed to produce the product and let the suppliers stock materials and deliver them as needed—was adopted by the thousands of convenience, department, and grocery stores in Tokyo. Visualize tens of thousands of vans and trucks creeping through the city streets to make their just-in-time deliveries—not just one or two a day, but 10 or 12! Inventory is often replenished every few hours. The result, per business writer Michael Schrage ("The Pursuit of Efficiency Can Be An Illusion," *The Washington Post,* March 20, 1992), horrible traffic congestion, wasted costly gas, and increased air pollution.

Myth: To start cost cutting, management should ask: "How can we make this operation more efficient?"

Reality: Peter Drucker poses, instead, what he considers to be a more appropriate question: "Would the roof cave in if we stopped doing this work altogether?" If the answer merits a response of "probably not," the operation should go. Drucker says that as many as one-third of all clerical and control operations could be shedded, either because they never served or have outlived their real purposes ("Permanent Cost Cutting," *The Wall Street Journal,* January 11, 1991).

Myth: The best goal for quality is a "zero-defects" program.

Reality: Although reaching zero may be a worthy goal, it implies that perfection is reachable and once that is achieved we thus can rest on our laurels. The better concept is *continuing improvement,* going beyond any established target, even a target of zero.

Management Consultant Pat McLagan ("The Dark Side of Training," *Training,* November 1991) points out a serious problem with the zero-defects notion:

> *. . . it also can create a fearful, risk-averse environment where people take safe avenues and play games to cover up errors. Furthermore, since zero defects (as many companies practice it) cannot routinely apply to new products, services, and processes, the concept can encourage people to stay with what they know. The long-term effect may be to stifle innovation and experimentation, and to lock people into their current thinking and ways of doing things.*

Myth: Problem solving entails a search for answers. Right?

Reality: Wrong. Problem solving entails a search for *questions*—the right questions. It's relatively easy to find staffers and others who can provide "answers." But what is really needed is a staff that can ask the right questions.

Myth: Satisfied people—those who feel good about what is going on—make the best problem solvers and decision makers.

Reality: Actually, the reverse is true. Dissatisfied people, unhappy with the status quo, are looking constantly for opportunities for improvement. Because they see the world as much less than perfect, they are able to spot problems more readily.

Myth: A bad mishap is a problem of catastrophic misfortune.

Reality: Not necessarily so. It can become an opportunity. For example, defective products, if remedied properly, can augment the loyalty of customers. John Rettie, editorial director for *The Power Report,* an automotive marketing newsletter, states: "There is an axiom in all industries that the most satisfied customers are those that have had a problem that has been resolved properly" (quoted by John Burgess, "GM to Replace 1,100 Saturn Sedans," *The Washington Post,* May 11, 1991).

Myth: The myth of competition holds that someone's out there who will take away what I have unless I grab it first.

Reality: Per marketing consultant Terry Mandel ("Marketing With Integrity," *Business Ethics,* September/October 1990), a radically different outlook merits our consideration:

> *. . . as long as we subscribe to the metaphor of 'them and us,' we're stuck in a mindset that diverts energy away from pursuing our uniqueness—which is our true competitive edge. We're also in danger of approaching customers as if they're 'them,' some anonymous group we must coerce into taking the action we want.*
>
> *By switching instead to a metaphor of 'we're all in this together,' we restore competition to its original meaning of 'striving together.' Then competitors become mirrors for us of where we need to strengthen our product or service and of how we can polish our uniqueness.*

Myth: If it ain't broke, don't fix it.

Reality: This prescription, which sounds good if looked at only on a surface basis, is a certain means for preservation of the status quo. For what is really needed in today's competitive world is to examine continually and carefully what is going on and to come up with new and better approaches, programs, products, or services.

The concept overlooks the all-important idea of looking for ways to make things better. If this philosophy, historically, had been followed to its logical conclusion, we'd still be reading from stone, riding to work on a horse, washing our clothes in icy rivers, roasting our entrees over an open fire, and bowing to kings.

So even if it ain't broke, let's fix it. Let's constantly assess, improve, revamp, update, and upgrade rather than glory in our past accomplishments.

Myth: Effective managers are able to get people to focus (pay attention to) on problems.

Reality: True enough. But the greater reality is that they can't necessarily get people *to think about them in a preferred way.* Like the media, it can tell you what to think *about,* but it can't tell you *what* to think. Hence the need to work with the team—group discussion, group decision—to ensure that the best thinking is tapped to solve problems. As the saying goes: "All of us are smarter than one of us."

Myth: Effective managers make a point of tackling all problems that have been identified.

Reality: All problems are not equal in severity, nor can all of them be tackled simultaneously. Hence the need to sort them out as to their gravity. Pareto's Law— the 80/20 principle—is a guide to help set priorities for problems that have surfaced or have been isolated.

Myth: "The Panacea Fallacy." It tells us that if a proposal/plan/program/procedure falls short of solving all problems, it must be flawed.

Reality: Progress is not to be equated with perfection. Small, step-by-step "victories" are to be preferred to waiting for the "perfect" solution. If we adopted the "Panacea Fallacy" philosophy literally, its logical conclusion would be that we would hesitate to buy a car or a house, choose a university or a mate, observe an ath-letic team, go to a restaurant or a movie, or vote for a politician.

"Perfection" is a worthy goal. But it should not be confused with what is attainable in the real world and how progress actually comes about.

Myth: In problem solving, "half a loaf is better than none."

Reality: Not very true if we really want high-quality decisions and results. Compromises due to limited resources, time pressures, and the like may be inevitable, but not necessarily desirable. Winston Churchill once stated pithily: "All attempts to bridge a 12-foot stream by an 8-foot plank are doomed to failure, and the plank is lost. It is a concession to bring forward a 9-foot plank, but again that may be lost."

Note: The Panacea Fallacy, referred to previously, relates to unrealistic waiting for total perfection before acting. The half a loaf myth relates to settling for a weaker solution than is dictated by the actual needs of the situation.

Myth: Wise problem solvers learn from their mistakes.

Reality: Of course. Why not? But more realistically, you and I can't afford to err with enough frequency to produce a lot of desirable learning. **A better approach:** Learn from the mistakes of others. It's much less expensive and painful. And, still better, learn from your successes. This course has the richest potential for worthwhile learning.

Actually, learning from mistakes is not always easy as the following story indicates:

Three hunters hire a small plane that lands them in a wilderness where they stalk caribou. The pilot says, "I'll return in a week, but remember what I said last year: planes like this can carry only three hunters and one caribou." When he returns he sees the three hunter—and three caribou.

The hunters say: "Last year we slipped you $100 and you let us load three caribou." The pilot says: "Okay, but this year it's $200." The hunters grumble but pay, jam the caribou aboard, the plane lumbers a few feet aloft—and plows into some trees. The hunters are scattered through the branches, and one shouts: "Where are we?" Another answers: "A hundred yards from where we crashed last year" (quoted from a column by George F. Will in *The Washington Post,* November 27, 1987).

Myth: Experience is the best teacher.

Reality: It depends on the experience for it is also possible to learn the wrong things, to let the dead hand of the past take over and influence decisions negatively. **Example:** Jennifer Runyeon, an investment banker in Dallas with no experience with automotive products, purchased in 1988 a Chapter 11 firm making high-quality windshield wipers. The new firm name was called Lifetime. While some learnings accrued from the mistakes of the sick firm, Runyeon made a huge success of her venture by developing new marketing strategies. The fact that Lifetime's officers were from outside the auto parts industry helped them make key decisions quickly. To quote Ms. Runyeon (Suein, L. Hwang, "Rescuers of Windshield-Wiper Manufacturer Clean Up," *The Wall Street Journal,* March 11, 1991), "Being naive helped me. I was willing to try things that I may not have if I was entrenched in the industry."

Myth: Once the symptoms of a problem are relieved, the problem is solved.

Reality: The problem is truly solved only if we go back to fix the system so the problem doesn't recur.

Myth: A problem once solved results in the demise of the problem.

Reality: Certainly desirable, but not necessarily so. Quite often the resolution of a problem comes back to haunt us, for it results in the creation of a new problem.

Example: Downsizings (layoffs) may produce significant cost benefits. But they may also leave an unwanted legacy: a surplus of costly unused office space that can't be subleased very readily. Because other firms may also be reducing the size of their workforces, the end result, community-wise, is a major glut of unwanted office space (Jim Carlton, "Excess Space Is a Big Expense for Many Firms," *The Wall Street Journal,* May 7, 1991).

In an article entitled "Downsizing Doesn't Necessarily Bring An Upswing in Corporate Profitability," (*The Wall Street Journal,* June 6, 1991), Amanda Bennett cited a five-year survey of downsizing results of 1,005 firms employing more than four million people. **The results:** Less than half of the companies with restructuring goals of cutting costs actually met that target. Only 32% improved profitability and 21% met expectations for improved return on investment.

One of the problems in downsizing efforts is that while staff may be cut, low-value work may not be eliminated. The downsizing puts the organizations under such pressure that as soon as financial results are better, people come pouring back into the firms. Also, savings on personnel often are not accompanied by other possible savings such as on travel. Some consultants favor a more global approach to efficiency; and only after the work is redesigned should staff size be looked at. And in some cases, staff size may not matter.

Also to be considered is that cutting staff doesn't necessarily mean a corresponding reduction in health-care costs. A 1992 survey by William Mercer, a New York benefits consulting firm, found that 21 of 65 downsized companies surveyed experienced a jump in worker-compensation claims leading to overall increased health costs. **The reason:** Cutbacks often require remaining workers to assume new duties and responsibilities. Older workers may become injured as they try to perform tasks they can't physically handle anymore. Added stress levels also can result in injuries, triggering added worker-compensation claims. All surveyed firms reported large increases in worker-compensation costs: 20% reported a doubling of costs since 1987, and another 20% said costs were up between 50% and 100%. The American Management Association advises that better ways to reduce costs are workplace safety education and immediate investigation of accidents ("High Costs Often Outlast Cutbacks in Work Force," *The Wall Street Journal,* August 17, 1992).

Myth: An effective, successful manager should have few, if any, problems.

Reality: Managerial success is not related to the absence of problems. Rather, because the existence of problems is a managerial given, success is more appropriately measured by the ability to identify actual problems and solve them economically, expeditiously, imaginatively, and hopefully, non-recurrently.

Myth: Worthwhile targets to cut during hard times are R&D, advertising and training.

Reality: Business guru Tom Peters advises that the opposite approach is preferred ("The Recession Squeezes Training," *Training,* April 1991). He believes that investments in quality improvement and customer service should be stepped up in hard times. The net effect should be that the company emerges from the recession stronger than when it began.

Myth: More is better than less.

Reality: Decisions that revolve around obtaining more—more budget, more equipment, more space, more staffing—aren't necessarily sound. **Example:** Consider Marriott's approach to room service staffing in the late hours. At their 1,200-room Chicago facility, self-service coffee makers, irons, and ironing boards were placed in every room. **The result:** There no longer is a need to keep room service staff available on a 24-hour basis. These manpower savings did not affect quality of service, said the hotel's general manager (Paul Farhi, "Keeping It a Family Matter At Marriott," *The Washington Post,* February 17, 1992).

Myth: Systems and procedures should be designed to be totally perfect or foolproof.

Reality: Perfect systems are likely to be too expensive. **Example:** An accounting office does not use the same accuracy checks on a $3 invoice as it does on a $150,000 one. **Example:** In one firm, small customer debts (under $50) are not pursued because of their greater cost of collection.

If we understand the significance of the above-described myths, we can see that we should solve problems and make decisions along the lines of the following themes (per management consultant Phil Hanford, "Good Managers Can Manage Anything," *Performance and Instruction,* July 1990):

- ☐ Use a holistic approach (not narrow or limited).
- ☐ Adopt a *results* orientation (not activities focused).
- ☐ Employ an integrated approach (not segmented).
- ☐ Strive to be outward looking (not insular).
- ☐ Constantly search for creative answers/solutions (not risk avoidance).
- ☐ Regard effectiveness as vital (not only efficiency).
- ☐ Be forward thinking (not past oriented).
- ☐ Employ a dynamic approach (not static).

"SELF-INFLICTED WOUNDS": PITFALLS AND PERILS IN PROBLEM SOLVING AND DECISION MAKING

We've met the enemy and it's us.

—Per Pogo, by cartoonist Walt Kelly

There are many traps and unhelpful detours in the problem-solving and decision-making process. Psychologists call them "dysfunctional behaviors": behaviors that hinder our effectiveness and thus derail the problem solving vehicle. They arise due to: **ego** or esteem needs—we want to look good in the eyes of others; **anxiety**—concerns about success, career, failure (actual or likely), strong criticism from the boss, withdrawal of affection by others; and needs for **power.**

These self-inflicted wounds operate, of course, below the level of awareness, so the behavior persists unless we receive feedback from others—bosses, peers, subordinates, customers, suppliers. Unfortunately, such feedback is not easy to come by, for the potential feedback-givers are uncertain how the recipients will react, and our prevailing culture typically does not support such candor.

A major influence as to how your subordinates (and others) see you as a manager—your image—depends upon your role (behavior, attitude) as a problem solver and decision maker. Be aware that what is certain to turn them off are these self-defeating behaviors described in this section.

The "Blame Game"

The person in this trap sees problems as opportunities to look for victims, villains, and enemies. It is more important that perpetrators of the "crimes" are tracked down than to look for causes of problems and to find cures for them. Staffers thus are reluctant to admit to error or to present the bad news lest they become scapegoats and they get their heads chopped off. Since time immemorial, messengers who arrive with bad tidings find their futures are short-lived. So a lot of covering up and alibiing takes place: "Gee, boss, I was on leave that day" or "I never saw that memo." Teamness is hard to develop for team members have greater needs to defend themselves, even at the risk of making others look bad: "We had all the paperwork done, but shipping held it up as usual."

In the marketing world, if products don't move off the shelf, the ad agency often becomes the scapegoat. To quote *The Wall Street Journal* (Joanne Lipman, "Blame-the-Messenger Mentality Leaves Scars on Madison Avenue," November 20, 1991):

In ancient times, messengers who brought bad news were summarily killed. On modern-day Madison Avenue, history may be repeating itself.

Advertisers facing bad news these days, whether from internal strife or recessionary pressures, are heeding a new battle cry: Fire the ad agency. It doesn't matter if the advertising is fabulous; no ad agency, it seems is safe. An unprecedented number have been unceremoniously dumped, or have watched their big accounts get put up for review, for reasons that seem to have almost nothing to do with their work.

Master adman David Ogilvy said in his *Confessions of an Advertising Man* (New York: Atheneum, 1963) that agencies "make convenient scapegoats. It is easier to fire your agency than to admit to your stockholders that there is something wrong with your product or your management."

TV networks faced with precipitous drops in viewers have responded by attacking the results and switching to a different mathematical sampling system. However, the new formulation doesn't alter the basic problem. An ad executive (quoted in "Inside Moves," *Business Month*, July 1990) stated: "Ratings are continuing to decline, and the networks are trying to kill the messenger."

In the broader, societal arena, the blame game also flourishes. To quote columnist William Rasberry ("Problems and Enemies," *The Washington Post*, November 4, 1991):

Give us a problem, and we'll find an enemy. The difficulties of the U.S. economy? Unfair competition from the Japanese. Inadequate schools? Tightfisted taxpayers. The discouraged and dangerous underclass? White racists.

It is not so much that the enemies we identify are innocent as that identifying them takes time and attention away from the search for solutions.

Skill pointer: Because you, as a manager, need authentic data for decision making, reward the messenger who brings bad news rather than punish him for it.

The Rationalization Malady

The manager who employs this device is trying to cope with reality by running away from it. Thus, he may engage in self-counsel which, if crises or problems have arisen, tells him to explain things away. His "quieting" self-talk can include alibis such as these: "We didn't have the staff," "Our competitors sure played hardball on that one," "We weren't the only ones who didn't see the change in the market," "The Post Office loused up our mailing of that promotion."

Philadelphia's fiscal crisis was initially described mildly as a "fiscal shortfall." It then became a "cash crisis"; later, a "calamity"; and, still later, a "catastrophe" (Michael Specter, "Philadelphia's Story Is a Fiscal Cliffhanger," *The Washington Post*, August 26, 1990).

Story: A lawyer defended a client before a jury in this manner: "TV was responsible for my client embarking on a criminal career—he didn't own a set, so he stole one."

The Minimization or the "Tuck It Under the Rug" Syndrome

This behavior entails a reluctance to face up to things due to the pain that reality brings. In this flight from reality, a phony optimism is projected about shortcomings obvious to everyone else. Thus, outdated policies, poor procedures, aging products, marginal staffers, and the like, are tolerated, their gravity minimized. Rationalizations by the bushel are trotted out to disguise what is really going on: "This isn't the time to get into it," "Let's not overreact," "We don't want to act too precipitously," "Things will probably work out by themselves," "We can probably live with it," "We have to stay within budget," "Let's bring it up at the next regional conference," and "Why not appoint a study group to look into it," and so on and on.

The Magnification or the "Making Mountains out of Molehills" Syndrome

This behavior entails a tendency to overreact to or exaggerate the significance of problems. All and any shortcomings or difficulties are equated with this being the end of the world. Mistakes, errors, or oversights are over-evaluated as to their importance, and the perpetrator of the miscue may never be forgotten or forgiven.

The unwanted incident thus may be brought to the attention of the errant one repeatedly. As the sign on the wall in a shipping room stated: "When I do something right no one remembers: when I do something wrong, they never forget."

Magnification may also relate to successes. A lot of mileage may be gotten out of certain victories, e.g., a fortuitous good fourth quarter may be cause to bring out the champagne even though the prior three were miserable and future prospects are on the uncertain side.

The "Ain't It Awful" Game

In this non-productive behavior, the manager, with great frustration, broods about what can't be done— "Ain't it awful." A much healthier approach, suggests education and training consultant David L. Hultgren ("Spheres of Influence: Doing What You Can Do," *Training and Development Journal,* July 1989), is to draw on his "sphere of influence" model when faced with a problem. It tells us that our influence or control extends to three areas: those we control, those we influence, and those we neither control nor influence. Obviously, attempting to control/decide things we can't is self-defeating, a sure route to submerge ourselves in a lot of stress. We can influence certain things (situations, people) via use of our good communication and interpersonal skills. And, finally, because none of us is totally powerless, there are things we can control. The trick is to sort out those areas where we can impact on results, and to not grieve about those we cannot. After all, even CEOs can't accomplish everything they would like to. They, too, recognize that what can't be cured must be endured.

The "Deep Deliberation Over Dimes" Syndrome

This behavior is essentially an organizational version of the "penny wise and pound foolish" phenomenon. Thus, discussions over major expenditure items are likely to produce relatively quick decisions. But minor matters (e.g., who gets the new parking space) may require interminable discussions. British management writer and humorist C. Northcote Parkinson has wryly observed (*Parkinson's Law,* New York: Ballantine Books, 1957) that there is an inverse relation between the importance of an issue and the time devoted to it!

The Denial Game

A non-productive way to deal with a problem is to deny that it exists or has real importance for us: "Oh, it's not that bad" or "No need to push the panic button." Recall the monkeys of "hear no evil, see no evil" fame? Delusions of this sort may provide temporary comfort, but over the longer haul the problem will catch up and corner us. The U.S. automotive industry is a perfect case of denial in the '70s and early '80s. By the '90s, they had crawled out of their cocoon and began to face the real world.

The answer to the denial game? Use staff, peers, the boss, customers, suppliers to conduct reality checks. This takes courage, of course. But, then, what is the alternative?

The "Magnifying Glass" Mentality

Management professor Roger Kaufman ("Some Cures for HRD Myopia," *Training and Development Journal,* December 1991) calls this syndrome a tendency to bring only one aspect of a problem into focus. It entails losing out on the "big picture." The pattern includes practices such as failing to ask whether problems are really symptoms of larger problems, being reactive rather than creative, dodging risk, settling for "damage control," assessing problems only at our particular organizational level, shining the magnifying glass harder and thus assuming that what's in focus is important.

The "Fact Fantasy" Malady

This behavior entails a tendency to overgeneralize from available information, i.e., taking a somewhat irrelevant, limited, or even isolated or unlikely fact and projecting it into a patently unwarranted conclusion. **Example:** In a recent college management class I conducted, a student, in a paper on EEO, asserted that Hispanics were not victims of discrimination as were blacks. His evidence? Our two Hispanic students did not make any references to such discrimination in our group-at-large discussions on that topic. But what the student conveniently overlooked was that our very reserved Hispanic students rarely spoke up at all in the class discussions.

Story: A couple met through a personal ad in the newspaper, dated, and soon married. But a problem immediately arose. It seems that when the husband retrieves the morning paper off the driveway, his spouse thinks he's cheating on her.

Principle: If we can deal with actual facts rather than imagined ones, we will make more rational and sounder decisions.

The "Drunkard's Search" Malady

This involves looking for information only where it is easiest to look. (Visualize the drunk who has lost his wallet in a tavern, but looks for it under the light of the lamppost because the illumination is greatest there!) **Example:** In the organizational realm, a personnel office may use the exit interview, because of its "convenience," to learn about the character of its supervision. But people who leave may be reluctant to level about the peccadillos of their former supervisors for fear of "bad" references at a later date. Anonymous questionnaires or the use of outside consultants are, of course, more likely to produce comprehensive and valid data.

The "Ignoring Differences" Syndrome

This behavior entails an inability to distinguish among various shades of gray, even though the distinctions are pronounced to others. Some verbal identifiers of the malady: "It doesn't make much difference which way we decide"; "They're really all alike, aren't they?"; "All of our products are the best." In its extreme forms, this syndrome leads to stereotypical thinking: "Women can't handle those kinds of jobs," "All those field people just don't get the point," "These young people are all alike—they don't know what it means to pay their dues."

The "One Size Fits All" Fallacy

As in the above-cited "ignoring differences" syndrome, managers may make all-encompassing decisions. **Example:** Multinational corporations operating in foreign countries may apply personnel policies that ignore local customs.

The "Indecisiveness" Malady

The manager may become a waffler due to high anxieties over outcomes and possible damage to his personal image. He wallows in vacillations even though his temporizing drives staffers and others up the proverbial wall. His verbal ploys take these forms: "We wouldn't want to move into this without exploring it in fuller detail," "We want to be sure of our timing before we rush into it," "We wouldn't want the front office to think we were a bit hasty on this." **The result:** He readily convinces himself that no decision is better than the wrong decision. Important decisions thus are shelved.

The "Value Rigidity" Trap

As an example of this pitfall, management writer Ron Zemke ("Predictions for the Decade of Doubt," *Training,* January 1991) raises the point that we can't realistically make great differences between product and service businesses because most are made up of a bit of product and a lot of service. Thus, quality of service counts to car makers and consumers alike; or filling prescriptions accurately is basic to A-1 healthcare service.

In the Great Depression years, famed British economist Lord John Maynard Keynes was chided by a colleague for shifting his position on free trade. In the '20s, he was a total free trader; in the '30s, he favored a protective tariff. Retorted Keynes: "When the facts change, I change my mind. What do you do, sire?" Of course, the new fact was the Depression. Keynes believed that protection would bear heavily on business confidence. He also favored a strong government spending response to stimulate consumer demand. His thinking became the basis for the famed Keynesian economics theory of "pump priming" (Alfred Malabre, Jr., and Lindley H. Clark Jr., "Changes in Economy Cause Much Confusion Among Economists," *The Wall Street Journal,* March 27, 1989).

In reference to staunch allegiance to "principle," the late Paul A. Freund, a constitutional authority at Harvard University stated it perceptively: "An absolute principle is as absurd as absolute power, and when you perceive a truth, look for the balancing truth" (quoted by Boisfeuillet Jones, Jr., "The Great Mind Not Appointed," *The Washington Post,* February 24, 1992).

Zemke cites this story (from Robert Persig's *Zen and the Art of Motorcycle Maintenance*) to illustrate how "value rigidity" adversely affects quality work and thinking:

Story: In the south of India, the monkey, a treasured delicacy, is eagerly sought via trapping. Visualize a simple trap, comprised of a hollowed-out coconut chained to a stake. Rice, which can be gotten out through a small hole, is put into the coconut. The aperture allows the animal's hand to enter, but it cannot be withdrawn if it has a fist full of rice. The monkey can become a permanent captive, not because of the nature of the trap but because of his own rigidity—an unwillingness to drop the rice. So only by looking at the rice and coconut in a different, non-rigid way—i.e., recognizing that the villagers are committed to having him for their dinner—can the monkey regain his freedom. Dropping the rice is a simple procedure, but it has a potentially tremendous payoff.

The "Ready-Fire-Aim" Syndrome

This is a managerial tendency, says training manager David L. Hobbs ("Training—Appropriations Process," *Training and Development Journal,* May 1990), to seek solutions before the problem is fully understood. It is akin to firing before aiming. Of course, jumping to conclusions—often a favorite form of managerial "exercise"—instead of gathering more badly needed data, is patently counterproductive. (Remember our 7-Step model of problem solving, which, among other things, is designed to slow things down.) While the staff may expect more emphasis on factual input and more identification of and discussion of alternatives, the group may be met by a "Damn the torpedoes, full steam ahead" stance.

"Action" is certainly commendable, but if it produces a "solution-minded" approach to problems, the end result inevitably will be less than what we're really capable of accomplishing.

The "Single-tool Problem Solver" Fault

In this self-inflicted wound, the manager steadfastly tackles and decides with single approaches. As psychologist Abraham Maslow phrased it, if your only tool is a hammer, every problem you encounter will be a nail. Thus, productivity problems are responded to with reorganizations; problem employees must be fired, which

may or may not be the best answer; sales people who are having trouble vending lousy products require more lectures and pep talks.

The antidote: Don't be a "Johnny One Note"; instead, vary your approach based on what the problem really requires.

The Group Decision-making Facade

Managers may present a counterfeit claim of team management and collective decision making when the reality, as one staff member put it, is that "he collects himself and makes all the decisions."

So what is really at work is an acute case of unilateralism. While the staff may feel that "no one is smarter than all of us," the unilateralist persists on going it alone, ignoring the potential richness of group input, group generation of and discussion of alternatives, and group decision.

The "Die-hard Consistency" Syndrome

This self-defeating behavior entails a reluctance to admit adoption of an erroneous position, that one may be wrong on an issue or approach, or that one may have blundered in some way. Instead, the self-vindicator may release a torrent of platitudes that insist "everything is going as planned," "things will turn around soon," "we're almost there," "we'll work it out," etc. (Recall the totally surrounded general who told his troops: "We have them just where we want them.")

The following story illustrates the "consistency" of the die-hard self-vindicator.

Story: A young woman entered a psychiatrist's office and stiffly advised her therapist that she had made this visit only to get her family "off her back." This dialogue ensued.

Doctor: "And why does your family want you to see me?"

Patient: "I presume it's because I'm dead."

Doctor (with good humor): "And how do you know you're dead?"

Patient, quickly one-upping the doctor, retorted: "How do you know you're *alive*?"

Doctor, taking another tack: "You will agree that dead people don't bleed, yes?"

Patient: "Of course."

The doctor then went swiftly to a wall cabinet, took out a needle, asked the patient to remove her jacket, and quickly pricked her right arm. Blood spurted, which the doctor picked up neatly on a slide. She then asked the patient to look at it and exclaimed to the patient in triumph: "See, it's real, red blood!"

Patient: "Good God! Dead people do bleed, don't they?"

Die-hard consistency is hardly a new phenomenon. Recall Ralph Waldo Emerson's statement that: "A foolish consistency is the hobgoblin of little minds, adored by little statesmen and philosophers and divines."

The "Being All Things to All Men" Syndrome

If we have extreme needs to receive affection from others, we are very likely to go all out to please them. So we may try to present an image of agreement and helpfulness to everyone. We do this by readily agreeing to requests, demands, and positions of others. Unfortunately, opportunistic decisions of this sort return to haunt us, for the staff and others see us as a "pushover," a person without convictions or principles, with one finger to the political wind—"Hey, the boss will give everybody what they want; all they have to do is smile and ask."

Syndicated columnist George Will ("The President's Own Worst Enemy," *The Washington Post*, January 30, 1992), commenting on President George Bush's mixed positions on free trade in the election year of 1992, recalled the 1903 House of Commons debate on protectionism. It seems that British Prime Minister Arthur Balfour stated that he had no "settled convictions" on the topic, which moved an opposing Member of Parliament to craft this pithy verse:

> *I'm not for Free Trade, and I'm not for Protection*
> *I approve of them both, and to both have objection*
> *In going through life I continually find*
> *It's a terrible business to make up one's mind*
> *So in spite of all comments, reproach and predictions*
> *I firmly adhere to unsettled convictions.*

The "Rigid Mindset" Syndrome

Here we have "one-option Ollie" who communicates an air of "don't bother me with the facts, my mind's already made up." New opposing information,

approaches, or options are strongly resisted because of one's need for certainty. Having to choose among a number of alternatives/options would be too anxiety-producing. Psychological comfort lies solely along one path to a decision.

The "Multiple-option" Obsession

While the above decision-making peccadillo relates to not pursuing added possibilities adequately, the converse is also certain to dismay the staff. Here the staff is presented with "the grand stall," disguised with a request for "Let's make sure we're touching all the bases." But if an endless search for more options is pursued, what is communicated loud and clear is not the need for fine tuning, but that the manager is, in truth, fearful of deciding at all. The metaphor for this behavior is that of the perfectionist artist who has a compulsive need to "touch up" his "masterpiece" and thus can never let the canvas go to the marketplace or exhibit hall.

In addition to the option obsession, there are various other ways (read "games") to duck decisions. Management consultant Stanley M. Herman, with tongue in cheek, suggests ("How To Duck Decisions," *Training,* September 1989) the following seven decision-avoidance techniques:

1. "The More Data Needed" Game

When a not-too-clear choice among possible decisions arises, the manager may deal with his anxieties by pointing to "inadequate information," opt for waiting until "trends are clearer," or ask for added staff work.

2. "It Never Should Have Happened in the First Place" Game

When facing an unpleasant situation and a certain solution is not apparent, the technique is to blame one's predecessor who had botched things. A variation of this ploy is the "It's not my problem, it's their game," providing the would-be decision maker with a basis for dodging the issue.

3. "Power, Power, Who Has the Power" Game

Used particularly in committees and advisory groups, it entails passing the buck when a new type of action arises, viz.,"We don't have the authority to act on this."

4. The "Waver" Game

This device, used in meetings, entails bouncing back and forth among alternatives, but never buttoning one down. When final action appears possible, the leader (and the group) seems to know when to shift to its reverse gear and not decide at all.

5. "What Will Harry Think?" Game

A decision can be avoided simply by worrying about what the boss or a peer may or may not favor. No one, of course, asks what Harry *would* think for that might end the game. And if someone does dare to speak for Harry, the game can be continued simply by asking what George or Mary would think!

6. "Yes, but" Game

The whole idea is to scuttle someone else's idea by providing a number of reasons why it won't work. Another version of the game is to ask for advice or help and then discount it by responding in "Yes, but" fashion.

7. "Wash Out" Game

This game is similar to the "Yes, but" game. But instead of waiting for the "Yes, but" response from someone else, the individual and/or group downgrades the value of the idea. The game is used by those who have little confidence in themselves or their outfit.

8. The "Pseudo-Certainty" Facade

This entails presenting an image of assuredness and knowledgeability when it is apparent to all ("The Emperor Wears No Clothes" phenomenon) that the manager is quite anxious and has grave doubts about the course of his action about to be taken. While the manager may feel he is presenting an image of assurance, in actuality he is communicating an adolescent, defensive pouting: "I know what I'm doing."

The "Management by Facade" Ploy

Instead of facing problems head on, and engaging in bona fide problem solving, it is not unusual for managers to try to muddle through by reorganizing. As one management consultant put it: "In the even years they centralize and in the odd years they decentralize." Changing organizational structure, under certain condi-

tions, is certainly a means of upgrading organizational capabilities. But it is hardly a tool to deal with deep-seated problems stemming from poor communication, old products, lack of training, outdated or murky policies and procedures, inadequate or even punitive reward systems, stifling of creativity, etc.

Interestingly enough, the urge to tinker with the organizational structure is centuries old as the following quote by Pertonius Arbiter, first century Roman satirist, indicates:

> *We trained hard . . . but it seemed that every time we were beginning to form up into teams we would reorganize . . . I was to learn later in life that we tend to meet any new situation by reorganizing; and a wonderful method it can be for creating the illusion of progress while producing confusion, inefficiency, and demoralization.*

The "Going in All Directions" Malady

Recall that in *The Wizard of Oz* Dorothy arrives at a fork in the road. She asks Scarecrow which way to go. Scarecrow points left, then right, and finally says, "Of course, some people do go both ways." What is at work, of course, is high anxiety, which creates a lot of nervous, uncontrolled energy.

Thus the manager in his hyperactivity attempts to do too much in too short a period of time. Meetings are called and cancelled; objectives are revised without notice; decisions are made too rapidly; projects are started but not followed through to completion; detours and loose ends abound; activity and motion appear to have a higher value than well-thought-out programs and clear-cut accomplishment.

The manager sees all this frenetic hustle and bustle as a "dynamic operation," whereas staffers view it as a form of "planned, determined chaos."

The "Worshipping of Yesterday's Breadwinners" Syndrome

This malady entails a love affair with what worked in bygone days. Thus, there is a reluctance to let go of products/services that were lucrative revenue producers at one time, but now, at best, please a few old customers. The rationalization for this behavior may be accompanied by statements such as these: "It still makes a good impression in the catalog," "You can't ignore your old customers," and "Let's give it a little more time."

Facing up to the new reality is difficult for the manager afflicted with a strong reverence for the past. Evidence as to its waste of resources—storage, inventory, money for promotion, staff time—is robustly resisted.

The "If It Doesn't Work, Do It Harder and More of It" Syndrome

But as performance technologist Clay Carr, ("More on Knowledge, Systems, and Motives," *Performance and Instruction,* December 1991) points out, systems tend to be in equilibrium, so their output can only equal what a system can produce. For a more logical endeavor, Carr cites the approach to processes adopted by today's quality movement: improve the process—competence, procedures, technology, plus their integration—for a better result/product.

The "Post hoc ergo propter hoc" Fallacy

This Latin phrase means, literally, "After this therefore because of this." (The rooster crows and the sun rises; therefore the crowing caused the sunrise.) *Example:* Sales were down badly in January. A new product was introduced in December. Therefore, by introducing new products in December we tend to reduce our January sales (!). The trap here is to confuse cause and effect, to assume that because one event follows the other, the latter was caused by the former.

The Language Trap

Managers and organizations often operate on the assumption that changing organizational and job titles and using elegant rhetoric has motivational or productivity value. But the reality is that decisions based on semantics are not effective. **Example:** The CEO who announces boldly that "We will now operate in teams." But because there is no preparation for the "change," especially training, let alone a change in the climate needed to operate in the new style, the rhetoric rings hollow to all concerned.

Similarly, changes in the names of organizational units don't by themselves create any magical improvement. **Examples:** changing the name of the Sales Division to the Marketing Department; or Training to

Human Resource Development; or Personnel to Human Resource Management.

The "name game" recalls Lewis Carroll's famous character Humpty Dumpty, who said scornfully: "When *I* use a word, it means what I choose it to mean, neither more nor less." But in the managerial world new labels are hardly a substitute for realistic, innovative decision making and programming.

The "CYA" Management Syndrome

In the CYA ("cover your anatomy") mode, the manager spends an inordinate amount of time and energy to protect himself against real or imagined criticism, complaints, or vendettas that may arise in the future. Common devices to deal with one's anxieties about what others will do to him are to "get everything in writing" and to "prepare a memo for the file." While the fear of potentially unfair criticism or other harassment may be justified, what gets lost in the CYA process is a failure to employ your higher-level interpersonal skills to strengthen your relations with the would-be "attackers," to defuse their hostility, and thereby reduce the likelihood of possible "attacks."

So if you find that your "solution" to a problem is of the CYA variety, before you "circle the wagons" you may wish to ask yourself these questions: How valid are my assumptions about my "enemy"? Am I overreacting, being paranoid? If my fear is truly valid is this the best or only road to take? Are there any other options? What are the possible losses as well as gains by CYA behavior? Am I going to let this person determine *my* actions?

CYA behavior may or may not have a touch of paranoia attached to it. It all depends on how real the "threat" is. As the quip has it: "Just because I'm paranoid, it doesn't mean they're *not* out to get me."

The "Closed Loop" Trap

One (poor) way to be "comfortable" about one's decisions is to avoid/reject feedback about them, either before the decision is made or thereafter. Ideally, the manager should be eager to elicit feedback—the open rather than the closed loop—as part of his learning and growth process.

Contrast the closed-loop approach to feedback with the eager quest for feedback by the very open and democratic Askar Akayer, first president of now independent Kirgizstan, a former republic of the defunct USSR. It seems that a journal editor had criticized Akayer, and the latter had called the editor about his comments. The editor stated (quoted by Margaret Shapiro, "Kirgizstan: New Freedom Amid Poverty," *The Washington Post,* April 4, 1992): ". . . when I wrote an article somewhat critical of him he called to thank me for pointing out his failings."

Added sources of traps in the making of decisions lie in the use of "heuristic principles," or rules of thumb, plus various biases these principles lead to, state management professors James A. F. Stoner and R. Edward Freeman (in *Management,* 4th Edition, Englewood Cliffs, N.J.: Prentice Hall, 1989). Several of these impairing heuristics or rules of thumb are:

Availability

The likelihood of an event taking place is based on frequent and recent events, thus producing vivid recollections of the event. **Example:** If one has been caught in a flood, or experienced a major accident, that history will be over-estimated in importance when buying insurance.

Representativeness or Past Association

Given a situation generally similar to a prior one, the same decision will be applied as previously. In taking this shortcut, no attempt is made, of course, to verify that the situation is indeed the same. (This is also an excellent example of the "don't bother me with the facts, my mind's already made up" syndrome). **Example:** prediction of the performance in the market of a new product by comparing it to other products with good track records. **Example:** a loan officer screens mortgage applicants using, in an iron-clad way, the principle that no more than 35% of income should go for housing.

Anchoring and Adjustment

The starting point or anchor influences strongly how a decision is made. Thus, an initial value is selected and adjustments are then made to that value in reaching the final decision. **Example:** In negotiation of a salary or a contract, the beginning points will influence the final outcome, with the bias leaning toward the anchor. More specifically, a salary decision is likely to be based on last year's salary (the initial value), an adjustment then

being made on it. Some common biases, per Stoner and Freeman, which stem from the above three heuristics, are these:

Easy Recall

The easier our recollection of examples of events, the more often we believe it takes place. This produces a bias, particularly if recentness and vividness are involved. **Example:** In the annual performance review, later behaviors or events tend to override in importance earlier accomplishments. This is very natural and common trap, of course. The employee's reaction? "Hey, he didn't give me any credit for what I did in the spring and summer. He just relied on the last three months."

Easy Search

Our approach to locating data is based on the assumptions we make about how the world is organized. **Example:** If we need information about computers, we go to the organization's MIS (Management Information System) office, even though worthwhile experience may exist elsewhere in the company.

Insensitivity to Prior Probability

We tend to overvalue the importance of representative data and underrate the importance of basic trends. **Example:** We may assume that an MBA graduate with a heavy interest in arts and music is more likely to seek a post managing the arts than as a general management consultant. Our stereotype of the student's interests leads us to ignore real-world facts or trends that should tell us that there are far more job opportunities in management consulting than in arts management.

Insensitivity to Sample Size

We tend to evaluate and accept quantitative data as presented, ignoring the statistical concept of size of sample. **Example:** Ads that tout such claims as "8 of 10 housewives surveyed favored the whiteness of Super-Duper Suds" may be influencing to us as consumers, even though the sample may not have been any larger than 10 or even 20.

Misconceptions of Chance

Again, basic statistics—probability occurrence—is misunderstood, an assumption being made that random events are indeed connected. **Example:** In a coin toss procedure, which produces a dozen tails in a row, the assumption that added tosses must favor heads popping up is statistically incorrect. Why? Because each toss is an independent event with a 1 in 2 (50-50) probability. Amateur decision makers in Las Vegas casinos may well surrender their shirts if they assume that the dice are "bound" to produce a desired 7 or 11.

Insufficient Adjustment

Final decisions may be arrived at by adjusting an initial value to fit a specific situation. **Example:** A year's salary plus a percentage increase is the usual formula for annual salary setting. What is ignored, obviously, is the correctness of last year's salary. The person's true worth may have been over- or undervalued. So if this biased procedure is followed each year, the person may never be compensated equitably.

Overconfidence

Strange as it may seem, when uncertainty is at its maximum, our overconfidence is likely to be highest. So the less our insight, knowledge or expertise we have about Situation X, the more overconfident we will be about it. (Psychologically, our reaction is one of denial accompanied by reassurance. We deny that we don't know what we should, and tell ourselves instead: "We're really on the right track.") The true expert is less likely to be overconfident. Overconfidence can be reduced by giving people feedback on their judgments or pushing them to reflect on why their response might be erroneous.

The Confirmation Trap

This entails making a decision tentatively and, then, very humanly, seeking out evidence to confirm its appropriateness. (Who wants to experience the pain of being proven wrong?) **Example:** We hire someone and seek out information to demonstrate that person's competence. Disconfirming or opposite data are not sought out.

Hindsight

We tend to believe that we could have predicted the outcome of our decision ahead of its actual accomplishment. (Not "if we knew then what we know now," but "why didn't we act on what we really knew?") The trap

is that we forget the many uncertainties we encountered before the decision was made. The unfortunate significance of this is that managers are assessed totally on their results even though the results often are out of their control. **Example:** A manager's hiring decision backfires. His bosses may assert (with "20-20 hindsight") that the data was at hand to predict the new hire's likelihood of failure. A major point of this, say management researchers, is that managers should be rewarded for the "how" of their decision making, not merely the outcome of the decision.

Significance of Heuristics

They often are great time savers, but they still may be loaded with pitfalls that bias our judgments. These biases, of course, are unconscious, which means they are hard to control. The net effect is that decisions are systematically and seriously distorted.

Psychologists Jonathan Baron and Rex W. Brown ("Why America Can't Think Straight," *The Washington Post,* August 7, 1988) enumerate a number of common tendencies and behaviors that thwart straight, logical thinking. They include:

The Endowment Effect: a classic decision-making fallacy, entailing an irrational tendency to favor the status quo, a rigid commitment to the past. Some verbal identifiers: "We've always done it this way." "But is it worth the risk?" "We're not doing too badly now, so why rock the boat?" "You must admit it's been working for us." The debate in the early '90s regarding national medical care exhibited considerable status quo thinking.

Shortsightedness: a tendency to over-evaluate the worth of the immediate presence. Some verbal indicators: "We already have a good share of the market." "Tomorrow will have to take care of itself." "We'll cross that bridge when we get to it." (Remember the song line, "Que sera, sera"—what will be, will be.)

Impulsiveness: "shooting from the hip" (or even lip!)—that is, a tendency to act and react without thinking things through carefully or at all. Some verbal identifiers: "Let's (or we gotta) move on this." "Let's not waste too much time talking about it." "This may be a once-in-a-lifetime opportunity."

Neglect of Probability: a built-in assumption that unwanted things can't happen to us. Ignored is the truism that choices set precedents for later choices and the probabilities thus mount. **Example:** Not wearing a seatbelt on one occasion may not create any harm. But if it sets a precedent for all the later rides, the odds favoring an accident move up.

"My-side" Bias: a tendency to justify our beliefs to ourselves with great certainty and enthusiasm. As one employee put it describing his boss: "He's rarely right, but never in doubt."

Single-mindedness: a tendency to make decisions oriented toward only one goal, when in actuality other goals should be considered. **Example:** In a downsizing, multiple goals should be considered, such as being certain to avoid giving pink slips to the best people; maintaining the goodwill of those laid off for we may want them back and we don't want them to "badmouth" the outfit; ensuring that our reputation in the community as a a good employer is not lost; and so on.

Researchers at the University of Chicago's Center for Decision Research (Paul J.H. Schoemaker and J. Edward Russo, *Decision Traps,* 1989) point out a number of common decision traps:

Frame Blindness: a tendency to make a decision from only one or two "frames," or perspectives. **Example:** Students in decision-making seminars evaluate a business venture with an 80% success probability; they usually vote to go ahead. But if another frame is presented—the venture has a 20% failure probability—they turn it down. **Significance:** Don't be trapped by failing to explore a problem from a number of angles.

Shortsighted Circuits: using mental shortcuts—rules of thumb—to help rapidly produce a set of givens. **Example:** availability bias, entailing a tendency to assume (most likely erroneously) that the data at hand is all that we require. Similarly, recency bias encourages use of the ideas most recently encountered/learned. So salespeople tend to vend the new product even though the customer's needs might be better met via an older item.

Overconfidence: a tendency to regard confidence and competence equally. So executives may over-evaluate opinions (of their own or of their subordinates) that are delivered in a highly certain, self-assured fashion. The danger is that confidence may be a cloak for eagerness, self-delusion, and other faults. Shoemaker and Russo suggest that subordinates tone down their level of confidence when presenting recommendations to their bosses, e.g., "I'm 80% certain we can increase our market share if . . ." **Key point:** Each proposed decision should have its *own* confidence level.

Failure to Audit and Improve Decision Making. While serious post mortems could augment decision making, egos seem to prevent them from taking place—executives see them as questioning their decision-making prowess. If post-mortems are done, it invariably turns out that the boss makes the good decisions, and you, the staffer, makes the bad ones.

Dropping the "Shoot Yourself in-the-Foot" Syndrome

For the manager who is willing and able to engage in candid self-examination concerning his possible engagement in any of the above problem-solving and decision-making traps and detours, tremendous rewards are possible—higher-quality decisions and results, better staff relations, and a more positive image being presented to others. The alternative? More self-inflicted wounds. And who needs that?

GUIDELINES AND ORIENTATIONS FOR THE EFFECTIVE PROBLEM SOLVER AND DECISION MAKER

To escape criticism: do nothing, say nothing, be nothing.

— Elbert Hubbard (1856–1915), American writer and author of "A Message to Garcia" (1899)

Not everything that is faced can be changed, but nothing can be changed until it is faced.

—James Baldwin (1924–) U.S. author of novels, plays, essays and short stories

Never be afraid to make a mistake.

—Soichiro Honda (1907–1991), the Japanese auto repairman turned auto magnate

Based on your reading thus far, you undoubtedly are aware that problem-solving and decision-making activities often are undermined by ineffective and unattractive behaviors. In fact, decision making is the kind of area where it is a lot easier to do things wrong or poorly than right or well. The challenge for the manager is to rise above the potential pitfalls and thereby elevate the quality of his skill. In this section, I will present a number of principles or guidelines to help you develop a highly effective decision-making/orientation style.

Analyze Your Assumptions

Decisions are never made in a vacuum. Rather, they are based on your experience, values, preferences, prejudices, perceptions, and all the rest. Based on our "world view," then, when we encounter a problem and endeavor to resolve it we proceed from a particular set of assumptions. **To illustrate:** Assume you or I have a problem with our boss. He has been inconsiderate in certain ways, and we are not too happy about it. If we have any smarts at all, we won't barge into his office and confront him with our difficulty or concern. Instead, we will make certain assumptions about how likely the boss is to respond favorably, when is the best time of day to do this, how a confrontation may affect our future relations, etc.

Similarly, when solving any other problem, we have to slow down the action and ask ourselves what assumptions are we employing in making the decision.

And in a more global sense, we might alter our assumption that a problem is something to be solved and that is it. Instead, we might make an assumption that a problem is a vehicle to seek out new opportunities. For example, customer complaints might cause us to examine our ongoing assumptions about customer service and customer relations, and possibly to develop some new and better approaches.

Consider Corporate Culture When Deciding

A key backdrop to any decision is an understanding of the culture or business environment relating to it. To illustrate, in the middle '70s, AAMCO, a large wholesaler of car transmission parts, diversified with Plum Tree, a chain of gift boutiques. AAMCO had bought parts centrally and resold them to its franchises. But this approach failed because it ignored the difference in the culture of the two operations.

Specifically, although AAMCO's ordering and inventory control system worked splendidly in the transmission business, it failed miserably in the gift store operations. Why? In respect to transmission repair, AAMCO could order and re-order large quantities of the more commonly used parts for repair and overhaul work. But boutique customers rarely purchase identical gifts more than once. Thus, the boutique customers might return to the store, browse a bit and, not finding any new gift items, would not return. (Cited in Arno Penzias, *Ideas and Information,* New York: Simon & Schuster, 1989.)

Ask/Decide What Business or Function You Really Are In

Basic to wise decision making is deciding things on the basis of your goals or mission. Let's assume, for example, that you are a producer of widgets, gizmos, and gadgets. You have a lot of capital tied up in your distribution system, both for delivery of product and maintenance of the vehicles that haul the stuff. But what if one day in a team-building session, a young MBA (probably a Harvard hotshot) raises these questions: What if we exited from the transportation and maintenance business by contracting out for these services? Could we not then concentrate on our real or proven business—widget/gizmo making—and free up capital for more modern plant equipment, more R&D to improve our product, and thus produce more, expand market share, and grow in size as well efficiency?

Note: *The Wall Street Journal* (Michael Selz, "Small Companies Thrive by Taking Over Some Specialized Tasks of Big Concerns," September 11, 1991) reported that in a survey of 1,005 of the largest U.S. firms, 86% had cut back operations over the prior five years and 35% were making greater use of outsiders. An executive at National Steel Corporation, which had farmed out a number of its administrative services, stated: "Our business is producing steel and whenever we can devote more resources to it, that's what we want to do."

Engage in Constant Evaluation

Free up resources—money, staff, equipment, space, time—by regularly posing the bold question Peter

Drucker asks business executives: "If you weren't already doing it, would you start?" The realistic thinking underlying this query is that few organizations can afford to bestow unending revenue on all prior decisions.

Pursue a Quest for Quality

In today's complex world, broad-gauged, far-seeing managers' decision making must be obsessed with quality—quality work/product, quality service, quality materials/parts/equipment, quality rendered by suppliers. In the latter connection, consider the severe impact on services delivered on only a slightly less-than-perfect basis (see box).

What You'd Get From "99.9%" Suppliers

- At least 20,000 wrong prescriptions each year
- Unsafe drinking water almost 1 hour each month
- No electricity, water or heat for 8.6 hours each year
- No telephone service or television transmission for nearly 10 minutes each week
- 2 short or long landings at O'Hare each day (also New York, Los Angeles, Atlanta, etc.)
- Nearly 500 incorrect surgical operations per week
- 2,000 lost articles of mail per hour

—Source Unknown

Choose the Long-Term Over the Immediate

Long-term investments—training, quality, R&D, A-1 customer service—often take a back seat to immediate concerns such as cash flow or getting the product out the door. This is understandable, of course. Yet long-term organizational health is usually dependent on long-term investment. Hence, at some point the manager has to be willing to decide on the long-haul objective and not be seduced by an immediate payoff nor be put off by what the fiscal people see with alarm as an expense.

Guard Against Decisions That Create New Problems

At times, resolving a problem can create new ones. For example, in the late '80s U.S. automakers tried to fight Japanese and European competition by, among other things, offering longer-term warranties. But the warranties typically had a deductible feature attached to them. **The result:** General Motors found that its $100 deductible irritated customers and was dropped for its 1992 models. Chevrolet's general sales manager in Dallas was delighted with the new decision: "It's a better program when you have something with no deductible rather than insulting the customer with a $100 fee. The consumer found the deductible quite petty" (quoted by Gregory A. Patterson, "GM to drop $100 Deductible Charges It Charges for Repairs Under New Car Warranty," *The Wall Street Journal,* June 3, 1991).

Airlines use many devices to reduce highly expensive fuel consumption, e.g., opting for a bumpier ride if it is more fuel efficient than a smooth one, flying at higher altitudes and in straight lines, slowing down as opposed to changing course when maneuvering into line for landing (course changing adds more distance and thus burns more fuel), and carrying less fuel. On the other hand, if fuel is cheaper at the departure point as opposed to the arrival point, extra fuel may be loaded at the former location (David D. Medina, "Airlines Resort to Penny-Pinching Ploys to Bring Their Fuel Bills Back to Earth," *The Wall Street Journal,* September 28, 1990).

And a final example of a boomerang effect: The citizens of Georgetown, Kentucky, population 12,910, were initially elated when Toyota built its auto plant there. Toyota created about 4,000 new jobs and increased the income of the area. But the downside is that Toyota seems to be producing a company town, and the city is losing its small-town ways (Thomas F. O'Boyle, "New Neighbor: To Georgetown, Ky., Toyota Plant Seems a Blessing and a Curse," *The Wall Street Journal,* November 26, 1991).

Reap More With Less

Much of our conventional wisdom supports the notion that the greater the input, the greater the output. Generally so, but not universally true. **Examples:**

☐ In the marketing area, pouring buckets of cash into advertising to reach everyone is hardly as effective as targeting ads primarily at likely prospects. Also to be considered is which form of promotion works best for certain products.

☐ Pension fund managers are raising questions about the wisdom of owning 2,000 stocks when 500 will do the job. Lilli Gordon, a Cambridge, Massachusetts, pension fund adviser, says, "It's impossible to keep an eye on every single company in your portfolio if you have 2,000 stocks" (quoted by James A. White, "Pension Funds Think Less May Be More," in *The Wall Street Journal,* October 23, 1991). Sampling procedures can be used to create a worthwhile portfolio of stocks.

☐ In the desire to upgrade public educational programs and results, one idea that keeps popping up is to lengthen the school year. But Robert M. Nielsen, Assistant to the President of the American Federation of Teachers, Washington, D.C., points out that "school time is simply too valuable to waste doing more of the same old things the same way. A longer school year without systematic curricular restructuring would be like running an automobile assembly line three shifts instead of two and expecting that change would make the American cars more competitive . . . School outcomes cannot be changed without changing what goes on in classrooms between teachers and student" (per "A Longer School Year? Not Yet," a letter to the editor in *The Washington Post,* August 31, 1991).

Capitalizing on Concurrent Engineering

New products and services all too often are designed in isolation from other vitally concerned parties. The Japanese, however, to overcome this form of managerial myopia, see design in opposite terms. They use "concurrent engineering," which entails teaming up design, production and marketing people well before the new model is on the drawing board. Daniel T. Jones, co-author of *The Machine That Changed the World* (New York: HarperCollins, 1991), puts it this way: "You have to think about manufacturing the product when you design it. And that means involving people on the shop floor at an earlier stage than they are used to" (quoted by Patrick Oster, "European Auto Industry in Race Against Imports," in *The Washington Post,* December 29, 1991).

The "Why didn't you let us know sooner?" complaint needn't arise if all who have a stake in the project/design/product are involved at the earliest possible date. In effect, what is called for is "systems thinking," recognizing at the conceptual stage the impacts our decisions may have on other units in the organization.

In dealing with municipal problems, politicians and the city fathers all too often try to resolve problems on a piecemeal, isolated basis (per Victoria Linton, "The Piecemeal Approach," letter to the editor, *The Washington Post,* September 19, 1990). For example, take the problem of pollution caused by heavy use of cars. Note that articles may appear periodically in the paper about the need to switch to less-polluting fuels, mammoth congestion caused by increasing auto traffic, environmental degradation caused by new road construction, the high cost of parking, the double parking nuisance, construction, and so on.

But what is overlooked or not faced up to is that all of these problems have a common cause—too many cars. So rather than searching for less-polluting fuels, the real remedies are expanded public transportation, the possible designation of bicycle lanes, more carpooling along with staggered work hours, designation of carless days, and even designing communities so that work, recreation, and shopping may be reached on foot or bike from home, all within easy reach of public transport.

Guard Against the NIH Syndrome

Good ideas and solutions can make your world go round. This is true regardless of where the idea originated—Plant X, Department Y, Company Z, or wherever. In other words, don't fall victim to the NIH (Not Invented Here) syndrome when decisions have to be made.

Recognize That People Respond to What They See

Decisions, which are made or not made, should take into account the degree to which they serve as models, examples, encouragers to or discouragers of behavior. **Example:** Take graffiti on urban walls or subways. If left alone, it not only will remain but will attract more. Criminologist James Q. Wilson labels this "the broken window syndrome." Thus, if one window in a building is not repaired, the window breakers naturally assume no one cares, and so they add to their "fun" by breaking more of them.

New York City and other municipalities have learned that graffiti has to be cleaned up promptly. If left alone, it becomes a symbol of urban neglect and decay. To subway riders it communicates: "No one is in control." And if the graffiti makers can do their vandalizing without apparent limits, would not muggers have the same freedom to do their thing, too? (per Edward T. McMahon, "Handwriting On the Wall," letter to the editor, *The Washington Post,* July 21, 1991).

Of course, park administrators have long recognized the psychology of litter-free park grounds. They thus provide good quantities of strategically placed trash cans and assiduously pick up litter and empty the trash cans before the refuse flows over.

Avoid Decision Making With a Rearview Mirror

What has always worked may or may not be a valid guide to a decision for today or, more accurately, for a decision with which you will have to live tomorrow. For approaches based on history, tradition, past experience, or the "tried and true" may well have outlived their usefulness in today's rapidly changing world. While it is quite comfortable to follow the path previously taken (really the dead hand of the past), a fresh, new route is more likely to be the means to avoid the doldrums. So pat questions such as "What have we done before?" and "Are there precedents to support this?" should give way to better questions. **Examples:** "What are some *new* ways to tackle this?" "Are we taking tomorrow into account in this decision?" "What has changed (e.g., the technology, the market, the competition, etc.) since we went that route?"

In the '80s and '90s, numerous American companies ran aground because of rearview mirror thinking, relying on the conventional wisdom of the prior decade. **For example:** In Detroit, the conventional wisdom of the '70s was that car buyers favored the big vehicle, had little interest in quality, and thought that Japan produced shoddy products. But Detroit executives were in error in all these assumptions. One union official saw his stagnant company analogous to a statement attributed to Winston Churchill: "You can always count on the American people to do the right thing after they've tried everything else" (quoted by Frank Swoboda, "GM's Deep Cuts Signal the End of A Work Force Era," *The Washington Post,* December 20, 1991).

An excellent example of rearview mirror thinking relates to the changed and changing field of retail selling. If you are into retail sales and understand the changes in the economy and resultant consumer behavior of the '90s compared to the '80s, you know quite

well that the 1980s consumer creed of "shop 'til you drop" has been converted in the '90s to "Why should we buy?" Accordingly, decisions about merchandise selection, promotion, pricing, including possible discounting, customer relations, etc., have to take into account new rather than past realities. The many retailers, large and small, who never caught up with this change in consumer behavior have paid the price.

Sheraton Corporation's CEO, John Kapioltas, inveighing against rearview mirror thinking, warned those in his worldwide hotel, inn, and resort network (owners, financiers, and general managers) at a management conference:

> *No company is immune to the fate of the dinosaur. (It) became extinct because its response time was so slow . . . because of its inability to respond to change fast enough. The demands of the marketplace call for cost and operations flexibility. Survival depends on timely response and appropriate action.*

Sheraton's Director of Marketing added: "If you're doing business today the same as even five or ten years ago, you're almost certainly doing it wrong" (quoted by Connie Goldstein, "Sheraton: New at 50," in *Corporate Meetings* and *Incentives,* May 1987).

The rearview mirror/dead hand of the past syndrome may, at times, be so severe that earlier rationales for a given decision may even be lost, yet the decision persists. The following anecdote illustrates this point.

Story: Mary Jane, observing her mother at work in the kitchen, asked: "Why do you cut off the ends of the ham before putting it into the baking pan?"

Mother: "Why I've always done it this way, Mary Jane, because that's the way *my* mother did it."

Mary Jane, persisting: "But why?"

Mother: "I don't know, dear. Let's ask grandmother."

Grandmother: "Why? For a very good reason. Because my pan was too small for the large ham." (!)

Beware of Tendencies Toward Unanimity

Unanimity of thinking should breed anxiety, not comfort. When everyone agrees instantly with a single approach, it's time for pause. *Look for and encourage dissent.* For it just may be that other possible options have not been considered. Also, the possible weaknesses in the course of action agreed upon may not have been explored adequately.

Mavericks, iconoclasts, against-the-grain types, devil's advocates, and dissenters should be encouraged and rewarded, not smothered. Management authority Dr. Warren Bennis states that seven (or more) out of ten people in U.S. business stifle their views when they clash with those of their bosses. He states: "This means that subordinates allow bosses to make mistakes even when the subordinates know better" (quoted by Frank Sommerfield, "Paying the Troops to Buck the System," *Business Month,* May 1990).

Bennis believes that the absence of dissent breeds an attitude basic to today's corporate problem. "Arrogance is not listening, and General Motors is suffering today for not listening in the 1970s."

Management writer Frank Dommerfield (*Business Month,* May 1990) believes that "yes men" should be discouraged and that the troops should be paid to buck the system. He states:

> *Hidebound companies that don't encourage dissent may not survive the 1990s. Figuring ways to reward naysayers is likely to be on the agenda of more compensation committees. But if corporations really do open up and encourage challenges from all sides, the question of how to reward dissent becomes moot. Big bonuses for bucking the boss may be big news today. A decade from now, challenging the boss will be what everyone is paid for in the first place.*

The bottom line: You can't yield to the unverified assumption that all team members see the problem alike or that everyone sees it as you do.

Shed Standard Solutions for Those Igniting the Imagination

One of the major traps in problem solving and decision making is a tendency to apply pat or standard remedies based on one's prior experience, preference, or comfort level.

As an example, assume people in the field are slow in forwarding their monthly reports to us at headquarters. What do we do? We may do what we always do—send them a memo that reminds them of the established deadline date, asks for their cooperation, etc. But ignored is the possibility that lateness may be a symptom that

a) the reports are too detailed and thus burdensome,
b) the deadline is unreasonable,
c) the purpose of the report is not clear, or
d) there is no evidence that the report actually is used in any significant way.

Overlooked, too, may be the approach of complimenting people when they get the report in on time—positive reinforcement—as opposed to complaining about lateness.

When we talk about shedding standard solutions, we also should guard against "operational ossification." If a plan or project has been in operation two or three years, the odds are that your subordinates—the operators/administrators of the plan—are trying to standardize and stabilize its modus operandi. Your job is to "destabilize" that urge to get comfortable with the status quo. This means a frequent review to accomplish an upgrading of what is being done.

Respect "The Law of Holes"

Wise advice to any manager is to observe "The Law of Holes." When you are in a hole, stop digging. Putting it more concretely, don't tolerate or aggravate situations that are already pretty bad, e.g., tolerating the fair-haired boys (and girls) who are essentially lightweights; supporting yesterday's breadwinners that are revenue eaters rather than revenue producers, e.g., keeping a marginal product, which should be phased out rather than repeatedly trying to resuscitate it with more costly marketing efforts; not facing up to the need to abandon assorted mud-stuck projects resulting in more throwing of good money after bad.

Companies and individuals get ensnarled in what Michael M. Miller and Patricia B. Gray ("Why Businesses Often Sink in 'Decisional Quicksand,'" *The Wall Street Journal,* December 15, 1986) called

> *. . . the corporate equivalent of fly paper—bad ideas they can't seem to shake quickly or gracefully.*

> *The harder they try, the more tightly glued they become. Over here, a clutch of banks is festooned with third-world loans; over there, utilities struggle with nuclear projects that will never produce a kilowatt. And they are all caught in what failure researchers call 'escalation dilemmas,' projects or strategies that*

appear doomed or highly dubious but into which they keep pouring more resources.

And if businesses have sunk into "decisional quicksand," the final cost may exceed the cash already gone down the tubes. These dilemmas may become black holes consuming managerial time for years, diverting funds from more worthwhile projects, and even damaging the firm's other enterprises to an uncertain degree.

The momentum propelling a bad decision may overwhelm good judgment: Failure is not kind to ego or self-esteem needs. And if things are going bad—via a slow hemorrhaging, not sudden death—managers learn to live with the negative results, even regarding it as "normalcy." Says Columbia University psychologist Dr. Harvey Hornstein: "People get comfortable with decline. When you live with dragons for a while, they don't look so bad close-up anymore. You persist because it is more terrifying to leap into the darkness" (quoted by Miller and Gray in *The Wall Street Journal,* December 15, 1986).

Rather than waiting for projects to go sour and then trying to rescue them, organizational psychologists Barry M. Staw and Jerry Ross ("Good Money After Bad," *Psychology Today,* February 1988) recommend the following preventive measures:

☐ Schedule regular intervals to step back and look at a project from an outsider's perspective.

☐ Establish a climate so that subordinates feel free to present the news, good or bad.

☐ Key staff members can meet regularly to evaluate hurdles facing a project and its likelihood of success.

☐ Invite a manager from another department to attend or even chair the above meetings.

And if the project is in trouble, say Staw and Ross, those responsible for the sinking ship should be replaced. A less drastic step is to assign initial and subsequent decision making to separate groups—a failing project would be turned over to a new team. A broader strategy: Move toward an "experimenting organization"—every program is reconsidered at regular intervals and all lines of business are available for sale at the right price. Managers would be evaluated not on their success/failure rates, but on how well they recognize and cope with problems in their functions.

Beside individual-oriented psychological factors that produce adherence to bad decisions, there is also a cultural factor at work. The American culture supports the frontier notion of sheer persistence as a virtue, thus making early bailout—cutting one's losses—difficult. As the maxim has it: "When the going gets tough, the tough get going." Similar cultural cliches are "weathering the storm," "staying the course," and "sticking to your guns." Business heroes of the past are those who stuck to their guns despite the odds and converted big losers into big winners. Hollywood has picked up this theme many times.

But if we understand the Law of Holes, the bottom line is to do what's right and logical, to bite the bullet and to deal aggressively with all the excess baggage that is crying out loudly to be thrown overboard. This also means not to "kill" the messenger bearing grim news; instead, facing up to glaringly bad situations and dealing with them now; not to use PR ("smoke and mirrors") to paper over reality, for it is in fact counterproductive—realism tells us that there are no $5 cancer cures. In sum, letting out one's belt to control obesity is a no-win solution. The cliche "no pain, no gain" still makes a lot of sense.

Go With the Winners

Because you are interested in decisions with high payoffs, your best strategy is to go (invest, support) with the winners. This is true whether we are talking about producing and marketing products or providing services such as, say, operating prisons. In the latter connection, the State of Maryland's Patuxent Institution, a prison that once tried to salvage the hard-core criminal (mostly sociopaths) has done a 180-degree turn. It is now focusing on younger, less-hardened criminals who can be reached more readily. Said the prison director: "Rather than invest . . . on this group of people that is likely to return, let's refine the system and look more closely at those who are most likely to be successful" (quoted by Howard Scheinder, "Md. Prison Shifts Focus to Less Hardened Inmates," *The Washington Post,* May 7, 1990).

So if we go with the winners, we avoid giving old responses to new challenges.

Study and Analyze, but Do Act

I advocate using a problem-solving, decision-making model to slow action down and ensure that all vital steps in the decision-making process are taken in logical order. However, it is essential to avoid delaying a decision when the needed facts already are assembled. Robert Goddard ("Viewpoint: The Vital Few and the Trivial Many," *Personnel Journal,* July, 1987) calls this "paralysis by analysis." Putting off a decision unnecessarily ignores an application of Pareto's Law; namely, if 20% of the facts will determine 80% of the outcome, and those facts are already at hand, it is self-defeating to wait for "all the facts" to come in.

One of the many traps of decision making is to let our anxieties over the "right" decision dictate super caution and thus delay action unnecessarily. We may do this by creating special study groups, task forces, ad hoc project teams, and the like. Actually, these study groups are great problem-solving tools when used with purpose. But if "send it to committee" translates into a means of taking refuge from reality, of studying something to death, it becomes counter-productive. The following anecdote about the ant and the centipede bears pointedly on this point.

Story: Ant to centipede: "I only have eight legs so I always admire the way you manage your 100 legs."

Centipede: "That is what I do."

Ant: "How do you know to move leg 7 after leg 98?"

The centipede reflected at length about the ant's question, and was never able to walk again!

Consider, too, the saying: "You can't jump over the river in two jumps," which means that either you do what has to be done with conviction and vigor or you don't do it at all.

So when we are tempted to become overly timid and delay things without end, we might jar ourselves into action with this bit of self-talk: "It is better to make things happen than to wait for them to happen." And we certainly don't want these assessments of our decision-making style by our subordinates and possibly others, too: "He has the knack of seeing six sides of every issue!" and per the old song line, "First you say you do, and then you don't. Then you say you will, and then you won't."

Finally, delayed decisions may mean lost opportunities. So don't wait until midnight has come and gone—recall Cinderella's fate for being late. And if the problem is one that requires resolution now, delay may produce what a colleague of mine calls "the fester factor," an aggravation of the situation.

But Patience is Still a Virtue

In decision making, it is all too easy to get caught up in the "let's move on this now" trap. The issue isn't really dilly-dallying as opposed to deciding. Rather, have we given enough thought to what we have to decide? And how sound is our diagnosis? A quote from Japanese-born George Tanaka, world-class art director for Dentsu, one of the world's largest ad agencies, who has to deal with American copywriters who complain that "things are going so slow," should help to put this issue into good perspective. Says Tanaka:

> *I understand well what they mean, because I felt keenly the cultural and philosophical differences between Asia and the West when I returned to Japan. In our culture, being swift isn't nearly as important as being right. Why hurry if your haste only means you'll have to do it over again? Our decision-making is, by Western standards, slow. But the objective is to reach a decision with which everyone can agree, not a quick decision that lacks support by those who must carry it out.*

—From an institutional ad in *The Wall Street Journal,* July 17, 1990

The bottom line: If we seek a "fast" solution, not doing our homework properly and gathering the data we need to identify the problem properly, we may well produce the proverbial "half-assed" solution.

Seek Solutions Rather Than Scapegoats

When problems occur, frustration may develop readily, and it becomes all too easy to think primarily in terms of who or what is at fault. However, pinning the blame on the "culprit" and fixating on the cause of the problem is much less useful than searching for a remedy. After all, the "blame game" is essentially a form of twisting logic into a pretzel. And who needs that?

An example of solution seeking in lieu of engaging in blaming behavior relates to the Complement, an Alexandria, Virginia-based specialty chain of luggage and leather goods. The owner-president, Arnold Bronfin, had to close his six-store lingerie chain (Arpres Peau) due to fierce competition in tough, recessionary times. **The result:** Mr. Bronfin found himself staring at vacant warehouse space, previously storing lingerie goods, and concerned about where to find some needed growth. Said Bronfin:

It was a soul-searching time and the easiest thing to do is to blame the recession or not to realize something was not working. Once you use those things as an excuse for losing, you focus on them and not on the things you need to do to improve.

Added growth within Bronfin's 11-store luggage chain was not too promising, for the luggage/leather goods business was saturated with rivals accompanied by consumer resistance to higher prices. But Bronfin assessed the explosion of new luggage products—wheeled lightweight and casual goods—and decided to experiment with a bigger warehouse store format of some 10,000 square feet compared to usual store size of 1,500 to 3,000 square feet. The large warehouse store can carry about three times the assortment of the established Complement stores. It can offer a greater range of colors and sizes. The warehouse luggage store, marked by concrete floor, simple fixtures, no-frills service, and open only Thursday through Saturday can discount prices greatly and provide volume sales (Sara Swisher, "Firm Turns to Discounting, Bag and Baggage," *The Washington Post,* April 25, 1992).

Shun the "Fairy-Godmother" Syndrome

When the problems mount and the solutions seem remote, it is all too easy to fall into the trap of hoping that someone in a gilded robe will suddenly arrive before us, wave a magic wand, and cause our headaches to vanish. Or worse still, we may fall into the trap of "redefining" a problem—more wishful thinking—if it seems too monumental or sensitive to tackle head on. One wag has described this as "Finagle's Constant": changing the objectives to fit what happened! **A sounder approach:** Get on the horn, call the staff together, catalog the worrisome events, set logical pri-

orities, and attack the problems one at a time. There may not be many things we can bet on in life successfully. But realism, rather than sprinkling pixie dust on a problem, is one we can take to the bank.

Deal Directly with Dereliction

If someone obviously is not doing what they are supposed to be doing and complaints are mounting because of it, we may be tempted to solve the problem by adding new checks, reviews, forms, controls, procedures, etc., to see that things get done properly. The danger, of course, is that by adding more controls, we may introduce more rigidity into the situation so that we have created a new and even more severe problem.

But sooner or later—preferably sooner—we may have to bite the bullet and decide to act, to level with the non-performer about job standards and our expectations regarding performance. The same thinking should hold true for other individuals who present us with unnecessary, unwanted problems such as sloppy suppliers, alibiing service people, fudging contractors, procrastinating peers, etc.

Avoid the Chaff from Staff

Specialists from various staff (advisory) departments can be useful in developing solutions to perplexing problems. So it is worthwhile to tap and listen to their special expertise. However, the listening should be done warily, for:

☐ Accountants may eagerly pull another control system out of their briefcases.

☐ Trainers may quickly endorse a pet training program.

☐ Systems and computer people, various personnelists, production engineers, quality control specialists, et al., may also have their pet projects available.

In sum, what you really need are tailor-made plans/solutions to meet your particular needs, rather than pre-packaged, predetermined panaceas to complex problems. To quote Winston Churchill: "It's not enough to say we are doing our best. We must do what is necessary."

Consider That Acting May Be Better Than Asking

Not every decision that you have to make will be based on precedent, experience, or past answers. At times your decisions may require plowing totally new ground. This may raise the following question: Do I act on my own now or do I "clear" this decision with my boss?

Obviously, if the boss has strong feelings about a problem area, it would seem that discretion rather than valor is called for. On the other hand, it may well be that your boss doesn't really have an answer to the problem or may not care that much about it. If that is the case, an immediate decision on your part may be the wisest course of action. This approach is based on this kind of "logic":

a) a well-thought out, innovative idea/solution on your part is quite likely to succeed

b) by asking for permission to act you may be communicating doubts about your proposal

c) providing the boss with an opportunity to mull over your desired solution may result in an unwanted turndown or simply a long drawn-out delay on his part in deciding, and

d) by acting (deciding), you prevent someone from scuttling or modifying (beyond recognition?) your plan, for you have presented him with *un fait accompli* (a completed act).

Even picky bosses are not likely to unravel what is already accomplished.

Avoid Decisions to Garner Love and Affection

The people feel no mercy: You do good and no one thanks you.

—Czar Boris Godunov (c.1551–1605) in a poem by Alexander Pushkin (1799–1837), Russian poet and prose writer

In the above quotation, the Russian czar expresses his hurt over the fact that his people did not appreciate his "good works." Maybe they should render such appreciation, but the odds are more likely that they won't. In fact, if anything, they are more likely to think that the decision maker is an easy mark and expect more largess: "What have you done for us lately?"

The wiser course of action, then, is to make decisions based on what is best for the organization. You will be respected for that—not loved, but respected.

Consider Your Projection of Style

It should be apparent after your reading of the above paragraphs that decision makers have different styles, temperments, and images. The question to ourselves is: What style/image/temperment am I projecting to peers, bosses and staff? Listed in the boxed item on page 553 are various statements and phrases of a non-flattering sort used by observers to describe what they see and feel about those who make decisions. Hopefully, these statements apply to others rather than to yourself. If any of them do relate to you, change is definitely recommended.

Final Rule

If the situation is totally murky, and the above rules don't "fit," abandon them and intuit. That is, call on your intuition, judgment, gut, and experience to assess the factors and forces in the situation and the people involved. Your "guesstimate," aided by staff input as to best possible outcome, should serve as a good substitute for "science," the "numbers," and the like.

An action-planning worksheet is provided on page 557.

QUESTIONS AND PROBLEMS FOR DISCUSSION

The questions and problems below are designed for discussion in management/supervisory training workshops or college/university classes in management. They may be discussed in (a) small groups with reports fed back to the group-at-large, or (b) in the total group.

1. Chapter 10 has two quizzes or instruments for thought stimulation and self-evaluation. They are:

   ☐ Problem Solving & Decision Making—A Quiz to Encourage Reflection

   ☐ Loose or Rigid? A Self-Assessment Opportunity

   They may serve as exercises for your participant group. Procedures:

   a. Have participants complete the quiz individually.

Managerial Decision Making: Is It Always Rational?

The statements and phrases below describe the ways managers often approach the decision-making process, as seen by others:

"Yesterday's breadwinners"	"Lets it sit in his in-box"
"Ego trip"	"A real penny pincher"
"Grandstanding"	"Painted himself into a corner"
"Just PR"	"Won't stick his neck out"
"Fair-haired boys (or girls)"	"Vested interest"
"Plays favorites"	"Has a death wish"
"Pet peeves"	"Throws his weight around"
"Pet projects"	"Knows it all"
"Strictly by the book"	"Simply won't listen"
"Division X gets anything they want"	"Don't bother me with the facts, my mind's already made up"
"Since he came up through (function . . .), he always sides with them"	"Easily swayed"
"Keeps an enemy list"	"Has no convictions"
"Conducts a vendetta"	"Like talking to a stone wall"
"You don't want to get in his black book"	"You can sell him on anything if you can corner him in his office after 5 o'clock"
"A long memory (about those who cross him)"	"If we don't do anything about it, maybe it'll go away"
"Off the top of his head"	"Sweep it under the rug"
"Fly by the seat of his pants"	"Afraid to lose face"
"Make mountains out of molehills"	"He is consistent in his inconsistencies"
"Afraid to make a decision"	"Sends it to committee"
"You can't get an answer out of him"	"Decides everything himself"
"Perfectionist (can't ever decide; won't let go)"	

b. Assign to small groups (3–5) to discuss their learnings from the quiz or possibly problems/difficulties with it (e.g., items not clear, too assumptive, etc.).

2. Assume that you have been asked to give a short talk on problem solving to the Supervisors' Club Monthly Luncheon Meeting. What main points would you make?

3. Assume that you are a member in a work group that has difficulty confronting its problems. What might you do to get the team to face up to its problems?

4. Using the guidelines given in the text, conduct a skill-building session via brainstorming. Possible topics:

☐ Items to consider when planning a trip to Europe.

☐ Ways to improve trust between a manager and his staff.

☐ Uses of a brick (or a paper clip).

☐ How to shop wisely for the family groceries.

5. How do you feel about the value/significance of intuition in decision making?

6. Have you used intuition in a recent decision? Explain.

7. It is not unusual for managers to stay with an obviously poor decision? Why might this be the case?

8. The Navy has this advice for new personnel: "If it waves, salute it; if it doesn't move, paint it." How does this statement relate to creativity in problem solving?

9. Do groups always make better decisions than individuals? Why or why not?

10. Assume one of the detriments of problem-solving groups is "groupthink," i.e., people rally around a proposed solution (high conformity) without engaging in enough dissent so that other options are generated and discussed. How can a work team overcome "group think?"

	Yes	No	Not Sure	
1.	☐	☐	☐	A decision involving plant rehabilitation
2.	☐	☐	☐	A decision involving hiring a new sales manager
3.	☐	☐	☐	A decision involving the switch to a new supplier of raw materials
4.	☐	☐	☐	A decision to install a new management information system (MIS)
5.	☐	☐	☐	A decision to switch from a formal suggestion system to an informal one
6.	☐	☐	☐	A decision to set new quality standards for our product/service
7.	☐	☐	☐	A decision regarding scheduling of summer leave
8.	☐	☐	☐	A decision re content of monthly progress/production reports
9.	☐	☐	☐	A decision re starting and quitting hours, including standards for flex time
10.	☐	☐	☐	A decision re the format, location and date for the next company picnic in the summer

Note: Items 1–4 probably would be decided best by the boss. Items 5–10 could be decided by the team.

11. What are the advantages of group decision making? The drawbacks?

12. Quiz on Group Decision Making

I would use the group decision technique as follows:

13. Could you turn any decision over to a group for its final resolution? Why or why not?

14. You manage a consignment shop. (People leave things for you to sell at a specified price, and you receive a 25% commission.) A customer brings in an old, complete and valuable set of china and says: "Just get me $200 for the stuff and I'll be happy." You know the china type very well and are certain you can get $400. What do you decide to do or say, if anything? What are your options as an ethical manager?

15. You have been to a management training program and learned about group decision making. You have tried it out for the past six months. Today you received a subtle complaint from your boss that you seem to be tied up in too many staff meetings. What do you do? What are your options?

16. Regarding the "Learning Organization": Put participants in small groups with half of them having this assignment: "Come up with a list of methodologies (policies, practices, protocols, etc.) that would most likely produce a creative, learning organization." The other groups are given the opposite assignment: "What methodologies might you employ, if you were so inclined or so ordered, to produce a stagnant, static, non-learn-

ing, bureaucratic organization?" Data can be captured on a flip chart sheet as follows:

Turn ons	Turn offs

17. You are a retailer of electronic equipment and home appliances. Your installer of gas appliances just installed a gas cooktop range. The customer smelled gas later that day. Also, the customer began to use the built-in wall oven (independent of the cooktop), but learned 30 minutes later that the gas in the oven for a beef roast had not come on. The customer, because of the gas odor and the failure of the gas oven to work, called the gas company. The serviceman from the gas company found that the pilot light in the oven was off, hence the odor. **The reason:** The installer had turned off the total gas system and failed to re-light the oven pilot. The gas company serviceman also found that the two pilot lights on the cooktop were set too high, causing its metal top to become very warm to the touch. Since these several problems were fixed by the gas company representative, the customer did not complain to the appliance company from whom the gas cooktop was purchased.

Questions: Since the gas company representative remedied the situation, does the company have a problem? Is there a training need? How can a company learn of service problems if the customer doesn't bother to complain?

18. **Memo from the Boss: Quality Circle "Overtime"**

You are the facilitator for a group of quality circles in your company. You have been conducting one of the circles yourself since the regular circle leader is away due to an extended illness. You recently worked with one group that got so engrossed in its problem that it ran over the allotted time by 30 minutes. (Meetings run for one hour per week, one-half hour on company time, the other half hour during the lunch period. Members brown-bag their lunch for the meeting.)

Your boss, who is not really sold on the Quality Circle idea, sent you this scorching note:

"The Quality Circle time has gotten completely out of hand. The meetings are for one hour only. Today we lost the production time of eight workers.

"This abuse will lead to disqualifying a circle. You are responsible for keeping it on track and observing the rules."

Questions: What is the likely impact on the receiver? If you were the facilitator, what would you do? What are your options? Which one would you select? Why? Would you show the memo to the participants? Why or why not?

19. **The Case of the Dirty Job**

You are the manager of a small food-processing plant. One of the jobs under your supervision is a real headache because of its constant turnover—employees last only 3–5 weeks. The duties involve handling the garbage, washing blood and other messy materials off the walls, and general janitorial work such as cleaning toilets and washing floors. The job is not demanding from a volume standpoint; in fact, the nature of the job is such that there are considerable slack periods in it each day.

What might you do to reduce turnover?

How Would You Respond? An Ethics Quiz

Personal	Decide in Your Favor	Decide in Other's Favor
1. You purchase a birthday gift (two shirts) for your son from an up-scale store. Cost: about $60. Several days later, you see an ad in the newspaper at another store offering identical merchandise for some $40. Because you still have the shirts (the birthday is next week), you can return them to the upscale store, buy the shirts at the other store at the lower price and save $20.	☐	☐
2. In a bank transaction the teller gives you an extra $10 bill. You wonder whether you should return it to her. You know that she will be held responsible for the shortage.	☐	☐
3. Your new car dealer overlooks a wheel alignment charge (a $50 item) on your $625 service and repair bill. You wonder if you should say nothing about it because you feel you have been getting gouged and wrenched right along by Mr. Good Sprocket.	☐	☐
4. When you return home from the above visit to the dealer, you discover two practically new and expensive hand tools on the floor of the passenger side of the car. You could use the tools, so you debate keeping them because the journey back to the garage is an inconvenient, 14-mile, roundtrip.	☐	☐
5. Your daughter delays preparing an important term paper for her high school social studies course. She asks you to write a note (a fictitious excuse of illness) to the instructor in her behalf so that she won't be penalized for a late paper. She states that a reduced grade in the course will affect her overall grade average and may jeopardize her chances of entering a college of her choice. She states further that "all the kids do this."	☐	☐
6. While parking you car in a restaurant parking lot, you inadvertently cause a deep scratch on a neighboring car. No one has noticed the incident.	☐	☐
7. You belong to a country club that subtly excludes blacks, Asians, Hispanics, and Jews.	☐	☐

On the Job

	Decide in Your Favor	Decide in Other's Favor
1. Your firm has a strict duties and responsibilities evaluation system. You have a secretary, a super, hard-to-replace employee, who will leave if she doesn't receive an upward reclassification. You could easily pad her job description to get her the higher grade and thereby prevent her departure.	☐	☐
2. You are a corporate meeting planner. A major hotel representative offers you a range of gifts—watches, cameras, VCRs—if you book rooms with them for your company's forthcoming annual conference.	☐	☐
3. You are recruiting for a top engineering position. You have a number of highly qualified applicants to consider. One of them drops clear hints that he has information about new design work under way by his current employer, a strong competitor of your firm.	☐	☐
4. You are a marketing director for a large toy manufacturing company. A group of your toys has been declared unsafe by the federal government. You could sell them overseas, however, which would make the difference between a bottom line that's black rather than red for this fiscal year.	☐	☐
5. You are the manager of a professional baseball team. You have found that you can increase you percentage of wins over losses by pilfering the opponent's signals.	☐	☐
6. Because you put in many hours of work and travel at no extra compensation, it is OK to take minor supplies (tape, paper, ballpoint pens) home and to use the office computer, copier, telephone, and secretary for non-business (personal, professional, community) purposes.	☐	☐
7. You are a banking executive responsible for processing interest payments on municipal bonds and dividend payments. You can save scads of money on corporate stocks for your bank by dating (meter mail) envelopes containing the checks on the first of the month, but mailing the envelopes on the second or third day of the month. Similarly, direct deposits of bonds and stockholders are processed on the first day of the month but are credited to their accounts on the second day.	☐	☐

Scoring

1. If all or nearly all decisions are made in favor of other people: You are eminently qualified to teach an advanced executive ethics course at the Harvard Business School.
2. If all or nearly all decisions favor gain for yourself: You probably should re-enroll in Sunday school for a hefty dose of ethical and moral development
3. If your decisions are mixed—some favor yourself, others favor others—you need to think through very carefully ethical and moral values so as to develop a firmer ethical philosophy.

Action Planning Worksheet for Improved Problem-Solving and Decision-Making Skills

The action plan which follows may be accomplished:

1. By the reader on his own, i.e., without reference to a training classroom situation.
2. In a training or classroom situation. If so, a) simply have each participant complete the form, either in or before class, depending on the available time. b) Assign participants to trios to discuss the Action Plans. Each person presents his plan to the other two participants (20–25 minutes) who serve as "consultants," i.e., they raise questions to clarify and strengthen the plan and give support and encouragement as needed.

My Action Plan for Improved Problem-Solving and Decision-Making Skills

1. My needs for improvement as a problem solver are:
   a. _____
   b. _____
   c. _____
   d. _____
   e. _____

2. My plans for improvement as a problem solver are:
   a. _____
   b. _____
   c. _____
   d. _____
   e. _____

3. Possible barriers/blocks to improvement as a problem solver are:
   a. _____
   b. _____
   c. _____
   d. _____
   e. _____

4. I can overcome such obstacles by:
   a. _____
   b. _____
   c. _____
   d. _____
   e. _____

5. My needs for improvement as a decision maker are:
   a. _____
   b. _____
   c. _____
   d. _____
   e. _____

6. My plans for improvement as a decision maker are:
   a. _____
   b. _____
   c. _____
   d. _____
   e. _____

7. Possible barriers/blocks to improvement as a decision maker are:
   a. _____
   b. _____
   c. _____
   d. _____
   e. _____

8. I can overcome such obstacles by:
   a. _____
   b. _____
   c. _____
   d. _____
   e. _____

12 The Manager as a Change Agent: How to Manage the Change Process

Don't change with the times—change before the times.

> —Author unknown

We cannot stop change and we cannot escape it. We can let it destroy us or we can embrace it. We must embrace it . . . Change is the force that causes us to take a look at the familiar in new ways. Change makes the adrenaline kick in and motivates us toward achievement.

> —Michael Eisner, chairman and CEO, The Walt Disney Co.
> (quoted in *Personnel Journal,* December 1994, p. 4)

We're trying to cope with the biggest economic change in two centuries. That truth is self-evident. But what does it mean to you? It means that to be scared out of your senses is sensible. To be comfortable is suicidal.

> —Tom Peters, management authority

It is not the strongest of the species that survives, nor the most intelligent, but rather the one most responsive to change.

> —Charles R. Darwin (1809–1882), English naturalist and
> formulator of the concept of evolution

It ain't instant pudding!

> —Advisory by quality improvement guru W. Edwards Deming to
> organizations looking for an instant cure to their problems
> (*Quality Digest,* July 1994, p. 79)

If we had to select one word that symbolizes the world we live in, it would be *change*. Certainly change was always with us, an inevitable fact of life. But it used to be incremental, a step-by-step phenomenon. Today we are confronted with change that is exponential; that is, change heaped upon change.

The forces driving change today are many and unrelenting—scientific and technological, e.g., computers, robotics, information systems; competition in the marketplace, both foreign and domestic; product changes (i.e, many new products and shorter product life cycles); market segmentation (as opposed to market homogeneity, the market fragmenting into highly volatile, "lifestyle" segments); economic uncertainty and all its impacts (e.g., inflation, changes in interest rates, recession, changes in employment rates); societal changes (e.g., in values, lifestyles, cultural diversity); political changes (electoral impacts); governmental pressures (e.g., new legislation, added regulations, taxation); internal organizational changes (reorganizing, centralizing, decentralizing, recentralizing, restructuring, divesturing, retrenching, re-engineering, downsizing, outsourcing); shareholder demands; employee/union demands; consumer demands (e.g., for safe, quality products and A-1 service); environmental demands (by private conservation organizations and government); demographic trends (e.g., change in composition of population groups by age, gender, ethnicity; geographical shifts of population); educational trends; the information age economy (the fundamental sources of wealth are no longer natural resources and physical labor, but knowledge and communication).

The result: The practices managers developed to work in a stable, predictable world often no longer apply, and indeed are outmoded. Yet the guideposts to manage today and in the future are far from clear.

As a reflection of our turbulent world, we are bombarded regularly by a lot of slogans and clichés about change—"Progress is our most important business." "For a better tomorrow." "You have to run twice as fast just to stay where you are." "Ahead of our time." "Everything changes." "There are no limits to change." "Building a better future." "The pride is back." "Quality is job one."

But while the world changes, organizations, managers, and employees within them may not always be able to foresee or adapt to change. In fact, there may be a deadly commitment to an obsolete policy or process, or a marginal product or service. As the British humorist/writer/journalist Hector Hugh Munro, pseudonym Saki (1870–1916), put it:

Some laud a life of mild content;
Content may fall, as well as Pride.
The Frog who hugged his lowly Ditch
Was much disgruntled when it dried.

(quoted by David McCord Wright, "The Administrative Fallacy," *Harvard Business Review*, July–August 1960)

So the big question for any of us who heads up an organization or a segment of one is: How can our operation become flexible and nimble enough to react to change/new demands and avoid the fate of the Frog (or of eminent companies long since gone or currently struggling to survive)?

Although statistics are often boring, here's one that should shake us up: Of this country's 25 largest companies in 1900, only about two are still in business today (David Fagiano, President and CEO, The Presidents Association of The American Management Association, in an August 2, 1994 promotional letter announcing a workshop on how to create a change-responsive organization). **Significance:** To survive necessitates the adoption of a mindset that accepts change as an ongoing phenomenon, as an opportunity and as a fundamental way of operating.

Additionally, managers must also be adept in introducing change in the organizations they manage. This chapter should arm you with a good fund of concepts and skill pointers to assist in becoming an effective implementor of change—a "change agent," if you will—who can accomplish changes rapidly, effectively, economically, and without any negative fallout (resistance).

CHANGE: YOUR INVOLVEMENT AS A MANAGER

The world is as it is and not as it should be.

—Virginia Satir, internationally renowned behavioral scientist and pioneering family therapist

We cannot direct the winds, but we can adjust the sails.

—Author unknown

—When it comes to the future, there are three kinds of people: those who let it happen, those who make it happen, and those who wonder what happened.

—Anon.

As managers we inevitably are involved with change in a number of ways.

First, we are expected to respond positively to change that comes from above, from our bosses. Organizations encounter new demands, develop and issue new policies, launch new programs, revise ongoing systems and operations, and the like. We thus become the instrument for the implementation of changes decreed from on high. It is our job to "rally the troops" to carry out the new requirements with enthusiasm, speed and precision.

Second, we ourselves may frequently encounter new needs and demands from inside or outside the organization, e.g., new technology, new systems, competition, etc. We thus may find it essential to inaugurate changes of our own within and for our own unit.

Third, we may *anticipate* the needs of our unit in a sensitive, looking-ahead manner. We thus may plan for change via the SWOT approach. That is, we assess our own STRENGTHS and WEAKNESSES and scan the environment for possible OPPORTUNITIES and THREATS. We then develop plans for change based on our SWOT survey.

Fourth, we may find it essential at times to prevail upon our boss to change, to accept a new policy, procedure, budget, staffing pattern, etc., that bears heavily on the success of our own area of responsibility. We thus have to use all our sophisticated skills of influence to effect that type of change.

Fifth, in all of the above activities we must secure the solid support of our staff to smoothly and enthusiastically execute the indicated changes. This means bringing about changes in staff attitudes and/or behaviors so that the shift from the old to the new proceeds without complaint or foot-dragging.

Sixth, we may be subject to change demands from our staff—more effective communication, more delegation, a greater sharing of the leadership role, more opportunities for training, growth, development, careers, etc. We also may be encouraged by our employees to adopt new policies, new goals, new systems, new procedures, even new products and/or services.

Looking at all of the above circumstances producing change, it is quite apparent that we do, indeed, have a heavy role to play in planning and implementing change.

SELF-ASSESSMENT AS TO YOUR CAPABILITY TO IMPLEMENT CHANGE

At this point in the chapter, it should prove helpful to you to obtain a reading on your own prowess (attitudes and actual or likely behaviors) as a change agent, i.e., your skill in dealing with situations that require the introduction and implementation of change. The quiz on page 580 should aid in this inquiry.

WHY RESISTANCE TO CHANGE?

If you want truly to understand something, try to change it.

—Kurt Lewin, pioneering social psychologist, founder of contemporary group dynamics and father of sensitivity training.

Misoneist (mi-se-ñe-ist)—one who has a hatred, fear, or intolerance of innovation or change.

In our highly dynamic culture one might assume that not only is change a fact of life, but that it is universally regarded as a fact of life and thus readily accepted. However, the reality is that change is all too often regarded with resentment, suspicion, fear, and anxiety. The likely result, then, is resistance to change. In more specific terms, change is likely to be resisted due to one or more of these types of feelings and perceptions:

Current comfort. If people feel that that what is, is OK—"We're doing all right now, aren't we? Why don't they leave well enough alone?"—there will be a negative reaction to attempts to undo the very comfortable status quo. Some may even feel that the forthcoming change is "change for the sake of change."

Skimpy information. If only small pieces of information are received about the change, doubt about its worthiness is certain to result. ("They're not telling us much about it. We need to know a lot more before it might make some sense.")

Ambiguity/uncertainty. Anticipate resistance if the purpose and/or impact of the proposed change is very cloudy. People naturally seek a high degree of predictability and certainty in their future. We may have some discontentment with what we now have. But at least we know what it is. An indeterminate future is scary, indeed.

So a good guide to adopt is this: Change isn't opposed/resisted because "the new order" will be worse than the ongoing one. Rather, the change is resisted because "what is" (the status quo) is understood and predictable whereas the new setup is not understood and hardly predictable.

Mixed messages. If the purveyors of change deliver messages perceived as inconsistent, illogical, incomplete, or unbelievable, acceptance of the change is not too likely.

Burdensome demands. People are likely to resist change if they perceive it to be burdensome and overwhelming. ("This looks like a lot of coolie labor to me. Why do they want us to do it the hard way?")

Long time frames. Change is more likely to be resisted if the process takes a longer rather than a shorter time. ("I don't know. Looks like we'll be at this two or three years before something will come of it, if then.")

Indefinite time frame. If the change seems to have no specified ending time (target date), resistance is likely. A totally loose time boundary does, indeed, provoke anxiety.

Attainability. The forthcoming change may be perceived as unattainable. So "why should we knock ourselves out, working at it?"

Control concerns. All of us need to feel that we are in charge of our destiny. We need to feel that we have the power to direct our lives as we best see fit. So if a change that comes our way is seen as arbitrary, inappropriate, harassing, ambiguous, or overwhelming, we inevitably feel that our world is caving in, that we have lost control.

Unfamiliarity. If people have rarely been exposed to or have only encountered one or two minor changes, it is understandable that their limited experience will cause difficulty in coping with more sweeping change.

Misunderstanding. Despite care in communicating the objective and possible impact of a change, there is always the possibility that its legitimate, lofty purpose may be perceived erroneously. ("I know they've explained it several times, but I still don't understand why they're doing it.")

Little or no involvement. People will respect and go along with a change if they had a role in it. Conversely, if they were merely on the outside looking in, rather than being an active player, they inevitably will resist the change. In general, the case for participation rests on this premise: It's hard for people to resist their own ideas.

"Surprise, surprise." Being suddenly subject to new conditions is a hard-to-cope-with irritant. (Visualize coming to work every day wondering if you will have a new boss, a new program or function to operate in, a new location for your desk, etc.)

Competence anxiety. Will the change require me to learn new procedures, master new skills, cope with hard-to-fathom problems? If so, will I be up to the new set of requirements? What if I don't make it? Anxieties of this sort will loom large if there is a threat to one's current repertoire of skills/abilities/knowledge.

Absence of rewards. When change looms on the horizon, people naturally ask: "What's in it for me?" So if the risks are great and the future is uncertain, anticipate resistance. People need to feel that they will end up as winners rather than losers when the dust settles.

Vested interests. If people (an individual or group) have a huge stake in the status quo (i.e., what is), we can expect an intense effort to hang on to what they have. This may be power, authority, responsibility for a pet project, budget, staff, space, etc. Change, in essence, is equated with loss or deprivation, hardly with opportunity.

Financial/economic impacts. If the contemplated change will clearly reduce skill levels or responsibility and thus lead to a possible reduction in pay or rank, we can anticipate negative reactions. ("You can bet that they won't pay me what I'm getting now if most of my authority goes to the field.")

Status reduction. The possible or certain loss of "ego-building perks" that go with our job—a large and/or private office, a secretary, attendance at the boss' staff meeting, attendance at the annual organizational meeting, field trips, and the like—will likely cause disenchantment.

Constant change. Change in minor ways or infrequent doses of it ordinarily are quite acceptable. But if people are put repeatedly in severely changed circumstances, acceptance/adjustment may be hard to come by. ("Stop this treadmill, I want to get off.")

Doubts by the boss. If the supervisor/manager (the change agent) is lukewarm about the change, subordinates can hardly be expected to rally behind it.

Credibility of the change champion. The change agent's job in the introduction of change is to provide reassurances that everything will be OK. ("In three months we'll be on top of things again.") But what if the purveyor of change is a person of low trust? How can people accept what they're told to believe?

Personal appeals. The weakest possible rationale for acceptance of a change is for the manager to ask for it on the basis of personal reasons. Change—the new order of things—is serious business. There thus must be a clear-cut, substantive reason for the change. "Do it for my sake" is the weakest reason one can offer anyone to accept totally new circumstances.

Disregard for group norms. Changes that seem counter to group/team standards, traditions, values, and expectations will meet resistance.

Missing "bridges." Change is most likely to be accepted if there are significant ties/bridges/connections to the old system. Conversely, if all of the old order is swept away without any link to the past, the natural reaction is that of dismay or anger.

Informal relationships. If the proposed change is likely to undo the social relationships people have held for a long time, we can anticipate negative reactions to it. After all, people spend half their waking hours with their associates. So if these relationships are to be abolished, resentment if very likely to rise.

Personal criticism. If the change is considered as a device "to straighten one out," it will be resisted. A proposed change, then, should be totally objective and related clearly to policies, programs, systems, procedures, product, etc., and not be directed at anyone personally.

Past experience. If people's prior experience with change has been traumatic, expect the new change to be perceived with doubt, suspicion, and possible hostility.

Mode of introduction. If the change is introduced or implemented in a way perceived as arbitrary, uncaring, too rapid, too far-reaching, ill-timed, etc., the change will most likely be resisted.

Personality factors. The "strong" personality can "roll with the punches" and accept change. For such persons, change is not perceived as a threat but as one of life's "inevitables." Conversely, others less secure in their makeup may have a low tolerance for change and thus regard it with fear, suspicion and/or resentment. ("They're always changing things just to make our jobs more difficult.")

Ideological issues. A person who has long advocated certain policies, management philosophies, or modes of operation will be upset if "the new order" changes everything he has long held near and dear to his heart.

Values and priorities. Related to the above, certain resistance is to be expected if a proposed or actual change is in conflict with an individual's or a group's values, beliefs, or priorities. So it's not that people are necessarily difficult, nasty, or stupid, they just see the world differently.

Rational resistance. Although it may be difficult for us as agents of change to admit, resistance to change may, indeed, be quite appropriate. Ill-conceived, inappropriate, or ill-timed change ventures certainly may merit employee opposition. For management it is a clear signal to return to the drawing board. Employee involvement should be tapped to develop a new and proper direction.

Obviously, every change effort is different and thus will be perceived differently. Factors of purpose, magnitude, frequency, rapidity, clarity, impacts, trust in the change agent, and so on will influence the likely degree of acceptance/resistance. No single attempt at change will trigger all of the numerous reasons for resistance cited above.

But if we were to make a somewhat global generalization concerning the most important bases for individual resistance to change, we would cite the viewpoint of behavioral scientist/management consultant Dr. W. Warner Burke (in "Managers Get a 'C' in Managing Change," *Training and Development,* May 1991), who has found in his experience and research that individual resistance stems from two conditions:

1. Loss of the known and tried—when certainty is exchanged for uncertainty, people necessarily spend a lot of effort to learn the new situation and to cope with initial frustration.
2. Loss of personal choice—people don't necessarily resist change but the *imposition* of change.

Hence the need for heavy and early participation in the change effort by those affected by it.

How Do People Resist Change?

Resistance to change may take a number of forms. Management consultants Bob Hunter and Mark LaLeike of Arthur Andersen and Company (in a presentation before the Potomac Chapter of the National Society for

Performance and Instruction, September 1987) classify them into two modes: *active* (fight) and *passive* (flight).

The active mechanisms are these:

- ☐ Attack directly
- ☐ Confront in meetings
- ☐ Send "killer" memos
- ☐ Use sneak attacks
- ☐ Stand on rules
- ☐ Ask for detailed plans, schedules
- ☐ Plan and organize a "resistance" movement

Anticipate, too, arguing, name calling, changing the subject, plus various other forms of emotionality.

The passive devices include the following:

- ☐ Cancel appointments (unavailability)
- ☐ Always present oneself as "too busy" (more unavailability)
- ☐ Maintain silence in meetings (withdrawal)
- ☐ Withhold critical information (polite sabotage)
- ☐ "Sign off" without discussion (withdrawal)
- ☐ Agree without commitment (lip service)

Anticipate, too, assorted excuses and promises, possibly in ambiguous language.

An added form of passive resistance is *denial,* to turn one's back on the change: "Hey, this doesn't affect me, does it?" Or: "Another bright idea from mahogany row. This, too, shall pass." If the proposed change turns out to be for real, the denier may embark on more active resistance—griping, tardiness, absenteeism, reduced quality or output, request for a transfer, possibly even departure to another organization.

Another writer categorizes resistance behavior into these four categories: *withdrawal, experiencing a loss of identity, feeling disoriented,* or *expressing negativity* (Gary Topchik in *Perspectives On . . .,* November–December 1993, adapted by *Training and Development,* January 1995). More specifically, management consultant Topchik suggests the following:

Withdrawal entails a loss of interest, initiative, energy and drive, maintenance of a low profile; silence (non-talking) about the change. **Your best action:** Draw the worker out to provide a talking out opportunity; provide assurances that it's OK to talk freely about the change and even to question it; do a lot of listening; and avoid being judgmental.

Loss of identity. This generally results from a job change. The past, when things were secure and stable, is very important to the person. Feelings encompass being stranded, hurt, frustrated, incompetent, possibly betrayed. **The result:** a strong reluctance to pick up new methods and make new associations. **Your best action:** Pose queries to highlight the particular emotion. Aid the worker to transfer acquired skills/knowledge/old system values to the new setup. Skip reasoning with the "injured" one, for it won't help at all.

Disorientation. These persons are experiencing confusion: Where do I fit in? Where am I going? What should I be doing? What is expected of me? There is a non-productive expenditure of energy plus a misdirection, for goals/priorities are unclear to these workers. Sad to relate, posing questions and seeking information do nothing to produce a healthy forward movement. The energy expended is simply to attain personal comfort, not to meet the new goals. **Your best action:** Provide information and direction, for that is their quest. Initially provide information in relation to the new vision, objectives, and goals. Then move from the big picture to the worker's particular goals, the new standards/expectations, and finally develop some joint plans.

Negativity. Behaviors include expression of anger, adopting the victim role, talking about it to anyone they can corner, and generally spreading their dissatisfaction with the new order. **Your best action:** Let people blow off their steam. Assure them it's OK to be upset. Once their anger is vented, the feelings of withdrawal, identity loss, or disorientation will most likely take over. So help them restore order by giving direction and setting priorities.

HOW DO PEOPLE COPE WITH CHANGE?

As indicated above, we can anticipate that change will often be perceived as a scam, as threatening, even as a dangerous phenomenon. Management consultants Cynthia D. Scott and Dennis T. Jaffee, in *Managing Organizational Change* (Los Altos, CA: Crisp Publications, 1989, reported in *The Pryor Report,* Vol. 10, No. 2A, 1994) suggest that when your organization under-

goes change, watch for the following four-stage sequence of employee reactions:

1. **Denial** (stage one). Initially people may not believe the change has occurred. So no reaction may be forthcoming at the outset. Production remains unchanged. But as the new reality sinks in and the change becomes real, a productivity loss may develop. **Significance:** Resistance is taking place. So the organization must respond to it.

Diagnostic key: Look for withdrawal or a focus on the past.

2. **Resistance** (stage two). Feelings of various sorts arise; e.g., self-doubt, anger, depression, anxiety, frustration, uncertainty. Anticipate reduced productivity, concern, negativity. Some may want to exit the outfit. **Possible remedies:** Let people express their anxieties and negativity. Organize group rituals, e.g., award ceremonies and celebration parties, to help employees share their experiences and thereby weather the storm.

Diagnostic key: Look for anger, blame, anxiety, depression, apathy. These clues represent the low point of the cycle before there is some upward movement toward acceptance.

3. **Exploration** (stage three). Anticipate that people's normal resilience will become operative. They begin to draw upon their internal resources and creativity to ascertain their new roles and responsibilities, and look toward their new future. People embark on a new adventure, bonding with their fellow pioneers.

Diagnostic key: Look for concern about details, possible confusion, new energy, helpful ideas, possible lack of focus.

4. **Commitment** (stage four). People are now ready to make solid long-range plans and to act on them. There is a willingness to re-create their mission, roles and expectations.

Diagnostic key: Real cooperation, improved focus, a healthy anticipation of the next challenge.

Note: Managing change would be relatively easy if all those affected by the change reacted in a like manner.

But sad to relate, change affects people differently. So people are likely to go through these stages at different speeds. Some may not go through the above stages at all, but will accept change enthusiastically at the outset. Others, conversely, may have a hard time "getting with it" for long periods of time. ("You know, way back before the change over we really had it good. But now . . .")

Another conceptualization re reaction to change is offered by management consultant Richard McKnight and management trainer Marilyn Thompson (in "Navigating Organizational Change," *Training and Development Journal,* December 1990). Their model, which they use in training employees to cope effectively in change situations such as in the case of mergers and acquisitions, depicts three responses:

The Victim

Despite the facts, victims see themselves as threatened by overwhelming, hostile situations with which they simply can't cope. They respond with an ineffective fight-or-flight mechanism. They typically are fatalistic. With great oversimplification they divide the world into good or bad, black or white, thereby shrinking their alternatives. Typically, they complain a lot, develop pessimistic outlooks and regard management's intentions in a cynical vein. In their passive or even frozen posture, they wait for the change to reach them and crush them.

The Survivor

Many people will go through the victim stage but quickly move on the the survivor stance. They tell themselves that they are at the mercy of unchangeable circumstances, events, forces. But they do believe they can live through it all (survive) if they can just hold on, tough it out or get competitive with colleagues—for gossip on the ongoing change, for available jobs, or for the good graces of their bosses. So, as the survivors see it, all these grasping and clinging behaviors are essential for self-protection as the change proceeds. The survivors have developed a (gloomy) scenario as to what is coming and they behave accordingly.

The Navigator

This mode or style is the effective one. Navigators face change with courage, they calm themselves and take a proactive rather than a reactive stance. This means they create a vision of a desired future, collect positive data relevant to it, and pursue it assertively. These types are excellent at personal stress management, which is developed due to a strong belief in their coping ability.

Note: The training designed and presented by McKnight and Thompson is intended to help people move from the stressful roles of victim and survivor to the more constructive and healthy navigator mode.

Figure 1, a conceptualization regarding response to change, sums up how people react/respond to a change.

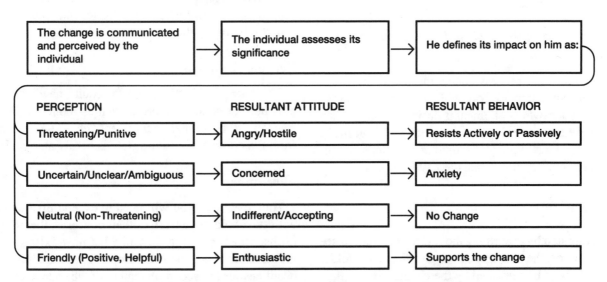

Figure 1. A conceptualization regarding response to change.

HOW TO INTRODUCE CHANGE SYSTEMATICALLY AND SUCCESSFULLY

If you only look at what is, you might never attain what could be.

—Author unknown

The management job consists largely of the management of change, if not of taking the lead in change.

—Peter Drucker, management authority, consultant, and author

Change can't be introduced successfully by hope, chance, magic, surprise, or smoke and mirrors. What it takes is careful, systematic, well-thought-out implementation. Management consultant Byron A. Stock offers this incisive six-step, reality-based approach (presented in "Leading Small-Scale Change," *Training and Development,* February 1993):

1. Assessment

Your first order of business is to make a critical analysis of the magnitude and difficulty of the change plus all the risks involved. You must ascertain the chances for success. Consider, then, these two factors:

The Number of Stakeholders Involved

Obviously the smaller the number, the easier your challenge will be.

The Complexity of the Process/Task/Operation to be Altered

The simpler the process and/or the fewer the tasks, the easier our change effort will be. Thus, a change involving your own department is easier to pull off than one involving several other departments. Similarly, establishing a new policy for summer vacations is simpler than computerizing a manual payroll operation.

2. Description

Start this step by describing the future you want to see as a result of the change. Also, list the stakeholder groups likely to be impacted by the change.

3. Current Factors Influencing the Possible Change

Your change efforts, says Stock, will succeed or fail depending on these critical six elements:

Dissatisfaction with the Current State

Successful change requires enough "pain" by the stakeholders, which emanates from the status quo (what now exists). The greater the pain, the greater the likelihood of real gain (change). So an early task, then, is to clarify the pain or dissatisfaction that exists at present.

Benefits from the "New Order"

Pain may exist, but the stakeholders are not likely to favor (and work for) a new scheme of things (the change) unless they see greater benefits on the horizon. This means working closely with the stakeholders to develop, establish, and articulate a rewarding, positive vision of the future state. This step answers the expected questions of "Why change?" and "What's in it for me?"

Individualized Benefits

Anticipate that different stakeholders will experience risk in differing forms and degrees. So each stakeholder must envision clearly how the change (the future state) will provide gains/benefits that are greater than the risks taken to bring the change about.

Sound Strategies/Action Steps

Stakeholders must feel that the route taken (steps, procedures, stages) will be workable, i.e., lead successfully to the new future scheme of things.

Rallying Resources

The change effort is likely to require new processes plus new or added resources such as money, added or specialized personnel, equipment, etc. The transition from the current to a future state is hardly automatic.

Time Frame

Anticipate that you will need to expend time to work with stakeholders to learn of their concerns, their degree of disenchantment (pain) with what now exists, and to garner their ideas about the hoped-for future state. Set deadlines for the accomplishment of the change carefully, for if it is too short (i.e., too close to today) the stakeholders may not see any possibility of success. Conversely, if it is too far out, they may not have the patience and stamina to see all the action steps through to a conclusion.

4. Taking Actions to Improve Conditions to Inaugurate Change

Accepting a program for change may not be an easy thing for the stakeholders to do. So your job is to work with them in several areas, says Stock, elevating current dissatisfaction, painting a promising picture of the future, stressing targeted benefits, pointing out the soundness of the proposed strategies/action steps, evaluating essential resources, and estimating properly the time stakeholders will have to program for the wanted change. Here are some specifics on these six tasks, per consultant Stock:

Elevating Dissatisfaction

If you encounter low dissatisfaction with existing conditions, amass *quantitative* data to clarify that there is, indeed, a sorry state of affairs; e.g., provide present statistics on accidents, production, order returns, employee turnover, etc. Also, gather qualitative data that bear on the situation, such as cumbersome procedures, inadequate reward systems, outdated equipment, etc.

Enhancing the Future

If the stakeholders hold only a hazy vision of the future, possess misconceptions about it, or are not fully satisfied with it as initially outlined, work with them so it can become more clear or more desirable. As appropriate, show them how the new order will, for example, improve/solidify relationships among individuals and groups. Remember, the stakeholders must rally to the proposed new future, be strongly in accord with it. Not all stakeholders will perceive it in the same detail, but they need to achieve consensus about its salient features.

Publicizing Potential Gains

Recognize that stakeholders may find it difficult to assess statements about the new future and the tangible benefits to be derived from it. So show the pluses/advantages via success stories, testimonials, site visits, and the like. Encourage other influential, verbal stakeholders to talk to the doubters.

Pursue the Correct Steps

You want the stakeholders to concur that the action steps you favor will certainly reach the hoped-for future state. If the stakeholders can suggest superior alternatives or amendments, by all means incorporate them in your plan. The wisest course of action is to consider strategies to implement the action steps in a number of stages.

Evaluate Required Resources

Be prepared to justify new costs with cost-effectiveness data. Point out instances where early payoffs are likely. If necessary, spread commitments over longer time periods. Work with stakeholders to eliminate unnecessary steps. Consider other resources to facilitate the change implementation.

Appraise Time Involved

Inform stakeholders of the time they will have to set aside to accomplish the change. Working with stakeholders, eliminate time-consuming steps wherever possible. Offer alternatives for greater commitment of resources, programmed for shorter time frames.

5. Appraising Your Readiness

In Step 3 above, per management consultant Byron A. Stock, we listed six change factors of concern to stakeholders that can increase/decrease the possibility of the desired change taking place: dissatisfaction with the status quo; perception of the future state; benefits from the change; perceptions regarding action steps; available resources; and time. Consider this helpful exercise: Respond aloud (assume you are talking to the stakeholders) to the following statements. They will assist you greatly in moving ahead. The statements are these:

☐ Spell out stakeholder dissatisfactions (pain).
☐ Outline the future state.
☐ Show how the change will affect work lives for the better.
☐ Outline action steps in relation to each stakeholder's personal interest.
☐ Show how you will tap stakeholders' ideas in the action steps.
☐ List major objections of stakeholders and respond to them.
☐ List and explain required resources for the change.

□ Explain time commitments needed to implement the change.

□ Highlight examples of a like change elsewhere that worked well.

Note: If you're shaky (not too confident) on the first seven statements, go back to the drawing board: Gather more data and query stakeholders further.

6. Act

We have no choice but to respond to the changes that have to be accomplished. This is the only route to a better future. We thus must work closely with the stakeholders concerned with the possible new future, to "liberate" them from the less-than-satisfactory status quo.

To do this we must allow the stakeholders to participate fully in the change effort, readying them gradually for the desired change. This is the only way they will buy into the action steps that lead to the change.

HOW TO STAY ON TOP OF (MANAGE) THE CHANGE PROCESS

There is one thing stronger than all the drives in the world—and that is an idea whose time is come.

—Victor Hugo (1802–1885), French poet, novelist, and dramatist (This quotation is the last entry in his diary).

There is nothing permanent except change.

—Heraclitus (circa 535 B.C.–circa 475 B.C.), Greek philosopher

In introducing change we have a number of options. We can do it by *fiat* or decree—"This is it." We can "play it loose" (laissez-faire) and let nature take its course. Or, as indicated above, we can do it on a planned and organized basis. The latter approach is essential and realistic if we are to prevent/overcome resistance to the change. These basic concepts, per behavioral scientist Dr. Gordon L. Lippitt in *Organizational Renewal* (Engelwood Cliffs, N.J.: Prentice Hall, 1982), should be followed:

Opt for Employee Involvement

The wise change agent wants to avoid lip service, foot-dragging, and other forms of resistance to an essential change. He thus strives for maximum participation in planning for the change. By involving people early on, understanding of and support for the change are more likely. As stated elsewhere in this volume, this all-important principle thereby becomes operative: *People support what they create.* Also, by talking things through, misunderstandings, doubts, and assorted anxieties are overcome.

Share Information Fully

People have a need to know the rationale for the change. They want to know the why of it plus its magnitude, its timing, its possible impact—positive or negative—on them. In the absence of full and honest information, mistrust is certain to arise. In the absence of trust, doubt, fear, and resentment will bedevil the implementation of the change.

Allow Airing of Concerns

Part of the process is to allow people to blow off steam. Listening to the ventilation of anxieties can provide useful data to the change agent. One can't allay fears if one doesn't know what they are. **Note:** Change is likely to be perceived as much more scary than it actually is.

Consider Established Group Norms/Habits

Obviously, people have developed a variety of rewarding interpersonal relationships—close-knit work teams, carpools, coffee and luncheon companions, and the like. A proposed change should take such factors into account to the extent practicable.

Introduce Only Vital Changes

People do have a limit as to how much change can be assimilated. Hence the need to key in on major or essential changes and avoiding change overload, which may arise by confronting people with trivial, minor, or too-frequent changes. One management writer uses the sponge as a metaphor to describe the effect of too many changes: People, like a sponge, can only absorb so much. So the advisory is to avoid operating "the change-of-the-month club" in your organization.

Look for Ways to Provide Motivational Opportunities

While initial reactions to change may entail doubt and even fear, added reflection may indicate that there are opportunities for new job challenge, including added personal growth and development.

A number of added helpful pointers for you, as a careful change agent, are offered by Walter D. St. John, educator and communication authority (in "Plain Speaking," *Personnel Journal,* June 1985). He advises that people need clear-cut data regarding these key changes that are likely to affect them:

☐ **Job impact:** How will my job be affected?

☐ **Goal clarity:** What are the actual goals of the proposed change?

☐ **Control:** Will the change(s) increase or reduce the control I have over my future?

☐ **Work demands:** Will I have to work harder?

☐ **New learning:** Will I need new or added training?

☐ **Possible problems:** What are the possible negatives of the change and what problems may arise?

☐ **Gains:** How and why is the change a plus or an improvement?

☐ **Success/non-success:** What will happen to us if the change bombs?

St. John also offers several helpful dos and don'ts:

☐ Change isn't easy, so anticipate an extended, tough job, and don't take possible resistance personally. (As you know, sophisticated and successful sales personnel expect a certain amount of rejection, but then go on from there.)

☐ Learn all you can about the process of change, and the strategies and possible problems.

☐ Rely on small groups as your best communication media.

☐ Avoid frightening statements such as "We have a radically new plan/policy/procedure that I'd like to launch a crash program for." Or: "This downsizing will give us that mean and lean stance we've been looking for."

☐ Don't turn off the group by criticizing its established standards. **A better tack:** Talk about *improvement.* Also, keep the change focus on the group, not on a single worker.

☐ Listen carefully to reactions to your change proposals. You can't navigate the riled waters successfully without feedback.

☐ Don't "pull rank" (using your power/status) to win support. Instead, rely on the power of the new idea.

☐ Be positive, but don't overwhelm people with hyper enthusiasm. Don't underestimate people's ability to discern phoniness.

☐ Stress advantages to the organization and the employees rather than to yourself.

It also helps to think in advance in terms of possible *losses* employees may experience—or fear they will experience—as a result of the change. Management consultant William Bridges (in "How to Manage Organizational Transition," *Training,* September 1985) suggests that these five be considered:

Identity loss: "Who am I since, for example, I no longer am a customer service representative or a member of the payroll office."

Control loss. I didn't ask for this and I don't need this. Are they forgetting that this is my life? And what will come after this?"

Meaning loss. "Why is this being done to me after all my years of dependable, loyal service?"

Belonging loss. "Look at all these new people we now have. I don't know a soul here, not even my boss."

Future loss. "I thought I had a future in this outfit. Now I'm at the bottom of the ladder and have to start all over."

When the change has be inaugurated and complaints from employees surface loudly, how do you respond? Management consultant Peter Yensen suggests ("Managing Before Change," *Training News,* June 1986) that you have these choices:

The "bully" role: "Look, I told you at the outset we were going to do this. And we did. I can tell you it's not going to go away. So forget the gripes and just get with it."

The "buddy" role: "Yes, it's rough on all of us. They probably didn't realize how terrible it would be. But we'll just have to make the best of it, won't we?"

The "better tomorrow" role: "I agree that it's rough on all of us right now. But in two or three weeks (or months) when we get the hang of it, we'll forget these startup problems. And once things are in high gear, we'll all enjoy the benefits of the change."

Key point: Alter the gripes and groans to cheers of encouragement by keeping the gains/benefits of the change in the forefront of all conversations about the change. This is certainly the time to stress the positives and thereby override the understandable uncertainties, fears and anxieties. ("Let's not throw in the towel. Hang in there. Things will work out, as we planned, soon.")

The author would add the following skill pointers to help you manage the introduction and transition through the change:

- [ ] When communicating about the need for the change, don't neglect to stress the consequences of *not* implementing the change.
- [ ] Phase in the new change programs gradually. People need to get adjusted to "the new." So,
- [ ] Consider the use of task forces to secure credibility/support/momentum for the forthcoming change. Or,
- [ ] Use pilot or trial runs, wherever practicable, prior to making the change final. Experimental runs can help to "debug" the change effort before the total change is implemented. Also, successful trial runs will provide solid evidence that the new approach is realistic and workable.
- [ ] Don't forget to regard the organization as a total system. So a change in one part, or even one individual's role in it, will have repercussions in other segments, too.
- [ ] Keep in touch with people while the plan is in its transitory stage. Use frequent meetings and rely heavily on "management by walking around" to sense how people are coping with the change. In the absence of follow-up, you may be communicating that the change isn't that important.
- [ ] Share information fully and candidly. If you hoard information, anticipate that rumor and the grapevine will take over. And the odds are that in the absence of information, people will imagine the worst and fill the grapevine with their own tidbits of gloom and doom. Psychologist Albert Ellis terms this phenomenon *catastrophizing* —that is, in the absence of contrary information, the worst is

assumed and people act as if their worrisome assumptions are legitimate, factual data.

- [ ] Support the change by enabling people to put it into effect. Forms of enablement include training; clear-cut assignment of responsibility; provision of needed resources including information; realistic time frames.
- [ ] Locate people who are progressing toward the new goal or have already reached it. Use them as role models to tout their success.
- [ ] Don't overlook your customers. Change not only impacts on those inside the outfit (the employees), but also on those on the outside who may be surprised, inconvenienced, or frustrated in big or small ways.
- [ ] When the change effort proves to be a success experience, celebrate its success. Reward people for their patience, support, and cooperation.
- [ ] Resist the temptation to belittle or bad-mouth the past. After all, people undoubtedly identified strongly with history, the old ways certainly being part of them. **A better tack:** Treat the past with honor and respect, and allow opportunities for staff to express sadness and grief for the loss. Dutiful deference to the old will pave the way for appreciation and anticipation for the new.
- [ ] Make certain that mechanisms are in place to assess the effectiveness of the new way of doing things. Communicate the evaluation of results as a device to solidify support for the change. If things are working out as promised, the doubters and fence-straddlers will be enabled (psychologically/emotionally) to switch their old allegiances to "the new order."

CHANGE AND LEADERSHIP STYLE

All of us, as managers, have a distinct leadership style. Organizational psychologist Dr. Hank Karp suggests that our unique style is composed of a combination of these four commonly observed styles: *autocratic, participative, supportive,* and *laissez-faire* ("Understanding Change from the Gestalt Perspective," *The 1995 Annual, Vol. 1, Training,* San Diego: Pfeiffer and Co., 1995). Thus, the perceptive manager as change agent will employ a particular style as circumstances best indicate. Examples of when to use each style follow.

Autocratic (Command/Directive Style)

Telling the team/group/unit that "This is it" is best used when

(a) the group has no reason to oppose the change, or
(b) when the leader feels that discussion/negotiation is inappropriate (e.g., when it is essential to save time), or
(c) when the change comes from above or from an outside source.

An example of (a) above might be a change in the location of the bins to salvage waste paper. An example of (b) might be a demand for special packaging and delivery by a large, important, long-standing customer. When a (c) type change occurs, e.g., a change in the hours to service customers, the best course of action is to let everyone "ventilate" their displeasure with the directed change, and then get on with the job and the new requirement.

Participative (Involvement/"Join In")

This style is best used when

(a) input from the group is essential to stimulate thinking about the best way to implement the change or
(b) when resistance is likely and acceptance is wanted.

An example of (a): a marketing unit is ready to participate in a trade show exhibit for the first time.

An example of (b): various changes affect the job/employment situation such as maintaining new/added records, submitting extra reports, changing the vacation schedule, altering the coffee break plan now in vogue, developing new safety rules, etc.

Supportive (Emphatic/Facilitative)

In this mode/style, the leader helps the staff, typically a new group, develop a process to deal with the forthcoming change. In this scenario the group has the skills and interest to deal with the change, but the trust levels and interpersonal relationships among group members are low. So the leader serves as a facilitator, ensuring that all have a chance to be heard, that conflict is handled so that group discussion is not impeded, and that the group atmosphere is a reasonably safe and cooperative one.

Laissez-faire

Here the leader leaves the group to its own devices so that it can independently use its own high-level, sophisticated interpersonal skills/resources/insights. The leader wisely recognizes that he has no special expertise to offer the group, so he adopts a "hands-off" policy. **Example:** A production team is asked to meet a special demand of an important customer, and the team has the skill, know-how, and motivation to implement the change.

WHEN CHANGE EFFORTS DISAPPOINT

Not all attempts at change will prove successful. But a failure can prove to be of positive value. Management professor Dr. Rita McGrath studied 18 corporate ventures of a large U.S. bank and concluded that sweeping failures under the rug to avoid looking like a loser wastes an enormous resource. As reported in "Make Your Failures Work for You," *Harvard Business Review,* November–December 1993, McGrath found four ways disappointing results can serve as catalysts to aid in securing successful innovation.

1. Re-evaluation

McGrath states that "People don't change unless they get bad news. By showing that the old routines aren't working, disappointments can gain legitimacy for new ways of doing things." So a disappointment can force reassessment of the status quo.

2. Attention Getting

If a stalled project was a result of lack of needed resources, the disappointment can serve to prod senior management to provide added support. Distress signals can serve as a spur to turn the situation around.

3. Motivation

A disappointment can encourage the advocates of an idea to rally to prove its worth. So a setback can prove to be a helpful invigorator for the change proponents.

4. Symbols

If an organization stays solidly with a venture that is doing poorly, it accomplishes two things:

- ☐ It shows its ability to take a beating, thus becoming a symbol that can discourage competitors from entering the field, and
- ☐ Internally, it serves as a strong symbol of management's commitment to stay with its innovators.

So McGrath sums up her concept of capitalizing on current failures thusly: "You've already paid for the disappointment; you might as well use it."

And Gerald C. Meyers, the former chairman of American Motors, sees failure in these terms (quoted in "How to Manage Change [It Won't Be Painless]" *Business Month,* September 1989):

One of the penalties for living in an uncertain world is occasional failure. The issue is, can you tolerate losing once in a while? If you can't, don't play. Failure is a part of progress. Failure is a part of testing limits. Failure is a part of creativity. It's going to be messy. Capitalism is messy. Birth is messy.

KEY CONCEPTS: SOME PRINCIPLES OF CHANGE TO LIVE BY

There is nothing more difficult to take in hand, more perilous to conduct, or more uncertain in its success, than to take the lead in the introduction of a new order of things.

—Niccolo Machiavelli (1469-1527), Italian statesman and political philosopher, in *The Prince* (1532), published five years after his death

Try not to become a man of success, but try to become a man of value.

—Albert Einstein (1879–1955), American (German born) theoretical physicist and winner of Nobel Prize in Physics (1921)

Every organization must prepare for the abandonment of everything it does.

—Management guru Peter Drucker (quoted in *Washington Business Journal,* September 9–15, 1994)

I have a colleague who quips that if you or I were to ask five "experts" on change to list their single most important change principle, you'd probably get six answers. Why? Because, he says with a smile, one would undoubtedly change his mind! Nevertheless, let me advance some principles—ideas or concepts, not necessarily iron-clad rules—that seem to make a lot of sense as guides for any manager who wishes to deal with change effectively:

- ☐ To succeed as an agent of change, think in terms of "friends" and "foes." Your most horrific foe? Previous victories/successes/accomplishments. Why? Because it will encourage you to (smugly) rest on your laurels, to let the dead hand of the past keep you from looking for new approaches, new mountains to conquer. Also, forget about longing "for the good old days" or brooding about "what could have been."

And your most worthy friend? Change itself. Why? Because this is where the new challenges and opportunities lie. So don't complacently ask yourself "What have I done well lately?", but introspectively ask "What am I going to do for myself (my unit, my function, my operation) in the on-rushing future that will have real payoffs?" Recognize that yesterday's strengths are likely to be today's weaknesses.

- ☐ In connection with the above advisories, don't fall victim to clichés in the culture that inhibit healthy attitudes toward change. **Examples:** "Don't rock the boat," "Don't mess with success," and "If it ain't broke, don't fix it." Also, don't succumb to the "NIH" factor, that is, to shun an opportunity because it was "Not Invented Here."
- ☐ Change may require a new humility, an admission that prior strategies/behaviors were inadequate. Thus, the Hechinger hardware chain in the Washington, D.C., area, a traditional, somewhat conservative home-grown company, had to reshape itself in this decade to meet competition from national chains such as Home Depot and Lowe's. One top Hechinger official candidly said, "We definitely started out late and we should have moved more quickly. We believed in our own PR for a little too long and did not look at the industry or ask who we were or where we were going." The president of the firm stated that "We are changing from being sales-driven to being customer-driven. We used to stock the store to our convenience, not the customers'" (reported in *Washington Business,* March 29, 1993).

I also like the quote by a VP of Xerox: "Benchmarking is nothing more than admitting that someone else is capable of doing something better than you" (quoted in *Personal Selling Power,* October 1992).

☐ In today's world, you have to build the concept of change into the very fiber of your organization. This means that you and your staff have to seek it out, salute it, and live by it. Change is not something you do only when the outfit is in trouble. Rather, change is the way you control your future. **The alternative?** Let the rest of the world pass you by.

☐ Think constantly in terms of making worthwhile changes, but don't make them as fast as you think of them. In other words, your team has to digest what it took in before it can consume more of it.

☐ You certainly want the latest and the newest, whether it's a new product, service, system, procedure, or management idea. But it has to make sense before you launch the change in terms of your own organization's standards for high quality, customer service, and general direction/character/style of what it does and is capable of doing. So don't jump aboard every bandwagon that drives by, but do pay serious attention to them.

☐ When introducing change think in terms of **influence,** your *personal* power, as opposed to **authority,** your *position* power. The former will more likely lead to commitment and cooperation. The latter will run the risk of engendering resentment, resistance, even retaliation. A coercive change may have the merit of speed, but it is less likely to produce real acceptance and be self-sustaining.

☐ Visualize, then, long-term as opposed to only immediate or short-term gains in productivity. Sure, pressure and shaking things up can garner prompt results, but what if there are negative reactions over time? Anxiety, frustration, resentment, and hostility can result in increased errors, waste, scrap, rejects, returns, absenteeism, turnover, theft, and all the other indices of an unwanted decline in productivity.

☐ Your own behavior can serve as a model for or against change. If you resist change your bosses favor or look askance at new ideas proposed by staff, your people will correctly see lip service rather than a true belief in the importance of change. One practical test to gauge your staffers' perception of you as a positive force for change is to tally the number of change proposals/ideas/recommendations that come to you each month. Are they few or many? Are they offered timidly or vigorously? Are they bold or merely "nibbling at the edges?" If change suggestions are rare and/or very cautious, it would seem that you have a lot of work to do to turn your image as a change agent around, for people sense that it is wise to "play it safe" rather than to innovate.

☐ Don't disguise or sugar-coat changes that must be made. Deception can only produce bitterness, for people can very readily detect a "con job." Their natural reaction: "Why doesn't he level with us? Doesn't he trust us to do what has to be done?" A sensible precept to adopt is that one can't be an effective change agent if truth-telling is not part of the change repertoire.

☐ Acceptance of change by staff will be facilitated by an atmosphere/climate/culture that respects and demands change. Actually, today's newer workforce favors a workplace that is on top of things, moves with or is ahead of the times, is flexible and innovative and is a fun place in which to work. It is axiomatic that positive change provides a stimulant to most people.

☐ One way to show your interest in and support for change is to encourage your people to attend courses, seminars, workshops, etc., that enable them to return with new approaches, concepts, ideas, techniques, and enthusiasm. Training has the potential to shake up existing mindsets. Conversely, keeping people in isolation, insulated from new or other thinking is a perfect recipe for retention of the status quo.

☐ You can also show your change orientation by how you conduct meetings. Consider doing these things: rotate responsibility for developing distribution of the agenda; rotate the chairperson role (where is it written that only the boss must conduct all meetings?); insist that everyone take a different seating location at each meeting; hold meetings in different locations besides your office (in other staffer's offices, in the conference room, in the cafeteria, at a nearby restaurant, possibly outdoors, etc.).

☐ When introducing change, think in *systems terms.* That is to say, a change of any sort—be it equipment, scheduling, budget, organization, key appointments or promotions—may well impact other parts of the organization or operation. So don't conceive of a change as something that occurs in isolation. Rather, anticipate that it may have ramifications—ripple effects or even shock waves—elsewhere or even throughout the total organization. Organizational psychologist Dr. Saul Eisen (in "Redesigning Human Systems—A Holistic-Humanistic Framework," in *AHP Perspective,* Newsletter of Association for Humanistic Psychology, November/December 1994) points out that *simple* changes can take place at one system level, impacting minimally, if at all, on other levels. *Moderate* change is likely to impact other levels, requiring them to adjust appropriately. *Fundamental* change impacts all levels, its reverberations creating crises and pressures to find new ways of functioning.

☐ Time and timing are key tools in introducing change. In respect to *time,* the admonition of "make haste slowly" is sound advice. People need time to internalize (digest) the new, be it policy, procedure, process, product, technology, or whatever. Integrating or incorporating a change into the existing value system takes time. Regarding *timing,* it makes good sense to avoid introducing a change when a prior one has not yet become totally part of the ongoing operation. In general, you don't want to introduce too much, too fast, too soon.

☐ When contemplating the introduction of a major change, think of the process as you would a mammoth ocean liner. You don't turn it around on a dime—it takes time, often a lot of it.

☐ On the other hand, you should ordinarily strive to achieve specific, measurable operational outcomes within a short time frame, say a few months. You build on what works and abandon what does not. By achieving quick successes you develop appropriate skills and garner support for future changes from staff. So take that somewhat "grand," long-term vision and convert it into workable, short-term goals.

☐ Anticipate that you are very likely to overestimate how well people understand and support the new change/project. Don't let your own vision of and enthusiasm for the change blind you to the fact that you can't take their stated concurrence (lip service?) for granted. Hence the need for their fullest possible involvement in the change effort, communication to them about the new goals, and securing of feedback about their perceptions of what they see, believe, and are willing to commit to.

☐ Anticipate and accept resistance because it is a natural, inevitable part of the change phenomenon/ process. So develop and apply your workable change agent skills to treat the resistance. Dealing with (working through) the resistance is the more likely part of wisdom, as opposed to getting frustrated by it with possible attempts to squelch it.

☐ When introducing change, think of non-threatening ways to do so, such as an experiment or offering people options. These types of devices help people avoid feeling "This is it," that the boss has rigidly decided there's only one way to go.

☐ Stay on top of a change by securing feedback about its actual operation. Successful implementation in the real world may require debugging, alteration, adaptation, or even abandonment in whole or in part. It is unrealistic to presume that a change can be so perfectly conceived and introduced that it requires little or no monitoring as to its success or impacts elsewhere in the organization.

☐ Change is too important and potentially complex to let it be a one-man band kind of thing. The wise change agent will involve the team in all aspects of the change process—conceptualization/visioning, depicting the desired outcome, implementation, monitoring progress, assessing actual end results/outcomes, and making adjustments/fine tuning as indicated.

☐ Move quickly at the outset to separate the change idea from yourself and move to make it group property.

☐ Use the team to develop support for the change idea, should there be any foot-dragging. Let the group put the pressure on the doubting Thomases and the reluctant dragons. Why do all the "heavy lifting" yourself?

☐ Planning/working carefully with staff for change, in all its phases, takes time. But as one witty observer put it, "If you don't have time to plan to *prevent* a nasty problem, how will you find time to do the necessary cleanup when the stuff hits the fan?"

☐ Recognize, too, that not all changes bring intended results or are for the better. Anticipate that "The Law of Unintended Consequences" may dominate your change effort. **Example:** Automated teller machines (ATMs) were supposed to reduce cost and thus make more money for the banks. But a Florida State University study (John M. Berry, "ATMs: The Machines Are Automated, But Are the Profits?", *The Washington Post*, June 2, 1994) found that the convenience of the ATM encouraged more transactions. Depositors used the machines twice as often as they formerly used a banking office. So while the per transaction cost at the machine equaled about half the cost of a teller transaction, depositors increased their transactions leaving total costs unchanged or slightly higher.

☐ Recognize that some people may experience losses or setbacks as a result of a change. Do everything possible to help them experience soft rather than harsh landings. People have a need to maintain their self-esteem: Regard it as your job to help them maintain and enhance it.

☐ Don't let the uncertainty of a change allow you to move into total inaction—paralysis by analysis:

Story: An invitee to a meeting, conducted by an important outside organization, engaged in heavy soul-searching concerning his proper arrival time. The would-be participant feared that if he showed up early, he would be regarded as *anxious*. If he arrived late, he might be perceived as *hostile*. And if he came on time, he would be classified as *compulsive*. So he didn't attend at all!

☐ In sum, seek to master change rather than let it control you. Presenting a positive vision of the new future; planning carefully for it; creating an open, free-wheeling climate that involves your staff fully; taking risks, stressing likely benefits initially and frequently thereafter; showing confidence in people's ability to adjust to the change; and securing feedback about the change while in process are skill factors you should employ to manage change successfully.

And the Bottom Line: If you're not thinking about the need to change things or to shake things up now and again, you run the big risk of being left far behind.

CHANGE: OTHER ASPECTS ELSEWHERE IN THIS TEXT

Although this chapter presents a systematic overview of the leadership skill area of introducing and managing change, other chapters also have addressed various aspects of it. Specifically:

☐ Diagnosing the forces at work in a given problem situation before embarking on a change strategy; that is, considering whether to increase the driving forces, to remove or weaken the restraining forces, or possibly to do both. See Chapter 10, What Managers Get Paid For: Problem Solving and Decision Making, Step 2: Gathering Information About the Problem, Problem Diagnosis "Using Force Field Analysis."

☐ Changing/altering the situation as opposed to working on the person(s) via training, coaching, or counseling to bring about a change in behavior. See Chapter 10, What Managers Get Paid For: Problem Solving and Decision Making, Step 5: Choosing (Deciding) Among Alternatives, Changing the Situation for Better Solutions.

☐ Setting high expectations can bring about a change in behavior. See Chapter 4, The Manager as a Motivator, "The Pygmalion Effect: The Power of Expectations."

☐ Bringing about change in behavior/performance through behavior modification techniques such as the use of positive reinforcers, prompting and shaping. See Chapter 4, The Manager as a Motivator.

PLANNING FOR A CHANGE EFFORT: USING A GUIDESHEET TO PLAN AND INTRODUCE A CHANGE

One of the great errors organizations make is shutting down what is a natural, life-enhancing process— chaos. We are terrified of chaos. As a manager, it signals failure. But if you move out of control and into an appreciation of natural order, you understand that the only way a system changes is when it is far from equilibrium, when it moves from the "quiet" we treasure and is confronted with the choice to die or reorganize. And you can't reorganize to a higher level unless you risk the perils of the path through chaos.

—Margaret Wheatley, a management consultant and author of *Leadership and the New Science: Learning About Organization from an Orderly Universe* (San Francisco: Berrett-Koehler, 1993), quoted in *Total Quality*, November 1994, p. 7)

Now that you have come to the end of this chapter, it should be apparent that introducing change successfully is not an easy thing to accomplish. Pitfalls may exist for you at each step of the way. However, with adequate analysis and planning, you can prevent things from going awry. The worksheet on page 583 can assist you in the successful planning and implementation of a change.

EXERCISES, PROBLEMS AND QUESTIONS FOR DISCUSSION

1. One way to begin a session on change is to ask the total group to respond (free associate) to this question: "When you think about change, what thoughts/ feelings come to mind?"

   Enter responses on flipchart.

   Then enter a P (Positive Reaction) or an N (Negative Reaction) after each item on the flipchart. Note whether there is a positive (opportunity) or a negative (disaster; gloom and doom) pattern. Discuss with the participant group the significance of the data.

2. A possible follow-up to question 1 above is to ask participants to form pairs and discuss the following question: What change are you undergoing in your personal or professional lives? Are they planned or unplanned? Minor or major? Satisfying or anxiety/stress producing?

   Then enter responses from pairs in the table below. (Use tick marks: 7H/ ///).

	Number
Planned	
Unplanned	
Major	
Minor	
Satisfying	
Stress/anxiety	

Discuss the above table with the group as to possible patterns.

3. **Small group discussion question**

   In small groups assign this task: How are you experiencing change at home, at work, in the community, in relationships? Discuss. We then will ask you to report back to the total group any generalizations, conclusions, patterns that your team can offer.

   Note: This question might serve as an alternate to 1, above.

4. **Exercise: Resistance to change**

   Create a fun-type competition by breaking down your total group into teams of 3 or 4 participants. **Task:** Develop a list of as many reasons as you can for resistance to change. The team that comes up with the most reasons gets this prize (you decide). Have the teams list their reasons on a large flipchart sheet, using felt markers, and then post their big sheets on the wall. Each team then presents its reasons to the total group.

   The discussion leader/trainer then tallies each sheet to select the winner.

5. **Small group discussion question**

   Ask participants in small groups to come up with different styles/attitudes managers might adopt in respect to change. (**Examples:** the ostrich; the saboteur; the enthusiast; the skeptic; the advocate.)

   Secure reports from the groups and discuss.

6. **Exercise:** On the scale below, have participants in small groups rate their key staffers regarding their attitudes toward change. Have them enter (position) their staffers' names on the rating scale to indicate their general attitudes toward change.

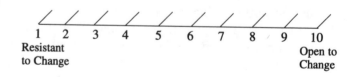

| 1 | 2 | 3 | 4 | 5 | 6 | 7 | 8 | 9 | 10 |

Resistant to Change   Open to Change

Then ask them to think of strategies which might be used to move "the reluctant dragons" from the left side of the scale to the right.

Secure reports from the teams regarding learnings from the activity.

7. **Small group discussion question.** Assume you are president of the New Age Washing Machine Corporation. Assume you wanted to introduce a change. Assume further that you wished to totally foul up the change, to ensure failure. What might you do?

Have the teams enter their ideas on flipchart paper. Secure reports from the teams, with their flipcharts posted on the wall. Ask: What does this exercise tell us?

8. **Exercise: Introducing a change to your staff.**
Procedure: Working individually, ask participants to think of a change they would like to introduce. (If a "real" one cannot be thought of, have them think of a likely one or an imaginary one).

Then ask them to consider how the change would be communicated, that is, how it would be stated or described. Ask: Would you anticipate objections? If so, how would you deal with them? What motivational approach/strategy might be used to garner staff support?

Then assign participants to small groups to share what they accomplished. Conclude the exercise by securing reports from each team as to what was learned about introducing change.

9. **Exercise: Force Field Analysis**
a) Ask each participant to develop force field analysis regarding a change they tried to introduce. They are to show forces at work for the change (driving forces) and the forces against it (restraining forces).
b) Or alternately, have them select an area of change they *wish* to accomplish.

In either case have them use the Force Field Analysis diagram. Then have them discuss their work in pairs. Secure reports from several pairs as to learnings from this exercise.

10. **Small group activity**
Recall a recent change you (or you and your staff) experienced.

Question 1: Was it an elevating, enriching, rewarding experience, or was it painful, punitive, confusing, frustrating? Or did it not engender any particular feeling, positive or negative?

Question 2: If the change effort was more harassing than exhilarating, what could have been done to make it a higher-level experience?

Force Field Analysis

Guide Sheet for Force Field Analysis

I (we, the work team) WANT TO ACCOMPLISH THIS CHANGE (improvement, new level, goal, result, etc.):

Driving Forces

Restraining Forces

11. Exercise: Feelings About Change

Procedure: Ask participants to draw a rectangle like the one below.

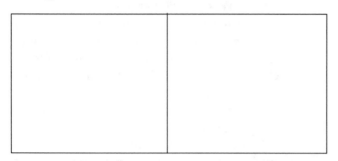

Then ask them to think of a recent change experience they encountered. On the left half of the rectangle have them depict graphically (draw) how the person, persons, or groups affected by the change seemed to respond/react. On the right side of the rectangle describe in a graphic or illustrative way your own feelings about the event.

Assign participants to trios and have them share their drawings. Secure comments from the trios (as many as time allows) about learnings from the exercise.

12. Exercise: Introducing Change

Provide the assignments below to two groups (or to two sets of groups):

(a) Recall a recent change you and your staff were asked by higher authority or your boss to implement. What were your feelings about it? Was it easy to do? Difficult? Traumatic? Or what? Why?

(b) Recall a recent change you introduced. Was it readily accepted or was there resistance? If it was well accepted, why? Did you take any actions that facilitated acceptance? If so, what were they? If there was resistance, what were the negative factors/forces at work? Were you able to overcome them? If so, how?

Secure reports from the (a) and (b) groups. Was it easier, harder, or the same to introduce change type (a) vs. change type (b)?

13. Exercise: "Accomplishing Change"

Objective: to point out the difficulty of change.

Group size: small or large—the interaction takes place in pairs, both partners standing up.

Source of exercise: presented to an audience of several hundred people by management consultant Ken Blanchard at the 41st National Conference of the American Society for Training and Development at Anaheim, CA (1985).

Procedures: Instruct your participants to pick a partner. Then ask them to observe each other without speaking, for one minute. The partners then are to turn their backs on one another and think about 5 things they would like to change about themselves.

When both partners are ready, have them turn around again and tell what changes each noticed in the other.

Now have them turn back to back again and this time ask them to change 10 more things about themselves.

Then have them turn around and each tells the other what was seen.

Processing: The exercise points out how hard it is to change. Blanchard points out that most people, when trying to choose five things to change about themselves, began to think about taking things away. People have a natural reaction to associate change with loss. Most people think they have only limited resources for this exercise, but people who used their imaginations added instead of taking things away.

14. How important is it for a manager to be skilled in introducing/managing change? Why?

15. In transitional periods, i.e., moving into a change situation, what might you, as a manager, do to ease/reduce stress?

16. Discuss the degree of difficulty involved in changing knowledge, attitudes, individual behavior, team behavior, and organizational behavior?

17. Comment on the significance/value of the use of field testing a change on a *small scale* and/or conducting one or several *pilot runs* before formally introducing a change.

18. In introducing change, how important is it to have developed and communicated a vision of the future—the desired state? Why?

19. How essential is it to establish a reward system to create or maintain desired changes in behavior?

20. Acme Publishing Company has a longstanding tradition of holding a lavish Christmas party for all

employees in a lush downtown hotel. A new CEO enters on duty around Labor Day. Cost cutting becomes an early program of the CEO, and the annual Christmas party, sad to relate, is eliminated.

(a) Discuss possible employee reactions and the wisdom of this action.

(b) What might the CEO do to accomplish this change without a possible boomerang effect?

Note: This problem may be presented to the total group or small groups for discussion.

My Skill in Introducing Change—A Self-Test

Please respond (via checkmarks) as candidly as you can to the 20 quiz items below. Provide a "yes," "no," or "sometimes" response. "No" means rarely or not at at all. "Yes" means means most of the time or always. "Sometimes" means occasionally or infrequently.

Quiz Items	Yes	No	Sometimes
1. Do I assume that a highly desirable change will be readily accepted by those affected by it?			
2. Do I consider that there may be various kinds of resistance to the proposed change?			
3. Do I seek out in advance of introducing a change reasons for possible resistance to the change effort?			
4. Do I assume that all (or nearly all) recipients of the change will react to it in the same way?			
5. Do I ask my staff for support for the change on the basis of a personal support for me?			
6. Do I consider ways of gaining acceptance for the change via survey data, pilot runs, special study groups, benchmarking, etc.?			
7. Do I seek to involve fully those affected by the change so that the change effort is joint or common property rather than mine alone?			
8. Do I approach those affected by the change with the kind of data that will enable them to see "what's in it for us?"			
9. Do I try to win over informal leaders to the change idea to help pave the way for acceptance by the total group?			
10. Do I seek out individual (one person at a time) as opposed to total group (team) support for the change?			
11. Is my relationship with those affected by the change based on a high degree of trust, openness, closeness, and mutual respect?			
12. Do I assume that it is of little importance whether the proposed change may alter well-established informal, social/interpersonal relationships?			
13. If the change is adequately radical and thus has a high potential to be perceived as traumatic, is attention paid to people's need for "support systems" to aid in adjustment to the change?			
14. Where opposition to the change exists, do I give people a chance to "talk out" their anxieties, concerns, fears, resentments, possible misconceptions?			
15. Do I release information about a change in a complete and candid way so that surprise, rumor and hostility are minimized?			
16. If the change involves serious cost, have I budgeted adequately for it?			
17. If the change itself (goal/purpose) is acceptable, do I assume that the means of implementation is of secondary importance?			
18. Again, if the goal is "right," do I assume that the speed of implementation—that is, too fast or too slow—is of secondary importance?			
19. As a step in implementation, do I try to phase out gradually "the old" and ease in "the new"?			
20. Is the plan for change so comprehensive and complete that adjustments need not be made to it once the plan is implemented?			

Scoring

Point values for each of the 20 responses in the quiz are as follows:			
	Yes	**No**	**Sometimes**
1.	0	3	0
2.	3	0	1
3.	3	0	1
4.	0	3	0
5.	0	3	0
6.	3	0	1
7.	3	0	1
8.	3	0	1
9.	0	3	0
10.	3	0	1
11.	3	0	1
12.	0	3	0
13.	3	0	0
14.	3	0	1
15.	3	0	1
16.	3	0	0
17.	0	3	0
18.	0	3	0
19.	3	0	1
20.	0	3	0

Using the above table, enter your point score for each test item in the matrix below. Then tally the points you have received in all three columns.

(*continued on next page*)

	Yes	No	Sometimes
1.			
2.			
3.			
4.			
5.			
6.			
7.			
8.			
9.			
10.			
11.			
12.			
13.			
14.			
15.			
16.			
17.			
18.			
19.			
20.			

TOTALS

My total number of points for all three columns is _____.

Interpretation of Your Score

50–60 points.	Go to the head of the class. Your understanding of the change process should help make you an effective change agent.
40–49 points.	You are on the right track, but have some distance to go. Further reflection on the change process should help to build upon the understandings you already possess.
39 points and below.	Be careful. Your efforts at introducing change may well backfire. Further study of the dynamics of the change process appears to be indicated.

Note regarding your scoring:

1. Be advised that your score is only a general indicator as to how you perceive the change process. More important than the score, are the twin activities of *introspection* (an inward look at one's beliefs/attitudes/values/ perceptions) and *reflection* (an attempt to make meaning of what one has learned in introspection). For maximum value the data (score) and the quiz items should be shared and discussed with colleagues and/or possibly one's boss and the work team.

2. It might also be helpful to you to ask your work team members to rate you on the quiz. Their perceptions of you as a change agent should have significant educational value for you.

   In any case, armed with the quiz data, your continued reading in this chapter should serve to strengthen your interest, understanding, and skill in implementing change.

Guide Sheet to Plan and Introduce a Change

1. Nature of change project/program/effort.

Describe the change you believe is required. Also indicate when the change should be initiated/introduced and when it should be fully implemented.

_____

_____

_____

2. Impetus for the change effort.

List the factors that have produced the need for the change.

_____

_____

_____

_____

3. Future outcome.

What will "the world" look like after the change has been introduced?

_____

_____

_____

_____

4. What forces in the situation are now driving/encouraging/supporting the possible change?

_____

_____

_____

_____

5. What forces in the situation now are discouraging/restraining/limiting the possible change?

_____

_____

_____

_____

(continued on next page)

6. In respect to the restraining forces or barriers to change that you have described above, what might be done to remove or reduce/weaken them?

Restraining Forces (List)	Strategy to remove/weaken/reduce them
A. _____	A. _____
B. _____	B. _____
C. _____	C. _____
D. _____	D. _____
E. _____	E. _____
F. _____	F. _____

7. In respect to the positive forces listed in 4 above, what might be done to enhance or strengthen them?

Encouraging Forces (List)	Strategy to remove/weaken/reduce them
A. _____	A. _____
B. _____	B. _____
C. _____	C. _____
D. _____	D. _____
E. _____	E. _____
F. _____	F. _____

8. Who are the stakeholders (critically concerned parties) in the proposed change?

A. _____	E. _____
B. _____	F. _____
C. _____	G. _____
D. _____	H. _____

Now rate the degree of change readiness and support each stakeholder represents on a 10-point scale, 1 meaning totally uncommitted/disinterested, 10 meaning totally committed/enthused/supportive. Enter the numerical rating after each stakeholder listed above.

_____	_____
_____	_____
_____	_____
_____	_____

(continued on next page)

9. List the stakeholders with the lowest ratings and indicate the strategy you have in mind to get their support/commitment.

Stakeholder	Strategy
A.	A.
B.	B.
C.	C.
D.	D.
E.	E.
F.	F.

10. Resources:

A. What are the resources essential to accomplish the change successfully? (List in column a. below)

a. Resources	b. Availability	c. Strategy to secure/strengthen/increase availability
1.		
2.		
3.		
4.		
5.		
6.		
7.		

B. Rate (in column b., above) the availability/adequacy of each resource listed above on a 10-point scale:
   1 = highly scarce or inadequate; 10 = totally available or plentiful
C. For resources in short supply, indicate (in column c., above) your strategy to increase their availability.

11. Based on the above analysis, what are the risks involved in the change effort?

_____

_____

_____

_____

_____

(continued on next page)

12. What procedures/strategies will be followed or used to minimize/neutralize the risks? (Consider use of survey data, benchmarking, task forces, pilot runs, self-directed teams, cross-functional teams, etc.)

_____

_____

_____

_____

_____

13. What procedures/strategies will be used to monitor the progress of the change activity?

_____

_____

_____

_____

_____

14. How will the change program be evaluated? What evidence or indicators will be used to measure success? (**Note:** Consider the use of "baseline" data as a basis for before and after measurement).

_____

_____

_____

_____

15. What procedures should/must be introduced to maintain the change after its implementation? (**Example:** A new standard of qualities may be introduced, but without continuing motivational efforts slippage may occur.)

_____

_____

_____

_____

The Manager as a Creative Force: How to Manage Innovation/ Creativity—The Art of Tapping and Unleashing "Possibility Thinking"

Vision is the art of seeing things invisible.

> —Jonathan Swift (1667–1745), Anglo-Irish author and satirist; author of *Gulliver's Travels* (1726)

Genius is but childhood recovered at will.

> —Charles Baudelaire (1821–67), French poet

People should think things out fresh and not just accept conventional terms and the conventional way of doing things.

> —Buckminster Fuller (1895–1983), U.S. architect and engineer

Organizations cannot create creative people, but they can help employees discover whatever creativity and potential they already have.

> —Douglas B. Gehrman, VP/Human Resources, Reading and Bates Drilling Co., Houston, in "Employees Thrive with Responsibility, Decision-Making," advertising supplement to *The Washington Post*, May 4, 1986, reprinted from the *Personnel Administrator*, American Society for Personnel Administration, Alexandria, Virginia

The strategic resources are no longer just the ones that come out of the ground, like oil and wheat and coal, but they are ideas and information that come out of our minds.

—John Sculley, former Chairman, Apple Computer Inc.

An acquaintance of mine wondered whether the above title—*How to Manage Innovation/Creativity*—is a contradiction of terms. After all, she asked, isn't all creativity innate, gifted, intuitive, inspired, wild, self-motivated, and self-implementing? **My reply:** Not really, for the organization and the manager can establish a climate that either stimulates or stifles creativity. Also, there is now enough available research data for us to know that creativity exists more widely in the working population than was formerly thought to be the case. The task for the manager, then, is to tap and unleash peoples' creative potential as opposed to letting it lie dormant.

But before I introduce you to the ideas on creativity, let's have a little fun and stimulate your creativity by focusing on two puzzles.

Duplicate the figure below with 24 toothpicks (or matches or nails). There are 12 toothpicks down (verticals) and 12 across (horizontals). **Your task:** Make two squares by removing (not moving) 8 toothpicks. An answer appears at the chapter's end.

The second puzzle is composed of 9 toothpicks. **Your task:** Move 3 toothpicks and come up with 5 triangles. Two answers appear at the chapter's end.

This chapter will try to put to rest some of the myths/misconceptions surrounding the creative process. We will then examine what managers, sad to relate, often do to stifle creativity and, conversely, what they can do to turn it on. Management consultants Eva Sonesh-Kedar and John Geirland (in "Developing More Creative Organizations: A Model for Consultants," *The 1995 Annual*, Vol. 2—Consulting, San Diego: Pfeiffer & Co, 1995) use the metaphors of "brake pedals"—inhibitors of creativity—and "gas pedals"—incentives to creativity.

We will also look at "risk taking" and "whole brain" concepts as they bear on creativity. The final topics will relate to how we, as individuals, can get our own creative juices flowing more freely and the techniques we, as managers, can employ to increase team creativity. We have also provided a self-quiz to help you gauge your own "CQ" (creativity quotient).

As in previous chapters, I will present a number of problems, exercises, and discussion questions for use by management trainers in workshops in organizational settings and by management instructors in college and university classes.

EXPLODING THE MANY MYTHS SURROUNDING CREATIVE BEHAVIOR

According to the theory of aerodynamics, and as may be readily demonstrated through wind tunnel experiments, the bumblebee is unable to fly. This is because the size, weight, and shape of his body in relation to his total wingspread makes flying impossible.

Yet the bumblebee, being ignorant of these scientific truths, goes ahead and flies anyway.

—Sign in an auto plant

Everyone sits in the prison of his own ideas.

—Albert Einstein

My father's longstanding appeal was to show how the simplest task, such as opening a garage door, can be complicated by machines and that human ideas are what really make things work, not the machine itself.

—George W. George, theatrical and film producer and son of the late, great cartoonist Rube Goldberg (quoted in *The Wall Street Journal*, June 15, 1990)

A lot of misconception and myths surround the field of creativity. Let's see if we can put to rest these many "old wives' tales."

A High I.Q. is Basic/Essential to Creative Behavior

Not true. I.Q. relates primarily to the ability to *acquire* information. Creativity, conversely, requires the ability to *reorganize one's knowledge* to solve new problems. Organizational psychologist Dr. Rosabeth Moss

Kanter (in "Creating the Creative Environment," *Management Review*, February 1986), uses a kaleidoscope as a metaphor for the creative process. She states:

In a kaleidoscope, a set of fragments forms a pattern, but it isn't locked into place . . . Shake it, twist it, change [the] angle, change perspective, and the exact same fragments form an entirely new pattern. Reality, the kaleidoscope tells us, is only a temporary arrangement. Creativity consists of rearranging the pieces to create a new reality.

So creativity is seeing what exists in alternate ways, and all of us have the capacity to perceive anew.

There is general agreement among leaders in the field of creative thinking that the potential for creativity is widely, not narrowly, distributed among the population. This means that reorganizing your own knowledge is something that most people can do. As the late Albert Einstein put it, "Imagination is more important than knowledge."

Consider the syndicated newspaper column by Heloise. She shows us with great certainty that all of us have the capacity to engage in possibility thinking to improvise, modify, rearrange, revamp, remodel, revise, even invent. Her columns are chockfull of ideas from trained householders who solved a vexing problem in a way which elicits from us the reaction, "Gee, why didn't I think of that?"

The following anecdote illustrates the point of widespread possession of potential for creativity.

Story: A motorist was traveling along the outskirts of town when a tire was punctured. He pulled over to the curb and proceeded to remove the wheel with the now defective tire. Unfortunately, in the course of this operation the motorist kicked into a drain the five nuts he had removed from the wheel. After he finished bawling himself out and cursing his luck, he looked around and noticed that he was parked near an iron fence that surrounded a large, red brick building several hundred yards away from the street, up a hill. He also noticed a man leaning on the fence who was watching his botched operation. This conversation ensued:

Motorist: I just had a flat tire and in changing the wheel I carelessly kicked the five nuts down the drain. Can you imagine that?

Observer: I know. I saw what happened.

Motorist: Is there a gas station or repair shop anywhere near here?

Observer: You don't need that. I can help you.

Motorist: You can? How?

Observer: Just take one nut off the other three wheels and put them on the wheel that has your good tire. That should hold you until you get to a service station.

Motorist (appreciative): Splendid! Very creative of you. Thank you very much. By the way, what is that big building up the hill?

Observer: The county mental hospital.

Motorist: Are you associated with it?

Observer: Oh yes, I'm an inmate. Have been for nine years.

Motorist: You mean you're a patient here, but you had this creative idea to help me out of my fix?

Observer: Look, mister, I may be crazy, but I'm not stupid.

We might add two more examples of creative problem solving ability by two "ordinary" people.

☐ At the big Thanksgiving dinner, the mother triumphantly marched from her kitchen into the dining room carrying the big holiday bird on a large silver platter. Unfortunately, she tripped over the rug and the golden turkey unceremoniously hit the floor. Without missing a beat, the mother scooped up the fallen bird, flashed a big smile, turned toward the kitchen, and reassuringly said to her expectant guests, "No problem at all. I'll be back in a minute with another one (!)"

☐ The high school English teacher was having a problem with four of her male seniors who frequently came 10–15 minutes late to her post-lunch period class. So when they arrived 20 minutes late on one occasion, she asked them what the problem was. Their spokesman replied: "We had a flat tire." Being skeptical of their story, she asked each of them to take a position in a corner of the room and write an essay about the incident, specifying

a) which wheel had the flat tire and b) precisely where the flat tire took place (!) **The result:** Future tardiness by the boys ended.

To put the issue of intelligence in relation to creativity in fuller and better perspective, we should certainly recognize that intelligence is very much a multi-faceted phenomenon. Thus, Howard Gardner in *Frames of Mind: Theory of Multiple Intelligences* (New York: Basic Books, 1983) enumerates seven kinds of intelligence. This means that any one of us has the potential to be intelligent and thus creative in one or more ways. The seven forms of intelligence are:

1. Logical, mathematical, or sequential-linear (e.g., a computer programmer or an engineer)
2. Linguistic or verbal (e.g., a political leader or TV personality)
3. Bodily-kinesthetic (e.g., a ballerina or a basketball player)
4. Visual-spatial or the ability to see patterns (e.g., an interior decorator)
5. Musical (e.g., a rock musician)
6. Interpersonal (e.g., a salesperson, a meeting facilitator)
7. Intrapersonal, or being smart about how you work (e.g., any one of us)

And, of course, there is a lot of difference between academic vs. practical intelligence, e.g., "street smarts." So, all in all, we shouldn't be too hasty in judging ourselves as unable to be creative.

Creativity is Innate

As the above discussion indicates, the view that you must be born with creative capability or you can't be creative is outdated. Many skill aspects of creative behavior are learnable, such as suspending/deferring judgment about ideas until they are all in; opting for quantity of ideas, for out of quantity will come quality; using intuition as opposed to relying solely on logic; using divergent, lateral thinking, i.e., thinking that is open-ended, "illogical," non-linear, non-vertical, non-sequential, non-convergent. (Convergent thinking is the opposite: orderly, logical, sequential, heavily fact-oriented, traditional.)

Psychologist Ellen Langer of Harvard University makes a distinction between *mindfulness* and *mindlessness* (reported by Marjory Roberts in "8 Ways to

Rethinking Your Work Style," *Psychology Today,* March 1989). In the former, the title of her book (Addison-Wesley: New York, *Mindfulness,* 1989), she states that mindfulness is seeing something new/novel/unique in the familiar. This is a kind of flexible, creative style that turns "stumbling blocks to productivity into building blocks." Mindfulness can also ease burnout by motivating people to locate innovative answers/solutions to their usual problems. Langer believes mindless people burnout when they see their job as old hat. She says that in their single-minded view their thinking is that "'We've always done it this way' and they give up. With mindfulness, you know there are multiple solutions."

People can learn to be mindful. Langer stresses what she terms the power of uncertainty or the need to keep one's mind open to the many ways information can be understood. Believing in uncertainty leads to more risk taking which, in turn, leads to innovation.

New Ideas are Produced by Special Brilliance or Cleverness

Not necessarily. More typically, ideas arise by such behavior as changing your viewpoint about something (abandoning old assumptions); reorganizing/rearranging the facts we have to produce a new assumption or approach; taking risks; learning from non-successes; overcoming fear of making mistakes, fear of failure and fear of criticism; adding new dimensions to a problem as opposed to merely adjusting things to fit old ideas/concepts/approaches; dropping temporarily the search for a solution when you hit an impasse and returning to it with new vigor and approaches later on; talking to others about the problem—stimulating their curiosity/thinking may stimulate new thinking on your part.

Prior Experience is Essential for Effective, Creative Problem Solving

Not necessarily. Actually it may be less than helpful because it only directs thinking along experienced paths. Experience may help to solve *familiar* problems. Creativity, contrariwise, requires abandoning past experience.

As Arthur Koestler, author of the scholarly work *The Art of Creation* (New York: MacMillan, 1964), put it, "The prerequisite of originality is the art of forgetting, at the proper moment, what we know."

Albert Einstein also offers some sound advice: "The important thing is not to stop questioning."

As an illustration of creative thinking and action, obviously not based on prior experience, the following story merits citation.

Story: A firm's employment officer was interviewing a large number of applicants for the position of assistant director of marketing. The first applicant, a young woman, appeared and sat down.

Employment Officer: We're looking for a person with a lot of spunk and, even more important, a lot of creativity.

Applicant: I'm sure I can qualify. I'm highly innovative.

Employment Officer: Can you show me some of that?

The applicant arose quickly from her chair, opened the door, and said in a loud, authoritative voice: "Okay, you folks can leave now. The job's just been filled."

Education is an Essential Route to Innovation/Creativity

Hardly so. Why not? As management writer Edward C. Schleh points out (in "Eureka Management . . . How to Generate Innovative Thought and Action," *Management Review,* May 1983), the actual thought processes used in the schools may be in opposition with creativity. Specifically, education often stresses memory and analysis, not developing new relationships, so schools may often stifle creative impulses. This may be because they must teach the fundamentals first. Note that, for example, engineers are specialists who require training in the basics of their specialties, and training usually follows an analytical or logical format. Creativity, of course, often requires taking a new tack, departing from the established logic.

As Adults We are Completely Adult

Part of our self-image and our self-talk relates to our assumption of total adultness. We tell ourselves (subconsciously, of course) that we must be adults because we have graduated from this school or that, have this degree or that, have a paying job, work with other adults, have a house (of one sort or another), have a spouse, have offspring, have adult neighbors whom we

are careful not to offend, have a driver's license, and can vote. And most important, we are quite careful to avoid unconventional, non-adult behavior.

Sure we're adults. But there are parts of us that are also adolescent, even childlike. The child part of ourselves is the portion that (potentially) is curious, excited, happy, carefree, funloving, playful, inhibition-free. Our adolescent self is independent, irreverent, rebellious, risk-taking, adventuresome, and experimental.

Our real makeup, then, is a grand and glorious mixture of child, adolescent, and adult. So what we must do, if we want to be creative, is to release the freer, less-rigid, more curious side of ourselves. It's certainly there. Why keep it corked up in the bottle that we have inappropriately labeled "for adult use only"?

Key point: Something wondrous and exciting happens when staid adults arouse their childlike, playful side. They loosen up, become more of their total self, and begin to break out of the societal and cultural constraints of adulthood.

Creativity is Essentially a Flash of Insight

Not necessarily so. More typically, they are systematic innovations in a supportive environment, says management consultant Alan Jay Weiss (in "Innovation—the Learnable Skill," *Training News,* February 1987). He cites as an example Thomas Edison's invention of the incandescent lightbulb. It took Edison more than 40,000 separate experiments to perfect it. A flash of insight? Hardly. Systematic hard work? Yes, indeed!

Edison's positive attitude toward trial and error, especially error, which often is essential to creativity, triggered this query by a colleague: "Why do you persist in this folly? You have failed 9,000 times." Replied Edison, "I haven't failed once. 9,000 times I've learned what doesn't work" (quoted by management consultant Jim Collins in "Creativity and the Personal Computer," *Managing Your Career,* Winter/Spring 1989).

Conflict in a Group Will Stifle Discovery of New Ideas

Totally incorrect. Disagreement/differences/conflict will cause the sparks to fly, get people's attention, and stimulate them, all of which can generate new, vibrant, creative thinking. Conversely, a calm, laid-back, contentedly coasting group will merely generate an atmosphere of contentment, pleasantness, of getting along. In the latter type of group, people will suppress their views, rather than to project them.

Key point: Disagreement can lead to hard feelings *or* creativity/innovation, depending on the facilitating skills of the team leader. The manager who has developed an open, enthusiastic, hard-hitting team can count on high team ideation (creation of ideas) and need not worry too much about anyone sulking or withdrawing because they were disagreed with.

Creativity is Serious and Sober Business

This approach to creativity is as out of date as the rumble seat, the buggy whip, the vacuum tube radio, or you name it. Creativity depends on people being loose, irreverent, status-free, friendly, relaxed but energized, challenged to think fresh and big; having fun; interacting with others; and the like. Edward R. McCracken, CEO of Silicon Graphics, Inc., put it this way (in Steven E. Prokech, "Mastering Chaos at the High-Tech Frontier—An Interview with Silicon Graphics' Ed McCracken," *Harvard Business Review,* November–December 1993) when he was asked about the importance of fun:

Very important. We've always said that Silicon Graphics is all about making technology fun and usable, and that means that working here should be fun. Too many companies in the United States and Japan have cut the fun out of their businesses. We think that if people are enjoying themselves, they will come up with better products in a shorter time. When people have fun, they bring more of themselves to the work environment. Irreverence is also important in a highly creative environment. If you're too reverent, your productivity decreases.

Fun and irreverence also make change less scary. For example, we recently replaced two old divisions with five new ones. We brought in a New Orleans band and held a wake on our Mountain View campus. We filled two coffins with paraphernalia from each division and then buried them. This ceremony reinforced our philosophy that we must view life as it is and how it might be rather than how it was.

British actor, film director/producer, and all-around funny man John Cleese (in "Serious Talk about Humor in the Office," *The Wall Street Journal,* August 1, 1988) believes humor stimulates creativity. Why? Because a joke involves a sudden switch from one frame of reference to another, essentially a form of lateral thinking. He cites the story of a woman who was interviewing an airplane pilot in connection with a survey of sexual behavior. Her final question to him was when had he last made love. "1956," he said. Very surprised at the response, since her assumption was that pilots were more dashing than that, she asked incredulously: "1956?" Replied the pilot, "Well, it's only 2216 hours now, ma'am."

Cleese makes a distinction between seriousness and solemnity, as follows:

When humor is present we lose not seriousness, but only solemnity. And the value of solemnity is overrated because it often induces in people feelings of pomposity, rigidity, and a corresponding loss of ordinary human warmth and easy, open communication. Solemnity has the effect of encouraging people—especially the most important ones—to feel even more important than they normally do. And I seriously doubt whether anything that tends to increase the egotism of our political and business leaders is healthy.

I'd go further and suggest that a lot of solemnity is due to the fact that the egotistical kind of leader fears humor in all its forms, since he or she knows that any kind of humor threatens self-importance. And what the usefulness of self-importance is I've yet to discover.

Creative Behavior Means Accomplishing Major Breakthroughs and/or Inventions

While blockbuster solutions to problems are great to achieve, in the real world most things get resolved in little doses. Bettering things one step at a time is more practical than always shooting for the moon. The Japanese are well known for their philosophy and practice of continuous improvement, or *kaizen.*

Dr. Theodore Levitt, marketing guru at Harvard University (in "Betterness," an editorial in the *Harvard Business Review,* November–December, 1988) states:

Big, prophetic leaps into sudden business successes are rare. That's why they make the headlines, as do similarly sudden and spectacular flops. Sustained success is largely a matter of focusing regularly on the right things and making a lot of uncelebrated little improvements every day. Getting better and better one step at a time adds up.

Expect Deterioration of the Aging Brain

A lot of tall tales exist regarding the aging process. Dr. Marion Diamond, neuroanatomist, University of California, Berkeley (in "Setting the Record Straight," *Modern Maturity,* June–July 1986) cites these research-based facts:

☐ Large numbers of brain cells don't start to vanish each year, starting at 21 and thereafter. Actually, the major loss of brain cells begins very early in life, not later.

☐ The healthy brain of an active adult is a terrifically resilient organ. So whether you're 35 or 85, you have no more need to anticipate senility than you would heart disease or lung cancer.

☐ A 55-year-old's basic thinking skills are nearly always vastly superior to that of a 25-year-old. **The reason:** A challenged brain never stops learning.

Ideas that Sound Good are Good

Not only are not all ideas created equal, but some of them may be downright impractical, real duds. Terry Dozier, the first classroom teacher to serve as an official advisor to the Secretary of Education in Washington, found herself providing much-needed "reality checks" at department policy meetings. Dozier, a former high school teacher from South Carolina, frequently pointed out practical flaws in various proposals.

For example:

At a recent department meeting, Dozier listened as colleagues proposed creating computer databanks that teachers could access via modem. Then she said, "I don't understand how teachers are going to use these centers . . . Teachers don't even have telephones . . . There may be a computer in every school in America, but the one with modem and a dedicated line is in the principal's office."

"They really had to stop and think," Dozier said later (quoted by Brooke A. Masters, "Teaching at a Different Level," *The Washington Post,* August 30, 1993).

Limit Training in Creative Thinking to Managers Because They Solve Problems and Make Decisions

This is, indeed, a narrow view of who might "benefit" from training. The better, more realistic view is that peo-

ple at all levels have the potential to be creative and thus can benefit from appropriate training. The best evidence for this is the training in problem solving given to millions of rank-and-file people, blue- and white collar, who participate effectively in Quality Circles and related problem-solving activities throughout the world.

Innovation is a Mystical, Magical, Mysterious, Divine Force

Actually, as the title of an article in *Total Quality,* March 1994, put it, "Inspiration for Innovation Can Be Found in Methodical Planning." The article suggests that innovation is essentially hard, consistent work. It is a function that needs managing, and this is done by basing new products on customer's needs, providing employees with incentives for successful innovation and refusing to punish those whose risks/gambles/ventures don't pay off. Added requirements are top management support, a culture that nurtures creativity, and a workforce fully involved in and convinced of the worthwhileness of "breakthrough thinking."

To structure/organize for innovation, these three areas demand a strong focus:

Structure

The organization must understand and acknowledge that it favors improving the manner of its innovation, and it must also know how to move toward increasing creativity. In some cases, a department for innovation may actually be established. In others, people may be permitted to work on their own ideas for a fixed percentage of their workday, e.g., 3M allows 15% of employee paid time for this.

Top Management Involvement

Senior management must involve itself early on in the innovative process. This means to study an idea not only to make a go or no-go decision, but to ascertain whether it is consistent with current corporate strategy and work to overcome any weaknesses/gaps it sees.

Environment

Being friendly to ideas by the organization is great. But added to this is a need to look at how well it encourages risk-taking and handles failure. If truly novel, breakthrough ideas are wanted, a higher level of risk must be encouraged and supported. Innovation consultant Robert

Johnston, Jr., says that "If you reward risk and have a positive approach to it, risk can actually become a motivator, a catalyst to higher levels of innovation."

Jim Thompson, manager of 3M's quality management services, says:

Innovation is about taking a problem that a customer or potential customer has and working to solve it on a commercial basis. I think you have to take an idea all the way through commercialization before you can say you're an innovative company. Otherwise, you're just a creator of things that don't go anywhere.

Thompson also points out that from a customer standpoint there are two kinds of innovation: to identify a problem customers are experiencing and to produce a solution, and to *anticipate* problems that *potential* customers will have and, again, find solutions for them. The second form of innovation obviously is more desirable and advanced than the first. It has the potential to give the firm an edge in the marketplace. **A great example:** 3M's now world-famous "Post-it Notes."

Creativity is Needed in Only Specialized Units of the Organization, Such as Advertising, Engineering, and R&D

Not so. All departments can profit from the infusion of new approaches and ideas, whether it's operations, administration, human resources management, finance, or sales and marketing. To quote Thomas Edison, "If there's a better way to do it . . . find it."

And as Thomas Watson, founder of IBM put it, "We are convinced that any business needs its wild ducks. And in IBM we try not to tame them."

Creativity is a Quiet, Lonely Process, Best Done in Isolation from Others

This is an old chestnut that should have been put to rest decades ago. Actually, it's a lot smarter to surround yourself with people who offer stimulation, excitement, fun, and inspiration. Harvey Mackay, head of Mackay Envelope Corporation and author of two best-selling business books, puts it this way (in "Great Minds: Surround Yourself with People Who Offer Inspiration," *Successful Meetings,* August 1993): "People enjoy being around others who care about the same things they care about. It's exciting, it's stimulating and it's fun."

Mackay tells a story of General William Westmoreland, who was reviewing a platoon of paratroopers in Vietnam. He went down the line and asked three of them a question:

General: "How do you like jumping, son?"

Paratrooper #1 (shouting back): "Love it, sir!"

General (to another paratrooper): "How do you like jumping?"

Paratrooper #2 (roaring back): "The greatest experience of my life, sir!"

General: "How do like jumping?"

Paratrooper #3: "I hate it, sir."

General: "Then why do you do it?"

Paratrooper #3: "Because I want to be around guys who love to jump."

Key point: Creativity is most likely to occur in the company of live-wire, fun-oriented, idea-seeking people. You want mentors and others—bosses, colleagues, subordinates—on whom you can bounce off ideas and vice versa, and this can rev up your excitement and thinking to new, imaginative levels. The observation "no man is an island" was never more meaningful than when applied to the creative process.

The More Precise, Pointed, and Close You Are to a Solution, the More Certain You Are to Solve It

Not necessarily so. Actually, the *starting point,* not the finishing point, is richest in solution possibilities. How's that again? Let's explain.

The closer you are to your stated goal—the finishing point—the fewer the options/alternatives now open to you. Think of the analogy of driving your car from New York to New Orleans. The farther you are from your destination point, the *greater* the number of possible routes available to you. Conversely, the closer you are to New Orleans, the lesser the number of new routes available to you. So, too, in creative problem-solving. The farther away you are from a solution, the more alternatives you have. You are less locked in and thus can increase the odds in your favor of finding an approach that is innovative. (I made this point to a group of students in a university management course, and one bright student responded by saying: "What you're saying, prof, is that if you firmly latch on to only one possible solution, you've really hemmed yourself in, pretty much closed the door to other creative possibilities." He was right, of course.)

You Can't Solve Problems While You're Asleep

Actually, there is a creative role of the subconscious mind, which has the capacity to solve problems during sleep and offers the solutions during a morning shower or after a midday nap. Nathaniel Wyeth, a one-time consultant for DuPont and principal inventor of the plastic soda bottle, has stated:

I once had a brilliant engineer working with me who insisted his best ideas came to him while he was napping. Certainly, there are examples of this from the lives of Descartes, Leibnitz, Milton, and Rossini who claimed that their best thinking took place under a blanket.

I mention this not because I am suggesting that every engineering lab should be equipped with beds, but rather that we ask ourselves whether we offer our colleagues or employees an environment which nurtures creativity.

—Quoted by Peter Behr, "Dupont Wraps It Up," *The Washington Post*, July 3, 1986)

Creativity is Synonymous with Action, Accomplishment, Results

Of course, as managers we want creative initiatives. But we are more likely to discourage creativity by pressing too eagerly for immediate achievement. So if we truly want creativity, we can't assume that demanding action will do it for us. **The reason:** The creative mind/process takes time to toy with fantasies, ideas, possibilities, free-wheeling thinking. Fun, play, relaxation, and reverie are more likely to beget creativity than the usual job pressures, demands, deadlines, schedules, crises, firefighting, and meetings in our daily organizational lives.

The Suggestion Box is the Key Tool for New Ideas in Organizations

While current suggestion systems may offer certain benefits, serious rethinking as to its actual value in today's organizations is now under way. Management consultants Robin E. McDermott, Raymond J. Mikulok, and Michael R. Beauregard, who are with Resource Engineering, a consulting company specializing in total quality (TQ) and continuous program implementation, offer an alternative in their book *Employee-Driven Quality: Releasing the Creative Spirit of Your Organization Through Suggestion Systems* (White Plains, N.Y.: Quality Resources, 1993), summarized in "How to Reap Organizational Creativity," *Supervisory Management*, April 1995).

The three authors point out that suggestion systems now in vogue typically focus on "big" ideas, providing a big return on investment via cost savings. Also, suggestion submitters often have a long wait before they receive a response on their contribution. Thirdly, the suggestor may get his reward, but his involvement ends. The implementation is usually accomplished by others at a higher organizational level.

An alternate approach, per the authors, is their Employee-Driven Idea System (EDIS). It has these characteristics:

- ☐ The focus is on identifying ideas to improve employees' work.
- ☐ All ideas are deemed to be equally important.
- ☐ Rewards take the form of recognition, not necessarily money.
- ☐ The idea creators are involved in the implementation of their own ideas and thus are recognized for both the idea and its implementation.
- ☐ Quick response time on submitted ideas, about five working days, is stressed.
- ☐ It is highly team oriented. The work team—the idea submitter plus his teammates—implements the idea.
- ☐ Its philosophy is that the only bad idea is one that isn't offered. This is an important concept because the EDIS system is intended to motivate those who have given up on traditional suggestion systems.

Smart People Always Do Smart Things

This would be nice if it were true. Actually, as management consultant Mortimer R. Feinberg points out (in "Why Smart People Do Dumb Things," *The Wall Street Journal*, December 21, 1992), presumed geniuses as well as bright people may do stupid things. Dr. Feinberg has formulated this principle: **Strong intelligence seeks to subvert itself.** Most people try and tend to follow a logical course. However, the exceptional brain may use the subconscious to find reasons to bypass logic. Feinberg cites these self-subverting mechanisms smart people may employ:

Recklessness

Motivated by a feeling of universal or complete knowledge, very bright people can become "risk junkies." It becomes a quick, short step from knowing more than most people to thinking you know everything. So if things come all too easily, the mind seeks greater challenges. Says Feinberg, "Boredom combined with brilliance make an explosive and self-destructive mixture."

Isolation

Smart people like to be surrounded by other bright ones. But if the extraordinary brilliant group relies totally on its own brilliance and ignores real-world experience, disasters may result. Smart people may fall into the trap of agreeing with one another strongly (groupthink) to the point of unwillingness to change, even though others have noticed their proposed course of action is faulty.

Feedback Deafness

Another trap is for bright people to become so impatient with their slower colleagues that they tune them out. But feedback is essential for everyone regardless of native brilliance. History is replete with instances of bright rulers and managers who flopped because of their inability to listen.

To get the most and the best out of the bright person, Feinberg suggests that their bosses do the following:

Focus on Results, Not Process

Anticipate that bright people will generate bright ideas. So give them a lot of freedom. But they can also produce some duds, too. So the manager has to sift carefully through their proposals to separate the wheat from the chaff.

Apply Uniform Evaluation Criteria to All Ideas

Don't fall into the trap of assuming that ideas from the exceptional ones require more favorable treatment. An idea from a smart guy or gal doesn't automatically make it a winner.

Feinberg quotes Lord Melbourne, Queen Victoria's first prime minister, who once stated, unhappily, "What all the wise men promised has not happened, and what all the damned fools predicted has come to pass."

So you certainly want to give the brainy ones leeway in the the way they produce ideas, but hardly as to how they are judged. Sure, they may resent being judged by someone less bright than they are, but the knowing manager will, nevertheless, stick to his standards.

Provide the Genius with Structure

These super-smart people may not like it, but they do need broad guidelines and limits like anyone else. So don't cancel the rules for the super brains: They'll do a better job within generally prescribed parameters. In essence, don't confuse freedom with total laissez-faire or license.

Key point: Smart people know *content,* but may lack understanding of *context,* something critically important in the Information Age, in a world of increasing change. It is their boss' job, then, to teach them context.

Manufacturers Create Most Innovations in Their Products

Not true. Innovations are more likely to come from consumers or product users who require something different or better. These advances are then adopted by manufacturers. Business writer Robert J. Samuelson (in "The Messy, Misunderstood Business of Innovation," *The Washington Post,* June 8, 1988) draws on an MIT study (by Eric Von Hippel, *The Sources of Innovation,* Oxford University Press, 1988), which found that product users are responsible for 77% of innovations in scientific instruments and 90% in certain plastics-making machinery.

Note that Japanese firms move products quickly into the market, secure customer feedback, and then make needed changes. This practice ties into Von Hippel's findings on users' innovations cited above.

Key point: Don't assume your outfit has a monopoly on creativity. Tap your suppliers and customers' experience and wisdom, either inside or outside the organization, as an added source of new ideas.

BARRIERS TO CREATIVITY: THE DEADLY HABIT OF LOOKING THROUGH THE WRONG END OF THE TELESCOPE

Don't say we've never done it that way before.

—Sign on the desk of James Lee Witt, Director of the Federal Emergency Management Agency (FEMA), quoted in *The Washington Post*, March 23, 1995

About any new idea, at the first moment, they say, "This is stupid." At the second, they say, "This is true but this is not important." And the third time they say, "This is nothing new; this is the same thing we have been saying all along."

—A reference by Jonas Edward Salk, U.S. physician, microbiologist, and developer of vaccine against polio, to early attitudes toward his vaccine, quoted in *The Washington Post*, February 27, 1986

Many ideas grow better when transplanted into another mind than in the one where they sprang up.

—Oliver Wendell Holmes (1841–1935), associate justice of the U.S. Supreme Court

If you take an idea to people, 9 out of 10 will tell you what is wrong with it. That's because we are taught to think critically instead of constructively. Most people start imagining all the reasons why things won't work or can't be done before they try to figure out how to make them work or get them done.

—Michael Michalko, creativity consultant and author of *Thinkertoys* (quoted in *National Report on Human Resources*, newsletter of the American Society for Training and Development, January/February 1993, page 3)

If you or I were to ask managers in organizations, at all levels, whether they favor creativity by their people, it would be extremely surprising if they responded in the negative. (They would also say they favor team management, open communication, deep delegation, etc.). Yet we know that roadblocks to creativity exist in many organizations. So what forms do they take? This question is important because we can't spark creativity effectively if we don't know what the impediments are.

Frank K. Sonnenberg, management consultant, and Beverly Goldberg, director of publications for New York-based think tank Twentieth Century Fund, helpful-ly categorize roadblocks to creativity as follows (in "It's a Great Idea, But . . .," *Training and Development*, March 1992): organizational culture, management style and operational style. Let's look a bit at each of these three obstructants.

1. Cultural Road Blocks

Because culture is what makes an organization what it is, barriers of these types are hardest to erase. Typical cultural blocks are:

Office Politics

It inhibits creative expression because of constant messages such as "What will the boss say?" or "Play it safe. Don't rock the boat." So people are likely to compromise, water down, or abandon their ideas totally.

Resistance to Change

This is the result of an enslavement by the dead hand of the past. Mottoes such as "If it ain't broke, don't fix it," "It's too radical a change," and "We're not ready for that" perpetuate adherence to the status quo, the tried and true. Innovation and growth can hardly emerge in this type of restrictive climate.

The Caste System

Only people in certain jobs can offer ideas. This is an A-1 idea suppressor. That is to say, ideas may be rejected because "That's not her job." So if you or I dismiss ideas/contributions of some workers, we'll never be advantaged by the one idea that could give us a big payoff. What is needed for real creativity to function is to recognize that people at all levels in the outfit are potential innovators/problem solvers/creative contributors.

2. Managerial Roadblocks

Management styles may also serve as creativity inhibitors. If managers create a work atmosphere marked by fear, conflict, constraints, controls, endless reviews, limited responsibility, narrowly defined jobs, plus all the other curbs on freedom and empowerment, fun, joy, and resultant creativity will rarely emerge.

Keeping People in the Dark

As opposed to sharing information freely, providing feedback and responding with interest to employee ideas, this is a sure-fire way to dim employee interest, enthusiasm, and creativity. A statement such as, "I can't tell you why, but I don't like it. I know what I want. When I see it, I'll let you know," will hardly excite the creative juices.

The Dictatorial Approach

This is another mechanism to scuttle possible creativity. "Here's my idea. Carry it out." Because the employee has not been involved in the idea, the response will only be an automatic salute rather than an enthusiastic assessment/joint exchange. Also, if the boss adopts an employee's idea and takes full credit for it, he will discourage future ideation by staffers. **Question:** Which leadership style will be best to unleash creativity: command and control, or energize and empower?

Unrealistic Timing

Setting arbitrary deadlines ignores the need to allow enough time for the creative process to develop. So work assignments coupled with insensitive constraints, such as "It shouldn't take more than an hour," will be counter-productive. Worse still, a manager may stall on providing the green light and then suddenly give the go-ahead signal with an expectation of instant results.

Procrastination

Delays in acting decisively are a certain means of inhibiting creativity. Delays in acting/deciding, until situations inevitably turn critical, result in fire fighting by staff. They may also produce the loss of needed momentum on a project with resultant lost opportunities.

3. Operational Roadblocks

Every outfit has its own way of doing business as reflected in its rules, protocols, and rewards. But consider these creativity squelchers:

Formalities and Rules of Protocol

If too rigid, they can kill initiative and ideation. **Example:** requiring all ideas to be put in writing and/or presented in a particular format. Also, rules that become dated and no longer make sense, but are inflexibly kept

on the books, stifle creative interest. Visualize the typical response by a customer representative to a customer who questions such a policy: "I really don't know why. It's just company policy, I guess."

Internal Bureaucracy

Its hallmarks are elaborate, time-consuming reviews of ideas, giving minor and major ideas the same amount of attention, plus other assorted red tape, all of which are handicaps to creativity. Getting multiple reviewers into the act, particularly if they are so far removed from where the idea applies, will serve as a certain idea stopper.

Negativism and Evaluation of Ideas

How a manager responds to an idea will go a long way in determining whether the employee will pursue the idea or return with another one. Consider these killer responses: "I personally wouldn't do it, but why don't you try it anyway?" Or, "I know I asked you to be creative. But this one is off the wall." The best approach to ensure continuation of creative inputs is to discuss fully and frankly with the employee why it is not quite on target. Even if the idea is rejected, most employees will still feel good about themselves if their idea gets a fair hearing. The response should also be prompt, for to sit on the idea for six weeks and then turn it down is another way to discourage creativity.

Key point: If an employee shows the interest to develop an idea, he is entitled to an early and appreciative response. If one can't act promptly, it's a good procedure to so advise the idea presenter. People need to know that their ideas/creativity are valued and that they, as idea contributors, can make a difference to organizational success.

Companies may create other obstacles to creativity inadvertently, per management writer/consultant Edward C. Schleh (in "Eureka Management . . . How to Generate Innovative Thought and Action," *Management Review,* May 1983):

Policies as Obstacles

Obviously, policies and the procedures that flow from them are essential to getting the organization's work done. But if people are encouraged to appraise carefully what they do solely in terms of those policies and procedures, these straight-jacket policies become discouragers of innovation. What is needed, then, is a culture or climate that (a) allows broad leeway to make adjustments within those policies and procedures, and (b) encourages challenges to the policies and procedures themselves.

Controls as Obstacles

Controls are designed to dampen deviation from usual/normal/expected operation. But because innovation obviously is a deviation, the innovator is likely to find that there are comptrollers and accountants who are ready to blow the whistle on deviations. So what every organization has to do is to weigh the import of adherence to rigid standards vs. the need to depart from them as new circumstances may demand. The dictum, "a rule once broken ceases to be a rule," is hardly a gateway to new thinking.

Budgets as Innovation Inhibitors

Financial blueprints don't ordinarily allow for a new departure to take advantage of new possibilities, opportunities, or directions. Departures from budget must be approved by someone or a board up the line. So the new idea might well be tabled until it can work its way through the budget mill. Obviously, some ideas can await the normal budgetary scheme of things to proceed, but others may suffer from being shelved.

Allied to the above may be the requirement to "submit a detailed cost estimate on the proposed new project," even on a small one. But what if the innovator can't do this because he isn't clear as to how to start or approach the problem? So if the innovator can't comply, the idea is likely to die before it even gets off the ground. And typically, even if approved, the first stage of a long project may be controlled identically to an established one. Ideally, from a creativity support standpoint, a distinction should be made between a newly launched and an ongoing project.

Organization-wide Requirements for Uniformity Can Inhibit Instincts for Innovation

Example: A product manager has a plan for marketing and selling for all field sales personnel in all sales districts. But if the product manager won't accept changes from the sales staff to deal with new local problems, not many new approaches will be tried.

Specialization May Frustrate Innovation

Specialists are very likely to ignore relationships outside their areas of expertise. Each technical expert is reluctant to compromise his discipline to blend it with another, but the most desirable solutions are more likely to result from combining various specialties. So if the specialists prevail, innovation will come out second best.

Note: The above paragraphs relate to how the organization's culture may affect creativity. We should also mention that the culture at large, particularly influences in the early child-rearing years, may inhibit the individual's creative potential. Specifically, consider these stultifying messages parents may transmit to their children and their possible role as creativity blockers:

- ☐ "Children should be seen and not heard."
- ☐ "If you can't say anything nice, don't say anything."
- ☐ "Don't speak unless spoken to."
- ☐ "Don't bite off more than you can chew."
- ☐ "Always look before you leap."
- ☐ "Don't stick your neck out unless you want to get it chopped off."
- ☐ "Do you want to make a fool out of yourself?"
- ☐ "You know that's not going to make you very popular."

The above preachments of caution, rationality, conformity, and deference to the standards and status of others, not surprisingly, over time, help develop our own adult-level cautionary admonitions:

- ☐ "I'm not the kind of person who . . ."
- ☐ "I wouldn't be caught dead (in or doing) . . ."
- ☐ "I would never . . ."
- ☐ "I've already tried . . ."
- ☐ "I'd look foolish if . . ."
- ☐ "What would the neighbors say (or think)?"

Some Added Roadblocks

Creativity in organizations can be readily stifled in a variety of other ways, too. Here are a number of them:

Treating Problem-Finders as Problem-Creators

Most of us would agree that resolving problems is a key managerial role. However, if the problem-finder is regarded as a problem-maker, creative endeavors by staff will become less frequent. So for the manager who treats problems as items to be deposited under the rug, placed on "the back burner" (indefinitely, of course), "sent to committee," or only meriting a "let's wait and see" attitude, the message will be that creativity may be wanted, but hardly with any great passion.

Dr. David P. Campbell of the Center for Creative Leadership (in "Inklings," *Issues and Observations,* Center for Creative Leadership, Greensboro, North Carolina, Vol. 12, No. 2, 1992) defines problem-finders as those who go beyond problem-solving. They have the knack of finding non-apparent problems and then presenting creative solutions for them. He cites these examples: Steve Jobs, who saw that many people could not afford a mainframe computer so he created the Apple personal computer; and Dr. Edwin Land, who observed that not everyone wanted to wait a week for their photos to be developed so he created the Polaroid camera.

Key point: Nurture those who recognize latent problems and those who zero in on problems not even regarded or identified as problems by others. The problem-finder may be "a maverick," an on-the-job irritant. But can we afford not to pay attention to his insights?

Communicating/Acting/Behaving in Ways to Indicate that You Want "Yes-Men" (or Women) Around

Recall the statement attributed to movie mogul Louis B. Mayer: "I don't want 'yes-men' around me. Tell me what you think even if it costs your job."

Judith Bardwick, management consultant and psychiatry professor ("Creating an Earning Environment," *Supervisory Management,* November 1991), states that creativity involves what psychologists call "breaking set." This means seeing things differently than they have been previously. But breaking set entails risk-taking because being different is initially regarded as being wrong. So the risk-takers need to feel respected for their accomplishments before they can abandon the safety of being "yes people."

The job of the creative manager is to communicate loudly, clearly, and frequently that it's OK to break rules because circumstances/situations are constantly changing. Staffers should be conditioned to ask: "Do we do as before or pick up something new? Do we stay with precedent or do we bend or abandon the rule?"

Key point: Don't let the cultural norm be (or develop into) "Don't propose unless the boss is already disposed."

Downgrading New Ideas with Gloom-and-Doom-Type Prognostications

New ideas may be perceived in a variety of negative ways, everything from scary and impractical to weird and wacko. A TRW ad (in *The Wall Street Journal,* September 26, 1985) cited these dishearteningly myopic views of innovative things to come:

Everything that can be invented has been invented.

—Charles H. Duell, Director of U.S. Patent Office, 1899

Who the hell wants to hear actors talk?

—Harry M. Warner, Warner Bros. Pictures, c. 1927

Sensible and responsible women do not want to vote.

—Grover Cleveland, 22nd and 24th U.S. President, 1905

There is no likelihood man can ever tap the power of the atom.

—Robert Millikan, Nobel Prize in Physics, 1923

Heavier-than-air flying machines are impossible.

Lord Kelvin, President, Royal Society of England, c. 1895

Babe Ruth made a big mistake when he gave up pitching.

Tris Speaker, (1888–1958), a superstar in baseball batting and fielding

The Washington Post staffer Mike McClintock ("Predictions and Prognosticators," *The Washington Post,* December 31, 1987) quoted two other pessimistic predictions:

Well-informed people know it is impossible to transmit the voice over wires, and that were it possible to do so, the thing would be of no practical value.

—From an editorial in *The Boston Post,* 1865

People will soon get tired of staring at a plywood box every night.

—Darryl F. Zanuck, head of 20th Century Fox Studios, 1946

How possibility thinking gets squelched very readily is illustrated in this story:

Story: Junior, eight years old, showed Dad a book filled totally with blank pages.

Dad (pained): This book says nothing, junior.

Junior: No, Dad, this book says *anything*.

Moral: Don't automatically put down new ideas. Try, instead, to visualize their possibilities.

Discounting New Ideas

Discounting is disparaging, putting down, or failing to affirm a new idea. Discounting may be indirect or unintentional, verbal or nonverbal, but the results can be devastating to the idea presenter, says Dr. Timothy Weaver of Boston University (in "When Discounting Gets in the Way," *Training and Development,* June 1993). Typical discounting behaviors include stressing one's rank, providing a silent response, and not offering ideas, responding with verbal putdowns, failing to listen, interrupting, avoiding mutuality by dominating or questioning, and transmitting negative, nonverbal responses.

Discounting messages can be very hurtful. People thus feel ignored, angry, defensive. They may then withdraw or withhold. Weaver offers these examples from actual meetings and conversations: "That makes sense, but . . ." "Be serious, will you?" "I have a problem with that." "Get your facts straight." "Let me challenge that." "I don't want to insult your intelligence, but . . ." "I don't know about that." The author would add one some old timers like to use: "If it could work, someone would have thought of it 30 years ago!"

The above statements are examples of very direct discounts. But they can also be more subtle or indirect, and equally as punishing. **Examples:**

Statement: "Let me tell you where I am on that."

Underlying meaning: "Where you are on this item is unimportant. What is most important is where *I* am."

Statement: "Permit me to clarify this for you."

Underlying meaning: "Obviously you are one person who has a real limitation in understanding the point/issue/item."

Statement: "You really believe that?"

Underlying meaning: "You're really out of touch with reality or you surely wouldn't have made such a foolish/crazy/wacko statement."

Statement: "That's interesting . . ." (and the receiver goes on to an unrelated topic).

Underlying meaning: "You're talking garbage so let me help you move on to more solid and interesting stuff."

Statement: "Wait–have you thought of this?"

Underlying meaning: "Drop it. You've missed the main point."

Bruce Smith of the University of Alaska at Fairbanks has conducted research on discounting and its impacts on group effectiveness. He thus believes it should be added as a fifth brainstorming guideline. (The standard four are *avoid judgment, seek quantity, welcome "free wheeling,"* and *combine and improve on the ideas of others.*) His research (reported in "Research Capsules—Avoiding Discounting," *Training and Development,* July 1993) used eight student volunteer groups. They were given 20 minutes to brainstorm a topic and to be as creative as possible.

Four of the eight groups faced assorted verbal and nonverbal discounting. The latter entailed rolling of eyes, folding arms tightly and scowling, drumming on the table, tapping of feet. Verbal discounts included statements such as "Wasn't that mentioned already?" "I'm having trouble with that." "What makes you think people want to hear that?"

The other four groups were discount free. In fact, two of them were given brief discounting training (ten minutes) about the definition, examples, and consequences of discounting.

The results: Based on the quantity of ideas produced and people's emotional response to the group process, the discounted groups produced statistically significant fewer ideas and its members recorded significantly more negative emotional-response scores. The most productive groups were those trained to shun discounting behaviors.

Key points: Group effectiveness/creativity depends on group processes that ensure a safe, supportive environment. If people feel unsafe, they become defensive and are less likely to produce new, worthwhile ideas. Understandably, if you or I are attacked, we will be so concerned with defending ourselves that we won't produce anything very creative.

Adhering to the "We've Always Done it This Way" Syndrome

For many of us, it's all too easy to seek the comfort of what has worked in the past. Old habits and old successes are comfortable hobby horses on which to ride. But when the world has changed, allegiance to "the tried and true" will no longer suffice. So what is really needed is to rally staff to generate new perspectives on the new problems that have emerged or are looming threateningly on the horizon.

Management writers use terms like "mindset," "mental models," and "paradigms" to point out how our traditional (and thus static) thinking keeps us from exercising our latent creative powers. Dr. Keshavan Nair describes the influence of the dead hand of the past as follows (quoted in "Controlling Strategic Diversity," *Management Letter,* The Bureau of Business Practice, September 25, 1991):

> *The conventional wisdom is to stick with what you know how to do. But this must be balanced by adopting new strategies and skills for new conditions. Circumstances change. What you know how to do may no longer be relevant. You must continually evaluate your business and all its components for obsolescence. Obsolescence can come from many sources— technology, customer preferences, regulations, and competition.*

Dr. Nair states, too, that to overcome the forces of obsolescence, a diversity of views must be developed. He says:

> *Old assumptions have to be challenged and new realities have to be developed. People who are mired in believing that there is one right strategy for achieving success will sooner or later lead you to failure. Without the presence of opposites, the organization will soon develop a system of decision-making that simply reinforces past decisions.*

If organizations are unable to see past their current success, they're unable to embrace the changes needed to ensure their future, says management consultant Alan Jay Weiss (in "Innovation—the Learnable Skill," *Training News,* February 1987). He cites these familiar but tragic examples:

☐ Addressograph Multigraph was unable to understand the threat of modern photocopying and tried to compete against the new technology by selling the merits of dated mimeography more determinedly.

☐ Friden, the mechanical calculator master, reacted to electronic calculators by trying to upgrade the mechanical technology.

☐ The Swiss watch industry was so bound to making analog watches that the Japanese were easily able to sweep the mass market with its newer digital technology.

Worshipping our Past Programs/Projects

Related to the above is a deep ego-involvement in established projects (products, services, policies, systems) that you may have personally created. Obviously, our own creations are very much near and dear to our hearts, so they may become very difficult to abandon— even when the facts and the logic dictate that their time has come. In this context, you may recall the powerful, dramatic movie "The Bridge on the River Kwai" (1957) wherein the British colonel, played by actor Alec Guinness, becomes so attached to the bridge he constructs for his Japanese captors that in the end he won't blow it up, even to help win the war.

Catering to Taboos

A subtle but common idea stifler is the existence of issues that simply can't be discussed openly. In some organizations, everything in the product line is too sacrosanct to question, particularly if the big boss favors totally and irrevocably products that he once launched. Or how can you challenge a product/service of a firm that believes with religious zeal that "We're the leader in the field?" In other organizations, established policies may be treated as holy writ. Times may change, but the policies are insulated from discussion or debate. So ongoing assumptions are never tested in light of new conditions or experience, and the status quo safely survives.

Key point: In a climate where policies, protocols or products are too sacred to be critiqued, people's energies to think creatively necessarily decline. Attitudes and statements of this sort thus surface: "Why knock your head against a stone wall?" "Sure, they want creativity. But they only want it in a centralized and carefully controlled way." "If it's 'new' it's OK, but not if it's 'new, new,' *really* new."

Bowing to History

If people have long encountered a reluctance to accept new ideas, their ardor for proposing new proposals/approaches will weaken. Lip service, stalling, side stepping, nit-picking, dropping projects that have promise, etc., are certain ways to raise staffers' doubts such as "Does anyone really want my commitment?"

Submitting to Peer Disapproval

If your peers have been conditioned over time to see the world through darkly-coated lenses—viz., "It won't work in our department," "We tried something like that before you were on the team," "That would make our whole system obsolete," "The union will give us a hard time on that," "We'd never get it in the budget, never"—it's difficult to always be the lone crusading knight on the white horse. So soon enough one senses that "the team" doesn't want any pesky "smart ass" to "rock the boat."

Listening Without Hearing

Essentially we are what we are because of our life experience, our beliefs, our values, and our perceptions. However, if they serve to create a mindset that blocks out new ideas from subordinates, we have what has been appropriately termed "a dialogue of the deaf." So instead of responding with all the usual negative alibis such as "Top management won't go for it," "We didn't budget for it," "They tried it in Department Y," "We're doing OK as it is," "Too much risk," etc., the manager oriented toward change and innovation will listen with a creative ear, as follows:

1. Withhold your judgment (premature evaluation) when an idea is presented. Don't engage in "ideacide," defined by psychologist Harvey A. Hornstein as "rejecting new ideas out of hand without adequate consideration or analysis" ("When Corporate Courage Counts," *Psychology Today*, September 1986). Instead, ask questions and seek out additional facts to be certain you fully understand what is being proposed. Recognize that overly prompt evaluation, as in brainstorming, will put a damper on people's creativity.

2. Listen with intent of altering or reshaping the idea so that it becomes usable.

3. Alternatively, one might respond thusly: "Your idea has potential. Let's bring it up with the rest of the team." The staff might be able to modify it appropriately or, if they decide it really isn't workable, the idea has at least received a full hearing.

And if the idea does have merit but requires upper-level approval, the manager should feel that it is his obligation to the creative staff member to present it to (and persuade) the bosses about the wisdom of the proposal. (The author once worked for a boss who was extremely resistant to subordinates' ideas, including mine. However, he typically would not say directly that he was opposed to an idea. Instead, he would cagily couch it in this type of language: "I'm not sure that I can sell this to my boss." In other words, he passed on the fiction that while he could support it, his tough, conservative boss wouldn't go for it!)

In passing, I might point out that reluctance to listen to staff is an ailment affecting managers at all organizational levels. For example, *The Wall Street Journal* ran a story (March 24, 1995) concerning a CEO who headed up a troubled national retail store chain. The executive, among other faults, "didn't think others could tell him much about the business." He bristled at criticism "and was known as 'Teflon-coated' because suggestions for change slid right off." And as might be expected, he avoided hiring managers from outside the firm who might challenge him.

Offering an Idea to Staff That Firmly Indicates "This is the Way to Go"

No one wants to knife the boss' pet project. (Bosses have tender egos, too.) So the better approach for the manager is to present the problem to staff for discussion; open-ended, solution-free, so as to produce a number of options. At a later point in the discussion, you, as a group member, can toss into the team's hopper your own idea. In this manner, your idea will be intermingled with the others (preferably on a flipchart) and all of them will become group property, subject to full and candid evaluation by the team.

Note:

1. It is quite possible that your own preferred approach also may be offered by a team member. If

so, great! Remember, you want full ideation by everyone and are not concerned with who gets credit for a particular idea, particularly yourself.

2. If you present your idea to staff and it is patently clear that you feel strongly about it, your staff now has a double problem—one is to evaluate your idea as an idea, and the other how to deal with your staunch feelings toward it.

Letting the Daily Rush of Activities Rob Us of "Think Time"

Managers typically find themselves on treadmills—countless meetings; interruptions by bosses, colleagues, and other telephonic demands; assorted crises; travel; making presentations; overflowing in-boxes; customer complaints; supplier foul-ups; and more. So it's hardly surprising that creativity may be forced to take a back seat. Yet, managers who understand the perils of the activity trap manage to rise above the daily routine, the hourly pressures, the incessant demands. They recognize that their real job is much more than fighting fires, signing papers, or attending meandering meetings. So they manage their day creatively by setting daily goals; delegating deeply to staff; using secretaries fully; going to another office, a conference room or the library to relax and reflect; working at home in lieu of the office occasionally; and so on. They also set aside time to attend workshops and training programs that can offer ideas and stimulate the creative juices.

"Bugging" People about "Watching Channels"

All too many managers have a fetish about staffers "cutting out the boss" (boss 1) and going to the boss' superior (boss 2) directly, even if done on a rare occasion. Sure, as a general rule, established channels should be observed. But if a staffer has a problem that can best be resolved by going directly to the next management level (boss 2), why not allow him the freedom to do so?

Of course, managers frown on anyone skipping channels for a number of reasons, some of which are rational and some certainly less so. These reasons are as follows:

☐ The organizational chart spells out the chain of command to ensure orderly discipline and communication, so they (channels) should be strictly observed. It would be a ragtag, undisciplined unit if everyone were free to run to boss 2 whenever they felt it was necessary.

☐ It is a matter of status and ego. How can one be the boss if people are free to decide when they will recognize the boss' authority?

☐ If staffers can run freely to boss 2, it makes boss 1 look bad. That is, the big boss (boss 2) surely will think that his subordinate manager (boss 1) can't handle things, so his people thus feel that they must "run around end." Or worse, boss 2 may feel that boss 1 isn't very interested in the problem so he naturally sends the subordinate "upstairs" directly.

☐ If an "end run" occurs, how will boss 1 know what his subordinate is getting into? Visualize the big boss (boss 2) later asking boss 1 a question about the problem the staffer brought him, and with boss 1 uninformed about it all. ("What, you mean you don't know why your people are coming up here to see me?")

I would suggest that if boss 1 is truly interested in people being creative and exercising their initiative, he should allow staffers the freedom to skip the channel in special situations and to see the big boss (boss 2) directly. This may be essential to save time, particularly if boss 1 is not available, or boss 1 may not have the authority to approve a particular action, or boss 2 may have superior or total knowledge about the issue or problem in question.

So how can the channel-skipping problem be resolved to meet the needs of all the parties involved (the subordinate, boss 1 and boss 2)? We would suggest that boss 1 allow staffers occasional freedom to skip the channel to go around end, with the understanding by the subordinate that he should inform boss 1 that he is going to see boss 2. This assumes that boss 1 is available to be so informed. And, in either case, the staffer subsequently informs boss 1, fully and promptly, in person or by a written note, about what was discussed or resolved in boss 2's office. Of course, the manager (boss 1) may have to trade off his "bruised ego" and "loss of deference/respect" for the self-propulsion and creativity he wants his employees to have.

In general, the challenge for the manager is to rise above ego and status considerations and simply say, "It's OK with me, Kim, for you to see my boss about this. Just let me know what you came up with."

A list of managerial actions/behaviors that are certain to zap any zest for creative problem solving is offered by business writer Leonard Silk ("On Managing Creativity," *Business Month,* April 1989) who draws on the work of Stanford engineer James L. Adams in his book *The Care and Feeding of Ideas* (Reading, MA: Addison-Wesley, 1986):

Assume no value, make no connections, be impatient, nit-pick, interrupt, be bored. Blame, name call, make fun of. Be dominant, command, order, direct, threaten, warn, demand. Be pessimistic, preach, moralize, misunderstand, disagree.

And: Give no feedback, be noncommittal, put on a stone face, be skeptical, correct. Take ball away from, pull rank, get angry, scare.

Silk adds the following to the above list: don't reply to ideas yourself, let someone else do it; steal the idea and claim its authorship; imply that the suggestion is a challenge to your leadership or an implied threat to your intelligence; advise the suggestor not to be such a wise guy; subtly tell others that he isn't a team player. If all else fails, fire the S.O.B. as an example to everyone else!

WHAT CREATIVE MANAGERS DO: GUIDELINES TO TURN ON YOUR OUTFIT'S LIGHTBULBS

Parachutes are like minds—they work best when they're open.

—Anonymous

The Lord gave us two ends—one to sit on and the other to think with. Success depends on which one we use the most.

—Ann Landers, U.S. syndicated columnist

We get nervous when we are satisfied. Then we are dead in the water.

—Bernard Marcus, Chairman of Home Depot (quoted in *Washington Business*, March 29, 1993)

Men grind and grind in the mill of truism, and nothing comes out but what was put in. But the moment they desert the tradition for a spontaneous thought, then poetry, wit, hope, virtue, learning, anecdote, all flock to their aid.

—Ralph Waldo Emerson (1803–1882), U.S. author, philosopher, poet

Creative thinking is simply the realization that there is no particular virtue in doing things the way they have always been done.

—Rudolf Flesch, U.S. author (1911–1986)

Your staffers bring to their jobs a variety of skills, behaviors, knowledge, and attitudes which, no doubt, contribute significantly to team results. However, that basic/latent ability can be enhanced many-fold by actions/interventions on your part that upgrade/convert everyday, moderate-level performance to truly high-level, creative accomplishment. Eugene Raudsepp, a long-time writer/consultant/trainer in the area of creativity, offers a powerful set of guidelines ("Establishing a Creative Climate," *Training and Development Journal*, April 1987) for the manager who conscientiously wishes to establish and nurture a highly creative climate:

Assume Personal Responsibility

While teammates may give each other support to encourage creativity, it won't be done over the long haul if you don't spearhead the encouragement for innovation. A key caution is to avoid counterproductive practices and procedures—overdirection, overobservance, and/or overreporting.

Encourage Freedom

People need a lot of wiggle room to function at their creative best. Encourage team achievement, but also celebrate individual contributors. Give the "creative loner" the freedom to follow leads the group won't pursue.

Communicate Loudly, Clearly, and Frequently that You Expect Innovation

Recognize that innovative behavior won't occur spontaneously. Anticipate that a certain amount of resistance and inertia will work against innovation. And you must walk the talk! So strive actively for commitment to clear-cut innovative goals.

Manage an Idea Factory

Provide an open, interactive climate so your staffers can stimulate ideas in one another

Opt for Growth

Drop products/services/programs that consume resources but don't produce payoffs in terms of growth. Budget properly to support the desired innovation.

Appreciate and Capitalize on Everyone's Uniqueness

Assess individual differences—needs, interests, values, strengths, weaknesses—and tap them while making task assignments. Build self-confidence, and capitalize on each person's desire to achieve/innovate/excel.

Vary Your Managerial Style to Meet Individual Differences and Changing Circumstances

But operate primarily in the participative mode: Lead by suggestion and indirect persuasion, allow full freedom to reach agreed-upon goals, avoid imposing your approach to a problem/task/operation lest it stifle initiative, and allow freedom to imagine as well as to err on occasion sans punishment. As may be appropriate, use traditional command and laissez-faire leadership styles, too.

Demonstrate Your People-identification Regularly

Strive to be a catalyst, a listener to new ideas, a resource person, a collaborator, a sharer of power. Drop traditional roles and behaviors of boss, controller, idea stopper, frustrator. Bring out the best in people by insisting on high standards. Match your serious side with an appreciation of humor and a capability to relax.

Encourage Maturity in Staff

This means supporting those who question ongoing assumptions, rock the boat as need be, take risks, offer ideas. Maturity equates with high motivation, freedom, action orientation, flexibility, and goal commitment. Operate so that these qualities rise to the fore in staff, rather than dependence and immaturity.

Assign Tasks That Provide Challenge and Growth

Use "stretch" in setting goals and assignments, that is, pitch them a bit above prior accomplishments and known capabilities. Encourage staffers to regard problems not as headaches, but as challenges and opportunities for innovative action.

Establish Standards That are Both High and Reasonable

High goals have the potential to produce innovative ideas. Support risk-taking as a mechanism to produce growth and innovation. (Stifling statements such as "we can't afford any risks" or "we must get payoff from this" are "no-no's.") Also, don't look at new ideas through negatively tinted lenses. Recall engineer and inventor Charles F. Kettering's (1876–1958) observation: "The typical eye sees the 10 percent bad of an idea and overlooks the 90 percent good." Hardly the route to unblocking creativeness, is it? (Incidentally, Kettering invented the automatic self-starter for the automobile.)

Tap Pent-up Creativity

Do this by learning the way individuals see themselves at their creative best and how their creative contributions could profit the outfit. Identify the creative ones and set them up as special "brain trusts" to produce creative solutions.

Prescribe Problems in Adequately Precise Terms so People Can Zero in on the Specific Nuances Involved in a Creative Way

Problems defined too broadly will defeat innovative responses. But approaches to problem solving should be open-ended and minimally structured. Expect possible messiness and disorder at the outset. Involve those who can identify strongly with the problem. Also, tap those who can offer skill/ideas/expertise or involve others in special ways.

Allow Adequate "Germination Time" for Ideas

Arbitrary time tables will stifle creativity. Give your creative people enough free time to ponder their solutions/ideas. Keep them from getting bogged down with the daily routine and minutiae so that they can reflect adequately on higher-payoff pursuits.

Identify Your Creative Staffers and Allow Them to Serve on Special Task Forces to Solve Your Most Vexing Problems

Allow these creative people full freedom to use their special talents for innovative problem solving.

Opt for an Open System

Strive for a climate that stresses and rewards openness, freedom, exploration, experimentation, the interaction of different individuals, team collaboration, and the mutual partaking of creative experiences. Recognize that a closed system—one marked by limited entry and exchange of ideas, and stifling of thinking, feeling, and imagining—establishes roadblocks to needed creativity.

Communicate That Mistakes are Learning Opportunities

Don't organize and operate to avoid the occasional "boo-boo." A heavy stress by the manager on error avoidance inevitably emphasizes a search for shortcomings in ideas and generates playing-it-safe attitudes and behaviors. So on your initial review of an idea/solution, zero in on its strong points. Shortcomings in ideas can always be worked on (strengthened) later. **A skill approach:** Assume at the outset that the idea is worthwhile and practical, and enumerate all its plus elements. Then, and only then, reality test it for possible flaws/weaknesses/shortcomings.

Establish a Safe Climate/Atmosphere/Environment for Non-successes

Don't let the penalties for failure exceed the rewards for success, says Raudsepp. **Your best strategy:** Reward success and ignore failure to the extent possible. Also, communicate that ideas that are not adopted or haven't panned out are not wasted. **The reason:** *Creative* types don't like to be identified with wasted activity for long time frames. (Remember that plaintive sign on the shipping room wall: "When I do something right no one remembers; when I do something wrong no one ever forgets.")

Involve People Fully in Decisions and Long-range Plans

Recognize that participation in decisions is a tremendous source of motivation and creativity. Also, higher-quality decisions are likely to result from actions taken by those on the firing line.

Stress Individualized Recognition for Achievement

Creative talent is too precious to ignore. Creativity feeds on recognition, praise, reward. Balance personal rewards against team/unit accomplishment, not letting the creative individual get lost in the rewards for the team.

Study and Upgrade the Ongoing Communications System

Keep all communication channels—up, down, across—open. Provide informational and job experiences that enrich your staffers' base for creativity. Break down barriers to communication that might exist with other departments. Be certain everyone knows where the outfit is going and how he can contribute to that end.

Provide for a Learning Organization

Use small study groups to discuss problems. Include people from other units to secure a greater mix of viewpoints. Assign staffers with promise to mentors to encourage development of their creative potential. If possible, have a special room where staffers can go to think creatively.

Tap the Talents of Those Who Can Help Your Staff to Be More Creative

Have them conduct workshops for your staffers. Also, increase your own creative potential by attending creativity workshops, reading up on the creative process, and interesting yourself in creative exercise, games and puzzles. Your own interest in the area of creativity will set a good example for your staff.

Encourage the Frequent Submission of Staffers' Ideas Up the Line

Make certain creative ideas move upward, and insist on a feedback mechanism from top officials to prevent future ideas from drying up.

Other ideas that managers can use to unleash creativity are:

Strive for a Creative Environment

While we should do all we can to teach people to be more creative, we should work, too, at building a creative environment, one "where ideas have a chance to bloom." This is essential because the individual can't readily rise above a stultifying climate. To quote management consultant Geary Rummler, "Put a good performer up against a bad system, and the system will win every time."

The creative environment is one where new ideas are encouraged, listened to, and rewarded; risk-taking is emphasized; mistakes are not punished, but are regarded as learning experiences; communication is open; trust is high rather than low; creative pronouncements pass the "walk the talk" test (that is, no hypocrisy); people are encouraged to interact widely with others, both within and outside the organization; group action is stressed; training is fully supported; ideation is expected/appreciated from everyone in the organization without regard to one's job title, gender, or organizational level; task forces/special study groups are used widely.

Added to the above is to preach and practice what Harry V. Quadracci, founder and president of printing giant Quad/Graphics, Peewaukee, Wisconsin, calls "The doctrine of assumed responsibility." This means to abandon the traditional practice of defining precisely and narrowly a person's responsibility. Instead, encourage people to behave in this mode: "You see something that has to be done, so you assume that you have the responsibility to do it" (quoted from an "Interview (with) Harry V. Quadracci," *Business Ethics,* May/June 1993).

Broaden the Team's Problem-solving Repertoire

Many of us are more capable than some of us . . . but none of us is as capable as all of us!!

—Per Ziggy, cartoon character

Most of us tend to rely on normal, traditional, logical problem-solving approaches. But some problems may be tackled better via creative methods. Here's how M.O. ("Mo") Edwards, a Palo Alto creativity consultant, helpfully differentiates between the two styles (in Jack Gordon and Rom Zemke, "Making Them More Creative," *Training,* May 1986):

The Logical Problem-solving Approach

☐ Start with a well-defined problem, i.e., one where a specific end result is wanted; e.g., the problem is to be resolved with a cost limitation, the regular situation is to be restored, a disaster must be avoided, etc.

☐ Use vertical thinking, i.e., the mode of attack is logical, sequential, convergent, and traditional. Facts and critical judgment are basic to the process.

☐ Few ideas/solutions are generated. Ideas are evaluated immediately when offered. Only those that fit the rigid criteria are discussed.

☐ The problem has some definite and identifiable cause.

☐ The solution is corrective, i.e., what was wrong now gets fixed. The applied solution produces predictable and measurable results.

The Creative Problem-solving Approach

☐ The problem typically is vague, ill-defined. Its definition is to be perceived in a novel or different way. Problems may be regarded as opportunities or challenges.

☐ Lateral thinking is applied, i.e., the mode is open-ended, "illogical," non-linear. The aim is for an "Aha," an intuitive response, a real breakthrough. Facts are used, but they are less critical than in the above-described logical approaches. A fuller description of lateral thinking is given below.

☐ Many ideas are generated, and they are evaluated only after all possibilities have been proposed.

☐ Problems have no single, precise cause; or this approach is used when seeking opportunities as opposed to fixing what is wrong.

☐ The solution, possibly a major breakthrough, may entail hitting upon a new challenge or opportunity.

So which approach is used when? Edwards advises to use the logical one first. But if you don't come up with a truly new departure, go on to creative thinking. Note that in the creative approach logic is not eliminated, only de-emphasized.

A word about convergent vs. divergent thinking: Convergent thinking requires the ability to recognize, to remember, to combine or link elements, features, or ideas in totally new ways, to solve by moving toward one more-or-less right answer. Intelligence tests measure this kind of intellectual/thinking ability.

But the divergent thinking approach, essentially elaboration, stresses searching activities with the ability to think in different directions, to elaborate, to expand, to develop and add details to ideas or products, to invent, to innovate. This freer-wheeling quality isn't measured by standard tests.

But note that those who are creative recognize the value of each thinking style and are comfortable using both of them.

We stated above that lateral thinking is part of the creative problem-solving approach (as opposed to the logical approach). The concept of lateral thinking (also referred to as zig-zag thinking) was developed by Dr. Edward de Bono, a British research physician and prolific writer on creativity. His theory ("Creativity and the Role of Lateral Thinking," *Personnel,* May–June 1971) is that we ordinarily think sequentially, that is to say, we take bits of information and assemble them to form logical patterns. This works for us most of the time, except when incoming information refuses to fit into a particular established pattern.

So what must we do? We need to rearrange patterns, think of new ones, and abandon old ones. What's needed, then, are imaginative sweeps of thought—breakthrough thinking—to liberate the mind from rigid, restraining patterns/habits into new, more useful patterns.

A key aspect of lateral thinking is what de Bono terms "direction." That is to say, wherever there is a direction, particularly one that is not producing anything for us, the opposite direction is implied. Reversal means taking the obvious idea and turning it inside out, upside down, back to front. Dr. de Bono (in "The Virtues of Zigzag Thinking," *Think Magazine,* May-June 1969) uses as an example the anecdote involving the 18th century Duchess of Devonshire, who was fat to the point that even her friends no longer could refer to her as plump. She called in various doctors for help on her weight reduction problem, but each recommended the same expected, traditional solution—a near-starvation diet. So she dropped all of them, because that wasn't what she wanted to hear.

Finally, one physician appeared who fussed over her, commented on her situation and recommended that in lieu of eating less she should have a big glass of malted milk 30 minutes before each meal! Note that the obvious remedy—logical thinking—was to recommend less food. But the Duchess' gargantuan condition really called for less appetite, not less food. So what was really needed was an appetite suppressant. The lateral approach, via reversal, says, "Yes, she eats too much. But let's not tell her to cut down on her food intake. Instead, let's tell her to eat more and see what results." Food as an appetite suppressor (food in) rather than some form of food deprivation (food out) was the magnificent reversal that really could make a difference. More becomes less!

de Bono thinks that lateral thinking, as a process, can be learned. All of us can escape from old ideas and generate new, more useful ones. Note that in logical (linear) thinking one must be right at each stage. Conversely, in lateral thinking one is allowed to be wrong, even to be wrong on purpose. With "permission" to be wrong, we can get far enough away from an old idea to locate a new one.

The most appropriate uses of lateral thinking, says de Bono, are these:

☐ at the outset of thinking about a problem.
☐ when one hits a brick wall via traditional, analytical thinking.
☐ when given a problem others have given up on.
☐ when one has enough time to seek for a solution better than the adequate one already on hand.
☐ when an assessment of the "adequate" ways indicate that much better ways can be turned up.

In essence, de Bono is telling us to stop bashing against a problem, but go around it, over it, or under it. **Note:** Many of de Bono's practical techniques are given in one of his early works, *Lateral Thinking—Creativity Step by Step* (New York: Harper & Row, 1970).

As we stated above, logical problem solving may be useful depending on the problem. But if improperly used it won't get us anywhere.

Story: In the Middle East a householder named Abdul was searching carefully for something on the ground. A neighbor came by and, wishing to help, asked: "What have you lost, Abdul?"

Abdul: "My house key."

Neighbor: "I will help you to find it."

So the neighbor joined Abdul on his knees. They both looked for the key, but with little success.

Neighbor: "My knees are getting sore. Where exactly, Abdul, did you drop your key?"

Abdul: "In my house."

Neighbor: "So, Abdul, please tell me why are you searching here?"

Abdul: "There is much more light here than in my house."

Make Room for the Iconoclasts

Organizational psychologist Dr. Harry Levinson (in "Why the Behemoths Fell: Psychological Roots of Corporate Failure," *American Psychologist,* Vol. 49, 1994) points out the need of organizations to take advantage of "creatively abrasive people . . . those sharp, scratch, harsh, almost unpleasant guys who see and tell you about things as they really are."

So how does one supervise mavericks—those creative, independent, and possibly difficult people who should be encouraged to offer their ideas but still meet organizational needs?

Management consultant James E. Seitz (in "Supervising Mavericks," The Pryor Report, October 1986) offers three key approaches:

Always be Available

Mavericks don't follow a rigid schedule, but they do need contact. They want others to show interest in them and their ideas. So initiate conversations with them, for they value communication opportunities to dispense or to gain insight. Contact is particularly important if the maverick has undertaken a high-risk project that flopped. They need solid support to bounce back.

Set Time Limits

Projects not only require beginnings but ends (completion points), too. So if a project isn't panning out in a reasonable time period, it is essential to communicate that time is now up. But this should be done with a full, reasoned explanation for the project's cessation and to be certain that the discussion ends up on a positive note.

Provide Adequate Resources

This should include everything from a workable (ample) budget to administrative support and help on paperwork.

Import New Approaches/Ideas

You undoubtedly want your staff and yourself to be highly creative, to be on the lookout for opportunities to innovate. But it also makes sense to shop the competition for better practices and improvement. Certainly few organizations have a monopoly on all the creative possibilities regarding their products or services.

In fact, it's also possible to upgrade performance/innovation by *importing* practices typically used in one field into another business operation that ordinarily doesn't use such techniques, says performance consultant Robert J. Kriegel, the author of *If It Ain't Broke, Break It!* (New York: Warner Books, 1991).

An example cited by Dr. Kriegel is the following: The head of a hospital chain wanted to upgrade the image and attitude people generally held about hospitals and his facilities in particular. So Kriegel advised the president to send its key personnel to different resorts and on cruises to learn about patient care from these other intensive (non-hospital) care setups. **The result:** The managers returned with more than 100 possible improvements—everything from altering the decor and meals to changing clothing codes and incentives for staffers. And by implementing many of these ideas, the organization's ranking among hospitals in its state rose dramatically (reported by Sheryl Silver, "Work Smarter: Import Innovations," *The Washington Post,* July 14, 1993).

Allow Informality in Dress

A growing number of firms are having one day, typically Friday, designated as a "dress-down day." The idea is to encourage people to be looser, to be more of themselves, even to de-emphasize status, all of which can bear on creativity. This one-day practice naturally raises this question: If it can work on Friday, why limit the policy to that one day of the week?

In any case, if it is OK to dress informally in your office, why not give it a whirl? But you might opt for other informal, fun-type activities, too, such as holding staff meetings outdoors, rotating the chairperson role at staff meetings, celebrating a goal accomplishment with a catered lunch or by going to a near-by restaurant, having a special cake and coffee for a staffer's birthday, holding added luncheon parties on Valentine's Day, the first day of spring, Halloween, or President Polk's birthday (!).

Also, allow people to work flexible hours. It's a lot easier to be creative in a less-rigid time frame. Recognize, too, that it may be a lot easier to ideate when the phones are no longer ringing and everyone else has departed for the day.

Use Inviting, Igniting Language

We, as managers, have a choice concerning the language we employ. We can turn people off with killer phrases such as "We're not budgeted for it," "The board won't go for it," "It's too political," "It needs a lot of committee study." Or we can turn people on with inviting statements such as "You're on the right track," "That could make a difference," "I see a lot of possibilities in that," "You're on target," "That's a blockbuster," "Let's give 'er a whirl," etc.

We also can get people out of their conventional thinking and performing modes by tossing challenging statements at them. **Examples:** "You know, there's gotta be another (more productive, better, faster, quieter, cheaper) way." "It's hard to imagine that we haven't changed anything on this since . . ." "I get the feeling that we're letting Company XYZ become the leader in this field."

Questions: Do we want to encourage or discourage communication? Do we want our people to think more or less well of themselves? Do we want to nurture or stifle creativity? The language we use can make the difference. Of course, language is more than mere borrowed words and phrases. It has to reflect our own innermost sentiments/feelings about the value of creative approaches to our problems.

Use Questions to Encourage Creative Thinking

Your job as a manager is not to solve all problems yourself—solo—but to get the staff to locate them and to propose constructive solutions. So when your staffers come to you with problems, your task is to encourage them to think in the greatest possible depth or breadth about them. You certainly don't want them to dump the problem onto your lap and run. Here, then, are some thought-provoking queries you can pose when problems are brought to you:

- [ ] What if we tried . . .?
- [ ] Could you give me some more of your reasoning about . . .?
- [ ] Who else will be impacted by this?
- [ ] Wouldn't it be great if . . .?
- [ ] Can you propose one or more alternate solutions?
- [ ] What if we were to brainstorm this with the rest of the team?

- [ ] Will this solution create new problems?
- [ ] If we don't act now, what is likely to occur?
- [ ] Could this be done in any way with no or lesser cost?
- [ ] Are there any "downsides" to your proposal?
- [ ] How does this relate to what the competition is doing?
- [ ] How soon can we implement this?

Adopt Roles Other Than That of "The Boss"

A leadership workshop I conducted had a session in it on "unleashing creativity." Two participants brought in ads from business magazines (neither the names of the journals nor their dates were indicated), which stated in very large, bold, black letters:

TALK BACK TO THE BOSS

WHEN EVERYONE THINKS LIKE THE BOSS, NO ONE THINKS VERY MUCH

The first ad, which had some text, was from the Dana Corporation, Toledo. The ad said, in part:

It's one of Dana's principles of productivity.

Bosses don't have all the answers. The worker who does the job always knows more about it than his boss. But all that he knows can't be used unless he's free to talk about it. Especially to his boss.

At Dana, bosses listen . . .

So we talked about the two statements in the ads. Some members of the group—certainly not all—made the point that the boss today has many roles to assume, most of which have little to do with managing as the traditional boss always has. These newer roles are encourager, enabler, empowerer, challenger, inspirer, praise-giver, cheerleader, supporter, risk tolerator, catalyst, listener, coach, facilitator, delegator, innovator, advocate (to his boss on behalf of the team), truth-seeker, change sponsor, negotiator/liaison (with other units), fun modeler.

These roles obviously have a lot to do with how creative the climate will be and the degree to which people will respond in a creative/innovative way.

Question: How do you feel about the messages in the two ads?

Tell Stories That Support Innovation

This idea is to inspire others to be creative by pointing out the special, innovative, exciting accomplishments of others. It is a great way to get people into new mindsets. It can introduce new people to the culture of the organization. Stories of creative successes can also help those who feel discouraged, disappointed, hemmed in, frustrated, or less than effective.

A story to be meaningful and inspirational to others, per research staffers Sylvester Taylor and Luke Novelli, Jr., of the Center for Creative Leadership, Greensboro, North Carolina ("Telling a Story about Innovation," *Issues and Observations,* Vol. 11, No. 1, 1991), has these key characteristics:

- ☐ The story presents the twin aspects of a novel idea, i.e., **creativity** and **innovation.** The former is the generation of a new and useful idea; the latter its successful implementation.
- ☐ **It is widely disseminated.** The intended audience must be reached, and the recipients must know that others know and believe the story. If these elements are present the story will be repeated, commented on, and its effect will be greatly enhanced.
- ☐ **It is vivid.** It must be about the stellar work of a real employee and have a strong sense of time and place. This will ensure credibility and aid retention of what is transmitted. The language used must be vivid, too.
- ☐ **It must inspire.** This requires presenting the whole story and suggesting one's desired behavior in light of the story.
- ☐ **It must stress uniqueness.** The story should point out that the organization is a special place in which to work. **The effect:** People feel they are special because they function in a super place and thus are drawn into the values and ideas of the story.

Key point: Telling a unique story can help us shape the organization's culture. Inspiring legend and lore will most certainly be passed along to others. An uplifting, well-told, well-timed story will accomplish more than several dozen memos. So if we can shape the culture toward creativity, we will encourage inspired/innovative behavior, because innovation won't occur unless the organization supports it.

Management guru Tom Peters (in "Training for Curiosity in Your Corporate Culture," *Washington Busi-ness Journal,* August 10–16, 1992), advises managers to keep their organization imaginative in these ways:

- ☐ As opposed to hiring "incurious" people, "hire a few genuine off-the-wall sorts—i.e., collect weirdos." Also, try to turn loose your creative types from time to time: "Bankroll them until they can invent a wacky project that will spark the whole organization."
- ☐ Weed out the dullards. You can't afford to harbor the mental deadwood on your payroll.
- ☐ Insist that everyone take vacations. Everyone needs a breather—all work and no play make Jack and Jane a dull boy and a dull girl. You can't expect curiosity to flourish among those in or near burnout.
- ☐ Opt for new staff interaction patterns, i.e., use space management as a tool (a) for project teams to be able to assemble with a minute's notice, (b) to allow people to express their diverse personalities, (c) to encourage people to mingle, talk, laugh, ideate, and (d) to abandon the usual functional groupings.
- ☐ Support off-beat, non-job-related educational activities such as clubs for hobbyists, lectures given by non-business types, taking of courses in non-business subjects. **Your goal:** to get people out of their tried-and-true, traditional, established, usual, limited-thinking patterns.
- ☐ Plump for curiosity by subjecting it to "measurement." Says Peters: At the usual semi-annual performance review time, have everyone submit a one-page essay on (a) the strangest thing I've done off the job this year, (b) the weirdest idea I've tried on the job, or (c) my most creative/novel/original foul-up, on or off the job. Then take these answers and "deal curiosity directly into the evaluation deck, near the top."
- ☐ Model curiosity. It's the best way to be sure it rubs off on the staffers.
- ☐ Teach curiosity. Use brainstorming and other creative thinking techniques.
- ☐ Make fun/laughter a workplace hallmark.
- ☐ Opt for change of pace. Declare a miniature golf day. Show a training film and pass popcorn all around.
- ☐ The bottom line, per Peters: You want to restore the child in overly patterned, uptight adults.

RISK-TAKING TO FOSTER CREATIVITY/ INNOVATION: "NO GUTS, NO GLORY"

One doesn't discover new lands without consenting to lose sight of the shore for a very long time.

—Andre Gide (1869–1951), French author and Nobel Prize winner in literature (1947)

. . . It is only by risking our persons from one hour to another that we live at all. And often enough our faith beforehand in an uncertified result is the only thing that makes the result come true.

—William James (1842–1910), U.S. philosopher and psychologist

Security is mostly a superstition. It does not exist in nature, nor do the children of men as a whole experience it. Avoiding danger is no safer in the long run than outright exposure. Life is either a daring adventure or nothing.

—Helen Keller (1880–1968), U.S. author and lecturer

The reasonable man adapts himself to the world; the unreasonable one persists in trying to adapt the world to himself. Therefore, all progress depends on the unreasonable man.

—George Bernard Shaw (1856–1950), Irish playwright, novelist, critic, and Nobel Prize winner in literature (1925)

Organizations and managers within them all too often strive for stability, predictability, doing things by the book, working from risk-free, "tried and true" formulas. The following anecdote makes this point.

Story: The administrative assistant was showing the bright, new, young MBA around executive row. The following dialog ensued.

Administrative assistant: This is what everyone calls "Head Harbor."

Bright new, young MBA: You mean this is where all the heads batten down the hatches and play it safe?

Administrative assistant (admiringly): Yeah, you're right on target. Sure, your bosses will tell you they want a lot of creativity; but if you're smart, you'll find out first where and how much they really want. If you check carefully, you'll find that they say they want innovation, but everyone knows that it should look a lot like what's already going on.

Bright new, young MBA (smilingly): You mean "new," but not "new, new"; "bold," but not "bold, bold."

Administrative assistant: Welcome to "Head Harbor," home of the nearly brave.

Part of engaging in creative thinking and behavior is to take risks. Of course, risk-taking understandably may be perceived as a scary process. Accordingly, here are some "rules" or ways to deal with (minimize) risk as suggested by educator Joe Agran (cited by Susan Morse in "You: Risk or Retreat," *The Washington Post,* July 24, 1984):

Affordability. Don't ever risk more than you can afford to lose. Watch "heat of the moment" decisions when large commitments are involved.

Practicality. Don't risk a great deal for a small gain/ return. (But weigh this advisory against the "no pain, no gain" dictum.)

Face loss. Avoiding loss of face is a poor basis for risk taking. Don't let anyone goad you into taking a risk you wouldn't normally take on your own. So be courageous and withstand possible loss of approval. (Real friends don't apply such pressures.)

Principle. Risks taken solely on the basis of principle may be dangerous to your health. There's little point in winning the battle and losing the war. **Example:** A bold confrontation with a key figure may wipe out a worthwhile relationship or even a career.

Calculation. Weigh/calculate your risks. Be clear on what you want and the possible price you're prepared to pay.

Most managers know that their organizations need new ideas and fresh approaches for them to remain vital and vibrant. But they also know that striking out in new directions, as we stated above, may be fraught with risk. Obviously the mindset of a risk-taker rather than the risk-avoider is needed to wrestle successfully with this dilemma. Consider, then, these concepts:

☐ Not taking risks may be more devastating than taking them. Playing it totally safe in today's world may well be the biggest risk of them all.

☐ Add to your repertoire of "rules to live by," these two:

1) The "Jesuit's Rule": It is far easier to ask for forgiveness than permission.

2) The "Rabbi's Rule": If you really want to eat it, don't ask if it's Kosher (!).

Key point: You'll get more done by moving ahead on what you strongly believe makes sense than to wait for "Big Daddy" to tell you it's OK to act on it. Recognize that one's bosses will fall into either of these two categories.

☐ The one who is always prone to ask: "What if it doesn't work?"

☐ The one who says "Why not? Let's do it. I'll support you on this."

If you have the "let's not rock the boat" type of boss, you can't afford to wait without end until he gets the courage to give you an OK on every action worth taking. So in either case, take the "full steam ahead" approach and accept the risk with a big, determined smile.

There are essentially two sides to risk-taking—success and less than success. In the latter case, it becomes a learning experience not necessarily a failure. So crank into your psyche or mindset this dictum: "It's OK for people to fail." Once you've given yourself permission to fail, the risk-taking process becomes much less scary. Use self-talk along this line: "We're going into unchartered waters. No one has done this before. But it's a real opportunity when (not if) we pull it off. Sure, it's new, unprecedented; but we have to do it."

More on mindset. Drop self-defeating queries such as "What am I likely to lose?" and adopt "Am I taking advantage of this opportunity?" and enthusiastic, inviting ones such as "What is the best outcome that's likely to happen?"

☐ Be clear about your definition of leadership. It certainly is not thinking of stratagems to stay out of trouble. Rather, as Chris Majer, president of Sportsmind, a consulting and training firm, puts it, "Leadership is the willingness to trust yourself enough to take certain risks—like empowering your people; letting go of control; and supporting people in their ideas, even new ones" (quoted in

"How Do You Get Managers to Be Risk Takers?", *Training and Development Journal,* July 1989).

☐ Assess risk-taking in light of what the competition and/or your customers might be up to. So if you don't move ahead, is there a possibility the competition will? Or your customers will behave in unwanted ways because of your reluctance to act?

☐ When considering a risk-taking move, anticipate that there will be a lot of naysayers and "stand-patters" who will be eager to slow you down. The world will communicate with great certainty "it's too risky," "it can't be done," "it's never worked before," and so on. But take all that negativism in stride. Simply override it with your own special brand of courage, faith, optimism, insight, and goal orientation.

☐ Be bold enough to take actions and make decisions even when all the facts are not in to form a neat, airtight pattern. **Note:** "All the facts" are rarely "all in."

☐ Don't rely solely on your own perceptions of your affinity toward risk taking. Instead, get some feedback from your staff, colleagues, and bosses regarding how they see you on this 7-point risk-taking scale:

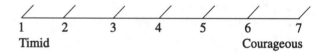

1	2	3	4	5	6	7
Timid						Courageous

Your staff can provide anonymous ratings. You might sound out your bosses on this leadership dimension at performance review time. Check with colleagues, too, assuming they know enough of your risk-taking style. If you're into team building, consider making this an agenda item.

☐ One helpful form of introspection is to ask yourself: "Where have I failed in the last 4–6 months?" No failures may mean that you've been totally skillful in everything you've undertaken. But conversely, it may simply mean that you haven't been taking any real risks, that you've been opting very carefully for risk avoidance rather than risk taking.

Risk-taking has the potential for valuable payoffs, as illustrated in this anecdote.

Story: The employment manager of a national chain of retail office supply stores was interviewing a young woman for a job of product manager. After chatting with her a while, he said: "We stress creativity, innovation, and risk-taking here. Here's my stapler. Show me a new use for this."

The job applicant very calmly picked up a scissors on the interviewer's desk and promptly cut his tie in half. While the interviewer looked on in disbelief, she deftly stapled the two parts of the tie together.

With a smile she asked, "Now that I have demonstrated my instant all-purpose mender, how many will you have?"

The risk-taking young woman got the job.

Note:

For material on risk taking in decision making, see Chapter 10, "The Manager as a Problem Solver and Decision Maker: What Managers Get Paid For," Step 5: Choosing Among Alternatives, Realizing Risk Reduction.

Adding "Whole Brain" Thinking to Our Problem-solving, Decision-making, and Creative-thinking Abilities

Not only our pleasure, our joy and our laughter but also our sorrow, pain, grief and tears arise from the brain, and the brain alone. With it we think and understand, see and hear, and we discriminate between the ugly and the beautiful, between what is pleasant and what is unpleasant and between good and evil.

—Hippocrates (460–c.370 B.C.), Greek physician and father of medicine (quoted in *The Washington Post*, September 6, 1982)

We can think differently about the mind now. It is not a mystical thing but something that can be understood.

—Dr. David Hubel, 1979 (quoted in *The Washington Post*, September 6, 1982)

Neurosurgeon Roger W. Sperry received the 1981 Nobel Prize in Medicine for his research in the differences in left vs. right brain hemisphere processing, essentially a "split-brain" concept (discussed in Roger W. Sperry, "Left-Brain, Right-Brain," *Saturday Review*, October 9, 1975). The management literature of the '70s and '80s used the concept of "left brain, right brain" frequently to explain the kind of thinking we do (or don't do).

Speaking broadly, the left hemisphere is the province of analytical thought, the right that of intuition and insight. More specifically, per the theory of hemispheric specialization, the left brain produces thinking that is objective, convergent, logical, orderly, factual, rational, linear, sequential, vertical, numerical/quantitative. Conversely, right-brain thinking is intuitive, emotional, non-linear, divergent, imaginative, experimental, non-judgmental, subjective, spatial, artistic, holistic, and marked by the ability to visualize and synthesize.

Ned Herrmann, pioneer of creative thinking in the corporation (at GE) and now a leading researcher, consultant, writer, and trainer in whole-brain technology, states (in "The Creative Brain," *Training and Development Journal*, October 1981) that the source of our creativity is our brain, particularly the aspect we call the mind. The mind, the most sophisticated portion of our brain systems, resides in the cerebral cortex of the two hemispheres.

For most of us, says Herrmann, the left cerebral hemisphere is much better at verbal, logical, sequential, analytical tasks—i.e., it is good at language, arithmetic, problem solving, and reason/logic. The right cerebral hemisphere, conversely, is artistic, better at non-verbal ideation, can perceive the big picture, can help us operate our autos and ski safely, receives wonderful flashes of ideas, and solves problems via the use of feelings (emotion) and intuition.

There is also another vital segment of the brain system that contributes further to brain function specialization, says Herrmann. This is the limbic system, also hemispheric, located deeper in the brain. Each half of the limbic system is nestled into the two cerebral hemispheres, near the corpus callosum, the main tie between the hemispheres.

How does the limbic system operate? It is the central point of the more visceral (instinctual) processing—emotional, interpersonal activities in the right limbic system, and structured, organized activities in the left limbic system.

In combination, the two hemispheres of the cerebral cortex plus the two parts of the limbic system form four quadrants of specialized mental activity, as the model on page 616 indicates (Figure 1).

Most of us, says Herrmann, are subject to a brain dominance condition with the two cerebral cortex hemispheres and other portions of the brain system working together, but with one or more elements taking charge. For creativ-

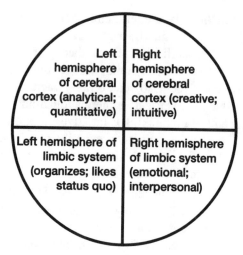

Figure 13-1. Conceptualization of the human mind.

ity to occur, the two left mode elements and the two right elements of the brain work together, cooperatively and repetitively. In the course of our creative work, our minds shift between the four quadrants, depending on the particular mental task requirements we face. In any case, creative thinking is "whole brained," with significant differences in the four processing modes. Most of us are dominant on one side of the brain; but fortunately, we can learn to tap our less dominant sides more often.

Note: Herrmann became manager of Management Education for GE in 1970. He created the Herrmann Participant Survey Form (1987) to describe workshop participants' thinking styles and learning preferences in line with his Brain Dominance Theory. With GE sponsorship, he developed and validated the Herrmann Brain Dominance Instrument (HBDI), the scored and analyzed Participant Survey. He heads up the Ned Herrmann Group, Lake Lure, North Carolina.

To understand the differences in the four processing modes, let's consider how problem-solving and decision-making strategies may take place. Drawing on a four-quadrant model developed by consultants of the Applied Creative Learning Systems, Inc., Largo, Florida (presented at the National Conference of The American Society for Training and Development, Anaheim, CA, May 21, 1985), consider (a) the strategic approaches in each mode, and (b) what may be overlooked in each of the four modes:

Cerebral, Upper Left Hemispheric Mode

Approaches: abstract, logical, analytical, theoretical-and-data based

May overlook: peoples' feelings and synergistic/holistic opportunities

Cerebral, Upper Right Hemispheric Mode

Approaches: intuitive, experimental, risk taking

May overlook: practicality, details

Lower Left Limbic Mode

Approaches: pragmatic, controlled, procedural, conservative, organizational

May overlook: the big picture, new ideas, other possible solutions

Lower Right Limbic Mode

Approaches: emotional, intuitive (feelings), interpersonal

May overlook: facts, logic, planning

To help us understand better the processing differences in each of the four modes, Herrmann suggests we look at the typical phrases we might use while in each mode and typical derogatory phrases used by others to describe those in the various modes (drawn from "Differences in Processing Modes," handout provided by Ned Herrmann at the 1993 National Conference of the American Society for Training and Development, Atlanta):

Typical Phrases We May Use

Upper left: "tools," "hardware," "key point," "the bottom line," "break it down"

Upper right: "the big picture," "conceptual," "innovative," "cutting edge," "play with the idea"

Lower left: "play it safe," "by the book," "sequence," "self-discipline," "we've always done it this way"

Lower right: "teamwork," "human values," "personal growth," "participatory"

Typical Derogatory Phrases Used by Others

Upper left: "number cruncher," "cold fish," "uncaring," "unemotional"

Upper right: "unrealistic," "off the wall," "ivory tower," "dreamer"

Lower left: "picky," "unimaginative," "one-track-mind," "stick-in-the-mud"

Lower right: "bleeding heart," "soft touch," "talk, talk, talk," "gullible"

The following anecdote illustrates free-wheeling, uninhibited right brain creativity.

Story: After an exhilarating lecture by Somerset Maugham, a young, first-time writer approached the renowned novelist. He showed Maugham his book, which the novelist ran through rapidly, and deferentially asked him for help to produce a sparkling title for his new novel. This conversation ensued:

Maugham: Any drums in your book?

Young novelist: No, sir.

Maugham: Any trumpets?

Young novelist: None at all, sir.

Maugham: Good. Then call it "No Drums, No Trumpets" (!)

Key points on whole brain thinking (based on a handout distributed by Ned Herrmann at the 1993 ASTD conference, Atlanta):

1. The Herrmann four-quadrant brain dominance model entails a blending of the four left and right brain learning/thinking styles.
2. The brain dominance concept is concerned with individual differences, rather than good or bad, right or wrong. So no one style is "best."
3. All of us have at least one primary learning/thinking style.
4. Our differences in our processing modes produce different skills for us:

Upper left: analytical, statistical, scientific, financial

Upper right: integrative, visualizing, conceptualizing, generating ideas, banking on our intuition

Lower left: planning, supervising, organizing, implementing

Lower right: expressing ideas, interpersonal, teaching/training

GROUP-IN-ACTION TECHNIQUES TO STIMULATE AND KEEP YOUR WORK GROUP'S CREATIVE JUICES FLOWING

Your team, obviously, can be a great source of creative problem solving. We say *can be* because its creativity is dependent on a number of factors. The most important factors are a climate that encourages candid, freewheeling thought plus the group-in-action techniques it uses to aid in unleashing its creativity. We discuss a number of these techniques below.

Brainstorming

This technique is easy to apply and thus is very widely used by work groups, committees, and task forces of all sorts. Its procedures are described in Chapter 10, "The Manager As a Problem Solver and Decision Maker: What Managers Get Paid For," Step 1: Identifying and Defining/Formulating Our Problem.

Role Storming. Also described in Chapter 10, Step 1.

Problem Identification—ABC Approach. Also described in Chapter 10, Step 1.

Force Field Analysis. Also described in Chapter 10, Step 2: Gathering Information About the Problem.

Brainstorming, a "Reverse Approach." Chapter 10, Step 3: Developing/Generating Alternate Solutions.

Card Posting Technique. Chapter 10. Same location as above.

The Slip Method. Same location as above.

Idea Writing. Same location as above.

Problem Onslaught. Same location as above.

Upside-Down Problem Solving. Same location as above.

Outcome Objective

Creativity consultant/author Bryan W. Mattimore ("Imagine That!", *Training and Development,* July 1994) stresses that creative, freewheeling, problem-solving sessions will benefit from clearly defined goals. An effective way to do this is via "time-track visualization." **Procedure:** Simply tell your participants to pretend their session has just ended and that everything went off terrifically. Then ask them what turned them on and what ideas were generated. Post the ideas on a flipchart. In effect, you are asking them to visualize "the future," i.e., the end of the session and what was accomplished. The result is establishing clear-cut goals (results, outcomes) for the meeting/session.

Then, when your session ends, use the visualized goals as a basis for assessing what was accomplished. Mattimore states that most groups are able to accomplish all the results they visualized.

Mindmapping (or Idea Mapping)

Developed by Tony Buzan of The Learning Methods Group, England (described in Tony Buzan in *Use Both Sides of Your Brain,* Revised Edition, New York: E. P. Dutton, 1983), many—not all—people find it helpful to dump out a lot of ideas in very short order. We simply start with a key concept in the center of a page or flipchart, circle it (the catalytic word) and then branch out from the trigger word in all directions. Creating a free-flowing web of ideas, as opposed to stacking them in the usual columns and rows, can be a great idea stimulator. The technique is useful for both groups and individuals.

The ideas may be related to causes, effects, solutions, lists of things to do or remember, etc. The important thing is to branch out from the core idea. The branches typically are areas to consider, with sub-branches flowing from the major branches.

As an example, why don't we plan Jane Jones' wedding? We'll start by putting "Jane's wedding" in the center of a flipchart sheet, Figure 13-2, page 619. We'll then randomly enter, as branches, the major areas of concern that have to be considered—announcements, invitation list, church service, reception, and so on. And for each of these branches we can add specific tasks (sub-branches).

So what we have, essentially, is an elaborate, king-size doodle with words. It is a non-linear, right-brain way of visually organizing thoughts, associations and/or rela-

tionships. Once a branch or two is identified as pertinent, it quickly triggers other related branches.

Storyboarding

Like brainstorming, this creative problem-solving device elicits ideas from a group very rapidly, but it does so along somewhat structured lines. A major theme or problem area, possibly with several sub-themes, are used to spark ideas. Here's how it works ("Eyes on Quality," *Performance,* March 1995):

1. Set up a large (4' × 4') storyboard (usually a black or green felt board) in front of the room.
2. State the purpose of the meeting and the ground rules, e.g., no blaming, no finger pointing, just generating ideas on the topics/problem areas at hand. It's a good idea to loosen up the group with fun warm-up exercises.
3. Post index cards (4" × 6") on the board, each bearing a key question. For example, Diane Elko, director of Quality for American Capital Management and Research Inc., brought 13 senior executives of a mutual bond firm together. **Their goal:** To enhance the firm's quality improvement process. The cards bore these four questions: How can we turn managers into quality leaders? How can we keep employees excited about quality? What quality improvements will grab the attention of every customer? What can we do to make us feel terrific about measuring quality?
4. As the participants then shouted suggestions, two participants wrote on smaller index cards, which were then pinned beneath the larger cards. All ideas had to be specific rather than vague.
5. The participants voted on the best and most actionable suggestions. **Note:** Storyboarding meetings must end with a commitment to action.

This particular meeting delivered these results: 80 ideas were generated, 20 being put into action. The visual information, posted up front, encouraged active responding. **Note:** The group was able to compress into one hour what could have been a daylong strategy session.

The McNellis Co., New Brighton, PA, which provides seminars on storyboarding, adds another procedure to aid in prioritizing the ideas for action. Using adhesive colored dots, each participant marks ideas that merit "floating to the top." The advantage of this procedure: It avoids politicking and time-consuming efforts at persua-

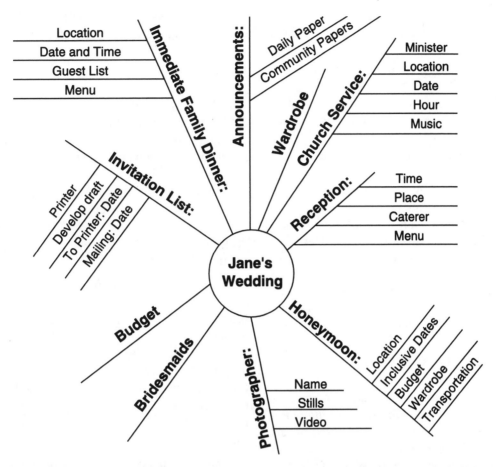

Figure 13-2. Illustration of a mind mapping diagram using the planning of a wedding as an example.

sion—ideas stand or fall on their own, separated from the egos of the contributors. The ideas with the most dots win their place on the storyboard (Julie Barker, "Get Outta Line!" *Successful Meetings,* October 1994).

Random Word Stimulation Technique

Much of our thinking is logical, i.e., we are only concerned with what is fully relevant. So we systematically discard elements not related to a subject. But, says management professor Dr. Thomas S. Isaack (in "Intuition: A Treasury of Knowledge," *Personnel Administrator,* July 1980), striving to freely associate unrelated things can jump-start the intuition (our right brain) to spot reasonable relationships among unrelated ideas.

How to do this? Simply select randomly a word from the dictionary and play with uncovering relationships between the random word and the topic/subject being worked on. **Example:** Dr. Isaacks says that the title for his article—"Intuition: A Treasury of Knowledge"— was produced by trying to connect intuition with the random word, "bullion." So by thinking about riches, gold, silver, pirates, buried treasure, and so on, Isaacks ultimately tied together *intuition* and *treasure.*

As another example, a group of product developers at Campbell Soup Company selected randomly from the dictionary the word "handle." Via free word association, one member suggested the word "utensil," which led to "fork." One group member joked about a soup that could be eaten with a fork. The group reasoned that you could only eat soup with a fork if it were thick with veggies and meat. Presto! Campbell's Chunky Soups line was created, a big seller for that firm (James M. Higgins, "Creating Creativity," *Training and Development,* November 1994).

Higgins suggests the following procedures, which he calls "Free Association: By the Numbers," to produce ideas that might trigger solutions to a problem:

1. Start with a random word; enter it in line 1 of a 10-line worksheet.
2. On line 2 enter the first word triggered by line 1.
3. On line 3 enter a word stimulated by line 2.

4–10. Continue the above procedure until you have 10 words. Higgins suggests that 20 or 30 words are better.

11. Now assess your word list. See if any word provides insight into your problem.

12. If you find one or more "hot" words, work with them: Brainstorm solutions, form new associations, or draw analogies.

13. Write your new ideas on 10 more lines.

Note that the stimulus (the random word) must be from the outside and truly irrelevant to the problem. If you or I were to select the stimulus, usually it most likely would be associated logically with the problem. This would defeat the intent of a random word, which is to depart totally from the problem situation. In sum, the idea is to disengage our thinking from logical patterns, to open up new routes for exploration, and to encourage full use of intuition to achieve breakthrough thinking.

Analogies and Metaphors

James M. Higgins, a consultant, management professor, and author ("Creating Creativity," *Training and Development,* November 1994, an article based on his book *101 Creative Problem Solving Techniques: The Handbook of New Ideas for Business,* Winter Park, FL: New Management Publishing Co., 1994) advises that analogies and metaphors can help us identify and understand our problems better. They also can be used to spark alternate solutions. **The concept:** Drawing an analogy between our problem and something else, or stating such a comparison as a metaphor, can provide us with real insight into how to solve a problem.

Definition

An analogy compares two dissimilar things, but through the analogy there is some similarity.

Procedure: For problem solving, think of an analogy between your problem and something else. Then ask: What insights/solutions does the analogy suggest?

Example: NASA had to design a satellite to be tethered to a space station by a thin wire, 60 miles long. But it was apparent that the motion of reeling in the satellite would produce a pendulum effect with an ever-widening arc. So what might be done? A NASA scientist came up with the analogy of a yo-yo. He determined that a small electric motor on the satellite would permit it to crawl back up the tether to the space station.

Definition

A metaphor is a figure of speech entailing two different kinds of thoughts linked by a point of similarity. It treats one thing as if it were something else to point out a resemblance we wouldn't ordinarily perceive. It takes place when an imaginative connection occurs between two unlike ideas/images that are normally regarded as very dissimilar. Some everyday examples: "paint yourself into a corner"; "the ship of state"; "ivory tower"; "cold turkey"; "Saturday night special"; "voodoo economics"; "basket case."

In general, metaphors permit us to go beyond standard thinking, thus allowing us to see a bigger picture. **Example:** If we are into team development or team management, we can draw on sports metaphors to give our team a better focus. We thus can talk about "team players," "not dropping the ball," "beating the competition," "hitting a home run," "grandstanding," "practice run," "full court press," "coming from behind," "let's not move the goal posts," "too much coaching from the sidelines," "out of bounds," and so on.

Here are two examples of changing our patterned or basic thinking by changing our metaphor. **Examples:** The firm is not being sold off, but is "up for adoption." People constantly complain that the elevator in our office building is slow. So do we spend a half million dollars or more to get a new one, or do we simply add mirrors on each floor so people can kill time by primping rather than griping? **Note:** We change the metaphor "Slower than molasses in January," to "Here's a chance to sharpen up a bit."

Using Checklists

A checklist is a tool to help participants focus on a list of categories related to the problem under review. The checklist, consisting of a series of verbs (also known as "trigger words"), is used to change the conventional approach or mindset to a problem. Three potent verbs for this purpose, per Alex F. Osborn, brainstorming inventor and author of the now classic work *Applied Imagination* (New York: Charles Scribner and Sons, 1957), are:

☐ Magnify ☐ Minify ☐ Rearrange

As a simple illustration of the way these verbs might be used to stimulate ideas, take the problem of space utilization in a shop, lab, office, or store. We can take the three verbs and expand them into questions relating to our problem.

Question 1: How can we increase *(magnify)* our space? Some answers are: knock down unnecessary walls and partitions; eliminate minimally used storage areas, closets; negotiate for more space with Divisions X and Y; rehabilitate the attic and basement; close in the porch; make two-story levels out of high ceilings wherever practical.

Question 2: How can we shrink *(minify)* our need for space? We could eliminate bulky furniture and unneeded file cabinets; use microfilm for files; reduce staff; drop unnecessary activities and operations.

Question 3: How can we *rearrange* our space more effectively? Some answers are: start with a floor plan; use wall space more imaginatively; reduce size of reception area; use modular furniture; stack file cabinets from floor to ceiling; use an open plan instead of partitions, and use potted palms for privacy; put all noisy operations in one section of our large room behind noise-proof walls.

Note: These three verbs represent only a partial list of those used by Alex F. Osborn. Others are modify, manipulate, substitute, combine, adapt, and reverse, with each category having several subquestions under it.

Two other types of checklists are area thinking and word stimulation (J. J. Mariotti, "Checklists in Problem Solving," *Management Review,* August 1971). Area thinking is the opposite of attribute listing. With this procedure we start with several major aspects of a problem, and then work toward details and specifics. In word stimulation, we use word lists to trigger creative ideas and solutions, e.g., see "Problem Identification—ABC Approach," cited earlier.

Note that these checklists, as well as attribute listing discussed below, are designed to unleash creativity. They are not to be confused with checklists that auditors, managers, and others might use to be certain that the right procedures are being followed in a given situation, such as in responding to a bomb threat in an office building, inspecting the effectiveness of a decentralized operation, or orienting a new worker.

Attribute Listing

This technique is intended to generate ideas about a product, service, or situation. After the list is developed, the various attributes, traits, or characteristics listed are analyzed for means of improving the product, service, or situation. Thus, each item may be subject to a special focus using the techniques of checklists (described previously) and forced relationship (described later).

Example: We may wish to improve the landscaping around our plant or office. We thus develop a list of its features or attributes such as the following:

- ☐ Lawn
- ☐ Beds, flower
- ☐ Beds, non-flower (e.g., ivy)
- ☐ Fences
- ☐ Flowering trees
- ☐ Other shade trees
- ☐ Shrubs
- ☐ Hedges
- ☐ Walks
- ☐ Stone walls
- ☐ Picnic/luncheon areas
- ☐ Signs
- ☐ Hazards

We may then develop checklists concerning one or more of these items; for example, in considering the picnic/luncheon areas, we may highlight benches, tables, trash cans, shade, shrubbery, flagstone, etc.

Morphological Analysis

This is a problem-generating and problem-solving approach that relates (or interrelates) all elements (independent variables) of a problem to aid in discovering fresh solutions. As will be apparent from the following discussion, it entails combining attribute listing with forced relationships in a matrix approach. The steps for conducting the analysis include:

1. Identifying the major elements (variables, parameters) of a problem.
2. Further identifying the sub-elements or factors that relate to the major variables.
3. Establishing a matrix to highlight the several variables and its sub-elements.

4. Choosing, generally on a random basis, the sub-elements in the matrix. One sub-element from each of the major variables is selected and combined with the others.
5. Analyzing the feasibility of combining the elements.
6. Selecting and analyzing the practicality of added combinations of elements.

In general, the whole process is designed to generate ideas. The combining and recombining of sub-elements provides numerous opportunities to look at a problem and come up with fresh, novel solutions, and our natural tendencies to ideate along habitual lines are upset.

To illustrate the process, let's assume we have developed a morphological matrix such as the one in Figure 13-3 relating to slow-moving products in a retail department store. Our objective is to design a program or campaign to help move these ten "slow-movers"—men's hats, toasters, suede jackets, half-inch garden hoses, portable first-aid kits, small electric fans, ladies' garter belts, porch paint, rolltop desks, and classical records. Our three key variables to accomplish this are internal management activities or programs, promotional approaches, and employee incentives.

Going to the three-columned matrix below, we might consider as our program the use of special sales or campaigns (column 1) via radio (column 2) coupled with special time off to employees who are the best performers (column 3). This tri-partite program, along with others selected similarly, would be evaluated as to possible pay-offs.

Forced Relationships Technique

To develop new combinations of ideas, participants may be given a new word, concept, phrase, or object and asked to relate it to the problem being studied. All senses may be tapped, attention being called to a sound or odor as well as items in view. Or the group may be asked to take an imaginary trip somewhere. In general, the idea is to find new stimuli to force creativity.

Example: Assume the group is working on a problem of tardiness. The moderator or supervisor introduces a bag of lemons (!) and asks participants to use it to help solve the problem. **Some possible solutions:** Using behavior modification principles, give the late-comer a glass of lemonade whenever arrival is prompt; add oranges to the lemons and set up a data display (visual feedback) for two weeks: give a lemon for tardiness, an orange for promptness; promise a cake (a lemon cake) and coffee party for the whole group if arrival time has improved materially at week's end; put a lemon on the employee's desk whenever he is late; add to the lemons a case of cokes as a reward for improved arrival time.

Another way to apply the forced relationship technique is to follow these procedures:

1. Cite your concern, problem, difficulty, e.g., customer complaints.
2. Enter "customer complaints" in a T-column (sample provided on page 623).

Internal Management Activities	Promotional Methods	Employee Incentives
Notices on bulletin boards	TV spots, radio spots	Contests with prizes ("Dog Mover of the Week")
Memos to employees with tips on selling the "dogs"	Newspaper ads	Special commissions
Boxed items in company newsletter	School newspaper ads	Supervisory praise
Encouragement of brainstorming sessions with employees	Suburban newspaper ads	Letters of commendation from top management
Pep talks at supervisors' meetings	Leaflets with customers' bills	Special time off
Review of pricing practices	Small catalog featuring "dogs"	Extra employee discounts on these items
Study of competitors' practices	Mail flyers to homes	Give some items away as prizes for perfect attendance
Special campaigns as "Discard Sale," "Overstock Sale," "Three-for-two" pricing, etc.	Leaflets on individual items at various points in store	Suggest these items for early Christmas gift buying (get your shopping done early!)
	Ads on store delivery trucks	

Figure 13-3. Example of a morphological matrix.

Customer Complaints— causes for	Baseball, attributes of
Poor selection of sales personnel	Hot dogs
Lousy products	Scoreboard
Unclear policies	Vendors
Lack of training	Bats
Ineffective reward system	Gloves
Lack of time to spend with customers	Stadium
	Coaches
Lack of feedback to reps	Diamond
Nasty customers	Tickets
	Players

3. Brainstorm or list by free association the possible causes for the problem. Enter them in the T-column.
4. Select an activity, totally unrelated, to customer complaints. Let's take "baseball."
5. Brainstorm or free associate a list of attributes of the game of baseball. Enter them in the T-column.
6. Try to tie together individual items in the two columns.
7. List on a flipchart the related ideas that have been generated. **Possible examples:** Hooking together "lack of feedback" and "scoreboard," we might have a daily display board regarding the number of complaints received; or tying together "reward systems" and "tickets," we might provide sales reps with tickets to the game for a complaint-free week or month; and "lack of training" and "coaches" might signify to us that we start doing a better job of coaching.

Movement—Talk While You Walk

Have pairs or trios take a 15–30 minute walk—down a shady path, across a meadow, around the block—to talk about an issue or problem. **Purpose:** To change perspectives. Most of do a lot of sitting, with a resultant quieting down (stagnation) of our creative juices. A "walking meeting" has the potential to stir us up and provide a fresh, possibly more imaginative view about the question at hand.

Guided Visualization

This is a form of communication for the purpose of stimulating creativity in a visual, pictorial, or graphic way. Participants use crayons or large, felt-tipped pens to draw pictures on large flipchart sheets. The drawings represent ideas about the themes raised by the session leader. Topics can relate to a description regarding what the firm is like, where it is, where it is going (visualize the future), or to solve current problems or clarify a long-term plan.

Procedure

1. After the individual drawings are completed, participants team up in pairs to explain their illustrations to each other. In unison, the task is to create a *new* picture that embraces the most significant aspects of the two original pictures.
2. Then each pair joins with another pair to create a new group (quartet) picture.
3. Each quartet then joins with another quartet to form an eight-person drawn graphic or picture.

Two rules govern the guided visualization activity:

1. Talking is allowed only when someone (individuals, pairs, groups) explains what has been drawn. The actual artwork is done silently.
2. Everyone must be involved in the drawing of the shared picture. Each person must ensure that what matters most to him gets carried over from his original picture to the new group picture.

Rationale

Very few of us have used drawing as a means of analyzing problems. But by creating the artwork, the right brain is engaged for greater creative output than is ordinarily the case via the written medium. Drawings help show relationships between things much more readily than when the usual writing is used. The process is also a good consensus-builder. Similarities emerge, overcoming the usual squabbling over details.

The process was developed by management consultants Chris Musselwhite and Cheryl De Ciantis (Julie Barker, "Get Outta Line," *Successful Meetings*, October 1994).

Diads/Triads Analysis

Working in diads (pairs) or triads (trios), one participant offers ideas about the assigned problem, issue, topic, or question. The other partner(s) uses the Journalist's Six Questions (What, When, Who, Why, Where, and How) to elicit more information from the idea presenter. Roles are reversed so that all members of the pair or trio get a chance to be an idea-offerer/generator.

After the work in pairs or trios, the class-at-large discusses what was learned or agreed upon in the small group meetings about the issue in question.

Principles for Collegiality at Meetings

Creativity consultant Michael Michalko, in "Einstein's Teamwork Secret," (*Training,* December 1993), describes why Einstein and his associates were able to collaborate so effectively. Their "secret": They avoided mistrust and suspicion and thus were able to share their work openly and honestly, unlike their contemporaries. How did they do it? They drew on the ancient Greek principles of in-group communication developed by Socrates and his colleagues.

Socrates and his fellow discussants had warm, free-flowing debates—known as dialogues—which rarely became overheated and personalized. They maintained their collegiality by observing seven discussion principles called *Koinonia,* or "spirit of fellowship." These principles are (1) establish dialogue, (2) exchange ideas, (3) don't argue, (4) don't interrupt, (5) listen carefully, (6) clarify your thinking, and (7) be honest.

Michalko offers these guidelines to set up *Koinonia* in your work group or in other meetings where creativity is important:

Build the Team

Hold several weekly practice sessions, agenda-free, at the same time each week. Let people talk on topics of their choice. Don't expect any particular results and don't worry about gripes about wasting time. Remind your participants that this is a team-building phase.

Create Dialog

The purpose of talking is to uncover truth, not to alter people's opinions. Everyone must focus totally on the speaker. This may be hard to accomplish at first, but with practice it's quite doable.

Be Clear in Your Thinking

Drop all untested assumptions. It's all too easy, for example, to tune out those we think are not creative. So suspend assumptions and thereby keep a bias-free view.

Speak the Truth

Be honest in expressing your thoughts even if they are controversial. People need to know who you really are and what you really think to feel comfortable—and thus open—with you.

Key point: If the *Koinonia* spirit is operative, you can anticipate honest, friendly collaboration and free sharing of information and ideas. Because ideation is encouraged, we can expect the group's potential for creativity to increase.

UNLOCKING DAY-TO-DAY, ON-THE-JOB THINKING OF YOUR WORK GROUP

There are a number of creative activities in which you can ask your team to engage. Creativity consultant Michael Michalko, author of *Thinkertoys: A Handbook of Business Creativity for the 1990s* (Ten Speed Press, 1991), suggests 15 ways to increase your staffers' energized thinking (presented in "Bright Ideas," *Training and Development,* June 1994).

1. Daily Task Improvement

As a daily activity, ask your staffers to try to improve one work area or an aspect of it. At day's end, meet with staff to learn what each did differently or better than previously.

2. Ensuring Positive Thinking

Overcome staffers' possible tendencies to worship negatives via this exercise: Ask staffers to come up with three work-related tasks or changes that *can't* be done. Then request them to create devices to "make them happen." In effect, the usual reasons why something can't be done are turned around with a positive focus.

3. New Idea Assessment

Reject the usual negative comments concerning new ideas. Instead, ask your staffers to come up with three or more ways to implement a new idea before they shoot it down.

4. Lunch Bunch

Set up once-a-week meetings over lunch, of three to five staffers each, at which they will discuss a previously assigned book on creativity. Each staff member presents the meat of the chapter about which he was given particular responsibility.

5. Job Swaps

Assign people to part-day work in other departments. The department heads then meet informally with the visiting part-timers to secure feedback—i.e., what they might do differently if they were full-timers.

6. Think Bank

Set up a special area of creativity stimulators: books, videos, games, toys, etc., all of which relate to creativity. Provide wall decorations as added brain stimulants.

7. Idea Board

Set up a bulletin board in a well-visited, well-lighted area to elicit ideas. To kick things off for staffers, post a major topic on colored paper in the board's center. Provide 3″ × 5″ slips for ideas on the major topic, which are then thumbtacked to the board.

8. Idea Exchange

Hold a "How I Did It" idea fest at which staffers tell and show how they made a recent first-rate accomplishment/contribution. Encourage the use of visuals (slides, photos, physical objects) to enhance the realism of each presentation. The aim is to stimulate creative thinking of others, to encourage borrowing of any of the ideas presented, and possibly for people of different departments to team up to do something of a creative sort. The event could be made into a gala family affair, too.

9. Rotational Coaching

Establish the rotating assignment of "creative coach." While in that role, the coach would encourage creative behavior of other staffers.

10. Committee Thrust

Set up a volunteer committee, representative of the several departments, to encourage, assess, and implement employee ideas. For motivational purposes, (a) post a chart of the number of ideas submitted, and (b) provide suitable rewards for employee contributions.

11. Lottery

Pass out numbered tickets to each staffer who produces a creative contribution. At month's end, share the ideas and draw a number from a box (or bowl or hat). The winning number gets the prize of the month.

12. Non-success Quotient

Query staffers regarding the outfit's three greatest non-successes (failures, if you will) over the past three years. If the answer is zero, it may be a good indicator that nothing new has been tried.

13. Assumption Assessment

Check out existing assumptions about everything the outfit holds near and dear to its heart: systems, policies, processes, procedures, methods, products. **Big question:** are they all really essential or working well, and might there be better ones?

14. Meeting Mart

Hold a total team, "no holds barred" meeting to discuss a current problem area and to garner ideas about it. Invite all in attendance to propose a pertinent issue on which they are willing to take responsibility. An issue's suggestor becomes its sponsor and then writes it on a flipchart, which is posted to the wall. Attendees "sign up" on a flipchart sheet of interest to join with others to discuss that particular issue. The idea sponsor and his study group (those who have signed a particular flipchart sheet) meet privately to ideate (project ideas) on their issue of concern. The idea sponsor serves as facilitator of the session.

15. Objects of Creativity

Have staffers come up with physical objects that epitomize their views/visions of creativity, which they can display on their desks. **Examples:** A heavy glove to symbolize "my ideas are so hot I can't handle them with my bare hand," a toy top: "to stay on top of things," an off-beat cap/hat: "my thinking cap."

Note: You may not wish to use all of Michalko's ideas. Just select those that fit your needs and personal style. Also, think in terms of implementation of several or more of them over a period of weeks or months, one at a time.

Planning for Greater Use of Group-In-Action Creativity Techniques

As an aid in planning greater use of the techniques described above, it is suggested that you complete the "Use of Group-In-Action Creativity Stimulation Techniques—Worksheet for Inventory and Planning," Figure 13-4.

HOW TO ACTIVATE AND KEEP YOUR OWN CREATIVE JUICES FLOWING

You will ask me where I get my ideas . . . they come unsummoned . . . in the open air, in the woods . . . at dawn . . .

—Ludwig von Beethoven (1770–1827), German composer

You can't find new ways of doing things by looking at them harder in the old way.

—Anon.

No problem can be solved from the same consciousness that created it. We must learn to see the world anew.

—Albert Einstein

I think and think for months and years. Ninety-nine times, the conclusion is false. The hundredth time I am right.

—Albert Einstein

Thinking always of trying to do more brings a state of mind in which nothing seems impossible.

—Henry Ford, American industrialist (1863–1947)

Being creative doesn't mean that we must have the insights and innovative capabilities to enable us to paint the Mona Lisa (or her brother, Manny Liso), to invent something like a lifetime car battery or to develop a truly grand plan for permanent, world-wide peace (and getting the Nobel Prize for it). Rather, it means tackling problems and situations in ways that challenge our curiosity and thus produce end results that are fresh, varied, exciting, spontaneous and/or novel, as opposed to the usual, routine, patterned, timid, limited, or old hat.

All of us can function at a more creative level if we adopt behaviors with that potential. The following paragraphs offer a number of ideas/approaches to upgrade your CQ (creativity quotient).

Creativity trainer/consultant/writer Charles "Chic" Thompson in his sprightly and meaty book *What a Great Idea! The Key Steps Creative People Take* (New York: HarperCollins, 1992) presents these "creative rules of thumb":

1. Great ideas come from quantity. So generate a lot of them and discard the bad ones.
2. Produce ideas that are workable in the next 15 minutes, not a generation ahead. Why? Because if they're light years ahead, they're very likely to be delayed or ignored.
3. Don't settle for one solution. Be open to many possibilities. Thompson quotes the French poet/philosopher Emile Chartier as follows: "Nothing is more dangerous than an idea when it's the only one you have."
4. When your "well" has run dry, simply stop. Switch gears. Give yourself a change of pace or a change of scenery. Then return with renewed interest and vigor.
5. Don't rely on memory to recall an idea. Instead, capture your idea, while it's hot, in your always-available notepad.
6. Don't succumb to the "Boo-leaders" (as opposed to the cheerleaders). There are hordes of people out there ready to tell you that you're on the wrong track, it'll never work, it's been tried before, and so on. So expect the skeptical laughs from those eager to predict failure. But if you're convinced you're on to something, stay with it. Don't let the naysayers talk you out of it.
7. If you have a problem, there generally is an answer "out there." It "pre-exists." Your task is to pose the

proper question to extract the answer/solution. This means that you have to define the problem properly and be able to generate causes for the problem and potential answers for it.

8. Ask basic, elementary "dumb" questions, and you'll get bright answers in return. Use the Journalist's Six Questions to help you pose your probes.

9. To solve problems creatively, drop your original perspective. Shift, instead, to a fresh look, a new angle, a different point of view.

10. Visualize a successful outcome before you tackle your problem. Picture in your mind a new result, an improved future, a reached goal. Conversely, don't envision a miss or a maybe. What you see is what you are likely to get.

11. To multiply possibilities, think in terms of opposites—in, out; hot, cold; up, down; sharp, dull; raise it, lower it; strengthen it, weaken it; and so on. You can capitalize on "The Power of Opposite Thinking" by stating the negative, producing a negative definition and ascertaining what everyone else doesn't do.

12. Challenge ingrained assumptions. Do this by reframing your problem or turning each assumption into a negative or the opposite (as above).

13. Put on someone else's moccasins. This will help you to see things from their point of view. And if the new shoes don't help, Thompson says to regard your problem from a helicopter or a spaceship.

14. By using metaphors and similes, you can help define problems and provoke possible answers. A powerful metaphor relates to nature (e.g., Darwin's "tree of life" and Newton's "the fall of an apple"). Sports metaphors ("are we playing the right game?") and music metaphors ("a new sound," "our section is out of tune") are great idea provokers, too.

15. Borrow/adapt ideas from others: Recognize that you don't have to re-invent the wheel. (Of course, you can do what McDonald's does, but you can't lift (steal) their logo. Or you can produce and market your own dictionary, but you can't copy someone else's and sell it.)

16. Failure/mistakes may be hard to accept. But doing nothing may result in a greater penalty. The best outlook: Regard failure as part of the learning process.

17. Typically we evaluate ideas as good or bad. But there also may be an intriguing, appealing, or interesting in-between factor in it. So don't abandon an idea outright. Let it sit on the back burner for several days and then return to it with a new look.

18. Store your ideas in some systematic way—in a notebook, in a recipe box, on a Rolodex, your computer, or on a magnetic board. **Key point:** Regard your ideas as treasure. Don't let them get buried or lost.

19. Launch your meetings with an ice-breaker or warm-up activity. You want to get people revved up lest they lapse into a quasi-somnolent state and remain that way.

20. Use your bathroom as your personal think tank. Ideas can come to you while showering, shaving, shampooing, or sitting on the commode. Keep that note pad near by.

Management consultant/trainer Gordon F. Shea in *Creative Negotiating* (Boston: CBI Publishing Co, 1983) offers these added suggestions:

Unleash questions. Use the Journalist's Six Questions—what, where, when, who, how, and why—to challenge the usual established assumptions. Probing with a lot of curiosity will ensure that you don't accept an idea whose time is not likely to ever come.

Avoid putdowns. Instead of knocking or downgrading the ideas of others, try to build on them. Provide praise and credit to people's ideas and you'll get a lot of "repeat business," i.e., more ideas will flow your way.

Challenge your own assumptions. If you are confident in your own reasoning powers, you can accept a lot of self-critique.

Opt for new angles. Challenge limits and constraints for they may be more imaginary than real.

Shop outside your own bailiwick. Look for ideas in fields of endeavor other than your own. Creativity is wherever you find it.

Stay with it. Persevere; leave no stone unturned. Good ideas don't necessarily come on the first try or two.

Exchange ideas with others. This will give you possibilities for new approaches now and later on as well.

Tap your subconscious mind. When you've hit a stone wall, just relax and let your subconscious mind go to work for you. This will give you a new, fresh look at things. Daydreaming is one way to tap the subconscious. In this regard, I like Thomas Edison's advisory:

As one grows older, one realizes the impossibility of imposing one's will on the chaos with brute force. But if you are patient, one day, while relaxing, or eating an apple, the solution presents itself and says, "Here I am."

Capture ideas on a notepad. You don't want to let a good idea get away. So have your pad handy to jot down what has just emerged. Do this regardless of where you are. (A colleague of mine tells me that he even takes his notebook along when he showers.)

Opt for constant idea flow. Move ahead from one idea to another. Let one idea trigger another.

Stay away from routines. Repetitive behaviors will put you where you don't want to be—in a rut. So keep thinking of new routines, patterns, etc., whether it's driving to work, where you have lunch and with whom, how and where you conduct staff meetings, how you conduct performance reviews, and so on. **The rationale:** New thinking about everyday matters will keep the ideation machinery well tuned up.

Implement Your Ideas

If you act on what you created, you'll be rewarded for that effort. Conversely, if you don't act and thus don't reward your creativity, it's very likely to taper off.

If you want to keep your brain sharp, young, and growing—the "evergreen brain"—exercise it each day with activities such as the following, per author Dudley Lynch ("Brain Aerobics," *Modern Maturity,* June–July 1986):

Future Forecasting

Practice anticipating the future in as many ways as you can. **Examples:** In your search for a parking space, imagine/anticipate where the first one will be; if dining with friends, guess what they'll be wearing. **Effect:** This will put your forward-thinking frontal lobes into gear.

Acting Actively

Expand your repertoire of activities, e.g., do volunteer work or go into political pursuits. **Effect:** If you put your body into action, your brain's limbic system does, too, where the powerful chemical controllers of your emotions originate.

Foreign Language Learning

This is intellectually challenging and of possible practical value, too, depending on your work/career. **Effects:** This will put new "muscle tone" in the language centers of your brain's left hemisphere.

Engage in Imagery

Imagine doing a job/task/activity *prior* to doing it. This will prime your mind for actually executing it. **Effect:** It will engage and exercise your right brain hemisphere's visualizing equipment.

Seek New Routes

When going to work, shopping, the movies, etc., find a new route. If you don't vary your route, the brain begins to miss segments of reality.

Stand Up for Unpopular Ideas/Opinions

This will stimulate your basic senses and idealistic sensitivities as well. **Effect:** You'll exercise the oldest and least adaptive structures of the brain.

Get Active with Music

Aerobics, dancing, swimming, and jogging to music forces your body to learn the rhythms of musical math.

Opt Seriously for Mental Challenges/Stimulators

Do crossword puzzles and engage in various games (spatial, manual-skill). **Effect:** It shakes up the brain's chemical and electrical mechanism.

Dudley Lynch, author of *Your High-Performance Brain: An Operator's Manual* (Englewood Cliffs, New Jersey: Prentice-Hall, 1984), presents in his book a lot of other suggestions to keep your gray matter in shape: master the piano; add 6,000 words to your vocabulary;

write a historical novel or one based on your family's generations; become an authority in something taboo such as erotic art; become a lay minister; bring a foster child or a foreign student into your home; run for office; redecorate or rearrange your home if you've been in it a decade or more; write 100 letters or more to the editor, keeping a scrapbook of those that make it; study journalism and contribute to a journal of your interest.

Finally, to restore and maintain your energy, creativity, and possibly your sanity, too, take a "joy break." Management consultant Ann McGee-Cooper, author of *You Don't Have to Go Home from Work Exhausted—A Program to Bring Energy and Balance to Your Life* (New York: Bantam, 1992), urges us to take joy breaks during the day. Periodically, take a two- to five-minute time out from work and focus on something else, something that can provide joy. So without feeling guilty about it, glance out the window, daydream, reflect on your forthcoming evening's activities. Or you might use one of the breaks to call a friend or chat with a colleague. Or just close your door and enjoy five minutes of relaxation, quiet, and solitude.

Also, use the joy break at home—take a bubble bath, call a good friend, recall a success or a fun thing from the past. Or playfully engage in fantasies.

McGee-Cooper also suggests taking a "vacation" every weekend. Not one to the Bahamas at a high cost, but one as brief as 20 minutes—start a book you've been putting off or go shopping for some new duds. Says McGee-Cooper, "A vacation is anything fun that makes you forget what time it is. If you're not losing track of time, you're not really there. A true vacation reaches (literally) the part of your brain that disengages you from monochromatic thinking."

And finally, per McGee-Cooper, get into a hobby. It can become an energy booster even when you're not doing it. In your breaks at work you can read about it or chat with colleagues about it. A real hobby is something you're passionate about. If it gets stale, move into a new one.

ASSESSING YOUR CQ (CREATIVITY QUOTIENT)

Now that you have read the materials in this chapter, you may wish to assess your own creative prowess with the following self-quiz.

What is Your CQ (Creativity Quotient)?

Using the 5-point scale (1 = low; 5 = high) below, indicate (by circling the numbers following the statements) the degree to which you perform in ways that encourage creative behaviors by your staff or yourself. Please try to be as candid as you can to ensure a meaningful result for you from this self-quiz.

1. When working on a problem, my staff and I systematically separate *idea generation* from *idea evaluation* (i.e., deferred judgment, our second step). 1 2 3 4 5
2. When working on a problem, I seek—and encourage my staff to seek—as many alternative solutions as possible, as opposed to settling early on for a single idea/approach/answer. 1 2 3 4 5
3. I operate my unit so that fun, playfulness, joy, and freewheeling—rather than formality, stiffness, dullness, and rigidity—become part of what we do. 1 2 3 4 5
4. I use delegation as a tool to empower my staff, encourage their risk-taking, and ignite their creativity. 1 2 3 4 5
5. I let my people try things out rather than prescribe a lot of procedures to carry out the task/job/operation. 1 2 3 4 5
6. I encourage my staff to come forward with new ideas, even those that are "off the wall." 1 2 3 4 5
7. When staffers present "off-beat" solutions, I listen to them attentively. 1 2 3 4 5
8. I encourage my staff to depart from or modify organizational policies/ standards/rules when it means getting the job done more effectively. 1 2 3 4 5
9. I provide a lot of praise to staffers who take risks and perform in creative (non-traditional) ways. 1 2 3 4 5
10. Our problem-solving and staff meetings are marked by humor and spontaneity. 1 2 3 4 5
11. I encourage disagreement/differences/ conflict to emerge at meetings with my staff. 1 2 3 4 5
12. I encourage my staffers to interact freely and frequently among them-

selves as well as with others outside
our immediate work unit.   1 2 3 4 5

13. At performance review time, I
    include "creativity/innovation/
    search for new approaches" as a
    topic for discussion.   1 2 3 4 5

14. At performance review time, I
    include risk taking as an element
    for discussion.   1 2 3 4 5

15. I feel comfortable when a staffer
    questions or challenges any of my
    ideas.   1 2 3 4 5

16. I take a keen interest in and work
    actively at problems that are open-
    ended, ambiguous, without precedent,
    even controversial.   1 2 3 4 5

17. I am interested in and get excited
    about problems outside my formal
    area of responsibility.   1 2 3 4 5

18. To release my inquisitive, creative
    self, I frequently depart from the
    logical step-by-step (sequential)
    method of problem solving and move
    into looser, wilder, more spontaneous
    thinking such as using analogies and
    metaphors.   1 2 3 4 5

19. I "bounce back" easily when I have
    goofed or produced a less-than-
    successful result and convert it into
    a learning experience.   1 2 3 4 5

20. I look for humor in disappointing
    situations.   1 2 3 4 5

21. I use "gut instincts" (intuition/hunches/
    impulses) in problem-solving
    approaches.   1 2 3 4 5

22. I regularly seek out opportunities
    for professional growth, develop-
    ment, and renewal.   1 2 3 4 5

23. I staff, in part, with people who
    might be described as mavericks/
    dissenters/risk-takers/iconoclasts.   1 2 3 4 5

24. To capture "stray" ideas, I carry a
    small notebook.   1 2 3 4 5

25. I push for new ideas with my bosses,
    even at some risk of "irritating" them. 1 2 3 4 5

Scoring Procedures and Interpretation

Procedures

1. Add the scores for each numbered column, e.g., if
   you circled item #5 eight times, give yourself a 40

($8 \times 5 = 40$); if you scored item #4 nine times, give
yourself a 36 ($9 \times 4 = 36$); and so on.

2. Combine your scores for the 5 numbered columns.
   This is your final or total score.

Interpretation of Your Final/Total Score

☐ A score above 100 indicates that you have a high
capacity for creativity. You are able to manage yourself and your staff so that new ideas are certain to
flourish in what most certainly is a truly creative
atmosphere.

☐ A score of 80–99 reflects an above average ability
for turning yourself and others on so that new and
promising ideas are generated, captured and prose-
cuted.

☐ A score of 65–79 suggests that you can do creative
things, but that you have a lot of "catching up" to
do to function more fully in a creative way.

☐ Scores below 65 indicate a low capacity to function
creatively or to get others to be creative. You might
find it helpful to reread this chapter to learn of the
new directions to take for greater creative behavior.

THE MANAGER AS A CREATIVE FORCE: KEY POINTS

1. In our efforts to unleash creativity, we should
   encourage a shift from an acquisitive emphasis
   (accumulating information) to an *inquisitive*
   emphasis (What if? Why not? How can we . . .?
   Who might help us? In what ways might we . . .?
   Do we need new assumptions?)

2. What creativity is all about is to arrive at new
   approaches, new departures, new directions; to
   shed the old "tried and true" for something imaginative and new. As one wag put it, "Insanity is
   expecting to get improved results when we continue to do things in the same way."

3. A basic principle of a creative organization is that
   it must be "risk-friendly," i.e., open to mistakes. If
   the reward system stresses punishment for errors,
   the wells of creativity will automatically dry up.

4. For creative problem solving, use "beginner's
   eyes," i.e., start from naivety, play "dumb." Drop
   standard assumptions and "play" with new ones.

5. Opt for divergent as well as convergent thinking.
   Divergent thinking is loose, freewheeling, unre-
   strained. It relies on risk-taking, visualizing, fanta-

sizing, imagining, associating randomly. Convergent thinking is structured, focused and evaluative. It encompasses the standard steps in the problem-solving process, including starting with a well-defined problem, evaluating alternative courses of action and choosing (deciding) among them. Both forms of thinking are useful, depending on the problem, i.e., whether patterned/unprecedented thinking is in order or intuitive, uninhibited, even "off-the-wall" approaches are needed.

6. Encourage your staffers to reframe/recast negatives into positives: "This won't work, but here's an alternative." Apply seriously the old maxim, "There's more than one way to skin a cat."

7. Operate on the assumption that "ideas are where you find them." So don't write off anyone as a possible source of creative thinking. Instead, garner ideas from other departments; peers; bosses; all staffers, irrespective of their seniority, salary level, type of job, sex, or age; competitors; suppliers; and most certainly, customers.

8. Revamp your action-oriented schedule and philosophy to allow for "thinking time." The old advisory of "Don't just stand there, do something" should yield to newer values related to time out for "possibility thinking."

9. Don't succumb to the many myths surrounding creative thinking. Put your trust in people's ability to see new possibilities if they are given the freedom to create and contribute.

10. Regard conflict/controversy/disagreement as vital sparks to ignite desired creativity. Differences in thinking, when expressed, can lead to hard feelings or new possibilities. Your job is to so manage that only the latter takes place.

11. And not only should "differences" be brought into the open, but so must "nondiscussables," the taboos, the "things we don't talk about here." Creativity unleashed means "putting everything on the table," "letting it all hang out," including policies, systems, procedures, products, and/or services. To do otherwise is to operate on one-half the available cylinders.

12. Be certain to try out the various techniques that can help make groups creative, everything from brainstorming and storyboarding to random word association and mindmapping.

13. Assess (or possibly reassess) your leadership style. Are you setting a climate that encourages growth, curiosity, exploration (possibility thinking), challenge, and risk taking? Are you listening fully when staffers come forward with new ideas? Are you (and your team) using the principle of "deferred judgment" to evaluate an idea, as opposed to promptly assessing it as to whether it's "good" or "bad"? Are you using your team as a vehicle for breakthrough thinking? Do you tolerate iconoclasts and mavericks? Would your staffers call your outfit a "fun place" to work or is it just a locale to spend eight hours and do no more than asked?

14. Assess your own lifestyle. Is there a balance of work, play, and family so that work routine, worry, and exhaustion don't sap your energy and creativity? In respect to worry about work, heed the advice of the way who says, "Stop it! You're not paid enough to worry."

PROBLEMS, EXERCISES AND QUESTIONS FOR DISCUSSION

The questions and activities given below are for use in in-house (government or corporate) management training workshops and in college/university management classes.

Note:

a. Non-managerial personnel such as technical, administrative, sales personnel, and others may also find training in creative thinking to be of value.

b. Most of the questions and problems can be used by individuals or groups. It is suggested that the group approach be stressed to point up how creativity/ideation can be stimulated by group-in-action activity.

1. To start your session on creativity (i.e., creative thinking or creative problem-solving), ask your participants to "free associate" with the word creativity—i.e., what words or phrases does it call to mind? (Anticipate a wide range of responses, everything from weird and off-the-wall to novel, curious, and spontaneous.) Don't try to assess the "correctness" of the words. Just treat them as stimulators to get thinking going on the subject. Enter the words on a flipchart and indicate that "We'll look at these words/phrases later in this session to see how they tie into what we may have learned."

2. As another type of "warm-up" activity ask each participant to come up with three things they "invented." Then share the inventions in small groups. (**Note:** The thrust of this exercise is to demonstrate that all of us are capable of engaging in creative thinking as evidenced by actual prior accomplishment).

3. As a possible fun warm-up activity, something to stir up the participants' creative juices, enter the items in the left-hand column below on a flipchart sheet. ("Correct" answers are provided in the right-hand column for the instructor or trainer's use).

Questions for Participants	Answers
1. How many days of the week begin with "T"?	4: T, Th, Today, Tomorrow
2. How many seconds are there in one year?	12: Jan. 2nd, Feb. 2nd, March 2nd, etc.
3. How many "d's" are there in "Rudolph the Red-Nosed Reindeer?"	110: Sing: Dee, dee, dee, dee, dee, etc.

Note to trainer/instructor: Anticipate "groans" that "this is a pretty sneaky exercise," etc. A possible response to that reaction: You may regard it as sneaky and it probably is. But it may also point out that if we're to engage in "breakthrough thinking," we may have to drop conventional, straight-forward approaches and shift to less traditional, wilder, off-beat modes.

4. **Exercise:** Traits Needed for Creativity

Step 1—Ask participants to study the following list of traits and characteristics and to mark with an "x" the ones that they think a creative person would or should exhibit.

___ Discontent	___ Approval of others
___ Risk-taking	___ Hard-working
___ Respect for tradition	___ Good listener
___ Willingness to collaborate	___ Cost conscious
___ Individualism	___ Broad interests
___ Status concerns	___ Broad interests
___ Neatness in dress	___ Rich fantasy life
___ Fear of criticism	___ Deviant
___ Preference for structure	___ Abstract thinker
___ Calmness	___ Deadline conscious
___ Method-oriented	___ Emphasis on detail
___ Concentration	___ Results-oriented
	___ Humorous

Step 2—Instruct participants that when they finish marking creative characteristics, they should go back and review the items, and circle the ones that best describe themselves. Approximately 10 minutes should be allowed for steps 1 and 2.

Step 3—Divide participants into groups of three and have them discuss their circled items for about 20 minutes.

Step 4—Reassemble the class and ask for volunteers to present the results of the small group work.

Step 5—Lead a summary discussion of the personal characteristics that help or hinder creativity.

5. Imagination stimulators:
   a. Come up with five new, dynamic names for the color beige.
   b. List 10 uses to which a hammer (or a coffee can, brick, or paper clip) could be put.
   c. Assume you are a mayor of your town or city. What might you do to solve the downtown parking problem?
   d. Voting in the U.S. is quite low compared to other countries. How might voting behavior be increased?

6. To stimulate imaginative thinking, ask participants in small groups to assess the impact of any of the following circumstances:
   a. All people, overnight, become double in width.
   b. The retirement age for everyone is moved up to age 75.
   c. Due to technological advances, the average work week declines to 20 hours.
   d. All cars now can go 70 miles on one gallon of gas.
   e. All foods can be refrigerated and stored indefinitely.

7. Exercise: Organizational Creativity

Step 1—Divide participants into small groups. Tell one or more groups that they are to draw up a list of characteristics, policies, and practices that would help ensure that a new organization is creative, innovative, and responsive to change from its outset. Then instruct the other groups to list characteristics and policies that would guarantee that a new organization will be static, nonresponsive, and resistant to change.

Step 2—Call time after 15–20 minutes and secure reports from the small groups. Post their ideas on flipcharts, using the T-column format below, and have the whole class discuss the contrasting characteristics.

Creative Organization	Static Organization
Extensive delegation Group decision-making Generous praise Etc.	No feedback on accomplishment Severe penalties for mistakes Lack of training opportunities Etc.

8. Comment on this incident. A new manager took over the Department of Operations. An early policy he declared was that all employees must arrive by 8:30 a.m. and cannot leave before 5 p.m. He also specified a 30-minute lunch period and two 10-minute breaks, a.m. and p.m. Since many employees had been working flexible hours, often longer than the required eight hours, people now began to leave at 5 p.m. sharp. Who were the winners and losers?

9. To introduce a group to brainstorming or as a warm-up activity before doing it, have them brainstorm the elements to consider in conducting a successful yard (garage, moving) sale.

10. Ask for a show of hands regarding answers to the following questions about "daydreaming":
   a. How many regard it as a waste of time?
   b. How many regard it as something that is nice to do occasionally; but has no real value or purpose?
   c. How many regard it as a fun thing to do and as also a good way to come up with new, interesting, different ideas?

Then discuss the merits of daydreaming from a creativity standpoint. Ask for possible examples of being helped creatively by daydreaming.

11. **Exercise:** Creative Problem-solving

Step 1—Divide participants into small groups and tell them that they have approximately 25 minutes to discuss the following problem:

You, as a manager, hold a weekly staff meeting from 10:30 a.m. to noon every Wednesday. You have picked this time period because your boss holds his own week-ly meeting with managers immediately before yours, and the quick follow-up allows you to communicate promptly to your subordinates the main ideas and other important items that emerged for the managers' session. Moreover, because everyone knows that Wednesday mornings are set aside for two meetings, people can readily plan their activities around the two sessions. One day, however, Jean, a key, young staff member, asks you to change your weekly meeting time because she has to leave early every other Wednesday to attend a Toastmaster's Club luncheon meeting that starts at 11:30 a.m. What would you do about Jean's request?

Step 2—Have each small group present its proposed solutions to the entire class.

Step 3—Conduct a general discussion about the importance of self-development efforts and managerial support for self-development in relation to organizational needs and objectives. In leading this discussion, the trainer might cover the following points:

Neither a production-oriented manager's quick refusal to change the meeting time, nor an immediate willingness to accede to the request would constitute a "creative" solution to the scheduling problem. Rather than a hasty "yes" or "no" the manager might turn the issue over to the whole staff for consideration as a "team" problem. The team then could devise solutions designed to meet everyone's needs. These, for example, might include: arranging meeting agendas so that the most urgent items are discussed early while Jean is still present; appointing someone to take notes for absentees or brief them orally; or exploring the possibility of Jean's attending a Toastmasters meeting that convenes on another day or evening.

12. **Exercise:** Seeing New Possibilities

Objective: To point out the idea that one aspect of creativity is the ability to see possibilities in the familiar.

Necessary materials. A 12-inch tall glass tube with a ping-pong ball in it. Objects spread alongside the tube are chewing gum, scotch tape, a straight pin, an open bottle of a soft drink, a ruler, a newspaper.

Task: Get the ball out of the narrow tube *without touching the glass.* The task may be accomplished with the total class or by several groups, depending on the availability of materials.

Note: This is a "classic" exercise that has been used widely in creative training programs.

Solution: Very few participants will solve the problem. It can be done by simply pouring the soda pop into the tube to float the ball to the top.

13. **Metaphors.** In groups, exchange data on the following: What animal might describe your job? What animal might describe your boss? What car (type or brand name) would describe your organization?

14. Comment on this situation as it relates to creativity: Kim Roberts heads up a headquarters function that frequently issues advisory and instructional booklets to the field. Kim is new on the job. When Kim presented her first manuscript for a booklet to the field to her boss, Bill Verne, he ruffled through its pages rather quickly and said: "It looks OK. Just be sure the artwork for the cover is in brown." This was a startling comment to Kim. But it became less so when she reflected on the fact that Mr. Verne only wore brown suits and previously prepared booklets also had brown covers.

15. **Exercise:** Write the capital letters I X on a flipchart. Ask your participants to add one line and make a "6." (Some see an i and ×. Others see the Roman numerals 9, i.e., IX. Still others see x as a multiplication sign and draw a six after the x and create an equation (1×6). More approaches are possible, e.g., simply putting an "S" in front of the numerals. (The S is a curved line which produces the word "six." No one said the line had to be straight). **Significance:** (a) more than one solution to a problem is possible, and (b) your particular point of view may influence your solution.

16. To make the point that creativity doesn't necessarily fade out with age, ask participants to cite well-known older creative people, past or present. **Examples:** Grandma Moses, Toscanini.

17. Ask for volunteers—two sets of individuals—to (a) recall a day when you felt particularly alive and creative. Visualize your events that day: walk yourself through that day and describe your activities, the persons with whom you were in contact, your feelings as you experienced the day and your feelings about yourself at day's end. (b) Recall a day when you felt very hemmed in, not creative at all. Visualize your events that day—what you did, with whom you were in contact, your feelings during the day and at day's end. **Question:** Can we create our days so they are more satisfying and creative?

18. How do the following factors bear on creativity in organizations:
    - ☐ the reward system
    - ☐ tradition
    - ☐ experts, specialists
    - ☐ flex time
    - ☐ fun, play, humor
    - ☐ the organizational dress code
    - ☐ opportunities for horizontal communication
    - ☐ past success
    - ☐ training
    - ☐ the subconscious mind (beliefs, behavior, attitudes)

19. Assume you become CEO of your outfit tomorrow. Assuming you want a lot of creativity, what would be your first step to get things going along creative lines?

20. How does "discounting" affect the creative process? Can you list some typical discounts? **Examples:** "I've heard that one before." "That doesn't make sense at all." "What makes you think it will work?" (**Note to trainer:** For an excellent article on this subject, see W. Timothy Weaver, "When Discounting Gets in the Way," *Training and Development,* July 1993, pp. 55–61).

21. What are some of the blocks any one of us might have that inhibit our creative talents?

22. Comment on the possible respective roles of pessimism and optimism in creative problem solving.

23. What is meant by a creative environment? How does it impact on creativity?

24. All of us have heard about playing "Devil's Advocate." What if, as has been suggested, we were to play "Angel's Advocate," seeking for

responses to this question: "What do I *like* about this idea?"

25. Assume you are stuck in a creative rut. How might you pull yourself out of it?
26. Our culture currently emphasizes teamwork or team collaboration. Are there any drawbacks to group work from a creativity standpoint?
27. Is it possible to shift subordinates' thinking from rational/convergent/logical to divergent/lateral/freewheeling? If so, how might you go about it?
28. a) Is it possible to learn how to be more creative, or is it more likely a matter of "some of us have it and some of us don't?"

    b) What might you, as an individual, do to make your daily work feel fresh and exciting, and thus expand your creative potential?
29. Question to group: How do you weigh a fidgety cat?

Procedures:

a. Ask everyone to jot down an answer on a slip of paper.
b. Collect answers and post them on flipchart or read them aloud. (**Best answer:** Grasp the animal firmly, step on a scale, and subtract your own weight from the scale reading).
c. Discuss the significance of this question and answer. (It necessitates a shift away from conventional thinking about the problem.)

30. **Exercise:** Creative Management Style

Step 1—Distribute the following quiz to participants and have them complete it on an individual basis.

Are You Using Your Creativity?

Candidly rate yourself on the following aspects of creativity and innovative problem-solving:

1. I tend to use groups to solve problems:
   Rarely 1 2 3 4 5 Often
2. I seek out new methods to improve our work:
   Rarely 1 2 3 4 5 Often
3. I believe it is important to establish a climate for innovation:
   Rarely 1 2 3 4 5 Often
4. I would rate may skill as a listener as:
   Poor 1 2 3 4 5 Good
5. My superiors see me as a creative person:
   Seldom 1 2 3 4 5 Usually
6. My peers see me as a creative person:
   Seldom 1 2 3 4 5 Usually
7. My staff sees me as creative person:
   Seldom 1 2 3 4 5 Usually
8. I see my staff as a creative group:
   Seldom 1 2 3 4 5 Usually
9. I emphasize delegation/empowerment as a means of encouraging risk-taking and creativity:
   Rarely 1 2 3 4 5 Often
10. I use praise as a means of encouraging self-motivation:
    Rarely 1 2 3 4 5 Often

Step 2—Divide participants into groups of three and have them discuss their quiz results.

Step 3—Reassemble the class and ask for volunteers to share their learning from the exercise.

Use of Group-in-Action Creativity Stimulation Techniques—Worksheet for My Inventory and Planning

The frequency rating scale given below will assist you in assessing how often you use the group-in-action techniques indicated on this worksheet. Enter your dots in the appropriate frequency column.

Procedure

1) Simply enter a solid dot after each technique to indicate:
   a) Current frequency of use
   b) Planned future use
2) In respect to "current use," connect all the dots with a ruler or straight edge. This will provide you with a profile or pattern of the frequency with which you now use the various techniques.

By completing the two columns under "Future Use," you now have a plan for greater use of these devices in the future.

Frequency of Use	Frequency Column
Don't use at all	1
Use rarely or occasionally	2
Use with moderate frequency	3
Use very often	4
Use regularly	5

| | Frequency of Current Use | | | | | Future Use | |
Technique	1	2	3	4	5	Will try out	Will use regularly
☐ Brainstorming							
☐ Role Storming							
☐ Problem Identification							
☐ ABC Approach							
☐ Force field analysis							
☐ Brainstorming, a reverse approach							
☐ Card posting technique							
☐ Slip method							
☐ Ideawriting							
☐ Problem onslaught							
☐ Upside-down problem solving							
☐ Outcome objective							
☐ Mindmapping							
☐ Storyboarding							
☐ Random word stimulation technique							
☐ Analogies and metaphors							
☐ Checklists							
☐ Attribute listing							
☐ Morphological analysis							
☐ Forced relationship technique							
☐ Movement—talk while youwalk							
☐ Guided visualization							
☐ Diads/triads analysis							
☐ Principles for collegiality at meetings							

Figure 13-4. Inventory/planning worksheet for greater use of group-oriented creativity techniques.

Solutions to Two Puzzles Given at Beginning of the Chapter

Solution to *first* puzzle:

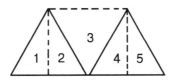

Eight toothpicks are removed from the figure, leaving two squares.

Solution to *second* puzzle.

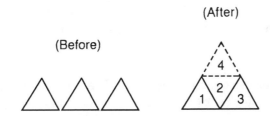

A solution to the puzzle involving the three triangles: Five triangles are created by placing the toothpicks from the right triangle in the positions shown by the dotted lines.

(After)

(Before)

A second solution to the triangle puzzle: The right triangle is placed on top of the other two triangles. The fifth triangle is the entire configuration

Glossary

ABC technique—A detailed checklist that serves as an aid in problem identification. Ideas, as stimuli, are offered in an A to Z format to provoke thinking about possible management problems.

Accommodation—(1) A conflict resolution style marked by giving in totally to the other party or group, smoothing over rather than confronting differences. (2) An adjustment in physical features of the workplace, equipment, work schedules, etc. to enable a person with a physical handicap to perform effectively on the job.

Action plans—Systematic, planned approaches/steps to achieve established goals/targets/objectives.

Action Research Model—A data-based form of problem solving entailing initial data collection, then operating or implementing a program/activity (action plans) based on that data, systematically securing feedback (data) about the actual results of the operation *while it is in process,* and then making necessary adjustments in the operation as indicated by the data feedback.

Active listening—An encouraging, empathic form of responding to another's communication (or problem) via feeding back (restating) what has been said; essentially, assuring the speaker that one understands what was stated, but not necessarily agreeing with the statement. **Note:** Active listening avoids probing, advising and disagreeing.

Activity—Action taken to accomplish an objective or end result; also used synonymously as a function, operation, and program.

Activity trap—Engaging in behaviors that emphasize activity rather than results; e.g., a surplus of meetings, memoranda, field trips, inspections, etc., having little or no impact on needed productivity.

Ad hoc committee (or group)—A special, short-term (limited time) committee (or group) assembled to study a particular problem or to plan/manage a special activity (e.g., the Xmas party). *See* **Standing committee.**

Allness—Assertions that are totally iron-clad or positive (an over-generalization) and thus likely to overwhelm/turn off people; e.g., "I worked at headquarters for eight years and I know those people." Victims of the disease of allness tend to ignore important distinctions and feel they have a corner on the "truth." *See* **Becauseness, Isness.**

Analogy—In creative problem solving making a direct comparison with a similar thing, object, idea; e.g., comparing the manager to a nurturing parent for both are concerned with the growth of people. *See* **Metaphor.**

Analytical listening—Ability/skill to distinguish fact from opinion, judgment, perception, bias.

Arbitrating—A skill/technique used to resolve conflicts between/among individuals or groups.

Attitude—A person's tendency to respond in a fixed way toward ideas, situations, groups, and individuals. Underpinning attitudes are values, perceptions, beliefs, experience.

Attribute listing—Compilation of a list of attributes (or characteristics) to create means for their improvement. Used to generate ideas about a product, service, or situation; e.g., to improve the landscaping around our building we develop a list covering lawn, shrubs, flower beds, benches, etc., and then list particular actions to be taken on each listed item.

Auditory communication style—Refers to those who use considerable references to hearing or sound in their speech, e.g., "That rings a bell with me."

Authentic communication—Unfiltered messages given to others that communicate honestly what one feels, sees, believes.

Authority—The formal power to act/decide granted formally to the manager by the organization; synonymous with formal power as opposed to informal power or influence.

Availability power—Power that accrues by virtue of being in the right place at the right time.

Autocratic leader—One who makes decision unilaterally, i.e., without eliciting team input. Command and control style.

Autonomy—Freedom to work out necessary procedures and to take other action on the job.

Avoidance—A conflict resolution style marked by withdrawal and flight rather than fight.

Back-up style—A mode of operating that is secondary to one's primary style used in conflict resolution, problem solving/decision making, or leadership.

Bargaining—In conflict resolution, a process of give and take to reach a solution agreeable to the parties involved. In the course of giving and taking, the best ("win-win") solution is likely to be overlooked.

Becauseness—A tendency to jump to conclusions on the basis of limited or incomplete data. *See* **Isness, Allness.**

Behavior modification—A motivational theory and technique wherein behavior is changed or maintained by managing the consequences that follow the behavior. So we say "Behavior is a function of its consequences." (Consequences relate to rewards or punishment.)

Benchmarking—Studying the competition so as to elevate the quality of your own product or service.

Body language—*See* **Kinesics**

Brainstorming—Free-wheeling ideation by a group; in the process, criticism is taboo so that no one is discouraged from contributing; after the group "runs dry," evaluation of the ideas is accomplished, either immediately or later on.

Breaking set—Seeing things differently than they have been previously, which allows for creative breakthroughs.

Bureaucracy—A term used to describe the formal organization; in more common parlance, a term to describe an organization marked by its most egregious characteristics: rigid, heartless, rule-bound, non-innovative.

Card posting technique—Posting ideas, written on slips of paper or index cards, on a board or wall for better visualization. Cards thus may be readily grouped, moved, removed, modified, prioritized. *See* **Story boarding.**

Career—A field of work marked by opportunities for growth, development, predictable upward movement, and resultant high satisfaction.

Career development—A formal plan by a manager or an organization to develop skill for orderly growth and progression in a given field of work, e.g., in finance, human resources, marketing, etc. This may be for oneself and/or staff members.

Career path—Logical stepping stones (jobs) in a field of work which lead to a worthwhile, satisfying career.

Career plateau—The point at which upward movement is no longer possible (or highly unlikely) for an individual.

Career stages—Varying points of work/job accomplishment that an individual passes through in his work life.

Catastrophizing—In the absence of contrary information, the worst is assumed and people act as if their worrisome assumptions are legitimate, factual data. This anxiety provides the grist for the rumor mill and grapevine.

Cause-and-effect diagram (ISHIKAWA fishbone diagram)—A device to systematically identify causes for a problem.

Centralization—A management system in which all or most of the organization's authority rests at top organizational levels rather than at lower levels.

Ceremonies—Special events designed to recognize/reward high or special achievement by an individual or group, often accompanied by food and drink such as at a banquet. *See* **Rituals** and **Culture.**

Chain of command—Based on military organizational principles, an organizationally established procedure rigidly defining the lines of responsibility (reporting relations) and communication that flow from the top to the lowest levels in the organization.

Change agent—One who consciously and systematically endeavors to introduce change.

Checklist—Via the use of "trigger words"—e.g., magnify, minimize, rearrange, modify, combine, substitute, adapt, reverse—new concepts or approaches become possible.

Checksheet—A simple, statistical (tabular) device to guide in gathering information about a problem.

Chronemics—An aspect of non-verbal communication in which the use of time communicates attitudes, values, respects.

Climate—The deep-seated tone or atmosphere in a group or total organization—based on its values, beliefs, history, precedents, formal and informal policies and practices—that guides and controls behavior. A climate may be supporting, encouraging, and rewarding, or discouraging and punitive.

Closed-ended questions—Designed to merely produce a "yes" or "no" response, e.g., "Is this the last batch of copy paper?"

Closed system—One that insulates itself from external inputs. *See* **Open system.**

Closure—The act of completing a task/activity/operation, which thus has high motivational value. Enriched and empowered jobs are characterized by opportunities for seeing a task through to completion.

Coaching—A manager's action to upgrade performance or to change a behavior. *See* **Counseling.**

Coalition power—Power that accrues to an individual by forming a coalition or alliance with others having similar needs and/or interests.

Coercive power—The ability to dominate other individuals or groups because of one's ability to provide punishment or withhold rewards.

Cognitive dissonance—An unsettling condition that arises when an individual is confronted with an apparent inconsistency or imbalance between his ongoing beliefs, knowledge, and values and his behavior. The individual thus is under psychological pressure to resolve the conflict by changing either attitude or behavior. Defense mechanisms such as rationalization or denial may be used to resolve the lack of harmony between beliefs and behavior.

Cognitive needs—People's need to know, to receive information so as to be able to predict and control their lives.

Cohesiveness—Attractiveness of a group by its members. The tendency of a group to bond together closely arises because of common goals and experiences, plus strong attraction of team members toward one another. Because membership is valued, members resist leaving.

Collaboration—A conflict resolution style ("win-win") marked by a sincere desire to arrive at a solution that makes winners of both (or all) parties involved.

Communication—A complex process that has for its end result an understanding of the messages transmitted between/among individuals and groups.

Competition—A conflict resolution style ("win-lose") marked by a total desire to win, to beat the other party.

Compromise—A conflict resolution style marked by "splitting the difference" rather than by confronting the issue and the other party to achieve a win-win decision.

Conflict—Differences or disagreements between/among individuals and groups that can promote change, high-quality decisions, and productivity if faced up to and worked through candidly.

Confrontation—In behavioral science terms, a *positive,* healthy action designed to face up to a problem, person, or group, thereby clearing the air and endeavoring to get one's legitimate needs met. **Note:** The term is not to be confused with its use in everyday parlance where it implies nasty or obnoxious aggression, attack, or belligerence.

Congruence—Agreement in (a) verbal communication (Do words support the behavior and vice versa); (b) overall behavior (Do actions taken relate to one's stated behavior, "walk the talk"?); or (c) team functioning, (Team members are "in sync" with—understand and support—team objectives and goals).

Consensus—A process in group decision making in which everyone's ideas are aired, debated, assessed, and ultimately a course of action is agreed upon. Total (100%) agreement is not essential. Free and open discussion, rather than voting, is key to reaching consensus.

Connective (associative) power—Power that accrues to an individual by the virtue of his connections with a powerful person. This may be a strong boss, mentor, or sponsor.

Contingency planning—Minimizing the impact of unforeseen, unwanted events by developing anticipatory plans before a catastrophe occurs.

Controls—Managerial actions/behaviors designed to ensure that delegation (or other performance) proceeds as intended; also, "red flags" to indicate that goals and standards are not being met. Also used negatively to indicate that people are not given the freedom to act properly on their own.

Coordination—A set of procedures that ensures an action taken is consistent with (a) other actions being taken, (b) existing policies, or (c) the needs/wishes of all concerned stakeholders who thus are involved (can provide input) or informed of action contemplated or already taken.

Counseling—A managerial skill designed to (a) overcome unwanted behaviors, (b) advise on career planning and development, or (c) advise on off-the-job, personal problems. In the best sense of the term, counseling means helping people reach informed, pragmatic decisions on their own. *See* **Directive counseling; Nondirective counseling.**

CYA (Cover Your Anatomy) Management—A defensive mode of operating, highly anxiety-driven, even paranoid, thus constantly necessitating the need to justify one's actions/decisions via explanatory memos for the file in case one might be questioned about an action taken.

Creative contact—Devices used to improve interpersonal communication and relationships such as MBWA, joining people for coffee or lunch, etc.

Creativity—The ability to take actions that are departures or breakthroughs in resolving a problem, or developing a product or service. *See* **Innovation.**

Crisis management—A "helter-skelter" or disorderly form of coping with problems as they arise; the opposite of planned management.

Cueing—Feedback that serves as an error-correcting device, e.g., as your rear-view mirror advises that your vehicle is moving out of the proper lane.

Culture—The fundamental beliefs, values, attitudes, assumptions, preferences, and prejudices shared by organization members, often operating below the level of conscious awareness, which serve as an unquestioned basis for action. Buttressing the culture is a blend of history, tradition, heroes, stories, rituals, and ceremonies that ensure that things are done in customary, expected patterns.

Decentralization—An organizational arrangement in which authority to take action is authorized at the lowest possible levels. **Rationale:** Those who are closest to the action should be empowered to decide what should be done.

Decision—An action to finalize a solution to a problem having consequences for the future. *See* **Problem solving.**

Decision making—The process of resolving a problem that entails seeking alternative courses of action, assessing the pros and cons of those options in terms of their possible implications/consequences for the future, choosing a course of action, and planning the implementation of the decision.

Deep delegation—Full—as opposed to partial or hesitant—delegation.

Defense mechanism—A coping device, often subconscious, designed to deal with frustration or anxiety, with the objective of maintaining self-esteem.

Defensive response—A reply to a message that the receiver interprets as an "attack," **Example:** "But, boss, I was on leave that day."

Delegation—Procedure in which the manager provides subordinates with the authority and responsibility to discharge assigned duties independently.

Deming's 14 Points—Major ideas advanced by the late, great management guru W. Edwards Deming, with particular emphasis on achieving quality management.

Denial—A defense mechanism used by individuals, groups and/or the total organization to avoid facing up to the existence or severity of a problem.

Descriptive feedback—The rendering of data, positive or negative, to another person, which describes the person's *behavior* rather than the person per se, e.g., "Your report has been late six of the last eight weeks." *See* **Evaluative feedback.**

Development—A conscious effort by an employee and/or his manager to broaden or upgrade the employee's skill or knowledge. *See* **Career development.**

Developmental feedback—Also termed formative or corrective feedback, it corrects, guides or improves the form or quality of performance. *See* **Motivational feedback.**

Devil's advocate (technique)—In a group problem-solving situation, a team member serves as a critic to point out possible weaknesses in group reasoning, decision making, or planning.

Directive counseling—A "counselor-centered" approach to resolving a worker's personal/emotional difficulties, wherein the counselor actively provides solutions or advice. Major techniques used are of the telling and selling type. *See* **Non-directive counseling.**

Disconfirmation—Feedback of data that is inconsistent with one's prevailing perceptions/beliefs, self-concept, etc., thus creating anxiety that may form the basis for changing one's behavior. **Example:** A climate survey "shocks" a manager with data that his delegation practices are highly "low trust."

Discounting—(1) To downgrade the significance of praise given by the boss or another person. (2) Disparaging or putting down an idea or failing to affirm it.

Dissatisfiers—In Herzberg's Motivation-Hygiene Theory, hygiene factors, such as pay, working conditions, supervision, and organizational policies may cause dissatisfaction when not adequate, but they do not bear on motivation. *See* **Motivators and Satisfiers.**

Distortion—An unintended (unconscious) interpretation or perception of a message by the message receiver at variance with that intended by the communicator.

Divergent thinking—A creative thinking device, used to stretch the minds of those attempting to resolve problems, that demands new, non-patterned possibilities.

Diversity of workforce—A work population, either of the whole organization or one or more segments of it, marked by a range of workers having different backgrounds, e.g., race, ethnicity, age, gender, physical attributes.

Downsizing—Deep staff reductions to save cost and possibly make for a more rational efficient operation.

Downward communication—Messages sent by those at the top of an organization to those below; essentially a form of one-way communication operating through the chain of command.

Driving forces—In Force Field Analysis, the forces that are encouraging, facilitating, or pushing an organization phenomenon (e.g., sales, costs, error rate) so that it remains at or rises above a particular level. *See* **Restraining Forces.**

Dual-career couple—A family in which both spouses are active members of the workforce.

Dual-career ladder—A two-track career system, one for management people and the other for technical or professional people who don't opt for a management career.

Dysfunctional behavior—Behaviors that retard rather than promote healthy group/organizational functioning, e.g., credit seeking, finger pointing, cliquing, nit-picking, protecting turf, excessive rationalizing.

Effectiveness—The accomplishment of a mission or activity that has sound, worthwhile objectives or high merit; doing the right thing(s). *See* **Efficiency.**

Efficiency—Literally, the ratio of output to input; more generally, the conduct of an activity with full and careful regard to the use of available resources such as budget, personnel, materials, equipment, time, etc; doing things right. **Note:** A mission or activity of little or no value can be conducted efficiently. *See* **Effectiveness.**

Empathic communication—Communication designed to allow employees to "ventilate" freely, to meet their need to be heard and really be listened to and feel supported.

Empathic listening—Allowing people to present "their view of the world," ventilating their feelings, without interrupting or passing judgment.

Employee assistance program (EAP)—A formal system of counseling which the organization uses to help employees resolve or face up to psychological problems which interfere with their on-the-job performance.

Employee involvement group—*See* **Quality circle.**

Empowerment—Organizational policy and practice which encourages and allows individuals and/or groups to make their own decisions, particularly those affecting customers/clients in a positive way.

Equal employment opportunity (EEO)—legally required system to ensure that all personnel transactions (hiring, advancement, training, etc.) are accomplished solely on the basis of merit and ability.

Equilibrium—In Force Field Analysis, a balanced state brought about by the equal strength of the driving and restraining forces. *See* **Driving** and **Restraining forces.**

Esteem needs—Innate, ego-satisfying desires to have one's needs met for status, reputation, recognition of accomplishment; an advanced stage in the Hierarchy of Needs.

Ethics—High-level standards and principles that guide individuals and groups to perform on the basis of fairness, equity, and morality, i.e., what is good and right. Ethics considers the needs of others as opposed to succeeding by besting others in any and all ways possible.

Evaluative feedback—Rendering a judgmental rather than a descriptive message, i.e., an evaluation of the person rather than the behavior, e.g., "you have a bad habit of . . ." *See* **Descriptive feedback.**

Evaluative response—In the directive counseling situation, an assessment by the counselor as to whether a proposed course of action by the counselee is wise or unwise, considered or impulsive, acceptable or unacceptable.

Expectancy—One's perception of the tie between effort and stipulated rewards.

Expectancy theory—A theory of motivation in which the individual will perform a reward-inducing behavior if he regards/assumes (a) the reward is worthwhile (significant, important), and (b) the appropriate performance/effort will actually provide that particular reward. So one's motivation is sparked by an estimate that effort can lead to the desired reward.

Expert power—The power that accrues to a person, managerial or non-managerial, because of his knowledge or high skill.

Expert systems—Knowledge-based systems consisting of computer software programs that assist decision making (or action taking) by asking totally pertinent questions.

Expressive communication—Communication by expressing one's feelings freely, "talking it out." *See* **Empathic Communication.**

Externalizer—Person who sees life's happenings—good or bad—as out of his control, "luck" being what determines the results. *See* **Internalizer.**

Extinction—The total elimination of an unwanted behavior achieved via punishment or removal of rewards (reinforcing consequences).

Extrinsic motivation—Motivation that may arise from external (non-job/work related) factors such as pay, fringe benefits, conditions of work, or threats, punishment.

Extroversion—An outward direction of one's feelings and attitudes, resulting in active relations with others. *See* **Introversion.**

Feedback—(1) Data received by an individual, group, or total organization which, if internalized, has the potential to change behavior or performance. (2) A check by a message sender to ascertain whether the transmitted message was fully understood—received as actually intended—by the receiver.

Flextime—A work schedule designed to meet the personal, off-the-job needs of employees. Typically, the organization establishes a midday core work period for all employees to observe, with freedom to decide arrival and departure time, done within the confines of the work week's total number of hours.

Force field analysis—A problem-solving device to assess the forces—driving and restraining—that bear on a problem (or situation) and, in combination, make for a level of equilibrium.

Forced relationship technique—To develop new combinations of ideas, participants are given a new word, concept, phrase, or object and asked to relate it to the problem being studied; or the group may be asked to take an imaginary trip somewhere.

Formal communication channels—Organizationally prescribed channels to give and receive information, generally following the established chain of command.

Formal groups—Groups set up by the organization to accomplish organizational goals. *See* **Informal groups.**

Formal organization—The nature of the organization as defined in mission statements, written policies, the formal reward system, written standards, procedure manuals, organizational charts, job descriptions, etc. *See* **Informal organization.**

Formal training—Planned training conducted in the classroom, generally in groups.

Frustration—An unwanted, dissatisfying emotional state that arises when goal achievement is subject to a block or barrier.

Gainsharing—Incentive pay based on sharing gains from employee involvement in productivity increases or cost reductions.

GASing people—Refers to behaviors which produce Guilt, Anxiety, or Shame. **Note:** The GASing may affect others or oneself.

Gatekeeper—In a problem-solving group or at meetings, one who invites others to "enter in," to offer ideas, opinions, information.

Goal—An end state; target.

Glass ceiling—An invisible but highly consistent and effective barrier to significant upward movement by women and minorities.

Grapevine—An informal, "unauthorized" system of communication that rises when the formal communication system fails to meet the needs of people "to know." Rumor as well as fact provide informational material for the grapevine.

Group dynamics—Behavior patterns of participants in a group as they interact with one another. The dynamics of a new group have been described as evolving via these stages: forming, storming, norming, and performing.

Group decision making—A tool used by managers to allow a group to act finally on a problem; used particularly when commitment for or acceptance of a decision is highly important.

Groupthink—Pressures within the group toward conformity/concurrence in thinking and action without appraising or seeking other, more realistic/appropriate alternatives.

Guided visualization—Using crayons or large felt-tipped pens, participants draw pictures (visual or graphic representations) on large flipchart sheets to develop ideas about themes raised by the manager or a trainer, e.g., what is the firm like, where is it going, what should the future be like, etc.

Haptics—In non-verbal communication, the messages we send, intentionally or otherwise, via touching another person.

Hedges—In interpersonal communication, a tendency to use qualifiers that may make the speaker appear overly tentative, e.g., "I guess you could say."

Heuristics—Devices ("rules of thumb") used to simplify decision making.

Hierarchy of needs—Per clinical psychologist Abraham Maslow, there are five need levels comprising the motivational system of individuals: physiological, safety (security), social (belonging), self-esteem (ego), and self-actualization (self-realization). The needs at any lower level must be met before an individual can ascend to a higher-level need.

Higher order of needs—In Maslow's Hierarchy of Needs, the esteem and self-actualization needs.

Horizontal communication—Lateral exchange of messages among individuals, groups, or other formal segments of the organization.

Hygiene factors—In Herzberg's two-factor theory, factors such as pay, supervision, physical conditions of work, and organizational policies, which are regarded as potential or actual dissatisfiers, not as demotivators. When these factors are present they produce non-dissatisfaction, but not motivation. *See* **Motivator.**

Ideation—Process of creating ideas; to be distinguished from *evaluation,* which follows after all ideas have been generated.

Idea writing—In small groups, individual ideation in writing, followed by written comments about those ideas by colleagues and total group discussion of ideas generated in each small group.

Idoiosyncracy credits—A form of "credit" or freedom to be oneself, which is acquired only with the (gradual) attainment of full membership in a group or organization. The "earned" credit may permit such "deviances" as speaking out freely, criticizing policies, procedures or products, performing in somewhat less conventional ways, etc.

"I" Message—A powerful technique for use in interpersonal communication. Messages, which can be declarative, responsive, preventive, or confrontive, entail candid expression of one's feelings in respect to the other party's (often) less-than-helpful behavior. Three elements comprise the message: the *behavior, tangible effects,* and one's *feelings* about the behavior and the effects.

Implementation—The final step in problem solving and decision making in which a decision is put into effect via a well-developed plan.

Impostors—Low-esteem people who thus see themselves as less than genuine, less qualified, or less able than others.

Influence—Informal or personal power (as opposed to *position* power, based on skill, knowledge, key contacts, information, and/or attractiveness of one's personality) that can be used to get others to respond to one's wishes. *See* **Authority; Legitimate power.**

Informal groups—Groups formed spontaneously by employees to meet member needs, but not officially sanctioned by the organization, e.g., carpools, luncheon groups, bowling teams, etc.

Informal organization—The way the organization actually operates in terms of authority (informal leaders, informal groups), communication (e.g., the grapevine), rewards (who really gets the promotions?), etc. *See* **Formal organization.**

Innovation—New applications, significant changes, or improvements in product, program, policy, procedure. *See* **Creativity.**

Instrument—A self-assessment device (self-quiz) to encourage introspection and reflection.

Instrumental communication—That which is essential to prescribe the execution of particular tasks.

Instrumented feedback—A device to measure team functioning, collected via self-quizzes. This provides the team leader and/or the team with input (team sentiment) concerning its effectiveness, e.g., on communication, climate, its creativity, etc.

Integrative listening—Accurately using the ideas presented by others and blending them with your own.

Intensifiers—Emphasizing words, usually adverbs such as "really" or "such," often used by women speakers (e.g., "really neat"), which male listeners are likely to regard as speech with little or no authority.

Interdependence—Joint or mutual dependence on other persons or groups.

Intergroup conflict—"Turf battles" designed to reduce the influence and/or goal achievement of other groups because of a presumption that one's own group has a higher priority or greater wisdom or importance.

Internalizer—One who sees life as well within his control. *See* **Externalizer.**

Interpersonal communication—Verbal or non-verbal communication between two or more individuals.

Interpretive response—In a counseling situation, an attempt by the counselor to uncover motives for a particular statement.

Intervention—A managerial action that intervenes in an ongoing organizational process, e.g., into delegation of work when it is not proceeding properly.

Intrinsic motivation—Motivation that meets a person's need for accomplishment, recognition, etc., typically as a result of the work itself rather than external factors such as pay, fringe benefits, physical conditions, punishment, etc.

Introspection—An inward look at one's beliefs, attitudes, values, perceptions, behaviors. *See* **Reflection.**

Introversion—An inward over-direction of one's attitudes and feelings, resulting in a decreased ability to relate well to others. *See* **Extroversion.**

Intuitive decision making—Making a decision based on hunches, gut feeling or intuition; often essential when policies, standards and/or outcomes are murky.

Isness—Assertions that give meaning to something "out there" when the meaning is actually in us, e.g., "Henry is simply out of touch with things." *See* **Allness, Becauseness.**

Job aid—A self-instructional tool for on-the-job learning, e.g., a checklist or a set of questions on a computer as a guide to proper performance.

Job design—The planning of work tasks to ensure the creation of jobs that are logical, efficient, and ego satisfying.

Job enlargement—The addition of like duties and responsibilities to an existing job with the objective of stimulating job interest; in effect, a broadening of scope but not depth.

Job enrichment—The addition of higher-level, more responsible, more varied duties and responsibilities to increase motivation.

Job empowerment—*See* **Empowerment.**

Job rotation—Switching of personnel among jobs to reduce fatigue and/or boredom, to increase job interest and motivation, and/or to provide added skills for greater flexibility in assignment of workers.

Job sharing (work sharing)—A formally established work schedule and work arrangement to meet the needs of two individuals who perform a single job.

Journalist's six questions—A device to aid in problem solving and creative thinking wherein one asks Who, How, What, Where, When, Why.

"JIC" (Just in Case) file—A defensive behavior involving maintenance of a file of memoranda to the file, in case one is questioned as to the basis for an action taken. *See* **CYA.**

Just-in-time (*Kanban*)—A system of inventory control that involves minimum inventory at the company with resultant heavy reliance on suppliers to deliver when needed.

Kaizen—In Japan, the never-ending quest for perfection that takes the form of continuous improvement.

Kinesics—An aspect of non-verbal communication, entailing body movement, which transmits messages, intentionally or otherwise. (Popularly referred to as "body language.")

Kinesthetic communication style—Refers to people who speak in terms of feelings and touch-related words, e.g., "We're up against the wall," or "in a bind."

Koinonia **("Spirit of Fellowship")**—Socratic dialogue based on collegiality, listening, exchange of ideas, candor; arguing and interrupting are taboo.

Laissez-faire—A leadership style marked by a "hands-off" policy and practice.

Lateral thinking—Open-ended, "illogical," non-linear, or "zigzag" thinking designed to produce an intuitive, "Aha" response; a real creative breakthrough.

Lateral transfer—A non-promotional but strategic career planning and development tool to (a) acquire new, desirable job experience/growth for a later upward move (a "stepping stone"), or (b) to remove oneself from an undesirable work situation, e.g., a dull job, impossible boss, etc.

Law of unintended consequences—A decision may backfire, causing new or added problems.

Leadership—Acts or actions that provide challenge and direction to team members so as to achieve new, established or changing goals.

Leadership style—A manager's distinct pattern of guiding and interacting with staff in respect to such leadership components as goal setting, assigning and reviewing work, communicating, innovating, approachability, etc.

Learning organization—An organization skilled at acquiring and using new knowledge to bring about essential change and/or to meet new challenges and opportunities.

Left hemisphere of brain—Province of analytical thought. It produces thinking that is objective, convergent, logical, orderly, factual, rational, linear, sequential, vertical, numerical/quantitative. *See* **Right hemisphere of brain.**

Legitimate power—The authority a manager receives from the organization, which provides sanction to direct and control subordinates. *See* **Influence.**

Line manager—One who is concerned directly with the administration or operation of a function or program basic to an organization's mission, e,g., production, sales, R&D, warehousing, etc; contrast with staff managers (e.g., finance, legal, PR, human resources), who advise and facilitate line operations.

Lose-lose—An outcome to a controversy in which all parties involved are losers.

Lower-order needs—In Maslow's Hierarchy of Needs, those needs that are termed physiological, safety, and social.

Machiavellian—One who sees the world as a place where one's needs for personal aggrandizment are to be met and thus operates accordingly; synonymous with manipulative behavior.

Maintenance roles—In meetings or problem-solving sessions, roles adopted informally/spontaneously by team/group members to meet social/emotional needs and relationships among group members/participants. **Examples:** harmonizing, gatekeeping.

Maldistribution rule—*See* **Pareto analysis.**

MBGOOTW—A "piggy-back" on MBWA (Management By Walking Around), meaning "Management By Getting Out of the Way" (or deep delegation).

MBWA (Management By Walking Around)—Visiting people at their desks or workstations to listen, seek suggestions, and/or maintain rapport with employees.

Management By Objectives (MBO)—A system of management that entails joint (boss and subordinate) goal setting plus quarterly and annual reviews to ensure that agreed-upon goals are met. The annual review is used to plan the next year's work.

Manipulative question—A loaded question designed to present a statement, feeling or decision, e.g., "You did know that regulation, didn't you?"

Mediation—In conflict resolution, the use of a third party who provides an advisory, facilitating role as opposed to making a decision that resolves the conflict.

Mentor—A senior, highly able manager who aids in furthering (and accelerating) the managerial career of a less-experienced person.

Mentoring—Counseling by a senior, experienced manager of a newer, less-experienced worker to upgrade more rapidly the latter's managerial knowledge and skills. The aim is to transmit experience-based know-how concerning organizational policies, programs and the culture generally. It is getting the "big picture" in a "hands-on" way.

Metaphor—A word or figure of speech involving two different kinds of thoughts linked by a point of similarity, e.g., "a can of worms"; a tool used in creative problem solving. *See* **Analogy.**

Mind mapping (idea mapping)—Starting from a concept or trigger word written in the center of a page (or flipchart), branches are drawn in various directions away from that center. Each branch then is subject to ideation.

Mindset—A particular predisposition, attitude, or "world view" toward a particular object (person, subject, idea).

Misoneist—One who has a hatred, fear, or intolerance for innovation or change.

Mission statement—The organization's high-level, written statement declaring its major purpose and ideals.

Mixed messages—Communication marked by an inconsistency between one's statement and behavior; also, an incongruity between one's verbal and non-verbal communication.

Modeling—Behavior, conscious or unconscious, by the manager, who sets a tone or style for subordinates to follow.

Morphological analysis—An idea-generating technique that entails relating several variables of a problem to aid in finding a new solution.

Motivational feedback—Relates to data that has the power to increase or decrease a particular performance, thus affecting the quantity of performance. *See* **Developmental feedback.**

Motivation—The will to do; largely a response to internal needs/drives to accomplish, to move toward a goal, to complete something.

Motivation-Hygiene Theory—The two-factor theory of Frederick Herzberg that postulates that people have two needs: to grow psychologically (motivation) and to avoid pain (hygiene). Motivators relate to the work itself (e.g., increased responsibility) whereas hygiene factors relate to work context (not work content) such as nice surroundings and good pay. Causes for satisfaction (motivation) and dissatisfaction (hygiene deprivation) are totally dissimilar and thus require different forms of management.

Motivator—A force that stimulates the will to do (or motivate). In Herzberg's Motivation-Hygiene Theory, motivators (also termed satisfiers) include added responsibility, recognition, and advancement. *See* **Hygiene factors.**

Multiple career pathing—Adding to (broadening) your skill repertoire to enhance (and possibly ensure) your employability/marketability.

Naive model of communication—A hypothetical, unrealistic assumption that (a) when A communicates to B, B hears accurately (unfiltered) what A said, and (b) A communicates accurately (unfiltered) what he meant to say. An added shortcoming: absence of feedback for a reality check.

Need—A source of psychological or physiological arousal (tension) due to some deprivation or deficiency, the tension existing until one acts to meet that need.

Needs system—The totality of motivations, drives, goals, hopes, etc. that drive our behavior, both rational and less than rational.

Negotiation—In the process of seeking a solution in a conflict situation, both (or all) parties are willing to confront the issue directly.

NIH factor—"Not Invented Here." **Significance:** A reluctance to adopt an idea or procedure because of its outside origin, which may mean a lost opportunity.

Non-verbal communication—Expression via facial, body and eye movements ("body language"). *See* **Paralanguage, Kinesics, Proxemics, Haptics.**

Non-directive counseling—A "client-centered" approach to help employees resolve their personal/emotional problems. Emphasis is on decision-making by the counselee based on new insight gained from the counseling process. Major techniques used are *active listening* and *reflecting feelings*. *See* **Directive counseling.**

Norms—Expectations/standards developed and shared by a group/team, providing guides to members/participants regarding their behavior in particular circumstances. Norms may be formal or informal, written or unwritten.

On-the-job training—A procedure for a subordinate to learn particular tasks from the boss or other workers in a non-classroom setting.

Open-door policy—A presumed "opportunity" for employees to visit the big boss and say or ask whatever one wishes. In actuality, a little-used procedure due to factors such as organizational climate and the boss' status and power.

Open system—A system that places great emphasis on the need to secure external inputs for survival and growth.

Open-ended questions—Designed to encourage thought, analysis, candor, e.g., "How might we turn things around?"

Orientation—Orderly introduction of a new worker to his job and the new environment to enable him to get into production more quickly and smoothly.

Outcome objective—A technique to encourage group creativity. The group is asked to assume the session has ended and things went very well. Next, the group discusses what turned them on and what ideas were generated. Ideas are then posted to a flipchart.

Paralanguage—An aspect of non-verbal communication that relies on how something is said rather than the words per se; in effect, how we use our voice: tone, volume, speed, inflection, pauses, etc. to communicate intentionally or otherwise.

Pareto Analysis—The 80/20 principle used in problem solving (20% of the effort contributes to 80% of the results). It can guide decisions regarding separating the significant few from the trivial many.

Pareto diagram—Bar chart used to show graphically the major problem or major causes for a problem.

Participative leadership—A style of management that stresses heavy participation/involvement of staff in all aspects of the problem-solving process, including group decision making.

Peak performer—A hard-working, high-producing individual who combines work with a balanced lifestyle—i.e., time for fun, relaxation and family, as well as with job demands.

Perception—Meaning from a message that accrues to an individual or group based on attitudes, values, expectations, self-concept. It thus may or may not be reality based.

Performance appraisal—A procedure to assess work performance, usually annually, and to develop plans for job improvement as indicated.

Performance gap—A discrepancy between desired/required performance and actual accomplishment.

Personality—The sum total of one's traits/characteristics that give a person his unique character. Because of the high stability of one's personal attributes, there is a tendency to behave in a predictable way in many situations.

Peter principle—Lawrence Peter's "principle" that employees tend to be promoted to their level of incompetence.

Physiological needs—Fundamental or basic biological needs such as for air, water, food, warmth, etc.

Pilot run—A trial run to test the worthwhileness of a new procedure, operation, etc., before its full implementation.

Plop—A term used in group dynamics to signify an idea or suggestion "falling to the ground with no one picking it up," i.e., the idea is discounted or ignored. The likely result: a "turned off" participant.

Polarization—Group interests and attitudes that become divided and fixed into rigidly held positions; refers to both intra- and inter-group behavior.

Policy—Guides or directives intended to bring about uniform action within an organization.

Positive reinforcement—The use of positive consequences (e.g., praise and other rewards) that tend to increase the likelihood of a behavior being repeated or maintained.

Postmortem critique—Critique made at the end of an activity to review and evaluate accomplishment in relation to stipulated evaluation criteria and desired outcomes.

Proactive—Taking the initiative firmly to control events rather than letting the events control you. *See* **Reactive.**

Probing response—In the counseling situation, an attempt by the counselor to secure more information by asking questions; used more commonly in directive as opposed to non-directive counseling. *See* **Directive** and **Non-directive counseling.**

Problem onslaught—Launching an all-out attack on a problem by throwing all the unit's talent on it.

Problem solving—A term used loosely to connote seeking a solution to a problem/difficulty and finalizing it. More precisely, problem solving relates to seeking a solution for a problem that has no or little future implication, e.g., buying a cabinet to store supplies. In contrast, decision making is marked by resolving a problem with future consequences, e.g., a promotion to a key position, a reorganization, a merger or acquisition, the launching of a new marketing program.

Procedures—Formally stated mechanisms and rules designed to execute enunciated policies.

Project team—A diverse or representative group set up to resolve a particular problem; also termed a task force.

Prompting—A tool to invoke a desirable behavior, e.g., a schedule, the yellow guidelines on a warehouse floor, arrows in a parking lot, a job aid.

Proxemics—In non-verbal communication, how we use our personal space ("territoriality"), thus communicating intentionally or unintentionally our attitude toward others.

Psychological size—Perception by employees that the boss is a "10-foot-tall giant," as evidenced by his status and power, and thus one is reluctant to communicate candidly with that person lest one be punished for that candor.

Punishment—The application of negative consequences (e.g., threats, put downs, "chewing out") to decrease or eliminate the possibility of a behavior being performed or repeated.

Pygmalion effect—A set of beliefs, positive or negative, that influences behavioral outcomes; also known as a "self-fulfilling prophecy."

Quality circle—A group of six to twelve workers who *voluntarily* meet regularly (e.g., once per week for one hour) to identify problems in their units and to produce recommendations to management for their resolution. *See* **Employee involvement groups.**

Quality of work life (QWL)—The general character of day-to-day experience people encounter in their workplace.

Random word stimulation technique—To overcome the dead weight of "logical" thinking, a word is selected randomly from the dictionary and group members free-associate words/concepts from this stimulus or "trigger" word.

Ranking—(1) A listing of problems ranging from most to least serious. (2) A listing of employees indicating the top-level, middle and low-order producers in a unit.

Rationalization—A defense mechanism in which one takes a "sour grapes" stance to avoid coping with the reality of a problem or an obviously serious event.

Reactive—A non-initiating, passive response style; responding only when events actually occur. *See* **Proactive.**

Reality testing—A process of sifting and weighing facts, opinions, attitudes, the internal and/or external environment, possible solutions to a problem, etc., to discern accurately what is prevalent in the real world; separating fact from fiction and fantasy.

Receiver—The one who receives a message from the sender.

Re-engineering—Changing work processes radically, not by "fixing" but by starting over; an antidote to behavior that persists beyond its point of usefulness.

Referent power—The power one has over another (or others) because of his attractiveness as a personality, that is, others readily identify with the one with the power.

Reflection—An attempt to make meaning of what one has learned in introspection. *See* **Introspection.**

Reframing—Readjusting thought processes to encourage breakthrough rather than static thinking. **Examples:** In problem solving, setbacks and negative feedback are learning opportunities; in delegation, the manager perceives himself as a coach rather than as a director; in motivation, joy in seeing others grow and accomplish as opposed to pride only in one's own achievements.

Reinforcement—A technique to elicit a desired behavioral response, using rewards or punishment, either of which can be applied or withdrawn as results dictate.

Reliability—The quality of data to be reproduced over time by other data collectors; consistency through a series of measurements.

Restraining forces—In Force Field Analysis, forces that discourage or resist movement toward a desired level.

Restructuring—Accomplishing major, strategic changes to ensure competitiveness and profitability, e.g., spinning off unprofitable units.

Reverse (or upward) delegation—The subtle technique used by staffers to get the boss to do their jobs.

Reward power—The ability to influence or control behavior via control (giving or withdrawing) of rewards or outcomes.

Reward system—The actions (behaviors) organization members must take to get positive payoffs and those that must not be taken to avoid punishment. The rewards may or may not be formally stated nor may they necessarily be in sync with written policy statements.

Right hemisphere of brain—Province of intuition and insight. Produces thinking that is intuitive, emotional, non-linear, divergent, imaginative, experimental, subjective, non-judgmental, spatial, artistic, holistic. *See* **Left hemisphere of brain.**

Risk—An adverse, unwanted outcome involved in making a decision. Note that the precise situation in which the negative event might arise is not known, but the probabilities of the events occurring can be anticipated.

Risk analysis—Procedure used to assess the nature and severity of unwanted outcomes and to arrive at means of reducing or eliminating that severity. Psychologically speaking, the opportunity for analysis and discussion of the presumed risk may in itself overcome the sense of risk severity.

Rituals—Guides to organizational behavior in the form of (routine) meetings, ceremonies, parties, social events, introduction of a new worker; part of the "glue" that helps to bind people to the organization. *See* **Ceremonies and Culture.**

Role—The set of expected behaviors to perform one's job properly and to have effective relationships with others.

Role ambiguity—Absence of clarity about expectations in a given role.

Rules/regulations—Requirements issued formally to ensure or forbid particular behaviors.

Role playing—A group-in-action training technique used to develop skills or to alter attitudes via the assumption of a role by a trainee and acting out particular behaviors.

Role storming—An offshoot of brainstorming, in which participants assume the role of another person, someone not in the group, and offer ideas as that person might provide them, given his values, attitudes, etc.

Rumor—Unauthorized, unofficial information—fact, fiction or fantasy—that feeds the grapevine.

Safety need—The need for such basics in daily living as security and stability.

Satisfice—In decision making, settling for a decision that satisfies (meets) most requirements for a satisfactory resolution of a problem, as opposed to seeking for an optimal (ideal) solution/decision.

Satisfiers (or motivators)—In Herzberg's Motivation Hygiene Theory, factors that make for motivation, e.g., increased responsibility, recognition, advancement. *See* **Dissatisfier, Motivator.**

Scatter diagram—A statistical procedure in problem solving designed to show graphically the relationship between two sets of data (variables), e.g., sales and tenure.

Scientific management—The management school of thought of the early 1900s developed by Frederic W. Taylor. **Key ideas:** workers are motivated by money alone, so pay should be based on piece rates. Jobs are to be broken down into simple, standardized tasks for greater efficiency. To analyze jobs, efficiency engineers use time-and-motion studies. In general, management does all the planning and thinking, workers merely perform as directed.

Selective perception—A tendency, usually subconscious, to select those elements in a statement or situation that reflect or are consistent with one's own attitudes, beliefs, needs, values.

Self-actualization needs—Highest level of needs to achieve self-fulfillment via growth, accomplishment, or contribution, thereby unleashing one's highest capability or potential.

Self-concept—Also known as self-image or self-worth, it is the amalgam or pattern of elements—attitudes, perceptions, feelings, success history, etc.—that one has about oneself, providing a mental image or perception of one's value as a person. For good mental health, a strong rather than a weak self-image is essential.

Self-inflicted "wound"—A style of operating or performing particular behaviors that is self-defeating, even punishing, and thus of limited utility or productivity. **Examples:** operating in a crisis mode, failing to "walk the talk," etc.

Self-managed (or directed) work team—A work group organized to perform a given task/activity/operation with full responsibility, authority and freedom to organize its work, assign work, review work, establish work schedules, deal with customers and suppliers, etc.

Semantics—meanings of words, particularly various meanings for the same word.

Sender—The one who transmits a message to the receiver.

Severity—A criterion to aid in identifying a problem properly, using such factors as cost, frequency, location, system, equipment.

Shaping—A behavior-modification procedure, using positive reinforcement, to shape or develop a desired behavior of a fairly complex sort, accomplished by having the worker, as learner, experience successive approximations of that desired behavior/performance.

Sharing—A key behavior essential to develop and maintain interpersonal effectiveness, involving providing freely to others one's feelings, attitudes, viewpoints, experience, etc., in addition to factual information.

Simplistic thinking—Taking a problem of considerable complexity and reducing it to a false unidimensionality; ignoring or downplaying significant, ramified factors.

Situational ethics—An approach to problem solving or decision making wherein when one is faced with an ethical dilemma, one rationalizes a less-than-ethical decision (e.g., "no one will really be hurt by this" or "it's only a one-time thing").

Slip method—A problem-solving tool wherein team members list individually on 3″ × 5″ slips ideas that relate to problem identification, causes for problems, or solutions to problems. Slips are then collected, grouped, and evaluated. *See* **Card-posting technique.**

Smoothing—In conflict resolution, playing down the event or importance of differences to ease tensions between the parties involved.

Social power—Social pressure used by a group, panel, or clique to accomplish its objectives. **Example:** A panel that decides on promotions.

Specialization—To become limited to a specific portion of a whole job; a key element in Taylor's Scientific Management Theory.

Staff manager—One who advises and facilitates line managers to get their job done more effectively. Staff positions include finance, human resources, legal, PR.

Span of control—The number of persons reporting to and managed by the boss. Five to seven subordinates is deemed to be a manageable number, although larger numbers may be supervised if the same routine work is performed by large numbers of workers.

Social need—The need for affection from others; the desire for affiliation or belonging; a heavy group or team orientation.

Stakeholders—Those who have a direct interest in the resolution of a problem or the outcome of a decision.

Standing committee—A formally established, permanent committee, e.g., suggestions, safety, credit union, etc.

Status—the degree of deference or prestige one can command from others, hence the terms "high" status and "low" status.

Stereotyping—Assigning of characteristics/qualities/traits to individuals because of their group membership as opposed to their actual, individualized qualities.

Storyboarding—A problem-solving procedure entailing the writing of ideas on index cards by team members, then posting the cards to a board and arranging them into groups. This helps achieve focus, creativity, and productivity (time saving). *See* **Card posting technique.**

Stress listening—In coping with an angry person, one uses active listening techniques to defuse the rancor and encourage a free flow of meaningful information.

Superordinate goals—The top-level goals of an organization, which, because of their key importance, readily override those of an individual or group; particularly important as a lever to resolve conflict between individuals and groups.

Supportive leadership—A leadership style in which the manager exhibits a high interest in and concern for the needs of staff members.

Supportive response—In the counseling situation, an attempt by the counselor to provide help, advice, comfort, assurance, or concurrence.

Surface language—In non-verbal communication, the psychology of first impressions based on dress, grooming, one's name.

SWOT analysis—A long-range planning tool used by a team or the total organization to assess Strengths, Weaknesses, Opportunities, and Threats.

Symbol—By virtue of its association or relationship to something else, an item that gives meaning to a particular idea, thought, belief, outlook; e.g., the "right" kind of dress symbolizes your intent to function properly at the office or at an event.

Synchrony—A phenomenon in interpersonal communication in which the communication pattern between the parties evolves into a rhythmic relationship as evidenced by proximity, body movement, voice (volume, pitch, rate), etc.

Synergy—Energy in which the whole is greater than the sum of its parts. **Example:** Team effort typically exceeds the productivity of individuals operating in isolation from one another.

System—An integrated, interrelated set of elements that functions as a significant whole.

Systems thinking—Looking at an organization holistically, that is, a number of integrated components that, when functioning in unison, make for a significant whole.

Tag questions—The use of questions at the end of a sentence that ask the listener for confirmation, e.g., "We should get reports from the field, shouldn't we?" Often used by female speakers. Males interpret this technique as seeking approval or lacking in authority.

Task force—A special team created to study and make recommendations on a particular problem or to coordinate activities; also termed *project team.*

Task roles—In meetings or problem-solving sessions, roles adopted informally by team/group members to facilitate work accomplishment. **Examples:** requesting information, giving information, clarifying, summarizing.

Team building—Planned, systematized activities to gather data about a team to augment its effectiveness, cooperation, communication, unleashing of creativity, and goal and policy clarification and development. A common way of beginning is via a distraction-free, off-site, two- or three-day retreat.

Theory—In behavioral science parlance, a set of rigidly proven, closely linked principles or concepts based on controlled experimentation, systematic collection of survey data, or systematically observed experience. Generally, a hypothesis (a presumption or supposition) proceeds a theory and is created for testing events. **Note:** A theory can provide a basis for predictability of behavior/performance, e.g., motivation theory, communication theory.

Theories X and Y—Developed by Douglas McGregor, Theory X assumes that people dislike work, have limited capacity for growth, are self-centered, are motivated primarily by money, and thus must be supervised very closely. Theory Y assumes people do like to work; can identify with work objectives; will seek rather than avoid responsibility; are capable of self-direction; and have capacity for growth, something that is widely rather than narrowly distributed among the work population. The particular outloook toward people one adopts then becomes a self-fulfilling prophecy.

Toastmaster's Club—A group that meets regularly for the purpose of providing its members with the development of public speaking skills.

Total Quality Management (TQM)—An all-out improvement effort marked by customer obsession, a systems view, an open system, teamwork, continuous improvement.

Trust—Feeling by a person that it is "safe" to communicate freely (honestly) with another (boss, peer).

Two-way communication—A form of transmission of messages in which senders elicit feedback from receivers, and receivers are permitted to ask questions of senders. *See* **Two-way flow.**

Two-way flow—Ideal state of interpersonal communication wherein there is "give and take," and no one person monopolizes the available air time.

Type A behavior pattern—A set of frenzied behaviors marked by constant movement, impatience, competition, and placing of great pressures/demands on oneself to achieve and be perfect.

Type B behavior pattern—A set of behaviors exhibited by individuals who are relaxed, laid back, easygoing, comfortable with themselves, and more cooperative than competitive.

Unanimity—Total agreement by group members on the nature of a problem, or issue, or the course of action to be taken. *See* **Consensus,** which relates to group agreement, but not unanimity.

Understanding response ("mirror response")—In the counseling situation, the counselor reflects back (restatement) what is said by the counselee, either content or feelings underlying it, or both. Its major purpose is to drain off feelings and encourage people to "talk it out."

Upside-down problem solving—Unconventional solutions to a problem may be obtained by abandoning "common sense" and thinking in opposite terms. **Exam-**ple: to lose weight, eat more (rather than less), but the "more" might be carrots, celery, etc.

Upward communication—A formal communication system, sometimes informal, which allows employees at the bottom of the organization to send messages up the line to those in higher-level positions.

Validity—Data that actually reflects or measures what it is supposed to.

Values—Our internal key guides to advise us as to what is ethical, moral, significant, good, bad, beautiful.

Visibility—Opportunities for career-conscious individuals to be seen by those in upper management via large projects or important task groups; making of presentations, attending social functions, etc.

Visual communication style—Refers to people who use considerable references to seeing in their speech, e.g., "Do you get the picture?"

Visualization—Developing a mental picture/image about a desired goal or end-result; useful for developing self-confidence.

Voting—A simple, quick way for a group to decide something, but not as profound and cohesive as achieving consensus. *See* **Consensus.**

"Wiggleroom"—Freedom to operate without the delegator constantly looking over the delegatee's shoulder; thus one decides one's style, pace, who to contact, procedures, sequencing of work, etc.

Win-lose—A highly competitive attitude or behavior involving a desire to best the other party; or a result from a highly competitive onslaught wherein one party wins big ("the winner takes all") and the other party is totally beaten.

"Win-lose" concept/model—As a result of either competition or collaboration (cooperation) one of these outcomes arises: win-win, win-lose, or lose-lose.

Win-Win—As a result of a high degree of cooperation/collaboration, everyone ends up as a winner.

Withdrawal—Leaving an undesirable situation, either psychologically (via silence) or physically (departing the room).

Worst scenario—A form of Risk Analysis in which team members ask: "What is the most horrendous thing that might occur if we did A (or B or C)?" It is a device to get the fears and anxieties out in the open and to then examine them realistically.

Index